Psychology:
Science and Understanding

Barry Smith

THOMSON

CUSTOM PUBLISHING

Editor: Nathan Anderson
Publishing Services Supervisor: Christina Smith
Manufacturing Supervisor: Donna M. Brown
Project Coordinator: Matthew Board
Graphic Designer: Krista Pierson
Rights and Permissions Specialist: Kalina Ingham Hintz
Marketing Manager: Sara L. Hinckley

Printed in the United States of America.

Thomson Custom Publishing
5191 Natorp Blvd.
Mason, Ohio 45040
USA

For information about our products, contact us:
1-800-355-9983
http://www.thomsoncustom.com

International Headquarters
Thomson Learning
International Division
290 Harbor Drive, 2nd Floor
Stamford, CT 06902-7477
USA

UK/Europe/Middle East/South Africa
Thomson Learning
Berkshire House
168-173 High Holborn
London WCIV 7AA

Asia
Thomson Learning
60 Albert Street, #15-01
Albert Complex
Singapore 189969

Canada
Nelson Thomson Learning
1120 Birchmount Road
Toronto, Ontario MIK 5G4
Canada
United Kingdom

Visit us at www.thomsoncustom.com and learn more about this book and other titles published by Thomson Learning Custom Publishing.

ISBN 0-759-34577-5

The Adaptable Courseware Program consists of products and additions to existing Custom Publishing products that are produced from camera-ready copy. Peer review, class testing, and accuracy are primarily the responsibility of the author(s).

Table of Contents

Chapter 1

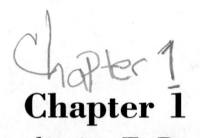

An Introduction To Psychology

Outline

Overview

WE ARE ABOUT to embark together upon a most interesting journey — a guided tour of the field of psychology, the discipline that studies *you.* We will see in this chapter that psychology is a scientific discipline, based in theory, grounded in research, and applied to many aspects of our daily lives. Psychology is rooted in older disciplines like physiology, medicine, and philosophy and has developed, mostly during this century, a solid base of knowledge of many aspects of behavior. Psychological theory and research are aimed at one chief goal: understanding the causes of behavior and underlying mental processes. To achieve this goal, psychology in the 21st century must also find definitive answers to a central question: How do biological and environmental factors work separately and together to influence behavior and mental processes, and to what extent is a given behavior influenced by each. In this chapter, we will explore the variety of perspectives from which psychology approaches the study of behavior, discuss the subfields that make up the discipline, and consider careers the field has to offer. We will also teach you how to study, take examinations, and think critically.

Human behavior is perhaps the most fascinating area of study ever subjected to scientific scrutiny. It probes the heights of creativity and the depths of depression. It strives to understand how we sleep and why we wake, how helpless babies become mature adults, and how we all learn, remember, and think. It studies *your* behavior—and mine. To get a better idea of the scope of psychology, consider the following questions:

- Do you have trouble sleeping? Psychologists have learned a great deal about the sleep process and the factors that affect how well people sleep. Some of their suggestions are discussed in Chapter 5.
- Are the behaviors of men and women different? Yes! We know that biological factors differentiate women and men in certain behavior patterns. Other gender differences in behavior are primarily due to social factors (Chapter____).
- Why do people kill? Why did 23-year-old Susan Smith kill her two children? For nine days, the South Carolina mother insisted that a car jacker had taken her car with her sons, aged 3 years and 14 months, in it. After police found her burgundy sedan at the bottom of a lake, she confessed to drowning the boys. What had happened? Read Chapter 16.
- Can memory be improved? Extensive psychological research has shown us how you can learn more efficiently and remember things better (see Chapter 9). In addition, Chapter 7 shows how aging people can improve their memories.
- What makes two people fall in love? Although it may seem impossible to study something as elusive as "love," social psychologists have done just that. We now have a good idea about what attracts people to each other and what causes friendship and love to grow (Chapter 19).
- Can a stressful job really cause ulcers? A major focus of psychology has been on mind_body interactions: how emotions can contribute to physical disorders, such as heart disease and ulcers. The answer is a bit complex, but fascinating. See Chapter 15.

These examples all fall within the general definition of *psychology* as *the scientific study of behavior and underlying mental processes.* Although this is a definition many psychologists would agree with, not all would include "mental processes." Some psychologists have carefully limited their research to the study of externally observable behaviors. In recent years, however, there has been an increasing tendency to focus on underlying processes, recognizing that such mental activities as thoughts (cognitions) and emotions may be crucial determinants of behavior. All psychologists would agree that pecking a key, pressing a bar, blinking an eye, mating, and eating are directly observable behaviors. Further, most would agree that other behaviors can easily be made objectively observable. For example, we can use an electrocardiograph (EKG) machine to measure heart rate.

But beyond such clearly observable behaviors, there is less agreement as to how we can study such underlying mental processes as thoughts, emotions, dreams, and motives. Ideally, we study these mental operations by making them as objectively observable as possible. We measure mental imagery, for example, by clocking how long it takes you to move from one point to another on a mental map, and we assess anxiety by using objective scales developed by researchers like Janet Taylor Spence. Despite disagreements regarding the study of mental processes, there is general consensus that psychology is *empirical,* where *empiricism* is the assumption that knowledge is best acquired through careful, precise observation. It is this assumption that makes psychology a science, a topic we take up in detail in Chapter 2.

Psychology Begins

Now that you have a partial sense of "the big picture" and of where psychology is likely to go in the 21st century, it is important to step back and learn something about where it came from.

If most of your friends were eighty years old, one who was only ten would seem very young by comparison. Among the major scientific disciplines, psychology is the youngster. Consider, for example, the biological and medical sciences. Hippocrates, dubbed by historians the father of medicine, lived between about 460 and 377 B.C. Wilhelm Wundt, who is usually credited with beginning psychology, established his laboratory in 1879, just over a century ago (Blumenthal, 2002). The youth of psychology as a discipline means that we have had little time to study behavior and thus have major gaps in our knowledge of how and why people and animals act as they do.

Although psychology as a formal discipline began in the late nineteenth century, interest in the behaviors that psychologists study is probably as old as the history of human thought. That curiosity is most clearly seen in two disciplines that provided the soil from which psychology eventually grew: philosophy and physiology. We will discuss their influence and also consider how psychology began, its early history in America and Europe, and the organization of psychology into a formal field of study. Finally, we will explore the origins of applied psychology, the important historical role of women in the field, and increasing concerns with understanding cultural and gender diversity.

Early Roots

The origins of psychology can be found some eighteen centuries ago in the work of the Greek Philosopher Socrates (470_399 B.C.) and particularly his successors, Aristotle (384_323 B.C.) and Plato (427_347 B.C.). Aristotle wrote extensively on the subject of human behavior, formulating a number of laws and discussing such topics as sensation and perception, learning, memory, motivation, and personality. Plato similarly contributed to the philosophical beginnings of psychology.

While many philosophers after the ancient Greeks addressed psychological issues, it was the seventeenth_century French philosopher Rene Descartes (1596_1650), known as the father of modern philosophy, who had the greatest impact in relatively modern times. Descartes focused on the relationship between mind and body. His approach, called *dualism,* held that the mind and body are distinct entities that function independently. The body obeys the laws of the physical universe, while the mind operates in a world of ideas. How, then, do thoughts—products of the mind—cause the physical actions of the body? How does thinking about food cause you to walk to the refrigerator to eat? How do erotic thoughts cause physiological sexual arousal and often sexual behavior? Descartes' answer was that mind and body interact in the pineal gland, a small structure found near the base of the brain.

The work of Aristotle, Plato, Descartes, and other philosophers dominated thinking about psychological matters for nearly 2000 years, but philosophy alone was not enough. Philosophies begin with basic assumptions that seem eminently logical, then use *reason* to arrive at conclusions. The missing element in achieving a full understanding of behavior is observation and the application of the scientific method.

It was the discipline of *physiology,* which studies the operation of body organs and systems, that provided the missing link. Although concerned primarily with the biological basis for the functioning of organisms, nineteenth_century physiologists began to demonstrate that psychological processes and behavior could be studied objectively. Of particular importance to the development of psychology was the work of German physiologists Hermann von Helmholtz and Johannes Muller and German physicist Gustav Fechner.

Trained initially as a physicist, Helmholtz turned his attention to the study of perception and the processing of sensations by the nervous system. Muller provided an initial understanding of how impulses are conducted along nerves in the body, information crucial to the eventual investigation of behavior. Fechner studied the translation of physical stimulation into psychological experience. How much brighter, for example, must a light get before it is perceived as brighter? Such questions became part of the field of *psychophysics,* which Fechner helped to found and which we will study in Chapter 4.

The years between 1875 and 1900 saw the birth and early development of psychology as a separate discipline. It arose out of the increasing need to apply scientific principles to the study of behavior. To say that we act on the basis of our free will—we simply decide what to do—is nonscientific because it suggests that our behavior is not a product of universal scientific principles. *Determinism,* the basis for science, holds, instead, that every behavior results from causes that conform to scientific principles. To understand the origins of behavior, we therefore need to study the scientific principles that determine it. The scientists who developed psychology in those early years included Wilhelm Wundt, William James, Ivan Pavlov, and Sigmund Freud (Pickren, 2002; Figure 1.3). We will consider their historical influence and also take up the major schools of thought—functionalism, structuralism, behaviorism, and humanism (Leahey, 2002).

Two Pioneers, Two Views

Two of the most significant of the major contributors to the early history of psychology were Wilhelm Wundt and William James.

Wilhelm Wundt. The greatest credit for establishing psychology as an independent discipline is usually given to Wundt, who is generally recognized as the founder of psychology. He formally opened a laboratory for the study of psychological phenomena in Leipzig, Germany, in 1879. A student of Helmholtz, Wundt was trained in both physiology and philosophy. He became interested in the study of human consciousness, and this study became the subject matter of the new discipline of psychology. It was possible, Wundt held, to apply the scientific methods of physics to the study of consciousness, thus using the methods of science to study the functioning of the mind (Danziger, 2002). His interest was in selective attention, and his method was to train students to introspect (Blumenthal, 2002). *Introspection* is a method of self-observation in which the subject focuses on his own individual sensations, analyzes his consciousness, and verbally reports the results of the analysis.

A hard worker and dedicated scientist, Wundt published over 50,000 book and journal pages in the course of his career and influenced many other psychologists, including a number of Americans, to follow his lead. In fact, Ludy Benjamin and several colleagues recently analyzed historical student archives at Karl Marx University in Leipzig and identified 33 American students who completed their doctoral degrees with Wundt (Benjamin et al., 1992). Among them were Edward Titchener and G. Stanley Hall, whose work we will discuss shortly. In addition, numerous researchers, including some Americans, traveled to his laboratory to learn introspective techniques and returned home to establish their own laboratories. The 1880s and 1890s saw the opening of twenty_four new laboratories for psychological research in the United States and Canada, most of them modeled after Wundt's. Interestingly enough, many of Wundt's books and journals are housed in a collection in Japan (Takasuna, 2001).

William James. The first major American psychologist was Wundt's contemporary, William James (1842-1910). He led a group of American psychologists who became interested in the practical applications of psychological research and in combining the direct observation of behavior with the use of introspection to study underlying mental processes. James trained in medicine but took a position on the faculty of Harvard University and taught his first psychology course in 1875. Fifteen years later he published the first major textbook in the field, entitled *Principles of Psychology.* Influenced by Darwin's theory of evolution, James concluded that psychologists should not study merely the *structure* of consciousness, as Wundt and others were doing, but its adaptive significance or *function.* As a result, the school known as *functionalism* was born (Leary, 2002). James proposed that people learn and continue to perform adaptive behaviors and tend not to repeat less adaptive or maladaptive actions. His books are among the most important in the history of psychology, and his functionalist approach continues to influence psychological theory and research.

Early Psychology in America

James was not the only early American psychologist of note, nor was functionalism the only school. Other schools included structuralism, behaviorism, and humanism.

Structuralism. After receiving his Ph.D. degree under Wundt, Edward Titchener brought Wundt's methodology to Cornell University and founded the school of psychology known as *structuralism.* Titchener and those Americans who joined him continued to experiment on conscious experience, dividing it into objective sensations, such as vision and hearing, and subjective feelings, such as memory and emotion. They trained subjects to objectively report these sensations and feelings. The structuralists hypothesized that mental processes are based on a combination of the elements of experience. Like Wundt, Titchener used introspection, but unlike Wundt he believed that sensory experience can be used to pull together all the basic elements of the mind.

Despite his contribution, Titchener's method eventually failed. Wundt had warned that introspection has limitations as a scientific method, and he was right. The problem is that introspection cannot be verified. It is private and specific to a given individual, and the data it produces cannot be observed independently by anyone else. As a result, modern psychology has no place for introspection as Titchener employed that technique and no place for his structuralist view.

Behaviorism. Another major American school of thought began with two blockbuster articles in 1907 and 1913 by John B. Watson. A student of William James, Watson conducted a series of experiments with animals, including dogs, cats, monkeys, frogs, and especially rats. He found that these animals could readily learn simple behaviors and that laws of behavior could be developed without reference to such nebulous concepts as mind. His studies convinced him that postulating mentalistic concepts to explain behavior—even human behavior—was both unnecessary and confusing. He concluded that the only proper focus of psychology as a science was on the externally observable behavior of the animal or human (Harris,2002). The goal of the field was therefore to understand the environmental conditions that produce specific behaviors. Watson called his view *behaviorism,* and it was soon enthusiastically embraced by many psychologists.

There were numerous early behaviorists in the United States, but it was Clark Hull (1884-1952) and B.F. Skinner (1904-1990) who emerged as the leaders of behaviorism. Hull's major work, *Principles of Behavior* (1943) outlined a mathematically precise theory of learning and established him as the major figure in the increasingly influential field of the psychology of learning. His dominance was, however, later overridden by Skinner, whose 1938 book, *The Behavior of Organisms,* became one of the most important works in the history of psychology. Skinner went on to actively led the behavioral movement of the next several decades (L. Smith, 2002). Like Watson, he focused on the externally observable behavior of the animal or human and rejected the use of such internal explanations as the concept of the mind.

Humanism. Not all American psychologists were happy with behaviorism. One result of this discontent was the development of the school of *humanism.* Although its origins can be traced to philosophy, humanism emerged as a school of psychological thought primarily as a result of the work of American psychologist Carl Rogers, beginning in the early 1940s. The humanistic view suggests that human beings are unique in the animal kingdom, not merely the highest rung on the ladder of evolution. Humans are uniquely capable of having a self-concept, a perception of their own characteristics. In addition, every individual is different, and this individuality is a central determinant of human behavior. Since the pioneering work of Rogers and another humanist, Abraham Maslow, humanism has come to have many advocates and is still an important influence in American psychology.

Early Psychology Abroad

At about the same time that Wundt and James began the work that led to structuralism and functionalism, the Russian Pavlov, the Viennese Freud, and the German Wertheimer went in quite different directions. Ivan Pavlov, a Russian physiologist, began the formal study of learning processes with his demonstration of how responses to new stimuli can be learned (Todes, 2002). He showed how a dog can be taught to salivate to the sound of a bell and established *classical conditioning* as an approach to understanding how learning takes place. We will study his contributions in Chapter 8.

Sigmund Freud, a physician trained in neurology and practicing as a psychiatrist in Vienna, was interested in the scientific study of the human personality or psyche, as he called it. His *psychoanalytic theory* is one of the most influential theories ever developed in psychology or any other field. Freud's theory describes the structure and functioning of the personality, emphasizing the impact of unconscious determinants on behavior (Hornstein, 2002). We will discuss aspects of his work in Chapter 2 and in several other chapters.

A third major European school of thought emerged in 1912 when Max Wertheimer (1890-1943) published an article suggesting that we perceive objects as whole structures, not as a set of separate parts. Wertheimer, together with Wolfgang K^hler, Kurt Koffka, and Kurt Lewin, went on to found the German school known as *Gestalt psychology* (Ash, 2002). The basic hypothesis of this new school was that our perceptions and mental operations can best be understood as organized wholes, not elementary parts. When we view a painting, we see it as an integrated totality, not a blue stripe here and a red dot there. Similarly, a melody is not just the sum of a series of notes, but rather is heard as a whole musical structure. As we will see in Chapter ____, Gestalt psychology has had a considerable impact on the study of how we view objects around us (Franz et al., 2001)

Many other theorists and research scientists have contributed to the development of our current fund of knowledge in psychology. We will explore the work of these later contributors when we delve into the various subfields of psychology in other chapters.

Getting Organized

Every new discipline, if it is to last, must eventually be organized, and it was G. Stanley Hall, Wundt's first American student, who performed that important function for psychology (White, 2002). Having also studied with Helmholtz and James, Hall was well qualified to establish the first American laboratory for psychological research at Johns Hopkins University in 1883. A few years later, in 1887, he founded the *American Journal of Psychology,* the first psychology journal published in the United States. And in 1892, Hall organized the *American Psychological Association* (APA) and became its first president. Only 31 psychologists attended the initial meeting. By 1993, APA had grown to over 75,000 members.

As is true of many other disciplines, there are differences of opinion among psychologists as to the relative emphasis that should be placed on research as compared with application. One result of this difference in psychology was the later formation of a second organization. It began in 1987 as the Assembly for Scientific and Applied Psychology (ASAP), and this small group of 450 psychologists worked to found, in August, 1988, the *American Psychological Society* (APS). Its mission is "...to promote, protect, and advance the interests of scientifically oriented psychology in research, application, teaching, and in the improvement of human welfare" (APS, 1993). This new organization had grown to over 15,000 members by 1993. Though both organizations recognize that both research and application are important, the emphasis on research is greater in APS.

The differences between APA and APS are reflected in virtually every chapter of this book. They are the differences between practice and science, between application and research, between clinical methods and experimental methods.

Applied Psychology Arrives

The term *applied psychology* refers to the use of scientifically developed knowledge of psychological phenomena to solve practical problems in the real world. The largest branch of the field involved in application is *clinical psychology,* which is concerned with assessing, diagnosing, and treating psychological disorders. Other applied specialties include counseling, industrial/organizational, health, and school psychology, which we will take up later in the chapter.

In its early years, psychology was largely a research field concerned with understanding the scientific principles underlying behavior. Applied psychology developed very gradually, beginning with the opening of the first psychological clinic in 1896. Few psychologists joined this new clinical branch until the recruiting of soldiers for World War I (1914-1918) created a need for psychological testing. Even though some psychologists fulfilled this need, a 1918 survey showed that only 4 percent of the APA membership at that time were interested in such pursuits (Finison, 2002). By 1937 that figure had grown to a still small minority of about 20 percent.

It took another war, World War II (1941-1945), and its aftermath to interest larger numbers of psychologists in application. The need to evaluate military recruits meant the development of additional psychological tests and the application of these tests by psychologists, many of them recruited from universities (Von Mayrhauser, 2002). These psychologists soon further applied their skills to the treatment of soldiers who had been psychologically traumatized by battle. The demand for such treatment continued after the war, when tens of thousands of veterans appeared at Veterans Administration (VA) hospitals with psychological problems. Since the number of clinical psychologists available was very small, the VA began to fund programs to train more, and soon nearly half the new Ph.D.'s in psychology were clinical (Shakow, 2002). By the 1950s, applied psychology came into its own, with clinical psychology solidly established. The other applied specialties then developed quite rapidly, reversing the balance in the field as a whole. Where most psychologists had been researchers in academic settings, a vast majority now spent much of their time providing professional services. However, it is important to note that the emphasis is on the application of principles derived through research.

Women in Psychology

It is apparent from what you have just read that historians have not typically included women among the major figures in the development of psychology (Riger, 2002). So it is important to know that women have made real contributions to the field (Table 1.1). The first woman to receive a Ph.D. in psychology and the second to serve as president of APA was Margaret Floy Washburn, who completed her degree at Cornell in 1894 (Furumoto & Scarborough, 2002). She became a member of the faculty at Wells College and later taught at Vassar College. She contributed significantly to the emergence of behaviorism as a major school, and her most important written contribution was *Movement and Mental Imagery* (1916). Other particularly accomplished women in the early history of psychology were Christine Ladd_Franklin, Lillien Martin, Eleanor Gibson, Mary Ainsworth, Mary Calkins, and Leta Hollingworth. Calkins founded one of the first laboratories in America and developed a widely used technique for the study of memory. As one of the most active members of the field, Calkins became the first woman to serve as president of the APA. Hollingsworth was a major earlier contributor to work on adolescent development and mental retardation. She was also the first to use the term "gifted" to refer to children with high intelligence and pioneered in debunking the myth that menstrual cycle phases are associated with decrements in performance.

Why did these and other women not achieve the status of Wundt, Hall, James, or Freud? First, it is important to realize that a vast majority of male psychologists also failed to achieve the prominence of these men. Second, women operated under social constraints and expectations that men did not. Women were generally expected to be religious, pure, submissive, and domestic, and some universities did not admit them as students. Society constrained them to marry, raise children, and care for their immediate family and elderly parents (Vande Kemp, 2001). Some commentators even held that women were not mentally or physically fit for the rigors of college education (Furumoto & Scarborough, 2002). In short, any woman who pursued a professional career began with two strikes against her. Despite these obstacles, a number of women did enter psychology in its early years, and they made important contributions.

Whatever the history, the future of women in psychology is assured (Raphael-Leff, 2001; Thompson, 2001). In fact, psychology has become increasingly "feminized" in recent years. As Patricia Ostertag points out, increasing proportions of graduate applicants in psychology are women, and increasing numbers and proportions of women are receiving doctorates in the field (Ostertag & McNamara, 1991). This is a positive and healthy trend for a profession that is concerned with all human behavior but whose practitioners have previously been predominantly male.

Psychology and Human Diversity

The psychological study of women's issues exemplifies the growing recognition within the field of the importance of human diversity. Men and women are different and in scientifically verifiable ways. So are African-Americans and whites, Asians and Hispanics, Europeans and Americans. Recognizing the importance of differences in cultural and subcultural background and experience is taking psychology increasingly in the direction of studying these individual differences systematically and of including them in theories of human behavior (Stevenson, 2002). It is important to note, however, that in psychology the emphasis is on the study of the individual, not the group. Cultural background is thus an individual difference variable that may affect the behavior of the person.

The idea that cultural differences are important is a relatively new one in psychology. Historically, the field has been dominated by white, middle-class males (Walker, 1991), who have tended to study other white, middle-class males, mostly college students (Choi, 2001). One problem with this historical situation is that we may not be able to generalize scientific findings in groups of white, male college students to, for example, black females from Africa. In fact, it is increasingly clear that different cultures—and different subcultures within American culture—teach very different patterns of behavior. Knowing how white, middle-class women communicate with each other may tell us very little about how either white or African-American women in ghettos communicate, let alone how men communicate. A middle-class American clinical or counseling psychologist who can effectively treat middle-class American patients may be far less effective with Asian, African-American, or Hispanic patients. The growing recognition of the importance of cultural variables will greatly inform and enhance theory, research, and clinical practice as we move rapidly toward the twenty-first century. A discussion of research on cultural diversity appears in Chapter 2.

Models and Perspectives in Psychology

Psychologists are all basically interested in the same thing: a better understanding of behavior and underlying mental processes. However, in much the same way that different cultures have different perspectives, psychologists differ in their views of behavior and its causes, and the result has been the development of several different models for understanding behavior.

These differing perspectives grow out of the varied backgrounds of psychologists and their basic philosophical assumptions about behavior. Among the philosophical issues on which psychologists differ are: the *nature_nurture* issue; whether behavior is primarily driven by the desire to maximize pleasure and avoid pain *(hedonism)* or by some other motive; whether behavior is essentially random or primarily purposeful *(teleology)*; whether the behaviors of an organism can be broken down into components for study or whether the organism must be studied as a whole *(holism);* and whether human beings should be seen as basically good or basically evil (see Table 1.2).

The positions psychologists adopt on these and other important issues determine what behaviors they will choose to study, what kinds of hypotheses they will be interested in testing, and what research methods they will use. A psychologist's basic assumptions will also determine the model she will use in formulating a conceptual basis for theory and research. A *model* is a way of organizing thinking about the various components of behavior and the ways in which they relate to each other. Individual psychologists operate from a wide variety of models, but five are currently dominant: Neuroscience (biological), psychodynamic, behavioral, humanistic, and cognitive science. Some of these have clearly grown out of the historical schools of thought (Figure 1-4).

The Neuroscience or Biological Model

Originally favored by such pioneers as Freud and Wundt, the *neuroscience* or *biological model* holds that an understanding of behavior requires knowledge of underlying physiological processes (Posner, 2000). We need to know how the structure and biochemistry of the brain and nervous system are related to behavior, how genetic inheritance influences behavior, and how a variety of physiological processes affect and are affected by psychological processes. Moreover, neuroscientific research provides a basis for understanding and treating neurological disorders that affect behavior. The biologically oriented psychologist usually believes that genetic factors can predispose individuals toward certain types of behavior patterns that can be modified to some extent by experience. This model clearly stands somewhat closer to the nature end of the continuum, although neuroscientists clearly acknowledge the important role of experience in the development of behavior (Wilson, 2001).

Suppose, for example, that we were interested in the study of skiers, a small proportion of the normal population who engage in a somewhat dangerous, thrilling sport. How might the biological psychologist study skiers? One good example is the work of Marvin Zuckerman, who has suggested that the same people who ski often sport parachute, drive racing cars, and engage in a variety of sensation_seeking activities. Interestingly enough, he has found that high and low sensation seekers differ in the levels of certain brain biochemicals (Zuckerman, 1984). Those at the sensation_seeking extremes also differ in certain aspects of their physiological functioning (Smith, et al., 1986), as do sport parachutists at various stages of the jumping process (Epstein & Fenz, 1965), and there appears to be a genetic predisposition involved.

The Psychodynamic Model

According to the *psychodynamic model,* powerful biological and psychological forces within the individual motivate all human behavior. The most noted proponent of this model was Freud, who suggested that most human motivations and drives are unconscious. Conflicts between these drives and environmental constraints against their satisfaction produce tension, and behavior results from the attempt to reduce that tension as the person strives to satisfy his needs. Like the neuroscientist, Freud is somewhat more interested in nature than in nurture. However, he nevertheless considers the role of parental and other environmental influences on the developing child.

According to Freud, heredity combines with early life experience to determine the personality and behavior patterns of the adult. Born with only the most primitive physiological and psychological drives, the infant soon begins to learn how to satisfy these drives through interaction with the environment. However, that interaction is often frustrating and unrewarding as the child repeatedly satisfies drives, only to have them recur. Moreover, the infant's path to satisfaction is often blocked by parents and other adults, who impose sanctions and demands, some of which the child eventually internalizes. In Freud's view, these experiences of infancy and early childhood stay with the individual for a lifetime. A psychodynamic researcher might choose to study highly anxious individuals in an effort to determine what unconscious motivations and conflicts underlie their problems.

Freud's psychodynamic model has always been controversial, but he has probably had a greater influence on psychology than nearly any other single individual. As we continue our study of psychology, we will frequently encounter Freud's ideas on such wide-ranging topics as dreaming, child development, memory and forgetting, unconscious motivation, emotion, sexuality, personality, abnormal behavior, psychotherapy, and reactions to stress.

The Behavioral Model

According to the *behavioral model,* the only proper subject matter for psychology is observable behavior. We cannot go inside the body or mind to explain behavior. Knowledge of the brain and other biological mechanisms is not essential to our understanding of the origins of behavior, and such ideas as unconscious motivation and internal conflict are virtually taboo. Behaviorists' experiments tend to be relatively simple and straightforward, and as objective as possible. A behaviorist might, for example, give a pigeon food for pecking a key, then observe how long it takes the bird to keypeck regularly.

Classic behaviorism clearly stands at the extreme nurture end of the continuum, emphasizing environmental effects and essentially eliminating biological factors. In fact, *environmental determinism* is a hallmark of the behavioral approach. Although modern behaviorists have begun to recognize the influence of biological factors, classic behaviorism sees virtually every behavior as resulting from environmental conditions. Reinforcers are things that cause the animal to learn the behavior, and they all come from the environment. The food that causes the pigeon to keypeck, for instance, is an environmental reinforcer. Stimuli are objects in the environment that guide behavior. The pigeon might learn to peck when a key is red but not when it is green: The color is the stimulus. Together, stimuli and reinforcers account for all aspects of behavior. The approaches of the major behavioral psychologists, including John B. Watson and B. F. Skinner, are discussed in Chapter 8.

The Humanistic Model

Psychologists who follow the *humanistic model* believe that human beings are innately good and that they strive to achieve goals and actively develop both physical and psychological potentials. According to humanists, people are not driven by unconscious forces, nor are they entirely controlled by environmental conditions. Rather, each human being is a unique individual who has a self_concept _ a picture of what he or she is like _ and a basic desire to become a better, more fully functioning person.

Behavior is controlled not so much by the external environment as by the subjective environment created by the individual's biased *perceptions* of what is going on around her. Each individual experiences the world a bit differently, and it is this subjective, individualized world that influences behavior. Biology also has a role, in that each person is endowed with biological motivations that greatly affect behavior. The best_known humanistic theorists are Carl Rogers and Abraham Maslow, and their approaches to personality are described in Chapter 14.

Cognitive Science and the Cognitive Model

The *cognitive model* suggests that people use such cognitive processes as thought, attention, and expectation to search the environment for needed information, then process that information and behave accordingly. Cognitive processes are used both to react to outside stimuli and to initiate behavior without an external stimulus being involved. Cognitions not only cause actions but also result from them, and there can, in fact, be a cycle of thoughts and actions.

The cognitive model has grown rapidly in recent decades and has begun to merge with other disciplines. In fact, the study of human cognition has led to the development of a relatively new interdisciplinary field called *cognitive science.* It includes researchers from linguistics, philosophy, computer science, engineering, and other fields, as well as psychology. Beyond cognitive science is a yet newer hybrid interdisciplinary field call *cognitive neuroscience,* which focuses on the neurophysiological bases of cognitive processes. Those who study cognition are interested in how information coming in from the environment is processed, how expectations of success or failure influence behavior, how the environment is interpreted as a basis for action, and how individuals make decisions. Cognitive science has arrived at a position near the center of the nature-nurture continuum and emphasizes the interaction of environmental factors with internal, neurological processes. We will take up cognitive psychology and cognitive science in more detail in Chapter 10.

Applying the Models

Different models lead to different hypotheses and often different conclusions about the causes of behavior. Consider the behavior and the anxiety of the skier about to plunge down a precipitous slope (Table 1.3). The biological model would emphasize the need to study the physiological changes that precede and accompany the anxiety. The psychodynamic model would focus on the early, unconscious precursors of anxiety more generally and might wonder what unconscious need is being met by seeking out the anxiety of skiing. The behavioral model would focus on the externally observable manifestations of the anxiety, such as sweaty palms. To the behaviorist, the skier is simply a "behaving organism," his ski behavior a product of reinforcement. The behaviorist could perhaps design a better training program by studying the specific behaviors associated with skiing and the reinforcers that help the individual learn those behaviors. He could study the history of reinforcement that might lead one person to ski and another to avoid skiing. The humanist would consider the conscious experience of anxiety and the extent to which that experience is consistent with the person's self concept. What kinds of self_conceptualization would lead one to attempt this risky sport? What does thinking of oneself as a skier add to the self_concept? And the cognitive scientist would examine the contribution of thought processes to the development and reduction of both the behavior and the accompanying anxiety.

As a second example, consider the disorder we call depression. If you have ever been depressed over a poor exam performance, the breakup of a love relationship, or the number on the scale when you weigh yourself, you have at least a small idea of how a severely depressed person feels. In attempting to understand depression, the biological model would lead us to examine the genetic and neurochemical correlates of depression, the psychodynamic model would focus on its unconscious origins, and the behavioral model would examine and treat the behaviors of the depressed person, such as crying and lethargy. The humanistic model would ask how discrepancies in the self_concept might lead to depression, and the cognitive theorist would ask what thought processes might be causing the depressive affect.

It must by now be apparent that there is no one "correct" way to view or study behavior. Five psychologists faced with precisely the same behavior can view it from 5 quite different perspectives, develop 5 different kinds of theories, study it with 5 different scientific approaches, and potentially reach 5 somewhat different conclusions. Each of the major models offers a valid way to approach the understanding of behavior, but the various models have not all been equally influential at any given time. The cognitive and neuroscience models have been very influential in recent times, and evolutionary psychology is receiving increasing attention as we move into the 21st century.

The Field of Psychology: Areas and Careers

Psychology is not a unitary field, even though psychologists share the same broad goals. Psychologists differ not only in the models of behavior they choose to adopt and the topics they choose to study but also in the types of work they do. Not all psychologists work in laboratories or see disturbed patients. In fact, there are a substantial number of specialty areas, each focusing on a different aspect of behavior and each having its own perspectives and methods.

Areas of Psychology

Some indication of the major areas of psychology—its subdisciplines—can be seen in the structure of the American Psychological Association (APA). APA contains forty-eight divisions, each representing an area of mutual interest to a number of psychologists, and some of these varied areas of expertise are reflected in the membership of APS as well. The APA divisions are listed in Table 1-4. Many psychologists belong to more than one division, as the areas often overlap. The major specialty areas are experimental, biological, health, developmental, social, personality, clinical, counseling, and industrial/organizational psychology (Table 1-5). Others include the environmental, school, and educational fields.

Experimental psychology focuses on the scientific study of basic processes that underlie behavior. Research in this area typically focuses on such topics as sensation, perception, learning, memory, cognition, and motivation. Most of the work of the experimental psychologist is done in the laboratory (Myers, 2002).

Neuroscience is an interdisciplinary field that studies the brain and associated physiological processes. Many psychologists are among the neuroscientists whose disciplines make up this important, broader field (Walfish, 2001). Now a part of neuroscience, *biological psychology* (or biopsychology) deals with neurophysiological processes that underlie behavior. Using drug, surgical, and other techniques on animal subjects, the biopsychologist attempts to further our understanding of the relationship between physiology and behavior.

The roles of the brain and nervous system and of brain biochemistry in behavior are the typical interests of the biopsychologist. Many psychologists who work in this area refer to themselves as comparative or physiological psychologists or as neuroscientists, and some work more specifically in the areas of sensation and perception, where they study how the senses function and how stimuli encountered in the environment are processed by the senses and interpreted by the brain.

Health Psychology is related to the more general field of *behavioral medicine* and is concerned with understanding how physical health and illness relate to individual behavior. With such earlier killer diseases as influenza and small pox largely conquered, attention has turned to cardiovascular disease, cancer, and AIDS. These and other chronic diseases can be greatly affected by stress and by such health behaviors as smoking, diet, exercise, alcohol consumption, and sexual practices. With 50% of deaths in the U.S. due to modifiable personal health behaviors (Smith, in press), the goal of health psychology is to develop and promote both preventive and treatment approaches that involve behavioral change (Smith et al., 1999).

Developmental psychology is concerned with the origins of behavior and the growth and change of the individual over the life span. Those specializing in this area originally focused almost exclusively on the study of children, investigating how development takes place from infancy through adolescence. More recently, developmental psychologists have broadened the scope of the field to include adolescence, adulthood, and the aging process.

Social psychology uses experimental techniques to investigate how people interact and what effects these interactions have on the behavior of the individuals involved. Social psychologists study the formation of attitudes and how they affect behavior, as well as the effects of thought processes on social behavior. They are also concerned with interactions in groups and with those that take place between two people.

Personality psychology focuses on the investigation of patterns of consistent behavior (often called personality traits), how these patterns develop and change, and what influence they have on behavior. This subfield of psychology has been responsible for the development of some of its most important and widely influential theories. Included are psychoanalytic theory, humanistic theory, and a number of trait theories. Personality and social psychology are closely related and are often treated together.

Clinical psychology is the largest single subfield of psychology and is primarily concerned with the assessment and treatment of individuals with psychological disorders. Clinical psychologists use various devices to aid in diagnosing disorders and conduct a variety of forms of therapy. Many clinical psychologists are involved in research programs that examine the effectiveness of psychotherapy, attempt to determine the causes of abnormal behavior, and in various other ways contribute to our understanding of psychological disorders.

Counseling psychology also provides assessment and treatment services for individuals. However, the counseling psychologist tends to focus on less serious problems. She may provide vocational, academic, or marriage counseling, or supportive therapy to help individuals deal with specific problems, such as drug abuse or grief. Like clinical psychologists, many counseling psychologists conduct research related to their specialty.

Industrial/organizational psychology deals with the realities of the world of business and government. Psychologists who specialize in this area measure employee attitudes, devise methods for personnel selection, suggest ways of improving employee productivity, and help design equipment better suited to human operation, among other activities. Many industrial/organizational psychologists conduct research, whether to solve a specific problem (such as a drop in work productivity at a particular company) or to address more general issues (how to improve employee morale in any organization).

There are also other specialties. *Environmental psychologists* examine ways in which the physical environment affects behavior and mental processes. They study, for example, how high temperatures increase stress and cause aggression (Anderson, 1989) and how crowded conditions can lead to violence (Paulus, 1988). *School psychologists* work in primary and secondary school settings, where they assess the intellectual and emotional functioning of students. They sometimes also counsel students who have problems. *Educational psychologists* are found primarily in colleges and universities. They conduct research aimed at understanding and improving educational processes and may advise school systems on educational programs.

The various specialty areas in psychology are by no means equally represented in the field. You can see in Figure 1_5 that clinical and counseling psychology account for the work of some 55 percent of all psychologists. The largest single number of psychologists (36 percent) are found in colleges and universities, where they teach, do research, and may also engage in the practice of clinical, counseling, or industrial/organizational psychology (Stapp, Tucker, and Vanderbos, 1985). Other relatively large numbers of psychologists are found in private practice or in hospital settings, and some are found in industrial and organizational settings.

Careers in Psychology

Careers related to psychology are possible at several different degree levels. We will discuss the options available with bachelor's, master's, and doctoral degrees (Figure1-6).

The B.A. or B.S. Degree. A recent study showed that most undergraduate psychology majors had heard someone say: "You can't get a job with a bachelor's degree in psychology" (Ware, 2001). However, that is not true. If you complete a bachelor's in psychology, there are many kinds of positions available to you. You can become a psychiatric assistant or a psychology technician in a community mental health center or a large hospital. There you are likely to help in administering psychological tests and may also assist in treatments such as biofeedback and in research. Vocational rehabilitation positions, in which you counsel handicapped persons preparing for new vocations, are also a possibility, although some states require a master's degree for this type of job.

Alternatively, a B.S. or B.A. in psychology also qualifies you for some research positions in the field. A survey of psychology graduates with bachelor's degrees indicated that a number had obtained research jobs in which they were performing a variety of tasks, such as running subjects in experiments, coding data, and conducting data analyses. Some even had the responsibility for entire research projects; they trained and supervised other people and had overall responsibility for carrying out the research and analyzing the data. Graduates with bachelor's degrees are also found in a variety of other jobs, including community relations officer, recreation worker, technical educator, and day_care center supervisor. In fact, there are numerous jobs for those with a bachelor's degree in psychology (Ware, 2001).

The Master's Degree. Another career path for someone interested in psychology is to obtain a Master's degree. Such individuals work in hospital settings, conducting psychological assessments and sometimes counseling under the direction of a Ph.D. psychologist (Perlman, 2001). A Master's degree will sometimes also get you a job working in a rese ratory or in such settings as prisons and school systems, and in many aspects of industrial/organizational psyc

The Doctorate. In order to actually be called a psychologist, you must obtain a doctoral degree (usually a Ph psychology. Most doctoral training programs require that you have a high undergraduate grade point average, and relevant research experience can be essential (Wiens & Hope, 2001). Clinical and counseling psychologists who graduate from APA_approved doctoral programs are required to complete a predoctoral internship, and most states require that psychologists be licensed before being allowed to administer psychological tests or treat clients (Denicola & Furze, 2001). It is important to note, however, that such nebulous titles as "therapist" are usually not protected by state laws, so care is required to determine whether or not you are actually dealing with a Ph.D. psychologist. Currently popular areas of training in doctoral programs nationally include health psychology and, within clinical psychology, family therapy, neuropsychology, and couples therapy (Walfish, 2001). Many students also receive Ph.Ds. in general experimental, biological, sensory and perceptual, counseling, cognitive, industrial/organizational, or social psychology or in such interdisciplinary fields as neuroscience and cognitive science. If you plan to go to graduate school, you might interested in reading a book called *Succeeding in Graduate School* (Walfish, 2001).

Psychology and Psychiatry. It is important to distinguish between Ph.D. psychologists and psychiatrists. *Psychiatry* is a *medical* specialty. Psychiatrists attend medical school and receive an M.D. degree, then complete about four additional years of training specifically in psychiatry. As licensed physicians, psychiatrists not only diagnose individuals with psychological disorders and conduct psychotherapy, but can also administer drugs and carry out such medical procedures as electroconvulsive shock therapy. A *psychologist* is someone with a doctorate in psychology rather than medicine. Psychologists cannot prescribe drugs or perform other medical procedures.

Conclusion

Psychologists focus on three major endeavors: theory, research, and application. Some psychologists have developed broad theories that attempt to provide comprehensive explanations for virtually all human behavior. Others have formulated models dealing with relatively narrow aspects of behavior, such as memory, learning, or schizophrenia. Some of these same psychologists and many others spend much of their time engaged in research to test the various theories and increase scientific understanding of the causes of behavior. Finally, some psychologists apply theoretical and empirical (research_based) knowledge in an effort to help individuals, groups, and society as a whole to function more effectively. The treatments administered by clinical and counseling psychologists and the organizational analyses conducted by industrial/organizational psychologists are examples of such applications.

You may have also realized in reading this first chapter that you are beginning your study of psychology at a particularly exciting time, a time when a new era has just dawned in this increasingly important scientific field. This new era—which will carry us into the 21st century—is marked by the growing recognition that behavior is strongly influenced by the neurobiological expression of genetic factors. From an evolutionary standpoint, this hereditary component is, in turn, a product of adaptive mechanisms developed in response to the demands of ancient environments. This new emphasis on understanding the genetic and neurophysiological underpinnings of behavior will be paired with a much more complete and accurate view of the role of environment. More important, we will come to understand, in a far more sophisticated way, how biology and environment *interact* to cause behavior. We will increasingly recognize that there are three sources of influence on behavior:

- Biology
- Environment
- The interaction

In each of the remaining chapters, we will strike a balance on the nature-nurture question. We will fully present both biologically and environmentally oriented theories of behavior and associated scientific research and let the evidence carry the day. You will certainly not come away from each chapter believing that behavior is entirely a product of environment. But you will also not believe it is entirely due to heredity. Rather, we'll tell you the whole story and let you—and of course your professor—draw your own conclusions.

Psychology is the new kid on the scientific block. Though it has deep roots in philosophy, physiology, and medicine, it began as a separate discipline only a little over a century ago. It's practitioners relied heavily on theories of environmental causation for much of this century, but have now begun to recognize the importance of biological factors as well. In Chapter 2 we will see how psychology uses the powerful methods of science to accomplish its goals, and we explore just what those methods are.

Summary

1. Psychology studies behavior and underlying mental processes.

Psychology Begins

1. Psychology had its origins in the disciplines of philosophy and physiology.
2. The science of psychology officially began in 1879, with the establishment of Wilhelm Wundt's laboratory in Germany. In America, William James began the school called functionalism.
3. Edward Titchener started the school of structuralism.
4. Watson's behaviorism denied the value of mentalistic constructs. Skinner later became the major theorist.
5. The humanism of Carl Rogers emphasized the uniqueness and goodness of humans.
6. Major early European figures in psychology included Pavlov (classical conditioning), Freud (psychoanalysis), and Wertheimer (Gestalt).
7. G. Stanley Hall started the American Psychological Association.
8. World Wars I and II stimulated the development of clinical psychology.
9. Major early women psychologists include Washburn, Ladd-Franklin, Martin, Calkins, Gibson, Ainsworth, and Hollingworth.

Models and Perspectives in Psychology

1. The major models currently used in psychology are the neuroscience (biological), psychodynamic, behavioral, humanistic, and cognitive models.
2. Each psychologist adopts a set of assumptions that determine the model to be used in formulating the conceptual basis for theory and research, The model adopted will heavily influence the theories to which the psychologist subscribes and the research she will conduct.

The Field of Psychology: Areas and Careers

1. The major subfields of psychology include experimental, biological, health, developmental, social, personality, clinical, counseling, and industrial/organizational psychology.
2. A bachelor's degree in psychology opens the door to a variety of jobs, but a doctorate is required to be called a psychologist; an M.D. degree and additional training are required to become a psychiatrist..

Ask Yourself

1. From what earlier disciplines has psychology arisen, and how have those disciplines influenced the current field of psychology?
2. What is psychology, and what are its major goals? Which goal is most important, and why?
3. Describe briefly the principal models that underlie the thinking of most psychologists.
4. List and briefly define the major specialty areas within psychology.
5. How might the neuroscience and cognitive science areas be related?
6. Discuss the "right" and "wrong" ways of asking the nature-nurture question. Why is the newer question a better one?
7. How does the model you adopt affect the research you do and the theories you develop?
8. Discuss the historical and current roles of women in psychology.

Further Readings

Benjamin, L. Durkin, M., Link, M., Vestal, M. et al. (1992). Wundt's American doctoral students. Special Issue: The history of American psychology. *Amer. Psychologist*, 1992, 47, 123-131.

The authors searched the records of the German university where Wundt taught and located the American students who had trained under the father of psychology.

Medick, M. (1991). Currents and futures in American feminist psychology. *Psych. of Women Quart.*, 15, 611-621.

Medick explores intellectual development in feminist psychology, tapping the views of 20 active psychologists.

Bogan, J. (1992). *Seldom seen, rarely heard: Women's place in psychology.* Boulder, CO: West view Press.

This book reviews the history and current status of women in psychology, noting their important contributions to the development of the field.

Burle, A., & Banks, W. (1992). *African American psychology: Theory, research, and practice.* Newbury Park, CA: Sage.

Another important cross-cultural contribution, this book contains a collection of articles from *The Journal of Black Psychology* dealing with important psychological issues for Afro-Americans and studies of Afro-American culture.

Moghaddam, F., Taylor, D., & Wright, S. (1993). *Social psychology in cross-cultural perspective.* NY: Freeman.

This important book deals with the role of culture in social psychology.

Schultz, D. & Schultz, S. (1992). *A history of modern psychology.* Fort Worth: Harcourt.

The Schultzes provide a solid overview of the history of psychology since its beginnings in the late nineteenth century.

Hergenhan, B. (1992). *An introduction to the history of psychology.* Belmont, CA: Wadsworth.

Beginning with the ancient Greek philosophers, this book traces the history of psychology long before it became a separate discipline.

Keys to Psychology 1

1. Psychology originated primarily in 2 other disciplines.
   - A. What they were?
     Philosophy and physiology
   - B. The major ancient Greek philosophers who contributed?
     Socrates, Aristotle, and Plato.
   - C. The major contributors from physiology?
     Helmholtz, Muller, and Fechner

2. Wundt and James were major early contributors.
   - A. Wundt's role?
     Began psychology in Leipzig. Developed introspection.
   - B. James' role?
     First major American psychologist.
     Developed functionalism

3. Several other major American schools of thought are also important.
   - A. What they are?
     Structuralism, behaviorism, and humanism
   - B. The major figures in each?
     Titchener, Watson and Skinner, Rogers

4. Europe also saw several major early developments.
   A. What they were?
      Classical conditioning, psychoanalysis, and Gestalt psychology.

   B. The major figure in each?
      Pavlov, Freud, and Wertheimer

5. Psychology now has two major organizations.
   A. What they are?
      American Psychological Association and American Psychological Society.

   B. Who started APA?
      Hall

6. Applied psychology developed after scientific psychology.
   A. The major events in the history of clinical psychology?
      First psychological clinic in 1896
      World Wars I and II

   B. The other applied areas?
      Counseling, industrial/organizational, health, school.

7. Women made important early contributions to psychology.
   A. The major women contributors?
      Washburn, Ladd-Franklin, Martin, Calkins

8. Psychology recognizes and studies human diversity.
   A. The emphasis regarding cultural factors?
      On individual differences and their effects.

   B. What is wrong with studies of white males by white males?
      Difficult to generalize to other groups.

Key Terms

American Psychological Association
American Psychological Society
classical conditioning
functionalism
introspection
structuralism

Key People

Aristotle
Mary Calkins
Rene' Descartes
Gustav Fechner
Sigmund Freud
Eleanor Gibson
G. Stanley Hall
Hermann von Helmholtz
Leta Hollingsworth
William James

Christine Ladd-Franklin
Lillien Martin
Johannes Muller
Ivan Pavlov
Plato
Socrates
Edward Titchener
Margaret Floy Washburn
John B. Watson
Max Wertheimer
Wilhelm Wundt

Keys to Psychology 2

1. The psychologist's model strongly influences his theory and research.
   - A. The major philosophical issues on which we differ?
     Nature-nurture, hedonism, goal-directedness of behavior, whether behaviors should be broken into components, whether humans are good or evil.
   - B. The major current models?
     Neuroscience, psychodynamic, behavioral, humanistic, and cognitive.

2. The relative emphasis on biology and environment varies with the model.
   - A. Which are more strongly biological?
     Neuroscience, psychoanalytic
   - B. Which are more clearly environmental?
     Behavioral
   - C. Which emphasize both?
     Humanistic, cognitive

Key Terms

behaviorism
Gestalt psychology
humanism
model
psychoanalysis

Key People

Carl Rogers
B. F. Skinner

Keys to Psychology 3

1. Psychology is not a unitary science.
   - A. The major areas?
     Experimental, biological, health, developmental, social, personality, clinical, counseling, industrial/organizational.
   - B. Some additional areas?
     Environmental, school, educational

2. Careers related to psychology occur at several degree levels.
   A. Positions available with a bachelor's degree?
      Psychology technician, psychiatric assistant, research technician, community relations.

   B. What is needed be called a psychologist?
      A doctorate, usually a Ph.D. Licensure is usually also required to perform services.

   C. Options available with a Master's degree?
      Conducting assessments and possibly counseling under supervision.

   D. What psychiatry is?
      A medical specialty requiring an M.D. degree.

Key Terms

psychiatrist
psychologist

Probe 1

Applications of Psychological Research

How To Get an A!

You can learn to be a more effective and successful student by following a number of guidelines derived from psychological research. Those guidelines apply to all five of the major components of college courses: Textbooks, lectures, discussions, laboratory sessions, and examinations. Of course, not all of these components apply to every course, but let's look at each in turn and see what psychology has learned about the more effective approaches.

Reading a Textbook

It does very little good to read a textbook passively or casually, perhaps highlighting a sentence here and there. To better retain what you read and to be an effective student, you must read actively. You must think carefully about the material as you read, constantly ask yourself questions, and make sure that you understand what you are reading. Psychologists have developed a number of methods aimed at more active, effective reading. One of these is called PQRST, an acronym for the five stages it involves: Preview, Question, Read, Self-Recitation, and Test. Let's see how you can use this approach in studying this or any book.

- Preview—If you are reading a chapter, the first step is to preview or look over the material before starting to read in depth. The idea is to get the big picture (Walfish, 2001). In this book, read the Networking overview and Outline that begin each chapter, then go over the Summary at the end of the chapter.
- Question—Leaf through one section of the chapter, noting the main headings and subheadings. Then turn the headings into questions that you think are likely to be answered in the text. Set these lists of questions aside for later use when you study for the exam. You can supplement your own questions by reviewing the questions in the Ask Yourself section at the end of the chapter.
- Read—Carefully read the section, highlighting or otherwise marking important points and attempting to answer the questions you formulated.
- Self-Recitation—Recall the main points made in the section and recite the information, either aloud or subvocally. Such recitation increases comprehension (Loxterman et al., 1994).
- Test—After reading the entire chapter, test yourself. Recall the main facts and see if you understand how they relate to each other. The "Keys To ..." summaries that appear throughout the chapter will be very helpful. Cover the answers and ask yourself the questions.

Beyond the specifics of the PQRST approach, studies show that you retain material better when you first establish an overall context—a big picture—rather than immediately plunging in and reading for detail (Walfish, 2001). In addition, distributed practice is better than massed practice (Krug et al., 1990). Spread your reading and study of the material over time. Chapter 9 presents an alternative to the PQRST method for learning and retaining information that you might want to look over.

Lectures

Some professors give fascinating lectures, others lectures that are—well—not so fascinating. In either case, however, lectures are a central and important part of most college courses, and studies have shown how you can use lectures to learn more and do better in your courses (Appleby, 2002). In fact, students with better lecture notes perform better on examinations (Baker, 2002). There are just a few basic rules:

Read Ahead—Whenever you can, read the relevant material before you hear the lecture. It gives you a frame of reference and makes the lecture more understandable.

Attend Lectures—Research shows that students who regularly attend lectures do significantly better in courses (Baker, 2002). It's simple: You have to be there to get the information and to learn what the professor emphasizes.

Pay Close Attention—It does no good to attend a lecture if you are reading the campus newspaper or the text for another course.

Take Accurate Notes—Good, accurate note-taking is related to better performance on examinations (Baker, 2002). If necessary, ask the professor for help to fill in important gaps in your notes or cross-check with another good student.

Listen Actively, Think Carefully—Madly scribbling down every word that ushers forth from the professor's mouth is not the best approach. Instead, listen to what he says, extract the important meaning from his words, and record that meaning (Spires, 1993). If you find you can't think fast enough to accomplish this, ask permission to tape-record lectures, and take careful notes later. Such note-taking helps you to recall importance material (Appleby, 2002; Sotiriou, 1993).

Ask (Reasonable) Questions—If something is unclear during lecture, ask questions (course size permitting). Most professors appreciate good questions because they also help other students who may need the same clarification. But restrict yourself to asking only a small number of good, reasonable, important questions.

Review and Summarize—After a lecture, review it, be sure you understand it, and summarize it (Appleby, 2002; O'Donnell & Dansereau, 1993). Set your outline aside for use in later exam preparation. Asking yourself questions about the lecture also helps.

Discussion Sessions

Many courses have either separate discussion sections or structured discussions during some or all lecture sessions. As with lectures, it is first important to *attend* these sessions. Some students adopt the inaccurate view that discussions, particularly if conducted by a teaching assistant (TA), are unimportant. However, the TA can often clarify the professor's points or the textbook material, and the discussion is a great opportunity to ask questions (Appleby, 2002). During discussions, it is important to *listen carefully* and *participate actively.* The more active you are, the more you will learn and the better you are likely to do.

Laboratory Sessions

Some courses also have laboratory sessions involving either demonstrations by a TA or active participation in conducting experiments. The rules for maximizing learning are the same as for discussion sessions, with one important addition. You must *understand* the purpose of the experiment, the principles it demonstrates or the points it makes, and its relationship to other course material. Prepare ahead for each session and ask questions as necessary to be certain of your understanding.

Sleep

Yes, sleeping well will also help you to learn more and do better on examinations. Studies show that 73% of students have occasional sleep problems and 15% have chronic problems and generally poor sleep quality. Poor sleep habits and lack of adequate sleep interfere with academic performance (Buboltz et al., 2001). Chapter ___ reviews the literature on good sleep habits and the importance of sleep.

Preparing For Examinations

The best students view exam preparation as a *continuous* process. It begins the first day of the semester and continues through the final exam. It does not take place mainly during the day or two prior to the exam, much less during the "wee hours" of the morning immediately preceding the test (Flippo et al., 2000). Basically, you prepare best by applying all the principles we have discussed for learning the text, lecture, discussion, and laboratory material. In addition:

Plan Ahead—Look at your overall schedule of examinations and other important tasks and plan ahead to make sure you can accomplish all you need to.

Start Early—Even if you are continuously preparing by following the principles we discussed, there comes a time for more concentrated preparation. Start this phase at least a full week before a major exam, by which time you should ideally have completed your reading and basic study of all chapters.

Get Organized—Start by pulling together all the text, lecture, discussion, and laboratory materials related to each chapter.

Determine What Is Important—Trying to learn every detail of every chapter is self-defeating. Pause to identify the most important points in each chapter and focus on these.

Summarize, Summarize, Summarize—Boil your now extensive notes and the reading material down as much as possible, outlining it under the important headings. The headings will serve as brief cues for remembering large amounts of material.

Ask Yourself Questions—Go back to the sets of questions you developed when reading the chapters and ask them again. In this book, review the "Keys To..." and Ask Yourself materials as well, and reread the Summary at the end of the chapter.

To Cram or Not To Cram?—You've always heard that you shouldn't cram for tests, but you also know that many students do it. Although cramming is a bad approach when used alone, some studies show that it can help when you also study in advance and when you study more total hours than non-crammers (Vacha & McBride, 1993).

You might want to read the *Handbook of College Reading and Study Strategy Research* (Lawrence Erlbaum Associates, 2000). It covers a number of topics relating to examinations.

Exam-Taking: TOP SECRET Strategies!

There are some "top secret" principles of examination performance known only to successful, testwise students. Millman defined testwiseness as the ability to use knowledge of the characteristics of tests and the testing process to improve one's performance (Millman, Bishop, & Ebel, 1965). Studies show that more testwise students do better in exams (Appleby, 2002). You can even take a test, the Gibb Experimental Test of Testwiseness, to see how testwise you are (Miller et al., 1990)! Here are the basic principles:

Know Your Stuff—The single most important point is to have a good, solid *knowledge* and understanding of the material being tested.

Schedule Your Time —Look the test over quickly and calculate the time you can afford to spend on each item.

Read Completely—Be sure to read the entire item. Try to answer it before looking at the alternatives so that you will know which is correct.

Eliminate Options—If you don't immediately know the answer, eliminate unlikely options quickly, then choose among the remainder. Your score may well be higher.

Look To Other Items—It is common for information in one item to provide an answer or partial answer to another.

Don't Think Too Much—If you don't know an answer, put down your best guess and come back later if time permits. Mark questions you are most uncertain of so that you can return to them later.

Don't Leave Items Blank—Despite rumors to the contrary, it is to your advantage to guess unless the professor will deduct substantial credit for guessing (Appleby, 2002).

Ask Questions—Ask the professor or TA to clarify an item if necessary.

Review Your Answers—Time permitting, go back over the entire test before turning it in. If you are short on time, concentrate on the difficult items you marked.

CHANGE YOUR ANSWERS—We emphasize this one because the idea that you should never change an answer is so widespread among students and faculty alike. It is a *myth* (Schwarz et al., 1991). Studies show that students change answers from right to wrong about 20% of the time, but change them from wrong to right 58% of the time (Benjamin et al., 1984). Other work shows that 3 points are gained for every 1 lost by changing answers (Geiger, 1991).

Most of the principles for learning new material and performing well on examinations boil down to using very active learning techniques and approaching each task in an intelligent, informed, systematic, organized fashion. The bottom line is that you will work harder but learn more.

The Critical Thinker

As scientists, psychologists apply *critical thinking* to both their work and their everyday lives. Indeed, all effective adults apply critical thinking in their everyday lives, and this important skill is arguably what makes them more effective. As you read this text, we will ask you to think critically in every chapter.

How To Think Critically

Cognitive psychology is basically the study of how people think and reason, a topic we will consider in detail in Chapter 8. One important application of the growing body of research and theory amassed by cognitive psychologists is in the area of critical thinking. *Critical thinking* means carefully examining the evidence underlying claims made by others, as well as the basis for your own ideas (Pithers & Soden, 2000). Put otherwise, it means not blindly accepting contentions, claims, or ideas, but rather first assessing the extent to which they are valid. Questioning, analyzing, judging, evaluating, and using clear logic are all elements of critical thinking (Messer & Griggs, 2002).

Critical thinking is a valuable tool. Every time you turn on the TV set or open a magazine or newspaper, you are deluged with advertisements: "Vitamin Q will make you a sexual dynamo!"; "With Insta-Slim, fat melts away like magic, and you are never hungry!" Likewise, you hear the claims of politicians, insurance salespeople, advocates for a wide range of causes, evangelists, and many others. Do you blindly accept their claims or do you evaluate about them? Scientists usually do not make outrageous claims, but they do develop theories and formulate hypotheses that they believe are correct, and you will read about many of these hypotheses in subsequent chapters. It is just as important that you think critically about scientific hypotheses as about the contentions of advertisers and politicians.

Critical thinking is typically a multi-step process, which begins with the claim to be assessed and ends with a logical conclusion (King, 2002); Millis et al., 1995). Psychologists have conducted considerable research on critical thinking (Royalty, 1994) and developed a number of different models that specify the steps it should involve (Bell, 1991; O'Flahanan & Tierney, 1991; Scott & Markert, 1994; Halonen, 1995). While there is some variation among models, there is general agreement as to what constitutes critical thinking. Moreover, studies have begun to show that it is possible to teach critical thinking skills Æ. Smith, 2002; Ellis, 2001; Allegretti & Frederick, 1995).

In an effort to show you how to think critically about scientific issues in psychology, each of the remaining chapters in this book will apply a five-step critical thinking approach to one hypothesis or issue, with the fond hope that you will apply it to many others. Hypotheses can be of scientific or pseudo-scientific origin, and any given hypothesis or claim can be evaluated by asking yourself a series of five questions:

- **What is the hypothesis or claim?**
  Ask yourself exactly what the scientist or pseudo-scientist is suggesting. Assess the clarity of the hypothesis. Is it clearly and unambiguously stated? Identify the underlying assumptions. What is being assumed to be true in order to formulate the claim? Analyze the arguments made for the hypothesis. How tight and logical are they? As an example, apply your analysis to astrology. One basic claim or pseudo-scientific hypothesis of that field is that an individual's behavior patterns or personality characteristics can be predicted from his astrological sign.

- **How good is the evidence?**
  Ask yourself what evidence is being offered to support the hypothesis, then evaluate that evidence. How credible is it? Is it based on a single study? Multiple studies? No studies? And how scientifically sound are those studies? The astrologer may offer anecdotal evidence for his hypothesis, citing several instances in which an individual's personalty characteristics follow from astrological predictions.

- **Is the evidence open to alternative interpretations?**
  The idea here is to look at the evidence from several different perspectives. Are other interpretations as good as or better than the hypothesis being offered? An important underlying question is whether there is better evidence for some opposing hypothesis than for the one being offered. If so, the hypothesis is considerably weakened. There is a substantial scientific literature showing that personalty characteristics are determined by the individual's genetic inheritance and past experience, beginning in childhood (Chapter 14). This evidence provides an alternative to the explanation offered by astrologers.

- **Do we need additional evidence?**
  Scientists almost always answer "yes" to this question unless the phenomenon being studied is extremely well established. The hypothesis that the earth revolves around the sun, rather than vice versa, is backed by centuries of evidence in the physical sciences, so current scientists are unlikely to say that more evidence is needed. However, we will rarely find instances of a hypothesis in psychology—a much younger science—in which no additional evidence is desirable. Ask yourself in each case what kinds of further evidence would be useful. You might correctly conclude with regard to personality characteristics that anecdotal evidence is not scientific evidence. What is needed to test the relationship between astrological sign and personality is a series of careful studies involving large numbers of people. It turns out that a few such studies have been conducted, and they provide no support at all for the astrological hypothesis (van-Rooij & Jan, 1994; Crowe, 1990; Carlson, 1985).

- **What conclusions can we reach?**
  Here, you are left with your powers of logical deduction. What can best be concluded? That the hypothesis is probably correct? That it is more likely not correct? Or that certain kinds of additional evidence are needed before any final conclusion can be reached? With regard to astrology, you might conclude that there is no scientific evidence to support its claims and that alternative explanations for personality characteristics have been supported by research.

This five-step approach to cases of scientific hypotheses, it can obviously be applied to everyday life as well. The life-insurance salesperson may persuasively claim that you must have more insurance because family disaster will otherwise ensue, that such financial disasters are very common, and that her policy is the best available at the lowest price. You can apply our five-step critical thinking approach to an evaluation of these claims and perhaps avoid buying something you don't need. You will be invited to be THE CRITICAL THINKER about one major issue in each chapter, and we hope you'll think critically about *every* issue.

Chapter 2
The Science of Psychology

Outline

Networking

PSYCHOLOGISTS constantly strive to better understand the causes of human behavior, and this chapter is about the methods we use and the approaches we take. In fact, there is really only one general method that is used by theorists and researchers across disciplines, and that is the scientific method. The virtue of this approach is that it is systematic, orderly, and precise, and it leads over time to an accumulation of increasingly accurate knowledge of the behaviors we study. We will also discuss the major research methods used by psychologists and examine the principles and practices commonly employed to ensure that the outcomes of research are accurate. You may have wondered just how scientific data are collected, analyzed, and reported. We will cover these topics and tell you how to locate and read journal articles. Finally, we will take up some sources of error that can distort the results of research and consider some of the major ethical issues with which psychologists are concerned.

A Leap of Faith

Most of what I remember about the charming little New England town of Orange, Massachusetts, is the small airport at its outskirts. I remember vividly the first time I arrived at that airport. It was a bright, sunny morning in September. A light breeze blew across the airstrip as I parked my car and headed for the small building that housed the office. If I tell you that I approached that building with some trepidation, you will understand when you learn that Orange is no ordinary airport: It is a sport parachuting center, and I had come there to learn to jump.

I tell this story because it is one of anxiety—mine and that of many other people—and anxiety is one of the things psychologists study. We want to know what anxiety is, what causes it, how it affects behavior, how it enters into abnormal behavior, and how it varies from one person and situation to another. My story also deals with a form of behavior, sport parachuting, and we will see that the scientific methods of psychology can be applied to study a number of aspects of this behavior.

My training class that September day consisted of instruction on how to exit the plane, ensure that the chute is functioning properly, and land, and a film showing experienced sport parachutists jumping. The instructor then announced that training was over. My anxiety took a quantum leap as I heard the distinctive sound of a nearby aircraft engine—that of the plane that would carry us to our first jump. The day was clearly just beginning.

I'll complete the story of "the first jump" later in the chapter, but for now think of yourself as a psychologist interested in the study of stress and anxiety. How would you go about assessing my anxiety and that of my companions as we completed training, boarded the plane, and then jumped? How might you design studies to learn something important about anxiety by using the sport parachuting situation and about the causes of sport parachuting as a form of behavior? Before we consider specific methods, however, we need to consider the goals that psychology has set for itself.

The Science of Pscyhology

"The whole of science is nothing more than a refinement of everyday thinking." ALBERT EINSTEIN, *Physics and Reality*, 1936

We all continually make observations about behavior and often come to conclusions based on those observations. In this case, you might observe and talk with some novice sport parachutists, with some who have had a fair number of jumps, and with some who are highly experienced. From what they say, it appears that experienced jumpers have a lower level of anxiety, and you therefore conclude that the major effect of parachuting experience on anxiety is to reduce it. Or you may observe a number of couples and conclude that most consist of two individuals who are very different from each other, thus supporting the old adage that "opposites attract." The basic difference between your personal observations and those of a researcher lie in the fact that your observations and conclusions are casual, whereas those of research scientists are as precise as they can make them. Let's consider just what the scientific method involves, examine the differences between basic and applied science, and outline the goals of psychological science. Finally, we will take up the roles of theory and research in science.

The Scientific Method

Casual observation often leads to inaccurate conclusions because it is not systematic, objective, or precise. In addition, it is usually based on just a few observations and is not cross-checked with observations made by others. Consider the casual, but common, observation that geniuses are "nerds," lacking in social skills and failing in sports. Scientific studies show that precisely the opposite is true: Geniuses have superior social and athletic skills (Terman & Oden, 1959; Lubinsky & Humprhreys, 1992). Similarly, the casual observation note above that "opposites attract" in forming romantic relationships turns out, with scientific study, to be patently wrong (Shaikh & Kanekar, 1994). It is because casual observation so often fails that you hope the surgeon standing over your anesthetized body, the engineer who designed the bridge beneath your car, and the physicist developing safety devices for nuclear bombs are not basing their work on a few brief observations but rather on scientific data.

The *scientific method* assumes that events follow lawful causal principles and uses objective, systematic observation to determine what those principles are (Hayes, 2002). Isaac Newton observed that an apple released from a tree falls to the ground. To explain his observation, he formulated the law of gravity, a general principle that explains why objects fall. Psychologists seek similar laws that explain the basis for behavior. They conduct scientific research to determine the causes of various behaviors, and we will see the results of that research throughout this book.

The scientific approach has several specific advantages over casual observation and personal experience:

- ***Science is systematic, formal, and objective.* Scientists seldom make casual observations. Rather, they follow a** set of rules that maintain a high degree of scientific formality and require that the scientist be as objective as possible in both designing studies and interpreting the results.

- *Science strives for simplicity and order.* Science insists that there is order to the universe. Physical scientists expect to find orderly movements of the planets and orderly arrangements of atoms and molecules. Behavioral scientists expect to find order in behavior.
- *Science is precise.* Science insists on careful measurement and on quantifying observations. Such precision is well worth the effort and time. In the long run, the scientific knowledge gained through precision will be of much greater value.
- *Scientific knowledge is repeatable.* Scientific studies are conducted in such a way that other scientists can follow the same procedures to see whether they arrive at the same results. Such replication—repetition of the research—ensures that results are carefully checked and thus more likely to be accurate and meaningful.
- *Science provides cumulative knowledge.* The results of scientific experiments are published in books and journals and taught to future scientists. In this way, scientific knowledge accumulates over time, with new information and ideas building upon an existing foundation.

We should hasten to note that science and scientists are by no means perfect. The highly trained surgeon with all her scientific data can still fail to cure your disease; the engineer's bridge will occasionally collapse; and the physicist cannot be absolutely certain that his nuclear safety device is fail-safe. Science is not perfect, but it is far superior to casual observation.

Basic and Applied Science

Scientific research is of two types, basic and applied. Basic research is research that addresses an important issue or problem but has no immediate practical consequences. A scientist like B.F. Skinner might believe that he can discover something about how behavior occurs by teaching pigeons to fly figure eights in a green-lit room (see Chapter 6). The immediate, practical application of such a study may not be at all obvious, even to the scientist doing it.

Applied research is research designed to deal with an immediate, practical problem that needs a solution. Psychologists are working hard, for example, to find ways of preventing and treating drug addiction, alcoholism, and a host of other psychological disorders (see Chapter 5 and 16).

Both basic and applied research are important. In the case of applied research, the benefits are usually obvious. The research may result in a more effective treatment for alcoholism or a way to increase worker productivity in an industrial plant. The virtues of basic research are perhaps less obvious, simply because there are no immediate benefits. However, basic research is essential because it provides background knowledge that will eventually be needed in order to develop practical applications.

The basic research of Skinner and his colleagues has led to many practical applications, such as the development of behavior modification therapies and teaching machines, as well as the use of pigeons to select imperfect drug capsules on an assembly line, spot lifeboats at sea, and guide missiles. Basic research on sources and effects of stress has been applied to the development of techniques to treat stress-related hypertension (Albright et al., 1991) and migraine headache (Blanchard et al., 1991). Research on sexual physiology and psychology has served as a basis for developing greatly improved treatments for sexual dysfunctions (Wilson & Wilson, 1991). And one very practical result of basic cognitive research on how humans think has been the use of artificial intelligence (AI) techniques to develop expert systems that help psychologists and physicians make more accurate diagnoses (Sumner & Schultz, 1992; Scott, 1993).

The Goals of Scientific Psychology

Consider these varied events:

- An otherwise quite normal person exhibits significant memory impairment and cannot retain newly learned material.
- The productivity of a group of workers decreases significantly over a six-month period.
- A man listens to a speech by a candidate for senator and decides to vote for her.
- A woman hears voices that tell her she is evil and is doomed to Hell.

Each of these complex behaviors, like the decision to try sport parachuting, has a *cause*—a specific reason or set of reasons why it occurred. The principal goal of psychology is to discover and understand such causes. The nature-nurture question, for example, asks to what extent a given behavior is caused by biological and to what extent by environmental factors (Chapter 1)? As they strive to determine causation, psychologists seek to attain the major goals of scientific psychology: to accurately *describe*, *predict*, and *control* behavior and to *apply* what they have learned to real-life situations. As these subgoals are achieved, they move toward the broader goal of *understanding* (see Figure 2-1).

Description. Tom was "sweating bullets" as he boarded the plane for his first jump and couldn't understand why Mark was so calm. After landing safely, Tom got a negative evaluation on his jump technique from the instructor, while Mark's evaluation was quite positive. Why did the anxious Tom do poorly and the calmer Mark do well? The first step in answering such a question is to *describe* what has happened. We can describe parachuting performance objectively by breaking it down into specific correct and incorrect actions, then counting the number of correct behaviors. Anxiety may be a bit more difficult. We might ask our *subjects* or *participants*—the people whose behavior we are studying—to rate their anxiety on a scale from 1 (not at all anxious) to 7 (extremely anxious). Alternatively, we might have their anxiety rated by trained observers or we might measure heart rate, breathing, and other physiological indicators. Each of these procedures would provide relatively objective information and allow us to arrive at a description of the relationship between anxiety level and jump performance.

The description we arrive at must include only *objectively observable* behaviors. The idea at this stage is to describe what we see or hear, not to infer or assume the existence or involvement of any internal processes that cannot be directly examined.

Prediction. Description allows us to comment on behavior that has already occurred, but psychologists often want to be able to look ahead and predict a behavior before it occurs. A *prediction* is a statement of expectation that a particular event will occur. It is grounded in prior observations and may be based on some overall explanation of certain aspects of behavior. Some people who take a parachute training class later refuse to jump out of a plane. If we could predict that result in advance, we could save the individual the time, trouble, and cost of taking the class.

But you don't have be a scientist to make predictions. We all use these statements of expectation every day. You predict that it will take you 15 minutes to get from home to your class or that eight hours of study will get you an 'A' on a particular exam.

In science, a prediction made about a particular type or instance of behavior is called a hypothesis. A *hypothesis* is a clear, specific proposition that can be tested to determine whether or not it is true. You might hypothesize that the person you are about to ask out on a date will accept your invitation. Similarly, having observed Tom and Mark, we might hypothesize that anxiety interferes with good sport parachuting performance.

Control. We *control* a behavior when we know how to cause that behavior to occur at will. The ability to control a behavior brings us substantially closer to the broader goal of understanding it. We know, for example, how to control the flow of electricity by flipping a light switch.

A good example of behavior control in psychology comes from experiments begun in the 1930s by American psychologist B.F. Skinner and his colleagues. They used *reinforcers*—rewards from the external environment—to control behavior, even fairly complex behavior. For instance, they could teach a pigeon to fly back and forth across a room when a red light is on and to fly in a figure-eight pattern when the illumination is green. They had established control over the behavior of their experimental participants. Using the same basic principles, a behavior therapist can treat a person with a very strong fear of flying so that she will be able to travel on airplanes.

Application. The goal of *application* refers to the use of knowledge and techniques derived from research to accomplish some practical purpose. If you have ever had psychotherapy, used a computer program that teaches you math, or taken an aptitude test like the SAT, you have experienced one of the many benefits derived from psychological research.

Research results on the effects of stress on the body have become important in health care. In law, research on mental disorders is used to determine the mental competency of defendants in criminal cases. Studies of memory are used by attorneys in cross-examining eyewitnesses to crimes. In the community, research findings on the effects of environmental factors like noise and crowding are used by urban planners and architects to design better environments. And in numerous other ways, the results of psychological investigations have found useful applications in our lives.

Understanding. Description, prediction, control, application—none of these alone gives us knowledge of the underlying causes of behavior, but together they may contribute to the development of full understanding. *Understanding* means that we have achieved accurate insights into the underlying *causes* of a behavior. Medicine, for example, understands how infections by specific microorganisms cause specific diseases, as when the streptococcus bacillus causes a "strep" throat. The secret to scientific understanding lies in the careful development of theory and the meticulous conduct of systematic research, often over a considerable period of time. In psychology, a true understanding of underlying causes is thus far rare, but we will achieve that understanding through continued scientific work.

The Roles of Theory and Research

In order to achieve the goals of psychology, we apply the scientific method to each aspect of behavior and underlying mental processes we study. We engage in research and develop scientific theories.

Scientific Research. Research is a process of inquiry or investigation in which scientists use careful, precise observation to arrive at a better understanding of some phenomenon. The observations made in conducting research take a variety of forms, depending on the purpose of the research, but they must be as meticulous as the psychologist can make them. A social psychologist interested in whether opposites attract might design a piece of research—a *study* —in which he attempts to control all relevant factors that might influence the results. He would conduct his study by collecting information from a set of subjects (participants), carrying out a statistical analysis of this information, and reaching a set of conclusions as to whether or not opposites attract.

Rarely is research a simple matter of conducting a single study to arrive at some final conclusion. Rather, scientists must systematically replicate their work to assure that the results are consistent. Research in any field is therefore an ongoing process that is carried out in many different settings by many different scientists.

Scientific Theory. To further understand how people are attracted to each other, the social psychologist might develop a theory of interpersonal attraction. A *theory* is an organized set of concepts and propositions designed to help scientists account for, predict and explain some set of phenomena. As a potential theorist, consider these observations: Obese people often eat no more than people of average weight; they regain weight quickly after losing it; and they usually have biological relatives who are overweight. Such observations led scientists to develop the theory that obesity is partially genetic (Cardon et al., 1994). On a larger scale, Darwin's theory of evolution helps us understand the biological relationships among animal species, and Freud's psychoanalytic theory explains how unconscious factors influence behavior (Chapter 1). The social psychologist studying factors in interpersonal attraction might find that successful relationships are more likely when the partners are quite similar in a number of important characteristics and incorporate this observation into a more general theory of interpersonal attraction.

Once we have a theory, we can derive hypotheses from that theory and subject them to testing through scientific research. The genetic theory of obesity might lead to the hypothesis that obesity is more likely to be seen in both members of a pair of identical twins (who are genetic duplicates of each other) than it is in both members of a pair of fraternal twins (who are genetically much less similar). The genetic theory of obesity might lead to the hypothesis that obesity is more likely to be seen in both members of a pair of identical twins than it is in both members of a pair of fraternal twins. The attraction theory might produce the hypothesis that similarity in attitudes and preferences increases the probability of attraction between two people. The theory will also include hypotheses about additional factors that might contribute to attraction.

All theories are not created equal. Some are far better than others. A good theory has four important characteristics:

- It incorporates into a consistent, logical framework what is already known all the existing facts and observations.
- It produces new hypotheses and thereby predicts new observations.
- It adheres to the *law of parsimony,* which says that the theory should be as simple as possible while still fully accounting for the phenomena it deals with.
- It is testable and falsifiable. That is, its hypotheses can be tested in the scientific laboratory and can potentially be shown to be false. Some theories are so vague and general that they seem to fit all observations and hence cannot be falsified. Astrology—the theory that behavior and events can be predicted from an individual's astrological sign—is a good example (van-Rooij & Jan, 1994). These are not good theories.

The Interplay of Theory and Research. Once a scientist has developed a good theory that deals with important phenomena, it can lead to a considerable amount of research. Every scientific field has such powerful theories. Well-known examples in other fields are the theories of Isaac Newton and Albert Einstein in physics, Darwin in biology, and Margaret Mead in anthropology. As you study psychology, you will see that there are major theorists in virtually every area: B.F. Skinner in learning; Freud in abnormal and clinical psychology; Jean Piaget in developmental psychology; Hermann von Helmholtz in sensation and perception; Leon Festinger in social psychology. You may not recognize quite all these names now, but as you read other chapters, you will see that each developed a theory that generated large amounts of research.

The results of research on a given theory typically lead to modifications of that theory, and the modified theory leads to further research. This cycle of theory and research, each building on the other, gradually increases the scope and accuracy of our scientific knowledge (see Figure 2-2). Even inaccurate theories are valuable if they lead to careful research, because they at least eliminate some possible explanations and may stimulate new research and the development of more accurate theories.

Why Bother? Why should we go to all the trouble and expense of formulating scientific theories and conducting research? Is all the work worthwhile? You bet! Consider the concept of biorhythms—recurring biological cycles, such as the sleep cycle and the menstrual cycle. Biorhythm theory suggests that a number of regularly recurring biological rhythms influence your performance on nearly any task. Performance is supposed to be systematically affected by highs and lows in your cycles.

Biorhythm theory may sound quite reasonable and scientific, but it isn't. It was based on casual observation and anecdotal examples that seemed to confirm the prediction. It appeared, for example, that heavyweight champion Muhammad Ali successfully defended his title when two of his important biorhythms were on the rise. However, when scientists undertook careful studies, they found no relationship between biorhythms and performance in any of a variety of areas (Bradshaw, 1982). Rising cycles do not predict good performance on examinations or in sporting events, and people are no more likely to perform poorly in these areas or to undergo a more difficult recovery from surgery when their cycles are at the lowest points. Nevertheless, the scientifically unsupported biorhythm theory has sold many books and computer programs! Yes, science is worthwhile.

Keys to Psychological Research 1

Research Methods

My sport-parachuting companions and I boarded the plane, which carried us to 3000 feet. There, the instructor designated a jumping order (I was Number 5), and our anxieties peaked as we moved, one at a time, to the door of the plane to push off into space. How can we study this anxiety and the behaviors associated with it? Psychologists use two principal methods. One is experimental in nature; the other is descriptive or correlational in nature. Each method, when properly applied, provides a basis for scientific observation. However, the kinds of observations that can be made and the kinds of conclusions that can be drawn vary considerably from one method to another.

The Experimental Method

The real backbone of psychological research is the *experiment*—a research method involving the manipulation of one or more variables under carefully controlled conditions and the measurement of its effects on one or more other variables. Properly carried out, such an experiment allows the researcher to determine actual *cause-effect relationships.* A recent example of applying the experimental method is a study in which each of 37 participants "drove" a driving simulator four times. On some drives they were randomly assigned to use a cell phone, on others not. Results showed that use of a cell phone was distracting and caused poorer driving performance. However, the authors also found that drivers slowed down to compensate when using cell phones and that the overall number of collisions was not affected by phone use (Haigney et al., 2000).

In experimental research, the investigator systematically varies conditions and records the effects of these variations on behavior. The conditions that can be changed in an experiment are called *variables,* as described above. Variables can be characteristics in which participants differ, such as age or gender, measures that can yield different values, such as the scores on a test, or situations that differ.

Variables that are set, changed, or otherwise manipulated by the experimenter are called *independent variables;* those measured to see whether they change as a result of experimental manipulations are called *dependent variables.* Dependent variables are so called because they *depend* on levels of or changes in the independent variables. A third type of variable is the *intervening variable,* which represents the researcher's hypothesis or best guess as to what it is that connects the independent variable with the dependent variable. Typically, an intervening variable is a hypothesized internal process, such as anxiety, depression, or thought.

The Use of Controls. In many experimental studies, participants are divided into two kinds of groups called experimental and control groups. In the simplest case, *experimental groups* are those that receive the treatment being studied and *control groups* are those that are otherwise identical to the experimental groups, but do not receive the treatment. The purpose of the control group is to assure that changes in behavior are, in fact, the result of manipulation of the independent variable. A study of the effects of a stressor on behavior might have an experimental group that receives the stressor and a control group that does not. In more complex studies, there may be two or more experimental and one or more control groups. We might have three levels of stress (low, medium, high), each administered to a different experimental group, and a no-stress condition administered to a control group.

The use of control groups allows us to reach firm causal conclusions. Suppose we simply place a group of participants under stress and observe some change in their behavior. Was the change due to stress or perhaps just to the passage of time? We cannot be certain that the behavior would not have changed even without the stress. If, on the other hand, the behavior of an experimental (stress) group changes and that of a control (no stress) group does not, we can conclude that stress caused the change.

To understand how experiments work, let's look at an example of an actual controlled experiment conducted by Hiroto (1974). This experiment was devised to test Martin Seligman's theory of *learned helplessness.* According to Seligman (1975; Nolen, Girgus, & Seligman, 1992), people who come to believe that their actions have little or no effect on what happens to them develop a feeling of helplessness that permeates their lives and may lead to depression (Chapter 16).

Hiroto tested Seligman's theory by assigning college students to one of three groups. The first two groups were *experimental groups.* In one of these, called the Escape Condition, the student heard a loud noise and could turn it off by pushing a button. In the other group, the No Escape Condition, the students heard the noise but could not stop it.

The third group was a *control group* that did not hear the noise at all (Figure 2-3). Assignment to experimental and control groups was done at random or by chance, a procedure we will discuss shortly.

In the next phase of the experiment all three groups again heard the loud noise sounded repeatedly. However, if the participants could learn to respond to a light signal by moving their hands from one side of a box to the other, they could escape the noise. Hiroto measured how long it took them to make this response. Participants in the Escape Condition and those in the control group quickly learned to move their hands to stop the painful noise. Those in the No Escape Condition— the ones who had been unable to stop the noise earlier—were slower to make the escape response when they made it at all. Hiroto's results, which are depicted in Figure 2-4, were interpreted as showing that being helpless in one situation (being unable to escape) caused participants to learn helplessness and therefore respond less adequately in other situations.

In this study, the *independent variable* was the ability to escape or not escape the noise in the first phase of the experiment; the *dependent variable* was the lag or "latency" of the hand- movement response—the amount of time subjects took to make a hand movement in the second phase of the experiment. The *intervening variable* was learned helplessness, a feeling that the researchers thought caused the participants to fail to try to stop the painful noise.

To assure that the results of an experiment like Hiroto's are accurate, the experimenter must be certain that his measurements are precise and that he has adequately controlled any variable that might possibly affect the results. Depending on the nature of the experiment, such factors as instructions, room lighting, temperature, and the recording of responses may need to be handled with precision and care. When all potentially influential variables have been carefully controlled, it is possible to draw cause- effect conclusions from the experiment.

Why do we need controls in an experiment? A good example is provided by the ongoing attempt to find better ways of lowering cholesterol. You might find a book advocating a diet that consists mostly of cottage cheese and water. The authors say they put 25 subjects on this diet for 30 days and observed that their cholesterol levels had decreased. This study, however, actually does *not* prove that the cottage cheese-water diet lowers cholesterol. At the very least, they would have needed a control group on some other diet to prove that this diet reduced cholesterol levels *relative to the other diets*. In the absence of such control data, it is entirely possible that cholesterol levels dropped for some reason unrelated to the diet, such as consuming fewer calories. By contrast to this fictional study, consider an investigation in which each of 72 healthy women was randomly assigned to one of two groups. Members of the experimental group ate a diet with only 15% fat (far lower than the normal American diet), while control group members ate their usual diets. After one year on these diets, the experimental group had significantly lower cholesterol levels than the control group (Kasim et al., 1993). Unlike the cottage cheese-water study, this study *does* demonstrate that lowering fat intake lowers cholesterol level.

Representative and Random Samples. Virtually all forms of research require that we obtain one or more groups of participants from whom we will collect data. We typically cannot test the entire population we might be interested in, such as all U.S. college students, all married women, or all men between the ages of 25 and 60. As a result, we must obtain a *sample*—a small number of people from a much larger population. The basic requirement is that the sample we draw must be *representative* of some population, meaning that it must have the same relevant characteristics as that population. If we want our results to apply to all middle-class women, our entire sample must consist entirely of middle-class women. Sometimes the population of which our sample is to be representative is not entirely obvious. There are many differences, for example, between men and women, between college students and the older population, and among people of differing cultural backgrounds. If we conduct a study of aggressive behavior in men, we can't be certain that the results will generalize to women. Studies of drug and alcohol use in college students would probably not generalize well to an older population. And research on family structure and child-rearing practices in the United States might not generalize to Eastern European countries. The implications of population diversity and its study are addressed in our 21 for this chapter.

The sample we use must also be *unbiased*, meaning that it contains equal proportions of participants with important differential characteristics. If, for example, we are trying to sample all men between ages 25 and 60 and we end up with 90% of the sample between ages 25 and 30, we have a biased sample. To obtain unbiased samples, we usually sample randomly from the population. A *random sample* is one that is drawn in an unbiased way from a specified population. In an experiment, we also place our participants randomly into the various experimental and control groups involved in the study. This unbiased way of placing people into the conditions in the study is called *random assignment*. We have already seen the use of random assignment in the Hiroto experiment, where subjects were placed randomly into the experimental and control groups. Suppose Hiroto had assigned only women to the Escape Condition in his study and only men to the No Escape condition—an example of nonrandom or biased assignment. If his results had then shown a difference in performance between participants in these two conditions, he would not have known whether the condition difference or the gender difference was responsible.

How do we draw random samples or make random assignments? We could toss a coin or draw numbers out of a hat. These approaches may be adequate, but there is always some chance of bias, as happens when a coin is weighted to more often turn up heads than tails. To reduce the potential for bias, we usually use a table of random numbers or a computer program that generates random numbers (Figure 2-5). We can then be quite certain that our assignments are unbiased.

When we are selecting subjects for a study, even random sampling does not always ensure that the sample will meet the most important criterion—representativeness. As a result, researchers sometimes resort to stratified sampling. A *stratified random sample* is one in which separate samples are randomly drawn from each of several subpopulations in order to assure that the overall sample is representative of the population of interest. Stratification is used because the population contains several subgroups defined on the basis of some crucial characteristic, such as age, gender, or socioeconomic level. In doing a political survey, for example, we might believe that political preferences are strongly influenced by age. Therefore we may use age to stratify our sample. If 15% of voters are between ages 21 and 25, we would want to ensure that 15% of our stratified random sample is in that age range. Figure 2-6 shows the steps followed in a typical experimental study.

The Quasi-Experiment. A *quasi-experiment* is one in which psychologists study independent variables that they cannot readily control or manipulate. Such independent variables are often called *natural* variables because they are based on pre-existing conditions. Gender, for example, is a natural or quasi-experimental variable. We can study differences between males and females, but we cannot manipulate gender; we cannot cause one person to be female and another male.

Another example is the study of the effects of front line combat stress on the body. You cannot ethically manipulate combat stress by randomly assigning some individuals to the front line and others to desk jobs. But you can measure the effects on the body of stress experienced by those who happen to be in front line combat and compare them with those who happen to be assigned to desk jobs. What you have done is a *quasi-experiment.* It is important to realize that this is not a *true* experiment because you do not manipulate the independent variable. Don't be confused by the fact that the term "experiment" is used here.

Our sport parachuting situation is a quasi-experiment. As experimenters, we do not decide who will parachute and who will not, and we are thus not manipulating the situation but rather measuring the effects of parachuting on anxiety in a group of people who choose to parachute. Seymour Epstein and Walter Fenz (1965) conducted a series of studies in which they examined changes in anxiety over time in experienced and inexperienced parachutists. In one experiment they tested two groups of parachutists, one with little or no sport parachuting experience and another with more than 100 jumps. Each group was tested for self- ratings of anxiety at a number of points prior to the jump and just after landing. The independent variable was prior experience in sport parachuting, the dependent variable was self- rated anxiety. Figure 2-7 shows some of the results of this study. Notice that the investigators did not actually manipulate prior experience, making this a quasi-experiment.

The inexperienced parachutists felt most anxious shortly before jumping. Interestingly enough, however, experienced parachutists reported their highest anxiety well before the jump (that morning), then became calmer as they approached the jump. The reduction in anxiety allowed them to concentrate on performing the jump correctly, a finding that has received further attention in more recent research (Schedlowski & Tewes, 1992). Although we do not actually manipulate the independent variable in a quasi-experiment like this one, it is reasonable to assume that the two groups are quite comparable on variables other than sport-parachuting experience (Graziano & Raulin, 1993). We still cannot draw strong cause-effect conclusions as we can when we manipulate the independent variable, but we can be fairly confident in our results.

Combining Quasi-Experimental And Manipulated Variables.

Many experiments in psychology combine natural variables with manipulated variables. An example is a study conducted in my laboratories and described in Probe 1. The natural or quasi-experimental variable in the study was extraversion- introversion, meaning basically how outgoing a person is. Since the experimenter did not cause the participants to be more or less extraverted, the variable is natural, not manipulated. The manipulated experimental variable was the administration of caffeine. Each introvert and extravert was randomly assigned to one of the four conditions in the experiment. A *condition* is simply an experimental situation created by the researcher and imposed on the participant through manipulation (usually random assignment). In this case, the experimenters decided to use three drug dosages and a placebo. These constituted the conditions, and they imposed them on the participants by randomly assigning each to one of the four. Put otherwise, they manipulated the drug dosage variable through random assignment of subjects to the various drug conditions.

Since manipulated variables permit true cause-effect conclusions and caffeine dosage was manipulated, we were able to draw causal implications regarding any result involving drug dosage alone. It turned out, for example, that when data were examined across the groups studied, the higher the caffeine dosage, the higher the physiological arousal. This result means that caffeine does, in fact, *cause* an increase in physiological arousal. Results involving the quasi-experimental introversion-extraversion variable, however, do not allow us to reach such strong cause-effect conclusions. You can find a full coverage of experimental methods in a recent book devoted entirely to that topic (Myers & Hansen 2002).

Descriptive and Correlational Methods

Alternatives to the experimental method include the descriptive and correlational methods, which can be collectively referred to as nonexperimental methods. A *nonexperimental* method is one in which behavior is observed and measured but not controlled or manipulated. Such methods are often used to accomplish the goals of description and prediction, and they permit us to carefully examine and precisely describe a variety of behaviors. They also provide us with a basis for making predictions concerning cause-effect relationships (Figure 2-8). The most commonly used nonexperimental methods include case studies, surveys, and naturalistic observation. We will discuss each of these, consider how they are applied, and then describe correlational designs.

The Case Study. A *case study* is an in- depth analysis of the behavior of a single person, whose thoughts, emotions, personality, attitudes, and life history are subjected to careful, detailed scrutiny. It is a scientific biography that probes the depths of the individual in an effort to better understand her behavior and its origins.

Case studies are useful because they give psychologists valuable insights into single individuals and can provide a basis for hypotheses about behavior more generally. For example, on the basis of a single case, that of a boy called Little Hans, Sigmund Freud formulated some of his hypotheses concerning the causes of a psychological disorder called phobia. Similarly, developmental psychologist Jean Piaget based his theory of development on case observations of his own children. However, because a case study provides us with information about only one person, it can never serve as a basis for firm, broad conclusions. It would be impossible on the basis of the Hans case alone, for instance, to determine whether Freud's hypotheses were correct.

The Survey. A *survey* is a device used to assess and predict the views, reactions, or standings of a large number of people on a limited topic. The researcher develops a list of questions and presents them in a standardized way to each participant, typically using either interviews or questionnaires. Survey studies often involve a relatively small number of people, sometimes one percent or less of a large population, with the goal of generalizing the findings to that larger population. We might, for example, survey 2000 married, middle-class women in order to assess the views on abortion of all married, middle-class women. Another good example is the political survey, including the vote count on election day:

"With 1 percent of the vote counted, CBS projects Clinton the winner,"

says Dan Rather. His colleagues on other networks make similar projections, usually accurate but always based on very small percentages of the vote.

Surveys have both advantages and disadvantages as research techniques. On the positive side of the ledger, a carefully designed and conducted survey can give us a substantial amount of information about the views, attitudes, opinions, or preferences of a large number of people. This information can help psychologists formulate hypotheses, politicians develop campaign strategies, and community planners decide where to locate the new incinerator or football stadium.

At the same time, we can arrive at incorrect conclusions if the people we survey are not very representative of the larger group or if they are reluctant to give us the information we need. Some survey participants, for example, may report what they think the researcher wants to hear or what seems "politically correct," rather than what they really believe. Some women in the abortion survey, knowing that the topic is both emotionally and politically loaded, might give what they consider the most acceptable answers, rather than the most accurate ones. In addition, participants may display a *self-report bias*, a tendency to give a positive impression of themselves, which can also make findings inaccurate. Results depend, in addition, on the specific wording of the questions. If you ask respondents the question: "Is abortion right or is it wrong?," those whose true belief is that it is right under certain circumstances and wrong under others will not be able to express that view, and your results will be distorted. A further limitation of surveys is that they are an indication of public opinion only for a specific point in time. Attitudes toward the space shuttle program changed dramatically, for example, after *Challenger* exploded in 1986 and again after a series of mishaps in 1993; public opinion polls taken before these disasters and mishaps would clearly have been an inaccurate representation of opinions afterward.

These various problems with surveys sometimes mean that the results will be off target. For instance, political polls, though often quite accurate, have been notorious for their classic failures. In 1936 the results of a telephone poll indicated that Alf Landon would win the presidency. However, it turned out that the sample was biased because at that time telephones were found largely in the homes of the well- to- do, who tended to be Republicans; Democrat Franklin D. Roosevelt won by a comfortable margin.

Naturalistic Observation. In *naturalistic observation*, the psychologist observes some naturally occurring behavior without attempting to modify or interfere with that behavior. Such observations can be conducted in the laboratory as well as the field. Next time you're in the Student Union, pick out some people you would judge to be very attractive, some of average attractiveness, and some who are unattractive. Do the attractive people seem to be happier (smile and laugh more)? Do they have more people with them? Are they more likely to be with a member of the opposite sex? Do they attract more attention from passers- by? Whatever your conclusions, you are conducting a naturalistic observation.

Other examples are seen in work with animals and children. Jane Goodall is well known for her observation of the behavior of chimpanzees in their natural environment. In a laboratory setting, we might sit behind one- way glass and observe a child trying to solve a puzzle or a group of children at play. In each case, we would decide in advance what kinds of behaviors we wanted to focus on, then make detailed recordings of our observations. In the case of children at play, our focus might be the effects of aggression. Will an aggressive child become more dominant? Be rejected? Elicit aggression from other children? Disrupt group play? Observing a number of instances of aggression and its effects may provide valuable information that could potentially be generalized to other situations.

Like other approaches, naturalistic observation has advantages and disadvantages. The principal advantage is that it permits scientific assessment of naturally occurring behavior. The principal disadvantage is that it is very difficult to be totally objective and hard not to interfere with the behavior being observed. A good example is the work of Margaret Mead, the famous anthropologist who studied adolescents on the South Sea island of Samoa and reported her observations in the 1928 book *Coming of Age in Samoa.* She concluded that Samoan culture was characterized by very low levels of competitiveness and violence and that the youth of Samoa were free of most of the problems and guilt that accompany American adolescence. Many years later, another anthropologist, Derek Freeman, challenged Mead's conclusions, suggesting that the Samoans had deceived Mead by allowing her to see only a limited sample of their behavior. Freeman observed that Samoan adolescents were often quite violent and competitive, showing high rates of suicide, sexual offenses, and delinquency (Freeman, 1983). Different scientists, each attempting to conduct careful naturalistic observations, reached quite different conclusions.

Applying The Nonexperimental Methods. What you already know about my first jump experience is at least the beginning of a case study. A psychologist might choose to conduct a more in- depth study by carefully assessing my anxiety level, the range of my emotions and cognitions relating to the jump, and aspects of my personality and attitudes that might relate to my reactions to jumping. *Naturalistic observation* would come into play if a team of psychologists decided to observe the behaviors of sport parachutists, perhaps accompanying them through training and jumping. Finally, a parachute manufacturing company interested in promoting the sport might decide to conduct a survey of a random sample from the population of middle- income Americans to examine their attitudes toward parachuting as a basis for attracting more people into the sport.

Correlational Research. Often we want to go beyond simple description to determine the relationship between two variables that we are interested in. A *variable* is any characteristic that can take on several different values. When we measure anxiety in sport parachutists, for example, it can take on values ranging from low to high. A *correlation* indicates the degree of relationship between two variables. We can, for example, calculate a correlation between our measure of anxiety and our measure of performance (number of correct behaviors) in the parachuting study. In the attraction study the members of each couple might be asked to indicate their degree of satisfaction with the relationship on a scale of 1 (not at all satisfied) to 7 (extremely satisfied). These results can then be correlated with the data on age differences to see whether there is a relationship. Suppose we found a correlation between age similarity and satisfaction: couples more similar in age report higher marital satisfaction. Would we then be able to conclude that greater age similarity causes greater marital satisfaction? The answer is no. Correlation can never tell us anything about cause and effect because we have done nothing to manipulate or control either variable. We will see shortly why manipulation is necessary if we are to make causal statements.

If correlations do not provide an indication of cause- effect relations, what good are they? The answer is that they often show us where we should look for such relationships. The earliest studies on cigarette smoking, for example, showed only that there was a correlation between smoking cigarettes and having lung cancer: People who smoked were more likely to develop the disease. This correlation sent researchers off to animal laboratories, where they were able to conduct cause- effect studies by systematically exposing animals to smoke or its components to discover the true nature of the relationship. (Correlation is explained in more detail in the appendix).

Keys to Psychological Research 2

Principles and Practices in Scientific Research

The more objective science can be, the more accurate will be its conclusions. Researchers therefore follow a number of general principles and common practices that cut across a variety of forms of both nonexperimental and experimental research. These principles are applied in an effort to assure that the results of the research are scientifically sound. Some of the major principles and practices include reliability and validity, standardization, generalization, operational definition, sampling procedures, generalization, replication, and the programmatic conduct of research (Table 2-1).

Reliability and Validity.

Findings based on an experiment or psychological test are useless if they are not reliable. Basically, *reliability* means consistency or stability. In controlled experiments, results are reliable if they can be repeated in other experiments.

Psychological tests are reliable if the score of a given participant remains reasonably stable over time. This is called *test/retest reliability*. A test of extraversion/introversion would be unreliable, for example, if the same individual came out as an extravert on one occasion and an introvert on another. Establishing the reliability of a test in advance works to ensure that this situation will not arise.

We also have to make certain that the results of our studies are valid. *Validity* is the extent to which a measure, a procedure, or a study does what it is supposed to do. A test that is supposed to measure extraversion/introversion has validity to the extent that it does accurately measure that construct. A study of the effects of caffeine on behavior is valid to the extent that it actually does measure the effects of caffeine. If any aspect of the experiment—something extraneous to the drug and other variables controlled in the study—affects the dependent variable, the results will be less valid. That is why researchers work hard to be certain that every study is done in a valid way and that every measure is a valid measure. We have more to say about both validity and reliability in Chapter 9.

Standardization

Standardization means that every aspect of an experiment is applied in a consistent, uniform manner to every participant. The experimental conditions are the same for each participant (unless there is a planned, systematic variation), and the data collection procedure never varies. In the study described in Probe 1, for example, every subject took the same test to determine introversion-extraversion, and the instructions, timing, and other aspects of testing were identical for all participants. It also means that caffeine doses were measured and administered in exactly the same way for all.

Generalization

A broad goal of psychological science is to formulate general principles of behavior, principles that *generalize* beyond the sample we have studied. The results of Hiroto's learned helplessness study would be of little use if they applied only to the students who served as his subjects. We would want the results to generalize to all U.S. college students and ideally to a much broader population. Using random, representative samples helps us to generalize. However, we also have to perform statistical calculations to demonstrate that any observed difference or relationship is extremely unlikely to have occurred by chance, a topic we will take up in more detail shortly.

Operational Definition

Every variable in an experiment must be carefully and clearly defined if we are to reach valid conclusions concerning that variable. In order to arrive at such precise specifications, the researcher much operationally define each variable used in the study. An *operational definition* is one that specifies the procedures or operations used to manipulate, control, or measure a variable. The Eysenck Personality Inventory (Eysenck & Eysenck, 1968), for example, is a test developed to measure extraversion/introversion; scores on this scale provided the operational definition of that variable in the extraversion-introversion study. Another example of a variable requiring operational definitions is hunger, a subjective term referring to some sort of internal condition. To define it operationally, we might simply say that a rat is "hungry" when it has been deprived of food for 36 hours. Operational definitions are essential because they permit the experimenter to reduce subjectivity and to report exactly how an experiment was done.

Replication

One study, no matter how carefully done, rarely if ever gives us a final answer in science. Rather, scientists want to see the results of a study or series of studies repeated or replicated. *Replication* refers to the repetition of a study to determine whether or not the same results can be achieved. The caffeine experiment showed that higher doses of caffeine caused higher levels of physiological arousal. However, researchers would not accept as final a result from a single experiment, even though this was a true experiment and cause-effect conclusions were possible. We would want to see the results replicated in other studies. To go a step further, it would be better if the result were replicated in a different laboratory. That way we can be more certain that some subtle aspect of the procedures used in any one laboratory was not responsible for the observed result (Neuliep & Crandall, 1993).

Programmatic Research

A final aid in assuring that findings are systematic and objective is *programmatic research*, a series of systematic, interrelated studies that all move toward the same broad goal of establishing a greater understanding of some particular aspect of behavior. The investigator becomes an expert in a specific area of research, learns the best and most accurate procedures for designing, carrying out, and controlling experiments in that area, and cross- checks results from one study to another. Such an approach permits replication of results from prior studies, while, at the same time, gaining additional new knowledge. Some of the conditions from previous studies are repeated and the results replicated, while new conditions or procedures are added to further extend the research.

The extraversion/introversion study is an example of programmatic research. This study was one in a series of investigations conducted over a period of years, all aimed at a better understanding of the biological underpinnings of certain personality dimensions. Each study provides only a small increment in our knowledge, but a series of systematic, programmatic experiments can yield a substantial amount of information on the issues in question.

Keys to Psychological Research 3

Collecting, Analyzing, and Reporting Data

Every study involves collecting data, analyzing it, and reporting the results to the scientific community. Let's take at look at some of the methods used to collect and analyze data. We will also outline the process by which reports of research are published in scientific journals and show you how to locate and read these articles.

Methods of Data Collection

Psychologists employ a number of different methods of data collection, depending upon the nature and purpose of the study. Included among the major approaches are self-report, behavioral, and physiological methods.

Self-Report. The *self-report* method is just what it sounds like: We ask participants to tell us something about themselves—to give a self-report. Two major forms of self-report are interviews and questionnaires.

An *interview* is a dialogue between an interviewer and an interviewee. You may have been interviewed by a potential employer, who asked questions designed to determine your interest in and qualifications for the job. The interview is used almost universally in clinical psychology to partially assess a person's psychological problems and as a basis for psychotherapy. In research, interviews are used as a method for collecting data and may be highly structured so that the interviewer is sure to cover a number of specific questions. The interviewer may also follow up answers with additional queries to ensure that she has all the data needed to answer the research question. In addition, she may record nonverbal behavior, such as shakiness in the voice, nail biting, or excessive shifting in the chair.

The interview has both benefits and drawbacks as a research device. On the positive side, it can provide far more in- depth information than can readily be obtained with other methods. It also allows the researcher to ask further questions based on the subject's answers— something that is not possible with other approaches. Daniel Levinson, a researcher who wanted to study the midlife crisis phenomenon, interviewed 40 middle- aged men for a total of 10 to 20 hours each in order to obtain detailed information on their midlife experiences (Levinson et al., 1978). The results of this research are reported in Chapter 11.

On the negative side, the interview typically yields highly subjective data because the interviewer must interpret what the participant is saying and determine what additional questions to ask and because the questions asked may vary from one participant to another. In addition, there is usually no check on the factual accuracy of what the interviewee reports, and he may inadvertently give false information or even intentionally lie. Finally, the quality of the interview and therefore the data obtained depend on the skills of the interviewer, and the information is often difficult to quantify reliably.

A *psychological test* is a standardized measure of a person's behavior or performance. It provides a sample of behavior and is used to assess individual differences among people. Psychological tests have been devised to measure intelligence, personality traits (such as anxiety or extraversion/introversion), values, attitudes, achievements, and aptitudes.

A test of a given characteristic consists of a number of statements, questions, or problems. The participant's score on the test is taken as an indication of where the person stands on the characteristic being assessed. Ideally, the test is carefully constructed and does indeed measure the trait it is intended to measure. An example would be the Taylor Manifest Anxiety Scale (Figure 2-9), developed by Janet Taylor Spence to assess the anxiety level typically characteristic of any given individual. A person with a high score on the test is anxious much of the time; one with a low score is not. The construction of intelligence tests is described in Chapter 9; personality tests are discussed in Chapter 14.

Psychological tests have the advantage of being more objective than interviews and of asking precisely the same questions of all participants. However, they are still influenced by both intentional and unintentional distortion, in part because many participants are motivated to give as positive a picture of themselves as possible.

Behavioral Approaches. Researchers who want a method less subject to distortion than the self-report may turn to *behavioral* measures, in which there is some direct assessment of the participant's actions. Participants in the learned helplessness study, for example, were given an opportunity to learn to avoid the loud noise. The experimenters could have simply asked the participants whether or not they thought they could escape the noise, a self-report measure. Instead, they directly observed this behavior. Did they, in fact, display the learned hand-movement behavior that permitted them to avoid the noise? Many experiments employ measures of behavior or change in behavior as the primary basis for the conclusions to be reached by the experimenters. The naturalistic observation is also a behavioral approach to data collection.

Physiological Measures. Biological measures of various aspects of body function have become increasingly common in psychology over the past four decades. We may need to know, for example, how aroused a person is, how memories are stored in the brain, or how stress affects the body. In these and many other instances, we employ *physiological* measures—measures that assess the internal functioning of the body.

The introversion/extraversion study in the Probe provides a good example of the use of physiological measurement to assess arousal. The experimenters recorded the skin conductance response (SCR), a good measure of arousal. As arousal increases, the SCR becomes larger. As an alternative, they might have used an electrocardiogram (EKG) to measure heart rate, which also increases under higher arousal. One advantage of such physiological measures is that the participant cannot distort or control the measure as he can potentially do with self-report approaches.

By measuring brain function, we can determine what parts of the brain are involved in a variety of psychological processes, such as memory. Some measures can be taken by using instruments that operate outside the body and without doing the participant any harm. These *noninvasive* measures can be used in humans. Other measures require that the experimenter place instruments inside the brain or remove and examine the brain. These *invasive* approaches usually require that animals be used as subjects. If we want to know where memories are stored, we can perform noninvasive experiments in humans and invasive experiments in animals. Together they will help us to understand memory storage. We discuss techniques for studying the brain in Chapter 3 and the brain mechanisms involved in memory in Chapter 7.

Another example of physiological measurement is its use in studying the effects of stress. Researchers began to suspect many years ago that psychological stress might be a factor in ulcers, heart attacks, and a variety of other illnesses. The question was how. What body mechanisms might permit psychological stress to cause physical illness? Again, physiological measures were essential. In this case, not only measures of brain function, but also measures of hormone levels have been taken in order to further understand how stress is processed physiologically. We discuss what has been learned in Chapter 15.

A final example is in the study of sleep. Is sleep a single state or are there various types or depths of sleep? What goes on in the brain during sleep? These and other questions about sleep have been addressed by using physiological measures, primarily measures of the electrical activity of the brain, in order to better understand sleep (Chapter 5).

Data Analysis

Once we have collected the data in a study, we typically subject it to a data analysis or statistical analysis. *Statistical analysis* refers to the application of mathematical calculations to describe, summarize, and account for the observed variability in numerical data. We carry out the analysis in order to quantify our observations, making them more precise and allowing us to better understand what we have observed. The analysis also helps us to better communicate our results to other scientists. We typically use two kinds of statistics, descriptive and inferential.

Descriptive Statistics. Descriptive statistics serve the function of condensing and summarizing data. Consider, for example, the situation faced by your professor when he has given a test to 200 students. He will likely use descriptive statistics to summarize the data (test scores) as a basis for determining what scores will constitute A's, B's. etc. His descriptive statistics will tell him how many students received each possible score and what the average score for the class was, among other things.

Inferential Statistics. Inferential statistics are designed to tell us whether our results can be generalized beyond the present experiment (Gliner et al., 2000). Can we reasonably expect that our results are reliable or replicable? In other words, if we repeat this experiment again on another group of participants, is it likely that we will get the same results? Do our results apply to the entire population of people from which our sample was drawn? In the extraversion/introversion experiment, we found that larger amounts of caffeine produce higher arousal, but is this a "true" or reliable result, one that is likely to hold up if we repeat the experiment with a new group of participants? We calculate inferential statistics to make that decision by determining whether or not the difference was statistically significant. A difference is generally considered to be *statistically significant* if the chances of finding a difference that large or larger are less than 5 in 100. If they are, we conclude that we can generalize the result to the population. In this study the difference was statistically significant, so we concluded that the caffeine results do generalize and should replicate in future studies.

A second example of statistical analysis is provided by the learned helplessness experiment. The graph of response latency in Figure 2-4 makes it clear that the Escape and No Escape conditions produced quite different results. However, such "obvious" differences do not permit us to conclude that there is a *real* difference between conditions that would be present virtually every time we repeated the experiment. The differences seen on the graph could be due to chance unless they are confirmed by a statistical analysis showing that they are significant and hence meaningful. Hiroto (1974) conducted such an analysis and confirmed the result in his graphs.

Appendix A discusses descriptive and inferential statistics in more detail. It describes some of the specific statistics often used in psychological studies, shows you how they are calculated, and discusses their uses and limitations.

A more recently developed approach to statistical analysis is one that can deal with data from a number of different studies simultaneously. It is called meta analysis and is described in Horizon 2.

Keys to Psychological Research 4

Sources of Error

Despite the "best laid plans" of psychologists and other scientists, error does creep into research and can fully or partially invalidate results. The best defense against invalid results is to be aware of the major sources of error and design studies to guard against them. They include experimenter biases, placebo effects, and the influence of demand characteristics in the experimental situation.

Experimenter Bias

You probably believe that the boyfriend or girlfriend with whom you are madly in love is very attractive, intelligent, warm, and kind. On the other hand, your roommate's boyfriend or girlfriend may seem to you to be a complete nerd. The point is, of course, that you are probably biased about the positive characteristics of your own dating partner and may see him or her quite differently from the way other people do. Well, experimenters are human too, and most humans are biased in one way or another. The problem is that when an experimenter is biased, the bias can affect the results of the study (Forster, 2000). For example, an experimenter might interact quite differently with some participants than with others. He might inadvertently act to calm down an anxious subject or to pep up a bored participant. These differing interactions could affect the outcome of the study.

A good example of the effects of such *experimenter bias* is provided in a classic study done by Robert Rosenthal (1966). He had groups of students run rats through mazes. Half the students were told that their rats had been especially bred to be slow learners ("maze- dull rats"), while the other half were told that their rats had been bred to be quick learners ("maze- bright rats"). The rats had actually been chosen at random, and there were no differences between the groups of rats. Nevertheless, it was found that the "maze- bright" rats learned the maze significantly faster than their maze- dull cousins. The student experimenters had somehow treated or observed them differently. Other studies have shown that experimenters with strong needs for social influence can affect the performance of participants and that children perform differently on some tasks if the experimenter takes a caring attitude as opposed to an indifferent one (Schneider, 2000; Hazelrigg et al., 1991).

Participant Expectancy: The Placebo Effect

Subjects can also be biased. One specific form of such bias is the *placebo effect,* in which behavior changes merely because the participant *expects* it to change (French, 2001). Placebo effects are perhaps most obvious when drugs are administered. A patient may, for example, repeatedly complain to her physician of heart palpitations. When a full diagnostic workup shows no evidence of heart abnormalities, he may give her a *placebo*—basically a "sugar pill" with no active ingredients—but tell her that it is a highly effective new heart drug. Miraculously, the palpitations stop. The patient has experienced the very common placebo effect. Suppose now that a pharmaceutical company has developed a new drug that is to be marketed as a tranquilizer—a drug that reduces anxiety. We give it to some patients, telling them that it should lower their anxiety, and they then report lower anxiety. Is the anxiety reduction due to a physiological effect of the drug or is it merely a placebo effect based on the participant's expectancy that his anxiety will be reduced? To find out, we might do an experiment in which we randomly assign patients to receive either the new tranquilizer or a placebo (in this case a "sugar" pill that looks exactly like the drug). We do not tell the patient what he is actually taking. We say that the participant is blind to the drug, and we thus far have a *single-blind* experiment.

Ideally, we will go a step beyond the single-blind control to ensure that people who interact with the patient, such as psychologists, nurses, and physicians, are also unaware of whether she is receiving the drug or the placebo (Dienstfrey, 2000). The reason for this precaution is that if they do know the condition, they can unintentionally affect the patient's behavior by treating drug and placebo patients differently. When both the patient and the people interacting with her are unaware of the experimental condition, we are using a *double- blind procedure.* If patients in the drug condition now show significantly greater reductions in anxiety than those in the placebo condition, we can reasonably conclude that the drug is effective. In the experiment described in Probe 1, the researchers used a double-blind procedure; neither the experimenter nor the participant was aware of the participant's personality group or drug condition (Krakow, 2000)..

In using placebo conditions, ethical considerations are especially important (Miller, 2000). Is there an ethical violation in withholding a psychiatric drug from an ill patient in the control (placebo) group? The answers to such ethical questions are not simple, but they must be considered in each individual study to be conducted (Roberts, 2001; La Vaque, 2001).

Demand Characteristics

Have you been a participant in an experiment? If so, what were you thinking about as the study got under way, and what were you consciously trying to do during the experiment? Many researchers used to think of subjects as people who just

blindly followed instructions and provided data. All that changed when Martin Orne began his classic studies on demand characteristics in the 1960s, demonstrating that participants are anything but passive data providers. *Demand characteristics* are cues in the experimental situation that the participant interprets as indicating the purpose of the study and what is expected of him. The problem with demand characteristics is that participants use them to formulate hypotheses as to what the experiment is about, then typically try to be helpful to the experimenter (Vartanian, 2001). Often the participant is actively trying to behave in ways that she believes will support the experimenter's hypotheses, rather than simply following instructions. Unfortunately for the unsuspecting researcher, the participant often focuses on the wrong cues or misinterprets what she sees, then proceeds in the now abortive attempt to be helpful. The result can be invalid data.

That participants will do whatever they think is necessary to be helpful was clearly demonstrated in one of Orne's (1962) classic studies. He placed 2000 sheets of paper in front of the participant, each filled with columns of numbers to be added. The participant was told to add the numbers on the first page, tear that page into not less than 32 pieces, then do the addition on the second page and tear up that page. This repetitive process of adding numbers and tearing up pages went on as long as the participant was willing to continue it. How long would you have continued? Five minutes? Ten? Maybe fifteen? Well, many of Orne's subjects continued for hours. They were clearly trying to be cooperative and helpful, even when faced with a boring, seemingly endless task.

A second study showed just how powerful demand characteristics can be in affecting perception as well as behavior (Orne & Scheibe, 1964). It was based on previous research in which participants had been placed in special sensory isolation chambers, where they received virtually no visual, auditory, or other sensory stimulation for hours. Subjects in such studies often exhibited impaired performance on intellectual tasks and reported anxiety, difficulty in concentration, and hallucinations in which they would see or hear things that were not there. In this study of demand characteristics, Orne introduced participants in an experimental group to the research by taking a medical history and having them sign forms releasing the hospital where they conducted the experiment from legal responsibility for its consequences. They also saw a clearly labeled display of emergency equipment and medications before entering what was described as an "isolation chamber." There they were shown a microphone that could be used to report hallucinations and other unusual experiences and a "panic button" that could be pressed if they needed to get out. The "isolation chamber" was actually an ordinary office with a desk, chairs, and a window. Such deception of participants has important ethical implications that we take up later in the chapter. Participants in the control group were not asked to sign the release form, did not see the emergency equipment, and were not told to expect unusual experiences like hallucinations.

Control subjects reported nothing unusual after several hours in the room, and none showed any impairment on intellectual tasks performed when they came out. However, one experimental participant pressed the panic button to be released and others reported excessive restlessness, anxiety, difficulty in concentration, disorientation, and hallucinations. The latter included objects on the desk moving around, the walls wavering, and colored spots on the walls. Their performance on the intellectual tasks was also impaired. All these effects were clearly based on the expectations of the participants and their attempts to help the experimenter by supporting what they thought were his hypotheses. More recent studies confirm the impact of demand characteristics (Bjorklund, 2000).

One way to reduce demand effects is to conceal the true purpose of the experiment. A second is to avoid or reduce experimenter contact with the participant so that he will be less likely to try to help the researcher. Instructions can be tape-recorded, responses made anonymously, and the entire experiment controlled by a computer. Finally, participants can be carefully questioned at the end of the experiment to find out exactly what they were thinking. What did they believe the study was about? Were they trying to be helpful? Did they follow instructions? Taking all these precautions, we can eliminate or substantially reduce the effect of demand characteristics.

A final—and very important—source of error in experiments is the positive effect of change. It is called the Hawthorne effect and is discussed in Horizon 3.

Now that you have analyzed your data and are aware of some important sources of error, it is important to carefully evaluate what you have found. That means engaging in critical thinking, a skill that we will try to teach you in a special feature of each chapter called Thinking Critically. Our Application for this chapter tells you how to develop this skill.

Keys to Psychological Research 5

Doing It Right: Ethical Considerations

You have volunteered to be a participant in an experiment. Upon arriving at the laboratory, the experimenter tells you that your task is to monitor the behavior of another participant who is performing a learning task. Whenever he makes a mistake, you are to punish him by pressing a switch that will deliver a shock to his arm. He makes a few mistakes at first, then progressively more, and the experimenter repeatedly instructs you to give shocks, turning the level up as the person makes more errors. The learner moans, groans, and cries out with each shock as the level increases, but the experimenter insists that you deliver up to 450 volts or more of shock. Would you do it? You might think not, but in 1963 65 percent of Stanley Milgram's subjects in his initial experiment "went all the way," not knowing that the learner was a confederate of the experimenter and that no actual shocks were being delivered (Milgram, 1963).

We consider Milgram's work in more detail in Chapter 18, but here the issue is *ethics*. Should Milgram have done what he did? Should he have deceived his participants into thinking that they were delivering shock when they were not? Should he have placed them under the stress of the experimenter's attempt to force them to shock the learner? Such questions have frequently been raised about the Milgram studies and others involving such conditions as deception or pain.

The broader issue is that psychologists, like physicians, lawyers, and other professionals, need a code of ethics. The code provides each practitioner with guidance that represents the collective wisdom of colleagues in that profession as to what is right and what is wrong. Without such ethical guidelines, professionals are more likely to engage in behavior that can be harmful to others. The World Medical Association has created the Declaration of Helsinki, now in its fifth revision, which outlines ethical standards for medical research (Tollman, 2001). Many of the same principles apply to psychologists, who operate under a code of ethics developed by the American Psychological Association (APA) and by Canadian and other national organizations as well (Adair, 2001). We will discuss here the issues of voluntary participation, deception, confidentiality, and animal research.

Voluntary Participation in Research

Human subjects are obviously needed for experiments in every area of psychology. The only question is how we obtain participants. Do we require that certain people—say all students in introductory psychology courses—participate in specific studies that we assign them to or do we instead allow participants to decide whether or not to participate in a given experiment? From an ethical standpoint, a *voluntary participation* guideline—one that allows subjects to choose the studies they will take part in—is obviously preferable, and most human research is now conducted on that basis. As an introductory psychology student, you may be required to either participate in some number of experiments or perform some alternative task, such as writing a paper. Participation in any given study will be voluntary.

The voluntary participation principle is typically implemented through an *informed consent* procedure. Before a participant serves in an experiment, the researcher tells him what participation will involve, allows him to ask questions, then obtains his signed consent to participate. The participant also has the right to withdraw at any point during the experiment and the right to be debriefed afterward. *Debriefing* means that the participant receives information about the purpose and nature of the experiment and has an opportunity to voice any concerns he had about the procedures.

Deception and the Protection of Individual Rights

Although participation is voluntary, researchers sometimes deceive participants in their experiments in order to study the phenomenon in question. The Milgram experiment mentioned earlier is an example. Psychologists have faked equipment dangers, fights, rapes, thefts, and epileptic seizures, among other things, in conducting their studies. Why? Because such deception is sometimes essential to provide the kinds of controls described earlier. If it is important to learn about the phenomenon of obedience, for example, how could we conduct experiments like Milgram's without deception? The basic issues and conflicts here should be clear: Are there important experiments that cannot be done without the use of deception? If so, is it more important to do the experiment or to avoid the use of deception? Obviously, some psychologists have concluded that deception should be used when absolutely essential. Others have seriously questioned its use (Misra, 1992).

One of the APA ethical principles states that psychologists must protect the *rights* of persons involved in experiments, taking into account the welfare of the participant as well as the value of the study. Critics of deception argue that it may violate the rights of participants and thus be inappropriate. They make three basic points (Baumrind, 1985; Kelman, 1982). First, deception is basically *immoral*, since it involves a lie. Second, deception imposes potentially high levels of stress on participants and could thus be *harmful*. Finally, the use of deception may undermine the *trust* of participants in others. Those who defend deception argue that the "lies" are minor ones, that the scientific investigation of many important issues would be impossible without deception, and that the benefit to society of the knowledge gained outweighs the cost (Aronson, Brewer, & Carlsmith, 1985; Trice, 1986).

Unfortunately, the horns of this dilemma are sharp ones, and there is no simple answer. The closest we have come to a solution thus far is to have all proposed experiments reviewed by knowledgeable individuals who are not involved in the study. Most psychology departments and universities, as well as hospitals and other institutions, now have committees, usually called Institutional Review Boards, that evaluate all proposed experiments before they are conducted. They work to ensure that participation is voluntary, that any deception is justified, and that other ethical guidelines are followed. Researchers must present and explain their procedures to the board, which gives permission to conduct the experiment, then monitors compliance with the guidelines.

Confidentiality

Another important principle protects the confidentiality of information collected by psychologists. It applies to participants in experiments, patients or clients in therapy, workers studied in industrial settings, and anyone else providing personal information to a psychologist. Few would question the importance of this principle. You would be shocked to hear someone at a party describe your progress in psychotherapy or mention the IQ score you attained in an experiment. Confidentiality is basically a protection of the individual's right to privacy. As such, it is an important protection of individual rights and is employed in other professions as well as psychology. The confidentiality protection is not, however, absolute. In fact, the psychologist may be ethically or legally obligated to violate confidentiality under certain circumstances, as when a person reveals ongoing child abuse or a plan to commit murder (Thompson et al., 1993).

Animal Research

"French Court Upholds Use of Animals, Fines Activists for Theft of Baboons."

This was the title of a news item in the journal Nature, and it points up the heated international controversy concerning the use of animals in research (Zola, 2001). Animals are used to conduct research on anatomy, neurophysiology, biochemistry, neurochemistry, cancer, heart disease, stress, drug effects— and more. Animal research has been crucial to the development of heart transplantation techniques, antibiotics to fight life-threatening bacterial infections, and drugs to treat victims of AIDS and many other illnesses. In psychology, drug treatments for depression, anxiety disorder, schizophrenia, and other serious psychological disorders would not now be possible were it not for extensive animal research.

Why is animal research so important? Because often the critical research—that absolutely required before an important behavior can be understood or a disorder treated—simply cannot be done on humans (Singer, 1993; Howe, 1993). We cannot, for example: cut out sections of the human brain to study its functions; subject humans to stress, then sacrifice them to study changes in brain chemistry; implant electrodes in the human brain to determine the locations of reward centers; or keep humans in separate cages for months in order to study the effects of social isolation. We can, however, employ these procedures more readily with animals. Animals are used in about 8 percent of all experiments conducted by psychologists (APA, 1984). A review of the journal literature since 1967 reveals that the research use of most species has remained stable, though the use of a few, including dogs and cats, has declined (Viney et al., 1990).

Animal rights groups object strenuously to the insistence of scientists that animals are required for some kinds of research. They accuse researchers of subjecting animals to serious and unnecessary harm and severe pain and point to poor housing and feeding conditions in some laboratories (Ulrich, 1991). They estimate that 20 million rats, mice, and other animals die each year in experiments and that additional millions are subjected to pain and discomfort (Cunningham, 1985). At the same time, groups of permanently disabled people argue that the animal rights groups do not take the plight of the incurably ill into account. Without continued animal research, they argue, their illnesses will never be treatable (Feeney, 1987).

The current animal rights issue is by no means a new one. There was a similar movement in Victorian times, and such famous researchers as Charles Darwin, William James, G. Stanley Hall, John B. Watson, and Ivan Pavlov were at various times at the center of animal rights controversies (Dewey, 1990). Nevertheless, the animal rights conflict has been particularly heated in recent years. Demonstrations, such as some at the National Institutes of Health (NIH) in Bethesda, Maryland, have become increasingly common, and some groups, like the French one headlined in *Nature*, have even broken into laboratories, stolen animals and destroyed equipment.

Animals will certainly continue to be used in research. However, the animal rights movement has made a major contribution in focusing national and international attention on *how* the animals are used, what is done to them, and how they are housed and treated (Hollands, 1989). Universities and other research institutions now carefully regulate animal research to ensure that the animals are properly housed, fed, and treated and that they are not subjected to inappropriate procedures. Each university has a special "animal care and use committee" that monitors all animal research on the campus. In addition, granting agencies that fund animal research insist on humane treatment of the animals and carefully review the proposed studies to ensure that the procedures are justified.

Keys to Psychological Research 6

Conclusion

Our discussion of the scientific goals and methods of psychology is an important introduction to all that follows. In every chapter, we will see how scientific methods have been used to gain new knowledge in some area of psychology and how these same methods will be applied in the 21st century to further increase our understanding of behavior and underlying mental processes.

Well, you might wonder what ever happened to sport parachuting. Needless to say, I landed safely on my first jump - and on many thereafter. I found the sport to be exhilarating and fulfilling, and I vowed after the very first jump to continue it indefinitely. By way of analogy, you have now completed in these first two chapters— I hope safely— your first jump into psychology. I sincerely hope you will find it as interesting and fulfilling as I have and that you do well in your course.

Summary

The Science of Psychology

1. Science has five main virtues: It is systematic, formal, and objective; it strives for simplicity and order; it is precise; its results can be replicated; and it provides cumulative knowledge.
2. Both basic and applied research are essential to the full conduct of the science of psychology.
3. The major goals of psychology are description, prediction, control, application, and understanding.
4. Theory and research interact to further progress in a science.

Research Methods

1. Descriptive and correlational (nonexperimental) methods of psychological research include case studies, surveys, and naturalistic observation. Each of these methods has advantages and disadvantages.
2. Correlations are used to determine the degrees of relationship among variables. They do not determine causation.
3. Data can be used to describe behavior, to examine correlations between factors, or to determine cause- effect relationships. Statistical analyses are performed on data to see whether the results could have been achieved by chance. If not, the findings are said to be generalizable.
4. In controlled experiments, the experimenter manipulates independent variables and measures dependent variables. The use of controls permits firm causal conclusions.
5. In quasi-experiments, we study variables that cannot be manipulated or controlled. Both experimental (manipulated) and quasi-experimental (non-manipulated) variables can appear in the same study.

Research Principles and Practices

1. Major research principles and practices include standardization, operational definition, sampling procedures, generalization, reliability and validity, replication, and the programmatic conduct of research.

Data Collection, Analysis, and Reporting

1. Principal data collection methods include self-report, behavioral, and physiological approaches.
2. Self-report techniques include interviews and psychological tests.
3. The two major types of statistical techniques are descriptive and inferential.
4. Inferential statistics tell us whether our results can be generalized beyond the sample in a given experiment.
5. Scientific results are typically reported in journal articles that usually include several sections: abstract, introduction, method, results, discussion, and references. They can be located by using PsycLIT or PsycINFO.

Sources of Error

1. Sources of error in research include experimenter bias, placebo effects, demand characteristics, and the Hawthorne Effect.

Doing It Right: Ethical Considerations

1. Psychologists conduct research and practice under a set of ethical principles formalized by APA. These principles include attention to the rights of the individual, maintaining confidentiality, and respecting animal rights.

Ask Yourself

1. Discuss the differences between a correlational relationship and a cause- effect relationship.
2. What are the major virtues of science, and how does a scientific approach to psychology and behavior differ from an everyday or common sense approach?
3. What are the major nonexperimental methods in psychology? Why are they called nonexperimental?
4. What are the principal experimental methods? Why are they called experimental?
5. What conclusions can we draw from experimental studies that we cannot draw from nonexperimental studies?
6. How can researchers make psychological studies more precise and objective?
7. Does deception have an appropriate role in psychological research?
8. Does the value of animal research offset the animal rights issues raised by activists?
9. How important is confidentiality in psychological research and why?
10. What is the role of operational definitions in psychological research?
11. How do quasi-experimental designs differ from experimental designs and how are they related to correlational research?

Further Readings

Fiske, D., & Fogg, L. (1990). But the reviewers are making different criticisms of my paper! *American Psychologist*, 45, 591-598. When a psychologist writes a journal article, it is reviewed by two or more reviewers. The authors describe the review process and discuss the common phenomenon of differing criticisms.

Bangert-Drowns, R. (1986). Review of developments in meta-analytic method. *Psychological Bulletin*, 99, 388-99. Meta-analytic methods are those used to summarize data collected by many authors across many studies. The author discusses how these methods are used to review the literature in psychology.

Hoshmand, L.T., & Polkinghorne, D. (1992). Redefining the science-practice relationship and professional training. *American Psychologist*, 47, 55-56. How do the conduct of scientific research and practice in clinical, counseling, and other areas of psychology relate to each other? The authors deal with this important question and how it relates to training in psychology.

Sieber, J., & Stanley, B. (1988). Ethical and professional dimensions of socially sensitive research. *American Psychologist*, 43, 49-55. The authors discuss the ethics of scientific research in some areas of psychology, addressing the issue of what the researcher must be aware of in order to conduct research that is socially sensitive.

Graziano & Raulin. (1993). *Research methods: A process of inquiry.* NY: HarperCollins. This book focuses on an integrated thought process that leads to a conceptual understanding of psychological research methods.

Ray, W. (1993). *Methods toward a science of behavior and experience.* Pacific Grove, CA: Brooks/Cole. This useful book provides an in- depth examination of the methodology used by psychologists in their research.

Rosnow, R., & Rosenthal, R. (1993). *Beginning behavioral research: A conceptual primer.* NY: Macmillan. This book on research methodology teaches basic methods and emphasizes the importance of critical thinking.

Sieber, J. (1992). *Planning ethically responsible research.* Newbury Park, CA: Sage. This book provides a solid review of the ethical considerations that enter into psychological research.

Psychology in the 21st Century

Human Diversity and Psychological Research

Human diversity **refers to the variability of human beings along many different dimensions. Psychological research in the first half of this century rarely took diversity into account, assuming, in effect, that it was not important. However, diversity promises to be an increasingly important consideration as we move into the 21st century. We will consider two ways in which psychologists have begun to approach this topic. First, we have come to recognize that we often cannot generalize research results across such groups as women and men or whites and African-Americans. Rather, we must take the diversity among these groups into account in designing and interpreting the results of our research. Second, psychologists have begun to study diversity itself—to directly address differences among the various groups that make up the dimensions of human diversity (Stevenson, 2002).**

Designing and Interpreting Research. **A researcher interested in the average height of the American population would likely arrive at an inaccurate conclusion if he did not take gender differences into account. He could not measure only men or only women and generalize to the entire population, and he would be missing an important element of physical diversity if he did not realize that the two genders have different average heights.**

While sex differences in height are obvious, psychological differences among groups are often not apparent, and their unrecognized presence can lead to seriously flawed generalizations. Among the many dimensions on which people differ are gender, race, ethnicity, culture, age, and socioeconomic level (Choi, 2001).

Gender differences are so widespread that they must be taken into account in virtually all psychological research. Men, for example, are more likely to be aggressive, though not under all circumstances (Swim, 1994; Clark et al., 1994), and to develop alcoholism (Dawson, 1993; Robins et al., 1984). Women are more likely to seek psychotherapy and to develop depressive disorders (Leadbeater et al., 1995). And there are gender differences in mathematical and perhaps verbal skills, as measured by the Scholastic Assessment Test (SAT; Feingold, 1994; Warrick & Naglieri, 1993), as well as spatial ability (Casey et al., 1995) and attitudes toward science (Wienburgh, 1995). Some of these gender dissimilarities are due to biological differences between the sexes, others to differences in social training.

Race, ethnicity, and culture are closely related dimensions that also represent important individual difference variables in research. *Race* is genetically determined and reflects the individual's ancestry. *Ethnicity* is learned and reflects the person's upbringing in such areas as religion, language, values, and interests. *Culture* refers to the influence of the broader social context in which a person is raised and includes such variables as race, work ethic, religious values, health attitudes, and interest in the arts. Hispanic-Americans, African-Americans, and Asian-Americans differ greatly from each other and from Caucasian-Americans in their views of the world. Asian parents, for example, place far greater value on education and academic achievement than do Hispanic or black parents (D'Ailly, 1992). And there are systematic differences among racial, ethnic, and cultural groups in such areas as aggressiveness, moral standards, attitudes toward children and elders, educational level, income, and patterns of language and thought (Miller, 1994; Steward et al., 1995). None of these group differences apply to every member of each group studied, but they do make it difficult and inappropriate to generalize many kinds of research results across such groups.

Age **is yet another dimension of human diversity that must be taken into account. The aging process brings with it a loss of neurons in some areas of the brain (Carlson, 1986), gradual changes in many other body systems, and a variety of psychological changes that affect preferences, activities, and interests. Reductions in hearing and visual acuity (Thomas et al., 1983; Long & Cranbert, 1990) are accompanied by a slowing of motor (movement) processes (Salthouse, 1993). Short-term memory is often impaired (Kliegl & Lindenberger, 1993). Clearly, we would be foolish to generalize across age groups in many kinds of studies.**

A final important variable is *socioeconomic level*—basically, the individual's income group. While U.S. society is not strictly divided into classes, as some societies are, the impact of socioeconomic status is still very substantial. Poor, middle-income, and wealthy groups live very different lives—usually from birth—and family income affects a wide variety of variables. Higher income is associated with better nutrition from childhood on, greater educational opportunities, higher intelligence, and more motivation to work and achieve, among other things (Oakland & Glutting, 1990; Lucas et al., 1992; Atkinson & Raynor, 1974). Such differences must be taken into account if research results are to be accurately understood.

The Study of Diversity. **Psychologists have also begun to study human diversity (Orbe, 1995). How do blacks, Hispanics, Asians, and whites differ from one another, and what can knowledge of these differences tell us about these varied subcultural groups? In what particular ways do men and women, young and old, or lower and upper income groups vary in their value systems, intellectual strengths, and proneness to various forms of abnormal behavior? Research examining such group differences gives us considerable basic scientific information about each dimension of diversity we study. It also helps us to better understand the motivations and predict the behaviors of the various groups. And it may, as we move into the 21st century, contribute to greater intergroup understanding, a reduction in discrimi-**

nation, and an optimization of the potential of each person, no matter what his or her group membership (Betancourt & Lopez, 1993; Camino, 1995).

Probe

Research in Psychology

Extraversion and Caffeine: An Experimental Example

Some studies involve both controlled experiments, with manipulated independent variables, and natural experiments, in which participants are chosen on the basis of some preexisting individual characteristic. In one such experiment, it was hypothesized that extraverts and introverts would react to stimuli with different amounts of arousal and that their differing responses would be affected by the amount of caffeine they had received.

Groups of 48 extraverts and 48 introverts were chosen by giving a standardized psychological test to a group of over 400 college students, then selecting those who had very high scores on the test (the extraverts) and those who had very low scores (the introverts). Each participant was then randomly assigned to one of four experimental conditions: a low dosage of caffeine, a medium dosage, a high dosage, or a placebo (a substance that looks like caffeine but does not have its arousing effects).

Once in the laboratory, each participant was given the caffeine or a placebo in the form of identical pills, then waited 45 minutes for the drug to take effect. After that, the participant entered an acoustic chamber. Headphones were attached to deliver auditory stimuli (tones), and electrodes were attached to fingertips to measure the skin conductance response (SCR). The SCR measures the firing of the autonomic nervous system (see Chapter 3) and serves as a measure of arousal. The larger the SCR, the greater the participant's arousal response to the stimulus.

After receiving careful instructions, each participant heard a series of tones, all of the same pitch and intensity. The response (SCR) to each tone was recorded, and the data were later analyzed statistically. One analysis examined the response of each participant to the first tone that was presented. You can see in the Figure 2-10 that the responses of extraverts and introverts were quite different, depending on the dosage of caffeine. Extraverts gave the smallest response when they received the placebo and the largest response under the highest dose of caffeine. Introverts responded in exactly the opposite way; they showed the largest response (most arousal) to the tone in the placebo condition and the smallest response at a high dosage of caffeine.

The researchers concluded that their major hypotheses were supported by this finding (and others in the study), and that a theory they were testing was confirmed by the data (Smith, Wilson, & Jones, 1983).

Horizona in Psychological Research

Multivariate Research

In the Hiroto study of learned helplessness, only the latency of hand movement was measured, making his study a *univariate* experiment—one with a single dependent variable. Had he also measured the distance the hand moved, he would have had two dependent variables, and we could say that he conducted a multivariate experiment. A *multivariate experiment* is simply one involving more than one dependent variable. In such research, psychologists often measure not just two but many dependent variables simultaneously.

Multivariate research is important because it often allows us to examine complex determinants of behavior that would not be discovered in univariate research. Multivariate research can be experimental, quasi-experimental, or correlational in nature. In a multivariate correlational study, for example, we might be interested in relationships among a number of variables thought to relate to abnormal behavior. We might therefore obtain scores on such variables as anxiety, depression, compulsive behavior, difficulty sleeping, suicide risk, happiness, life satisfaction, and self-esteem. We could use all these variables in any of a number of different kinds of multivariate analysis in order to determine the relationships among them.

Meta Analysis

One of the major advantages of science is its cumulative nature; each new study builds on prior work in the same area, and knowledge accumulates as multiple studies and theories become available. This means, however, that scientists are frequently faced with numerous studies on the same topic, some with conflicting findings, and a need to resolve discrepancies and reach conclusions. One solution to this need is meta-analysis, a set of statistical techniques used to synthesize the results of any number of studies.

The researcher conducting the meta-analysis first reviews all the studies done on the topic of interest and selects those that fit a set of criteria. Using statistical techniques, she combines the results of these studies to reach general conclusions and indicates the degree to which those conclusions are supported by the studies used. With its ability to integrate large numbers of studies (Windle, 1994), it is easy to see why meta-analysis has become such a popular weapon in the arsenal of science (Pollock, 1993).

There are many examples of meta-analysis in the psychological literature. One investigator, for example, located 20 studies of the effects of physical exercise on stress and conducted a meta-analysis. He concluded that there is only slight support for the hypothesis (Schlicht, 1994). Another example is of self-esteem in stepchildren as compared with those in nuclear families and those in single-parent households. A meta-analysis of 24 studies showed that the self-esteem of stepchildren is somewhat lower than that of children in nuclear families but not different from that of children in single-parent homes (Ganong & Coleman, 1993). Another meta-analysis showed that alcohol clearly impairs both reaction-time and memory performance (Maylor & Rabbitt, 1993), and an analysis of 38 studies showed that stress reduces immunity, impairing the ability to fight infectious diseases (Herbert & Cohen, 1993).

The Hawthorne Effect

Experimental results can sometimes be biased in ways that you might not expect. A good example first arose in the 1920s and 1930s when studies of worker productivity were conducted in the Hawthorne Plant of the Western Electric Company near Chicago. Researchers discovered that when they increased the brightness of lighting in the plant, worker productivity increased. However, they then found out that *decreases* in lighting also increased productivity. Both increases and decreases in rest periods and in work hours boosted productivity. This tendency of people to work harder or perform better simply because there has been a change or because they know they are subjects in an experiment is called the *Hawthorne Effect*. We still don't know exactly why it occurs, but we know that it does (Adair, 1984).

Keys to Psychological Research 1

Key Knowledge

1. The scientific method assumes lawful, causal principles and uses objective observation to determine them.
    - A. What its virtues are?
        - Simplicity and order, precision, replication, cumulative knowledge.
    - B. Two major types of research?
        - Basic
        - Applied
    - C. The major goals of psychology?
        - Description, prediction, control, application, understanding.
2. Sciences involve both theory and research.
    - A. What research involves?
        - Precise observation
    - B. What a theory does?
        - Accounts for, predicts, and explains.
    - C. The characteristics of a good theory?
        - Puts knowledge into a logical framework
        - Produces new hypotheses
        - Adheres to the law of parsimony
        - Has testable, falsifiable hypotheses

Key Terms

applied research
basic research
research
scientific method
theory

Keys to Psychological Research 2

Key Knowledge

1. Research methods fall in two general categories.
   - A. What they are?
     - Descriptive and correlational
     - Experimental
2. Descriptive and correlational methods are all nonexperimental approaches.
   - A. The major methods?
     - Case studies
     - Surveys
     - Naturalistic observations
   - B. The goals they typically accomplish?
     - Description
     - Prediction
   - C. What a correlation indicates?
     - The degree of relationship between variables.
   - D. A major limitation of correlation?
     - Does not determine cause-effect.
3. Controlled experiments manipulate variables and measure their effects.
   - A. Their advantage?
     - They determine cause-effect
   - B. What manipulated variables are called?
     - Independent variables
   - C. What variables affected by the manipulation are called?
     - Dependent variables
   - D. What explanatory variables are called?
     - Intervening variables
   - E. The role of control groups?
     - To assure that changes are due to the manipulation
4. Quasi-experiments are done when manipulation is not feasible.
   - A. Another name for quasi-experimental variables?
     - Natural
   - B. Some examples of quasi-experimental variables?
     - Gender, anxiety level, extraversion-introversion

Key Terms

case study
cause-effect
control group
correlation
dependent variable
descriptive methods
double-blind procedure
experimental group
experimental research
hypothesis
independent variable
intervening variable
interview

multivariate experiment
natural experiment
naturalistic observation
nonexperimental methods
placebo effect
quasi-experiment
survey
variable

Key Terms

inferential statistics
physiological measure
psychological test
self-report

Keys to Psychological Research 3

Key Knowledge

1. Scientific research must be objective and precise.
   - A. How objectivity is assured?
     - By applying standard principles and practices
   - B. Some major principles and practices?
     - Standardization
     - Operational definition
     - Random sampling and assignment
     - Reliability and validity
     - Replication
     - Programmatic approach
2. What a representative sample is?
   - One with the same characteristics as the population
3. How representative samples are obtained?
   - Random sampling
   - Stratified random sampling
4. What we mean by reliability?
   - Stability or consistency
5. What we can say about a measure or study that does what it is supposed to do?
   - It is valid.
6. The principal methods of data collection?
   - Self-report
   - Behavioral
   - Physiological
7. Statistical analysis describes and accounts for observed variability.
   - A. The two major types of statistics?
     - Descriptive
     - Inferential
   - B. What inferential statistics tell us?
     - Whether we can generalize

8. The typical sections of a journal article?
    - Abstract
    - Introduction
    - Method
    - Results
    - Discussion
    - References

Key Terms

generalization
meta-analysis
operational definition
programmatic research
random assignment
random sample
reliability
replication
representative sample
standardization
stratified random sample
validity

Keys to Psychological Research 5

Key Knowledge

1. Errors can invalidate scientific research.
    - A. Some major sources of error?
        - Experimenter bias
        - Placebo effects
        - Demand characteristics
        - Hawthorne effect
    - B. How the placebo effect works?
        - Expectation causes change.
    - C. Ways to reduce effects of demand characteristics?
        - Conceal purpose of experiment
        - Reduce experimenter-subject contact.

Key Terms

critical thinking
demand characteristics
experimenter bias
Hawthorne Effect

Keys to Psychological Research 6

Key Knowledge

1. A code of ethics guides professionals in conducting research and practice.
    - A. Who provides the code for psychologists?
        - APA
    - B. Some major ethical issues?

Voluntary participation
Deception
Confidentiality
Animal research

2. Voluntary participation in research is an important guideline.
   A. What it accomplishes?
      Protection of individual rights
   B. How it is usually accomplished?
      Through written, informed consent.
   C. The rights of the subject?
      To withhold consent
      To be debriefed
3. Deception in psychological studies is controversial.
   A. Why?
      It is sometimes necessary, but can be seen as inappropriate.
   B. The arguments against deception?
      It is immoral
      It can be harmful
      It can undermine trust
   C. The response to these arguments?
      The "lies" are minor
      It is necessary for important studies to be done.
      The benefit outweighs the cost.
4. The use of animals in research is controversial.
   A. Why?
      They are necessary but may be harmed.
   B. What proportion of psychological research involves animals?
      8 percent
   C. The effects of the animals rights movement?
      Has focused attention on how animals are housed and treated.

Key Terms

informed consent
voluntary participation

Chapter 3

Neuroscience: The Brain and Behavior

Outline

Neurons and the Nerve Impulse

Neuron Structure: Form Follows Function
The Nerve Impulse: Getting the Message Across
Neuron Interaction: Bridging the Gap
Summation: The Neuron as Computer

The Peripheral Nervous System: Acting and Reacting

Cranial and Spinal Nerves
The Somatic Nervous System: Sensation and Muscle Control
The Autonomic Nervous System: Internal Organs and Emotions
The Endocrine System

The Central Nervous System: Where You Live

The Spinal Cord: Communication To and From The Brain
The Brain
The Cerebral Cortex
Neural Networks
The Evolving Brain

A Brain Divided: Lateralization of Brain Function

Dividing the Walnut: Split-Brain Research
Asymmetry in the Normal Brain
Two Brains, Two Minds?

Immersed in Thought: Brain Biochemistry

Neurotransmitters
Brain Drugs: The Natural Opiates
Eat, Drink, and Be Functional: Nutrition and the Brain

Breaking the Code: Methods of Brain Study

Damaged Brains
Up Close and Personal: Tissue Examination
Cut It Out: Ablation and Lesioning
Stimulating Experiences
Electrical Recording
Brain Scanning: The Newest Kid on the Block
The Disease That Kills Twice: Alzheimer's

Networking

THE FUNDAMENTAL basis of all human behavior—and thus of psychology—is the functioning of the nervous system. Neuroscientists are an interdisciplinary group of psychologists, neurologists, physiologists, computer scientists, and others who are fascinated with the study of the brain. How we learn and remember, the emotions we feel, what motivates us to act, how we perceive the world around us—all may be influenced by a variety of internal and external events, but all are ultimately under the control of the nervous system. In this chapter we will see that electrical and chemical processes occurring at microscopic levels underlie the functioning of the nervous system. The brain, which directs the activities of the nervous system, contains billions of nerve cells. It is these nerve cells, grouped into functional components, that control specific aspects of behavior. How these components work as an integrated whole remains a fascinating mystery—one that neuroscientists are trying to solve by applying a variety of powerful new methodologies. We will cover the major components of the nervous system, the division of the brain into two halves, the role of brain biochemicals, and the methods by which we study the brain.

Life and Death: A Judgment Call

The scene in a Baltimore courtroom on May 9, 1986, was a grim one. A Presbyterian minister—an intensely religious man—had come to ask that his wife be removed from an artificial life support system that had kept her heart beating while she lay in a coma for 42 days. The chief of neurology at a Maryland hospital where the patient—we'll call her Ruth —lay comatose testified that she had given no response to painful stimuli and had contracted severe pneumonia in both lungs.

The problem had begun when Ruth collapsed on the floor of her kitchen, suffering from a stroke. Even as she went down, she told her daughter that she did not want her life artificially prolonged, and now, 42 days later, her husband was in court to ask that her wishes be carried out. Medical witnesses testified that her chances of recovery at this point were 1 in 100,000 to 1 in 1,000,000. They also pointed to a 1981 study of 500 coma victims, which showed that nearly 75 percent had died, with the remainder left in a vegetative state or with moderate to severe disabilities. More recent studies have used various diagnostic techniques (see p.____) in an attempt to predict which coma patients will return to reasonably normal consciousness, but have thus far achieved only about 75—80% accuracy in prediction (Whyte et al., 2001; Wong et al., 2001).

The judge was not convinced and postponed his decision, asking the minister's lawyer to come up with more convincing legal precedents. We'll return to Ruth's case later in the chapter and see what the eventual outcome was.

But you might be asking yourself why psychologists study the brain. The answer is that all human behavior and mental processes are controlled by the brain and nervous system. If we are ever to fully understand behavior, we must understand the role of the brain. To learn how we can accurately predict whether or not Ruth will recover and to see how the brain controls behavior, we must learn about far more than comas. Indeed, we must learn everything we possibly can about the human brain. What are all its parts, from the largest to the smallest, and what are their functions? How do the various parts interact to affect behavior? What chemical substances and processes are involved in the neural control of behavior and how do they function? How is the brain influenced by learning and experience?

All these and other questions about the brain and its relationship to behavior are the province of neuroscience. *Neuroscience* is an interdisciplinary science that pools the expertise and resources of psychology, neurology, zoology, physiology, biochemistry, computer science, and other disciplines (Bradley, 2002; Miller, 2002). Scientists from these fields work together to learn more efficiently and effectively how the human brain functions and how it interacts with behavior and human consciousness. Neuroscience is clearly one of the major scientific thrusts of the future, and we have every reason to hope that its efforts will lead to a rapid increase in our knowledge of brain function.

The human brain is the most complex three_pound mass of anything anywhere in the universe. That complexity is the result of the large number and great diversity of specialized cells in the brain, the intricacies of neurological organization, and the myriad interconnections and communications that take place among brain cells. The brain can be understood, but the task that we have set for ourselves as scientists, as teachers, and as students is both massive and fascinating. For what we are trying to do is to understand the human brain using the human brain.

Place your two index fingers on your eyebrows, then trace a line from there all the way around your head (Figure 3-1). Most of your brain is above that line. Constituting only about 2 percent of the total body weight of a 150_pound person, the brain, supported by a nervous system that extends throughout the body, controls virtually every behavior. As you read this page, for example, your eyes and head are moving, your hand may be holding a highlighter or pen, and you are thinking; you are conscious of the material you read, and your brain is constantly interpreting the words and storing their meaning in a series of memories that will eventually help you understand and retain what you have learned.

Like a successful college student, the brain accomplishes its complex task of behavior control through organization. That organization is hierarchical, not unlike that of a large corporation. In a corporation, individual workers make up small groups, which report to progressively higher levels, which in turn report to top management. Top management, in this case the brain, assigns tasks to lower levels and also integrates the information those levels provide. The individual workers in the nervous system are nerve cells and their component parts. These nerve cells form simple and then more complex networks. The networks at lower levels of the brain control relatively specific functions that are then integrated at progressively higher levels to permit the complex, intricate control that the brain has over behavior.

Through its hierarchical organization, the nervous system allows us to apply past experience in responding continuously and effectively to a constantly changing internal and external environment while anticipating the future.

Physically, the brain is a somewhat nondescript, walnut_shaped tissue mass. However, its complex structure contains billions of neurons. The neurons are intricately connected and function collectively to control all aspects of behavior. The high degree of interdependence and cooperation among individual nerve cells makes possible such uniquely human behaviors as the highly coordinated movements of a champion gymnast and the complex thoughts of a theoretical physicist.

The two main divisions of the nervous system are the central nervous system (the brain and spinal cord) and the peripheral nervous system (which transmits nerve impulses back and forth between the central nervous system and the body's senses, muscles, and organs). This complete nervous system contains more neurons than there are stars in the galaxy, somewhat over 100 billion, although we will see in Chapter ___ that there is a considerable loss of neurons as people age (Gur et al., 2002). In this chapter we will concentrate on understanding the nervous system, its structure, function, and biochemistry. But first we must take a closer look at the individual units, the nerve cells, in order to understand the basic electrical and chemical processes that underlie neural functioning.

Neurons and the Nerve Impulse

A *neuron* is a single cell in the nervous system that is specialized to receive impulses from other neurons, process those impulses, and transmit information to yet other neurons. Neurons have the same basic properties as other living cells, but they have modifications that specialize them for carrying messages throughout the body. The functioning of any nervous system, whether of an earthworm or a human being, depends on the structure and activity of neurons, the propagation of electrical impulses, and the complex interactions that take place among these nerve cells. We will take up each of these topics, then see how the neuron functions as a tiny computer.

Neuron Structure: Form Follows Function

Each neuron is an independently operating cell with a specific structure and set of functions. Special techniques have been used to determine that there are about 200 types of neurons (Muller, 1992). Let's consider the basic structures that make up a neuron, the major types of neurons, and the role of other cells found in the nervous system.

Most types have three main structures: a cell body or soma, dendrites, and an axon (see Figure 3-2). The *soma* contains the cell's nucleus, carries out the chemical processes involved in the metabolism and respiration of the cell, and serves to integrate information arriving at the neuron. The cell membrane surrounding the soma plays an important role in many of the chemical reactions in which the neuron is involved.

Dendrites are short, spidery filaments that receive information from other neurons. Together with the region of the cell membrane to which they are attached, they constitute the *dendritic zone.* Often the dendrites of a single neuron will receive input from hundreds or even thousands of other neurons. At the opposite side of the cell from the dendrites is the axon. The *axon* is a filament—often a long one—that serves to transmit nerve impulses from the soma to the dendritic zones of other neurons or to organs or muscles. It may extend a long distance from the soma, as in the case of giraffes, where a single axon can stretch from the spinal cord down to the toe. Some axons, especially long ones and those in the peripheral nervous system, are surrounded by myelin. This *myelin sheath* is a fatty covering that serves to insulate the axon and speed the transmission of nerve impulses. A given neuron receives information from its dendrites, integrates that information in the soma, and passes it on to other neurons through the axon.

The exact structure of a particular neuron depends on its function. There are three main functional types of neurons in the nervous system: sensory neurons, motor neurons, and interneurons. *Sensory neurons* are specialized to conduct impulses from receptors in the eyes, ears, and other sense organs toward the central nervous system. The receptor is sometimes part of the sensory neuron. Sensory neurons are essentially input cells. *Motor neurons* are output cells that activate the muscles of the body. The soma of a motor neuron is located in the spinal cord, and its axon terminates in a muscle cell.

Lying between the sensory and motor neurons are *interneurons,* which serve as relay stations between sensory and motor neurons, particularly in the spinal cord, and as connectors between other interneurons (Figure 3-3). There are perhaps 5,000 interneurons for every motor neuron, and they come in two basic types. One type has a very long axon and serves to transmit neural information over great distances within the central nervous system. The second type has a short axon and is specialized for entry into multiple relationships with other neurons. It might, for example, accept impulses from many sensory neurons and convey that information to a large number of motor neurons.

The differing functions of the three types of neurons can be seen when neuronal damage occurs. If sensory (input) neurons are damaged, the person may be unable to detect sights, sounds, or other stimuli. Damage to motor neurons can lead to paralysis or loss of muscular coordination. Injury to interneurons can lead to learning disabilities, memory loss, inappropriate emotional reactions, and the coma that Ruth experienced.

Far more numerous than neurons, by a ratio of ten to one, are the glial cells, or *glia,* that make up the other major structural component of the nervous system. Glia are much smaller and more numerous than neurons and are not involved in transmitting nerve impulses. Instead, the several different types of glia perform a number of other important functions (Figure 3-4). They fill vacant spaces between neurons, form scar tissue following brain damage, remove the waste materials that remain when neurons die, build myelin sheaths, fill spaces between neurons, and help to supply neurons with nutrients. They also produce the myelin sheaths that surround axons and help guide the axons to target areas during both the development of the nervous system and the regeneration process that repairs damage in the peripheral nervous system (Krarup et al., 2002). Finally, recent evidence suggests that glia may be actively involved in the transmission of nerve impulses (Haydon, 2001).

The Nerve Impulse: Getting the Message Across

Like an unplugged telephone, a neuron that was not connected to other neurons would be a complete, functional unit, but it would be rather useless. When plugged into its system, a phone transmits and receives messages electrically; a neuron communicates *electrochemically,* which simply means that both electrical and chemical processes are involved in neural transmission. The structure of the neuron makes it ideally suited to the transmission of such electrochemical messages. Transmission of neural messages requires two main processes: Generation of a nerve impulse within the neuron, and transmission of impulses from one neuron to the next. The first is an electrical process; the second is primarily a chemical one. We will consider resting and active states of the neuron, the nature of neural firing, and the refractory period that follows firing.

The Resting Neuron. Electrically, a neuron may be either at rest or active. The *resting potential* of the neuron is its unstimulated, inactive state, during which it has a negative electrical charge. Like a fully drawn sling shot, it is loaded and ready to fire. In this state, there is a relative predominance of negatively charged potassium ions inside the neuron and of positively charged sodium ions outside, and the cell membrane is said to be *polarized.* To make the neuron active, it is necessary to stimulate the cell in such a way as to reverse the electrical charges inside and outside the cell. So long as no incoming impulse stimulates its dendrites, the neuron will remain in this steady state.

Ready, Aim, Fire: The Action Potential. An appropriate stimulus causes the cell membrane to depolarize briefly, permitting the positively charged sodium ions outside the membrane to come rushing in. For a brief moment, the charge inside the cell becomes positive in relation to the outside of the cell, creating an *action potential,* which is another name for the nerve impulse (see Figure 3-5). The generation of an action potential occurs in only one small region of the membrane, but it starts a chain reaction down the axon. It stimulates the firing of an action potential in the adjoining region, which stimulates the next region, and so on, driving or *propagating* the nerve impulse down the length of the axon, like a flame along a fuse.

All or None: It's The Law. The "firing" of a neuron, causing the generation of a nerve impulse, requires an *adequate* stimulus. That is, an action potential will be generated only if the stimulus exceeds the *threshold,* or minimum level, for the particular neuron. If the threshold level for depolarization is not reached, the neuron will not fire. However, once the stimulus reaches the critical level, further increases in stimulus intensity will have no effect on the intensity of nerve firing. Thus, firing is said to follow the *all-or-none law:* The neuron either fires or doesn't fire. It's just like firing a gun. When you increase pressure on the trigger, nothing will happen until you pass the threshold for the hammer to be released, at which time the gun will fire. But no matter how hard you pull the trigger, the intensity of the firing will always be the same. The one element that *can* be varied with either a gun or a neuron is the rate of firing; that is, increased stimulation can cause the neuron to fire more frequently. An intense stimulus may thus cause the neuron to fire repeatedly, producing bursts of activity (sort of like firing a machine gun). In addition, more intense stimulation causes larger *numbers* of neurons to fire simultaneously or in rapid sequence.

The flow of the nerve impulse down the axon is somewhat like the flow of electricity through a wire when a light switch is thrown except that the nerve impulse travels at a considerably slower speed. The speed of the impulse depends on the diameter of the axon and the presence or absence of myelin sheathing. A greater diameter will speed up transmission, as will myelination. A myelinated nerve fiber (which looks like a string of sausages or hot dogs _ see Figure 3-6), transmits impulses much faster than an unmyelinated one because the fatty coating provides insulation; in effect, the nerve impulse jumps along the axon, pausing only at breaks in the sheathing (the breaks between the "hot dogs"), rather than plodding along the entire length of the axonal membrane. In general, the speed of transmission varies between 2 and 200 miles per hour (considerably slower than even the speed of sound, which is about 750 miles per hour).

The Refractory Period. After firing, the neuronal membrane enters a *refractory period*—a period of one or more milliseconds (msec.) time during which it cannot fire. Like a runner who's just completed a 440-yard dash at top speed, it needs a brief rest to replenish its resources. Its threshold is greatly increased, and it cannot discharge because of the ongoing influx of sodium. At this point a cellular process called the sodium-potassium pump goes to work to pump the excess sodium ions out of the neuron, restoring the chemical and electrical balance between the inside and outside of the cell so that the membrane will again be responsive to stimulation. The existence of the refractory period places a limit on the frequency with which a neuron can fire. If the refractory period is 1 msec., the neuron can fire no more than 1000 times per second.

Neuron Interaction: Bridging the Gap

If you accidentally touch a hot stove with your index finger, you will pull your hand away and shortly experience a sensation of pain. How does the nerve impulse generated by the sensory neuron in your finger wind up as a message to your arm muscles to yank the hand away, and how does the message almost simultaneously end up as a sensation of pain in your brain?

For the message to travel from your finger to your arm muscles and brain, the electrical impulse must be able to pass from neuron to neuron over various pathways in the body (see Figure 3-6). Because there are tiny gaps between neurons, the electrical transmission process is supplemented by a chemical transmission process that carries the electrical signal across the gaps.

The Synapse. Axons typically branch into several small filaments, each ending in a tiny swelling or knob (Figure 3-7). These knobs, known as *axon terminals* or presynaptic terminals, bring the axon of one neuron to a point very close to the dendritic zone of another. As recently as the 1950s, it was thought that, at least within the brain, the axon of one neuron connected directly to the dendrites of another and that the transmission of nerve impulses was a purely electrical process (Carlsson, 2001). It turns out, however, that there is typically no actual physical contact between the axon and the dendrites. Rather, there is a *synapse*—a tiny or space or cleft between the axon terminal of one neuron and the dendritic zone of another. Although studies show that synapses are more complex than originally thought, the basics of synaptic transmission are fairly straightforward (Devered and Wheland, 1988; Pender, 1989).

Consider how electricity works in your house. When you plug a lamp into a socket and turn it on, the electricity flows from the socket through the wire to energize the light. But suppose you were to cut the wire and separate the cut ends, leaving a tiny gap between the two segments. Flicking the switch would no longer turn on the light _ the electricity would not cross the gap. Similarly, the electrical nerve impulse alone cannot ordinarily cross the synaptic gap. How, then, does the message get relayed?

While some synapses do involve direct electrical connections between neurons (Leitch, 1992), most rely on chemicals to get the impulse across the synapse. These substances are called *neurotransmitters*—specialized chemicals that carry neural information across the synaptic cleft. They are produced in the soma of the neuron and travel down the axon to the axon terminal, where they are stored in the *synaptic vesicles*—tiny sacs within the axon terminal. When the action potential reaches the axon terminal, it depolarizes the presynaptic cell, and the vesicles break open, releasing the chemicals into the gap (Sollner & Rothman, 1994; Sihra & Nichols, 1993). Once released, the chemical diffuses across the gap and attaches to receptor sites on the postsynaptic membrane (Figure 3-7). After the nerve impulse has crossed the gap, the neurotransmitter is destroyed by an enzyme or reabsorbed into the presynaptic vesicles. We will have more to say about neurotransmitters later in the chapter.

Much of the complexity and flexibility characteristic of the human nervous system results from the fact that most neurons communicate not with a single neuron but with many. In fact, a given neuron may have synapses with 50,000 to 100,000 other neurons. It has been estimated that there are some 100 trillion synapses in the human nervous system (Hubel, 1979). These synapses are in a constant state of degeneration and regeneration; nerve cells themselves cannot be regenerated, but new synapses are formed every day. Ruth, in our opening example, undoubtedly experienced brain damage, leading to the loss of some synapses. Evidence suggests that even while she is in a coma, at least some of these synapses will begin to regenerate (Ross, 1994). The Probe further discusses the interesting phenomenon of synapse turnover.

Summation: The Neuron as Computer

When a single nerve impulse arrives at an axon terminal, it releases a small amount of neurotransmitter and causes a small electrical potential to develop in the postsynaptic cell. This electrical potential can be one of two types: excitatory or inhibitory (see Figure 3-8). An *excitatory postsynaptic potential* (EPSP) *depolarizes* the cell, increasing the likelihood that a new impulse will be generated. An *inhibitory postsynaptic potential* (IPSP) *hyperpolarizes* the neuron, making firing less likely. In either case, a single EPSP or IPSP is usually not sufficient to influence the neuron one way or another. Rather, it is necessary for many simultaneous or consecutive impulses to occur before a neuron will reach its threshold and fire. The soma (cell body) acts as a tiny computer, adding up all the impulses that are reaching the neuron. The cumulative process through which multiple impulses influence a postsynaptic cell is called *summation.*

There are actually two types of summation, spatial and temporal. *Spatial summation* occurs when the axons of many different neurons all conduct impulses that simultaneously affect one neuron. *Temporal summation* occurs when a number of impulses from a single axon arrive in rapid succession to repeatedly stimulate the postsynaptic neuron. This repeated stimulation can accumulate until it surpasses the threshold level and induces the neuron to fire. Such complex neuron interactions permit the skilled fingers of the surgeon to tie tiny knots in tiny spaces and allow the seasoned politician to a deliver a smooth, polished speech.

Although we have described summation in terms of the excitation of a neuron, both spatial and temporal summation apply to inhibitory potentials as well. Whereas the cumulative effect of EPSPs is to make it more likely that the neuron will fire, the cumulative effect of IPSPs is to make it harder for the impulse to be generated. The EPSPs and IPSPs occurring on a given neuron also summate with each other. In fact, whether or not a neuron reaches threshold and fires is a function of the balance between excitatory and inhibitory potentials as determined by the soma's "computer" function.

The Neural Hierarchy: Building On The Neuron

The billions of neurons in the human body are linked in a number of ways. Nerves (also called pathways or fiber tracts) are bundles of axon fibers that travel through the nervous system together. The cardiac nerve, for example, is a bundle of axons going to the heart, and the optic nerve contains axons that carry visual information from the eyes to the brain. Cell bodies also group together at many points in the nervous system to form ganglia and nuclei. A ganglion is a localized cluster of cell bodies, usually outside the CNS (see Figure 3-13). A nucleus is a cluster of neuron cell bodies within the CNS. Many fiber tracts, ganglia, and nuclei are functionally wired together to form systems. The two main nervous systems are the peripheral nervous system and the central nervous system, each of which is made up of several subparts (see Figure 3-9). We will take up each of these in turn.

Keys to Neuroscience 1

The Peripheral Nervous System: Acting and Reacting

The *peripheral nervous system* consists of all neural structures outside the brain and spinal cord and serves to carry neural information both to and from those structures. You stub your toe hard or overdo on pizza. Recognizing that the pain is in your toe or that the upset feeling is in your stomach requires that messages get from these structures to your brain. The means by which these messages are transmitted is the peripheral nervous system. The peripheral system also carries messages from the brain to the rest of the body, directing you, for example, to rub your hurting toe or to reach into the medicine cabinet for an antacid. Without the peripheral nervous system, the brain would be as isolated as a king on a mountain with no subjects to bring him information about his kingdom and no soldiers to carry out his commands. The peripheral nervous system provides the subjects and soldiers. It is directly involved in the functioning of both the muscles and the internal organs. The peripheral nervous system can be further divided into the somatic (skeletal) nervous system and the autonomic nervous system (ANS). After distinguishing between cranial and spinal nerves, we will consider each of these systems separately. Then we will take up the closely related functions of the endocrine system.

Cranial and Spinal Nerves

Some of the fiber tracts that make up the peripheral nervous system come directly from the brain, others from the spinal cord. Those that go directly from the brain to various structures located primarily in the head, face, and neck are called *cranial nerves.* There are 12 pairs of these nerves, most consisting of one sensory nerve and one motor nerve (Figure 3-10). The cranial nerves are involved in such activities as vision, eye movement, smell, taste, hearing, the operation of the vocal cords, and tongue movement. The *spinal nerves* originate in the spinal cord and *innervate* (carry nerve impulses to and from) the rest of the body. We will have more to say about them shortly.

The Somatic Nervous System: Sensation and Muscle Control

The *somatic nervous system* consists of all the nerves that carry impulses to the skeletal muscles and all those bringing information from the sensory receptors. Stroke patients like Ruth, even if not in a coma, often don't feel pain in one or more limbs and develop "motor" problems—difficulties in movement or even paralyses that make movement of some limbs impossible. The brain damage caused by the stroke has cut off the flow of neural information over parts of the somatic nervous system.

The somatic system contains sensory neurons and motor neurons. The axons of the sensory neurons group together to form *afferent nerves*—those that carry information from the senses to the central nervous system. The axons of the motor neurons form *efferent nerves*—those that carry impulses from the central nervous system to the periphery to control the external behaviors of the individual. The sensory information is carried up the spinal cord to the brain. The cell bodies of the motor neurons are located in the spinal cord, and the axons extend to the *neuromuscular junctions*—the points where nerves join muscles. There, a neurotransmitter called acetylcholine carries the electrical message across the synapse, causing the muscle to contract. It is in this way that the somatic system controls both voluntary behaviors, such as picking up a pencil or swinging a bat, and automatic ones, such as reflexively hopping when you stub your toe. But even spontaneous reflexes controlled by the somatic system can be influenced by *voluntary* control or intention. You could, for example, consciously suppress the reflexive hopping if you had to.

The Autonomic Nervous System (ANS): Internal Organs and Emotions

The autonomic system originates in a structure called the hypothalamus (see p. ___) and controls the activities of the internal organs and glands, regulating heart rate, respiration rate, digestion, and many other processes. The functions influenced by the ANS are not usually under voluntary or conscious control. You cannot, for example, consciously decide to speed up your heart rate in the same way that you can decide to move your arm. The autonomic system does not actually determine *whether* an organ will function but rather the level at which it functions. If, for example, the heart is surgically detached from the autonomic nerves, it will continue to beat; the ANS only influences the rate at which the it beats. Whether your heart speeds up because you are huffing and puffing around the track or because you have just fallen madly in love with someone you met in your psychology class, the increase in heart rate is mediated by autonomic nerves.

Notice the difference between the functioning of the ANS and that of the somatic system. The autonomic system serves to modify or *modulate* the actions of the muscles it acts on. The somatic system directly *causes* the actions of the skeletal muscles. Whereas the ANS influences the rate of the heart, the somatic system causes muscles to contract when you decide to extend your arm. Basically, autonomic functions are involuntary and somatic functions are voluntary (Janig & Habler, 2002).

The autonomic system consists of two subsystems, the sympathetic and the parasympathetic (see Figure 3-11). The *sympathetic nervous system* has sometimes been called the "emergency" nervous system because it tends to dominate in times of stress or extreme activity. In an emergency, sympathetic dominance readies the body to react to danger or otherwise deal with stress: heart rate and blood pressure increase, respiration quickens, and pupils open wide, while such "less important" activities as digestion are inhibited. The *parasympathetic nervous system* tends to be dominant during periods of relative relaxation. It enhances digestive processes, reduces heart rate and blood pressure, and inhibits the flow of blood to skeletal muscles.

Usually, the sympathetic and parasympathetic systems work together to keep the body in a balanced state. Activities that bring the two systems into conflict can cause problems. You may have wondered, for example, why you are commonly cautioned against swimming right after eating a heavy meal. The answer is that swimming produces sympathetic dominance, whereas digestion requires parasympathetic dominance, thus creating a conflict between the two autonomic functions. In this case the conflict might produce muscle cramps, which could make swimming difficult and might cause you to drown.

As you might guess, the autonomic nervous system is particularly important in reactions to stress and in emotional responses more generally (Buijs & Van Eden, 2000). Anxiety is a good example. When you feel anxious or "uptight" during an exam, your heart rate, blood pressure, and other indicators of arousal increase. The increment is produced by a shift to sympathetic dominance caused by the stress of the exam. The same is true for instances of anger, joy, excitement, and other strong emotions. Similarly, the physical stress of jogging causes the ANS to shift to sympathetic dominance, thereby again increasing heart rate and arousal more generally.

Sympathetic activity also occurs when you consume arousing drugs. Caffeine, for example, makes you feel wider awake and more alert, and you might have wondered how it does that. To address that question, the physiological effects of caffeine have been studied extensively (Smith et al., 2001). What we have found is that it produces sympathetic dominance and thereby increases blood pressure (James, in press) and often heart rate (Smith et al., in press).

Arousal involving sympathetic dominance is a normal result of many daily activities. However, when the arousal produced by the sympathetic system under stress is prolonged, it can be a causal factor in such physical disorders as ulcers, high blood pressure, and heart disease (see Chapters 12 and 15). It is because the autonomic system mediates emotion that disorders of the ANS can also result in serious emotional, as well as physical, problems (Benarroch & Chang, 1993).

Gaining Control: Biofeedback. Since the activity of the autonomic nervous system is involuntary, you cannot ordinarily control the functioning of your heart, kidneys, or digestive system. Since it would sometimes be helpful if you could, scientists have been attempting for years to help individuals gain some degree of control over autonomically innervated systems. We do this providing the person with *biofeedback*—consciously perceivable information about the operation of these systems. Stop for a second and put your fingers on the side of your neck over the carotid artery. The heartbeat you feel provides a crude form of biofeedback. Slightly better feedback would be provided by listening to your own heartbeat through a stethoscope.

A more sophisticated way to provide biofeedback about heart rate is to attach electrodes from an electrocardiograph (EKG) machine to the person's chest (Inoue & Sadamoto, 2002). The resulting information about heart rate is then fed through equipment to produce a tone that varies with the heart rate or that operates a meter indicating increases and decreases. With access to such feedback, people have been taught to accelerate or decelerate their heart rates. For example, an individual with tachycardia, an abnormally fast heartbeat, may be able to learn to slow the heart and avoid episodes of tachycardia. Cardiac biofeedback has also been successfully used to reduce the heart response to stressful situations. In one study experimental participants were given heart-rate biofeedback training while controls were not. All played a stressful video game, and the experimental participants were able to maintain a significantly lower heart rate (Larkin et al., 1992). Since stress is a contributor to heart disease, such training may have additional practical applications in the future.

Biofeedback has also been applied to brain waves. In this case, electrodes are attached to the skull, and changes in brain waves are recorded by an electroencephalograph (EEG) machine and fed back to the person as a change in sound or light. Some individuals have been able to use such biofeedback to improve their ability to relax by learning to produce more of the type of brain wave associated with a relaxed condition. In one case study, an alcoholic patient was given EEG feedback of alpha waves, which are associated with relaxation, and told to increase his alpha activity. After training, he was better able to relax, and since alcoholics drink in part to reduce anxiety, he had less craving for alcohol (Evers et al., 2002).

Other applications of biofeedback have included EEG feedback in the treatment of epileptic seizures, blood pressure feedback to help reduce hypertension, and muscle tension feedback to control chronic headaches (Silberstein & Lipton, 1994). In one such study, participants with tension-type headaches were given muscle feedback and told to use it to reduce muscle tension. The biofeedback therapy was successful in raising their pain thresholds and thereby decreasing the frequency of their headaches (Schoenen et al., 1991). Such uses of biofeedback should not be interpreted to mean that it is a cure-all. In fact, it doesn't work at all with some people, and it is seldom easy for the person to gain enough control over autonomic function to produce a clinically significant effect. It is simply one more useful tool in the treatment of some kinds of disorders.

The Endocrine System

The *endocrine system* is a set of glands in various parts of the body that release chemicals into the bloodstream to influence both physiological and emotional functioning. *Hormones* are the chemicals secreted by the endocrine system.

The functioning of the endocrine system is intimately connected with that of the autonomic nervous system. When you are under stress, your ANS not only speeds up your heart rate and raises your blood pressure but also triggers the release of hormones that support the stress response. Some of the more important hormones and the glands that secrete them are shown in Figure 3_12.

The action of neurons is brief, rapid, and limited; the action of hormones is more prolonged and diffuse. When a hormone is released by an endocrine gland, it is carried through the bloodstream to specific target tissues, where it exerts its effects (Buijs & Van Eden, 2002). The hormone testosterone, for example, is produced primarily in the male testes. It stimulates the development of secondary sexual characteristics (such as a beard), promotes sperm production in the testes, and influences overall sex drive. Some chemicals released by endocrine glands act only as hormones, and testosterone is a good example. It performs discrete functions in specific target areas of the body but has no direct neurological functions.

Other chemicals serve dual roles as both hormones and neurotransmitters. Good examples are epinephrine and norepinephrine. When these chemicals serve as a neurotransmitters, they are released across a synapse to carry the nerve impulse; when they serve as a hormones, they are released into the bloodstream to travel to target tissues and perform specific functions there (Tanaka et al., 2000). You can see that the nervous and endocrine systems are closely related in a variety of ways. Their interaction is explored in greater detail in Chapter 12.

Keys to Neuroscience 2

The Central Nervous System: Where You Live

Every organ system in the body is essential to living and functioning normally. However, the central nervous system (CNS) is you. It is the system that controls all the other systems, interprets the world around you, and tells you who you are.

The *central nervous system* consists of two structures: the brain and the spinal cord. Together these structures mediate all interactions between the body and the external environment. Incoming information carried by the peripheral nervous system is processed by the central nervous system, which then issues outputs and commands resulting in reflex actions, voluntary motor behavior, thoughts, and verbalizations, among other modes of action. We will take up the spinal cord first, then deal in more detail with the structure and functions of the brain, ending this section with a discussion of the cerebral cortex.

The Spinal Cord: Communication To and From The Brain

The crucial importance of the spinal cord was made tragically clear when actor Christopher Reeve—Superman—fell from his horse on May 27, 1995. He was riding in a jumping competition when his horse stopped abruptly at a jump, throwing him over its head. The fall injured his spinal cord so severely that he became quadriplegic (had no movement in any of his limbs) and was unable to breathe on his own.

The *spinal cord* is a thick neural tube surrounded by the protective spinal column and containing a small hollow center called the *central canal.* The canal is filled with *cerebrospinal fluid*, a colorless liquid that also circulates through the brain. As Figure 3-13 shows, the H_shaped central part of the spinal cord consists of *gray matter.* The gray color comes from the predominance of unmyelinated gray cell bodies in this area. The surrounding *white matter* consists of myelinated axons that travel up and down the cord.

The spinal cord contains two basic kinds of nerves, sensory and motor. The sensory fibers enter the cord on its *dorsal* (back) side, with one dorsal group of sensory nerves on each side of the spinal column. The motor nerves leave the cord on its *ventral* (front) side. In all, there are thirty_one sets of spinal nerves, each set containing one sensory and one motor nerve on the left side and one of each on the right side.

The spinal cord has two main functions. First, it acts as a neural switchboard, carrying messages back and forth between the brain and the peripheral nervous system. Ascending fiber tracts carry information to the brain, while descending tracts transmit instructions from the brain to the periphery. When you touch a hot stove with your finger, a signal is transmitted from the receptors in your finger up the ascending fiber tracts to the brain, which in turn sends out the pain message via the descending tracts (Cadden & Orchardson, 2001). The second function is to act as a center for processing *reflex behaviors*—automatic behaviors that need not involve the brain. The immediate withdrawal of your finger from the hot stove is a reflex act mediated directly by the spinal cord. When a physician taps your knee to test your reflexes, she is attempting to elicit a stretch reflex. The slight stretching of the muscle fibers caused by the tapping excites muscle receptors, which send information to the spinal cord. Interneurons in the cord relay the information to motor neurons, which are activated to produce the knee jerk reflex (see Figure 3_14). Another example of reflex behavior is the simple act of standing up. When you are standing, you don't have to constantly think about how to keep from falling over. The reason is that your postural stability is mediated by spinal reflexes. Interestingly enough, research shows that such reflexes can be modified by athletic training.

How do we know that reflexively withdrawing your finger from the hot stove doesn't require action by the brain? One way to prove the existence of spinal reflexes is to surgically separate the spinal cord from the brain. When we perform this operation in experimental animals, spinal reflexes continue to occur, proving that the brain is not essential to the reflex. We should note, however, that when the brain and spinal cord are intact, the brain can intervene in what is usually a reflexive process (Schnitzler & Ploner, 2000). For example, knowing that the physician is about to tap your knee, you can make a conscious effort to stop it from jerking when tapped.

The Brain

The brain is without doubt the most complex organ in the human body, and scientists have long believed that the mind lurks somewhere within it. So intricate and delicate are its structures that an alteration in the functioning of a few millimeters of brain tissue can mean the difference between movement and paralysis, between speech and muteness, even between life and death.

Fortunately, the brain is carefully protected from injury in several ways. Its most obvious protection is the bony skull, which can be struck reasonably hard without damaging its precious contents. In addition, the brain is surrounded by three layers of "insulation" called the *meninges.* These membranes both protect the central nervous system and supply it with nourishment. Circulating between the meningeal layers and throughout the brain and spinal cord is a third form of protection, the *cerebrospinal fluid,* which cushions the central nervous system and also provides nutrients.

One final protection is the *blood-brain barrier,* a special arrangement of cells in the walls of the tiny vessels that carry blood and nutrients to brain tissue. This barrier uses specific transport systems and enzymes to regulate the entry of all substances into the brain. Although the brain constitutes only about 2 percent of body weight, it receives 15 percent of the blood supply of the body because of its special needs for nutrients and oxygen. The blood-brain barrier allows these nutrients to enter the brain and spinal cord but bars most chemicals that might disrupt the brain's biochemical balance or damage its tissues. Unfortunately, the blood-brain barrier is not perfect and can be breached by harmful substances, like the bacteria that cause meningitis (Norinder & Haeberlein, 2002). At the same time, the barrier can keep out helpful drugs, such as some antibiotics, a problem that is the basis for considerable current research (Zhang et al., 2002).

Structurally, the well_protected brain can be divided into a large number of parts, representing a division of labor not unlike that in a symphony orchestra. Each part is responsible for special activities—vision, hearing, movement—and all act together in a grand concert that organizes and orchestrates behavior. The various parts make up three major subdivisions: the hindbrain, the midbrain, and the forebrain (see Figure 3-15 and Table 3-1).

The Hindbrain. Have you ever considered how fortunate you are not to have to decide when to take the next breath or how fast your heart should be beating? These important functions and some aspects of sensory and motor operation are controlled quite automatically by the *hindbrain*, highlighted in Figure 3-16. This most primitive of brain structures lies just above the spinal cord. Its major parts include the medulla, the pons, the cerebellum, and the raphe system.

As Figure 3-16 shows, the *medulla* is essentially an enlargement and extension of the spinal cord. It is involved in the control of such body processes as heart rate, breathing, and digestion and in such reflexive behaviors as sneezing, coughing, and vomiting.

As its name implies, the *pons* (meaning "bridge") is a structure that basically serves to connect lower parts of the brain. It contains nerve fiber tracts that come up the spinal cord and continue through to the cerebellum.

The *cerebellum* is basically a sensory_motor coordinating structure. The cat, well known for its graceful movements, has a highly developed cerebellum. Damage to this important structure produces abnormalities in the muscular system. In some instances of cerebellar damage, muscle tone is reduced; other kinds of damage lead to irregular, uncoordinated movements or to reduced speed of movement. The cerebellum is also very sensitive to the effects of alcohol, which is part of the reason that coordination is so impaired even after drinking small amounts.

A final hindbrain structure, the *raphe system,* is important in the control of sleeping/waking patterns. It consists of several nuclei lying between the medulla and the midbrain and contains virtually all the neurons in the brain that release the important neurotransmitter serotonin.

The Midbrain. Lying above the medulla and pons, the *midbrain* (highlighted in Figure 3-17) is a connecting formation that represents a further continuation of the spinal cord. It contains four structures of particular importance: the tectum, the tegmentum, the substantia nigra, and the reticular formation.

The *tectum* is a major way station at which messages from the senses stop on their way to further processing by higher brain centers. It includes two major structures, the *superior colliculus,* which processes primarily visual information, and the *inferior colliculus,* which processes primarily auditory information. More complex processing of visual and auditory stimuli also occurs at higher levels in the brain.

The *tegmentum* contains nuclei involved in the control of eye muscles and also contains ascending and descending fiber tracts connecting the hindbrain and the forebrain.

The *substantia nigra* processes motor information from higher brain levels and is involved in neuromuscular control. The precise muscular control that allows Mikhail Barishnikov to dance so perfectly and steadies the hands of Mario Andretti at 200 mph requires the participation and cooperation of several members of the "neural community," including the substantia nigra. Recent research has shown that this area is importantly involved in Parkinson's disease.

Horizons in Neuroscience: *Aids and the Brain*

The final midbrain structure is the *reticular formation,* or *reticular activating system* (RAS). Although it is classified as a midbrain structure, it is actually quite diffuse, running from the medulla and pons through the midbrain and on to the forebrain (see Figure 3-18). The RAS mediates attention and is particularly important as one of the centers controlling wakefulness and the integration of activation or arousal. Although input from the various senses goes primarily to special centers in the brain, each sense also sends collateral fibers to the reticular formation. For example, the sudden sight of the flashing red lights on a police cruiser stopping on your street might cause your heart to pump faster and your blood pressure to rise, both signs of an increase in your general level of arousal. A piercing scream from somewhere nearby would push your heart rate and general arousal level even higher. The arousal generated by the visual stimulus (flashing red lights) and by the auditory stimulus (the scream) is integrated to produce an arousal level higher than either stimulus alone would generate. Such integration is performed by the RAS.

Nerve fibers from the reticular formation ascend to the cortex and descend into the spinal cord. The ascending fibers activate the cerebral cortex, producing a diffuse state of arousal. The descending system affects muscular movement, as well as the functioning of the heart, stomach, intestines, and other organ systems.

The Forebrain. The largest and most complex section of the brain, the *forebrain,* begins just in front of the midbrain. It can best be conceptualized as divided into two areas, subcortical and cortical.vIf you were to slice down vertically through any portion of the forebrain, you would see that the thin top layer, the cortex, is gray because its cells are unmyelinated. Beneath this thin but crucial layer, there is white matter made up of myelinated tracts that connect the various areas of the cortex. The *subcortex* comprises all structures below the level of the cortex. These structures, shown in Figure 3_19, include the thalamus, the hypothalamus, the limbic system, and the basal ganglia. The cortex performs the most complex functions. It is important to remember that each of the subcortical and cortical structures appears on both the left and right sides or *hemispheres* of the brain. For example, there is a left thalamus and a right thalamus.

The thalamus. Lying just in front of the midbrain, the *thalamus* contains nuclei that receive information from the senses, process and integrate that information, and send it on to the cortex for further processing (Miller et al., 2002). In particular, the *lateral geniculate nucleus* is involved in visual processing and the *medial geniculate nucleus* deals with auditory processing (see Chapter 3). Other nuclei serve to connect the thalamus with the reticular formation and the limbic system. In addition to functioning as a neural relay station for incoming information, the thalamus is an important center for processing certain pain sensations (Sherman, 2001; Jones, 2001) and helps organize the sleep/wake cycle (Lugaresi, 1992).

The hypothalamus and limbic system. The hypothalamus is a tiny but very important structure lying just below the thalamus. Very near the hypothalamus is the *limbic system,* which separates the thalamus from the cortex. It is not a single structure but several separate entities, including the amygdala and the hippocampus. The limbic area is thought of as a system because its structures are all involved in the control of emotion and motivation. Together with the hypothalamus, it also regulates temperature, food and water intake, and the maintenance of a constant internal environment throughout the body (homeostasis). Let's consider what the hypothalamus and the major limbic structures do.

- Hypothalamus. The *hypothalamus* is one of the most fascinating structures in the entire human brain. About the size of a peanut, it makes up only three tenths of one percent of the brain. Nevertheless it is divided into a number of cell groups and is importantly involved in many functions, including eating, drinking, body temperature, consciousness, the sleep/wake cycle, and sexual behavior (Parmeggiani et al., 2000; Swaab et al., 2001). It is important in some forms of obesity and may be a factor in homosexuality, though that is not yet certain

(Schwartz, 2002).

To understand the "love affair" that neuroscientists have with the hypothalamus, imagine yourself working as a research assistant in the laboratory of James Olds and Peter Milner in 1954. Trained in social psychology and relatively new to the rat brain, Olds attempted to implant an electrode in the reticular formation to study the functions of that structure, but he missed. The errant electrode landed in the septum, a part of the limbic system near the hypothalamus. Olds and Milner attached the electrode to a stimulator, and allowed the rat to roam freely around a box. Whenever the rat went to a corner, the researchers stimulated the hypothalamus to see if the rat would find the stimulation unpleasant and avoid the corners. As the research assistant observing the rat, it was your solemn duty to report to Drs. Olds and Milner that precisely the opposite happened. The rat kept returning to the corner in order to get additional stimulation.

Following up on this observation, Olds conducted other experiments in which electrodes were implanted in various limbic structures and thereby located a number of reward centers. In one study, for example, implanted rats pressed a bar to stimulate their brains over 2000 times per hour for 24 hours until they dropped from exhaustion (Olds, 1958). Later research located additional reward centers in and around the hypothalamus and also demonstrated other important functions of that structure.

The hypothalamus is the neural origin of the autonomic nervous system, which is involved in emotion and motivation (see Chapters 12 and 13). In addition, it interacts with the pituitary gland to regulate the production of hormones by the endocrine system (Chapter ___). Because of its many important functions, disorders of the hypothalamus can cause such problems as diabetes, chronic drowsiness, depression, memory loss, hyperphagia (extreme overeating), and hypothermia (low body temperature).

- Amygdala.The *amygdala* is also involved in emotional behavior, particularly aggression. Stimulation of this structure in humans can produce agitation, anger, or rage, while ablation (destruction) can decrease aggressive behavior in violent patients (Buchanan et al., 2001). The amygdala also influences the experience of anxiety and appears to be a center for the processing of emotion. Finally, this tiny structure can be a causal factor in epilepsy (Kenworthy et al., 2001). Studies show that when the amygdala, along with the temporal cortex, is removed in epileptic patients, most remain free of seizures for many years after surgery (Feindel & Rasmussen, 1991).

- Hippocampus. The *hippocampus* is involved in learning and memory (Spiers et al., 2001). Studies show systematic changes in hippocampal firing while an animal is undergoing a learning task and important changes in synapses that may become long-term or permanent (Sela, 2001; McNaughton, 1993). Some evidence suggests that it may be the hippocampus on the left side of the brain that is most critically involved in learning. The hippocampus also appears to play a role in the storage of recent memories, so patients with hippocampal damage rapidly forget recently acquired information. We discuss some interesting cases of such patients in Chapter 9.

  The *basal ganglia.* The *basal ganglia* are located in the central area of each half or hemisphere of the brain, just below the cortex. They are nuclei made up of groups of cell bodies and are believed to be involved in the control of sensory and motor functions (Kaji, 2001). Damage to the basal ganglia can impair motor functions and produce repetitive, compulsive behavior.

  You can see that the exact effect of damage to the brain, such as that caused by Ruth's stroke, will depend, in part, on just what areas of the brain are affected. A stroke that affects the hindbrain could cause breathing or heart problems, while one in the forebrain could affect emotional, motor, and cognitive (thought) functions.

The Cerebral Cortex

The most complex structure in the brain is the very top layer of the forebrain, the *cerebral cortex*. In evolutionary terms, it is the most recently developed area of the brain and is far larger and more complex in humans than in other animals. This area contains three-fourths of the over 100 billion neurons that make up the human nervous system (Gazzaniga, Steen, and Volpe, 1979). Although the cortex is only about a quarter inch thick, its area is vastly increased by numerous convolutions in its surface. If its many overlapping folds and crevices were to be flattened out, the human cortex would have an area of about 2 square feet.

Structurally, the cortex is subdivided into four major areas or *lobes*, which differ in location and function (see Figure 3_20A). The divisions are created by a vertical groove (the *central fissure*) and a horizontal groove (the *lateral fissure*), which course like deep rivers through the mountains and valleys created by the convolutions of the cerebral cortex (Figure 3-20B).

The Frontal Lobes: Moving and Thinking. The *frontal lobes* are involved in the control of movement, and damage can result in such motor defects as paralysis and loss of coordination (Rizzolatti & Luppino, 2001). As you can see in Figure 3-21, there is a band along the rear of the frontal lobe called the primary motor cortex or motor strip. It is here that all fine motor movements are initiated and controlled, each part of the body having its own small area of cortex. The flying fingers of the concert pianist give you an idea of just how intricate and precise this control can be. As

Figure 3-21 shows, areas of the body involved in more precise movements (such as the fingers) have disproportionately large representation in the cortex. However, recent evidence that the motor strip may not be quite so highly organized as has long been thought (Schieber, 2001).

The part of the frontal lobe that lies in front of the motor cortex is called the *prefrontal cortex*, and it handles the most complex intellectual functions, including thought processes and probably self-perception (Gehring & Fencsik, 2001). Damage to some parts of the frontal lobes can therefore greatly reduce cognitive ability (Miller, 2000). As an example of what frontal damage can do to your ability to think, consider a recent study done by Paul Eslinger and Lynn Grattan (1993). They compared groups of patients who had damage to either the frontal lobes or one of two other brain areas with a normal control group. Each patient and control was given a test of spontaneous flexibility called the Alternate Uses Test. For each item, the experimenter named a common object, indicated its usual use, and asked the participant to generate as many other uses as possible. For example, the experimenter would say "newspaper," and give its most common use as "reading." The participant might then indicate that it could alternatively be used to start fires, wrap garbage, swat flies, cushion items packed in boxes, etc. How many more can *you* generate? Try generating as many alternative uses for *these* items as possible:

Hammer—commonly used to pound nails

Pencil—commonly used to write

Paper clip—commonly used to join pages together

How did you do? Well it's a good bet that you did better than most people with damage to the frontal lobes. They showed significantly less spontaneous flexibility than either control participants or those with damage to other parts of the brain. This and similar studies demonstrate the central involvement of the frontal lobes in complex and creative thought processes.

Horizons in Neuroscience: *And You Thought You Had a Headache!*

The Temporal Lobes: Hearing, Emotion, and Memory. The *temporal lobes*, which lie along the sides of the brain in the area of the temples, are involved in hearing; they interpret sounds that reach the ears. It is the temporal lobes that recognize the sound of a voice and let you know that the music you are hearing is Beethoven's Fifth Symphony (Tramo et al., 2002; Keenan et al., 2001). These lobes also have important language functions, as we discuss in Chapter 10. And they are a part of the neural systems that control our emotions and store some kinds of long-term memory (Gaffan, 2001).

The Occipital Lobes: Vision. The *occipital lobes*, at the back of the brain, are concerned primarily with vision and the interpretation of visual images (Sharon & Grinvald, 2002). If you glance around the room you are in right now and name several objects you see, you are using your occipital cortex to interpret and name the visual images. Areas of the temporal lobe also contribute to visual recognition. Damage to the occipital cortex can result in partial loss of vision or at least of the ability to interpret visual images and identify objects. We have more to say about their visual functions in Chapter 4.

The Parietal Lobes: Touch and Movement Sensations. The *parietal lobes*, found just in front of the occipital lobes, are concerned with the interpretation of body sensations, including touch and pressure. They also interpret feedback from your joints and muscles so that you know the position of your body and how it is moving through space. Close your eyes and have a friend hand you an object. By running your fingers over it, you can tell that it is a pencil because your parietal cortex interprets the sensory images transmitted to it from your fingers. Just as there is a motor strip in the frontal lobe, there is a sensory strip, called the *primary somatosensory cortex*, in the forward part of the parietal lobe (Figure 3-21). Let's take a look at how the sensory and motor areas of the brain are organized to deal with incoming information and the control of movement.

Projection and Association Areas. Of the total area of the cerebral cortex, about 20 percent is involved in receiving input from the senses and sending commands to the muscles. These areas of the brain are called sensory and motor *projection areas*, respectively (see Figure 3-21). The remaining 80 percent of the cortex integrates sensory and motor information in what are called *association areas*.

Projection areas. The localization of specific functions in the various lobes of the cerebral cortex can be more fully understood by considering the concept of projection areas. The projection areas for vision and hearing are straightforward. Visual images are carried through nerve fibers from the eyes via lower brain centers to the occipital lobes, while sounds entering the ear project to the temporal lobes. It is in these specific areas of the cerebral cortex that the interpretation of sights and sounds takes place. For example, the page you are staring at right now is seen by the eyes and lower brain centers as simply an object _ a visual stimulus _ but it is interpreted by the occipital cortex of your brain as a part of a textbook.

More elaborate is the breakdown of the areas dealing with information from the skin and body senses and with motor movement. As we have already noted, these areas lie on either side of the fissure that separates the frontal and parietal lobes and are called primary somatosensory cortex and primary motor cortex. Each projection area either receives certain kinds of sensory information or causes certain motor commands to be carried out. As Figure 3-21 shows, it is laid out like a map of the body with each tiny area corresponding to a part of the body. Stimulation of one sensory area may lead to a tingling sensation in the index finger, another to sensation in the lips. Stimulation of one small portion of the motor cortex controls the movement of the toes, another the wrist. Brain damage that affects the somatosensory cortex and related association cortex can cause a variety of sensory or motor problems.

Association areas. Association areas serve to connect the various projection areas together (Figure 3-22). Areas of sensory and motor cortex dominate the brains of lower animals, but the association areas are far larger in the human brain. These areas also appear to be involved in such complex processes as thought, memory, and language. The major association areas are the *frontal, somatic* or body (located in the parietal lobe), *visual* (in the occipital lobe) and *auditory* (in the temporal lobe). We have more to say about the functions of specific association areas in Chapters 9 and 10 where we discuss memory and language.

Neural Networks

From our discussion of the brain thus far, you might easily decide that all functions are entirely localized: specific aspects of vision in specific areas of the occipital cortex; right index finger movement in a small area of the motor strip; sound interpretation in the temporal lobe. It is certainly true that many functions are localized. However, one of the newest theories of neural activity suggests that other functions are often spread across several areas of the brain in what are called neural networks (Wiech et al., 2001).

A *neural network* is a set of neurons linked to each other at their synapses. The neurons in a given network may be close to each other but are more likely to be scattered across the cortex. Each network performs specific functions, and many networks are connected to form larger and larger networks that carry out coordinated activities. Your memories of numbers, names, and various aspects of your life, for example, may be contained in interlinked neural networks. The network concept has been applied particularly to such areas as learning, memory and thought processes, and we deal with it in Chapters 8, 9, and 10.

The Evolving Brain

We have been describing the structures of the human brain. However, as Chapter 1 suggests, we humans are basically animals that exist at the top of an evolutionary hierarchy. It will therefore be no surprise to learn that, like the behaviors it controls, the brain has evolved over the centuries and across animal species to its present human form. Lower animals do not have such elaborate brains.

Figure 3-23 shows how the nervous system has evolved. Both vertebrates—animals with backbones—and invertebrates have neurons. However, the structure of the nervous system in invertebrates like the jelly fish is very simple, and there is no true brain. Species slightly higher on the scale, like the flatworm, have a more advanced structure called a nerve cord, which is basically a sheaf of nerve cells that extends over the length of the body. They also have ganglia, including enlarged ganglia at the front of the body that serve as primitive brains.

Vertebrates have a spinal cord surrounded by the bony disks of the spinal column, and the vertebrate brain has evolved gradually as an extension of the spinal cord. The brains of animals lower in the hierarchy, such as reptiles, emphasize hindbrain and then midbrain structures. Early mammals have subcortical forebrain structures, including the limbic system, that deal with aggression and emotion more generally, as well as hunger, thirst, and other drives. Gradually, as mammalian species evolve, we begin to see the cerebral cortex being laid down as the top layer of the forebrain and the frontal lobe enlarging in relation to the other lobes. The human brain has by far the most advanced structure, with its extensive, convoluted cortex. The adaptive evolutionary developmental process is clear: The lowest animal species have only those neurological structures necessary for biological survival; more advanced species develop neurological mechanisms that permit a structure of drives and the experience of emotion; and the most advanced species are also equipped to think. Notice also how the intrauterine development of the human brain parallels the evolutionary process.

The biological evolution of the brain is seen by evolutionary psychologists and biologists as an adaptive process necessitated by environmental demands. Each species, as it evolved during ancient times, was faced with the need to survive and reproduce in the specific environment in which it existed. The environment posed problems, such as the need to obtain food and the need for self-protection, and the species evolved to solve those problems. Members of the species who responded successfully to these environmental demands were more likely to survive and reproduce, passing on their genes—and hence their brain structures—to future generations. Neural structures thus evolved in order to perform the functions required to adapt to the environment. More advanced structures were required to deal with more complex environments, and the human brain therefore gradually evolved over millions of years to its present state. We discuss in other chapters how this biological evolution of the brain is related to the evolution of psychological functions, such as emotion and thought.

Interestingly enough, the development of the human brain, beginning a few weeks after conception, roughly parallels its evolution across species. Within the first month of fetal development, three bulbous enlargements or swellings of the nervous system develop. As development progresses, the formation of the hindbrain is followed by that of the midbrain, then the forebrain. The development of the cortex continues well beyond birth, gradually ending during adolescence.

Keys to Neuroscience 3

A Brain Divided: Lateralization of Function

Remember we said that a grove running from the front of the head to the back divides the brain into two halves, which are called *hemispheres*. For some functions, such as motor control, each hemisphere affects the opposite side of the body. Control is thus *contralateral;* that is, the right hemisphere controls the left side, while the left hemisphere controls the right side. When you write with your right hand, for example, its movement is controlled by the left hemisphere of your brain.

Early scientists believed that the two hemispheres are identical in structure and function, but that has turned out not to be true. Just as your two hands may vary somewhat in size or shape, the two hemispheres vary in both size and function. The speech area in the left hemisphere, for example, is actually larger than comparable areas in the right hemisphere, and the left hemisphere is typically longer and wider than the right (Koff et al., 1986).

The two hemispheres are connected by a tract of fibers called the *corpus callosum* (see Figure 3-24). Like the old underwater telephone cables that crossed the ocean to connect the North American and European continents, the corpus callosum permits the two hemispheres to communicate with each other so that each knows what the other is doing. The result is coordinated activity, some controlled by the right hemisphere, some controlled by the left, and some by the interaction of the two. The amount of information transferred from one hemisphere to the other via the corpus callosum varies considerably from one area of the brain to another, probably because some kinds of information are processed primarily within a single hemisphere while other kinds require that both hemispheres be involved, or at least informed. Let's take up two bodies of research that have attempted to sort out the differing functions of the two hemispheres: studies of patients with no intact corpus callosum and studies of normal controls. We will then ask whether we really have two brains and hence two minds.

Dividing the Walnut: Split Brain Research

You might ask what would happen if someone were born with no corpus callosum. To answer this question, two patients in whom the corpus callosum was absent were carefully tested for the interhemispheric transfer of information. Interestingly enough, one showed only minor deficits and the other showed none at all. Other brain mechanisms had compensated for the missing structure.

The effects of disconnecting the two hemispheres have also been studied in people suffering from epilepsy, a neurological disorder characterized by seizures. Epilepsy can result from a stroke like Ruth's, from a blow on the head, or from a number of other causes. Neurosurgeon William Van Wagenen discovered in the 1940s that by severing the corpus callosum he could reduce the incidence of seizures in his epileptic patients. He noted that despite such seemingly radical brain surgery, the patient's day-to-day behavior was essentially unaffected. Two other neurosurgeons, Phillip Fogel and Joseph Bogen, refined the split-brain technique and obtained positive results for most of their patients as well.

Curious about the effects of this surgery on behavior, Roger Sperry (1964) and his colleagues began to test split-brain patients in a number of ways. Sperry discovered that the operation had little effect on general intelligence, personality, or temperament, and more recent research has shown little effect on memory.

But Sperry couldn't quite believe that severing the corpus callosum had such minimal effects, and he saw in the study of split-brain patients the possibility of learning whether or not the two hemispheres differed in their functions. He and his colleagues therefore devised some ingenious methods for discovering ways in which split-brain patients differ from "whole-brain" people. In a *visual half-field* experiment, for example, a picture is flashed briefly to either the left or the right side of the patient's visual field. Remember that control is contralateral, so a picture shown to the left visual field is projected to the right hemisphere and vice versa. The person is then asked to report what she sees. Sperry found that patients could easily identify and verbally report pictures shown to the right visual field, but they had difficulty naming items shown to the left field (see Figure 3-25). The reason is that the left hemisphere usually controls speech.

More recent studies confirm a right visual half-field (left hemisphere) advantage in naming objects. Take the example of N.G., a California housewife. She was briefly shown a picture of a nude woman in her left visual field (right hemisphere). She began to giggle, but when asked to report what she saw, she said she had only seen a flash of light. When the same picture was flashed to her left hemisphere, she laughed and described it correctly (Gazzaniga, 1967).

Interviews with split_brain patients have also revealed that there are other occasions on which "the right hand doesn't know what the left hand is doing." One man reported that on an occasion when he had been angry at his wife, he reached for her with his left hand, then noticed that his right hand had grabbed the left in an effort to stop the attack (Broca, 1970). Further studies of split_brain patients have shown that the left hand (right hemisphere) is better at performing spatial tasks. For example, the left hand can usually produce more skillful drawings than the right. Such findings suggest that the right hemisphere is superior to the left in visuospatial tasks. And more generally, Sperry and others began to discover that the two hemispheres are not identical in their functions. As we will see, the left side has primary control of some activities, the right side of others. This differentiation between to the two hemispheres is called *lateralization* of function.

Asymmetry in the Normal Brain

When studies are done only in a special patient population, such as epileptics with split brains, it is always possible that the results are not generalizable to the normal population. Research with normal participants has involved such techniques as Sperry's visual half-field method, already described, and a procedure called *dichotic listening.* In this approach, subjects hear two different messages spoken simultaneously, one presented to each ear. "Red flowers" might be the verbal message presented to the left ear, while "blue necktie" is simultaneously presented to the right ear. Participants are then asked to report what message they heard. In hearing one competing message over the other, subjects may show right-ear or left-ear dominance, depending on the nature of the stimulus (Christianson, 1992). This evidence supports the idea that one hemisphere is typically dominant over the other in normal controls as well as split-brain patients.

Two Brains, Two Minds?

Evidence suggests that there may be some real and important differences between the two hemispheres centering around the differentiation between *verbal* and *spatial* processes (Kenworthy et al., 2001). The left hemisphere appears to be specialized for the processing of verbal information. It contains the speech center in about 95 percent of all right-handed people and 70 percent of all left-handers. The right hemisphere is typically better equipped to deal with spatial tasks. Suppose you were to ride in a car over a new route to a distant location. If you then had to make the same trip on your own, you would find your way using the spatial abilities of your right hemisphere (provided you didn't use too many verbal cues to learn the route).

It also appears that the left hemisphere is more analytical than the right and is concerned with fine motor control and organization in time (see Table 3-2). The right hemisphere appears specialized for the perception of music and for less analytical and more global or holistic thought processes. It may also be specialized for personal relevance, maintaining and processing such information as familiar faces, voices and names, as well as your unique style of handwriting and otherwise expressing yourself (Perry et al., 2001).

Additional research on hemispheric differences has focused on the perception and expression of emotion. These studies show interesting, but inconsistent, differences between the two hemispheres. One theory holds that the right hemisphere is almost wholly responsible for emotion, and there is considerable evidence in support of this hypothesis (Borod, 1992). An alternative theory, based on somewhat different experimental results, suggests that positive emotions are handled by the left hemisphere and negative ones by the right (Davidson, 1992). A final theory divides the action of the two hemispheres differently, hypothesizing that emotional experiences have two components, content (happy, sad, angry, and so on) and intensity (mild, moderate, or strong). You can be mildly happy or extremely happy, and similarly a little sad or very sad. The theory holds that the content of the emotion is processed by the right hemisphere, which determines whether you will be happy or sad, while the intensity of the emotion is a left-hemisphere function (B. D. Smith, Kline, & Meyers, 1990; Smith et al., 1994). Obviously, we will have to do considerable additional research before we know which theory is more nearly correct.

Does the apparent functional difference between hemispheres suggest that we have two brains rather than one? In a sense, it appears we do. However, the point should not be overstated, for many functions are performed equally well by both hemispheres.

Keys to Neuroscience 4

Immersed in Thought: Brain Biochemistry

It was only a little over 100 years ago that Sigmund Freud, a medical student specializing in neurology, was studying the human brain in an attempt to understand how it controls behavior. He and his colleagues were greatly hampered by the belief that they could understand brain function by focusing solely on the anatomy of the brain and its electrical activity. What they did not yet know was that the brain is constantly bathed in a multitude of substances that we now call *neurochemicals*—chemicals involved in the functioning of the brain. In fact, the brain is a chemical laboratory, far more accomplished than those of Dupont or Parke Davis. Its cells constantly produce, store, use, and destroy a variety of chemicals that are crucial to the neural control of behavior. Indeed, the electrical activity of the brain and nervous system would be essentially useless if it were not for the presence of chemical codes that permit the same electrical nerve impulse to produce a variety of behaviors. We will focus on two major classes of brain chemicals, neurotransmitters and natural opiates. We will then consider the role of nutrition in brain chemistry and ask whether there really are drugs that make you smarter.

Neurotransmitters

In the simplest of neurological worlds, there would be only one or two of the neurotransmitters that carry nerve impulses across the synaptic cleft. It appears, however, that in reality there are at least 100-150 of these chemical substances. We don't know exactly why there are so many different kinds, but we do know that each transmitter is quite specific to particular locations in the nervous system (Table 3-3). Dopamine, for example, is found primarily in the midbrain, serotonin is concentrated mostly in the raphe system, and norepinephrine has its highest levels in the RAS, the hypothalamus, and the medulla. This specificity is also reflected in the behavioral effects of neurotransmitters. Serotonin, for example, appears to be involved in the control of sleep and perhaps some aspects of eating behavior, depression, and suicide (van Heeringen, 2001), whereas dopamine and norepinephrine are important in emotional responses. All three probably also have important roles in psychological disturbances, a topic we discuss further in Chapter 16. Other neurotransmitters deal with learning and memory or with addiction to alcohol and drugs.

So crucial are chemical transmitters to the normal flow of activity in the nervous system that any interference with these substances is likely to create problems. Some poisons, such as botulism toxin and the curare used by South American tribes on their blowgun darts, act by preventing the release of acetylcholine, which is found in axon terminals that end at muscle fibers. These poisons reduce or eliminate movement, including respiratory movement, thereby causing paralysis and death. Chorea, a serious disorder characterized by irregular, involuntary movement of muscles in the tongue, face, and hands, is associated with excessively high levels of dopamine. Parkinson's disease, with its tremors, slowed movements, and muscular weakness, appears to be caused by low levels of dopamine in particular areas of the brain. And a blow on the head can temporarily disrupt normal neurochemical activity, creating what we call a biochemical lesion and rendering the person unconscious. Fortunately, if the damage is entirely neurochemical, the patient can recover fully.

Brain Drugs: The Natural Opiates

Lying in a hospital bed after a horse-riding accident in 1970, biologist Candace Pert received numerous shots of morphine, a painkiller derived from the opium plant. As a result of her experience, she became curious about the brain mechanisms underlying the effects of morphine, and she returned to her research laboratory to find out. Three years later, she and Solomon Snyder published the striking discovery that morphine kills pain by binding to special receptors in the brain (Pert & Snyder, 1973). Since the brain would not likely have special receptors for a substance that comes from outside the body, they reasoned that morphine-like chemicals must occur naturally. They called these chemicals *endorphins* (endogenous morphines). The endorphins, and chemically similar substances called *enkephalins,* act in much the same way that morphine does, but are far more potent. They are *neuropeptides*—strings of amino acids—that occupy the same receptor sites in the brain as opiates do, and these sites are located along brain pathways known to carry pain information.

Evidence that the endorphins are natural pain-killers and stress reducers comes from a variety of sources (Drolet et al., 2001). First, a drug called naloxone, which is known to block the effects of morphine, also blocks the action of endorphins, suggesting that they are similar to the pain drug. In addition, acupuncture procedures used to reduce pain may do so by causing a release of endorphins (see Chapter), perhaps found in the cerebrospinal fluid (Shen, 2001). Other evidence shows that patients with severe pain following an acute myocardial infarction, or heart attack, have elevated levels of beta-endorphin (Bernardi et al., 1992), presumably in reaction to the pain. Still other research has focused on those born without the ability to feel pain, a dangerous condition that leads to burns and other serious injuries. These people have much higher plasma levels of beta-endorphin than do controls who feel pain normally.

A final body of research has long shown that physical exercise increases pain thresholds considerably, thereby reducing pain sensations. For example, a research associate who works with me played varsity soccer several years ago in college. She seriously sprained her ankle near the beginning of one game but played the entire day without experiencing much pain. Shortly after the game ended the pain became severe, and she was unable to walk or even sleep well for several weeks. The exercise of playing the game had produced elevated endorphin levels and protected her from the pain. Recent evidence suggests more generally that the pain-reducing effect of exercise is achieved by increasing levels of beta-endorphin. Thus, endorphins appear to be true natural pain killers that provide an internal supply of morphine-like substances when needed. Just how endorphins work is not certain, but it appears that they chemically stimulate descending brain stem mechanisms, which affect the spinal cord to inhibit the transmission of pain sensations from the body.

Interestingly, endorphins are often released in the brain under conditions in which the sensation of pain might be harmful to the individual. Soldiers wounded in battle, for example, often report no pain sensation until they are out of danger, and people injured in car accidents report similar experiences. Studies with rats appear to confirm these anec-

dotal observations: endorphins are released under stress to reduce pain. One group of investigators conditioned rats to fear their cage by giving them a series of electric shocks. After eight days of shock training, the researchers performed a "tail flick" test in which a rat's tail was heated with a light bulb and the reflex tail movement recorded. Rats that had been shocked were less sensitive to the pain induced by the heat and thus slower to flick their tails. When endorphins were administered to the rats, the delay in the tail-flick response increased markedly, suggesting less pain. In addition, when the brains of the rats were later examined, it was found that those with the shock-conditioned fear had released endorphins to a much greater extent than those without the conditioned fear.

Horizons in Neuroscience: *A Natural Brain Tranquilizer*

Eat, Drink, and Be Functional: Nutrition and the Brain

The more we learn about brain biochemistry, the more apt the adage "You are what you eat" becomes. Not surprisingly, the functioning of the nervous system can be influenced by the substances we take in as part of our diet. In particular, the quantity of specific neurotransmitters available for use at synapses may be in part a function of the intake of dietary substances that are important in the synthesis of those transmitters. For example, dopamine and norepinephrine (collectively referred to as catecholamines) are synthesized from an amino acid in protein_rich foods. A dietary protein deficiency can therefore result in changes in neurological functioning due to inadequate levels of catecholamines. Similarly, consuming choline, which is found in egg yolk, liver, and peanuts, increases brain levels of acetylcholine. There is some animal evidence that a choline-rich diet may actually enhance memory. This effect is also seen in those with senile memory deficits or memory impairment following brain concussions who are given choline. The evidence to date is, however, minimal and may well not hold up. Therefore, don't eating lots of eggs and liver to increase affect your memory; such a diet might only serve to clog your arteries!

A further example of dietary effects is seen in work on the consumption of tryptophan, an amino acid that can increase the level of serotonin in the brain under some circumstances. Tryptophan is found in such protein-rich foods as meat, chicken, and fish. When these foods are eaten in combination with carbohydrates, which help the tryptophan enter the brain, levels of serotonin increase. Since serotonin is involved in sleep and pain sensitivity, it is not surprising that some studies show positive effects of tryptophan ingestion on mild insomnia and chronic pain. However, tryptophan has been identified as a possible causal factor in at least one fatal disease, called eosinophilia-myalgia syndrome, and is therefore potentially dangerous (McKinley et al., 1993).

What happens when the diet does not contain sufficient amounts of substances necessary for the manufacture of neurotransmitters? One possible answer comes from the observation that countries with large amounts of corn in the diet have the highest murder rates). Because corn contains little tryptophan, a high-corn diet might lead to a deficiency of serotonin in the brain. It has been found that serotonin levels are below normal in people with a history of violent behavior (Virkkunen et al., 1994). So it is possible that a high-corn, low-serotonin diet increases violence and hence the murder rate in some countries. However, this is so far only a hypothesis that will require considerable further research.

A final example of the role of diet in brain chemistry is Korsakoff's psychosis, a severe disorder characterized by memory loss, confusion, and disorientation, which results from a deficiency of B vitamins. The vitamin deficiency itself is usually caused by alcoholism and occurs because the alcoholic eats a very poor diet and consumes relatively little vitamin B, while the alcohol creates an abnormally high need for this nutrient. The vitamin deficiency produces brain damage, which causes the Korsakoff psychosis.

If nutrition affects the brain, could we use specific nutrients or perhaps drugs to improve intellectual functioning? We ask you to Think Critically about that question.

Keys to Neuroscience 3

Breaking the Code: Methods of Brain Study

Over the years, brain researchers have used a number of methods to try to discover how the brain works. The older, but still important, methods of brain study include examination of brain-damaged persons, microscopic examination of brain tissue, ablation (destruction of brain tissue), electrical and chemical stimulation, and electrical recording. Newer methods include computerized axial topography (CT), magnetic resonance imaging (MRI), positron emission tomography (PET), single photon emission computed tomography (SPECT), and a variety of others (Mazziotta, 1994). These methods are used both in research and to assess brain damage in cases like Ruth's where we need to know what treatment might be most appropriate. Let's look at each approach briefly.

Damaged Brains

One way to localize brain functions is to correlate damage to certain areas with specific impairments in behavior. Brain damage may be caused by blows to the head, tumors, oxygen deprivation, stroke, bacterial infections, the HIV virus, excessive alcohol consumption, and a variety of other agents (Brady et al., 2001).

Damage to some parts of the parietal lobes reduces the ability to perform even fairly routine motor tasks. Depending on the area damaged, the person may be unable to use colored blocks to copy a pattern shown in a drawing or be incapable of dressing properly. If damage occurs in certain areas of the left parietal lobe, the patient will not attend to most objects or events to his right. In addition, the right half of a picture he is asked to draw will be poorly drawn, whereas the left half will be relatively well executed.

Speech disturbances have been found to result from damage to specific areas of the frontal and temporal lobes (Lytton and Brent, 1989). A variety of disorders, ranging from muteness to relatively minor speech difficulties, can result from damage to these areas. The major speech disorders, referred to as *aphasias*, are discussed in greater detail in Chapter 10.

Damage to yet other areas of the brain can result in memory problems (Hodges and Ward, 1989). Difficulty in recognizing objects occurs, for example, when areas that store sensory memory are damaged. These parts of the cortex are located near the primary sensory areas for vision, hearing, touch, and smell. If the visual memory area is damaged, the person may not recognize a book presented visually, although careful feeling of the object with the fingertips may allow her to identify it. Another kind of memory problem that can occur with damage to the right hemisphere is *prosopagnosia*, in which the patient is unable to recognize faces but otherwise functions quite normally.

It was long thought that damage to neurons in the central nervous system is permanent, since it appeared that there was no regeneration of CNS cells. However, exciting new findings show that neurons in the brain and spinal cord can regenerate under certain conditions and that this regrowth process can be furthered by using newly developed drugs and procedures (Woerly et al., 2001; Guo et al., 2001). These advances in knowledge have important implications for the eleven thousand Americans who are paralyzed each year. In fact, we may soon be able to cure some paralyses by producing and supporting nerve regeneration (Evans, 2001; Ramer et al., 2000).

Up Close and Personal: Tissue Examination

Perhaps the most obvious method of study is to directly examine the tissue of the brain after autopsy. This approach, employed by early neuroscientists, is still used in updated form by modern researchers, who examine the tissue under a microscope. To prepare brain tissue for such examination, the researcher removes the tissue to be studied, places it in formalin to fix and preserve its features, hardens it by freezing or embedding it in wax-like substances, then sections it into extremely thin slices. The tissue is then stained to allow ready identification of specific features. The prepared tissue can now be examined under a microscope to determine its characteristics.

In animal research, tissue examination is the final phase of a study in which the animal has been subjected to various experimental conditions. In human studies, the researcher can examine suspected sections of the brains of people who have died natural deaths to determine whether there is any evidence of damage that could have caused some unusual behavior or disorder. The brains of psychotic patients, mass murderers, and other groups with some particular behavioral deviation can be studied in this way.

Ablation and Lesioning

In using ablation or lesioning techniques, researchers observe the animal's behavior, then remove or destroy a specific bit of brain tissue to see what effect it has on behavior. ***Ablation*** techniques involve surgically removing a part of the brain, while *lesioning* involves destruction of tissue.

An example of the use of lesioning and ablation techniques can be found in the study of aggressive behavior. Early researchers found that destruction of the amygdala greatly reduces aggression (Galef, 1970). More recent studies have shown that only one specific nucleus within that structure must be ablated to reduce aggressive behavior. Based on the animal studies, human patients who exhibit uncontrolled aggressive behavior have been successfully lesioned (Mark, Sweet, and Erwin, 1975; Treiman, 1991). Our peek into the next century deals with an exciting newer technique that involves implanting new tissue in the brain—essentially the opposite of lesioning.

Stimulating Experiences

An alternative to destroying brain tissue is to stimulate it, either electrically or chemically, and we have already noted how stimulation can affect areas of the hypothalamus and amygdala. In investigations involving brain stimulation, researchers deliver a mild electrical current through an implanted electrode to a specific brain area (see Figure 3-26). In order to study blood pressure responses to stress, for example, electrodes were implanted in the amygdalas of a group of hypertensive rats. Stimulation of the amygdala reduced the arousal response of the hypertensive rats to stressful stimulation, possibly suggesting a role for the amygdala in the arousal response of human hypertensive patients (McBride et al., 1999).

Electrical stimulation can also be applied to the human brain. During brain surgery, the surgeon can open the skull, then electrically stimulate areas on and surrounding the diseased tissue to determine what must be removed. Some surgeons have used stimulation techniques to map human brain functions, especially of the somatosensory and motor areas of the cortex. One investigator was even able to elicit specific memories by stimulating precise areas (see Chapter 9).

Jose Delgado has been a pioneer in electrical stimulation of the brain. His early studies involved implanting chimpanzees with up to 100 electrodes through which he could deliver stimuli to the brain, causing a chimp to turn its head, yawn, open or close its eyes, or move its arms and legs. More dramatic has been his work with bulls and humans. Delgado implanted electrodes in the amygdala of a bull, then put the bull in a ring with a matador. When the bull was in full charge toward the matador's red cape, Delgado used a remote control stimulator to stop the enraged animal in its tracks. He has also implanted electrodes in the brains of humans in an effort to control rage attacks, epileptic seizures, and pain (Delgado et al., 1975). The implanted patient carries a small transmitter that he can use to activate the electrode himself. Such treatments are quite controversial, but the future nevertheless holds fascinating possibilities for using implanted electrodes to treat a variety of human nervous system maladies.

A good example of the potential human benefits of brain stimulation is seen in work on *Parkinson's Disease.* First described by the English physician James Parkinson in 1817, the disease is characterized by muscular tremors, rigidity, and movement problems that become progressively more severe. Studies implicate the neurotransmitter dopamine, which is found in the midbrain (Tooyama et al., 1993) and drugs related to dopamine are used to treat Parkinson's with some success. One recently developing alternative treatment involves the permanent implantation of stimulating electrodes. The electrodes are implanted in the thalamus, the sensory relay center in the forebrain. A recent study of 10 Parkinson's patients with these electrode implants showed that tremors were reduced or eliminated in eight of the ten cases when stimulation was regularly delivered (Caparros-Lefebvre et al., 1993).

We also now implant electrodes in the human brain and spinal cord for other therapeutic purposes. A patient with severe pain can use a remote control to turn on an implanted electrode that reduces the pain, and some epileptic patients have implants that can stop seizures. We can also record from human implants to study the functioning of the brain during such activities as thought and face recognition (Allison et al., 1994).

An alternative to electrical techniques is the use of chemicals to stimulate small areas of the brain. The researcher inserts a cannula (tube) instead of an electrode. Drugs, neurotransmitters, and other chemicals can then be delivered through the cannula and their effects on brain and behavior can be observed. Results of this type of research have been difficult to interpret because the same chemical delivered to different areas of the brain may produce quite different results.

Electrical Recording

The *electroencephalogram* (EEG) is a measure of the electrical activity of the brain. It was first developed by Hans Berger in the 1920s. As a young German soldier, he fell off his horse one day and was surprised to get a telegram from his father that evening saying that his sister had a sense that he was in danger. Berger thought that this was an instance of telepathy and became interested in the relationship between mental phenomena and the brain. Later, as a doctoral student at the University of Jena, he began a long series of attempts to record electrical activity from the brain. Finally, in 1924, he placed two metal electrodes on his son's head and successfully recorded wave forms that he reported were correlated with conscious experience.

Berger's EEG and its far more sophisticated modern counterpart involve attaching electrodes to specific points on the scalp to record the electrical activity of several brain areas simultaneously. As each EEG electrode picks up neuroelectrical activity the signal is amplified by the electroencephalograph and written out as a "squiggly" line on a moving strip chart or recorded on a computer disk. The squiggles represent *brain waves* (Figure 3-27). Characteristic brain waves are associated with each state of consciousness, from alertness to deep sleep (see Chapter 5). Experienced clinicians and researchers can "read" the EEG recordings of a person to determine what activity is taking place in the brain, and it is used in diagnosing epilepsy and other disorders, as well as in research on the brain (Schutter et al., 2001).

One EEG study involved professional soccer players who might have brain damage caused by hitting the ball with their heads for many years. EEG recordings showed abnormalities in 35% of active players, as compared with only 13% of matched control samples (Tysvaer, 1992). Other researchers have used EEG to study epileptic children with possible brain tumors (Sjors et al., 1993) or to confirm the presence of brain damage that often follows whiplash injuries in automobile accidents (Ettlin et al., 1992).

The brain waves recorded on the EEG represent the activity of large numbers of neurons. It is also possible to record the activity of a single neuron. This is accomplished by inserting a *microelectrode*—an electrode too small to be seen by the human eye—into the soma of the neuron or just outside the neuron. The electrode used for such recording is typically a glass capillary tube with a tip that is less than 0.0002 mm in diameter. The microelectrode is usually filled with a potassium chloride solution to permit electrical contact with the interior of the cell, and wires attached to the electrode allow the amplification and recording of electrical activity within the neuron. Microelectrode recording has helped us understand the mechanisms involved in neuron firing that we discussed earlier.

Brain Scanning: The Newest Kid on the Block

The medical use of computers and other sophisticated equipment has given rise to several very useful noninvasive methods for studying the brain (Bassarath, 2001; Mazziotta, 2001). In each case, the brain is scanned from outside the skull to determine whether or not there are abnormalities that may underlie either neurological or psychological symptoms (Honey et al., 2002).

***Computerized Axial Tomography* (CT). Ordinary X-rays typically take a single picture of the three dimensional body and print it on two-dimensional film. With *computerized tomography* or CT (sometimes also abbreviated CAT), researchers are now able to produce what is essentially a 3-D X-ray. The scanner accomplishes this feat by taking a number of different photos of the internal structure of the brain, then using mathematical techniques to construct a picture of the brain's interior (see Figure 3-28A). CT scanning, the first of the newer techniques to be fully developed, revolutionized both neurological research and the clinical evaluation of central nervous system disorders.**

The CT scanner reconstructs slices of the brain for diagnostic examination. It is the primary imaging technique for patients with head trauma and is routinely employed in detecting a wide variety of brain disorders, such as abscesses, tumors, intracranial bleeding, degenerative diseases of the brain, and congenital abnormalities (Prayer & Rametsteiner, 2001). It can be used to determine the extent of brain damage caused by a stroke or to guide the injection of radioactive materials into malignant brain tumors. CT is also commonly used to evaluate psychiatric patients for possible neurological involvement and may eventually be a useful tool in diagnosing such disorders.

***Magnetic Resonance Imaging* (MRI). Another of the relatively new brain imaging techniques is *magnetic resonance imaging* (MRI). The person is placed in a magnetic field 4,000 times stronger than that of the earth. Coils surrounding him pulse radio waves into the body, which responds by bouncing the radio signals back to the machine. The resulting scan provides important information about biochemical and metabolic activity (see Figure 3-28B). It has the unique ability to provide information about tissue chemistry without invading the patient's body. A more recent upgrade of the "old" MRI technique is called *functional MRI* (fMRI). It adds to basic MRI a mapping of blood volume and blood flow patterns in the brain (Miki et al., 2001; Menon, 2001).**

Magnetic resonance imaging has rapidly become one of our most important research and clinical diagnostic tools. Its use for diagnosis of tissue disorders shows considerable promise, but its primary use at this time is in studying and diagnosing such neurological disorders as tumors and epilepsy. MRI is already considered one of the most accurate tools for diagnosis of some brain disorders, and some believe it is more generally the most useful of all the neurological diagnostic techniques. MRI is also used in brain research. An example is provided by a study of the effects of boxing, which is known to produce brain damage. Thirteen boxers who agreed to participate were given MRIs before and after each of several fights. All eventually showed neurological signs, documenting the destructive effects of the sport (Holzgraefe et al., 1992).

***Positron Emission Tomography* (PET). One of the newest tools in the little black bag of the neurologist and neuropsychologist is *positron emission tomography* (PET). This exciting method provides intricate pictures of the inside of a living brain. The operation of the PET scanner is complex but interesting. The person is given a dose of radioactively labeled glucose. The glucose passes the blood_brain barrier and circulates through the blood supply of the brain, where it is scanned by the PET machine. The radioactive substances are positron_emitting isotopes that are incorporated into neurotransmitters and other brain biochemicals. The positrons collide with electrons. Both particles are destroyed in the process, but their mass is converted to energy that can be recorded by the PET scanner. A computer then determines the distribution of positron_electron collisions and generates images of slices of the brain (see Figure 3-28C). These images can be examined to determine chemical and metabolic changes in brain tissue.**

PET scans are highly sensitive to blood flow changes in the brain and even respond to changes in mental activities. Robert Beck, a PET scan researcher, feared that he had a brain tumor after a scan of his own head revealed an asymmetry of blood flow. It turned out that the asymmetry was apparently the result of his thought processes during the scan. He had been counting, a process that activates the left temporal lobe (remember those hemispheric differences), thereby causing a difference in blood flow between the right and left sides of the brain.

Researchers at the University of Chicago are studying blood flow and metabolism in people without brain damage to establish baseline indications of just what the normal brain looks like on a PET scanner. Other laboratories are investigating the use of PET scanning in diagnosing and studying brain tumors, epilepsy, the aging process, and stroke (Fahey, 2001). One long-standing problem in the treatment of stroke victims has been that of predicting the final neurological outcome of the stroke: How much damage will there be and to what extent will the patient be impaired? PET scans are now being used to increase the accuracy of this prediction. Researchers at the University of California are doing PET studies of schizophrenics. Other PET scanners are being used to study the functioning of the upper part of the spinal cord and to better understand the formation and use of serotonin in the brain. As research continues, PET scanning is expected to provide not only a considerably improved means of detecting brain abnormalities, but also a revolution in our knowledge of many aspects of brain function.

***Single Photon Emission Computed Tomography.* Single photon emission computed tomography (SPECT) is a still newer scanning technique. It is related to PET and CT but uses a radioactive tracer that emits only a single**

photon. The person is given a dose of radioactive xenon-133, and a camera then revolves around the head to obtain a three-dimensional picture of blood flow in the brain. The resolution, which determines the smallest area of brain tissue that can be seen clearly, is not as good as that of PET. However, SPECT has the advantage of being faster and less expensive, and the radioactive tracers are easier to obtain than those used in PET.

SPECT is already being widely employed in diagnosis and research. It has been used, for example, to locate the lesions caused by such poisons as organic solvents (Callender et al., 1993), to study the brains of patients with traumatic brain injuries caused by blows to the head, and to diagnose such problems as Alzheimer's, epilepsy, and tumors Beekman et al., 2001). SPECT is also being used in an effort to understand how multiple sclerosis affects the CNS and has already demonstrated that it causes reduced blood flow in certain regions of the brain. Finally, SPECT has been used in the ongoing attempt to better define brain death, which is generally regarded as the most definitive way to determine death (Masdeu et al., 1994). The primary method to date has been EEG, but initial studies suggest that SPECT may provide a simpler and more reliable definition in the long run (Beekman et al., 2001).

You might be wondering at this point which of the brain scanning methods is "best." The truth is that there is no simple answer to that question. One technique may be better for one problem, a different technique for another, and only more research comparing the various scanning approaches will resolve that issue. In addition, some applications may profit from combinations of various scans. For example, PET has been combined with CT to help guide neurosurgeons in performing biopsies of some kinds of brain tumors (Levivier et al., 1993) and with SPECT to study the opiate and dopamine receptors that may be involved in Alzheimer's and other diseases (Frost, 1993). MRI has been combined with CT to evaluate brain tumors, with each scan adding information not provided by the other.

Repetitive Transcranial Magnetic Stimulation (rTMS). In TMS, a magnetic coil is used to deliver pulses of electromagnetic energy through the skull to the brain and the cortial responses f the brain recorded. This relatively new technique was introduced in 1985 and has been used primarily to assess and learn about motor functions of the spinal cord and brain, contributing greatly to our understanding of how movement is produced and controlled (Weber & Eisen, 2002). TMS is also used to evaluate the effects of drugs on the brain, help determine the amount of damage from strokes, better understand migraine headache, and study the neurological changes associated with Parkinson's disease (Cantello et al., 2002; Bohotin et al., 2002; Padberg et al., 2001). Interesting new, experimental applications of TMS include its use to actually treat clinical depression and movement disorders (Schiffer et al., 2002; Weber & Eisen, 2002).

Microarray Scans. In this very new approach, "DNA chips" are used to perform a genetic analysis of brain tissue. Using new knowledge derived from the Human Genome Project (see Chapter ___), the microarray technique performs a genetic analysis of brain tissue to determine just where and how specific genes are expressed in the brain (Luo & Geschwind, 2001). With further study, it should increase our understanding of both the functioning of the healthy brain and the origins of disease (Dougherty & Geschwind, 2002; Prolla, 2002).

The Disease That Kills Twice: Alzheimer's

A good example of the application of brain study techniques to a very real problem is *Alzheimer's disease*—a degenerative neurological disorder that gradually leads to severe loss of memory and skills. Though a vast majority of Americans 65 or older—85-90%—have no neurological problems of any kind, about 4 million do currently suffer from some form of brain disorder. Most of these are eventually diagnosed as having the neurological disease that has affected President Ronald Reagan, actress Rita Hayworth, actor Edmund O'Brien, artist Norman Rockwell, director Otto Preminger, and several million other Americans over age sixty-five. The disorder is called Alzheimer's disease because it was originally described by German neurologist Alois Alzheimer in 1906 when he treated a fifty-one year old woman with severe memory loss and other symptoms. Although Alzheimer's disease can occur in the fifties or even the forties, it is most often a disease of those over age sixty-five and is more likely at more advanced ages. In fact, Alzheimer's occurs in at least 4 to 6 percent of those over 65 and in 20 to 30 percent of those who reach their mid-eighties, killing about 120,000 people each year (Bickel & Cooper, 1994). Unfortunately, death follows slow torture, since Alzheimer's lasts an average of about ten years.

The disease begins gradually, first affecting short-term memory and immediate recall. Speech then begins to ramble, and there is a loss of language skills and comprehension. These symptoms are typically followed by disorientation, more severe memory loss, and eventually hallucinations and an inability to recognize even close relatives or familiar aspects of the environment. Eventually, Alzheimer's patients lose the ability to do such simple things as tie their shoelaces, cut up their food, and tell time. The disease is thus far incurable and so difficult to recognize that a firm diagnosis must sometimes await autopsy (Burggren et al., 2002). In addition, 61% of Alzheimer's patients are have 3 or more other diseases, and those with more diseases show greater cognitive impairment (Doraiswamy et al., 2002).

Microscopic examination of the brains of Alzheimer's patients reveals widespread neuron degeneration, especially in the hippocampus and cerebral cortex. The destroyed cells are replaced by tangles and plaques, which are patches of dying axons and dendrites. Many of the dying neurons are those that produce acetylcholine, and this neurotransmitter is currently being studied to further understand its role in the disease. Experiments show that drug_induced reductions in acetylcholine levels are associated with memory loss, a further clue to the mechanisms underlying Alzheimer's.

Recent research suggests that actually there is far more involved in Alzheimer's than acetylcholine deficits (Cutler & Sramek, 2001). Other important neurotransmitters, including norepinephrine, serotonin, and dopamine, have been implicated, and there is evidence that brain iron levels may also be a factor. In addition, some studies point to possible defects in the blood-brain barrier.

What causes the neuron degeneration and acetylcholine reductions we see in Alzheimer's? A number of theories have been developed to answer this question, and part of the answer lies in genetics (Sloane et al., 2002). About one case of Alzheimer's in three appears to be hereditary and involves chromosome number 21, which codes for a specific protein found abundantly in the neural plaques seen in the disease (Tractenberg et al., 2000). Other research shows that Alzheimer's may sometimes result from a slow virus that damages the blood_brain barrier and allows toxins to enter and poison the brain, causing declines in memory and vocabulary. Finally, excessive aluminum in the brain has been implicated as a possible factor, though its causal role remains controversial (Langauer, 1994).

As more and more people live to reach advanced ages, finding a cure becomes increasingly important, but at this point, we must settle for treatments that provide some relief. Adequate nourishment and exercise are often advised; drugs can be used to relieve such symptoms as agitation, depression, and hallucinations; support groups provide a degree of emotional comfort; and memory aids can be helpful (see Chapter 9).

Keys to Neuroscience 6

Conclusion

The human brain is, indeed, a miraculous organ. It works continuously throughout life, controlling states of sleep and waking, monitoring such critical bodily functions as respiration and heart rate, and permitting us to learn, think, formulate ideas, and solve problems. Through the wonders of the brain, concrete facts become abstract ideas, simple observations lead to scientific knowledge, and initial attraction grows to profound love. The brain also interprets what is going on in the outside world. Information about the world must reach the brain before it can be interpreted, understood, and acted upon. The task of receiving input about events around us belongs to the senses—vision, hearing, and so on—and it is the operation of these sensory systems and the perceptual processes associated with them that we address in Chapter 4.

And what about Ruth, whom we left in a coma following a stroke? Well, six days after the judge refused to order the removal of life support, a friend who had come to visit Ruth in the hospital called her name, and Ruth opened her eyes. Her husband, who was standing at the foot of the bed, said, "I went over and kissed her and she kissed me back.... a miracle, that's indeed what it was" (Washington Post, September 28, 1986). Ruth lived to complete a rehabilitation program and go home. Her case points up the still inexact nature of our understanding of the principles of neuroscience. With chances described as only 1 in 100,000, she lived. We don't know why she lived—or why most others with her condition die.

Summary

Neurons and the Nerve Impulse

1. Neuroscience is the interdisciplinary study of the brain and nervous system.
2. The nervous system contains over 100 billion neurons.
3. The basic unit of the nervous system is the neuron. The typical neuron is composed of a cell body (soma), dendrites (which accept input from other neurons), and an axon (which transmits information to other neurons or to muscles or organs).
4. The major types of neurons are sensory neurons, motor neurons, and interneurons.
5. When inactive, the neuron membrane maintains a resting potential with a negative charge inside the cell and a positive charge outside. A sufficient stimulus depolarizes the membrane, producing an action potential, which is propagated down the length of the axon membrane.
6. Neuron firing is all-or-none. There is a brief refractory period after firing during which the neuron cannot fire again.
7. Neurotransmitters, contained in synaptic vesicles, carry the impulse across the synapse.
8. Spatial and temporal summation in the soma determine when a neuron will fire.

9 Axons typically travel in bundles called nerves. Somas collect in clusters called ganglia. Nerves and ganglia form systems. The major systems are the central and peripheral nervous systems.

The Peripheral Nervous System

1. The peripheral nervous system carries all neural information to and from all parts of the body except the brain and spinal cord.
2. The cranial nerves go directly from the brain to structures in the head, face, and neck. Spinal nerves originate in the spinal cord.
3. The peripheral nervous system divides into the somatic (controlling external behaviors) and autonomic (controlling internal organs) systems. The sympathetic division of the ANS is dominant in periods of stress, the parasympathetic division in periods of relaxation.
4. Afferent and efferent nerves carry information to and from the CNS, respectively.
5. The somatic system is voluntary and the autonomic system is non-voluntary.
6. The nervous system interacts with the endocrine system to control behavior.

The Central Nervous System

1. The central nervous system consists of the spinal cord and the brain. The spinal cord carries messages back and forth between the brain and the peripheral nervous system and acts as a center for processing reflex behaviors.
2. The brain is protected by the skull, meningeal layers, cerebrospinal fluid, and blood_brain barrier.
3. Structurally, the brain consists of three main parts: the hindbrain (medulla, pons, cerebellum, and raphe), the midbrain (tectum, tegmentum, substantia nigra, and RAS), and the forebrain (subcortex, cortex).
4. Subcortical forebrain structures include the thalamus, limbic system (hypothalamus, amygdala, and hippocampus), and basal ganglia.
5. The cerebral cortex is divided into frontal (movement and thought), temporal (hearing, emotion, memory), occipital (vision), and parietal (touch and movement sensations) lobes.
6. Neural networks are hypothesized to link together sets of neurons to perform specific functions.
7. The nervous system has evolved from that of the invertebrates, with no true brain, to the lower vertebrates, with primitive brains, to the mammals, with subcortical forebrain structures and later cortex, to humans, with a large, complex cortex.
8. Evolution is an adaptive process required by environmental demands .

A Brain Divided: Lateralization of Brain Function

1. The brain has left and right hemispheres, and control is contralateral.
2. The hemispheres are connected by the corpus callosum.
3. Studies of normal split-brain people suggest that the left hemisphere is somewhat specialized for verbal and analytical processes and the right for spatial and holistic processes.
4. The processing of emotion may also be lateralized.

Immersed in Thought: Brain Biochemistry

1. Neurotransmitters are specific to particular locations in the nervous system and particular types of behavior.
2. There are about 100-150 neurotransmitters.
3. The endorphins are involved in pain control. They are natural opiates.
4. The maintenance of normal brain biochemistry is dependent on nutritional intake.
5. Nootropic drugs may improve memory, but perhaps only in rats and in humans with memory deficits.

Breaking the Code: Methods of Brain Study

1. Among the major methods used to study the brain are observation of brain_damaged people, tissue examination, ablation, lesioning, electrical and chemical stimulation, and electrical recording (EEG).
2. Brain scanning techniques include computerized axial tomography (CT), positron emission tomography (PET), magnetic resonance imaging (MRI), and single photon emission computed tomography (SPECT).
3. Alzheimer's disease involves extensive neural degeneration. It may result, in part, from a genetic predisposition combined with a virus.

Ask Yourself

1. What are the major parts of a neuron, and what function does each part serve?
2. What are the steps involved in the transmission of a nerve impulse? Describe the role of electrical and chemical processes at each step.
3. What roles do summation and the all_or_none law play in the firing of an individual neuron?
4. Entering a pitch dark room, you feel along the wall for a light switch, identify the switch by touch, and turn on the lights. What major areas of the brain and nervous system are involved in the process of locating and turning on the light switch, and how does the brain function to control this action?
5. What are the major differences between the right and left hemispheres of the brain? What evidence do we have to support the existence of these differences?
6. What can the study of patients with brain damage tell us about how the normal brain functions?
7. What advantages do CAT and PET and SPECT scanning and MRI have over ablation, stimulation, and recording techniques for studying the brain?
8. Discuss three principal functions served by the biochemicals that occur naturally in the nervous system.
9. What is Alzheimer's disease, and what are its possible causes?

Further Readings

Churchland, P., & Sejnowski, T. (1992). *The computational brain.* Cambridge, MA: MIT Press.

This book deals in detail with how neurons interact to form and function as neural networks in the brain. It represents the newest approach to neuroscience.

Corbalis, M. (1991). *The lopsided ape: Evolution of the generative mind.*

In this fascinating treatment of lateralization, Corbalis explains clearly how the two hemispheres of the brain came to have different functions.

Kimble, D. (1992). *Biological psychology.* Ft. Worth: Harcourt.

Kimble's book is a clearly written text that expands greatly on all the topics we have covered in Chapter 2.

Knight, R. (1992). *The neuropsychology of degenerative brain diseases.* Hillsdale, NJ: Lawrence Erlbaum.

If you are interested in Alzheimer's disease and other dementias, this book deals thoroughly with what is known about the neurological bases, effects, and treatments.

Levitan, I., & Kaczmarek, L. (1991). *The neuron: Cell and molecular biology.* N.Y.: Oxford University Press.

This book provides a fascinating look at the unique inner workings of the neuron and how neurons communicate with each other.

Nicholls, J., Martin, A., & Wallace, B. (1992). *From neuron to brain.* Sunderland, MA: Sinauer Assoc.

How to higher brain functions arise out of the functioning and interactions of neurons? This interesting book attempts to answer that question.

Noback, C., Strominger, N., & Demarest, R. (1991). *The human nervous system: Introduction and review.* Philadelphia: Lea & Febiger.

This heavily illustrated book provides a clear, readable coverage of the complex subject of brain anatomy and function.

Rodgers, J., (1992). *Psychosurgery: Damaging the brain and saving the mind.* N.Y.: HarperCollins.

In this interesting look at psychosurgery, Joann Rodgers explains how intentionally damaging the brain to treat certain psychiatric disorders is done and what the legal and ethical implications of such surgery may be.

Neuroscience in the 21st Century

Brain Grafts

In 1985, neurosurgeon Olof Backlund had a patient at the Karolinska Hospital in Stockholm, Sweden, who had such severe Parkinson's disease that he could not move without medication. Because this disease involves reduced production of the important neurochemical dopamine, Backlund searched for a way to provide an increased dopamine supply to the patient's brain. He knew that the adrenal gland produces dopamine outside the brain and reasoned that transplanted adrenal tissue might produce it within the brain. He removed tissue from the adrenal gland and grafted it into a nucleus of the patient's brain in a dramatic attempt to treat the disorder. After recovering from the surgery, the patient showed some improvement and required less medication than previously. However, the improvement was not as marked as Backlund had been hoped (Backlund et al., 1985).

Mexican researchers soon grafted dopamine-producing tissue from the adrenal medulla into the brains of two Parkinson's patients and reported dramatic improvements. This success triggered a number of additional attempts in both Mexico and the United States, and fetal brain tissue from therapeutic abortions has been used in many cases (Silani et al., 1994). Moreover, Backlund has developed new techniques that are more successful. Overall results from the several hundred patients implanted to date show modest improvement in about 30-50% (Broadwell et al., 1994).

With these improved graft techniques come serious ethical questions. Who should receive grafts, and under what conditions? Might some kinds of grafts change the individual's personality, and if so would he be the same person? Should tissue be taken from aborted fetuses? Will some women conceive babies for the express purpose of using the fetal brain tissue for grafting? In fact, one woman asked to be artificially inseminated with her father's sperm so that the fetal tissue could be used to treat his Alzheimer's disease (Lewin, 1987). One possible answer to some of these concerns is to grow the needed tissue in cultures. Ethical issues not withstanding, researchers are exploring a variety of brain grafting possibilities. Some work, thus far primarily in animals, has focused on treating brain damage associated with memory loss by using raphe nucleus and hippocampal grafts to increase levels of such neurotransmitters as acetylcholine and serotonin. Other studies have involved grafts that might lead to improvements in Alzheimer's patients or reduce the problem of obesity, which can be based in brain function. It seems clear that the future of brain grafting is an exciting one. Ethical considerations will have to be dealt with carefully, but it is likely that brain grafting will become fairly common within a decade.

Probe: Research in Neuroscience

Synaptic Plasticity

The many synapses that exist in the central and peripheral nervous systems are not necessarily constant throughout life. Rather, the nervous system demonstrates *synaptic plasticity*, a process of synapse turnover in which old synapses degenerate and new ones develop (Finney et al., 2001). Synapse turnover has long been known to occur when synapses are damaged. The chest of the frog, for example, contains two broad, flat muscles known as cutaneous pectoris muscles. These muscles can be made nonfunctional by cutting the axons of the motor neurons that control them. When the axon feeding one of the two muscles is severed, the muscle on the opposite side sprouts between 12 and 30 percent new synapses (Holloway et al., 2000). Synapses have also been grown in cell cultures, and their development has been observed and measured (Basarsky et al., 1994). Some studies have shown that the growth of new synapses can begin as early as 4 to 5 days after lesioning in the central nervous system and within as little as 2 days after lesioning in the peripheral nervous system. When the human brain is damaged, neural compensation, which can permit some return of function, may involve synaptic plasticity (Frackowiak, 2001).

More recent evidence suggests that synapse turnover occurs not only after injury, but also in the normal nervous system in response to such stimuli as environmental change (Huntley et al., 2002). Such normal growth has been observed in the ciliary muscles (fibers that control eye movement) of monkeys. Under the electron microscope it has been observed that about 2 percent of these muscles are degenerating and an additional 2 percent are regenerating at any given time (Townes_Anderson and Eaviola, 1978). This suggests turnover of synapses as well and would mean that half the total number of synapses in the ciliary muscles are being replaced by new ones about every 18 days (Cotman et al., 1981).

The relatively new discovery that synapse turnover is a continual and substantial process requires some reconsideration of our understanding of how the nervous system functions to control a wide variety of behaviors and how information is stored in the brain (Calverley & Jones, 1990). Turnover may be a factor, for example, in the storage of memories in neural networks and in complex thought processes. In addition, as we learn more about it, we may be able to cause selective synapse turnover in order to repair damaged or diseased parts of the brain.

Application

Think Critically: *Can Drugs Make You Smarter?*

You may soon be coming up on that first exam in your introductory psychology course and wondering how best to prepare for it. Suppose you could take a drug that would make you smarter? Some believe that such drugs do exist.

The Basic Hypothesis or Contention

John Morgenthaler, co-author with Ward Dean of the 1991 book *Smart Drugs and Nutrients*, says he has taken certain *nootropic* drugs—those aimed at improving memory—and gotten smarter as a result. Others have made similar claims and advocated the use of specific drugs and nutrients to improve memory and hence, in effect, make you smarter. In fact, you can now buy such drugs in "smart bars." But do they work?

What Is the Evidence?

If smart drugs make you smarter, it would very likely be through an effect on brain chemistry. Early studies suggest that the nootropics may, in fact, have some effect on neurotransmitters and on memory. Several animal studies have shown that one of the most widely touted drugs, piracetam, does appear to have neurochemical effects that improve memory (Stancheva et al., 1993). In addition, Alzheimer patients show some memory benefits from the drug (Croisile et al., 1993). Other, newer nootropics that show positive effects on cognitive functioning in animals include nefiracetam, pramiracetam, and oxiracetam. The animals' scores on memory tasks do show significant improvement in some studies when these drugs are given, and animals in experimental groups receiving the drugs perform better than those in control groups not receiving nootropics.

Is The Evidence Open To Alternative Interpretations?

Although the nootropics do show some apparent cognitive benefits, neuroscientists consider the evidence to be preliminary, at best (Evenson, 1993). There are three basic reasons for this skepticism. First, the positive results have been seen almost exclusively in studies of rats and mice. While these species certainly do have some physiological similarity to humans, it is a considerable leap to conclude that a drug that improves performance on simple, mechanical tasks in rodents will improve memory for complex information in humans.

A second concern relates to the initial evidence that humans with cognitive deficits resulting from Alzheimer's disease or other neurological disorders seem to improve with nootropics). Even assuming that they do—and there is thus far very little evidence—we cannot readily generalize from people with brain damage to those with normal brain function. This means that we have little idea what effects these drugs might have in a person with normal memory. They may well have none at all. Suppose you have no headache but take two aspirin anyway or you have no strep throat but you take antibiotics. What benefits will you see? None! So even if the so-called smart drugs do eventually prove beneficial for patients with cognitive deficits, they may be of no value at all to a person with no deficits.

A final concern is that there is simply not yet enough evidence to convince most scientists that the nootropics are effective, even in animals. Early studies in any field are often flawed because we don't know just what variables need to be controlled or how to control them. As these variables become known and new experimental procedures are devised, it is common for findings to change. A drug that seemed highly effective in initial studies may prove less effective or totally ineffective in later studies. Since there have thus far been few studies of the nootropics, most scientists remain skeptical.

Do We Need Additional Evidence?

We clearly do need further evidence. For one thing, we need more animal studies in order to increase the weight of the evidence and extend the findings to other species, such as primates. In addition, we need studies showing just what variables need to be controlled in order to reach valid conclusions. Through such investigations, we can be more certain that the conclusions we reach are accurate and therefore more certain that the drugs are effective—if they are. Finally, those who advocate the use of these drugs to improve memory in normal humans must directly demonstrate their effectiveness. Carefully controlled studies of college students, as well as older and younger people, are needed. We might, for example, randomly assign each of 100 students to either an experimental group receiving one of the nootropics or a control group receiving a placebo. The students might then prepare for and take one or more exams to determine whether or not the experimental group can outperform the controls. Many such studies, systematically varying drugs, dosages, age groups, and types of memory tasks, will be required before final conclusions can be reached.

What Can We Conclude?

Well, don't rush to your neighborhood "smart bar" just yet, as about 5% of college students in one study were doing (Canterbury & Lloyd, 1994). There are as yet no proven benefits of the nootropics in normal people. Moreover, any drug can potentially be harmful. So experts advise against using these drugs, at least for now.

Horizons in Neuroscience

Aids, Brain, and Behavior

Scientists are trying to determine just how AIDS—the increasingly prevalent disease that always kills its victims—causes abnormal cerebral blood flow and brain damage. One mechanism already known is infection, which can be partially prevented by certain drugs (Gray et al., 1994). The virus that causes AIDS inactivates T4 lymphocytes of the immune system and thereby virtually eradicates the body's defenses against viral and bacterial infections. As a result, various infectious agents can affect the brain, causing meningitis, encephalitis, tumors, and vascular hemorrhage. In addition, the HIV virus directly enters the brain and infects the glial cells that normally remove the waste materials created when neurons die. The effects of these brain insults can include loss of motor coordination, personality change, and intellectual deterioration.

And You Thought You Had a Headache!

In 1848, railroad construction foreman Phineas Gage was injured when some blasting powder went off accidentally. It drove a 3 1/2-foot iron rod up through the left side of his face and out the top of his head just in front of the center. Studies of his preserved skull using modern neuroimaging techniques show that the damage was primarily to the right and left prefrontal cortex (Damasio et al., 1994). Gage remained conscious, was able to speak rationally, and soon regained all his physical strength, but he underwent a significant personality change. Previously a rational, calm, quiet individual, he became loud, impulsive, stubborn, and moody (Barker, 1995). Similar changes in less dramatic cases were the basis for inaccurate early theories of frontal lobe function. Such theories suggested that each aspect of human functioning (e.g., thought, personality, emotion) has its own, independent basis in the brain. The underlying neural mechanisms were seen as separate and distinct, never interacting with each other to affect behavior and mental processes. Since only Gage's personality seemed to be affected, his case was taken as confirmation of this view, which we now know is incorrect. Although we have more accurate knowledge in 1998, we still do not know just how the frontal lobes affect personality functioning and how thought processes are carried out.

A Natural Brain Tranquilizer

The tranquilizer diazepam (Valium) was the single most widely prescribed drug in the 1970s, with over 8000 tons (yes, that's tons!) consumed annually (Tallman et al., 1980), and it is still widely used. It now appears that just as the brain produces natural pain killers, it may also produce substances similar to tranquilizers like Valium—anti-anxiety neurochemicals with their own specialized receptors. The key substance is a natural polypeptide called diazepam binding inhibitor or DBZ. This brain tranquilizer is released when you are under stress and activates the hypothalamus, autonomic nervous system, and endocrine system to respond to the stress. The new discovery is already leading to a better understanding of how anxiety is affected and controlled by a complex set of neurotransmitters.

Key Terms 1

action potential
all-or-none law
axon
axon terminal
cell body
dendrite
depolarization
excitatory postsynaptic potential (EPSP)
hyperpolarizeinterneuron
inhibitory postsynaptic potential (IPSP)
innervate
ganglion
motor neuron
myelin
nerve
neuron
neurotransmitter
propagate
refractory period
resting potential
neuroscience
nucleus
sensory neuron
soma
summation
synapse
synaptic plasticity
synaptic vesicle
threshold

Key Terms 2

afferent nerve
autonomic nervous system (ANS)
biofeedback
cranial nerve
efferent nerve
endocrine system
neuromuscular junction
parasympathetic nervous system
pituitary gland
peripheral nervous system
somatic nervous system
spinal cord
spinal nerves
sympathetic nervous system

Key Terms 3

amygdala
association areas
basal ganglia
blood-brain barrier
central canal
central fissure
central nervous system (CNS)
cerebellum
cerebral cortex

cerebrospinal fluid
corpus callosum
dorsal
forebrain
frontal lobe
glia
gray matter
hindbrain
hippocampus
hormone
hypothalamus
inferior colliculus
lateral geniculate nucleus
lateral fissure
limbic system
medial geniculate nucleus
medulla
meninges
midbrain
neural network
occipital lobe
parietal lobe
pons
prefrontal cortex
primary motor cortex
primary somatosensory cortex
projection areas
raphe system
reflex
reticular formation
reticular activating system (RAS)
subcortex
substantia nigra
superior colliculus
tectum
tegmentum
temporal lobe
thalamus
ventral
white matter

Key Terms 4

corpus callosum
dichotic listening
hemisphere
lateralization
visual half-field study

Key People 4

Roger Sperry

Key Terms 5

diazepam binding inhibitor
endorphins
enkephalins
neurochemical
neuropeptides
neurotransmitter
nootropic

Key People 5

Candace Pert

Key Terms 6

ablation
Alzheimer's Disease
aphasia
brain graft
computerized axial tomography (CT)
electroencephalogram (EEG)
lesioning
magnetic resonance imaging (MRI)
Parkinson's Disease
positron emission tomography (PET)
prosopagnosia

Key People 6

Alois Alzheimer
Olof Backlund
Hans Berger
Jose Delgado
Peter Milner
James Olds

Keys to Neuroscience 1

Key Knowledge

1. **The brain is a highly complex structure.**
   - A. **How the brain is organized?**
     Hierarchically
   - B. **How many neurons it contains?**
     About 12 billion
2. **The neuron is the basic unit of the nervous system.**
   - A. **Its major parts?**
     Soma, axon, dendrites.
   - B. **About how many types there are?**
     200
   - C. **What the axon and dendrites do?**
     Transmit and receive, respectively.
   - D. **The major types of neurons?**
     Sensory, motor, and interneurons

E. What the glia do?
   Fill spaces, form scar tissue, remove waste, supply nutrients.

3. Nerve impulse carry information through the nervous system.
   A. How transmission occurs?
      Electrochemically
   B. What the resting potential is?
      An inactive, polarized state with a negative charge.
   C. What happens when the charge becomes positive?
      Action potential is generated.
   D. The law governing neuron firing?
      All-or-none
   E. What the myelin sheath does?
      Insulates and speeds transmission.
   F. What follows firing?
      A refractory period.

4. The synapse is a space between an axon and the dendrites.
   A. How messages get across this gap?
      Chemically—with neurotransmitters
   B. Where neurotransmitters come from?
      Manufactured in the soma and stored in synaptic vesicles.
   C. How many synapses there may be?
      100 trillion

5. Many impulses are typically required to fire a neuron.
   A. Where summation occurs?
      In the soma.
   B. The types of summation?
      Temporal and spatial
   C. The types of potentials?
      Excitatory and inhibitory

5. Neurons are linked to perform functions.
   A. How axons travel?
      In bundles called nerves
   B. What clusters of somas are called?
      Ganglia
   C. The major subdivisions of the nervous system?
      Peripheral and central.

Keys to Neuroscience 2

1. The peripheral nervous system innervate all structures outside the brain and spinal cord.
   A. What nerves in the head and area are called?
      Cranial
   B. The major divisions of the peripheral system and what they control?
      Somatic (external behaviors) and autonomic (internal organs).
   C. Which division is under conscious control?

Somatic

D. The divisions of the autonomic system and when they dominate?
Sympathetic (under stress) and parasympathetic (relaxation).

E. What other body system interacts closely with the ANS?
Endocrine.

Keys to Neuroscience 3

1. The CNS has two major parts.
   A. What they are?
   Brain and spinal cord
2. The spinal cord carries messages to and from the brain.
   A. What is found in the central canal?
   Cerebrospinal fluid.
   B. What nerves exit the dorsal and ventral sides of the cord?
   Sensory and motor, respectively.
   C. The major functions of the cord?
   As a switchboard for the brain
   Processing reflex behaviors
3. The brain is heavily protected.
   A. The majors forms of protection?
   Meninges, cerebrospinal fluid, blood-brain barrier.
4. The brain has three major subdivisions.
   A. What they are?
   Hindbrain, midbrain, and forebrain.
   B. The structures of the hindbrain?
   Medulla, pons, cerebellum, raphe
   C. The structures of the midbrain?
   Tectum, tegmentum, substantia nigra, RAS
   D. The subcortical forebrain structures and their functions?
   Thalamus—integrate and relay information
   Limbic system—emotion, motivation, temperature, food and water intake, maintain homeostasis.
   Hypothalamus—Eating, drinking, body temperature, consciousness, sleep/wake cycle, sexual behavior.
   Amygdala—Rage, anxiety
   Hippocampus—learning, memory
   Basal ganglia—sensory and motor
5. The cerebral cortex controls the most complex functions.
   A. The lobes and their functions?
   Temporal—hearing, emotion, memory
   Occipital—vision
   Parietal—touch and movement sensations
   Frontal—Movement and thought
   B. The role of the projection areas?
   Process sensory input and motor output.
   C. The role of the association areas?
   Connect projection areas.
6. The brain has evolved over millions of years.
   A. The order of development of structures from lowest to highest species?
   Hindbrain to midbrain to forebrain

B. What the brain has evolved?
Adaptation to environmental demands

Keys to Neuroscience 4

1. The brain divides into two sides.
   A. What they are called?
   Hemispheres
   B. Which side of the body is controlled by the right hemisphere?
   Left
   C. What connects the hemispheres?
   Corpus callosum
2. The two hemispheres have somewhat different functions.
   A. What functions the right hemisphere may control?
   Musical, spatial, global
   B. The major left hemisphere functions?
   Speech, verbal information, analytical
   C. One method Sperry used to study split-brain patients?
   Visual half-field

Keys to Neuroscience 5

1. Neurotransmitters account for most synaptic transmission.
   A. About how many there are?
   100-150
   B. Where they are found in the brain?
   Each in specific locations, performing specific functions.
   C. What happens when they are interfered with?
   Problems occur: Movement difficulties, paralysis, weakness, unconsciousness.
2. The endorphins reduce pain.
   A. What drugs they are similar to?
   Opiates
   B. What their chemical nature is?
   Neuropeptides—strings of amino acids
   C. When they are released?
   Under pain or stress
3. Nutrition influences neurochemistry.
   A. Examples of food-neurotransmitter relationships?
   Proteins—dopamine, norepinephrine
   Egg yolk, liver—acetylcholine
   Tryptophan (from meats)—serotonin
4. Nootropics may improve memory.
   A. Where positive results are seen?
   In rats and in humans with deficits

Keys to Neuroscience 6

1. Older methods of brain study are still used.

A. What the methods are?

Study of brain-damaged people
Microscopic study of tissue
Ablation
Stimulation
Recording

B. Why ablation and lesioning are used in studies?

To identify the functions of areas of the brain.

C. The types of brain stimulation?

Electrical, chemical

D. What the EEG records?

Electrical activity of the brain.

2. Various brain scanning techniques are the newest tools.

A. Some major types of scans?

CT, MRI, PET, SPECT

B. The basic nature of CT?

It's a 3-D X-ray

C. Which scan is considered most useful overall?

MRI

D. What the PET scan measures?

Blood-flow patterns

E. What technique may provide an improved definition of death?

SPECT

3. Alzheimer's is a degenerative disorder.

A. Some major symptoms?

Memory and skill loss

B. What percentages of the population are affected?

Over 65: 4-6%
Mid-eighties: 20-30%

C. A neurotransmitter that may be involved?

Acetylcholine

D. What may cause it?

Genetic predisposition, slow virus, excessive aluminum.

Chapter 4

Sensation and Perception

Outline

Sensation and Perception: Characteristics, Methods and Theories

Sensation

Perception: Knowing What You Sense

The Evolution of Sensory and Perceptual Mechanisms

Vision: The Sense of Sight

The Visual Stimulus: Light

The Eye: Structure and Function

The Retina: Window To The Brain

Visual Adaptation

The Neurophysiology of Visual Sensation and Perception

Color Vision

Visual Perception: Knowing What You See

Bottom-Up and Top-Down Processing

Perceptual Organization: The Gestalt Laws

Perceptual Constancy

Depth Perception

Moving Experiences: The Perception of Movement

Optical Illusions

In The Mind's Eye: Perception and Mental Imagery

Audition: Sensing and Perceiving Sound

The Auditory Stimulus: Sound Vibrations

The Ear: Structure and Function

Vibration Becomes Information: Auditory Pathways

Auditory Perception: Major Theories

Auditory Perception: Localizing Sounds in Space

Hearing Disorders

The Chemical Senses: Taste and Smell

Gustation: The Sense of Taste

Olfaction: The Sense of Smell

More Senses, More Perceptions: Touch, Balance, and Movement

Somesthesis: The Skin Senses

Proprioception: Perceiving Movement and Balance

Networking

IN ORDER TO understand and respond to the environment—and to our own bodies—we must constantly sense, recognize, and interpret a large number of different stimuli. These stimuli range from sights and sounds to odors, heat, cold, and our own body positions and movements. We detect them through the process of sensation and recognize them through perception. We will learn how each sense detects and processes stimuli and how the brain interprets them. We will see how we perceive objects as having the same shape, size, and color no matter what their distance, orientation, and lighting conditions. We will learn about newly discovered "color channels" in the brain, sounds emitted by the ears, and implants that can improve hearing. And we will find out what causes those tricky visual illusions that so fascinate us.

Near Miss!

You have just stepped off the curb at a street corner when a sports car suddenly comes roaring out of nowhere. You leap out of the way. The situation may seem simple—if dangerous—but consider the complexity of the process by which you have reacted so quickly to it. Your ears—your auditory sense-detected the sound of the engine, then your eyes —your visual sense—detected an image of a speeding vehicle. How do you know it is a sports car? How do you know it is moving at high speed? And, indeed, how do you know that you are in danger? Clearly, the sensation alone—the sound and image of the car—does not yield all this information. In fact, *sensing* is not *perceiving*. Not until the image is transmitted to the brain and compared with past experience do you actually perceive the object. Thus, whereas sensation refers to the process of taking in an image and preparing it for transmission to the brain, perception refers to the active process of interpretation through which we come to understand the meaning of the image.

Both sensation and perception begin with stimuli, and we can distinguish two general classes of stimuli: A distal stimulus is an actual object or event located in the real world, such as a person we are looking at or a piano we are hearing; a proximal stimulus is the information received by the sensory apparatus. The task of perception is to accurately interpret the distal stimulus on the basis of the proximal stimulus. Often, however, the proximal stimulus is not ideal for this purpose, and such factors as context and past experience must be brought to bear in order for accurate perception to occur.

Sensation and Perception: Characteristics, Methods, and Theories

Hearing, seeing, and identifying the sports car and recognizing the danger it presented required both sensation and perception. Let's take a look at each of these two important processes before dealing with each of the major senses in turn.

Sensation

The purpose of the senses is clear: to provide us with an absolutely essential and reasonably accurate picture of what is going on both inside and outside our bodies. We need this picture to survive—to locate food and avoid predators—and to enjoy our lives—to experience the sights, sounds, smells, tastes, and touches that contribute to life's richness.

Most people believe that there are just five senses: vision, audition (hearing), olfaction (smell), gustation (taste), and somesthesis (touch). But there are more. Somesthesis is actually several senses, including touch, pressure, and pain. In addition, there are kinesthetic (movement) and vestibular (balance) senses. Somehow, that seems to add up to more than five! We will consider some general characteristics of the senses, see what is known about thresholds for sensations to occur, and discuss the laws that relate physical stimuli to psychological interpretation. Finally, we discuss sensory adaptation.

General Characteristics of the Senses

You may describe a fruit as having a "sickeningly sweet" taste, the color of someone's shirt as "hot pink," the sound of your neighbor's motorcycle as "deafening," or the feel of an unshaven face as "scratchy." For you to be able to make these verbal responses, three steps must occur. First, the stimulus activates *sensory receptors*—cells specialized to detect specific types of stimuli. These receptors, in turn, transduce the incoming stimulus energy. *Transduction* is the process of converting physical stimulus energy into electrochemical messages for transmission as nerve impulses to the brain. For example, photoreceptors in the eye generate a train of impulses over the optic nerve and into the brain. Finally, stimulus information must be coded in some way to describe the quantity, or intensity, of the stimulus and its quality. In general, a more intense stimulus, such as a loud sound or a strong odor, causes more frequent firing of neurons, and the brain interprets this increased frequency as increased intensity. Qualitative differences are detected by special structures characteristic of each sense. Different colors of light, pitches of sound, and tastes of food are given special processing by the sensory structures involved.

Sensory Thresholds and Psychophysics

Psychophysics is the science that studies the relationship between a physical stimulus and the sensory experience it produces. Over the years, psychophysicists have been particularly interested in sensory thresholds (Hellstrom, 2000).

A *threshold* is the level at which someone can detect either a stimulus or a change in a stimulus. The *absolute threshold* is the lowest level of stimulus intensity to which a sense will respond (Table 4-1). You will hear the sound of the approaching sports car when it gets close enough to cross your absolute sensory threshold. The *difference threshold*, also called the *just-noticeable difference* (JND), is the smallest difference between two stimuli that can be reliably detected or discriminated. It is, for example, the smallest difference in pitch between two musical notes that a participant can detect, and it is expressed in physical units, such as millilamberts of light illumination or decibels of sound intensity.

As an example, suppose you are charged with developing a new display for air traffic controllers to use in monitoring the altitudes of planes. The altitude of each plane is represented by a vertical bar of light, and it is important that the controller be able to tell the difference between the altitudes (bars) of any two planes. So that you can represent as great a range of altitudes on the screen as possible, you need to determine the difference threshold so that the controller can tell the difference in length between the two bars without using too much space on the screen to display them. Other important applications of psychophysical methods include assessing pain threshold, hearing loss, and recognition memory, and the improvement of acoustics in concert halls (Heinz et al., 2002; Okono, 2002). Psychophysical methods have also been used to determine severity of illness as rated by psychologists, physicians, and nurses (Kamizaki et al., 2000).

There are three traditional methods for measuring sensory thresholds. In the *method of limits*, the researcher gradually reduces a clearly detectable stimulus until the observer can no longer detect it. In the method of *constant stimuli*, several stimuli to be detected or discriminated are given repeatedly in random order, and the participant must report each detection. In the *method of average error*, the participant adjusts a stimulus until it becomes just detectable or until the difference between a pair of stimuli disappears. Thresholds for taste and smell have also been measured using a maximum-likelihood procedure (Linschoten et al., 2001), and additional methods are being developed (Leek, 2001).

Psychophysical Laws. The ultimate aim of psychophysics is to arrive at basic laws that specify the relationship between physical stimulation and psychological experience. In particular, what is the smallest reliably detectable difference between two stimuli, such as the bars representing planes on the air traffic control screen? In other words, what is the best formula for the difference threshold over a range of starting stimulus intensities? The answer to this question would constitute the basic law of psychophysics, and the three principal answers have been competing laws formulated by Weber, Fechner, and Stevens.

The first answer was formulated as a law of psychophysics by the German physiologist Ernst Weber in 1834. *Weber's law* states that the smallest detectable increase in the intensity of a stimulus is a constant proportion of the intensity of the original stimulus. The constant proportion referred to is known as the Weber fraction or difference threshold (the JND). The *Weber fraction* for light is typically about 1/60. That means that subjects can detect a difference in intensity between 60 and 61 candles (a measure of light intensity). If the starting intensity is 120 candles, however, you would not be able to detect the difference between that initial intensity and 121 candles. Why? Because the JND for 120 candles is 2 candles (1/60 of 120). You must thus increase the intensity from 120 to 122 in order to detect the difference. The Weber fraction is different for each sense, as Table 4-2 shows.

Weber's Law holds for a variety of psychophysical measurements, including intensity discrimination and the visual discrimination of spatial intervals. It also applies to the range of human hearing and the discrimination of the heaviness of objects. And it pertains not only to intensity but also to the discrimination of sensory quality. For example, it holds for tone frequencies (pitches), as well as intensities (loudness). However, it fails in some threshold judgments, as Weber's brother-in-law, Gustav Fechner, discovered.

Fechner found that Weber's law breaks down for sensations at the extremes, particularly the lower end, and he therefore revised the law. *Fechner's law* states that constant increments in the intensity of the *physical* stimulus create progressively smaller *perceived* increases in intensity (Figure 4-1). Put otherwise, the more intense the initial stimulus, the larger the increment required to produce a perceptible change. Thus, while physical stimulus intensity increases geometrically, psychological intensity increases logarithmically. As physical intensity goes from 2 to 4 to 8 units, for example, experienced intensity goes from 2 to 3 to 4 units. As a practical matter, turning on a 100-watt bulb in a pitch dark room produces a large increment in perceived light intensity—the room seems much brighter. Turning on a second 100-watt bulb will not, however, be perceived as doubling the brightness of the room, even though the physical intensity of the light has doubled from 100 to 200 watts.

S.S. Stevens (1955) found that Fechner's law did not hold well across all senses, and he therefore formulated a third law. *Stevens's power law* states that the perceived magnitude of a sensation is equivalent to the magnitude of the physical stimulus raised to a power. The power for a given sense can be determined through research. He arrived at this law by using a method called *magnitude estimation*, in which the participant assigns some value to an initial stimulus, then scales other stimuli relative to the value assigned to the initial stimulus. If the subject assigns a value of 50 to an initial tone, a second tone that is perceived as twice as loud would be given a value of 100. The Stevens law holds for a variety of stimuli across all senses and also appears to apply to learning and memory (Anderson, 2001).

The magnitude estimation approach has some very practical applications. Consider, for example, the old axiom that "Beauty is in the eye of the beholder." Using the Stevens method, we could scale "the eye of the beholder" by beginning with a standard stimulus and having participants scale other stimuli (for example, men, women, or paintings) relative to that standard stimulus. In another interesting application, psychophysicists asked young adults to perform magnitude-estimation scaling of their relative preference for different pieces of rock music (Fucci et al., 1993). The most recent work concerning the basic law of psychophysics has focused on the neural mechanisms involved in the relationship between physical and subjective intensity. While this research is ongoing, it thus far appears to demonstrate a direct, linear relationship between subject intensity and the underlying neural activity (Johnson, et al., 2002).

Signal Detection Theory. John Swets (1964) pioneered another psychophysical approach when he focused on sensory thresholds for the detection of stimuli and found that detection and perception are influenced by far more than the intensity of the physical stimulus (Green, 1993). *Signal detection theory* holds that stimulus detection involves both sensory processes and decision processes and that both are influenced by a number of factors (Green & Swets, 1966). In effect, signal detection theory replaces the simple concept of an absolute sensory threshold with the concept of *detectability*—the ability of a participant to notice a stimulus under a given set of circumstances.

We often need to detect a *signal*—the important or central stimulus—while faced with *noise*-distracting sensory and cognitive information. The noise may involve external, physical stimuli (flashing lights, loud construction work), and individuals differ in their sensitivity to noise (Ellermeier et al., 2001). Noise can also involve a variety of internal response biases. For example, when a tone close to the auditory threshold is presented, some participants tend to say "yes" when not certain whether they have heard a tone, while others tend to say "no." This response bias is affecting the participant's judgment. The practical importance of signal detection is apparent to the radiologist, who must try to detect a tumor (the signal) on a mammogram or chest x-ray in the presence of considerable noise (surrounding normal tissue).

A subject in a signal detection experiment receives numerous trials on which background noise is constantly present and signals occur periodically. There may, for example, be a constant background "hissing" sound (the noise) on which a signal tone, or *target*, is occasionally superimposed. There are four possible detection outcomes on a given trial: a *hit*—correctly detecting a target stimulus; a *miss*—failing to detect a target; a *false alarm*—reporting a target when no target tone was sounded; and a *correct rejection*—not reporting a target when there was, in fact, no target (Figure 4-2). The experimenter can use the percentages of these various outcomes in combination to determine just how good the participant's detection performance is under a given set of circumstances (Parasuraman et al., 2000). Such determinations have been made for memory (see Chapter 9), facial expression during painful stimulation, and the judgment of whether a series of tones are coincident with the participant's heart beats (Harver et al., 1993).

The original work of Swets provides a good example of the practical application of signal detection theory. He wanted to test and improve the sensitivity of air traffic controllers to planes that appeared as blips on their radar screens. He reasoned that in detecting signals (blips indicating planes), operators could have hits, misses, false alarms, and correct rejections. By using signal detection techniques and modifying the radar displays, it was possible to improve the hit rate and hence improve the safety of air travel. A second example is provided by recent studies in which signal detection is used to help experts detect abnormalities on functional MRIs (fMRIs) and other scans of the brain (Petersson et al., 1999). Ongoing research on signal detection theory has demonstrated its usefulness across a wide variety of practical applications (Heffernan et al., 2002).

Perception: Knowing What You Sense

Look at an object—perhaps a coffee cup—a few feet away from you. How do you know it's a coffee cup? The sensory image is simply that of a cylindrical object with something protruding from its side. If you move closer to the cup, its image gets larger; if you move farther way, the image gets smaller. Looking at it from different angles changes its apparent shape. Yet you interpret all these varying stimuli as representing the same object. How is that possible?

Understanding the nature of the real world through perception involves two basic processes, interpretation and categorization. In the *interpretation* process, basic information about the physical object, such as its size, shape, and color, are integrated and compared with an existing "data base" in your brain—a body of knowledge that permits you to identify the object. In the *categorization* process you place the object in a hierarchical scheme of increasingly broader categories of objects. Coffee cups are cups (a larger class), which are among several subcategories of vessels from which people drink, which is one of several classes of objects used in human consumption. This knowledge of categories tells you the function of the object and how it relates to other objects.

The interpretive role of the brain in perception is demonstrated when the sensory image of an object does not provide all the relevant information (Poirier & Gurnsey, 2002). The two college students in Figure 4-3 are standing in a library. Do they have legs? You assume they do because your brain interprets them as standing up. Actually, though, the image you see shows no legs. An even more striking example of the how the brain can complete a partial image is seen in the case of *subjective contours*, which are shapes or lines that appear to be present but actually are not. You see two triangles in Figure 4-4, one pointing up and one pointing down. But look more closely, and you will see that neither of the triangles is actually present! Recent evidence points to specific areas of the visual cortex that complete the subjective contours (Lee, 2002).

The brain is clearly capable of performing what might be considered perceptual miracles—accurately interpreting complex sensory stimuli of many kinds. But can it perceive events and situations that are beyond the known limits of the usual senses? Can the brain engage in extrasensory perception, the controversial topic of our Thinking Critically box?

The Evolution of Sensory and Perceptual Mechanisms

You may have wondered why humans have the particular senses and associated perceptual mechanisms they do. Why do we have vision, audition, and the other senses? Why color vision? Why certain taste preferences?

One theoretical answer to these questions comes from the biological theory of evolution and its modern extension, evolutionary psychology. From this point of view, we are dealing with two aspects of evolution: the *biological* evolution of sensory mechanisms—those that receive stimuli—and the *psychological* evolution of perceptual processes—those that permit us to interpret the sensory stimuli. Each component of our sensory and perceptual systems evolved in order to fulfill some specific function important to survival or reproduction. In order to accomplish that evolutionary purpose, each solves an adaptive problem presented to humans by ancient environments. Examples would be obtaining water and nutritious food, reproducing the species, and avoiding many kinds of danger, such as predators, falling from heights, and drowning.

Adequately adaptive sensory and perceptual systems are crucial to the ability of any species to survive and reproduce. Evolutionary psychologists John Tooby and Leda Cosmides (1990, p. 408) make this point succinctly but strongly:

> *Animals subsist on information. The single most limiting resource to reproduction is not food or safety or access to mates, but what makes them each possible: the information required for making adaptive behavioral choices.*

The senses provide the information so essential to survival and reproduction, and the perceptual mechanisms in the brain interpret that information, enabling the individual to act on it.

To solve adaptive problems, humans must be able to sense both close and distant stimuli and have information about body position, movement, and balance. The evolved mechanisms deal with all these problems. Vision, audition, and olfaction detect stimuli at a distance, permitting us to seek a desirable object or avoid a dangerous one. Gustation and the skin senses permit detection and evaluation of objects that come into contact with the body. And the kinesthetic and vestibular senses provide the information necessary for locating the body in space and maintaining balance. All can be seen as adaptive products of the evolutionary response to environmental demands.

One good example of an evolved mechanism is *sensory adaptation*—a progressive decrease in sensitivity to continuing or recurrent stimuli. It is adaptive in the evolutionary sense because survival usually means paying more attention to a changing environment than to a constant one (Peterson & Kramer, 2001). To an ancient human, a sudden crackling sound—perhaps a large animal in nearby bushes—required alertness, but a continuous stimulus could be ignored. In fact, becoming less and less aware of continuing stimuli is adaptive because it frees up awareness for attention to new stimuli (Remington & Folk, 2001). Sensory adaptation is an everyday experience. For example, bath water that feels very hot at first as temperature receptors fire rapidly soon feels just warm as you adapt and the receptors fire less rapidly. Participants in one study listened to pure tones of differing pitches. When the tones were presented repeatedly, they showed sensory adaptation in that their auditory thresholds increased; in effect, they couldn't hear as well (Miskiewicz et al., 1993). Sensory adaptation is characteristic of all the senses except pain.

Other examples of evolution at work include color vision and natural camouflage. Why do humans (and many other animals) have color vision? To make color television more pleasurable, perhaps? Probably not! But color vision very likely did evolve to serve such specific adaptive functions as identifying foods that provide nutrients needed by the species, locating animals that provide nourishment and comfort, and avoiding animals that are dangerous (such as snakes with particular color markings). It is interesting to note, also, that not all mammals have good color vision. Those that do, including humans, tended in ancient times to forage for food during daylight hours, when colors are readily differentiated. Nocturnal animals, like owls, generally have poor color vision. Natural camouflage is also adaptive. The chameleon, for example, avoids predators by changing colors to closely match its background.

Evolved mechanisms are also found in audition and taste. Auditory perception evolved to a high level in humans in part because it is essential to complex communication. Humans communicate most efficiently through articulate speech, an evolved ability that would be of little value without the auditory mechanisms necessary to process it. Similarly, bats evolved sonar to locate prey. Taste mechanisms, which provide information about the chemical composition of substances in the mouth, are also highly evolved. Not everything that might enter the mouth is food—indeed, some substances are toxins—and not all that are foods are equally nutritious. Animals therefore evolve taste mechanisms that permit the selection of foods needed by the body. Why, then, you might ask, do most humans prefer high-fat foods, which we now know promote heart disease and cancer? Probably because food was relatively scarce in ancient environments, so foods dense in calories were needed to sustain life and provide the energy needed for activities.

Now that you know the general characteristics of sensation and perception and the likely evolutionary origin of these important functions, let's take a look at the individual senses. For each, we will examine transduction, coding, and neural processing mechanisms, as well as perceptual processes. Some important information about the senses is summarized in Table 4-3.

Vision: The Sense of Sight

Most people would agree that if they were limited to the use of only one sense, they would choose vision. We will take up the nature of light, the visual stimulus, then consider the structure of the eye, the transduction of the light stimulus, and the neural processing of the sensation to permit perception. Finally, we will discuss color vision.

The Visual Stimulus: Light

When the electricity went off while I was walking down an interior hallway in our psychology building, I literally could not see my hand in front of my face. Why? Because of the lack of electromagnetic energy. All senses are stimulated by energy sources, and the stimulus for vision is *light*, which is one form of electromagnetic energy.

When you see a sunbeam illuminating particles of dust in the air, you might think that light is continuous and travels in a straight line. Neither of these observations would be correct. In fact, light energy is broken up into tiny units or particles called photons (from the Greek word meaning "light"), which travel in waves. These waves vary in amplitude (intensity) and wavelength (color).

***Amplitude* is measured as the total amount of radiant energy received in a unit of time and is a major factor in perceived brightness. It is analogous to the height or amplitude of an ocean wave (Figure 4-5). *Wavelength* affects the perception of color and is analogous to the distance between the crests of successive ocean waves. We typically see light that is a mixture of wavelengths and hence a mixture of colors, so light can also vary in *purity*—the extent to which the wavelengths are varied.**

Wavelengths of light—and hence colors—are distributed along the *electromagnetic spectrum*, a continuum that ranges from gamma rays and x-rays at one end to AC current at the other (see Figure 4-6). The *visible spectrum* is one narrow band of wavelengths running from about 400 to 700 nanometers (nm) and encompassing the range of colors between violet and red. Since a nanometer is one billionth of a meter, the visible spectrum runs only from 400 billionths to 700 billionths of a meter, a very small distance on a meter stick.

The Eye: Structure and Function

Figure 4-7A shows the basic structures of the eye and the pathway the light travels through these structures. To understand how the eye works, imagine that you are looking at a person. Light reflected from the person first passes through the transparent entryway to the eye, the *cornea*, then reaches the pigmented (colored) *iris*, which surrounds the *pupil*. The pupil is a hole in the iris that dilates as light becomes dimmer and constricts as it becomes brighter in order to regulate the amount of light entering the eye, much as the diaphragm regulates the amount of light entering a camera. The *lens* is a transparent sac filled with gelatin-like material that serves to focus objects at varying distances more sharply. The light, and the image it carries, is finally focused upside-down on the *retina* (Figure 7B), from which it is transmitted to the brain.

The Retina: Window To The Brain

For all its complexity and splendor, the brain cannot directly "read" or interpret light waves. It is the job of the all-important retina to convert the light waves into signals that the brain can understand. The *retina* is the specialized tissue at the back of the eye that senses light and transduces it to nerve impulses, thus sending images to the brain. Derived from the Latin word for "net," the retina is a network of blood vessels, visual receptor cells, cell bodies, and neuron fibers (Provencio et al., 2002). It contains about 130 million receptor cells and many millions of neurons. In fact, the retina is considered by many experts to be a part of the central nervous system (Penfold et al., 1993).

As Figure 4-8 shows, there are several different types of cells, positioned in layers. The receptor cells of the innermost layer convert the electromagnetic energy of light to nerve impulses. After further processing by other cells, the impulse reaches the *ganglion* cells, whose axons leave the eye in a bundle that makes up the *optic nerve*, carrying information to the brain.

The point at which the axons meet is called the *optic disk*. Because it contains only nerve fibers and blood vessels, you cannot see the part of a visual image that falls on it, and it is therefore also called the *blind spot*. You are normally unaware of the blind spot because the receptors in one eye usually pick up what those in the other eye miss and because the brain compensates for the blind spot and fills in the hole in your vision with an image that is appropriate to whatever surrounds the hole. To locate your blind spot, close your left eye and look at the hot-air balloon in Figure 4-9; watch the jet disappear as you move the book. Notice that there is no hole in your visual field. Instead, the brain simply continues the white background to cover the area that actually contains the jet.

***The Rods and Cones*. The receptor cells in the retina are called rods and cones. Both are sensitive to light and process the light stimulus in about the same way (Burns & Baylor, 2001), but they differ in shape, number, and function. Rods are thin, cylindrical structures, while cones are thicker and have a cone_shaped tip (Figure 4_10A). Rods are also much more numerous than cones and are found throughout the retina, but the major difference between the two is in their functions.**

***Rods* are visual receptors that are highly sensitive to light and are involved in night vision. They are also important in peripheral vision, which allows you to detect objects at the edges of your visual field, where they are almost—but not quite—out of sight. They lead to *achromatic* perceptions, which is why we become unable to distinguish among colors at night or in a darkened room, when only the rods are operating.**

***Cones* are visual receptors that dominate in daylight vision and color vision. They are concentrated primarily in**

a small central area of the retina called the *fovea*, where there are no rods at all (see Figure 4-7A). The fovea is only about the size of the period at the end of this sentence, but it is the area of greatest *visual acuity*, or sharpness, the part of the retina capable of the clearest vision and with the ability to distinguish the finest details. Animals that function primarily during the day, such as pigeons, may have nothing but cones in their retinas, whereas nocturnal animals, like bats and owls, have a predominance of rods. Evidence shows that rods and cones interact, with certain cones affecting the sensitivity of rods to light (Shapiro, 2002). It has also been found that both rods and cones decrease in number as we age (Curcio, 2001).

Recent evidence suggests that we will need to go beyond the rods and cones fully understand how light is processed. In fact, it now appears that there may be non-visual mechanisms in the eye that are also involved in the transduction process (Van Gelder, 2001).

Visual Adaptation

You can't see so well immediately after stepping from a dark room into bright sunlight or vice versa because your visual mechanisms must undergo sensory adaptation. *Light adaptation*, which occurs when you move from a dark theater into bright sunlight, takes place in a few seconds. *Dark adaptation* is much slower process, with cones taking about 10 minutes and rods nearly an hour to adapt (Bouman, 2002; Figure 4-10B). That is why airline pilots should dark adapt for at least 30 minutes before taking off at night.

The Neurophysiology of Visual Sensation and Perception

Nerve impulses from the retina travel over special optic pathways to the brain. There are actually several pathways and several areas of the brain involved, but we will consider only the most important ones.

Pathways To The Brain

A given cell in the retina responds only to light originating in a specific, circumscribed area of the visual world. This area is called the *receptive field* of the cell. If you are in a darkened room where the only visual stimulus is a tiny pinpoint of light to your left, it will stimulate certain cells in the retina; if it is to your right, it will stimulate different cells.

Stimulation of its receptive field increases firing of the cell. Stimulation of a neighboring cell while continuing to record from the first cell *reduces* the firing of the first cell. This effect is called *lateral inhibition* because it involves inhibiting the firing of cells beside a stimulated cell. It accounts for an effect called *brightness contrast*, which can be observed and measured in both infants and adults (Davies & Morland, 2002).

Each of the one million ganglion cells in each eye sends an axon to the brain via the optic nerve. The two optic nerves converge at the *optic chiasm*—a crossover point at which the axons from the inside half of each eye cross to the opposite side of the brain (see Figure 4-11). This means that each eye projects to both hemispheres of the brain (M. Smith, 2001).

Continuing into the brain, the optic nerves form two pathways. The main tract enters the *lateral geniculate nucleus* (LGN) of the thalamus (Figure 4-11). The neurons next to each other in the LGN have receptive fields that are next to each other in the retina. This match-up means that there is a *map* of the retina in each layer of the LGN, and we call this arrangement a *topographic* organization (Krahe et al., 2002). The LGN sharpens the resolution of light patterns striking the retina, much as a computer enhances images transmitted to the Kennedy Space Flight Center from outer space.

The remaining optic fibers go to the *superior colliculi*, a pair of nuclei in the midbrain. These structures also receive information from the touch and hearing senses and from some areas of the cortex. They organize visual, auditory, and touch information into maps so that we can determine just where a stimulus originated (Stein et al., 2001).

Light Becomes Information: The Visual Cortex

After processing in the LGN, information is passed directly to the visual (occipital) cortex. Again, the relationship is topographic, and an integrated model of the neural processing of visual information has been developed (Bullier, 2001). It shows that each retinal cell is connected to one specific cell in the lateral geniculate nucleus, and that cell, in turn, sends fibers to specific cells in the occipital lobe (Hasnain et al., 2001).

It is in the visual cortex that sensation becomes perception, and researchers have begun to discover some of the biological bases for the complex perceptual processes that take place there (Julesz and Schumer, 1981; Kovacs & Julesz, 1993). Visual pathways have been mapped in considerable detail, and neural locations for the perception of motion and direction have been studied (Ghazanfar & Nicolelis, 2001). In addition, we have learned *top-down processes*, in which prior knowledge and expectations affect perception, involve not only the occipital cortex, but also areas of the frontal cortex (Kostandov, 2001; Engel et al., 2001).

Feature analyzers. But just how does the visual cortex turn sensory images into perceptual information? David Hubel and Torsten Wiesel (1962) won the Nobel Prize for taking a significant step in the direction of solving this puzzle. They discovered specialized nerve cells called *feature analyzers* or feature detectors—occipital neurons that respond only to highly specific aspects of a complex stimulus, such as its shape or orientation. There are a number of specific feature analyzers, of which Hubel and Wiesel emphasize three: *Simple cells* react only to lines or edges with a particular orientation, such as horizontal or vertical; *complex cells* respond only to lines of specific orientations when the lines are moving; and *hypercomplex* cells respond to such perceptual features as right angles or lines of certain lengths. Basically, this suggests that the further we go from the retina to the brain, the more specific the stimulus needed to cause a given neuron to fire.

Feature detectors are essential but primitive units for pattern recognition—the identification of stimulus patterns. Even the hypercomplex cells can account for only the most basic aspects of pattern recognition. These simple units of specific information are somehow integrated by the brain so that we can recognize such complex patterns as the words you are reading now.

Color Vision

Have you ever watched a perfect sunset, rushed outside to see a rainbow in the clouds, or been struck by the beauty of a painting? You perceive and differentiate many colors every day, but can you verbally describe the color blue? Give up? Color is a highly evolved property of the visual system (Yokoyama & Radlwimmer, 2001), and a subjective experience difficult to describe except by way of example: the blue of a clear sky, the red color of blood, the green of grass. Nevertheless, experimental psychologists, defining color in more technical terms, have been able to gain considerable knowledge of its properties and of the processing of color by the visual system.

In 1671, Isaac Newton cut a tiny hole in one of his window shutters, allowing a thin beam of sunlight to pass through a prism, thereby projecting rainbow colors on the wall. This proof that white light is composed of many wavelengths became the basis for understanding color. Let's take a look at the nature of the stimulus for color and its transmission to the brain, consider several theories of how color perception occurs, and see what is involved in color blindness.

The Color Stimulus. Color is a psychological experience, a perceptual interpretation of light, which is the physical stimulus. It has three psychological properties—hue, brightness, and saturation—that correspond to the three physical properties of light—wavelength, amplitude, and purity. *Hue* is the psychological interpretation of the wavelength of light that an object produces or reflects. Light reflecting from a car at a dominant wavelength of 580 nm, for example, will be perceived as yellow, while green and blue, respectively, will be perceived at wavelengths of 515 nm and 475 nm. All the colors of the spectrum are found around the outer edge of the *color circle* that can be made by joining the ends of the rainbow (Figure 4-12A).

A given hue can vary considerably in brightness and saturation, as the color solid shows (Figure 4-12B). *Brightness* is primarily the psychological interpretation of amplitude. More intense hues are perceived as brighter. Yellow, for example, can be very bright or relatively dull. *Saturation* is the psychological result of the purity of light—the extent to which it has been mixed with white or gray. Saturated (undiluted) colors look deep and strong. Desaturated colors are diluted and weak. By using all three properties, a person with normal color vision can distinguish at least a million shades of color (Boynton, 1990).

Although we occasionally see pure wavelengths, most light is a mixture, and the perceived hue depends on that mixture. You no doubt recall mixing primary colors of paints in elementary school to obtain derivative colors. Yellow and blue, for example, make green. Since the pigments (color components) in paints achieve their final color by absorbing most wavelengths, you were engaging in what is called *subtractive color mixing*—extracting some wavelengths to leave less total light in the mixture (Figure 4-12C). A second possibility is *additive color mixing*—adding more light to the mix (Figure 4-12D). Shine a yellow light and a blue light on the same white surface, adding one color to the other. Do you get green? No! You get something closer to white light. Since pure white light contains the full visible spectrum—as Newton demonstrated with his prism—adding one color to another shifts the perceived color of the mixture toward white. Additive and subtractive mixing thus yield quite different results.

Color Channels in the Brain. Recent evidence shows that color and brightness are processed somewhat separately beyond the retina (Snowden, 2002). Color processing follows one channel from the LGN to the cortex, while information regarding brightness follows another. The color channel enters small, oval-shaped areas of the visual cortex called *blobs*—that's right, *blobs* (who ever said all scientific terms are sophisticated?)! Cells of the brightness channel project to areas between the blobs (you guessed it, *interblob regions*). Recent studies have begun to show how the two channels interact to permit more complex sensations to be processed (Billock et al., 2001).

Theories of Color Vision. Do we need a million different kinds of receptors to differentiate a million colors? No, perhaps only three different types. Formulated by Thomas Young and Hermann Von Helmholtz in the nineteenth century, the *trichromatic theory* suggests that color vision involves only three different receptor mechanisms that respond to different regions of the spectrum (Figure 4-13A). One of these responds to long wavelengths (roughly the red region of the spectrum), one to medium wavelengths (green), and one to short wavelengths (blue). You can see all the colors of the rainbow because visual mechanisms mix these primary colors by varying the ratio of one to another and transmitting that ratio to the brain (see Figure 4-12D). Until recently, most research confirmed that there are, indeed, three different types of cones, each with a different pigment (color base) and each specialized for a somewhat different region of the spectrum. However, current studies show that a substantial percentage of women possess genes for four or more types of cones and that those with more cone types are better able to differentiate colors (Jameson et al., 2001). One type responds best to short wavelengths (the blue region of the spectrum), one to medium (the green region), and one to long (the red region).

A second theory of color vision, originally proposed as an alternative to trichromatic theory, is called *opponent-process theory*. Developed by German physiologist Ewald Hering, also in the nineteenth century, and revised more recently by DeValois and DeValois. The final version of the theory hypothesizes three pairs of cones: red-green, blue-yellow, and black-white (a brightness dimension). They are called opponent or *complementary colors*—colors that when mixed together result in shades of gray (see Figure 4-12A and Figure 4-12C). The gray can range from nearly white to nearly black, depending on the intensity of the light. The members of each of the opponent pairs inhibit or oppose each other. Our experience of hue or color is determined by the interaction of these pairs (DeValois and DeValois, 1975, 1993). In each pair only one of the two opposing colors can be transmitted to the brain at a time.

For nearly a century, scientists assumed that one of the two theories was right and the other wrong. However, there research showed that each of the two is partially correct. In fact, it now appears that the best understanding of color vision comes through the *dual-process theory*, which combines the trichromatic and opponent-process theories. It suggests that color information is processed in multiple stages. Wavelengths of light are first transduced by the cones, and research confirms that there are three types of cone receptors in the retina. Beyond the cones, however, an opponent_process mechanism takes over at the ganglion cell layer and continues to the LGN and occipital cortex (DeValois and DeValois, 1975, 1993).

At each of these later stages, there are some cells that are excited by yellow and inhibited by blue, others that show the reverse pattern. Other opponent pairs respond differentially to red and green. Color vision thus ultimately depends on both trichromatic and opponent-process mechanisms. Figure 4-13B compares the three theories.

The *retinex theory* adds a third mechanism and has more recently been integrated with the dual-process theory (Zeki et al., 1998). This approach suggests that both the retina and the cortex (hence the term "retinex") contribute to color processing and perception. In particular, the cortex compares patterns of light originating in different areas of the retina and integrates them to perceive color.

Each of these theories is based on the assumption that color and its perception are based in the brain. An interesting alternative idea is that color is actually based in the external environment, not the brain (Ross, 2001). This new view has not yet been widely accepted and is, in fact, actively opposed by some experts (Revonsuo, 2001).

Color Blindness: Do You "See Red?". You can partially test yourself for color blindness by examining the patterns in Figure 4-14A. Our mini-test probably showed that you see color normally and are therefore a *trichromat*—one who can differentiate all three primary colors. However, 8 percent of men and less than 1 percent of women are genetically colorblind, sometimes as a result of a genetic defect, sometimes due to exposure to neurotoxins (Gobba, 2000; Neitz & Neitz, 2000). Most of these are called *dichromats*—people who can differentiate only two of the three basic hues (Figure 14B). A dichromat is typically missing either red cones or green cones and therefore sees colors at the blue-green end of the spectrum as blue and colors at the red-yellow end as yellow. Only one person in 40,000 is a monochromat—one who has so few cones that he is totally colorblind.

Visual Perception: Knowing What You See

The process by which the eye senses a complex stimulus—a form or pattern—and transmits the information to the brain is quite straightforward. However, the *perception* of such a stimulus—its interpretation—is much more *subjective and* can be influenced by a variety of factors. Some of those factors represent properties of the stimulus itself; others arise within the brain and are a function of the perceiver—the individual viewing the stimulus. After considering these factors, we will see how visual perception is organized and how it tends to be constant. We will then learn how depth and movement are perceived but will find that the normally accurate processes of visual perception can be fooled, creating optical illusions. We will also see how mental imagery parallels the visual perception of the external environment. And, finally, you may be interested in the fascinating, but controversial, topic of subliminal perception—perception without awareness—the subject of our 21 for this chapter.

Bottom-Up and Top-Down Processing

Bottom-up processing begins with the individual elements of a stimulus and integrates those elements to form a whole—an overall perceptual interpretation of the stimulus. Any form or pattern you observe is made up of such features as edges, lines, angles, and corners. According to bottom-up theories, the brain analyzes each of these elements, then assembles them to form a whole. In effect, we identify simple features, then put them together to recognize the complex stimulus of which they are parts. The process is somewhat like putting a puzzle together by fitting all the pieces into their proper positions to form the complete picture (Figure 4-15A). The concept of bottom-up processing is consistent with the discovery by Hubel and Wiesel of feature detectors in the occipital cortex, and this theoretical approach to perception is therefore often referred to as *feature analysis.*

Although feature analysis is important, it cannot entirely account for perception. Theories have long suggested that we also engage in *top-down processing,* in which preexisting concepts, knowledge, ideas, and anticipations influence the interpretation of the stimulus. Also known as conceptually-driven processing, this approach suggests that the brain doesn't just analyze a stimulus and label it. Rather, it goes beyond the elements of the stimulus to impose its own organizational principles, concepts, and prior expectations. If you know that the picture in Figure 4-15B is that of a young woman with her head partially turned, you can easily see her. Prior knowledge of this ambiguous picture influences your perception. Had you been told, instead, that the picture is that of an old woman in profile, you would more likely have perceived it that way.

We can probably best conclude that any complete theory of perception must take into account both bottom-up and top-down processing. Although one or the other may be dominant on a given occasion, it is likely that most instances of perception involve both.

Perceptual Organization: The Gestalt Laws

One major approach that emphasizes top-down processing is *Gestalt psychology,* which insists that perception is an *active* process in which the brain imposes organization and interpretation on incoming stimulus information. Gestalt theory says that we perceive objects as *wholes*—complete forms—and emphasizes that the whole is greater than the sum of the parts. The series of lines in the two panels of Figure 4-16, for example, have exactly the same number of dashes of exactly the same length, but you would probably describe one of the lines as straight and the other as curved. The "sum of the parts" is quite literally identical, but the whole in each case has what the Gestaltists call *emergent properties*—attributes that cannot be found in any one component part.

Gestalt (German for "form") psychology began in Germany just after the turn of the twentieth century under the leadership of Max Wertheimer and Wolfgang Kohler.

The Gestalt psychologists believed that the basis for organizing parts into wholes is innate: the brain comes equipped to perceive certain kinds of wholes or patterns. A concept of "roundness," for instance, is built into the brain. You have to learn that the object is a coffee cup, but the perception that it is round is inborn. Gestalt theory remains a major top-down approach to understanding perception.

Figure-Ground Relationships. Do you see a vase or two faces in Figure 4-17? The reason you see one or the other is that one serves as the *figure*—the central feature or object you are viewing—while the other serves as the *ground*—the backdrop against which the figure is perceived. The coffee cup sitting on your desk is a clear figure that stands out against the ground formed by the desk, walls, and other surrounding objects. But if you refocus your attention so that you are concentrating on a pencil lying on the desk, the coffee cup recedes and becomes part of the ground.

The vase-face picture is a different story. To Gestalt psychologists, it is an example of an ambiguous figure-ground relationship in which figure and ground represent reversible perspectives. Such reversible perceptual organizations tend to be unstable and to shift back and forth as you look at the picture.

Despite considerable research, psychologists still don't fully understand the reversible figures effect and, more generally, how figure and ground are differentiated. The four principal factors that seem to contribute are area, symmetry, familiarity, and orientation. Smaller areas and more symmetrical areas are more likely to be seen as the figure. We are also more likely to perceive a familiar stimulus as the figure, and horizontal and vertical orientations are more likely to be seen as figure than are diagonal orientations.

Going beyond these basic factors, Ann Treisman (1986) proposes a *feature-integration* thesis, in which the determination of figure and ground takes place in two stages: a *preattentive stage,* in which the stimulus is quickly and automatically broken down into its basic properties, called primitives; and a *focused attention* stage, in which primitives are combined in a process that requires conscious attention and effort. She argues that is isolated features are processed automatically, a target feature should "pop out" of a display even when surrounded by objects that it differs from. Her research has supported this role of preattentive processing (Treisman & Souther, 1985), as has more recent research on top-down processing (Sarter et al., 2001); Miyashita & Hayashi, 2000).

Gestalt Principles. Figure-ground relationships provide one example of the more general issue of part-whole relationships—the relationship of any given element to a total perceptual picture. Wertheimer and other Gestalt psychologists concluded that certain general perceptual tendencies govern how we group parts to form wholes or "gestalts:"

- *Simplicity.* Any stimulus pattern will tend to be perceived as simply as possible (Figure 4-18A)
- *Proximity.* The closer two figures are to each other, the more likely they are to form a perceptual group. There are a number of ways you can view the six dots in Figure 4_18B _ as pairs of two or sets of three, for example. The difference is in the proximity of the dots.

- *Good continuation.* We tend to perceive contours as continued along smooth perceptual lines. In Figure 4-18C, you probably tend to group segments A and D and segments C and B. The principle of good continuation is the basis for some types of camouflage, both in nature and in human endeavors.
- *Similarity.* We tend to group similar items together (Figure 4-18D).
- *Common Fate.* Elements tend to be grouped by coordinated movement or common fate (Figure 4-18F). If two fighter jets moving faster and two moving slower are flying in the same area of the sky, you tend to perceive the faster jets as one group and the slower jets as another.
- *Closure.* One of the most interesting of the Gestalt principles suggests that our perceptual system strives to attain closure, meaning that it tends to complete or close figures that are incomplete. A glance at the circle and triangle in Figure 4_18E will make the closure principle clear.

Relying on Gestalt principles to explain results, one recent study showed that ancient cave drawings are recognizable because the artists conformed to the principles of closure and good continuation, as Figure 4-19 shows. Other studies show how these same principles allow you to perceive a whole object when you can see only a part of it (Kovacs & Julesz, 1993). In a final example, Robert Frick (1987) asked college students to rapidly but accurately count a series of digits. The grouping and good continuation principles accounted for the fact that digits spaced evenly along one row were more difficult to count than digits presented on three different levels.

Perceptual Constancy

A passenger jet flying toward you from a great distance first throws a tiny image on your retina, and the image grows larger and larger as the plane lands and taxies to where you are standing. But do you perceive the plane as getting larger? Of course not. This tendency to perceive objects as being consistent in lightness, size, shape, and other characteristics under a wide variety of viewing conditions is called *perceptual constancy.*

Lightness Constancy. A white car always looks white, despite the fact that the amount of light falling on it—its *illumination*—varies markedly, resulting in a variation in the amount of light reflected by the car, or its luminance. This effect is called lightness constancy. It can be affected by perceptual organization and experience (Paradiso, 2000).

Size Constancy. A man 6'4" tall standing 50 feet away from you will look taller than a man 5'6" standing 10 feet away. Despite the fact that the more distant man projects a much smaller image on your retina, the size constancy phenomenon allows you to correctly determine that he is taller. Size constancy can be understood by noting that the perceived size of an object is a joint function of the size of the retinal image and the apparent distance of the object from the person. When a known object is farther away, the brain estimates the distance and automatically increases the perceived size of the object accordingly.

Size constancy can break down under certain circumstances. It is likely to fail when you are at very great distance from an object, when distance cues are minimal or absent, and when a person has had little or no experience with the use of distance cues. Blind people whose vision is restored in adulthood and people raised in jungles, where objects are rarely viewed at great distances, often exhibit impaired size constancy. Studies of size constancy continue as we attempt to understand it better and determine its neural basis.

Shape Constancy. If you hold this book in front of you and rotate it at various angles, it does not appear to change shape, although the retinal image changes considerably. Similarly, you easily see the coin facing you on the left side of Figure 4-20 as round, but you also see a round coin on the right side of the figure, where it is at an angle and actually presents an ellipse to the retina.

The constancy phenomenon is not limited to size, shape, and lightness. It is also seen in other aspects of perception, such as color, the velocity of moving objects, and distances judged by touch alone (Novak, 2001).

Why Perceptual Constancy? Despite the occasional occurrence of some illusions that we will consider shortly, constancy is the general rule. Why? German physiologist Ewald Hering long ago suggested that at least lightness constancy is a result of *innate* visual mechanisms. He hypothesized that changes in illumination affect both the object being viewed and the background against which it is seen, resulting in both brightness contrast and lightness constancy, and more recent evidence points to color constancy mechanisms in the visual cortex (Foster et al., 2001). However, attempts to explain other types of constancy, especially size constancy, in terms of similar innate visual mechanisms have been largely unsuccessful.

The alternative approach is to emphasize the role of *experience* in constancy phenomena. Hermann von Helmholtz suggested that the size-distance relationship that appears to underlie size constancy is acquired through learning. Considerable research has tended to support this view, showing, for example, that cultural experience affects constancy illusions. A case in point is the Zulu tribe, a primitive South African culture. Shown the Muller-Lyer illusion (see Figure 4-22), most Zulus see the two lines as about equal in length or one line as only slightly longer than the other. The probable reason is that the Zulus live in a culture that emphasizes curved lines. Their eating utensils and tools are invariably curved, their huts are round and have round doors, and they even plow their fields in curved rows. The lack of experience with straight lines seems to eliminate the distortion in the Muller-Lyer demonstration.

Depth Perception

Only the two-dimensional image of an object that falls on the retina is transmitted directly to the brain. Nevertheless, we live in a three-dimensional world and must have *depth perception,* which tells us how far away an object is. Depth perception relies on two kinds of cues: *binocular cues,* which require the use of both eyes, and *monocular cues,* which need only be viewed with one eye (Read, 2002).

Using Both Eyes: Binocular Cues. The most important depth cues are those provided by retinal disparity and convergence. *Retinal disparity* refers to the slightly different locations of an image on the right and left retinas resulting from the separation of the eyes. The farther away an object is (up to about 25 feet), the greater will be the difference in retinal locations, giving the brain its major depth cue.

Retinal disparity can be demonstrated with a stereoscope, a device for viewing 3-D pictures. When you look through a stereoscope, your left eye is presented with one scene and your right eye with another. The slightly different images are transmitted to the brain, and specific portions of the right occipital cortex then interactively interpret these images to achieve a perception of depth (Andrews et al., 2001). Similarly take a pencil in your left hand and hold it at arm's length in front of you. Close your left eye and hold another pencil in your right hand in such a position that it blocks your view of the first pencil. Now open your left eye and you should be able to see both pencils.

Convergence results from the differences in the strain on the eye muscles as you view objects that are far away or close up. Stand in front of a mirror and watch your eyes turn inward as you move a pencil closer to your face. Convergence is useful in perceiving depth up to a distance of about 10 feet. Beyond that you rely on retinal disparity and on monocular cues.

Using One Eye: Monocular Cues. Even a person who is blind in one eye from birth can perceive depth. Thus, some monocular depth cues must exist. One set of such cues is the relative size and height of objects. Smaller objects appear to be farther away, while larger objects appear closer. Adelbert Ames had observers view illuminated balloons in a dark room. When he pumped more air into one of the balloons, the observers reported that it appeared to be moving closer. Relative height also provides a set of depth cues: Objects that appear to be higher in the field of view usually appear to be further away. Other monocular cues include interposition, perspective, texture gradients, aerial perspective, and motion parallax (Ujike & Ono, 2001), all shown in Figure 4-21.

Moving Experiences: The Perception of Movement

We can readily determine not only whether an object is moving but in what direction and at what approximate speed. Such movement perception begins in peripheral vision, where you perceive some forms of movement even when you can't identify the object (Geisler et al., 2001). This suggests that movement perception may have appeared earlier in evolutionary development than shape perception because it promoted survival by detecting potential enemies. The edge of the retina serves as an "early warning device," detecting movement and causing the head and eyes to turn in the direction of the object in order to center it on the retina and identify it. There are two basic kinds of movement perception: real movement and illusory movement.

Real Movement. The perception of objects that really are moving is called *real movement.* Three factors involved in this form of perception are the size of the object, its *distance* from the observer, and the nature of the *background.* The bigger the object is and the further away it is, the faster it must move in order for us to notice the movement. Thus, a horse moving across a large field must travel considerably faster than a rabbit for both to appear to be moving at the same speed. The background also makes a difference. A spot traveling across a background of vertical lines will be perceived as moving faster than a spot moving across a uniform background. The perceptual apparatus is highly sensitive to real movement. In fact, even a very minimal change in the position of an object can be perceived as movement, and the direction of motion can also be readily detected (Geisler et al., 2001).

An especially interesting form of real movement that is currently being studied is *biological motion*—the movement of the human body. Gunnar Johansson (1973) pioneered the effort to determine just how we perceive the movement of other humans. In a fascinating series of studies, Johansson and his colleagues have shown that observers can easily identify complex human movement patterns even when they cannot see the person. In one study, they taped a flashlight bulb to each major joint (shoulders, knees, etc.) of a person, who was then filmed while moving around in a dark room. Observers who watched the film saw only moving lights but could readily identify the pattern as a person walking or running after .1 second (Johansson, von Hofsten, & Jansson, 1980). Other studies have shown that observers can quickly determine whether the pattern of moving lights is that of a woman or a man and even identify specific individuals they know (Crowell & Andersen, 2002).

Illusory Movement. Have you ever slammed on your brakes while sitting at an intersection, only to discover that your car was not moving at all, but that the truck next to you was moving? It is easy to fool the brain into perceiving movement when there actually is none. The false perception of stationary objects as moving is called *illusory movement*, and there are three major forms. *Induced movement* occurs when the actual movement of one object causes the perceived movement of another. The moon appears to be moving rapidly through clouds on a windy night, when it is actually the clouds that are moving. Apparent motion or *stroboscopic movement* occurs when there is a rapid progress of images of stationary objects across the retina. The lights around the edge of a theater marquee appear to be moving rapidly in one direction, though they are merely flashing on and off in rapid sequence. Neurons corresponding topographically to points on the retina are stimulated sequentially as the series of stimuli march across the visual field. There is similarly no real movement in a motion picture. Rather, movies consist of individual, stationary images shown at the rate of 16_22 frames per second. The rapid succession of these frames provides the illusion of movement. Stroboscopic movement can be affected by the past experience of the observer and the shape, size, and color of the object being observed, as well as the brightness of background lighting. Both top-down and bottom-up processes appear to be involved.

Another type of illusory movement is based on the *autokinetic effect*—the perceived motion of a stationary point of light in a dark environment. If you darken a room, place a penlight at the opposite side of the room, and stare at it for a while, it will appear to move. Autokinetic movement is probably a result of *eye drift*, the automatic movement of the eyes that occurs when you attempt to fixate. This involuntary movement causes a repositioning of the retinal image of the light that is incorrectly interpreted by the brain as movement. Autokinetic movement is easily affected by suggestion, as was demonstrated by social psychologist Muzafer Sherif in a famous 1935 experiment. Participants placed alone in a room reported that a dot of light moved anywhere from 0.8 to 7.4 inches, but participants placed in the room in groups of three all reported about the same amount of movement, approximately 4 inches. The observers clearly influenced each other's perceptions—or at least their reports of what they saw.

Virtual Reality and Cybersickness. Among the most striking of all visual effects involving depth and motion are those created with computer-based *virtual reality* environments. A helmet tracks head and eye movement and feeds this information to a computer, which instantly changes the scene, creating the sensation that you are operating in three-dimensional space. This relatively new—and still imperfect—technology has proven extremely useful in such applications as the training of surgeons, pilots, and drivers. However, many of those exposed to virtual reality develop a form of particularly potent form of motion sickness that has been termed *cybersickness.* It may result from the compelling feeling of self-motion or *vection* when there is no actual motion. Alternatively, virtual reality may cause cybersickness because it elicits eye-movement patterns that are associated with motion sickness (Kennedy et al., 1997).

Optical Illusions

An *optical illusion* or visual illusion is a distorted perception that does not accurately represent the real object you are viewing. Illusions occur when the brain applies inappropriate perceptual assumptions to misleading sensory cues. Illusions are more than just tricks or party games because they provide important insights into the basis for perceptual constancy and related processes. They also vividly demonstrate the subjective nature of perception by showing that the perceptual hypotheses we regularly formulate about the real world are sometimes strikingly wrong (Plodowski & Jackson, 2001).

A number of illusions have been studied. Each involves a violation of one or more of the major principles of perception, such as size and shape constancy. However, the exact reasons for some illusions are not yet well understood. Among the illusions investigated to on those called the Ebbinghaus, Moses, mega-Moses, and Armstrong illusions (Hanisch et al., 2001; Shafto & MacKay, 2000). Far more research has been done, however on several other illusions that we will consider here.

- **The Muller-Lyer Illusion.** Which line in Figure 4_22 is longer? The line on the right looks longer, although in reality they are the same length. This *Muller-Lyer illusion* is an example of inaccurate application of the size constancy principle, possibly combined with misperception of depth cues. Studies to further understand its implications are ongoing (Franz et al., 2001; Predebon, 2001).

- **The Ponzo Illusion.** A second line illusion depends primarily on mis-perceived depth cues. Even though the two horizontal lines in the *Ponzo illusion* (Figure 4-23) appear quite different in length, they are actually identical. The reason for the illusion is that the linear perspective cue provided by the converging lines suggests depth, making the apparently more distant line seem longer (Prinzmetal et al., 2001).

- **The Horizontal-Vertical Illusion.** Figure 4-24A shows a striking line illusion. Which line is longer? The vertical line appears longer, but it is actually much shorter, and the illusion probably relies primarily on depth cues. This *horizontal-vertical illusion* causes us to overestimate the heights of many vertical objects, such as trees, buildings, and parking meters, on a daily basis. Look at the Gateway Arch in St. Louis, Missouri (Figure 4-24B). Believe it or not, the height and width are identical (630 ft.).

- **The Geographical Slant Illusion.** It is a common observation that people tend to overestimate the steepness of hills, slanted roofs and mountain slopes. This slant illusion has been confirmed in studies in which subjects give visual or verbal estimates of the slopes of various hills. Both tend to be substantial overestimates of steepness, and some investigators have argued that this illusion has adaptive evolutionary value; it allows people to avoid attempting climbs that are beyond their ability and hence reduces the likelihood of injury (Proffitt et al., 1995).

- **The Ames Room Illusion.** An area illusion that tricks size constancy mechanisms is the *Ames room illusion* (Figure 4_25A). Viewed from the angle in the figure, three men of quite different heights appear to be standing a few feet apart. Actually, the men are all the same height but the left corner of the room is nearly twice as far from the camera as the right corner (see Figure 4-25B). In addition, the windows are actually trapezoids, though your brain attempts to preserve good form by making then appear square. So effective is the illusion that a person walking across the room from left to right will appear to grow rapidly from midget to monster.
- **The Margin Illusion.** Look at the page you are reading. What proportion of its total area is taken up by margins? Few people guess that the answer is typically about one-third. The area of print appears much larger than twice the total area of the top and bottom margins.
- **The Moon Illusion.** Figure 4-26 shows the interesting *moon illusion*, in which the moon appears to be much larger when it is at the horizon than when it is overhead. This variation in perceived size has been noticed for centuries, and the best explanation to date seems to be the phenomenon of *apparent distance.* According to this idea, the sky appears as a flattened dome in which the point directly overhead seems closer than the horizon. The visual system compensates for the perceived difference in distance by making the moon appear larger at the horizon (Kaufman & Kaufman, 2000).
- **Impossible Figures.** Among the most striking of illusions are *impossible figures*—two-dimensional objects that look three-dimensional but could not actually exist in three dimensions. Figure 27A shows several classic impossible figures, but perhaps most dramatic is my favorite illusion, rendered more recently by Roger Shepard (1990; Figure 4-27B). At first glance, all of the figures appear to be feasible structures, but the impossibility of actually constructing them quickly becomes apparent. The illusion probably relies on a violation of the brain's bottom-up processing mechanisms. Many of the elements needed to form a meaningful, three-dimensional whole are present, but the missing ones make completion impossible.

Illusion and Culture: Experience Affects Perception. The optical illusions are not universal; some may be products of life in Western cultures. The Muller-Lyer illusion, for instance, appears to be based on a lifetime of experience with angles and straight lines, common elements of Western cultures, but not of all others. A case in point is the Zulu, a primitive South African culture. Shown the Muller_Lyer illusion, most Zulus see the two lines as about equal in length because they live in a culture that emphasizes curved lines. Their eating utensils and tools are curved, their huts are round and have round doors, and they even plow their fields in curved rows. The lack of experience with straight lines seems to eliminate the distortion in the Muller_Lyer demonstration. Others have shown that the Ponzo illusion is absent in cultures where visual distances tend to be short and where there are few railroad tracks and roads (Berry et al., 1992). All of this does not mean that built-in neurological factors, like those hypothesized by Gestalt theorists, have no role. Indeed, recent research suggests that changes in the perception of vertical and horizontal orientations induced by visual cues may underlie the neural misinterpretations that lead to illusions (Prinzmetal & Beck, 2001). Overall, it seems clear that both biology and environmental experience are important in perception.

In the Mind's Eye: Perception and Mental Imagery

We can perceive not only objects in the external environment, but pictures or images of objects that we have stored in memory. The study of such mental imagery can tell us more about how perceptual processes take place. Form an image of an elephant far off in the distance and imagine that you are walking toward it. Does the image seem larger as you get closer, and do you reach a point at which you are so close that you can no longer see the entire animal? Most participants in Steve Kosslyn's experiments answer "yes" to both these questions. Proving what? Proving that mental images appear to closely mimic our actual perceptions of objects in the environment.

This similarity of mental images and perceptual objects has been demonstrated in a number of ways. Roger Shepard and his colleagues have done experiments to show how objects can be imagined, mentally rotated, and mentally compared (Shepard & Hurwitz, 1984). Similarly, Kosslyn had participants view a map of an imaginary island containing seven specific objects, such as a hut, a tree, and a rock, with distinctively different distances between each pair of objects. The map was removed, and participants mentally focused at some specific location on the map, such as the rock. They then moved mentally from that object to another specific object and pushed a button when they reached the second object. They took longer to "reach" objects further from the starting point than to reach objects that were closer. We must conclude that the same neural structures—at least at the highest levels—involved in actual perception are involved in mental imagery.

Audition: Sensing and Perceiving Sound

Your auditory sensation and perception of that speeding sports car allowed you to identify it before you saw it. Sounds are important to all of us. They provide pleasure, warn of impending danger, and give us a variety of important information about our environment.

An important general characteristic of *audition*, or hearing, is that it provides us with information about events occurring at a distance, often before any other sense can come into play. Audition also has a unique role in language functions. Recent research has substantially increased our understanding of auditory functions. We will discuss some of the most important and interesting new findings. Let's begin by looking at the stimulus for audition, the structure of the ear, and the role of the brain. We will then take up the major theories of how sound is perceived, see how we localize sounds in space, and discuss hearing disorders and their treatment.

The Auditory Stimulus: Sound Vibrations

The basic physical stimulus for audition is *vibration*. This is obvious when you strike a metal object, such as a tuning fork or guitar string, that visibly vibrates at the same frequency as that of the sound it produces. Sound travels in *waves*, which can vary in amplitude, frequency and purity (Figure 4-28A). *Amplitude* (intensity) is measured in decibels (dB), and Figure 4-28B shows the decibel levels of a variety of common sounds. *Loudness*—the perception of sound amplitude—approximately doubles each time the physical intensity increases by 10 dB. If you are engaged in a normal conversation at 60 dB and a radio increases the sound level to 70 dB, the overall perceived loudness will be twice what it was before the radio came on. Very loud sounds, particularly when heard repeatedly, can seriously damage your hearing, as the Probe demonstrates.

Frequency is measured in cycles per second or *hertz* (Hz). When you strike a tuning fork, the prongs of the fork move in and out at some particular frequency, and each in and out movement constitutes one cycle. If the tuning fork vibrates at a rate of 256 cycles per second, you will hear a middle C on the musical scale, and we would say that middle C has a frequency of 256 Hertz (Hz). The psychological interpretation of frequency is called *pitch*, and we must triple the frequency of a tone in order to double its pitch. Perceived pitch is also influenced by amplitude (Kishon-Rabin et al., 2001).

The span of human hearing is quite wide, ranging from about 20 to 20,000 Hz, although age substantially affects the range. Selective loss of hearing for high frequencies begins around 20 years of age, and very few people older than 60 can hear frequencies above 13,000 Hz. Some animals have a much wider range, with bats hearing sounds up to at least 100,000 Hz. Most humans have their best hearing in the range from about 400 to 4000 Hz. To give you a better idea of the frequencies we typically hear, a piano can play notes from about 30 to 4000 Hz; bass and soprano singers can hit notes as low as 100 Hz and as high as 1000 Hz, respectively; and human speech usually occurs in the range of about 200 to 800 Hz. Not surprisingly, musicians, particularly those with years of experinece playing classical music, are better able to differentiate pitches than the average person (Kishon-Rabin et al., 2001).

Sounds also vary in *purity*—the extent to which they contain a mixture of frequencies. The psychological result of purity is *timbre* (pronounced tamber)—the perceived quality of sound. Middle C played on a piano sounds quite different from middle C played on a trumpet. Each instrument has a different timbre.

The Ear: Structure and Function

We divide the ear into three areas: the outer ear, middle ear, and inner ear. The visible, external ear is the *pinna*. It serves as a funnel that collects incoming sound vibrations, which travel down the *auditory canal* to the *tympanic membrane*, or eardrum, a taut membrane that vibrates when struck by sound waves (Figure 4-29). The auditory canal and eardrum constitute the *outer ear*.

Beyond the eardrum is the *middle ear*, which contains three small bones called the *malleus*, the *incus*, and the *stapes*. They are often nicknamed the hammer, anvil, and stirrup. The stapes connects directly to the *oval window*, a membrane that separates the middle ear from the inner ear (Figure 4-29). Vibrations in the eardrum are transmitted mechanically to the bones, which concentrate and amplify the incoming sound waves to a force of more than 20 times that of the sound entering the outer ear.

The *inner ear* includes the cochlea and the semicircular canals. The *cochlea* is a curled, bony, fluid-filled tube that contains the auditory receptors and transduces sound vibrations into electrical energy. Cochlea means "snail," and you can see why in Figure 4-30A.

The cochlea divides into three canals, the vestibular canal, the tympanic canal, and, between these two, the cochlear duct. The cochlear duct is separated from the vestibular canal by Reissner's membrane and from the tympanic canal by the *basilar membrane*. Attached to the basilar membrane is the *organ of Corti*, a gelatinous structure about 1.5 inches long that contains nearly 25,000 auditory receptor cells called *hair cells* (Figure 4-30B). Waves in the cochlear fluid stimulated by the mechanical vibrations of the oval window cause the basilar membrane to vibrate in a wavelike motion that travels along the length of the membrane. The traveling wave causes the hair cells to bend, producing an electrical potential that can initiate a nerve impulse. The impulse is transmitted via the *auditory nerve* to the brain (Moore et al., 2002). It is the cochlea that can be seriously damaged by loud noises, as the Probe describes. We will discuss the semicircular canals when we take up the balance sense.

Some fascinating recent research shows that two kinds of hair cells on the cochlea may have quite different functions. The single row of *inner hair cells*, found on the inner side of the organ of Corti, serve as the primary transducers of sound preparatory to the transmission of the signal to the brain. The three rows of *outer hair cells* serve mainly to *modulate* or fine-tune the transmission, providing the brain with the information it needs to interpret the nuances of the sound (Tsuprun & Santi, 2002). Further fine-tuning may be the function of *efferent* (outgoing) stimulation from the brain to the hair cells. While the hair cells are sending information to the brain, it is sending other information to the hair cells.

Did you realize that your ears not only receive sound but *emit* it? The sounds produced by the ear are called *otoacoustic emissions*. They are probably a product of cochlear functioning. Some appear to be generated by the outer hair cells as they work to make signals to the brain more precise. Others occur when the basilar membrane fails to respond precisely to the simultaneous occurrence of differing frequencies.

Vibration Becomes Information: Auditory Pathways

When the receptors in the cochlea fire, they transmit impulses via the auditory nerve to a number of locations in the brain (Figure 4-31). In particular, there are synapses in the *medial geniculate nucleus* of the thalamus, from which the pathway continues to the primary auditory cortex of the *temporal lobe* (Tramo et al., 2002). Just as the visual system demonstrates topographic organization, the auditory system shows *tonotopic* organization: both the hair cells of the cochlea and the neurons of the auditory cortex that are sensitive to particular frequencies are close to each other. The auditory cortex of the right hemisphere is dominant in the perception of nonverbal stimuli, such as music, whereas the left hemisphere is more active in processing the verbal stimuli of speech and language. Recent evidence suggests that the parietal cortex may also be involved in some aspects of audition (Lewald et al., 2002).

Auditory Perception: Major Theories

The basis for loudness perception is fairly well understood. Increases in the amplitude of sound waves cause the basilar membrane to move more vigorously and over a larger area. This increases the number of hair cells, and thus neurons, stimulated. The more neurons firing, the greater the perceived loudness. So intricate is this intensity coding mechanism that the ear can respond over a range of some 100 trillion sounds (Uttal, 1973).

The basis of pitch perception, however, is not so well understood. As a result, two major theories, called place theory and frequency theory, and a third, combined theory, have been developed.

Place Theory. The first theory was proposed by Herman von Helmholtz in the 19th century. He hypothesized that the 25,000 hair cells spread along the cochlea divide the task of processing sounds of different frequencies. His *place theory* holds that different areas or places on the basilar membrane respond to sound waves of different frequencies. A Middle C note causes vibrations in hair cells on one part of the membrane; a B note vibrates other hair cells. It's much like plucking one guitar string to get one note and another to get a different note. The stimulated hair cells fire corresponding neurons, and the brain interprets pitch according to the specific neurons fired. Georg von Bekesy (1960) won the Nobel Prize for research on guinea pigs that partially supported place theory. However, a low-frequency stimulus will excite virtually all the receptors on the basilar membrane, making it difficult or impossible for place theory to explain how we discriminate low frequencies. Another mechanism must clearly be involved.

Frequency Theory. August Seeback and others saw this and other problems with place theory even in the 19th century and worked to develop an alternative. More recently championed by E.G. Wever (1937), *frequency theory* holds that the entire basilar membrane vibrates at a frequency that matches that of the stimulus (e.g., 256 times per second for a middle C). Pitch perception is determined by the frequency of impulses traveling up the auditory nerve to the temporal cortex.

The problem with frequency theory is that a neuron can fire only about 1000 times per second, while humans, as we saw, can hear frequencies up to 20,000 times per second (20,000 Hz). As a result, Wever offered a modification of frequency theory called *volley theory*, which suggests that groups of neurons fire alternately in rapid succession. One group fires while another rests. The result is a volley of impulses that exceeds the 1000 Hz limit (Wever, 1949) and could theoretically account for hearing at higher frequencies. But the apparent upper limit of volley theory is about 4000 Hz, so even this more recent theory doesn't fully account for pitch perception.

Place Plus Frequency: A Scientific Compromise. We are left with two conflicting theories—place theory and the volley version of frequency theory—each partially accounting for the processing of sound frequency. As often happens in science when there are opposing theories, a combination of the two may be the best approach. We have already seen one example of this in the integration of the opposing trichromatic and opponent-process theories to arrive at the dual-process theory of color vision. A similar theoretical compromise occurred in hearing when Wever (1970) and others proposed that place theory holds for some pitches and frequency theory for others. Up to about 500 Hz, pitch is coded according to the frequency principle; between 500 and 4000 Hz, both place and frequency coding take place; and above

4000 Hz, all coding is in terms of place. This place-frequency compromise is currently the most widely accepted theory, and it has thus far been well supported by a number of studies. However, it may still not represent the final answer to pitch perception, and research continues.

Auditory Perception: Localizing Sounds in Space

Your visual system has access to an entire painting at any given moment, but your auditory system must process the sounds of a symphony *sequentially*. This makes auditory analysis harder than visual analysis and makes it very difficult to locate sounds in space.

If you look at an object, you know immediately whether it is to your right or your left. With sound, however, there is often a question. When you hear that sports car coming, can you immediately tell whether it is coming from your right or your left? Two basic kinds of cues permit at least some degree of sound localization in space: monaural cues and binaural cues.

Monaural cues are those that involve only one ear; they provide information about the *distance* the sound source lies from the listener. Louder sounds are usually perceived as closer, softer sounds as farther away.

The ability to perceive the *direction* of a sound is primarily a function of *binaural cues* provided by sounds reaching both ears and involves two specific cues: timing and intensity. A sound originating to your right will reach your right ear slightly before your left ear, yielding a difference in *timing*. While the time difference is very small (about 600 microseconds), the brain can discriminate differences as brief as 10 microseconds, or 1/100,000 of one second. There is also an *intensity* difference between the two ears. A sound to the right is farther from the left ear and hence loses more intensity before reaching that ear. A more important factor is that your head acts as a sound barrier or *shadow* and reduces the intensity further before it gets to the second ear. The inferior colliculus of the midbrain (see Chapter 4) processes sound cues relevant to localization, and the auditory cortex takes the small differences between the two ears into account in attempting to localize the sound (Litovsky & Delgutte, 2002). Areas of the hindbrain may also be involved (Riedel & Kollmeier, 2002).

Even with the monaural distance cues and the binaural direction cues, sound localization is often poor. As a result, we tend to supplement the ears with the eyes, using vision to help locate sound sources. If the sound initially seems to come from the right, you are likely to look to the right, searching visually for an obvious sound source. If it is not there, you look elsewhere. The direction of the approaching sports car may not be apparent until you see it coming.

Hearing Disorders

As they age, many women and especially men experience significant hearing losses, particularly at higher frequencies. Progressive hearing loss has a number of effects, including the increasing isolation of the person from his most important informal means of communication with others. At best, growing deafness is an unpleasant reminder of the aging process, and in some cases it has more serious consequences. Some older people with hearing problems become at least mildly paranoid, suspecting that other people are talking about them behind their backs.

There are two major types of deafness. In *conduction deafness*, structures in the outer or middle ear become defective and interfere with sound transmission to the cochlea. Conduction deafness may be caused by wax accumulation in the auditory canal, a defect in the eardrum, or damage to the ossicles of the middle ear. Hearing aids or surgical procedures can often correct this form of deafness. *Nerve deafness* occurs when there is damage to the hair cells of the cochlea or to the auditory nerve itself. Most often, it results from damage to the hair cells caused by frequent exposure to intense sound or is a product of the cochlear degeneration that can occur as part of the aging process. Disease processes also cause loss, as can happen when a child has severe, repeated ear infections. Studies show significant high-frequency losses in adults with a childhood history of this disorder (Lopponen et al., 1992).

In addition, some people experience *tinnitus* or ringing in the ears, which may be worsened by taking aspirin and certain other drugs (Cazals, 2000).

Can hearing loss be treated? The answer is a qualified "yes." Some forms of loss can be dealt with by using hearing aids, which have become increasingly sophisticated. In addition, exciting work in recent years has led to the development of a *cochlear implant* that is essentially a "computer ear". Tiny electrodes are implanted in or near the cochlea, with wires leading to a microphone located behind the ear. The microphone transmits sounds to a small computer in the person's pocket, and the signal processed by the computer then goes directly to the auditory nerve, bypassing the damaged cochlea. Patients often report hearing only robot-like speech, but implant techniques and devices are improving, and some people with total hearing loss achieve nearly 100 percent understanding of sentences presented with the cochlear prosthesis in place.

The Chemical Senses: Taste and Smell

If your university encourages you to be a participant in experiments while you are taking introductory psychology, you might consider a taste study. One investigator, for example, fed subjects party dip (free of charge, of course!) with varying amounts of salt in order to study taste discrimination (Stillman, 1993).

Taste and smell are both important senses. They are called *chemical* senses because they are stimulated by chemicals from the environment, and both evolved as essential mechanisms for locating and sampling food. Together, these important senses often protect us from eating poisons and help us select foods containing substances that are needed by the body. Animals fed a diet deficient in salt, for example, will seek out foods high in salt (Pfaffmann, 1963). The receptors for taste and smell, called *chemoreceptors*, are specialized for transducing chemical messages into neural impulses.

Gustation: The Sense of Taste

Known technically as *gustation*, the sense of taste involves the processing of chemicals in solution by specialized receptors in the mouth.

If you stand in front of a mirror and stick out your tongue, you will be able to see numerous tiny projections called *papillae* (Latin for "nipples") on the surface. The sides of each of these tiny bumps are lined with the receptors for taste, which are contained in *taste buds* of which there are some 10,000, mostly on the upper surface of the tongue (Figure 4-32). The actual number varies from person to person. In general, those with numerous taste buds are "*supertasters,*" people who are more sensitive to a variety of tastes than are those with few taste buds. Whether you're a supertaster or not, when you slide a velvety spoonful of chocolate mousse into your mouth, chemicals in the pudding enter the taste pores and stimulate the receptors, which in turn transmit neurological signals along fibers that travel via the medulla and thalamus to the somatosensory cortex of the parietal lobes and the frontal lobes (see Figure 4-33). Some studies show that certain proteins are involved in the transduction of taste sensations (Margolshee, 1993) and that hormones and other neurochemicals are essential to the transmission of neural taste impulses (Gilbertram, 1993).

Taste Qualities. Most evidence points to the existence of four basic taste qualities: sweet, bitter, salty, and sour. Compounds that come closest to eliciting these qualities in pure form are sucrose (sweet), quinine (bitter), sodium chloride (salty), and hydrochloric acid (sour). Studies show that we recognize salty tastes most rapidly and bitter tastes least rapidly.

Most substances produce taste sensations representing a mixture of these four qualities. Chocolate mousse would clearly produce a sensation of sweetness, but it is not pure sugar, so the chocolate flavoring must be conveyed by a combination of the other taste qualities. The next time you eat a meal, experiment a little. Taste one food, concentrating on its flavor, and see if you can tell what combination of the four taste qualities seems to be present. Rinse your mouth thoroughly with water, then try a different food.

We are not sure just how tastes are discriminated at the receptor level. However, it does appear that taste receptors are differentially distributed on the tongue. As Figure 4-34 shows, receptors specialized for sweet substances are located near the tip of the tongue, those for salty and sour substances along the side, and those for bitter near the back. The central part of the tongue has no taste receptors, which is why you can place an aspirin tablet toward the middle of your tongue and avoid tasting it.

The idea that there are four distinct taste qualities might suggest that there are four types of nerve fibers entering the nervous system. However, Carl Pfaffman, a pioneer in taste research, found evidence for only two types of nerve fibers, one specialized for salty, the other for sweet tastes (Pfaffman, 1984). Two types may do the job, however, because two receptors often connect to a single nerve fiber and, conversely, a single receptor may attach to several nerve fibers. Thus, taste coding is probably based on the interaction of multiple nerve fibers. This view fits with *across-fiber pattern theory*, which holds that a given taste sensation depends on a pattern of neural firing across a number of taste neurons. Overall, it is likely that taste sensations depend on the combined responses of some narrowly tuned neurons that react to specific qualities and on across-fiber patterns of neurons that respond to several qualities.

Taste Perception. How do we interpret or perceive tastes? How do you know whether the food you have just eaten is chocolate mousse or cheese dip? It appears that the molecules of a given food fit into specific sites on the receptor cells (much in the way that a key fits only into a specific lock). A molecule of chocolate will fit some receptor sites and a molecule of cheese dip will fit different sites. Once the receptor site has been triggered by a molecule that fits it, the receptor sends a message to the brain, which must then determine what chemicals are present in your mouth and thereby tell you what you have eaten.

Food identification and preference involve touch and smell, as well as taste. Your mouth has tactile or touch receptors, and you therefore also *feel* the food you eat. Size, shape, and hardness all help you to identify a food and influence your liking for it. Although good French bread has great flavor, for example, I don't particularly like it because the crust is too hard. In addition to texture, smell is involved in what we usually think of as the flavor of food. Try pinching your nose closed while you eat an apple or drink some coffee and notice how different it "tastes." And vision plays a role in how good food "tastes," which is why chefs in elegant restaurants go to great lengths to prepare visually appealing plates.

All in Good Taste. You probably know someone who actually likes the taste of raw fish, calf's liver, anchovies, limburger cheese or some other food you can't stand. More generally, there are many individual differences in *taste preference*, and both genetic factors and learning appear to be involved in their development. There is some evidence that adults with higher body weights may show a stronger preference for sweet and fatty foods and that taste preferences vary systematically as a function of sex, race, and smoking (Drewnowski, 1993) . A progressive decrease in taste sensitivity frequently accompanies aging, as taste receptors are lost and not replaced.

Olfaction: The Sense of Smell

"Only the nose knows" is an aphorism that describes a variety of sometimes important situations in which the sense of smell will provide the best clues to the nature of some object or situation. I was skiing several years ago at Taos Ski Valley in New Mexico when just ahead of me I heard the rushing, thundering sound of an avalanche cascading down a steep side slope to block the trail. Ski patrollers brought in "avalanche dogs," whose highly developed olfactory sense allows them to smell humans even beneath the snow (as it turned out, there were none). Dogs are also used to locate explosives and drugs. Many animals, in fact, depend on olfaction more than on sight or hearing. It also helps newborn babies to differentiate their mothers from other people and allows animals to locate food, avoid predators, and find partners for mating. In addition, the sense of smell permits humans to obtain chemical information at a distance and thus helps us to seek out food and to avoid fires, gas leaks, spoiled foods, and poisons (Dalton, 2001). If you still don't believe the smell sense is important, ask an executive in the multi-billion dollar perfume industry!

Types of Odors. The stimuli for smell are, of course, odors. That perfume or cologne that you find so attractive on your dating partner is composed of a set of molecules that travel through the air until they reach the smell, or *olfactory,* receptors. About 100 million of these receptors are located in each nasal passage. The receptors for smell are unique because they are, in fact, *neurons.*

Beginning with Aristotle, there have been attempts to classify odors as we have colors and tastes. In one major attempt, John Amoore (1977) sampled over 600 chemical compounds and derived seven primary odors, such as musky and floral; he later expanded the total to 32. However, his scheme has not held up well in subsequent research. At the same time, there is evidence of odor specificity. Some receptors fire in the presence of one chemical, some in the presence of another (Dalton, 2000), so we may eventually find a way to classify odors.

The nose also contains specialized receptors that serve specific purposes. One set of receptors triggers protective reflexes in response to irritating and potentially dangerous chemical vapors. They may cause you to back away from the odor, turn your head, or momentarily stop inhaling. Other specialized nasal receptors appear to be involved in sexual activity, where they sense the presence of *pheromones*—chemicals related to sexual attraction. They are discussed in Horizon 2.

The Nose Knows Not. As with other senses, the structures in the nose are not capable of interpreting smells but only of receiving the odors and transducing them for transmission to the brain. The 30 million receptor neurons in each nostril are located in the *olfactory epithelium* at the top of the nasal cavity. Their axons come together to form the *olfactory nerve,* which carries smell sensations directly to the *olfactory bulb,* a part of the limbic system with a structure similar to that of the retina (Nikonov et al., 2002; Figure 4-35). Unlike the other senses, smell shows no topographic organization of the projections from olfactory receptors to the olfactory bulb. From an evolutionary standpoint, this is probably because odor localization was less necessary in ancient environments, where vision did an adequate job (Cloutier et al., 2002). The bulb sends fibers via other brain structures to the hypothalamus, the amygdala, and, ultimately, the temporal cortex, which is considered to be the *primary olfactory cortex.* There neurotransmitters appear to be involved in differentiating odors (Treloar, et al., 2002).

More Senses, More Perceptions: Touch, Movement, and Balance

Our knowledge of the external world is completed by the skin senses, which often step in where vision and the others fail. But we must also be able to know the internal world of our bodies by perceiving how we are moving and whether or not we are balanced.

Somesthesis: The Skin Senses

Have you ever stopped to think how important a structure your skin is? It keeps your organs and fluids inside your body, protects your internal systems from a variety of physical and chemical dangers that lurk in the outside world, and insulates you, thereby helping to regulate internal temperature.

Equally as important as the protective and insulating functions of the skin is the information it provides about what is going on in the outside world. Helen Keller, who was deaf and blind from infancy, was able to learn to interact very effectively with the external world primarily through her skin senses, which are also called cutaneous or *somesthetic senses.* The term *somesthesis* comes from the Greek for "body knowledge." Research suggests that this body knowledge comes from four basic skin senses: pressure, warmth, cold, and pain.

As Figure 4-36 shows, several types of receptors are found in the skin. *Free nerve endings* are simple nerve cells that spread like the barren branches of a winter tree just beneath the surface of the skin. They are found in most areas of the body, and they sense pain and perhaps pressure and temperature. The other major receptor types are *Pacinian corpuscles*, the largest sensory end organs; *basket cells*, which look a bit like tiny wicker baskets and are found in hairy areas of the body; and *Meissner corpuscles*, tiny, rounded receptors found primarily in hairless areas, such as the palms of your hands. Others include Ruffini endings, Merkle discs, and end bulbs of Krause.

Each of these different types of receptors responds somewhat better to some stimuli than to others, but they do not have unique functions. In fact, there appears to be no clear relationship between the type of sensation found in a given skin area and the types of receptors found there. It appears likely that the perception of a given kind of skin sensation, such as warmth or pressure, occurs when the brain interprets a pattern of activity occurring across several different groups of receptors.

Touch and Pressure. The touch and pressure senses allow us to determine where a stimulus is coming in contact with the skin (localization) and to differentiate simultaneous stimuli (discrimination). If you close your eyes and someone touches a point on your body, you can immediately identify the area touched and discriminate the magnitude or intensity of the touch stimulus. Touch two pencil points to your skin. The distance that you have to separate the pencils in order to tell that there are two separate points being touched is called the *two-point threshold.* On your index finger the required distance is only about 3 millimeters; on your arm it can be 40 millimeters or more.

Fibers carrying touch and pressure sensations up the spinal cord synapse in the medulla, then cross over to the thalamus and the primary and secondary somatosensory projection areas of the parietal cortex on the opposite side of the brain (Figure 4-37). Current evidence suggests a topographical relationship between touch and pressure receptors on the body and the arrangement of corresponding sensory neurons in the thalamus and cortex.

Temperature. The perception of warmth or coldness depends on both the actual temperature of the stimulus and your existing skin temperature. Try an experiment. Fill three bowls with water: one with hot, one with cold, and one with warm. Put one hand in each of the first two bowls, allow them to adapt for a few minutes, then put both hands in the third bowl. The hand that was in the hot water will feel cool, and the hand that was in the cold water will feel warm.

Thermal signals leave the receptors to synapse in the spinal cord. They travel upward and cross over to terminate in the opposite brain stem, the thalamus, and the somatosensory cortex. As with most other senses, the organization of projections from the receptors upward into the brain is topographic. An interesting disorder involving skin temperature is Raynaud's disease, in which the fingers are highly sensitive to cold and show changes in skin color (O'Connor, 2001).

Pain. Pain is perhaps of more interest to us than the other somesthetic senses because it is so demanding of attention and because—well, it's painful! Questions about the sensation and perception of pain have been addressed in recent years with a variety of physiological and psychological research methods. Let's see how pain is sensed, transmitted to the brain, and perceived.

Pain sensation. The sensation of pain is quite variable, depending on the stimulus, the area of the body, and the individual. One study compared the effects of pain produced by four different kinds of stimulation. Pain produced by heat or electric shock was rated by participants as less unpleasant than pain caused by extreme cold or exercise (Rainville et al., 1992). There are also individual differences in the perception of pain. And gender differences have often been reported, with women showing lower pain thresholds for some kinds of painful stimulation than men. Finally, recent studies confirm what you already know from personal experience: Unlike the other senses, pain shows little sensory adaptation—little decrease—with repeated noxious stimulation, primarily due to the continued firing of neurons (Fredriksson et al., 2000). The endorphins, however, may help to alleviate pain (Chapter 3).

The transmission of pain. The pain from a toothache or surgical incision is sensed and transduced primarily by the free nerve endings. From these receptors, two types of pain signals travel over two pathways. Acute, sharp pain is transmitted by fast-conducting fibers that operate at velocities between 6 and 30 meters per second. Dull, chronic pain is transmitted over slow-conducting fibers that carry the signals at a rate of 0.5 to 2 meters per second. The fast fibers are myelinated, while the slow fibers are not.

The fast pain fibers travel up the spinal cord to carry the signal primarily to the reticular formation, the thalamus, and areas of the somatosensory cortex. The slower fibers travel up the cord to terminate almost primarily (but not entirely) in the reticular formation of the brain stem (see Figure 4-37). The reticular system activates higher levels of the brain, creating the general sense of arousal or activation that often accompanies chronic pain.

The Gate-Control and Neuromatrix Theories. For a long time, the dominant theory of how pain is transmitted was the *gate-control theory,* developed by Richard Melzack and Patrick Wall (1965). It says that we sense and perceive pain when pain sensations get past a "gate"—a pattern of neural activity—in the spinal cord. The gate opens only when there is damage from disease or injury to certain nerve fibers.

Recent work suggests that this theory is incomplete, and Melzack (1993) has proposed an alternative theory, the *neuromatrix theory* of pain. It hypothesizes that there is a complex network of neurons in the brain—a neuromatrix—that constantly monitor neural firing to detect incoming pain signals. Certain abnormal patterns of neural activity are generated when there is pain, and the neuromatrix interprets these patterns correctly as indicating disease or injury in some specific part of the body.

Proprioception: Perceiving Movement and Balance

You can easily close your eyes, stand on one foot, and spread your arms without losing your balance. But none of the senses we have explored so far would be very helpful in doing this. The receptors involved in movement and balance are those that detect sensations originating within the body. They are called *proprioceptors*, and they sense body position and motion and thereby control balance and help coordinate movement. There are two proprioceptive senses: kinesthesis and the vestibular sense.

***Kinesthesis: Perceiving Movement. Kinesthesis* provides neural feedback concerning position and movement. The joints and ligaments of the body are surrounded by special receptors. As limbs move, these receptors are deformed to varying degrees, causing transduction and creating a neural impulse (van Wezel et al., 2000).**

You could easily eat a meal or tie a knot in a rope while blindfolded because kinesthetic receptors make it possible to virtually "see" without your eyes. Participants in studies of kinesthesis are able to quite accurately reach toward and grasp a known object and judge the size of unseen gaps by "feeling" them with a metal rod (Darline & Miller, 1993). In addition, researchers in one study showed subjects a target object, then blindfolded them and moved them along a track that passed the object. They were able to press a button to quite accurately indicate when they were passing the target (Israel et al., 1993).

Kinesthetic messages are carried over nerve tracts via the medulla and thalamus to the primary somatosensory area of the parietal lobe. The route is similar to that taken by the skin senses, and there appears to be a topographical arrangement of cortical cells that code for kinesthesis.

***The Vestibular Sense: Balance.* Individuals who become skilled in sports like gymnastics can rapidly change body positions without losing their balance. This control of balance is achieved through the vestibular sense. The dizziness you experience when you spin rapidly around in a circle is caused by overstimulation of the vestibular apparatus. Dizziness can also result from a disturbance of vestibular functioning caused by toxic chemicals, disease processes, or changes that occur naturally with aging. The motion sickness many people experience on boats or planes is a vestibular and cortical phenomenon (Koch, 1999).**

Although both visual and kinesthetic senses contribute to our ability to maintain balance, the principal balance apparatus is located in the inner ear, where receptors detect rotary and linear motion. The *vestibular sense*—the sense of balance—has been studied quite extensively, and we know that the receptors for rotary motion are contained in two kinds of structures, the semicircular canals and the vestibular sacs (see Figure 4-38). There are three *semicircular canals*, each approximately perpendicular to the others. Each contains a viscous fluid that moves when the head rotates. The fluid compresses a gelatinous glob of tissue at the base of the canal, which bends hair cell receptors, causing transduction of a neural impulse. The receptor discharges from all three canals are "read" by the brain to provide an accurate perception of the rotation that has occurred.

The position of the head at rest or in linear motion is detected by two tiny bags called the *vestibular sacs*. Each contains hair cells surrounded by a gelatinous substance containing tiny, hard particles, rather like grains of sand. Linear or straight-line movement of the head stirs up the "sand," causing the gelatinous tissue to bend the hair cells and send a signal to the brain. If you are sitting in a car with your eyes closed and the driver rapidly accelerates or decelerates, you will immediately know that the change in speed has taken place. That is because the crystals in the fluid_filled canals of the vestibular sacs have depressed the receptor cells, signaling the change in head motion.

Conclusion

The senses only receive and transduce information. Perception involves interpretation of that information by the brain. You also know that there are considerably more than five senses and that all the senses share several common characteristics. You also now know that sensory receptors take in and transduce stimuli, but that perception—interpretation—takes place only in the brain. And you have now been introduced to the major characteristics of all the senses and their perceptual components. You know that there are several major theories of color vision and of auditory frequency perception and that all perception likely involves both bottom-up and top-down processes. In addition, you should now have a good, basic understanding of the major aspects of visual perception, including the Gestalt laws and the principles of constancy and of depth perception. Finally, it seems clear that evolution has produced a set of sensory and perceptual mechanisms and processes that allow humans to quite optimally interpret both the external environment and our own, internal body sensations. In other chapters, it becomes apparent that advancement in virtually every major field within psychology depends, in part, upon knowledge of basic sensory and perceptual operations.

Summary

Sensation and Perception: Characteristics, Methods, and Theories

1. Sensation of a stimulus occurs in three main steps: detection by a sensory receptor, transduction of physical stimulus energy into a nerve impulse, and neurological coding of the signal to provide information about the quantity (intensity) and quality of the stimulus.
2. Psychophysics is concerned with quantifying relationships between the characteristics of a physical stimulus and the sensory experience that is produced.
3. The absolute threshold is the lowest level of stimulus intensity to which a sense will respond. The difference threshold (just noticeable difference) is the smallest difference between two stimuli that can be reliably detected or discriminated.
4. The relationship between a stimulus and its perception has been expressed in three major psychophysiological laws: Weber's law, Fechner's law, and Stevens's power law.
5. Signal detection theory recognizes that many factors can influence individual psychophysical judgments and attempts to take these factors into account. 6. Perception is the active process by which the brain interprets and categorizes sensory stimuli to determine their nature and meaning.

Vision: The Sense of Light

1. Light, the stimulus for vision, is a form of electromagnetic energy. It travels in waves that vary in intensity and length.
2. Light striking the eye passes through the cornea and the pupil to the lens, which focuses it on the retina. The axons of the ganglion cells make up the optic nerve, which connects the retina to the brain.
3. Black-and-white and color vision are mediated, respectively, by rods and cones. The rods are thin, cylindrical structures that operate primarily under conditions of low illumination and "see" only black, white, and shades of gray. Cones are fatter, operate under high levels of illumination, and detect color. The fovea at the center of the retina contains only cones and is the area of highest visual acuity.
4. Each retinal cell responds only to a certain area of the visual world, called its receptive field.
5. The ganglion cell axons (the optic nerve) exit at the blind spot. The two optic nerves converge at the optic chiasm, then travel to the lateral geniculate nucleus (LGN), the superior colliculi, and the occipital cortex. The visual cortex has a one_to_one topographical relationship with cells in the LGN and the retina.
6. Color has three major psychological properties: hue, brightness, and saturation. There are three types of cones, each specialized to respond to different regions of the spectrum.
7. The trichromatic and opponent-process theories have been partially combined in the dual-process theory.

Visual Perception: Knowing What You See

1. Bottom-up processing integrates individual elements of a stimulus to form a whole. Top-down processing influences perception by imposing preexisting knowledge and expectations.
2. Gestalt psychologists identified several principles of perceptual organization that lead us to group parts of a stimulus into a perceptual whole, or gestalt. These perceptual laws include simplicity, proximity, good continuation, similarity, common fate, and closure.
3. The tendency to perceive objects as being constant in size, shape, lightness, and color under a wide range of viewing conditions is called perceptual constancy.
4. There are two major kinds of cues for depth perception, binocular cues and monocular cues. The most important depth cue is binocular disparity.
5. There are two basic kinds of movement perception: real movement and illusory movement. There are three types of illusory movement: induced, stroboscopic, and autokinetic movement.

6. Optical illusions can occur when perceptual mechanisms, such as constancy, fail. They help us better understand the principles of perception

7. Mental images are quite similar to actual perceptions, a relationship that is most likely the result of sharing the same brain structures.

Audition: Sensing and Perceiving Sound

1. The basic physical stimulus for audition is vibration. Sound travels in waves, which vary in amplitude, frequency, and purity. Psychologically, we interpret the amplitude of sound as loudness, the frequency as pitch, and purity as timbre.

2. Sound waves enter the ear through the auditory canal, causing the eardrum to vibrate. This sets in motion three small bones, which pass the vibration on to the oval window. Movement of the oval window creates waves in the fluid that fills the cochlea, where hair cells on the organ of Corti transduce the mechanical waves into nerve impulses, which are carried over the auditory nerve to the brain.

3. The intensity of sound is coded in terms of the number of hair cells stimulated.

4. The three major theories of auditory frequency perception are place theory, frequency theory, and a combination of the two.

5. Auditory localization involves monaural cues for distance and binaural cues for direction.

6. Hearing disorders include conduction deafness, nerve deafness, and tenets.

The Chemical Senses: Taste and Smell

1. The main receptors for taste are the taste buds on the tongue. There are four distinct taste qualities: sour, sweet, bitter, and salty.

2. The receptors for smell, are unique in that they are neurons. So far schemes for classifying odors have proved inadequate in explaining how odor receptors function.

Sensing and Perceiving Touch, Balance, and Movement

1. The somesthetic, or skin, senses, include pressure, warmth, cold, and pain.

2. Sensations that originate within the body are dealt with by two proprioceptive senses, kinesthesis and the vestibular sense.

Key Terms

absolute threshold
apparent motion
audition
auditory nerve
autokinetic effect
basilar membrane
binaural cues
binocular cues
binocular disparity
blind spot (optic disk)
bottom-up processing
center-surround organization
cochlea
color channels
color constancy
cones
convergence

depth perception
dichotic listening
difference threshold
dual-process theory
electromagnetic energy
extrasensory perception (ESP)
feature analyzers
Fechner's law
figure-ground relationship
fovea
Gestalt psychology
gustation
hair cells
hue
illusory movement
induced movement
just-noticeable difference (jnd)
kinesthesis
lateral geniculate nucleus (LGN)
lightness constancy
monaural cue
monocular cues
olfaction
olfactory bulb
opponent-process theory
optic chiasm
optic disk
optic nerve
organ of Corti
perception
perceptual constancy
pheromones
precognition
proprioceptor
protensity
psychophysics
purity
receptive field
retina
rods
saturation
sensation
sensory adaptation
sensory receptors
shape constancy
signal detection theory
size constancy
somesthetic senses
Stevens' power law
stroboscopic movement
subliminal perception
superior colliculi
telepathy
threshold
top-down processing
transduction
trichromatic theory

vestibular sense
visible spectrum
visual acuity
wavelength
Weber's law

Key Names

Gustav Fechner
Ewald Hering
David Hubel
Wolfgang Kohler
Carl Pfaffman
Muzafer Sherif
S.S. Stevens
Ernst Weber
Max Wertheimer
E.G. Wever
Torsten Wiesel
Thomas Young
Herman Von Helmholtz

Ask Yourself

1. What are the similarities and differences among the various senses in the process of transduction?
2. What are the major advantages of perceptual constancy? What problems can it sometimes create?
3. In what important ways are the retina and cochlea similar?
4. What are the roles of monocular and binocular cues in vision and of monaural and binaural cues in audition?
5. What are the major similarities and differences among the neurological pathways of the various senses?
6. Why is it necessary to use somewhat different principles to explain perception of illusory movement than to explain real movement?
7. On what factors are taste preferences based?
8. What is the relationship between mental imagery and perception? Why?
9. How does time perception differ from other forms of perception?
10. What is the difference between bottom-up and top-down processing?

Further Readings

De-Valois, R.L., & De-Valois, K.K. (1993). A multi-stage color model. *Vision Research*, 33, 1053-1065.

These widely respected theorists, whose theory has long influenced work in color vision provide an update of their model.

de-Jong, B., Shipp, S., Skidmore, B., Frackowiak, R., et al. (1994). The cerebral activity related to the visual perception of forward motion in depth. *Brain*, 117, 1039-1054. The authors show which areas of the visual cortex are involved in motion perception.

Smith, K., & Rogers, M. (1994). Effectiveness of subliminal messages in television commercials: Two experiments. *J. Applied Psychol.*, 79, 866-874.

Fowler, C. (1991). Auditory perception is not special: We see the world, we feel the world, we hear the world. *J. Acous. Soc. Amer.*, 89, 2910-2915.

Janal, M.N., Clark, W.C., & Carroll, J.D. (1993). Multidimensional scaling of painful electrocutaneous stimulation: INDSCAL dimensions, signal detection theory indices, and the McGill Pain Questionnaire. *Somatosens. Mot. Res.*, 10, 31-39.

In this pain study the authors applied current techniques to the study of individual differences in pain sensitivity. The paper also exemplifies the use of psychophysical measurement.

!Matlin, M., & Foley, H.J. (1992). *Sensation and perception.* Boston: Allyn & Bacon.

This is a current textbook in sensation which covers virtually all the topics we have touched on in much more detail.

O'Regan, J. (1992). Solving the "real" mysteries of visual perception: The world as an outside memory. *Canadian J. Psychol.*, 46, 461-488. The author points out some significant flaws in major theories of visual perception.

Stein, B.E., & Meredith, M.A. (1993). *The merging of the senses.* Cambridge, MA: MIT Press. Barry Stein's book is the first detailed account of how information from the various senses is combined to provide us with a coherent, overall view of the world around us.

Wouterlood, D. & Boselie, F. (1992). A good-continuation model of some occlusion phenomena. *Psychol. Res.*, 454, 267-277. This study uses the Gestalt law of good continuation to explain how we perceive as a whole an object that is partially hidden from view.

Wenderoth, P. (1994). On the relationship between the psychology of visual perception and the neurophysiology of vision. *Austral. J. Psychol.*, 46, 1-6. This interesting study deals with the Hubel-Wiesel feature detectors in the visual cortex.

Sensation and Perception in the 21st Century

Beyond The Senses: Subliminal Perception

Suppose you don't detect a stimulus because it doesn't reach threshold. Can it still affect your behavior? That is the question at the heart of the controversial subject of *subliminal perception*—the perception of sensory input without consciousness awareness. *Limen* is another word for threshold, so subliminal simply means below threshold. In subliminal perception, a sensory stimulus is not intense enough to cross the threshold, so you don't realize that it occurred. Nevertheless, it registers at an unconscious level.

Continuing interest and increasing research make subliminal perception a topic for the next century. The first work on this interesting topic began about four decades ago not in the scientific laboratory but in the offices of marketing executive James Vicary. In 1957, he superimposed hidden messages, such as "Eat popcorn," on just a few frames of a movie, so that they flashed by too quickly to be consciously perceived by viewers, and claimed that popcorn sales increased by 58%. The ensuing controversy about the ethics of influencing defenseless consumers in this way became more heated when Wilson Bryan Key (1980) published a series of books suggesting that sexual messages were frequently embedded in magazine advertisements.

Research on subliminal perception began in the 1960s. The basic idea is to show that: (a) A sensory stimulus has not registered consciously, usually by demonstrating that the participant cannot verbally report it; and (b) the stimulus nevertheless does have some effect. Initial studies were poorly controlled, as often happens in early scientific research on a new subject, but a series of more recent studies have clearly demonstrated the phenomenon (Kunimoto et al., 2001). Many of these studies employ a *tachistoscope*—an instrument that can present visual stimuli too briefly to be consciously perceived. Any demonstrable effect of such brief, imperceptible stimuli on the participant's behavior or physiology would have to be a result of subliminal perception—and studies do confirm such effects. In fact, its occurrence is now generally accepted in cognitive psychology, where theories have been developed to explain it (Klinger & Greenwald, 1995).

Does the laboratory demonstration of subliminal perception mean that it affects behavior in important ways? There are certainly many claims to that effect: consumers can be influenced to buy Coke rather than Pepsi; unsuspecting potential sexual partners can be seduced by hidden messages in tapes; subliminal passages in rock music, when played backwards, encourage devil worship and sexual abandon; and, for a mere $30.00 or $40.00, you can greatly improve your memory, stop smoking, lose weight, or sleep better by listening repeatedly to a tape with embedded, below-threshold messages.

Well, not to worry, at least not yet! Research to date shows that the effects of subliminal perception on behavior are actually quite small. Anthony Greewald and his colleagues (1991) had over 200 participants listen for a month to subliminal self-help tapes designed to improve self-esteem or memory. They showed no improvement at all on laboratory tests in either area. Interestingly enough, however, the participants nevertheless *believed* that they had improved, providing a clue as to why many people continue to purchase such useless tapes. Weight-loss tapes have similarly been shown to be ineffective, as have advertising messages embedded in television programming. And backward speech in rock music cannot be interpreted and has no effect on behavior. Bottom line: Subliminal perception does occur, but it has only short-term effects that are so subtle as to be detectable only by precise measurement in laboratory settings. The long-term persuasive effects appear thus far to be nonexistent.

The question for future research is whether or not it is possible to make subliminal persuasion a reality. If theorists and researchers can combine increased understanding of the underlying perceptual processes with new approaches to subliminal stimulation, the 21st century may well see subliminal persuasion become a successful technique. It could be used not only in advertising, where there are serious ethical questions, but also in such areas as psychotherapy. Even there, we would have to answer serious questions regarding the ethical nature of approaches in which the therapist influences a client with subliminal techniques. In that case at least the intent would be to help the individual, rather than to sell a product.

Application

Thinking Critically: *Is Extrasensory Perception Real?*

Hold it! Let me try to read your mind. You're thinking "This topic sounds kind of interesting. I've always wondered about ESP." Well, maybe that's not what you were thinking, but there are certainly those who believe that they have experienced *telepathy*—the transfer of thoughts from one person to another. Telepathy is one form of *extrasensory perception* (ESP), which is more generally the ability to perceive things without apparently employing the usual senses. Other forms of ESP include precognition, clairvoyance, and psychokinesis. *Precognition* is the sense that an event is going to happen before it actually does, while *clairvoyance* is the ability to perceive objects or events that do not act directly on the senses, such as being able to predict the next card to come up in a randomly shuffled deck. *Psychokinesis*, or telekinesis, is the mental control or movement of objects—bending a spoon or causing a chair to fly across a room, for example. And *parapsychology* (meaning "beside psychology") is the field that studies all of these phenomena. The practical applications of ESP, like communicating with others, predicting the future, and the like are abundant—provided that ESP is a reality.

The Basic Hypothesis or Contention

Proponents of ESP have long maintained that such parapsychological phenomena like precognition occur on a regular basis. Some insist that every individual is equipped to use these abilities but most have not had the necessary experience. Others suggest that ESP occurs only in those who are endowed with this capacity. In either case, they maintain that it does occur and that it can be scientifically documented.

What Is The Evidence?

Anecdotal evidence for ESP abounds. Numerous books and magazine articles have recounted ESP experiences, and many self_proclaimed "psychics" have received publicity for their precognitive and clairvoyant feats. Moreover, experiences of ESP are reported by many people, and these reports have increased in recent years. It is perhaps therefore not surprising that studies repeatedly confirm a widespread public belief in ESP (Gallup & Newport, 1991). Thomas Gilovich (1991) concludes that this blind faith is a product of the continuing barrage of anecdotal evidence provided by TV psychics, reports of unexplained events (particularly in the tabloid press), and books written by proponents of parapsychological phenomena.

But is there any *scientific* evidence? Formal studies began in the late 1920s with the work of J.B. Rhine at Duke University. Rhine used a deck of 25 cards, each printed with one of five symbols: a star, square, circle, cross, or wavy lines. In assessing telepathy, the experimenter would look at one of the randomly shuffled cards while the participant attempted to guess the symbol on the card by "reading the experimenter's mind." A subject was considered to possess telepathic or clairvoyant abilities if she scored significantly above chance on this task over the course of numerous trials. With over 100,000 responses collected, Rhine reported that subjects had an average of 7.1 correct identifications out of a possible 25 cards. This was significantly above chance and convinced him of the validity of ESP. Hundreds of additional studies followed. Some supported Rhine's contention, but many others did not, and laboratories often could not replicate each other's findings.

More recent research has used the *Ganzfield procedure*, in which a "sender" focuses for thirty minutes on a visual stimulus—perhaps a photo or drawing—while a "receiver" continuously reports his thoughts. The receiver later rates the extent to which each of four stimuli matches his earlier thoughts. To assure no direct use of the usual senses, the receiver sits in a soundproof chamber, a red light shining on split ping-pong balls that cover his eyes. Receivers have been reported to achieve an average 32% hit rate on the four stimuli, which is significantly more than the 25% that would represent chance (Bem & Honorton, 1994).

Is The Evidence Open To Alternative Interpretations?

Although many of the studies have been based on the scientific method, they have been strongly criticized. For one thing, most such studies use large numbers of trials, which has the effect of increasing the likelihood of statistical significance (see the Appendix). A second problem has been the lack of adequate controls. In Rhine's original studies, for example, participants were frequently allowed to handle the cards, which had tears and physical marks that could allow them to be identified. Worse, the symbols could be faintly seen through the cards when they were held up to the light. Even Rhine's best participant, who had very high "hit" rates for correct identification, could not reproduce the feat when tested in other laboratories. Moreover, when newer studies have employed better control procedures, the likelihood of significant results and the number of participants identified as "sensitive" have both declined substantially). In addition, some researchers have been accused of not reporting negative findings when they occur.

Further evidence suggests that claims of ESP are often patently fraudulent. Here, science owes a debt to a magician. He is James Randi, who began many years ago to show how supposed feats of ESP could be accomplished through standard stage magic. In one case, he took on Uri Geller, a self-proclaimed Israeli psychic who insisted he could divine the content of sealed packages and bend spoons, among other things. He was so convincing that physician Andrew Weil (1974), after investigating Geller, concluded that his feats were genuine. Imagine Weil's amazement, then, when Randi showed him that he could use the magician's stage techniques to duplicate Geller's tricks. In fact, Randi publicly offered $10,000 to anyone who could demonstrate ESP under scientific conditions. That was in 1964, and Randi still has the check (Randi, 1987)!

If ESP is poorly supported, what kinds of people most strongly believe in its existence and why? Some investigators have marshalled evidence that childhood trauma, including physical and sexual abuse, is strongly associated with paranormal beliefs (Irwin, 1994). Others have found evidence for abnormal subcortical functioning, similar to that seen in epileptics, in the right hemispheres of those reporting paranormal experiences. While these findings are not final answers, they suggest that paranormal phenomena may eventually be understandable in fully scientific terms.

Do We Need Additional Evidence?

Proponents clearly need more evidence if they are to convince the scientific community that ESP is a valid phenomenon. It is essential that foolproof scientific methods be developed, methods with controls ensuring that no alternative explanation of results is feasible.

In the meantime, many scientists are ready to give up on additional ESP research. Marks (1986) points out that, despite extensive efforts, not a single subject has ever been able to replicate ESP feats when tested by a second laboratory. Results also break down under close observation by nonbelievers and when studies are more carefully controlled. Perhaps, some argue, we've gone far enough.

What Can We Conclude?

Many honest scientists have made Herculean efforts to demonstrate ESP. However, there is still no good evidence to support its existence. That was also the conclusion of a group of scientists chaired by John Swets, who reviewed all the available evidence for the U.S. Army (Swets & Bjork, 1990). No wonder, then, that the National Research Council has severely criticized research on ESP and concluded that the phenomenon remains to be demonstrated.

Research in Sensation and Perception

Probe

Noise Annoys—and Destroys

Attended a lot of rock concerts lately or spent a summer using a jackhammer? Exposure to high-intensity noise can produce significant hearing loss and actually destroy hair cells in the cochlea, as the accompanying figure shows. This was shown in one classic, long_term study of women jute weavers who were exposed to mill noise of 98 dB for eight hours a day, five days a week (Taylor, Pearson, Mair, and Burns, 1965). The effects of noise exposure were examined by testing both recently hired workers and those who had been employed for periods of up to 40 years. The researchers found that progressive hearing loss occurred up to about 10 years of employment. For a 4000 Hz tone, workers with 10 years or more of exposure showed a threshold increase of about 35 dB, a substantial hearing loss.

Other studies confirm these results. In one interesting investigation, rock musicians were given audiometer tests before and after playing a heavy metal concert. All showed temporary upward threshold shifts, indicating poorer hearing after the concert. More important, there was evidence of long-term damage to the cochlea in these young men. Aircraft noise causes similar damage. Moderate to severe hearing losses were found in 41.9% of all airport employees and in 65.2% of aircraft maintenance workers, who have the greatest noise exposure (Chen et al., 1993). And automobile stereos, which can generate extremely loud sounds measured at up to 138 decibels, can also damage the cochlea.

Individuals vary considerably in susceptibility to noise-induced hearing loss due primarily to genetic factors. If, for example, we put two individuals side by side in the same noisy factory environment, one may experience much greater hearing loss after years of exposure than the other. Recent research has shown that individuals who experience greater temporary hearing losses and changes in measures of brain functions associated with hearing are also likely to show greater permanent losses. Thus, it is now possible to predict, to some degree, the extent to which a given individual is in danger of experiencing a significant hearing loss if exposed to a noisy environment over a long period of time.

Even short-term loud noises can produce permanent hearing loss. Hunters who are periodically exposed to the loud noise of their guns firing, for example, can show a substantial hearing loss. Similarly, a firecracker exploded near the ear can cause a partial loss of hearing, as in the case of a college student who suffered a permanent 50 dB rise in threshold following just one such explosion.

The basis for these hearing losses is revealed by studies of the inner ears of individuals who have died following years of exposure to high noise levels, and we are now beginning to understand the mechanisms. There is typically noticeable damage to the delicate cochlear structure, including cellular degeneration. The cochlea of one steel mill worker showed severe damage, and the organ of Corti had actually collapsed, leaving no receptor cells. It is now possible to assess the damage caused by noise by measuring otoacoustic emissions (see text).

Noise is also a major factor in the ability of those who already have a significant hearing loss to understand normal conversation. In particular, background noise interferes with the ability of hearing-impaired individuals to understand low-frequency cues that are a part of normal speech. When noise is absent, people with hearing impairment pick up low frequencies better, and their understanding of an overall conversation is much greater.

Noise also interferes with the ability to concentrate on tasks, as you know if you've ever tried to study in a dormitory while others are playing stereos and having loud conversations. Research shows, in fact, that performance on standardized tests is significantly better under low-noise than under high-noise conditions (Edmonds and Smith, 1985). The bottom line is that loud noise can be, at the very least, annoying. And in many cases, it is downright destructive.

Horizons in Sensation and Perception

Time Perception: A Sixth Sense?

Stop reading for a minute—*exactly* one minute. Have someone time you, and you will probably find that your estimate is not very accurate. But you may be able to estimate the passage of somewhat longer periods of time more accurately. Although humans do not have any specific sensory receptors for time, we do have some perception of time passing, a subjective sense that is called *protensity* (Grondin, 2001). How does it work? There are two theories, one biological, the other cognitive.

Time perception may be a function of some form of internal, *biological clock* mechanism, possibly involving neurological, biochemical, or endocrinological activity. Support for this idea comes from the observation that many of the body's activities are periodic or rhythmic (and hence time-related): the beating of the heart, the regularity of respiration, the electrical activity of the brain; and sleep-wake cycles. Evidence that time perception is based in these biological rhythms comes from research showing that increases in body temperature shorten a person's estimate of time intervals. Why? Because a temperature increase speeds up such activities as heart rate, which means the "clock" is ticking faster and making time seem to pass more quickly (Carr et al., 2001).

Another theory sees time perception as a cognitive (thought) activity, involving information processing. In one experiment, Ornstein (1969) hypothesized that greater amounts of information entering consciousness require more cognitive processing and therefore lead to greater perceived time durations. He presented subjects with three tape recordings of repeated tones. Each recording lasted exactly 9 minutes, 20 seconds, but the tones occurred at different rates: 40 per minute, 80 per minute, or 120 per minute. The greater the rate, the longer the participants perceived the tape to run. More information processing and hence more cognitive activity had lengthened the time estimates.

Smell: The Sexy Sense?

In many animals the principal sense involved in sexual stimulation is olfaction. These animals release chemicals called *pheromones*, which cause sexual behavior when smelled by members of the opposite sex. The pheromones serve as *releasers*—chemicals that trigger off sexual behavior. They are very powerful sexual stimulants and can be effective over great distances. For example, the pheromone bombykol, released by the female silkworm moth, can attract a male over 3 kilometers (nearly 2 miles) away. A single female, releasing about .01 millionth of a gram of bombykol, can potentially attract a *billion* males.

Pheromones are also found in humans. Their role in human sexual behavior, if any, is not yet clear. However, they may be responsible for *menstrual synchrony*. Some studies confirm the common observation that women who live together, such as mothers and daughters or college roommates, often have nearly identical menstrual cycles, with periods starting on the same day (Weller & Weller, 1993). If so, pheromones may be responsible.

Needling People: Acupuncture

Acupuncture is one of the world's oldest treatments for pain. Practitioners insert needles at special points on the body determined by using detailed charts developed over the centuries by Eastern practitioners. The needles are then usually twirled and often heated.

Acupuncture is used by the Chinese to treat a variety of problems, and many Eastern studies have supported to its effectiveness. It has been found to improve respiratory function in asthmatic patients and to produce faster, more complete recovery following stroke. Acupuncture also appears to make ovulation more regular in some women and even to aid in weight loss (Sun & Xu, 1993).

The principal question raised by Western investigators is the extent to which acupuncture is effective in the treatment of pain. Many studies suggest that it is and that it can often replace anesthetic drugs or reduce required dosages following major surgery (Kho et al., 1993; Nissel, 1993). However, some Western scientists maintain that the scientific basis for acupuncture is still weak. As a result, additional research will be needed before firm conclusions can be reached (Johnson, 1993).

Keys to Sensation and Perception 1

1. The senses share a number of important characteristics.
   - A. What they are?
     Sensory receptors, transduction, thresholds, adaptation.
2. Psychophyics studies the relationship of physical stimuli to sensory experience.
   - A. The types of thresholds?
     Absolute, difference
   - B. The methods?
     Limits, constant stimuli, average error
   - C. The major laws?
     Weber, Fechner, Stevens
   - D. What signal detection theorists study?
     Detectability under various circumstances.
3. Perception permits us to know what we see.
   - A. The two basic processes?
     Interpretation, categorization.

Keys to Sensation and Perception 2

1. The visual stimulus is light.
   - A. What it consists of?
     Photons traveling in waves.

B. The characteristics of light waves?
Amplitude, wavelength, and purity

2. The retina processes the visual stimulus.
   A. How visual information leaves the eye?
   Axons of ganglion cells form the optic nerve. It leaves the eye at the optic disk.
   B. The characteristics of rods?
   Cylindrical shape, operate under low illumination, sense only black, white, and shades of gray.
   C. The characteristics of cones?
   Cone-shaped, operate under high illumination, detect color.

3. The retina connects the eye to the brain.
   A. The path taken by the optic nerves?
   To the optic chiasm, the LGN, the superior colliculi, and the occipital cortex.
   B. The nature of the organization of cells?
   Topographic at all levels.
   C. What feature analyzers are?
   Occipital cells that respond to specific charactistics of a stimulus.

4. Color is psychological, not physical.
   A. Its major properties and the corresponding physical characteristics of light?
   Hue—wavelength
   Brightness—amplitude
   Saturation—purity
   B. Two major ways to mix colors?
   Additive
   Subtractive
   C. The role of color channels?
   Transmit color and brightness separately to different cell groups in the visual cortex.
   D. The major theories of color vision?
   Trichromatic, opponent-process, and dual-process.

Keys to Sensation and Perception 3

1. Perception involves two basic processes.
   A. What they are?
   Bottom -up and top-down.

2. Gestalt psychology suggests that the whole is greater than the sum of its parts.
   A. The major factors in figure-ground perception?
   Area, symmetry, familiarity, orientation.
   B. The Gestalt principles?
   Simplicity, Proximity, Good Continuation, Similarity, Common Fate, Closure.

3. Perceptual constancy maintains consistency under varied viewing conditions.
   A. Some major constancies?
   Lightness, size, shape

4. Depth perception provides knowledge about distance to an object.
   A. The major types of depth cues?
   Binocular, monocular
   B. The types of binocular cues?
   Retinal disparity, convergence

5. **Movement perception begins in peripheral vision.**
   - A. The types?
     Real and illusory.
   - B. Three factors in real movement perception?
     Size, background, distance
   - C. The types of illusory movement?
     Induced, stroboscopic, autokinetic
6. **Optical illusions are distorted perceptions.**
   - A. Why we study them?
     To gain knowledge of constancy and related processes.
   - B. What some major illusions are?
     Muller-Lyer, Ponzo, Horizontal-vertical, Ames Room, Margin, Moon, Impossible Figures
   - C. What influences the occurrence of illusions?
     Cultural experience and biological mechanisms.

Keys to Sensation and Perception 4

1. **Sound vibration is the stimulus for audition.**
   - A. The physical characteristics of sound and the corresponding psychological properties?
     Amplitude—loudness
     Frequency—pitch
     Purity—timbre
   - B. The effect of very loud sounds on hearing?
     Potentially permanent damage
   - C. The frequency range of human hearing?
     20-20,000 Hz
2. **Ear structure is important to the processing of sound.**
   - A. The major divisions?
     Outer, middle, and inner
   - B. The outer ear structures?
     Auditory canal, tympanic membrane
   - C. The middle ear structures?
     Malleus, incus, stapes
   - D. The inner ear structures?
     Cochlea, semicircular canals
3. **Major cochlear structures and their functions?**
   Inner hair cells—primary transduction
   Outer hair cells—modulation
4. **The auditory nerve carries information to brain.**
   - A. The principal lobe involved?
     Temporal
   - B. The differing roles of the right and left hemispheres?
     Right—processes nonverbal stimuli
     Left—processes verbal stimuli
5. **Pitch perception is not entirely understood.**
   - A. The major theories?
     Place, frequency, and the combination of the two.

B. What the updated version of frequency theory is?
Volley theory

6. Localization is much more difficult for auditory than visual stimuli.
A. Why?
Sequential processing
B. The cues involved in sound localization and their functions?
Monaural—distance
Binaural—direction
C. The principal binaural cues?
Differential timing
Differential intensity

7. Hearing disorders affect many men and somewhat less women.
A. The types of deafness?
Conduction, nerve
B. Causes of conduction deafness?
Wax, eardrum defects, damage to ossicles
C. Causes of nerve deafness?
Intense noise
Cochlear degeneration with age
Disorders like ear infections

Keys to Sensation and Perception 5

1. The taste buds serve as receptors for taste sensations.
A. The distinct taste qualities?
Sour, sweet, bitter, salty
B. The structures containing the taste receptors?
Papillae

2. Taste perception is not well understood.
A. How we identify a food through taste?
Molecules fit specific sites on receptors.
B. What is involved in taste perception besides taste?
Smell, texture
C. A major theory of taste perception?
Across-fiber pattern theory

3. The chemical stimuli for smell are odors.
A. The unique characteristic of olfactory receptors?
They are neurons.
B. The success of odor classification attempts?
Poor, so far.
C. The neural mechanisms involved in smell?
Axons of receptors for the olfactory nerve, which goes to the olfactory bulb and the temporal cortex.

Keys to Sensation and Perception

1. Somesthesis provides additional information about the outside world.
A. The major skin senses?
Pressure, warmth, cold, pain

B. The types of receptors?
   Free nerve endings, Pacinian corpuscles, basket cells, and Meissner corpuscles.

2. Pain is the most demanding of the skin senses.
   A. The amount of sensory adaptation it shows?
      Very little
   B. The principal receptors?
      Free nerve endings
   C. The types of pain and associated fibers?
      Acute pain—fast fibers—myelinated
      Chronic pain—slow fibers—not myelinated
   D. The brain area involved in pain perception?
      Somatosensory cortex of the parietal lobe

3. Proprioception deals with the perception of internal sensations.
   A. The major proprioceptive senses?
      Movement, balance
   B. Where kinesthetic receptors are located?
      Joints and ligaments
   C. Where the vestibular apparatus is located?
      In the inner ear
   D. The major components of the vestibular system?
      Semicircular canals, vestibular sacs

Key Terms 1

absolute threshold
bottom-up processing
difference threshold
extrasensory perception
Fechner's law
just-noticeable difference
perception
psychophysics
sensation
sensory adaptation
sensory receptors
signal detection theory
Stevens' power law
threshold
top-down processing
transduction
Weber's law

Key People 1

Gustav Fechner
S.S. Stevens
Ernst Weber

Key Terms 2

blind spot (optic disk)
color channels

color constancy
cones
dual-process theory
electromagnetic energy
feature analyzers
fovea
hue
opponent-process theory
optic chiasm
optic nerve
protensity
purity
receptive field
retina
rod
saturation
superior colliculus
trichromatic theory
visual acuity
wavelength

Key People 2

Ewald Hering
David Hubel
Torsten Wiesel
Thomas Young
Herman von Helmholtz

Key Terms 3

apparent motion
autokinetic effect
binocular cue
binocular disparity
convergence
depth perception
figure-ground relationship
Gestalt psychology
illusory movement
induced movement
lightness constancy
monocular cue
perceptual constancy
shape constancy
size constancy

Key People 3

Wolfgang Kohler
Muzafer Sherif
Max Wertheimer

Key Terms 4

audition
auditory nerve
basilar membrane
binaural cue
cochlea
dichotic listening
frequency theory
hair cell
inferior colliculus
lateral geniculate nucleus
monaural cue
organ of Corti
place theory
purity

Key People 4

Georg von Bekesy
Hermann von Helmholtz
E.G. Wever

Key Terms 5

gustation
olfaction
olfactory bulb
pheromones

Key People 5

Carl Pfaffman

Key Terms 6

hair cell
kinesthesis
proprioceptor
proprioception
semicircular canals
somesthesis
vestibular sacs
vestibular sense

Chapter 5

Consciousness

Outline

Human Consciousness

The Evolution of Consciousness
The Study of Consciousness
Features of Consciousness
Modes of Consciousness
Determinants of Conscious Experience
Selective Attention
The Fifty States (of Consciousness)

"To Sleep, Perchance to Dream"

Stages of Sleep
REM Sleep
Functions of REM sleep
Sleep Schedules and Biological Rhythms
Dreams: Windows To The Unconscious?
Sleep Problems and Disorders

More States: Hypnosis, Meditation, Relaxation, and Daydreaming

Hypnosis
Meditation and Relaxation
Daydreaming

Alcohol and Other Psychoactive Drugs

Alcohol Dependence and Abuse
Other Psychoactive Drugs

The Neurophysiology of Consciousness

The Waking State
Sleep and Dreaming
The Sleep-Waking Cycle
Drug Effects

Networking

CONSCIOUSNESS is more than just being awake and aware. It exists along a continuum, from the unconsciousness of deep sleep to the full alertness of intense concentration. Consciousness also occurs in many forms, or states. The most common states of consciousness that we encounter on a regular basis are sleep, dreaming, and daydreaming. In addition, various altered states of consciousness, varying one's receptivity, perceptions, or mood, can be induced by techniques of meditation, relaxation, and hypnosis, as well as by a wide variety of drugs.

Terror in the Night

Seana's breath came in short gasps and her heart pounded in her chest as she turned into a very narrow, flagstone-paved tunnel that seemed to spiral off into a dark abyss. She fought through the sticky cobwebs that clung to her clammy skin, as she continued to run faster than she ever had before. She had made so many turns that she'd lost count, each into a yet narrower tunnel. At 3:00 a.m. she heard only the clip-clopping echo of her own shoes on the flagstone as she glanced over her shoulder to see that the huge man in the dark overcoat and hat was gradually gaining on her. She turned again, this time into a dirt alley filled with a gray, hazy fog, strewn with debris, and so narrow that it seemed like a mere slot. She could barely run. Her terror became outright panic as she saw that the end of the alley was blocked by a latticework wall and knew that she was going to die. Her piercing scream cut through the night and she awoke abruptly in a state of utter panic as her husband shook her.

We will return to Seana's bad dream later in the chapter, but before you read on, stop and spend about three minutes focusing on your own thought processes. Write down each successive thought as it occurs. Hold nothing back; say everything that comes to mind.

Done? In doing this brief exercise, you have been a participant in your own study. You have engaged in the process called *introspection*, in which you look in upon and report your own conscious thoughts. To put it in more popular terms, you were recording what William James called your *stream of consciousness*—the continual flow of information in and out of awareness.

One person's response to this exercise might sound something like this:

> ***I wonder if this exercise is worth doing. What's he trying to get at? This chapter sounds pretty interesting, but I've got to get it read. Don't have much time. Got to study for that physics exam. Physics! That course is impossible. The equations don't make much sense at all. That sounded like Bob's voice in the hall. Hope he's not coming here. I've got to study. Three minutes is a long time. Got to stop this exercise. Need to finish this chapter so I can study physics.***

Your stream of consciousness, like that of the student in this example, is probably quite normal. Even young children, in fact, are aware of the normal flow of conscious thought. However, not all consciousness has this normal waking quality. We all experience altered states of consciousness, as when we sleep and dream. And for some people the waking stream of consciousness is highly abnormal:

> ***Hitler stood swaying in his room looking wildly about him. "Ha! Ha! He's been here!" he gasped. Suddenly Hitler began to reel off figures, and odd words and broken phrases, entirely devoid of sense, using strangely composed and entirely unhyphenated German word formations. He shouted confused and totally unintelligible phrases. "There, there! In the corner! Who's that?" He was shown that there was nothing out the ordinary in the room. He stood quite still, only his lips moving (Rausching, 1940).***

This behavior, representative of Adolph Hitler's stream of consciousness, was certainly not normal. He was apparently experiencing a hallucination, an altered state of consciousness that we will discuss later in this chapter.

Human Consciousness

***Consciousness* can be defined as awareness of one's own thoughts and of stimuli in the external environment. In most cases, if something is in consciousness, you can report it verbally, draw a picture of it, or in some other way demonstrate behaviorally that you are aware.**

Consciousness can also be seen as a continuum of states of awareness (Matsuno, 2002). At one extreme is the state of alert wakefulness that you are experiencing as you read this chapter—I hope! You are acutely aware of what you are reading and can readily become aware of stimuli in the environment around you. At the opposite end of the continuum are states of deep *unconsciousness*. One such state is sleep, a normal condition that we experience nightly.

According to Sigmund Freud, we are also influenced during waking states by an unconscious part of the mind containing memories that cannot easily be brought to awareness. Some of these memories are unconscious because they occurred in infancy, before the appearance of verbal abilities. Others have become unconscious through the process of *repression*, in which thoughts and memories that produce high levels of anxiety are forced out of consciousness but remain in the unconscious indefinitely. Freud believed that these unconscious memories motivate both normal human behavior and abnormal psychological states (see Chapters 14 and 16).

Somewhat distinguishable from unconscious states are *nonconscious* processes. These are bodily conditions of which we are typically unaware, even though they are constantly going on. They include the electrical activity of the brain, the growth of hair, the digestion of food, and the passage of oxygen via the bloodstream to various parts of your

body. Let's see how consciousness has evolved and take a look at the various modes and features of conscious experience, then examine its determinants and explore the role of selective attention. Finally, we will see how consciousness is studied by scientists and learn about its major states.

The Evolution of Consciousness

We have asked you to think critically about issues we deal with in the various chapters of this book. So here is some food for critical thought: Why do human beings have consciousness? Why are we aware of the surrounding environment and of our own thoughts and feelings? One answer is that consciousness provides substantial adaptive benefits. Like other aspects of behavior and its underlying neural mechanisms, consciousness has evolved over millions of years because it has adaptively solved problems presented by ancient environments (Stanford et al., 2001). Being aware of their surroundings allows humans to react quickly and effectively in both positive and negative situations. Consciousness makes it easier to avoid predators, to gain pleasure by appreciating the beauty of nature, and to interact cooperatively with other humans to achieve common ends (Jones & Blackshaw, 2000). It also permits us to react to the needs and behaviors of other people and to achieve self-awareness—the all-important knowledge of our own characteristics. Consciousness, in fact, even allows us to ponder and understand the phenomenon of *consciousness*, as we are attempting to do now.

Some recent theorists have argued that consciousness may be thought of as a sensory modality, like vision and audition (Chapter ___). Instead of bringing in information from the external environment, consciousness provides information about the brain and thus about the functioning of the organism and its environment. It integrates knowledge from the other senses, then provides that organized perspective to higher levels of the brain for final interpretation (Tannenbaum, 2001).

But is consciousness a uniquely human characteristic? Probably only in degree. From an evolutionary perspective, we might expect some amount of awareness in at least immediately sub-human species, particularly primates, but scientific evidence of animal consciousness is very difficult to obtain. Much of what we know about human consciousness derives from the verbal statements of other people ("Look at that incredibly beautiful sunset" or "I just don't feel like myself today") and from our own sense of personal awareness. The possibility of consciousness in other animals is much more difficult to assess (Dubrovsky, 2002). Although some investigators have claimed to have evidence of awareness in some primates, particularly chimpanzees and orangutans, it is virtually all anecdotal. Famous anthropologist Jane Goodall (1971), who has observed chimpanzees in the wild for many years, reports such an anecdotal observation. She hid a banana in a tree, then observed a young chimp named Figan. He appeared to see the banana, but also noted that an older chimp, Goliath, was sitting near it. Figan waited until Goliath left, then immediately retrieved the banana. Goodall interpreted Figan's behavior as evidence of conscious thought and intent. While her account of the events is no doubt accurate, the "evidence" is clearly anecdotal and subject to alternative interpretations. For example, Figan's behavior may have been purely instinctual, Goliath serving as a stimulus to trigger an inborn avoidance response. More generally, while it may be likely that primates show some degree of consciousness, the anecdotal evidence for it remains highly controversial. We have more to say about animal consciousness, intelligence, and language in Chapters 8 and 9. However, there is little doubt that human consciousness, as we usually understand it, is an evolved characteristic, and there is evidence that individual differences in both waking and sleeping states are a product of genetic predispositions (Toth, 2001). Moreover, sleep is also a product of adaptive evolution. It very likely evolved from earlier rest/activity cycles, as a result of its survival value for the species (Staedt & Stoppe, 2001).

The Study of Consciousness

Over the past century, interest in the study of consciousness has waxed and waned. Psychology began with Wilhelm Wundt's studies of human consciousness, using introspection (see Chapter 1). Sharing Wundt's view of the importance of consciousness, William James (1890) defined psychology as "the science of mental life, both of its phenomena and their conditions." He then went even further by adopting George Ladd's definition: "Psychology may be defined as the description and explanation of states of consciousness as such" (Hilgard, 1980).

When John Watson and the behaviorists came along shortly after the turn of the century, they rejected the idea of consciousness as the focus of psychological study because, they said, consciousness cannot be studied scientifically. The individual's verbalizations about awareness, they argued, are not valid, scientific raw data. As a result, psychologists rarely studied consciousness during the long reign of the behavioral approach, focusing instead on externally observable behavior. In more recent decades, beginning in the 1950s, the pendulum has reversed its swing, and psychologists have once again begun to wet their feet in the stream of consciousness. Indeed, the stream has grown to become at least a small river, and a kind of "modern introspectionism" has risen from the waters. Psychologists have intensively studied the phenomena of sleep and dreams, hypnosis, meditation, drug_induced states, and even daydreaming.

A good example of research on consciousness is provided by the study of *self-awareness*. Carl Rogers, the major theorist in the area of humanistic psychology (Chapter 14), suggested that each individual formulates a self-concept, which is basically an integrated body of personal knowledge about one's own characteristics. In his view, self-awareness has a significant influence on behavior (Rogers, 1959).

One interesting approach to the study of self-awareness is the Experience Sampling Method (ESM). In one study, each of 107 individuals was given a pager to use for one full week (Csikszentmihalyi and Figurski, 1982). The beeper sounded at random on seven to nine occasions each day, for a total of fifty-six times over the seven-day period of data collection. Whenever the beeper sounded, the person recorded his thoughts, activities, and moods. This approach yielded some 4800 reports of conscious experience. Among the findings were that people experience more positive emotion when an activity is voluntary (e.g., working on a hobby) than when it is obligatory (e.g., doing a homework assignment) and that self-awareness is a clear component of voluntary but not of obligatory activity. Other methods in current use include psychometric (measurement) approaches to establish normative data on conscious experience and signal-detection paradigms to study the ongoing stream of thoughts.

Features of Consciousness

Research on states of consciousness requires that we impose some degree of structure on the stream of consciousness so that we can analyze it. A helpful framework for such analysis was provided by Caryl Marsh (1977), who suggests examining four principal features of awareness: focus, structure, attributes, and flow.

1. *Focus.* The focus of the individual's attention may be outward (to the environment) or inward (to thoughts and physiological states). Marsh likens the focus of consciousness to a moving spotlight.
2. *Structure.* The structure of consciousness can be determined by examining it from three points of view. The foreground of consciousness is typically momentary, consisting of passing reactions, desires, impressions, and thoughts that capture attention. Background refers to continuing, constant thoughts relating to time and place, personal identity, and the functioning of the body. The *aerial* perspectivel[1] is the view from outside: your awareness of the fact that you are obseving your conscious thought processes.
3. *Attributes.* The images and actions in your awareness have varied attributes. They may be viewed as significant or meaningless, organized or disorganized, clear or blurry, and so on.
4. *Flow.* Flow refers to the continual changes that occur in conscious awareness—the stream of consciousness.

To see how Marsh's analysis works, imagine that you are walking through a park on a beautiful spring Saturday. The *focus* of your attention is directed outward, taking in the trees, the flowers, the birds. *Structurally,* the foreground of your awareness changes continually as you focus briefly on each stimulus: a stand of tall birch trees, a squirrel scampering across the path, a bed of daffodils. The *background* may include your thoughts about the beauty of nature and the serenity of your break from the hubbub of the week. You may also at times be aware that you are observing your own peaceful reactions to the beauty of the setting (an *aerial perspective*). The *attributes* of your experience may include a sense of the setting as restful, peaceful, beautiful, and happy. Finally, the *flow* or stream of your consciousness will continually change as the environment changes and as you shift back and forth between observations of the natural setting around you, thoughts about the setting, and your own emotional reactions to the experience.

Modes of Consciousness

Normal, waking awareness is characterized by two basic modes of consciousness: passive consciousness and active consciousness. The basic feature of *passive consciousness* is receptivity: The person receives information from both the external environment and the internal workings of the body but takes little or no action. During this receptive state, consciousness is rather like a sponge, quietly soaking up information. A state of tired relaxation would be an example. A good example of passive consciousness is the "mindless" absorption you may experience while watching television.

If someone were to yell "Fire!" while you were watching TV, you would probably shift to a more alert mode of awareness. In *active consciousness,* you typically seek information from either external or internal sources and prepare to act on this information. Other examples of active consciousness include studying for an exam, planning a vacation, and solving a puzzle. More generally, *attention* is a state of active consciousness; when you are attending to a stimulus or thought, you are actively processing it in consciousness (Driver & Frackowiak, 2001).

Determinants of Conscious Experience

Both internal and external factors influence conscious experience. *Internal factors* are of two types: biological and psychological. *Biological* determinants include all aspects of body functioning that enter into awareness. Pain, for example, can often interfere with other thought processes. *Psychological* influences on consciousness come from your own thoughts and emotions. The anxiety of an upcoming exam or the pleasant anticipation of a party this weekend can affect awareness as well. And unconscious motivations may also have significant effects on conscious thought processes.

External factors include nearly any object or event in the outside environment that can serve as a stimulus by activating one or another of your senses. The sight of an acquaintance or the sound of her voice may start you thinking about that person. Some research has suggested that nearly 60 percent of reported thoughts are directly related to current environmental activities (Marsh, 1977).

Selective Attention

Much of The time, the contents of consciousness are largely a product of *selective attention*—intentionally focusing on a relatively narrow aspect of the environment. A good example is the *cocktail party effect,* in which attention is selectively focused on one of a number of simultaneous auditory stimuli. Attending closely to the conversation you are having with someone at a party, even though many other conversations may be going on around you, is the classic example. Selective attention is an important determinant of how we process sensory information and what we perceive (Dayan et al., 2000). It is active in the early stages of perception and slows perceptual processing as information is selected (Giard et al., 2000).

The focus of selective attention at a given moment is influenced by several interacting factors. Various physical characteristics of a stimulus, such as its *intensity* and *size,* are important. We are more likely to attend to a bright light than a dim one, for example. *Motives* and background may also affect attention. At a crowded party, a hair stylist may be focusing on heads, a shoe salesperson on feet, and a photographer on interesting expressions. Other determinants of selective perception include one's *physiological* and *psychological state.* Hunger, for example, produces selective attention to food, while depression may predispose you to notice negative events. Finally, a stimulus with *abrupt onset,* as when a car on a crossing road suddenly approaches an intersection you are about to enter, tends to capture attention (Giard et al., 2000).

Selective attention, and hence consciousness, is strongly influenced by preexisting expectations that constitute a perceptual set imposed during the neural processing of a stimulus. A classic demonstration of *perceptual set* was designed by Jerome Bruner and Leigh Minturn (1955). They showed one group the test stimulus in Figure 5-1 following a series of numbers, while another group were first shown a series of letters. Of those who first saw numbers, 83 percent said the test stimulus was a 13. Of those who first saw letters, 92 percent said it was a B. The induced perceptual set clearly influenced participants in naming the ambiguous test pattern.

The Fifty States (of Consciousness)

Well, there may not be 50 states of consciousness, but there are certainly numerous states different from the normal waking state that characterizes most of your typical day. An *altered state* of consciousness is one that deviates from the normal, waking state. Some altered states, such as sleep and daydreaming, are universal. Others, like hallucinations, occur in only a small proportion of the population. And still others, including meditation, hypnosis, and drug_induced states, are achieved through willful acts. Let's take a look at some of these altered states, beginning with the most common one, sleep.

"To Sleep, Perchance to Dream"

This quote from Shakespeare's *Hamlet* is perhaps the most famous of all passages concerned with sleep and dreaming, but Shakespeare was not alone in his interest in sleep. In fact, scholars point out that the Bible contains numerous references to sleep and that the ancient Hebrew tradition saw sleep as restorative and pleasant and sleep deprivation as harmful (Ancoli-Israel, 2001). More generally, popular literature abounds with passages on sleep and dreaming. These references reflect the virtually universal human fascination with what goes on beyond the silent veil of sleep, and scientists often literally stay up all night studying its vicissitudes. Let's take a look at what we know about sleep and then turn to the equally interesting topic of dreaming.

We spend about a third of each day in the altered state of consciousness known as sleep—actually, college students sleep more than that on weekends. Yet what do we know about it? The answer is "quite a bit." Scientists have studied the process by which we fall asleep, the several stages of sleep, and how we sleep on a typical night. We will also explore the relationship of sleep schedules to natural, biological rhythms and take up such sleep problems as insomnia.

Falling asleep is typically a two-step process. As you lie in bed and begin to feel sleepy, you pass into a *hypnogogic state*—a transitional stage in which thoughts are loose and disorganized and dreamlike images are experienced. This state lasts for about one to ten minutes and involves important changes in brain chemistry that are essential to the onset of normal sleep. John Pappenheimer (1976) isolated a sleep_inducing biochemical in the brains of goats and rats. When the animals are deprived of sleep, the level of this brain biochemical increases. Moreover, injecting the chemical into the brains of other animals produces increases in the duration and frequency of sleep.

The transitional stage ends with an abrupt change in your state of consciousness when you fall asleep. In one sleep study, the eyes of participants were taped open and a strobe light flashed repeatedly a few inches from their faces; the participants pressed a response button every time the light flashed (Dement, 1978). When sleep came, it was sudden. The button-pressing stopped abruptly and the eyes began to drift slowly from side to side, a change long known to indicate the onset of sleep. Now that we know something about falling asleep, let's explore sleep stages and the interesting phenomenon of REM sleep. We'll then turn to sleep schedules, biorhythms, the mysteries of dreaming, sleep disorders.

Stages of Sleep

When people fall asleep, they do not drift into a single state and remain there for the next eight hours. Rather, they experience a series of qualitatively different stages of sleep, each repeating several times during the course of the night (Erman, 2001). Sleep researchers have recorded the electrical activity of the brain during sleep and, more recently have used neuroimaging techniques, particularly positron emission tomography (PET) to study the brain during sleep (Maquet, 2000). One result of these studies is the finding that each sleep stage is characterized by a particular EEG or brain wave pattern (Cantero et al., 2002; see Figure 5-2). Prior to falling asleep, the predominant EEG frequency is the *alpha wave* (8 to 12 cycles per second), which is often associated with feelings of pleasant relaxation (Chapter 3). In the pre-sleep alpha state, you experience reduced responsiveness to sensory stimulation, coupled with disjointed, dreamlike images and often a floating sensation. Once you have fallen asleep, you typically go through four distinct stages:

- *Stage 1.* During Stage 1 sleep, the predominant brain wave frequency shifts from alpha to slower *theta* (5 to 7 cycles per second). The hypnogogic imagery of the pre-sleep period continues into Stage 1 as the person falls into a light sleep from which he can easily be awakened.
- *Stage 2.* In Stage 2, there is again a change in the EEG pattern, now characterized by waves of about 12 to 14 cycles per second. These bursts of EEG activity, typically lasting from second to 2 seconds, are called *sleep spindles.* There are also some large, slow EEG changes referred to as *K-complexes.* Sleep is now sound. There is greater muscular relaxation, and thoughts are virtually absent.
- *Stage 3.* Sleep deepens still further, and the EEG pattern typically shows the presence of delta waves (1/2 to 2 cycles per second) of relatively low amplitude (height). The sleeper may show some muscular movement during Stage 3 but is difficult to awaken and can be said to be in a state of deep sleep.
- *Stage 4.* The deepest sleep state is characterized by delta waves of relatively large amplitude and virtually total muscular relaxation. Awakening a sleeper during Stage 4 sleep is nearly impossible. It is often during this deepest stage of sleep that such unusual sleep activity as night terrors, sleepwalking, and sleep talking occur.

Interestingly enough, studies of identical twins reared apart show that the exact nature of Stage 2, 3, and 4 sleep are heavily influenced by genetic factors, while Stage 1 sleep is perhaps more strongly affected by nongenetic factors (Linkowski, 1994).

REM Sleep

At times during Stage 1 sleep, the eyes move rapidly beneath the lids, causing researchers to refer to this type of sleep as *rapid eye movement* (REM) sleep. Because these eye movements do not occur in the other stages, the latter are collectively referred to as *non-REM* (NREM) or slow-wave sleep. The eye movements of REM sleep come in short bursts and may represent a scanning of the visual events that occur during a dream (Dement, 1974; Nielsen, 2001). The EEG record is similar to that of Stage 1 NREM sleep except that saw-toothed waves are also present (see Figure 5-3). Newborns spend about 50% of their time in REM sleep, decreasing to the adult level of about 20% or 2 hours by age six months.

REM sleep is often referred to as *paradoxical sleep* because in some ways the sleeper acts almost like a person who is wide awake. The EEG pattern is quite similar to that of a waking person, and there is also considerable body activity. On the other hand, when these bursts of activity are not taking place, the action of the voluntary muscles is greatly reduced, to the point where the body is virtually paralyzed. But perhaps the most significant feature of REM sleep is the occurrence of dreams—most people awakened during a REM period will report having been in the midst of a dream. We will take up dreaming shortly.

Neurophysiologically oriented theories suggest that REM sleep does more than simply facilitate dreaming (Cirelli, 2002). One hypothesis is that REM sleep is essential to the *development* of the nervous system, which is not complete at birth. This would explain why the percentage of REM time decreases substantially over the first four years of life. Research partially supporting this idea comes from work showing increased protein synthesis, which would support neural development, during REM sleep. However, the hypothesis has proven difficult to test definitively.

An alternative idea is that REM sleep represents the physiological processes involved in the consolidation of long-term *memory* (Stickgold et al., 2001). When we learn something new, it first enters short-term memory. If we are to remember it more than very briefly, it must somehow be incorporated into long-term memory, where it is stored with memories that can last a lifetime. Protein synthesis, neurotransmitter production, and other neurophysiological events during REM may support the process by which long-term memories are consolidated (Hoffman & McNaughton, 2002). There is research support for this idea, but some reviewers conclude that there is still no solid evidence the REM sleep consolidates memory (Siegel, 2001; Vertes & Eastman, 2000).

NREM Sleep

If REM sleep provides dreams and perhaps memory consolidation, what does NREM sleep do for us? There are two basic theories. The first suggests that the slow EEG waves of NREM are associated with the *preservation and protection* of the species. An evolutionary account of sleep, this theory suggests that sleep evolved in order to protect members of the species from harm during that part of the day when there was danger in moving around in the environment (usually at night when it is dark). Humans continue this pattern of sleeping each night, even though it might now be more adaptive to sleep less hours and accomplish more (Webb, 1982).

The alternative approach is *restoration theory,* which suggests that deep, slow-wave sleep serves to is, to borrow a phrase, "the pause that refreshes." Both the brain and other body systems require rest in order to continue to function properly over time. Deep sleep provides time for the body to repair itself and may, in fact, involve neurological processes that actively promote the restoration of bodily functions. Cells in some organs can regenerate, while those in others get the "downtime" they need to survive and operate the next day (King et al., 1997).

A Typical Night

When you fall asleep, you do not simply pass through the four sleep stages, then remain in Stage 4 the rest of the night. A more typical pattern begins by initially falling asleep and passing through Stages 1, 2, and 3 to Stage 4 NREM sleep. The sleeper then usually returns to Stage 3, then Stage 2 and then to Stage 1, where the first REM period takes place. It begins about 70 to 90 minutes after the onset of Stage 1 and lasts about 3 to 7 minutes. A return to delta sleep and then to Stage 2 is followed by a second, longer, REM period. A typical night's sleep usually consists of four to six of these *sleep cycles,* with proportionately longer REM periods and shorter Stage 4 periods in each subsequent cycle (see Figure 5-4). Each REM period after the first may last for 40 minutes or more.

Because there are longer and longer periods of the more intensive REM sleep as the night progresses, physiological and psychological activity increase over the course of the night. Body movements and brief awakenings are characteristic even of those who sleep well. Both too many and too few movements may interfere with sleep. The soundest and "best" sleep occurs in those who move once every 10-20 minutes.

While Stages 3 and 4 predominate during the early part of the night, they drop out almost completely as the night progresses. As a result, about 20 percent of the night is spent in these two stages, 5 percent in Stage 1 NREM, and 20-25 percent in REM sleep. The remaining 50 percent of the night is characterized by the sleep spindles and K_complexes of Stage 2. Children spend relatively larger portions of the night in REM and Stage 4, while elderly people show somewhat less REM sleep and much less Stage 4 sleep.

Sleep Schedules and Biological Rhythms

The average adult sleeps 7-8 hours per night, with virtually all normal adults falling within the 6-10 hour range. Typical sleep patterns do, however, change with age (see Figure 5-5), and a significant reduction in overall sleep accompanies the aging process (Dijk et al., 2000). Although some people, like Benjamin Franklin, remain healthy on 3 hours of sleep or less, people who sleep less than 6 or more than 10 hours per night generally have a higher incidence of mortality than those who sleep within that range. The ideal now appears to be about 7 hours. There are, however, considerable variations in actual sleep schedules and particularly in the periods of time at which individuals are the most alert and can think and otherwise function optimally. You may know some people, for example, who say they work best at night, others who are more alert in the morning. Studies confirm that such morning types and evening types do exist, as Figure 5-6 show. These variations probably reflect differences in biological rhythms that may be modified by experience (Folkard, 1994).

Sleep is, of course, simply one major part of the daily cycle of activities. Biological activities that occur on a daily cycle are said to follow a *circadian rhythm*—a roughly 24-hour cycle involving consistent biological changes (Rivkees, 2001). But to what extent is this apparently biological rhythm affected by environmental factors, such as the change from light to dark? Not very much, probably because the circadian rhythm is based in an array of genes that regulate physiological systems throughout the body (Vitaterna, et al., 2001). In some studies, people have been fully isolated from all external time cues and day/night cycles for days or even weeks by putting them in rooms or caves with no clocks or windows. Their circadian rhythms persist. However, interestingly enough, their sleep gradually shifts later and later (Figure

5-7), and they tend to adopt a 25-hour sleep-wake cycle. Similarly, one blind person had a circadian rhythm of 24.9 hours, and efforts to modify his daily cycle in a sleep laboratory were unsuccessful (Miles, Raynal, and Wilson, 1977). Such observations suggest that the "natural" biological clock may be somewhat longer than the global clock and that the sleep-wake cycle and overall circadian rhythm may be, in part, regulated by somewhat different mechanisms (Dijk & Lockley, 2002).

Departures from normal cycles make it difficult for the individual to sleep normally, as is often seen in airline passengers who experience jet lag after crossing multiple time zones. People take about one day to adjust for every time zone crossed. However, there is less jet lag when traveling westward than eastward, probably because shortening the day is a greater violation of natural circadian rhythm than lengthening it (Figure 5-8). The effects of jet lag are thus apparently due not to sleep loss but rather to a disturbance of the normal circadian rhythm.

Dreams: Windows To The Unconscious?

All we see or seem
Is but a dream within a dream.
EDGAR ALLAN POE

To many people, dreams seem to be rather mundane, disorganized replays of everyday life, having no great importance. To Sigmund Freud, however, dreams provide an all-important window to the unconscious, a partially veiled view into the forbidden desires that lurk in the dark world beneath consciousness.

The earliest empirical work on dreaming was done by Eugene Aserinsky and Nathaniel Kleitman (1953). These researchers, who had discovered REM sleep, also found an association between REM periods and dreaming. When participants were awakened during REM sleep, they reported experiencing vivid dreams 74 percent of the time, as compared with only seven percent during NREM. When dreaming does occur during NREM sleep, its content is similar to that found in REM sleep on the same night, though there are gender differences (Soper et al., 1994).

Everyone dreams nightly, but only about half the population remembers dreams regularly. If you don't remember your dreams but would like to, try this little experiment: Buy a loud, raucous new alarm clock that is likely to awaken you suddenly. Sound the alarm a number of times while you are awake and try to condition yourself to think about dreams any time the alarm sounds. Now set the alarm, and the very moment it awakens you think: "What was I dreaming?" *Immediately* write down as much dream detail as you can recall.

Why Do We Dream? Just as we must all eat and drink, it appears that we must all dream. Food and water keep us alive. Does dreaming have a similarly important function? Sigmund Freud certainly thought it did. In a little-known commentary, he described some of his own dreams, which may have been a partial basis for his theory of dreaming (Blum, 2001). He hypothesized that dreams provide an outlet for intense, dangerous anxieties and impulses that otherwise become "dammed up" in the unconscious mind. In Freud's view, many of our needs or wishes are perceived as psychologically unacceptable and therefore dangerous. In our dreams, such unacceptable, repressed desires are translated into symbolic form as the *latent content* of the dream, which is then converted to *manifest content*, or the actual dream as it appears to us. Manifest content is now often called simply dream consciousness (Cicogna & Bosinelli, 2001). If, for example, a man dreams of ice skating with a queen (the manifest content), a Freudian analyst might interpret the latent content to be an incestuous wish for sexual relations with the man's mother: The queen is symbolic of the mother, and the slipping, sliding motion of skating is symbolic of sexual intercourse.

Freud's own evidence for his dream theory came primarily from his experience in doing psychoanalytic therapy. While his careful observations of his patients' dreams do constitute a systematic basis for dream theory, others might have interpreted the dreams differently. Critics of Freudian dream theory have also noted that the content of dreams, whether symbolic or not, may have little to do with the actual purpose of dreaming, which may be totally physiological. Moreover, some evidence suggests that people can make up dreams that are indistinguishable from the real thing. Despite these criticisms, Freud's theory has been the principal basis for most dream content analysis. Moreover, recent research does point to the usefulness of the dream in psychotherapy and provides evidence that dreams have an unconscious origin (Glucksman, 2001).

One way to study the value of dreaming is to systematically deprive subjects of dreams for an extended period of time and see what happens to their physiology and behavior. Because most dreams occur during REM sleep, investigators have done studies in which they awaken experimental participants whenever they enter a REM period. Subjects in a control group have their sleep interrupted an equal number of times during the night, but only during NREM periods. A number of studies have shown that after a few nights of REM_sleep interruption, participants begin to show heightened anxiety, irritability, agitation, and a variety of mild neurotic symptoms not seen in the control group. In addition, when allowed to sleep without interruption, the REM_deprived participants show a considerable increase in the amount of REM sleep time for one or more nights (Cicogna & Bosinelli, 2001).

An alternative theory suggests that dreaming is simply a product of normal neurophysiological processes. Formulated by Alan Hobson and Robert McCarley (1977), *the activation-synthesis hypothesis* suggests that a biological clock mechanism in the brainstem periodically activates neural circuitry in a random fashion during sleep. The activation also arouses higher brain centers in the cerebral cortex, and these centers attempt to synthesize the random sensory, motor, and emotional information being generated within the circuitry of the brain (Hobson et al., 2001). The result may be random dreams or dream fragments. If this theory is correct, the content of the dream is a relatively unimportant side effect of rhythmic neuroelectrical activity in the brain.

Other theorists have criticized the Hobson-McCarley hypothesis, noting that dream content is not as disorganized as they imply. In fact, the content is organized, selective, and often negative, suggesting that the dream may be a product of evolution. Its function is to simulate threatening events and rehearse threat avoidance, an adaptive function in ancient times, when life was short and filled threatening waking events (Revonsuo, 2000).

A final theory is Rosalind Cartwright's *cognitive* approach (Cartwright, 1993). She hypothesizes that dreams are extensions of waking thought and involve *problem-solving* activities. The dream has the advantage of being less constrained by logic than are waking thought processes and therefore potentially able to bring creative solutions to real-life problems. Women in the process of divorce, for example, dreamed repeatedly about problems related to the divorce in one of Cartwright's studies. Those whose dreams dealt directly with divorce issues showed better adjustment to the divorce than those whose dreams did not.

Dream Content. Psychologists since Freud have attempted to study dream content in three principal ways. Some have used the clinical method, in which the patient is asked to recall dreams that have occurred since the last therapy session. The dreams are then recorded and interpreted by the therapist. The second approach is the *diary method*, in which participants are asked to record every dream they remember as soon as possible after waking up. Calvin Hall (1951) conducted a classic study of this type in which he collected some 10,000 dreams and analyzed their content. A third approach is the *laboratory method*, in which participants sleep in a dream laboratory and are awakened at the end of REM periods and asked to relate their dreams, which are then recorded.

The results of all three types of studies suggest that dreams tend to be populated by familiar people, objects, and places. Hall found, for example, that most reported dreams dealt with events that might equally as well have happened to the person during waking hours. The dreams usually involved places the person frequented regularly, and the people were usually relatives or acquaintances. A more surprising result was that the majority of dreams involved predominantly negative emotions, and more recent work also shows that pain is often experienced in dreams (Nielsen et al., 1993). Pleasant feelings were reported in only 18 percent of Hall's dreams, while anxiety and anger were found in 64 percent, a finding consistent with Freud's dream theory. Aggressive and hostile acts were also far more common than more positive acts.

A number of studies have pointed to factors that may influence dream content, including events happening just prior to falling asleep. Subjects who come to a sleep laboratory, for example, often have dreams that contain both direct and symbolic references to the laboratory and the experimenter. Dream content can also be influenced by events that occur *during* sleep. In one study, experimenters waited for the beginning of a REM sleep cycle in their laboratory participants, then exposed the sleepers to a variety of stimuli, such as tones and flashing lights. About 25 percent of the subjects reported dreams incorporating these stimuli in some way (Dement and Wolpert, 1958).

Additional influences on dream content include current stresses and cultural norms. People worried about losing their jobs dream about seeking work or about rejection by potential employers; competitive athletes dream about winning or losing a contest; hungry people dream about food; and those with problems dream about possible solutions. In addition, the amount of hostility and aggression found in dreams tends to be correlated with the amount of actual aggressiveness found in the dreamer's society. Sex differences also occur, with American men more likely to have dreams characterized by aggression, sex, and achievement and American women dreaming more about family, emotionality, and friendship.

Special Dream States. Some dreams involve special dream states that are relatively rare but particularly interesting. In a *lucid dream*, the sleeper suddenly becomes aware of the fact that she is dreaming, then establishes an almost conscious degree of control over the content of the dream. Experimental evidence shows that lucid dreaming tends to take place relatively late in the night and that the controlled imagery of this special dream is probably a product of the left hemisphere of the brain (Wolpin et al., 1992).

An extension of the lucid dream is the out-of-body experience, in which the dreamer seems to become an outside observer who can see himself in bed or in some other circumstances as another person might view him. Such dreams are also very rare.

Night Terrors and Nightmares. So far we have called Seana's experience a bad dream, but technically she had a *night terror*, an extremely frightening dream that causes the person to awaken in a state of panic. Night terrors are rare but are far more likely to occur in someone who has a family history of night terrors and are more frequent in children than in adults. They are usually associated with other sleep disorders, including insomnia (who wouldn't rather be awake!), sleep talking, and sleepwalking (Pagel, 2000). They typically occur during Stage 3 or 4 sleep and are often associated with high levels of stress or the use of antidepressant drugs. Virtually all adults with night terrors have other significant psychiatric symptoms.

Far more common and less severe than Seana's night terror is the nightmare. *Nightmares* were reported at least as long ago as 2000 to 3000 B.C. in the epic poem *Gilgamesh.* The mother of Gilgamesh interpreted his nightmare about a star falling toward him as a sign that a friend would come to him. Nightmares peak at ages 3-6, but are also seen in adults. They are formally referred to as *anxiety dreams* and are characterized by experiences of threat and fear that are often fairly direct continuations of more usual dreams (Pagel, 2001). Unlike night terrors, nightmares occur during REM sleep and involve relatively small changes in body physiology. They can be brought on by periods of REM sleep deprivation, are often caused by sleeping pills or physical illnesses, and are particularly common in narcoleptics. In one study of 1,695 students between the ages of 5 and 20, 37.2 percent were found to have had nightmares, though most no more frequently than once a year (Fisher and Wilsons 1987). The frequency of nightmares increases with stress, but those afflicted with these negative dreams can often be effectively treated with psychotherapy in a few sessions. Those with particularly distressing nightmares are likely to have underlying psychological disorders (Levin & Fireman, 2002).

In the Middle Ages people thought that nightmares were brought about by demons as a form of punishment for their sins. The Henry Fuseli painting "Nightmare" (Figure 5-11) depicts such a demon sitting on the chest of a woman who is experiencing a nightmare.

Sleep Problems and Disorders

Hippocrates, the father of medicine, noted that "sleepiness or wakefulness when immoderate constitute disease." His statement recognizes the fact that sleep disorders can include sleeping either too little or too much. Despite the fact that these problems were recognized even in ancient Greece, it was not until the 1970s that the intensive study of sleep disorders began. We can now identify at least 88 different sleep disorders. The major, general classifications are *insomnia,* involving too little sleep, *hypersomnia,* where the patient sleeps too much, and *parasomnia* or disturbances during sleep. Here we will focus on four specific sleep disorders: insomnia, hypersomnia, narcolepsy, and sleep apnea, later taking up others relating to dreaming.

Insomnia. If you have experienced *insomnia*—the failure to get adequate sleep—even the word may be enough to keep you awake. In most cases, insomnia occurs for no more than a few days at a time and is not serious enough to be called a disorder. In fact, between 30 and 45 percent of the general population experience some degree of insomnia. However, for 10_15 percent the insomnia is severe and may require treatment, and 7 percent express general dissatisfaction with sleep quality and quantity (Ohayon & Zulley, 2001). According to some estimates, over 30 million Americans suffer from insomnia at any given time, and the problem accounts for at least 3.3 million visits to physicians each year (Radecki & Brunton, 1993). Moreover, chronic daytime drowsiness, a common result of true insomnia, is a factor in 15-30% of traffic accidents, involving three times as many fatalities as other accidents (Haraldsson & Akerstedt, 2001). While there are a number of specific types of insomnia, the two most basic are *sleep-onset insomnia*—difficulty in falling asleep—and *sleep-maintenance insomnia*—difficulty remaining asleep throughout the night.

Interestingly enough, many people who complain of insomnia actually sleep no less than individuals who say they sleep normally and show no daytime impairment indicative of sleep loss. Some studies show that only about half of a group of self-described insomniacs actually stayed awake in the sleep lab as long as 30 minutes throughout the night (Carskadon, Mitlar, and Dement, 1974). Most of them were apparently bothered more by their *perceived* lack of sleep than by any actual sleep loss.

True insomnia can have a variety of causes and correlated problems. Three sets of factors appear to enter to be involved: *predisposing tendencies,* which make it more likely that the individual will develop insomnia under the right conditions; *precipitating circumstances,* which trigger the insomnia; and *perpetuating factors,* which may cause the insomnia to continue over a relatively long period. The predisposing factors may include a variety of medical conditions, as well as personality factors and the physiological state of the individual. For example, insomniacs have high levels of muscle tension, anxiety, and depression. They also show higher levels of autonomic activity (indicative of high arousal) when they try to sleep, are more depressed, and have more physical complaints than good sleepers do (Riemann et al., 2001). Our friend Seana might be subject to insomnia because she has experienced a series of bad dreams and is afraid to fall asleep. A precipitating incident typically involves stress, such as a death in the family. Perpetuating factors can include spending too much time in bed (attempting to sleep), daytime napping, the use of sedatives or alcohol, irregular times for retiring and getting up, and excessive worry about sleeping.

By now you should be wide awake and ready to hear just what it is that helps insomniacs to sleep better! First, in serious cases the insomniac is best treated in a sleep disorder center, where a complete medical and psychological workup can be used to pinpoint and treat the causes of the sleep problem. A combination of several treatments is often better than any one alone. One of the newest methods is *light therapy,* in which the sleep of some insomniacs improves when they are exposed to extremely bright lights during the morning hours (Mishima et al., 2000). Beyond formal diagnosis and treatment, the best approach to better sleep is to develop better sleep habits. Establishing a pattern of getting no more and no less sleep than one really needs and of going to bed and getting up at about the same time each day is particularly important. The Probe offers other suggestions for avoiding or dealing with sleep difficulties.

Many people try to relieve their insomnia by taking tranquilizers and other drugs, particularly barbiturates (Silber, 2001). However, there are two basic problems with this approach: (1) the drugs are dangerous, and (2) they don't really work. Some of the drugs commonly prescribed for insomnia are physically additive and can even be lethal. In addition, these drugs tend to rapidly lose any initial tendency to produce sleep because the user builds tolerance to their effects. Furthermore, they interfere with REM sleep and may actually do more harm than good (see Figure 5-9). Over-the-counter medications are also a poor bet. The drugs they contain are of questionable efficacy and can be quite toxic (Wing, 2001). Nevertheless, there is hope. New drugs are constantly under development, and two of the newer candidates, zolpidem and zalephlon, do seem promising in that they appear to be relatively effective with few side effects (Lippmann et al., 2001).

There has also been considerable publicity about the use of the hormone melatonin. Some preliminary studies did show that it may help some people with sleep disorders to sleep better, and it may turn out to be a useful drug (Richardson & Roth, 2001). However, more recent work suggests that it may be helpful only in the elderly, and even there its value has not been clearly demonstrated (Olde & Rigaud, 2001). In addition, we don't really yet know that it is safe, particularly for long-term use, and some adverse effects have been reported (Benca, 2001). Moreover, melatonin is sold primarily in health food stores and is not currently regulated by the FDA. As a result, there is no way to be certain that samples are pure, and the dosages recommended by manufacturers may be far higher than necessary. It must therefore be considered a drug of questionable safety and efficacy until more research is done and the manufacturing process is monitored.

Hypersomnia. Meaning excessive sleepiness, hypersomnia should be distinguished from fatigue, which refers to a lack of energy. In hypersomnia, which affects 2-5% of adults, the patient sleeps long hours, takes involuntary naps, and reports a constant craving for sleep, difficulty working, and often involvement in accidents. The condition is sometimes associated with sleep apnea or chronic sleep deprivation (Bassetti & Gugger, 2000).

Narcolepsy. Where the insomniac has trouble falling asleep, the narcoleptic has trouble staying awake. *Narcolepsy* is a disorder characterized by sudden attacks of sleep. It most commonly begins in the late teens and is estimated to affect over 800,000 people in the United States (Brooks & Guilleminault, 2001). The person may be reading a book, engaging in conversation, or driving a car and suddenly fall asleep with little or no warning. He typically sleeps for 10 to 15 minutes and awakes refreshed but often falls asleep again within 2 hours. Fifteen or more narcoleptic attacks a day is not unusual. Narcoleptics fall asleep quickly in the laboratory, and studies show that they sleep significantly more hours per day than do normals (Overeem et al., 2001). Often, however, they deny that they have fallen asleep or claim that they were awake much longer than they were. This discrepancy between an objective EEG indicator of sleep onset and the subjective reports can be seen in Figure 5_10 (Bierbrauer et al., 2000). Unlike insomnia, which is most often a result of psychological problems, narcolepsy appears to involve neurological abnormalities that may be hereditary and probably involve low levels of a neuropeptide called hypocretin that is found in the lateral hypothalamus (Krahn et al., 2001).

Sleep Apnea. About 40% of adults are habitual snorers and, about 2% of women and 4% of men have additional sleep-disordered breathing, primarily sleep apnea (Ullmer & Soler, 2001).

In ***Obstructive sleep apnea***, the sleeper stops breathing for a short time, awakens slightly, emitting a gasp and a loud snore, then falls asleep again. Once asleep, the cycle is repeated _ in some people over 500 times in one night. Apnea is most likely to occur during REM sleep, and the stoppage of breathing is due to closure of the upper airways resulting from a loss of muscle tone (Balcerzak, 2001).

The surest sign of apnea is snoring so loud that it "can reach levels of intensity associated with industrial noise pollution" (Allen, 1986). There is frequently also considerable daytime fatigue. Sleep apnea is a serious disorder that is associated with neurological disturbances, hypertension, cardiac arrhythmias, strokes, and sudden, fatal heart attacks (Escourrou et al., 2000). In addition, the automobile accident rate of sleep apnea patients is seven times that of the general population (Strollo & Rogers, 1996). In some cases, the problem is so serious that nasal and oral surgery are needed to remove airway obstructions (Greeg et al., 2000). The disorder runs in families and may have a genetic component (Douglas et al., 1993).

More States: Hypnosis, Meditation, Relaxation, and Daydreaming

Among the most interesting states of consciousness are those that are very common and those that are quite uncommon. Let's explore such common states as daydreaming and relaxation and such relatively uncommon states as meditation, and hypnosis. Our 21 is concerned with research on another interesting altered state—hallucination.

Hypnosis

Hypnosis is a very old phenomenon. It was developed by Viennese physician Anton Mesmer in the eighteenth century and soon came to be called *mesmerism.* Mesmer exposed his patients to magnetic objects and fluids in order to restore their bodies to a "magnetic balance" that seemed to cure many ills. He was apparently unaware that his "cures" where actually a result of hypnotic suggestion. In 1784, a French government commission investigated Mesmer, concluded that his technique was a hoax, and closed his popular clinic in Paris. Later, a Portuguese priest proposed that the effects of mesmerism were due not to magnetic changes but to suggestion, and a Scottish surgeon then coined the term *hypnosis,* from Hypnos, the Greek god of sleep. Although William James (1890) discussed hypnosis late in the 19th century, research did not begin in this country until 1920.

Hypnotic States and Phenomena. Hypnosis is a state in which the participant displays heightened suggestibility and distortions of perception or memory (Kirsch, 2001). The induction of hypnosis involves two major elements: deep relaxation and imagery. Deep relaxation is achieved either by directly suggesting that the participant relax or by describing relaxing imagery, such as beach scenes or reclining in an easy chair, or by using both techniques together. George Mitchell and Richard Lundy (1986) found that the combination of relaxation and imagery produced the best hypnotic induction and that relaxation alone was better than imagery alone.

Not everyone is equally susceptible to hypnosis. In a classic study, Ernest Hilgard (1965) found that about 25 percent of 533 college students quite readily achieved a hypnotic state, 5-10 percent were totally unresponsive, and the rest were moderately susceptible. To assess susceptibility, researchers developed the Stanford Hypnotic Susceptibility Scale (SHSS). In using this test, the hypnotist makes a series of suggestions to the participant and then systematically observes the extent to which his instructions are followed. Those who conform most closely are the most susceptible. Hypnotizability is a reasonably stable characteristic of the individual, adult scores remaining about the same over a ten year period, but it can be modified with training.

Measures of hypnotizability, like the SHSS, are frequently used in hypnosis research. An example is the Mitchell and Lundy (1986) study of relaxation and imagery. The 63 undergraduates in the study were divided on the basis of a suggestibility measure into high, medium, and low levels of hypnotizability. Participants higher in hypnotic susceptibility showed a greater degree of hypnosis and differed on a number of dependent variables on which data were collected during the hypnotic trance state. Figure 5_12 shows the distribution of resistance to hypnosis (the opposite of hypnotizability) in over 400 college students.

Theories of Hypnosis. What is going on when a hypnotic state occurs? According to the *neodissociation theory* of Ernest Hilgard (1992), hypnosis causes the subject to focus his attention selectively on one thing, typically the hypnotist's suggestions. Other stimuli are still processed subconsciously, but the conscious and subconscious are *dissociated*—separated—and the dissociation is mediated by brain systems that become isolated from each other. To demonstrate dissociation, Hilgard had hypnotized participants immerse their left hands in buckets of ice water. As instructed, they verbally reported no sensation, but, through automatic writing with the right hand, they reported coldness to the point of pain. More recent theorists have recent similar conclusions (Kirsch, 2001).

In an alternative theory, Martin Orne hypothesizes that hypnosis is primarily a matter of *role playing.* The participant knows that a hypnotized person is supposed to lose consciousness, appear to be in a trance, lose inhibitions, and follow the instructions of the hypnotist (Whitehouse, Orne, Orne, & Dinges, 1991). A "good" hypnotic subject is one who plays this role effectively, and Orne has mustered data to support his position.

A third theory is offered by Theodore X. Barber (1970), who proposes that hypnosis is the result of *suggestibility* and *motivation.* According to Barber, the hypnotic suggestion produces a set of motives and expectations to which the subject responds by following the instructions of the hypnotist. Thus, hypnosis is no more than a state of heightened suggestibility—a hypothesis supported by the finding that conscious suggestion is often equally as effective as hypnosis, as we will see. Similarly, Jerome Singer and Kenneth Pope (1981) have suggested that the state of consciousness achieved through hypnotic induction is similar to that seen in ordinary daydreaming. Recent studies continue to support this theoretical approach (Lynn et al., 2002).

Uses of Hypnosis. Hypnosis has been successfully used to reduce the pain of childbirth, surgery, and dental work, particularly in highly hypnotizable subjects (Patel et al., 2000). However, it may get a lot of help from the natural distribution of pain receptors in the body, since many tissues beneath the skin, including major body organs, are totally or largely insensitive to pain. Only the skin is highly pain sensitive, and local anesthetics are ordinarily used to numb it during surgery under hypnosis. It is therefore not surprising that analgesia (pain reduction) suggestions given without hypnotic induction are equally as effective as those given under hypnosis.

Hypnosis has also been used to reduce blood pressure, help people stop smoking, reduce itching, and improve the functioning of the immune system (Covino & Bottari, 2001; Nash, 2002; Rucklidge & Saunders, 2002). However, there are few studies supporting such uses and they are often flawed by inadequate controls. Indeed, hypnosis is often found to be no more effective than no treatment (Abbot et al., 2000).

In yet another application, *hypnotherapy*—psychotherapy using hypnosis—has been widely used in the treatment of a number of psychological problems (Noble, 2002). Some therapists, for example, would use it in an effort to relieve Seana's night terrors. However, it is no more effective and is less thoroughly documented than other forms of therapy.

The Thinking Critically box asks you to carefully analyze other claims made for hypnosis.

Although hypnosis is widely used by professionals, a word of caution is in order concerning its use by amateurs. Hypnosis is easy to do, but the state of heightened suggestibility it induces can be dangerous. The participant can become emotionally upset, and there is some danger of precipitating more serious emotional problems. It should therefore be used only by a fully qualified psychologist or other mental health professional.

Meditation and Relaxation

Many people, particularly in Eastern cultures, intentionally alter their state of consciousness by engaging in meditation. A similar state—or at least one with similar benefits—may be attainable through relaxation. We will consider the altered states of meditation and relaxation, then turn to an assessment of their effects on the individual.

Meditation is "A family of techniques which have in common a conscious attempt to focus attention in a nonanalytical way and an attempt not to dwell on discursive ruminating thought" (Shapiro, 1982, p. 268). It moves thought processes away from their usual, analytical mode, in which external stimuli and internal thoughts are actively dealt with on a moment_to_moment basis. Analytical thought is replaced with a more passive, receptive, quiescent state. If you would like to learn how such meditative states are achieved, you can either pay $500 or so to take a class in some form of meditation or you can simply read the paragraphs that follow!

Meditation came to be of particular interest to many people during the 1960s and 1970s because of the claims made for its positive effects on mental health. Advocates that meditation can produce such positive changes in personality and behavior as greater creativity, energy and wisdom, a sense of inner peace and unity, and increased, self_esteem, self_actualization, and spontaneity. Who could resist the promise of such psychological riches? Unfortunately, it appears that many who did not resist probably should have, particularly those who spent large sums of money learning meditation techniques.

Take Your Choice: An Eastern Potpourri. Meditation can be divided into two main types: concentrative and opening up. In *concentrative meditation* the meditator focuses totally on one particular word, object, or picture. In Transcendental Meditation (TM), for example, you concentrate on a *mantra*, a short, sacred term taken from Sanskrit, such as "om." The basic goal is to achieve a kind of mental void, a complete clearness in which all active thought processes and perceptions of the external environment are temporarily excluded from consciousness. In *opening-up meditation* the goal is a dramatically heightened awareness of the environment. An example is Zazen, a form of Zen Buddhist meditation in which the meditator seeks a state of total alertness without interference from troubling thoughts.

The Relaxation Alternative. One of the chief benefits claimed for meditation is relaxation, which may have positive psychological and physiological effects. Herbert Benson, a pioneer in research on relaxation, considers it a response that can be achieved quite readily through learning (Benson et al., 1994). Benson describes the relaxation process as having four basic elements: (1) the use of a mental device, such as a word (like "om"); (2) a passive attitude, in which the person disregards any potentially distracting thoughts; (3) muscle relaxation; and (4) a quiet environment (Beary and Benson, 1974). Participants are taught to go alone to a quiet room and sit in a comfortable, relaxed position. They concentrate on a chosen word to clear the mind of other thoughts, and they systematically relax their muscles. Beary and Benson found that participants could learn a simple relaxation technique with about one hour of self_instruction. After mastering the technique, they were able to maintain a state of self_induced relaxation for a period of time, producing physiological changes comparable to those achieved with TM.

Do simple relaxation techniques really produce the same results as the intense meditation of a Zen master? Let's look at the physiological and psychological evidence.

Effects of Meditation and Relaxation. Among the changes said to occur during meditative states are shifts in neural and metabolic functions. Some studies have shown that brain electrical activity and cerebral blood flow during meditation are indicative of relaxation and drowsiness (Arambula et al., 2001; Newberg et al., 2001). In fact, meditators appear to be in sleep Stages 2, 3, and 4 during about 40 percent of their meditation time. Additional changes include slowing of heart rate, decreased metabolic rate, and lowered blood lactate levels (Barnes et al., 2001; Travis et al., 2001). However, the changes seen during TM and other forms of meditation are found to occur equally under conditions of relaxation as well (Benson et al., 1994).

Meditation is also said to reduce stress, increase happiness, and alleviate painful neuromuscular symptoms. Stress reduction through meditation has often been reported (Jacobs, 2001). Those who teach TM also claim increases in happiness and in effectiveness of functioning, but the empirical literature has been mixed. In one study, an experimental group of emotionally disturbed people participated in a three_month program of TM, while a control group did not (Kline, Docheerty, and Farley, 1982). TM produced no clinically significant improvement. Similarly, some believe that TM may reduce blood pressure and decrease hospitalizations for heart disease, but experts believe that more work is needed before we can be at all certain of these benefits (King et al., 2002). However, we have no solid data supporting these claims. Finally, research shows that meditation may help reduce the pain of fibromyalgia, a chronic illness characterized by widespread muscle and joint pain (Kaplan et al., 1993). Again, however, relaxation may achieve the same benefit, as has been the case with essentially every benefit claimed for meditation.

Meditation may also have adverse effects. One investigator studied a number of subjects who had meditated regularly and found that many of them reported negative changes (Otis, in press). These included anxiety, depression, withdrawal, boredom, confusion, and restlessness. Interestingly enough, it was found that individuals who had meditated longer were more likely to show adverse effects.

Daydreaming

One student reported that at least once or twice each week he dropped whatever else he was doing and imagined himself to be a famous movie star. The fantasy was played out in great detail, as he saw himself on stage, in movies, attending White House dinners, and luxuriating in the jacuzzi of his mansion attended by beautiful women. He was disturbed about the fantasy because it included a strong erotic element and was often accompanied by masturbation. His daydream, however, were quite normal, as daydreams are a common part of the everyday experiences of many people (Ray & Faith, 1995).

Daydreaming takes a variety of forms. Jerome Singer (1978), whose pioneering research has done much to increase our knowledge of this state of consciousness, notes that daydreaming can involve any shift of attention away from immediately demanding tasks. Singer and his colleagues have surveyed large numbers of people to determine the frequency and nature of daydreams. In one such study they found that 96 percent of participants reported daydreaming daily, with the highest frequency occurring in young adults between the ages of 18 and 29 (Singer and McCraven, 1961; Singer, 1975a).

Based on his studies, Singer (1978) has identified three major patterns of daydreaming. The first involves *poor attentional control*—the mind wanders rather aimlessly, and there is little extended thought. The second type consists primarily of *negative emotional fantasies* involving guilt or hostility. And the third type is an emotionally *positive fantasy* in which the primary content is wishful, playful, and fanciful. The first type has been shown to be related to measures of psychological instability, and the second type is clearly uncomfortable to the individual. The third kind, on the other hand, is indicative of a positive, healthy mental status.

What about sexual daydreams? In a Canadian survey of single women between the ages of 18 and 47, only 2 percent said that they never had sexual fantasies, and the most active fantasizers were the older women in the group. The women fantasized about intercourse with a boyfriend or husband (90 percent), being undressed by a man (79 percent), a specific prior sexual experience (78 percent), intercourse in some exotic locale (72 percent), undressing a man (71 percent), and oral sex (66 percent). Most said that they engaged in these fantasies in order to become sexually aroused, fall asleep, or simply have a pleasant interlude (Pelletier and Herold, 1983). Such sexual daydreams are more common in women with higher sex drives and decrease with increasing age. Men, of course, also experience these sexual fantasies.

The exact causes of daydreaming are not yet well understood. Psychologically, daydreams may fulfill the theoretical Freudian need to discharge dammed up drives and anxieties, though less vividly and less effectively than night dreams. Alternatively, daydreaming may be an inevitable consequence of the normal firing of brain cells, primarily in the right hemisphere.

Alcohol and Other Psychoactive Drugs

The use of drugs to alter consciousness is nothing new. Archaeological findings suggest that mescal has been used for over 10,000 years in Mexico and the southwestern United States. Written accounts of opium use date back to at least 4000 B.C. And the consumption of alcoholic beverages goes back 6,000 years or more. Some mind-altering drugs are used in connection with sacred rituals by members of certain cultures, but it is the recreational use of these powerful substances that has been of increasing concern in recent decades as drug abuse approaches worldwide epidemic levels (Vetulani, 2001). We will consider what is known about alcohol—the most widely abused of all drugs—then consider the several other major drugs of abuse, including depressants, stimulants, marijuana, and the hallucinogens.

Alcohol Dependence and Abuse

Did your activities last Saturday night include drinking? If so, you are a potential future alcoholic. "Can't happen to me!?" Well, perhaps not, but that is undoubtedly what all alcoholics once said to themselves (Table 5-1) Even short of alcoholism, drinking is by far the largest single drug problem today, other than nicotine (Chapter 15)—far worse than marijuana, cocaine, and other drugs. Well over 80% of the population have used alcohol, compared with 37% for marijuana and much lower percentages for other drugs (SAMSHA, 1995).

Humans have been abusing alcohol for centuries, and modern times are certainly no exception. The number of Americans who drink regularly rose from 30% in 1940 to 84% in 1994 (SAMSHA, 1995), with men drinking about twice as much as women. In fact, 11 million Americans admit to being heavy drinkers (SAMSHA, 1995). Over 80% of high school seniors and 55% of 8th graders have used alcohol, with nearly 63% of seniors and 26% of 8th graders having been drunk (NIDA, 1995). Of those who drink, nearly 6.0% drink every day and 9.4% binge on 10 or more drinks fairly often. More generally, heavy drinking (5 or more drinks in a row) has become very common, even in high school (Figure 5-13). A more frightening figure is that 5% of females and fully 20% of males become diagnosable alcoholics at some time in their lives (Enoch & Goldman, 2002). That's *one-fifth* of the male population!

Alcohol abuse takes its toll on both the individual and society. It is responsible for at least 700,000 hospital admissions (20-30% of all admissions) and 100,000 deaths annually in the United States and for greatly reducing even more life spans. Drinkers suffer from a number of ailments, ranging from impaired memory and concentration to sleep disturbances, malnutrition, cirrhosis of the liver, brain damage, and alcoholic psychosis (Brower, 2001). In addition, alcohol consumption is a causal factor in various forms of cancer (Bardou et al., 2002; Noda et al., 2001).

The cost to society can be measured in both lives and dollars. Alcohol consumption is a major factor in 38% of all traffic fatalities, 25% of suicides, 50% of homicides, 20% of teenage deaths, and 40% of all crimes that result in conviction (McCannon et al., 2002; Woodward et al., 2000; Martin, 2001). Alcohol_related motor vehicle accidents cost the American economy $5.14 billion annually, and the treatment of drinking problems costs the United States over $12 billion each year.

The effects of alcohol are highly correlated with its concentration in the blood. It is for this reason that *blood alcohol level* is used as a legal guideline for determining intoxication (Table 5_2). In most European countries and most states in the U.S., a person is legally intoxicated when the blood alcohol level reaches O.10 or more. Statistics show that the chances of an automobile accident are six times greater when the alcohol level is .10 than when it is half that amount and that most of the 5500 pedestrians killed and the 96,000 injured by cars each year are victims of alcohol intoxication (MMWR, 1994; Table 5-3).

The immediate effects of alcohol on the individual are widely recognized. Social inhibitions often appear to decrease, and the person may become boisterous, depressed, or hostile. However, the loss of inhibitions is more a function of the individual's *belief* that he has consumed alcohol than of the actual effects of the drug. Alcohol also causes blackouts and affects sexual performance, as William Shakespeare was aware: "Lechery, sir, it provokes, and it unprovokes: it provokes the desire but it takes away the performance" (*Macbeth*, Act II, Scene 3). Research confirming the Bard's observation shows that alcohol reduces the ability of men to achieve an erection and inhibits vaginal blood flow, an index of sexual arousal in women (McCannon et al., 2002).

Why Drink? Given these dramatic individual and societal costs, why do people drink, and what causes some drinkers to become alcoholics while others do not? A number of biological and psychological factors seem to be involved.

Beginning to drink is largely a social phenomenon involving peer pressure. The modeling of drinking behavior by parents is also a significant factor. And expectations may contribute to the decision to drink. A particularly powerful expectation held by a vast majority of people is that drinking reduces anxiety or tension. Although alcohol may help reduce tension, there is evidence that the expectation is more important than any actual pharmacological effects of the drug, and alcohol actually increases tension in some individuals (Martin, 2001). Along these same lines, many people believe that alcohol consumption can serve as a valid excuse for what would otherwise be socially inappropriate behavior. Studies, show, however, that such uninhibited behaviors can easily be avoided under the influence of alcohol if the person is rewarded for avoiding them (Enoch & Goldman, 2002).

Alcoholism. The most serious effects of alcohol are those associated with *alcoholism*—a disorder in which the individual consumes excessive amounts of ethyl alcohol and is unable to control his drinking. Alcoholism and alcohol abuse rank among the three most frequently diagnosed psychiatric disorders and affect nearly every organ in the body (Volpicelli, 2001). Because the alcoholic gets his calories by drinking, he eats very little and may suffer severe malnutrition, including a B-complex deficiency that can produce permanent brain damage (Mann et al., 2001; Thomson, 2000). In addition, he may develop cirrhosis of the liver, in which cells die, blood flow is impeded, inflammation occurs, and death may result (Schmidt et al., 2002). Other damage is often seen in the heart, pancreas, and endocrine glands (Haber et al., 2001; Spies et al., 2001). Overall, in fact, alcoholics have a mortality rate that is 5.6 times that of nonalcoholics and live an average of 19 years less (Spies et al., 2001; Ojesjo et al., 1998).

Alcoholics are found at all levels of society and in all walks of life. It has been estimated that at least 70 percent are salespersons, teachers, homemakers, physicians, and the like. Only a small proportion fit the stereotype of the homeless. Could you be on the way to alcoholism? Check Table 5-4. Like most psychological disorders, alcoholism has no one, simple cause. Rather, it is a product of multiple biological and psychosocial factors that work together to create an alcoholic (Jacob et al., 2001).

Biological factors. If you drink but believe you could never become alcoholic, consider this: There is a definite genetic predisposition toward alcoholism, and there is no way to be certain that you do not have it. Individuals who inherit this tendency have a much greater chance of becoming alcoholic than those who do not (Gianoulakis, 2001).

Both classic early studies and recent research demonstrate that alcoholic adoptees are significantly more likely to have biological than foster parents who are alcoholics (Goodwin et al., 1973; Allen et al., 2001), and the concordance (agreement) rate for alcoholism is 55 percent in identical twins as compared with 28 percent in same-sex fraternal twins (Buckland, 2002). More recent work confirms these findings for both men and women and shows that there may be a predisposing factor that is common to alcoholism and drug abuse (Mann et al., in Press). Finally, some specific genes linked to alcoholism have been identified (Schuckit, 2000). Neurochemical studies suggest that the genetic tendency may be expressed in neural structures containing receptors for dopamine, serotonin, and norepinephrine (Kranzler, 2000). It may take the form of a taste preference for alcohol or a physiologically based positive feeling that results from drinking (Brooks & Lipsky, 2000).

A second predisposing biological factor is alcohol consumption during fetal development. You can be predisposed if your mother drank even in small amounts during pregnancy (Alcohol Research and Health, 2000). But do women really abuse alcohol and other drugs during pregnancy? Unfortunately, they do. Indeed, almost a third of all women—31% of them (Mann et al., in Press)—drink and abuse other drugs while they are pregnant.

Psychological factors. Although alcoholism is partially a product of inheritance, psychological factors are also important in determining whether a person will actually start and continue to drink. Several major theories have hypothesized the influence of various kinds of psychological factors. Freud's *psychoanalytic* theory proposes that the alcoholic has a history of unsatisfied dependency needs—desires to be helped and cared for by others, including parents. These can stem from problems experienced even in the first year of life. The result is that alcoholics drink in order to satisfy their unmet needs and to have others care for them.

Behavioral theory suggests that drinkers may become alcoholics because alcohol reduces anxiety (Kushner et al., 1994). According to this *tension-reduction hypothesis*, everyone experiences some anxiety and guilt and searches for ways to alleviate these unpleasant emotions. Because alcohol is a central nervous system depressant, it can reduce tension somewhat, and the tension reduction is rewarding. When drinking is reinforced (rewarded), it is likely to be repeated. In this way, the use of alcohol for tension reduction can eventually lead to alcoholism. Behavioral theory is discussed more fully in Chapters 6 and 14.

Cognitive theory hypothesizes that certain kinds of thought processes may be directly involved in alcoholism. In particular, the pre-alcoholic may develop *expectancies* related to drinking, such as the idea we noted earlier that drinking will make him feel better by reducing his anxiety. These expectancies can become cognitive motivations for drinking and hence be a causal factor in alcoholism. Cognition is the topic of Chapter 8.

Research has not yet determined that one of these theories is clearly more valid than the others. In fact, it is likely that the factors hypothesized in all three theories can contribute to the development of alcoholism. What has been determined is that both family interaction patterns during childhood and a variety of factors and experiences in the larger society are important. It is more likely, for example, that alcoholism will occur in higher socioeconomic groups and in metropolitan areas. Personality factors are also involved. A report of the National Academy of Sciences (1983) concluded that impulsiveness, sensation seeking and antisocial personality are often associated with alcohol and drug abuse. And cultural factors can be important. One expert notes, for example, that findings regarding alcoholism in one tribe of Native Americans may not validly apply to another tribe (Westermeyer, 2001).

Other Psychoactive Drugs

Alcohol, although clearly dangerous, is a legal drug for those over state minimum ages. Most other drugs of abuse are illegal and undeniably dangerous, causing both short- and long-term psychological and physiological problems and sometimes death (Amano et al., 2002). Yet over 50% of both high school and college students report at least some experience with illicit drugs, and 20 million people reported heavily using and abusing these drugs in 1994 (NIDA, 1995). In fact, 27% of all Americans abuse drugs at some time in their lives, and drug use and abuse appears to be more likely when a person is under stress (Sinha, 2001). As Figure 5-14a shows, illicit drug use decreased somewhat between 1985 and 1992, but is now rapidly increasing (NIDA, 1995; SAMSHA, 1995). The relative levels of use of the various drugs, topped by alcohol and marijuana, is shown in Figure 5-14b.

While we will focus primarily on illegal drugs, it is worth noting that many perfectly legal substances can also produce altered states of consciousness. Many common medications, including both prescription and over-the-counter drugs, can cause you to feel drowsy, highly aroused, or "spaced out." The difference is that these drugs are legal (when properly prescribed and used), have usually been shown to have beneficial effects, and are typically quite safe when used strictly according to instructions.

Drug abuse and the crime it brings with it are clearly among the major social problems in the United States today (Gordon, 2002). The National Crime Index shows that drug abuse violations increased 54.5 percent between 1978 and 1987. This increment is at least partially responsible for an increase of 25.3 percent in violent crimes and 15.9 percent in property crimes in recent years (Blanc et al., 1994). These statistics are reflected in our common daily experience, making crime the "number one domestic issue" in public opinion polls and leading to the passage of the $30 billion crime bill in 1994. Recognizing the central role of drugs in crime, the bill committed several billions of those dollars to drug prevention and treatment (Rawson & Obert, 2002). Abuse also contributes to suicide, heart disease, stroke, brain damage and workplace inefficiency (Bush & Autry, 2002; Rowan, 2001; Neiman et al., 2000).

Drugs that alter consciousness and thereby affect the psychological functioning of the individual are referred to as *psychoactive drugs*. When taken over time, most of these drugs can produce *tolerance*, in which continued use of the drug causes the body to adapt to it, such that ever increasing doses are required to produce the desired effect. Some psychoactive drugs can also produce physiological dependence, or *addiction*, in which biochemical functioning is altered in such a way that the body needs the drug in order to function "normally." Withholding the drug from an addicted individual will result in *withdrawal symptoms*, which may include severe physiological and psychological disturbances as the body attempts to adapt to the absence of the drug. In addition, most psychoactive drugs can produce *psychological dependence*, in which the individual comes to need the drug to maintain a comfortable level of emotional functioning.

Psychological dependence is an extremely common form of addiction to which some people are particularly prone. Louis Lasagna (1986) relates an interesting case study of a woman in her forties who was given a new tranquilizer to reduce her severe anxiety. She was initially very satisfied with this treatment, but she seemed to gradually develop tolerance and therefore increased her dosage over time to 12 and eventually 25 tablets per day. Interestingly enough, the "tranquilizer" she was taking was actually a *placebo*, a completely inert substance that was not really a drug at all. Some people will abuse *anything*, even a placebo!

The causes of drug abuse are both genetic and environmental. The Harvard Twin Study and others have shown that there is a broad genetic factor that makes the individual prone to drug abuse and also drug-specific genetic predispositions that contribute to the preference for a given drug (Tsuang et al., 2001; Kuhar et al., 2001). In addition, such environmental factors as parents, peers, cultural norms, and early childhood stress, as well as current stress, significantly influence the likelihood that a given individual will abuse drugs (Gordon, 2002; Heath, 2001)

Unfortunately, recreational drugs are not placebos. They really do alter consciousness, as Figure 5-15 shows, and they often have serious negative consequences for both the individual and the society, causing 20,000 deaths in 1994 (SAMSHA, 1995). Since they are so widely abused and of such great concern in our society, we will consider each of the several major classes of psychoactive drugs, including depressants, stimulants, hallucinogens, marijuana, and opiates (Table 5-5).

Depressants. Drugs that inhibit or depress the activity of the central nervous system are called *depressants*. Alcohol, which we have discussed separately, is a depressant, as are a number of other drugs often referred to as sedatives. While small doses of these drugs can produce sleep, larger doses can have severe negative effects on thought processes, memory, speech functions and coordination. An overdose can lead to unconsciousness and even death. The most widely used of the depressants, other than alcohol, are the *barbiturates*, including phenobarbital, amobarbital, seconal, and nembutal. Commonly referred to as "downers," they have great potential for physiological dependence, and withdrawal produces a severe, life-threatening illness.

Even when used in small doses, the barbiturates make patients sleepy during the day and typically lose their effectiveness after short periods of use. Moreover, they reduce the amount of REM sleep and interfere with normal sleep patterns. Finally, they are associated with 12% of all suicides, and when the suicide is committed by overdosing, barbiturates are used about one-third of the time (Mendelson & Rich, 1993).

Stimulants. Stimulants are drugs that speed up body activities, often increasing heart rate, blood pressure, and other aspects of physiology. Psychologically, these drugs can provide a "lift," ranging from heightened wakefulness to feelings of power and invulnerability. The most commonly used stimulants are nicotine (Chapter 15), caffeine, amphetamines, and cocaine.

As I sit writing this chapter, I am using a (perfectly legal) stimulant. The drug is, of course, *caffeine*, a powerful stimulant present in the coffee I made before starting to write. Virtually everyone uses caffeine in one form or another. It is found in tea, soft drinks, chocolate, many over-the-counter medicines, and, of course, coffee. It reduces drowsiness and feelings of fatigue, promotes clearer thinking, reduces reaction times, and increases levels of physiological arousal.

Although small amounts of caffeine seem to do little harm, large amounts (e.g., ten cups of coffee per day) can have negative physiological and psychological effects. For example, *caffeinism* is a psychological syndrome that initially appears to be much like an anxiety disorder (see Chapter 16). The person is extremely anxious and upset much of the time and may experience a variety of physiological symptoms, such as heart palpitations. High caffeine consumption is also associated with significantly lower grade point averages in college students and with increased tension, sleep disturbances, and problems with intellectual functioning. Long_term consumption of large amounts of caffeine has been linked in some studies to such serious disorders as heart disease, though the findings are mixed (Smith et al., in Press).

Methamphetamines, popularly known as bennies, speed, or uppers, are far more powerful stimulants than caffeine and are strictly illegal, yet their abuse has reached epidemic proportions (Rawson et al., 2002). Originally prescribed as diet pills and sold under such names as Dexedrine, Methedrine, and Benzedrine, these drugs are often used and abused by people who want to stay awake and alert for long periods.

The currently popular drug is methamphetamine hydrochloride or "Ice" can be injected, smoked, or snorted. It can permanently alter brain biochemistry and is often neurotoxic (Cho & Melega, 2002). Amphetamines quickly build tolerance, and small doses become insufficient to achieve the desired effect. As a result, the user increases the dose. Psychological dependence then develops, and she may switch from taking pills to mainlining (injecting) the drug, producing a "rush" of euphoria. The abuser may continue to inject large doses every time the effects begin to wear off, staying awake for several days at a time before crashing and sleeping, only to awaken and repeat the cycle.

Among the negative effects of large doses is an increase in risk-taking behavior. Users are likely to share needles and neglect to use condoms during intercourse. They also suffer hallucinations and delusions, and prolonged use of amphetamines can induce permanent psychotic states. Physiological effects include degeneration in some areas of the brain, elevated blood pressure, heart failure, and death (Forrest et al., 1994).

Cocaine, also a stimulant, was used by no lesser a light than Sigmund Freud, who entitled an 1884 article on cocaine "Song of Praise." He had used the drug to fight a bout of depression and found that it greatly lifted his spirits. A year later another famous institution, the Coca-Cola company, introduced Coke it actually contained cocaine. But Freud soon gave the drug up, recognizing its negative effects, and "coke" was also removed from Coke.

Cocaine is a white, crystalline powder derived from the leaves of the coca plant. Historically, it was used by the Indian people of Peru in religious ceremonies, and coca leaves are regularly chewed by Andean Indians in South America today. The drug is also abused by 1.8 million Americans, 70% of whom are male (Quinones-Jenab et al., 2001). Most cocaine abuse in earlier years involved inhaling or injecting the drug to achieve a highly energetic, euphoric state in which the user often feels that she can take on the world. Many abusers now smoke *crack*, the highly concentrated pellets of cocaine that result from the chemical process called "freebasing." This most potent form of cocaine provides an instant, short-lived high and is extremely addictive.

In 1986, Len Bias, a basketball player here at the University of Maryland, where this is being written, died of a heart attack after using cocaine. His case was one of an increasing number of cardiac deaths that have been directly attributed to cocaine use in apparently healthy individuals (Dackis & O'Brien, 2001; Woods et al., 1994). Cocaine use rose rapidly during the 1970s and again in 1986, when it reached 12.7% of the population, decreasing to 3.1% in 1992 and 3.6% in 1994 (SAMSHA, 1995). The number who had used the drug within the previous month increased from 1.6% in 1977 to 5.8% in 1985, then dropped again to 1.5% in 1994.

Even when cocaine doesn't kill, it often has other adverse effects. In fact, over 50% of users report significant problems related to cocaine abuse (SAMSHA, 1995). Callers to a national telephone help line, 1-800-COCAINE, have reported a wide variety of negative—sometimes devastating—effects. Among the psychological effects are chronic anxiety, depression, irritability, lack of motivation, and absence of sex drive. Many males cannot perform sexually at all on cocaine. The most commonly reported physical effects are sleeplessness, chronic fatigue, headaches, and nasal bleeding. Some users also report seizures. The drug can also damage the fetus during pregnancy, causing later cognitive, emotional, and motor symptoms in the child (Frank et al., 2001).

If cocaine produces such severe adverse effects, why is it so widely used? The answer is that it can initially produce pleasurable effects. Users of multiple drugs often report that cocaine produces the "best" effects, including euphoria and a sense of excitement. Cocaine is also highly addictive. Some users become addicted after trying the drug only once, and the often severe withdrawal symptoms can include depression, chills, nausea, and sleep disturbances. Current research suggests that the rapid, powerful addiction develops because cocaine directly affects reward centers in the brain (Uhl et al., 2002). The hypothalamus, pituitary gland, and adrenal glands are among the systems affected and contribute to the "rewarding" experience of ingesting cocaine (Goeders, 2002). Many users also become psychologically dependent on cocaine and report that they simply have to have it either to do their most effective work or to enjoy their social lives or both.

Hallucinogens. The powerful *hallucinogens* are drugs that cause people to have hallucinations. They first gained international popularity following 1943, the year in which Albert Holmann, working at Sandoz Pharmaceuticals in Basel, Switzerland, accidentally—and later purposely—ingested a small quantity of a drug called lysergic acid diethylamide or LSD. By the 1960s, LSD was in widespread use as a recreational drug, and cases of adverse reactions to this powerful hallucinogen began to mount. A 16-year-old on the drug drove a knife into the heart of another student who accidently bumped into him at a high school dance; and a Brooklyn medical student stabbed his mother-in-law to death—both typical incidents. In the early 1970s LSD usage began to decrease nationally, but it has been rising rapidly in whites and African-Americans since 1985 (NIDA, 1995; Figure 5-16). About 14% of young adults had tried LSD as of 1994, and about 5% were using it at least annually (NIDA, 1995).

Many hallucinogens are derived from organic substances. Mescaline comes from the peyote cactus, and psilocybin is a derivative of mushrooms. LSD is obtained by processing an ergot fungus, which is a wheat disease. It is the most potent psychoactive drug: a nearly microscopic 50 micrograms can produce a 10 to 15_hour "trip." The trip typically begins with visual hallucinations and extreme mood swings. Next come perceptual distortions _ small objects appear large, sounds seem louder. Judgment is severely impaired, and users may experience panic attacks or severe depression.

LSD is commonly associated with the development of psychopathology that lasts for years after the drug is stopped. Flashbacks to LSD experiences are common, as are panic attacks and lengthy or permanent psychotic disorders.

Phencyclidine (PCP) is a powerful drug that cannot be readily classified as a depressant, stimulant, or hallucinogen, since it may have the effects of any of these drug categories, depending on the individual and the dosage. It can be injected, snorted, swallowed, or smoked. The immediate effects of PCP, commonly referred to as "angel dust," are mixed. They range from hypersensitivity to stimuli, giddy feelings, and numbness at low doses to generalized anesthesia, convulsions, coma, dramatic elevations in blood pressure, respiratory depression, and death at high doses.

Long-term use of PCP can produce significant chronic symptoms. Neurologlcal problems, including memory lapses, speech anomalies, and visual disturbances, have been reported, and over half of chronic users show impairment on neurological tests. Behavioral problems associated with chronic use include anxiety, depression, states of confusion, violence, and PCP psychosis, a disorder with symptoms similar to those of schizophrenia (see Chapter 16; Gillet et al., 2001).

Marijuana. The most commonly used of illegal psychoactive substances is cannabis or *marijuana.* A continuing rise in use peaked in 1980 at nearly 60% of high school seniors, then declined every year through 1992, when 33% reported having tried it. Unfortunately, usage has been rising sharply since that time (NIDA, 1995; Figure 5-17). Similarly, where 11% of seniors (1 in every 9) used marijuana daily in 1979, only 1.9% reported daily use in 1992, rising to 3.6% in 1994 (NIDA, 1995). Studies of minority groups show higher usage levels, longer usage histories, and more drug-related problems in African Americans than in Hispanics (NIDA, 1995).

When marijuana is smoked, it enters the bloodstream rapidly. Its effects typically begin within about 15 minutes and last up to 4 hours or so. The psychological effects depend on dosage, mood state, expectations, and social setting. In general, they range from a light-headed, giddy state of relaxation at low doses to anxiety, panic, hallucinations, and irrational behavior at higher doses. Perception is distorted, time and space expand, motor reflexes are impaired, and appetite is increased. In addition, 47% of users report significant problems related to the drug (SAMSHA, 1995), and marijuana intoxication is associated with a higher incidence of automobile accidents.

Chronic effects have also been observed. Marijuana is associated with abnormal menstrual cycles, and the incidence of fetal death is four times higher in nonusers. Pregnant users also endanger the physiological stability of the baby and increase the likelihood of birth defects, and decrease its cognitive functioning (Fried & Smith, 2001). In addition, the drug may cause brain damage, psychosis, lung damage, and weight gain (Tashkin, 2001; Nunez & Gurpegui, 2002). It has also been associated with homicide and may lead to the use of more damaging intravenous drugs (Spunt et al., 1994). And marijuana use is a causal factor in cancers of the lung, digestive system, brain, and neck (Carriot & Sasco, 2000). On a more positive note, it is often argued that marijuana may have medical applications in dealing with pain and nausea. However, the evidence is very weak, and there are safer drugs that serve these purposes better (Balint, 2001).

Opiates. Often referred to more loosely as narcotics (from the Greek word for "numbness"), opiates are capable of producing the strongest forms of physiological addiction. True *opiates* are derived from the opium poppy. Chemically similar drugs made synthetically are called *opioids.* The opiates include opium and morphine, but the primary street drug is heroin, a more concentrated and powerful form of morphine. When first used in small doses, heroin produces a state of euphoria that addicts say is comparable in intensity to orgasm. While abuse of narcotics begins in a social context under peer pressure, there is also a genetic tendency to underproduce the pain-killing endorphins that may contribute to addiction in some individuals.

Heroin and other narcotics cause drowsiness, loss of appetite, depression, constipation, and constricted pupils. With continued used, tolerance develops, dosages must be increased, and the addict begins to use the drug more to avoid such withdrawal symptoms as severe pain and nausea than to achieve pleasure.

The Neurophysiology of Consciousness

Among the most important challenges for 21st-century neuroscience is the discovery of just how the brain controls states of consciousness and the patterns of behavior associated with them. What neural mechanisms put us to sleep and wake us up? What happens when a dream occurs? Do unique brain states characterize meditation, relaxation, and the hypnotic trance? We don't yet know the answers to these questions, but neuroscientists have already begun the research that will provide them.

We know that all states of consciousness involve complex, diverse mechanisms throughout the brain and that circadian rhythm is control by specialized brain circuits (Aston-Jones, 2001; Cote et al., 2001). However, certain structures and certain neurotransmitters appear crucial to the maintenance of waking states and are subject to the factors that produce altered states. Let's turn to the neurophysiology of the waking..

The Waking State

A major structure in the maintenance of the waking state is the *reticular activating system* (RAS), shown in Figure 5-18 (see Chapter 3). It has long been recognized as the principal arousal system of the brain, receiving and integrating

input from the various senses, as well as the cortex, and maintaining the arousal level characteristic of waking states. Lesions in the RAS produce a state of continuous sleep, although wakefulness may return under certain circumstances, suggesting that additional brain areas are involved.

The other major mechanisms of waking consciousness are the posterior nucleus of the hypothalamus and the prefrontal cortex (Salin-Pascual et al., 2001). Lesions of the posterior hypothalamus produce continuous sleep in cats. Interestingly enough, fairly normal EEG sleep/waking cycles are maintained in these cats, although the animals appear to be in a state of sound sleep at all times and cannot be aroused. Integrative activity relating to wakefulness appears to take place in the prefrontal cortex (Stephan et al., 2002), and new theories showing how the brain more generally deals with consciousness are emerging (LaBerge, 2001). Among these is the idea that *microtubles*, which are components of specialized proteins called *tubulins*, may store and process information that the brain uses to form its integrative sense of consciousness (Hameroff et al., 2002). In addition, recently discovered peptides, called *hypocretins*, appear central to the production and maintenance of waking states (Espana et al., 2001).

Sleep and Dreaming

Not surprisingly, different mechanisms control NREM and REM sleep. It appears that NREM sleep involves three principal areas of the brain: the anterior hypothalamus, which is critical in the induction and maintenance of sleep states; the basal forebrain, which, when lesioned, virtually eliminates NREM sleep; and the Raphe nucleus of the pons (Figure 5-18; Nofzinger et al., 2002). Cells in this nucleus show high concentrations of the neurotransmitter serotonin, and it is hypothesized that this important chemical is crucial to the initiation and maintenance of NREM sleep states. More recent research suggests that other substances, particularly uridine, are also involved (Kimura, et al., 2001).

The primary subcortical mechanism involved in REM sleep is the small area of the pons called the locus coeruleus (Figure 5-18). Lesions of this structure decrease the occurrence of REM sleep patterns. Norepinephrine, the principal neurotransmitter associated with the locus coeruleus, also appears to be centrally important. Finally, there is some evidence that dreaming is mediated predominantly by the cortex of the right hemisphere of the brain (Serafetinides, 1993) and that neural networks are involved. The latter are sets of neurons linked by connecting fibers that provide feedback when nerve cells in the set are stimulated. The neural network may supply the selective memories found in dreams. We have more to say about *neural networks* in Chapter 7.

How do the mechanisms of REM and NREM sleep interact? The best neurological explanation to date is that the Raphe system initiates NREM sleep by inhibiting the action of the RAS with serotonin. The locus coeruleus, at least in part through the action of norepinephrine, then inhibits the Raphe system, thereby releasing inhibition of parts of the RAS and causing the onset of REM sleep. The alternating periods of REM and NREM sleep that characterize the normal sleep cycle can thus be seen as the result of fluctuating relative levels of serotonin and norepinephrine in the Raphe and locus coeruleus systems.

The Sleep-Waking Cycle

What causes us to cycle between sleeping and waking states on a daily schedule? The best answer to date lies in the biological clock mechanism governed by the suprachiasmic nucleus of the hypothalamus (Herzog & Schwartz, 2002; Figure 5-18). This structure operates in much the same way as a 24-hour timer that turns lights on and off when you are away from home. In this case, however, the timer is set to turn on one light (the waking state) for a number of hours, then turn that light off and turn on another light (the sleeping state) for several more hours, maintaining this cycle (with some obvious variations) throughout life.

There are also significant genetic and neurochemical substrates for sleeping and waking states (Brown & Schibler, 2001; Harmer et al., 2001). Certain peptides, similar to the endorphins (see Chapter 3), appear to be natural sleep-inducing "drugs." The neurotransmitter serotonin also helps in achieving sleep states, and both dopamine and norepinephrine are important to activity and alertness in the sleep-waking cycle. Finally, many scientists hypothesize that acetylcholine may have the most important neurochemical role of all in states of consciousness. It may initiate and maintain REM sleep and thus be somehow involved in dreaming. It may be cholinergic neurons—those involving acetylcholine—in the pons and forebrain that are primary in maintaining consciousness.

Drug Effects

The many different neurotransmitters all act to carry nerve impulses across synapses (Chapter 3). Each neurotransmitter system is found in limited areas of the brain and acts to help control specific aspects of physical or psychological functioning. Most psychoactive drugs achieve their effects by interacting with specific neurotransmitters to enhance or block synaptic transmission.

Psychoactive drugs can enter the body in a variety of ways—by swallowing, smoking, or injecting them, among others—but they all end up in the bloodstream, which carries them to the brain. Like most fat-soluble substances, they pass

the blood-brain barrier to enter brain tissue. Beyond that point, the specific effects of a given drug depend on the neurotransmitter it interacts with, the ways in which it affects the transmitter or its receptors, and the functions normally performed by that transmitter.

Some drugs affect primarily the *presynaptic* neuron by facilitating or impairing the release of the neurotransmitter from the axon terminals. Amphetamine, for example, causes increased output of norepinephrine and dopamine to achieve its arousing effects (Figure 5-19b). Other drugs act by blocking the reuptake of a neurotransmitter after the synapse is completed. *Reuptake* is the process by which the neurotransmitter is reabsorbed into the axon terminals of the presynaptic neuron. When it is blocked, the effects of the transmitter are enhanced. Cocaine, for example, inhibits the reuptake of norepinephrine, thereby acting as a stimulant to increase arousal (Figure 5-19c and d). We might note that it also blocks the reuptake of epinephrine, dopamine and serotonin, providing an example of another important point about drugs: a single drug often affects more than one neurotransmitter.

Other drugs act by binding to receptors on the *postsynaptic* neuron. They can attach to these receptors—normally reserved for a particular neurotransmitter—because they are structurally similar to the transmitter. Think of a lock and a key: the receptor is like a lock, and its neurotransmitter is the key that fits and turns it. An *agonist* is a drug that also fits and turns the lock, thereby enhancing the effects of the normal brain chemical (Figure 5-20b). Nicotine, for example, is an acetylcholine agonist; it attaches to acetylcholine receptors and thereby increases arousal. Alternatively, an *antagonist* is a drug that attaches to a postsynaptic receptor but cannot produce the same effects as the neurotransmitter; it fits the lock but doesn't turn it (Figure 5-20c). This blocks the action of the transmitter because it cannot attach to the receptor while the drug is in its way. An example is LSD, a serotonin antagonist that is structurally similar to the natural neurotransmitter and hence fits the lock but fails to turn it, causing hallucinations. Notice that the same general effects can be achieved in different ways by different drugs. Amphetamine, cocaine, and nicotine are all stimulants. Cocaine achieves this effect by blocking norepinephrine reuptake and amphetamine by increasing its output. Nicotine does it by enhancing the output of a different transmitter, acetylcholine.

Other drugs also achieve their effects by acting on neurochemical systems in various parts of the brain. Alcohol, barbiturates, and other sedatives depress activities in a number of neural structures, including the reticular activating system. The opiate drugs act on special receptors in the central nervous system that exist to receive the body's natural pain killers, the endorphins. And marijuana may achieve at least some of its effects by blocking the activity of the hippocampus, the limbic structure that is involved in the control of some aspects of emotional functioning and memory.

Most of this knowledge of the neural mechanisms underlying states of consciousness is very preliminary. It represents just one step along a lengthy path to full understanding. However, once we gradually achieve that understanding, we will reap not only scientific, but also practical benefits. We will learn how better to help people sleep, how to safely maintain states of alert wakefulness, and what dreams really represent. We will be able to diagnose and treat insomnia, narcolepsy, and the other sleep disorders more effectively. And we may be able to directly treat drug dependencies by correcting the affected neurotransmitters. Indeed, research in the 21st century should provide much better answers than we now have to virtually every question we have raised about the basis for human consciousness.

Other Altered States

The neurological mechanisms involved in the remaining altered states of consciousness are poorly understood. During hypnosis, the hypothalamus, reticular system, and other subcortical centers apparently become dominant and inhibit the functioning of higher brain centers in the cortex. Hallucinations appear to involve the frontal lobes, the thalamus, and the temporal lobes. But beyond these generalities, a clear understanding of the mechanisms underlying these and other altered states awaits future research.

Conclusion

In the short space of one chapter, we have trekked through the vast, relatively uncharted reaches of human consciousness in all its varied states. Our journey has taken us from the glaring sunshine of total awareness to the very shadows of our minds. We know something now about how we stay awake and asleep, how we dream and daydream, and how very delicate our normal waking consciousness really is. And we can now ask—and each answer for ourselves—ßwhether the personal consciousness of the individual is merely a product of a complex neurobiological process or whether, perhaps, it is something more, something unique to each and every person.

Summary

The Nature of Consciousness

1. Thoughts typically flow in a continuing stream of consciousness. You can examine your own consciousness through introspection.

2. Consciousness can be conceptualized as a continuum ranging from deeply unconscious states to alert wakefulness. Normal waking consciousness occurs in two major modes: active and passive.

3. Consciousness can be seen as an adaptively evolved function of the brain and behavior.

4. Four major features of consciousness are focus, structure, attributes, and flow. Determinants of conscious experience include both internal and external factors.

5. Selective attention focuses consciousness and is influenced by a variety of internal and external factors.

"To Sleep, Perchance to Dream"

1. There are four stages and two main types of sleep, REM sleep and NREM sleep. REM involves rapid eye movements and an EEG pattern similar to that of the waking state. NREM and REM periods alternate in a sleep cycle. REM sleep may be important in neural development, memory, or both.

2. The daily, or circadian, rhythm includes a 25-hour sleep-wake cycle.

3. Sleep problems and disorders include insomnia, narcolepsy, and sleep apnea.

4. Everyone dreams. REM dreams are more vivid and better organized, but some dreaming also occurs during NREM periods.

5. Freud hypothesized that dreams provide an essential outlet for intense, dangerous impulses. The activation_synthesis hypothesis says dreams are an important side effect of rhythmic neurological activity. Cartwright's cognitive theory holds that dreams involve problem-solving activities.

6. Special dream states include lucid dreams, out-of-body dreams, night terrors, nightmares and sleepwalking.

More States: Dreaming, Meditation, Relaxation, and Hypnosis

1. Virtually everyone daydreams, and Singer identifies three patterns of daydreaming.

2. There are two main types of meditation: concentrative and opening up. The physiological changes that occur with meditation are similar to those of relaxation, as are the psychological and physical benefits.

3. People vary in their susceptibility to hypnotic induction.

4. Theories of hypnosis include neodissociation theory, role playing, and suggestibility.

6. Many of the widely cited accomplishments of hypnosis are not unique to the hypnotic state, and hypnosis may not be a unique state.

Alcohol and Other Psychoactive Drugs

1. Alcoholism causes damage to The brain, liver, heart, and other organs and shortens life. Biological factors include a genetic predisposition and drinking during pregnancy.

2. Psychological theories of alcoholism include psychoanalytic, behavioral, and cognitive approaches.

3. Psychoactive drugs can produce dependence and tolerance.

4. Depressants included the barbiturates—highly addictive prescription sedatives.

5. Stimulants speed up body activities and include caffeine, amphetamines, and cocaine.

6. Hallucinogens include LSD, mescaline, and psilocybin, and PCP. There is considerable controversy over marijuana's detrimental effects.

7. Opiates are derived from the opium poppy and are extremely addictive.

The Neurophysiology of Consciousness

1. The RAS is central to the waking state. Other structures include the posterior nucleus of the hypothalamus and the prefrontal cortex.
2. NREM sleep is controlled by the anterior hypothalamus, basal forebrain, and Raphe nucleus.
3. REM sleep is a function of the locus coeruleus.
4. The sleep-waking cycle involves the suprachiasmic nucleus of the hypothalamus.
5. Some drugs act on the presynaptic neuron to facilitate or inhibit neurotransmitter release, others affect reuptake after the synapse occurs. Still others act as agonists or antagonists at the postsynaptic receptor.

Ask Yourself

1. How can knowledge of the various modes and features of consciousness help us in studying the ways in which states of consciousness affect behavior?
2. What do sleep deprivation studies tell us about the functions of sleep?
3. What appear to be the major functions of dreams, and what is the evidence for these functions?
4. What does research suggest concerning the similarities and differences between states of deep meditation and states achieved through systematic relaxation?
5. What appears to be the relationship between hypnosis and the normal, waking state as far as what can be accomplished in each state?
6. Discuss the major problems that can be created by each of the principal classes of drugs.
7. What would you tell your own 12_year_old child about marijuana use? What are the risks and benefits?
8. Discuss the neurophysiological bases for sleep. What are the major brain structures and biochemicals involved?

Further Readings

Cohen, D.B. *Sleep and Dreaming: Origins, Nature, and Functions.* Oxford: Pergamon Press, 1979. The author presents an in_depth treatment of most aspects of sleep, including the physiological and psychological aspects of REM and NREM sleep, as well as results of research on dream content and recall.

Dement, W.C. *Some Must Watch While Some Must Sleep.* San Francisco: San Francisco Book Company, 1976. One of the pioneers in sleep research provides a readable description of the discoveries about sleep and dreaming he and his colleagues made.

Farthing, W. (1992). *The psychology of consciousness.* Englewood Cliffs: Prentice-Hall. The author provides a book-length treatment of the topics we have covered in this chapter. If you are fascinated by states of consciousness, Farthing is a good choice for further reading.

Ford, K., & Norris, A. (1994). Urban minority youth: alcohol and marijuana use and exposure to unprotected intercourse. *J. of Acquired Immune Deficiency Syndrome,* 7, 389-396. An added danger of alcohol and marijuana use is that it may increase the likelihood of intercourse without condoms and hence of contracting AIDS, as this study of minority youth shows.

Johnson, F.H. *The Anatomy of Hallucinations.* Chicago: Nelson_Hall, 1978. This book deals with the history of hallucinations and with the various theories and types of research that have been carried out.

Kendler, K.S., Neale, M.C., Heath, A.C., Kessler, R.C., & Eaves, L.J. (1994). A twin-family study of alcoholism in women. *Amer. J. Psychiat.,* 151, 707-715. One of the major contributors to literature in behavior genetics, Kendler reports a study showing that alcoholism in women has a partially genetic basis.

Leung, A.K., & Robson, W.L. (1993). Nightmares. *J. of the National Medical Association*, 85, 233-235. This interesting article reviews what we know about nightmares, particularly in children, and what we can do about them.

Levitt, F. *Drugs and Behavior.* New York: Wiley, 1982. This work provides an excellent overview of all major classes of drugs that affect behavior. It deals with drug actions, dangers, and possible benefits, plus the use of drugs in connection with psychotherapy.

Singer, J.L. (1993). Experimental studies of ongoing conscious experience. *Ciba Foundation Symposium*, 174, 100-116. One of the major figures in this field, Jerome Singer explains how research on consciousness is done.

Key Terms

activation_synthesis hypothesis
active consciousness
addiction
alcoholism
altered states
amphetamines
anxiety dream
Barbiturates
biological rhythms
caffeinism
circadian rhythm
cocaine
consciousness
daydreaming
depressants
hallucination
hallucinogens
hypersomnia
hypnagogic state
hypnosis
insomnia
introspection
latent content
lucid dream
manifest content
marijuana
meditation
mesmerism
narcolepsy
narcotics
night terror
nightmare
non_REM sleep
nonconscious
out_of_body experience
paradoxical sleep
passive consciousness
phencyclidine (PCP)
psychoactive drugs
psychological dependence
REM sleep
repression
reticular activating system (RAS)
selective attention

sleep apnea
stimulant
stream of consciousness
tolerance
Unconscious
withdrawal symptoms

Key People

Eugene Aserinsky
Theodore X. Barber
Rosalind Dymond
Sigmund Freud
Ernest Hilgard
Alan Hobson
Nathaniel Kleitman
Robert McCarley
Anton Mesmer
Martin Orne

Consciousness in the 21st Century

Hallucinations

One of the most fascinating of the altered states of consciousness is the *hallucination*—a perception that occurs in the absence of any actual stimulus. The person is literally seeing things—a hairy monster that's not actually there—or hearing things—a voice when no one has spoken. And there are tactile, olfactory, and gustatory hallucinations as well. Most hallucinations are vivid and seem very real to the person experiencing them. Consider the description given by William James of the hallucinatory experience of a friend who had been working at his desk late at night:

> *About eleven o'clock, as I sat there buried in sines, cosines, tangents, cotangents, secants, and cosecants, I felt very distinctly upon my left shoulder a touch, and a slight shake, as if somebody had tried to attract my attention by other means and had failed. Without rising I turned my head, and there between me and the door stood my wife, dressed exactly as I last saw her, some five weeks before. As I turned she said: "It is a little Herman; he has come." Something more was said, but this is the only sentence I can recall. To make sure that I was not asleep and dreaming, I rose from the chair, pinched myself and walked toward the figure, which disappeared immediately as I rose. I can give no information as to the length of time occupied by this episode, but I know I was awake, in my usual good health. The touch was very distinct, the figure was absolutely perfect, stood about three feet from the door, which was closed, and had not been opened during the evening. The sound of the voice was unmistakable, and I should have recognized it as my wife's voice even if I had not turned and had not seen the figure at all. The tone was conversational, just as she would have said the same words had she been actually standing there. (James, 1890, p. 119)*

It is difficult not to be struck by the convincing quality of the hallucination. James' friend was clearly certain, for a few minutes, that his wife had entered the room and spoken to him.

People have known about hallucinations for centuries, but it is only relatively recently that scientists have begun to systematically study their nature and causes. Hallucinations have most commonly been studied as a frequent symptom of certain psychological disorders, especially schizophrenia—a severe disorder in which the person loses normal contact with reality, is unable to think clearly, and displays other serious symptoms as well (Chapter 16). One study showed that 94 percent of chronic schizophrenics hear nonexistent voices (Goodwin, Alderson, and Rosenthal, 1971), and other research confirms this finding (Johns & van Os, 2001). However, hallucinations are not limited to schizophrenics. They are also fairly common in Alzheimer's disease and occur as well under conditions of migraine headache, sensory deprivation, high fever, and the use of such drugs as LSD, peyote, and alcohol (Bailbe et al., 2002). Accidental ingestion of jimson weed, a plant containing powerful, poisonous hallucinogens, has also produced hallucinations in Texas, New York, and California in recent times. Even more interesting is the fact that perfectly normal people sometimes experience hallucinations even without drugs. Long-distance runners, truck drivers alone on monotonous highways, isolated explorers like Admiral Byrd, and several Apollo astronauts have reported brief hallucinations, including flashes of light, huge animals, cars, and floating colors. Overall, the rate of hallucination in the general population is about 20 per 1000 men per year and 13 per 1000 women per year (Johns et al., 2002).

Some religions and some cultures encourage and openly reward hallucinations, which are consequently more common among these groups. Anthropologists report, for example, that many normal Malaysians experience *latah*, a state of mind in which hallucinations are common. Latah may occur under stress, but it also appears quite frequently under normal circumstances.

Ronald Siegel (1985), who has conducted a number of investigations of hallucinatory experiences, points out that hallucinations need not be imbued with any mysterious qualities. Like other psychological phenomena, they can and should be subjected to scientific investigation. Siegel and others have carried out such investigations and find that hallucinations display some remarkably consistent characteristics. In particular, most are characterized by geometric forms, including lines, curves, webs, lattices, tunnels, and spirals. There are also consistent patterns of color, especially black, violet, and blue, and a variety of movement patterns, including vertical, horizontal, and concentric. It might occur to you that many of these elements were also present in Seana's night terror—cobwebs, lattices, tunnels, the black of night—suggesting that hallucinations are qualitatively similar to some other altered states of consciousness.

Siegel and others conclude that there are straightforward, scientific explanations for the occurrence of hallucinations (Siegel, 1992). The consistency of their characteristics suggests a common neurological origin. In particular, there is some evidence that they may represent sensations arising from neural discharge activity in visual or auditory receptors and corresponding centers in the brain. The hallucinations that sometimes accompany migraine headaches, for example, probably result from electrical excitation of cell groups in the occipital (visual) cortex, and some studies have shown that direct electrical stimulation during neurosurgery can produce geometric forms and colored lights similar to those frequently seen in hallucinations.

Studies of hallucinatory phenomena will clearly continue well into the next century. As they do, they will not only tell us more about the nature and causes of this altered state, but also provide better treatments for patients chronically experiencing it. In addition, the study of hallucinations in the 21st century will help us to better understand the functioning of the human brain and its role in behavior.

Application

Probe

Sleeping Better

The average college student today sleeps one hour less than he did twenty years ago, and up to 74.5% of adolescents need more sleep than they are getting. Perhaps some scientifically based information on how to sleep better would be helpful. Fortunately, sleep research has yielded not only a technical knowledge of the sleep process but also some very practical information on how to sleep better. The following list of sleep hints was compiled by P. Hauri (1977) and is also consistent with more recent research:

1. Sleep as much as you need to feel refreshed and healthy during the following day, but not more. Curtail time in bed a bit to solidify sleep; excessively long times in bed seem related to fragmented and shallow sleep.

2. A regular rising time in the morning strengthens circadian cycling and makes it easier to fall asleep at a regular time each night.

3. A steady daily amount of exercise deepens sleep over the long run, but occasional one_shot exercise does not directly influence sleep during the following night.

4. Occasional loud noises (for example, aircraft flyovers) disturb sleep even in people who do not awaken. Soundproofing the bedroom is advisable for people who have to sleep close to excessive noise.

5. Although an excessively warm room disturbs sleep, there is no evidence that an excessively cold room solidifies sleep, as has been claimed.

6. Hunger may disturb sleep. A light bedtime snack (especially warm milk or a similar drink) seems to help many individuals sleep.

7. An occasional sleeping pill may be of some benefit, but the chronic use of hypnotics is ineffective at most and detrimental in some insomniacs.

8. Caffeine in the evening disturbs sleep, even in people who do not feel it does.
9. Alcohol helps tense people to fall asleep fast, but the ensuing sleep is then fragmented.
10. Rather than trying harder and harder when you are having difficulty falling asleep, switch on the light and do something else for a while.

Thinking Critically

Probe 2

How Unique Is the Hypnotic State?

There is little doubt that a hypnotist can put a participant into a trance in which she appears to be in a different state of consciousness— neither awake nor asleep in the usual sense. Moreover, she is typically attentive to the hypnotist's voice and will often carry out his wishes. There remains, however, the question of what unique accomplishments are possible under the influence of the hypnosis.

The Basic Hypothesis or Contention

Advocates of hypnosis have long contended that the hypnotic trance is a unique state of consciousness that makes possible a number of feats that could never be accomplished in a normal, waking state. Participants can, they say, remember better, be regressed (taken back in time) to an earlier age, and be made temporarily deaf or blind. Otherwise impossible muscular feats are easily accomplished. Eyewitnesses to crimes have much more vivid and accurate memories of the crime scene. And participants are so completely under the control of the hypnotist that they will do whatever he commands, even commit murder.

What Is The Evidence?

Scientific studies of the various claims about hypnosis have usually involved comparing the behaviors of hypnotized subjects (experimental groups) with those of waking subjects who are highly motivated to comply with the experimenter's suggestions (control groups). If the waking participants perform as well as those who are hypnotized, the claims are not valid.

What have researchers found? When it comes to muscular feats, such as remaining stiff as a board when suspended between two chairs, highly motivated waking participants perform as well as or better than hypnotized participants (Barber, 1969b). Similarly, no differences have been found in the performance of hypnotized and motivated participants on various learning tasks. What about the claim that subjects can be made hypnotically deaf or blind? Controlled studies show that participants told they are deaf actually do hear sounds but suppress their reactions (Barber et al., 1974). Similarly, subjects made hypnotically "blind" can see but may not react to visual stimuli.

Another claim is that hypnosis produces unique physiological states. In particular, it is said to modify brain functions, changing the dominant EEG frequency patterns in a unique way. Research does not support this contention (Raz & Shapiro, 2002). One interesting study was conducted on an epileptic patient at the University of Milan in Italy. She had EEG electrodes implanted deep within her brain, where recordings are better than those from surface electrodes on the skull. Hypnosis produced an increase in alpha and beta activity and a decrease in slower brain waves. However, investigators found that the very same changes could be induced in a waking state (DeBenedittis, 1986).

Yet another hypothesis is that memory is greatly improved under hypnosis. This contention quickly led to the widespread use of hypnosis in the criminal justice system. It is used to jog the memories of eyewitnesses to crimes and of others involved in criminal cases. Martin Reiser (1980) developed one widely use technique, in which the hypnotized witness is told that he is watching a video of a TV report of the crime. He can control the VCR, rewinding and replaying the scene as necessary, and he reports to the hypnotist what he is seeing. Jurors told that eyewitness memories were elicited under hypnosis are more likely to believe the memories are accurate. As we discuss in more detail in Chapter 7, however, evidence shows that hypnosis does not even slightly enhance the accuracy of recall (Loftus, 1993). Both waking and hypnotic recall tend to be highly inaccurate. In fact, the issue became so important and controversial that the Council on Scientific Affairs of the American Medical Association established a panel chaired by Martin Orne to review the evidence. The AMA group concluded that recollections produced under hypnosis are too inaccurate to serve as valid evidence in court (AMA, 1986).

Now we come to the most dramatic claim of all: Hypnotized subjects can be induced to commit murder, engage in sexual activities, or perform other acts against their will. Some studies have indeed shown that hypnotized participants will comply with orders to commit antisocial acts. In one study, for example, six hypnotized subjects were instructed to throw "acid" in the face of an experimenter. Five of the six complied. However, six participants told to *pretend* they were hypnotized all threw the acid, as did five of six other participants told nothing about their mental state. Hypnosis made no difference in compliance with the antisocial request (Orne and Evans, 1965). More generally, it appears that the hypnotic trance is no more effective than strong suggestion in inducing someone to commit an act that violates her social values. In fact, one investigator who read through medical literature and case histories spanning 150 years could find *not a single case* in which a violent crime was proven to have been committed under hypnosis (Wolberg, 1972). Moreover, these older findings continue to be supported by more recent studies of hypnosis (Lynn et al., 2002; Kirsch, 2001).

Is The Evidence Open To Alternative Interpretations

Some of the early studies of hypnosis lacked adequate controls, and questions were raised about the ability of the hypnotists involved and the depth of the trance states achieved. If the trance state were not deep enough, it could be argued, the subject would show little improvement over performance in a waking state. While that may be true, more recent studies have been carefully controlled. The hypnotists are well trained and experienced, and participants have been randomly assigned to the hypnosis and waking control conditions. As a result, it is difficult to arrive at alternative interpretations of their results.

Do We Need Additional Evidence

We probably need very little additional evidence against the hypothesis that unique accomplishments are possible under hypnosis. However, those who advocate its use certainly need to muster evidence to support their position. There may, for example, be critical variables in hypnosis, such as the depth of the trance, the hypnotizability and suggestibility of the participant, and the exact ways in which suggestions are presented, that could make a difference. Perhaps some yet unrecognized combination of such variables and conditions would permit hypnosis to yield unique accomplishments. If so, further research will be needed to demonstrate it.

What Can We Conclude?

It seems clear on the basis of evidence to date that all or most of the feats accomplished with hypnosis can be achieved through strong suggestions given to participants in normal waking states.

As a result, we must conclude that hypnosis is not unique. Interestingly enough, Sigmund Freud, who developed psychoanalytic theory, reached essentially the same conclusion a century ago without the benefit of the scientific data we have now (Bachner-Melman & Lichtenberg, 2001).

Horizons in Consciousness

Do We Have To Sleep?

William Shakespeare seemed to have little doubt about the need for sleep:

Sleep that knits up the ravel'd sleeve of care,
The death of each day's life, sore labor's bath
Balm of hurt minds, great nature's second course
Chief nourisher in life's feast.

However, scientists are far less certain. New York disc jockey Peter Tripp stayed awake for 200 hours in a glass booth in Times Square and experienced delusions and visual hallucinations but no other ill effects. Randy Gardner, a 17-year-old San Diego high school student, stayed awake for 264 hours —a full 11 days —and experienced nothing more than fatigue. In fact, Wilse Webb (1972) studied sleep deprivation for 20 years and decided that basically "It makes you sleepy," a conclusion with which other researchers agree. On the other hand, when animals are forcibly and indefinitely deprived of sleep, they show severe effects and eventually die, and this fits better with the evolutionary view that sleep is essential. In earlier evolutionary history, when there were no artificial lights, humans and other visual species engaged in few activities at night because it was dangerous—you could fall off a cliff or become hopelessly lost. Sleep was the most adaptive response (Berger & Phillips, 1995). Evolution also accounts for species differences. Cats sleep a lot because they can exist on one of two meals a day, whereas horses need more food and thus may graze most of the day. Similarly, animals like birds that are likely to be attacked sleep lightly, often with one eye open (Rattenborg et al., 1999).

Sleepwalking: Myth and Reality

Sleepwalking, also known as somnambulism, occurs in 15% of children, where it is typically not considered abnormal (Ipsiroglu et al., 2001). However, it is rare in adults, where it is usually related to underlying psychological problems, particularly to dissociative and conversion disorders (Hartman et al., 2001). It involves abnormal brain activity during deep sleep, may be accompanied by hallucinations, and can actually be lethal, since sleepwalkers have been known to fire guns, drive cars, and commit murders (Espa et al., 2000; Broughton et al., 1994). In fact, the number of legal cases of sleep-related violence has increased substantially in recent years (Cartwright, 2000). In addition, we know that it runs in families and has been shown to have a substantial genetic component (Hublin et al., 2001). But what little research we have suggests that some common beliefs about somnambulism are not true. Sleepwalkers typically avoid objects in their paths, will not walk out an open window, and do not have their eyes closed and their arms extended. Their eyes are at least partially open and their arms swing normally as they walk. Further, the sleepwalker is probably not acting out a dream, since most sleepwalking episodes occur during NREM sleep when dreaming is minimal. And there is no particular danger in awakening a sleepwalker. Episodes of somnambulism increase following sleep deprivation but we still need to know why sleepwalking occurs, what triggers it on some nights and not others, and how to treat it (Joncas et al., 2002). Scientific studies will give us these answers as researchers pursue yet another interesting issue behind the veil of sleep.

The Near-Death Experience: Afterlife or Hallucination?

> *I believe that it was at the very instant when I felt myself die that I started moving at a very high speed toward a net of great luminosity and brilliance. (Siegel, 1981, page 70)*

Near-death experiences are reported by 30%-40% of individuals who survive a close call with death. They include such commonalities as bright lights, dark tunnels, glowing human shapes, out-of-body experiences, and meeting spirits or dead relatives. They are often taken as evidence that there is an afterlife (Greyson, 1993), but researcher Ronald Siegel (1980, 1981) says they are not. He believes these individuals are simply victims of hallucinations, because their descriptions are very similar to hallucinations and could result from depriving the brain of adequate blood and oxygen. Other scientists agree, pointing out that near-death experiences vary from one society to another (Gomez-Jeria, 1993) and appear limited to cultures whose religious beliefs include an afterlife (Kellehear, 1993). Future research will give us the answer: a glimpse of Heaven or a hallucination? Of course, even if near-death experiences are hallucinations, this does not mean there is no afterlife.

Keys to Consciousness 1

1. Consciousness involves a continuum of states of awareness.
   - A. What the extremes are?
     Alert wakefulness
     Deep unconsciousness
   - B. The major theorist hypothesizing the importance of the unconscious?
     Freud
   - C. Why we have consciousness?
     It is adaptive and has evolved.
   - D. The modes of consciousness?
     Passive
     Active
2. The stream of consciousness can be structured for purposes of analysis.
   - A. The major features?
     Focus, structure, attributes, flow.
   - B. The types of determinants?
     Internal, external
   - C. The internal factors?
     Biological, psychological
3. Selective attention focuses consciousness.
   - A. What the cocktail party effect is?
     Attention to one of several auditory stimuli.
   - B. Some influences on selective attention?
     Stimulus intensity and size
     Background and motives

Physiological and psychological states
Perceptual set

Keys to Consciousness 2

1. Sleep cycles among its several stages.
   A. The transitional state between waking and sleep?
      Hypnogogic
   B. The stages and associated EEG ranges?
      Stage 1—Alpha shifting to theta
      Stage 2—Waves of 12-14 cycles, sleep spindles, K-complexes.
      Stage 3—Delta
      Stage 4—Large-amplitude delta
   C. When REM occurs?
      During Stage 1
2. Sleep is often divided into REM and NREM.
   A. Another name for REM sleep?
      Paradoxical
   B. Possible functions of REM?
      Dreaming
      Neural development
      Memory consolidation
3. Sleep disorders have been recognized at least since Hippocrates.
   A. The general classes?
      Insomnia, hypersomnia, parasomnia.
   B. The types of insomnia?
      Sleep-onset
      Sleep-maintenance
   C. Some causes of insomnia?
      Predisposing: Medical conditions, physiological states, personality factors.
      Precipitating: Stress
      Perpetuating: Excess time in bed, worry, daytime naps, alcohol, sedatives.
   D. Some other major disorders?
      Narcolepsy
      Sleep Apnea
4. There are several theories of dreaming.
   A. The major theories?
      Freud
      Activation-synthesis
      Cognitive
   B. Why we dream according to Freud?
      To release dangerous impulses
   C. Why according to activation-synthesis?
      Random neural firing.
   D. Why according to cognitive theory?
      To aid in problem-solving.
5. Some dream states are relatively unusual.
   A. The major special states?
      Lucid, out-of-body, night terrors, nightmares.

B. When during sleep night terrors occur?
Stages 3 and 4

C. When nightmares occur?
REM sleep—Stage 1

Keys to Consciousness 3

1. Daydreaming is an essentially universal experience.

   A. Three patterns Singer reported?
   Poor attentional control
   Negative emotional fantasies
   Positive fantasy

   B. The percentage of single women reporting sexual fantasies?
   98%

2. Hallucinations seem real to those who have them.

   A. Some causes
   Migraines, sensory deprivation, high fever, certain drugs, and schizophrenia

   B. Some consistent characteristics
   Geometric forms (lattices, tunnels, spirals)
   Color patterns (black, violet, blue)
   Movement patterns

   C. A likely mechanism?
   Visual sensations due to neural discharge in retina and visual brain centers.

3. Meditation is widely practiced, particularly in Eastern countries.

   A. Its focus?
   Toward passive and away from active, analytical thought.

   B. Claims as to its unique benefits?
   Creativity, energy, wisdom, inner peace, self-esteem, etc.

4. There are a number of types of meditation.

   A. The two general categories?
   Concentrative, opening-up

   B. A major example of the concentrative school?
   TM

5. Relaxation can have positive benefits.

   A. Benson's four elements?
   Mental device, passive attitude, muscle relaxation, quiet environment.

   B. How the relaxation response is acquired?
   Through simple learning

6. Both meditation and relaxation are said to have physiological and psychological benefits.

   A. The neurological state during both meditation and relaxation?
   About 40% Stage 2-4 sleep.

   B. Other physiological changes?
   Heart rate slows, metabolic rate decreases.

   C. Some claimed benefits of meditation?
   Reduces stress, increased happiness, alleviation of pain.

   D. Whether these benefits are unique to meditation?
   No—relaxation has the same effects.

E. Some adverse effects of meditation?
Anxiety, depression, withdrawal, etc.

7. Hypnosis distorts perception and makes the subject more suggestible.

A. Who first used it and what it was called?
Anton Mesmer—Mesmerism

B. The major theories and theorists?
Neodissociation—Hilgard
Role-playing—Orne
Suggestibility—Barber

8. Hypnosis has been said to have a number of uses.

A. What some are?
Reduce pain
Reduce blood pressure
As a form of psychotherapy

B. Whether it is dangerous?
It can be.

C. Whether its accomplishments are unique?
In general, no.

Keys to Consciousness 4

1. Alcohol is an extremely dangerous drug.

A. The percent of males and females who become alcoholic?
20% and 5%

B. How many deaths it causes?
100,000 plus each year

C. How much shorter the lifespan of alcoholics is?
19 years

D. Some effects of alcohol on society?
Occupies 40% of hospital beds
50% of auto accidents
50% of homicides and 30% of suicides
$12 billion in treatment costs

2. There is multiple reasons for starting to drink.

A. What the major ones are?
Parents model drinking
Peer pressure
The idea that it reduces tension
As an excuse for inappropriate behavior

3. Alcoholism is caused by both biological and psychological factors.

A. The major biological factors?
Genetic predisposition
Alcohol consumption during fetal development.

B. The major psychological theories?
Psychoanalytic—dependency needs
Behavioral—tension-reduction
Cognitive—expectancies

4. Psychoactive drugs are very dangerous and widely abused.

A. The major types of drugs?
Stimulants, hallucinogens, narcotics, Barbiturates

B. Some general properties of these drugs?
Develop tolerance
Often addictive

C. The major types of addiction?
Physiological, psychological

5. Stimulants speed up physiology.

A. Some major examples of stimulants?
Caffeine, amphetamines, cocaine

B. Which of these are legal without prescription?
Only caffeine

C. Some major problems with cocaine?
"Instant" addiction
Cardiac death
Chronic anxiety, depression, and lack of motivation.
Chronic fatigue, headaches, nasal bleeding

6. Hallucinogens produce hallucinations.

A. Some major examples?
LSD, peyote, psilocybin, , marijuana, PCP

B. Some dangers of LSD
Permanent psychosis
Flashbacks

C. Dangers of marijuana?
Automobile accidents
Abnormal menstrual cycles
Fetal death and birth defects
Brain damage, lung damage, weight gain
Homicide

D. Dangers of PCP?
Convulsions, hypertension, respiratory depression
Death
Neurological damage, memory problems, speech and visual disturbances
Anxiety, depression, violence, psychosis

7. Narcotics and Barbiturates are highly addictive.

A. The major narcotics?
Opium, morphine, heroin

B. What Barbiturates are used for?
Sedation

Key Terms 1

active consciousness
altered states
consciousness
introspection
nonconscious
passive consciousness
repression
selective attention
stream of consciousness
unconscious

Key Names 1

Sigmund Freud

Key Terms 2

activation-synthesis hypothesis
anxiety dream
biological rhythm
circadian rhythm
hypersomnia
hypnagogic state
hypersomnia
insomnia
narcolepsy
latent content
lucid dream
manifest content
night terror
nightmare
non-REM sleep
paradoxical sleep
REM sleep
sleep apnea

Key Names 2

Eugene Aserinsky
Alan Hobson
Nathaniel Kleitman
Robert McCarley

Key Terms 3

daydream
hallucination
hypnosis
latah
meditation
mesmerism
out-of-body experience

Key Names 3

Theodore X. Barber
Ernest Hilgard
Anton Mesmer
Martin Orne

Key Terms 4

addiction

alcoholism
amphetamine
barbiturate
caffeinism
cocaine
depressant
hallucinogen
marijuana
phencyclidine (PCP)
psychoactive drug
psychological dependence
stimulant
tolerance
withdrawal

Key Terms 5

EEG
Neural Network
agonist
antagonist
reticular activating system
reuptake

Chapter 6

Learning

Outline

Networking

LEARNING IS a part of almost every aspect of psychology, from developmental psychology (how we acquire behaviors throughout the life cycle) to social psychology (how we learn to interact with others) to abnormal psychology (how we develop such behaviors as phobias and depression). It has evolved over the course of genetic history as a set of adaptive mechanisms that allows us to acquire new behaviors and modify old ones. In order to understand this most complex of human behaviors, we need to know more about the basic processes fundamental to all learning. In this chapter, we will study these basic processes and also consider more complex ways in which people learn. We will examine exciting new work on the neurological basis for learning and applications of research to such practical realities as the effect of televised violence on aggressive behavior.

Everyday Learning

Don't Needle Me

Cold sweat beaded on Chuck's forehead as he sat on the edge of his chair in the physician's waiting room. His tightly clasped hands were clammy, every muscle in his body was taut, and he could almost feel his hair turning gray. Chuck was not afraid that he had a terminal disease; he was afraid he had an infection severe enough to require an injection of antibiotics. His fear of "the needle" was so great that he had avoided this visit to the doctor for as long as possible. The physician soon confirmed his own diagnosis. The sound of syringes rattling around as the nurse retrieved one from the sterilizer and the sight of the small bottle impaled on the needle as she filled the syringe produced such severe anxiety that Chuck closed his eyes and literally shook while awaiting the injection. What had produced such severe anxiety?

Seven, Come Eleven!

Jenny pumped yet another dollar into the slot machine, pulled the lever, and immediately lost. Undaunted, she quickly inserted more money and again operated the machine. She had already lost $200 tonight, but last week and on a few other occasions over the years she had won some money. Now she would persist until her funds were exhausted. How did Jenny become a compulsive gambler?

Fire Away

Sam had accompanied his friend Ron, a policeman, to a local firing range to watch him practice. Somewhat leery of handguns, Sam had never fired one and initially declined Ron's offer to try his gun. However, he finally picked up the gun, assumed a firing position very similar to the one Ron had been using, and fired, hitting one of the outer circles in the target. How did Sam know how to hold the gun, how to stand, and how to fire at a target when he had never even held a gun before?

Chuck's, Jenny's, and Sam's very different experiences are similar in some important ways. In fact, what has happened to them has happened to all of us. People do it. Rats do it. Even planaria do it. It is easy and difficult, stimulating and boring, unavoidable, essential, and virtually universal. It is, of course, learning.

Learning is usually defined as a set of relatively permanent changes in behavior that result from prior experience. You are learning as you read this chapter, listen to your professor's lectures, and study for exams. Learning is also involved in many other aspects of life. You learn to ride a bike, recognize a song, drive a car, smile when someone smiles at you, repair a stereo, and tune out your mother when she complains for the umpteenth time about your hairdo. In fact, learning influences behavior to such a great extent that it is one of the most important concepts psychologists study.

The complex learning that humans engage in can be seen as an adaptive product of millions of years of evolution. From an evolutionary standpoint, we expect those mechanisms that permit organisms to adapt to environmental conditions to be selected for survival. Learning is clearly such a mechanism. This means that organisms capable of more effective learning have survived, while those not so capable have not. The highly evolved learning mechanisms of humans allow us to adapt to a wide variety of environments—hot and cold, flat and mountainous, urban and rural—and to acquire many survival skills. However, other organisms are also capable of learning. Even such primitive creatures as the flatworm can learn, and we will see that psychologists have often used lower animals to study learning processes. We will have more to say about evolution later in the chapter.

The experiences of Chuck, Jenny, and Sam illustrate three major forms of learning. Chuck's fear of the sights and sounds associated with injections is based on *classical conditioning*. Jenny's gambling is based on *operant conditioning*. Sam's ability to hold and fire a gun without previous training is based on *observational learning*. Most of the skills we have as adults and most of the behaviors we exhibit are based, at least in part, on one or more of these forms of learning.

Classical Conditioning: Ivan Pavlov

Many important scientific discoveries have been made quite accidentally through careful observation and just plain curiosity. Classical conditioning is a good example. We will consider the initial classic studies, the components and processes of classical conditioning, some recent developments, and applications of this form of learning to real problems.

Pavlov's Classic Studies

The name Ivan Pavlov may "ring a bell." He was not a psychologist, but a Russian physiologist who won the Nobel prize in 1904 for his work on digestion. Pavlov developed a method for measuring and analyzing the secretion of saliva. He surgically implanted a tube in the salivary gland of a dog, then gave it meat powder. The meat caused the dog to produce saliva, and Pavlov collected and measured it. Pavlov spent many long hours in his laboratory, driving his assistants to do the same, and he often watched as the dogs went through his experimental procedures. After a while, he began to notice that the dogs often salivated before the food was even placed in their mouths. It appeared that this early salivation could be triggered by such things as the sight of the food, the click of the equipment, or the sound of approaching footsteps as an assistant prepared to start the experiment. This observation so fascinated Pavlov that he changed the whole focus of his research in order to explore it.

In Pavlov's best known experiment, he taught dogs to salivate to the sound of a bell. His experimental setup is illustrated in Figure 61. The dog was strapped in the harness and the tube inserted to collect saliva. When meat powder was placed on the dog's tongue, saliva would flow—a biological response requiring no learning. Pavlov then rang a bell before placing the powder on the tongue. After this procedure had been repeated a number of times, he rang the bell without supplying any food. The dog salivated. The mere sound of the bell had come to cause the response—the association of the bell and the meat powder had produced learning.

Components of Classical Conditioning

What Pavlov observed is now called classical conditioning, or learning by association. It is essentially a matter of forming associations or relationships between objects or events in the external environment (Rescorla, 2002). To accomplish classical conditioning, we simply arrange two events in such a way that the learner can form an association between them. A college student who sees a physics text he used in a course he failed may again experience the sick, tight feeling in his stomach that he got during exams for the course. Our friend Chuck also acquired his fear of needles through classical conditioning. The doctor's office and the syringe became associated with the pain of injection and thereby came to elicit the anxiety originally caused by pain.

Each of these instances of classical conditioning, like Pavlov's famous experiment, involves several important elements. The *unconditioned stimulus* (UCS) is any stimulus that evokes a response without prior conditioning taking place—the meat powder in Pavlov's experiment. The *unconditioned response* (UCR) is the unlearned reaction to the UCS—salivation in Pavlov. The *conditioned stimulus* (CS) is a previously neutral stimulus that comes, through association with the UCS, to evoke a response very similar to the UCR—Pavlov's tone. The *conditioned response* (CR) is the newly learned reaction to the CS—also salivation in Pavlov. Notice that the CR is an adaptive response; salivation prepares the dog to consume the food. Figure 6-2 shows the sequence of events in classical conditioning. It is interesting to note that Pavlov originally used the term "conditional" in designating the key elements of his experiments, but it was incorrectly translated as "conditioned" instead.

By now you may be wondering why we use different terms to designate the unconditioned response and the conditioned response, since they may appear to be the same reaction—salivation in Pavlov's experiment. The answer is that the UCR and CR are very similar, but may actually not be identical. This is a good example of scientific precision: Pavlov realized that the two responses might not be identical, so he used different terms. With further observation, he learned that the UCR and CR were, indeed, different. There was less total saliva produced in the CR than in the UCR, and the levels of certain digestive enzymes were lower. Differences between the UCR and CR in other types of classical conditioning experiments have also been observed (Hermans et al., 2002).

Classical Conditioning Processes

Classical conditioning involves several different processes. We will discuss five: Acquisition, stimulus generalization, stimulus discrimination, extinction, and spontaneous recovery.

Acquisition: Learning Something New. The initial process in classical conditioning is response *acquisition.* In Pavlov's view, it is the gradual formation of an association between the CS and the UCS, and it is based on *stimulus contiguity*—the pairing of the stimuli in time—with the CR as a consequence (Figure 6-3). He thus believed that the essential element in conditioning is that the two stimuli occur very close together in time. We will see, however, that more recent theorists do not all agree with Pavlov on this point.

To see how acquisition occurs, let's take Pavlov's classic experiment as an example. At first the bell (the conditioned stimulus) is a *neutral* stimulus. If it is sounded before conditioning begins, it produces nothing more than an orienting reflex—the dog may prick up its ears and turn its head toward the source of the sound. During conditioning, the bell is followed shortly by the presentation of meat powder (the unconditioned stimulus), causing the dog to salivate (the unconditioned response). Acquisition consists of repeating this sequence of events a number of times. Each repetition is termed a *trial.* The dog soon salivates to the bell even when the food is withheld (the CR).

A second example of acquisition is provided by both human and animal experiments in *eyelid conditioning.* The participant hears a tone, followed by a puff of air blown into the eye. The air puff causes an eyeblink, and repeated pairings of the tone with the air puff cause the participant to blink at the sound of the tone. The tone is the CS; the air puff is the UCS; the eyeblink to the air puff is the UCR; and the eyeblink to the CS is the CR. The tone is a neutral stimulus that becomes a conditioned stimulus by pairing it with an unconditioned stimulus that elicited the reflexive eyeblink response.

The acquisition of classically conditioned responses is not limited to salivating dogs and blinking human eyes. A famous example of classical conditioning in humans is the case of Little Albert, an 11-month-old child whom John B. Watson and Rosalie Rayner (1920) conditioned to fear rats. While Albert played, Watson and Rayner placed a white rat (the CS) in front of him. He showed no fear of the animal. But when he reached out to touch the furry white rat, the researchers made a loud noise (the UCS) directly behind him. The noise produced a startle reaction and crying (the UCR). When Albert recovered and again reached for the rat, the experimenters repeated the loud noise, again resulting in crying. After a number of pairings of the rat and the loud noise, Albert began to show fear of the rat alone (the CR). Little Albert had learned an emotional response (fear) to a previously neutral stimulus through classical conditioning. As Watson suggested, this may be the way in which many emotional responses are learned, though some more recent researchers have not been able to replicate his findings. Moreover, it is no longer clear that Watson accurately reported his experiment (Harris, 2002). A common human example of classical conditioning is seen in Figure 6-4.

As Pavlov surmised, one of the most important factors in the successful acquisition of classically conditioned responses is the *timing* of the stimuli (Kemenes et al., 2002). Figure 6-5 shows five temporal arrangements of stimuli in classical conditioning experiments. In *standard* or short-delay conditioning, the CS begins shortly before the UCS (often about one-half second) and remains on until the UCS starts. In *delay conditioning* the CS begins several seconds or more before the UCS and remains on until at least the onset of the UCS; we might thus turn on a tone (the CS) and keep it on until the meat powder is placed on the tongue. In *simultaneous conditioning*, the two stimuli are presented at exactly the same time. In *trace conditioning* the CS is turned off and a fixed interval is allowed to pass before the UCS is delivered (Rodriguez & Levy, 2001). In *backward conditioning* the UCS is presented before the CS.

The best learning occurs with delay conditioning involving a very brief delay, about one-half second in some kinds of conditioning, between CS and UCS (Balsam et al., 2002). Far less effective are simultaneous conditioning (Rescorla, 2002), trace conditioning (Staddon et al., 2002), and backward conditioning (Rubeling, 1993). One comparative study examined how humans learn to evaluate works of art by pairing pictures of well-liked sculptures (the UCS) with those of neutral sculptures (the CS). Participants trained with delay conditioning showed an increased liking for the previously neutral pictures, while those experiencing backward conditioning did not (Hammerl & Grabitz, 1993).

You might wonder whether a subject in a Pavlovian experiment must become aware of the CS-UCS connection before the association is learned so that the CS alone elicits the response. Awareness has been the subject of considerable research, which shows that awareness is probably necessary for conditioning to occur but that it is not sufficient because some essential aspects of the learning process take place outside conscious awareness (Lovibond & Shanks, 2002; Field, 2001).

Extinction: Eliminating Learned Responses. Suppose that after Chuck's early experiences with the pain of injection, he had a number of additional visits to the doctor's office in which he felt no pain. What would happen to his conditioned fear response? As you might suspect, he should gradually lose it because the CS (sights and sounds of the doctor's office) was no longer followed by pain. Pavlov made the same discovery: continued presentation of the CS *without* the UCS reduces and eventually eliminates the conditioned response. This phenomenon is referred to as *extinction*—the reduction in responding that occurs whenever the CS is repeatedly presented without the UCS (Figure 6-3). But note that extinction does not occur simply with the passage of time. Rather, the CS must be presented repeatedly. Thus, the college student who has a deathly fear of speaking in front of groups will experience no reduction in that fear by simply putting off that speech course. Like acquisition, extinction has evolved as an adaptive response. For example, if a well-established source of food becomes unavailable, the animal must abandon the responses needed to obtain that food and acquire new responses or it will starve to death.

Spontaneous Recovery. Extinction does not mean that the learned association is necessarily lost forever. Pavlov trained a dog to salivate to a tone CS. He then extinguished the CR by repeatedly presenting the CS alone. The dog then heard no tones for several days, after which it was again presented with the tone CS. The salivation CR was once again present, and Pavlov labeled this phenomenon *spontaneous recovery*—the weakened return of responding following the passage of time without exposure to the CS (see Figure 6-3). He noted that the CR was considerably weaker (there was less salivation) and it re-extinguished very quickly. More recent work confirms the occurrence of spontaneous recovery with the passage of time after extinction. For example, Herbert Kimmel and his colleagues paired a tone with shock to produce a conditioned increase in blood pressure in dogs, then presented the tone repeatedly without shock. The blood pressure increase disappeared, but after four days it returned, showing spontaneous recovery (Kimmel et al., 1992).

Watson and Rayner could have extinguished Little Albert's fear of the white rat by repeatedly presenting the animal (CS) without the noise (UCS). However, they never attempted extinction even though they knew that he would soon be removed from their research project. By current standards their behavior would be considered unethical because researchers are not supposed to cause a participant harm or discomfort. They also conducted no follow-up, so we have no way of knowing whether there were lasting effects of the procedures they used.

Stimulus Generalization. A dog taught to salivate to the sound of tone of a specific pitch will also salivate to tones with somewhat different pitches. The response is carried over to stimuli that are not quite the same as the original conditioning stimulus, a widely demonstrated phenomenon called stimulus generalization (Till & Priluck, 2000). *Stimulus generalization* means that a response originally conditioned to one specific stimulus also occurs when similar stimuli are presented (Figure 6-6a). The importance of generalization is that it greatly broadens our ability to react to a wide range of related stimuli in the environment.

A good example of generalization is again the case of Little Albert. Once Watson and Rayner had conditioned him to fear the rat, they introduced other white furry objects to see how Albert would respond. A white rabbit, a fur coat, and a Santa Claus mask all made Albert cry and attempt to escape. His fear response to the rat had generalized. A second example is seen in a recent study in which college students generalized their brand preference for one product to a preference for other products of that same brand (Till & Priluck, 2000).

Stimulus Discrimination. While stimulus generalization can be helpful, overgeneralization can be a problem. A dog conditioned to respond to a specific tone might begin to salivate to the ringing of any door bell or telephone, and Chuck might experience anxiety in every office he enters. Such problems are avoided by learning to discriminate among similar stimuli. *Stimulus discrimination* means learning to respond to a specific stimulus and not respond to other stimuli that are similar to the original one (Figure 6-6b). The similarity between two stimuli is the key to generalization; the differences between stimuli are the key to discrimination (Brandon et al., 2000).

Pavlov taught his dogs discrimination by giving them meat powder in association with sounds of a certain pitch but withholding the food when other tones were sounded. The dogs learned to salivate only to the original CS tone. Similarly, Albert showed no signs of fear when colored blocks were placed in his crib, since he was able to clearly discriminate between the blocks and the white rat. More recent studies have demonstrated discrimination learning in preschool children who learned to discriminate among fictitious animal figures.

Beyond Pavlov: Modern Developments in Classical Conditioning

Since Pavlov's initial discoveries, there have been some interesting developments. They include the development of new theories of just how classical conditioning takes place, and they have generated some differences of opinion (Pearce et al., 2002; Wagner & Brandon, 2001; Williams & Ben, 2001). One ongoing debate is concerned with what associations are actually learned in classical conditioning (Gallistel & Gibbon, 2002). A second is the recognition that biological characteristics of the organism may impose constraints on its ability to learn and perform tasks. And a final issue deals with the effect of repeatedly exposing an individual to the same stimulus.

The Great Debate: S-R or S-S? A classic difference of scientific opinion is the ongoing debate as to whether classical conditioning involves primarily the learning of stimulus-response (S-R) associations—those between the CS and the CR—or of stimulus-stimulus (S-S) associations—those between the CS and the UCS. Pavlov hypothesized that the S-S association is what underlies learning; the connection between CS and CR is an indirect result. However, the S-R view—that the CS-CR connection is the primary one—soon became dominant and was the favored explanation for many years (Stock & Hoffmann, 2002; Fezzani et al., 2000). More recently the S-S hypothesis has once again begun to receive considerable support. In its current form, which differs from Pavlov's original view, it suggests that the important association formed during conditioning is between the CS and a mental image of the UCS, which then elicits the CR (Yin & Knowlton, 2002). This version of the S-S theory is an essentially cognitive explanation of conditioning, and we will have more to say about cognitive elements later in the chapter. Figure 6-7 compares the three theories.

Learning As Adaptation: Biological Preparedness. Gregory Kimble, a major learning researcher, asserted in 1956 that any response of an organism can be conditioned to any stimulus it can perceive. This *equipotential* view means that any conditioned stimulus has equal potential for becoming associated with any unconditioned stimulus.

This strongly environmental theory of learning was later challenged by findings suggesting that genetic tendencies may influence learning processes (Newcombe & Huttenlocher, 2000). A given organism may be genetically programmed in such a way that certain conditioned stimuli can much more readily become associated with some unconditioned stimuli or conditioned responses than with others. This phenomenon is called *biological preparedness,* meaning that there are species-specific genetic predispositions (inborn tendencies) to form some kinds of learned associations and not others (Skre et al., 2000). So strong is the evidence for biological preparedness that Kimble was moved to write in 1981 that the equipotential theory had simply been wrong.

A good example of preparedness is phobia, an irrational fear. People have phobias for a wide variety of things—flying, heights, water, darkness, snakes, cars, and many others—and phobias often involve a combination of genetic predispositions and classical conditioning. For example, one patient had a water phobia so strong that he experienced severe anxiety if faced with a swimming or boating scene in a movie and could not go near any body of water. As a child, his father had repeatedly forced him to go boating, reacting with anger and putting him on restrictions when he expressed an initially mild fear of the water. Later, his father pushed him out of the boat a number of times in an effort to teach him to swim, pulling him back in only after he had gone under. The water became a conditioned stimulus through its association with the unconditioned stimuli: the father's anger, the restrictions, and the respiratory distress of nearly drowning. Fear—the phobia—was the conditioned response. Even if you don't have a phobia, you may have milder anxiety responses to certain objects or situations, and these anxieties can also involve classical conditioning.

Because phobias are subject to biological predispositions, some will develop much more readily than others. Water is one for which humans are biologically prepared. Others include phobias for darkness, snakes, injury, spiders, and heights. For example, the heritability for phobic fear of small animals and of social situations was .47 in one study, meaning that about 47% of the determinants of these phobias are genetic. Why are we predisposed to more easily develop fears of these particular objects and situations than of others? Because these fears had real survival value in our ancestral past—and many still do. You can fall off a cliff in the dark, drown in the water, or die of a snake bite. Thus, the adaptive value of these fears is of evolutionary origin (Dellarosa & Cummins, 1999). Early humans who more quickly and strongly learned to fear these particular situations and objects were more likely to survive, and their genes were therefore more likely to be passed on to future generations. Thus, as Martin Seligman (1971) points out, humans are genetically programmed to easily acquire fears that will potentially save their lives and hence further the survival of the species. If a fear of heights saves you from a fatal fall or a spider phobia protects you from a deadly bite, the fear is adaptive. This doesn't mean, however, that no learning is involved. It means that when a biologically predisposed CS, like darkness or snakes, is associated with a UCS, like pain or difficulty breathing, the association is more readily formed. In this way, some people may develop a mild fear of darkness or snakes, others a very strong fear—a phobia.

Work on biological preparedness actually began not with phobias but with the phenomenon of conditioned taste aversion, in which a strong aversion to a particular flavor develops because that flavor has been associated with nausea (Cailhol & Mormede, 2002). The Probe discusses the important work of John Garcia on this interesting and important phenomenon.

The Mere-Exposure Effect

What would happen if you were to repeatedly present a CS to a subject without any UCS ever being presented. Would her preference for the CS over other stimuli increase? The answer, documented by many studies across cultures and species, is "Yes," and this acquisition process is called the *mere exposure effect*. Robert Zajonc argues that the effect is the result of a classical conditioning process in which the UCS is the absence of aversive events. Benign repetition thus enhances positive feelings and associates those feelings with the stimulus (Zajonc, 2001).

Applications of Classical Conditioning

Classical conditioning is not merely a laboratory demonstration; it also affects important aspects of human life. In addition to the development of phobias, it is involved in the learning of a wide range of normal behaviors, in helping smokers stop smoking, and in understanding decreases in the immune response to disease.

There are many examples of classically conditioned responses in humans (see Figure 6-4). Perhaps you smile and feel happy upon seeing your significant other approaching, cringe at the sound of the dentist's drill, and salivate at the sight of a banana split. Why do we have these reactions? The answer in each case is that we have formed a classically conditioned association between two stimuli, such that a previously neutral stimulus has come to elicit a reaction (sometimes an emotional reaction) that is naturally or automatically produced by the unconditioned stimulus.

People who smoke are often encouraged to stop because it endangers their health (see Chapter 15), and some studies suggest that classical conditioning can help (Field & Duka, 2001). One team of researchers had smokers inhale an extract of black pepper, then inhale smoke. They found that inhaling the pepper reduced the effects of nicotine withdrawal when the smokers then stopped smoking. The black pepper provides sensory cues that serve as CSs for the physiological satisfaction response experienced by smokers. The pepper relieves anxiety and produces sensations in the chest similar to those produced by smoking. As a result, the pepper may be able to substitute (at least partially) for the nicotine in cigarettes and help smokers stop smoking (Rose & Behm, 1994; Carter, 2002). However, further research is needed before we can be certain about the safety and effectiveness of pepper.

The body's immune response to disease, though basically biological, can also be affected by classical conditioning. Horizon 2 discusses the implications of the relevant research.

Operant Conditioning: B.F. Skinner

Jenny's penchant for gambling is not elicited by any conditioned stimulus. Rather, she originally tried gambling, periodically won some money, and thereby acquired a "gambling response." This response was not acquired through classical conditioning, but through an alternative form of learning called operant conditioning. We will consider the history of operant conditioning in the work of Edward L. Thorndike and B.F. Skinner, how learning can occur through reinforcement, and the differences between positive and negative reinforcement. We will also take up the role of biological preparedness in operant conditioning and the applications of Skinner's approach.

Edward L. Thorndike: The Law of Effect

Working at Columbia University at about the same time Pavlov was studying classical conditioning in Russia, Edward L. Thorndike set out to determine whether animals could solve problems by thinking. His basic approach was to present a hungry animal with a problem that it could solve in order to obtain food. In one of his classic experiments, he put a cat in a special "puzzle box." The cat had to find a way to open a latch on the box so that it could escape and reach food placed outside the box. If the cat pulled a string or pressed a lever, the latch was released, the box opened, and it could get to the food (see Figure 6-8). Because the string-pulling response was instrumental to obtaining the food, Thorndike called the form of learning exhibited by the cat *instrumental conditioning* (Chance, 1999).

Thorndike's cats clearly learned in a trial-and-error fashion. The cat in the box did not simply look around, calmly stroll over and pull the string. Rather, it gave what appeared to be random responses until it accidentally pulled the string. Once it had done so a few times, this response became more frequent because it was the only one that led to the food. The cat would take less and less time on each trial to make the string-pulling response. Thorndike was forced to conclude that the cats were not thinking, since they learned the response only gradually and mechanically. However, based on his experiments he was able to formulate what is perhaps the most basic "law" in psychology, the *law of effect*. It states that a behavior is more likely to be repeated when it is followed by satisfaction or reward (Halvor-Teigen, 2002).

The law of effect applies to a wide range of organisms and behaviors because it helps the organism to survive in and adapt to its natural environment (Nevin & Grace, 2001). From a Darwinian standpoint, in fact, such a behavioral law is essential because it causes the organism to seek out and approach objects and events that promote survival (Gallistel et al., 2001).

B.F. Skinner: Consequences Determine Behavior

Thorndike's experiments on instrumental learning and his law of effect served as the basis for the operant conditioning theory of the most influential of all American psychologists, B.F. Skinner. Skinner was a college English major and frustrated writer, who sought a new career by attending graduate school and receiving a Ph.D. in psychology in 1931. Seven years later he published *The Behavior of Organisms* (Skinner, 1938), which sold a grand total of 80 copies in its first four years. Undaunted, he continued his work, later publishing many articles and books detailing and defending his theoretical approach to understanding how behavior is acquired and modified (Skinner, 1953, 1957, 1969, 1971).

Skinner was influenced by the writings of the philosopher Francis Bacon and consequently adopted a rather technological and reformist orientation (L.D Smith, 2002). He hypothesized that behaviors are acquired primarily through operant conditioning. The term derives from his distinction between acts that are *elicited* by a known stimulus (such as salivating to food placed in the mouth) and those that are spontaneously *emitted* without the need for any particular stimulus to be present. Skinner called elicited responses, such as the salivation, eye blinking, and fear in classical conditioning studies, *respondent* behaviors. They involve primarily involuntary or reflexive reactions, and classical conditioning can account for them. He called emitted behaviors, such as the smile of a child or the spontaneous pecking of a pigeon, *operants*, and held that they cannot be accounted for by classical conditioning, since there is no eliciting stimulus. Instead, they are controlled by events that *follow* the response and can be accounted for by a different learning process that he called operant conditioning. *Operant conditioning* is a form of learning in which responses are controlled by their *consequences*. The money that Jenny occasionally won served as a pleasurable consequence that caused her to repeat the gambling behavior.

Living With The Consequences. Skinner's basic thesis is that any behavior is entirely a function of its consequences. Simply stated, behaviors associated with desirable consequences will likely be repeated, while those associated with neutral or no consequences will not (Colwill & Triola, 2002). This idea, also seen in Thorndike's law of effect, is the basis for the centerpiece of Skinner's theory, the principle of reinforcement: *Reinforcement* occurs when the consequence of a response increases the likelihood or probability that the response will be repeated). When Jenny wins money gambling, the money increases the probability that she will repeat the behavior, and the money is therefore reinforcing.

Skinner and his colleagues have studied the effects of reinforcement extensively. In a typical experiment, a pigeon (Skinner's favorite laboratory subject) is first placed in a *Skinner box.* The box is a specially designed chamber in which the pigeon can be systematically reinforced, usually with food pellets, and its responses recorded. The pigeon is typically deprived of food, then placed in the box. The box contains only two items: a translucent disk with a light behind it (called a *key*) on one wall, and a hopper fed by a magazine (dispenser) that contains food pellets. While it is moving and pecking around the box, the pigeon may accidentally peck the key. In conditioning jargon, the pigeon is said to have "emitted an operant key pecking response." The key peck operates the dispenser, giving the pigeon food. As a result, the frequency of pecking increases. Skinner would say that the food serves to *reinforce* the key pecking response, which accounts for the increase in its frequency). Skinner boxes have also been designed for work with other animals. In one designed for rats, the animal learns to press a bar for reinforcement.

To conduct a specific study, the experimenter establishes a set of *reinforcement contingencies*—circumstances or conditions under which the reinforcer will be delivered. He then delivers the reinforcements and records the frequency with which the pigeon pecks the key—its *response rate.* In reporting the results of the study, the experimenter typically provides graphs of the response rate as it changes over time. Figure 6-9 shows the operant conditioning process.

Direct Observation. Also basic to Skinner's thinking is the insistence that psychology focus only on those aspects of behavior that can be directly *observed.* We can observe that Jenny's gambling increases when she wins money. We cannot, however, infer from this that winning the money gives her "pleasure." We must stick with the basic behavioral observation: Money, when it is a direct consequence of gambling, increases the probability that the gambling behavior will be repeated. We can similarly observe that the pigeon has been deprived of food, but we cannot infer that it is "hungry." And we can record the increased frequency of key pecking, but we cannot say that the pigeon has "learned" the response; learning, like pleasure and hunger, is a construct that we cannot directly observe.

This thesis—that psychology should study only directly observable behavior and ignore internal, mentalistic constructs like anxiety, thought, and consciousness—is an extreme one. It has been termed radical behaviorism or simply *behaviorism* and can be traced back to the views of Galileo (1564-1642) and the philosopher Francis Bacon (1561-1626). In Skinner's hands, it gradually became a major school of thought in psychology. However, it has also been widely criticized as too extreme because it suggests that we need not, at least for now, understand thought processes and neurological functioning to understand learning (Malone & Cruchon, 2001).

Operant Conditioning Processes

The reinforcement principle is powerful because it can explain not only the behavior of pigeons and rats, but much of what we humans know and do. You become an extravert because you are repeatedly reinforced for outgoing behavior and an honest person because your honest responses are rewarded. You work because you are reinforced by money and praise. And you are reading this chapter because you have been reinforced by grades and perhaps parental plaudits for studying in the past. However, even the almighty reinforcement principle cannot alone explain behavior. Rather, it operates in the context of a set of processes similar to those seen in classical conditioning (Hausken & Moxnes, 2001). We will consider acquisition, and the associated phenomena of shaping and autoshaping, as well as extinction, spontaneous recovery, generalization, and discrimination.

Acquisition: Shaping Up. The basic process by which new behaviors are acquired is *acquisition*—an increase in response frequency with repeated reinforcement. The increased key pecking of the pigeon, for example, is an indication of acquisition (see Figure 6-9).

One problem experimenters run into is that they cannot reinforce a response until the participant emits it. Skinnerian experimenters may have to wait a long time for the pigeon to peck the key accidentally, just as parents may have to wait patiently for their baby to smile in order to reinforce this behavior. The solution is to reinforce a series of behaviors that are increasingly like the desired behavior. When we do this, we say that we are reinforcing *successive approximations* to the behavior. We may initially reinforce the pigeon with pellets for simply standing near the key, then for turning toward the key, for approaching it more closely, and finally for pecking it. When we reinforce successive approximations and thus make the response more and more nearly correct, we are *shaping* the desired behavior, a procedure that can lead to much more rapid learning than if trial and error is simply allowed to take its own course. Skinner used shaping to teach pigeons to apparently play ping pong, and others have used it to show how maladaptive behaviors can develop in rats, among many other demonstrations.

Shaping is not just a laboratory convenience; it is used by parents every day. Shaping can teach children to eat, dress themselves, or ride a bicycle. In the latter case, parents may reinforce the child with praise for just approaching the bike, then for sitting on the seat with someone holding the bike, making a series of initial failed attempts to ride, riding successfully a short distance, and finally for mastering the skill. In adults, shaping is used for many purposes, such as improving the task performance of children with a serious disorder called autism (Sundberg & Michael, 2001). In fact, human applications go back at least to the seventh century A.D., when ancient documents describe the use of shaping to teach mute people in Saxon, England to talk.

Superstitious pigeons (and humans). Did you know that even pigeons can be superstitious—or at least exhibit superstitious behavior? Pigeons trained to key peck for food rewards often develop unique patterns of pecking. One pigeon will turn around completely in the Skinner box before pecking the key, while another may develop the habit of hitting the key with the side of its beak rather than the front. The pigeons accomplish nothing by these added flourishes, so why do they perform them? Skinner explains that they are superstitious behaviors that are unplanned but lawful effects of operant conditioning procedures. A *superstitious behavior* is one that becomes established because it happens to be associated with the correct response and is therefore accidentally reinforced when the experimenter is attempting to reward only the correct behavior.

Superstitious behaviors are common among humans as well as pigeons. The woman who purchases a lottery ticket at the third checkout stand in a certain supermarket and wins $1,000 may subsequently buy all her lottery tickets at that checkout stand, even though it is extremely unlikely that this behavior has anything to do with winning. Can you think of any rituals you go through that might be considered conditioned superstitious behaviors?

Autoshaping. But the shaping process is not quite as straightforward as it might at first seem because a phenomenon known as *autoshaping*—shaping without reinforcement—has been demonstrated (Papini et al., 2001). In the original, classic study, the key in a Skinner box was illuminated briefly and then food was delivered whether or not the pigeon in the box pecked the key. After a few such trials, the pigeon began to spontaneously peck at the key even though the keypeck was not required to obtain the food (Brown and Jenkins, 1968). The relationship in this experiment is between the light and food reinforcement, not between the keypeck and the reinforcement. Rats have similarly learned to self-administer cocaine without reinforcement (Carroll & Lac, 1993). The phenomenon is called autoshaping because the key pecking is readily established or shaped, even though it produces no reinforcement (Ploog, 2001).

Autoshaping substantially blurs the distinction between classical and operant conditioning. In fact, the best interpretation of autoshaping is that the keypeck is actually a classically conditioned response. The key, lighted just before allowing the pigeon to eat, becomes a conditioned stimulus for pecking at the food. The pigeon goes on to peck the lighted key because it is closely associated with the actual pecking of the food. Interestingly enough, if the light on the key closely approximates the shape of a kernel of food, conditioning is more rapid, and autoshaping produces faster learning than shaping by successive approximation. So powerful, in fact, is autoshaping that pigeons will peck the lighted key even if the experimenter actually reinforces them for not pecking it (Pearce et al., 2002).

Extinction and Spontaneous Recovery. If we withhold the food reinforcer, the key pecking or other acquired behavior will gradually decrease in frequency because it is no longer being rewarded. This gradual reduction in responding in the absence of reinforcement is called *extinction.* Consider the case of a child who frequently throws temper tantrums. Tantrums can recur because the parents are reinforcing them by giving the child their attention. If the parents consistently ignore the tantrums, they may decrease in frequency or stop: They have been extinguished by withdrawing the reinforcer.

If we return the pigeon to the box a few days after its key peck response was extinguished, we may find that it will once again display the response. Skinner called this return of responding *spontaneous recovery.* It has also been demonstrated in a variety of other animal species, including rats, dogs, monkeys, and even the opossum. If the child's temper tantrums extinguish through nonreinforcement, they may later spontaneously return, but they can usually be extinguished with ease by again simply failing to reinforce them.

You might now look at Table 6-1. It compares the basic procedures and results in operant conditioning with those in classical conditioning.

Stimulus Control: Discrimination and Generalization. If Jenny finds that slot machines with red levers sometimes pay off while those with blue levers never do, she will quickly come to choose the red-lever machines. Operant psychologists would say that the color of the lever has become a *discriminative stimulus*—one that permits a differentiation between a response that will lead to reinforcement and one that will not. Unlike the CS in classical conditioning, the discriminative stimulus in operant conditioning is *not necessary* for learning. However, when it is present, it can serve to bring the behavior under *stimulus control,* a condition in which the specific stimulus can reliably produce the behavior.

Much of our behavior as adults is under such stimulus control. For example, college students are likely to talk aloud and initiate conversations at a party but not in a classroom. The classroom situation is a discriminative stimulus for quiet behavior, the party situation for more informal behavior. To study discriminative stimuli, we might give a pigeon food reinforcement for pecking a red key but not for pecking a green key. It will soon learn to peck only the red key, which leads directly to primary reinforcement (food). In addition to pigeons, discrimination has been demonstrated in rats and humans, as well as other species.

The establishment of stimulus control involves the processes of stimulus generalization and discrimination. *Stimulus generalization* occurs when the organism responds to a stimulus that differs to some degree from that originally involved in the acquisition of the response. The pigeon that learns to peck a red disk may also peck a pink disk, and Jenny may choose gambling machines with levers that are various shades of red and pink. *Stimulus discrimination* occurs when there is an increase in the probability of a response to one stimulus and a decrease in the probability of response to another. We achieve discrimination by selectively reinforcing responses in the presence of one stimulus and not of another. If we reinforce pecks on a ruby red key but do not reinforce pecks on a key that is a different shade of red, the pigeon will learn to peck only the ruby red key.

Principles of Reinforcement

Reinforcement is the principal mechanism through which the biologically adaptive law of effect operates. It is the crucial element in operant conditioning because it determines what behaviors will be acquired, maintained, and extinguished. Jenny was reinforced by money, the pigeon by food pellets, and the child learning to ride a bicycle by praise.

But what is reinforcement more generally? As we have seen, *reinforcement* takes place when an object or event following a response increases the likelihood of future occurrences of that response. Correspondingly, a *reinforcer* is an object or event that increases the probability of a response. Sometimes reinforcers are entirely obvious. Chocolate candy will successfully reinforce the five-year-old for putting away his toys only if he likes chocolate candy. Otherwise, cookies, praise, or TV privileges might be more effective reinforcers. Let's see how reinforcers are identified and how positive and negative reinforcement modify behavior.

Experimental Analysis of Behavior. It is sometimes difficult to immediately identify effective reinforcers. To solve this problem, Skinner developed a simple approach called the *experimental analysis of behavior* (EAB). In EAB, the experimenter follows a behavior with a stimulus that is a potential reinforcer. If it increases the probability of the response, it is defined as a reinforcer. If we follow key pecks with standard laboratory food pellets, we will very likely find that the frequency of the key peck response increases, and the pellets are therefore reinforcers. If we follow key pecks with pieces of gravel and response probability does not increase, gravel is not defined as a reinforcer. Sometimes a less desirable reinforcer can be substituted for one that is more desirable (Gaynor & Shull, 2002). For example, suppose the pigeon's preferred reinforcer is food pellets, but we deliver caviar instead. Will it substitute? Well, you'll have to answer that question by testing your own pigeon!

A human example of EAB is seen in a study done by Christine Chambers and her colleagues. Before children aged 8-12 were exposed to a task that produced mild pain, their mothers were trained to engage in either a pain-promoting or pain-reducing interaction with them. Girls whose mother promoted pain reported more pain than those whose mothers reduced pain, although boys were unaffected (Chambers et al., 2002).

An alternative to EAB in identifying reinforcers is the "Premack Principle," developed by David Premack (1965). It states that reinforcers can be identified by simply noting those activities that are performed most frequently when participants are given a free choice among a number of different activities. More frequently performed activities can be used to reinforce less frequently performed activities when access to the more frequent activities is blocked. For example, we might observe that when given a choice of leisure activities, including gambling, lying on the beach, water skiing, and hiking, Jenny chooses gambling most frequently. According to the Premack principle, Jenny's boyfriend should be able to increase the frequency with which she will be willing to lie on the beach by following a day on the beach with an evening of gambling. Similarly, parents can reward a child for studying by allowing him to go out and play, assuming that playing is higher on the preference list than studying. But the Premack principle has been criticized because it cannot readily explain the occurrence of low-frequency behaviors, such as washing the windows of your house. Why do such behaviors occur at all? The answer is that when we have experienced prolonged response deprivation for some activity, the opportunity to engage in it can, itself, be reinforcing, allowing us to maintain an equilibrium among our many activities (McFarland & Lattal, 2001).

Primary and Secondary Reinforcement. Primary reinforcers are those that have a direct relationship to some known biological drive. Food and water, for example, are primary reinforcers for animals that have been deprived of these necessary items. *Secondary reinforcers* are those that become reinforcers as a result of being associated with primary reinforcers. We can condition a secondary reinforcer by arranging the Skinner box so that every time a thirsty rat presses the bar, a light comes on and water is delivered. The light will eventually become a secondary reinforcer capable of rewarding responses even when the primary reinforcer, water, is no longer available.

Secondary reinforcers are particularly important in humans, and money is a good example. In childhood it is paired with such primary reinforcers as food and drink and with such previously conditioned reinforcers as social praise. Money thereby becomes such a powerful reinforcer that most people expend great effort to maintain an adequate supply of it. A classic study of the power of money as a reinforcer was a laboratory investigation involving chimpanzees in which coins were paired with grapes and thereby became conditioned reinforcers (Wolfe, 1936). The chimps learned that inserting the coin in the slot would produce a grape, and they then learned to perform a variety of tasks in order to get coins.

Schedules of Reinforcement

When rewards are given after each response, the procedure is called *continuous reinforcement*, and it leads to rapid acquisition of operantly conditioned responses. However, behaviors can also be acquired and maintained when the correct response is reinforced on every other trial, every fifth trial, or even every hundredth trial. This procedure is called *partial reinforcement*.

The Partial Reinforcement Effect. Continuous and partial reinforcement differ in the ease with which the acquired behavior can be extinguished. *Resistance to extinction* is seen when the organism continues to respond for a time after reinforcement stops. Interestingly enough, a response learned on a partial reinforcement schedule is more resistant to extinction than one learned on a continuous schedule. This high resistance to extinction is called the *partial reinforcement effect* (PRE). Gamblers like Jenny are always on partial reinforcement schedules, so failure to win on any given occasion does not imply that there will never again be a reinforcement. On the other hand, who hasn't on one or two occasions pumped quarters into a soda machine only to receive no "reinforcement" for doing so. You don't stand there and continue to feed quarters to the machine because you are on an essentially continuous reinforcement schedule with such machines—you have always gotten soda in the past.

Many persistent human behaviors may be the result of the partial reinforcement effect. Motor skills, such as those involved in riding a bicycle or swimming, can be learned through partial reinforcement (Engel et al., 2001). A person may fish hour after hour, day after day, even if he only occasionally catches a fish. And a woman may continue to stay with a husband or lover who drinks heavily and regularly abuses her because occasionally he is loving and kind.

Scheduling Partial Reinforcement. One of Skinner's great insights was that partial reinforcement typically does not occur entirely at random. Rather, it is delivered on schedules, and the schedule on which a behavior is reinforced is a very powerful determinant of the nature of that behavior. A *schedule of reinforcement* designates the particular instances of the correct response that will be reinforced (Mazur, 2002). There are two major classes of schedules, ratio schedules and interval schedules (Figure 6-10).

In a *ratio schedule,* the delivery of reinforcement depends simply on the number of correct responses emitted by the participant. Reinforcement may be delivered every second, eighth, or twentieth correct response or in some other ratio chosen by the experimenter. Ratio schedules are further divided into fixed and variable schedules. A *fixed ratio* (FR) schedule consistently delivers reinforcement at the same ratio, such as every five responses, a 5:1 ratio (Figure 6-10). A good example is frequent-flyer miles, a reinforcer delivered by the airlines on a fixed ratio of points to miles flown. The effectiveness of FR reinforcement has often been demonstrated (Kelley et al., 2002).

The *variable ratio* (VR) schedule varies the ratio of reinforcements to responses. The variation (often random) occurs around some mean or average ratio, usually with set outer limits. A variable 5:1 ratio schedule might mean that the reinforcer would be randomly delivered after 4, 5, or 6 correct responses since the last reinforcement, with an average of 5.

Response patterns vary from one schedule to another. When ratio schedules are used, animals tend to respond with high rates or "bursts," probably because the high response rate leads to more frequent reinforcement (Figure 6-10). Jenny's gambling behavior is reinforced on a variable ratio schedule because the slot machine pays off once every one hundred times or so.

Skinner points out that variable ratio schedules are predominant in the development of human social behavior. Simply stated, the reinforcement of most social actions is a function of the number of occurrences of the response rather than the passage of time. The spontaneous smile of the child, for example, may occur over and over again and is reinforced whenever an attentive adult hugs the child, comments positively, or otherwise reinforces it. The amount of time between smiles is irrelevant. Sexual behaviors and preferences can be acquired in this way, and mathematical models can predict current behaviors on the basis of the reinforcement history of the behavior.

With an *interval schedule,* reinforcement follows a response that occurs after a specified time period has elapsed. On *fixed interval* (FI) schedules, the time period is constant from one experimental trial to the next. A rat might be reinforced for the first bar press after each five-minute period has passed. The response pattern on FI schedules is "scalloped;" the rate of responding typically increases to its highest level just before reinforcement, drops to near zero afterward, then gradually rises again until the next reinforcement occurs (see Figure 6-10). Notice how different the response pattern in FI schedules is from the high-rate responding of the ratio schedules (Figure 6-10).

*Variable interva*l (VI) schedules use a range of varied intervals around some average time and tend to be characterized by stability rather than scalloping. They have been used to demonstrate an acquired button-pressing response in college students. Learning that takes place on a VI schedule is extremely resistant to extinction. The fisherperson who sits patiently in his boat dangling a line in the water hour after hour tends to be rewarded on a VI schedule. The fish are likely to strike periodically but unpredictably. The person must therefore engage in fishing behaviors on a fairly steady basis in order to be rewarded.

Positive and Negative Reinforcement

Table 6-2 shows the various ways in which pleasant and aversive consequences can be used to modify behavior. In general, a *positive reinforcer* is one that produces pleasure or satisfaction, while a *negative reinforcer* is one that removes displeasure or dissatisfaction. Both are reinforcers because they increase the likelihood of a response.

A monkey will learn to pull a lever to obtain food (positive reinforcement) or to escape electric shock (negative reinforcement). Notice that it is the *presentation* of the positive reinforcer and the *removal* of the negative reinforcer that produce reinforcement and increase the probability of the behavior. When the monkey pulls the lever for positive reinforcement, it is presented with food, and food is therefore *present after* the response is made. Positive reinforcers in humans include money, praise, attention, and approval. When the monkey pulls the lever to turn off the shock, the negative reinforcer (shock) is *absent after* the response is made.

Negative reinforcement has some applications in human behavior. For example, every time you get into your car that aversive buzzer comes on. It stops when you fasten your seat belt, providing negative reinforcement to increase the probability that you will fasten it the next time. Other human examples include working hard to accomplish an aversive task just to get it over with and developing a psychological disorder (a so-called "nervous breakdown") to escape a bad marriage. However, negative reinforcement is not very useful in teaching desirable behaviors to children because you would have to subject the child to an aversive stimulus that would stop only when he made the correct response.

Punishment. When seven-year-old Margie beats her little brother to a pulp, she may be yelled at or put on restrictions. These are punishments, the most common form of parental discipline. *Punishment* refers to a consequence that follows a response and decreases its probability. It is easy to confuse punishment with negative reinforcement. Just remember that in negative reinforcement the aversive stimulus occurs *before* the response and *increases* its probability, while in punishment it occurs *after* the response and decreases its probability.

When Skinner (1953) punished rats for pressing a lever in a Skinner box, he found that the probability of the behavior decreased with punishment but quickly recovered when punishment stopped. He concluded that punishment basically doesn't work because it only temporarily suppresses the undesirable behavior. As a result, he said that parents who punish children for unacceptable behaviors are wasting their time.

It turns out that in this instance Skinner may have been wrong. Many more recent studies have clearly demonstrated that punishment works just as well as reinforcement under certain circumstances. Its effects can be lasting when the punishing stimulus is intense, frequent, immediate, and inescapable.

There are nevertheless several problems with punishment that revolve around its undesirable side effects. First, since punishment must be harsh to be effective, it often leads to the development of *negative emotional responses.* For example, when Margie is sent to her room for refusing to eat breakfast, she is likely to become anxious or angry, and these negative emotions may cause more trouble than the behavior that was punished. The second problem is that punishment can suppress general behavioral activity. Instead of just stopping the undesirable behavior, the punishing stimulus may reduce activity overall. Rats shocked for bar-pressing often stop all activity, and children who are severely punished can become inhibited, withdrawn, and shy. A third difficulty is that punishment may *increase aggressive behavior.* An abusive parent often produces an eventually defiant, abusive child. Finally, attempts at punishment may actually *result in positive reinforcement* of the undesired behavior. Margie may find that when she is a "good girl" she gets very little attention, and when she is a "bad girl" she gets punished, providing at least some form of attention. Since attention is positively reinforcing, her undesirable behavior is positively reinforced through punishment—not exactly what her parents had in mind!

A final possibility is called *negative punishment.* It occurs when we withdraw a pleasant stimulus. A parent can discipline a child by taking away TV privileges. A coach can negatively punish a first-string player by making her sit on the bench during a game for missing a practice.

It appears that operant research has identified a parental dilemma: Negative reinforcement is difficult to apply in many human situations; punishment is effective only under limited circumstances and has unfortunate side effects. What to do? Skinner's answer is that parents should emphasize positive reinforcement, which is relatively free of negative consequences and is often associated with such emotions as pleasure and joy. Basically, rather than waiting for the child to misbehave and then punishing him, we should wait until he does something right and then positively reinforce him.

Escape Learning. Negative reinforcement occurs in the laboratory as well as the home. Consider an experiment in which we place a dog in a *shuttle box* that is divided down the middle by a low partition so that the dog can move from one side of the box to the other by jumping over the barrier. If we give the dog electric shocks when it is on one side of the partition, it will learn to jump to the other side to escape them. The shocks serve as negative reinforcement for the jumping behavior—they cause it to increase. This procedure, in which the organism acquires a response that ends or decreases an aversive stimulus, is called *escape learning.*

Avoidance Learning. Related to escape learning is avoidance learning, in which the acquired response prevents an aversive stimulus from occurring. Dogs and rats can be taught to avoid the shock administered in a partitioned chamber by moving from one chamber to another when they receive a cue, such as a tone, indicating that shock is imminent. Humans are also responsive to avoidance learning techniques. A child, for example, soon learns that the approaching footsteps of her father mean she had better stop playing with his computer before he returns to the den and catches her.

O. Hobart Mowrer (1947) argued that avoidance learning, like autoshaping, blurs the distinction between classical and *operant* conditioning. Accordingly, he developed a *two-process theory* to explain how avoidance learning takes place. He argues that the operant conditioning of the dog's jumping response is accompanied by the classical conditioning of the emotional state of fear (Mowrer & Solomon, 1977). During the avoidance learning procedure, the fear response elicited by the shock is classically conditioned to the tone that warns of the coming aversive stimulus. The fear response then serves as a stimulus for the operant conditioning of the avoidance response of jumping the partition. This provides another explanation for human phobias, such as fear of darkness. Darkness (the CS) is first paired with some terrifying event (the UCS) through classical conditioning. An avoidance response (turning on the lights) is then operantly conditioned because it reduces the fear. In short, the fear response is classically conditioned and then becomes a stimulus for the operant conditioning of an avoidance response.

Although it provides a good explanation for avoidance learning, two-process theory does present some problems. In particular, if reduction of the conditioned fear reinforces the operant development of the avoidance response, then the two should be closely related: greater fear should mean better avoidance learning. However, this has not proven true, creating a need to further develop and refine the theory.

Evolution At Work: Biological Preparedness

Just as in classical conditioning, biological factors that are adaptive products of the evolutionary process limit the power of reinforcement to produce operantly conditioned responses. A good example is *instinctive drift*, in which operant response acquisition is impaired by inborn predispositions. The phenomenon was discovered by Keller and Marion Breland (1961, 1966), Skinnerian psychologists who used operant techniques to teach animals tricks. In one case they conditioned raccoons to "save money" by picking up coins and depositing them in a "bank" (a small box). However, after several occasions on which they gave the raccoons two coins, they found that the animals sat and rubbed them together, rather then depositing them, even though they would have received food reinforcement for doing so. The Brelands attributed the failure of conditioning to instinctive drift. Raccoons innately rub objects together to clean them. Associating the coins with food triggered this genetically based response: A biologically prepared behavior that is a product of evolution had interfered with an operantly conditioned response.

A second example is seen when rats are subjected to painful electric shock that they can escape by learning to make a specific response. They have no difficulty learning to run from one chamber of a box into another or to freeze in place to escape the shock. However, they have great difficulty learning to press a lever, even though they easily acquire a lever-pressing response to obtain food or water. Why? Again, because evolution has biologically prepared them to acquire some defensive responses much more easily than others.

Applications of Operant Conditioning

Operant conditioning affects many aspects of human behavior. We smile, help others, and go to work every morning because we are reinforced for these behaviors. Welfare payments reinforce sometimes able-bodied adults for not working, and politicians shake thousands of hands and kiss babies because they are reinforced by the advantages of elective office. Operant conditioning can also be responsible for the development of abnormal behaviors and can be systematically used in very positive ways. Indeed, in his book Walden II, Skinner (1948) details the use of operant techniques to construct an ideal society, though his approach to the design of cultures has been controversial (Lamal, 2001; Wyatt, 2001). To see how operant approaches are applied, let's consider one theory of how depression develops, then see how operant psychology is used to modify a variety of behaviors, enhance the educational process, and develop new drugs.

Learned Helplessness and Depression. Martin Seligman (1975) has shown how one form of abnormal behavior, depression, can be acquired through operant processes. He delivered electric shock to two dogs simultaneously. The Group A dog could turn off the shock by pressing a button and thus had some control over the situation. The Group B dog simply stood there and received the same shocks as the Group A dog but had no control; it was helpless. Both groups were then moved to a shuttle box. The dog was placed in one compartment, where a signal was followed by shock. Group A dogs soon learned to jump the barrier when the signal sounded and thereby avoid the shock, but Group B animals did not. Why? Because the Group B dogs had learned that they had no control over the shock and thus did not try to make the avoidance response. Seligman called this phenomenon *learned helplessness.*

Other studies have demonstrated that lacking operant control over the environment can produce helplessness in humans as well as animals and that it is often associated with depression. The secretary who is repeatedly overruled by her boss when she tries to be more efficient and by her family when she tries to improve home life may eventually come to feel helpless more generally. Such learned helplessness can be a major factor in depression, a phenomenon discussed in Chapter 16.

Modifying Human Behavior. The intentional application of Skinnerian principles in an effort to alter human behavior is called *behavior modification.* Skinnerian approaches have been applied to parenting, education, therapy, decreasing chronic pain, and the development of new drugs (Vargas, 2001; Flor et al., 2002).

Operant techniques can be helpful in correcting problem behavior in children. In one study, frustrated parents whose children watched an average of 21 hours of TV per week agreed to a Skinnerian behavioral program. The child received 20 tokens per week; each could be turned over to mom or dad in exchange for a half hour of TV viewing time. If the children watched no more than the 10 allotted hours, they received a gold token that could be exchanged for some special reinforcer, like a trip to an amusement park or a party for friends. The children cut their TV viewing time to 10 hours and kept it there over a period of eight months after they stopped receiving the tokens (Wolfe, Mendes, and Factor, 1994). Walter Mischel (2001) provides a history of the behavioral therapies are now used extensively in both children and adults, and we have more to say about their use in Chapter 17.

A second application of Skinnerian techniques has been *programmed instruction.* Developed by Skinner in 1954, it applies operant techniques to the teaching of various school subjects. One early device presented addition problems and allowed a child to type the answers on a keyboard. The machine reinforced correct responses by moving on to the next problem. Such reinforcement is immediate and accurate to a degree that can never be achieved by a teacher working with many children at once. Current computer-based instructional systems are the modern products of Skinner's genius.

Skinnerian approaches have also been applied to the modification of abnormal behavior. Hospitalized mental patients suffering from such serious disorders as schizophrenia (see Chapter 16) typically have few of the social skills needed to obtain reinforcement in the world outside the institution. Behavioral programs called *token economies* teach them social skills through operant techniques. Specific behaviors to be changed (e.g., keeping a neat room and going to meals on time) are identified and appropriate reinforcers (e.g., candy, movie attendance, and TV watching) are determined. When patients perform the desired behaviors, they receive tokens, such as poker chips, that can later be exchanged for the reinforcers they want. Operant techniques are also used to reduce the occurrence of psychotic symptoms, decrease problem behaviors in elementary students, reduce stuttering, and teach independent living skills to visually impaired and retarded people.

Testing New Drugs. Before a new drug becomes available, we need some way to be certain that it is safe and effective. Operant techniques can be used to teach an animal a new behavior. A drug is then administered to see how it affects the behavior. The effects of new tranquilizers and of anti-psychotic drugs—those that reduce the symptoms of psychotic patients—have been evaluated in this way (Wiley et al., 1994). Similarly, the effects of withdrawal from narcotics have been assessed, as has the interaction between narcotics and the antidepressant drugs used to treat clinical depression (Kovera et al., 1994). Finally, Skinnerian techniques have been applied to show that cocaine decreases response rates and reduces the consistency of behavior (van Haaren, 1994).

The Current Status of Operant Psychology

It is important to put behaviorism in historical perspective. This major school of thought at first took psychology by storm. Many psychologists became behaviorists, and operant explanations of both human and animal behavior were predominant for many years. Behaviorism rose to such prominence not only because of B.F. Skinner's work, but because psychologists were ready to largely abandon the "soft," mentalistic explanations of earlier eras. In order to become a harder science, it seemed essential that the field become more precise. Psychologists needed to deal with what could be seen and measured—with externally observable responses—and avoid getting further mired in the complex, invisible vagaries of the human mind.

More recent times have seen the decline of behaviorism. Most psychologists are no longer satisfied with the total denial of mentalistic concepts. In fact, the very issues that allowed behaviorism to become such a powerful force have also been responsible for its decline. Psychology has returned to the study of internal constructs, particularly those involving thought or cognition, because the emphasis on external behavior became too sterile and simplistic. This does not mean that operant psychology is gone; certainly its techniques live on in such areas as drug testing and behavior therapy. Moreover, current proponents of behaviorism have revised it to make it less radical and argue that is should continue to be an important theoretical approach (Staddon, 2001). But it is no longer the major guiding force in the field.

Cognitive Factors in Learning

Many psychologists who see both classical and operant conditioning as too mechanical and too simple to account for the learning of complex behavior argue that a variety of *cognitive* processes—those involved in acquiring, modifying, and acting upon knowledge and more generally in thought processes—affect learning. Although most of the theoretical models developed to date are not full-blown cognitive theories of learning, several do include cognitive factors, such as cognitive maps, other cognitive and associative elements, and insight.

Cognitive Maps

Edward Tolman, a pioneer in cognitive psychology, argued that learning is based in cognitive or thought processes, not merely in the formation of associations. He made his point by conducting experiments on maze learning in rats. Previous investigators had concluded that rats learning over many trials to find their way through a maze were simply acquiring a series of turning responses. Tolman argued that instead rats develop a *cognitive map* as they repeatedly negotiate the maze. The map provides a mental representation of the maze that becomes increasingly accurate with experience. The rats are thus undergoing *place learning*: they use the cognitive map to identify the place in the maze where food is found. The process Tolman imagined is very similar to what can happen when you start a new semester. You find your way from a dorm or parking lot to a classroom building on the opposite side of the campus. As you repeat this process, you develop a mental map of the route you take.

To test his theory, Tolman ran three groups of rats in his maze. One group received food reinforcement in the goal box on every trial and made few errors after training. Another group received no food and made many errors. The third—and critical—group received no food for ten trials and made numerous mistakes, but after they got food on Trial 10, they quickly stopped making errors and performed as well as the group that had always received reinforcement (Tolman & Honzik, 1930b).

Tolman concluded that the rats demonstrated *latent learning*, which is learning that is not apparent when it takes place. That is, they had actually been learning all along but had not shown what they knew because there was no reward for doing so. This is important because it means that learning can take place without reinforcement. What the rats had learned, Tolman argued, was a cognitive map of the maze, which allowed them to perform almost perfectly as soon as reward was introduced.

In an extension of this cognitive formulation, Anthony Dickinson has shown that conditioning can be mediated by knowledge (a cognitive concept) concerning the association between a behavior and its outcome and by learning the value of the expected outcome. For example, children receiving gold coins for reducing TV watching will condition more quickly and effectively if they understand that reducing TV time produces the coins and if they know the redemption value of the coins (Wolfe, Mendes, and Factor, 1994). Even newborn infants appear to use cognitive mechanisms in acquiring conditioned responses.

Cognitive Elements in Classical Conditioning

Pavlov and most early psychologists theorized that classical conditioning is an essentially mechanical process in which simple associations are automatically formed under certain conditions. More recent developments suggest that cognitions are involved. The cognitive view holds that the stimuli in classical conditioning have meaning for the learner. To predict responses to these meaningful stimuli, we must know how the learner will interpret the stimulus and thus what is going on in his mind—what he is thinking about. Thoughts are cognitions, so this makes conditioning a cognitive process (Chapter 8).

Blocking. Leon Kamin (1969) long ago demonstrated a phenomenon called *blocking*—interfering with the association between a CS and a UCS. He conducted a three-stage experiment:

- First, a CS (noise) preceded a UCS (shock), and conditioning occurred.
- Second, the same tone CS and also a light CS preceded the UCS on a series of conditioning trials, after which the tone and light presented together, but with no shock, elicited the expected fear response.
- Third, he presented the light alone to see if it elicited the fear response.

What outcome would you expect when the light was presented alone? The traditional prediction would be that the light would elicit fear, since it had, after all, been paired with shock. What Kamin found, however, was that the light alone produced either no fear response or a very weak one. Why? Because the association of the second CS with shock was blocked by the first association. The tone alone provides the rat with all the information it needs to predict the shock. The light is therefore a redundant stimulus; it doesn't improve the rat's ability to predict the UCS.

This finding has great significance for our understanding of the classical conditioning process. It means that the rat does not just mechanically form associations. Rather, it uses stimulus (CS) information to form expectancies and predict the shock. In effect, these are cognitive processes that apparently occur during classical conditioning, even in the lowly rat!

Rule Generation. Forming *rules* governing a likely sequence of events is also a cognitive process, and it is prominent in another classical conditioning model. It suggests that what the animal is doing during conditioning is generating a set of rules about the likely sequence of events. When two unexpected events, such as a light and shock, occur close together, the rat begins to generate the rule that shock follows light, and further pairings strengthen that rule. Again, we see that conditioning may involve elements of cognition (such as applying rules) to a much greater extent than Pavlov imagined.

Forming Complex Associations: The Rescorla-Wagner Model. Robert Rescorla and Allan Wagner (1972) theorize that even lower animals like the white rat form relatively complex mental associations between the CS and UCS during conditioning. In a series of important experiments, Rescorla demonstrated that animals seem to learn an *expectancy*, which allows them to *predict* a second event when the first event occurs. Rather than simply forming mechanical associations between events, the dog or rat processes information about the relationship between CS and UCS and forms a mental representation of that connection which subsequently guides its responses (Rescorla, 1988). Rescorla's model provides one explanation for Kamin's blocking phenomenon, but Rescorla, one of the leading researchers in classical conditioning, has conducted many studies of his own.

In one important study, Rescorla (1967) compared contiguity and predictability explanations of conditioning. He tested several groups of dogs, using a tone CS and a shock UCS, but two groups were of particular importance:

- **Group 1**—Though not all tones were followed by shocks, every shock was preceded by a tone. Thus the tone predicted the coming of the shock reasonably well.

- **Group 2—The number of pairings of CS and UCS was the same as for Group 1, but the shock was equally as likely to be preceded by no tone as by a tone. Thus, the tone did *not* predict the shock.**

And the outcome? Rescorla's results showed that fear conditioning did occur in Group 1. The dogs learned to respond to the tone in order to avoid the shock. Group 2 animals showed no conditioning because, unlike Group 1, they were unable to use the tone to predict the shock. Results for other groups followed this same pattern: the amount of conditioning was related to the predictive value of the CS, not to simple CS-UCS contiguity.

The Rescorla-Wagner model suggests that animals rehearse information they are acquiring. When the association of CS and UCS is new, there is active rehearsal and learning is rapid. Later, when the UCS can be completely predicted by the occurrence of the CS, learning slows down and stops.

What Rescorla is basically saying is that learning does not occur just because two stimuli occur in close temporal proximity—close together in time. Rather, it occurs because one stimulus comes to predict the occurrence of another. Since expectancy and predictability are cognitive concepts, we can conclude that the Rescorla-Wagner includes cognitive elements in its associative explanation of conditioning. However, this theory is not as cognitive as some of the others.

Work related to the Rescorla model, as well as that on blocking and rule formation, along with other recent bodies of research, clearly favor a cognitively oriented S-S understanding of classical conditioning (Rescorla, 2002). However, there is by no means total agreement, and research in this area continues. We have more to say about cognition in Chapter 8.

Aha!: Insight Learning

You have no doubt had insights. For example, you are faced with a complex new concept, perhaps in a math course, and decide that you will never fully understand it. You put the book away and come back to the problem hours later. After ten minutes of renewed study, you suddenly say "Aha!" as the concept becomes clear. This is insight learning.

While Skinner was promoting the behavioral school in the United States, Gestalt psychologist Wolfgang K^hler was studying the behavior of chimpanzees in Europe. His most intelligent chimp, Sultan, had learned to use a stick to pull in bananas placed outside his cage. One day K^hler put the bananas too far out to be reached with the short stick in the cage, but he placed a longer stick outside the cage that Sultan could reach with the shorter stick. Sultan first tried and failed to reach the banana with the short stick. He then looked around the cage and the outside area for some time. Suddenly, he grabbed the short stick, used it to pull in the long stick, then used the long stick to reach the banana. K^hler's explanation was that Sultan had engaged in *insight learning,* which is characterized by sudden resolution or action after a period of study during which there is no action or apparent understanding.

How can insight learning be explained theoretically? A partial answer is that it appears to involve two stages. The first is a process of problem-solving, a kind of mental trial-and-error, in which solutions are tried out and rejected without any actual behavior being displayed. The second stage is storing the final solution in memory, where it is available for retrieval later.

Are cognitive processes the best explanation for conditioning and learning? Some psychologists clearly believe they are, but others are not convinced. They argue that the proposed cognitive processes cannot be directly observed and must be inferred. When cognitive psychologists do not fully understand how a conditioned association takes place, their critics argue, they propose constructs like expectancy, prediction, and cognitive maps to fill the gaps in understanding (Uttal, 2001). The danger is that such constructs may be difficult to test empirically. This theoretical battle represents a scientifically healthy difference of opinion and promises to continue for many years to come.

Observational Learning: Albert Bandura

Have you ever fired a pistol? If not, you probably nevertheless feel, like Sam in our opening example, that if you were called upon to do so, you would know how to hold it, aim it, and pull the trigger. That's because you have often seen guns being fired in movies and on television. In the same way, you acquire a large repertoire of social and other behavioral abilities by seeing your parents and others perform these behaviors as you grow up. You are engaging in a cognitive learning process that theorist Albert Bandura (1965, 1992) calls observational learning. *Observational learning* takes place when the ability to perform a behavior is acquired or modified by observing others. Those performing the behavior and being observed are called *models.*

In a classic study of observational learning, Bandura (1965) showed young boys and girls a short film depicting an adult model behaving aggressively toward a Bobo doll, an inflated toy that bounces back whenever it is knocked down. After the film, the children were taken to a room containing a number of toys, including a Bobo doll. Results showed that the children tended to reproduce the model's aggressive behaviors toward the doll rather than engage in other types of behavior. A control group of children who did not see the Bobo doll film did not display the modeled behaviors toward the toy. The behavior of children in the experimental group could not readily be accounted for by operant conditioning principles, since they had not been reinforced for playing with it. The modeled behaviors had been learned by observation alone. And what would happen if the child saw the model actually being rewarded for his aggressive behavior? A second Bandura study answers that question (Figure 6-11).

Studies suggest that even lower animals learn by observation. Chickens that have observed chicken models pecking a key to obtain grain learn the response themselves more quickly than chickens that did not observe the model. We will take up the basic processes involved in observational learning, the role of reinforcement, and applications of Bandura's approach to the understanding of human social behavior.

Four Basic Processes

Bandura explains instances of observational learning as involving four basic processes:

- *Attention.* You must attend to the model in order to learn by observation.
- *Retention.* If you are to later use what you have learned, you must store it in memory.
- *Reproduction.* You must be capable of reproducing the learned response. Watching Bruce Lee or Chuck Norris expertly executing a series of karate moves doesn't mean that you can reproduce them accurately.
- *Motivation.* You will reproduce observationally acquired behaviors only if you are motivated to do so. You need to have some expectation that making the response will be rewarding. Sam picked up and fired the gun because his friend offered to give him five dollars.

The Role of Reinforcement

Observational learning can take place without reinforcement. In fact, Bandura emphasizes that the reinforcement seen as so essential in classical and operant conditioning theories is totally unnecessary in an observational learning theory. Learning occurs by simply observing a model. The model performs the behavior, you observe it and "copy" it into your behavioral repertoire. You may display it immediately, as in the Bobo doll study, or not until many years later, as when someone invites you to fire a gun at a target range.

Although not necessary for learning, reinforcement does have at least two functions in Bandura's approach. First, it plays a role when the person actually *performs* the behavior. Bandura suggests that an observed behavior may be incorporated into an individual's repertoire but never actually exhibited until reinforcement is available for that behavior. Unfortunately, watching people or cartoon characters fire guns and beat each other up, activities that many children see every day in violent TV programs, may also lead to observational learning and perhaps later to violent behavior when reinforcement is available (see Thinking Critically).

The second role of reinforcement is to enhance the learning process. If, for example, the adult model is rewarded for a particular response, the child is more likely to learn that response rapidly than if the model is not rewarded or is actually punished.

Self-Efficacy and Human Agency

Observational learning and reinforcement result in the development of a sense of *self-efficacy*—the individual's belief about his own ability to perform behaviors that lead to desired or expected outcomes (Bandura et al., 2001). Those with high self-efficacy are confident that they can engage in behaviors that will be successful in gaining reinforcers. However, low self-efficacy leads to anxiety and can contribute to ineffectual behavior. To some degree, feelings of self-efficacy are specific to particular situations and aspects of life, and they can influence which problems an individual chooses to deal with and which ones she doesn't (Horn et al., 2002). In general, greater feelings of self-efficacy are associated with greater success in such areas as coping with pain, academic achievement, athletic competition, smoking cessation, and career choice (Bandura et al., 2001). In fact, so important are these feelings that Bandura and his colleagues have developed a scale to measure them (Steffen et al., 2002).

By applying self-efficacy to everyday situations, the individual exercises *human agency*—the ability to control one's own life (Conte, 2002). The degree of control that actually is exercised varies from person to person and is also influenced by external situations. However, Bandura sees human agency as the essence of humanness and hence of life itself (Bandura, 2001).

Human Social Behavior

Bandura (1992) argues that observational learning is the basis for the development of most human social behaviors. A little boy who starts "shaving" with a plastic razor learns to do so by observing his father. We also learn negative and dangerous behaviors through modeling. For example, a model's fear of snakes is quickly learned by an observer, and child abuse is seen primarily in people who apparently learned this behavior by observing their own parents. In addition, there is evidence to support the common notion that children learn to become drinkers and sometimes alcoholics in part by observing their parents (Lang & Stritzke, 1993).

The Neurophysiology of Learning

When you read a chapter or take a tennis lesson, the learning process produces changes in your brain. Knowing what these changes are and how they take place is basic to a full understanding of what learning involves. We will examine the evolutionary basis for learning processes, changes that take place at the synapse when learning occurs, the major brain structures involved in learning, and the neurochemistry of response acquisition.

Evolution: Learning As An Adaptive Mechanism

Neural mechanisms have evolved over time and across species from the simple nervous systems of such organisms as the jelly fish to the complex human brain (Chapter 3). This neural evolution has been accompanied by the evolution of mechanisms that help each organism to survive and reproduce in its natural environment. Clearly, one of those mechanisms is learning, and evolution has favored learning as an important survival tool.

From the perspective of evolutionary psychology, the learning mechanisms of a given species are best understood as being related to the natural environment in which the species has evolved. As we saw in Chapter 1, natural selection means that the species-specific behavior patterns seen in animals are those that have historically allowed them to best survive and reproduce in their natural environments. What must therefore evolve is both a set of innate behavioral tendencies and a set of innate mechanisms for modifying those tendencies. For example, a person might inherit a genetic tendency to be more extraverted than introverted. She also inherits mechanisms that permit this tendency to be modified by her experiences in the natural environment. If her parents and others reinforce primarily extraverted behavior, she may become more extraverted; if more introverted behaviors are reinforced, she may become somewhat less extraverted. See Chapters 1 and 10 for a discussion of how genetic predispositions interact with environmental experience.

Simpler behaviors in lower animals—avoiding dangers, foraging for food, selecting mates—evolve in the same way. Some songbirds, for instance, inherit neural mechanisms that allow them to make sounds but learn or modify their songs by hearing their parents sing. Both a genetic tendency toward a certain behavior pattern and mechanisms through which environmental experience can modify that pattern are thus inherited. The collective mechanisms for changing behaviors in response to the environment are what we call learning.

We have already seen examples of the interactive roles of heredity and learning in connection with our discussion of biological preparedness. Phobias for darkness and snakes but not for flowers or trees are genetically predisposed because they have adaptive value for the species. However, not every human being has darkness and snake phobias. Only those who also undergo relevant learning experiences actually develop the phobias.

Food Preference: Genetics and Learning. Another good example of the evolution of both hereditary predispositions toward patterns of behavior and hereditary flexibility mechanisms is the development of food preferences. Why is it that we prefer certain foods over others? The answer is that we inherit tendencies to prefer foods that satisfy nutritional needs, but these tendencies are modified toward preferences for specific foods through learning and experience. For example, protein can be obtained from either fish or red meat, but you may learn to prefer one over the other (Figure 6-12). The genetic factor works to ensure that the body will periodically replenish a variety of vitamins, minerals, and other substances to survive and maintain normal functioning. If you are deprived of a certain nutrient—say vitamin C—you will tend to select foods containing that nutrient. When the vitamin C need is met, your preference will change to foods containing other substances for which there is now a greater need.

To test this idea, suppose we could stop feeding infants foods that adults know are good for them and let them choose their own foods. We might do this for six months or more and see if the infants fulfilled their own nutritional needs and remained healthy. In modern times, we would seriously question the ethics of such a study and would very likely not approve it. However, pediatrician Clara Davis actually did this experiment in the 1920s (Davis, 1928). She put 35-week-old babies in a hospital and let each baby feed itself for at least six months. At each meal the baby received a tray containing about a dozen natural foods, including fruits, vegetables, meats, eggs, fish, and cereals. It selected and ate the foods it wanted. In order to remain healthy, the infant had to vary its diet, since no one food contained all necessary ingredients.

What happened? Typically, an infant would eat only two or three foods at a given meal and might continue to eat these foods for a week or so. It had thus developed a food preference. However, it would soon switch to other foods containing different nutrients, supposedly because those nutrients were now needed. In one particularly striking case, a baby entered the study with a vitamin D deficiency, which had produced rickets, a disease involving muscle pain and bending of the bones under muscle tension, among other symptoms. Included on its tray was a dish of cod-liver oil, which infants usually hate but which contains large amounts of vitamin D. Interestingly enough, this particular infant regularly chose the cod-liver oil until the rickets disappeared, then never ate it again. It had cured its own nutritional disease!

Research done since the Davis study has confirmed the tendency to seek foods needed by the body. Both people and animals selectively deprived of salt prefer salty solutions and foods. Animals deprived of the B-vitamin thiamine and those deficient in vitamin A also preferentially select foods containing the nutrient they need.

Foods can also be deselected when they are no longer adaptive. The best case in point is milk. Most newborn babies —and, more generally, mammals—survive entirely on milk but stop nursing when they are older, and most adults actually drink very little milk. Why? Because levels of the intestinal enzyme lactase decline with age and lactase is needed to metabolize lactose, the sugar in milk. Without it, mammals can experience nausea, cramping, and vomiting. About two-thirds of adult humans inherit the recessive gene that produces low lactase levels (Flatz, 1987). If you think about it, you will quickly realize that very few Chinese, Thai, or Japanese foods contain dairy products. That is because Asians (and also Africans) have the most difficulty with lactose intolerance, while Europeans and European-Americans have less. Although many adults do consume cheese and other dairy products, most cannot eat large quantities without distress. The declining levels of lactase beyond infancy may well be an evolved mechanism that serves to motivate the child on a milk diet to learn to eat foods containing a wider variety of nutrients.

The Lowly Aplysia

To understand how learning takes place in the highly evolved human brain, with its 100 billion neurons, it might be best begin by studying a much simpler nervous system. Eric Kandel (1985, 2001) and his colleagues therefore decided to study the sea snail *Aplysia*, a simple invertebrate with less than 100,000 neurons in its nervous system, some large enough to be seen by the naked eye.

Kandel began by studying the two simplest forms of learning, habituation and sensitization. ***Habituation*** is a decrease in responding that occurs when a stimulus is repeated, and ***sensitization*** is an increase. When Kandel repeatedly touched the snail, its natural withdrawal reflex decreased or habituated. When, however, he first delivered an electric shock to the head or tail, the reflex increased or sensitized. He found that the primary neural changes taking place during these simple forms of learning were at the synapses between sensory and motor neurons. Habituation was accompanied by a decrease in the release of neurotransmitters at the synapse, while sensitization involved an increase.

Kandel went on to study classical conditioning, a more complex form of learning. He found that touching the sea snail with a nylon bristle produced little or no response. Delivering an electric shock to its tail, however, produced a vigorous withdrawal response. He therefore used the bristle touch as a CS and the shock as a UCS. After repeated pairings the animal developed a conditioned withdrawal response to the bristle touch. Kandel found that the neural mechanism associated with the development of this CR was increased release of the neurotransmitter at the synapse (Kandel & Schwartz, 1982; Kandel, 2001).

Kandel's pioneering work has led to a large body of research on *Aplysia* that demonstrates one specific neural mechanism—presynaptic change in neurotransmitter release—through which learning may take place (Mayford et al., 1992). We cannot reasonably expect that learning processes in the far more complex human brain will be entirely based on this same mechanism. However, we now know of at least one likely neural basis for learning.

Learning in More Complex Brains

Much of the work on neural processes underlying learning in vertebrates has focused on the brain structures that may be involved (Kandel & Squire, 2000). Confirmed by recent studies using functional magnetic resonance imaging (fMRI; see Chapter 4), they include the hippocampus, the cerebellum, and areas of the motor, temporal and somatosensory cortex (Corbit et al., 2001; Toni et al., 2000). Other work has identified neurochemicals that appear to be involved in learning.

The Hippocampus: Long-Term Potentiation. Recent research has shown that the *hippocampus* (Figure 6-13 and Chapter 3) may have an important role in learning. This discovery came through classical conditioning studies conducted primarily by Berger and Thompson (1978a, 1978b). They conditioned rabbits to blink to a tone (the CS) by pairing it with a puff of air directed at the eye (the UCS). As conditioning took place, the researchers observed increased firing in response to the tone in certain hippocampal cells that had initially responded only to the airpuff. Interestingly enough, the increase in firing rates occurred a number of trials *before* the corresponding behavioral changes took place, suggesting that the neurological changes involved in learning must precede the behavioral change.

More recent research has included direct study of the brain and computer simulations of the learning process. It confirms the role of the hippocampus in both classical and operant learning (Munera et al., 2001; Beylin et al,. 2001). One theory is that response acquisition may involve the development of neural networks—sets of interacting neurons—that mediate the learned response (Keil et al., 2001). These networks are described in our 21 for this chapter. It appears that as the CR develops, both changes in synapses and increased connections among neurons lead to a gradual reorganization of neural connections. In addition, important changes take place within the single neuron.

Learning in the hippocampus—and perhaps elsewhere in the brain—may involve *long-term potentiation* or LTP. LTP refers to a measurable increase in the size of a neural response following brief, intense electrical stimulation. The electrical bombardment makes the neuron highly sensitive and responsive to the same type of stimulation for days or even weeks. LTP can also be classically conditioned. The researcher delivers a very weak stimulus that elicits no potentiation (the CS) followed by the strong electrical stimulus that causes LTP (the UCS). After repeated pairings, the CS alone will elicit LTP).

LTP has been demonstrated primarily in the same areas of the hippocampus that are otherwise associated with learning processes. It appears to involve a combination of chemical, electrical, and structural changes at specialized synapses. It thus appears that learning may take place, in part, by modifying synapses in specific areas of the hippocampus.

The Cerebellum. Richard Thompson and his colleagues (Thompson, 1991; Logan et al., 1994) have discovered that the cerebellum, which coordinates motor activity, is also involved in learning. They find that the acquisition of classically conditioned responses is associated with measurable changes in groups of cerebellar neurons. It appears that these changes serve to store the information acquired during conditioning.

The Cerebral Cortex. Much of the research on structural changes during learning was stimulated by work on discrimination learning in monkeys. Measuring the electrical activity of the brain, researchers have found that cells in the *motor cortex* (see Chapter 3) increase their firing rates during and just before the occurrence of an avoidance response but show no increase when there is no response (Sakamoto et al., 1987). Other research has confirmed that changes in firing rates in the motor cortex typically accompany some kinds of learning.

The *temporal cortex* also appears to be involved. In one study, lesions were made in areas of the right temporal lobe. The animals were then operantly conditioned to make simple learned responses and also to discriminate between two stimuli. The simple conditioned responses were unaffected by the lesions. However, the discrimination responses were significantly impaired. It may be that the learning of the simple responses can be mediated by the hippocampus and other subcortical structures but that the more complex discrimination learning requires involvement of the temporal cortex. The *somatosensory cortex* also undergoes important changes when learning takes place, and damage to this area impairs some aspects of learning processes (Wozniak et al., 1989).

The Neurochemistry of Learning. A variety of *biochemicals* known to exist in the brain and nervous system have also been implicated in learning. These biochemicals include neurotransmitters, such as acetylcholine, as well as DNA, RNA, and various proteins and glycoproteins. Because most of the work related to the biochemistry of learning and retention has focused more specifically on memory, the details of this research are described in Chapter 7, which deals with memory processes.

Conclusion

Both genetics and learning are involved in the acquisition and modification of behavior. Neither alone can account for the relatively simple learning that takes place in the animal laboratory or the vast repertoire of behaviors that humans acquire over a lifetime. Learning is clearly both an important process and a complex one. It is most basically a set of mechanisms that have evolved over the course of genetic history to allow us to adapt to environmental conditions by acquiring new behaviors and modifying old ones.

We have also seen in this chapter that there are several major theories of learning, each suggesting somewhat different key processes by which knowledge is acquired. Classical conditioning approaches hypothesize the gradual formation of associations through which the CS comes to elicit the CR. The operant model holds that emitted behaviors are reinforced, causing an increase in the probability of the behavior. More recent theoretical interpretations of both classical and operant conditioning suggest the involvement of cognitive factors. The broader reality is that all three forms of learning—classical conditioning, operant conditioning, and observational learning (as well as cognitive learning more generally) work together in everyday situations as we all develop a broad repertoire of behaviors. It seems likely that in the foreseeable future the psychology of learning will move more and more toward the study of cognitive factors and the nature of the neurological processes underlying learning. Both these issues are discussed further in Chapters 7 and 8.

Summary

1. Learning is usually defined as a set of relatively permanent changes in behavior that result from prior experience. Learning is what one is capable of doing, whereas performance is what one is currently doing.

Classical Conditioni

1. Classical conditioni ...) with a neutral stimulus, such that the neutral stimulus be ... ditioned response (CR).
2. The best results a ... ortly before the unconditioned stimulus (delay conditionin
3. Extinction is the ... d UCS are no longer paired. Spontaneous recovery is the re ... d.
4. Generalization m ... o the CS. Discrimination involves learning to distinguish be ... propriate one.
5. There is an ong ... est understood as S-S or S-R learning.
6. The equipotent ... ome associated with any UCS. Work on biological prepare ... organism has genetic predispositions to form some kinds of asso...

Operant Conditioning

1. Edward L. Thorndike developed the Law of Effect, which says that a behavior is more likely to be repeated when it is followed by satisfaction or reward.
2. B.F. Skinner developed the view that behavior is determined by its consequences.
3. Responses are elicited in classical conditioning and emitted in operant conditioning. Operant conditioning involves trial-and-error learning in which responses are acquired through reinforcement of operant behaviors.
4. Skinner holds that only directly observable behaviors should be studied.
5. Acquisition involves shaping by reinforcing successive approximations. Withdrawal of reinforcement leads to extinction. The passage of time can lead to spontaneous recovery.
6. A response can be generalized to similar stimuli, become specific through discrimination procedures, or come to occur only in the presence of a particular discriminative stimulus.
7. A reinforcer is any object or event that increases the likelihood of a response occurring. Reinforcement occurs when the consequence of a response increases the likelihood or probability that the response will be repeated.
8. Primary reinforcers have a direct relationship to some known drive; secondary reinforcers are learned on the basis of primary reinforcers.
9. Positive reinforcers are present and negative reinforcers absent following the response. Punishment is a consequence that follows a response and decreases its probability.
10. In escape learning the organism acquires a response that ends an aversive stimulus. In avoidance learning, the response prevents the aversive stimulus from occurring. Mowrer's two-process theory says that avoidance learning involves both classical and operant conditioning.
11. The four types of reinforcement schedules are: fixed ratio, variable ratio, fixed interval; and variable interval.
12. Biological preparedness limits the power of reinforcement. Instinctive drift, in which operant response acquisition is impaired by innate predispositions, is a good example.

Cognitive Factors in Learning

1. Cognitive maps are used even by rats running a maze, according to Edward Tolman.
2. The Rescorla-Wagner model suggests that classical conditioning involves learning a cognitive expectancy that permits the prediction of a second event when the first occurs.
3. Blocking is important because it shows that learning involves the use of expectancies to predict outcomes.
4. Insight learning is characterized by sudden resolution after a period of study without action.
5. In observational learning behaviors are acquired by watching another person (the model) perform that behavior. A model displays it and the learner observes it.
6. Four basic observational learning processes are attention, retention, reproduction, and motivation.
7. Reinforcement is not necessary for observational learning. It is needed, however, for the behavior to be repeatedly performed at some later point. In addition, reinforcement of the model can enhance learning.

The Neurophysiology of Learning

1. Kandel has shown that learning in Aplysia involves presynaptic changes in neurotransmitter release.
2. The hippocampus appears to be importantly involved in both classical and operant conditioning. Long-term potentiation may be involved.
3. Areas of the cerebellum, temporal cortex, the motor cortex, and the somatosensory cortex may also be involved.
4. A variety of neurotransmitters, DNA, RNA, and proteins may be involved in learning.
5. Learning can be seen as a set of evolved mechanisms that permit organisms to adapt to their environments and thus survive.
6. Food preference development is a good example of the inheritance of both predispositions toward certain behavior patterns and flexibility mechanisms.

Ask Yourself

1. What are the major similarities and differences between classical and operant conditioning?
2. Describe recent developments in both operant and classical conditioning.
3. What cognitive factors have been proposed as elements of conditioning processes? Do you think they are important?
4 Discuss the role of reinforcement in classical conditioning, operant conditioning, and observational learning.
5. What have we learned from studies of aplysia?
6. Does the evolutionary view of learning conflict with any of the other major theories?
7. How can human social behavior be explained by Pavlov, Skinner, and Bandura?
8. What do we know about the role of the brain in learning?
9. How does biological preparedness limit the power of reinforcement in operant and classical conditioning?
10. Describe some useful applications of the various forms of learning.

Further Readings

Bandura, A. *Social Learning Theory.* Englewood Cliffs, N.J.: Prentlce-Hall, 1977. A definitive treatment of observational learning and Bandura's social learning theory more generally. The book deals with research and applications as well as basic theory.

Corrigan, P.W., & Storzbach, D.M. (1993). Behavioral interventions for alleviating psychotic symptoms. *Hosp. & Commun. Psychiat.*, 44, 341-347. The authors show how behavioral techniques can be used even with severely disturbed patients to enhance the effects of medication, decrease symptoms, and increase coping skills.

Pavlik, W.B. & Flora, S.R. (1993). Human responding on multiple variable interval schedules and extinction. *Learning and Motivation*, 24, 88-99. This study provides a good example of human operant conditioning.

Lieberman, D.A. (1993). *Learning: Behavior and Cognition.* Pacific Grove, CA: Brooks/Cole. This is a solid basic text that examines in more depth most of the topics we have covered in this chapter.

Murre, J.M. (1992). *Learning and categorization in modular neural networks.* Hove, England: Lawrence Erlbaum. If you are interested in some more advanced reading about neural models and the neurological basis for learning, this book will give you what you need.

O'Brien, C.P., Childress, A.R., McLellan, A.T., & Ehrman, R. (1992). A learning model of addiction. O'Brien provides evidence that learning processes may be involved in The development of addictions to psychoactive drugs.

Rubeling, H. (1993). Pavlovian conditioning in human skilled motor behavior. Integr. Physiol. Behav. Sci., 28, 29-45. This article provides a good, recent example of human classical conditioning in the important area of motor skill acquisition.

Skinner, B.F., *Walden II*. New York: Macmillan 1976 (originally published 1948). In this provocative novel, Skinner applies conditioning principles to human behavior and creates a utopian community.

Squire, L.R. (1992). *Encyclopedia of learning and memory.* NY: Macmillan. As the title implies, this book may contain "everything you ever wanted to know about learning but were afraid to ask." It compiles 189 articles covering virtually every aspect of the learning field, and many are good examples of how research is done.

Key Terms

avoidance learning
classical conditioning
conditioned response
conditioned stimulus
continuous reinforcement
discrimination
discriminative stimulus
escape learning
extinction
generalization
higher order conditioning
instrumental conditioning
interval schedule
law of effect
learning
negative reinforcement
observational learning
operant conditioning
operant
partial reinforcement
partial reinforcement effect
positive reinforcement
primary reinforcement
punishment
ratio schedule
secondary reinforcement
shaping
Skinner box
spontaneous recovery
stimulus control
successive approximation
token economy
trial-and-error learning
two-process theory
unconditioned response
unconditioned stimulus

Key People

Albert Bandura
John Garcia
Eric Kandel
Gregory Kimble
Wolfgang K^hler
O.H. Mowrer
Ivan Pavlov

David Premack
Robert Rescorla
Martin Seligman
B.F. Skinner
E. L. Thorndike
Edward Tolman
Allan Wagner
John B. Watson

Psychology in the 21st Century

Neural Networks

Learning clearly involves the formation of associations. In classical conditioning, there is an acquired association between the previously neutral CS and the UCS. In operant conditioning, the association is between the operant response and the reinforcer that causes it to increase in frequency. We see these associations in behavior when Pavlov's dog learns to salivate to a bell or Skinner's pigeon increases the key pecking that results in food. But what is going on in the brain? What neural changes take place as learned associations form?

Several decades ago, Donald Hebb (1949) theorized that when learning takes place, it causes the formation of groups of neurons that serve to maintain the memory of what has been learned (see Chapter 7). His hypothesis anticipated a major current theory suggesting that *neural networks* form as the learning process proceeds. Each network is a set of neurons linked to one another through synaptic connections. The neurons may be physically close to each other in the brain, but often they are widely scattered, linked only by the synapses of their axons and dendrites. In essence, then, the theory suggests that as the rat, pigeon, or human undergoes repeated trials of a learning task, linkages are gradually formed among a number of neurons, and these networks form the neural basis for learning. Connections that are weaker increase in strength more rapidly (Keil et al., 2001), which is consistent with typical behavioral learning curves —rapid early learning, followed by slower learning, finally reaching maximum strength of association.

Consider the word "cat." We learn the basic meaning of the word at an early age, then gradually learn a variety of additional meanings and associations over time. In the accompanying figure, the concept "cat" is neurally linked directly to such learned associations as meow, pet, and scratch. Each of these is, in turn, linked to other concept categories that may be triggered off by the word "cat." For example, scratch is associated with pain, which is linked with injection, dentist, and blood. Ultimately, many interrelated networks form our body of acquired knowledge if this model of the neural basis for learning proves correct. In any case, it will surely remain a major basis for research in the 21st Century.

But not everyone agrees that neural networks can entirely explain learning. One objection is that a network may quickly lose old information when it gets new information, a phenomenon called catastrophic interference. However, studies show that human learning doesn't really work that way. Rather, the loss of learned information tends to occur gradually over a period of time. A second problem is a lack of definitive evidence that learning networks are actually found in the brain. It may, in fact turn out that they are not even neurologically possible. Despite these concerns, neural networking and connectionism continue to become increasingly popular and important ways of understanding how learning takes place.

Probe

Ugh! It's Avocado: Taste Aversion

As a teenager, I was once invited to the home of family friends for a dinner that included an avocado salad. Several hours later I became violently ill, with nausea, vomiting, and diarrhea. I remembered the taste of the avocado in the salad. It turned out that in reality I was coming down with the flu. Nevertheless, I had associated avocado with nausea, and to this day I avoid it at all costs. I had developed a *conditioned taste aversion* (Kimball, 2002).

John Garcia (1989) and his colleagues have done a series of studies that explain why I can't stand avocado. They give rats a particular sight, sound, or taste, then used radiation to make them nauseous (Garcia & Koelling, 1966). In one study, rats were exposed to a loud buzzer, a bright light, and water sweetened with saccharin (all potential conditioned stimuli), then shocked or made nauseous with radiation (the unconditioned stimuli). The rats developed a conditioned fear response only to the buzzer and light, not to the sweet water. They developed conditioned avoidance of the sweet water—a taste aversion—only when made nauseous in the presence of that stimulus (see the figure). It thus appears that only certain associations can be learned, namely, those for which the organism is biologically prepared (Massei & Cowan, 2002). Only when a taste is paired with nausea will the taste aversion develop (Risenger et al., 2002).

Garcia went on to conduct a series of animal studies clearly demonstrating the constraining role of biological preparedness in classical conditioning (Garcia & Rusiniak, 1980; Garcia, Rusiniak, & Brett, 1977). Other studies have shown that taste aversions can sometimes be extinguished, though with considerable difficulty (Sorge et al., 2002; Lopez et al., 2002).

Taste aversion has also been studied in humans (Batsell, 2000). Studies of human cancer patients show that they develop taste aversions for food eaten just before X-ray therapy or chemotherapy, which makes them nauseous (Flaherty, 1985). Ilene Bernstein (1978, 1991) gave children with cancer a unique flavor of ice cream she called "Mapletoff" just before chemotherapy. Only 21% of these children would eat the ice cream again later as compared with 67% of a control group who had not experienced the taste aversion manipulation.

Evolutionary theory provides one explanation of taste aversion. It suggests that this food-avoidance response is a biologically adaptive reaction that can stop you from eating a potentially dangerous food. This biological preparedness permits us to easily acquire at least some kinds of protective taste aversions. The evolutionary result is enhanced survival of the species, and taste aversion is an excellent example of the adaptive value of learning mechanisms. When you consume a food that will make you ill, the nausea and other symptoms usually come not immediately but hours later. Taste aversion or food-avoidance learning allows you to detect the toxic food immediately through its smell and taste, thus avoiding the illness.

One practical application of taste aversion has been to help sheep farmers. They are often plagued by coyotes killing and eating their sheep, so researcher Garcia (1974) laced sheep carcasses with lithium chloride, a drug that causes nausea. Coyotes ate the carcasses, became ill, and avoided eating sheep thereafter. Unfortunately, in some cases the coyotes continued to kill the sheep but did not eat them.

Think Critically: *Does Television Promote Violence?*

Television is a very powerful medium because so many people spend so much time watching it. For that reason, cigarette advertising was banned from TV after extensive studies clearly documented the deadly consequences of smoking (see Chapter 15). Is there good reason to similarly ban or greatly reduce violence in television programming? Studies show that children spend 15,000 hours watching TV by the time they graduate from high school, compared with 11,000 hours in the classroom. Moreover, they see 5 violent acts every 60 minutes, over 20 per hour during Saturday morning cartoons, and an average of 122 per hour in such shows as "Superman" (Radecki, 1990). Indeed, by age 15, the average child has observed a whopping 24,000 televised shootings and virtually countless other acts of violence!

The Basic Hypothesis or Contention

Bandura's observational learning theory clearly suggests that the daily modeling of violence on TV can cause children observing the models to become more aggressive. In addition, repeated viewing of such programming may make children (and the adults they become) less sensitive to violence. Finally, the violence may produce emotional arousal and increase the likelihood of violent reactions to frustration. If observational learning theory is correct, televised violence should clearly be reduced or eliminated.

What Is The Evidence?

Evidence supporting the Bandura hypothesis has been developed over the past thirty years and is a good illustration of several types of studies discussed in Chapter 2: Case, correlational, experimental, and quasi-experimental studies. Case studies include claims by adults on trial for murder that their violence was prompted by watching TV. In addition, there have been news reports linking specific violent programs to violent behavior over long periods of time following the airing of the program (Johnson et al., 2002; Anderson & Bushman, 2002). One, for example, documented cases in which children poked out each other's eyes after seeing the Three Stooges do it (Associated Press, 1984).

The many correlational studies are quite consistent in showing a link between television violence and personal aggressiveness. For example, a study that followed people from age 8 to age 30 found that those who watched more TV violence as children were convicted of more violent crimes as adults (Centerwall, 1989). Moderate, but significant, correlations of this type have been found in at least five different countries.

Experimental studies have added weight to the evidence (Walsh et al., 2002). Such studies randomly assign children to view more or less violence, then record their subsequent aggressive behavior. In one study, children systematically exposed to violent movies become more aggressive than those in a control group exposed to nonviolent movies (Leyens et al., 1975). Similarly, boys shown violent movies were more aggressive when they later played field hockey than those who first saw nonviolent films.

Finally, quasi-experimental studies, involving designs in which random assignment to different groups is not possible, are supportive. In one study three such groups were compared:

- A town with no TV station before one became available in 1974.
- A town with a TV station both before and after 1974.
- A town with four stations before and after 1974.

A count of the change in number of aggressive acts by children in the three towns between 1973 and 1974 showed a significantly greater increase in the town that had just acquired TV (Joy, Kimball, & Zabrack, 1986).

Is The Evidence Open To Alternative Interpretations?

Each type of evidence can be questioned on scientific grounds. We know, of course, that we cannot rely on case studies for final conclusions. Some people may report that viewing violence caused them to become more aggressive. Others might say that violent TV has no effect on them or even that seeing the destructive nature of the acts causes them to become less violent. In cases of criminals blaming TV, we must, of course, question their motives.

Correlational studies are much more convincing, but we still cannot ignore their usual limitations. First, the link between TV viewing and violent behavior may be due to a third variable. Perhaps, for example, parents who prohibit their children from watching violent TV shows also discourage aggressive behavior, though studies do not support this conclusion. Another possibility is that unemployment and attendant poverty cause people to watch more TV and also cause them to be more violent. Secondly, we can seldom be certain of the direction of causation in correlational studies. Does viewing violence cause children to become more aggressive or do children with more aggressive personality traits (perhaps in part for genetic reasons) prefer to watch more violent TV? Again, studies to date do not support these alternatives, but correlational research alone is still not sufficient.

Even the experimental and quasi-experimental evidence must be interpreted with caution. We can ask how valid the experimental studies are. They are necessarily short-term studies, such as those exposing children briefly to violence, then testing its effects. Do they prove that long-term viewing has the same effects? The quasi-experimental studies present the problem that random assignment is not possible. The towns in the study we discussed could not be randomly assigned to the television viewing conditions. Can we therefore be certain that the observed effects were really due to observational learning and not to some biasing factor?

Do We Need Additional Evidence?

Further correlational and experimental evidence would certainly be welcome. However, the best studies, from a scientific viewpoint, would have to randomly assign children to view larger and smaller amounts of violence over a period of years, then assess differences in aggressive behavior. Such studies would be impractical because accurately monitoring the viewing habits of many children over time would be very difficult. In addition, they would raise serious ethical questions because they would intentionally expose some children to an agent that is widely thought to be harmful.

What Conclusions Can We Reach?

The consistency of evidence across several types of studies supporting the observational learning hypothesis is quite convincing. There can be little doubt that watching violent television can be a causal factor in violent behavior, a conclusion shared by researchers from the National Institutes of Mental Health, the American Psychological Association, and the American Academy of Pediatrics (American Academy of Pediatrics, 2001). As this evidence becomes more convincing to the general public, federal and state governments, television networks, and advertisers, we may eventually see a real and practical application—a systematic reduction in televised violence. At the same time, we must recognize that observational learning through television viewing is by no means the only factor in aggression. Observing violent behavior in parents, peers, and the community at large probably also plays a role. In addition, personality traits and cognitive interpretations of violence no doubt influence the ultimate behavioral outcome.

Horizons in Learning

Do Guns Kill People?

Guns killed 35,000 people in the United States in 1990 and injured countless others, despite a National Rifle Association slogan which asserts that "Guns don't kill people, People kill people." The slogan suggests that guns may be used as weapons but do not actually elicit aggressive responses. Is a gun really a neutral stimulus, as the NRA implies, or is it perhaps a powerful cue that can cause violent conditioned responses? After all, we learn early in childhood that guns are associated with violence. One study showed that angry participants delivered more shocks to partners if there were guns lying on the experimental table than they did if the table contained badminton racquets. That is, the gun *elicited* aggression. In other studies, college students threw more wet sponges at a clown when there was a rifle lying nearby and more people honked their horns at a stalled pickup truck when there was a gun displayed in the truck (Berkowitz, 1981). Do guns kill people? It appears that they do, at least in the sense that the weapon itself can be a conditioned stimulus for aggressive responses.

Learning to Be Immune

Your immune system includes white blood cells called B-lymphocytes that fight bacterial infections and T-lymphocytes that attack foreign tissues, viruses, and cancer cells. It now appears that the immune response involving these cells can be enhanced and suppressed through classical and perhaps operant conditioning. Robert Ader and his colleagues had mice taste sweetened water, then made them nauseous by injecting a drug called cyclophosphamide. When later forced to drink the sweetened water, some mice became ill and died. Apparently the sweet water had become a CS that suppressed the immune response, making the mice more susceptible to infections. Other studies confirm this effect of learning on immunity (MacQueen & Siegel, 1989). It may thus eventually be possible to use conditioning techniques to enhance the human immune response, even for such deadly disorders as AIDS.

Food, Pleasure, and Your Amygdala

Food is often associated with pleasure, an emotional experience, and neuroscientists are beginning to track down the neural basis for this food/pleasure reaction. Have you ever come home after a very busy day during which you ate absolutely nothing? You're starved, so you open the refrigerator and discover that it contains a delicious steak or some other favorite food. You probably have a positive emotional reaction to seeing the food. Although you might not have delay your meal to wonder what is taking place in your brain, neuroscientists do. Some studies have demonstrated that cells within the *amygdala*, a part of the limbic system, fire at the sight of desirable food presented to hungry animals (Parkinson et al., 2001). The researchers hypothesize that the firing of the amygdala represents the affective or feeling-state response to a reward object like food. Your joy at seeing the steak was mediated by an amygdalar response. The next time you are very hungry, you will surely go to your refrigerator expecting a reward.

Key Terms 1

backward conditioning
biological preparedness
classical conditioning
conditioned response
conditioned stimulus
delay conditioning
equipotential view
extinction
generalization
higher order conditioning
learning
simultaneous conditioning
spontaneous recovery
stimulus contiguity
stimulus generalization
stimulus discrimination
trace conditioning
unconditioned response
unconditioned stimulus

Key Terms 2

avoidance learning

behaviorism
behavior modification
continuous reinforcement
discrimination
discriminative stimulus
escape learning
experimental analysis of behavior
extinction
fixed schedule
generalization
instinctive drift
instrumental conditioning
interval schedule
law of effect
learned helplessness
negative punishment
negative reinforcement
operant
operant conditioning
partial reinforcement
partial reinforcement effect
positive reinforcement
primary reinforcement
punishment
ratio schedule
reinforcement
reinforcement contingency
respondent behavior
schedule of reinforcement
secondary reinforcement
shaping
Skinner box
spontaneous recovery
stimulus control
stimulus generalization
successive approximation
token economy
trial-and-error learning
two-process theory
variable schedule

Key Terms 3

blocking
cognitive map
insight learning
latent learning
place learning

Key Terms 4

model
observational learning

Key Terms 5

aplysia
cerebellum
habituation
hippocampus
long-term potentiation
motor cortex
neural network
sensitization
somatosensory cortex
temporal cortex

Key Names 1

Gregory Kimble
John Garcia
Ivan Pavlov
Martin Seligman
John B. Watson

Key Names 2

O. Hobart Mowrer
David Premack
B.F. Skinner
E.L. Thorndike
Martin Seligman

Key Names 3

Wolfgang Kohler
Robert Rescorla
Edward Tolman

Key Names 4

Albert Bandura

Key Names 5

Eric Kandel

Chapter 7

Memory

Outline

Networking

IT SLIPPED MY MIND. Remind me to do that. It's right on the tip of my tongue. If memory serves me. . . All these everyday phrases refer to the operation of memory, and they may somehow imply that memory is a fairly straightforward matter. You remember something or you don't. And you tend to remember things that are simple, important, and recent better than you remember things that are complex, unimportant, or in the past. Right? Well, not really. In fact, memory is a complex process. There is much more to it than being able to remember phone numbers, course material, or where you left your car keys. Psychological research has addressed a number of fascinating questions about how we remember and why we forget. For example, is there more than one type of memory? Is the capacity of memory limited? Are pictures easier to remember than words? How can memory be improved? Can there be false memories of events that never actually occurred? How accurate are eyewitness memories? Is there such a thing as photographic memory? Are memories stored in specific locations in the brain? This chapter explores these and many other memory-related topics. You might try applying the memory principles we discuss as you read and study this chapter. After carefully applying them, think back to the recall of material from chapters you have read previously. Did applying memory principles help you to recall the material better?

Memories . . .

"Let's see now, so Boyle's Law says..." Willi was studying at the home of his neighbors and good friends, the Everetts. Mrs. Everett had asked him to stay for a few hours with her husband, who had recently had a heart attack. Suddenly, Mr. Everett began to gasp, clasped his chest, and passed out. Boyle's Law was gone and forgotten. Very upset, Willi wasn't immediately sure what to do, but after a minute remembered a CPR course he had taken two years ago. He immediately placed his hands in the correct position and began the rhythmic compressions, alternating with breaths. Trouble was, he couldn't remember the counts—the number of compressions between breaths. Then he suddenly remembered he should call 911. As he resumed the CPR, waiting for the ambulance, he remembered some of the good times with Mr. Everett. There was the time that only Mr. Everett had been able to fix his bike, the time he had grabbed Willi just in time to pull him from the path of an oncoming car, and all the fun playing catch. An approaching siren broke into his thoughts and he realized that he should call Mrs. Everett as soon as the ambulance crew arrived. She had given him a phone number as she left the house. He had repeated it to himself twice but not written it down. Now he just couldn't remember it: 738-94__; or was it 387-94__; or ...? He still couldn't remember as the ambulance crew came through the door.

We'll return to this story and learn just how important a role Willi's memory played on this dramatic day in his life.

Human Memory: Origins and Basic Processes

Who are you? What are you like as a person? What kinds of life experiences have you had? Only memories can provide you with the information you need to answer these questions. We will consider the evolutionary origins of memory, the processes of encoding, storage, and retrieval, and the ways in which psychologists use three types of memory to learn just how it works.

The Evolution of Memory

Evolutionary theory hypothesizes that memory, like learning, arose as a response to environmental demands and serves an adaptive function. It allows the animal to retain information about its environment and thereby survive. Remembering the locations of food sources, the identity of a mate, and the association of a certain stimulus with impending danger can be important to the survival and reproduction of a species. It is for this reason that evolution has favored those species that develop adequate memory functions. Memory exists because it is an adaptive mechanism that permits the animal to repeat helpful behaviors and avoid repeating harmful behaviors.

The specific nature of memory mechanisms, processes, and capacities varies from one species to another. This variability reflects the differing environmental demands to which different species have had to adapt over the course of evolution. Birds can recall the location of the nest; squirrels remember for months where they stored food; and antelope retain the association of the lion's roar with danger. Each species is using memory to adapt to its environment (Klein et l., 2002).

Human memory has also evolved adaptively. For millions of years after the evolutionary beginnings of the human species, speech as we know it now did not exist, and the verbal memory so essential to modern existence was not needed. Instead, early humans relied on such spatial cues as gestures to communicate and on spatial orientation to move about in their environment. As a result, spatial memory represented a necessary adaptation, fulfilling the need to recall the locations of food, shelter, and other essentials. One modern-day evolutionary result of this adaptive need may be the superior spatial-location ability of females; it may have arisen as an adaptation to the crucial role of women in gathering food and living materials during ancient times (Barkley, 2002).

More generally, humans now live in a far more complex physical, social, and emotional environment than other animals, and our highly evolved memory mechanisms reflect the need to survive and function adaptively in that environment. We will examine the types of human memory that have evolved over the centuries and the ways in which they operate to permit the continuing adaptation and survival of the human species.

The Memory Process: Encoding, Storage, and Retrieval

Before reading on, try this brief exercise. Memorize the number for the Federal Trade Commission's Consumer Inquiry Office, which you might call with a serious consumer problem: (202) 326-3430.

Having memorized the number, you should now cover it, try to recall it, and write it down on a separate piece of paper (no cheating!).

Now let's see how you went about doing this task.

Encoding. The process by which information is converted into a form in which it can be placed into memory (a code) is called *encoding*. Just as the numbers and letters you type into your computer must be appropriately coded for transmission over telephone lines to a mainframe, the digits of the FTC telephone number must be encoded for entry into your memory. Three principal types of codes appear to represent information in memory. *Acoustic encoding* uses the sounds of words to encode the material. *Visual encoding* uses images, such as the visual image of a word or picture. And *semantic encoding* represents the information in memory in terms of its general meaning.

Though not usually thought of as one of the major types of encoding, *motor encoding* also occurs. It is involved in learning and remembering physical skills. Swimming is easy once you've mastered it, but try to describe to someone who doesn't swim just how you do it. The specific muscular movements involved cannot easily be verbalized due to motor coding.

Storage. The retention of memorized material over a period of time is called *storage.* Storing information like the FTC number in memory is a bit like putting file folders into drawers under an appropriate set of categories. Your memory of an apple may be stored in an "apple" folder, which is under a larger category called "produce," which, in turn, might fall under "food."

Retrieval. Retrieval is the process by which previously encoded, stored memories are brought back for current use. A particular cue, like "FTC", for example, can cause you to retrieve information that you had previously encoded and stored. One way to think of these basic memory processes is in terms of information-processing theory, which sees human memory processing as analogous to the operation of a computer. Information enters through the senses (keyboard), is stored somewhere in the brain (hard or floppy disk), and is retrieved (brought up on the monitor) when needed (Figure 7-1). We have more to say about information-processing theory in Chapter 8.

Now, let's put it all together. It's time to retrieve the FTC telephone number that you previously encoded and stored. Write it down, then check to see if you got it right.

The Study of Memory: Recognition, Recall, and Relearning

How are memories encoded, stored, and retrieved? What factors contribute to successes and failures? The answers to these and other questions can come only through careful research, and three principal approaches account for most of that research: Recognition, recall, and relearning (Table 7-1).

Recognition. Try this little experiment: First, study the list of words in Table 7-2A for 30 seconds. Then, turn the page and check off the words in the Table 7-2B list that were in Table 7-2A What you have just exhibited is *recognition memory*—the ability to identify something you have seen before. Every time you take a multiple-choice exam, you are undergoing a test of recognition.

Recognition memory may seem to be a relatively simple process. However, understanding just how recognition takes place and what factors affect it has not proven easy. For one thing, the process is subject to age differences. In fact, it is so involved that researchers have found it necessary to develop special theories in an attempt to better understand it (Yonelinas, 2001).

Recall. Let's make your task a little more difficult. Without looking back, write down as many as you can remember of the words you memorized from Table 7-2A. This is a recall task, which is considerably more difficult than recognition. *Recall* means that you are asked to remember something you have previously learned without again seeing the material. In a recognition task, you see the word and simply have to remember that you have seen it before, whereas the recall task provides no such cues.

In a test of free recall, participants are initially given material to memorize and later asked to recall as much as possible. An essay exam is a free recall test (Higham, 2002). In a test of cued recall, participants are given a hint or cue. Suppose you run into someone you went to elementary school with but cannot remember her name. Given the cue that her father owns Harper's Music Store, you may immediately recall that her name is Jackie Harper. If we want to make your test on the words in Table 7-2A a cued recall task, we might give you the following cues: sit; cardboard; text; light; folder. Is recall easier with these cues?

Relearning.

If you don't already recall the names in Table 7-2A perfectly, go back now and try to relearn them. You should be able to do so very quickly. *Relearning* means that you re-study the material to be learned and learn it again (Snowden & Neary, 2002). A familiar example of relearning (also called the *method of savings*) is studying for final exams. Assuming you have studied the course material throughout the quarter or semester, it should take you much less time to relearn the material in preparing for finals.

The Three-System Memory Model

We can think of memory as a box or boxes in which we store information, and these boxes constitute the structure of memory. The real question is just how many boxes there are and what each contains.

There are actually several theoretical views as to the structure of memory. During the first half of this century, the predominant view was that memory is a single system. The dominant—though by no means onl—approach more recently has been the three-system model developed by information-processing theorists Richard Atkinson and Richard Shiffrin (1971). It hypothesizes that there are three separate components of the overall memory system. The first of these, called sensory memory, is specific to one sensory modality and is very brief. Short-term memory is memory of limited capacity that also stores information briefly, though for longer than sensory memory. Long-term memory holds information indefinitely or even permanently. These systems can best be viewed as separate but continuously interacting (see Figure 7-2). We will discuss each in turn and also consider some alternatives to this three-system model.

Keys to Memory

SENSORY MEMORY

A *sensory memory* is one that is specific to a particular sensory modality and very briefly continues the sensation of a stimulus after that stimulus ends. The sensation of a sight or sound remains for just a moment after the stimulation is over. The major types of sensory memory are iconic and echoic.

Iconic and Echoic Memories

Iconic memory occurs when a visual stimulus produces a brief visual memory trace called an icon (Figure 7-3). *Echoic memory* is the brief registration of sounds or *echos* in memory (Pekkonen et al., 2001).

George Sperling (1960) first documented the very brief duration of sensory memory in a classic experiment in which subjects saw three rows of letters for only 1/20th of a second (Figure 7-4). After variable periods of time up to one second had passed, the participant had to recall one of the rows. The greater the delay before reporting, the less accurate the reports. Why? Because the subject had to retain an afterimage of the very brief stimulus in order to recall it, but such sensory afterimages decay and fade out very quickly. The duration of iconic memory has been directly measured in experiments in which a narrow slit, one-eighth inch wide, is moved rapidly back and forth across an opaque screen. Behind the screen is a picture, and at any given time the viewer can see only the part of the picture revealed by the slit. If the slit is moved at a rapid rate, the viewer can soon describe the entire picture. If it is moved at a slower rate, he cannot. The reason is that the iconic memory traces of each portion of the picture left as the slit moves back and forth are lost after about a quarter of a second.

Iconic viewing is also common in normal visual perception. When you look at a picture like the one in Figure 7-5, you probably believe that you are seeing the entire picture simultaneously and that your eye movements are smooth and continuous. In reality, your eyes cross and recross the picture in a series of irregular movements, as the recordings of eye movement patterns show. The icons may last for only 20-400 milliseconds. Auditory echos are slightly longer—up to 4000 milliseconds (4 seconds).

Neuroscientists have shown that there are very brief memory traces in the brain corresponding to sensory memories. These neural traces can to transferred to more durable memory storage in short-term memory.

Attention

In order for something to be registered in sensory memory, it must first be attended to. Attention is a focusing of consciousness on a limited range of stimuli or events. It is often an active, conscious process, though it can also be more automatic. You can, for example, attend to a single conversation at a party despite the sound of other people talking or focus your attention on a book even though there is background noise.

Research indicates that attention is a major factor in determining what is later remembered and what is not (Gasper & Clore, 2002). In one study, for example, participants were shown an array of items in two colors and asked to attend to and remember only those of one color. They later recalled virtually all the items in the attended color and very few in the other color (Russell & Hollosy, 1992). In another study, subjects remembered significantly more when they gave full attention to a memory task than when they gave divided attention (Jennings & Jacoby, 1993). The recent work of Fergus Craik shows that attention is far more important during encoding than during retrieval (Craik et al., 2000).

Short-Term Memory

Short-term memory (STM) is a system that retains a limited amount of information for a brief time. While of considerably longer duration than sensory memory, STM typically holds information for no more than 30 seconds (Xu, 2002). If you have ever had the frustrating experience of forgetting a number by the time you got from the phone book to the phone, you have experienced a loss of information from short-term memory. Let's consider how encoding, storage, and retrieval take place in short-term memory.

Encoding

A classic study of short-term memory showed that encoding is most often *acoustic*. Robert Conrad (1964) showed people random strings of six letters, then asked them to write down the letters immediately. He found that the errors they made involved primarily replacing the correct letter with one that sounded like it. For P they would substitute V, D, or T, but not F, S, or M. He concluded that they had encoded the letters acoustically, even though they were presented visually. His conclusion has been supported by other research (Baddeley, 1966), though there is also evidence for at least some visual encoding in STM.

Storage

In the three-system model, shor-term memory is defined primarily in terms of its capacity—the amount of information that can be stored—and the length of time that the information can be retained. The success with which memories are stored is dependent on both the amount and the type of rehearsal or practice engaged in.

Storage Capacity: Just Chunking Along. George Miller (1956) entitled his summary of work on the capacity of short-term memory: "The Magical Number 7, Plus or Minus Two." He concluded that the average person can retain approximately 7 items in short-term memory. Some people can remember only 5 items, others up to 9 (hence, the "Plus or Minus Two"), and capacity decreases with increasing age (Haarmann & Usher, 2001). However, more recent research has raised questions about Miller's "magic number." In fact, most work now points to an average capacity of only about 4 items, rather than 7 (Cowan, 2001). This capacity is also subject to individual differences; some people can recall more and some less than 4 bits of information (Tuholski et al., 2001).

But you can remember much more total information if you break it up into meaningful *chunks*, which are recognizable units of knowledge. Each of the letters E H and T is a separate item. However, the letters T H E, because they form a word, constitute one chunk.

The beauty of chunking is that each of the seven items retained by the average person can be a chunk containing a considerable amount of information (Gobet et al., 2001). For example, your social security number consists of nine digits, but you easily remember it because it is actually presented in three chunks. It is not 294418347, but 294-41-8347. Similarly, your best friend's phone number is remembered not as 2155554158, but as (215) 555-4158. By extending this chunking process, even complex bodies of information can be stored, as long as only about seven chunks need to be retained at a time (Figure 7-6).

Research suggests that the optimal size of any one chunk is three or four items and that memory operates much more efficiently when chunks are of this size. This applies to long-term as well as short-term memory capacity (Koch & Hoffman, 2000).

You can easily demonstrate the power of chunking by trying an experiment similar to those done by psychologists who study it. Try to learn the items in Table 7-3 then chunk them into categories, like tools and animals, to see if they are easier to memorize.

Short-term memory capacity can also be understood as a part of your total capacity to deal with current information. Overall capacity is referred to as *total operating space.* This total is divided into short-term memory space and operating space. The latter is the space needed to process current information. The more efficiently you process information, the more space you have left for short-term memory.

How Long Is Short? The Brown-Peterson Paradigm. We can objectively measure the length of time you retain information in short-term memory.

Try this experiment. Look up an unfamiliar telephone number, wait 20 seconds, then write the number down. Look up a second number, count backwards by threes for 20 seconds, beginning with 999, then write the number down. If you repeat this process about ten times, you should have considerable difficulty remembering the numbers, especially on the later trials.

The experiment you just carried out is called the *Brown-Peterson paradigm.* The participant is given a series of trigrams, each consisting of three consonants, such as "FMP." She is also given a set of 3 starting digits, such as "387." During an interval of 0 to 18 seconds, she then counts backwards by threes from the starting number to prevent her from rehearsing the trigram. After that, she tries to recall the trigram. As Figure 7-7 shows, the subject's short-term memory allows about 20 percent retention after 15 seconds and practically none after 18 seconds. More generally, research has shown that people retain information in short-term memory without rehearsal for no more than about 15-30 seconds. Those with less education tend to have shorter retention times (Bherer et al., 2001).

Alternative Models. Some cognitive psychologists have pointed out flaws in the three-system model and, as a result, alternatives to this standard model have been developed (Nairne, 2002). One model emphasizes the nature of the rehearsal engaged in, while another hypothesizes a working memory that is similar to short-term memory but more complex.

Levels of processing theory and rehearsal. Rehearsal—repetitively practicing or thinking about the information to be remembered—can keep it in memory for longer periods of time. Simple repetition is called *maintenance rehearsal,* and it can serve to keep information active in short-term memory indefinitely (Cheung & Wooltorton, 2002). Had Willi, in our opener, rehearsed Mrs. Everett's telephone number more, he might have recalled it later.

To facilitate the transfer of information from short-term to long-term memory, it is far more effective to employ *elaborative rehearsal,* in which we analyze new information and relate it to patterns of information already stored in long-term memory (Figure 7-8). To demonstrate this point, Fergus Craik and Endel Tulving (1975) performed an important experiment that you might like to try: Examine the words in Column A of Table 7-4. For each word, answer the following three questions:

1. Is the word printed in capital or small letters?
2. Does the word rhyme with "more"?
3. How many letters does the word have?

Now try to recall the words in column A. After that, examine the words in column B, and do the following:

1. Decide whether the word is a noun or a verb.
2. Give a synonym for the word.
3. Determine whether or not the word fits into of any of the following sentences:
   The meeting took place in a ____
   The detective worked on his first ____
   He carefully hung the picture on the ____
   The baseball player swung a ____

Now try recalling these four words.

Like the participants in the Craik_Tulving experiment, you probably recall more words from column B, where you used elaborative rehearsal, than from column A, where you used maintenance rehearsal. The rehearsal helped you remember, though not all types of rehearsal are helpful under all circumstances. The results of the classic Craik-Tulving study are shown in Figure 7-8.

The Craik-Tulving experiments are basic to the *levels-of-processing theory* that Craik and Robert Lockhart developed in 1972. It is an alternative to the three-system model and holds that there is really just one memory storehouse, which contains information at differing levels or depths (Figure 7-8). The depth at which incoming information is stored is partly a function of the way in which it is encoded (Rhodes & Anastasi, 2000). *Structural encoding* is superficial because it relies primarily on physical properties of the stimulus, such as whether the words you learned were in capital or small letters. You achieve greater depth when you use *phonemic encoding,* in which you repeat the word and note what it sounds like. But the greatest depth comes with *semantic encoding,* which is accomplished through elaborative rehearsal, in which you think actively about the word and understand its meaning. The deeper the level of processing, the better will be the recall of the stored information (West & Craik, 2001).

Craik and Lockhart do not actually argue against the existence of separate short-term and long-term memory stores. However, they do de-emphasize these structures in favor of a focus on the *process* by which memories are stored (Craik, 1990).

Working memory. Alan Baddeley and Graham Hitch (1974; Baddeley & Wilson, 2002) have developed another alternative view in which short-term memory is seen as a *working memory.* It is more complex and more active or dynamic than the short-term memory of the three-system model and contains several substructures that take in visual and auditory information and hold it while processing takes place (Hutton & Towse, 2001). Working memory serves as a central processor that controls the flow of information in and out of the memory system (Kanashiki et al., 2002).

Baddeley (2001) has further expanded his theoretical ideas to offer a partial integration of the three-system and levels-of-processing theories, which incorporates the working memory concept. He suggests that working memory serves a *central executive* function, moving information in and out of short-term memory. The levels-of-processing framework is seen as basically an extension of the three-system model, specifying the types of processing that take place as material moves through the three memory stores (Baddeley & Wilson, 2002; Osaka et al., 2002).

Retrieval

Researchers have studied how we retrieve information from STM and what factors affect the success of retrieval. How do we search for information to be retrieved? Do we examine all potentially relevant items or stop when we find the correct one? When we scan multiple items in memory, do we scan all of them simultaneously or do we examine them one-by-one? Finally, does the position of an item in a series to be remembered affect the success of its later retrieval?

Saul Sternberg (1966) studied retrieval by presenting subjects with a series of memory sets; each set consisted of several digits or letters. The participants were then shown an individual item and asked whether it was a member of the set. Experimenters recorded the accuracy of the answers and the reaction time between the presentation of the test item and the response.

In Search Of: How Do We Scan Memory? Sternberg found that reaction time did not systematically increase as the number of digits in the original set increased. He therefore concluded that subjects scan the entire set in memory, even if it is quickly determined that the test item is part of the set. This means that the search tends to be *exhaustive* rather than *self-terminating.* Why such inefficient processing of information? Sternberg suggests that it probably takes very little time to make a comparison of the test item with each item in the set and that most of the time is spent making the decision to respond "yes" or "no." However, other researchers have reported evidence that the search is self-terminating, and the issue has not been resolved (Rojas et al., 2000).

Parallel and Serial Processing. A second issue is whether we examine all the digits at once (*parallel processing*) or one item at a time (*serial processing*)? Sternberg attempted to answer this question by varying the size of the memory set. More digits would add little to the time required to perform a parallel search, but would noticeably increase the time needed for a serial search (Figure 7-9). Sternberg's original results suggested were consistent with a serial search process. However, some studies suggest that parallel processing can also account for his findings, and we will see later that newer memory models emphasize such parallel processing.

The Serial Position Effect. The probability of retrieval is affected by the position of any given item in a list or series relative to the other items in the set—its *serial position.* The effect of serial position has been studied in free-recall experiments, in which participants are presented with a long series of unrelated words and later asked to recall as many as possible. The experimenter determines the relationship between the serial position of each word and likelihood that it will be recalled (Surprenant, 2001). The result is a serial position curve, such as that in Figure 7-10. Two effects are typically seen. The *primacy effect* means that words near the beginning of the list are recalled best. The *recency effect* means that words near the end are recalled best. These effects have been routinely demonstrated both in humans and in nonhuman primates, such as rhesus monkeys. In fact, human infants exhibit them within one day of birth (Gulya et al., 2001).

Serial position experiments can be used to distinguish between short- and long-term memory. We modify the free-recall experiment by dividing the subjects into two groups. The first group recalls the list of words immediately; the second group performs a distracting task, such as mental arithmetic, before recalling the words. If there is only one type of memory, the mental arithmetic task should affect both early and late words equally. However, results show that the intervening task affects primarily the later words in the list. Other research shows that if more rehearsal is allowed, the earliest items tend to be remembered even better, whereas later items are unaffected (Farrand et al., 2001). The most widely held conclusion is that the primacy effect reflects the contribution of long-term storage, since there is greater opportunity for rehearsal of words earlier in the list. The recency effect is seen as due primarily to short-term storage, since distractions can easily interfere with it. There are, however, alternative explanations of primacy and recency (Tan & Ward, 2000).

Keys to Memory 2

Long-Term Memory

If you can still recall that FTC phone number, you have transferred it to long-term memory. Although the transfer process is not well understood, we do know that a number of factors can affect it (see Figure 7-2). The more meaningful and more novel the information, the more likely it is to be entered into long-term memory (LTM), which may involve two or more stages beyond STM (Kemps, 2001). In addition, long-term storage is more likely to be achieved when smaller amounts of information are presented. And more active, intensive rehearsal may facilitate long-term storage, although the evidence here is somewhat more mixed (Kellogg, 2001). All of this assumes, of course, that there really are separate long-term and short-term memories, as the three-system model hypothesizes, and we don't yet know if that is true. In any case, we certainly do store some memories for long periods of time, and we will therefore explore just what encoding, storage, and retrieval processes are involved in long-term memory.

Encoding

The primary form of encoding for information entering long-term memory appears to be semantic, although visual encoding is also used. Some theorists have suggested that semantic and visual codes are often used together in preparing information for storage, and others have shown that the size of a visual image affects the ability to recall details of the image. We will also see that the encoding of a given memory is so specific that only a limited set of cues can later be used to elicit it. Finally, prior experience can influence the encoding process by affecting how we formulate or construct the specific memory to be stored.

Semantic Encoding. As we saw earlier, the Craik-Lockhart model sees semantic encoding_encoding in terms of meaning—as achieving the greatest depth of storage and the best recall. Semantic encoding for storage in long-term memory was first demonstrated by William Bousfield (1935). He asked participants in his experiment to memorize a list of 15 personal names, 15 professions, 15 animals, and 15 vegetables. The 60 words were randomly interspersed, and participants were not aware that they fell into the four categories. Nevertheless, when asked to repeat them back, they tended to recall them in categories, giving several animals, then several professions, and so on. Subjects were clearly taking the meaning of the words into account as they memorized them, and Bousfield concluded that they were therefore encoding semantically.

Visual Encoding. Millions of years before the evolutionary process introduced verbal encoding in humans, they used images to encode information for long-term memory—and you can too. For example, if one of the words in Bousfield's list of professions was "doctor," you might improve your memory by picturing a person in a white coat with a stethoscope. Visual encoding reliably enhances memory when a concrete object is involved. However, if asked to memorize an abstract term like "patriotism," visual imagery is hard to generate (Paivio, 1969).

To better understand just how encoding typically takes place, Allan Paivio (1986) has formulated a *dual-coding theory*, which holds that memory performance is dependent on both verbal and nonverbal cues. The visual cues enhance memory by providing a second code so that you now have two ways of recalling the memory. High-imagery words and sentences (such as "The sweating brown horse jumped the stone wall") are much more easily remembered than low-imagery ones (such as "Being and essence are fundamental constituents of reality"). This suggests that dual-coding may indeed take place (Toichi & Kamio, 2002). Further evidence shows better recognition and recall of ambiguous pictures when the original presentation is accompanied by a verbal interpretation than when it is not (De-Santis & Haude, 1993).

The power of visual coding is also clear in studies confirming the old saying that "A picture is worth a thousand words." If we give one group of participants a list of 100 words and another group a corresponding series of 100 pictures, then conduct a recognition test, the picture group will always have a much higher memory score. We also know that memory for pictures is better than memory for the labels on those pictures.

Visual memory may be superior to verbal memory, but how much detail does it store? Raymond Nickerson and Marilyn Jager Adams (1979) showed participants drawings of pennies and asked them to identify the correct drawing (Figure 7-11). Before you look at the correct answer in the footnote, try it for yourself. Only 50% of the participants got it right.

In a fascinating series of studies, Stephen Kosslyn has shown that the amount of detail you recall from visual encoding depends on the size of the image your brain generates. Larger images are easier to inspect for detail than smaller images. Close your eyes and picture a rabbit standing beside an elephant; try to inspect the rabbit for details. Now picture a rabbit standing beside a fly and again look at the details of the rabbit image (Figure 7-12). Kosslyn's participants found it far easier to inspect for details when the rabbit was next to the fly (Kosslyn, 1975).

Encoding Specificity. As Fergus Craik points out, memories are encoded so specifically that only specific cues originally associated with the memory will readily lead to retrieval (Hannon & Craik, 2001). The situation is somewhat like a bank vault containing separate safety deposit boxes for each customer. Each memory is stored in a separate box, which can be opened only by a certain set of keys. This idea that memory is best when specific cues present during encoding are available at recall or recognition is called the *encoding specificity principle.*

In one important study, subjects read each of 67 sentences, focusing on an adjective-noun phrase that was capitalized and underlined. An example would be: The *STRAWBERRY JAM* tasted great. Later they saw 134 adjective-noun phrases and had to indicate whether or not the noun in each phrase had been in the original list. They were much more likely to say that JAM had been in the list if it was presented as STRAWBERRY JAM than if it was presented as TRAFFIC JAM. Their encoding had been specific to the word STRAWBERRY, even though all they had to remember was JAM.

Effects of Prior Experience: Constructive Memory. Our discussion of short-term and long-term memory has thus far implied a *bottom-up* process, in which incoming information produces a memory that is encoded, stored, and retrieved. However, memory, like perception, is also affected by *top-down* processes, in which we use our prior experience to modify the information as it is encoded and retrieved (see Figure 7-13). This use of existing knowledge, expectancies, or biases to modify new, incoming information is called *constructive memory* (Huron & Danion, 2002).

We use memory construction constantly as we read and hear new information (Woike et al., 2001). Suppose, for example, that you turn on the radio to hear the announcer say: "The ball was hit out of the park." Hearing nothing else about this event, answer the following questions:

- What game was being played?
- What did the player do next and why?
- What gender was the player?
- Where was the game being played?

You would probably answer: baseball; ran around all the bases; male, and baseball stadium. None of this information was in the sentence you heard, so how did you answer the questions? You imposed a *memory construction* in which you used your prior knowledge of baseball to make an *inference* based on the sentence you heard.

Constructive memory is accomplished through the use of schemas or schemata. A *schema* is a mental representation of a category of objects, people, or events. Your baseball schema allowed you to answer the questions in the example.

There are many kinds of schemas. The baseball schema is a script—a schema that represents memories derived from repeated experiences with common events. Scripts cover such situations as going to a class, attending a surprise party, and shopping. *Person schemas* are mental representations of specific people with whom you have had experience. Your mother schema, for example, may include such characteristics as socially skilled, easily upset, and hard-working; it helps you to predict your mother's behavior and to construct memories of new events involving your mother. *Self-schemas* represent your knowledge and beliefs about your own characteristics. You may see yourself as strong-willed, kind, and athletic, and this schema will affect how you encode and retrieve memories involving your own behavior.

Schemas are often valuable because they increase our cognitive efficiency by telling us what to expect and how to act. However, this efficiency has a substantial price-tag: schemas also act to distort memories. Frederick Bartlett (1932), a pioneer in schema theory, conducted a classic series of studies to demonstrate distortion. In some he asked British college students to listen to a rather bizarre story taken from a North American Indian folktale. Called "The War of the Ghosts," the passage tells about spirit warriors who take one of two young men into a ghostly battle with them (Figure 7-14). After hearing the story, the students were asked to retell it from memory. Bartlett reported numerous inaccuracies in the retellings. He interpreted the incorrect memory constructions as reflecting schemas the students had acquired in their own culture that were different from those of the Native American culture, and his work has continued to guide much of the research on constructive memory (Johnston, 2001). Another striking example of how schemas can distort memory comes from research showing that eyewitness accounts of crime can be extremely inaccurate, as the Thinking Critically box discusses.

Clearly, our memories are not simple, accurate encodings of real events in the real world. Rather, they are modified by existing knowledge and biases.

Storage

Your long-term memory store provides you with a wealth of information that is essential as you interact with others, do your job, and more generally conduct everyday life. We will learn something about the capacity of this important store, the permanence of memory and some of the kinds of information that are stored. In addition, we will look at some cases of people with exceptionally good memories.

The Capacity of Long-Term Memory. Have you ever wondered whether long-term storage of new information is likely to somehow push old information out, like over-filling a glass with water? Should you perhaps stop reading right now before the new material on this page forces some important old information out of your long-term memory?

Well, not to worry. Research suggests that the capacity of long-term memory may be virtually unlimited, somewhat like a bucket so large that we are unlikely to ever put enough water in it to cause an overflow. Fry (1977) has estimated that the long-term memory system of an average individual can retain 1,000,000,000,000,000 items of information. However, there are substantial individual differences in how much people actually do store in long-term memory.

Is Memory Permanent? Seventy-five percent of respondents in one survey said they believe that we remember all our experiences—that all memories are permanently stored somewhere in the brain (Loftus and Loftus, 1980; Figure 7-15). Is there evidence to support this widely held belief?

Studies using hypnosis and drugs often called "truth serums" to tap early memories provide some apparent support. In studies of hypnotic age regression, the hypnotist tells subjects to go back to some earlier period in life. They are usually able to do so and often describe childhood experiences in great detail. However, it turns out that these memories are often very distorted and inaccurate (Macrae et al., 2002). For example, the recall of college students regressed to their sixth birthday does not match well with information from parents and other sources. The same results are seen when participants receive drugs like sodium amytal. These drugs supposedly release unconscious memories and remove inhibitions against telling the truth. In reality, however, they provide memories that are no more accurate than those achieved under hypnosis.

Further apparent evidence regarding the permanence of memory comes from the work of noted brain surgeon Wilder Penfield. Patients are often wake during neurosurgery, with local anesthetics used to eliminate pain, because the surgeon may need to ask them questions in order to determine very precisely where the damage is located. Taking advantage of this waking state, Penfield electrically stimulated areas of the brain during surgery and reported that patients gave detailed verbal descriptions of events in their past. The time period involved and the specific events they talked about depended on just where he stimulated their brains (Penfield, 1969, 1975). His results were later called into question, however. For one thing, only 3.5% of some 1,100 patients produced memories during stimulation. For another, the reports were typically very inaccurate and often appeared to be fantasies or dreams, not true memories (Barbizet, 1970; Squire, 1987). And more generally we have no convincing evidence that all memories are stored permanently.

One example of memory that seems to have permanence—though it may be distorted—is autobiographical or everyday memory. It is the memory that lets us recognize faces at a 25th high school reunion, estimate dates of personal or political events, and recall our first year of college. It includes memories of early childhood and our body of knowledge about ourselves (Giffard-Quillon et al., 2001; Herz & Schooler, 2002). How does this autobiographical memory affect such decisions as our choice of significant others and our understanding of how memory functions in our own lives. ((Heaps & Nash, 2001; see Horizon 1).

Facts and Skills: Declarative and Procedural Memory. According to some theories, we can differentiate two basic types of memory (Figure 7-16). *Declarative* memory is memory for specific facts and personal experiences (Weiss et al., 2001). You remember that George Washington was the first President of the United States and that long-term memory has a very large capacity, and you remember your very first kiss. *Procedural* or nondeclarative memory is memory for motor, cognitive, and perceptual skills (Gupta & Cohen, 2002). Swimming and driving a car involve procedural memory, as do tying your shoes and skiing. The memory involved in such skills is more implicit than explicit, and we have more to say about it in the 21 for this chapter.

Specific Events vs. General Concepts: Episodic vs. Semantic Memory. Endel Tulving (1972) further subdivided declarative memory into two types that he called episodic and semantic. *Episodic* memory stores facts relating to information we have received or experiences we have had (Tulving, 1993; Senkfor et al., 2002). You store the fact that your birthday falls on March 2, that you were in San Francisco last Friday, and that you ate lunch in the Student Union yesterday. Tulving (2002) has suggested that episodic memory may be a relatively new evolutionary development and may be unique to humans, where it is important in social interaction and social communication. It is less essential to the environmental adaptation of other species, where social communication, if it exists, is much less extensive or complex (Tulving, 2001). For the same reason, it was less necessary to humans millions of years ago than it has become more recently.

Semantic memory is less specifically focused on particular times and places and deals with a variety of meaningful information, such as general concepts and rules. You know how to perform addition, the rules of a variety of games, and the courses that make up your current schedule. Such complex cognitive activities as recognition, perception, and language comprehension are dependent on semantic memory.

Retrieval

The recovery of information stored in LTM is heavily dependent on the presence of cues associated with the remembered material. It is also affected by the broader context in which retrieval is attempted and by such factors as mood state.

Cues Aid Retrieval: The Role of Priming. The recall of information from long-term memory can be greatly facilitated by *priming,* which means giving the participant some cue to facilitate recall (McKone & French, 2001). If a subject learns a number of word pairs, including **dine-TABLE,** we can give her the cue **dine** and thereby facilitate her memory for **table.** This is called a *paired-associates* memory task. A second approach is to have the participant learn a list of single words, then use some common associate of each word as the priming cue. If one of the words on the list is GRASS, we might prime the participant's response by saying "green."

Priming may be especially effective for material that can be organized in a hierarchical fashion, with categories and subcategories of information. The theoretical breakdown of long-term memory provides a small example (see Figure 7-16). A more extensive one is the hierarchical organization of the human nervous system that we discuss in Chapter 3 (Figure 7-17).

Tulving (1983) has suggested that priming effects may actually be under the control of some memory system other than the episodic (factual) and semantic (conceptual) systems. He found that recognition accuracy for a word list decreases greatly over a seven_day period, but priming effects remain unchanged. Priming facilitates recall just as much seven days later as it does one hour after learning the list. In addition, patients with amnesia, a disorder involving memory loss, perform as well as normals on priming tasks, though their memories are far below those of normals on other tasks (Malapani et al., 2002).

Priming is not merely a phenomenon of the laboratory. You may considerably improve your performance on an examination through priming. Many students summarize substantial amounts of information under single words or phrases, which serve as cues. The words "short-term memory" might become a cue that elicits an organized set of associates: working memory, Brown-Peterson paradigm, rehearsal, chunking, serial position effect, and so on. Each of these terms, in turn, may serve to prime responses concerning the details of their meaning. Our 21 discusses the role of priming in eliciting implicit memories—those you do not intend to recall.

Some studies of cue-facilitated retrieval have focused on the interesting tip-of-the-tongue (TOT) phenomenon. In a classic TOT study, Roger Brown and David McNeill (1966) gave participants definitions of such uncommon terms as caduceus and sextant and asked them to provide the words associated with the definitions. Their experiment produced over 200 TOT states in which subjects were sure they knew the word associated with the definition but couldn't quite produce it. They got the sound of the word's first letter right over half the time, and that first letter was sometimes able to serve as a cue for retrieval of the entire word.

Studies more generally suggest that participants often retrieve partial information about a memory before having complete access to the word they are searching for (Metcalfe et al., 1993). One implication of this finding is that long-term memories are stored in an interconnected set of locations, each containing only partial information. Complete retrieval means that information from the various locations must somehow be brought back together, a process that can be triggered by a cue.

Distinctive Cues: Flashbulb Memory. Whenever the assassination of President John F. Kennedy is mentioned, I immediately recall exactly where I was and what I was doing when I heard the news: I was on a coffee break from a course I was taking. Tony Randall remembers that he was in the bath tub, and Julia Child distinctly recalls that she was eating soup de poisson in the kitchen (Brown & Kulik, 1982). Studies of the assassinations of Robert Kennedy and Martin Luther King in 1968 and of the Senate confirmation hearings of Supreme Court Justice Clarence Thomas have also turned up flashbulb memories in large numbers of people (Morse et al., 1993; Christianson, 1989). You may have similar flashbulb memories relating to the disastrous explosion of the Challenger or the bombing of the federal building in Oklahoma City in 1995 (Figure 7-18). *Flashbulb memories* are graphic, detailed remembrances of striking events. Although such memories are sometimes not perfectly accurate, they demonstrate the effects of cues on retrieval and may help us to better understand retrieval processes more generally (Davidson & Glisky, 2002). What flashbulb memories do you have?

The Influence of Context. Retrieval depends not only on specific cues, but also on the broader *context* in which learning took place. In one study, subjects were presented with a series of problems to solve. They later remembered more of the unsolved than solved problems, so long as there were fewer total unsolved items. When the task was made more difficult and the numbers of solved and unsolved problems became about equal, there was no difference in memory (Patalano & Seifert, 1994). Context made a difference: The unsolved problems stood out when there were fewer of them.

The broader environmental context is also important. Information is generally recalled better when testing takes place in the same situation in which the original learning occurred. Steve Smith and his colleagues showed that students have better recall on an exam when they take it in the same room in which they heard the lectures (Smith, Vela, & Williamson, 1988). In another important and innovative experiment, divers learned a list of unrelated words either on the beach or 15 feet under water and were later asked to recall them (Figure 7-19). The divers recalled the list material better when tested in the environment in which they had originally learned it (Godden & Baddeley, 1975; Baddeley, 1976). A final study showed that undergraduates performed better on a word recall test when the same music was playing during both learning and recall (Balch et al., 1992).

State-Dependent Memory: Physiology, Mood, and Retrieval. Context is not always external. Even physiological conditions can provide a context for retrieval. Alcoholics who have hidden liquor while intoxicated recall its location better when intoxicated than when they are sober. Similarly, word lists learned under the influence of marijuana are better recalled when the participants are again under the influence of the drug. The same effect occurs with alcohol. This phenomenon is called *state-dependent memory*, and it refers to the improvement of recall when physiological or emotional conditions are the same as they were at the time of learning.

In one systematic study of state-dependent memory, subjects learned word lists under one of four randomly assigned conditions. One group became intoxicated by drinking vodka and fruit juice before learning and were again intoxicated during the recall task. A second was intoxicated during learning but not recall. The third was sober during learning but intoxicated during recall. And the fourth, a control group, learned and recalled while sober. Recall was best when participants were in the same state during learning and recall (Weingartner et al., 1976).

Other research has shown that *mood state* affects memory in two ways. First, material learned while you are in a particular mood or emotional state is better recalled when that same state recurs. Information acquired when you are happy (or sad) is more easily retrieved when you are again happy (or sad). Current mood state may not, however, influence very long-term memory, such as the memory for childhood events. Many studies support the occurrence of such effects (); however others do not (). Researchers are now attempting to determine the circumstances that might facilitate mood effects.

The second influence of mood on retrieval is seen in the more reliable *mood-congruence effect*, in which memory is better for material that is consistent with your current mood state. You retrieve pleasant information more readily when you are happy and unpleasant information when you are unhappy (). In effect, your mood serves as a priming or context cue for information previously associated with that mood state. In one study, both normal subjects who had been exposed to an experimental induction of temporary depression and clinically depressed participants had better recall for negative events and poorer recall for positive events than did nondepressed individuals (Blaney, 1986).

Enhancing Retrieval: Mnemonics. Mnemonic devices are organizational memory schemes that help you retrieve information from memory. They enhance retrieval by providing cues, meanings or images associated with the material to be retrieved (McNamara & Scott, 2001). For example, you know "Thirty days hath September, April, June, and November" and "I before E, except after C."

Like all mnemonic devices, these rhymes aid memory by providing a well understood framework that has the effect of limiting the number of alternative responses that can be made. Mnemonics thereby often change a recall task into a far easier recognition task.

A number of different mnemonic schemes can be used to aid retrieval. The *pegword system* provides a scheme for retrieving complex information in a relatively simple form. You first learn a list of rhyming words, which serve as "pegs" upon which to hang a new list of items to be learned. The pegword list in Table 7-5A is a classic one (Miller, Galanter, and Pribram, 1960; Bower, 1973), but any similar rhyming list would do. The learner initially memorizes the pegword set—one-bun, two-shoe—and so on—then learns new lists by associating them with the pegwords. You can remember the grocery list in Table 7-5B by associating the items with the pegwords in Table 7-5A. The system works well, particularly when you use vivid imagery to associate the two lists.

In the *method of loci* you memorize a series of locations, such as rooms in your house, then use them to remember new information. If you are now learning a new list of words that includes "cat," you might picture a cat in the living room. When you mentally walk through the house later, you will picture a cat in the living room and thereby recall the word.

In the *link method*, you form associations among otherwise unrelated words or objects, with the result that recalling one word in the list allows you to recall the next word because the two have been linked in some fashion. For example, you might learn the first few words in Table 7-3 by forming the following associations: The cat jumped on the table with the dog, knocking the hammer off. The hammer crushed the loaf of bread that the lion was eating. Studies show that the link method is far superior to simply trying to memorize the list of words.

Exceptional Memories

Both long-term and short-term memory are subject to wide individual differences. Some people seem to have very good and others very poor memories. In discussing exceptional memory and memory improvement, we need to clearly distinguish between the terms mnemonist and mnemonic. A *mnemonist* is a person with a truly exceptional memory, and the term *mnemonic*, as we have already seen, refers to the use of memory aids to improve recall. However, mnemonists often do not appear to use special mnemonic devices, and there is thus some contradiction in the usage of the root term.

Laboratory-Created Mnemonists. K. Anders Ericsson and his colleagues (1980) set out to create a mnemonist in their laboratory, thereby showing that exceptional memory ability can be, at least sometimes, acquired. They selected a single subject whose initials were S.F. He began with a normal 7-digit short-term memory span, and Ericsson trained him by reading random digits to him at the rate of one per second. The number of digits was increased by one if he correctly recalled the prior series and decreased by one if he did not. After 230 hours of training over a period of one-and-a-half years, S.F. had a short-term memory capacity of 79 digits (Figure 7-21). He accomplished this feat by chunking the digits into meaningful subsets that represented running times. For example, 3 4 9 2 was stored in memory as "3 minutes and 49 point 2 seconds, near world_record mile time."

True Mnemonists. There are also cases of exceptional long-term memory, and many of these appear not to be based primarily on training. Consider the famous conductor, Arturo Toscanini. Estimates suggest that Toscanini had memorized the music and words for 100 operas, knew every note for every instrument in 250 symphonies, and had also committed to memory a variety of chamber music, concertos, and other pieces (Marek, 1982). On one occasion, an understandably upset bassoon player approached Toscanini just as a concert was about to begin to report that the key for the lowest note on his bassoon was broken. Toscanini thought for a few moments, then told the musician that he could relax because the note did not appear in the concert for that evening!

A less prominent mnemonist was Rajan Mahadevan, a graduate student in psychology at Kansas State University. His exceptional memory for numbers was reported by Washington Post staff writer, T. R. Reid, who interviewed him (Washington Post, June 18, 1989). He could apparently commit to memory and retain indefinitely virtually any number sequence. Perhaps his greatest reported accomplishment was memorizing and accurately repeating the first 31,811 digits of the constant, pi. Most people remember only the first few digits, 3.14159—or something like that!

A more scientifically documented case was that of an artist named Elizabeth, who could reproduce any material she saw after only a brief study period (Stromeyer, 1970). She could, for example, examine a page of poetry printed in a foreign language that she did not speak and reproduce it perfectly minutes or years later. An even more striking feat was superimposing patterns of dots. Presented sequentially with two separate, seemingly random dot patterns, each consisting of 1,000,000 dots, Elizabeth was able to mentally superimpose the two patterns to correctly form the images of three-dimensional objects.

Another interesting case was that of a Russian newspaper reporter studied by Luria (1968). Given a table of more than 50 numbers arranged in random order in four columns, this man, known as S., could store the table in memory after only three minutes exposure. He could then recall any column in backward or forward order and retained the stored information in long-term memory for many months.

Eidetic Imagery. The exceptional memories of these subjects were based, in part, on their use of eidetic imagery. *Eidetic imagery* is a form of visual coding and storage in which a highly detailed visual image of the stimulus is retained.

The person can later literally "see" the information before him and scan it as though it were physically present.

Ralph Haber (1979; Haber & Haber, 1988) has long studied eidetic imagery. He often uses the *picture elicitation method*, in which a participant scans an unfamiliar picture like the one in Figure 7-22 for 30 seconds. The picture is then removed and the subject continues to look at the easel that held it, reporting what he sees. Haber knows when a subject has a true eidetic image because it differs from other visual images. It stays in one place, rather than moving around like other images. It also disappears gradually and involuntarily, lasting only a few seconds to a few minutes; it usually cannot be immediately retrieved. And the eidetic image is typically imperfect—not a true, photographic reproduction of the actual picture.

Eidetic imagery is certainly an interesting phenomenon, but don't expect to run across too many people with this capability. Researchers have concluded that it appears to occur primarily in children, and even there is seen in only about 2 to 15 percent of the population (Haber & Haber, 1988). However, it may be present in more adults than has generally been recognized. Some studies have shown that it appears not to decrease between the ages of 7 and 12 and that children who display eidetic imagery between those ages still have it 7 years later (Leask et al., 1969).

You now know a lot about both short-term and long-term memory. Table 7-6 will help you to organize, rehearse, and retain that information.

Keys to Memory 3

Forgetting

The old professor who informed his students that he had forgotten far more than they had ever learned may well have been right because memory is really a two_sided coin—or maybe a leaky bucket (Figure 7-23). One side of the coin is concerned with what we remember, the other with what we forget. The major question addressed by psychologists is how forgetting occurs.

Experiments aimed at answering this question began in the late nineteenth century with the work of Hermann Ebbinghaus, a pioneer memory researcher. He developed 2300 nonsense syllables—strings of letters that mean nothing—each consisting of three letters with a vowel between consonants. Examples might include: ZIK, CEX, HOJ. Using himself as a subject, he then selected groups of 7—36 nonsense syllables, learned them, and tried to recall them. He found that after 20 minutes he could remember 58% of a list, after 48 hours less than 40%. When he relearned a forgotten list, it took him fewer trials than it had taken to learn it in the first place. By relating savings on relearning to time since learning, a forgetting curve can be obtained (Figure 7-24). As this *Ebbinghaus curve* shows, forgetting is rapid at first, then becomes more and more gradual. More recent studies have shown that other types of memory tasks typically follow this pattern but vary in forgetting rates and that memory for words is lost more quickly than memory for pictures (Hart & O'Shanick, 1993).

There are a number of possible explanations for forgetting: the limits of short-term memory may be exceeded; the encoding of information may be inadequate or incomplete; information stored briefly in short-term memory may not have been transferred to long-term memory; or the material may have been stored in long-term memory but still be inaccessible because cues necessary for retrieval are absent (Bauml & Hartinger, 2002; White, 2002). There are two general classes of theories of forgetting. One class is based on the idea that information can be lost from LTM. We refer to these as *availability* theories. The second—and currently dominant—approach suggests that information is not permanently lost from LTM but may become difficult to retrieve. These can be called *accessibility* theories. The forgotten information is there but is inaccessible (Table 7-7).

Availability Theories of Forgetting

The older, but still active, theories of forgetting were based on a concept of true information loss. If you can't remember it, it is simply gone—deleted from the brain and no longer available. The four major theories of this type are trace-decay, disuse, interference, and encoding failure.

Trace-Decay Theory. The emphasis in trace-decay theory is on the failure to store information permanently in memory. Trace-decay theory holds that forgetting results when memory traces in the brain weaken and disappear with the simple passage of time. Rehearsal can strengthen a trace, but failure to rehearse allows it to deteriorate.

The Greek philosopher Plato was one of the earliest writers to suggest a trace-decay explanation of forgetting. When a memory is initially formed, he argued, it is like imprinting a seal on a piece of wax. With time, the imprint gradually loses its shape and finally disappears completely. In similar fashion memory loss begins with a fading of details and ends with a total failure of the memory (Altman & Gray, 2002). There is evidence that decay may account for losses from short-term memory when there is no rehearsal, but decay from long-term memory has not been shown (Sakai & Inui, 2001).

Disuse Theory

A new version of this view, disuse theory, (Bjork & Bjork, 1992), suggests that it is not the mere passage of time, but rather the repeated retrieval of similar information that leads to memory loss. You eventually forget your former home phone number because you have learned and retrieved numerous other phone numbers since last using it. From an evolutionary standpoint, a major adaptive value of loss due to disuse is that old information becomes increasingly less likely to impair your ability to retain new information.

Interference Theory

Trace-decay theory depends entirely and disuse theory partially on the passage of time to produce forgetting. An alternative is interference theory, which suggests that some *active* process must interfere with the learned material, causing it to be unlearned (Melton & Irwin, 1940). Basically, interference theory holds that we retain everything we learn unless other memories either prior to or following current learning compete with the information to be retained. The more *similar* the competing material, the more likely it is that forgetting will occur (McGeoch & McDonald, 1931). Thus, you may incorrectly call someone Janet because you have met a similar-looking woman with that name.

There are two basic types of interference: retroactive and proactive. *Retroactive interference* means that exposure to new information impedes the recollection of previously memorized material. In an ingenious experiment to test for retroactive interference, Jenkins and Dallenbach (1924) used just two subjects. They learned lists of ten nonsense syllables and then either engaged in normal waking activities for eight hours or slept for eight hours. Recall proved to be greater after the sleep period because interference from new learning is much more likely during normal, waking activities. Retroactive interference easily explains why Mr. Everett's heart attack interfered with Willi's memory of Boyle's Law.

In the basic paradigm for retroactive interference studies (Figure 9-25A), two groups of participants learn the same task, such as a list of words. Then the experimental group is given a similar task to do, while the control group engages in some unrelated activity. The experimental group might learn a list of birds, then learn a second bird list, then be tested on the first list. The control group learns the first bird list, then learns a list of vegetables, then is tested on the bird list. On retesting, the control group shows greater recall.

Many studies confirm the occurrence of retroactive interference (Howe, 2002). It can even occur across sensory modalities. Performing an auditory task, for example, can interfere with a visual memory and thereby enhance forgetting, particularly when the auditory and visual materials are closely related (Koster et al., 2002). A series of bird pictures will interfere with memory for a verbal list of bird names.

The retention and recall of information can also be hampered by interference that occurs before the learning task—*proactive interference* (Figure 9-25B). In basic studies, the experimental group learns related material prior to memorizing the critical information, while the control group engages in irrelevant activity. In this case, the experimental group might first learn a bird list and the control group a vegetable list. Both then learn a second bird list and are later tested on that second list. The control group shows better memory performance because of the lack of proactive interference (Humphreys, 2001).

Exam preparation provides a real-life example of proactive and retroactive interference. Suppose you are studying for your psychology exam and you study first Chapter 3 on neuroscience, then Chapter 4 on sensation and perception. If having studied Chapter 4 later impairs your memory for Chapter 3, you are experiencing retroactive interference; if Chapter 3 decreases your recall of Chapter 4, that is proactive interference.

How Does Interference Work? There are several ways to explain how interference produces memory loss. One possibility is that interference is a function of *cue confusion.* If similar cues are associated with different memories, a confusion of cues may occur, and processing the cue stimulus may thus lead to interference.

Salame and Baddeley (1982) presented subjects with nine random digits. During that presentation, some participants heard a series of one-syllable words (oat, bun, pad), while others heard nonsense syllables (cag, dak, jun). Although they were told to ignore these sounds, the nonsense syllables and words both interfered substantially with memory for the digits. Interestingly enough, both types of sounds produced equal amounts of interference. However, either words or syllables that *sounded* similar to the digits being presented—and hence constituted cues that were confused with the digit cues—produced more interference than those that did not sound like the digits. "Bun" and "jun" would be more likely to interfere with the digit "one" that would "cag" and "dak." This phenomenon is called *phonological similarity.*

A *classical conditioning* explanation of interference suggests that it causes unlearning of material because it is no longer reinforced and becomes extinguished. In a typical experiment to demonstrate this theory, participants learn one list of words, called the A-B list (one pair might be CAT-SUN) then a second, called the A-C list (for example, CAT-BOOK). The participant is given the A term and has increased difficulty recalling the B term. The reason is that while learning the A-C list, the B responses to the A stimuli are extinguished because they are no longer reinforced and are thus unlearned. SUN is difficult to recall in response to CAT because it has extinguished while learning BOOK.

The *response competition* hypothesis holds that whenever someone learns two different responses to the same stimulus, the responses will compete when the participant is attempting to recall one of them, and the stronger of the two responses will prevail. If you have two acquaintances named Nancy and someone says "Nancy called," the one you are most likely to think of first is the one you know better or have had the most recent contact with. In one study of response competition, subjects were presented with a series of stimuli having three properties: form, color, and mode (Ceraso, Timmerman, and Belk, 1982). As Figure 7-26 shows, some items had the shared property of mode in that both, although of different form and color, had lines made up of stars. Other items had no shared properties. Recall was better for items of the second type, where no properties were shared.

Encoding Failure. A final availability theory suggests that recall failure may occur because the original encoding of the information was inadequate. We call this *pseudoforgetting* because there never really was a memory. Either there was no encoding, probably due to inattention to the memory task, or the encoding was so inadequate that a clear memory was never formed.

Accessibility Theories of Forgetting

Availability theories have become increasingly unpopular in recent years, though they are by no means dead. The currently dominant view is that memories are retained in LTM—stored somewhere in your brain—but that some become inaccessible. Two major accessibility theories are retrieval failure theory and motivational theory.

Retrieval Failure Theory

The retrieval failure theory of forgetting suggests that memories, though stored, cannot be recalled because the appropriate retrieval cues—words or images that are associated with a memory and can elicit it— are not present. Suppose an exam question asks you to discuss the major structures of the central nervous system. If you can't remember the retrieval cues—for example that "forebrain," is a subcategory under "brain," you will have great difficulty remembering the specific structures in the forebrain (see Figure 7-17).

A considerable amount of research suggests that the best cues for retrieval are distinctive events (Williams & Zacks, 2001). "Tool" would be a distinctive and therefore excellent retrieval cue for "hammer" if all the other items in the memory list were fruits and vegetables; it would be a virtually useless cue if all the other items were also tools.

Although distinctive cues are best, it is also important that the cue be a well-learned associate of the item to be recalled. When it is not, retrieval failure can again occur (Butler et al., 2001). A good example is hiding valuables when you go away on vacation. You put the diamond bracelet in the light fixture, where no burglar would look. It is "obviously" an excellent storage place because it is distinctive and unusual, so you'll easily remember it. Or will you?

Eugene Winograd and Robert Soloway (1986) found that when participants hide special things in unusual places, they usually don't remember the locations. Why? Retrieval failure: The association between the retrieval cue and the location is so unusual that the link between cue and memory is very weak. You had hoped that "diamond bracelet" would be a cue for the association "light fixture," but actually it is much more likely to cue off such places as jewel box, dresser, or drawer _ more common associates. If you ever do remember where you put the bracelet, you may be in for the further shock of finding that it is gone. As Jay MacLean (1983) notes in his book Secrets of a Super Thief, it's quite likely that if you think of a "distinctive" hiding place for your valuables, professional burglars will have already thought of it.

Perhaps there will eventually be an easy answer to the problem of forgetting, whether it involves availability or accessibility: a memory pill. Such a pill would, indeed, be a miracle drug. Drugs that enhance acetylcholine effects might be expected to help, since this neurotransmitter is important in memory, but results with such drugs as choline and lecithin are thus far inconclusive On the other hand, physostigmine and tacrine, which prolong the effects of acetylcholine at the synapse, do improve memory in some older adults with deficits (Johannson & Nordberg, 1993), as does tyrosine (Shurtleff, 1994). With continued research, we may eventually have safe drugs that can improve normal memory.

Motivational Theory

So you've forgotten once again where you left your notes for that impossible math course, the specific criticisms the boss mentioned when he called you into his office last week, and the name of the girl in high school who repeatedly rejected your dating requests.

Such forgetting appears to be motivated by our needs and desires. We tend, for example, to remember positive aspects of our experience better than negative ones. Gamblers remember times they have won and forget times they have lost, and students have more detailed memories relating to courses they did well in than courses they did poorly in.

Sigmund Freud argued that *selective forgetting*—forgetting certain kinds of information and not other kinds—is the result of repression, in which painful or anxiety-producing information is forced out of consciousness. The worker criticized in a subtle way by the boss may repress the criticism and place a positive or neutral interpretation on what the boss said. In an extreme case, a person who is very unhappy and anxious about important aspects of his life may repress his own name and undergo a period of amnesia. Repressed material does not simply "go away," but rather remains in the unconscious, where it can have considerable impact on behavior.

Some interesting research has confirmed Freud's suspicions about repression. Penelope Davis and Gary Schwartz (1987) asked individual undergraduate students to first recall any experiences they could remember from childhood, then to recall childhood experiences specifically associated with each of five emotions: happiness, sadness, anger, fear, and wonder. Students who had previously been classified as repressors—those who tend to engage in selective forgetting more readily—recalled significantly fewer childhood events, particularly negative ones, than did students who were not repressors. Thus, as Freud hypothesized, the greater the tendency to repress, the fewer negative memories the individual will have. Repression and the unconscious are discussed in greater detail in Chapter 14.

False Memory Syndrome: The Sexual Abuse Controversy

Although decades of research leave little doubt that repressed memories do exist and can motivate behavior, it may also be possible to "remember" something that never actually occurred (Kaplan & Manicavasagar, 2001). According to The False Memory Syndrome Foundation, established in 1992, that may be exactly what happens in some reported cases of childhood sexual abuse.

There has been a dramatic rise in public awareness of child sexual abuse and an apparent increase in the frequency with which women (and occasionally men) report that they were sexually abused as children. A recent national survey of over 700 women, aged 26-54 years, showed that 15% reported being sexually abused as children. About one-quarter of these (i.e., about 4% of the total sample) said they had forgotten the abuse for some period of time, then remembered it (Wilsnack et al., 2002). However, statistics have varied considerably across studies, and some of the most carefully done investigations report much lower figures. In fact, when asked specifically about incest in which there is physical sexual contact between father and daughter, major studies report figures of 1.4% to 5% (Cole & Putnam, 1992). While sexual abuse may thus not be as common a problem as some have thought, it is certainly an important one because there is no doubt that it can lead to serious psychological problems when it does occur (Heskestad, 2001).

In some cases of reported abuse, the individual indicates that she was unaware of the abuse for many years—suggesting that she had repressed it—but finally recalled it during adulthood. This recall sometimes comes during therapy after the occurrence of such symptoms as sexual dysfunction, intrusive thoughts, eating disorders, depression, and relationship problems. Suspecting sexual abuse, the therapist suggests this possibility to the patient. The result may eventually be a more or less vivid memory of abuse, called a *recovered memory.* The question is whether memories arrived at under these circumstances are real memories or whether they are fantasies created by the patient in response to suggestion, and studies do show that the conditions often present in therapy increase false memories (Zaragoza et al., 2001). Indeed, therapists are frequently later sued for "planting" a false memory (Gothard & Ivker, 2000), despite the fact that only 1.8% of women who reported recovered memories in a national survey did so during therapy (Wilsnack et al., 2002).

It was experts on human memory, experimental psychologists experienced in the study of recall accuracy, who first began to question the validity of clinical reports of recovered memories of abuse. They point out that the "memory" may be induced by the therapist's questions and suggestions (Kimball & Bjork, 2002). A simple question like "Do you recall ever having been touched sexually by a man during childhood?" could easily plant in a woman's mind the idea that she might have been sexually abused. With further encouragement, she could then report a "memory" of abuse that is actually an *illusory memory*—a fantasy—triggered off by the therapist. This is the *false memory syndrome.*

Both anecdotes and the experimental literature on human memory clearly show that memories can be distorted and even "planted" in the mind of a participant (Macrae et al., 2002). For example, the famous developmental theorist Jean Piaget (Chapter 10) reported a vivid memory that someone had attempted to kidnap him as a child; but the incident never actually took place. So widely recognized are such false memories that the author Mark Twain observed: "It isn't as astonishing the number of things I can remember, as the number of things I can remember that aren't so" (quoted in Ceci & Bronfenbrenner, 1991, p. 29).

Published studies support this anecdotal evidence by showing that an individual's beliefs and expectations can easily distort her recall of events (Cleary & Greene, 2002). Moreover, memories can be distorted by suggestion (Roediger et al., 2001). In fact, Loftus and her colleagues recently demonstrated that false memories can be induced even when the event initially seems implausible to a participant in the experiment (Mazzoni et al., 2001). In typical experiments, the subject witnesses some event on videotape, then is given misleading information suggesting that certain events occurred in the taped scene. Actually they did not. Many participants "remember" the distortions as part of the actual scene they witnessed. This is particularly true when false suggestions are made by an authority figure, when they are made repeatedly, and when there is a long delay between the event in question and the attempt to recall it (Belli et al., 1992). All of these conditions are clearly met when recall of sexual abuse occurs during therapy (Schooler, 1994).

Experimental subjects not only report false memories, distorted by misleading information, but have great confidence that the fabricated event actually took place (Lindsay, 1994). In fact, one study showed that subjects not only remembered false details suggested to them, but were willing to bet substantial sums of money that their inaccurate recollections were, in fact, accurate (Weingardt et al., 1994).

Although false memory syndrome remains a controversial topic, it clearly does occur (Loftus, 1999; Del Monte, 2000). In fact, there are numerous cases in which individuals make accusations of sexual abuse, then later retract them as false memories (Rybin, 1993). The cost to both the individual and their family in these cases is tremendous, in part because these cases often end up in the court system, which is still evolving its approach to recovered memories of abuse (Gothard & Ivker, 2000). One study of 20 families showed that family relationships in such cases were destroyed, with members forced to choose sides and enter the battle (Goldstein & Farmer, 1992). As major memory researcher Elizabeth Loftus (1993) points out, there is also a more subtle effect of false memory syndrome: When instances of illusory memory receive publicity and retractions are made, many people become very skeptical of future cases in which the memories may be real. The False Memory Syndrome Foundation reports that it is aware of about 140 such retractions as of 1993 (FMS Foundation Newsletter, November, 1993).

After all this discussion of forgetting, you may be ready for some ways to improve the duration and accuracy of your memory. The Probe deals with this practical application of memory research.

Keys to Memory 4

The Neurophysiology of Memory

Memories are obviously stored in a brain that has evolved to include modules for that purpose, and a complete understanding of memory therefore requires knowledge of the neural structures and processes involved (Duchaine et al., 2001). What changes take place in the brain when a memory is established, retrieved, or forgotten? The general answer is that both structural and biochemical changes appear to underlie the processing of memories. We will examine some neural theories of memory, the major structures and neurochemicals involved, and the effects of brain damage on memory processes.

Neural Structures in Memory

Karl Lashley (1929, 1950) suggested that a memory trace, which he called an *engram*, is left in the brain whenever learning occurs. He hypothesized that engrams are not stored in any one location and that virtually all areas of the cortex are equally important for memory. More recent research generally does not support Lashley's hypothesis. Some studies show that disconnecting an entire hemisphere has less effect on memory storage than tiny lesions in specific areas of the brain (Ledoux, Wilson, and Gazzaniga, 1978).

At about the same time that Lashley developed his engram theory, Donald Hebb (1949) proposed a two-stage neural theory of memory formation. During the first stage, corresponding to short-term memory, learning causes the formation of *cell assemblies*, groups of neurons in which electrical impulses reverberate. These reverberations can change the strength of synaptic connections among cells in the assembly so that when the reverberations stop, the memory is maintained, completing the second stage of the model.

Memory At The Synapse. More recent research confirms that memory storage may involve the synapse (Chapter 3), where a number of possible changes could account for it. Two recently studied phenomena, synaptic plasticity and long-term potentiation, are of particular interest. Synaptic plasticity, which refers to the fact that synapses change over time (Finney et al., 2001), is discussed in Chapter 3.

Long-term potentiation occurs when the response of a neuron to later stimulation is enhanced by an electrical stimulus. This means that when certain neural pathways are stimulated, the response of the neuron is potentiated or increased for long periods of time, ranging up to weeks or even months (Laroche, 2001). Long-term potentiation may be the process by which memory traces are consolidated and stored. It is discussed further in Chapter 6.

The Hippocampus and Other Subcortical Structures. How is memory established above the neuronal level? As Endel Tulving (1992) points out, there appear to be multiple memory systems in the brain. At the subcortical level, the *hippocampus* has evolved to facilitate memory storage and retrieval (Rodriguez et al., 2002). It appears to be particularly important in long-term memory and in the memory for sequences of events, but it may also play a role in short-term memory as well (Fortin et al., 2002). In fact, it may be that long-term potentiation occurring in the hippocampus is the basis for the consolidation of relatively new memories (Hasselmo et al., 2002). Interesting recent research suggests that an area near the hippocampus may be responsible for deja vu experiences, in which you have the feeling that a current situation or event has occurred before (Spatt, 2002). Other subcortical structures that may contribute to memory included the thalamus and amygdala.

The Cortex. The *temporal cortex* appears to play a substantial role in memory, including visual memory. It may also play an important role in the consolidation of memories (Picton et al., 2001). Once consolidated, memory stores may be established in other areas, including the *frontal lobes* (Stebbins et al., 2002) and the *association areas* of the brain (Figure 7-27). The location of specific memories may depend on the principal sensory modality involved in a given memory (Fletcher & Henson, 2001). Visual memories involve visual association cortex, auditory memories auditory association cortex, and so on (Mottaghy et al., 2002).

Connectionist Models

Going beyond the idea that specific areas of the cortex mediate specific memories, one current set of theories suggests that most memories are stored in sets of interconnected neurons that are often widely scattered or *distributed* across the brain (Carpenter & Grossberg, 1993). According to *connectionist models*, a memory consists of a set of associations formed through such processes as classical and operant conditioning. In a paired-associates memory task, you might learn a list of word pairs that includes the pair: **cat-FUR**. On recall, **cat** will be the cue for **FUR**. Your memory for the pair will not be simply stored in one location. Rather, it will be distributed over a number of neurons, which encode the letters **c-a-t** and **F-U-R**, as well as the cue-response connection between the two words (Figure 7-28).

Neural Networks. The distributed neurons for your **cat-FUR** association are interconnected to form a *neural network*—a set of neurons linked together through synaptic connections to form a circuit (Schluter et al., 2002). Stimulating one element or set of elements in the network can trigger off the others (Nadeau, 2001). Thus, the cue cat can elicit the response FUR only because the necessary network has been established. This idea that memories are distributed is consistent with the concept of multiple memory systems—the observation that memory storage seems to involve a number of different areas of the brain (Soumireu-Mourat, 2001). Theorists believe that we begin to establish neural networks during childhood, while the brain is still developing (Nyberg et al., 2000). They continue to grow as new information is added, and new networks may form throughout life.

We have already seen that memories are typically formed and strengthened through rehearsal of the associations involved. Connectionist models take rehearsal into account by noting that each time you practice the association, the neural connections in the circuit are strengthened and the probability of a correct response to the cue therefore increases (Kesner et al., 2000). By estimating the current strength of each link in the network, we can thus predict the likelihood that you will respond with **FUR** when given the cue **cat**. The general rule here is that the weaker the connections, the greater will be the increase in strength on a given practice trial. Early in the process of establishing a neural network—say on the first few trials of rehearsal—connections are weak and the increase in strength is rapid. Later in the practice series, the connections are already quite strong, and increments are smaller. This principle corresponds well with typical learning curves that represent gradual increases in memory (see Chapter 6).

Connectionist models propose that numerous memory circuits in the brain are interconnected to form a complex of networks. The network that contains **F-U-R** connects not only to **c-a-t**, but also to numerous other associates of **FUR** (dog, coat, soft, warm, etc.). When a cue elicits **FUR**, these associated memories may also be activated.

Parallel Distributed Processing. When multiple networks are triggered, they tend to be activated simultaneously, rather than sequentially. We call this concurrent operation parallel processing, in contrast to the sequential or *serial* processing assumed by older models of memory, including the three-system model (Collette et al., 2002). The occurrence of many simultaneous operations distributed across many locations in the brain is called *parallel distributed processing* (PDP). It is far more efficient than sequential processing and better accounts for the speed and complexity with which the brain operates (Prut et al., 2001). By way of analogy, think of the telephone system. Your telephone can be connected through switching circuitry to any of millions of other phones, and thousands of conversations can be conducted simultaneously.

One result of PDP is that new experiences can establish or modify multiple memories simultaneously (Haberly, 2001). For example, suppose that when he is lecturing on flashbulb memories, your professor relates a specific memory that he was eating his favorite food, chocolate, and studying a navigational map at the moment his helicopter was shot down many years earlier in Vietnam. You can store this information simultaneously in several different memory networks, including those dealing with the definition of flashbulb memory, the Vietnam war, favorite foods, chocolate, and your professor. Later when someone mentions the cue "chocolate," one of the memory networks triggered may remind you that your psychology professor likes chocolate too.

Parallel distributed processing means that acquiring new information not only establishes or modifies information-specific memory, but also alters your overall understanding of some general part of your world. Hearing your professor's lecture not only provides a number of specific memories about the material, but also updates memory networks dealing with your view of professors in general. Similarly, each new person you date alters your overall understanding of members of the opposite sex, the dating process, and romantic relationships.

There are actually a number of different connectionist models, which vary in their specifics but share the basic concepts of neural networks and PDP. Thus far, they have proven difficult to test experimentally and are not as widely accepted as the more traditional three-system model. However, experimental evidence, including some from positron emission tomography (PET) scan studies in humans, has provided at least partial support for the network concept of memory, and ongoing studies may well make these models quite popular in the future. Other aspects of neural networking, parallel distributed processes, and connectionism are discussed in Chapters 6 and 8.

The Biochemistry of Memory

The cortical and subcortical structures that mediate memory contain a number of neurochemical systems that are intimately involved in memory processes. Included are certain neurotransmitters, brain proteins, hormones, and RNA.

Neurotransmitters. The neurotransmitter acetylcholine (ACh) increases in quantity when memory storage takes place and appears to be crucial to the formation of memories (Pekkonen et al., 2001). Studies of ACh show that enriching the environment of rats produces an increase in brain ACh levels (Rosenzweig, 1970). In addition, drugs that increase levels of active ACh improve animal performance in conditioning tasks, whereas drugs that inhibit ACh decrease performance (Scali et al., 1994). Perhaps most interesting are human experiments in which participants have been given drugs to inhibit or facilitate the action of ACh. Inhibiting drugs appear to impair the performance of people with memory disorders on neuropsychological memory tasks, while antidotes that increase ACh levels seem improve their memory performance in some studies. It may well be the that ACh is the principal biochemical involved in the establishment and maintenance of neural networks. However, evidence to date is not consistent enough to permit firm conclusions.

Proteins, Hormones, and RNA. The operation of the nervous system depends greatly on the presence and action of a number of protein substances, and any important structural change in the brain requires protein synthesis. Evidence confirms that when memories are stored, there are specific changes in protein synthesis (Lisman et al., 2002). Research also suggests that these changes are selective and specific to areas of the brain that may be involved in memory, such as the hippocampus (Kida et al., 2002). Furthermore, inhibition of protein synthesis impairs long-term memory. A protein called protein kinase C, in particular, appears to be critically involved in the formation of new memories.

Certain hormones, such as norepinephrine, are found in the brain and may affect memory. James McGaugh (1992) has studied the influence of hormones at specific kinds of synapses and receptor sites. Some hormones appear to facilitate memory storage at these sites and others appear to inhibit it.

A final biochemical is RNA (ribonucleic acid). It exists in every cell in the body and may act to encode individual memories within neurons. The idea is that the neurological activity involved in learning modifies the chemical structure of RNA in such a way that the new information is held and hence remembered. Evidence for the role of RNA comes from studies of imprinting, in which a young animal follows the first moving object it sees during a critical period (Chapter 10). Shortly after hatching, chicks imprint on the mother hen; they stay close to her and follow her around. At that time there is an increase in RNA in the region of the brain associated with imprinting. In addition, agents that inhibit the synthesis of RNA impair long-term memory, although they have little effect on short-term memory (Grabowski & Black, 2001). Work on the biochemistry of memory is exciting but far from complete. In fact, researchers have only begun to delve into the mysteries of how these complex substances support memory storage and how they interact with the structural components of memory.

Memory Pathology

Much has been learned about the role of the brain in memory by studying patients with brain damage. We will describe two famous cases, then discuss the major types of memory loss and their causes.

Brain Damage and Memory Loss. Most brain-injured patients suffer relatively little loss of information from long-term memory but are often unable to incorporate new information into long-term storage. One famous case is that of H. M., who has been studied by Brenda Milner and her colleagues since 1953 (Milner, 1970; M. Smith, 1988). H. M. had a history of severe epileptic seizures. Drugs provided no relief, and at age 27 he underwent brain surgery in which both the hippocampus and amygdala were removed. The operation was successful in reducing H.M.'s convulsions, but it left him with a severe memory deficit. He had no problem with old memories and could readily carry on conversations, do arithmetic problems, remember a span of digits for a short time, and recall events that occurred prior to the operation. However, he had lost the ability to remember most things that happened after the surgery. New learning seemed to be impossible. He could, for example, reread the same magazine every day and have no memory that he had ever read it before. And a full year after his family had moved he could not remember the new address. He basically has normal memory for knowledge acquired prior to surgery but virtually no memory for information to which he has been exposed since surgery. Other studies support the role of the hippocampus, and a review of 147 cases of memory problems following hippocampal damage or removal confirms the likelihood of deficits in anterograde episodic memory, with working memory and procedural memory remaining largely intact (Deweer et al., 2001; Spiers et al., 2001). Other evidence shows that the amygdala is also involved in memory (Adolphs et al., 2001). N.A., a fencer whose opponent's foil went through a nostril and penetrated his brain, damaging the amygdala (Teuber, Milner, and Vaughn, 1968). Like H.M., N. A. suffered a significant loss, particularly in the ability to transfer information from short-term to long-term memory. After the injury he was unable to acquire new memories, though his memory for earlier events was unimpaired. A third interesting case, that of K.C., is described in Horizon 3.

More recent studies suggest that encoding may be virtually unaffected by brain damage, leaving short-term memory relatively intact. The problem is the transfer of newly acquired information to long-term memory (Watson, 2001). Other research shows that new information often does affect behavior, even when the patient cannot recall it. For example, patients who read a set of sentences once will read them faster the second time even though they cannot recall or recognize the sentences. Similar results have been attained with H. M. This may suggest that there are two separate long-term memory systems or that there is one system with multiple components that are differentially sensitive to various aspects of memory.

There are two general types of memory impairment, anterograde amnesia and retrograde amnesia, and both have been studied extensively. In *anterograde amnesia*—the type suffered by both H.M. and N.A.—the patient experiences a loss of memory for events *following* a trauma. In *retrograde* amnesia, the memories lost are for a period *preceding* the trauma. A mild blow on the head may cause a loss of memory for a few seconds before the blow, and a severe blow can cause memory loss for a period of hours or even years prior to the blow. At least some instances of retrograde amnesia involve a disruption of the memory storage mechanisms in the temporal lobes (Malapani et al., 2002).

Memory pathology can result from brain injury, brain surgery, the aging process, alcoholism, and a number of other causes. The nature and degree of impairment depends, in part, on the area of the brain that is damaged. Removal of a portion of the left temporal lobe, for example, tends to cause selective impairment of performance on verbal memory tasks (Milner, 1970). A particularly interesting case more recently reported by Endel Tulving (1993) appears in **Horizon 3.**

The aging process produces systematic memory losses. Many older people (beyond age 65 or so) display deficiencies on memory tasks, and a small percentage experience much more severe memory problems due to senile brain disease (Ishihara et al., 2002). The loss is typically greatest for declarative memory and may be due to frontal lobe or hippocampal damage that can occur with aging (Collie et al., 2002; Stebbins et al., 2002). Senile brain diseases disorder is caused by cerebral arteriosclerosis (narrowing of the arteries) in the brain, which leads to a reduction in the supply of oxygen to the cerebral tissues (West et al., 2002). The problem is found more often in women than in men and seldom occurs before age 65, and some recent evidence suggests that hormone replacement therapy after menopause may slow brain aging in women (Resnick & Maki, 2001). Another small percentage of aged people experience severe memory loss as a part of Alzheimer's disease, in which there is widespread degeneration of neurons (Chapter 4). The effects of aging on memory are discussed in more detail in Chapter 11.

Memory pathology can also result from the physiological effects of alcohol consumption. Alcohol interferes with the transfer of information from short-term memory to long-term memory (). Interestingly enough, it is not the total amount of alcohol consumed over a lifetime that affects memory so much as the amount consumed on a typical drinking occasion (Brower, 2001). The individual who has one drink every day will experience less memory impairment than the person who drinks seven drinks every Saturday night and none at other times. Excessive drinking to the point of alcoholism often causes irreversible brain damage that can have radical effects on memory, the most serious being a disorder called *Korsakoff's syndrome.* The typical patient with this disease shows both anterograde and retrograde amnesia. He has all but lost the ability to incorporate new information into long-term memory and also suffers from remote memory loss.

Not all cases of memory impairment have physiological origins. Certain types of psychological disorders, such as psychogenic amnesia, also involve clear memory losses. These disorders are discussed in Chapter 16.

And speaking of memory impairment of nonphysiological origin, Mr. Everett made it to the hospital and was fine, but Willi's memory for the telephone number was gone, and he had to re-learn Boyle's Law.

Keys to Memory 5

Conclusion

There may well come a day when we fully understand the psychological and neurophysiological processes involved in the encoding, storage, and retrieval of human memory. At that point we will able to develop efficient and effective ways of enhancing memory in normal individuals and treating cases of memory pathology. In the meantime, both the three-system memory model and its alternatives, including the levels-of-processing and working memory theories, have generated substantial amounts of research, giving us considerable knowledge of memory processes. The structure of memory is reasonably well understood, though none of the existing models can fully account for what is known about it. We also have at least a rudimentary understanding of the role of organization in memory, with chunking and mnemonics providing ways of improving it. And the availability and accessibility theories give us some good clues as to how forgetting takes place, though they do not fully account for motivated forgetting.

The 21st century holds great promise for rapid progress in our understanding of memory. We will learn much more about its neural substrates and very likely revise our understanding of its structure. We will also see progress in the area of autobiographical memory, where researchers are already working hard to learn just how we retain everyday events and how those memories accumulate over a lifetime. Finally, our knowledge of memory pathology should accrue by leaps and bounds over the next several decades. With new brain imaging and neurochemical technologies, we should soon know more about the amnesias, how they occur, what their neurological bases may be, and by what means we might better treat them.

Summary

Human Memory: Origins and Basic Processes

1. Memory is an evolved, adaptive mechanism that makes it possible to repeat helpful and avoid repeating harmful behaviors.
2. Memory involves three steps: encoding, storage, and retrieval.
3. The main methods used to study memory are recognition, recall, and relearning.
4. The three principal memory systems are sensory memory, short-term memory, and long-term memory. Sensory memory includes iconic memory and echoic memory.

Short-Term Memory

1. Short-term memory holds information for no more than 30 seconds and a has capacity of about seven bits of information. Rehearsal facilitates short-term memory but may or may not help transfer information to long-term memory. Retrieval involves a serial search, rather than a self-terminating or parallel one.
2. Encoding in STM is usually acoustic.
3. Chunking enhances STM by permitting more total information to be remembered.
4. The three-system model is only one of several alternatives. Levels of processing theory emphasizes elaborative rehearsal. Another approach focuses on working memory as an alternative to STM.
5. Serial position studies show that the primacy and recency of materials may affect memory.

Long-Term Memory

1. The transfer of information to long-term memory is facilitated by the presentation of relatively small amounts of meaningful, novel information and by active rehearsal.
2. Long-term memory is affected the encoding process, the availability of cues, the effects of context, the complexity of the material, and cognitive schemes.
3. Visual encoding is superior to verbal, but may store limited detail.
4. The encoding specificity principle suggests that memory is best when cues present during encoding are also present at recall.
5. Constructive memory, involving schemas, existing knowledge to modify new information. It is a top-down process.
6. The capacity of LTM is virtually unlimited.
7. We have little solid evidence that most memory is permanent.
8. We differentiate between declarative (factual) and procedural (skill) memory. Declarative memory breaks down into episodic and semantic memory.
9. Mnemonists have exceptional memories that may involve eidetic imagery, a form of visual coding.
10. LTM is elicited by cues, as seen in priming, TOT, flashbulb memory, context, and state-dependent studies.
11. Mnemonic devices, such as pegwords, method of loci, and link method, can enhance memory.

Forgetting

1. Availability theories of forgetting include trace-decay, disuse, and interference theories.
2. There are two main types of interference: proactive and retroactive. Interference has been explained by phonological similarity, classical conditioning, and response competition hypotheses.
3. Accessibility theories include retrieval failure and motivational theories.
4. There is clear evidence that false memory syndrome does occur. The difficulty is in determining when the memory is false and when it is real.

The Neurophysiology of Memory

1. Early theories included Lashley's engram and Hebb's cell assembly.
2. Memory may involve synaptic plasticity and long-term potentiation.
3. Major structures in memory are the hippocampus, temporal cortex, frontal lobes, and association areas.
4. Connectionist models theorize that memory is established in a complex set of neural networks. Each network is a set of interconnected neurons that.
5. Parallel distributed processing permits the simultaneous processing of multiple memories.
6. The biochemistry of memory involves certain neurotransmitters, proteins, hormones, and RNA in the brain.
7. Memory pathology usually involves either anterograde or retrograde amnesia.
8. Brain injury, brain surgery, aging, and alcohol consumption may all cause memory loss. Memory loss can also occur without physical causes, as in the cases of amnesia and fugue states.

Ask Yourself

1. What are the three major methods of studying remembering and forgetting? Describe each one.
2. What evidence is there that short-term memory and long-term memory are separate?
3. Discuss several factors that affect long-term memory.
4. What is the relationship between memory for verbal material and memory for pictures?
5. How does interference produce forgetting, and what is the supportive evidence for interference theory?
6. What are the effects of context on memory?
7. What are the major neural structures and biochemical substances thought to be involved in memory?
8. What does connectionism have to say about the storage of memories in neural networks and the role of parallel distributed processing.

Further Readings

Baddeley, A.D. (1990). *Human Memory: Theory and practice.* Boston: Allyn and Bacon. A solid treatment of memory by one of the fields long-standing experts.

Casey, P.J. (1993). "That man's father is my father's son": the roles of structure, strategy, and working memory in solving convoluted verbal problems. *Memory and Cognition,* 506-518. An interesting, well-designed study of the involvement of short-term memory in solving verbal problems.

Cohen, G. (1989). *Memory in the real world.* Hillsdale, NJ: Erlbaum. This book deals with real-life situations and how they affect and are affected by memory.

Hermann, D.J. (1991). *Super memory.* Emmaus, PA: Rodale Press. A good book on how to improve your memory.

Larsson, M., & Backman, L. (1994). Did I unplug the iron or did I only look at it? External source monitoring across the adult life span. *Aging,* 35-42. A solid study of the effects of aging as they apply to practical memory problems as well as laboratory tasks.

Loftus, E., & Ketcham, K. (1991). *Witness for the defense: The accused, the eyewitness, and the expert who puts memory on trial.* NY: St. Martin's Press. Elizabeth Loftus, a leading memory researcher, relates stories of her own experiences as an expert witness on the fallibility of memory and ties them to the research she has done.

Medin, D.L., & Ross, B.H. (1992). *Cognitive psychology.* Fort Worth: Harcourt Brace. Douglas Medin is one of the leading figures in cognitive, and his book contains two excellent chapters on memory.

Ochsner, K.N., Chiu, C.Y., & Schacter, D.L. (1994). Varieties of priming. *Current Opinion in Neurobiology,* 189-194. An interesting study of the nature and role of priming in brain-damaged and normal people.

Key Terms

accessibility theories
acetylcholine
acoustic encoding
amnesia
anterograde amnesia
autobiographical memory
availability theories
cell assembly
chunking
connectionist models
consolidation theory
constructive memory
cued recall
declarative memory
dual-coding theory
echoic memory
eidetic imagery
elaborative rehearsal
encoding
encoding specificity principle
engram
explicit memory
false memory syndrome
flashbulb memory
free recall
elaborative rehearsal
episodic memory
hierarchical organization
iconic memory
implicit memory
interference theory
levels-of-processing
long-term memory
long-term potentiation
maintenance rehearsal
memory storage
metamemory
mood congruence effect
mnemonic device
neural networks
parallel distributed processing
parallel processing
primacy effect
priming

proactive interference
procedural memory
pseudoforgetting
recall
recency effect
recognition
relearning
repression
retrieval
retroactive interference
retrograde amnesia
RNA
schema
script
semantic encoding
semantic memory
sensory memory
serial organization
serial position effect
serial processing
short-term memory
simultaneous acquisition retention phenomenon (SARP)
state-dependent memory
storage
synaptic plasticity
trace-decay theory
visual encoding
working memory

Key People

Alan Baddeley
Frederick Bartlett
Fergus Craik
Hermann Ebbinghaus
Sigmund Freud
Donald Hebb
Graham Hitch
Steven Kosslyn
Karl Lashley
Robert Lockhart
Elizabeth Loftus
George Miller
Brenda Milner
Allan Paivio
Saul Sternberg
Endel Tulving

Psychology in the 21st Century

Implicit Memory

Most of the work on memory in the 20th century has focused on explicit or declarative memory. *Explicit memory* is established when you remember something intentionally, as in the mini-experiment you tried with the FTC phone number, and it begins to develop early in infancy (Carver & Bauer, 2001). Recalling material you studied for an exam is another example of explicit memory. It is this type of memory that was studied almost exclusively until relatively recently (Chiu, 2000). As a result, we know quite a bit about the encoding, storage, and retrieval of explicit memory but very little about implicit memory, a phenomenon of that has begun to receive considerable attention and promises to be a major focus in the 21st century.

But what is implicit memory? Maybe a personal experience will help to make it clear. When my kids were very small, my wife and I took them to Disney World, where they met Mickey and Minnie, rode all the rides and saw all the shows. As the day wore on, I realized that I felt unusually calm, relaxed, and happy, and I suspected that my very positive mood was affected by more than the kids and the vacation. The fact was that I had grown up myself with Mickey and his friends as primary fantasy characters, pleasant companions throughout childhood. Disney World was a return to some of the happy but largely unconscious memories of my own early life, and even though I didn't immediately realize it, these implicit memories were significantly affecting my mood state at Disney World that day so many years later.

Implicit memory occurs when you unintentionally recall something, an unconscious memory affects your mood or behavior, or you engage in some activity without consciously knowing how you are doing it. In effect, implicit memory is automatic. Like explicit memory, it is subject to priming in that it is often elicited by cues, though you may be unaware of the specific cues at the time (Zeelenberg et al., 2002).

Implicit memory is perhaps most obvious in memory for skills. If you learned to ride a bike as a child and haven't ridden one in ten years, you can easily climb on now and ride, but you will have difficulty verbally describing exactly how you do it. Swimming and tying your shoelaces are other examples. You remember a motor skill, but the memory is implicit. Willi had no difficulty doing CPR because of his implicit motor memory, but he had trouble remembering the counts, which are explicit.

Implicit memory is involved in more than motor skills. For example, you may not be able to figure out why you find yourself getting anxious on a walk with your girlfriend in a wooded park on a beautiful day. The reason is that as a child you were once very frightened when you became lost in the woods for a few minutes, even though you have no conscious recollection of that incident now. The implicit memory is producing your anxiety. It has also been demonstrated in a variety of verbal tasks, and memory for visual objects (McKone & French, 2001). A striking experimental example of implicit memory is seen in work on surgical patients. One team of researchers presented words to patients who were under general anesthesia during surgery. Although they later had no recollection of being presented with the words, they performed significantly better on an implicit memory recall task than did a control group (Jelicic et al., 1992).

It appears that implicit and explicit memories may involve separate systems functioning on somewhat different principles (Rajaram et al., 2001). Suppose you were to read a long list of unrelated words once, then try to remember them a week later. You probably wouldn't do very well because your explicit memory for the words is gone. However, studies show that if you are given fragments of the words, you can often remember them. For example, you may be given the fragment **I-p-I-it.** Figure it out? The word is, of course, **implicit.** Such experiments support the idea of two different memory systems (Lustig & Hasher, 2001). Explicit memory is gone a week after learning a list, but implicit memory remains, permitting you to complete the word. Studies of patients with amnesia have also supported the differentiation. Such patients have difficulty with conscious learning and memory but clearly have unconscious or implicit memories that affect their behavior (Tulving, 1993). For example, they can be shown the word **IMPLICIT** a number of times and have no explicit recall, but given the letters **IM**, the first word to come to mind will be **IMPLICIT.**

Think Critically

Do Eyewitnesses Give Accurate Testimony?

A few years ago the author was called for jury duty and selected to be on a jury to try a rape case. The prosecutor at one point showed the victim a series of twenty slides that included a photo of the man on trial for her rape. Although she had some months earlier identified his picture, she was now unable to do so—even though he was sitting ten feet from her in the courtroom. Although most jury members were convinced by other evidence that the accused man was the rapist, some felt that he should not be convicted because the victim—obviously an eyewitness to the crime—had been unable to identify his picture. Gottesman (1992) relates a similar incident in which an eyewitness in an arson case was asked on the stand to identify the man she had seen leaving the burning building. With great confidence, she pointed toward the defense table—at an assistant defense attorney!

Eyewitness errors like these occur in field settings, in police lineups, and in courtrooms and are especially important because the courts often rely heavily on the testimony of such witnesses in reaching verdicts (Behrman & Davey, 2001). One study reviewed all the police lineups conducted in England and Wales during 1973 and the outcomes in terms of convictions. It turned out that in 347 cases in which eyewitness identification was the only evidence against the defendant 74 percent were convicted (Loftus, 1973). Experiments revolving around a hypothetical murder case with subjects serving as

jurors confirm this observation. Only 18 percent of these "jurors" found defendants guilty on the basis of circumstantial evidence alone, while 72 percent gave a guilty verdict when the testimony of just a single eyewitness was included.

The Basic Hypothesis or Contention

Memory researcher Elizabeth Loftus (1993) and other psychologists hypothesize that eyewitnesses to crimes very often have moderately to extremely inaccurate memories of those crimes. If Loftus is right, this would obviously mean that whenever judges and juries rely heavily on eyewitness testimony, there is substantial risk that innocent people will be convicted. Agreeing with this hypothesis on the basis of his experience, noted attorney F. Lee Bailey contends that the single major basis for the conviction of innocent people is eyewitness testimony. Do you agree with this hypothesis? How could you test it?

What Is The Evidence?

Considerable research suggests that an eyewitness cannot tell a jury what she *sees*, only what she *perceives* and *remembers* (Loftus, 1993). Since perception is influenced by the focus of attention, the complexity of the scene, the response biases of the observer, the familiarity of the witness with the perpetrator, and other factors, it is no wonder that eyewitnesses often give inaccurate descriptions of a crime (Asai, 2001). In one study, each of sixty undergraduate students saw one of two similar videotapes that depicted a man approaching a woman. One tape showed a violent mugging, while the other showed the man asking for directions. Those who saw the nonviolent tape were later able to select the man from a set of photos 40 percent of the time, while those who saw the violent tape could identify the same man only 30 percent of the time. Thus, less than half the witnesses could identify the individual in either case, and even fewer were accurate when violence was involved. Other studies confirm that violence reduces eyewitness accuracy (Burke, Heurer, & Reisberg, 1992), as does high anxiety (Dobson & Markham, 1992).

In addition to showing that eyewitnesses have poor memories for faces and events, research indicates that memory can be influenced *after the fact* by even minor variations in the questions used during interrogation. For instance, one group of people who had viewed an automobile accident film were asked, "Did you see *a* broken headlight?" while a second group were asked, "Did you see *the* broken headlight?" Even though there was no broken headlight in the film, 15 percent of the people in the second group reported seeing one, while only 7 percent of those in the first group did so (Loftus, 1974). Another study showed that eyewitness accounts given by children can be greatly affected by what their parents tell them (Poole & Lindsay, 2001).

The fact that misleading information distorts memory for an event is a serious problem that goes beyond the nature of the questions asked (Belli et al., 1994). Later mention of an object that was not actually present at the crime may cause the witness to incorporate it into his perception. This phenomenon is termed the *misinformation effect.* For example, a police interviewer might mistakenly tell the witness that she believes there was a knife several feet from the body. Later the witness is quite likely to recall with confidence that he saw a knife at the scene, even though there wasn't one (Gordon et al., 2001). Similarly, studies show that the expectations of a police lineup administrator, who may think he knows who the criminal is, can influence the eyewitness's identification of the suspect (Garrioch & Brimacombe, 2001). The dominant explanation for the misinformation effect is that the witness's original memory is impaired—perhaps overwritten—by the new, inaccurate information (Wright et al., 2000). The memory is thus modified to incorporate the new object. When asked to recall the scene, as when he is testifying, the witness remembers the new object in the same way that he remembers what he actually saw at the time of the crime (Loftus, 1992).

Perhaps one way to increase accuracy would be to have witnesses indicate how confident they are in their memories. Sounds good, but, in fact, confidence levels are typically unrelated to accuracy of recall. To make matters worse, jurors are much more likely to believe eyewitnesses who are highly confident.

Juries are also more impressed when a witness gives a very detailed account of the crime, rather than a more general one. Although that bias appears to make sense, evidence suggests that a witness who focused on minute details may have less accurate recall of such important items as the suspect's facial features and clothing (Bradfield & Wells, 2000). So strong is the evidence of errors by eyewitnesses that there is 80% agreement on the nature and sources of these errors among 64 experts who regularly testify in court (Kassin et al., 2001).

Another way to improve accuracy might be to warn subjects about possible misleading information. In one such study, college students saw a series of twenty-four color slides depicting a wallet-snatching incident. Each then read one of two paragraphs providing information that was either consistent or inconsistent with the slide presentation.

In addition, some participants were warned before viewing the slides that there might be misleading information in the paragraph, some were given this warning after viewing the slides, and some were not given the warning at all.

The researchers found that the greatest accuracy occurred when the warning was given after seeing the slides and before reading the paragraph. Warnings given at other times had no effect on accuracy, and the presentation of misleading information still considerably reduced the accuracy of recall, despite the warning (Greene, Flynn, and Loftus, 1982).

Perhaps a final ploy would be to warn the jurors about the possible ways in which eyewitnesses can make mistakes and instruct them to take this into account. However, research shows that jurors have very inaccurate memories for instructions (Deutsch, 1992)! For example, 75% of 238 people on jury duty in one study seriously misinterpreted important elements of instructions regarding the death penalty (Hayes, 1992). Instructions on eyewitness testimony would probably also be mis-remembered.

Is The Evidence Open To Alternative Interpretations?

The studies of Loftus and others have been carefully done, with random assignment of participants to conditions and appropriate controls. Moreover, the consistency of the evidence across studies and laboratories is quite compelling, though some have raised questions about specific studies.

Perhaps the principal basis on which we might question the results is the artificial nature of the situation in which they are obtained. The work supporting the Loftus hypothesis is predominantly laboratory research and therefore involves only simulated situations. The crimes are not *real* crimes, the eyewitnesses are not *real* eyewitnesses, and the jurors are not *real* jurors. It is possible that things are different in the real world outside the laboratory. Subjects are obviously well aware that they are simply viewing a videotape and answering questions as part of an experiment. Their motivations and states of mind are probably quite different from those of an eyewitness to an actual crime in progress. Perhaps knowledge that the crime is a real one somehow makes perceptions more accurate and memories more reliable. However, there is no evidence to that effect and no reason to believe it is true.

Do We Need Additional Evidence?

It would certainly be helpful to have more evidence concerning the accuracy of eyewitnesses to actual crimes. For example, when we know with certainty who the criminal is based on other definitive evidence, do eyewitnesses identify her correctly? Is the rate of inaccuracy the same in witnesses of real crimes as it is in laboratory studies? What kinds of errors do real eyewitnesses make and under what circumstances?

What Conclusions Can We Reach?

As always, our conclusions should be cautious, pending further research. However, despite the artificial nature of the laboratory studies, it is difficult to argue with the weight of the evidence. It clearly appears that the inaccuracy of eyewitnesses is well-documented, and it is reasonable to conclude that the courts would be well-advised not to rely too heavily on such testimony.

Eyewitness memory is, however, clearly an area in which practical application has not yet caught up with empirical findings. Perhaps the future will see decreased reliance on eyewitness testimony, coupled with further attempts to increase its accuracy. Some hope for improvement is that eyewitness researchers and experts participated in writing a national guide for dealing with eyewitnesses and their testimony that has been released by the Justice Department (Wells et al., 2000).

Probe

Slipped My Mind! Improving Your Memory

There are a number of strategies you can use to improve your memory. Some approaches work better for some people, others for other people, so the first thing to do is to follow the mandate of Socrates to "Know thyself." *Metamemory* refers to your knowledge of your own memory and how it works. This chapter can provide you with some general knowledge about memory, but only you can assess the best approaches to improving yours. A serious attempt to improve memory is most likely to succeed if you take a comprehensive approach (Tekcan & Arturk, 2001). Look at all the strategies, decide how they will best work for you, then choose multiple strategies, try them out and modify your approach if necessary.

Some Useful Strategies

- *Pay Attention.* It may be obvious that you will not establish a memory for material unless you pay close attention, and studies have supported this observation (Jennings and Jaccoby, 1993). However, it is quite another matter to establish attention as a *principle* of memory improvement. Among other things, this principle means that you will study more efficiently in a relatively isolated environment free from distractions—perhaps alone in a room—rather than in the student lounge or even the library.

- *Spend More Time.* Spend more time studying and you will learn more. Sounds just like a college professor, doesn't it! But it's true. The more time spend on a block of material, the more you will recall later. Sorry about that.
- *Practice, Practice!* How you spend your time is also important. You need to practice what you are trying to commit to memory, often over and over. And the kind of practice makes a major difference. *Distributed* practice is far better than *massed* practice (Bahrick & Hall, 1991). This means spreading out your studies. For example, if you are taking this course and have a job, do part of your study before work and part after. Alternatively, study math for a while, then psychology, then back to math. Another aid is to *practice retrieval* of the information. You might, for example, go over the material on short-term memory in this chapter several times, then practice retrieving by trying repeatedly to recall it without looking at the book.
- *Process Deeply.* Simple maintenance practice does relatively little good. To really make your practice time count, you must engage in *elaborative practice.* Make the material meaningful. Go beyond what you read to integrate. For example, ask yourself questions about the long-term and short-term memory material in the text and about how they are related.
- *Be Organized.* Encoding something that is organized is always far better than trying to encode a chaotic mass of separate facts. One good approach is to use an outline of the material you are studying. For example, you might use the section headings in this chapter as a way of organizing your study. It helps you to get a sense of the "big picture," which in turn aids effective encoding of the details.
- *Chunk.* Whenever possible, chunk the information you need to remember. If the material is not already conveniently chunked for you, as in the case of phone and social security numbers, create your own chunks. Try it with your credit card or driver's license numbers. Break the number into chunks, learn each chunk, then put them together. Remember that you can much more easily increase the size of each chunk than the number of chunks.
- *Use Imagery.* Remember the old "picture is worth a thousand words" axiom that much research supports. Whenever possible, use imagery to aid your memory. Study the charts and graphs in this chapter carefully and commit them to memory as visual images. Retrieve them later (for example, during an exam) and they will give you much useful information. Mnemonic devices like the pegword method often use imagery to enhance memory. They can be very useful in limited situations, though you should not attempt to use these devices alone to improve your memory (Herrmann, 1991).
- *Use Context Cues.* Context serves as a cue for retrieval (Balch et al., 1992), so try to re-create the learning context as much as possible when you need to retrieve what you have learned. It may be hard to get your psychology professor to let you take the exam in your room at home, where you learned the material. However, you can try to mentally re-create the context during the exam by picturing yourself in your room studying or even by wearing a specific piece of clothing that you wear while studying.

SQ3R and PQRST

Putting it all together, memory experts have devised formulas for effectively learning from a book—for example, this one. There are two similar methods, and both rely primarily on the memory principles of organization, elaboration, and practice. One method goes by the convenient mnemonic SQ3R: Survey, Question, Read, Recite, and Review (Thomas & Robinson, 1972). The other, method is PQRST: Preview, Question, Read, Self-Recitation, and Test. The PQRST steps would apply to learning the material in any chapter of this book:

- *Preview.* Preview by reading the Networking section, going over the chapter outline, skimming the chapter, noting especially the section headings and overall organization, and reading the Keys To Knowledge summaries.
- *Question.* Study the section and subsection headings, then turn them into questions you can ask yourself after reading the material.
- *Read.* Experts have astutely noted that it is important to actually *read* the chapter! But there is a trick to reading: read while keeping in mind and answering the questions you have formulated.
- *Self-Recitation.* In this stage you practice retrieval of what you have learned. You recall the central points in each section, using the chapter outline and your questions to help you.
- *Test.* Test yourself over the chapter as a whole. Recall the central points, and engage in elaborative rehearsal, asking yourself how the various points relate to each other.

One More: I AM PACK

A third technique is call Interactive Images, Acronyms, Method of Loci, Pegwords, Acrostics, Categories, and Keywords (I AM PACK). The basic principle here involves the organization of information into meaningful chunks. You group new materials to be learned into categories (e.g., vegetables, tools), devise acronyms (IQ, SSN), and use acrostics—initial letters of items that form a sentence. You also use interactive images (e.g., to memorize the items Lamp, Book, Tree, and Towel, you might picture a lamp wrapped in a towel sitting on a book hanging from a tree). You add the pegword system the method of loci, described in the text, and also use keywords (individual words to which you link larger amounts of information.

Horizons in Memory

The Autobiography in Your Brain

How do we remember the wide variety of events that occur every day and accumulate over a lifetime, forming a kind of autobiography in the brain? How, for example, did Willi remember the good times he had experienced with Mr. Everett?

The concept of *ecological validity*, increasingly important in psychology, suggests that research should apply to real life occurrences. As a result, memory researchers have begun to turn their attention to *autobiographical* or everyday memory. How do we recognize faces at a 25th high school reunion, estimate dates of personal or political event, or recall events from our first year of college? What are our memories of early childhood and how do they affect our behavior now? How do we develop self-knowledge and self-conceptualizations in memory, and how does this autobiographical memory affect such decisions as our choice of significant others? Through this exciting new research, we will gradually enhance our understanding of how memory functions in our own lives.

A Memory Pill?

Could you take a drug before that next exam that would actually improve your memory? Clearly such a drug would be particularly useful for older people with memory deficits, in amnesia cases, and probably in reducing retroactive interference more generally (Ellis & Nathan, 2001). That is why scientists are searching for this "magic bullet." Drugs that enhance acetylcholine effects might be expected to help, since this neurotransmitter is important in memory. Some of these drugs do help in some studies, but choline and lecithin—biochemical precursors that increase ACh levels—have no effect on memory in other studies. On the other hand, physostigmine and tacrine, which prolong the effects of acetylcholine at the synapse, do improve memory in some older adults with deficits, as does tyrosine (Ellis & Nathan, 2001).

How about an alternative approach? Some hypotheses suggest that increased arousal enhances memory consolidation in the brain, so perhaps drugs that increase arousal would improve memory—and they do. Amphetamines, vasopressin, norepinephrine, and adrenaline do enhance memory—but the effect is small and temporary. Glucose also has at least a small positive effect on memory in mice (). However, none of these drugs represent breakthroughs in memory enhancement, and memory drugs are not likely to be ready for your next exam. But don't give up. This is a "hot topic" in memory research, and it is likely that we will see significant progress in this exciting field.

Memory Loss: An "Exceptional" Case

What we almost always find following brain injury is anterograde amnesia—the inability to retain newly learned information. However, exceptions can be as important as rules in teaching us about the brain, and Endel Tulving (1993) has recently discovered one. He reports the case of K.C., who suffered severe brain damage in a motorcycle accident. Unlike most patients, he has essentially complete anterograde and retrograde amnesia for specific facts and events. On the other hand, he can read, write, and communicate normally with others. Moreover, he does not know that his personality changed substantially as a result of the brain damage, but he can quite accurately describe himself both before and after the accident. In effect, K.C. has virtually no episodic memory, but his semantic memory is intact. Because his case is so unusual, K.C. will be studied very carefully for many years. If we can in this way differentiate brain structures involved in semantic memory from those mediating episodic memory, we may move significantly closer to understanding the neurological bases of memory.

Keys to Memory 1

Key Knowledge

1. Memory can be seen as an adaptive product of evolution
   - A. What the species-to-species variability in memory functions reflects?
     The need to adapt to differing environments.

2. Memory is viewed as a 3-step process
   A. What the 3 steps are?
      Encoding
      Storage
      Retrieval
   B. The 3 principal forms of encoding?
      Acoustic
      Visual
      Semantic
   C. The form of encoding involved in bike riding?
      Motor encoding
3. Memory is studied experimentally using 3 major methods.
   A. What the 3 methods are?
      Recognition
      Recall
      Relearning
   B. The major types of recall experiment?
      Free
      Cued
4. Dominant memory theory postulates 3 types of memory
   A. What the 3 types are?
      Sensory
      Short-term
      Long-term

Keys to Memory 2

Key Knowledge

1. Sensory memory briefly continues the sensation of a stimulus after that stimulus ends.
   A. Two major types of sensory memory?
      Iconic (visual)
      Echoic (auditory)
2. Short-term memory stores very limited information for brief periods.
   A. The probable maximum duration of STM?
      Probably about 30 seconds.
   B. The average amount of information stored in STM?
      Seven items
   C. How capacity can be effectively increased?
      By chunking
   D. The optimal size of a chunk?
      3 or 4 items.
   E. What the Brown-Peterson Paradigm is?
      A method for studying the duration of STM
3. Rehearsal is a major factor in retention.
   A. The major types of rehearsal
      Maintenance
      Elaborative
4. There are alternatives to the three-system theory.
   A. The name of the theory developed by Craik and his colleagues?
      Levels-of-processing theory

B. The alternative theory specifying an executive memory function?
Working memory—Baddeley

5. We scan memory in order to retrieve items.

A. The type of scan conducted in short-term memory according to Sternberg?
Exhaustive, rather than self-terminating.

B. The kind of processing Sternberg specified?
Serial

6. There is empirical evidence for the distinction between STM and LTM.

A. The two major serial position effects?
Primacy
Recency

B. What primacy reflects?
Long-term memory

C. What recency reflects?
At least short-term memory

Keys to Memory 3

Key Knowledge

1. Encoding in LTM is of at least two types.

A. What the two types are?
Semantic
Visual

B. What theory incorporates both types of encoding?
Paivio's dual-coding theory.

C. What the encoding specificity principle says?
Memory is best when cues are highly specific.

2. Constructive memory uses existing knowledge to modify new information entering memory.

A. The major types of schemas?
Scripts
Person
Self

B. A major advantage of memory schemas?
Cognitive efficiency

C. A major disadvantage of memory schemas?
Distortion

3. The storage capacity of long-term memory is virtually unlimited.

A. Two types of memory devoted to facts and skills?
Declarative
Procedural

B. Tulving's 2 major types of declarative memory?
Episodic
Semantic

4. Some individuals with exceptional memories have been studied.

A. What eidetic imagery is?
A form of coding and storage involving a detailed visual image.

B. Who developed the picture elicitation method?
Ralph Haber

5. Priming with cues aids retrieval.
   A. The significance of the TOT phenomenon?
      Suggests memory is stored in multiple locations.
   B. The name of memories cued by dramatic events?
      Flashbulb.
6. Context affects retrieval
   A. Some types and examples of context effects?
      State-dependent memory
      Mood affects memory
      Alcohol and drugs states affect memory
7. We have methods to enhance memory.
   A. Some major mnemonic devices?
      Pegword
      Method of loci
      Link method

Keys to Memory 4

Key Knowledge

1. Hermann Ebbinghaus
   A. What he did
      Conduct first studies of forgetting.
2. Availability theories hypothesize real information loss.
   A. What these theories are called?
      Trace-decay theory
      Disuse theory
      Interference theory
   B. The major types of interference?
      Proactive
      Retroactive
3. Accessibility theories hypothesize that all memories are stored but some are inaccessible.
   A. What the major theories are?
      Retrieval failure theory
      Motivational theory
   B. The cause of selective forgetting in Freud's theory?
      Repression
   C. The meaning of false memory syndrome?
      Recalling childhood sexual abuse that never occurred.

Keys to Memory 5

Key Knowledge

1. Karl Lashley
   A. His theory of memory?
      Engrams (memory traces) are stored throughout the brain.
2. Donald Hebb
   A. His theory of memory?
      Cell assemblies reverberate to cause anatomical changes at the synapse.

3. Memory storage may begin at the synapse.
   A. What synaptic processes may help account for memory?
      Synaptic plasticity
      Long-term potentiation
4. It appears that memory storage involves a few predominant neural structures.
   A. Some major structures storing memories?
      Hippocampus
      Temporal cortex and possibly other cortical areas
5. Connectionist models hypothesize that memory storage is distributed across the brain.
   A. The type of processing hypothesized by connectionism?
      Parallel distributed processing.
   B. The storage mechanism for memories?
      Neural networks.
6. Neurochemicals are probably also involved in memory.
   A. The major biochemicals implicated thus far?
      Neurotransmitters, particularly acetylcholine
      Proteins
      Hormones
      RNA
   B. The major types of memory pathology
      Anterograde
      Retrograde
   C. Some common causes of memory loss or pathology?
      Brain injury
      Brain surgery
      alcoholism
      aging

Key Term 1

encoding
recall
recognition
relearning

Key Terms 2

echoic memory
iconic memory
sensory memory

Key Terms 3

chunking
constructive memory
parallel processing
primacy effect
recency effect
priming
schema
script

serial position effect
serial processing
short-term memory
working memory

Key Names 3

Alan Baddeley
Frederick Bartlett
Fergus Craik
Graham Hitch
Robert Lockhart
George Miller
Saul Sternberg
Endel Tulving

Key Terms 4

autobiographical memory
declarative memory
eidetic imagery
episodic memory
explicit memory
flashbulb memory
implicit memory
long-term memory
mnemonic device
procedural memory
semantic memory

Key Names 4

Steven Kosslyn
Elizabeth Loftus
Alan Paivio

Key Terms 5

false memory syndrome
interference

Key Names 5

Hermann Ebbinghaus
Sigmund Freud

Key Terms 6

amnesia
cell assembly
connectionism

neural network
parallel distributed processing

Key Names 6

Donald Hebb
Karl Lashley
Brenda Milner

Chapter 8

Higher Mental Processes: Cognitive Science

Outline

Networking

AMONG THE most complex and fascinating of all human behaviors are those based on cognitive (thought) processes. How do we think? How do we solve problems, reason, make decisions? How do we acquire language? In the past three decades or so, cognitive psychology—a part of the broader fields of cognitive science and cognitive neuroscience—has become a dominant emphasis in psychology. Several major theories have been developed in an effort to understand how thought processes take place and how language is acquired, produced, and comprehended. Important cognitive research has addressed the development and use of concepts, the ways in which we solve problems and make decisions, and the structure and acquisition of language. Most recently, cognitive neuroscientists have developed interesting and powerful connectionist models of thought and language.

Cognitive processes and language are closely linked to learning (Chapter 6), memory (Chapter 7), and intelligence (Chapter 9). When we think in order to make a decision or solve a problem, we depend on memory to provide much of the information we need to carry out the cognitive processes. That information is acquired through learning. In addition, we may need to use learning processes to acquire new information needed to fully engage in a thought process, and that newly acquired material will be stored in memory. Language, in turn, is dependent on thought processes that rely on learning and memory. Intelligence is basically an indication of cognitive capacity and hence also closely linked to cognition. It reflects individual differences in the abilities to learn new material, retain that information, and process thoughts effectively. The associations among these phenomena—cognition, language, intelligence, learning, and memory—are thus virtually endless.

The Triumph of Pure Raason

Helen Keller became blind and deaf at the age of eighteen months. When Helen was seven years old, her teacher, Anne Sullivan, tried to show her language by writing letters in the child's hand. At first the task seemed hopeless. One day, however, Helen experienced a sudden insight into the connection between the finger-spellings and the objects they represented:

> *. . . we walked down the path to the well-house, attracted by the fragrance of the honeysuckle with which it was covered. Someone was drawing water, and my teacher placed my hand under the spout. As the cool stream gushed over one hand she spelled into the other the word water, first slowly, then rapidly. I stood still, my whole attention fixed upon the motions of her fingers. Suddenly I felt a misty consciousness as of something forgotten—a thrill of returning thought; and somehow the mystery of language was revealed to me. I knew that "W-A-T-E-R" meant the wonderful cool something that was flowing over my hand. That living word awakened my soul, gave it light, hope, joy, set it free! (Keller, 1954).*

Helen Keller's discovery of the connection between the word "water" and "the wonderful cool something" she was feeling demonstrates, in one dramatic moment, the human capacity for acquiring language and the link between thought and language.

On the one hand, language is the expression of thought. On the other, language may help to structure thought.

Among the most complex of all human activities is the process of cognition or thinking. *Cognition* means "to know" and refers to the mental activities involved in acquiring, processing, and using knowledge (Boreham, 1994). Without perceiving any immediate external stimuli or making any outwardly observable responses, a human being can solve mathematical problems, organize a series of tasks to be completed, create a poem, or develop a scientific theory. Amazingly enough, however, psychology largely ignored cognition until nearly 1960, principally because the field was caught up in the behaviorism of B.F. Skinner and his colleagues (Chapter 6). Behaviorism rejected any attempt to deal with internal constructs, making the study of the "mind" virtual heresy. But the mid-1950s saw the beginnings of change. George Miller (1956) began to study memory, a clearly internal, cognitive process, and published the famous paper that we discuss in Chapter 7. Rebel psychologist Herbert Simon (1957) insisted on the importance of understanding the role of thought processes in behavior. Linguist Noam Chomsky (1957) proposed a new theory of language, introducing biological and cognitive concepts that were virtually unheard of in psychology. And French psychologist Jean Piaget (1926, 1954), who had actually begun to examine thought processes in children many years earlier, published some of his most influential works on cognition. At about the same time, Jerome Bruner began his classic cognitive work on the formation of concepts (Bruner, Goodnow, & Austin, 1956), Donald Broadbent (1954) developed a cognitive model of human performance in work settings, and George Kelley (1955) proposed a thoroughly cognitive theory of human personality and behavior. The revolt was on, and the new baby of the field—cognitive psychology—was born. It would go on to become one of the most central and influential forces.

Modern cognitive psychologists are scientists interested in how we gain new knowledge, incorporate that knowledge into existing frameworks, and use information to solve problems, arrive at decisions, and engage in effective behavior. The broader field of which cognitive psychology is a part is *cognitive science*, which studies the nature, components, and development of thought and knowledge. It is interdisciplinary, crossing the fields of cognitive psychology, linguistics, computer science, anthropology, artificial intelligence, and philosophy (Hunt, 1989). Adding to this list such fields as biological psychology, neurology, and neurochemistry has resulted in the newer, hybrid interdisciplinary field called *cognitive neuroscience.* It studies the origins and processing of thought in the brain (Kosslyn & Koenig, 1992).

The study of cognition has become an increasingly central—some would say dominant—part of psychology in recent years. It is a major focus of the work of not only those interested in learning and memory, but also many developmental, social, and clinical psychologists. In fact, a 1990 survey showed that 75 percent of psychologists in U.S. colleges and universities identify themselves as cognitive psychologists (Eysenck & Keane, 1990).

Before we begin to examine the elements of cognition, let's look for a moment at the idea of writing a chapter on cognition and language, something that is certainly on my mind at the moment. The process is quite similar to the one you might have engaged in while writing a paper for your English course. You have to decide on the general nature of the topic, collect information, plan and organize the paper, and then turn your thoughts into words and sentences. These complex processes are based on our ability to form concepts, develop propositions, and solve problems in a systematic way.

Elements of Cognition

When you have a specific thought, it is the end product of a process that involves one or more of several elements. These components are important both because we could not engage in cognitive activities without them and because they help us to understand how those activities take place. Among the principal elements of cognition are concepts and propositions.

Concepts

A *concept* is a mental representation of the central properties of a class of like objects or instances that serves to group or classify them into categories. Helen Keller eventually learned that "water" falls under the concept "liquid." Similarly, "dwelling" is a concept that includes such varied items as igloos, tents, huts, apartments, houses, and palaces. A good example of a widely used concept is color. The human visual system is capable of discriminating some 7.5 million colors (Brown and Lanneberg, 1954). However, we commonly use just eight basic categories or specific color names (red, green, and so on) under which we classify all the colors in the spectrum.

When we think, we use concepts and the categories they involve to deal with both concrete objects and abstract ideas (Fodor, 1994). "Would you rather have a hot dog or a hamburger?" You answer this question by referring to your mental concepts of these two concrete items without having to see a real hamburger and hot dog in front of you. "Would you rather have health or wealth?" Again your cognitive concepts of these more abstract ideas allow you to formulate an answer.

Concept Types. Cognitive scientists have identified two principal types of concepts: artificial and natural. *Artificial concepts* are those defined by a specific set of rules and are relatively concrete. The elementary school teacher defines a triangle as a closed figure with exactly three sides and sharp corners, and you thereafter classify all such figures under the concept "triangle." *Natural concepts* are more abstract. They have shared properties that are less fixed. Fish have fins, live in the water, and swim. However, not all creatures that have fins or swim or both are fish. Humans swim and are clearly not fish, and porpoises, which have all three properties, are mammals, not fish.

Acquiring Concepts. Concept formation is a cognitive process through which we learn major categories of information and the members of those categories. We acquire concepts gradually, learning the identifying characteristics of members of the class and examples of objects that fit that class (Demetriou et al., 1993). Over time, we refine our knowledge of the concept and learn more and more clearly what to include and exclude.

Concepts can be learned through either experience or teaching. Many are initially acquired through experience with *prototypes,* which are examples or instances of the concepts (Massaro & Ferguson, 1994). Water was Helen Keller's first prototype for the concept liquid. Similarly, a child may over time see a robin, a blue jay, a cardinal, and a sparrow and learn that each is a bird. He may now see an eagle and easily classify it as a bird, since its characteristics are typical of the bird concept. If shown an ostrich or turkey— atypical examples—the child will have more difficulty classifying them correctly.

The reason the child has difficulty in correctly classifying the ostrich or turkey is that he has not yet learned the *core* of the concept, which tells him just what properties are essential. Birds, for example, are living and animate, have wings, two feet, hollow bones, and feathers; many fly and sing. The cores of concepts are often acquired better through direct *teaching* than through experience with prototypes. Once a parent has pointed out the core properties of the bird concept, the child will have much less difficulty in categorizing the atypical turkey or ostrich.

Of course, not all birds have all the core properties. As a result, some theorists believe that we operate on a *probabilistic* basis. We classify an object as belonging to a concept category if it has properties that are *typical* of that category (Medin & Smith, 1984) or bear a *family resemblance* to typical members of the category. A robin is a bird that has most of the core bird properties. A penguin is missing some important properties, but older children and adults quite easily classify it as a bird because it has some of the typical properties and bears a family resemblance to bird prototypes (Medin & Ross, 1992).

Models of concept formation include mediation and hypothesis-testing theories. Mediation theory suggests that we acquire concepts by forming associations between stimuli and responses. A specific instance (daisy) is thus linked to a concept category (flower). This older theory made concept formation a passive process of building stimulus-response associations through reinforcement. It has been largely replaced by hypothesis-testing theory, which sees concept formation as an active process, particularly for the acquisition of more complex concepts. When faced with such complex concepts as patriotism or love, we hypothesize or speculate as to what the critical properties of the concept may be, then test a potential instance to see whether or not the hypothesized properties apply. If our classification is correct, we apply that hypothesis to future instances. If not, the hypothesis will be modified. A physician may initially hypothesize that your stomach pain is due to an ulcer. If he finds no ulcer when he examines you, he may then hypothesize that you are taking too much aspirin, which can also cause stomach pain. In future cases he may be more likely to offer that hypothesis initially.

Concept Hierarchies. Robins are birds; birds are vertebrates; and vertebrates are animals. The point, of course, is that we learn hierarchies of concepts. Vertebrates are a subset of animals, birds a subset of vertebrates and robins a subset of birds.

The value of concept hierarchies is that they allow us to infer properties that may not be directly or immediately associated with the lower level concept. We know that animals have the property of life. We therefore know that birds, which are animals, must also be living things.

Propositions

Concepts are typically combined in various ways to form the basis for thought. We commonly link concepts by formulating a proposition about the relationship. A proposition is a statement that links mental elements in ways that allow us to use those elements for purposes of thought. For example, "Trees often have branches" and "Health is preferable to wealth" are propositions suggesting a relationship between the concepts of tree and branch or between the concepts of health and wealth. By creating many propositions representing associations among a variety of concepts, we can engage in complex thought processes that allow us to plan and cook a meal, study for an exam, or create a scientific theory.

Concepts and propositions are vital to human cognition (Fodor, 1994). Without concepts, we would simply experience an unending flow of apparently unrelated information. Each object and situation would be unique, and the information we were taking in would be of little value. Fortunately, we tend to place each incoming bit of information under some existing concept, and concepts become the foundation upon which all thought processes are built. But just how objects are identified and categorized is still a matter of considerable theoretical speculation and empirical research (Nosofsky, 1987).

Combining The Elements: Cognitive Processes

We all regularly engage in a variety of cognitive processes, including problem-solving, decision-making, and reasoning. When we do, there are actually two different kinds of activities going on simultaneously. First, there is the primary cognitive process you are engaged in, such as solving a problem. Second, there is your awareness of your own processing of the problem. This latter activity is called metacognition, and it is essentially your cognition of your cognitions. It may be accurate or inaccurate. As you finish studying for an exam, you think about how you have gone about studying and how well prepared you are. If your metacognition is on target, you will do well in the exam.

While metacognition is important, it is the basic thought processes themselves that have attracted most of the attention of cognitive scientists. We will focus here on three of these forms of cognition: problem-solving, decision-making, and reasoning.

Keys to Higher Mental Processes 1

Problem-Solving

A problem is a difficult situation that has at least one—often more than one—possible solution and in which the "correct" resolution is uncertain. Problem-solving is the active effort to resolve such problems and occurs when a barrier blocks the path to a goal. How do people go about solving problems? Are some problem-solving strategies more efficient than others? What interferes with our ability to solve problems? These are some of the questions cognitive psychologists explore.

Theories of Problem-Solving and Cognition

In their classic work on problem-solving, Allen Newell and Herbert Simon (Newell, Shaw & Simon, 1958; Newell & Simon, 1972) saw it as a cognitive process of choosing among alternative solutions. More generally, problem-solving takes place through thought processes. Thought involves the internal representation and manipulation of the external world through mental models or representations of that world (Johnson-Laird, 1994). As a result, cognitive scientists try to understand problem-solving by developing theoretical approaches to understanding how these mental models work (Radvansky et al., 1993). The principal approaches include Gestalt theory, information-processing theory, and connectionism.

Gaining Insight: Gestalt Theory. A classic problem-solving model is provided by Gestalt theory, which suggests that we solve many problems through insight. When faced with a problem, we actively integrate all available information into an overall whole, or gestalt. When the gestalt is complete, we may achieve insight—a sudden recognition of the correct solution, usually after a period during which we are not consciously thinking about the problem. As we discuss in Chapter 6, even Wolfgang Köhler's chimps were able to achieve insight. Perhaps you have experienced insight while attempting to write a computer program or solve a math problem. You ponder the various elements of the problem for some time, put it aside to do something else, then come back to it later. Suddenly the correct approach comes to you, and you quickly complete the program or problem. Helen Keller provides a classic example of insight: "Suddenly I felt a misty consciousness as of something forgotten . . ."

One of the most famous examples of human insight was that of chemist Frederick Kekùle in 1865. Kekùle had been trying to devise an overall theory of the structure of organic molecules. One afternoon he was dozing before his fire and had a dream in which "atoms gambolled" before his eyes, forming "long rows, sometimes more closely fitted together; all twining and twisting in snakelike motion." As the dream continued, Kekùle noted that "One of the snakes had seized hold of its own tail, and the form whirled mockingly before my eyes. As if by a flash of lightening, I awoke." In the vision of the snake biting its own tail, Kekùle saw that important organic compounds consist of closed rings of atoms. He had made a discovery fundamental to the understanding of organic chemistry.

Theorizing that problems are commonly solved through insight is one thing; demonstrating it has proven to be quite another. Although many studies have been completed by Gestalt psychologists, they have been unable to provide convincing support for this insight theory.

The Brain As Computer: Information-Processing Theory. If you've ever wished you had a computer for a brain, information-processing is the theory for you. It suggests that the human brain is like a computer and that the person more generally is a system for processing information (Massaro & Cowan, 1993). Events in the external environment provide information (input) through the senses, the brain (the central processing unit or CPU) manipulates that information, and behavior (output) occurs (Figure 8-1).

To see how information is processed, let's take the example of reading this textbook. Its content is represented internally as a set of symbols to be stored, retrieved, and manipulated (thought about) by your computer (brain) to solve the problem of preparing for the next exam. You can outline the content of a chapter, formulate questions about the material, and decide what points are most important. You are processing information in order to solve the problem.

According to one information-processing approach, there are four main stages involved in solving most problems: preparation, production, judgment, and incubation (Bourne, Dominowski, and Loftus, 1979). During the preparation stage, the person gathers information about the problem and formulates an interpretation of what it involves. Preparation for a move in a chess game, for example, may involve scanning the board to determine the locations of all pieces and formulating a goal for the next few moves. In the production stage, possible solutions are generated, and recent evidence suggests that there may be individual differences in the ability to generate alternatives (Newstead et al., 2002). The third stage is judgment, during which the possible solutions are evaluated. The final stage is incubation, during which the person does not actively work on the problem, but may do so unconsciously. The incubation period often helps in arriving at a novel solution to a complex problem (Figure 8-2).

Information-processing theory is important because it has long served as a principal organizing force for much of cognitive psychology and because it has generated a large body of research (Stratta et al., 1994). It remains a major theory, but has been joined in more recent years by connectionism.

Problem-Solving Networks: Connectionism. In 1986, James McClelland, David Rumelhart, and their research group published a two-volume book called Parallel Distributed Processing that has become of the most influential works in the field of cognitive science. They present a connectionist model and hypothesize that problem-solving and other thought processes take place through the establishment of systems of neural associations or connections (Chapter 7). These connections, or neural networks, engage in parallel distributed processing (PDP), which means that multiple cognitive activities can take place simultaneously. As you build knowledge of the members of a concept class, such as liquids or colors, you are building and modifying a neural network in which the developing concept is stored (Tsuzuki et al., 2002).

Older theories, including information-processing theory, hold that the processing of information is at least largely sequential or serial, such that only one mental operation occurs at a time. PDP theorists point out that serial processing cannot readily account for the complexity and speed of neural activity (Ohayon, 1990). To understand their point, glance at a picture on your wall. You immediately perceive the entire picture, even though your retina sends to the cortex perhaps a million distinct bits of information that must all be processed before you perceive the picture. Moreover, different areas of the brain process information about the forms, colors, and distances represented in the picture. Such speed can only be explained in terms of parallel processing; serial processing would be too slow (Martindale, 1991).

The information-processing and connectionist models have somewhat different implications for how thought processes take place in the brain. Information-processing theory hypothesizes the existence of a single central-processing unit that analyzes and integrates data, drawing from other units, such as memory, which contain needed information. Connectionist models spread cognition throughout the brain by hypothesizing wide-ranging neural networks. The much faster processing postulated in these models takes place not in a single, central area that draws from other areas but in scattered neural circuits that span the brain. Memory, which is necessary for thought, is also stored throughout the brain in interconnected neural networks. The two neural theories of cognition thus operate on quite different models of the brain and how it functions.

They are increasingly helping us to understand the basic nature of cognition, as well as important aspects of perception, memory, language, and vision (McClelland & Plaut, 1993). In addition, they are currently being introduced into other fields, such as psychiatry and clinical psychology (Rialle & Stip, 1994; Olds, 1994). Other aspects of the connectionist approach are covered more fully in our discussions of learning and memory in Chapters 6 and 7.

Problem-Solving Strategies

Research growing out of information-processing and other theoretical models has identified a number of strategies that people often use to solve problems. They include algorithms and heuristics, working backward from the endpoint of the problem, reducing the differences between the starting point and the endpoint, analyzing the differences between means and ends, and applying approaches you have successfully used before.

Algorithms and Heuristics. One approach to solving problems is to use algorithms, which provide mechanical, step-by-step solutions. If you need to multiply 2005 by 1995, you can use the usual multiplication algorithm to get 3999975. However, the calculation is somewhat laborious, so if you just need an approximation, you might use a heuristic, a short-cut rule-of-thumb that can be a powerful aid to efficient cognition (Natsopoulos et al., 1993; Metcalf et al., 1993). In this case, the heuristic might be to look for a round-number approximation. Knowing that 20 X 20 is 400, you note that the problem involves two numbers around 2000, suggesting the square of 2000 or 4,000,000 as an approximate answer. Many people apply a common heuristic in voting for politicians. They assume that all politicians of a given party hold similar views. Therefore, it becomes unnecessary to learn the specific views of each candidate; you can just vote the party slate.

Working Backward. When you approach a problem by working backward, you simply start at the endpoint or goal and move back toward the starting point. The idea is that knowing where you want to end up will guide you in planning how to get there (Best, 1991). You might plan a ski trip by picturing yourself on the slopes, then determining what you will need to get there: What equipment and clothing? Where will you stay and eat? What airline will you take? When will you depart? What has to be done at home before leaving? Working backward is a particularly useful strategy when there is a well-defined goal.

Difference Reduction. In using a difference reduction strategy, you establish a set of sub-goals that will get you to the goal. You then reduce the difference between where you are now and where you want to be (your goal) by accomplishing the subgoals. If you are in high school and want to become a physician, your major subgoals may include getting admitted to college, graduating with a high GPA, getting into medical school, and successfully completing your M.D. degree. You reduce the difference between high school senior and M.D. by achieving each subgoal. Difference reduction is often a better strategy when you do not know the precise nature of the endpoint.

Means/Ends Analysis. Means/ends analysis is a more advanced kind of difference reduction. In means/ends analysis, you determine your present state and your goal state, assess the difference between them, then decide on the best means for achieving the goal. Let's say you already have a B.A. degree in chemistry but decide you would like to be a psychologist. Means-end analysis may suggest that you would best move backward—perhaps getting a second bachelor's degree in psychology—rather than immediately applying to graduate school. The end justifies the means, even though it requires a temporary backward step.

Finding Analogies. A final strategy is to find analogies to problems you have faced before (Medin & Ross, 1992). How similar is this problem to previous problems? You may find a conflict with college roommates to be analogous to a situation you faced with your brother while living at home. Would the strategy you used to resolve that earlier conflict apply to the new situation as well? Finding analogies can be a very useful and efficient way to solve problems, since it avoids "re-inventing the wheel" (Gick & Holyoak, 1980).

The Problem-Solving Process: Success or Failure?

A variety of factors can contribute to the success or failure of the problem-solving process. Among the more important are the way in which the problem is represented, prior knowledge, memory, selective attention, and planning (Table 8-1).

Representing The Problem. Your success in solving a problem can depend on your conceptualization—your representation—of the problem (Koenig & Griggs, 2001). Any given problem can potentially be represented in a variety of ways—verbally. mathematically, graphically, pictorially, and so on. Consider this problem:

> *Precisely at sunrise one morning, a Buddist monk began to climb a high mountain. He ascended a narrow path that spiraled around the mountain to a temple at the summit. His speed varied from time to time, and he stopped many times along the way to rest and eat. He reached the temple at exactly sunset. After fasting and meditating for several days, he began his journey back down the same path, starting exactly at sunrise, walking at variable speeds, and pausing frequently. His average speed of descent was, of course, greater than his average climbing speed, but he reached the bottom precisely at sunset. Show that there is a point along the path that the monk will reach at precisely the same time of day on both trips (Glass, Holyoak, and Santa, 1979).*

A good way to solve this problem is to represent it graphically and think of the situation as involving two monks, one ascending and one descending simultaneously. This makes it obvious that there must be some place on the path where the two monks will meet and it must be at precisely the same time (see Figure 8-3).

Using Prior Skills and Knowledge. You would probably call an architect to design your house and a psychologist to get help for depression. You recognize that they have differing skills and bodies of knowledge. The same principle applies to solving any problem: Prior skills and knowledge affect the likelihood of success (Reid and Evans, 1987).

The cognitive skills involved in solving problems can be acquired through experience or teaching or a combination of the two. You've often heard "experience is the best teacher." But studies show this is only partially true. When problems are solved on the basis of experience alone, initial solutions are typically weak. Applying these weak solutions and observing the results gradually leads to the acquisition of problem-solving skills (Anderson, 1987). Cognitive skills can also be taught, either as general problem-solving strategies or as approaches to dealing with only specific types of problems. Richard Herrnstein and his colleagues have developed specific courses that successfully teach thinking and problem-solving skills to 7th-grade students (Herrnstein, Nickarson, deSanehez, and Swets, 1986).

Memory. A third factor in problem-solving is memory, which can affect ability to solve a problem by providing both relevant factual information and strategies that might be useful (Palalavo & Seifert, 1994). You might also store and retrieve information that you develop as you attempt to solve the problem. And you must, of course, store the details of the problem itself in memory. Consider the following problem:

> *Three hobbits and three orcs are standing on one side of a river. Two of the orcs are blue and one is green. Two of the hobbits are red and one is blue. Near them is a boat that will hold one or two creatures. All six must be transported to the other side of the river. However, if hobbits are outnumbered by orcs at any time on either side of the river, the orcs will eat the hobbits. How can you transport all six across the river without having any hobbits eaten by orcs? (Solso, 1979)*

After working on this problem for a while, you might check Figure 8-4 for a solution.

To solve the problem, you must represent its details in memory: Three hobbits and three orcs must cross the river, the boat holds a maximum of two creatures, and orcs must not outnumber hobbits on either side of the river.

Attending Selectively. Selective attention also plays a role in problem solving. When faced with a problem, you must determine which information is really needed to solve the problem and which is extraneous (Remington, 2001). Remember how Helen Keller focused on the word that Sullivan was spelling ("my whole attention fixed upon the motions of her fingers"). And in the hobbit-orc problem, the colors of the hobbits and orcs turn out to be irrelevant.

Planning. If you approach a problem in a disorganized fashion, haphazardly looking first at one element, then another, you will probably not solve it very efficiently. If you use mental trial and error in the hobbit problem, for example, it will take you a long time to solve the problem. But if you formulate a plan to make a pictorial representation of the problem and to use a systematic series of steps in the search for a solution, you are more likely to be successful. Planning is especially important when we move from orcs and hobbits to solving real social problems, which follow basically the same problem-solving rules (Heidrich & Denney, 1994).

Problems in Solving Problems: Doing Things The Hard Way

You can picture the problem-solving process as moving along a path from a starting point to a goal point, and you often run into barriers that block the path (Table 8-2). Research has identified several of the most common of these obstacles to effective problem-solving: functional fixedness, irrelevant information, psychological sets, and confirmation biases.

Functional Fixedness. Gestalt psychologists were the first to identify one of the most common constraints on problem-solving (Duneker, 1945). Functional fixedness is a failure to realize that an object can have a use other than the one with which it is most commonly associated. A good example is the two-string problem shown in Figure 8-5 (Maier, 1931). The object is to tie together the two strings, which are too far apart to reach at one time. How would you solve this problem? If you answered that you would tie the pliers to the end of one string and then set that string swinging toward the other one, you have overcome functional fixedness. Most participants see the pliers as a tool, not as a weight, and therefore have difficulty solving the problem.

Irrelevant Information. The hobbit-orc problem presents irrelevant information concerning the colors of the creatures. This may seem unfair, but the reality is that many problems in everyday life include such irrelevancies. Their effect on problem-solving has been addressed by a number of information-processing researchers, including Robert Sternberg (1986). Consider one of the problems he has presented to participants in some studies:

> *The Thompson family includes five brothers. Each brother has one sister. Counting Mrs. Thompson, how many females are there in the family? (Sternberg, 1986, p. 215).*

The answer is two: Mrs. Thompson and her daughter. This problem may seem simple, but many participants fail to recognize that information concerning the number of brothers in the Thompson family is irrelevant. More generally, irrelevant information, particularly in numerical problems, is often a barrier (Ben-Shakhar, and Gati, 1987).

Psychological Set. Problem-solving also becomes less efficient when the individual adopts a mental or psychological set that is inappropriate to the problem at hand. A psychological set is a tendency to persist in the use of previously successful strategies, even when they may be inappropriate for the current problem. A good example of set is the classic water jar problem used by Gestalt psychologist Abraham Luchins (1942). He gave a participant three jars of different sizes, and she had to use only these jars to measure out a specified amount of water. Several of Luchins' problems are shown in Table 8-3.

In one sample problem, the participant is told that Jar A holds 21 quarts of water, Jar B 127 quarts, and Jar C 3 quarts. The task is to obtain exactly 100 quarts. A good solution in this case is represented by the formula B—A—2C. When given a series of problems that could be solved with this formula, participants quickly became adept at the solution. However, when the nature of the problems changed so that they could be solved more simply ("Obtain 20 quarts when jar A = 23 quarts, jar B = 49 quarts, and jar C = 3 quarts"), participants continued to use the more difficult solution. A second example is the nine-dot problem (Adams, 1980) (Figure 8-6). Try to solve it before turning the page to find some solutions (Figure 8-7).

Confirmation Bias. Another problem is the inclination to be defeated by preconceptions. A confirmation bias is the tendency to interpret new information as verifying a pre-existing hypothesis. You face a problem, formulate a hypothesis, then gather information. You may proceed to interpret the information in a biased way that confirms your initial hypothesis (Ditto & Lopez, 1992). A man may, for example, experience chest pain and guess that it is caused by indigestion. He repeatedly confirms this hypothesis by observing that the chest pain seems to follow heavy meals and spicy foods—until one day he has a heart attack.

The Expert As Problem-Solver: How Does He Do It?

You take your sore throat to a physician, she immediately knows what to do, and you are soon cured. You see a mechanic about your squeaking brakes and a plumber about your leaky pipes. They are experts and can usually solve problems in their own areas of expertise far better than you can. But how do they do it? The brief answer is that they store information in meaningful chunks, process deeply, and have highly organized bodies of knowledge (Gobet et al., 2001).

Chunking A Chess Board. Adriaan de Groot, a Dutch psychologist, was the first to take an active interest in just how experts solve problems. In research that began in the 1940s, master chess players and ordinary players were shown a chessboard containing about twenty-five pieces for 5 or 10 seconds. The master could thereafter reconstruct the location of any piece, while the ordinary player could recall the location of only 5 or 6 pieces. Further work showed that the master gains his advantage in part by chunking the chessboard into several familiar small groups of pieces. Chunking is a great aid to memory (Chapter 7) because the master now has only five or six bits of information to remember, while the ordinary player has twenty-five. Later research showed that the chunks used by expert chess players grow larger with experience and that masters may retain about 50,000 chunks in long-term memory (Huffman et al., 2001). Research in other areas of expertise confirms the findings for chess (Masunaga & Horn, 2001).

Depth of Processing. Micheline Chi studied expertise in physicists, rather than chess players. In some studies, she gave novices and experts sets of problems to sort into categories. Novices categorized the problems on the basis of superficial characteristics, such as whether they involved wheels, pulleys, or inclined planes. Experts classified on the basic of the underlying principles of physics, such as gravity or inertial force. In other words, they used the *meaning* of each problem and hence were processing more deeply (Chi, Feltovich, & Glaser, 1981). Studies in such areas as physics, chemistry, orienteering, educational evaluation, and art have confirmed that expertise is characterized by greater depth of processing (Sanford, 2002; Eccles et al., 2002; Kozbelt, 2001; McCombes-Tolis, 2001; Engeman, 2000).

Getting Organized. You may have noticed that as you learn a new body of material better and better, it becomes easier to organize the information in meaningful ways. It is not surprising, then, that an additional cognitive advantage of experts over novices is organization. Experts in chess, physics, finance, and other areas that have been studied differ from novices in having much more organized bodies of knowledge (Chi, Glaser, & Farrm 1988). They use this organized information as a basis for planning. Unlike the novice, the expert does not immediately begin to solve a complex problem. Rather, she first examines the problem carefully, checks her ordered body of knowledge, then develops a plan—an organized series of steps—before pursuing the actual task. Studies of financial experts, for example, show that they will first carefully analyze a complex financial problem to determine its elements, then formulate a sequence of steps to be taken. Only when this plan is in place do the most effective experts even attempt to solve the problem (Kozbelt, 2001).

Experts also have other advantages over the ordinary person. The expert has a global view, seeing the entire problem—the forest—rather than the individual trees (Medin & Ross, 1992). She also relates the current problem to similar past problems much more easily (Crook, 2001) and discriminates among types of problems, categorizing each on the basis of possible solutions.

The Computer As Problem-Solver: Artificial Intelligence

Human beings are not the only ones who can engage in problem-solving activities. Computers can too, and they are not affected by such factors as functional fixedness and psychological set. Artificial Intelligence (AI) refers to the use of computer hardware and software to solve complex problems in much the same way as humans are thought to solve them.

There are three reasons for developing computer software that mimics human cognitive processes. First, psychologists and computer experts have long recognized that humans and computers are similar in certain important respects.

Both have "brains" that are made up of basic units _ neurons in humans and chips in computers. Both also solve problems systematically on the basis of a set of rules and procedures. Both have memories and move information in and out of these memories as they solve problems. And both accept information from the external environment as input, process it centrally, and produce output. Second, if we can develop computer models that simulate human cognition, we will clearly learn something about how humans solve problems. Finally, as we develop more and more sophisticated software, the programs become "experts" and may actually solve important problems or at least help human beings deal with problems that would otherwise be difficult or impossible to solve.

Workers in the field of artificial intelligence began the development of problem-solving computer programs by having humans solve problems while they talked out loud and explained how they were solving those problems (Johnson, 1993). Human problem-solving rules and approaches derived from these verbal explanations served as the basis for the set of instructions that comprises a computer program. The programs were then developed, tried out, and modified to make them more and more sophisticated problem-solvers, often capable of beating humans at their own game. Among the newest of these programs are those that employ computer-based neural networks to solve complex problems. Such software is designed to operate in the same way that actual neural networks are theorized to do (Hampson, 1994). Our 21 for this chapter discusses the fascinating application of AI to the development of expert systems.

Keys to Higher Mental Processes 2

Decision-Making and Reasoning

Thinking involves not only problem-solving, but also decision-making and reasoning. We will consider just what cognitive psychologists have learned about how we make decisions and how we go about the complex process of reasoning.

Decisions, Decisions!

Some cognitive psychologists have carefully studied the final phase of problem-solving, in which you must often decide among several feasible solutions. Which one should I marry? Should I be a psychologist or a physicist? Do I want the hamburger or the hot dog? Decision-making is the process of evaluating two or more alternatives and choosing one of them. It is the bottom line when solving problems. So how do we make decisions? Often poorly. For example, most policy makers in business, government, and education said in one study that their decisions are made quite subjectively, "by the seat of their pants" (Janis, 1986).

In making decisions, most people use a variety of strategies (Johnson, 1993), and some studies have focused on how these strategies are applied when the person is faced with uncertain or risky decisions (Shafir & Tversky, 1992; Zacks, Tversky, & Iyer, 2001). Perhaps many of those policy makers learned the hard way what cognitive psychologists have discovered through this research—that making decisions is a complex, difficult, and often flawed process. Factors that have been identified as often leading to difficult or simply incorrect decisions include inaccurate use of heuristics, inadequate framing of questions, aversion to loss, overconfidence, and biased probability estimates.

When Heuristics Fail. Heuristics are usually very helpful rules-of-thumb, adaptively increasing the efficiency of cognitive operations beyond what is typically possible with algorithmic approaches. However, heuristics are only general rules that do not validly apply to every instance of decision-making. Sometimes an otherwise useful heuristic can lead to a bad decision. Cognitive psychologists Amos Tversky and Daniel Kahneman (1974; Zacks & Tversky, 2001; Kahneman, Slovic, and Tversky, 1982) have identified three heuristics that can sometimes lead to incorrect conclusions or wrong decisions.

- *The Representativeness Heuristic.* We use this common heuristic to determine how probable something is based on the extent to which it matches a prototype. Have you ever been in a store and asked a well-dressed woman where the shoelaces are, only to find out that she doesn't work there? She fit your prototype of a store clerk, but she wasn't. Similarly, you are introduced to a man who is shy, wears glasses, speaks softly, and is tidy and small in stature. Is he more likely a farmer or a librarian? Tversky and Kahneman (1974) found that most subjects said librarian because the description matched that prototype. However, probability theory would say that because there are many times more farmers than librarians, it is much more likely that the man is a farmer. The representativeness heuristic, a form of bias, has led to an improbable conclusion.

- You must often make judgments of probability (Gavanski & Hui, 1992). In using the anchoring heuristic, you estimate the probability of an event by modifying an earlier estimate on the basis of current data. A smoker, for example, may believe that the probability of developing lung disease from smoking is only 5%. If she reads statistics suggesting that it is actually 50%, she may then decide that her own actual probability is 10%. She has adjusted it upward, but has not adopted the more factual statistic.

- *The Availability Heuristic.* Given the need to formulate a hypothesis or make a decision, we often use the first alternative that comes to mind, the one that is most readily *available*. For example, you must decide whether to fly or drive on an upcoming trip. Hearing about a plane crash in which 135 people died, you immediately decide that it would be safer to drive. Had the plane crash information not been immediately available, you might have remembered that it is statistically safer to fly. Counting on the availability heuristic, the life insurance salesperson may describe for you in gory detail cases of people in the prime of life who have died, leaving grieving families in penniless squalor. She then shows you the insurance policies and points out what a bargain they are. If your availability heuristic is operating, it may influence your decision to buy, even though the scenario described by the salesperson is a very rare one.

Further research confirms that these heuristics can lead to inaccurate decisions. However, it appears that they are much more likely to be used when the decisions to be made are relatively minor ones in which errors would not be very costly. When the stakes are high and accuracy is centrally important, people tend to use algorithmic or other systematic approaches (Chaiken, Liberman, & Eagly, 1989).

Not all cognitive psychologists entirely agree with Kahneman and Tversky. Gigerenzer, for example, argues that the three heuristics should not be thought of as producing errors or fallacies, but rather as perhaps simply biasing responses. Vranas (2000), however, questions Gigerenzer's analysis, suggesting that it is based on faulty assumptions.

Framing The Question. The slightly modified version of the old axiom that "If you don't ask the right question, you won't get the right answer" becomes important in decision-making. The framing heuristic (Tversky & Kahneman, 1991) refers to how you structure the questions and pose the issues involved in making a decision. Suppose you are the head of a government and must make a decision in the following situation:

> *Imagine that the U.S. is preparing for the outbreak of a dangerous disease, which is expected to kill 600 people. Two alternatives to combat the disease have been proposed. Assume that the exact scientific estimates of the consequences of the programs are as follows:*
>
> - If Program A is adopted, 200 people will be saved.
> - If Program B is adopted, there is a one-third probability that all 600 people will be saved and a two-thirds probability that no people will be saved.

Which alternative would you choose? Now consider this framing of the problem:

> - If Program C is adopted, 400 people will die.
> - If Program D is adopted, there is a one-third probability that nobody will die and a two-thirds probability that all 600 people will die.

When Kahneman and Tversky (1984, p. 343) asked participants to choose between Programs A and B, 72% chose Program A (a "certainty") over Program B (a "risk"). When choosing between Programs C and D, on the other hand, 78% of subjects selected Program D. Notice, however, that the probabilities in A and B are *exactly* the same as the probabilities in C and D. The difference lies only in the framing of the choices. The participants chose "certainty" when the framing referred to lives saved and the "risky" alternative when framing referred to lives lost. It turns out, in fact, that this appears to be a general principle: When seeking gains, people avoid risk; when seeking to avoid losses, people take risks.

Loss Aversion. People don't like to lose what they have. Seems logical, but did you know that aversion to loss is greater than pleasure from gain? Tversky and Kahneman (1991) call this phenomenon loss aversion. You will probably expend considerably greater effort to recover $50 that someone owes you than to win $50 in a contest. Similarly, you may well spend several hours trying to find a $10 bill you have misplaced, even if you could be working and earning $10 an hour during that time. Loss aversion often affects our judgments.

The phenomenon is magnified disproportionately when we perceive losses as large. If you have reason to believe it will cost $1000 to repair your car, you may expend considerable effort to avoid the loss. You make many phone calls, get several estimates, check with friends who might do the job for less, and buy repair books in hopes of doing it yourself. If the cost is likely to be $500, you may only confirm it with a second estimate, then have it done, expending far less than half the effort.

Overconfidence. Your friend is absolutely certain he'll do well on that next test in Introductory Psychology. The first one was a snap, and he understands the material with no problem. Result: He is overconfident, doesn't study much, and fails miserably. Your stockbroker tells you with great confidence that you should immediately sell your stock in IBM. Problem is that someone else's broker is telling him, with equal confidence, to buy IBM.

Our decisions are often plagued by *overconfidence.* In one study, students interviewed a person about his background, interests, aspirations, and the like, then predicted his answers to 20 questions. They were 75% confident in their predictions but only 63% correct (Dunning et al., 1990). In other research people were asked to estimate the answers to factual questions, such as the number of nuclear power plants in the world in 1980 (189) and indicate their confidence in their answers. They were wrong about one-third of the time, but were nevertheless 98% confident that they were right (Kahneman & Tversky, 1979). Finally, 98% of entering freshmen are virtually certain they will graduate in 4 years (Astin, 1991) (Figure 8-8). The truth is that nearly 50% will not graduate within 5 years!

Probability Biases. Another way to make incorrect decisions is to succumb to common biases about probabilities. One example is the gambler's fallacy. Over the past 3 years, you have bought a total of over 300 state lottery tickets and never won a nickel. You "obviously" should hit big any day. Right? Wrong! The gambler's fallacy is that random events are self-correcting. If you have flipped a coin 5 times and all 5 have been heads, it seems as though the next one just has to be a tail. However, each toss is independent, and the probability is always 50%.

A second probability bias is the common tendency to overestimate the likelihood of rare events and correspondingly underestimate frequent ones (Kahneman & Tversky, 1984). We tend to overestimate the low probability of an airline crash and underestimate the potential for a much more likely car crash. Another good example is the lottery. Knowing that the probability of winning is often 1 in 10,000,000, why does anyone ever buy a ticket? You guessed it, the overestimate bias. Interestingly, a good mood state enhances this positive bias; a bad mood enhances estimates of negative outcomes, such as a plane crash (Wright & Bower, 1992).

Human Reasoning

Problem-solving and decision-making both involve reasoning, a broader set of cognitive activities. Reasoning is the process by which we generate, examine, and evaluate information. It involves manipulating and transforming the information in order to arrive at conclusions and is often further defined as thinking that relates to a specific goal (Rips, 2001). It is the most complex of all cognitive abilities. We will consider the adaptive value of reasoning, the distinction between autistic and realistic reasoning, and the use of deductive and inductive logic.

The Evolution of Reasoning. Early humans were faced with increasingly complex environments fraught with both possibility and danger. Food was sometimes plentiful, sometimes scarce. Traveling repeatedly through dense underbrush was necessary but difficult. Living in the open was both uncomfortable and perilous. Large animals could be good sources of food but were often dangerous predators. These were among the many problems posed by ancient environments. Some could be partially solved by simple trial and error, but not easily and not well.

One answer to solving such problems and thereby increasing the probability of the survival and reproduction of the human species was reasoning (Suddendory & Whiten, 2001). A carefully reasoned consideration of the periodic food scarcity problem—gathering relevant information, generating and evaluating solutions—might lead to the establishment of methods for storing food in times of plenty. Reasoning about the difficulties of living in the open might lead to living in caves and closing the entrances with boulders at night or using available materials to construct primitive dwellings. From an evolutionary standpoint, it is likely that those early humans who used reasoning more effectively were more likely to survive and their genes more likely to be passed on to later generations. It now appears that these gradual genetic modifications may have led to the development of distinct systems for deductive and inductive reasoning in the right and left hemispheres, respectively, of the brain (Parsons & Osherson, 2001).

Reasoning more generally permits us to adapt to a complex physical and social environment that would otherwise threaten the survival of the species. In modern times, how do we deal with the high level of violence in society? How do we assure the safe use of nuclear power and genetic engineering? Although it does not always allow us to immediately reach the correct conclusions, reasoning helps us to resolve these and many other issues and thereby to survive as a species. We will examine the evolutionary basis for cognition more generally later in the chapter.

Types of Reasoning. There are two types of thinking upon which reasoning can be based: autistic thinking and realistic thinking. Autistic thinking is an unrealistic, illogical process based on fantasy and wish fulfillment. Daydreaming is a common type of autistic thinking. Realistic thinking is based on the realities of the external world and involves testing ideas against evidence available in the environment (Markman & Gentner, 2001).

When we engage in realistic thinking, we formulate rational arguments that involve premises and conclusions. The premises are logical antecedents [RTF bookmark start: }2[RTF bookmark end: }2that ideally lead to and justify the conclusion. Such reasoning can be deductive or inductive.

Deductive Reasoning: Thinking Logically. In deductive reasoning we use logical relationships to determine the validity or truth of our conclusions. We begin with relatively general propositions in order to reach more specific conclusions. The result is a syllogism made up of premises and the conclusion. For example:

Ripe bananas are yellow
This banana is yellow
Therefore, this banana is ripe.

Such logic prevents you from eating a banana that is not ripe and, of course, serves many other purposes in everyday life. It is important when the repairman uses deductive reasoning to diagnose the problem with your TV and when a scientist develops a new theory. Ongoing research may show us how to better teach high-level deductive logic (Pillow, 2002).

We do, however, have to be careful. If the premises are wrong, the conclusion will be wrong even though the structure of the syllogism is still logical (Johnson-Laird, 2001). Consider:

Ripe bananas are yellow
This is yellow
Therefore, this is a ripe banana.

Not quite! It could be a peach, a golden delicious apple, or even a yellow car.

Another logical error is to assume that syllogisms are symmetrical, meaning that valid reasoning in one direction permits valid reasoning in the other (Knauff et al., 2002). For example, it is correct to say that all pediatricians are physicians, but the reverse—all physicians are pediatricians—does not follow.

Inductive Reasoning: Estimating Probabilities. When we engage in inductive reasoning, we move from the specific to the general—just the opposite of deductive reasoning. We start with specific pieces of knowledge, then put these together in an effort to reach a more general conclusion. Anne Sullivan, for example, provided Helen Keller with repeated instances in which some object that Keller touched was associated with a word spelled into her hand. Keller used inductive logic to put these specifics together and arrive at a general principle. As another example, consider:

Ron drinks liquor every day
Ron has cirrhosis of the liver and brain damage
Therefore, Ron is an alcoholic.

You begin with specific information about Ron's drinking. Since cirrhosis and brain damage are frequently consequences of alcoholism, you then reach the more general conclusion that he is an alcoholic. Your conclusion has considerable inductive strength and may well be correct. However, notice that it basically depends on *probability theory* for its validity (Heit, 2000). You believe there is a high probability that someone with Ron's characteristics is alcoholic. In fact, of course, they *could* be independent of alcohol consumption in Ron's case.

A more serious case in which inductive reasoning can fail is prejudice. Company superiors might deny promotion to an employee in his mid-sixties because they assume someone that age can't do the job. Inductive reasoning has failed because many older people are just as capable as younger ones. Cardiac surgeon Michael DeBakey, for example, was 88 years old in 1996 when he played a major role in the decision to perform coronary bypass surgery on Russian Premier Boris Yeltsin. We have more to say about stereotyping and prejudice in Chapter 19, where we discuss how people form impressions of others. More generally, all inductive reasoning involves probabilities, not certainties; solid deductive reasoning, when the premises are correct, can result in certainties.

Using Logic. Science uses both deductive and inductive logic in an interactive way to formulate and revise theories. After observing that you can readily describe a picture you have seen only for a moment, for example, a theorist might infer or inductively reason that your brain dealt with the information too rapidly to be accounted for by serial processing. Aware that parallel processing is much faster than serial processing, he might then deductively reason that most information processing must be parallel. Experiments would then test this hypothesis, providing data that might lead inductively to the modification of the theory.

Keys to Higher Mental Processes 3

Language: Its Structure and Function

Most of us tend to take for granted our ability to communicate verbally with others. But have you ever stopped to think just how complex language is? The average college student has a vocabulary of some 200,000 words and produces numerous novel sentences every day. Where does this complex ability come from?

Language has been spoken for at least 1 and perhaps 3 million years and written for about 6000. Perhaps the earliest recorded study was conducted by an Egyptian king, Psammetichus, who wanted to resolve a longstanding controversy over which was the older race, the Egyptians or the Phrygians. The king ordered a shepherd to raise two infants from birth in an isolated cabin and never to speak in their presence. He reasoned that when the children started talking, whichever language they spoke would be the one of the "older" race. Legend has it that the shepherd was once absent from the cabin for longer than usual, and when he returned, both children came running toward him saying, "Becos, becos." Because "becos" is the Phrygian word for bread, the king concluded that the Phrygians were the older race. By modern standards this experiment would be unethical because the children may have been harmed by the isolation.

Fortunately, language studies have become a bit more sophisticated. The study of the psychological nature of language is called psycholinguistics, and most of the findings we will discuss are products of this field (Taylor & Taylor, 1990).

What is language? Language is a structured system of symbols that can be combined according to a set of guidelines to produce virtually infinite messages. George Miller (1981) suggests that language has three major properties:

structure, process, and use. In terms of *structure*, language consists of a series of word sequences. When you use word sequences to communicate, you are engaging in a *process* involving a set of skills that permit you to both use and understand the sequences. In terms of *use*, language is a set of social conventions that shape the word sequences you select and the skills you employ in using them.

Language has two other properties as well. First, it is semantic or meaningful. Each word has a specific meaning or set of meanings, and meaning is also conveyed through the patterns in which those words are used. Consider these two sentences: "People water plants"; "Plants water people." The sentences use exactly the same words, but the meaning is very different. Finally, it is generative, meaning that a limited number of words and syntactic rules can be used to generate a virtually infinite variety of novel communications. Although any given person calls on the same vocabulary over a period of time, he constructs and understands new sentences every day.

If someone wants to point out, for example, that a plant needs watering, she can convey this idea through a wide variety of sentences: "That plant needs to be watered"; "I must water the plant"; "The plant needs watering"; "That plant looks awfully dry"; "If I don't water that plant soon, it will probably die"; and so on. She has not previously memorized these sentences; rather, she has learned a vocabulary of words and the rules for putting those words together in a wide variety of ways. Another term for this ability to produce novel sentences is *productivity.* That memorization is not involved is pointed up dramatically by Postal's (1968) estimate that the English language contains 10 million different sentences of twenty words or less. Anyone attempting to memorize all these sentences would master only a small proportion in a lifetime.

Language and Thought

When we think, we often speak, and when we speak we are thinking. But what is the actual relationship between cognition and language? Are they one and the same thing? Do thoughts determine language? Or does language somehow structure thought?

John Watson (1913) hypothesized that language and thought are basically the same thing. That is, thinking is essentially covert speaking, and speaking is thinking aloud. We can dispose of Watson's hypothesis rather quickly, since evidence simply does not support it. Humans who cannot speak, like the young Helen Keller, are nevertheless quite capable of thought.

An alternative hypothesis was offered by Jean Piaget (see Chapter 10), who held that language is a reflection of thought processes. He suggested that linguistic development follows or accompanies the stages of cognitive development and that although language can facilitate cognition, it does not in any way *determine* thought processes. In short, thought determines language; language does not determine thought.

Benjamin Whorf (1956) adopted exactly the opposite point of view. He hypothesized linguistic determinism, which means that language determines thought, and linguistic relativism, meaning that speakers of different languages perceive and experience the environment differently. This latter idea is often called the Sapir-Whorf hypothesis because it was also championed by Edward Sapir (1949).

To support his ideas, Whorf marshalled evidence that cultures with different languages have different concepts and differing views of the world. He noted that English has only one term for "snow," whereas the Eskimo language has many, each one describing a particular type of snow. This causes speakers of the two languages to think about snow in different ways. Similarly, the Hanunoo of the Philippines recognize some 92 different kinds of rice, and Arabic speakers have about 6000 terms to describe camels. To Whorf, these differences in language mean differences in thought processes.

In a well-designed, direct test of the Sapir-Whorf hypothesis, Eleanor Rosch (1973) studied the Dani people of New Guinea, whose language, as Whorf had earlier pointed out, contains only two words for color (light and dark). Since earlier research had shown that English speakers, whose language has 11 basic color names, learn nonsense names for these eleven more easily than for nonbasic colors, she presented the same task to the Dani. She found that they also learned the nonsense names for the eleven basic colors quite easily, a finding that clearly does not support linguistic relativism.

Critics of the Sapir-Whorf hypothesis cite Rosch's study and others to point up some apparent weaknesses in the theory. In particular, the lack of a special term does not seem to make it impossible for speakers of a given language to think about a more differentiated concept. English-speaking skiers, for example, certainly differentiate among various types of snow. Moreover, Laura Martin (1986) and other experts on Eskimo language point out that it does not actually have a very large number of terms for snow. In addition, it is not that difficult to create new terminology whenever it is needed. The advent of the automobile, for example, brought to the English language a variety of terms to distinguish among types of cars (sedan, coupe, turbo, and so on). Similarly, we have added such terms as rocket, missile, and laser to describe technological innovations that came into being long after the English language was developed.

Despite these criticisms, the Whorf hypothesis was revived and quite intensively discussed again (Imai, 2000). Alfred Bloom (1981) has shown Chinese speakers have much more difficulty than English speakers in understanding counterfactual reasoning—reasoning that starts with a statement known to be false. "If John had gone to college, he would have a better job" is a counterfactual statement because John did not go to college. Chinese speakers do not readily grasp such reasoning because their language has no straightforward way to produce counterfactual statements. They are much more likely to make and understand factual statements: "John didn't go to college, and therefore he doesn't have a good job." Bloom's studies support the linguistic relativism hypothesis by demonstrating that a characteristic of the Chinese language affects how speakers of that language think. We must be cautious, however, because his research is correlational and hence cannot directly demonstrate a causal relationship. It is possible that the differences in understanding counterfactual arguments reflect differences between cultures, not just between languages.

Additional supportive research has shown that it is easier to think certain thoughts in one language than in another (Johansen-Berg, 2001). In fact, the work of Curt Hoffman and his colleagues (1986) shows that a bilingual speaker thinks differently in the two languages. It appears that each language evokes a different set of concepts, which then influence the bilingual's thought patterns, depending on which language she is currently reading or speaking. Does this mean that her thoughts and perceptions are likely to be confused? The Critical Thinker box asks you to focus on this controversial issue.

Cognitive skill acquisition and social perception are also affected by language background. Language differences may at least partially explain, for example, why Asian children surpass Americans on tests of mathematical ability (see Chapter 9). As Irene Miura points out, Asian cultures typically use a base-10 number system, and their languages reflect that system. Thus, the number 15 is "ten-five" and the number 25 is "two tens-five." These linguistic labels may produce more effective mathematical learning in Asian children (Miura & Okamoto, 1989).

Gleitman and others have recently suggested an interesting extension of the Sapir-Whorf concept to the area of spatial reasoning (Li & Gleitman, 2002). They point to a series of studies showing that spatial terminology and reasoning are affected by the language culture. English speakers, for example, typically refer to nearby directions from the perspective of the viewer ("to the right"), whereas some other language cultures usually refer to spatial coordinates (e.g., "to the south"). These differences in preferred spatial systems may, in turn, reflect the nature of the landscape or availability of landmarks in a given culture.

Social perception is similarly influenced by linguistic processing. In fact, it can often lead to bias, as we discuss in Horizon 3.

The Structure of Language

The 4000 or so human languages have been grouped by linguists into about 50 language families (Nadasdy, 1993). Even across the different family categories, the languages all share the characteristic of having a basic structure involving a set of sounds, rules for combining those sounds, and meanings. They also share some common characteristics that may have to do with the perception of language (Hura et al., 1992). We will examine the basic components of language, how those components are put together, and the ways in which these linguistic elements convey meaning.

Basic Components. The three basic components of language are phonemes (sounds), morphemes (meanings), and lexemes (words) (Table 8-4). A phoneme is a distinctive speech sound. For example, the letter *h* in *hat, head,* and *hold* produces the same initial vowel sound and is thus a phoneme that we label with the symbol *h*. The English language has about forty phonemes representing thirteen vowel sounds, twenty-five consonant sounds, and the additional sounds of *sh* and *th*. The number of phonemes varies from as few as twelve to as many as eight-five across the world's languages (Miller, 1994). We can speak and understand about 16-20 phonemes per second in normal conversation.

The combining of phonemes in a language is governed by certain phonological rules. These rules tell us which phonemes can be combined and which cannot. If you decided to coin a new word in English, you would probably not come up with "gpers" because English words never begin with *gp*. Considerable recent work has demonstrated that phonological awareness—knowledge of the key sounds of one's language—is important in learning to read (Lundberg, 2002).

Several phonemes, combined in certain sequences, make up morphemes, the smallest linguistic units that actually carry meaning. Some morphemes are words: *door, light, make*. Others are prefixes such as *pre-*, or suffixes, such as ing. There are an estimated 100,000 morphemes in English, of which the average speaker knows about half. Morphology, the study of how phonemes are combined to produce morphemes, has shown that each language has definite rules governing the formation of morphemes (Boudelaa & Marslen-Wilson, 2001). English, for example, has no morphemes that begin with more than three consonant sounds. A morpheme may begin with *thr*, as in *throw*, but not with *thrk*. More generally, a given morpheme is appropriately used in certain positions within English words, and the words would not look right to an intelligent English speaker if the phonemes were arranged differently. Since morphemes are more complex than phonemes and put more demands on memory, it is not surprising that children master phonemes at an earlier age than they do morphemes (Roelofs & Baayen, 2002).

The third structural component is the lexeme, or word. There is obviously an overlap between morphemes and lexemes. *Dream*, for example, is both. However, words such as *dreamed* and *dreaming* consist of more than one morpheme. All the words that make up a given language are collectively termed the lexicon for that language. Some indication of the lexicon of the English language is the fact that *Webster's Third New International Dictionary* contains over 450,000 entries. An intelligent English speaker may well have a vocabulary of 100,000 to 300,000 words and can speak and understand at the rate of 250 words per minute (Carroll, 1968).

Getting Organized: Syntax. The organization of language does not stop at the level of individual words. Rather, we group words together in systematic ways. Syntax is the set of rules that govern the arrangement of words into phrases and sentences. It appears to be processed in a separate neural system from that which deals with morphemes and lexemes (Frazier et al., 1993). In the sentences "The girl petted the cat" and "The boy held a candle," the syntax is correct and the meaning is clear. The sentence "The rock helped the door" is nonsense, but its syntax is basically the same as that of the two "normal" sentences. So it would be easier to remember than "Door the helped rock the," which is syntactically incorrect.

Clearly, syntax influences our ability to understand the meaning of a spoken or written sentence. The sequence "boy candle the a held" has all the words we know can be used to form a meaningful sentence. However, the meaning of these scrambled words is not as immediately obvious as their meaning when placed in correct syntactical order. In fact, the syntactic context can even make a difference in whether words are correctly recognized (Hahne et al., 2002). In one study, researchers presented participants with twenty syntactically related pairs of words (such as *we-paid*) and twenty unrelated pairs (such as *it-planet*). The words were presented so rapidly that the subjects could barely perceive them, and for each pair the participant had to decide whether a word or nonword was being displayed. It was found that words in syntactically correct pairs were recognized more quickly than words in unrelated pairs (Goodman, McCalland, and Gibbs, 1981). Thus, the context in which a given word was presented affected its recognition. More generally, when you have a thought that you would like to encode into language, you must access words from your lexicon and arrange them according to the rules of syntax (Gordon & Dell, 2002).

Semantics: Noam Chomsky

Every child probably has a moment of tremendous insight very much like that of Helen Keller. It is the moment at which he first realizes that words have meaning. Semantics is the study of the meaning of language and particularly of its individual words and the relationships among them. Even if the child had an excellent knowledge of the structure of language, it would do her little good if she did not know the meanings of the words she heard and used. Through semantics, we learn how the child acquires these meanings, how they relate to the formation of meaningful thoughts, and how those thoughts are put into words that convey the intended ideas (Kraut et al., 2002).

Language is essentially an organized hierarchy of component structures beginning with bits of sound at the bottom and ending with complete thoughts at the top. Most of the work of psycholinguists has concentrated on the upper levels of this hierarchy—phrases and sentences—and hence has focused on syntax. Linguist Noam Chomsky (1957) formulated the theoretical basis for most of the work being done on the structure of phrases and sentences and the relationship of this structure to meaning.

Transformational Grammar. Chomsky theorized that there are two levels of structure in language: surface structure and deep structure. The surface structure of a sentence is the relatively obvious and superficial form that the sentence takes. For example, the sentence "The boy held a candle" consists of a noun phrase ("The boy") and a verb phrase ("held a candle"). The deep structure of a sentence is essentially its meaning. Thus, the sentence "A candle was held by the boy" would have the same deep structure as "The boy held a candle," even though their surface structure is different.

According to Chomsky, surface structure is derived from deep structure by rules referred to as transformations. If we know the deep structure and the appropriate transformation rule, we can readily derive the surface structure of a sentence. For instance, the transformational rule governing the production of questions allows us to construct the sentence "Is the boy holding a candle?" and the rule governing the formation of negatives allows us to formulate "The boy is not holding a candle." Because of Chomsky's emphasis on transformational rules, his theory is called transformational grammar (Figure 8-9).

Deep structure is more important in determining the listener's understanding of a sentence than is surface structure. In one study participants listened to stories, then indicated whether isolated sentences presented to them had been in the story (Sachs, 1967). Consider the following three sentences:

1. He struck John on the shoulder.
2. John struck him on the shoulder.
3. John was struck on the shoulder by him.

Assume that sentence 1 was in the original story but the other two were not. Given these three choices, subjects were generally quite sure that they had never heard sentence 2, but they often chose sentence 3 as one they *had* heard. Notice the difference. Sentence 2 has the same surface structure as the original sentence, while sentence 3 has a different surface structure but the same deep structure, or meaning, as the first sentence. As this study illustrates, people tend to remember the meaning of a sentence rather than its surface structure.

Even when the same statement has two possible meanings or deep structures, most people will tend to interpret it correctly, as a function of the context in which the sentence is presented (Danks and Glucksberg, 1980). The sentence "Can you pass the salt?" may be a question about your physical ability to pass the salt or a request to hand over the salt. When such a sentence is presented in isolation, participants take somewhat longer to process it than they do to process a sentence with an unambiguous meaning. But if the sentence appears in the context of an appropriate story, it is interpreted without delay (Gibbs, 1979). Thus, when a sentence has more than one possible deep structure, context determines interpretation.

Government and Binding Theory. Transformational grammar theory can be a bit cumbersome because it specifies a number of different rules, some for transforming a sentence to a question, others for negatives, and so on. The applicable rule depends on both the type of sentence you start with and the type you would like to end up with. In an effort to simplify these syntactic rules, Chomsky (1981) modified his theory substantially . In the new approach, called government and binding theory, he has shifted much of syntactic structure to individual lexical items, such as lexemes and morphemes. An example is provided by verbs, which form a class of items in the lexicon. Government and binding theory assumes that each individual verb contains information as to whether it requires a direct or indirect object. The verb "take" requires a direct object: "He takes the apple." However, the verb "dream" does not require a direct object: "She dreams every night." This observation eliminates the need for special syntactical rules determining the relationship of verbs and objects and thereby simplifies the transformational grammar. In fact, Chomsky's new theory hypothesizes only one transformation, called "transformation X," an abstract reference to the concept of a generalized transformation.

Chomsky has long been the leading psycholinguistic theorist, and his government and binding approach remains the guiding theoretical light in that field, generating many studies (Bolta, 1990). Most have supported the theory (McElree & Bever, 1989; Droste, 1992), though some point to problems that may require revision (Kim, 1989; Hacker, 1990). In fact, some investigators have already begun to offer modifications and extensions (Vigliocco & Hartsuiker, 2002; Hornstein, 1991), and the theory continues to evolve.

Language Acquisition

You're in a delivery room and have just observed the birth of a baby. The obstetrician addresses the infant: "Well, how are you feeling? Any pain or discomfort? The baby replies: "No, I'm fine, but these lights are awfully bright, and I wish you wouldn't shout when you talk to me."

Convenient though it would be, we all know that newborns can't talk. However, language development beyond the delivery room is actually quite rapid. Let's take a look at how we move from the cooing of infancy to the articulate speech patterns of adulthood. We will also consider the major theories of language acquisition. They address the important question of the extent to which language ability is inborn and the extent to which it is a product of learning.

The Sequence of Language Development. Neonates may not speak in coherent sentences, but they do begin to make sounds within moments after they are born. The initial crying is supplemented, at the age of one or two months, by cooing and, at about six to eight months, by babbling (Batchelder, 2002). Early babbling consists primarily of vowel sounds, with consonants being added somewhat later. Many linguists believe that babbling is cross-culturally universal and that the language environment of a given culture causes some sounds to drop out and others to be retained. The babbling gradually becomes more systematic, and the child begins to engage in lalling—deliberately repeating the same sounds, as in "mamamamama." This repertoire of vocalizations progresses to the point where the child can contribute actively to cooperative interaction with her mother before the end of the first year (Papaeliou et al., 2002). At about age one, children begin to utter meaningful single words, called holophrases. Although the vocabulary is small to begin with, each word in it has a number of meanings (Jusczyk, 2002). "Go" may mean "I want to go," "Are you going?" "Go away," or "Do we have to go?" Some words take on quite broad meanings. Thus, "cookie" may mean "I am hungry," rather than simply "I would like a cookie."

At around age two, the child begins to use two-word phrases. She then progresses quite rapidly to the point where she knows many individual words and many two-word combinations, shortly thereafter graduating to the use of multiword sentences. "Ball" becomes "My ball" and later "That's my ball." Two-word speech has often been described as telegraphic, since it expresses a potentially complicated idea in a few words. It is actually a highly efficient form of speech. When Bobby says "My ball!" the listener quickly gets the message: "That's my ball and you can't have it." Of course, some chidren develop language competence relatively late. Recent evidence suggests this late acquisition may be a result of several factors. First, the mothers of late developers do not respond to or reinforce speech adequately (Girolametto et al., 2002). Second, the child's diet may be deficient; children whose diet is low in protein, cholesterol, and polyunsaturated fats at early ages develop language late (Rask-Nissila et al. 2002). And, finally, being raised in poverty impairs the achievement of language competence (Lock et al., 2002). These are important findings because late talkers perform relatively poorly on most language measures until at least age 9 (Rescorla, 2002).

The most significant linguistic development involved in the use of two-word expressions is the acquisition of the rules of syntax (Braine, 1992; Gerhen et al., 1994). Almost invariably, the child places words in the correct order. If she wants her father to drive the car, she will say "Daddy drive" or "Drive car," but not "Drive Daddy" or "Car drive." More generally, the child achieves at least a rudimentary understanding of the variety of syntactic rules, such as possession ("my ball") and attribution ("big ball"). With further development, he begins to acquire more complex aspects of syntax, including plurals, more advanced possessives, and past tense. By age three or so, he is using auxiliary words ("I am helping") and can ask simple yes-no questions ("Can I help?"). As he approaches age 4, the child becomes quite expert in transformational grammar, forming and transforming increasingly complex sentences. Chomsky would be proud!

A final and fortunately temporary development between the ages of 3 and 4 involves the use of overregularization, in which the child over-applies the syntactic rules. She may now use the past-tense rule indiscriminately, attaching the *ed* ending to all verbs and making such errors as "goed" and "breaked." Neural network theory has an explanation for this phenomenon, as we will see a bit later when we take up theories of language acquisition.

The child's increasing ability to apply rules correctly and formulate more and more complex sentences is, of course, accompanied by a developing vocabulary. Typically, his vocabulary increases rapidly from a few words at age one to over 2500 words at age 6 and, by age 18 or so, about 200,000 words in college students (Lenneberg, 1969; Moskowitz, 1978) (Figure 8-10). Thereafter, he progresses gradually toward the 200,000 word vocabulary that *you* possess.

An interesting question raised in recent research is whether children can later verbalize events that occurred before their vocabularies included terms needed to describe the early event. For example, a child falls down and breaks his arm at age one, when his vocabulary is very small and may not include such words as "break," "pain," and "bone." When he knows these words at, say, age 3 or 4, can he then verbalize the events involved in the broken arm? The answer so far is "no." He will never be able to verbally describe the event, except insofar as parents or others describe it to him at later ages. This phenomenon is called *childhood amnesia* and is apparently based, at least in large part, on the lack of vocabulary terms needed to verbally encode experience (Simcock & Hayne, 2002).

Theories of Language Development

We now know the sequence of events involved in language development, but how and why do we acquire linguistic ability? There are two basic approaches to explaining how humans acquire language. The *environmental* approach suggests that language is entirely or largely learned from parents and others, while the *biological* approach emphasizes the role of genetic factors (de Geus et al., 2001). *Interactionist* theories combine the two perspectives to provide a third.

Environmental theories. There are two principal environmental approaches to language learning: reinforcement theory and social learning theory. Reinforcement theory hypothesizes that language is acquired through conditioning processes based on reinforcement (Skinner, 1957; Staats and Staats, 1963). All the elements of Skinner's operant approach—acquisition, extinction, shaping, punishment, discrimination, and generalization—apply as much to the development of language by the child as they do to the development of key peck responses in the pigeon (see Chapter 6). When the child utters the first sound that approximates a word, the parents reinforce this verbalization with smiles, hugs, and other rewards. Further word-like verbalizations are similarly reinforced. As the infant develops, specific words become attached to specific rewards. If the child says "milk," his parents may reward this utterance with the desired food. As the child grows older, he is reinforced for using more and more complex speech patterns and thus learns to use language entirely through reinforcement processes.

An alternative approach, social learning theory, suggests that children acquire language primarily by observing and imitating the verbalizations of adults. The child hears her mother say "It's time for bed" and may echo "time for bed." After repeating this phrase over and over again, she learns it. Other verbalizations are acquired in the same way. Consistent with Bandura's (1965, 1992) more general observational learning approach (Chapter 6), this theory of language acquisition hypothesizes that reinforcement is not required for learning to take place. Research has shown that children do imitate adults, sometimes for the specific purpose of communicating important information (Snow, 1983). However, imitation may play a relatively minor role in language acquisition, since only about 20% of children studied imitate as much as 30-40% of what their parents say; the remainder imitate less than 10% (Snow, 1981).

Both approaches are subject to criticism. For one thing, older children and adults are capable of generating a virtually infinite variety of sentences that are grammatically correct and accurately convey meaning to others. How can this multitude of sentences have been learned through reinforcement or observation? Other problems with learning theory revolve around the role of the parent in teaching language. Considerable research suggests that children do not frequently imitate the language of adults, at least not at early ages. A three-year-old is not likely to have heard an adult say "I breaked it" or "All gone Daddy."

A related problem is that parents do not attend regularly to the grammatical structure of their children's sentences (Slobin, 1975; Gleason & Ratner, 1993). And most parents will not routinely correct a child for saying "I breaked it." Instead, they may openly reward such incorrect usage simply out of a desire to reinforce the continued development of meaningful speech. Another problem with the parental role is that parents vary considerably in their patterns of applying reinforcement, which should lead to considerable variability in language development. Yet children actually show little variation in patterns of language acquisition (Brown and Hernstein, 1975; Gleason & Ratner, 1993).

Although learning theories do not appear to provide an adequate theoretical basis for the development of language, this should not be taken to mean that the environment plays no role (Palmer & Donahoe, 1992). The language that parents use in addressing children (called "motherese" or "infant directed speech") can enhance or hinder language development (Hampson & Nelson, 1993). The child's vocabulary of auxiliary verbs, for example, grows faster when the care giver tends to ask yes-no questions than when she tends to make imperative statements, probably because the child must generate internal phrases in order to formulate answers to the questions (Newport, Gleitman, and Gleitman, 1977). On the other hand, use of complex sentences does not seem to be influenced by the nature or quality of motherese. At a more general level, studies suggest that *simpler* care giver speech leads to more rapid language development (Furrow et al., 1979).

Biological theories. An alternative to learning theory, advocated primarily by Eric Lenneberg (1967) and Noam Chomsky (1968), is that language acquisition is based primarily on innate biological factors. They basically see language as an evolutionary adaptation to the environment that humans inhabit, where survival is enhanced by linguistic capability (Nowak et al., 2002). The early phases of this neural evolution have been found in great apes, suggesting that they originated at least 5 million years ago, though they are fully developed only in humans (Cantalupo & Hopkins, 2001). Some have gone so far as to argue that the unique language capability of humans may be responsible for the high intelligence of the human species (Macphail & Bolhuis, 2001). In essence, the evolutionary theory suggests that children are born with a predisposition to learn language.

Called *nativism*, Chomsky's biological approach suggests that humans have a built-in language acquisition device (LAD)—an inborn mechanism that encourages and facilitates language learning. It is assumed to consist of some set of neural structures and processes that are maximally ready to acquire language.

The three principal arguments favoring this theory are that language is species uniform, that it is species specific, and that it involves critical developmental periods.

- Species Uniformity. According to biological theory, the capacity for language is species uniform, meaning that it is present in all normal human beings. This point certainly has some validity, since no group of humans ever discovered has been without language. In addition, the pattern of early language acquisition is similar in children throughout the world, even in different cultures with different languages (Williamson, 1979).

  In all cultures studied, children move from learning single words to 2-word phrases to increasingly complex sentences. In fact, even when no language users are present, children appear to go through a normal process of language acquisition. Speaking parents of deaf children, for example, sometimes choose not to have their children immediately learn sign language. Evidence shows that under these circumstances the child develops his own sign language, called home sign, moving gradually from one sign to two-link signs and then to more complex sign language sentences. Moreover, this individually developed sign language has a structure similar to normal language, including morphemes and syntax (Feldman, Goldin-Meadow, and Gleitman, 1978). Arguing further for species uniformity, Chomsky (1965) points out that all languages have similar components, such as nouns and verbs, and that each has an identifiable transformational grammar.

- Species Specificity. Biological theory also suggests that language is species specific, meaning that only human beings have the capacity for spoken language. Many animal species can communicate in one degree or another, indicating the location of food or the presence of danger, and some can even identify themselves individually to other members of the species. However, not even primates have a complex language system that allows for the construction of novel sentences to express new ideas. In fact, those apes that have been taught to use language to communicate have been taught forms of *human* language.

- Critical Periods. Further supporting the biological nature of language is the observation of critical or sensitive periods for language development. A critical period is a limited span of time early in life during which language acquisition is possible or optimal (Weber-Fox & Neville, 2001). Lenneberg (1967) points to the phenomenon of accent in a second language as an example of critical periods. If a second language is taught to a young child, she will speak it without an accent, but if the language is acquired after the age of approximately 13, it will almost invariably be spoken with an accent. More generally, Lenneberg hypothesizes that the ability to acquire language decreases sharply with the onset of puberty.

More recent studies point instead to a gradual decrease in language acquisition capacity that begins before puberty and continues its downward course into adulthood (Mayberry et al., 2002). Older adults certainly can learn new languages, but not as easily as children. The Probe describes some fascinating case studies of attempted language acquisition in "wild" children raised with no human contact.

Interactionist Theories. Both learning and biological explanations have been criticized for not providing a full understanding of language acquisition. One major result has been the development of *interactionist* perspectives, which adopt the view that both learning and biology have important roles to play. There are two basic interactional approaches. The *cultural-context* or social communication perspective of Jerome Bruner (1983) and his colleagues hypothesizes that the social environment is structured to incorporate the child into an ongoing language-using group. This typically means that the parents, as agents of the culture, speak slowly to the child, using simple vocabulary and careful enunciation, in order to intentionally promote language development. Bruner refers to this linguistic cultural climate as a *language acquisition support system* (LASS), the environmental counterpart to Chomsky's LAD. Language acquisition results from the interaction of the LAD and the LASS.

The second interactionist approach is the *cognitive* theory of Jean Piaget (Chapter 10) and others. Piaget hypothesized that cognitive development is a lengthy process that takes place in a series of stages over the course of childhood. It begins at birth, when the child has no cognitive skills, and enters its final stage at about age twelve, when she begins to use more abstract concepts and to formulate and test hypotheses about the world. Cogntive theorists believe that language acquisition is simply one part of this overall cogntive developmental sequence, which depends on both biological maturation and environmental experience.

What can we conclude about the roles of learning and biology? Since Chinese children do not "automatically" acquire the ability to speak Swahili and German children are not found jabbering in Japanese, it seems clear that learning is involved in language acquisition. However, it appears that adaptive, inborn, biological mechanisms provide the all-important basis for language. Since most current evidence points to the involvement of both nature and nurture, the interactionist theories may provide the best understanding of language acquisition. However, considerably more research is needed to determine the exact nature of both biological and environmental components and just how they interact (Ratner & Gleason, 1993).

Talking to the Animals: Was Dr. Doolittle Right?

Perhaps as a child you read some of Lofting's famous stories of Dr. Doolittle, who was able to communicate fluently with a variety of animals. If we could "talk to the animals," we could gain much valuable information not only about life as a dolphin or an ape, but also about the acquisition and use of language. Primates have long been studied because they are so similar to humans in many ways and can therefore tell us much that is relevant to human behavior. The Yerkes Regional Primate Center in Atlanta, for example, houses over 3000 monkeys, apes, and other primates. It spreads over a 117-acre area, has a staff of more than 140 people, and even breeds its own primates, with over 500 born each year (Skolnick, 1994). At centers like Yerkes across the country, there have been at least 20 language-acquisition experiments in progress simultaneously at times. The basic questions underlying these studies are simple: Can animals acquire language skills? And how similar are language and underlying thought processes in animals to those in humans?

Language Acquisition and Use. The first published attempt to teach language to an ape involved a chimpanzee named Gua, who was raised in a home for nine months (Kellogg and Kellogg, 1933). Gua learned to understand about 70 words, but never spoke. Another couple were able to teach a chimp named Viki to speak four words: *mama, papa, cup,* and *up* (Hayes and Hayes, 1951). It became clear from these experiments, however, that chimps are not physically equipped to use spoken language, and subsequent attempts focused on American Sign Language (ASL).

The best known attempt to teach sign language to an ape was the effort of Allen and Beatrice Gardner (1969). They raised a chimp named Washoe in their home for several years, and she has since been studied at the Institute of Primate Studies in Norman, Oklahoma and a chimp colony at Ellensberg, Washington.

During her first seven months of training, Washoe learned four signs that she was able to use quite reliably: "sweet," "more," "up," and "come-gimme." By the age of twelve, Washoe could use more than 180 signs and understood several hundred more (Fouts, 1977). Although this vocabulary is impressive for a chimp, it does not compare with that of an average four-year-old child, who has a vocabulary of some 3,000 words.

Other chimps at the Institute of Primate Studies have also been taught to use sign language. Lucy, at age seven, had a vocabulary of some 75 signs and used them to communicate quite effectively with humans. Some of the chimps in the colony acquired certain signs from Washoe, who remained the most language-sophisticated chimp in the group, and the chimps communicated with each other using sign language (Gardner et al., 1992).

In another laboratory, David Premack (1970; Premack & Premack, 1994) taught a chimp named Sarah to communicate by using plastic chips that varied in color, shape, and texture. She learned to construct sentences by placing these chips on a magnetized board. Her "chip vocabulary" consisted of about 120 words. Another chimp, Lana, housed at the Yerkes Primate Research Center in Georgia, communicated by typing out her requests on a computer keyboard; she learned at least 74 word symbols and was taught to use grammatical sentences (Rumbaugh, Gill, and von Glaserfeld, 1973). Koko, a gorilla housed at Stanford University, us[RTF bookmark start: }1[RTF bookmark end: }1ed over 400 signs and was reported to converse quite effectively with humans (Patterson, 1977).

Primates are not the only animals given language training. The other notable species has been dolphins, who appear to be more intelligent than most other animals. Louis Herman and his colleagues have carried out a series of studies dealing with dolphin language and intelligence (Herman et al., 1993; Herman & Forestell, 1985; Herman et al., 1990). They find that dolphins can learn languages consisting of sounds or visual images and use the language to communicate in meaningful ways. They can indicate when objects are missing from their tank and comprehend sentences. However, far less work has been done on dolphins than on primates, so many of the answers regarding dolphin language learning and usage are not yet in.

The Creative Urge. True language usage should involve creativity. It clearly does in humans, but what about primates? There is some observational evidence that they do occasionally use language creatively (Dore and Dumas, 1987). Washoe, for example, once had a fight with a Rhesus monkey and afterward signed "dirty monkey." She had previously used the sign "dirty" only to refer to soiled clothing and the like, suggesting a creative and appropriate use of the term for a different purpose. Having never learned a separate sign for watermelon, Lucy tried it and then signed "candy drink" or "drink fruit." She also ate a radish one day, quickly spat it out, and signed "Cry, hurt, food." A chimp named Moja once drew a picture of a bird, then signed "bird" to name her artistic creation. And Koko, an ape, signed "I hate" for a mask, "white tiger" for zebra, and "finger bracelet" for ring.

How Good Is The Evidence? Despite such observations, a number of psychologists have questioned the conclusion that apes actually use language in a human-like fashion (Sidenberg and Petitto, 1979); Sebeck and Uniker, 1980). One critic, Herbert Terrace (1979), was originally a firm believer. He spent four years teaching sign language to a male chimp with the tongue-in-cheek name Nim Chimpsky. Virtually convinced that Nim was "sounding" more and more like a child, combining words into meaningful sentences, Terrace conducted a more formal analysis of his data and found out otherwise. Unlike children, whose sentences rapidly increase in length, complexity, and syntactic accuracy, Nim produced primarily simple sentences that often had notably poor syntax. In addition, his grasp of syntax did not improve much over time, and he often merely imitated what his teacher had just said. In short, he did not acquire language in the way a child does.

Terrace and others point out that much of the primate language research has employed questionable research methods. For one thing, investigators tend to rely on anecdotes. When Washoe signed "water bird" for duck, was this a valid indication of actual language use or was it a random occurrence of signing behavior? If Washoe also sometimes signed "water banana" or "cookie bird," it would considerably weaken the argument that she was using "water bird" in a meaningful way. A second problem is that language-trained apes may produce many essentially uninterpretable sign language strings, which researchers tend to ignore. Might the "meaningful" strings be random occurrences embedded among inappropriate strings? Furthermore, researchers have often freely interpreted the signing of their subjects. In many cases, the experimenter's interpretation has been based more on the context than what the ape has actually signed. Washoe's once signed "open lollipop please" with no lollipop in sight, and her signing was therefore interpreted to mean simply "open."

Finally, some have questioned whether apes actually learn words in the human sense at all. It may be that their use of signs is just an operantly acquired response. The animal is shown a banana, makes the banana sign, and is rewarded. Even pigeons are capable of learning to "name" objects through such conditioning techniques (Hernstein, Loveland,and Cable, 1977), and no one argues that *pigeons* can talk!

There is, however, some evidence for the meaningful use of language by primates (Patterson, Patterson, & Brentari, 1987; Bernstein, 1987). Sue Savage-Rumbaugh and her colleagues at the Yerkes Center at Emory University have worked with a rare species called the pygmy chimpanzee (Savage-Rumbaugh, McDonald, Sevcik, Hopkins, & Rubert, 1986; Nelson, 1987). These more intelligent chimps are reported to show more convincing language capability than the common chimps used in most other studies.

Savage-Rumbaugh notes that even when common chimps know a symbol that they can use to request an object, they ordinarily cannot name the object when it is shown to them. Washoe, for example, can use the sign for banana to request the fruit but if shown a banana cannot name it. A normal child acquires this labelling capacity without difficulty. The more intelligent pygmy chimpanzees acquire the ability to label objects without special training (Savage-Rumbaugh, 1990). In addition, they learn signs for specific objects much more readily than do common chimpanzees.

A further observation is that pygmy chimps appear to be capable of acquiring language socially. That is, they can acquire symbols by simply observing other chimps or humans associating those symbols with particular objects, whereas common chimps have much more difficulty with this task. And, finally, pygmy chimps at the Yerkes Laboratory quite unexpectedly showed an ability to understand a substantial number of spoken English words even when they were not directly taught the meanings of these words. They actually learned the word meanings from hearing humans around them engaging in normal conversation, something that has never been demonstrated in common chimps. So do pygmy chimps use language symbolically? Savage-Rumbaugh and her colleagues believe they do, but others disagree (Seidenbaugh & Petitto, 1987).

It is probably reasonable to conclude that apes have some capacity for learning language but that their ability to use language in abstract ways has not yet been clearly demonstrated. The work with pygmy chimpanzees may constitute something of an exception, and studies may eventually confirm that in this species we have evidence for more human-like linguistic capabilities. However, to date, a reasonable interpretation may be that the rote, rather than creative, nature of chimp language may represent a logical step in the overall evolutionary process that culminates in creative human language (Fouts & Waters, 2001).

Keys to Higher Mental Processes 4

The Evolution and Neurophysiology of Cognition and Language

As you might imagine, the neural basis of human thought and language is exceedingly complex. We will begin with a consideration of how cognitive and linguistic processes and their underlying mechanisms may have evolved. Then we will turn to what is known about the neurophysiology of cognition from electroencephalographic studies of normal people and from studies of the effects of brain damage on cognitive processes. Finally, we will look at how the brain deals with language.

Cognition and Language Evolve

We have observed that human beings are unique in their ability to formulate highly complex thoughts and to use spoken and written language creatively. Such abilities imply the presence of certain kinds of underlying neural mechanisms, and a central question for cognitive psychology is what those mechanisms are and how they developed.

One answer comes from an increasing number of theorists who suggest that cognitive science can best cast its theories of mind in the context of a broader theory of evolution (Cosmides & Tooby, 1994; Knight, 1994). As Leda Cosmides and John Tooby (1994) put it: "Cognitive psychology is the study of the design of minds that were produced by the evolutionary process" (p. 47). That process is one of designing mechanisms to solve specific problems faced by our ancient ancestors, thereby promoting the survival of the species. To look ahead, then, we must first look back. Accordingly, the initial focus is on *function*, and we must ask just what functions our current cognitive processes and their neural mechanisms were designed by evolution to serve. The rule is that *form follows function.*

By way of analogy, the task of guessing what piece of equipment (it could be anything) I am thinking of right now is easier the more you know about its functions. It can receive signals from afar (TV, radio, radar detector?); it is used to communicate with others (two-way radio, computer, telegraph, telephone); it transmits and receives speech sounds (two-way radio, telephone?); it is used for immediate communication between virtually any two people in nearly any homes or businesses (telephone). Even if you had never used a telephone, you would know from its functions that it must contain components to send speech, receive speech, and transmit signals that would alert another person to your attempt to communicate. Knowledge of its functions thus tells you what to look for inside the phone.

From this evolutionary perspective, the neural mechanisms that permit human cognition are a product of natural selection, which "'chooses' among alternative designs on the basis of how well they function" (Cosmides & Tooby, 1994, p. 45). The designs chosen and passed on to future generations are those that have historically performed important functions and solved important problems of survival and reproduction. Thus, the structural and neurochemical properties of the current human brain are those that best solved the problems imposed on ancient peoples by their environments (Brune, 2001).

An important implication of this evolutionary perspective is that cognitive functions and underlying brain mechanisms are *specific*, rather than general. That is, cognition is carried out not by one broad set of mechanisms that are content-free or *domain-general*, but rather by a number of separate modules, each solving particular kinds of problems. The distinction is an important one because domain-general cognitive theories—including those we have already discussed—have been the more common approach since Aristotle originally described the mind as a *tabula rasa*, or blank tablet, to be written on by experience. Modern evolutionists adopt the opposing view that the neural mechanisms of cognition "provide not a blank sheet for individual mental and cultural development, but a sheet at least lightly scrawled with certain tentative outlines to assist survival and reproduction" (Shaw & Wong, 1989, p. 84). Just as the heart is specifically designed by natural selection to pump blood and the liver to detoxify poisons, each cognitive mechanism in the brain has evolved to solve particular kinds of problems. They include predator avoidance, locating food, incest avoidance, mate choice, sexual jealousy, language acquisition, and social exchange, among others (Cosmides & Tooby, 1994).

Consider the example of *social exchange*—cooperation among people for mutual benefit—which is a crucial feature of hominid evolution that is substantially enhanced by language capability (Tooby & DeVore, 1987). You help your friend paint her apartment, and she takes you out to dinner. You have undergone a social exchange, a universal phenomenon in all human societies for at least hundreds of thousands of years. In fact, even primates, representing an earlier phase of evolution, appear to engage in some degree of social exchange (Quiatt & Reynolds, 1993). Gift-giving, barter, mutual helping, and buying food at a grocery store are all common examples of human social exchange. Evolutionary theory assumes that early humans found such cooperation necessary for survival. As a result, natural selection built a set of domain-specific neural, cognitive mechanisms by choosing and passing on those that promote social exchange and thereby the survival of the species (Cosmides & Tooby, 1994). The structures involved are specialized for cognitions necessary for social exchange; they differ from the structures that have evolved for language acquisition, mate choice, and other functions.

The evolutionary view of language and its neural basis is a straightforward extension of what we have said about cognition. Our human ancestors had an increasing need to communicate in order to locate food, avoid predators, and otherwise survive. Early communication involved primarily gestures and later simple sounds (Joseph, 1993). Over hundreds of thousands of years, supportive neural structures further evolved to permit spoken and written language. Spoken language appeared about 40,000 years ago in Europe and Africa (Joseph, 1993), and written language came along at least six thousand years ago in Mesopotamia (Bradshaw & Rogers, 1993). Evolutionary theory is consistent with Chomsky's concept of a language acquisition device in the brain.

Cognitive-Neuroscience: The Neurophysiology of Cognition

The marriage of cognition to neuroscience to produce the relatively new hybrid known as cognitive-neuroscience appears to be a permanent one promises increasing insights into the brain functions that underlay cognition and language (McIntosh et al., 2001). Much of what we know about the neural basis of cognitive processes comes from work involving the electroencephalogram or EEG and, more recently, several scanning techniques, including fMRI (Chapter 3) in normal humans and from studies of brain-damaged individuals. Working with normal subjects Emmanuel Donchin has focused on the relationship of event-related brain potentials (ERPs) to the processing of information. The ERP is an electrical change in an EEG measure of brain activity that occurs when some event affects the individual. One component of the ERP is a large, positive, momentary increase in electrical activity called "P300." It occurs 300-500 milliseconds (about one-third to one-half second) after the event and appears particularly relevant to information processing (Figure 8-11).

When you are presented with a stimulus, that stimulus represents potential information. This information must undergo neural evaluation before you can produce a response. A driver who sees a red light must evaluate that stimulus as meaning "stop" and respond by stepping on the brake. Apparently, the P300 component of the ERP is an index of the time it takes to process the information provided by such a stimulus and thereby evaluate its meaning (Duncan-Johnson and Donchin, 1982; Donchin & Coles, 1988). Evidence amassed by Donchin and his colleagues suggests that P300 is closely related to the processing of surprising or unexpected events; that is, the P300 response is greater when an event is unexpected than when it is expected.

All of this does not mean that Donchin has necessarily discovered the neurological basis for information processing. What he has done is move us one step closer to the beginning of a rudimentary understanding of the neurology underlying cognitive processes. More important, this research provides the cognitive psychologist with a tool for studying the processing of information.

A second set of data comes from studies of individuals with brain damage arising from injury or disease. Damage to areas of the *frontal cortex* produces relatively specific deficits in the ability to solve problems without causing an overall reduction in intelligence as measured by IQ tests (Holyoak, 1990). With frontal damage, we typically see reductions in the ability to plan ahead and to give novel answers, both aspects of problem-solving; with prefrontal damage, there is a breakdown in the integration of cognition with emotion (Gray et al., 2002). Moreover, areas of the prefrontal cortex fire in response to spoken language (Romanski & Goldman-Rakic, 2002). In addition, there is emerging evidence that the right frontal lobe may be somewhat more involved in visual problem-solving and the left more in verbal problem-solving (Kolb & Whishaw, 1990). However, few cognitive neuroscientists believe that we can localize thought in any small area of the brain. In fact, current models increasingly follow the neural network concept. According to this approach, thought processes probably involve parallel distributed processing in a network of interlinked neurons that may be scattered over wide areas of the cortex (Pulvermusser, 2001; Philipson, 2002). Some have gone so far as to suggest that the self-concept—your view and understanding of your own personal characteristics—arose in evolution as neural networks that coordinate a variety of body signals were developed (Churchland, 2002). Do such neural models accord more generally with an analysis of function from the viewpoint of evolutionary theory? Only further research can answer that question.

The Neurophysiology of Language

Most of what we know about the neurophysiology of language also comes from the study of brain-damaged patients (Scherzer et al., 1993). The basic form of speech pathology that results from brain damage is aphasia, which involves difficulty in producing or comprehending meaningful speech. The problem is not in the physical ability to produce speech sounds but rather in using language in a meaningful way. The aphasic has difficulty turning thoughts into meaningful speech or understanding what someone else is saying.

Studies of aphasics show that the neural circuits necessary for language and speech functions are located primarily in the left hemisphere (Chapter 3). In fact, damage to this side of the brain results in aphasia in about 95 percent of cases (Geschwind, 1970). However, recent evidence suggests that parts of the right hemisphere are involved in the reasoning that helps us understand the topic of a conversation and its meaning (Caplan & Dapretto, 2001; Ince & Christman, 2002). There are, however, some differences in the neuroanatomy of speech between left- and right-handed individuals (Springer & Deutsch, 1993). In right-handers, the left hemisphere is dominant for speech in over 95% of the population. In left-handers and those who are ambidextrous (have no dominant hand), the left hemisphere is dominant for speech in only about 70% of the population (Rasmussen & Milner, 1975). Some of these individuals even show speech capacity in both hemispheres.

There are three basic types of aphasia, called Broca's aphasia, Wernicke's aphasia, and conduction aphasia. Around 1865, Paul Broca, a French physician, reported speech problems in patients suffering damage to a specific area of the cortex in the frontal lobe of the left hemisphere, now known as Broca's area (Figure 8-12). Patients with damage to this area have Broca's aphasia or non-fluent aphasia—difficulty in producing meaningful speech. They speak in short phrases, consisting mainly of nouns, verbs, and major modifiers, and their speech lacks correct grammatical structure. In addition, the speech is usually slow, effortful, and distorted, and there is a great reduction in total speech output (ter Keurs et al., 2002). Here, for example, is one patient's effort to describe a picture in Figure 8-13. Times required to produce the speech are in parentheses:

> *girl is . . . falling falling (6 sec) c-cookie/tsar/fall . . ah man ok/ lady washin' . . .eh . . ./tfitfiz/ ah man. . .boy . . .ah. . . (7 sec) fall. . .fall. . .fall. (Caramaza and Berndt, 1982, p. 485)*

The patient probably understood quite well what was going on in the picture but could not meaningfully describe it. Interestingly enough, many patients with Broca's aphasia can *sing* words that are correct and fluent, probably because a different part of the brain mediates singing.

In 1874 Carl Wernicke, a German neurologist, observed that speech difficulty could also arise from damage to the posterior region of the temporal lobe of the left hemisphere, a spot now known as Wernicke's area (see Figure 8-12). Patients with damage to this area have dramatically different symptoms than those with Broca's aphasia. A patient with Wernicke's aphasia or fluent aphasia usually maintains speech fluency but has great difficulty in *comprehending* the speech of others. Voice quality is also quite normal, and the person articulates words without difficulty. The problem with this fluent, articulate speech is that it tends to be meaningless. Here, for example, is an excerpt from one such patient's description of the scene in Figure 8-13:

> *he f-fall down/ yeah it's fall down its gonna fall down now..see it's got the jar he's trying kno-knock it out/ an he's gonna/fct/ it . . . see he's getting/aet/down/rai/he's grabbin' a thing. (Caramaza and Berndt, 1982, p. 486)*

The Wernicke patient also often misspells words when writing, and the misspellings are not random; they tend to reflect interchanges of letters with similar sounds. "Tip" may be written as "dip" or "horse" as "morse."

Wernicke's area is quite specific to symbols that represent *sounds*, as opposed to pictures. Perhaps the most striking demonstration of this fact is seen in Japanese patients. The Japanese language uses three kinds of written symbols: two, *hiragana* and *katukana*, represent phonemes or sounds; the third, *kanji*, are pictographs and are thus visual in nature. Japanese patients with left temporal lesions have difficulty writing with the phoneme symbols but no problem with the pictographs. Patients with damage in areas of the brain that deal with vision have trouble with the *kanji* symbols but not the others (Sasanuma, 1975). It thus appears that the Wernicke area stores memories for the sounds of words and their association with ideas, while the Broca area stores memories for the patterns of muscular movements of the vocal chords that are necessary to translate thoughts into meaningful words. In addition, recent research suggests that Wernicke's area is divided into several subsystems that perform specific speech functions and that other areas of the temporal cortex are active in comprehending visual aspects of speech, such as lip-reading (Bernstein et al., 2002; Wise et al., 2001).

The Broca and Wernicke areas are connected by a fiber bundle called the *arcuate fasciculus*. This tract is crucial for the transfer of information between the two speech areas, and the patient in whom this bundle is damaged exhibits conduction aphasia. In this disorder, the primary symptom is an inability to repeat words. One patient tested during the early 1960s was asked to repeat the word "president." His response was, "I know who that is—Kennedy" (Geschwind, 1965). He was unable to repeat the word, but it obviously elicited an appropriate association. Conduction aphasics can usually express thoughts meaningfully in words, have reasonably fluent speech, and appear to comprehend the meanings of the words they cannot repeat.

Recent neurological findings suggest that it may be necessary to modify our understanding of the exact involvement of brain areas in aphasia (Ingvar, 1993). One striking finding comes from cases of young children in whom disease or injury has damaged one hemisphere so severely that a hemispherectomy (complete removal of half the brain) may be necessary. Studies show that these children can go on to develop language even when it is the left hemisphere that is removed (Curtiss et al., 2001). Other major findings are that the area of the frontal cortex involved in Broca's aphasia may be considerably larger than originally thought, extending well beyond Broca's area (Grodzinsky, 2000) and that the prefrontal cortex is involved in the semantic aspect of language (Chee et al., 2002). It has also been found that the brain damage involved in aphasia may extend below the level of the cortex to the subcortical *basal ganglia* and even into the hindbrain cerebellum (Duffau et al., 2002; Marien et al., 2001). There are even some cases in which injury to certain subcortical areas appears to produce aphasia without any cortical involvement at all (Bares, 2001). Finally, researchers have discovered that there is substantial variation in brain structure from person to person and that the localization of brain functions can vary markedly from one individual to another (Ojemann and Whitaker, 1978). This discovery may indicate that aphasia can result from damage that is not precisely located in the Broca or Wernicke area (Roder et al., 2002). These findings may lead to a more complete understanding of the causes of aphasia, new approaches to diagnosis, and perhaps better methods of treatment.

Neural Networks For Language. David Rummelhart and Jay McClelland (1986) have extended their connectionist model involving parallel distributed processing to explain some aspects of language acquisition. In addition, Gary Dell (1988) has proposed that both linguistic structure and syntactic rules involve the development and operation of neural networks. The phonemes (sounds) that form morphemes (meanings) and the morphemes that form lexemes (words) must somehow be linked together in the brain as learning takes place. The hypothesis is that they are connected by ever more complex neural networks (Westen & Gabbard, 2002). For example, when you speak a sentence such as, "I'm almost done reading this chapter," the first words activate word nodes in the appropriate networks, which trigger off later words in those networks. The activation spreads through the networks, stimulating other sounds, meanings, and words as it goes. The rapid result is your spoken sentence.

Keys to Higher Mental Processes 5

Conclusion

It is difficult not to note while writing a chapter on cognition that humankind has been fascinated for centuries with the phenomena of thought and language. You can easily imagine great thinkers like Aristotle, Plato, and Hippocrates wondering how they themselves thought and talked. But it is almost entirely in this century—primarily in the past four decades—that we have begun to systematically learn about cognition. And now you know, at least in brief form, much of what cognitive psychology and cognitive science have discovered. If we have learned nothing else in this chapter, it is that humans are unique members of the animal kingdom. True, some animals can run faster, others have more acute senses, and still others are physically stronger. But humans are the only animals capable of complex cognition and creative, meaningful speech.

Fascinated by the human capacity for complex cognitive activity, scientists have created two major theories—information processing and connectionism—in an attempt to understand cognition. Its major elements have been at least tentatively identified and applied to such major cognitive activities as problem-solving, decision-making, and reasoning. The structure of language has also been defined and theories of language development proposed. And we have at least begun to understand the rudiments of the neurophysiological substrates of cognition and language.

Our knowledge is thus far very incomplete—indeed primitive—but we have at least moved a giant step closer to understanding human thought and language. Clearly, the 21st century will begin with a great emphasis in psychology and allied disciplines on cognitive science and cognitive neuroscience and likely end with a correspondingly great increase in our knowledge of cognitive functioning.

Summary

Elements of Cognition

1. Cognition, or thought, includes two major elements: concepts and propositions.
2. Cognitive science and cognitive neuroscience are interdisciplinary fields that study human cognition and its neurophysiological bases.
3. Concepts group like objects into categories and are acquired through teaching and prototypes. The two principal types of concepts are artificial and natural.
4. Concept hierarchies permit us to infer properties that are not directly associated with the lower level concepts in the hierarchy.
5. Two major theories of concept formation are mediation theory and hypothesis-testing theory.
6. Propositions combine concepts to form the basis for thought.

Problem-Solving

1. Gestalt theory hypothesizes that problem-solving takes place through insight.
2. Information-processing theory says that human behavior depends on the information available to the person and how that information is processed.
3. The major stages of problem-solving in one model are: preparation, production, judgment, and incubation.
4. Connectionism postulates that cognitive processes take place in neural networks that engage in parallel distributed processing.
5. Major problem-solving strategies include algorithms and heuristics, working backward, means/ends analysis, difference reduction, and finding analogies.
6. Factors that affect the problem-solving process include the way in which the problem is represented, prior knowledge and memory, selective attention, and planning.
7. Factors that can hamper problem solving include functional fixedness, irrelevant information, psychological set, and confirmation bias.
8. The advantages experts have in solving problems include: chunking, deep processing, organization and planning, taking a global view, relating the current to past problems, and categorizing problems on the basis of solutions.

Decision-Making and Reasoning

1. Decision-making can be impaired by the inaccurate use of heuristics, inadequate framing of questions, loss aversion, overconfidence, and probability biases.
2. Three heuristics that are often used inaccurately are representativeness, anchoring, and availability.
3. Human reasoning can be seen as an adaptive product of millions of years of evolution.
4. Reasoning, or thinking that relates to a specific goal, may be autistic or realistic.
5. Deductive reasoning involves logical thinking and moves from the general to the specific.
6. Inductive reasoning involves probability estimates and moves from the specific to the general.

Language: Its Structure and Function

1. Three major aspects of language are structure, process, and use. Language is also meaningful and novel.
2. Major theories relating language to thought include Watson's, Piaget's, and Whorf's.
3. The Whorfian hypothesis suggests that all thought processes are determined by language (linguistic determinism) and that the speakers of different languages perceive and experience the environment differently (linguistic relativism).
4. The basic components of language are phonemes, morphemes, and lexemes. The arrangement of words into phrases and sentences follows the rules of syntax. Semantics is the study of word meanings.
5. Chomsky hypothesizes two levels of structure in language: surface structure and deep structure. Transformational grammar is the set of rules that relate surface structure to deep structure. Government and binding theory does away with most transformations in order to simply the theory.
6. Early language acquisition typically begins with prelinguistic babbling and lalling, then moves to holophrases, two-word expressions, the use of syntax, and overregularization.
7. Environmental theories of language development suggest that acquisition is based on conditioning processes or observational learning. Biological theories hold that language is species uniform and species specific and that the major language structures are inborn.
8. Some primates have been taught to communicate through the use of sign language or other nonverbal means, though they may not have any substantial degree of linguistic ability.

The Neurophysiology of Cognition and Language

1. The neurophysiological basis of cognition has been studied by examining event-related brain potentials and brain-damaged individuals, and the neural network concept has recently been applied.
2. Damage to Broca's area results in difficulty in producing meaningful speech. Damage to Wernicke's area results

in difficulty in comprehending speech of others. A number of other brain areas, both cortical and subcortical, appear to be involved in language as well.

Ask Yourself

1. What are the basic elements of thought, and how are they put together?
2. Can the information-processing approach to problem solving explain how insight takes place? How about connectionsim?
3. How could the information-processing approach be applied in solving the Buddhist monk problem?
4. What factors would be helpful to someone trying to solve the hobbits and orcs problem? What factors would hinder someone trying to solve this problem?
5. How are problems solved? What factors determine the effectiveness of problem-solving and what interferes?
6. What are the main attributes of language?
7. What roles do surface structure and deep structure play in conveying meaning? Which is more important?
8. What is the Whorfian hypothesis? Do you agree or disagree with this hypothesis? Give reasons for your answer.
9. What have studies of various aphasias revealed about the brain mechanisms involved in language?
10. Discuss the sequence of language development and its relationship to environmental and biological theories of language acquisition.

Further Readings

Barsalou, L.W. (1992). *Cognitive psychology:* An overview for cognitive scientists. Hillsdale, NJ: Erlbaum. Lawrence Barsalou provides a thorough, book-length overview of the entire field of cognitive psychology.

Fisher, C.M. (1993). Concerning mind. Can. J. Neurol. Sci., 20, 247-253. Fisher thoughtfully addresses the nature of thinking from a neurological standpoint.

Gleason, J.B., & Ratner, N.B. (1993). *Psycholinguistics.* Fort Worth: Harcourt. A solid overview of language production, comprehension, and development.

Johnson-Laird, P.N., & Byrne, R.M.J. (1991). *Deduction.* Hove, Great Britain: Erlbaum. This book contains everything you ever wanted to know about deductive logic, including syllogisms and conditional reasoning. A good review of relevant research.

McClelland, J.L., & Plaut, D.C. (1993). Computational approaches to cognition: top-down approaches. *Curr. Opin. Neurobiol.*, 3, 209-216. One of the major theorists in connectionist modeling, McClelland reviews the use of such models in understanding cognition and language, as well as brain disorders affecting cognitive processing.

Nelson, T.O. (Ed.). (1992). *Metacognition: Core readings.* Boston: Allyn & Bacon. This is a good collection of articles by top experts in the field of metacognition.

Owens, R.E., Jr. (1992). *Language development: An introduction.* New York: Merrill. A very readable review of the field of language development from babbling and lalling to pragmatics and bilingualism.

Shafir, E., & Tversky, A. (1992). Thinking through uncertainty: nonconsequential reasoning and choice. *Cognit. Psychol.*, 24, 449-474. One of the most prominent theorists and researchers in cognition, Amos Tversky and his colleague present an excellent of how we think through and arrive at decisions when we are uncertain.

Shortliffe, E.H. (1993). The adolescence of AI in medicine: will the field come of age in the '90s? *Artif. Intell. Med.*, 5, 93-106. If you are interested in artificial intelligence, this article provides a good sense of where we are, not only in medicine but in other fields. What is the state of the art in AI?

Spelke, E.S., Breinlinger, K., Macomber, J., & Jacobson, K. Origins of knowledge. *Psychol. Rev.*, 99, 605-632. Elizabeth Spelke, a major figure in cognitive research, and her colleagues address research and theory on an important cognitive topic: Where does our knowledge come from? How do we develop a body of knowledge?

Key Terms

algorithm
aphasia
artificial intelligence
autistic thinking
Broca's area
chunking
cognition
cognitive science
cognitive neuroscience
concept
confirmation bias
connectionism
creativity
critical period
deductive reasoning
depth of processing
difference reduction
deep structure
event-related potentials (ERPs)
functional fixedness
heuristic
hypothesis-testing theory
gambler's fallacy
g factor
gestalt
government and binding theory
inductive reasoning
information-processing theory
insight
intelligence quotient (IQ)
intelligence tests
language acquisition device
lexeme
linguistic determinism
linguistic relativism
loss aversion
means/end analysis
mediation theory
metacognition
morpheme
nativism
neural network
overregularization
parallel distributed processing
psycholinguistics
phoneme
pragmatics
proposition
psychological set
realistic thinking
reliability
selective attention
semantics
species specificity
species uniformity

standardization
surface structure
syntax
transformational grammar
validity
Wernicke's area

Key People

Donald Broadbent
Paul Broca
Jerome Bruner
Noam Chomsky
Leda Cosmides
Emmanuel Donchin
Daniel Kahneman
George Kelley
Wolfgang Kohler
Eric Lenneberg
Jay McClelland
George Miller
Jean Piaget
David Rummelhart
Edward Sapir
Sue Savage-Rumbaugh
Herbert Simon
B.F. Skinner
Robert Sternberg
Herbert Terrace
John Tooby
Amos Tversky
John Watson
Carl Wernicke
Benjamin Whorf

Psychology in the 21st Century

The Computer As Expert

"Go to warp speed. We need to know exactly how many aliens there are, what weapons they possess, and how we can take over without endangering the Enterprise. There are over 200 parameters to consider. Mr. Spock, make a computer run to determine the best approach." "Yes, Captain." The computer that Captain Kirk of Startrek fame refers to is, in fact, an expert system, a computer program developed to solve problems in a limited area—in this case space invasion.

While we don't yet have expert systems as advanced as these, we are developing increasingly sophisticated computer expertise in many areas. Imagine arriving at your physician's office to be ushered into a small chamber, where a technician attaches electrodes. A computer then asks you questions about your complaint and activates equipment to obtain blood and urine samples and measure the activity of your heart, lungs, brain, and other organs. It analyzes the data and prints a diagnosis. Later that same day, you go to your clinical psychologist for therapy. There you sit in front of another computer, which asks you questions, determines a diagnosis, and goes on to conduct therapy.

Although we do not yet have expert systems capable of a full medical or psychological diagnosis or therapy, we are rapidly moving in that direction in medicine, psychology, and many other fields. We already have, for example, expert systems that learn the English language, play chess, aid in medical diagnosis, and conduct psychotherapy. In developing these programs, scientists use *knowledge engineering*, in which human expertise is translated into computer language to form an extensive knowledge base. They add an *inference engine*, which is a set of computer instructions for drawing information from the knowledge base to solve problems (Hix, 2002).

Language acquisition programs actually learn English without ever being given the symbols and rules that we have traditionally believed are necessary for children to acquire language, suggesting that perhaps language is learned in different ways than was originally thought (Kolata, 1987). Chess-playing programs have taught us much about how experts solve problems. Chess is a complex game that requires experts to learn sophisticated rules and remember large numbers of board patterns. The best chess-playing programs today can actually beat master and even grand master chess players (LeFraneois, 1983). In 1996, international champion Gary Kasparov defeated the most sophisticated program, Deep Blue, though he did lose two games to the computer.

More serious expert systems have been created for medical diagnosis and psychotherapy. The medical programs are fed large quantities of information based on blood and urine samples, EKGs and other medical tests. The programs can quickly integrate all this information—often better than a typical physician—and suggest a diagnosis. Expert systems are now increasingly used to interpret electrocardiograms and monitor patients in intensive care facilities (Satava et al., 2002). These systems are not just machines that spew out numbers, but highly sophisticated computer software that processes volumes of information and makes or suggests decisions—much as a physician does. Expert medical systems also monitor and automatically adjust anesthesia during surgery (Schulte & Mollenberg, 1994), prescribe eyeglasses (Madsen et al., 1993), and conduct complete hearing tests (Ozdamar et al., 1994).

Psychotherapy programs—which you may someday find at your college counseling center— are capable of actually conducting some kinds of therapy (Ford, 1993). ELIZA is a program developed at the Massachusetts Institute of Technology to simulate the behavior of a psychotherapist. ELIZA actually interacts with a human therapy client in much the same way as a psychotherapist might (Murphy & Pardeck, 1988). The program "listens" to the client's problem and responds. Of course, it is difficult for a machine to achieve the warmth or understanding that one would hope to find in a good human therapist, but ELIZA does further our understanding of just how psychotherapy takes place and may help us to improve the process. ELIZA's author believes the program should not actually be used as a substitute for the human psychotherapist except for research purposes (Weizenbaum, 1976), and others have used it to help in teaching psychotherapy to graduate students (Suler, 1987). Other psychological expert systems aid the therapist in psychological assessment, history-taking, and health education (Bloom, 1992).

How expert are the experts? Well, even experts are not perfect, and expert computer systems are no exception. In fact, we have a long way to go in this field. The major medical systems, for example, are very useful in providing the physician with integrated information and in suggesting diagnoses. However, they are often not entirely on target. Two of the major diagnostic systems, Iliad and QMR, are still not expert enough to perform final diagnoses (Sumner & Schultz, 1992). In one study, ten expert clinicians provided information on over 100 actual cases, and these were given to four expert systems for diagnosis. The computer programs agreed with the human experts a little less than half the time, though the programs did provide additional possible diagnoses that the physicians had not thought of (Berner et al., 1994).

Despite their utility, then, expert systems obviously have limitations. First, they still cannot reason as well as a human. Second, they must depend on relatively simple logic: "If the patient has a sore throat, do a strep culture." And, finally, the computer program does not "know enough" to link up multiple knowledge bases even when that might be useful. An expert system examining a patient with chest pain and heart palpitations will not look into a separate psychological data base to determine whether the cause might be an anxiety disorder, which can also produce these symptoms (see Chapter 16).

The near future will see some solutions to this problem. The fact is that many large but separate information data bases already exist in a variety of fields. The National Library of Medicine, for example, produces Medline, a general database of medical literature referencing over 6 million journal articles. It also produces a number of more specific data bases in such areas as cancer, AIDS, and toxicology. New expert system programs are now being "taught" to automatically access these and other data bases when the problem requires more information than the expert program contains (Berman et al., 1993).

Computers are still not quite human. But stay tuned. The neural network concept is already being applied to the development of ever better expert systems, and the future holds considerable promise of increasingly sophisticated software that will gradually become more and more capable of engaging in human-like reasoning. Indeed, it is virtually certain that some expert systems developed in the 21st century will match or surpass human expertise.

The Critical Thinker

Think Critically: *Is Bilingualism a Disadvantage?*

Quiz: Answer True or False to each of the following items:

____Learning two languages simultaneously is confusing to children.

____Bilingual children show slower intellectual development.

____Bilinguals do not perform as well on IQ tests.

____Only a small percentage of people world wide speak more than one language.

As usual, we can arrive at the best answers to these items by developing relevant theories and conducting research.

The Basic Hypothesis or Contention

Some early theorists in the areas of thought and language argued that cognitive capacity is quite limited. This led them to the conclusion that thought processes become less efficient when the brain stores two linguistic systems (Lambert, 1990). As a result, some hypothesized that bilinguals—those who speak two or more languages—have decreased capacity for learning other things and therefore display slower intellectual development (Jespersen, 1922). They may be confused by having to deal with two competing languages and have lower IQs. Bilingualism is therefore a significant disadvantage.

Such a hypothesis has educational, social and political implications. It might be expected to influence our school systems, which must decide whether or not to teach second languages to children. In addition, it could well have an impact on immigration policies and the society's view of the intellectual functioning of bilingual immigrants.

What Is The Evidence?

Early studies supported the hypothesis that bilinguals are intellectually disadvantaged. Their cognitive development was shown to be slower, and they scored lower on IQ tests than did monolinguals. Theorists and researchers concluded that the hypothesis was supported by the evidence: learning two or more languages impairs intellectual functioning (Lambert, 1990).

Scientists later reexamined these initial findings and discovered that the early studies were flawed in several ways (Reynolds, 1991). The tests used were given in English, even when that was not the child's primary language. The bilinguals were often first- or second-generation immigrants who were usually not proficient in English and frequently had lower socioeconomic backgrounds. And test scores were compared with norms developed on monolingual, English-speaking, middle-class children (Diaz, 1983).

More recent studies have been done more carefully, and the results are substantially different. In fact, it appears that bilingualism may give a child several specific advantages. Learning a second language seems to provide a better understanding of the structure of the first language (Lambert et al., 1991). A Spanish-speaking child often shows enhanced understanding of Spanish language structure when he later learns English. Bilinguals also show greater cognitive flexibility on creativity tests, where they may be asked to list all the possible uses of a hammer or a rubber band, including unusual ones. Another advantage of learning a second language is that it allows the child to better understand that the names we assign to concepts are arbitrary—that a hammer could just as easily have been assigned the name "muffin" (Jordaan et al., 2001).

Some studies of bilinguals quite directly refute the early hypothesis and have even turned up some broader advantages of learning a second language. They show that children who learn two languages do not show confusion and that they perform as well as their monolingual counterparts on tests of intelligence and cognitive functioning more generally (Rosselli et al., 2000). In fact, some results suggest that children raised from early life in a bilingual environment actually perform better in both languages than monolinguals (Hakuta & Garcia, 1989) and do better in school (Peal & Lambert, 1962). Even if not exposed to the second language until after the age of three, such children often attain fluency in about one year (Reich, 1986). Those who achieve *balanced* bilingualism, with equal facility in both languages, actually show superior performance on tests of concept formation and creativity (Padilla et al., 1991), perhaps because the two languages permit more flexible thinking. Interesting recent studies show that the neural representation of the two languages is the same when both are learned at an early age (Hernandez et al., 2001). However, when one is learned after age 7, it is represented quite differently in the brain (Fabbro, 2001).

One more observation—and the answer to our last quiz item—is that a majority of people in the world speak at least two languages; Americans are the exception, with most speaking only one (Grosjean, 1982). Most European countries, for example, routinely teach English, as well as the languages of surrounding countries, and the norm is to achieve fluency in each language.

Is The Evidence Open To Alternative Interpretation?

Clearly the more recent evidence concerning the advantages and disadvantages of bilingualism appears to refute the disadvantage hypothesis. However, we cannot fall into the trap of assuming that what we now seem to know is right in some absolute sense.

One set of questions revolves around the comparability of the monolingual and bilingual samples used in some studies. For one thing, it is possible that those who become fluent in a second language, particularly in countries like the United States where that is uncommon, may be more intelligent than those who do not. Their higher level of intellectual functioning may make it more likely that they will learn the second language. If so, their advantage on aptitude tests given in studies of bilingualism might be due to higher general or verbal intelligence, not to learning the second language.

A related sampling concern is that people who leave some countries to come to the United States tend to be those with better educations and incomes. As we discuss in Chapter 9, higher parental socioeconomic and educational levels are both associated with better child performance on intelligence and aptitude tests (Oakland & Glutting, 1990; Capron & Duyme, 1989). This means that the children of some immigrants—who make up the bilingual samples in some studies—may have advantages over the monolinguals.

A further consideration is that some studies still show disadvantages of bilingualism. There is evidence, for example, that bilinguals process language less rapidly than monolinguals (Taylor & Taylor, 1990). They are also slower to make decisions about the use of language, often taking longer to turn thoughts into words and formulate sentences (Taylor & Taylor, 1990). A third disadvantage is that bilinguals take longer to determine whether or not a string of letters actually is an English word, probably because of interference from the second language (Ransdell & Fischler, 1987). And speaking two or more languages may alter pronunciations of some words in both languages, making some bilinguals harder for other people to understand (Caramazza et al., 1973).

What Conclusions Can We Reach?

Despite the cautions we have noted, it appears that the weight of evidence to date does not favor the disadvantage hypothesis. The disadvantages that have turned up, such as reduced language processing speed, appear to be relatively minor and are offset by evidence of higher performance in other areas. Perhaps the appropriately cautious conclusion is that there appears to be no overall disadvantage of bilingualism and that further research should determine whether or not there are clearly documented advantages in well-controlled studies.

Probe

The Wild Child: The Case Study Approach

Case studies involve an in-depth analysis of a single person. They cannot be the basis for final scientific conclusions, but they are very useful in generating hypotheses and providing insights into psychological phenomena. In psycholinguistics, one of the major questions is whether language must be learned early in life or whether it can be acquired just as easily at later ages. Case studies of "wild" children, raised with little or no human verbal contact, help to offer hypotheses and partially answer this question.

Imagine going on a hike in a forest, perhaps in the South of France, and quite accidentally discovering a 12-year-old child who has grown up with no human contact whatsoever. That is exactly what happened in a forest near a village in southern France in 1800 (Shattuck, 1980). Known as the Wild Boy of Aveyron, the 11- or 12- year-old child had apparently never had human contact. A young physician named Jean-Marc Itard undertook the task of socializing the boy and partially succeeded in teaching him to read and write, but he never did learn to speak more than a few words. He had apparently passed the critical period for language acquisition.

Another interesting case is that of two girls found in the den of a wolf mother in India in 1920. The younger, dubbed Amala, was about 1-1/2 years-old, and the older, Kamala, was about 8. Roger Brown (1958) described them as "wolfish in appearance and in behavior." They moved their nostrils to sniff food, had sharp teeth with which they ate raw meat, and often prowled and howled at night. Amala, who lived to be 18, eventually learned to walk upright and wear clothing, but she was able to speak only a few words.

Somewhat less dramatic cases of social isolation are those created by parents who have kept their children away from normal social contact. One of the best documented cases is that of Genie, a child discovered in California at the age of fourteen. She had lived in apparently complete isolation from everyone but her parents since the age of about twenty months. At that time, she had been tied to a chair and placed in a closet, where she remained for twelve years. Apparently language was never used in her presence (Fromkin et al., 1974). After years of language instruction, Genie developed a basic vocabulary and some essential language skills. She became able to formulate meaningful ideas and put them into words, but she could not combine propositions to form complex sentences and her language usage remained quite primitive (Curtiss, 1977).

A second case is that of Isabelle, who had been kept from all outside social contact by her parents and was never spoken to until she was discovered at age six (Brown, 1958). After about a year of language training, Isabelle learned to speak quite normally, and she quickly caught up with her age peers. She soon began school and appeared to progress normally. It is probable that Isabelle learned language better than Genie because she was discovered at an earlier age.

Collectively, these cases offer the hypothesis that normal language development requires children to have human linguistic contact from a reasonably early age. It may be that only during these early years is the brain "ready" for the acquisition of language. However, as we explain in the text, more recent studies—going beyond the case study method—do not entirely support this hypothesis.

Horizons in Cognition and Language

Computer Neural Networks That Learn

Imagine a computer program that not only simulates a human neural network but actually learns from experience—just like a human! While this is largely an idea for the 21st century, it is by no means science fiction. Preliminary programs of this type have already been developed. A computer-simulated neural network is a program that can detect complex patterns found in input data. Much like the human brain, the network is "trained" by giving it a variety of input patterns and corresponding expected output patterns. The network can then generate correct output from data never before encountered.

One such program has been developed to predict the probability of survival for patients who come to the emergency room with knife wounds. After being trained on the records of 3500 previous patients, the network correctly predicted survival 97% of the time (McGonigal et al., 1993). A second neural network program, LiverSoar, was developed to help in diagnosing liver diseases. When LiverSoar "sees" a case, it not only suggests a diagnosis, but learns from its experience in solving the problem and accordingly updates its knowledge base, becoming more and more expert with experience (Bayazitoglu et al., 1992).

Making Great Decisions

President George Bush made the decision to invade Iraq. President Bill Clinton made the decision to invade Haiti if necessary (a peaceful landing was finally made). And many years earlier President John F. Kennedy made the Bay of Pigs invasion decision. Although presidents are kept well-informed by a large cadre of advisors, these and other presidential decisions vary considerably in how good they are. But suppose the presidents and their advisors could all be trained in decision-making on the basis of a large body of scientific research that had determined quite precisely how to best make decisions. Well, they can't because we simply don't know enough about decision-making—yet. The question for future research, then, is how we can make those decisions better.

While we have a long way to go, studies are already underway to determine how we think through uncertainty to arrive at conclusions (Shafir & Tversky, 1992), how we can improve our judgements about probability (Gavanski & Hui, 1992), how we can engage in more effective reasoning (Bonati, 1994), and how memory processes can be enhanced to improve thinking and decision-making (Patalano & Seifert, 1994). Increasingly sophisticated computer-simulated neural networks will help us by processing large amounts of information about a decision and giving us possible alternative decisions and their consequences (Hampson, 1994; Olds, 1994).

For Men Only: When is a Person Not a Person?

This question is for men only because women know the answer: when the pronoun "he" is used to refer to a generic person. Historically, English language writers and speakers consistently used the male pronoun as the neutral pronoun whenever the person referred to could be either male or female. The problem is that this practice can bias our social perceptions, conveying the idea that men are more important or that women don't count. Our linguistic usage has influenced our thinking.

Now that the problem has been recognized, change is under way. This book alternates the male and female pronouns in examples. Sometimes the participant in an experiment is identified neutrally as "he," sometimes as "she." Such changes in linguistic usage are important because studies show that when children or adults use "he" in the context of a gender-neutral sentence, they actually think only of men (Hamilton, 1991; Henley, 1989). The linguistic choice has thus influenced thought in a very direct way.

Key Terms 1

cognition
cognitive science
cognitive neuroscience
concept
mediation theory
metacognition
proposition

Key People 1

Jerome Bruner
George Kelley
George Miller
Jean Piaget
Herbert Simon

Key Terms 2

artificial intelligence
autistic thinking
chunking
confirmation bias
difference reduction
functional fixedness
heuristic
information-processing theory
insight
loss aversion
means/end analysis
psychological set
selective attention

Key People 2

Wolfgang Kohler
Robert Sternberg

Key Terms 3

deductive reasoning
gambler's fallacy
inductive reasoning

Key People 3

Daniel Kahneman
Amos Tversky

Key Terms 4

aphasia
Broca's area
critical period
deep structure
government and binding theory
language-acquisition device (LAD)
language-acquisition support system (LASS)
lexeme
linguistic determinism
linguistic relativism

morpheme
nativism
overregularization
psycholinguistics
phoneme
semantics
syntax
transformational grammar

Key People 4

Noam Chomsky
Eric Lenneberg
Edward Sapir
Sue Savage-Rumbaugh
Benjamin Whorf
B.F. Skinner
John Watson

Key Terms 5

connectionism
event-related potentials (ERPs)
neural network
parallel distributed processing
Wernicke's area

Key People 5

Paul Broca
Leda Cosmides
Emmanuel Donchin
Jay McClelland
David Rummelhart
Herbert Terrace
John Tooby
Carl Wernicke

Reference

Skolnick, A. (1994). Neuroscientist/Psychiatrist takes helm at flagship primate research center. JAMA, 272, 907-909.

Piaget, J. (1926). *The language and thought of the child.* N.Y.: Harcourt.

Piaget, J. (1954). *The construction of reality in the child.* N.Y.: Basic Books.

Bruner, J. (1983). *Child's talk.* N.Y.: Norton.

Moskowitz, R.A. (1978). The acquisition of language. *Scientific American,* November, 92-98.

Adams, J.L. (1980). *Conceptual blockbusting.* San Francisco: W.H. Freeman.

Chapter 9
Intelligence

Outline

Testing . . . Testing . . .

Test Construction

Defining Human Intelligence

The Origins of Intelligence Testing

Intelligence and Beyond: Current Cognitive Testing

Theories of Intelligence

Intelligence As A General Capacity

Intelligence As A Set of Factors

Intelligence As Information Processing

Intelligence As A Componential Triararchy

So What IS Intelligence?

The Ups and Downs of Intelligence

Mental Retardation

The Gifted

Creative Genius?

Lifespan Stability and Change

Issues in Human Intelligence

Gender Differences: Real and Imagined

The Mysterious, Declining SAT

Nature vs. Nurture

Controversies in Human Intelligence

Minority Groups Have Lower Average IQ Scores

Test Scores: Use or Abuse?

Are Tests Fair?

The Evolution and Neurophysiology of Intelligence

The Evolution of Intellect

The Neurological Basis of Intelligence

Intelligence As a Neural Network

Networking

INTELLIGENCE. You know approximately what it is. You know it is important. But what do you *really* know about this widely used construct? To what extent is it influenced by heredity and by environment? Can it be tested accurately? How are tests developed? Are they biased? Are they unfair to some groups? We will review the evidence concerning both hereditary and environmental influences on intelligence. We will also examine differences in measured intelligence among racial and ethnic groups and learn something about their likely origins. And we will see how tests are constructed, what happens to intelligence as we age, what we know about retardation and giftedness, and how creativity relates to intelligence.

As we note in Chapter 8, cognition involves the processing of information in the brain, drawing on memories acquired through learning. What we do not discuss in any detail in that chapter is the fact that different people have quite different capacities for learning, remembering, and processing information. Some learn a new task very quickly, others slowly; some retain much of what they learn, others relatively little; and some solve cognitive problems easily, while others have more difficulty. These differences in cognitive ability represent differences in intelligence, and knowledge of an individual's level of intellectual functioning tells us much about her likely performance in many areas of life. It is for that reason that psychologists have developed intelligence tests and expended considerable effort studying human intelligence and its relationship to learning, memory, and cognition.

Sweating It

Jose sat hunched over the papers in front of him, almost literally on the edge of his seat, very alert, very focused. In fact, he had never in his life concentrated so hard on any task. Jose was taking the SAT, and he knew it would have a lot to do with getting into college and choosing the college he wanted. Besides, he and two close friends all wanted to go to the same college if possible, so he hoped they did well too. As fixed on the test as he was, he couldn't keep out the occasional thoughts about how important this test could be. He remembered the IQ test in elementary school, that had so obviously been used to split the kids into ability groups for reading and math and that his parents had said would influence how teachers viewed him. And all year the guidance counselor had been talking about how important the SAT was. There were a lot of answers he wasn't sure of, and time was running out. Someone sneezed and broke his concentration. College was looking further and further away.

We'll come back later and see how Jose made out in his test, but first we need to find out just what testing involves and what it is we are testing.

Testing . . . Testing . . .

People exhibit many *individual differences*—variations from person to person in such physical characteristics as height and weight and such psychological dimensions as anxiety, depression and intelligence. A *psychological test* is a standardized measure of some aspect of the behavior or performance of an individual. It provides a sample of your behavior and thereby an indication of your anxiety, intelligence, or some other characteristic. When you go to your physician with a sore throat, she immediately knows that it could be due to the streptococcus bacillus—a "strep" throat—but she can't be sure. As a result, she will probably do a strep culture to make the diagnosis. She is performing a test, a way of getting a more accurate idea of what is wrong with you. The test is physical in this case, but the basic idea is the same.

Psychologists develop and give tests to understand and predict behavior and to improve the accuracy of their findings. Some of the tests measure normal or abnormal personality functioning (Chapter 14); others are tests of intelligence and cognitive ability more generally. A test of abnormal personality functioning may help us to better understand its nature and help diagnose the problem. Using cognitive tests, we may be able to better predict the future GPA of a student hoping to enter college or medical school or the performance of a future police officer on the job.

Intelligence testing is one of the most controversial topics we will consider, primarily because of racial and ethnic group differences in scores. However, testing also has some very real advantages. If, for example, your physician decides incorrectly without a culture that your sore throat is not strep, there could later be very serious medical consequences. In a similar way, a psychologist could get a fairly good idea of how intelligent you are by just talking to you and your teachers, but the accuracy of his judgment would be greatly improved if he gave you the test. Thus, one advantage of testing is improved *accuracy.* A second advantage is that tests are generally more *efficient* than other means of assessment. We can test hundreds of people at a time, whereas each individual assessment might require hours of work. Third, tests provide a *quantitative* measure of ability, allowing us to make a comparative judgment. Where do you stand relative to your peers? And, finally, tests are *standardized,* meaning that everyone who takes the test will be subject to the same procedures, the same scoring, and the same score interpretation. We will consider how tests are constructed and how we define intelligence. We will also take up the interesting history of intelligence testing and the development of major aptitude and achievement tests, including the SAT.

Test Construction

Any test, whether of intelligence or personality, must have three basic characteristics. It must be standardized, reliable, and valid.

Standardization. When our friend Jose took the SAT, the tester followed a very set procedure. She read the instructions aloud and started and stopped everyone at precisely the same time. In addition, everyone was given the same items, and, of course, every test was scored in exactly the same way. Without such *standardization,* the results of the test would be virtually useless. If, for example, one person had two hours and another had three to work on the test, their scores would clearly not be comparable.

The key to standardization is the development of norms for each test. *Norms* are comparative statistics that tell us the characteristics of a test and allow us to determine where a given individual stands. We calculate the average score for the test on some group of people—say, all U.S. college students—and the frequency with which each possible score occurs in the population. We can then determine how far above or below the average your score is. That is, we know where you stand *relative* to the standardization sample of all people in your group. Jose, like every college-bound student, hopes to be well above average, but, of course, not everyone can be. It is always important to make sure that the person whose score we are comparing with the test norms is, in fact, a member of the normative population. If a test is normed entirely on college students, for example, it may not be a valid indicator for someone who has never attended college.

Reliability. Your bathroom scale is a test of your weight. If you step on the scale twice in rapid succession, you expect to see the same weight. If the second weight is 10 pounds more than the first one, your scale is inconsistent and hence not very useful. By the same token, if you are well above the average on a psychological test today and well below average when you retake it in a month, the test would not be very useful. To be of any value, the test must have high *reliability*—the ability to yield consistent scores for an individual relative to the group.

There are several ways to check reliability. The most obvious is *test-retest reliability* (Figure 9-1), in which we give the same test to the same group twice, then calculate a *correlation coefficient* to determine the degree of relationship between the two testings (see Appendix ___). If it is above .80 (a perfect correlation would be 1.00), the test is judged to be adequately reliable. The problem with test-retest reliability is that there may be a *practice effect*; you may remember some of the items and therefore perform differently the second time. To avoid this problem, we can use *alternate form reliability*, in which we develop two statistically identical forms of the test, giving one now and the other to the same group later. A third approach is *split-half reliability*. Here, we give the test just once, then divide it in half (often using odd-numbered items as one half and even-numbered as the other), then correlate the two halves.

Validity. Let's assume that you find your bathroom scale to be highly reliable. However, you now visit your physician and his scale says you weigh twenty pounds less. If his scale is right, yours is clearly wrong, and we would say that your scale is reliable, but not valid. *Validity* is the extent to which a test measures what it is supposed to measure. If the test is supposed to measure intelligence, we must prove that it does measure intelligence. Any test can be highly reliable without being valid, but you can never have a test that is more valid than it is reliable. A test with a reliability coefficient of .90 isn't necessarily a valid measure of intelligence or any other variable. On the other hand, a test with only .70 reliability can never have a validity coefficient of more than .70. That is, reliability places an upper limit on validity.

There are three principal ways in which validity is established. *Content validity* is the ability of the test to measure what it is supposed to be measuring. If you stepped on the bathroom scale and it said three and a half inches, you would probably conclude that it was not a valid measure of weight. If you examined a test that was supposed to measure intelligence and found that it contained only mathematical items, you might similarly question its content validity. A more formal approach to determining content validity is to have experts rate each item as to its appropriateness for inclusion in the test.

Criterion-related validity, or concurrent validity, involves a comparison of the test in question with some criterion, which is often an established test that measures the same construct. Suppose a professor assigns you to develop a brief intelligence test. To determine the validity of your new test, you might compare it with a well-established intelligence test of known reliability and validity. If the correlation between the two is high, your test is considered valid, at least by this measure.

Predictive validity involves determining how well the test predicts future performance. We might develop an aptitude test like the SAT, give it to a group of high school seniors, then later compare the test scores with their college GPAs. In one predictive validity study, vocational training students were given achievement tests at the beginning of their program in an effort to predict how well they would do. When they finished, their test scores were correlated with two measures of performance in the program, grades and supervisor ratings. The correlations between test scores and the two performance variables indicated that the test did have adequate predictive validity (Schmidt-Atzert & Deter, 1993).

A final approach is *construct validity*, which is established by determining the extent to which the test scores are related to a particular theory that underlies the intelligence construct. If, for example, our theory says that intelligence is related to learning ability, the test should be correlated with learning ability.

Constructing A Test. Reliability, validity, and norms are established by applying a carefully developed set of test-construction procedures. We would typically begin development by defining the construct the test will measure—intelligence, for example. We also determine the population we would like to be able to test—say, college students. Next, we develop or select items that might collectively provide a test of the construct in question and we devise a standard set of instructions. The set of items is then given to a large group of people from the population. Its reliability is determined, and items that are not reliable or that add nothing useful to the test are dropped. After further testing to ensure that reliability is adequate, we begin to examine validity. This can be done by comparing the new test with related tests of the construct (criterion-related validity) and by determining how well it predicts performance or behavior (predictive validity). The test is then normed on the population in question. Finally, after many studies, we may be able to determine its relationship to underlying theory (construct validity).

Defining Human Intelligence

There is no one, universally accepted definition of intelligence. However, most experts agree that *intelligence* is the capacity for adaptive, goal-directed behavior. More intelligent people adapt better to their environments by reasoning clearly and solving problems in order to attain goals.

Beyond these basics, some experts believe that intelligent behavior may take a variety of forms. It can be seen in the exceptional social skills of the successful politician, the tracking ability of the primitive hunter, and the survival skills of the embattled soldier or inner city gang member. It is present in the deep wisdom of the aged grandmother, the creativity of the scientific theorist, and the diagnostic acumen of the exceptional physician. We will return later to the question of what intelligence is when we discuss the major theories of intelligence.

The Origins of Intelligence Testing

It became apparent just over a century ago that such an important construct as intelligence could be assessed, even if scholars were not exactly sure how to define it. This realization started the intelligence testing movement, which was pioneered by Sir Francis Galton in England, Alfred Binet in France, and Louis Terman in the United States.

Sir Francis Galton. A British mathematician and naturalist, Sir Francis Galton (1822-1911) became interested in intelligence even while still in college, where he often noted the superior performance of certain students across a variety of courses. When his cousin, Charles Darwin, proposed his natural selection theory of evolution, Galton applied it to his own developing notions about differential proficiency and is credited with coining the term "nature-nurture." Although he recognized that both biology and environment can potentially affect intelligence, he came down heavily on the nature side of the argument. In particular, he noted that such characteristics as problem-solving ability and social prominence run in families and hypothesized that these families (like his own!) pass on their superior intellectual traits genetically. Intelligence was thus largely inherited, and high intelligence assured superior performance across a variety of endeavors. As a member of the British aristocracy, the "obvious" conclusion was that men and women with high mental ability should be encouraged to marry each other and bear superior children, thus furthering the progress of the society. Galton's *eugenics* (meaning "well-born") movement promoted this end.

Galton developed an assessment battery that included measurements of head circumference, body proportions, auditory thresholds, visual acuity, reaction time, and memory. He administered his tests to 10,000 people who attended the London Exposition in 1884, charging a fee for the service. His assumption was that some or all of his tests would clearly differentiate between more and less accomplished people. To his dismay, they did not. Eminent scientists and superior students scored no differently than ordinary citizens. He had failed, but in doing so had stirred interest in developing tests of intelligence.22 Galton also developed the correlation coefficient, a statistic widely used in psychology and other fields (see Appendix).

Alfred Binet. French psychologist Alfred Binet (1857-1911) saw the possibility of applying Galton's testing concept in a different way. Binet's attempt began when the French government discovered that a new law requiring all children to attend school brought in children with a very wide range of academic ability. Some kind of uniform assessment procedure was needed, and Binet was commissioned to develop it.

When Binet and his colleague, Theodore Simon, began their work, they reasoned that a measure of intelligence or relative ability could be calculated by comparing a child's mental age (MA) with his chronological age (CA). This was accomplished by developing a scoring system in which the average MA across a large number of children was the same as their CA. The average MA for all chronological 8-year-olds, for example, was set at 8.0. Thus, an 8-year-old with an MA of 6.5 was below average and hence "dull" and one with an MA of 10.0 was above average and hence "bright." The items used to arrive at Binet's measure of mental age involved primarily reasoning, problem-solving, and memory.

Galton had theorized that intelligence is innate. Binet had little to say about the origins of intellectual ability, but he clearly believed that academic performance could be improved. He thus subscribed to a more environmental view than Galton's.

Lewis Terman. A professor at Stanford University, Lewis Terman (1877-1956) theorized that Galton was right about the hereditary basis of intelligence but had simply arrived at the wrong ways of measuring it. Binet's approach, he thought, provided the needed method and thus measured innate intelligence.

Terman revised Binet's test for use with American school children and called the new test the *Stanford-Binet.* It is still one of the major tests of intelligence. He modified some of Binet's original items and added others of his own. He also adopted a measure of intelligence developed by the German psychologist William Stern called the *intelligence quotient* or *IQ* (Kreppner, 1992). It is simply the ratio of mental to chronological age multiplied by 100. The multiplier is arbitrary and simply serves to provide more manageable numbers that are never fractional. The formula is:

$$IQ = \frac{\text{Mental Age}}{\text{Chronological Age}} \times 100$$

Since the average child has an MA that is the same as her CA, the average IQ is 100. A 5-year-old child with an MA of 7.0 would have an IQ of 140. A child the same age with an MA of 4.0 would have an IQ of 80 (Table 9-1).

Originally published in 1916, the Stanford-Binet (Figure 9-2) has been revised and re-standardized several times. In revisions published in 1937, 1960, and 1973, Terman was joined by a female psychologist, M. A. Merrill, who made major contributions to those revisions (Terman & Merrill, 1937, 1960, 1973).

More recent versions of the Stanford-Binet do not yield an IQ but rather Standard Age Scores. These are percentile scores that show the percentage of subjects at each age in the standardization sample falling above and below that of the individual being tested.

Intelligence and Beyond: Current Cognitive Testing

As we end a full century of cognitive testing, we see a tremendous expansion in the number and types of tests being developed and used. You have no doubt taken many tests, from preschool or early school readiness tests to the SAT, and you may well take more, particularly if you decide to go for an advanced degree. We will distinguish between aptitude and achievement tests, then explore some widely used group and individual tests and their reliabilities and validities.

Aptitude and Achievement Tests. We typically distinguish between two types of ability tests, aptitude and achievement. An *aptitude* test is one that predicts your ability to accomplish something if you are given proper educational opportunities. Intelligence tests, for example, are aptitude tests. They test general learning or academic ability. A more specific aptitude test might measure mechanical aptitude and thereby predict your performance in training as an automobile mechanic. An *achievement* test measures not what you can accomplish but what you have already accomplished. The examination you take covering the material in this and other chapters, for example, will indicate your level of achievement in this part of your introductory psychology course.

The distinction between aptitude and achievement seems simple and straightforward—right out of the dictionary. But is it? Let's give a test of musical aptitude to two college students. One comes from a family in which both parents are musicians and has himself played piano since age three. The other has had no exposure to music training. We would not be surprised if the first person has a higher musical aptitude, even though this would ideally be a "pure" measure of ability.

The truth is that the distinction between aptitude and achievement lies on a continuum defined by the amount and relevance of prior experience. Aptitude test scores rely relatively little on relevant prior experience, while achievement test performance is more heavily dependent on such experience. But the distinction is not absolute. You might tend to think of an IQ test as being uninfluenced by experience, but if you speak only English and someone gives you a test written in French, you will quickly see the point. In more subtle ways also, aptitude test scores are affected by prior experience.

The Wechsler Intelligence Scales. David Wechsler (1939), a Romanian immigrant to the United States, published what is now the single most widely used set of individual intelligence scales. He developed his principal test, the *Wechsler Adult Intelligence Scale* or *WAIS* (now WAIS-III), because he felt the Stanford-Binet was too dependent on verbal ability and was not adequate for adults. The WAIS is split into a *verbal* scale and a *performance* scale, a division generally supported by research (Ringe, 2002). The verbal scale has a series of subscales measuring such things as information, vocabulary, and comprehension, while the performance scales measure such abilities as picture completion, block design, and object assembly (Table 9-2). Unlike the Stanford-Binet, the WAIS scores are not a function of age. Rather, the test yields a separate score for each subscale, separate verbal and performance IQ scores, and an overall or full-scale IQ (Figure 9-3).

In devising his scales, Wechsler developed a scoring system that employs a *deviation IQ* score—one in which the score of a given person is located relative to the mean, using the standard deviation as a measure of distance from the mean. If we calculate IQs for a very large number of people, we find that they vary in a systematic way. Like many other individual difference variables, such as weight and height, IQ scores form a *normal distribution*—a bell-shaped curve like that shown in Figure 9-4. Notice that most of the scores cluster near the center of the distribution, which represents the mean (average), median (middle), and mode (most frequently occurring score) of the distribution. Since the normal distribution of IQs is based on some particular population (for example, all U.S. college students), the deviation IQ shows where the person stands relative to the population of which he is a member. Most other tests now use this system, in which the mean is arbitrarily set at 100 and the standard deviation at 15. A person with a score of 115 is exactly one SD above the mean and falls at the 84th percentile; one with an 85 is exactly one SD below and falls at the 16th percentile (see Figure 9-4).33You may want to review the material on the mean and standard deviation in the Appendix

Wechsler and his colleagues have also developed a test for children, the *Wechsler Intelligence Scale for Children* (WISC), and one for pre-schoolers, the *Wechsler Preschool and Primary Scale of Intelligence* (WPPSI). Examination of subscale scores on these tests can lead to a tentative identification of school-related problem areas in a given child (Watkins, 2002). The Wechsler tests have all been widely evaluated in concurrent validity and other studies and found to be both reliable and valid (Burton, 2002; Axelrod, 2002).

Group Tests. Group tests can simultaneously assess the aptitudes of hundreds or thousands of people. They are *paper-and-pencil tests* that can be computer scored, printed, and mailed.

You have no doubt taken—and apparently survived—either the Scholastic Assessment Test (SAT) or the American College Test (ACT) as part of your college admission process. The SAT, which our friend Jose is sweating out, is almost universally used on both coasts of the United States, while the ACT dominates testing in the Rocky Mountains, the Southeast, and the Midwest. The SAT has been modified in recent years. Its name has changed from Scholastic Aptitude Test to Scholastic Assessment Test because it measures both aptitude and achievement. The format has also changed. It long consisted of two major sections, testing verbal and mathematical aptitudes (Table 9-3). The most recent revision provides two separate math scores and adds an essay section.

The SAT was originally standardized on a group of over 10,000 students who took it in 1941 (the annual number now is over 1.5 million). Like IQ scores, SAT scores are arbitrary, and the developers decided on an average score of 500 on each section of the test. It is important to note, however, that 500 on a section of the SAT is not equivalent to an IQ of 100. Those who score 500 on the SAT would score considerably above 100 on an IQ test (probably about 120) because the standardization samples for the two types of tests differ. The IQ tests were normed on samples from the general population, while the SAT was normed on a college-bound population. Anyone who scores above 600 on each section of the SAT (1200 total) is considered quite exceptional.

The ACT has 12 subtests, covering such areas as scientific reasoning, writing skill, and math. It yields separate scores for each and an overall score.

Many other standardized ability tests serve a variety of groups and purposes. If you decide to work for the Federal Government, you will probably take the Professional and Administrative Career Examination (PACE), more popularly referred to as the Civil Service exam. It was originally developed and mandated by the U.S. Civil Service Commission to provide a more uniform way of selecting government employees. Another series of tests was developed to help select recruits and is used by all the military services. The series began with a test developed by Arthur Otis and later modified to become the Army Alpha and Army Beta. The more recent version is the Armed Services Vocational Aptitude Battery (ASVAB).

Reliability and Validity. The major intelligence scales are highly reliable. The WAIS, has a retest reliability coefficient of about .91 and the Stanford-Binet a reliability of about .90.

Validity is more complex. As a general rule, the WAIS correlates about .50 with school grades, but the specific correlations vary considerably with age. Overall, participants with higher WAIS and Stanford-Binet IQ scores get better grades, complete more years of high school, express greater satisfaction with school, and show better job performance, all indications of the predictive validity of the scores. The validity coefficients decrease in size with age and schooling (Laurent et al., 1992), in part because the range or spread of the scores decreases. However, they remain useful as partial predictors of academic performance.

Keys to Intelligence 1

Theories of Intelligence

Basically, intelligence is a *construct*—something abstract that we have to infer from observations we make. As we have seen, those observations often include such things as scores on an IQ test and performance in school. Beyond that, and the idea that we are dealing with the ability to perform on cognitive tasks, psychologists are divided as to the nature of intelligence. There are a number of major theories, each adopting a position on this important issue. Some hypothesize that intelligence represents some kind of *outcome*, either a general ability to reason or several separate factors, each representing a specialized ability. Other theorists view intelligence as a *process*. It may then be seen as the general effectiveness with which the brain processes information or as a set of processing components arranged in a hierarchy.

Intelligence As A General Capacity

In their recent book, *The General Factor of Intelligence: How General Is It?*, Sternberg and Grigorenko (2002), as well as other authors attempt to answer the title question. As they note, many psychologists have theorized that intelligence is best understood as one, general capacity. It can be thought of as overall cognitive ability, global intellect, or simply general intelligence. From this point of view, it is unnecessary, and perhaps inappropriate, to think of it as consisting of more specific components, such as verbal and mathematical intelligence. Alfred Binet certainly subscribed to this school of thought. He was convinced that intelligence is a general capacity for thinking and reasoning that affects the ability to perform well on a wide variety of tasks. His IQ test, though it contained a number of specific subtests, was based on this premise. So was David Wechsler's. The WAIS and its child counterparts also contain a series of subscales, but their developer thought of these as merely a way of tapping into various aspects of global intellect. Research continues to show that general intelligence is an important correlate of performance in a variety of academic and work settings (Tenopyr, 2002).

Intelligence As A Set of Factors

Many psychologists have long questioned the view that intelligence is a general capacity for reasoning and problem solving. Some have allowed for the possibly of general intelligence, but they all believe that it can be broken down into a number of relatively independent parts called *factors*.

Factor analysis is a statistical technique that is used to determine the component parts of intelligence. We typically begin by having each of a large number of participants answer many items or perform on a number of tests designed to tap various aspects of cognitive functioning. We then use factor analysis to identify groups or clusters of items that go together, and these clusters become our factors.

Charles Spearman (1904), who developed factor analysis, also offered a theory of intelligence. He hypothesized that each person possesses both general and specific intelligences (Figure 9-5). Accordingly, when Spearman factor analyzed his data, he found a general intelligence factor that he called g. Your score on this general factor tells us how bright you are overall, across a variety of cognitive tasks. He also found factor analytic evidence for a number of specific factors, each designated as an s. One s might be verbal ability, another spatial perception, and so on. Given Spearman's view, how would we predict your performance in an academic course with a strong verbal component, such as English Literature? We would use your score on g and your score on the s that measures verbal ability.

Louis Thurstone (1938), also a factor analyst, disagreed. He theorized that the emphasis in intelligence testing should be on specific abilities, not general functioning. His *primary mental abilities* approach focused on these specifics. Using factor analysis to search for clusters among 56 different tests, he identified up to a dozen factors in early studies. Eventually he reduced the total to seven that constituted primary abilities. They included verbal comprehension, reasoning, word fluency, number, memory, spatial ability, and perceptual speed (see Table 9-4. Thurstone used his list to develop a battery of tests to measure the seven aspects of intelligence. Called the *Test of Primary Mental Abilities*, it is still used in revised form.

More recent studies have shown that the independent abilities are not quite as autonomous as Thurstone thought. In fact, these studies provide evidence that there is also a general intelligence factor of the sort found by Spearman and assumed in the work of Binet and Wechsler.

Why does the same statistical approach, factor analysis, lead different researchers to arrive at different conclusions? The answer is that the numbers and types of factors you derive from a set of data depend on the type of factor analysis you do and the way you conduct and interpret it. Among major current batteries developed in this way, the Differential Aptitude Test measures eight factors, the General Aptitude Test Battery taps nine, and the Armed Services Vocational Aptitude Battery contains ten. Others go as high as 150 factors.

Intelligence As Information Processing

One of the major current theories of how people reason and solve problems is *information processing theory* (Stratta et al., 1994). It suggests that the person is basically a system for evaluating and acting on information and that the brain, operating like a computer, provides the highest level of processing. We discuss this theory more generally in Chapter 8, but here let's see how it applies to human intelligence.

Binet and Wechsler viewed intelligence as an *outcome*, a kind of final common pathway that is a product of reasoning. We think, we reason, and the outcome is the solution to a problem or the score on an IQ test. But perhaps intelligence is not so much an outcome as the *process* of reasoning itself. If so, a measure of intelligence should focus not so much on a final result as on the manner in which the person goes about solving the problem. That is the view of information processing theory, which must then ask just what aspect of information processing might be the key to intelligence. Is it the speed with which we process information or perhaps our ability to attend closely to the information we are dealing with?

The idea is to get inside the thinking brain and find out how it is going about the process of reasoning in order to solve problems. To get a better sense of information-processing theory, pause for a moment and answer one of the Ask Yourself questions at the end of the chapter. What reasoning *process* did you go through in order to arrive at a response? An extension of this approach might be to conduct a junior high school science fair project: Give some intelligence tests to other students in your school; ask the students to explain how they actually went about thinking in order to answer the questions; report your findings at the science fair. That, in fact, *was* a science fair project conducted by seventh-grader Robert Sternberg, now one of the major intelligence theorists.

Sternberg was basically asking: How do we think? How do we reason? How are such mental processes as memory and attention involved? One possibility—originally Galton's idea—is that what we have long called intelligence is, in fact, primarily the *speed* with which people process information (Jensen, 1993, 2002). Higher processing speeds would allow people to process more complex information and thereby lead to higher IQ scores. In the simplest case, then, speed would essentially define intelligence. Nice idea, but not quite on the mark. Sternberg (1985) found, in fact, that people with higher overall intelligence actually take *longer* to think about each question but do recognize the correct answer more quickly. In other words, it takes them longer to fully comprehend the nature of the problem but then less time to solve it. The overall result may be a faster response, in part because they retrieve needed information from memory more rapidly (Jensen, 2002).

Another possible information-processing answer to the intelligence puzzle is that differences in *attentional capacity* are involved. Perhaps more intelligent people are those who are better able to focus on a task. Our capacity for attending is limited. You can focus on this page, for example, but a favorite song on the radio may cause your attention to shift. A person with greater attentional resources might have a real advantage in solving problems, and this might translate into higher measured intelligence, as Earl Hunt (1980) has suggested. He has some data to support this hypothesis, but we still don't know how large a role attention may play in IQ.

Is intelligence basically the ability to process information? There is certainly evidence that various aspects of our processing capacity at least partially account for IQ (Miller & Vernon, 1992). However, much more research will be needed before we can reach firm conclusions.

Intelligence As A Componential Triararchy

But we are not yet quite finished with the work of Robert Sternberg. In a recent article entitled "In Search of the Zipperump-a-Zoo," Sternberg (2002) points out that intelligence theorists have often asked the wrong questions about IQ and have therefore come up with the wrong answers. His attempt to ask the right questions has led him to take an information-processing approach to building a general theory of intelligence. His view, often called the *triararchic theory of intelligence*, views intelligence as consisting of three major aspects: componential, experiential, and contextual (Sternberg, 1993, 2002; Sternberg et al., 2002). The *componential* or internal world aspect has three major components: metacomponents, knowledge-acquisition components; and performance components (Figure 9-6). *Metacomponents* are the top-level, coordinating components. They transcend the other elements and are involved in such processes as goal-setting and planning. When you have an exam coming up, you are dealing with a problem to be solved. The metacomponents of your intelligence will define the problem, design strategies for solving it, and formulate a general plan of attack.

The *knowledge-acquisition components* subserve the metacomponents to help solve the problem. They include learning and related processes that allow you to acquire new information. In Sternberg's theory, learning is an active process. Ideally, you do not simply "absorb" knowledge; rather, you initiate and carry out active strategies that will help you produce new knowledge and retain it. You will likely do better when preparing for a test if you don't just memorize the book. Instead, you should ask yourself questions about the material, outline what you know, and think about what the author is saying. Intelligence also requires *performance*, and people differ in their ability to perform—to solve mental problems. A good plan, based on the metacomponents, and awareness of relevant information, based on the knowledge-acquisition components, will not be very useful without effective performance components. You need to be able to carry the process all the way through to the final solution of the problem. There are a variety of specific performance components, depending somewhat on the nature of the problem. *Encoding* involves the ability to consider each aspect of a problem and form a symbolic, mental representation of it (usually in words or images). *Inference* is the ability to formulate or discover a general rule that will guide you to a conclusion. *Application* involves mentally using the general rule to explore possible solutions. And *comparison* is the step at which you relate the mentally derived resolution back to the problem and its possible solutions.

The *experiential* aspect interacts with all three of the information-processing components. More familiar tasks are carried out more automatically, whereas novel tasks make heavier demands on intelligence. The *contextual* or external world aspect involves applying experience to the information-processing elements to accomplish three things: adapting to the existing environment; modifying that environment to create a new environment; and choosing new environments. Depending upon the specific situation you face, one or more of these approaches may be more effective than the others.

A highly intelligent person is one who is strong on all three components of the triararchy and therefore has a substantial capacity for processing information. Such a person has unusually good planning ability, acquires new knowledge rapidly and effectively, and uses encoding, inference, application, and comparison to perform exceptionally well in solving problems. People who are strong in one component or another but not in all will be less intelligent than those with strength in all areas. In addition, there is a range of individual variability in the strength of each component. Recent studies have shown that a secondary school curriculum based on the triarchic theory is more effective in improving student performance than more traditional approaches (Grigorenko et al., 2002).

One other theory of intelligence is very new. It is Howard Gardner's interesting hypothesis that we have not one, but several different intelligences. It is called the theory of multiple intelligences and is discussed in our 21 for this chapter.

So What IS Intelligence?

If the wide variety of intelligence theories leave you a bit baffled, be assured that psychologists are also somewhat confused. To conclude that we believe intelligence is probably either one general thing or many specific things—or perhaps both one general and many specific things —hardly clarifies the confusion. What does help is to know that the careful thinking and extensive research done by psychologists has given us considerable understanding of the range of theoretical possibilities. The theories we have outlined are guiding further research, which will lead to a continuing revision of theory. We will move gradually toward an even better understanding of intelligence and its measurement.

Keys to Intelligence 2

The Ups and Downs of Intelligence

A vast majority of people fall fairly close to the middle of the normal distribution of intelligence. What about those who don't, those who fall at the extremes or "tails" of the distribution (see Figure 9-4)? They constitute two relatively small groups in the population, the mentally retarded and the gifted. In addition to considering what is known about these extremes of intellect, we will discuss the relationship of IQ to creativity. Finally, the ups and downs of intelligence can potentially apply to the same individual. In particular, you might wonder whether intellectual functioning varies with age and perhaps whether yours is likely to change as you become older.

Mental Retardation

We used to classify people as retarded entirely on the basis of IQ. In 1959, the American Association on Mental Retardation (AAMR) established a cutoff score of 85, below which anyone was officially considered to be retarded. In 1973 it dropped that cutoff significantly to 70, in part to reduce the number of children federally mandated to receive special education. The change makes it obvious that the criterion is arbitrary and that perhaps IQ alone should not be used to establish a classification of retardation. Indeed, it is easy to observe that some people with a score of 70 (or 85) manage their everyday lives fairly effectively, while others do not. Moreover, some retarded individuals exhibit relatively high levels of social functioning, while others do not.

These observations led the AAMR to add *adaptive behavior* to IQ as a classification criterion, and Federal law now requires that more than IQ be taken into account. Children have their hearing and vision tested, are observed to see how well they can carry out everyday tasks, and undergo a health assessment. In addition, their cultural and language histories are considered. Only if the child has a low IQ and also exhibits deficiencies in the ability to take care of herself and otherwise function on a day-to-day basis should she be classified as mentally retarded.

There are four major ranges or subclasses of retardation. They are based on IQ ranges for simplicity, but behavior must again be taken into account. The subclasses are *mild* (IQs of 50-70), *moderate* (35-49), *severe* (20-34), and *profound* (below 20) retardation (Table 9-6). They constitute 86%, 10%, 4%, and less than 1% of the retarded population, respectively (American Psychiatric Association, 1987). The majority of retarded people can conduct their everyday lives reasonably well, though they rarely develop high levels of skill. They perform mental operations slowly, have less knowledge of the world, and have difficulty solving problems.

Major Causal Factors. It may surprise you to learn that we know very little about the causes of retardation, despite extensive studies (Dosen, 2001). *Organic* retardation, which involves a neural defect, can be clearly diagnosed in only about 25% of all cases (Nass, 1994). Some of these neurological problems are due to conditions that occur during pregnancy, especially the first trimester. Rubella (German measles) in the mother commonly causes damage to the fetus. Other infectious diseases that are dangerous include herpes simplex, syphilis, toxoplasmosis, and cytomegalovirus. Noxious substances consumed during pregnancy can also produce retardation. These include not only alcohol and various illicit drugs, but also such prescription drugs as thalidomide, a morning sickness pill that caused massive damage to fetuses in mothers who took it during the 1960s (Baumeister, 2000). It is for this reason that a vast majority of prescription drugs are not approved for use during pregnancy; there is no safe way to test them in pregnant women. Following birth, retardation can result from blows to the head or infectious diseases like encephalitis and meningitis, which can damage the brain. Such environmental hazards as mercury, found in some fish, and lead, found in some paints, can also produce retardation.

Overshadowing all other organic causes of mental retardation are those involving genes, chromosomes, and their effects on brain structure and neurochemistry (Nokelainen, 2002). The most commonly diagnosed organic cause is trisomy 21 or *Down syndrome.* Named for Langdon Down, the British physician who first described it, this disorder is the result of a chromosomal abnormality in which the individual has one extra chromosome on the 21st pair (Figure 9-13). It is diagnosed in about 1 infant in every 700. The Down child can be mildly or more seriously retarded and will exhibit a defining syndrome of physical characteristics (Dykens, 2000). These include a rounded face, thick tongue, and upward-slanting eyes, as well as congenital heart and motor problems. Behaviorally, the child tends to be friendly and affectionate.

A second genetic cause is *fragile X syndrome,* so-called because the X chromosome can actually break in two in those who inherit this characteristic. Affected children usually have long, thin faces, underdeveloped ears, and, in males, enlarged testicles.

Phenylketonuria (PKU) is inherited on a recessive gene. The infant is normal at birth but soon develops a deficiency of a liver enzyme needed to convert the amino acid phenylalanine to tyrosine. The phenylalanine builds up in the body and causes extensive brain damage, resulting in profound retardation. Several hundred other genetic diseases are also associated with retardation in small percentages of cases.

Some have hypothesized that there are also non-organic cases of retardation involving primarily environments severely lacking in intellectual stimulation and educational opportunity. However, many children exposed to such environments are not at all retarded, raising serious questions about this hypothesis. It is much more likely that in the long run we will be able to identify biological factors that are the primary causes of virtually all retardation.

Dealing With Retardation: Effects on Individual and Society. The American educational system has long spent many hundreds of millions of dollars each year educating retarded children and adults, and a wide variety of programs and strategies have been tried. Unfortunately, however, educators have never found a program that works well for a majority of retarded children beyond simply providing very small classes and massive amounts of individual attention (Turner et al., 1994).

The Gifted

Sir Francis Galton knew the alphabet when he was 18 months old and could easily read any adult book by age 5 (Terman, 1917). He was probably *mentally gifted*—a genius. And the same can be said of such luminaries as Sigmund Freud, Albert Einstein, and Madame Curie. But what is giftedness? It is formally defined as an IQ greater than 130, combined with high scores on tests in one or more areas of achievement, such as reading or mathematics (Fox, 1981). Gifted people also have different styles of thinking than those of average intelligence (Simpson, 1999).

There is some evidence pointing to two different forms of giftedness, general and specific. Most gifted children have a high level of broad intelligence that cuts across a range of abilities and academic subject areas. Some, however, are *prodigies*—children with domain-specific talents. Mozart, for example, was a prodigy; he showed a very high level of musical talent from an early age. From the standpoint of evolutionary psychology, broadly gifted children and prodigies may represent two distinct evolutionary developments that together maximize the probability of human survival (Dewitte, 2002).

We know that gifted people are highly intelligent, but what do they accomplish? A famous case is that of William James Sides, who was admitted to Harvard at age 11 in 1909 and soon became widely known as a "boy genius" (Montour, 1977). Although he later took a faculty position at Rice Institute in Houston, he soon resigned and spent the rest of his life in menial jobs.

While there are certainly other sad stories of genius gone awry, studies show that mentally gifted people do, on average, excel in jobs and in life more generally. The gifted appear to particularly excel in the area of complex reasoning (Simpson, 2002). People with very high IQs often quickly solve perplexing problems that others will work out much more slowly if at all. This ability may account for a number of the reported differences between the gifted and those of normal intelligence.

The most famous research on giftedness is that of Lewis Terman, who selected 1500 California school children with minimum IQs of 135 and a group average of about 150. He and others followed them for sixty years, with periodic tests and interviews (Cravens, 1992). Of the total group, all but 11 graduated from high school, and there were eventually over 240 who received doctorates or law degrees. Beyond these accomplishments, the group as a whole was both physically and mentally healthier than the average person, a finding confirmed by other studies (Devlin, 2002). In addition, Terman's studies put to rest the old stereotype of geniuses as "nerds," social "klutzes" who could not interact appropriately with others. In fact, Terman's gifted people had better social skills and adjustment than the general population (Terman & Oden, 1959).

Similar results come from a more recent longitudinal study of mathematically gifted children. Conducted by Camilla Benbow and Julian Stanley from Johns Hopkins University, the *Study of Mathematically Precocious Youth* set up special programs for adolescents scoring over 700 on the SAT mathematics subtest. A followup ten years later showed that the group had much greater educational accomplishments than the average person. It also confirmed Terman's conclusion that these gifted individuals displayed good social and psychological adjustment (Barnett & Durden, 1993). These results are further supported by studies showing that gifted children do not feel socially isolated and have superior social skills (Sayler & Brookshire, 1993).

Although gifted people have more overall success than others, there are certainly differences within the gifted group, some based on level of education. Michael Pyryt (1993) studied the 100 most and the 100 least successful men from Terman's original sample of geniuses. He found that there was very little difference between the average IQs of the two groups and that they were also similar in most other characteristics. The best single differentiator was educational attainment. The highly successful gifted had significantly higher levels of education than those who were unsuccessful.

Intellectually superior children, like retarded children, have special needs. They can easily become bored with ordinary classroom education and are often pressured by parents to excel. In addition, these bright children are still children. They do not know how to maximally realize their own intellectual potentials, and they do need special help. However, it is only in recent years that we have seen a real effort in the American educational system to address the needs of this group. Research has already demonstrated that many students profit from the programs that have been developed, and the future will no doubt see an intensified effort to address the needs of the gifted.

Creative Genius?

Surprisingly enough, the most intelligent people are not necessarily the most creative. In fact, correlations between IQ and scores on tests of creativity are rarely above +.30 (Rushton, 1990). On the other hand, there is evidence that creativity is unlikely to be high unless the person's IQ is at least 120 (MacKinnnon & Hall, 1972). Some minimal level of intelligence—well above the population mean of 100—is required for creative thinking, but beyond that creativity is fairly independent of general intelligence.

What Is Creativity? Creativity is the ability to develop novel ideas that have some value in the society. Attend any show where inventors display their products and you will see many unusual—but not necessarily useful—devices. For true creativity, both qualities must be present. J.P. Guilford (1959) captured creativity in his classic, three-dimensional model of the structure of intellect (Figure 9-14).

A common way of measuring creativity is in terms of *divergent thinking*, which involves generating multiple, different solutions to the same problem. An item from The Uses Test (Guilford, 1959), for example, might ask you to rapidly generate a list of as many different uses for a hammer as possible. Try it! You no doubt came up with pounding nails and breaking up old furniture, but how about using the hammer as a paper weight or a weapon to be thrown at an intruder. Divergent thinking is also required for the Consequences Test: "Think of what might happen if air travel were suddenly banned."

There is, of course, more to creativity than just divergent thinking. Robert Sternberg (Sternberg & Lubart, 1993), Teresa Amabile (1989) and others have identified several characteristics of the creative intellect.

- *Creative Skills.* To be creative, you must be able to define a problem clearly, engage in divergent thinking, and not be bound by existing or common approaches. You must be capable of considering novel solutions to both old and new problems—going beyond traditional or established ways of viewing situations.
- *Risk Taking.* You must be willing and able to take intellectual risks and persist in your attempts to solve problems. Sigmund Freud, for example, failed in his first major attempt to develop a theory of personality but persevered and started over. He also took the risk of introducing the idea that virtually all behavior is motivated by that of which we are not aware—the unconscious—and insisted, in the face of massive opposition, that his idea was of value.
- *Expertise.* Albert Einstein was one of history's greatest geniuses. His theory of relativity was a highly creative set of propositions that spanned most aspects of the physical sciences. Although Einstein was clearly both intelligent and creative, none of this would have been possible had he not developed expertise in physics.
- *Motivation.* Both Freud and Einstein often worked far into the night to develop their theories, as did inventor Thomas Edison. They were no doubt motivated by interest in their work and the sheer satisfaction they derived from what they were creating. Amabile's research confirms that such *intrinsic motivation* is a component of creativity. In fact, when she offered children extrinsic rewards for producing collages or stories, they were less creative than when she asked them to perform the same tasks without any promise of reward.

Putting these ideas and others together, Robert Sternberg and Todd Lubart (1992) have proposed an investment theory of creativity. They suggest that the most creative people are those who have a novel idea and are willing to invest their time and energies in it, despite the fact that others consider it to be odd or strange. They refer to such a creative process as "buying low" in developing an out-of-favor idea, then later "selling high" after developing their concept further. Based on their approach to creativity, Sternberg and Lubart developed a test that includes assessment tasks covering the domains of drawing, writing, advertising, and science. They have data demonstrating the reliability and construct validity of their instrument.

Lifespan Stability and Change

We have already seen that the major IQ tests have high reliability, but what about stability in the same individual over time? In other words, does IQ change? This question can really be subdivided into two others. First, both parents and educators would like to know whether intelligence measured at an early age can be used predict later scores. The second question is whether intelligence changes over the lifespan. In particular, is there a decline in intelligence in old age?

Early Measurement and Stability.

Consider this testing session:

Examiner: What color is an apple?
Infant (age 2 weeks): Red
Examiner: What is 2 + 2?

Infant: 4
Examiner: Who was the first president of the United States?
Infant: Lincoln

Well, the infant made only one mistake, but....

These might be items from an IQ test for infants that would ideally provide an accurate prediction of their IQs at later ages. Unfortunately, the flaw is that even the most precocious infant cannot give us meaningful responses to anything that resembles a traditional IQ test. We are thus left with the options of either doing nothing or finding some IQ measure that does not involve verbal responses. Since scientists rarely do nothing when an important problem presents itself, psychologists have made many attempts to find some indicator that is measurable during infancy and accurately predicts later intelligence. The Probe describes some of the major efforts.

The Aging IQ. Many older people fear that their intelligence will decrease with increasing age. Early studies addressing this issue were cross-sectional, involving different subjects in each age category, and some later studies were longitudinal, reassessing the same individuals as they aged. The cross-sectional studies showed a definite decline (Doppelt & Wallace, 1955; Wechsler, 1972), but longitudinal designs have yielded aptitude scores that are stable or even increase over the lifespan (Sands, Terry, & Meredith, 1989; Schaie & Geiwitz, 1982) (Figure 9-15). Two Duke University longitudinal studies showed that those who go against the trend and show declining WAIS scores are less likely to survive for the duration of the study than those who maintain their IQs (Busse, 1993).

Both cross-sectional and longitudinal designs have their flaws, so we cannot definitively conclude that IQ does or does not decline with age. However, most authorities currently believe that there is little decrease, at least in most abilities. Warner Schaie, a major theorist and researcher, concludes that there is tremendous individual variability in the tendency for IQ to drop with age (Schaie, 1990). For some, there is a decline in the 50s. For others, no drop is seen until the 60s, 70s, or 80s. In still other cases there is never any apparent falloff at all. This latter group includes primarily those who can process information more rapidly (Hertzog, 2001).

This variability has made it possible to study the causes and effects of decline. On the causal side of the equation, genetic factors are substantial. The Swedish Adoption/Twin Study recently showed that the heritability for IQ accounts for 80% of the variance in aged twin pairs (Pedersen et al., 1992). Another study confirms this genetic component and adds that education is also important (Anstey et al., 1993). More educated people and those who continue to exercise their intellectual talents show less decline. Still other studies show that the only significant factor in maintaining cognitive functions into old age is high socioeconomic status (Aartsen, 2002), which is related to education. Verbal intelligence shows less decrease than nonverbal, and declines tend to show up primarily on timed tests (Schaie & Willis, 1993); Figure 9-15).

Anecdotal evidence that IQ need show no decline is also abundant. Several years ago, for example, the author invited a well-known psychologist to give a talk at his university. Though the psychologist was in his mid-eighties at the time, his talk on highly complex subject-matter was well-organized, accurate, and clearly presented. Moreover, he had published six books and a number of journal articles in the five years prior to his talk. Suffice it to say that no decrease in his intellectual functioning was evident! Similar cases were those of architect Frank Lloyd Wright, who designed the Guggenheim Museum in New York City at age 89, and artist Grandma Moses, who continued to paint even after she had passed age 100.

To further understand the relationship between age and intelligence, Raymond Cattell (1987) identified two factors that represent different kinds of intellect. *Fluid intelligence* is the ability to reason and manipulate information. *Crystallized intelligence* is a base of acquired knowledge and skills, together with the ability to apply this accumulated intellect in solving problems. Your fluid intelligence may have already peaked; Cattell says it reaches its maximum point by age 20. However, crystallized intelligence continues to rise into old age so long as the person is intellectually active (Ryan et al., 2000; Figure 9-16). Thus, a 20-year-old may solve an unfamiliar problem faster than an 80-year-old, but the older person will perform much better within his own area of expertise than the inexperienced 20-year-old is likely to perform in any area. In fact, the 80-year-old may well have much better problem-solving skills than his younger counterpart.

Keys to Intelligence 5

Issues in Human Intelligence

Once aptitude and achievement tests had been developed, they were quickly put to widespread use. School systems, universities, industries, and many other organizations developed assessment policies and often required that everyone be tested initially or periodically. The importance of cognitive testing grew as its applications expanded, and this led to the recognition of a number of issues relating to intelligence. Three of these—gender differences in specific aptitudes, a decline in population aptitude scores over time, and the role of heredity and learning in intelligence—have become centrally important in cognitive psychology.

Gender Differences: Real and Imagined

Do men and women differ in aptitude? There is a certainly a consistent gender bias—a set of stereotypes—that views men as having greater mathematical and spatial skills and women higher verbal intelligence (Quaiser-Pohl, 2002; Saucier, 2002). It causes problems in part because it affects the kinds of jobs for which men and women are viewed as prime candidates and can affect teacher attitudes in school settings.

There is some factual basis for the stereotype (Colom, 2002). Over many studies girls have tended to score higher than boys on the verbal section of the SAT, but boys have higher math scores. They average about 50 points higher, which essentially means that boys give on average four more correct answers than girls. These score differences appear to reflect primarily greater problem-solving performance in boys, since the two groups show little difference in computational ability.

Recent studies suggest that these male-female differences are decreasing (Olszewski-Kubilius, 2002). Both verbal and math scores on some tests have come together, so that neither sex has an advantage. The one exception is the SAT math test. Boys and girls now have approximately equal scores on the verbal section, but boys continue to have significantly higher scores in math (Halpern, 2001).

What do these score differences mean? Do they reflect biological differences between males and females? Perhaps, but then how do we explain the fact that scores on most tests have come together over the years? And what about the observation that girls have higher grades in math courses than boys? These findings and others suggest that the observed sex differences probably reflect, at least in part, differences in social expectations and educational practices (Halpern, 2001), with some basic biological differences still a very real possibility. Both parents and teachers expect boys to have higher math aptitude and may therefore treat the two genders differently.

The Mysterious, Declining SAT.

If the SAT is a valid yardstick of our educational system, we may be in some trouble because scores declined significantly between 1963 and 1980. Since then, verbal scores have flattened out somewhat, while math scores have risen slightly (Figure 9-7). Both scores continue to have some predictive validity for performance in college, but both are still lower overall than they were in earlier decades. Is our educational system really in cardiac arrest or are people just getting less intelligent?

The Flynn Effect. A partial answer to that question is that intelligence is not dropping. Quite the contrary, if anything it appears to be rising. We know this because the major IQ scales are re-normed periodically so that the average score in the population remains at about 100. When the scores of a recent standardization sample were compared with those of the original sample tested in the 1930s, it was found that IQ test performance had *increased,* not decreased. A score of 100 on today's norms would have given you a score of about 130 in that original sample. This increase is called the *Flynn Effect,* after the psychologist who discovered it (Flyn, 1984, 1999).

How do we explain what caused IQ scores to rise while SAT scores were falling? This is a bit like an Agatha Christie mystery, but without the neatly unambiguous ending. Probably part of the answer is that the general population is better educated now than it was in the 1930s. In addition, there is less malnutrition in children, and technological advances, including computers and TV, may be contributing to the upward march of IQ scores (Williams, 1998). However, this is not a simple matter. Given the factors we are aware of, it is very unlikely that human intelligence—however we define it—has actually increased by 30 points in 50 years. Among other things, that would mean that the average person of 50 years ago had an IQ (by current norms) of about 70 and was hence retarded (see Mental Retardation below). The average individual would thus have been hardly able to take care of herself, which we know was not the case. As a result, we must consider the possibility that IQ scores are rising but intelligence is not. After all, our IQ tests are only attempts to measure intelligence, and they may be inadequate.

But Why the SAT Decline? None of this explains why, in the face of rising IQ scores, SAT scores have declined. One factor may be family size. In fact, Robert Zajonc actually predicted in advance that a decrease in family size would stop the drop in SAT scores because parents would have more time to devote to each individual child. Specifically, he predicted in 1976 that the SAT decline would stop in 1980 because by then the "baby boom" generation would have graduated and those taking the SAT would be from smaller families (Zajonc, 1976). Most experts believe that shortcomings in our educational system were also responsible for the decline. Grades became inflated, homework loads were reduced, and textbooks were written at lower levels. In addition, many teachers became disaffected as their ability to maintain discipline was legally reduced, their salaries remained low, and classroom violence became increasingly common. At the same time, there was an increase in households headed by a single parent or with both parents working and a simultaneous increase in student time spent watching television. A formula for educational disaster? Well, it certainly appears that way, and educators are now struggling to bring the SAT scores back up.

Nature vs. Nurture

One of the most important issues in the intelligence field today is the relative role played by genetic and environmental factors. In order to determine the extent to which nature and nurture contribute to intelligence, psychologists and behavior geneticists have carried out a long series of careful scientific investigations. We will consider the results of family, twin, and adoption studies done to arrive at estimates of heritability and environmentality.

Family studies. Considerable evidence supports the conclusion that genetic factors are heavily involved in intelligence. The first line of evidence is from family studies, which confirm that level of intelligence runs in families. Brighter parents have brighter children, and the closer the genetic relationship, the more similar biological relatives are in intelligence (Plomin, 2002). Siblings are more similar to each other than to cousins but closer to cousins than to biologically unrelated people. Of course, this does not prove that the family similarity or *familiality* is hereditary. It may simply be that similar family environments produce similar IQs. However, the high degree of familiality opens the door to behavior genetic studies.

Twin studies. Twin studies have examined intelligence in identical and fraternal twins. A controversial set of early studies was carried out by Sir Cyril Burt (1883-1971), using British twins. He found much higher intelligence correlations in monozygotic (identical) than in dizygotic (fraternal) pairs and concluded that intelligence is predominantly a function of heredity. Many years later, Leon Kamin (1974) undertook a very careful reexamination of Burt's data. Burt had published three separate studies, reporting a correlation of exactly .771 for identical twins in all three cases. Kamin points out it is extremely unlikely that all three correlations would have been precisely the same and that other patterns of results in Burt's studies were also very improbable. He concludes that Burt probably falsified the data. Although the issue was never fully resolved, many psychologists are convinced that the data were very likely fraudulent.

We cannot, of course, allow the problems with the Burt studies to cause us to ignore the possibility that his conclusion was correct. Other psychologists have therefore taken it upon themselves to conduct additional twin studies. These more recent studies, which appear to be scientifically sound, clearly show that agreement (technically called concordance) between IQ scores is significantly higher in identical twins than in fraternals, as Figure 9-8 shows. This means that there is substantial heritability (the influence of heredity) for intelligence. One recent study tested IQs in 209 twin pairs at ages 5, 7, 10 and 12. High concordance was found in identical twins, and IQ was shown to be highly heritable at all ages (Bartels, 2002). The Minnesota Twin Study found a correlation of .71 between the IQs of pairs of identical twins, far higher than correlations for fraternal twins (Lykken, 1982). Another team reported a correlation for monozygotic twins raised together of .86 (Bouchard et al., 1990). In fact, even when identical twins are separated at birth and raised by different parents, their IQs are more highly correlated (above +.60) than those of fraternal twins reared together (Neubauer, 2000).

Adoption Studies. Further evidence comes from adoption studies, which compare the IQs of people who were adopted early in life with those of their biological and adoptive relatives. A genetic contribution to intelligence is indicated when the IQs of biological relatives are closer to those of the adopted person than are the IQs of adoptive relatives. A study of French children showed that their IQ scores correlated much more highly with those of their biological parents than with those of their adoptive parents (Capron & Duyme, 1989). Similar results have been obtained in other studies (Fulker et al., 1988). Moreover, after adopted children have lived with their foster parents for a number of years, the correlation of their IQs with those of their biological parents does not decrease—in fact, it *increases!*

A careful investigation called The Colorado Adoption Study showed that the heritability of intelligence was only .09 at age 1 but had gone up to .36 by age 7 (Fulker et al., 1989). The Texas Adoption Project has reached similar conclusions (Loehlin et al., 1989). In older adults, heritability can be .80 or above. More generally, the IQs of adopted children correlate significantly more highly with those of biological than foster parents (Petrill, 2001). Heredity clearly makes a larger contribution to intelligence than does environment (Tsai, 2002).

Heritability. The overall conclusion from genetic studies of IQ is that heredity accounts for over 50 and perhaps at least 60 percent of the variance in general intelligence (Plomin, 2002). These group heritability estimates do not, however, apply directly to your own IQ score. If your IQ is 120 (the college average), does a heritability of .50 mean that 60 of those IQ points are due to heredity? No. We cannot apply heritability to the IQ of any one person in this way; it is an estimate of the genetic influence on the variability of IQs among many people.

Further research has shown that not only general intelligence, but also specialized verbal, mathematical, and spatial abilities are highly heritable (Quaiser-Pohl, 2002). Other studies have focused on possible genetic mechanisms, with some pointing to the dopamine D2 receptor gene, which influences brain dopamine activity (Tsai, 2002). A further question is just how the genetic predispositions involved in intelligence are expressed. Just what is affected by these "IQ genes?" One answer is that they may influence brain volume or size, and, indeed, smarter people do appear to have bigger brains (Gibson, 2002; Posthuma, 2002). Additional studies, concerned with likely future trends in intelligence, show that people with lower IQs have higher rates of reproduction. This may mean a long-term decrease in the average IQ in the population. However, statistics thus far show that intelligence is slowly rising, and authorities believe there is no cause for alarm (Lam, 1993).

Environmental Factors. How can environment affect something so seemingly basic as intelligence? Let's begin with a classic study done not with humans but with rats. Mark Rosenzweig and David Krech randomly assigned rats to two groups. The animals in one group were housed in a communal cage with other rats and various "toys" to play with. Each rat in the second condition was housed alone in a bleak, isolated cage with nothing but food and water. They found that the neurons of the isolated rats had smaller cell bodies and that the cortex of the brain was not as thick in this group (Rosenzweig, 1984). The enriched environment had actually modified the structure of the brain.

Environmental effects in humans can be seen in some of the same adoption studies that demonstrate the role of genes. The French study that reported evidence of heritability also noted the occurrence of substantial environmentality (the influence of environment). Children from impoverished backgrounds who were adopted into educationally enriched home environments showed IQ increases of 12-15 points (Capron & Duyme, 1989). In the Minnesota Adoption Study, African-American children adopted by white parents of higher socioeconomic status had average IQs of 110, as compared with an average of 90 in similar children reared by their biological parents (Scarr & Weinberg, 1976; Sangwan, 2001) (Figure 9-9). In the same fashion, orphaned children raised by foster parents show higher IQs than do those raised in institutions, presumably because of the more enriched environment of the foster home (Tabassam & Hamayun, 1993). And, finally, facing larger numbers of risks during childhood—a mother with poor mental health, occurrence of major stressful events—has been shown to lower a child's IQ (Sameroff et al., 1993).

Other studies have shown that even the general sociocultural setting in which a child is raised can affect his intelligence. Children raised in rural environments have significantly lower IQs than those who grow up in urban and suburban settings (Coon et al., 1992). Family income is positively correlated with the IQs of children. And children from lower socioeconomic families are 14-17 IQ points below those from higher socioeconomic levels (Bacharach et al., 1998).

These differences may arise from a variety of factors. For one thing, lower incomes are associated with lower parental educational levels. This means that the parents are less likely to be interested in the child's education and less capable of helping with academic work. In addition, even the parent who might want to provide a more educationally enriched environment for her children will not be able to do so if her income is too low to permit purchasing books, educational toys, and the like. A further factor is the existence of motivational differences. Studies show that middle-class families convey to their children a higher degree of motivation to excel in school and to succeed more generally (Hout, 2002). Poverty also brings with it such conditions as poor nutrition, stress, chaotic home and community environments, violence, and less adequate schools, all of which can impair intellectual functioning (Horn, 2002).

We turn finally to the physical environment to learn that toxins and nutritional deficiencies can lower intelligence. Environmental toxins, like the lead in some house paints, have long been known to impair cognitive functioning (Mchaffey, 1992). In addition, deficiencies of vitamins, minerals, and other substances associated with malnutrition during infancy and early childhood impairs neurological development and lowers IQ (Ricciuti, 1993). There is, however, some evidence that healthy eating somewhat later in childhood, combined with an intellectually stimulating environment, can at least partially reverse this early loss (Molfese, 2002). The Critical Thinker describes Project Head Start, which can also produce at least temporary improvements in IQ by enriching the environment.

The Heredity-Environment Interaction. Just to make things a bit more complicated, genes and environment do not each act entirely on their own. As Urie Bronfenbrenner and Stephen Ceci (1994) point out, heredity imposes limitations on the effects of environment. As Figure 9-10 suggests, you inherit a predisposition—an intellectual potential—that places you somewhere on a continuum of intelligence. A highly enriched environment can move you up the continuum somewhat, and a very impoverished environment can move you down. However, there is a limit to how far environmental factors can push you, and the range of potential movement is determined by the heritability of the characteristic, in this case intelligence. A heritability coefficient of .80 would permit little flexibility, and environmental effects would be minimal. A .10 coefficient would provide a very wide range for environmental impact. If heritability is .50 to .60 or so, as with intelligence, the range is fairly narrow, but environment can still have considerable influence (Dickens, 2001).

Beyond the range effect, nature and nurture interact in other ways. Your hereditary characteristics affect the ways in which you experience the world. Your intelligence level, for example, is a major factor in how you process information and thus in what you learn on a day-to-day basis. Suppose we observe two children. Mary inherits a predisposition toward very high intelligence; Beth has a much lower intellectual potential. Both watch an episode of Sesame Street covering the concept of personal safety and the corresponding rules for children. Mary will not only remember the rules better, she will also understand the concept of personal safety more fully and be able to apply it to new situations not specifically covered on Sesame Street. Your intellectual potential also affects the way others treat you. Mary's parents will likely perceive that they can talk to her in more adult language at an earlier age and discuss with her complex concepts and ideas that Beth's parents would not expect her to understand. Thus, Mary's genetic potential will indirectly provide her with better learning experiences from an earlier age.

The Bottom Line. There is clearly good scientific evidence that intelligence is strongly influenced by heredity. We inherit genetic potentials that predispose both our general level of cognitive functioning and our specific abilities, and these predispositions restrict the extent to which environment can affect intelligence (Molfese, 2002). Of course, in somewhat the same way that eyeglasses can correct for genetic nearsightedness, environment can, to some extent, modify intellectual functioning. The bottom line is that scientific research leads us to a three-factor model of influences on cognitive functioning:

- Heredity
- Environment
- The Heredity-Environment Interaction

Keys to Intelligence 3

Controversies in Human Intelligence

The major controversy in the field of human intelligence revolves around the extent to which racial and ethnic differences reflect genetic differences among the groups. To be blunt, are some groups genetically inferior to others? We have already seen that heredity does contribute heavily to intelligence test scores, but that conclusion tells us nothing directly about *group* differences. We will therefore consider how nature and nurture contribute to such group disparities in IQ as those between African-Americans and whites. We will also take up two other controversial issues: Do we abuse test scores by using them improperly; and are tests fair to all who take them?

Minority Groups Have Lower Average IQ Test Scores

African-Americans average 15 points lower on intelligence tests and 100 points lower on both verbal and math sections of the SAT than whites (Bracken et al., 1993; Ogbu, 2002). Mexican Americans, American Indians, and Hispanic Americans also score lower on average than whites, and these differences are highly consistent across studies (Figure 9-11). Moreover, minority subgroups in other areas of the world often have lower intelligence test scores than the majority groups in their countries. A Japanese minority called the Burakumin typically have lower scores than do other Japanese, the Maori in New Zealand score lower than the Europeans in that country, and there are similar discrepancies between Israeli Jews of Middle-Eastern and European descent (Zeidner, 1990).

There is one notable exception to the finding of lower average scores in minority groups. Asians and Asian Americans score slightly higher than white Americans on some IQ tests and on the math section of the SAT (D'Ailly, 1992). Caucasian children also perform poorly in mathematics courses as compared with Asian children, as Harold Stevenson discovered. He and his colleagues studied groups of American and Asian children in the cities of Minneapolis, Taipei in Taiwan, and Sendai in Japan. Americans and Taiwanese started out with almost identical average scores in kindergarten, but American children went down and Taiwanese children up by the fifth grade. Japanese children were well above Americans from the start (Stevenson et al., 1986).

Before examining the basis for these IQ variations, it important to note that the reported differences are *group* differences and tell us nothing about any given individual. Consider coronary heart disease. On average men have heart attacks at earlier ages than their wives. However, in any given married couple, the wife may have a heart attack and her husband may not. By the same token, an African-American teenager may have higher SAT scores than his white classmates, even though group averages for African-Americans are lower.

The major question about racial group differences is whether they are partially or wholly genetic. Let's take a careful look at the genetic and environmental views, then consider the evidence relating to each.

The Genetic Viewpoint: Goddard, Jensen, Shockley, Rushton. Following Galton's lead, Henry Goddard greatly favored a genetic view. In 1912, he became director of intellectual assessment at Ellis Island in New York Harbor, where immigrants to the U.S. were processed. He concluded that most immigrants were of genetically inferior intellect because 83% of Jews, 79% of Italians, 87% of Russians, and 80% of Hungarians scored in the "feebleminded" range on American-developed tests translated into their languages (Goddard, 1917). He later revised his conclusions to suggest that perhaps a mere 40% of these groups were feebleminded! On the basis of Goddard's findings, many immigrants were deported, though the mayor of Chicago, who reportedly also scored in the feebleminded range, was not. It had evidently never occurred to Goddard that poor translations of the tests and differences in cultural and educational backgrounds could account for the group differences in measured IQ.

In much more recent times, Arthur Jensen also argued that racial and ethnic differences in cognitive functioning can best be accounted for by differential heredity. In a 1969 article in the *Harvard Educational Review,* he concluded that the heritability for IQ is about .80, which, he said, means that group differences are attributable to genetics, not environment. This, of course, creates a kind of permanent, genetic second-class citizenry, and Jensen's article lit a firestorm of controversy. He was accused of racism, and there were demonstrations against him when he spoke on college campuses.

But he also had supporters. One of the most vocal was William Shockley (1972), who was not a psychologist but was widely known because he had earlier won the Nobel Prize for his invention of the transistor. Adopting Galton's eugenics, he joined a small cadre of other Nobel winners in donating his sperm to a sperm bank to be used to inseminate highly intelligent women and thereby produce intellectually superior children. He also advocated that the government pay individuals with below-average IQs $1000 per IQ point below 100 to allow themselves to be sterilized. Because this segment of the populace was disproportionately black, Shockley was accused of being not only a racist but a latter day Hitler, trying to create a super race.

While the genetic viewpoint is currently unpopular, Phillippe Rushton (1992) is a strong and vocal advocate for this theory. He points to DNA studies suggesting that the races diverged at different times in evolutionary history, leading to physiologically based differences among them. These include temperament, social organization, and, perhaps most important, brain size, which he sees as substantially accounting for differences in IQ. In a similar vein, Richard Herrnstein and Charles Murray, authors of a controversial book, *The Bell Curve*, support the genetic theory of racial differences in intelligence. They suggest that such hereditary differences between the races determine who in America prospers and who does not, though we should point out that this book has been widely criticized (Shanklin, 2002; Cohen, 2002).

Galton, Goddard, Brigham, Jensen, Shockley, Rushton, Herrnstein, Murray: Were they right? Is the best explanation for group differences in intelligence a genetic one? Before reaching a conclusion, let's look at the environmental view of intellect.

The Environmental Viewpoint. Consider the example of height, a highly heritable characteristic. Around the time of World War II, American men were significantly taller than Japanese men. Now, American and Japanese men have about the same average height because the Japanese have become taller by 3.5 inches (Angoff, 1989). The likely explanation? A change in the Japanese environment that includes much improved nutrition in the decades since the war. In other words, the earlier difference in height was probably due to differences in nutrition and other environmental conditions.

The message in this height example also applies to intelligence and is an important one: Heritability estimates apply to differences among the individuals *within* a group but do not necessarily apply to differences *between* two groups. Variation in height among Japanese men is strongly influenced by heredity: Those with taller parents are likely to be taller. And the same is true for American men. However, the difference in average height between the two groups can be due as much to environmental as to genetic, variation. This means that differences in IQ or aptitude between African-Americans or Asians and Caucasian Americans could be strongly influenced by environmental factors (Block, 2002).

The Jensen controversy helped to generate a variety of empirical studies. Research in the United States has most often focused on the origins of the IQ difference between African Americans and whites. We will touch on two kinds of studies: those relevant to the issue of genetic differences between the groups and those that address environmental differences.

The Genetic Evidence. Rushton cites considerable evidence to support his genetic view. However, a direct attack on this perspective was launched by Sandra Scarr and her colleagues (Scarr et al., 1977). They hypothesized that if racial differences in IQ are genetic, blacks with greater percentages of European ancestry, as compared with African ancestry, should have higher IQ scores. To find out, they used a blood test to determine percentage ancestry for 362 black children in Philadelphia.

They then ran analyses to determine the correlation between degree of European ancestry and scores on several tests of intellectual functioning. The result? There was essentially no relationship between ancestry and any measure of intelligence or aptitude. They therefore concluded that their study did not support a genetic hypothesis. We must caution, however, that it was a correlational study and therefore did not prove any cause-effect relationship (Appendix ___).

A second study was based on the fact that following World War II German women had children fathered by both white and black American soldiers. There was no difference in the average IQs of the two groups of children, again providing no support for a genetic hypothesis (Mackenzie, 1984). A final genetically relevant study focused on differences in skin color within the African-American population. If the genetic hypothesis is correct, we should see higher intelligence in the lighter skinned sample. Results, however, showed no relationship between skin color and IQ).

The Environmental Evidence. Can differences in the average environments of the two racial groups account for discrepant scores on tests of cognitive functioning? The relevant evidence comes primarily from data on group differences in poverty, education, and motivation (Fish, 2002)

Census statistics have consistently shown that African Americans have lower incomes than white Americans. About 8% of white, European-American families have incomes below the poverty line, as compared with about 28% of African American families. Moreover, 33% of African American children as compared with 11% of white children live below the poverty line. And we have already seen that family income is correlated with IQ (Block, 2002).

A second important environmental factor is education. Ceci (1991) reviewed nearly 200 studies and found that the amount of time spent in school can significantly affect IQ scores. Up to 6 points can be lost for each year of school missed. In addition, children who enter school late or attend only sporadically have lower IQs, and those raised in poverty are more strongly affected. Combine these findings with the fact that African Americans have, on average, poor educations as compared with whites and you have another environmental factor that contributes to group differences (Fish, 2002).

Similar environmental factors may also at least partially account for the IQ differences between Asians and Caucasians. Studies show that Asian parents are typically much more attentive to the early education of their children. They create an educational environment in the home, teach children academic skills early, and stress the importance of achievement in school. They also help more with homework and monitor the child's progress closely. The results are apparent in studies of high school graduation rates (Figure 9-12).

If differential education is important, we might expect that more similar educational opportunities will decrease group differences in cognitive test scores—and that is what appears to be happening. The substantial aptitude and achievement differences between African Americans and whites have begun to disappear over the past forty years, perhaps as a function of greater educational equality under desegregation. Both the SAT scores and the reading and math achievement test scores of the two groups are now closer together (Fish, 2002).

A further group difference reflecting environmental factors may be in the area of motivation. One team of scientists studied 15,000 European-, African-, Hispanic-, and Asian-American high school students (Steinberg, et al., 1992). Parents of European- and Asian-American students provided considerably more encouragement for academic achievement than did black and Hispanic parents. Moreover, peers of these latter two minority groups actively *dis*couraged achievement. Doing well in school was considered "selling out" to the white value system.

Group Differences: What Can We Conclude? A recent book entitled *Race and Intelligence: Separating Science From Myth* (Fish, 2002), presents extensive reviews of the literature and the views of a number of experts on this topic. However, even these experts find it difficult to reach firm and final conclusions regarding the origins of group differences in intellectual functioning. It does seem clear that genetic factors alone are unlikely to account for the observed discrepancies and that environmental differences between minority and majority groups can play a substantial role. However, to obtain the scientific answers needed to reach firm conclusions, we must either eliminate the environmental differences or be able to understand and measure them more precisely. Only then can we draw final conclusions concerning the degree of involvement of nature and nurture.

Test Scores: Use or Abuse?

We know that intelligence and aptitude test scores are not flawless: They are not perfectly valid, do not measure all the factors that may be important in school or job settings, and vary from one group to another. In particular, the fact that minority groups tend to have lower scores than Caucasians means that the tests could potentially discriminate against them in some settings, even though the predictive validity is the same for whites and minorities. Ironically, we are therefore forced to ask whether tests developed to reduce subjectivity and thereby discrimination and other forms of abuse may, in fact, be abused. Sources of potential abuse include the use of tests to place and label elementary and high school students and to admit college students. One solution may lie in the use of multiple criteria.

Placement Effects. Children are commonly assigned to achievement-related subgroups on the basis of test scores. The child may be placed in a high, medium, or low reading or math group (barely disguised as "red," "green" and "blue" or "bears," "rabbits" and "squirrels," as though the children don't know the real difference!) on the basis of a test score. Decisions regarding placement in a regular classroom vs. one for "slow learners" or the "gifted and talented" also involve scores.

These obviously important decisions can substantially affect not only the child's short-term educational exposure but her long-term achievement. You will probably one day be the parent of a first-grader—or perhaps you already are. Your child walked early, talked early, knew her colors at age 3 and the alphabet at age 4, and you know from observation that she is a fast learner. Now you find in her backpack a note indicating that she has been tested and placed in the "low" reading group. You may feel that the test was in error or that it should not be the sole basis for this important decision about your daughter—and you could be right.

Placed on a fast track, a child with high intelligence will have maximal opportunity to develop intellectually. In the top reading group or the class for gifted students, he will often have the best available educational materials, the top teachers, and the greatest encouragement to achieve. He will be in a group of other bright students where the educational process moves rapidly, more material is covered, he learns more, and his creativity is encouraged and supported. That very same child placed in a slow group, perhaps because of a testing error, would not progress anywhere nearly as rapidly. The opposite situation is also potentially detrimental. A student placed in a reading group or special classroom that is well above her aptitude level will be likely to struggle unnecessarily and become discouraged. And intelligence test scores alone do not necessarily predict achievement with great accuracy. As Horizon 3 suggests, test scores may also create teacher expectancies, which can affect the child's learning.

College Admissions. In a somewhat different way, concern about the use of scores also applies to the SAT and ACT. These tests are almost universally required as a part of the college admission process. The only question is how they are used, and the truth is that a college admissions office can easily put too much or too little emphasis on the test scores. If heavily emphasized, scores on the standardized tests can reduce admissions of students whose primary talents lie in such areas as art or music or perhaps the creative student who worked through the night before taking the SAT to complete his first-place science fair project. Underemphasizing SAT scores, on the other hand, can admit too many students who will have difficulty keeping up in tough college courses that require high aptitude. Similar concerns apply to job settings. David McClelland (1993), replying to authors who held aptitude testing up as the best predictor of job performance, points out that a number of other important predictors must also be examined.

Improving Prediction: Multiple Criteria. We can improve the accuracy of prediction—at all levels of schooling and on the job—by applying a balanced, multiple-criterion approach to selection and placement combined with periodic reassessment. A teacher, for example, should never rely on test scores alone to place or label students. Rather, she should also look at the student's past performance, review her current work, and periodically reassess each student.

Are Tests Fair?

One possible explanation for group differences in test scores is that the tests themselves are biased. Based on that possibility, in fact, some people have gone to court to argue that IQ tests are unfair and should therefore not be used to place children in special-education classes (Larry P. v. Riles, 1975). Some sources of potential bias in tests include the vocabulary terms employed, group differences in life experience, and the effects of cultural background on item interpretation. We will see, however, that even though tests are often blamed for group differences, they may not be unfair.

Possible Biases. One argument for bias in testing is that the test items may require knowledge of vocabulary that is much more likely to be familiar to members of a cultural majority group. This point is brought home in the reverse situation by items from a test developed in the 1970s specifically for African-Americans (Table 9-5) (Matarazzo & Wiens, 1977).

A similar argument suggests that differential experiences in life may disadvantage minority groups on tests designed by members of the majority group. An African-American growing up in the inner city has a very different set of life experiences than a white growing up in the suburbs (Suzuki, 2001). He may be less likely, for example, to grow up learning that the fork goes to the left of the plate when setting the table, and such differences could cost him points on aptitude tests.

A final problem is that some items may be open to interpretation, depending upon the test-taker's background. This raises the possibility that the correct answer as keyed by the majority-group member writing the test item is not the only correct response. Suppose you were asked to sort into categories a group of objects that included a tomato, a knife, a carrot, a head of lettuce, a machete, a turnip, and a hatchet. You would probably put the vegetables in one group and the cutting implements in another. However, rice farmers in Liberia routinely placed the knife with the vegetables because they commonly use knives to cut vegetables (Segall et al., 1990). Their reasoning was based on their cultural experience, and we can hardly say they are less intelligent because their rational grouping of objects is different.

Killing The Messenger. We are told that in ancient times a messenger who brought bad news was sometimes killed, even though he had nothing to do with creating that news. Many psychologists argue that this is exactly what has happened in the realm of aptitude testing. The tests, as messengers with bad news for certain groups, have been inaccurately blamed. In reality, the test is simply an indication that there are, in fact, group differences. They argue that we should spend our time looking for possible causes of those differences, not blaming the test.

Taking the argument a giant step further, some psychologists have noted the ironic fact that intelligence and aptitude tests were developed specifically to *reduce* the operation of bias. If we allow teachers, college admissions officers, and personnel departments in corporations to make entirely subjective decisions, we are likely to both increase bias and reduce the accuracy of decisions. It is precisely for that reason that the French government originally commissioned Binet to create a standardized intelligence test and that psychologists have continued to develop such tests.

Reducing Bias. Some psychologists have attempted to develop tests specifically intended to reduce or eliminate bias. Early scales contained items that tested primarily spatial and perceptual abilities, thereby eliminating bias due to differences in vocabulary (Davis & Eels, 1953). The Raven Progressive Matrices test, for example, avoids group differences in vocabulary by presenting the person with a series of matrices to be completed by selecting an appropriate pattern from a set of several patterns. This test, however, is also subject to racial group differences, and culture-fair tests more generally have not proven to be the solution psychologists had sought (Pascual-Leone, 2000).

Biased But Not Unfair: The Validity Criterion. Actually, test bias is not nearly the problem some have thought. In fact, a test is biased only to the degree that its validity—its ability to predict performance—is lower for some groups than for others. Intelligence tests are most often normed to predict success in academic settings, and the fact is that they do—across a variety of cultural and ethnic groups. Tests like the SAT have about the *same predictive validity* for African-Americans and other minority groups as they do for whites. People who score higher on the SAT in high school—whether they are black, white, or Hispanic—do better in college than those who score lower. The test predicts academic performance equally well for all ethnic groups.

Based on the extensive data showing equal predictive validity, we can reasonably conclude that aptitude tests may be biased but are not unfair. They may be biased in the sense that certain items can be more easily answered by whites than by minorities. However, these items appear to reflect the realities of the culture: a higher score on an aptitude test does, in fact, predict better school and job performance. It is for that reason that the Committee on Ability Testing of the National Research Council concluded that these aptitude tests are not unfair (Wigdor & Garner, 1982).

The Evolution and Neurophysiology of Intelligence

Intelligence is clearly based in the structures and neurochemistry of the brain. Hereditary factors determine the basic nature of neural structure and function, and environmental experience introduces modifications. Let's examine the evolutionary basis for intelligence and what little we know about the role of the brain.

The Evolution of Intellect

The human brain is a product of millions of years of evolutionary development, so human intelligence is clearly an evolved function (Dewitte, 2002). The question is how and why it evolved and where it may go from here.

The first multicellular, oxygen-breathing species, which inhabited the earth nearly four billion years ago, had no brain at all. However, by about one-half billion years ago, the bony fish appeared. They were equipped with a primitive brain, which further evolved by 250 million years ago, when the reptomammals—creatures with characteristics of both reptiles and mammals— appeared. True mammals, with much more advanced brains, first lived 75-100 million years ago. And the apes—far more intelligent than earlier mammals—evolved about 30 million years ago. They were able to communicate feelings and needs through gestures and facial expression.

Most authorities believe that the earliest humans evolved as one of at least a dozen different types of apes (Joseph, 1993). Ramapithecus, an ape-human that evolved from about 30-15 million years ago, ranged through parts of Africa and Asia. She was probably able to devise such primitive tools as sticks sharpened for digging, a clear sign of increased intellect. After Ramapithecus, the brain underwent very rapid advancement as the evolving human species experienced new and more complex environments to which it had to adapt. About 500,000 years ago, the brain underwent further significant enlargement, with considerable development of the cerebral cortex. Eventually, Homo sapiens (the wise man) appeared, diverging into two human species, Neanderthal and Cro-Magnon, between about 130,000 and 40,000 years ago. Tool-making was now routine, and both species lived in cultural groups. Cro-Magnon, the more intelligent of the two, had a much enlarged frontal cortex and was capable of complex speech, artistic expression, and self-consciousness. He built houses, lived in villages for mutual protection and benefit, devised clothing and weapons, became an accomplished hunter, and developed spiritual beliefs (Figure 9-17).

As humans have been forced to adapt to changing environments, the enlargement of the brain, and particularly the development of the cortex, has continued since Cro-Magnon. Some theories suggest that such neurological evolution may occur as neuron structures and synapses are modified by learning and environmental interaction more generally (Adams, 2002). The frontal cortex—the seat of complex thought—has evolved rapidly as humans have met the demands of diverse social, cognitive, and physical environments. Indeed, social interaction alone—whether in maintaining a friendship or avoiding global war—involves a complex interplay of cognitions and emotions. One interesting theory suggests that the neural development underlying human intellect is, in part, a product of the need for Machiavellian intelligence—the ability to deceive and plot against others in order to survive (Bradshaw & Rogers, 1993). More positive social demands must also be met, and cortical structures and functions that effectively serve such needs have survived the adaptive test of evolution.

Intellect has evolved for millions of years, and there is every reason to predict that it will continue to do so. The only question is whether the rapid evolutionary pace of the past 500,000 years will continue.

The Neurological Basis of Intelligence

There is no doubt that evolution has provided a genetic basis for the brain functions involved in intelligence, as we saw earlier in the chapter. The questions are just what brain structures and functions are affected by this hereditary factor and how they are modified by learning and experience.

Unfortunately, we thus far have no good answers, in part because intelligence is such a complex construct and in part because of the likely intricacies of the brain functions involved. However, there are two ongoing attempts determine the neural basis for intelligence.

Brain Structure and Intelligence. Much of what we know about brain structures that may be involved in intelligence comes from studies of learning, memory, and cognition. First, it is likely that the *prefrontal cortex* is heavily involved in the complex cognitive processing that we call intelligence. Differences in the size or form of this important area are almost certainly one product of differential heredity for intelligence. In addition, environmental experience probably produces systematic changes in the prefrontal area.

A number of other brain structures also seem to be involved Figure 9-18). The temporal cortex appears to be important in the learning of complex responses and probably in consolidating memories, the somatosensory cortex has also been implicated in some studies (Gur et al., 1993). In addition, a number of subcortical structures may contribute to intelligence: The hippocampus is active in the learning of simple responses and in at least short-term memory, both of which contribute to measured intelligence; the cerebellum may be important in learning motor responses, which contribute to the performance aspects of IQ; and such other structures as the amygdala and thalamus have also been implicated in some studies. A final structural feature is the individual synapse. Changes in the structure of the synapse as learning takes place may partially account for the contribution of environmental factors to intelligence (Adams, 2002). In addition, overall brain volume is correlated with IQ (Gibson, 2002)

Neurochemistry. Intellectual functioning also appears to involve the complex neurochemical substrates of the brain. In particular, acetylcholine is the neurotransmitter at many of the synapses in areas likely to be involved in intelligence (Diaz-del-Guante et al., 1993). Other brain chemicals may include DNA, RNA, and quite likely a number of other neurotransmitters.

Intelligence As A Neural Network

Most neuroscientists are now convinced that intelligence does not lie in any one, small area of the brain. Rather, it is spread over a number of structures, including those we have just discussed. But how do these scattered areas operate in concert to mediate intellectual functioning? The principal answer to date comes from *connectionist models,* which suggest that we acquire, process, and store information by establishing systematic neural associations or connections, such that one element of the network can provide a cue that triggers off the others. From this perspective, variations in intelligence may involve the differential formation, complexity, and interconnection of neural networks (Posthuma, 2002). The highly intelligent person may be one who forms networks more rapidly, is capable of developing more complex networks, forms appropriate connections among networks more readily, or some combination of these.

And what about Jose, who was sweating out the SAT as the chapter began? Well, if we had known that he was consistently placed in the highest reading and math groups in school and that his parents were both hard-driving professionals, we might have predicted that he would do well. We would have guessed that his SAT scores would be easily high enough to get him admitted to the college he had chosen—and they were.

Conclusion

Since the very beginnings of interest in intelligence and its measurement in the work of Galton and Binet, we have learned much. We know that IQ is strongly influenced by heredity but is also subject to environmental effects. We know how to test aptitude reliably and validly. We know that test scores can greatly improve our accuracy and objectivity, though they should not be the sole basis for important decisions. And we know that the differences among groups are influenced by environmental factors, though heredity may also be involved. What we do not yet know—or at least agree on—is just what intelligence is. What comprises human intellect? How can we even better test for it? And what are the best uses for IQ in situations involving decisions about individuals? These are among the major questions for our continuing work on this important construct in the 21st century. We will test the various theories we have outlined and perhaps develop some new ones, and we will continue to work on direct neurological testing and other new approaches.

Summary

Testing . . . Testing . . .

1. Psychological tests provide standardized measures of individual differences. Tests are given to predict behavior and improve accuracy.
2. Advantages of testing include accuracy, efficiency, quantitative comparisons, and standardization.
3. Test standardization involves the development of norms. Tests must be reliable and valid. Types of reliability include test-retest, alternate form, and split-half. Types of validity include content, criterion-related, predictive, and construct.
4. Major early contributors to the development of intelligence testing were Galton, Binet, and Terman. The Stanford-Binet remains one of the major, individual IQ tests.
5. Aptitude and achievement tests measure what you can accomplish and what you have accomplished, respectively.
6. The Wechsler scales, with their verbal and performance subscales, are the most widely used of modern, individual intelligence tests.
7. Group tests like the SAT permit the efficient testing of large numbers of people. They have good reliability and reasonable validity.

Theories of Intelligence

1. Binet and Wechsler hypothesized that intelligence is a general cognitive capacity, an outcome that is a product of reasoning.
2. Spearman opted for one general and several specific factors, while Thurstone found seven specific factors but no general factor.

3. **Information-processing theory sees intelligence as a process of reasoning, with differences reflecting such variables as speed and attentional capacity.**
4. **Sternberg proposes a triararchic, componential theory. The three aspects are metacomponents, knowledge-acquisition components, and performance components.**
5. **Gardner hypothesizes multiple, separate intelligences that operate independently.**

Issues in Human Intelligence

1. **SAT scores have declined, probably as a result of our educational system. IQ scores have risen, probably in part because the general population is better educated.**
2. **Boys score higher on standardized math and girls on verbal tests. Both biological and environmental explanations have been offered.**
3. **Family, twin, and adoption studies all show that genetic factors account for 50 to 60 percent of the variance in IQ. The role of environment has been shown in adoption studies and in work relating IQ to family income. Heredity and environment also interactively influence intelligence.**

Controversies in Human Intelligence

1. **Minority groups have lower IQ test scores, and this has been the basis for a major controversy in intelligence.**
2. **Arthur Jensen and others have argued that group differences are due primarily to genetic factors. Some evidence does support that view.**
3. **Currently more popular is the environmental view of group differences: Blacks have lower incomes, poorer educations, and fewer sources of positive motivation than whites. Sandra Scarr and others have mustered considerable evidence to support this view.**
4. **We cannot yet draw firm conclusions as to the roles of heredity and environment in group differences.**
5. **Some tests are biased due to group differences in vocabulary, life experience, and background relative to the items. However, the major tests are still fair in that they reflect the realities of the culture and have the same predictive validity for African-Americans and whites.**
6. **Tests can be used to mislabel children or be overemphasized in college admissions or other settings. It is therefore important to use multiple criteria in any setting where testing is employed.**

The Ups and Downs of Intelligence

1. **Mental retardation is determined by considering both IQ and adaptive behavior. The subclasses of retardation are mild, moderate, severe, and profound. Most retarded people are in the mild range.**
2. **The organic causes of retardation include Down Syndrome and fragile-X syndrome, and phenylketonuria, all involving genes and chromosomes, as well as effects on the fetus during pregnancy caused by the mother's illness or use of noxious substances.**
3. **The two forms of giftedness are general and specific. Gifted people excel in jobs, social skills, and in generally.**
4. **Gifted children, like retarded children, have special needs, and the American educational has only recently moved toward effectively addressing those needs.**
5. **Creativity requires some minimal but high IQ. However, the overall correlation between creativity and IQ is not great.**
6. **Characteristics of the creative intellect include creative skills, risk taking, expertise, and motivation.**
7. **Developing tests that can be used in infants to predict later IQ has proven difficult, though there are some promising possibilities.**
8. **Cross-sectional studies show declines in IQ with age, while longitudinal studies generally do not.**
9. **Overall, evidence suggests that IQ declines with age in some people but not in others and that some aspects of IQ decline more than others.**

The Evolution and Neurophysiology of Intelligence

1. **Mammals first appeared bout 75-100 million years ago and apes about 30 million.**

2. Significant brain enlargement began about 500,000 years ago.
3. Homo sapiens diverged into Neanderthal and the more intelligent Cro-Magnon between about 130,000 and 40,000 years ago.
4. The principal brain structures involved in the most complex aspects of intellectual functioning may be the prefrontal cortex.
5. Other structures may include temporal and somatosensory cortex, the hippocampus, and the cerebellum.
6. Neural networks may interlink the various brain areas to provide for overall intellectual functioning.

Ask Yourself

1. Discuss the major considerations in developing a "good" test.
2. Discuss the difference between IQ score determination in Binet's original test and the current method for deriving IQs.
3. What are the advantages and disadvantages of individual and group IQ tests?
4. Is intelligence a general capacity or a set of components? Take and defend a position.
5. In what ways does Sternberg's componential triarchy differ from the earlier theories of Spearman and Thurstone?
6. What implications does evolutionary psychology have for the current neural mechanisms of intelligence and the future of human intellectual functioning?
7. Why does the fact that intelligence is strongly influenced by genetics not necessarily mean that racial differences in IQ represent differing racial heredities?
8. How can we conclude that tests can be biased but not unfair?
9. What is the likely relationship between IQ and creativity?
10. Does intelligence decline in old age? Take and defend a position.

Key Terms

Achievement test
alternate form reliability
American College Test (ACT)
Aptitude test
Connectionism
Construct
Construct validity
Content validity
Creativity
Criterion-related validity
Crystallized intelligence
divergent thinking
Down syndrome
Environmentality
eugenics
Factor analysis
familiality
Fluid intelligence
Fragile-X syndrome
Giftedness
Heritability
Individual differences
Information-processing theory
intelligence quotient (IQ)
Intelligence

knowledge-acquisition components
Mental retardation
metacomponents
Multiple intelligences
Neural network
Norm
normal distribution
Parallel distributed processing
performance components
Phenylketonuria
Predictive validity
Primary mental abilities
Prodigy
Psychological test
Reliability
savant syndrome
Scholastic Assessment Test (SAT)
split-half reliability
Standardization
Teacher-expectancy effects
test-retest reliability
Triararchic theory
Validity
Wechsler Adult Intelligence Scale (WAIS)

Further Readings

Anstey, K, Stankov, L., & Lord, S. (1993). Primary aging, secondary aging, and intelligence. *Psychology and Aging*, 8, 562-570. The authors report a well-designed study of the factors that contribute to declining intelligence with age.

Brody, N. (1992). *Intelligence.* San Diego: Academic Press. In this useful book, Nathan Brody provides a detailed review of much of what we currently know about the origins and nature of intelligence.

Coon, H., Carey, G., & Fulker, D. (1992). Community influences on cognitive ability. *Intelligence*, 16, 169-188. Using the Colorado Adoption Project sample, the authors demonstrate an effect of specific community variables on IQ over and above the influence of heredity.

Davis, R. (1993). Biological tests of intelligence as culture fair. *American Psychologist*, 48, 695-696. Commenting on another article, Davis makes a solid case for the eventual use of neurological tests of intelligence as the culture-fair standard.

Hamilton, S. (1993). Identifying African American gifted children using a behavioral assessment technique: The Gifted Children Locator. *Journal of Black Psychology*, 19, 63-76. The author reports on the development and use of an interesting new instrument that provides a possible alternative or adjunct to IQ testing for locating the gifted.

Locurto, C. (1991). *Sense and nonsense about IQ: The case for uniqueness.* N.Y.: Praeger. Locurto puts IQ in perspective, trying to strike a balance between heredity-oriented and environment-oriented views of IQ.

Pyrrt, M. (1993). The fulfillment of promise revisited: A discriminant analysis of factors predicting success in the Terman study. *Roeper Review*, 15, 178-179. The author provides an interesting, recent followup on the work of Lewis Terman with his sample of geniuses.

Richardson, K. (1991). *Understanding intelligence.* Milton Keynes, England: Open University Press. In this interesting book Richardson provides a critical review of what we know about intelligence, contrasting popular views with a view from a rigorous, scientific perspective.

Sternberg, R., & Lubart, T., (1993). Investing in creativity. *Psychological Inquiry*, 4, 229-232. This article by one of the major theorists, Robert Sternberg, details in clear language his new theory of creative intelligence.

Psychology in the 21st Century

Multiple Intelligences

You may have seen the movie *Rain Man*, the true story of a person who did not display high traditional intelligence but was exceptionally skilled in limited areas. It is, in part, from such cases that Howard Gardner's (1985, 2002) theory arises. Gardner studied cases of people with *savant syndrome*, in which the person has one or two exceptional abilities but low general intelligence. Some savants can recall long strings of numbers, others have exceptional musical or artistic skills, and still others have extremely good spatial memory or calculation abilities. Each, Gardner says, is displaying a form of intelligence.

Gardner argues that there are *multiple intelligences*, each independent of the others (Gardner, 2002). This may sound a bit like Thurstone, but Thurstone's theory is based on factor analysis and calls for multiple abilities that together make up a more general form of intelligence. Gardner maintains that his multiple intelligences operate quite independently; they are truly separate kinds of intellect. In fact, his is a *modular* approach. It suggests that each separate intelligence will eventually be found in a separate module or area of the brain, which has evolved multiple intelligences as a way of better adapting to a complex, multi-component environment. His approach is consistent with more general evolutionary theories of cognition that hypothesize neural modules performing specific functions (Cosmides & Tooby, 1994; see Chapter 8). Gardner and the evolutionary theorists present 21st-century cognitive neuroscientists with the task of identifying these neural modules.

What Gardner is saying is that we cannot accurately or usefully conceptualize intelligence as one, single thing—the kind of general ability implied by the single IQ score on traditional tests. Instead, there are a number of different competencies, each of which can reasonably be called a form of intelligence. You can be successful in life to the extent that you are high in the particular intelligences that are valued by your culture.

How many intelligences are there? At least seven, according to Gardner (see Table). Three of them are not new. They have long been assessed by the major IQ tests and include linguistic, logical-mathematical, and spatial intelligences. The remaining four are not traditionally tested, yet they are equally as important as the others in carrying out life's tasks. A person with high musical intelligence—someone like Beethoven or Mozart—can carry on a most productive and effective life even if relatively low in some other areas. Similarly, someone with high interpersonal intelligence may compensate for other shortcomings by easily maintaining effective relationships with others. It may well be that we will be required to rethink our entire conceptualization of intelligence. In fact, if Gardner's theory—still too new to be fully evaluated—is right, we may have been walking for many years down a path of general intelligence that leads to a dead end!

The Critical Thinker

Does Head Start Give IQ a Head Start?

In 1965, Congress approved funding for Project Head Start, a part of President Lyndon Johnson's War on Poverty. Head Start began as an 8-week summer program for a small number of children; it had grown to a year-round enrichment program that now targets about 600,000 children each year, primarily from poverty-stricken families.

The content of Head Start programs varies considerably. Most provide basic medical and dental checkups and immunizations, as well as hot meals. In some programs teachers and other professionals regularly go into the home to work with the preschooler and the parents. The child's environment becomes more orderly and predictable, and she is directly educated from an early age in somewhat the same way that middle-class parents educate their children. In other programs the child goes off to nursery school and gets an early start on both academic and social education. Health and nutrition are often also emphasized, and the low-income child is treated more like a child from a higher-income family. Parents may or may not actively participate in the program, and this seems to make little difference in the child's later academic achievement (White et al., 1992). In early programs children learned rhymes, were read to, and spent time drawing and coloring with crayons, learning about birds and animals, and playing with puzzles, blocks, and educational toys. More recent offerings have included intensive, direct-education programs, where children learn reading, arithmetic, and language.

The Basic Hypothesis or Contention

Project Head Start was based on the theory that environment, particularly early environment, significantly affects intelligence. The more specific hypothesis is that enriching the environment of an impoverished child 2-5 years old can boost his level of intellectual functioning. Measured IQ should increase significantly, and the child should do better in school and perhaps other areas of life as well.

What Is the Evidence?

One of the earliest studies of Head Start, conducted by the Westinghouse Learning Corporation and Ohio University (1973), demonstrated a statistically significant increase in the IQs of children in the program. Other early studies showed that Head Start children were better able to learn language, showed greater intellectual curiosity, and were more attentive than neighborhood children not in Head Start. Head Start students were also shown to have higher reading and math scores, exhibit less antisocial behavior, and be less likely to be held back in school (Watkins-Emonet, 2001; Locurto, 1991).

Other findings are more mixed and less hopeful. On the positive side, some studies show that Head Start participation is associated with more constructive attitudes toward achievement and perhaps with reduced delinquency and less welfare assistance. On the other hand, the Westinghouse/Ohio University (1973) study showed that the IQ gains did not hold up over time. Moreover, even at their IQ peak following the program, Head Start children continue to score 5-15 points below the national average and below their grade level on achievement tests.

Large-scale studies are also discouraging (Warr-Leeper, 2001). A review of over 1000 programs confirms that the positive effects of Head Start on IQ decrease after one to two years (Lee et al., 1990), perhaps in part because of decreases in motivation. If that is the principal result of Head Start interventions, we might well question the advisability of spending billions of taxpayer dollars on such programs. A gain that lasts for only a short time, one could argue, is not a real gain at all, and the money would be better invested in some other way. Moreover, programs other than Head Start have also failed to make a lasting difference. The Infant Health and Development Program, which uses a variety of early interventions in an effort to raise intelligence and prevent retardation has failed to make any difference (Baumeister, 2000).

Is the Evidence Open to Alternative Interpretations?

The harshest interpretation of the evidence—the one we have already hinted at—is that early intervention programs simply cannot produce long-term gains in intellectual functioning. An alternative explanation might consider the possible reasons for that finding. Head Start personnel may provide external motivation while the child is actually in the program. However, after he leaves it and goes off to school, he remains in an environment of parents, siblings, and peers who may not encourage achievement, causing his scores to drop. Moreover, we cannot realistically expect a part-time program to substitute for full-time parenting. The middle-income child is typically provided with educational opportunities and encouragement seven days a week, whereas the low-income Head Start child is afforded such advantages only a few hours a week (Schnur, 2000).

Based on this explanation for the IQ loss in Head Start followups, the Carolina Abecedarian Project took on the challenge of providing a much more intensive intervention. Children were chosen from welfare families, usually headed by a single mother who had a low IQ (70-85). Children entered the project by the time they were 12 weeks old and stayed in it for five years. Half the children—the control group—received only medical care, dietary supplements, and social services. The other half—the experimental group—received these same interventions, but also participated in an intensive, educational day-care program that ran from 7:15 a.m. to 5: 15 p.m. five days a week.

Early results showed substantial IQ gains in the experimental group. Children in that condition had IQs considerably above those of the control group. Moreover, by age 3, the daycare children were slightly above the national average IQ. It thus appears that the program raised IQs and kept them up for at least five years. The overall implication is that longer-term, more intensive early educational efforts might produce the lasting gains Head Start had hoped for.

Do We Need Additional Evidence?

Programs like the Carolina Abecedarian Project are very expensive. This means that it would be unwise to attempt such programs on a national scale until we can be sure that they will produce substantial, meaningful, lasting gains. We need to know that the IQ increases will hold up over many years and that the child will do better in and beyond school. We also need to know about other possible program benefits, such as reductions in teen pregnancy, delinquency, welfare usage, and school dropout, and enhancements of educational attitudes and career potential. Finally, it would be helpful to know whether there are more efficient, less costly ways to accomplish the same ends. Could we potentially raise IQs just as much and achieve other gains with programs costing far less than the intensive Carolina project?

What Conclusions Can We Reach?

Head Start has clearly not met the original challenge of permanently raising the levels of intellectual functioning of children born in poverty. Moreover, its results have by no means provided unqualified support for the role of environmental factors in intelligence. However, we must be cautious in reaching final conclusions because of the nature of typical Head Start programs. It may eventually be possible to show that intensive educational programs that start very early in life and continue for long periods can produce lasting IQ gains.

Probe

The Intelligent Infant: How Can We Know?

Ever wonder how intelligent an infant is? Well, psychologists have because it would be helpful to parents and educators alike to know early in life just how intelligent a person is likely to be later on. Many potential predictors of later intelligence have been examined. For example, a larger head and hence perhaps a larger brain might be predictive of higher IQ. Head circumference during infancy might therefore be indicative of later intelligence. Interesting idea, but it didn't work, even though brain size later in life is correlated with IQ [RTF bookmark start: }BM_1_[RTF bookmark end: }BM_1_(Gibson, 2002). What about birth weight or the age at which the infant sits up, crawls, or walks? Unfortunately, these measures also fail to predict IQ at later ages. Another approach uses a set of measures called the Bayley Mental Development Index (BMDI). In one study Linda Siegel (1992) administered some of the BMDI subscales to infants at ages 4, 8, 12, 18, and 24 months. They provided some prediction of IQ measured with the WISC at ages 6, 7, and 8 years, but again the prediction was not very accurate. A book dealing with the issue of intellectual stability and containing several relevant reviews makes it quite clear that most attempts at measuring infant intelligence have failed (Bradley-Johnson, 2001).

Despite the string of failed attempts, one recent approach does show promise. It is based on the hypothesis that attention to and memory for novel auditory and visual stimuli during infancy may predict later IQ. One measurement method is based on the idea that more intelligent infants will become bored more easily. Hence, infants who prefer to look at new pictures rather than pictures they have just seen may be more intelligent, and it appears that they are. Such infants have higher IQs on intelligence tests administered years later (Sigman, 2000). Similarly, visual memory performance at 6 months of age predicts IQ at 6 years of age quite well. While these must still be considered preliminary results, they do give some hope that we can develop fairly accurate infant predictors of later IQ.

In an effort to further explore the stability issue, investigators have conducted longitudinal studies in which IQ is measured annually from age 1 through age 18. Intelligence measured at age 18 was considered to be a good indication of what IQ would be throughout adulthood and therefore was used as the criterion to be predicted by earlier IQ measurements. Test scores at very early ages (1-3) were not good predictors of the age 18 criterion IQ. However, by age 4 the correlation of about .45 is fairly predictive, and it continues to rise, becoming a good predictor by age 7 and a very good one by age 9. These findings have been confirmed by more recent research testing children at ages 4 and 13. This basically means that IQ measures taken in kindergarten and the first 3 grades are reasonably good to very good indicators of later intelligence, while measurements in the first 3 years of life are not. Of course, the new approaches involving attention and memory may soon provide better early estimates.

Some investigators have compared aptitude scores within the range of adulthood. Suppose we tested students at age 18 and then tested them again at least four years later. How stable would the aptitude scores be? We can easily find out because many students take the SAT in the senior year of high school and the Graduate Record Examination (GRE) in or after their senior year of college. Taking advantage of this convenient situation, one investigator obtained SAT and GRE verbal and math scores on 23,000 students (Angoff, 1988). The SAT verbal score correlated +.86 with the GRE verbal scale, and an identical correlation of +.86 was found between the SAT and GRE math subscales. This clearly indicates a high degree of aptitude stability.

Horizons in Intelligence

The SAT Coach

We have football coaches and baseball coaches. Why not SAT coaches? When you were about to take the SAT in high school, you may well have studied for it. Perhaps you even took a course to prepare yourself. But does such coaching actually work? The answer is that it may help, but only in some very basic ways. It teaches you some test-taking techniques and familiarizes you with the nature of the items, the answer sheet format, and the testing procedures. Did you know, for example, that it is better to guess the answer on an SAT item if you can narrow it down to 2 or 3 possibilities because a correct answer scores +1 point, while an incorrect answer scores only -1/4 point? Or did you know that it's OK to choose the obvious answer in the early part of any SAT section because the obvious answer is the correct one. However, late in the section, nearly 80% get the answer wrong, and the correct answer is usually not the obvious one.

Beyond these basics, the effect of SAT coaching or study is typically minimal because the skills and knowledge needed to answer test items must be learned over a period of years. Early studies did suggest gains of 50-80 points from coaching, but they used no control groups and gave participants lengthy, intensive training courses of several months duration (Pallone, 1961; Marron, 1965). More recent studies show average gains of only about 14 points on the verbal section and 30 points or less in math. Remember that each section goes up to 800 possible points, so these gains are unlikely to make the crucial difference in getting you into college.

Brains and IQs

We would probably all agree that intelligence is located somewhere in the brain. If so, perhaps some direct measurement of neural functioning could provide an unbiased test of just how intelligent you are (Davis, 1993). The most recent attempts to develop unbiased tests are accordingly based on the assumption that differences in IQ may be reflected in structural or functional differences in the brain. One possibility is that the corpus callosum, which connects the two hemispheres of the brain, is larger in more intelligent people, presumably because cognitive processing would improve with better or more extensive connections. Preliminary studies, in which the size of the corpus callosum is assessed using magnetic resonance imaging (MRI), does support such a positive relationship (Strauss et al., 1994). Other studies find relationships between IQ and measures derived from single photon emission computed tomography (SPECT) scans of the brain or electroencephalography (EEG; Kao et al., 1994).

This is a very new approach to intelligence testing, and it will be many years before routine practical applications are possible. However, if reliable, valid neurological measures of IQ can be developed, we will have made a major advance in both the assessment and understanding of human intelligence.

Can Teacher-Expectations Bias Learning?

Might a child do better—or worse—in school just because a teacher *thinks* he will? Robert Rosenthal and Lenore Jacobson (1968), in a classic but controversial study, hypothesized that test-score *labels* also affect how children are treated. They gave elementary school students a test that teachers were told could identify those who were about to enter a period of "blooming," during which they would show rapid academic progress. The children listed as "bloomers" were, in fact, randomly selected. About two-thirds of them nonetheless showed an IQ increment of twenty points or more by the following year, while most children in a control group did not. The authors concluded that being told the children were "bloomers" had produced *teacher expectancy effects*—changes in a teacher's behavior toward a child based on knowledge of the test scores.

Although some studies have found expectancy effects to be minimal or nonexistent, others do show them. Children identified to teachers as exceptionally bright are encouraged more and provided with a wider variety of achievement experiences, while those labeled as dull are not (Blatchford et al., 1989). Since results are mixed, we have no final answers concerning labeling and expectancy effects in the classroom. However, it seems likely that at least some busy teachers with limited time and large classes may provide better educations for students they believe are bright and interested. Since minority students on average have lower test scores, such score-based teacher-expectancy effects may have implications for unintentional differential treatment of minority and majority group children.

Key Terms 1

achievement test
alternate form reliability
American College Test (ACT)
aptitude test
construct validity
content validity
criterion-related validity
individual difference
intelligence quotient (IQ)
intelligence
norm
normal distribution
predictive validity
psychological test
reliability
Scholastic Assessment Test (SAT)
split-half reliability
standardization

Key People

Alfred Binet
Lewis Terman
David Wechsler
Sir Francis Galton

Key Terms 2

construct
factor analysis
information-processing theory
knowledge-acquisition components
metacomponents
multiple intelligences
performance components
primary mental abilities
savant syndrome
triarchic theory
validity
Wechsler Adult Intelligence Scale (WAIS)

Key People

Howard Gardner
Charles Spearman
Robert Sternberg
Louis Thurstone

Key Terms 3

eugenics
familiality

Key People

Sir Cyril Burt

Key Terms 4

teacher-expectancy effects

Key People

Henry Goddard
Arthur Jensen
Phillipe Rushton
William Shockley

Key Terms 5

creativity
crystallized intelligence
divergent thinking
Down syndrome
fluid intelligence
fragile-X syndrome
mental retardation
phenylketonuria (PKU)
prodigy

Key People

Langdon Down
Warner Schaie
Raymond B. Cattell

Key Terms 6

connectionism
Cro-Magnon
Homo sapiens
Neanderthal
neural network
prefrontal cortex

Referencces

Darlington, K. (1991). *The long-term effects of model preschool programs.* In L. Okagaki & R. Sternberg (Eds.), Directors of development: Influences on the development of children's thinking. Hillsdale, NJ: Erlbaum.

Horn, J., & Donaldson, G. (1980). *Cognitive development II: Adulthood development of human abilities.* OM P/G/ Bro, & K/ Lagam (Eds.). Constancy and change in human development: A volume of review essays. Cambridge, MA: Harvard U. Press.

Kaufman, A., Reynolds, C.R., & McLean, J.E. (1989). Age and WAIS-R intelligence in a national sample of adults in the 20-74-year age range: A cross-sectional analysis with educational level controlled. *Intelligence*, 13, 235-253.

Schaie, K., & Strother, C.R. (1968). A cross-sequential study of age changes in cognitive behavior *Psychological Bulletin*, 70, 671-680.

Schaie, K., (1989). Age difference pasterns of psychometric intelligence in adulthood: Generalizability within and across ability domains. *Psychology and Aging*, 8, 44-55.

McGue, M., Bouchard, T., Iacono, W., & Lykken, D., (1993). Behavioral genetics of cognitive ability: A lifespan perspective. In R. Plomin & G.E. McClearn (Eds.), *Nature, nurture, and psychology.* Washington, DC: American Psychological Association.

College Board. (1994). Highlights of the 1994 college-bound seniors national report. N.Y.: College Board.

Sue, S., & Okazaki, S. (1990). Asian-American educational achievements: A phenomenon in search of an explanation. *American Psychologist*, 45, 913-920.

Schaie, K., & Willis, S. (1993). Age difference patterns of psychometric intelligence in adulthood: Generalizability within and across ability domains. *Psychology and aging*, 8, 44-55.

Chapter 10

Life-Span Development: Infancy and Childhood

Outline

Lifespan Development: The Journey Begins

A Lifetime of Development

The Lifespan Emphasis

Nature Versus Nurture

Developmental Continuity

Individuality: Are We Unique?

Nature and Nurture in Human Development

Heredity vs. Environment: Opposing Camps Find a Middle Ground

One-Half Plus One-Half = One: Genetic Principles

Behavior Genetics

Evolution and Development: Genes and Environments Interact

From Zygote to Newborn to Infant: Early Development

Where Danger Lurks: The Uterine Environment

The Newborn: Sensing and Perceiving the World

Responsiveness and Intellectual Development

Learning in the Newborn

Forming Emotional Bonds: Attachment

Cognitive Development in Infancy and Childhood

Jean Piaget: The Child's Approach to the World

Piaget's Stages of Cognitive Development

Was Piaget Right?

Beyond Piaget: Cognitive Development in the 1990s

Lawrence Kohlberg: The Development of Moral Reasoning

Personality Development in Infancy and Childhood

Freud's Theory of Psychosexual Development

Erikson's Theory of Psychosocial Development

Are There Discrete Stages?

Contexts of Development: Parent and Child

The Neurophysiology of Development

Prenatal Neural Development

Physiological Maturation

Critical Periods

Networking

WE BEGIN life as single cells, the products of genetic material contributed by our mothers and fathers. But even as early as the first few days of embryonic development, environmental forces begin to affect how this simple aggregate of cells will become a fetus and then a viable infant. Thus, from the moment of conception both heredity and environment interact to produce a human being. Throughout infancy and childhood this interaction continues, playing a role in physical, cognitive, and emotional development. In this chapter we examine the basic genetic and environmental factors involved in the development of the fetus, the newborn, the infant, and the child. But development continues over the entire lifespan, so we address issues of development in adolescence, adulthood, and aging in Chapter 11.

The Drama Unfolds

Mark could hear the urgent screams of at least two approaching ambulance sirens as he brought his ancient Ford to a quick, jerky stop in front of the large electric doors of the emergency room. Beside him, Valerie sucked in her breath and tensed as yet another labor pain racked her body. The drama of human birth had begun.

Once inside the hospital, a nurse produced a wheelchair, and a young doctor asked about the spacing of the pains. Val was then whisked off to one of the hospital's modern birthing rooms. A few hours later, dressed in gown and mask, Mark held Val's hand as the obstetrician instructed her to "push," and the drama of birth itself was under way. Finally, the tiny baby was expelled from the dark, warm, protective prenatal environment of the uterus into a bright, cold, noisy world. As soon his head appeared, the obstetrician aspirated mucus from his mouth by suction so that the newborn could breathe. The umbilical cord, through which the baby had received oxygen and nutrition during intrauterine life, was clamped and cut. Since bacteria naturally occurring in the vagina can cause eye infections, silver nitrate was dropped into the baby's eyes, and he was given an injection of vitamin K so that his blood would clot properly if he should bleed.

Val and Mark were not concerned about possible birth defects because of the tests performed early in the pregnancy. They were more concerned about ensuring that the baby would grow up to be a bright, emotionally stable child.

Life-Span Development: The Journey Begins

With conception and birth, we all embark—as did Val and Mark's baby—on what Raymond Cattell has called "a strangely brief pilgrimage from oblivion to oblivion," a dramatic journey through time and space, a journey that will last precisely one lifetime. The journey is continuous, but it is punctuated by special events—first steps, first words, first days of school, first loves, first jobs, perhaps marriage and divorce—and death.

You have probably seen an infant, an older child, an adolescent, an adult, and an aged adult together. Did you realize that each represents, in a sense, a stage in your own development? The infant, who cannot walk or talk, will become a walking, talking child, the child an accomplished adolescent, the adolescent a mature adult, and the adult an aged citizen.

The Lifespan Emphasis

You could not step twice into the same river.
HERACLITUS, *On The Universe*, Fragment 20

In this famous line, Heraclitus (540-480 B.C.) captured the essence of human development—and the reason we study it. Like a flowing river, each human being is continuously changing, never the same, as the developmental process goes forward.

Until the 1970s, the focus of the field of developmental psychology was on infancy and childhood. Then came a pronounced upswing in research on development over the entire life span, including adolescence, adulthood, and aging. As a result, modern developmental psychology deals with patterns and sequences of change in behavior over the full span of life (Kagan, 2002; Lewis, 2000). So important is this new emphasis that one of its pioneers, Warner Schaie, has received the prestigious Award for Distinguished Scientific Contributions given by the American Psychological Association (*American Psychologist*, 1993).

It was William Wordsworth who gave us the famous line "The child is father of the man." Wordsworth was a poet, but he could well have been a developmental psychologist, for his statement succinctly expresses the theme and basis for the study of human development. The adult human being is very much the product of her childhood. Every accomplishment, every thought process, every moral value, every emotional tendency is, in part, a developmental product of early life. The child is indeed the "parent" of the adult.

Although developmental psychology spans a great breadth and depth of concerns, three classic theoretical issues are part of virtually every discussion of developmental processes: the nature-nurture controversy, the continuity of development, and the uniqueness of the individual.

Nature Versus Nurture

In 1970 most U.S. psychologists were convinced that the development of human cognition, emotion, and personality is influenced almost exclusively by such environmental factors as learning and stress. By 1990 it had become clear that genetic and related biological factors are at least equally as important. Both personality and intellect are clearly interactive products of heredity and environment (Smith et al., In Press). This change reflects current thinking about one of the oldest and most pervasive questions in the history of philosophical, physiological, and psychological thought: Is a given aspect of human behavior due to heredity, to environment, or to some combination of the two? In brief, to what extent is it a product of nature and of nurture? We raise this centrally important question in Chapter 1 and will address it here in more detail.

Developmental Continuity

Is development continuous or discontinuous? Be careful! Before you answer, think about what you were like five years ago and what you are like now. Do you have the same basic traits and skill areas? If you were generally better in English composition than many of your classmates but not as good in math, is that still true? If your answer to these questions is yes, it would seem that development is continuous. If no, it would seem to be discontinuous, as in the moth that was once a cocoon and before that a larva.

Jerome Kagan (1980), a widely respected developmental psychologist, notes that there are several ways of defining continuity. First, continuity may imply sameness on a given trait over time. If you were an extravert as a child and still are now, that implies continuity. Continuity can also refer to your own relative standing on different characteristics. If you had better verbal than mathematical skills in elementary school and now excel in your English course but struggle in your math course, that would imply continuity. Finally, continuity may be defined in terms of your standing relative to other people. If you were among the two or three most extraverted children in your second-grade class and are now among the most extraverted people in your peer group, that would imply continuity.

On an anecdotal level, you might conclude that you have always been better at English than math, implying continuity, but that you have become much more extraverted in recent years than you were as a child, implying discontinuity. Some psychologists have argued that continuity is really not very plausible when we compare individuals of very different ages (Baltes, 1982). For example, infants seem to focus their time and effort on playing, often do "socially inappropriate" things, and are not very fluent in language. Adults, of course, exhibit the opposite characteristics. To some, it seems clear that these observations imply discontinuity. At the same time, psychologists like Raymond B. Cattell (1973) have carefully studied the same traits in children and adults and found evidence for a high degree of consistency. You can see why the continuity-discontinuity issue continues to be controversial.

Individuality: Are We Unique?

Growing up in the late twentieth century, you have already heard the axiom that "Every individual is a unique, living being. No two people are alike." We certainly like to think of ourselves as unique, as having our own special qualities. However, the question is not as simple as it might seem. Perhaps you don't look *exactly* like anyone else you know, and perhaps no one else seems to have *exactly* your particular set of personality traits. However, if everyone were truly unique, it would be impossible to formulate general principles of developmental change. The fact that we can formulate such principles forces us to conclude that individual uniqueness occurs primarily because people exhibit different *patterns* of the same basic attributes. The elements of development are the same in all people, but they may be combined in unique ways in a given individual.

Although the continuity and individuality questions are certainly central in developmental psychology, the nature-nurture issue is really the overriding concern. If we can determine the relative roles of heredity and environment, we will go a long way toward a full understanding of the developmental process.

Nature and Nurture in Human Development

Developmental psychology now clearly recognizes that both genetics and learning—both nature and nurture—play significant roles in human development. Each human being enters the world already equipped with a set of genetic tendencies, then undergoes a lifetime of experience that interacts with those tendencies to influence behavior. Indeed, the aging process itself is subject to both genetic and environmental influences (Finkel et al., 1995). Let's examine two broad, opposing historical theories before exploring the interrelated roles of heredity and environment. We will then consider the field of behavior genetics and the interaction of evolution with individual development.

Heredity vs. Environment

My son and I sound almost exactly alike on the telephone, a source of some amusement when unknowing callers begin to conduct a conversation with the wrong person. More generally, we often hear people say "He has his mother's eyes" or "She has her father's nose." You no doubt attribute such physical similarities at least largely to genetic factors. But what about: "He comes from a musical family" or "She's obstinate, just like her mother"? You may tend to attribute such parent-child similarities in skills and personality primarily to environmental factors: The child learns from the parent. But is that the best explanation?

Historical Positions: Environmentalism. For most of the twentieth century, psychology has been dominated by environmentalism, which insists that behavior is learned and that environment largely determines human personality and behavior. This view can be traced back to the influential writings of the seventeenth-century English philosopher John Locke, who theorized that the mind of a newborn child is a *tabula rasa*, or blank slate, ready to be written on by experience. Locke's concept reappeared early in this century in the writings of several psychologists, particularly the noted behaviorist John B. Watson. Watson explicitly rejected heredity and asserted that learning is the source of all behavior. His brand of behaviorism is captured in a famous statement made in 1930:

> *Give me a dozen healthy infants, well formed, and my own specified world to bring them up in and I'll guarantee to take any one at random and train him to become any type of specialist I might select—doctor, lawyer, artist, merchant-chief, and yes even beggarman and thief, regardless of his talents, penchants, tendencies, abilities, vocations, and race of his ancestors (Watson, 1930, p. 104).*

Watson studied infants, becoming the first to film newborn reflexes, like the startle reflex. He also wrote a book on child rearing and made a movie teach medical students about child development. Following Watson's lead, many psychologists began to develop theories and carry out research based on the assumption that behavior is acquired. Those few who continued to insist that biological factors might be important were branded as heretics. Learning-oriented theories gained great momentum, and for decades environmentalism almost totally dominated the field.

Historical Positions: Instinct Theory. If environmentalism is the extreme view that learning causes all behavior, *instinct theory* is its opposite: heredity is the source of most behavior. The most prominent early psychologist to subscribe to this position was William McDougall (1908), who held that by far the most important determinants of individual conduct are instincts—inherited tendencies to perceive and behave in particular ways. He believed, for example, that people have instincts for curiosity, self-assertion, gregariousness, and pugnacity (aggressiveness), among many others.

The form of instinct theory advocated by McDougall and such other noted psychologists as William James was soon rejected because studies began to show clear environmental effects. However, modern *ethologists*—researchers who study the origins of complex behavior patterns in animals—remain interested in the study of instinctual bases for both simple and complex behaviors. Their basic position is that both instinct and learning play important roles in development. For example, birds instinctively attack potential nest predators, but how do they "know" a predator when they see one? The answer appears to be that they learn to recognize predators by observing the actions of other birds. In one study a German ethologist put two groups of blackbirds on opposite sides of a hall where they could see each other. Between the two groups he placed a box divided in such a way that one group of birds could see an owl (which blackbirds commonly attack) while the other group could see only an unfamiliar bird called an Australian honeyguide. The birds seeing the owl immediately attempted to attack it. The birds on the other side followed suit by trying to attack the honeyguide. These birds then passed on to future generations of blackbirds the practice of attacking honeyguides (Gould, 1982). Both genetics and learning were involved at various points in the process. But do humans have instincts defined as the ethologists define them? Probably not. There is currently no good evidence for the influence of instincts on human behavior.

One-Half Plus One-Half = One: Genetic Principles

Since ancient times, human beings have been fascinated with the question of how living organisms transmit characteristics to their offspring. In the fifth century B.C., Hippocrates hypothesized that tiny elements from all parts of the parental body are concentrated in the semen and thereby passed on to the child. Less than a century later, Aristotle offered an alternative view that was a remarkably insightful and modern genetic theory. He suggested that the semen contains not body elements but rather a *design* for the formation of offspring. Unfortunately, this essentially accurate theory was ignored for some twenty-three centuries. Even the Renaissance, which saw major scientific developments in other fields, produced a most inaccurate theory of heredity. Called *preformation theory*, it suggested that human development begins with a tiny preformed midget, or *homunculus* (little person), present in the semen of the father or the blood of the mother. Finally, in the mid-nineteenth century, the Augustinian monk Gregor Mendel performed his classic experiments with pea plants and formulated the basic principles of modern genetics. We'll briefly discuss such important genetic concepts as genes and chromosomes, dominant and recessive transmission, genotypes and phenotypes, and the roles of mutation and polygenic transmission.

Genes and Chromosomes: The Human Genome. Genes are segments of DNA (deoxyribonucleic acid) that constitute the basic units of genetic transmission and are found in every cell in the body. Thousands of genes are grouped together on each *chromosome*—a long, coiled strand of DNA that carries and organizes genetic information. As would be the case with Val and Mark's baby, every cell in the body contains 23 pairs of chromosomes (Figure 10-1). One chromosome in each pair comes from the mother, the other from the father. Since over 8 million random combinations of sex cells (sperm or eggs) are possible in each parent, there are about 70 trillion potential patterns when egg and sperm join. That is why no two siblings, other than identical twins (which are produced from the same fertilized egg), have the same characteristics.

Dominant and Recessive Genes. Since chromosomes are in pairs, so are the genes they contain. For each genetic characteristic, there are thus two possible genes, one contributed by each parent. The *dominant* gene is the one that will be expressed when the two genes are different (Figure 10-2). The *recessive* gene is the one that will not. The simplest case is one in which a single gene pair determines a characteristic. The pair is *homozygous* if the child receives the same gene from both parents and *heterozygous* if he receives the dominant gene from one parent and the recessive gene from the other. Eye color is a good example. If both genes in the eye-color pair code for the same color, the child's eyes will be that color. If the two genes code for different colors, the dominant gene will be expressed. Brown, for example, is dominant over blue, so the child with a brown-blue gene pair will have brown eyes. Table 10-1 provides other examples of dominant and recessive characteristics.

While the dominance principle applies to many instances of genetic transmission, it is not universal. Sometimes both genes are expressed, as in the case of type AB blood. Sometimes two genes merge to produce an intermediate characteristic, as when you cross certain red and white flowers of the same kind and get pink flowers.

Genotype and Phenotype. Just to complicate matters a bit, two parents with brown eyes can have a child with blue eyes. But how is that possible? Because it is not the parents' actual eye color but their *genes* that determine the child's eye color. Brown-eyed parents can have recessive blue-eye genes, which can pair in some of their offspring to produce blue eyes, whereas other offspring will have brown eyes. If we see someone with brown eyes, then, how do we know whether their color is the result of pairing two brown-eye genes or one brown (which is dominant) and one blue? The answer is that we don't. That realization forced geneticists to distinguish between genotypes and phenotypes.

Your *genotype* is your basic genetic makeup. It is determined at conception and can never change. Your *phenotype* consists of your actual, manifest characteristics—the expression of the genotype. Phenotypes can, to some extent, be modified by the environment. Height, for example, is highly heritable, but it is also influenced by nutrition and other factors, so two people with identical hereditary (genotypic) heights could end up somewhat different in actual (phenotypic) height. The phenotype is what we see, the genotype is what we do not. We know the person's eyes are brown (her phenotype), but we do not know whether the underlying genotype involves two brown genes or one brown and one blue.

Mutation and Polygenic Transmission. Unfortunately, the basic Mendelian principles account for only a relatively small proportion of human characteristics. Others are affected by *mutations*—modifications of the genetic code that represent errors during DNA replication (Zhang et al., 2002). They can occur as apparently spontaneous changes or under the influence of environmental factors, such as radiation. Many geneticists believe that mutations are ultimately responsible for all genetic variation that occurs over the course of evolution.

Another complication is *polygenic* transmission, in which a number of gene pairs act together to determine a single phenotypic trait. One difference between single-gene and polygenic transmission is that the latter produces much more variable trait heredity. If eye color is transmitted on one gene, is likely to be either brown or blue, not some color in between. However, a polygenic trait can vary along a continuum that ranges from low to high. Height and skin color, for example, are polygenically transmitted and therefore variable (Figure 10-3).

Most genetically influenced human characteristics are transmitted polygenically (McKusick & Amberger, 1993). Many physical traits, like motor coordination and susceptibility to heart disease, pass polygenically from generation to generation (Zdravkovic et al., 2002). And virtually all psychological traits, like extroversion-introversion and susceptibility to depression, involve multiple genes.

The Human Genome Project. Our understanding of genetic transmission has advanced to the point where we now have not only a good understanding of the process but a complete gene map that will tell us exactly which genes affect which characteristics. In order to complete that map, Victor McKusick (2001) and many other investigators pursued one of the largest international scientific endeavors ever undertaken, the Human Genome Project (van Ommen, 2002; Chiche et al., 2002). The map of the genome is helping investigators determine which specific genes and combinations of genes cause each normal and abnormal characteristic of the individual (Aldrich, 2002).

Behavior Genetics

Direct investigation of the heredity/environment interaction has depended heavily on work over the past several decades in the field of behavior genetics. Researchers in this discipline study a variety of behavior patterns in an effort to determine the relative influence of heredity, environment, and their interaction (Pedersen, 2002). Research suggests, for example, that alcoholism may be influenced by genetic factors, as we discuss in Chapter 5. This does not mean, of course, that alcoholism can occur without consuming alcohol. Genes do not alone cause the behavior to occur, but they can produce a neural sensitivity to alcohol, and an individual with this sensitivity who does drink is more likely to become an alcoholic. Behavior geneticists determine the heritability and environmentality of a trait using family, twin, and adoption methods.

Heritability and Environmentality. Your temperament, emotional reactions, and cognitive abilities are all significantly influenced by the tendencies you inherit from your parents. The extent to which a given trait or characteristic is determined by genetic factors is called *heritability*. In the language of the behavior geneticist, it is the proportion of variability in the phenotype of a population that can be attributed to variations in genotype. Put simply, it is the amount of influence genetic factors have on the trait in question. Heritability can vary from 0.00 to 1.00. A heritability of 0.00 would mean that there is no genetic influence, 1.00 would mean that all the influence is genetic, and 0.50 would mean that half the variance is genetic. *Environmentality* is the proportion of phenotypic variation that can be attributed to environmental variation.

Combining the heritability and environmentality concepts, which are really two sides of the same coin, we can see how individual differences are explained by the behavior geneticist. For a given trait or characteristic, studies may show, for example, that heritability is 0.60 and environmentality 0.30. This means that the extent to which you have that trait is determined 60 percent by genetic factors and 30 percent by environmental factors. The remaining 10 percent of the determinants remain unexplained.

It appears that many aspects of behavior are influenced by genetics (Glazier, 2002; Rijsdijk et al., 2002). Important examples include your level of social anxiety, your capacity to handle stress, your level of empathy—your ability to feel what another person is feeling emotionally—and the extent to which you are extraverted or outgoing (Stein et al., 2002; Bouchard & Loehlin, 2002). The term "extroversion" is actually used to denote the full continuum running from extreme extroversion to extreme introversion.

Psychologists can measure the degree to which you are extraverted by having you answer the items on a personality scale like the Eysenck Personality Questionnaire. Studies show that this personality trait is highly heritable, with rates ranging from .50 to .74 (Bookman et al., 2002; Eysenck, 1992; Eaves and Eysenck, 1977). More generally, research suggests that at least 50% of the variation in personality is genetic (Borkenau et al., 2001; Bouchard, 1994). Research has also confirmed that even your basic tendency to respond to the environment—your temperament—is strongly influenced by genetic factors, as the Probe describes.

Family Studies. Although there might be days when you would like to deny it, you probably have many personality and behavioral patterns that are very similar to those of one or both of your parents. One approach used by behavior geneticists to study the heritability and environmentality of a trait is to select a person who displays the trait in question and investigate his relatives to discover the degree of family resemblance or *familiarity* for the trait.

Unfortunately, simple estimates of familiarity cannot tell the researcher for certain just what contribution heredity makes, since it is impossible to rule out the influence of environmental factors. Because family members live together, interact regularly, and are subject to the same environment, they are likely to be similar regardless of genetic background. Thus, family studies are not generally regarded as final evidence of the degree of genetic contribution but rather as providing an estimate of the *upper limits* of heritability. In other words, heritability is unlikely to be greater than familiarity.

Consider the example of schizophrenia, a severe psychological disorder in which the person loses contact with reality and has hallucinations (such as hearing voices) and delusions (such as believing that people are out to get him). Family studies show that siblings of schizophrenics are about seven times more likely to exhibit this disorder than people who are not related to schizophrenics (Wickham et al., 2002). Similarly, 71% of obsessive-compulsive children have at least one parent with that diagnosis (Byrne et al., 2002; Riddle et al., 1990). Both disorders clearly have substantial familiarity and thus may have a hereditary component.

Twin Studies. Twins are perhaps as special to the behavior geneticist as they are to their parents, for they are essential to most major studies of heritability. There are two kinds of twins, *monozygotic* (identical) and *dizygotic* (fraternal). Monozygotic twins develop from a single fertilized egg and are genetically identical; dizygotic twins develop from two separately fertilized eggs and are no more similar genetically than any two non-twin siblings (Figure 10-4).

The basic question asked in twin studies is whether the degree of agreement, or *concordance*, for a given trait is greater in identical twins than it is in fraternal twins. The difference in concordances between the two types of twins can be used to determine the heritability of the trait in question (Sullivan & Eaves, 2002). Consider height and weight as examples. The heights and weights of two identical twins are much closer than the heights and weights of two fraternal twins (Coady et al., 2002). As a result, the heritability for height is about .90 and that for weight is about .85, demonstrating that genetic factors strongly influence these two physical measures (Choy et al., 2002; Arya et al., 2002).

In a representative study of schizophrenia in twins, concordance rates of 48% for identical twins and only 4% for fraternal twins were found (Onstad et al., 1991). In other words, in pairs of identical twins where one twin is schizophrenic, there is about a 48 percent chance that the other twin will also be schizophrenic, but in fraternal twins, the chance is only 4 percent. A variety of other psychological disorders, as well as normal personality traits, similarly show higher degrees of concordance in identical twins, even when they are reared apart (Hur & Bouchard, 1995). Behavior geneticists interpret such data to mean that there is evidence for genetic factors in whatever trait is being studied (Cardno et al., 2002).

Adoption Studies. The other major approach used in behavior genetic research is the *adoption study.* The basic procedure is straightforward. The researcher begins with a large group of adopted people and selects those with the particular trait being studied. She also chooses a control group of adoptees who do not have the trait. Because all the subjects are adopted, each has two sets of parents, biological and adoptive, who might be called "environmental parents." The task is to find out whether the biological or environmental parents exhibit the particular behavior in question (Tienari et al., 2000).

To conduct an adoption study of schizophrenia, Kety and his colleagues (1976) identified a group of adoptees who had previously been diagnosed as schizophrenic and an otherwise similar control group whose records showed no history of abnormal behavior. The researchers examined both the biological and adoptive parents and siblings of all participants and found that 12 percent of the biological relatives of schizophrenics but only 3 percent of adoptive family members had it. For control participants, there was no difference between biological and adoptive relatives. These results strongly suggest the presence of a genetic factor in this disorder, and other studies have achieved similar results (Kety & Ingraham, 1992; Cannon & Mednick, 1993).

Evolution and Development: Genes and Environments Interact

The development of the individual human being and the evolution of the human species are intricately interrelated, but they are not the same. The distinction we make is between *ontogeny*—the lifelong growth and development of one person—and *phylogeny*—the evolutionary history of the species. Individuals *develop*, but do not evolve; species *evolve*, but do not develop. Nevertheless, individual development is a product of the phylogeny of the species and contributes to its continued evolution.

The process of individual development involves an ongoing interaction between genes and the environment. The individual's genetic endowment—her genotype—is immutably established at the moment of conception. From that point on, genetically programmed development takes place in an ecological context, and the developmental process therefore proceeds as a joint function of the genotype and the environment. Some environmental factors are found within the individual (but outside the genes themselves). Hormones like testosterone and estrogen would be an example. Both physical and psychosocial elements in the external environment are also important. Temperature, for example, can affect the way genes are expressed. If the temperature in the egg containing an American alligator is less than 30o C, the alligator will be female; if greater than 34o, it will be male. Other environmental factors include nutrition and the presence of toxins. A person with a genetic tendency toward obesity will more easily gain weight if he consumes a high calorie diet (see Chapter 12), and puberty in girls requires having a minimum total of body fat, which is also affected by diet. The effect of environmental toxins is dramatically seen in cases of *fetal alcohol syndrome*, in which prenatal exposure to alcohol causes reduced brain size and retardation (Hankin, 2002). Finally, intellectual and social experience can affect developmental sequences that are genetically programmed. Intellectually enriched environments, for example, can produce higher IQs (Rosenzweig, 1984; Weinberg et al., 1992), as we discuss in Chapter 9).

The interactive developmental process means that phenotypes will be similar to the degree that both genetic inheritance and environment are similar. This is perhaps most obvious in the case of identical twins. Their behavior patterns are more nearly identical when they are raised together than when they are raised in separate foster homes, even though their genotypes are exactly the same.

It seems clear that the genetically designed lifelong developmental process involves a continuing effort to adapt to the environment. The success of that adaptation hinges on genetic endowment, and successful adaptation means greater reproductive success: those who survive and adapt are more likely to reproduce. The end result is that those genes contributing to increased reproductive success are passed on selectively and disproportionately to future generations. The ontogenetic development of the individual has contributed to the phylogenetic evolution of the species. And, coming full circle, later generations of individuals will be born with modified genetic endowments that interact with new environments in an unending process of evolution.

Most psychologists have now come to share the view that patterns of behavior typically develop as interactive products of genetics and environment (see Figure 10-5). Although this view represents a dramatic departure from the strict environmentalism of an earlier era, it does not suggest that most human behavior is inherited, as some critics have implied (Markon et al., 2002). Rather, it proposes that individuals may inherit a *predisposition*—a tendency—toward certain behavior patterns. That predisposition limits the range of environmental effects: The stronger the hereditary predisposition, the less environment can affect the behavior (see Chapter 9). To the extent that environment can have an effect, it influences the degree to which and the ways in which the predisposition is expressed. A person who has a hereditary tendency to be extraverted may be raised by extraverted parents or reinforced for outgoing activities and therefore be highly extraverted as an adult. But if that same person is raised by more introverted parents or rewarded for primarily nonsocial activities, she will be somewhat less extraverted as an adult. How much environmental factors can affect the trait depends on the strength of the hereditary tendency.

From Zygote to Newborn to Infant: Early Development

You began life not as a baby, a fetus, or even an embryo, but as just one cell called a zygote, the result of the union of egg and sperm. Once the infant-to-be has embedded in the uterine wall nine or ten days after conception, it is referred to as an embryo. During the next six or seven weeks, the embryo develops from a ball of cells into a recognizable little one-inch creature, with arms, legs, fingers, toes, and a very large head. Beginning with the third month, the organism is referred to as a fetus. By this time, rudimentary versions of all organ systems have appeared, and the rest of prenatal life is devoted to growth and the maturation of these systems to a point where survival outside the mother's body is possible. After reviewing the nature and role of the uterine environment, we'll turn to the motor development of the infant, the sophisticated perceptions of the newborn, her intellectual development, and the role of learning and attachment.

Where Danger Lurks: The Uterine Environment

Under normal conditions, the uterus provides an ideal environment for prenatal development. In this warm, comfortable setting, the embryo is provided with nutrients and protected from many sources of potential harm. However, harm can come from a number of maternal conditions and teratogens—environmental agents that can cause damage or death. Among these potentially harmful factors are maternal malnutrition, drug use, drinking, smoking, and stress (Schubert et al., 2002; Ivanovic et al., 2002; see Table 10-2).

The teratogenic effects of drugs were dramatically demonstrated in the early 1960s, when babies with grossly deformed limbs and other defects were born to thousands of women (primarily in Europe) who had taken the tranquilizing drug thalidomide early in their pregnancies. Although 70% of developmental defects are still of unknown cause, we now know that many drugs can have adverse effects on the fetus (Campistol, 2002). Included are heroin, methadone, cocaine, antibiotics, aspirin, anticonvulsants, and anticoagulants. Powerful adverse effects of another common drug, marijuana, include congenital abnormalities, stillbirth, and abnormal neurological functioning (Holmes, 2002). And smoking during pregnancy produces low-birth-weight babies with impaired cognitive development and increased risk of psychiatric problems (Ernst, 2001). Despite these strong negative findings, 60% of pregnant women continue to use potentially harmful drugs (Lo & Friedman, 2002).

Certain maternal diseases and conditions can also adversely affect the developing fetus (see Table 10-2). Among the most dangerous are diabetes and rubella (German measles). In diabetes, the high blood sugar levels in the mother and the insulin used in her treatment increase the risk of the fetus being spontaneously aborted, stillborn, or born with physical or neurological abnormalities. Rubella can produce blindness, deafness, heart defects, and mental retardation. Other diseases that can affect the fetus include syphilis, gonorrhea, and genital herpes.

Excessive stress during pregnancy is also associated with a variety of adverse outcomes (Huizink et al., 2002). It appears to cause fetal distress at birth (Sosa et al., 1980) and is a factor in various forms of later psychopathology (Ward, 1991). In primates, it even impairs motor development (Schneider & Coe, 1993).

The Newborn: Sensing and Perceiving the World

Have you ever watched a very young infant like Val's, its eyes roving about and periodically fixing on objects, and wondered just what the infant actually sees and perceives? The noted psychologist William James (1890) believed that the perceptions of the newborn were very different from those of adults - that the world of the infant was "one great blooming, buzzing confusion" (p. 488). It appears, however, that James was wrong. The newborn has a considerable array of both sensory-perceptual and emotional capabilities and responses (Table 10-3).

The normal response of the pupil to spatial objects is not present until about one month of age (Cocker et al., 1994), visual acuity at birth is poor (Courage & Adams, 1990), and the retina is immature (Johnson, 1990). Nevertheless, empirical evidence suggests that the eye movements and fixations of infants are not at all random (Lipsitt, 2002). In fact, they scan the environment *selectively*, focusing their attention on limited regions of a visual stimulus, and by age three months they select preferred objects and focus on them (Maurer & Lewis, 1991). Consider the classic study of an infant tested *3 minutes* after birth by Wertheimer and Michael (1961). The researchers sounded a toy "cricket" near her right or left ear on 52 consecutive trials. On 22 of the trials she moved her eyes, and 18 of those times eye movements were toward the click. This simple but powerful study demonstrates that newborns come equipped with a certain amount of auditory-visual coordination and spatial perception. Other important research has demonstrated a much more complex and dramatic response in which newborns raise their heads and turn toward a sound source. Given the difficulty that even adults have with auditory localization (Chapter 4), such findings make it clear that the newborn comes equipped with a complex sensory-perceptual system. Interestingly enough, the highly reliable head-turning response decreases in strength at about one month and reappears at about four months of age.

Many studies of early perceptual skills in infants have used methods developed by Robert Fantz (1961). He placed two visual stimuli above the infant, than recorded how much time the baby spent looking at each one. Fantz found that babies have a preference for more complex stimuli and particularly for the human face, a finding that has been confirmed (de Haan, 2002). They also prefer the shape of the human body over other objects (Slaughter, 2002). Others have shown that the preference for greater complexity and for novelty increases with age (Cassia et al., 2002; Figure 10-6).

Infants can also distinguish the human voice from other sounds and even detect slight differences between speech sounds by as early as one month of age. In addition, three-day-old babies prefer the voices and faces of their mothers to those of other women (Montague & Walker-Andrews, 2002; Bushnell, 2001) and display a definite preference for sweet tastes and smells. By three months, the infant can distinguish and selectively attend to three-dimensional objects (Bhatt & Bertin, 2001) and can tell the difference between closed and open containers (Hespos & Baillargeon, 2001), and by six months, some can evaluate complex, moving random dot patterns (Leat et al., 2001). Somewhat later, the infant shows a fear of strangers that occurs at about the same time even in very different cultures. While the fear may be inborn, its expression clearly requires that the infant have the ability to differentiate faces.

A particularly interesting body of infant research has been that on depth perception, where studies have involved a device called the visual *cliff,* developed by Eleanor Gibson and Richard Walk (1960). The "cliff" consists of a checkerboard design placed a foot or more below a sheet of transparent glass. An adult looking through the glass perceives a cliff-like dropoff. The transparent sheet is part of a table top that also has the checkerboard pattern. Infants six months and older placed on a central strip between the transparent side and the checkerboard side of the table top will crawl around on the checkerboard side but will rarely move toward the "cliff" side, suggesting that they have depth perception (Adolph, 2000). Other evidence suggests that depth perception is probably present even earlier—at least by one month of age.

Overall, results of studies with infants suggest that innate mechanisms are responsible for rather sophisticated early perception. However, these innate mechanisms are supplemented by early exposure to stimuli and by learning (Rovee-Collier, 2001).

Responsiveness and Intellectual Development

Are all infants alike in their responsiveness to the environment? Clearly not. John Worobey and Michael Lewis (1989) have shown that the degree of reactivity of infants to such events as PKU testing two days after birth and vaccinations at two months varies greatly. Levels of reactivity are relatively consistent within any one infant across events, but they vary considerably from one infant to another. Infants are even born with differing susceptibilities to stress. Both genetic influences and early environmental experiences dictate that some will tolerate a stressful event or environment well, others poorly (Schissel, 1993).

Perceptual and intellectual development, although heavily dependent on genetic factors, is definitely affected by parental stimulation and responsiveness. When 35 pairs of mothers and their infants were observed in one study, it was found that the intellectual development of the babies was positively related to the amount of smiling the mother did, her eye contact with the infant, and her responsiveness (Crockenberg, 1983). Research more generally has shown that development progresses best when the mother is verbally and emotionally responsive to the infant, is heavily involved with the child, avoids unnecessary restrictions and punishments, and provides a variety of daily stimulation. In addition, the physical environment should he safe and well organized, and the child should have a variety of appropriate play materials available. Finally, a variety of positive and negative parental behaviors are apparently learned by infants, who will display those same behaviors when they become parents later in life (Fleming et al., 2002).

Learning in the Newborn

Two types of learning, classical and operant conditioning (see Chapter 6), have been investigated in newborns. In classical conditioning experiments, researchers repeatedly present a neutral stimulus that does not elicit a reflex response (like startle or sucking) and follow it with one that does. The idea is to condition the newborn to respond to the neutral stimulus. Elliot Blass paired stroking the infant's face with a sweet taste that elicited sucking and demonstrated classical conditioning: Stroking alone came to elicit the sucking response (Blass, Ganchrow, & Steiner, 1984). While a number of studies have failed to obtain classically conditioned responses (Sameroff and Cavanaugh, 1979), some do support it, and many developmentalists are convinced that this basic form of learning is important in infants (Coyle et al., 2000; Ikovich, 1999).

Operant conditioning methods, in which a desired response is selectively rewarded, have been more successful (Wilk, 2001). The response of sucking on a nipple, for example, can be made stronger by rewarding only strong sucking (Standley, 2000). Similarly, newborns can be conditioned to turn their heads to the right (or left) more frequently by rewarding them with sugar water only when they turn in that direction. Such findings indicate that operant conditioning processes (learning from rewards) may provide the infant with its early repertoire of behavior.

A particularly interesting example of learning in the newborn is provided by research on sleep patterns. While otherwise a joyous time for many parents, the first months of an infant's life are typically marked by 3:00 a.m. feedings and sleepless nights. Indeed, the new parent arriving at work bedraggled, with bloodshot eyes and unkempt hair, is classic. Well, there may be hope! Despite evidence that early sleep patterns are substantially affected by the maturation of the forebrain, some scientists have attempted to teach newborns to sleep better. In a recent study, parents in an experimental condition learned ways to teach their infants to sleep through the night. They fed them just before going to bed themselves, gradually lengthened the intervals between night feedings, and substituted other caretaking behaviors, like diapering, for feeding on some awakenings. Control parents did nothing unusual. By 8 weeks of age, 100% of the experimental infants were sleeping all night, while only 23% of the controls slept through (Pinilla & Birch, 1993). This is a good example not only of learning and the effects of preparation for sleep in the newborn but of experimental research with a direct, practical application.

Forming Emotional Bonds: Attachment

Attachment refers to the development of lifelong emotional bonds between infants and their mothers or other caregivers. Val's baby stayed with her from shortly after birth because earlier theories suggested that this bonding process occurs primarily during the first few hours or days of life birth (Klaus & Kennell, 1982). Most studies, however, have not confirmed this hypothesis. Instead, it appears that attachment takes place between about six and eight months of age and usually occurs even in the face of severe mistreatment by the parent (Carlson, Cicchetti, Barnett, and Braunwald, 1989).

That attachment does take place is demonstrated by the behavior of the infant toward the mother. In fact, neuroscientists have even identified neural pathways in the thalamus and prefrontal context of mothers that may underlie and promote the attachment process (Lorberbaum, 2002). The baby will spontaneously approach the mother for affection, and his exploratory behavior will be interrupted if she leaves the room. Even brief separations in strange situations can produce considerable distress in the infant, and the mother may also suffer (Clarke-Stewart & Alison, 2001). The distress of separation often causes toddlers to show attachment to a favorite toy or some other transitional object, which provides temporary security (Goldberg, 2001). These transitional attachments are not, however, the same as the longer term attachments of some older infants to soft objects like blankets or teddy bears. One team of researchers conducted a longitudinal study in which they followed 33 infants and their mothers over time. They found that infants who were attached to a soft object at the age of 30 months had earlier shown secure attachments to their mothers. Thus, the "security blanket" was not a substitute for the mother or a sign of insecurity but rather an extension of the secure attachment relationship (Lehman et al., 1992).

Security of attachment appears to be affected by characteristics of both mother and infant (Stams et al., 2002). Isabella (1993) observed mother-infant pairs at infant ages 1, 4, and 9 months, then assessed the quality of attachment in each pair at 1 year. It was found that both mother and infant behaviors affected bonding. More secure attachments were present when the mother was more sensitively responsive and less rejecting toward her baby, behaviors that may be genetically predisposed (Perusse et al., 1994). It was also more secure when the baby was happy and at ease most of the time, as opposed to tense and uncooperative. In fact, infants who showed excessive distress in reaction to the withdrawal of a pacifier at 2 days of age were significantly more likely than others to show insecure attachments to their mothers at 14 months of age. But how does attachment occur? What are the underlying mechanisms?

Attachment Through Reinforcement? Behaviorists theorized that mother-infant attachment is a product of reinforcement. Mothers are associated with food, which satisfies the primary hunger drive, and the mother becomes a conditioned reinforcer. The early work of Harry Harlow 1958) however, called that view into question.

Harlow (1958) separated newborn monkeys from their mothers and put each one in a cage containing two surrogate (substitute) mothers, one made of wire, the other of terry cloth. Half the monkeys were fed by a bottle held by the wire mother, the other half by a bottle held by the terry cloth mother. Although all monkeys drank the same amount and gained weight at the same rate, they clearly preferred the terry cloth mothers. Those fed by the wire mother would go to her only for nutrition, then return to the soft comfort of the terry cloth mother.

In later work, Harlow and his wife Margaret (Harlow & Harlow, 1969) waited until adequate time for attachment had passed, then confronted the infant monkeys with some strange situation—a mechanical teddy bear that marched and beat a drum. Frightened by this intruder, the infants ran to the cloth mother and clung to her, even if they had been fed by the wire mother. After rubbing against the cloth mother for comfort, they seemed to lose their fear and turned with apparent curiosity toward the bear that only moments earlier had frightened them.

Over a long series of studies, the Harlows clearly demonstrated that reinforcement theory could not explain attachment in infant monkeys. If attachment had occurred because the surrogate mother was associated with food, monkeys fed by the wire mother would have preferred her and turned to her when faced with a strange situation. However, they invariably preferred the cloth mother, even when she had never been a source of food reinforcement. Harlow concluded that bodily contact and comfort were important elements of attachment formation.

Evolutionary Attachment Theory. Harlow's results were consistent with the evolutionary attachment theory of John Bowlby (1980) and Mary Ainsworth (1992). Observing that human infants become distraught when separated from their mothers, they first separately and then jointly hypothesized that mother-infant attachment is an evolved mechanism that developed in order to protect the infant and thereby promote the survival of the species. Harlow's cloth mother was preferred because it provided comfort more similar to that biologically associated with a real mother and could therefore better fulfill the evolutionary goal of survival. Given its evolutionary origins, Bowlby and Ainsworth consider attachment to be a centrally important aspect of early development, and their theory suggests that security of attachment during infancy affects later personality development and social relationships (Ainsworth, 1992).

This important theory has generated numerous studies, which have often confirmed the security hypothesis. Early effects are seen in the preschool years, where studies show that children who were more securely attached to parents during infancy have more friendships with other children and are less likely to be lonely or aggressive in preschool classrooms (Berlin et al., 1995). Other work shows that adolescents who were securely attached to their mothers as infants achieve a better sense of independent identity, are less likely to develop eating disorders, have better scholastic skills and social competence, and are more likely to be leaders and to be more active and curious (Aviezer, 2002; Fass, 2002). As adults, they may be less likely to experience anxiety disorders and better able to develop loving, romantic relationships (Roisman, 2002). Even in the elderly, there is less anxiety and depression among those who had secure early attachments (Dawson, 2001).

How Special Is Mom? Is Val more important to her baby's development than Mark? Most research concerned with attachment has focused on the relationship between infant and mother. However, the mother-infant bond may not be as essential as Bowlby and Ainsworth believe. In fact, it may not even be a unique social-affectional relationship, since we now know that infants form attachments to their fathers, to siblings, and to other people around them (McCormick & Kennedy, 2000). Some findings indicate that infants are as likely to approach and touch their fathers as their mothers, and other research suggests that the infant may be more likely to prefer its mother only in stressful situations, if at all (Grossmann, 2002). Researchers who have gone into family homes report few or no differences between attachments to mothers and to fathers for infants between the ages of twelve and thirty months. And studies in both homes and laboratories have shown that by the age of eighteen to twenty months children are attached to both the mother and the father and often also to siblings (Genuis, 2000; Ryan, 2002).

Despite the clearly important role of parents and the traditionally more important role of the mother in the rearing of children, relatively recent years have seen significant increases in the return of mothers to the work force. In fact, at least 65% of women have regular jobs (Rosenthal, 1992). Does this situation mean that infants and children are being deprived of adequate parenting and are likely to develop psychological problems or experience other difficulties? This issue is discussed in The Critical Thinker.

Cognitive Development in Infancy and Childhood

Perhaps right now as you read this chapter, it is Tuesday afternoon or Thursday evening. Whatever the actual time, chances are that you *planned* ahead to study at this time, that you are *thinking* about the material as you read it (I hope!), and that you are studying in order to *solve the problem* of getting the grade you want in your introductory psychology course. As adults, we are capable of such complex mental processes as planning, thinking, and problem solving. But even the most capable newborn seems totally unable to engage in these thought, or *cognitive*, processes. How, then, does an infant develop into a cognitively competent adult? In other words, how does cognitive development take place? Let's look at the fascinating and powerful cognitive theory of Jean Piaget, modern information-processing theory, and Lawrence Kohlberg's theory of moral development.

Jean Piaget: The Child's Approach to the World

Imagine publishing your first article in a scientific journal at the age of 10 and having your scientific writings recognized internationally by age 15! These were the experiences of Jean Piaget, a Swiss biologist and psychologist who studied and wrote about the thought processes of children for some 60 years, becoming the world's most influential theorist in the area of cognitive development. He died in 1980 at the age of eighty-four, leaving behind a powerful legacy of scientific observation and theory. Piaget was a scientific observer of the first order, and he focused his attention on children, particularly his own three, Jacqueline, Lucienne, and Laurent. He observed their behavior from birth onward, carefully recording his observations in great detail, and he formulated his theory on the basis of these observations.

Piaget concluded that the child's ways of understanding the world are very different from those of the adult. He emphasized that the child is not initially capable of logical reasoning, and that the development of this capacity is a central feature of a cognitive learning process that takes place as he grows up. A second emphasis was on the active role of the child in the learning process. Prior to Piaget's work, children had generally been seen as passive recipients of information provided by parents and others. He hypothesized that children actively seek knowledge and work hard to find ways to integrate that knowledge into their existing body of information to gain a better understanding of the world. A final important emphasis in Piaget's work was his belief that cognitive development is interactive. That is, as the child's ways of knowing about the world change, his view of the world changes correspondingly.

Schemes For Viewing The World. According to Piaget (1936, 1983), the child has unique ways of approaching and knowing the world, which he called schemes. A *scheme* (also called a schema) is a mental structure that constitutes a basic unit of knowledge. For the infant, all schemes are patterns of action, such as the sucking reflex that occurs when a nipple is placed in its mouth. Such reflexive schemes are present even at birth, but schemes constantly develop and change, growing more highly organized and complex and becoming differentiated from and integrated with other schemes (Nichols, 2002). Beyond early infancy, schemes may include an image of an object, such as the infant's mental picture of a toy that has been hidden from her view, a complex concept, such as a belief or a plan, or a logical operation like addition or multiplication.

Assimilation and Accommodation. The constant state of change that characterizes the child's schemes involves two important processes, assimilation and accommodation. *Assimilation* refers to taking in an aspect of the environment and making it conform to existing schemes. *Accommodation* involves the modification of existing schemes in response to new information from the environment. Through these twin processes, the child is able to adapt to the world in which it lives.

To understand how assimilation and accommodation work, consider the sucking reflex, a basic scheme with which the newborn reacts to objects in its environment. At first, the infant will suck nearly anything that enters or touches its mouth. In this way, sucking is used to assimilate new objects. However, before too long there comes the discovery that sucking on a thumb or the corner of a blanket requires a slightly different mouth shape than sucking on a nipple. Through accommodation, the infant is able to produce new sucking schemes suitable to each of these different objects.

It might appear that through assimilation and accommodation the child will eventually develop a rather random collection of schemes for knowing the world. Piaget suggested, however, that the development and modification of schemes is by no means a random process; rather, schemes become highly organized into an increasingly logical conceptual framework. The child may, for example, learn something about the top of its milk bottle through the use of its sucking scheme, the shape of the bottle through touching schemes, and the appearance of the bottle through visual schemes. Eventually the child will put these schemes together in an organized fashion so that it can readily identify the bottle and recognize it as a source of food.

Piaget's Stages of Cognitive Development

Piaget (1983) theorized that the cognitive developmental processes that transform a helpless, unknowing infant into a knowledgeable, thinking, adult take place over a series of four stages. These stages unfold on the basis of physiological maturational processes and occur in a set sequence that can be found at about the same ages in all cultures.

- The sensorimotor stage - birth to two years.
- The preoperational stage - ages two to seven.
- The concrete-operational stage - ages seven to eleven.
- The formal-operational stage - age twelve on.

Each of these stages is characterized by different cognitive methods for dealing with the world (Table 10-4). Let's consider each stage.

The Sensorimotor Stage. For about the first two years of life, the infant is not able to deal with the world in terms of verbal labels for objects because she has not yet learned language. As a result, she comes to know her world entirely through sensory impressions and motor responses, and it is for that reason that Piaget dubbed this early period the *sensorimotor* stage. The newborn deals with the world primarily through reflex actions, such as grasping, sucking, and crying. Through the process of accommodation, the reflexes are modified, and the child begins to repeat interesting actions in what amounts to the beginning of goal-directed behavior. At about six months of age, she begins to recognize that her own actions can modify events in the outside world, and at the end of the first year she develops a primitive understanding of cause-effect relationships. At about twelve months, the infant not only relies on old, reflex-based schemes to solve problems but begins to evolve new schemes specifically for the purpose of solving novel problems (Cook, 2001).

By the end of the sensorimotor period, the infant is exploring mentally as well as physically. He can examine a problem situation, internally consider alternative solutions, choose a solution, and try it out. Suppose, for example, that a two-year-old carrying a toy in each hand approaches a closed door. He contemplates the door momentarily, then puts down one of the toys, turns the knob with his free hand, picks up the toy, and goes through. He has successfully planned and carried out a unique (for him) solution to a novel problem. In other words, even before he is two years old, the infant can actually *think!*

Throughout the sensorimotor period, the child is gradually developing a sense of the general properties of objects. Early in this period, he has no sense of *object permanence*—of the fact that objects continue to exist when they are out of sight. When objects are hidden, he does not search for them or otherwise indicate an awareness that they still exist. Midway through the sensorimotor period, the child may reach for a partially hidden object, and by age one he may continue to search for an object in the location where it was last seen but not look elsewhere. By about eighteen months of age, however, the infant appears to have definite mental representations of particular objects and will search widely to find an object that has disappeared (Keenan, 2002).

The Preoperational Stage. During the *preoperatiomal stage*, the child becomes more effective at using the mental problem-solving mode developed near the end of the sensorimotor period. She is now able to deal with the world symbolically: Objects can be imagined or symbolized internally, and one object can come to stand for another. A pile of blocks becomes a fort, the crib becomes a jail for teddy, and dolls become children and friends.

Despite her newfound effectiveness in dealing with the environment, the preoperational child still lacks a sense of logic and any real comprehension of cause-effect relationships. Piaget (1976) asked preoperational children, who could walk and had long since mastered crawling, how they crawled. The children could demonstrate crawling with no problem but could not accurately describe the motions involved in this behavior. They told Piaget that they crawled by moving the right hand and foot together, then the left hand and foot. Actually, the opposite hand and foot must be advanced simultaneously. Try it!

Another characteristic of preoperational children is *egocentrism.* They are unable to look at things from another person's point of view and assume that everyone else sees things from *their* point of view. A four-year-old talking on the phone, for example, will assume that the person at the other end of the line can see what he sees. Being egocentric does not mean that the child is selfish; it simply means that he is not yet able to mentally put himself in someone else's shoes. Would Piaget have been surprised at the behavior of the 3-year-old in Horizon 2?

The Concrete-Operational Stage. During the *concrete-operational stage,* which begins at about age seven, the child develops the ability to reason logically about concrete things. Cause-effect relationships and other logical connections that previously escaped her now begin to become clear. Instead of dealing with the environment primarily through schemes, the child is now using operations—mental manipulations of objects. A *concrete operation* is a reversible mental manipulation of concrete objects. The child can imagine, for example, squashing a clay ball into a flat circle and then reshaping the clay into a ball again.

To better understand the level of concrete operations, try this little experiment: Fill a short, fat glass with water, then pour the water into a tall, thin glass, and ask your friends which contains more water. They should all quickly answer that the two contain the same amount of water, since the quantity of liquid has obviously been conserved; only the shape of the container has changed. *Conservation* is the understanding that the quantity, length, weight, number, mass, area, and volume of a substance do not change by merely changing its appearance (see Figure 10-7).

All normal adults have a good understanding of conservation, but preoperational children do not. Presented with the experiment you just tried on your friends, they will focus on the height of the liquid and say the tall glass has more. Children who have reached the concrete operational stage will say that the amounts are the same.

A similar Piagetian experiment tests for the conservation of mass. Children are shown two balls of clay and asked to add clay to either ball until both are of the same size. The experimenter then rolls one ball into a snake and asks the child whether the snake and the remaining ball have the same amount of clay. Preoperational children say the snake has more clay because it is longer; concrete operational children reply that the amount of clay has not changed. Some recent research continues to support Piaget's original hypotheses about the capabilities of the concrete operational child, but other research questions the cognitive basis for conservation (Caroff, 2002).

The Formal-Operational Stage. In the final stage of cognitive development, which begins at about age twelve, the ability to reason logically expands to involve more abstract concepts, such as "truth" and "justice." Only in this period of *formal operations* does the full power of reasoning, of which human beings are uniquely capable, come to the fore (Rips, 2002). The budding adolescent begins to understand abstract concepts and their logical interrelationships. He can formulate hypotheses about the world, test those hypotheses, and reformulate them if necessary (Kelley, 1999). Philosophical and moral principles are a function of formal operations, as are the theories developed by scientists to explain a wide variety of phenomena—including cognitive development!

Was Piaget Right?

Does the typical child develop systematically through the four major stages specified by Piaget, and do the abilities displayed at each age coincide with what Piagetian theory would predict? The answer is no—and yes!

First, the results of a number of studies have led many psychologists to conclude that some aspects of Piaget's theory are incomplete, incorrect, or ambiguous (Flavell, 2000; Wolfe, 2000). For one thing, Piaget tended to picture young children as less accomplished and knowledgeable than they actually are. It was his belief that very young children are incapable of sorting objects on the basis of a consistent criterion—that they are limited in their ability to classify objects systematically. Yet a number of investigations have shown that even three-year-olds are able to complete simple sorting tasks as effectively as an adult. Furthermore, the mental operations that Piaget specified may not be as general or as central to cognitive development as he suggested. And the mental structures that supposedly arise at the various stages do not always occur as clearly and consistently as Piaget asserted (Morris, 2001). Studies of 6- and 7-year-olds, for example, show them to be much more capable of carrying out number conservation tasks than Piaget theorized (McEvoy & O'Moore, 1991).

An additional difficulty is that the problems Piaget used in his studies are not always solved by the particular operations he postulated. For example, conservation tasks are not necessarily always solved through concrete operations.

Finally, where Piaget believed that his stages and their associated operations were a product of physiological maturation, recent studies suggest that children can be successfully trained to carry out a given operation before they reach the appropriate Piagetian stage (Pasnak et al., 1991).

Some theorists and researchers who are in general agreement with Piaget have addressed specific criticisms of the theory and modified it. These psychologists are sometimes called *Neo-Piagetian developmentalists.* A major figure in this movement is Jerome Bruner (1973), who has combined Piaget's theory with learning theory to emphasize how the child processes information about the environment and how that environment rewards and punishes specific behaviors. Where Piaget emphasized the developmental stages of the *person,* Bruner emphasizes the level of development of the individual's *behavior.* Others have insisted on the importance of recognizing that the teaching/learning process takes place in a sociocultural context. The child brings to the learning experience an individual, subjective perspective and a cultural background that influences her interpretation of meaning and hence what she ultimately learns on a given occasion or about a particular topic (Bickerton, 2002).

Two other Neo-Piagetian emphases are on the concept of stages-within-stages and on individual differences (Welch-Ross, 2000). The Neo-Piagetians have attempted to examine more fully just how transitions within and between cognitive stages take place (Al-Wattban & Soliman, 2002) and have found evidence for distinct developmental levels *within* the individual Piagetian stages (Niaz, 2001).

They have also recognized much more fully than Piaget did that there are significant differences among children at any given stage of development (Jacobs, 2002). One four-year-old may be much more capable of using symbolic representation than another, and one 8-year-old may solve conservation problems much better than his classmate. More recent studies confirm this observation and even find some evidence that individual differences in the functioning of the frontal lobes of the brain may underlie individual differences in performance (Segalovitz, 1992).

Beyond Piaget: Cognitive Development in the 21st Century

Despite the continued influence of Piaget's theory, cognitive psychologists have begun to study the development of thought processes, learning, and memory from quite different perspectives. *Information-processing theory* likens human cognitive processing to a computer, with "data" input through the senses, analysis of information by a central processing unit (the brain) and output in the form of behavior. All cognitive capabilities develop through information-processing, and Albert Bandura (Chapters 6 and 14) sees even social learning and personality development as products of the information-processing model of cognition (Pury, 2002).

We examine cognition more fully in Chapter 8 and consider memory as a separate topic in Chapter 7, limiting our discussion here to the study of cognitive development from the information-processing perspective. The basic question is: How does the child develop the ability to process information in the way that an adult does? The general answer is that through neurological maturation and experience the child gradually develops an increasing ability to remember larger and larger amounts of information and to make use of this memory store in processing new, incoming information.

The Development of Information Processing Ability. Three cognitive changes over the course of childhood are particularly important in the development of memory and the ability to process information effectively. The first is the capacity to *reason logically.* Very young children make few or no logical connections among bits of knowledge in their memory stores, while older children make such logical leaps quite readily. For example, you might tell a child that Tom is taller than Jane and later tell her that Ruth is taller than Tom. The older child can quickly reach the logical conclusion that Ruth is taller than Jane; the younger child cannot.

A second change is in the *body of knowledge* available to the child. It is an old adage that the more you know, the more capable you are of acquiring and retaining new knowledge. The child who develops a substantial body of knowledge about computers will have a far easier time acquiring and retaining new knowledge about computers than will the child without that body of information. More generally, the older child, who has more experience and has acquired more knowledge, will both learn and retain new information more readily than will the younger child.

The third change is in memory and learning *skills,* which improve with age as the child acquires new strategies for learning and remembering. The older child has learned to *organize* new information for entry into memory, *pay attention to details,* and *rehearse* or practice to improve retention.

Recognizing Individual Differences. A final important observation about cognition in childhood is that there are considerable individual differences in learning ability even at very early ages. In fact, information processing in infancy is statistically predictive of mental status later in childhood (Bornstein, 1989). One study used information-processing measures of cognitive ability, such as the visual recognition of objects, to test a group of 109 children at the age of 7 months and again at one year. Performance on the information-processing tasks at these early ages was predictive of cognitive development and performance when the same children were tested at age 6 (Rose et al., 1992).

Individual differences in cognitive ability are important in part because they are a major factor, if *not* the major factor, in later educational achievement (Stodden, 2001). At the upper end of the scale are children who will be recognized as geniuses; at the lower end are those with learning disabilities. Statistics concerned with this latter group show that about 20 percent of the school population performs below age-appropriate levels, and the Center for Disease Control estimates that between 5 and 10 percent of all children—some two to four million—are diagnosable as learning disabled. The neurological deficits that underlie much of this disability may have a genetic basis (Scott, 2001; see Chapter 9).

Other factors can also affect cognitive development and capability. One of these is *low birth weight* (LBW), which is a generally negative indicator. Babies are normally born weighing an average of about 3500 grams (7.7 lbs). Those weighing less than 2500 grams (5.5 lbs) are called LBW babies, and those weighing less than 1000 grams (2.2 lbs) are called extremely low birth weight (ELBW) babies. Maternal smoking, drinking, narcotic drug use and malnutrition, as well as multiple births, intrauterine infections, and chromosomal abnormalities, are causal factors. The consequences for cognitive development can be substantial. Low and extremely low birth weight children often exhibit long-term cognitive deficits, particularly when they are raised in socioeconomically deprived or unstable homes (Melnyk, 2001; Sajaniemi, 2001). In fact, LBW is associated with low cognitive functioning at ages 8, 11, 15, and 26 and with reduced education (Richards, 2001). A final factor influencing cognitive development is the way the child is fed. Breast-fed babies show statistically significant advantages over bottle-fed babies in cognitive performance in later childhood and adulthood (Mortensen, 2002; Quinn, 2001).

Lawrence Kohlberg: The Development of Moral Reasoning

Why are college professors so dead set against cheating on examinations? If the answer seems obvious, it is because you are a normal adult who is capable of *moral reasoning*. Piaget (1983) considered moral reasoning to be simply one aspect of overall cognitive development. He suggested that children have a concrete approach to morality that eventually evolves into more abstract approaches. During the sensorimotor and preoperational periods, moral thinking is highly concrete. If we tell a four-year-old that Johnny broke five plates accidentally while Linda broke one plate on purpose, the child will say that Johnny was more "wrong" than Linda. The number of plates is the central issue for this child. A youngster who has reached the formal-operational stage will arrive at the more abstract conclusion that Linda, who intentionally broke a plate, is more deviant than Johnny.

Kohlberg's Stages of Moral Development. Consider this moral dilemma: A woman is dying of cancer, and a local druggist has developed a drug that will cure her. However, he is selling the drug for an extremely high price—about ten times what the drug costs him to make. The woman's husband, Heinz, cannot borrow enough money to purchase the drug and asks the druggist to sell it to him for a lower price or wait until later for the money. The druggist refuses. Should Heinz steal the drug in order to save his wife's life? A person who follows the strict rules of society would say that Heinz would be wrong to steal the drug. One better able to engage in complex moral reasoning might argue that if all possibilities have been exhausted and death can only be prevented by stealing, then Heinz should steal the drug. This is one of the moral dilemmas that Lawrence Kohlberg has presented to children and adults in an effort to test his theory of moral development. A modern and very real example of such a life-or-death dilemma is that facing Jack Kevorkian, many other physicians, and society itself: When should a patient be helped to die—if ever?

Kohlberg proposes that there are three levels of moral development, each with two stages. The final stage involves an ideal and rarely-achieved form of moral reasoning. Table 10-5 shows what Kohlberg expects at each stage and level and how his levels corresponds to Piaget's. At the first, or *preconventional*, level, morality is a function of obedience and punishment. The basic moral reasoning is that one must obey authority figures to avoid punishment or gain reward. This level contains Stages 1 and 2 and lasts until about age six or seven, when the child achieves the *conventional* level of moral reasoning. Conventional morality (Stages 3 and 4) centers around the need to be approved by others, and the child at this stage will act to obtain approval and to avoid disapproval. The highest form of moral reasoning, the *postconventional* level (Stages 5 and 6), does not appear until age eleven or twelve. Individuals at this stage are able to understand the concepts of rights, laws, and justice and the morality of individual conscience.

Most evidence indicates that the transitions from one moral stage to another are not abrupt. That is, the person doesn't suddenly change completely from Stage 1 to Stage 2 or from Stage 3 to Stage 4. Rather, the transition is gradual and cyclical (Commons, 2002). The child may move, for example, from Stage 1 to Stage 2 in some situations, then switch back to Stage 1 for others. In this way, he gradually makes the full transition to Stage 2. However, Kohlberg (1969) found that, on the whole, moral stage increases with age (Figure 10-8).

Unlike Piaget's cognitive stages, Kohlberg's moral stages are only in part a function of age (Bergman, 2002). In fact, some evidence suggests that moral development increases with age up to a point, then decreases somewhat (Dawson, 2002). Such factors as parental training, self-confidence, and intelligence may also determine the rate at which morality develops and the level achieved. One study involved testing 120 children and adolescents aged 10-16 to determine the extent to which the stage of moral reasoning is dependent on mental capacity. The researchers gave their participants a measure of moral reasoning and two visual information-processing tasks designed to assess intellectual capacity. Stage of moral development was heavily dependent on mental capacity. Those who scored higher on the information-processing

tasks had also attained higher levels of moral reasoning, but many had not reached the highest stages. In fact, Kohlberg has suggested that many people never go beyond the conventional level, and research supports this observation. Even graduate students have typically reached only Stage 4 (Mwamwenda, 1991).

Does Moral Stage Affect Behavior? **If the Kohlberg stages have practical value, we would expect the moral reasoning they represent to provide a guide to behavior in various situations. Does it? Well, the evidence is mixed. In one interesting study, Kohlberg reexamined data gathered in 1964 over twenty years later (Candee & Kohlberg, 1987). The data were originally collected from students at the University of California when the Free Speech Movement held a sit-in to protest what they believed to be violations of their rights. Kohlberg hypothesized that students who had attained higher levels of moral development would be more likely to participate in the demonstration. Results supported this hypothesis. At each higher stage of moral reasoning, a higher proportion of students sat in:**

STAGE 3 — 10%
STAGE 3/4 — 31%
STAGE 4 — 44%
STAGE 4/5 — 73%

Although moral stage was clearly an important determinant of behavior in this situation, it was not the only one. The political identification of the student and other factors also influenced the decision to participate.

A study involving more recent events tested 91 college students during two tense days in the Persian Gulf War. The question was whether level of moral development would affect attitudes toward the war. The researchers found that a belief in the unity of humanity and previous war experience both decreased the likelihood that students would approve the war, while a belief in the importance of law and order was associated with greater approval. However, the student's level of moral reasoning did not affect his approval or disapproval of the war (Westman & Lewandouski, 1991). It appears that stage of moral reasoning may importantly influence attitudes and behaviors in some situations but not in others.

Criticisms of the Kohlberg Theory. **Critics have argued that moral development does not progress in the stagewise fashion Kohlberg proposes (Rest, 1983; Derryberry, 2002). They point out that individuals in a particular age group express moral values and judgments that cut across all three of his levels, and these variations may be so common as to invalidate the theoretical model. The specific things that parents teach their children at a given age may have far more to do with moral stage than some more general developmental model. A related criticism is that a person's apparent stage of moral reasoning may be influenced by the specific social or cultural situation (Dawson, 2002). One study supporting this hypothesis tested 40 men aged 18-45 (Carpendale & Krebs, 1992). Each was asked to indicate how he would respond to several moral dilemmas (a test of moral reasoning stage) and randomly assigned to one of two conditions. In one condition, he was told to direct his responses to a business audience. In the other, the responses were to be directed to a group of philosophers. Results showed that scores indicating stage of moral development were significantly influenced by the social situation (i.e., the audience to which responses were directed). This suggests that moral decisions are based on more than an overall, set stage of development.**

Critics have also pointed to studies failing to verify that the attainment of logical reasoning is a necessary condition for moral development, a key idea in Kohlberg's theory (Colby, 2002). An additional criticism holds that Kohlberg's stages are not as universal as he suggests and are unlikely to be found across a wide variety of cultures. However, after reviewing 45 studies of moral reasoning, John Snarey (1985) concluded that the sequence of moral development proposed by Kohlberg is, for the most part, found across a variety of cultures. Moreover, several longitudinal studies, in which subjects have been tested over a number of years, have confirmed a general upward movement in moral development that coincides with the theory (Carroll and Rest, 1982).

Perhaps the most serious criticism comes from Carol Gilligan (1982), who suggests that the theory is sexist in its bias toward male responses and suggests. Gilligan points out that men and women differ psychologically in important ways that affect their moral reasoning. Men are more concerned with individual achievement, separateness, and distinctiveness; women are more focused on relationships among people. The personal identities of men come primarily from their work; those of women rely more on personal relationships. These differences suggest that men are likely to be more morally concerned with individual rights and obligations, whereas women will probably be more concerned with how people are connected, interrelated, and obligated to one another.

Based on her observations and studies, Gilligan contends that Kohlberg's scheme automatically disadvantages women, who are likely to achieve lower ratings on his scale of levels. She provides an example of responses from two 11-year-old children, a boy and a girl, to the dilemma faced by Heinz and his sick wife. The boy said he should steal the drug. The girl's response was that Heinz probably should not steal the drug but rather try to find some means of borrowing the money in order to buy the drug. Stealing, she argued, might save his wife, but Heinz would then go to jail, his wife might get sick again, and this time he would be unable to help. Gilligan argues that the girl, who would come up with a lower score on the Kohlberg scale, is focusing more on human needs and relationships, a legitimate moral position.

Gilligan agrees with Kohlberg as to the three levels of moral development. However, she offers an alternative interpretation of the basis for the stages. She focuses on who it is that the person at a given level is concerned with—who she

cares about: Preconventional morality focuses on the self, conventional on others, and postconventional on both (see Table 10-5). Several studies have shown support for this approach (Caputo, 2001; Belknap, 2000)

Kohlberg and others have challenged Gilligan's criticism. Anne Colby and William Damon (1983) point out that Gilligan's study lacked adequate controls to support her contention that Kohlberg's theory is biased. They also note that women do not really score lower than men on Kohlberg's system when the educational and work backgrounds of the subjects are controlled, and other studies have also failed to support Gilligan's position (Shimizu, 2001). There is clearly no final answer as yet.

Personality Development in Infancy and Childhood

If all we developed during infancy and childhood was the ability to think, our lives might be productive, but they would certainly be dull. Fortunately, each individual develops not only cognitions but also a personality. You may have one friend who is very open and honest, another who reveals little of himself or seems a bit dishonest at times; one friend who accepts the blame for everything that goes wrong, another who blames others; one friend who is always anxious, another who is laid back. These differing patterns of behavior can be thought of as personality characteristics or traits. More generally, *personality* is a construct used to refer to the complex but reasonably consistent pattern of thinking, feeling, and behavior we see in an individual.

In Chapter 14 we describe various theories of the structure and functions of human personality. Here our focus is on how personality develops. Physiological maturation and the occurrence and resolution of crises have been proposed as possible causal factors in personality development. Even the number of brothers and sisters you have may significantly influence development, and some believe that it is a disaster to be an only child (Horizon 3). Two of the most influential theories devised to explain personality development are those of Sigmund Freud and Erik Erikson. After outlining these approaches, we turn to the role of the parents in personality development.

Freud's Theory of Psychosexual Development

Without the benefit of a word processor, a computer, or even electricity at first, Sigmund Freud wrote books and articles that fill twenty-six volumes and formulated one of the most influential psychological theories of all time. His theory describes how the human personality functions, how it can become disordered, and how the disorders can be treated. We describe Freud's monumental theory of human behavior in more detail in Chapter 14, but here we focus on his theory of how the human personality develops.

Freud hypothesized that personality development has a biological basis in physiological maturation. These processes take the individual through a series of *psychosexual stages*—discrete periods during which events significantly influence specific aspects of personality development (Table 10-6). They occur sequentially as the child's inborn sex drive moves from one area of the body to another. Freud's main focus was on the earliest years of life, for he felt that much of personality is already formed by the time a child reaches school age. He identified three separate psychosexual stages that occur in the first five years of life: the oral stage, the anal stage, and the phallic stage.

The *oral stage* is so-called because the mouth and lips give the infant his greatest pleasure. This stage is initiated by the feeding process, in which the infant must suck on a nipple in order to derive nourishment. So pleasurable is oral stimulation that the infant will often indiscriminately suck on virtually any object, including his own thumb. Clearly, the baby derives far more than nourishment from oral stimulation. In fact, Freud believed sucking to be the prototype for every kind of sexual satisfaction that an individual will ever experience.

The *anal stage* begins when stimulation of the anal region through the retention and expulsion of feces becomes pleasurable, and the pleasure can be increased by learning to delay bowel movements. Toilet training typically occurs during this stage, and the learning and stress associated with that process may affect personality development in important ways. More recent theorists have tended to interpret the transition from oral to anal stage as representing not just a maturational process but also a shift in parental concerns toward matters of continence and cleanliness.

At about age 3, the zone of greatest pleasure shifts to the genital region, and the *phallic stage* begins (Bergmann, 1995). Pleasure is derived from stimulation of the genitals ("phallic" comes from the Greek *phallus*, meaning "penis"). Masturbation begins, and the child soon faces the conflict of what Freud called the universal "family romance," in which he or she adopts the opposite-sex parent as a love object. Freud called this family romance the *Oedipus complex*. For a boy, like Val's baby, it begins with feelings of strong love or lust for his mother and fear of his father. For the girl, it is the opposite. Eventually, both sexes at least partially resolve the conflict, identify with the same-sex parent and begin to imitate some of that parent's behaviors.

The *latency* stage, which lasts from about age 6 to age 12, is a period of relative tranquillity. The child seeks contact with same-sex peers and gradually learns important social skills involved in peer interaction. Identification with the same-sex parent continues and sexual desire is minimized (Cincotta, 2002).

The final phase is the *genital* stage, which begins at puberty. The period of sexual neutrality comes to an end, and sexual desires, focused once again in the genital area, become dominant. As the genital stage continues, the adolescent seeks heterosexual attachments and moves into normal adult sexual relationships.

Each developmental stage serves as the basis for certain kinds of adult characteristics. An infant who is frustrated in his need to chew and bite during the oral stage, for example, may grow into an *oral sadistic* adult, who is argumentative and sarcastic; a child who undergoes unusually harsh toilet training may develop into an *anal retentive* adult, whose characteristics include stinginess and overconcern with orderliness and punctuality.

Many psychologists and psychiatrists have criticized various aspects of Freud's developmental theory, suggesting that development really does not take place in set stages, that the theory has a sexist orientation and tends to degrade women, and that there really is no latency phase of the sort Freud suggested. Although there is some evidence to support these criticisms, there is also research supporting the occurrence of a stage-wise process of personality development similar to that described by Freud (Tellings, 2001; Blass, 2001). Any resolution of this controversy will have to await further research.

Erikson's Theory of Psychosocial Development

Erik Erikson (1956, 1968), disagreeing with Freud's emphasis on the physiological basis for personality development, focused on the child's social environment. He hypothesizes that personality develops through a series of eight *psychosocial stages*. The first five stages parallel Freud's stages and span infancy, childhood, and adolescence, while the last three go beyond Freud and deal with the adult years (Table 6-7). Erikson envisions these stages as a series of crises, each characterized by a conflict between new attitudes or abilities and opposing tendencies. When the conflict is successfully resolved, the individual experiences an increased sense of competence in a particular social ability.

The first stage, called *trust versus mistrust*, occurs during the first year of life. The infant faces and resolves a conflict between opposing tendencies to trust and mistrust a world about which it knows very little. The second stage, corresponding roughly to Freud's anal stage, involves the conflict of *autonomy versus shame and doubt*. The crisis here pits individual autonomy (independence) against the shame and doubt that can be fostered by continued, forced dependence. Development will proceed most effectively if the parents gradually allow the child to achieve more and more freedom and independence. Otherwise, the sense of shame and self-doubt will predominate. The third stage, which corresponds to Freud's phallic stage, involves the conflict of *initiative versus guilt*. Favorable resolution of this conflict means that the child will learn to take a reasonable amount of initiative in order to achieve goals. If the child is consistently punished or criticized for taking initiative, a sense of guilt may result.

Erikson's fourth stage of development, *industry versus inferiority*, corresponds to the time period of Freud's latency phase. When the child is rewarded for hard work and diligence, the conflict is resolved positively, creating a sense of industry—a feeling of personal competence and a desire to achieve. Failure to reward the child's efforts leads, instead, to feelings of inferiority. As the child reaches adolescence, he enters the stage of *identity versus role confusion*. The conflict at this stage is the *identity crisis*, which arises as the adolescent realizes that he has a need to form an integrated sense of personal identity. Positive resolution of the identity crisis means that he will have an integrated body of self-knowledge; negative resolution means that he will suffer from identity confusion, which is characterized by anxiety, indecisiveness, and loneliness.

Stage six, which occurs in early adulthood, revolves around the conflict of *intimacy versus isolation*. Ideally, the conflict is resolved when the young adult learns to experience deep, loving relationships. Failure to become committed to intimate relationships results in isolation. The seventh stage (middle adulthood, ages 25 to 65) presents the conflict of *generativity versus stagnation*. Generativity is concern for the next generation and the society in which that generation will grow up. If this sense of mature concern for others and for the future of society is rejected, the result is stagnation and a sense of hopelessness and meaninglessness. The final stage, which occurs in old age, is the stage of *ego integrity versus despair*. A sense of ego integrity develops when the individual experiences satisfaction with prior accomplishments. If, on the other hand, she sees her prior life as a series of unattained goals and unrealized potentials, the result may be despair.

Erikson's theory has been widely questioned and criticized but remains a major theory of development (Cote, 2002; Levine, 2002). Like Freud's, it provides a logical framework through which we can interpret observations about developmental processes. Unfortunately, both theories have proven difficult to validate experimentally, though they have generated considerable research (Hoare, 2002).

Are There Discrete Stages?

You have no doubt noticed that all the major theorists discussed thus far—Piaget, Kohlberg, Freud, and Erikson—postulate that development occurs in discrete stages. Does it? The truth is that we don't yet know for sure. Some scientists interpret research as supporting the stage theories (Baumrind, 1989; Wilson, 1989). However, others are increasingly challenging this approach, suggesting, instead, that development is an ongoing process that cannot be broken up into meaningful, discrete phases (Springer & Keil, 1989; Slater, Cooper, Rose, & Morison, 1989; Sroufe & Jacobritz, 1989). We may eventually conclude that, in fact, some aspects of development are continuous, others discontinuous.

Contexts of Development: Parent and Child

When my son and later my daughter were born, I was absolutely fascinated—and a little scared—as I held these tiny packages of life in my hands and realized that they were now my responsibility. As much as I cared for them at birth, I found that my love for them grew with each passing day and month and year. As they grew, I grew with them, and to my love and fascination were soon added understanding and respect.

Stop for just a moment and think carefully about your parents. To most observers, they are probably fairly average, ordinary people. They live in a house or apartment, hold jobs, and have an income fairly comparable to that of other people they associate closely with. But chances are that your view of your parents is quite different from that of the general public. To you, they are very special people, and you probably have at least fairly strong feelings toward them—positive, negative, or both. Your view of your parents as unique individuals and your strong feelings toward them derive from the fact that they have greatly influenced the development of your personality.

There is little doubt that the developmental process is strongly influenced by the contexts in which it takes place, including the family. Freudian theory says that children are greatly affected by the emotional experiences they have in the context of their relationship with their parents in the early stages of life. Behavioral theorists believe that children develop a personality through a series of rewards and punishments administered primarily by parents. And much of modern developmental theory emphasizes the role of the parent as the teacher who imparts to the child a vast fund of knowledge, skills, attitudes, and emotional reactions. Whatever the approach, this emphasis on the importance of the family is well supported by scientific research, including studies of the effects of physical and sexual abuse, described in our 21 for this chapter.

Mother and Child. Research on the relationship between mother and infant has shown that the response of the parent to the needs of the child has effects on the later development of the child's personality. One study showed that children between the ages of 3 and 7 whose mothers respond in a sensitive way to their needs in infancy are more satisfied, have better relationships with others, and are more resourceful than children of less responsive mothers (Brody and Axelrod, 1978). Another found that more sensitive mothers produce more sociable, competent babies (Clarke-Stewart et al., 1980). And a third, which followed 44 mothers and babies from infancy through age 12, showed that children of more responsive mothers had more positive self-concepts, fewer behavioral and emotional problems, and even higher IQs (Beckwith et al., 1992). Still other investigations indicate that smiling, which is the best indication of infant social competence, increases when the parent includes active tactile stimulation in her caretaking.

As with bonding, the baby also influences the interaction pattern and thus partially determines the outcome. Babies who are more irritable, more subject to startle reactions, and less responsive are more difficult to care for. This reduces the ability of the mother to respond sensitively to their needs. On the other hand, conflict between parents and inconsistencies in their interactions with the baby can make the child more difficult to care for. The mother-child relationship, as it influences personality development, is clearly an interactive and reciprocal one. The Critical Thinker describes what happens when mom goes back to work and puts her baby in daycare.

Does Father Know Best? Fathers can also be very influential, and the extent of their influence is correlated with the degree of their involvement in child-rearing (Kryslova & Novakova, 1995). Greater father involvement contributes to the development of traditional gender role orientation, particularly in boys, and has many other effects as well (Hardesty et al., 1995; Yogman et al., 1995). In fact, the absence of a father during childhood can produce considerable distress, with more negative outcomes in Hispanic than in White or African-American families ©. Smith & Krohn, 1995).

The father is likely to be more involved and hence have more impact when the mother is working and when he has a flexible view of the male role in the family (Radin & Harold-Goldsmith, 1989; Hall, 1994). Going a step further, in fact, the number of single-father families more than tripled between 1970 and 1990 (Burgess, 1995; Greif et al., 1995), and increasing evidence shows that parental adjustment and parenting skills, not gender, are the important considerations (Burgess, 1995; Tillitski, 1992). Whether father knows best or not, he greatly influences the child's development.

Child-Rearing Practices. It is possible that different child-rearing practices—specific ways of raising the child—have differing short-term and long-term effects on development. Research involving 32 mothers tested five times over a period of eight years showed that the child-rearing practices of a given mother tend to be quite stable over time (McNally et al., 1991). But do different practices actually have differential effects?

A classic study of parental influence was based on 379 interviews with mothers of kindergarten children (Sears, Maccoby, and Levin, 1957). Each mother was rated on 100 childrearing practices, and the personalities of the children were assessed. The researchers concluded that the relationships between specific childrearing practices and personality were minimal. Later, David McClelland and his associates (1978) located 78 participants from this study (who were now 31 years old), gave them a battery of psychological tests, and interviewed them. Like the original researchers, McClelland concluded that there were no clear-cut relationships between specific child-rearing practices and the participants' personalities.

Parenting Styles: Love May Be The Key. If specific child-rearing practices are not the answer, perhaps broader parental disciplinary attitudes and styles influence child development. Dianna Baumrind (1977, 1991) hypothesizes that there are three styles of parenting involving different patterns of discipline. *Authoritarian* parents are firm, unsympathetic, unaffectionate, and punitive. They tend to be detached and seldom praise their children. *Permissive* parents give their children maximal freedom. They tend to be loving but exert little control. *Authoritative* parents reason with their children, listen to their objections, and are firm but loving and understanding. Their demands are rational and consistent, and they set limits but encourage independence.

The three styles have differing effects on the child's personality. Authoritarian parenting tends to foster children who are withdrawn, unfriendly, and discontented, but it yields better control over the child's behavior (Querido et al., 2002. Permissive parenting produces children who are immature, unhappy, dependent, and lacking in self-reliance. Authoritative parenting tends to result in children who are self-reliant, friendly, independent, happy, achievement-oriented, and cooperative (Lin & Fu, 1990). It may be that this style works better because it is more likely to be exhibited by parents who are more competent and better adjusted, characteristics that have been shown to contribute to the child's ability to adapt to stress and function more effectively (Melamed, 1993). What type of parent are you or would you be?

Despite its appeal, there are two possible problems with Baumrind's classification of parenting styles. First, preexisting temperamental differences among children may well influence parenting styles. Parents may respond much differently to a relaxed, easy baby than to a tense, difficult one. The second problem is that Baumrind did not have a broadly representative sample of families. Most were white, middle-class, suburban, two-parent families, and it is not clear how her observations would apply to the population as a whole. In any case, many researchers are now attempting to determine the relationship between parenting styles and the development of the child (Pychyl et al., 2002; Scarr, 1992).

A related line of research suggests that the predominant patterns of parenting in Western societies have changed over time. Duane Alwin (1988) compared 1924 data indicating the traits parents desired in their children with similar data collected in 1978. He found that earlier parents were more authoritarian, emphasizing obedience to parental authority, whereas the later parents preferred more autonomous children and hence were permissive in some cases and authoritative in others. It seems clear that the reciprocal causality seen in parent-infant interactions is also at work in parent-child interactions. Children who are cooperative, mature, sociable, and competent make it easier for parents to adopt a moderate, authoritative style.

Baumrind (1991) and other researchers have concluded that it is probably not highly specific child-rearing practices but rather the general style of parent-child interaction that influences the child's developing personality. Basically, it appears that the parent who is guided primarily by a loving, caring attitude toward the child is most likely to have well-adjusted offspring. Further research may uncover more specific variables that are important in childrearing, but for the moment, love appears to be the key

The Neurophysiology of Development

Neural processes underlie all aspects of development. The ability to walk and later talk, the capacity to engage in complex thought, and the formation of the personality all depend upon the central nervous system. So also do the infant's basic responses to stimulation, the learning processes that provide knowledge and experience, and the early emotional attachments that he forms. The neurophysiological bases of many of these aspects of development are covered in other chapters: cognition and language in Chapter 8, personality in Chapter 14, emotion in Chapter 13, learning and memory in Chapters 6 and 7, and the response to stimulation in Chapter 12. We will not repeat that information here. We will, however, take up the development of the prenatal development of the brain, the process of physiological maturation, and the occurrence of biologically based "critical periods" for developmental events.

Prenatal Neural Development

About two weeks after conception, the human embryo begins to form the nervous system. Interestingly enough, the ontogeny of neural development within the individual parallels the phylogenetic evolution of the brain across species (Chapter 3). First to differentiate is the spinal cord and hindbrain, followed by the midbrain (Figure 10-9). By the third week, the basic structure of the forebrain is also in place, and new neurons are being rapidly produced. At first, they look like other cells in the body, but soon they form axons and dendrites, some myelinate, and axons then begin to find their way to the dendrites of other neurons with which connections are needed.

By about the 35th day the thalamus, limbic system, and other subcortical structures are fairly complete and ready to receive axons from the cortex. However, cortical neurons do not appear until about the 7th week. At that point they begin to proliferate rapidly, continuing to increase in number until the 16th week and perhaps beyond that. The process of forming the connections between cortex and subcortex then begins, and some have argued that neural networks begin to form at this time (Prakash, 2002). By birth the brain has the same basic structure as that of an adult, but growth continues at a fairly rapid pace during the first year of life and more slowly after that.

Physiological Maturation

"Oh, grow up!" an exasperated Val might exclaim as her now 11-year-old son once again persists in teasing his 6-year-old sister. Val means, of course, that she would like her son to become psychologically more mature, but *maturation* is actually a biological process in which genetic factors direct an orderly sequence of changes that occur with age. Although these changes occur throughout the body, they are basically neurophysiological in nature.

Reflexes and Motor Development in Infancy. The newborn comes equipped with a set of reflexes that provide a starting point for responding to the outside world. These are soon supplemented or replaced by increasingly complex and sophisticated motor skills.

Primary reflexes are innate, unlearned responses to stimuli; they are present at birth to promote the infant's survival. Most disappear within the first year of life. The *Babinski reflex* is a curling upward and outward of the toes when the sole of the foot is touched. The *grasping reflex* is the closing of the hand around an object that touches it, and the *sucking reflex* similarly occurs in response to an object touching the lips. The *Moro reflex* is a sudden cry accompanied by outstretching of the arms and legs in response to an unexpected loud sound or environmental change. Finally, the *rooting reflex* is the turning of the infant's head toward a breast, hand or other stimulus that touches the cheek or lips.

The primary reflexes provide the first instances of patterned motor movement, but *motor development*—the innately programmed, progressive increase in muscular coordination—requires further maturation of the nervous system. The infant advances through a series of *developmental milestones*—motor skills—from lying prone to lifting its head, raising its chest, then rolling over (Figure 10-10). Later, it can sit, crawl, stand, and, finally, walk. The *developmental norm* for each of these activities is the median age—that at which 50% of infants have achieved the milestone—and there is considerable normal variability around the median. Thus, the *sequence* of maturational events is the same for all children, but the *timing* can vary from child to child. The median age for walking alone, for example, is just over 12 months, but 40% do not achieve this milestone until 14.5 months of age (Lejarraga et al., 2002; Piper et al., 1992).

The orderly sequence of motor development is based on the continuing maturation of the nervous system and follows two general principles. It is *cephalocaudal*—moving downward from head to foot—and *proximodistal*—moving outward from the center of the body toward the periphery. These principles probably reflect, in part, the pattern of myelination of nerve fibers, which begins at the brain and spreads downward and outward. At the same time, the developing cerebellum brings increased coordination, the hippocampus improving memory, and the frontal cortex complex motor control.

The regularity of maturational sequences is maintained even when environmental conditions would seem to make variability likely. Take Hopi Indian babies, for example. These infants are bound to a cradleboard and carried about by their mothers during the first year of life, which would seem to put them at a disadvantage in learning to walk. Yet once they are given the opportunity to move about on their own, they progress rapidly through the developmental sequence and are soon walking (Wayne & Dennis, 1940).

The Hopi example illustrates that once a child is physiologically ready to learn a particular skill, he will learn it rapidly and without undue difficulty. Conversely, it is nearly impossible to teach a child to do something for which he is not physiologically ready. You cannot teach a child to walk or talk until certain physical changes have taken place. The most basic of these modifications are those involving the brain and nervous system.

It seems clear that the development of the brain and central nervous system is by no means complete at birth. In fact, considerable neural development takes place well after birth, during childhood and adolescence. Children have only about 25 percent of their adult brain weight at birth, 75 percent at age two, and 90 percent at age five (Tanner, 1970). After that, neural growth is more gradual, and much of it centers around the development of the neurophysiological mechanisms that underlie complex thought processes. That aspect of neural growth continues beyond childhood, with some evidence for major maturational advancement in the frontal lobes into late adolescence (Hudspeth & Pribram, 1992).

Although developmental psychologists once thought that only biological factors determine maturation, it is now clear that learning can play a role in developmental timing. African infants display more rapid motor development than European or American infants, apparently because African mothers actively rehearse their infants in such motor skills as sitting, standing, and walking. In one experiment infants less than three months old practiced the stepping reflex, a natural motor response, for eight weeks. They were able to walk alone six to eight weeks earlier than a control group of infants who did not practice (Zelazo, Zelazo, and Kolb, 1972), a finding consistent with other studies that have shown positive effects of practice on a number of motor abilities.

Critical Periods. What would you think if you saw a man walking along with a string of newly hatched ducklings following him? You might think he had trained the ducklings to follow him and perhaps that he was an "odd bird" himself. However, the man we have in mind is Konrad Lorenz, an ethologist who discovered a curious but important fact: that the development of some behaviors and skills is limited not only by the body's level of physical maturation but also by the *timing* of certain key external events.

Lorenz noted that if he walked around and quacked like a duck soon after a group of ducklings had hatched, they would follow him rather than the mother duck. What he observed is called *imprinting*—an instinctual tendency that produces a sudden and irreversible attachment to some object. A duckling imprints on the first moving, quacking object to which it is exposed during a short period about sixteen hours after hatching. It turns out that ducklings will imprint on a variety of objects, including footballs and green boxes. Imprinting has been found in a wide variety of animals, including insects, birds, fish, and at least some mammals.

A very brief, single time in the lifespan of an organism during which an external stimulus has an effect beyond that observed at other times is called a *critical period.* A *sensitive period* can be a longer but still limited time span during which the stimulus can have its effect. A more detailed definition comes from Mark Bornstein: "The sensitive period reflects a developmental phase of built-in competence for specific exchange between organism and environment whose consequences presumably endure for the organism" (1989, p. 189). Before the emergence of the biological system and its full maturation, the organism is not physically capable of the behavior in question.

Are there critical periods in human development? Two pediatricians, Marshall Klaus and John Kennell (1976), observed in their clinical practice that the mother-infant relationship seemed to be greatly affected by contact between the two during the first few hours or days after birth. Early studies appeared to support these observations.

In one study researchers followed a group of mothers who had prolonged early contact with their newborns and a control group of similar mothers who did not (Kennell et al., 1974). When the babies were one month old, early-contact mothers watched and soothed their infants significantly more, engaged in more eye-to-eye contact during feeding, and fondled the infants to a greater extent than did the control mothers. These differences persisted when the infants were a year old, and additional differences were seen at age two. However, more recent research suggests that attachment may not occur in the ways that Klaus and Kennell thought (Kenny & Gallagher, 2002).

Eric Lenneberg (1967, 1969) has hypothesized that a sensitive period also exists for language acquisition. It begins at the age of about two and ends at the age of twelve to fifteen. If no language learning has occurred within this time, it becomes difficult if not impossible to learn language. Although the exact critical periods for the development of various aspects of language are not known, there is increasing evidence that the overall critical or sensitive period ends at about the time of puberty (Newman et al., 2002; Komarova & Nowak, 2001).

Conclusion

In this chapter we have followed the developing human being from conception through childhood to the very edge of adolescence. We have seen the tiny embryo, with nothing but its basic biological apparatus and genetic predispositions, become a baby and that baby interact with its environment to become a growing child. You know now how the evolution of the species interacts with the development of the individual to produce an adult human being, how cognitive, moral, and personality development take place, and how parents influence virtually all aspects of the process. And you know that infancy and childhood are only the beginning of a lifetime of growth and development. The remainder of that developmental process—adolescence, adulthood, and aging—is the subject of Chapter 11.

Summary

Lifespan Development: The Journey Begins

1. Among the major issues in developmental psychology are nature-nurture, developmental continuity, and individuality.

Heredity and Environment in Human Development

1. Environmentalists have long held that human behavior is largely a function of experience, while instinct theorists have placed heavy emphasis on heredity.
2. There are 23 pairs of chromosomes, yielding 70 trillion potential patterns in the offspring.
3. Phenotypes are expressions of genotypes and may be affected by the environment.
4. Mutation and polygenic transmission account for most human traits.

5. Modern behavior genetics emphasizes the interaction of heredity and environment in determining behavior.
6. Behavior geneticists use family studies, twin studies, and adoption studies to assess the extent to which a given behavior pattern is influenced by heredity. Recent evidence shows strong genetic influences on a variety of behavior patterns.
7. The ontogenetic development of the individual contributes to and is a product of the phylogenetic development (evolution) of the species.

Very Early Development: The Prenatal and Newborn Periods

1. Development begins when sperm meets egg, producing a zygote, which becomes an embryo, then a fetus.
2. Maternal malnutrition, drug use, drinking, smoking, and even stress can create significant problems for the fetus and may have long-term effects.
3. The newborn baby is much better equipped to sense and perceive the world than was formerly thought. It is also capable of learning through at least operant conditioning.
4. The attachment that typically develops between parent and infant appears important to the child's emotional development. Security of attachment is affected by both mother and infant characteristics.

Cognitive Development in Infancy and Childhood

1. Jean Piaget formulated the most important and influential theory of cognitive development. He suggested that such development takes place in a series of four stages: sensorimotor, preoperational, concrete-operational, and formal-operational.
2. While not all research supports Piaget's theory, it has nevertheless been the principal guiding force in the study of cognitive development. Information-processing theory offers an alternative approach.
3. Building on Piaget, Kohlberg has formulated a stage theory of moral development. He suggests three general levels of development, including preconventional, conventional, and postconventional. His theory has been criticized as inaccurate and sexist.

Personality Development in Infancy and Childhood

1. Personality development is influenced by a variety of genetic and environmental factors. Freud hypothesized that development takes place in a series of psychosexual stages, which he called oral, anal, phallic, latency, and genital.
2. Erikson theorized that development takes place in a series of stages based on the occurrence and resolution of important crises. His stages parallel Freud's but go beyond them to deal with development during the adult years.
3. Both parents clearly play significant roles in personality development, as does the child himself.
4. Baumrind's parenting styles include authoritarian, permissive, and authoritative. General style of parenting, rather than specific child-rearing practices, appears to influence the developing personality.
5. Infants differ at birth in temperament, which appears to be strongly influenced by genetic factors. Infant temperament influences and, in turn, is influenced by interactions with the parents and may have implications for the adult personality.
6. Parents differ in the way they treat their children, and these differences can substantially affect the child's developing personality. Baumrind has suggested that the three principal styles of parenting are authoritarian, permissive, and authoritative.

The Neurophysiology of Development

1. The physiological maturational sequence is the same for all children, but the timing of sequential events can vary from one child to another.
2. Neurological development continues into adolescence.
3. Some animals exhibit critical periods for such developments as imprinting and attachment. Some human studies suggest that there may be a sensitive period for bonding between mother and infant, but more recent research does not support that conclusion.

Ask Yourself

1. What are the major factors affecting development, and how do they have their effects?
2. How do events during critical periods affect later behavior in animals and in humans?
3. What major aspects of early experience affect later functioning?
4. What is the nature of the early relationship between mother and child, and how does it affect later development and functioning?
5. How did Piaget see cognitive development as taking place?
6. What are the principal criticisms of Piaget's theory, and how have they been dealt with?
7. How does the development of moral reasoning relate to cognitive development, and what may be the major steps in developing moral reasoning?
8. What are Freud's major developmental stages, and how do they influence the adult personality?
9. How do Erikson's developmental stages relate to Freud's stages?
10. How do varied patterns of parenting differentially affect the developing child?

Further Readings

Ambert, A. (1992). *The effect of children on parents.* NY: Haworth Press.

We discussed briefly how infants and children can affect their families. Using case studies and a review of the research literature, Ambert considers in detail the role of the child in the family.

Badcock, C. (1991). *Evolution and individual behavior: An introduction to human sociobiology.* Oxford: Basil Blackwell, Inc.

If you find sociobiology fascinating, you will enjoy reading what is perhaps the clearest published presentation of this major and controversial theory.

Flavell, J. (1993). *Cognitive development.* Englewood Cliff, NJ: Prentice-Hall.

Authored by a leading developmental psychologist, this book details the development process from each of the major, current theoretical perspectives.

Fogel, A. (1991). *Infant, family, and society.* St. Paul: West Publishing.

This fascinating book taps the wealth of research on infancy to describe in detail the infant at each stage of its development.

McShane, J. (1991). *Cognitive development: An information processing approach.* Oxford: Basil Blackwell, Inc.

Information-processing is a major cognitive approach (see Chapter 10), and McShane shows how it applies to human development.

Vander-Zander, J. (1993). *Human development.* N.Y.: McGraw-Hill.

This up-to-date general text in human development covers all the topics we have covered in this chapter, but in much greater detail.

Wren, T. (1991). *Caring about morality.* Cambridge, MA: MIT Press.

Wren explores the philosophical assumptions about human motivation that underlie major theories of the development of morality, such as Kohlberg's.

Psychology in the 21st Century

Physical and Sexual Child Abuse

The hospital intercom clicked on and crackled: "Pediatric resident to emergency. Pediatric resident to emergency." Rushing into the emergency, the young pediatrician found an unconscious girl about seven years old, her body covered with bruises. Her anxious mother, standing nearby, quickly explained that the girl had fallen from a second-story window while playing with some other children. An investigation initiated by the suspicious pediatrician revealed that the girl had in fact been severely beaten by her father.

Child abuse is both an old and a new phenomenon. It was widespread in the ancient Greek and Roman civilizations, and infanticide (killing infants) was a common practice in medieval times (Langer, 1972). However, evidence of child abuse—particularly sexual abuse—has often been suppressed (Olafson et al., 1993). Indeed, it was identified as a problem in this country in the 1940s (Caffrey, 1946) but has only recently received careful attention.

Did you know that one or two children are killed by abusive parents in the United States every single day (Durfee et al., 2002)? Moreover, according to the U.S. Department of Health and Human Services, at least 1 in every 43 children under the age of 14 is seriously abused, an estimated 500,000 each year—and this is no doubt a substantial underestimate (Hicks & Gaughan, 1995; Kasim et al., 1995). One study showed that up to 41% of children are physically abused at some point in childhood, and other data show that one specific form of abuse—sexual abuse—is seen in at least 11-26% of the population (Avery, 2002; Bugental et al., 2002). Anne Walsh and W. Eugene Broadhead (1992) found that of 147 female patients in a family practice, 47.6% reported some type of sexual victimization and 25.2% reported rape or attempted rape. Similarly, 57% of student health service patients reported sexual victimization and 28.7% reported rape. More generally, it appears that 2-5% of boys and perhaps three times that many girls are sexually abused during childhood. Such statistics can be substantial underestimates, since many people are unwilling to admit that they were abused. On the other hand, some children (or adults speaking on their behalf) may falsely allege sexual abuse (Wardinsky et al., 1995). Since there are rarely eyewitnesses, and physical evidence of abuse is found is only 15 percent of confirmed cases, care must be taken in evaluating reports of child sexual abuse.

What Causes Child Abuse? The causes of child abuse are found in the society at large, the individual parent, the family situation, and the children themselves. Society in the United States condones and promotes violence. Homicides involving firearms have reached the almost unbelievable level of 27.7 deaths per 100,000 population in metropolitan areas, increasing at a rate of up to 35% per year in the late 1980s and early 1990s, though they have declined considerably in recent years (Blumstein, 2002; Fingerhut et al., 1992). There are over 1.5 million violent crimes, including 20,000 murders, each year (Sak, 1992). These statistics are much higher than for most other Western countries. Two frequently cited reasons for some of this violence are television and video games (Anderson & Bushman, 2001; Cantor, 2000). In a recent survey, all families owned at least one TV set, and 57% owned two or more, with the sets turned on all day in 16% of cases and during mealtime in 54.5% of cases (Bernard et al., 1991). About 70% of children's TV shows and 67% of prime time shows depict violence (Wilson et al., 2002; S. Smith et al., 2002). In addition, 97% of urban children in one study had witnessed violent acts in their homes or communities and 49% had been victims of violence (Purugganan et al., 2000). No wonder over 80% of children say they like to play with guns!

The background, characteristics, and expectations of the individual parent also contribute to violence in the home (Eisenhower, 2002). First, most reported abusers are male, though recent evidence suggests that the frequency of abuse by females may be significantly underestimated. Secondly, it is consistently found that one-third of child victims become abusing parents themselves and another third may abuse their children under stressful conditions (Glasser et al., 2001). Being neglected during childhood also predicts later child abuse (Bevan, 2002). In addition, abusive parents are typically young, come from lower socioeconomic levels, and are more likely than nonabusing parents to have a history of mood disorder, alcohol and drug abuse, or personality disorder (Windle et al., 1995). Finally, these parents are often people who have never learned to be patient. They have unrealistic expectations for their children and feel that the child should be sensitive to the parent's problems and provide emotional support and gratification. When the child does not live up to these expectations, abuse follows.

The immediate family situation also contributes to child abuse. The child is in far more danger when the family is under stress and when the parents are frustrated by life events. Alcohol abuse is often also present (Bevan, 2002). In the specific case of sexual abuse, family circumstances and practices are often factors. Lack of personal privacy, excessive nudity in the home, physical contact that is not entirely affectionate, and an inadequate marital sexual relationship all increase the likelihood of sexual abuse.

A final causal factor is the child himself. A baby that is premature, for example, is likely to be more difficult to care for—and more likely to be abused. Excessive crying also leads to parental violence, and children who chronically misbehave beyond the norm are more likely to be victims of abuse. Overall, it appears that abuse is most likely to occur when parents are young, were abused in childhood themselves, have a difficult child, and are living in a family environment characterized by disorganization, failure, and violence between the parents (Woodward, 2002).

Abuse Can Be Devastating. Whatever its causes, child abuse can have devastating, long-term consequences for the child. Major reviews of child sexual abuse undertaken by Joseph Beitchman and by Kathleen Kendall-Tackett point to several common sequels of such abuse. Victims are often sexually promiscuous and have long-term sexual dysfunctions, higher frequencies of homosexual contact, depression, excessive fears, and poor self-esteem (Romans, 2002), as well as increased risk of poor physical health (Thompson, 2002) They may also have a heightened sense of anxiety and helplessness and are more likely to develop several different kinds of psychological disorder (Simpson, 2002; Mazzeo, 2002; Becker & Rickel, 1995). The likelihood and severity of these problems is increased when force is used and when the frequency of abuse is high. However, the victim does not necessarily exhibit psychological disturbances. Symptoms occur in about two-thirds of sexual abuse victims, but not in the other third (Levitt & Pinnell, 1995).

So what do we do about this serious problem? That is the question for research that will surely continue well into the 21st century. First, we study it further because we still do not have a clear idea of all the causes. Second, we attempt to prevent and treat it. Self-help groups like Parents Anonymous can be effective, and various treatment programs have used such approaches as parent aides, who assist in the home, foster care for abused children, crisis nurseries, and short-term residential treatment for parents or entire families. As we learn more, we will be able to devise more effective interventions (Benger, 2002).

Probe

Temperament and Personality

All infants act pretty much the same, don't they? Not so! Ask any nurse who works in a maternity ward or for that matter any experienced parent with several children, and they will quickly tell you that infants vary dramatically in how they act. Some are placid and inactive, while others are irritable and seem to be constantly wiggling and squirming. These differences, present at birth, represent variations in temperament, the physiologically based tendency to respond to the environment in particular ways. The fetus may move a little or a lot in the uterus, and this variability is due largely to differences in temperament (DiPietro et al., 2002). Similarly, infants may differ at birth in their levels of motor activity, their autonomic physiological responses to stress, and the extent to which they show behavioral inhibition (slow down or stop what they are doing) when presented with unfamiliar people or situations (Ullrich et al., 2002; Kagan, 2001). And there are consistent EEG characteristics of more and less active children (McManis et al., 2002).

These important biological differences in temperament can affect the development of personality and emotionality and the life-long behavior patterns of the individual. In fact, the existence of temperamental differences at birth raises several important questions:

- Are these early differences in temperament stable over time?
- Are they influenced by heredity?
- Do they influence the development of the adult personality?

The Stability of Temperament. The principal work on infant temperament has been that of Stella Chess and Alexander Thomas. They began their New York Longitudinal Study (NYLS) in 1956 with a group of 236 newborns and since that time have been following 141 children of middle-class parents and 95 children of Puerto Rican working-class parents. Other groups have also been added to the sample in more recent years. The newborns were initially studied by trained observers, and, as they grew up, information was gleaned from extensive data provided by parents and teachers (Thomas and Chess, 1977, 1981, 1990).

On the basis of their research Thomas and Chess concluded that there are nine basic aspects of temperament (see Table 6-6), which group together to form three major patterns. The first type they called the *easy baby.* She is generally cheerful, seldom fusses or cries unnecessarily, smiles frequently, and shows regular, predictable patterns of hunger and tiredness. The *difficult baby* tends to be unhappy and uncooperative. He throws temper tantrums, spits out new food, cries loudly and frequently, and fails to establish regular eating and sleeping patterns. The *slow-to-warm-up baby* may be difficult and uncooperative when presented with new objects or situations but eventually "warms up" and enjoys the novel additions. Of the babies in the NYLS, 40 percent were easy babies, 10 percent were difficult babies, and 15 percent were slow-to-warm-up babies. The rest could not be easily classified. More recent studies confirm these observations (Rubin et al., 2002).

Are these and other temperamental differences stable over time? Chess and Thomas (1990) and others (Gasman et al., 2002) conclude that the differences are quite stable, though in extreme cases they can be modified by an environment that consistently runs against the initial tendencies. For example, a difficult baby raised in a very warm, supportive environment may, over time, become a much less difficult child. With these kinds of exceptions, Jerome Kagan (1989) concludes that temperamental tendencies are highly stable. He and his colleagues measured behavioral inhibition at the age of 21 months, then again at ages 4, 5.5, and 7.5 years. The children who showed a high degree of inhibition in response to strange situations at 21 months were the same children who were inhibited at the later ages. Correspondingly, uninhibited babies became uninhibited children.

Genetics and Temperament. Most studies find support for strong genetic involvement in temperament (Saudino & Eaton, 1995). When two people are presented with a stressful stimulus, for example, one may show a much larger change in heart rate or in some other measure of physiological arousal than the other. Studies show that the magnitude of such physiological reactions is significantly more consistent in identical than in fraternal twins, supporting the idea of a genetic component (Schmidt & Fox, 2002; Gabbay, 1992). Other studies using the twin or adoption methods find substantial evidence of hereditary influence on such aspects of temperament and personality as motor activity level (Saudino & Eaton, 1991), extroversion (Braungart et al., 1992), empathy, and negative emotionality (Emde et al., 1992). And twin studies have confirmed a strong role for genetics in behavioral inhibition (DiLalla et al., 1994).

Temperament and Personality. Finally, do temperamental characteristics influence adult personality? Interestingly enough, we have very little solid evidence with which to answer this question. We do know that a number of personality traits demonstrate moderate to strong heritability (Bouchard, 1994) and that temperament is clearly influenced by genetic factors. It thus seems likely that temperament is a factor in the development of the adult personality. However, it is important to remember that other hereditary tendencies, parental behavior, and life experience more generally also help to shape the personality and behavior patterns of the older child and adult.

The Critical Thinker

Microwave Mothers

In 1940 it seemed obvious to most parents that the development of their children would suffer great harm if the mother worked outside the home. As a result, fewer than 10 percent of mothers with school-age children were the work force. By 1982, with the potentially harmful effects of maternal employment no longer so obvious, 60 percent of mothers with preschool children were in the labor force and (Hoffman, 1984). Today, at least 65% of American women work outside the home (Rosenfeld, 1992). As maternal employment figures began to climb, the daycare industry burgeoned, and psychologists began to address the question of whether placement in daycare is somehow harmful to the child. In particular, what effect does daycare have on cognitive functioning, security of attachment, and social adjustment?

The Basic Hypothesis or Contention

Advocates of the traditional family model have argued that the return of women to the work force is having negative effects on the children they leave behind. Jay Belsky (1988, 1990), for example, points out that the daily absence of the mother, particularly during early infancy, may significantly reduce the attachment security of her offspring. Other areas in which harm may be done include the cognitive functioning and social adjustment of the child. If true, this contention would mean that responsible parents should agree to make the mother's primary role that of child care, keeping her out of the work force.

What Is The Evidence?

Evidence has been rolling in for some years now. Two longitudinal studies in Sweden are providing some general answers. One reported results after following children for two years (Broberg, Lamb, & Wang, 1990), the other for seven years (Andersson, 1989). Both report that children in daycare generally fare as well as or better than those raised entirely at home, and results from other studies support this conclusion (Vander Ven, 2001; Kalil, 2001).

Studies focusing specifically on cognitive functioning show that the IQs, verbal abilities, and other intellectual characteristics of children raised in daycare centers are at least equivalent to those raised at home by unemployed mothers (Caldwell, 1993) and may actually be higher (Beyer, 1995). Indeed, when the welfare system was reformed in 1996, forcing more mothers to work, the children of those mothers performed better in school and displayed less behavior problems (Gennetian, 2002). However, some studies do show that when the mother is employed by the time the child is only nine months old, the child later shows lower school readiness scores (Brooks-Gunn, 2002). There is also evidence that children who spend much of the time during their early years in daycare exhibit higher levels of social skill and social adjustment than those who are raised in the home. Carollee Howes (1991) found, in fact that the earlier children were enrolled in daycare programs, the higher their levels of social competence.

Some studies have addressed the question of whether the child's security of attachment to the mother is affected by her absence from the home during the day (Harrison, 2002). Most data indicate that maternal employment has no effect on attachment security, and some studies actually find that children in daycare are more securely attached to their mothers than those whose mothers do not work (McKim, 1999). Exceptions occur when there are too many infants per caregiver in daycare settings, potentially leading to an ambivalent attachment (Scher, 2000; Sagi, 2002).

Is The Evidence Open To Alternative Interpretations?

Despite the evidence that mother absence is not harmful, Belsky (1990) believes there may be circumstances under which it is. Not all studies have taken into consideration the baby's age when the mother returned to work. When mom departs for work very early in her child's infancy, the effect on attachment security may still be quite negative. On this premise, Belsky (1988, 1990) reviewed the relevant evidence and concluded that there is a high likelihood of insecure attachment when the infant goes into daycare at a very early age, increasing the risk of later developmental difficulties.

Concerned about Belsky's contention, both Alison Clarke-Stewart (1988, 1992) and Lori Roggman (Roggman et al., 1994) reviewed basically the same studies that he had examined and reached a quite different conclusion. They interpreted the results as indicating that there is only a mild tendency toward insecure attachment, which would not necessarily affect later emotional adjustment. Supporting that position, one team of researchers examined cases in which children were placed in daycare no later than age 7 months and found no negative effects on attachment security and even some enhancement of the infant-mother relationship (Burchinal et al., 1992).

Do We Need Additional Evidence?

This is an area where we clearly do need additional evidence. At very least, the impact of beginning daycare in early infancy is controversial and remains unresolved. Respected research scientists simply do not yet agree, a clear indication that more evidence is needed. In particular, we need well-controlled studies that examine the effect on attachment security of the mother's return to work at various points in time after the child is born. We then need to follow these babies at least to adolescence to look for long-term effects.

What Conclusions Can We Reach?

While further studies in this area are clearly necessary the important point is that the "microwave mother" and the daycare she requires for her child are a reality. Even without counting the millions of intact families in which both parents work, one out of every four children in the United States lives with a single parent, who must ordinarily work. Louise Silverstein (1991) points out that 75 other nations have policies that help parents balance work and family needs. It is time, she believes, that we stop searching for the negative consequences of daycare and start examining the negative consequences of not providing high quality, affordable daycare. We must therefore face not the task of determining whether or not mothers should work, but the task of devising the best possible systems and methods of providing daycare (Elly, 1993).

Horizons in Development

Before It's Too Late: Genetic Disorders

A vast majority of babies are completely normal. However, some inherit severe disorders, and for most of the history of the human species they could not be detected until the baby was born. Now we can detect many of these disorders before birth, giving parents an opportunity to prepare or to consider abortion as an option. Medical geneticists have now learned how to recognize several hundred disorders by examining genetic material and are rapidly identifying more. Safe techniques for assessing the presence of these disorders before birth have been developed. One is *amniocentesis*, performed in the second trimester, in which cells are removed from the fluid surrounding the fetus and examined for genetic abnormalities. A more recently developed technique, *chorionic villous sampling* (CVS), can be performed even during the first trimester and has the advantage of making abortion a simple procedure without hospitalization.

Florida Toddler Goes for a Spin

This small headline appeared in the Washington Post with the following article.

> *Land O'Lakes, Fla., Oct. 3 —"I go zoom!" was all a 3-year-old boy had to say after grabbing his parents' car keys as they slept, firing up the 1979 Mercury and taking a midnight joyride.*
>
> *Florida Highway Patrol troopers remain stumped as to how Mikey Sproul, who stands just 30 inches tall, was able to hit the gas pedal and maneuver at the same time.*
>
> *The toddler's steering was a bit suspect. He hit three cars in less than a half-mile during the ride Friday. While backing out of the driveway and shifting into drive, he hit two cars at an auto repair shop next door. After a spin through a convenience store parking lot, he swerved onto busy U.S. Highway 41 and hit a car whose driver saw the car coming and had pulled into a ditch to avoid a collision. No one was hurt. (Washington Post, October 3, 1993).*

What would Jean Piaget say about this early preoperational child? Precocious perhaps? While it is unlikely that you will see many 3-year-olds on the interstates, such incidents provide examples of what may be quite common violations of Piaget's stage "rules."

The Only Child: A Sad Case?

If you are an only child, many people believe that you are greatly disadvantaged by being raised without the benefit of siblings. In fact, one early authority wrote that "Being an only child is a disease in itself" (Fenton, 1928, p. 547), and another wrote, "It would be best for the individual and the race that there should be no only children" (Brill, 1922, p. 28). Historically, psychologists and psychiatrists joined the general public in believing that only children are far more likely than those with siblings to show abnormal patterns of development and to display undesirable personalities and social behaviors.

Well, if you are an only child, you can breathe a sigh of relief, because more recent research does not support the stereotype. Toni Falbo and Denise Polit (1986) reviewed and analyzed 15 studies that provide data on the only child in comparison with children who have siblings. They conclude that the only child is not at any disadvantage and may have advantages in some areas.

Key Terms 1

environmentalism
instinct

Key Terms 2

behavior genetics
chromosome
concordance
dizygotic
environmentality
ethologist
familiarity
gene
genotype
heritability
human genome
monozygotic
mutation
ontogeny
phenotype
phylogeny
polygenic transmission
preformation theory

Key Terms 3

attachment
embryo
fetus
low birth weight
zygote

Key People 3

Mary Ainsworth
John Bowlby
Stella Chess
Alexander Thomas

Key Terms 4

accommodation
assimilation
concrete-operational stage
conservation
formal-operational stage
object-permanence
sensorimotor stage

Key People 4

Carol Gilligan
Lawrence Kohlberg
Jean Piaget

Key Terms 5

anal stage
egocentrism
fetal alcohol syndrome
Oedipal conflict
psychosexual stage

Key People 5

Erik Erikson
Sigmund Freud

Key Terms 6

critical period
imprinting
maturation
sensitive period

Keys to Child Development 1

1. **We now study development over the life span.**
   - A. **Some major issues in developmental psychology?**
     - **Nature-nurture**
     - **Continuity**
     - **Individuality**
   - B. **The historical positions regarding heredity and environmental?**
     - **Environmentalism**
     - **Instinct Theory**

2. **Basic genetic principles account for some aspects of heredity.**
   - A. **How many pairs of chromosomes there are?**
     - 23

B. The two major types of genetic transmission?
Dominant, recessive

C. What genotypes and phenotypes are?
Genotype: The basic genetic makeup determined at conception.
Phenotype: The manifest characteristic

D. The major form of transmission of human characteristics?
Polygenic

3. Behavior geneticists study the heredity/environment interaction.

A. The terms for the influence of genetics and environment?
Heritability, environmentality

B. The major types of studies done?
Family
Twin
Adoption

C. The measure of similarity between twins?
Concordance

4. Species evolution and individual development are interrelated.

A. The technical terms that differentiate the two?
Ontogeny, phylogeny

B. Where environmental factors are found and some examples?
Within the individual: Chemical composition of cells
Outside the individual: Temperature, diet, intellectual and social experience.

C. The typical basis for patterns of behavior?
Interaction of genetic predispositions and environmental factors.

D. Some developmental processes that involve the gene-environment interaction?
Maturation, critical periods, stages

Keys to Child Development 2

1. A person begins as a single, microscopic cell.

A. The steps in intrauterine development?
Zygote, embryo, fetus

B. Some prenatal conditions and behaviors that can negatively affect the fetus?
Drugs, alcohol, smoking, rubella, diabetes, stress

2. Newborn perception is more sophisticated than was earlier thought.

A. How infants scan the environment?
Selectively

B. The kinds of stimuli babies prefer, according to Fantz?
Complex

C. Some factors in early responsiveness and intellectual development?
Genetic influences
Parental stimulation

D. What kind of conditioning has been most clearly demonstrated in newborns?
Operant

3. Attachment may be an important factor in emotional development.

A. When attachment takes place?
Between about 6 and 8 months

B. What affects attachment security?
Mother behaviors: sensitivity, responsiveness
Infant characteristics: Happy, at ease

C. Who developed attachment theory?
   Bowlby, Ainsworth

D. Their major attachment hypothesis?
   Attachment security influences personality and social relationships.

E. Whether the mother-infant bond is unique?
   No. Bonds to the father and others also develop.

Keys to Child Development 3

1. Piaget's is the major theory of cognitive development.

   A. The major emphases of his theory?
      Cognitive learning leads to logical reasoning.
      The child is active in learning.
      Cognitive development is interactive.

   B. The child's unique ways of approaching the world?
      Schemes

   C. How the child interacts with the world using schemes?
      Assimilation: making the environment conform to existing schemes.

   D. The major stages of development?
      Sensorimotor, preoperational, concrete-operational, formal-operational.

   E. Some problems with Piaget's theory?
      Children are more accomplished than he believed.
      His mental operations may not be as general or central as he thought.
      The stages aren't as set as he believed.
      The problems he used are not always solved by the specified operations.
      Accommodation: modifying schemes

2. Information-processing theory likens human cognitive processing to computer processing.

   A. Three cognitive changes needed to process information effectively?
      Logical reasoning
      Increased body of knowledge
      Acquisition of learning and memory skills

   B. Some important individual difference variables affecting cognition?
      Learning ability
      Low birth weight
      Feeding method

3. Moral reasoning is an important aspect of cognitive development.

   A. Piaget's view?
      Concrete moral reasoning becomes more abstract with age.

   B. The major theorist, other than Piaget?
      Kohlberg

   C. Kohlberg's levels of moral development?
      Preconventional, conventional, postconventional.

4. Kohlberg has been widely criticized.

   A. Some of the criticisms?
      The stages don't progress as he suggested.
      Apparent stage is influenced by social situation.
      Logical reasoning may not be essential to moral development.
      Stages not universal
      Theory is sexist.

Keys to Child Development 4

1. Freud based personality development on physiological maturation.
   - A. The major stages?
     - Oral, anal, phallic, latency, genital
   - B. Some examples of adult characteristics associated with the stages?
     - Oral: oral sadistic
     - Anal: anal retentive
2. Erikson based development social factors.
   - A. How many stages he specifies?
     - 8
   - B. Their relationship to Freud's
     - First 5 parallel Freud, others go beyond.
   - C. What takes place as each stage?
     - A crisis occurs and must be resolved to produce a sense of social competence.
3. The mother significantly influences personality development.
   - A. Characteristics of children with more sensitive, responsive mothers?
     - Better relationships, more resourceful, more positive self-concepts, less emotional problems.
4. The father can be very influential also.
   - A. When fathers have more impact?
     - When more involved.
     - When mothers work
     - In single-father families
5. Child-rearing practices have been studied.
   - A. The influence of specific practices?
     - Minimal
   - B. Baumrind's major parenting styles?
     - Authoritarian, permissive, authoritative.
   - C. How Western parenting patterns have changed?
     - Now less authoritarian and more permissive and authoritative.
   - D. A possible key to successful child rearing?
     - Love

Chapter 11

Life Span Development: Adolescence, Adulthood, and Aging

Outline

Evolution and Adulthood

Heredity and Adulthood
The Ongoing Nature of Evolution
The Study of Developmental Processes

Adolenscenc: Transition to Adulthood

Puberty and Adolescent Sexuality
Personality Development: The Identity Crisis
Social-Emotional Development

Adult Development: From Maturity to Old Age

Stages of Adult Development
Biological Change: Ups and Downs
Cognitive Development
Personality Development: Stability is the Rule
Leiben Und Arbeiten
Social Development: Marriage and Family
Career Development: The Adult at Work

The Older Adult: Living Longer and Living Better

The Mythology of "Elderly"
The Graying of America
Cognitive Aging: Loss May Be Minimal
Personality Change: Stability is *Still* The Rule
Aging and Psychopathology
Family and Social Changes
As Certain As Taxes: Death and Dying

The Biology and Neurophysiology of Aging

The Life Span
Why Do We Age? Theories of Aging
The Dying Brain

Networking

THE process of development and change does not stop with the arrival of puberty. Puberty brings the awakening of sexuality and the search for a personality identity. Does this mean that adolescence is always a time of crisis and of conflict with parents? We will answer these questions before moving on to adulthood, a period of development during which the individual regularly encounters and resolves crises, becomes ever more mature, and takes on new responsibilities. Among the developmental tasks of adulthood are establishing intimate relationships and perhaps raising a family, entering an occupation, and achieving financial independence. Most adults are now living to retirement age and beyond and must also confront the issues of old age, including physical changes, changes in family and social relationships, and the deaths of loved ones. The final challenge of life is, of course, to deal with one's own impending death and to accept the life that one has lived.

Development over the Life Span

ADOLESCENCE. The principal of Everson High School took the microphone in the crowded auditorium: "Ladies and gentlemen, "I'm pleased to announce that Everson's valedictorian and the recipient of the award for excellence are, for the first time, one and the same person. He is Michael "Dirk" Carson. A star in track and captain of the football team, Dirk has maintained a 4.0 average and has been accepted in pre-med at several major universities. He has also been a member of Everson's highly rated debate and math teams and was recently given the city's Special Service Award for his work in the community."

ADULTHOOD. It was just after 11 P.M. and the crowd of political supporters were bleary eyed as just-elected new Congresswoman Pamela Blair took the microphone to thank them. President of the engineering firm she had started 15 years earlier, she was a self-made millionaire and served on the boards of directors of three banks, two hospitals, and several large corporations. She had received a long series of business and community awards, including an honorary doctorate, and had published articles in several major business magazines.

AGING. Graduate and undergraduate students, as well as faculty, quieted down as the Department Chair rose to introduce the speaker. He was an internationally renowned psychologist with over 700 publications, including 40 books. Six of those books, they were told, had been published in the previous five years - and the speaker was 86 years old. He proceeded to give a fascinating talk about his theory and research.

These three examples were carefully chosen to make the important point that a vast majority of people in modern society are able to function normally and effectively. Most teenagers are not crisis-driven drug addicts; most adults are not alcoholics in midlife crises; and most elderly people are quite capable individuals. The examples were also chosen to span the entirety of life beyond childhood, reflecting the life-span perspective increasingly emphasized in developmental psychology over the last three decades.

Researchers have discovered that life beyond childhood does show distinct developmental patterns, often best described in terms of the challenges and tasks that must be faced during particular life periods. In this chapter we begin by examining the role of evolution and genetics in adulthood. We then move on to the unique tasks of adolescence, the transition period between childhood and adulthood. Next we discuss some of the major challenges of adulthood, including the establishment of a career and the formation of relationships and a family. Going on to the last phase of development, we will explore the aging process, the changes and challenges of old age, and coming to terms with the reality of death and the process of dying. Finally, we will take up the biological and neurophysiological aspects of the aging process.

Evolution and Adulthood

We discuss in Chapter 10 the role of evolution in physical and psychological development, pointing out how genetics and environment interact to affect individual development. It would be easy to conclude that evolutionary influence, passed on to individuals as a part of their genetic makeup, affects only child development. After all, the genotype is determined at conception and present at birth. The truth is, however, that development throughout the life span continues to be affected by the genes - which are, of course, a product of the evolutionary history of the species (McClearn, 2002; Hughes et al., 2002).

Heredity and Adulthood

Consider the example of human social cooperation - working together in coordinated activities for the common good. Evolutionary theorists hypothesize that this tendency has a partially hereditary basis and has evolved over the centuries because it promotes survival and reproduction (see Chapter 8). Yet we rarely see much cooperative activity in very young children; it appears in later childhood or adolescence. And there are many other physical and psychological examples. Heart disease and cancer, though subject to genetic predispositions, usually do not show up until well into adulthood, as is also true of male pattern baldness (Graham et al., 2002; Donati & Iacoviello, 2001). Personality traits like extraversion, anxiety, and aggressiveness are more apparent somewhat later in life than in early childhood. And there is even evidence that the likelihood of an individual ever being divorced is influenced by genetics.

The Ongoing Nature of Evolution

You might conclude that such negative characteristics as tendencies to have heart disease or to be very aggressive hardly sound like adaptive products of evolution. However, it is important to remember two things. First, each of these negative tendencies is just one point on a continuum: Some people inherit predispositions *not* to have heart disease or *not* to be hyper-aggressive. Second, evolution is not complete in 1998! It is an ongoing process. We can expect the human species to continue to evolve, very gradually making its characteristics more and more positive and adaptive. The day may well come when coronary heart disease will "evolve out," though that day may be millions of years in the future. Beyond these observations, it is important to always keep in mind that we are not talking just about genetics. Evolution itself is a product of environmental factors, and the development of the individual is a joint, interactive result of environmental and genetic influences.

The Study of Developmental Processes

It is this overall development across the lifespan that defines for developmental psychology its principal task of examining the nature of the changes that take place throughout life. To accomplish this end, psychologists have used three major research designs: cross-sectional, longitudinal studies, and sequential.

In a *cross-sectional study* comparisons are made between groups of different ages. For example, the memory skills of a group of 25-year-olds might be tested against those of a group of 65-year-olds. Because cross-sectional studies are relatively easy to carry out, they have made up the bulk of developmental research.

Suppose we administer a test of complex reading skills to groups of 15- and 65-year-olds and find that the 15-year-olds are the better readers. Do the results of this cross-sectional study mean that reading skills have deteriorated with age, or do they perhaps reflect a change in educational practices across generations? This question reveals the major problem with cross-sectional studies: We can never be certain whether differences found between age groups are a function of age or of *cohort effects* - the effects of being a member of a particular generation.

So substantial are cohort problems in the interpretation of cross-sectional studies that developmental psychologists have long advocated increased use of *longitudinal studies*. In these designs, which can involve children or adults, a single group of participants from the same cohort is followed for a long period of time. The reading skills of the same subjects could be tested, for example, at age 15 and at regular intervals until age 65, and any observed differences would be attributable to aging and not to cohort effects.

But there are also some problems with longitudinal studies. They are slow, difficult to conduct, and expensive. In addition, testing the same person over and over again may familiarize her with the testing procedure and cause a practice effect that influences scores. Finally, society changes over time, and the participants in any longitudinal study may change along with it. Thus, if we were to study changes in sexual attitudes in the same group of people between 1940 and 1980, we might conclude that individuals become more liberal about sex as they grow older, even though the observed changes may reflect the general change in social attitudes during that time period.

To overcome these problems, Warner Schaie (1977; Schaie& Willis, 2000) has suggested what he calls a "most efficient design." It is called a *sequential design* and involves the cross-sectional comparison of two or more groups of subjects who are followed longitudinally over time. A sequential design thus begins with a cross-sectional study. The several cohorts involved in the study are each tested over a period of years, providing longitudinal data, and additional new groups of participants from a second cross-sectional study may also followed longitudinally over time. The whole process can be repeated every 5 or 10 years to provide an ideal combination of cross-sectional and longitudinal sequence data, thus theoretically eliminating all the problems inherent in both types of studies. We might initially test groups of 15-, 25-, 35-, 45-, 55-, and 65-year-olds on our reading task. We could then retest each of these groups every five years and make both cross-sectional and longitudinal comparisons.

Adolescence: Transition to Adulthood

Adolescence is a time of transition and includes important biological, social, emotional, and cognitive changes that take place quite rapidly over a relatively short period. The teenager is no longer a child, but not quite an adult. He is sexually mature and capable of reproduction, but has not yet attained the emotional maturity or economic independence of the adult. The range of ages spanned by adolescence is somewhat arbitrary and has changed with changes in society. From World War I through World War II, a period of about thirty years, it was regarded as ending at about age 16 because teens were needed to fight the wars and work in war-related industries. The exception during these years was the Great Depression that followed the crash of the stock market in 1929. Economic conditions defined the society, and adolescence was extended into the twenties so that teenagers would not take scarce jobs away from adults. Currently, adolescence is generally regarded as beginning at about age 13 and ending at about age 21. Is this period a time of crisis and turmoil? Are teens usually at loggerheads with their parents? We will try to answer these questions as we take up the physical, personality, and social aspects of development during adolescence. Let's consider the effects of puberty on the adolescent, then take up personality and social-emotional development.

Puberty and Adolescent Sexuality

- "I'm *never* going to have breasts?"
- "It seems like *all* my friends shave."
- "Gee, maybe girls (guys) aren't so bad after all."

If any of these moments from adolescence sound familiar, it is because they are common reactions to the physical aspects of this challenging time of life.

One of the major tasks of adolescence is to deal with the remarkable physical changes that occur in rapid succession. During the late pre-teen or early teen years, the body undergoes a *growth spurt*, in which there is a significant increase in height, and full adult size and proportions are attained rapidly. It begins on average at age 11 in girls and 13 in boys. In addition, the maturation of the brain becomes complete during adolescence, and the sexual organs become functional. The result is that the adolescent must cope with both a growth spurt that can make her feel gawky and uncoordinated and new-found sexual attributes and feelings. We will take up the general biological changes that mark puberty, then consider teen sexuality, including pregnancy and AIDS.

The Biology of Puberty. In girls, the onset of *puberty* - sexual maturity - is signaled by the *menarche* - the first menstrual period. In the early nineteenth century, it occurred at an average age of 16; now the average is about 12.5, substantially extending this physical aspect of adolescence, and the trend toward earlier onset appears to have stopped, although, although not all physicians agree (Apter & Hermanson, 2002; Finlay et al., 2002). In boys, sexual maturation is heralded by the enlargement of the penis and testes that begins at about age 12, just preceded by pubic hair development. Initial sperm production occurs in about 50 percent of boys by age 15. Interestingly enough, boys and girls who mature unusually early or late are more likely to smoke (Shi et al., 2002). The more noticeable sexual changes that mark puberty are the development of *secondary sex characteristics*, which include pubic and underarm hair growth in both sexes, breast development in girls, and a lowering of voice pitch and growth of facial hair in boys. Girls begin to show these secondary characteristics earlier than boys, and the ages at which the changes occur can vary greatly from individual to individual (Herter et al., 2002).

Exploding Hormones: Sexuality Begins. However you spell it, S-E-X becomes a hot topic during the teen years. Sexual curiosity and exploration are virtually universal. By the age of 15, 70 percent of boys and 45 percent of girls have begun masturbating, most of them at least once a week (Leitenberg, Detzer, & Srebnik, 1993).

The sexual revolution that began in the early 1960s has produced, until recently, a continuing rise in sexual activity among teenagers; adolescents are now practicing a wider variety of sexual behaviors at younger ages. Nationwide, nearly 7% of students have sexual intercourse before age 13 (MMWR, June 28, 2002), and one recent study done in urban schools with primarily ethnic minority students found that at age 13, 27% of girls and 62% of boys reported sexual intercourse experience (Aten et al., 2002). As Figure 11-3 shows, this represents a very substantial increase over the past several decades (Laumann et al., 1994), but educational programs have begun to pay off (Kirby, 2002). As a result, there was a 16% decrease in the prevalence of sexual experience and a 24% decrease in those reporting multiple sexual partners in high school students between 1991 and 2001 (CDC, 2002). Teens who report better relationships with their parents are less likely to have had intercourse (Karofsky et al., 2001; Feldmann & Middleman, 2002). Figures for college students show that 80% have had intercourse, with women having an average of about 6 partners and men an average of 11 (Reinish et al., 1992). Girls who first experience love-making by age 14 are 4 times as likely to have had 5 or more partners in the past year as those who start later.

The principal determinants of who does and who doesn't engage in sexual activity and who doesn't appear to be biology, friends, and parents. Teens with sexually active friends are more likely to become sexually involved. In addition, teens whose parents are either very lax or very strict about sex are more likely to be sexually active than those whose parents are moderately strict. A final factor is the personality of the adolescent. Shy teens, for example, are less likely to be sexually active than are those who are more outgoing.

Teen Pregnancy: A Rude Awakening. Despite the relatively high level of sexual activity, over one-third of adolescents do not use contraceptives (Ventura et al., 1995). The result has been a dramatic increase in pregnancies among unwed teenagers. The rate of nonmarital births was 6 times as high in 1993 as in 1940, rising from less than 90,000 to over 1.23 million (Figure 11-4; NCHS, 1995). In fact, just in the decade between 1980 and 1990, there was a 49% increase (Clarke & Ventura, 1994), but there was a substantial decrease in the late 1990s to an all-time low for the U.S. of 48.5 births/1000 teenage females (Wackett, 2002; NCHS, 2002 [HEALTH, U.S., 2002]). Currently, 12.8% of all births are to teenage mothers, about 30% of current nonmarital births are to adolescents, and 72% of all births to teen mothers are nonmarital (Figure 11-5; NCHS, 2002). In addition, there are ethnic and nationality variables in nonmarital birth rates: Rates are higher for Hispanics and African-Americans and lower for Asian-Americans than for whites and much higher in the U.S. than in many other countries (NCHS, 1995; Hou, 2002). Finally, babies born to teens are more likely to be of low or very low birth weight, often resulting in reduced cognitive functioning and other problems later in life (see Chapter 10; Chandra et al., 2002).

We certainly know *how* teenagers become pregnant, but *why* is there such a high pregnancy rate? It appears that there are several factors. First, many teens lack adequate knowledge about the reproductive process and contraceptive use. Second, parental role models and peer group norms regarding the desirability of sexual activity are influential; and sex may fulfill important psychological needs, as well as the physiological sex drive. Lack of adult supervision is an additional factor. Most teen sexual activity now occurs in the home at times when parents are at work. And somewhat older men often impregnate teenage girls. In fact, a study of over 280,000 adolescent girls showed that 70% of their male sex partners were over age 20, and 15% were over age 25 (Males, 1992). Finally, at a societal level, many have cited the increasing availability of welfare for unmarried mothers as a factor. Both teens and older women are aware that if they should become pregnant and need financial help, they will receive it from the welfare system. However, the Welfare Reform Act has reduced this expectation and had some positive effects as a result (Chase-Lansdale & Pittman, 2002).

Teen pregnancy carries with it considerable risk to the mental health and educational progress of the adolescent mother. One study of pregnant Hispanic teens showed devastating effects on mental health (Zayas & Busch, 1992). Another study, this time involving African-American teen mothers, showed that pregnancy greatly increased the risk of dropping out of school (Prater, 1992). Unfortunately, standard school sex-education programs do not delay sexual activity, improve contraceptive use, or reduce the pregnancy rate (Moore et al., 1995). However, more intensive programs offer hope for the future: recent studies show a reduction in the drop-out rate from 43% to 10% when such programs are in place.

Teens and AIDS. Beyond education, the one factor that has some potential to produce a further decline in adolescent sexual activity is the increasing frequency of AIDS in the general population. The Centers for Disease Control (CDC) reports over 816,000 current cases of AIDS in the U.S. Of these, 4428 are in the 13-19-year age range, and 28,665 are found in 20-24-year-olds. The latter were largely acquired during the teen years (CDC, 2002). Worldwide, 42 million people have HIV/AIDS, and 3.1 million died of AIDS in 2002 infection (CDC, 2002). While AIDS was originally seen primarily in injecting drug users and homosexuals and predominantly in men, transmission is increasingly a heterosexual phenomenon, and about 50% of all HIV/AIDS cases are now women, who acquire the disease primarily through sexual intercourse (CDC, 2002).

Although the steady increase in teen sex could obviously increase the risk of HIV infection, the good news is that both AIDS education and condom use have risen substantially in recent years. AIDS education in the schools has increased to the point where 67% of school districts now require it (Healthy People 2000, NCHS, 1995) and 82% of teens report that they have received such education. In addition, 69% of adolescents say their parents have discussed AIDS with them (Vital and Health Statistics, NCHS, 1995). Condom use has gradually increased from 24% in 1965 to 42% in 1988 and to 46% of females and 59% of males in 1993 (Healthy People 2000, NCHS, 1995), though these figures are somewhat lower in other studies (Corwin et al., 2002). While many adolescents still don't use this protection, there is clearly considerable improvement.

Personality Development: The Identity Crisis

Most adults have a reasonably good sense of such personal characteristics as strengths and weaknesses, likes and dislikes, and goals in life. In short, they know who they are. But children do not, and it is during the transitional period of adolescence that this sense of self or personal identity is established.

G. Stanley Hall, a well-known turn-of-the-century psychologist, believed that adolescence is basically one long crisis. He characterized it as a period of "Sturm und Drang" - storm and stress - as the adolescent undergoes the emotional and behavioral transition from childhood to adulthood (Hall, 1904). A number of other personality theorists, including Sigmund Freud and, most notably, Erik Erikson, have basically agreed with Hall. According to Erikson (1959, 1962/1988), adolescence is characterized by the crisis of *identity versus role confusion.* The basic question the adolescent is trying to answer is "Who am I?" The sense of self developed during childhood is called into question as a result of the sexual changes of puberty, the development of new physical and intellectual capabilities, and pressures from parents and society at large. The adolescent is expected to become more independent and more responsible, and the result of these combined physical, psychological, and social pressures is the *identity crisis.* Until and unless this crisis is successfully resolved, the adolescent will be in a state of "role confusion" or "identity diffusion" (Erikson, 1980). More recently, James Cote has extended Erikson's ideas to include an understanding of how the personality develops in the context of the larger culture (Cote, 1993).

Also working from Erikson's formulation, James Marcia (1966; Stephen, Fraser, & Marcia, 1992) has argued that identity formation involves two principal elements. The first is a *crisis* during which previously developed values and choices are reexamined and new decisions made. This process may involve a true crisis with all the negative emotions implied, or it may be more gradual and less traumatic. The second element is *commitment* to some particular role in life. Marcia's system has permitted researchers to apply a classification scheme for determining the extent to which a given adolescent is experiencing or has experienced a crisis and the extent to which it has been resolved.

Is there really a turmoil-filled adolescent identity crisis? There is certainly good reason to believe that the potential for crisis is ever present. The growing confusion about adult roles is no doubt furthered by the relative unavailability of parental guidance in modern Western society. In fact, of the 97.1 million households in the U.S. in 1994, 9.9 million were headed by single mothers and 1.6 million by single fathers. Single parents accounted for 25% of all white parents and 65% of all black parents, with 60 percent of all children now spending at least some of childhood and adolescence with a single parent (Report to Congress, NCHS, 1995; Murry et al., 2001). Some of these children are among the 1.3 million born out of wedlock each year (Waldman & Perlman, 2001)

Single parenthood brings with it far lower family incomes, with 46% of single-mother families, as compared with 8% of two-parent families, living in poverty (Report to Congress, NCHS, 1995). In addition, single mothers are more likely to exhibit depression and poor health (Brown & Eisenberg, 1995). Not surprisingly, the children of these single parents, particularly when the parent is an adolescent, sometimes suffer considerably (McKenry & Fine, 1993). They are less happy, have home environments of lower quality, and have lower average scores on tests of intelligence and achievement (Moore, Morrison, & Greene, 1995). Moreover, many other families have two parents who work during the day and are too tired at night to be available. Finally, there is considerable evidence of the erosion of the family as a social support network, and striking data show that 2.5 million adolescents (10 percent of the total) actually hit their parents each year (Agnew & Huguley, 1989).

Adding to all this evidence the increasing frequency of suicide among teenagers (see the Probe), one would be tempted to offer an unqualified "yes" to the turmoil question. But actual research based on Marcia's approach has yielded a different answer (Larson & Reed, 1993). Reed Larson and Mark Ham (1993) asked teenagers to provide reports of their daily emotional states and obtained data from both the teens and their parents on major events in their lives. They found that most teens were not in a state of crisis and that those who did experience more negative feelings were likely to be undergoing more negative life events. Other research suggests that the identity crisis is more likely to take place between the ages of 18 and 22 than between 12 and 16. More generally, it seems clear that adolescents as a group do not have poor mental health and are not undergoing a period of excessive stress. The reality is that adolescence is a period of self-examination, reorganization, and change, producing an increasingly clear sense of self.

Social-Emotional Development

The physical and sexual changes of adolescence are among the many factors that influence social and emotional development. Biological factors interact with sociocultural influences (peers, parents, cultural standards) and individual factors to affect the adolescent's behavior (Gavazzi, Anderson, & Sabatelli, 1993). We will consider the roles of peers and parents in teen behavior, then discuss the development of gender identity and the influence of ethnicity.

Peers and Parents: A Classic Tug of War. Peer group influence begins in childhood and becomes increasingly stronger as the individual approaches and reaches adolescence. Peers provide a source of social support, give continuing feedback about the adolescent's behavior, and serve to legitimize a variety of activities in which the teenager might otherwise be hesitant to engage. The peer group also adds to the adolescent's sense of security as he attempts to move toward increasing independence from his parents.

At a more general level, the peer group serves as a source of relaxation, entertainment, enjoyment, and reinforcement. In some cases, it becomes a clique in which members must meet certain selection criteria to be accepted. In other cases, the peer group is a more formal organization, such as an athletic team, a church youth group, or a sponsored club. Involvement with such organized groups, which typically have adult supervision, is often encouraged by parents, but these groups seem unable to fulfill all the functions of the informal peer groups that form spontaneously.

So advantageous is the peer group for the individual adolescent that teenagers have been found to spend more time with friends than with parents, and we might expect that this would mean the peer group is more influential than the parents. It can be, as one study of sexual behavior in Hispanic teens showed (Christopher, Johnson, & Roosa, 1993). However, parents remain very influential, with greater and more positive influence when good parent-child relationships as established by age 7, long before adolescence (Flouri & Buchanan, 2002). Parents influence such superficial behaviors as choice of clothing but have a far more significant impact at the deeper level of attitudes and values (Figure 11-6; Jackson, 2002). A study of over 3700 teens showed that parental practices affect not only such areas as academic achievement and drug use, but even the choice of adolescent groups with which their teenager associates (Brown, Lamborn, & Steinberg, 1993). In fact, although they will typically not admit it to peers, teens frequently agree with their parents on such important values as "work before play," independence, and self-reliance (Kasser et al., 2002).

But all that parents bring to their teens is not "goodness and light." They also influence the development of such unhealthy behaviors as drinking, drug abuse, risky sexual activity, and smoking (McNeely et al., 2002). Parental alcohol consumption strongly influences the development of drinking in the adolescent. Drinking parents also influence their children to abuse alcohol and drugs in at least three ways. First, the parent models the behavior, and the adolescent learns by observing. Secondly, the heavy drinker puts the child under added stress, causing negative feelings that may be temporarily offset by drinking. Finally, drinking parents usually fail to monitor their child's behavior (Chassin, Pillow, Curran, & Brooke, 1993).

Beyond drinking itself, studies show that parents who permit or encourage aggressive behavior or display low standards of personal moral behavior are more likely to end up with teens who drink (Brook, Whiteman, Cohen, & Tanaka, 1992). Parents are joined by friends of the adolescent and, interestingly enough, by doctors in introducing their teenager to drugs. In fact, these three groups have more influence on drug use than do drug dealers (Khavari, 1993)! The adolescent's perception of the social norms is also a major influence. "How many of my peers," he asks himself, "drink heavily and use drugs?" His subjective and often inaccurate answer can greatly affect his own behavior, and teens often substantially overestimate peer drug use.

Parents are also more responsible than peers for juvenile delinquency, violence, and the 18 percent school dropout rate (Report to Congress, NCHS, 1995; Gavazzi, Anderson, & Sabatelli, 1993), and family values are a major factor in teen pregnancy (Rodriguez & Jimenez, 2001). Moreover, parents influence teen smoking, though a review of 27 major studies suggests that other factors may be considerably more important. They include low socioeconomic status, low self-esteem, peer smoking, and peer approval (Conrad, Flay, & Hill, 1992). The media also strongly influence such behaviors as smoking, not to mention violence and sex, a topic we take up in Chapter 6 (Anderson & Bushman, 2001; Blumstein, 2002).

Gender Role and Gender Identity. Differences between males and females in either behavior or mental processes are referred to as *gender differences*. It has often been suggested that such differences are minimal, which bolsters the argument that the two sexes are equal. Alice Eagly (1995) points out, however, that this assertion grew largely out of political agendas aimed at raising the status of women in society and that it is not entirely supported by empirical studies. The moral observation that men and women should be *treated* equally does not necessarily mean that they *perform* in equivalent ways in all areas (see Chapter 9). Two important aspects of gender differentiation are gender role and gender identity.

Sex role or *gender role* refers to a wide range of behaviors, attitudes, and emotional states that are commonly seen as associated with an individual's gender. Boys and girls begin to learn the components of their gender roles in early childhood, and adolescence forces them to recognize and largely finalize their understanding of these roles. The problem is that many people engage in *gender role stereotyping*, in which they come to believe that certain behaviors and only those behaviors are appropriate for members of a given gender. "Real men don't cry," "Women are more sensitive," "Men are stronger and more assertive," and "Women are more socially skilled" are examples of stereotypes.

Psychologists have long known that stereotypes are often inaccurate and tend to narrow thinking. In the case of sex role stereotypes, one major effect has been on the jobs women and men choose - and the jobs they are chosen for. Male nurses and elementary school teachers are still rare because these jobs are not perceived by either men or women as gender-appropriate for men. Similarly, people who hold to female stereotypes may have difficulty seeing a woman as a physician, police officer, automobile mechanic, corporate executive, or engineer - or as President of the United States. While more and more women are entering such professions as medicine, law, and business, they still tend to earn less than men. Moreover, while 50% of law students are women, only about 15% of partners in law firms are, and only 7% of senior corporate executives are female. The good news is that there is considerable improvement over prior decades.

Gender identity is the set of self-perceptions that make up the individual's personal sense of being male or female. It is an important part of his or her overall identity as a separate, independent person. In fact, *gender schema theory* holds that gender identity acts as a central focus around which children and adolescents organize social perceptions of themselves and other people (Bem, 1988). Their own sense of self-esteem is often strongly influenced by the extent to which their physical and psychological characteristics appear similar to those of older adolescents or adults of their own gender. Adolescent boys, for example, are often concerned about when they will start growing beards, and girls may watch anxiously for the appearance of breasts.

Gender identity actually appears by about the age of 3, when it is common to see girls try to mimic mom's gender-role behaviors, such as putting on makeup, and boys try to imitate dad by "shaving." By age 5, the child has a definite perception of gender differences and realizes that the gender role is a permanent part of his or her identity. Late childhood and early adolescence may bring an exaggerated attempt to behave in gender-appropriate ways, with girls acting overly submissive and using too much makeup and boys becoming highly aggressive and rowdy.

Current social norms encourage both genders to also engage in some behaviors that represent violations of traditional stereotypes. These *androgynous* behaviors - those that may appear in either sex - make life more complicated for the adolescent. There is pressure not only to develop a traditional gender identity, but at the same time to exhibit some degree of androgyny. Girls, for example, are often encouraged to be assertive and boys to be sensitive. Both sexes are also exposed to the increasingly widespread view that jobs should not be gender-stereotyped. The girl's gender identity should ideally include the possibility of becoming a physician, engineer, or auto mechanic, and the boy's should accept the possibility of doing housework or becoming a nurse.

Ethnicity and Adolescence. Ethnicity also influences the experiences of adolescence, which is treated in Western cultures as a time of transition. During this period, the individual must move from dependence to independence, from relative lack of responsibility to mature responsibility. In many other cultures, however, adolescence is brief or nonexistent. In these cultures, the transition from childhood to adulthood is marked by a *rite of passage*, a ceremony that may include some sort of physical trial or mutilation. Once the culturally specified rites have been completed, the individual is treated as an adult.

There are also ethnic differences within U.S. society. Black teens, for example, are more likely to experience poverty and discrimination than are whites, and behavioral norms in black and Hispanic communities often differ from each other and from those of the majority culture. Moreover, all minority adolescents must decide on the balance between their *ethnic identity* - adopting the values and characteristics of their own ethnic group - and *acculturation* - adopting those of the broader culture.

Adult Development: From Maturity to Old Age

Adulthood is usually defined as that portion of the life span that occurs after maturity is reached. There are at least three kinds of maturity: biological, psychological, and social. *Biological maturity* is attained when the individual becomes capable of reproduction in the early teen years. *Psychological maturity* typically comes later when we begin to routinely engage in such adult behaviors as planning, thinking through the implications of our actions, adapting more rapidly to new situations, and becoming involved in continuing intimate relationships. *Social maturity* arrives when stable family and work roles are established. Obviously, the ages at which these various forms of maturity are attained vary from one person to another. Some may become mature in every sense by the late teens, while others do not reach psychological or social maturity until their thirties - if at all. We will consider the stages of development during adulthood and the biological changes that take place, then take up, in turn, the issues of cognitive, personality, social, and career development.

Stages of Adult Development

Although adults do not undergo the dramatic changes seen in infancy, childhood, and adolescence, they do enter and resolve crises, become yet more mature, and take on new responsibilities. Psychologists who believe that the basic challenges of adulthood occur in a predictable fashion have tried to delineate stages or phases in adult development. The idea of adult developmental stages originated in Erik Erikson's psychosocial theory of development, described in Chapter 10. Erikson divided adulthood into three stages: young adulthood (about ages 18 to 25 or 30), characterized by the issue of *intimacy versus isolation*; middle adulthood (approximately the thirties and forties), characterized by *generativity versus stagnation*; and maturity (age 45 on, especially old age), characterized by *ego integrity versus despair*. A more recent theorist, Daniel Levinson (1978, 1986), conducted an intensive study of 40 men, then outlined three stages of early adulthood, three stages of middle adulthood, and a final stage of old age. At each stage there are developmental tasks to be accomplished. The period of early adulthood between the ages of 22 and 28, for example, is marked by marriage and the establishment of a home; the midlife transition of the early 40s involves a reexamination of prior accomplishments in light of future possibilities. Despite the fact that Levinson used a small, all-male sample, his theory has received wide attention and is the approach to adult development popularized in Gail Sheehey's best-selling book *Passages* (1976). Levinson's theory has been criticized because it suggests clear breaks between stages, an idea that has yet to be substantiated. His emphasis on the widespread occurrence of a *midlife crisis*, discussed in Horizon 1, has also come under fire.

Biological Change: Ups and Downs

It is no secret that adulthood is a period of very gradual physiological decline. Arteries begin to lose their elasticity and to become blocked. Muscle strength, visual acuity, lung capacity, and reflex speed peak at about age thirty, then progressively decline. And all organ systems show a gradual decrease in functioning. Adults are also subject to neuron loss, which we will take up later when we look at the neurophysiology of aging, and women eventually experience the menopause.

Menopause - the point at which the ovaries cease to produce estrogen, menstrual periods end, and the woman is no longer fertile - is one major biological reality of adulthood. It begins at an average age of 51 - somewhat earlier for those who smoke, eat a high fat diet or are vegetarians, and somewhat later for those giving birth before age 25 (Przegl, 2002). Some women experience such physical symptoms as "hot flashes" (sensations of heat, mostly in the upper body), nausea, dizziness, and headaches. Psychological symptoms, like anxiety, depression, and irritability, can also occur (Anderson & Posner, 2002). However, both physical and emotional symptoms are typically mild and often virtually nonexistent, explaining why 70% of women report that they either perceive no change or feel relieved when the menopause arrives (McCoy, 2002). The reduction in estrogen levels can be a major causal factor in osteoporosis - the loss of bone tissue and consequent weakening of bones. Estrogen loss also increases the likelihood of heart attacks. However, the estrogen supplements commonly given to post-menopausal women can reduce or eliminate these effects.

Cognitive Development

Jean Piaget, whose theory has guided most work in cognitive development, initially hypothesized that adults engage primarily in the formal operational thinking first seen in adolescence (Chapter 10). They use abstract concepts to produce logical reasoning. However, later evidence forced him to revise his theory to suggest instead that adults use formal operations for only some of their thinking. In particular, he believed that this sophisticated logical mode of reasoning might be used primarily within the individual's primary areas of expertise and interest (Piaget, 1972). The engineer thinks logically about the designs of computer chips (her job) and about gourmet cooking (her hobby), but not about the national crime problem.

Neo-Piagetian theorists have proposed models of postformal thought. They point out that the formal operational thinking of the adolescent and young adult is limited to logical operations *within* one situation or system. Knowledge is absolute and does not vary from one setting to another. *Postformal* thought crosses situations and involves a number of diverse systems and their interrelationships. For the postformal thinker, reality consists of numerous, integrated, dynamic systems. The systems are interdependent, and knowledge thus depends on context. What these Neo-Piagetian theorists are saying, in effect, is that many adult thinkers go beyond formal operations to a higher form of cognition that is both more complex and more effective (McBride, 1999).

Personality Development: Stability is the Rule

There are two basic, related questions regarding personality development during adulthood: (1) Does the personality continue to develop or is it fully formed earlier in life? and (2) Does the personality of the adult remain stable throughout adulthood or does it change?

Theorists differ markedly on the issue of continued development. Some, like Sigmund Freud, believe that the personality is formed primarily in childhood; the experiences of early life determine what the personality of the adult will be. Others, like Erik Erikson, hypothesize that development continues throughout adulthood and into old age (see Chapter 10), a position that Levinson's stage theory also supports. While a majority of developmental psychologists now subscribe to the view that development does continue into adulthood, the issue remains unresolved.

We are closer to answering the stability question. Most research suggests that central personality characteristics remain quite stable throughout adulthood. The extraverted young adult will be an extraverted older adult. The anxious late adolescent will remain an anxious elder. We will have more to say on this issue when we discuss the aging personality later in the chapter.

Leiben Und Arbeiten

When asked what a healthy adult should be able to do, Sigmund Freud replied, "Leiben und Arbeiten" - "love and work." These two themes - relationships and careers - recur in all the major approaches to adult development. For most people in our society, one or another intimate relationship typically leads to marriage, and middle adulthood is often concerned with maintaining the marital relationship, raising a family, and advancing in one's job or career. In later adulthood, intimate relationships change as children leave home, and working life changes as retirement approaches. From time to time throughout adulthood individuals question whether they are doing the right thing - whether they have chosen the right spouse, the right occupation, the right lifestyle. Such questioning may result in a decision to make changes - divorce, career switch, relocation to a new city - or in an acceptance of the status quo, for better or for worse. But with age, fewer changes are made, and most individuals come to terms with the life they have chosen.

Because issues of love and work are central to adulthood - by far the longest developmental stage in the human life cycle - we will focus next on relationships and careers in an effort to further understand how the adult develops.

Social Development: Marriage and Family

Bernice Neugarten (1979) suggested that most adults are quite concerned about the loud ticking of a *social clock* - a set of cultural norms that specify the major tasks of adulthood and their appropriate timing. When should we be leaving home, beginning a career, getting married, becoming involved in the community? The normative timing varies from one culture to another and from one generation to the next. In the U.S. society of the 1950s, it was appropriate to marry as early as 19 and as late as 24 and to start a career in the mid-twenties. Now, it is "OK" to marry much later. In fact, between 1955 and 1992, the percentage of unmarried people aged 25-29 years increased from 30% to 54% for men and from 14% to 41% for women. Careers may also now begin in the late twenties or early thirties.

This cultural specification of social timing is a source of both satisfaction and stress. When we meet the guidelines of the social clock, we experience the pleasure of "doing it right." When we do things at the wrong hour, we often undergo stress and anxiety. Those who marry at age 18 or remain single at 35 feel the pressure to conform to the social clock. To make matters worse, the times on the clock are constantly, if gradually, changing. The ideal family of recent decades (working dad, housewife mom, married at age 21, with two bright-eyed kids) now makes up only about 15% of the population. Families headed by single parents, two working parents, and unmarried parents have become the more mixed and complex norm.

Marriage: Cure For Many Ills. For most people, the single greatest lifetime source of intimacy and social support is marriage, and the benefits of marriage are statistically quite substantial. Studies show that the marital partner may be an important source of emotional support, particularly in times of stress and that married people have better physical and mental health than their unmarried counterparts (Bolger et al., 2002; Tower et al., 2002). In fact, studies have shown that the companionship provided by marriage even protects men and women statistically from death. Cancer mortality, for example, is 15% higher in single than in married patients (Kravdal, 2001). Married people also display higher morale, greater happiness, a stronger sense of psychological well-being (Wilson, 2002), and less alcohol consumption (Prescott & Kendler, 2001) than do singles. Perhaps these benefits are among the major reasons why over 95 percent of people marry at some time during their lives.

Men who are high in self-confidence and women who are high in nurturance are more likely to have happy marriages (Furukawa et al., 2002), and middle-aged women are happiest in marriages where they have children and work outside the home (Baruch, Barnett, and Rivers, 1983). Other studies have found that the happiest marriages among older couples are those involving egalitarian relationships, those in which the husband is older than the wife, and those in which the spouses have similar levels of intelligence. There is also variability over time in just how happy the couple tends to be. Studies show that couples are typically happiest before the first child is born and after the children grow up and leave home, with the greatest tensions likely to occur during the child-rearing years (Findel & Hansen, 1992). Income level appears to have little or no effect on marital satisfaction, but perceived adequacy of income does have an effect.

The Dark Side of Marriage: Divorce. When marital satisfaction reaches a low ebb, *divorce* becomes an increasingly likely possibility. During the mid-nineteenth century, only about 4 percent of marriages ended in divorce. However, the divorce rate climbed steadily until World War II, then remained stable until the late 1960s. By 1975 the rate had climbed to

43 percent, and by 1991 it had reached nearly 50% for first marriages (Schoen, 1987; U.S. Bureau of the Census, 1991; NCHS, 1995; see Figure 11-8). There were about 1.2 million divorces in 1994 (Monthly Vital Statistics, October, 1995, NCHS). Of particular interest is a substantial increase over the past 15 years in divorce among couples in their sixties and beyond (Hammond & Muller, 1992). And estimates suggest that up to 56% of those now married will eventually be divorced (Monthly Vital Statistics, October, 1995, NCHS). Studies also show substantial racial and ethnic differences. In particular, African-American women tend to have less stable marriages than white women (Bramlett & Mosher, 2002).

Remarriage after divorce, as happens in 85% of cases, is also risky. Marital satisfaction is lower in second marriages, and they are less stable (Booth & Edwards, 1992). As a result, the divorce rate is about 25% higher for remarriages than for first marriages.

Why has the divorce rate increased so dramatically? For one thing, changes in the very fabric of society have made divorce much more acceptable. In addition, the increased entry of women into the labor force, combined with the easy availability of welfare assistance, has made women less financially dependent on husbands. Looking within individual marriages, Lynn Gigy and Joan Kelly (1992) surveyed over 400 divorced men and women. Their participants reported that unmet emotional needs, conflict, boredom, and differences in preferred lifestyle were the most frequent factors in arriving at the decision to divorce. Other studies add stubbornness, defensiveness, and withdrawal from interactions to this list (Gottman & Levenson, 1992). One final factor is genetics. Matt McGue and David Lykken (1992) studied over 1500 pairs of identical and fraternal twins and found that concordance for divorce was significantly higher in the identicals, confirming the importance of heredity. In effect, you can inherit tendencies that make you a much more likely candidate for divorce, probably by influencing your personality and the ways in which you treat and interact with your spouse.

The effects of divorce on both the adults and their children vary from negative to devastating. Marital breakup is associated with increased rates of illness, disability, homicide and suicide. The initial effects of divorce on children can also be substantial. Common effects include decreased self-esteem, lower grades in school, and increased depression (Isaacs, 2002). The long-term effects are less well understood. Some studies show that adolescents whose parents are divorced are more likely to have mental health problems, drop out of school, and become pregnant (Wolchik et al., 2002). However, other studies find no such long-term effects, and Joan Kelly, after reviewing the literature, concluded that it is exposure to marital conflict, not divorce, that has the most serious effects on children (Kelly, 2000). The child is worse off with two parents who have severe, ongoing conflicts than with a single parent (Amato, 2001).

Parenthood and Family Life. Did you know that your parents have spent, on average, a quarter of a million dollars raising you (Waldman & Perlman, 2001)? So why do people have children? Many couples expect children to be a source of pleasure and fulfillment. Others succumb to social pressure from parents and friends who insist that having children is an expected part of marriage. And there are those who have children to pass on the family name, prove their femininity or masculinity, and bring stability to a shaky marriage. The latter is a particularly unsound reason for parenthood and may eventually contribute to the increasingly common one-parent family.

The birth of a child creates a family, and that family is a *system* because a change in any one of its parts is likely to affect all the other parts. The basic purpose of the family is to satisfy the needs of its members, a role that it fulfills well only when the family is cohesive and the parents supportive.

The Empty Nest: Loss or Gain? The departure of the last child from home leaves the parents with an "empty nest." Popular articles and books have often suggested that the empty nest creates a difficult transition period for the mother in particular, who is expected to experience depression and loneliness. However, the empty nest syndrome turns out to be largely a myth. Studies have shown that both women and men are actually happier after the children leave the home. Moreover, women who do experience emotional problems when children leave home typically have a prior history of such problems.

Children who have left home are likely to keep in touch with their parents on a regular basis. One study found that 34 percent of parents, including elderly parents, lived within 10 minutes of their children, and that did not include the 19 percent of women and 7 percent of men over 65 who actually live with family members (Shanas 1980). About half of the older parents had seen at least one of their children on the day of the interview or the previous day, and an additional 25 percent had seen one of their children the previous week.

Career Development: The Adult at Work

You may be reading this chapter as a small part of your preparation for a career, and, indeed, you may already have a job. If not, you probably soon will. Most adults - 77 percent of men and 59 percent of women - are either working or looking for work (Sepielli & Palumbo, U.S. Bureau of the Census, 1996).

Choosing an occupation is not an easy task. Personality, social background, sex, and luck can all be significant factors in making the choice. Timothy Owens (1992) examined occupational choice data on over 2200 recent high school graduates to see what variables best predicted each young man's job decision. He found that the most important factors were family background and preferences, school performance, and peer influence. Attitudes toward self and toward society had little effect. Other data show that only about 20 percent of working people are in jobs they have actively chosen.

Working Women. Over the past several decades, women have entered the work force in ever-increasing numbers, even as the percentage of working men has decreased. The percentage of women in the work force climbed from 30% in 1950 to 57% in 1990 (Figure 11-9). During that same period, participation rates for men dropped from 82% to 74%. Not only are a majority of women now working, but they have come to dominate some previously "male" occupations and to increasingly gain high positions in business, government, and other areas. For example, women now hold a majority of the positions in such work categories as bill collector, real estate agent, insurance adjuster, and production line assembler.

Work and job status patterns of women have been widely studied. One common finding is that the salaries of female workers are still generally lower than those of their male counterparts. The salary discrepancy can be attributed to active discrimination by some employers, highly socialized career choices, and career interruptions. One study showed, for example, that no married women in their sample had experienced the continuous career pattern typically found in men. In fact, about 30 percent of married women had quite unstable careers, with as many as five interruptions. Some women are highly motivated and dedicated to their careers, while others put their households first and their careers second (Tangri & Jenkins, 1992).

A particularly interesting study of the occupational concerns of women was conducted by Betty Walker and her colleagues. They asked 201 intellectually gifted women, who spanned the decades from the 1910s through the 1980s, to indicate their major concerns regarding personal, educational, and vocational growth. The concerns were quite consistent across the eight decades. The women were disturbed about the vague expectations of schools and the society and the lack of helpful occupational counseling. In addition, they noted the significant lack of role models - highly successful older women - and the virtual absence of mentoring by superiors. Finally, they felt that they were hurt by being taught few networking skills and, as a result, by not being "in the know" concerning career advancement possibilities (Walker, Reis, & Leonard, 1992). Fortunately, there is evidence of change in some of these factors, with reductions in role conflict and greater work place support for career women.

One Household, Two Careers. The massive entry of women into the work force has obviously meant that there are many dual-earner career households. This means a higher income for the family and also changes family work habits and interaction patterns. Housework becomes an issue in dual-earner families. Principles of equity would certainly suggest that when the wife is working full time, the husband should take on a significant proportion of the housework, ideally one-half. Studies show, however, that he doesn't: Wives clearly do most of the housework, though there is evidence that husbands are beginning to do more.

Although generally viewed as essential, jobs often interfere with family life. Both men and women report that their jobs often get in the way of family activities, though the opposite is rarely true. Some of these job effects are indirect. Job conflict and insecurity cause depression and difficulty in concentration, which, in turn, reduce sexual satisfaction and interfere with overall marital fulfillment (Barling & MacEwen, 1992).

Jobs and Mental Health. Job satisfaction can be a source of happiness, and job dissatisfaction and resultant stress can be causal factors in poor mental health (Buunk & Janssen, 1992). One study examined the relationship between jobs and psychological distress and showed that poor job role quality is significantly associated with psychological distress in both women and men (Barnett, Marshall, Raudenbush, & Brennan, 1993). Other data show that this effect is heightened in men who have troubled relationships with their significant others (Barnett & Marshall, 1992).

Unemployment. Having no job can be far worse than having a bad job. One recent investigation showed that mental well-being was greatly reduced in 46% of the 700 unemployed people in the study. When they were re-employed, only 17% showed a reduced sense of well-being (Lahelma, 1992).

The effects of unemployment go well beyond mental health. Some cases of depression induced by job loss end in suicide. In fact, there is a significant increase in the suicide rate among unemployed people (Pritchard, 1992). Moreover, unemployment is associated with increased crime. Both property crime and homicide rates are higher in the unemployed, and this is true of both African-Americans and whites (M. Smith, Devine, & Sheley, 1992).

Adult: Living Longer and Living Better

The Indian Summer of Life should be a little sunny and a little sad, like the season, and infinite in wealth and depth of tone.

--Henry Brooks Adams, *The Education of Henry Adams*, 1918, Chapter 35.

Before you start reading about the aging process, pause for a moment and conjure up an image of your grandfather at age 75: gray hair, wrinkled skin, perhaps somewhat impaired hearing and vision, maybe some new aches and pains. Chances are pretty good that you will reach age 75 or beyond, that you will live longer than your parents and your grandparents before them, and that you will live to see the substantial changes likely to take place as the American population grows older.

Population change statistics can be fascinating because they tell us just what has happened in the past and what is likely to happen in the future. For example, life expectancy - the length of the average person's life at birth in about 500 BC in ancient Greece was 20. You might not have lived to read this chapter! In 100 AD in ancient Rome it was 22 years. By 1900, life expectancy at birth in the U.S. had climbed to 47 (a 22-year-old college student would be middle-aged!), reaching 68 years by 1950 and 76.9 by 2000 (Figure 11-11; Health, United States, NCHS, 2002). And all the indications are that the U.S. population is destined to rapidly grow larger and grayer. Since 1900, the size of the general population has tripled, while the elderly population has increased elevenfold. Between 1950 and 2000, the proportion of the population that is elderly rose from 8 to 12%, and mortality in that group decreased by one-third (Health, United States, 2000, NCHS, 2002). The total population is expected to increase from 252 million in 1994 to 302 million in the year 2040 (Knickman & Snell, 2002), and the proportion that is elderly should rise to 20% (NCHS, 2002).

Whereas a majority of people were under age 30 a few years ago, a majority are now over 30, and the median (middle) age, which was 20 at the time of the Revolutionary War and 32 in 1987, should be 42 by 2030. This increase in median age reflects the steady increase in life expectancy and, correspondingly, the proportion of the population that is over 65. That proportion has moved steadily upward to 12% in 1990 and will rise to 20% by the year 2000. In actual numbers, only 3 million Americans were age 65 or older in 1920, but by 1970, 20 million were in this age group, and the number should reach 35 million by the year 2000 and 59 million by 2030 (Wegman, 1987; NCHS, 1995).

Equally interesting are life expectancy data for various age groups. The basic rule is that the longer you live, the longer you are likely to live. Those born in 1986 should reach an average age of 76, with 45 percent reaching 80 and 30 percent reaching 85. However, those who have already reached the age of 65 still have 17 years to live (see Figure 11-11). Those who reach 75 should live another 11 years, and an 85-year-old can expect another 6 years of life (Vital and Health Statistics, NCHS, 1995).

The Mythology of "Elderly"

What does it mean to be "elderly?" When my father was 80 years old, he mentioned one day that he and my mother might not travel to Florida as they had done each winter for many years. It was just too much trouble, he said. I pointed out that all they had to do was pack, be driven a short distance to the airport, and board a plane. His reply was an insightful commentary on the aging process in the older adult: "All I can tell you," he said, "is that being 80 is a lot different than being 70." What he meant was that being elderly typically means being slower to move, having less energy and more aches, and often being saddled with one or more chronic disorders. Under these circumstances, one's priorities for life activities change, perhaps of necessity. However, even at age 85, participants in one recent study reported generally good health and a good quality of life (Michel, 2002).

The myths, however, go far beyond this reality. Cicero, the lawyer in Shakespeare's *Julius Caesar*, listed the "sins" of old age that had represented beliefs about aging as far back as Biblical times. He indicted old age on four charges:

- It weakens the body
- It virtually eliminates the enjoyment of life
- It makes great accomplishments impossible
- It is near death

Was Cicero right? Well, we'll see that he wasn't. Most older people do not have the severe deficits that Cicero speaks of (only about 4-6% have Alzheimer's disease, the major cause of deficit), do not live alone, and are not living in nursing homes or other institutions (Deck et al., 2002). Moreover, most are not sick at any given time, and the chronic disorders they may have are often not debilitating. Finally, many are happy and satisfied, and significant accomplishments by elderly professionals are common (Butler, et al., 1991).

The myths nevertheless persist in Western cultures. They are harmful because they create a significant disadvantage for older people, who are often viewed as unhealthy, demented, and useless. The result is a bias against the aged that can result in *ageism* - a form of prejudice and discrimination based on age. It can be seen in discrimination against older people on the job, in the lower priority given to the elderly by physicians and other health care practitioners, in the stereotypes of the elderly that are common in society, and in the abuse of older people. Fortunately, we have begun to move away from the stereotypes with educational programs in such fields as nursing (Pohl & Boyd, 1993) and optometry (Rumsey, 1993), as well as the development of fields like geriatric psychology and psychiatry (Blazer, 1992). There is also an increasing governmental effort to help aging Americans. The Administration on Aging (AOA) has developed two major programs. The Aging Network, with 25,000 local service providers spread across the 50 states, and the National Eldercare Campaign, which provides such services as information, transportation, housekeeping, repair and health screening. An evaluation of the program by the U.S. General Accounting Office suggests that it is quite effective (GAO, 1994).

Despite these positive changes, many continue to accept the myths as truths. Worst of all, the biggest believers in the stereotypes are the elderly themselves, and that can be literally unhealthy. Studies show that those who have more positive self-perceptions of the aging process report better health than do those with more negative views (Levy et al., 2002), and health status is an important contributor to perceived quality of life (Deck et al., 2002). In addition, those who are proactive in pursuing regular exercise, avoiding tobacco, and drinking only in moderation are healthier and live longer (Kahana et al., 2002). In what follows, you will learn that the myths are just that. Indeed, we will likely soon see an increasingly optimistic view of the 70s and 80s as truly "golden years" or, as Henry Adams said, the "Indian Summer of Life."

The Graying of America

As the graying of America continues, psychologists are struggling to understand its implications for both the individual and society. What do we mean by the terms "young" and "old" in our society? Age is not just a matter of chronological years. In fact, Birren (1964) defined three types of age, like the three types of maturity mentioned earlier in this chapter. *Biological age* is the person's present position relative to his potential life span. It is assessed by determining the functional state of the vital organ systems and is reflected in behavior.

Psychological age refers to the ability of the individual to adapt to changing environmental demands. It involves a combination of cognitive, emotional, and motivational capacities. The individual's psychological age, like her biological age, can be younger or older than her chronological age.

Social age refers to the individual's habits and roles relative to the society of which he is a part. It is determined by assessing language habits, mode of dress, and deference to those in leadership positions. A 70-year-old who continues to ski and play racquetball may also have attitudes and clothing preferences similar to those in their thirties or forties.

Cognitive Aging: Loss May Be Minimal

To put it bluntly, does older mean dumber? Do our cognitive abilities deteriorate as we grow older? Is aging associated with a lower IQ, a reduced ability to think, slower learning, and poor memory? The answer in 330 BC, given by the great Greek philosopher, Aristotle was "Yes." Memory, in particular he said, suffers with age. The brief answer in 2002 AD is that there are certainly cognitive changes with aging but that these are not as consistent or severe as many people fear they will be. In fact, there are many examples of high-functioning, productive older people. I know a dentist who is still practicing daily at age 79, a physician seeing patients at age 92, and a 93-year-old psychologist who continues to publish his research each year. And you may be aware of more famous cases: Frank Lloyd Wright, who designed New York's Guggenheim Museum at age 79; Marian Hart, who flew her single-engine plane across the Atlantic at 84; Grandma Moses, who painted at age one hundred; and actor George Burns, who performed until his death, also at one hundred. Even the cognitive losses that do occur may be reversible with training (Edwards et al., 2002). However, there is evidence for a rapid cognitive deterioration, called the terminal decline, that occurs in some very old people shortly before death (Hagberg, 2001)

Sensory, Motor, and Physiological Processes. You may have a grandfather who is hard of hearing or a grandmother whose vision is severely impaired. Such sensory losses make it more difficult for the elderly to deal with the world around them. Studies confirm widespread sensory deficits in the older population. Hearing is impaired in 46%, and hearing loss reduces the ability to recognize and comprehend speech (Schneider et al., 2002), though newer treatments for hearing impairment produce considerable improvement (Junker et al., 2002; James et al., 2002). Similarly, there is a significant decline in visual acuity with age, and the ability to discriminate colors decreases as well (Faubert, 2002). Since our cognitive processes are in part dependent on the ability of our senses to take in environmental information, these sensory losses are likely to result in cognitive impairment unless they are corrected.

Studies also show a slowing of motor processes and a reduction in physiological functions in older adults (Ranganathan et al., 2001; Ketcham et al., 2002). Reaction time increases (slows) with age, primarily as a result of changes in brain function. Comparing college students and older adults, Timothy Salthouse (1993) found that the elderly participants showed impaired processing speed as compared with the college students. Motor impairments occur throughout the body, but are more likely and more severe in the lower extremities (Onder et al., 2002). Such findings mean that it may be possible to reverse or partially reverse some of the effects of aging on perceptual-motor processes. In fact, there appear to be no differences in processing between older and younger adults when the older adults are healthier or both groups have had extensive practice on the task. In addition, there is evidence that regular aerobic exercise, which increases neural blood flow, may increase processing speed and decrease reaction times, though some studies find no exercise effect (Hill, Storandt, and Malley, 1993).

Old Dogs and New Tricks: Learning. Researchers have generally found that declines in verbal learning ability (such as learning lists of words) are small until about age 65, after which the losses are greater (Marquis et al., 2002). However, even these later declines may not occur if the elderly person is free of chronic disease. In more complex types of learning, such as problem-solving and complex decision-making, older adults tend to use less efficient strategies, are not as likely to arrive at correct solutions, make more errors, and often fail to modify their strategies after making incorrect responses.

What might account for age-related declines in learning? The answer seems to lie in three areas: pacing, motivation, and distractibility. *Pacing* refers to the rate at which experimental tasks are presented to the participant. In general, elderly subjects take more time to learn a task and to respond after learning has taken place. In fact, *slowness* in learning, as in perceptual processing, appears to be the major behavioral indicator of the aging process. It has been called the "most pervasive" characteristic of the elderly.

A second factor may be *motivation*. Older subjects may be more cautious when confronted with learning tasks and therefore make no response at all rather than risking an incorrect one. The third possible factor is an *attention_deficit*. Studies show that older adults are more easily distracted during learning, possibly as a result of reduced levels of arousal and alertness. Recent research suggests that neurological deterioration, particularly in the frontal lobes, may underlie many some of these age-related changes (Parkin & Walter, 1992).

Whatever the causes underlying learning deficits in aging populations, there may be some help. In particular, participating regularly in learning activities may improve performance. Barbara Clough (1992) studied 332 older adults and found that such learning activities as reading, traveling, and watching educational TV helped. Similarly, a continuing education program had positive effects on learning, social satisfaction and symptoms of aging in a sample of older people, but the effects lasted only a few weeks (Panayotoff, 1993).

Memory. Donald Hebb, a well-known psychologist, complained at the age of 75 that he sometimes had difficulty remembering words when he was lecturing to introductory psychology classes (Cohen, 1980). Hebb is not alone in observing that memory declines with age. Certain aspects of memory are quite clearly deficient in older populations (Hasher et al., 2002), and coronary bypass procedures, more common in the elderly, further impair memory (Bergh et al., 2002). Research suggests that elderly people store information in memory just as efficiently as younger ones. The problem appears to lie in the process of getting the information into memory (called encoding) and the process of retrieving it (Wingfield & Kahana, 2002). Their performance improves when they are presented with highly structured tasks and when they use memory strategies or "crutches" (Mackay et al., 2002). In fact, the famous behaviorist B.F. Skinner (Chapter 6) used such strategies successfully on himself in his later years. Memory clinic studies show, more generally, that deficits can often be reversed with treatment (Hejl et al., 2002).

Intelligence. Does intelligence also decline in old age? The general answer is "not usually." There appears to be no set rule, but probably a majority of older people experience no decrease (Shilling, 2002). In fact, a longitudinal study has shown that the "oldest old" actually show an *increase* in verbal IQ with aging (Field & Gueldner, 2001). We take up this topic in more detail in Chapter 9.

Wisdom. Older means wiser. Or does it? Most people believe that wisdom increases with age, but until recently this was an untested hypothesis. Paul Baltes and his colleagues recently began collecting data on *wisdom*, which they define as a body of expert knowledge regarding the practical issues of life (Baltes & Staudinger, 1993; Smith & Baltes, 1990). Wisdom means having deep, factual knowledge about life matters, exhibiting good judgment, being aware and accepting of the inherent uncertainties of life, and understanding the implications of the past for the present and future.

Baltes presented four hypothetical problems to young, middle-aged, and elderly adults and asked them to think aloud about how to deal with each problem. He found that only 5% of the solutions given could be considered wise, and these superior answers were no more likely to come from older than younger participants. In fact, young and middle-aged subjects had higher wisdom scores than older subjects, though usually not high enough to be considered truly wise. In another study, both older and younger adults were nominated by others as "wise people," then tested on wisdom tasks. The older wise people performed just as well as the younger ones, but no better (Baltes et al., 1995). Bottom line? Older does not necessarily mean wiser - but it doesn't necessarily mean less wise either.

Personality Change: Stability Is Still The Rule

The stereotype of elderly people commonly includes the idea that they tend to be rigid and irritable, suggesting a negative change in their personalities. Even psychiatrists and graduate students, and older people themselves held to this view in early studies (Thomas, 1980; Woodruff and Birren, 1972). Research findings, however, are largely at odds with the idea that personality changes with aging. Some studies do show age-related increases in such characteristics as self-confidence, autonomy, and humanitarian concerns. However, most current work in this area demonstrates the *stability* of the personality over time. Paul Costa and Robert McCrae have examined data from the Baltimore Longitudinal Study of Aging (BLSA), an ongoing investigation of adult development that began in 1958. They report that such major personality traits as anxiety, neuroticism, openness, and extraversion tend to remain quite stable throughout life (Costa et al., 1991; McCrae, 1991). Others have found evidence of stability for a number of additional traits, such as amiability, assertiveness, self-control, and hostility.

Why does personality remain so stable over time? Part of the answer lies in genetics. Empirical studies have established that personality has a substantial genetic basis. You inherit a set of predispositions to develop specific traits in particular ways. Your experience, beginning in childhood, then interacts with the genetic tendency to produce the final personality trait. Some traits are very strongly influenced by genetics, others moderately or slightly (Kendler et al., 1992). An example of a trait dimension with strong genetic influence is extraversion - introversion (usually just referred to as *extraversion*). A study comparing identical twins reared together with those reared apart found a strong genetic basis for extraversion. Even those twins reared apart had very similar scores on the dimension (Plomin et al., 1988). The same study found that neuroticism, a dimension very similar to anxiety, also has a substantial genetic basis. Beyond the genetic factor, there is evidence that most people tend to view themselves as consistent over time, which probably helps to stabilize personality and make substantial change less likely.

Aging and Psychopathology

We take up the topic of abnormal behavior in more detail in Chapter 16, but here it is important to note the nature and frequency of mental health problems in the elderly. It is commonly assumed that older adults are especially prone to mental health problems, and some early cross-sectional studies supported this assumption. However, recent work does not. Overall, National Institutes of Health (NIMH) statistics show that about 20% of Americans are experiencing some form of psychopathology at any given time, and the overall frequency of abnormal behavior does not vary with age. One team of investigators is conducting a longitudinal study of mental health in which over 2,000 men have been followed for an average of 17 years. Results show no change in the overall frequency of psychological symptoms with increasing age (Aidwin, Spiro, Bosse, and Levenson, 1989). Basically, a vast majority of older people are in good mental health (Cohen, 1992).

While the overall rate of mental disorder does not vary with age, the relative frequency of specific diagnoses does, and statistics indicate that *depression* is quite common in the elderly (Johnson et al., 2002). The NIMH statistics suggest that major depression rises in early adulthood (ages 20-25), decreases through the middle years (21-60), then increases again to reach its highest rates at age 80 and beyond (Krishnan et al., 2002). Other disorders, such as schizophrenia, are less common in the aged than in younger groups.

Depression is the single most common cause of *suicide*, and this may account for the fact that suicide rates are higher in the elderly than in any other age group (Devanand, 2002). The suicide rate for those over age 65 is 20 per 100,000 population, as compared with an overall rate across all ages of 12 per 100,000 (Health, U.S., 1994, NCHS, 1995). Based on data from the National Center for Health Statistics (NCHS), those over age 65, who make up about 13 percent of the population, account for 18% of all suicides (Health, U.S., 1994, NCHS, 1995). Contributing factors in the aged no doubt include poor health, widowhood, and social isolation (Koenig & Blazer, 1992).

In earlier decades, the treatment of depression and other disorders in the elderly received no special attention, and older Americans often avoided mental health services. However, the increasing proportion of older adults in the population has led to the development of a research agenda that addresses the special treatment needs of older people (Baker, Lebowitz, Katz, & Pincus, 1992). In addition, the new fields of geriatric psychology and psychiatry now focus specifically on the treatment of elderly Americans (Blazer, 1992), and the use of antidepressant drugs in older adults is being carefully studied (Salzman, 1993).

Family and Social Changes

As people grow older, the dynamics of their family and social lives change. Children grow up and leave home, get married, and have children of their own, and thereby add new members to the family constellation. Other members may die, leaving the survivors to adjust to life without them. In addition, retirement creates major changes in lifestyle and a need for social adaptation.

The combination of changes means that those beyond age 65, and even those beyond middle age, lead quite different lives than they did when they were younger. Couples must rely more on each other for social contact and support, and the spouse remains the number-one confidant for both men and women. A process of establishing and maintaining relationships with extended family, including daughters- and sons-in-law, must usually also take place.

Relatively recent developments in family structure include the increasing prevalence of the single-parent household following divorce in the middle years or before. In 1994, 12% of all adults - a total of 24 million people - lived alone. That number represents a 94% increase in women and a whopping 167% increase in men since 1970. This change has, of course, also begun to affect the aging population, in which 52% of women and 21% of men over the age of 75 live alone (Saluter, 1996, Bureau of the Census). When the last child leaves home, the single parent must adjust to a lifestyle in which there is no mate to provide the close contact and social support characteristic of good marriages. We do not yet have enough information to know whether those who divorce and never remarry are able to adapt as well to the process of aging as are married people.

Is The Watch Really Gold? Retirement. Despite the stereotypical image of the 65-year-old-man stepping up in front of friends and coworkers to receive a gold watch at his retirement dinner, many people retire much earlier or later than 65, and some never retire at all (Hadnagy, 2002). Overall statistics show that the proportion of retired people in the United States has increased considerably during this century. Approximately 70% of men over age 65 were still employed in 1900 as compared with 35% in 1960 and 11% in 1988 (Pienta & Hayward, 2002). In fact, about 65% of workers retire *before* age 65 (U.S. Senate Special Committee on Aging, 1987-88), and many couples plan well ahead to coordinate their retirements (Henretta et al., 1993).

Retirement is a new and very different situation for which many people are not adequately prepared, and there is considerable evidence of ambivalence and anxiety (Drentes, 2002). Financial security is a particularly important factor in adjustment to retirement, as is health status (Kim & Moen, 2002). Other factors include personality characteristics, prior attitudes toward retirement, and marital status (Reis & Gold, 1993). Retirees who harbor significant regrets about their lives have lower overall levels of satisfaction. Adjustment to retirement can be increased by retirement counseling, by continued engagement in a learning process, and by remaining active in organizations, volunteer work, and the like (Okun, 1993).

Grandparenthood. Conducting formal psychological studies of grandmothers may seem a bit like blasphemy, but some psychologists have done just that, and they find that styles of grandparenting vary considerably. One study of 125 grandmothers identified grandmothering styles. The *apportioned* grandmother is very involved with her grandchildren. The *remote* grandmother is detached from her grandchildren and has low social and personal expectations. The *symbolic* grandmother has strict moral standards that govern her grandparenting role. And the *individualized* grandmother emphasizes personal aspects of grandparenting, with a focus on the gratification and pleasure that can be derived from her role. Other studies have noted the relatively recent phenomenon of the *custodial grandparent*, who assumes full-time care of a child while the parent works. One study showed that custodial African-American grandparents enjoy their role but also find it stressful (Burton, 1992).

Interestingly enough, recent research shows that the role of grandmother may be of evolutionary origin. When a woman reaches menopause, she can no longer reproduce and hence fulfill a major goal of evolution. This suggests that evolution may have produced some other important adaptive function for older women, and that function may be grandmothering (Jamison et al., 2002). By supporting her grandchildren, the women may increase their survival and likelihood of reproduction, thus passing on her genes through them. Society considers this role to be so important that grandparents have increasingly received legal rights to see their grandchildren (Hill, 2002).

Studies show that grandchildren quite uniformly report positive feelings toward their grandparents (Clingempeel et al., 1992). However, grandparents are not so uniformly positive. Some welcome the role and derive satisfaction from it. Others do not see grandchildren as a source of pleasure and resent being asked to baby sit on a regular basis.

Widowhood. It is a hard fact of life that marriages not ending in divorce will end in death. Given the generally greater life expectancy of women, there are far more widows than widowers. In fact, more than 50 percent of women over age 65 are widowed, while 80 percent of older men have a living spouse.

The loss of a spouse is probably the greatest psychological trauma that most people ever endure. Immediately following the death, the surviving spouse undergoes a period of *bereavement* and high stress that usually involves feelings of loneliness, depression, and despair. After a period of feeling somewhat numb, the individual feels a strong *yearning* for the spouse, usually accompanied by anxiety and tension. There is then typically a period of *disorganization*, during which the person experiences depression and anger. Finally, there is a stage of *reorganization*, in which the loss is finally accepted, permitting the person to adjust to the reality of life without the spouse. However, individual differences in reactions to the death of a spouse are substantial. In particular, recent research shows that those whose marriages were conflicted experience less anxiety and adjust to the loss more quickly than those reporting a high degree of marital closeness (Carr et al., 2000).

Widowhood means far more than grief and bereavement. The death of a spouse eliminates or greatly reduces many sources of social interaction. Friends are often couples, and many social organizations are structured to accept couples only. Moreover, the income of the survivor tends to decline to about one-third of what the couple had before the husband died, and some 25% of elderly widows have incomes below government-defined poverty levels. Finally, there is typically a decline in health following the death of the spouse, though women with a history of work outside the home are less susceptible to this effect (Aber, 1992).

As Certain As Taxes: Death and Dying

I was 17 and in high school when my grandmother, who had always baked me sugar cookies, came to live with us. She had cancer, and it soon became apparent that there was no hope. Many years later a friend and colleague of mine was delivering a talk to a group of faculty and students when he had a heart attack. Even as I tried desperately to save him with CPR, his life seemed to seep away beneath my hands. His death felt no less tragic than had my grandmother's, and both losses merely served to once again confirm the universal human understanding that life must one day end.

Nearly everyone experiences the death of a loved one, and we must all come to grips with the reality of personal mortality. What death means and how we deal with it as individuals and as a culture is a central issue in the study of adult development and aging.

Definitions of Death. In the days of my grandmother's childhood, death could be determined quite simply. A finger on the pulse or a stethoscope on the chest could quickly ascertain whether the person was alive or dead. But times have changed.

With the advent of sophisticated life-support techniques, we must now differentiate between clinical death and brain death. *Clinical death* occurs when there is no longer a spontaneous heartbeat and when breathing stops. *Brain death* is characterized by a flat EEG, showing no cortical activity, a complete lack of reflexes, and a total failure to respond to stimuli or to breathe without a respirator (Wang et al., 2002). Even the EEG definition of death has been questioned, and new brain scanning techniques may eventually replace it.

"Doctor, Am I Dead?" This question is the title of an article in which Helen Sweeting and Mary Gilhooly (1992) discuss *social death*, a death that occurs when the body is still technically alive. This increasingly common situation involves a terminally ill patient who undergoes a long period of institutional care before dying. Social death is a child of technology, and it keeps many patients who would surely be dead without elaborate life-support equipment - patients who are simply waiting to die - alive. They have reached social death but not yet clinical or brain death. In fact, some have argued that we should define death as occurring when the person loses the capacity for consciousness (Persson, 2002). Whether the society should keep such patients alive is an ongoing ethical issue that is discussed in our 21.

The Meaning of Death. The progressive increase in life expectancy, together with a variety of changes in cultural attitudes and beliefs, has led to considerable changes in prevailing views of death and dying in American society. Death was common in all age groups in earlier centuries and was therefore widely accepted. However, the twentieth century has been characterized by what Philipp Aries (1981) calls *invisible death.* It has become common to deny the possibility of death, to ignore the subject whenever possible, and to conceal the certainty of impending death from gravely ill patients. One partial explanation of this change is higher anxiety about death. David Lester and DeAnne Becker (1993) found that death anxiety was much higher among college students in 1991 than it had been in 1930.

Stages of Dying. Some people die suddenly, but many others learn that they are dying and then go through a period before death actually occurs. In a classic analysis of the process of dying, Elizabeth Kubler-Ross (1969) proposed five stages to dying:

- *Denial and isolation.* The person first denies the possibility that she is dying and may isolate herself from others.
- *Anger and resentment.* When denial becomes impossible, the patient becomes angry that she is faced with death while others are healthy. She may lash out at relatives, friends, and professionals who are caring for her, but the anger is really against her own death.
- *Bargaining.* The person next tries to find some way of staying alive, perhaps by trying to persuade a physician to find a new cure or treatment for her condition or by bargaining with God ("If you'll just let me live, I'll be a better person").
- *Depression.* When bargaining fails, the person becomes depressed. The depression is a preparation for the impending loss of everything and everyone she has and loves.
- *Acceptance.* After working through the first four stages, the dying person finally accepts the inevitability of impending death. But even with acceptance she maintains a thread of hope. When that thread is severed - when hope is gone - death comes without further delay.

Kubler-Ross's theory dominated thinking on death and dying for many years, making it difficult to look beyond the idea of dying as a series of stages. More recent research, however, has called this theory into question (Corr, 1993).

Rituals of Mourning. For the individual, death is the end of existence as we know it. For the society, the death of one of its members leaves a gaping hole in the fabric of humankind, and each society has its own rites and rituals for mending that hole. These rituals - funerals, wakes, memorial services - provide an opportunity for family and friends to grieve, allow the society to express social support for the bereaved, thereby maintaining its integrity, and outline a period of mourning that allows for a return to normal community activities. Open expression of grief is an important part of working through the loss. Often bereaved persons can benefit by just being able to talk to someone about the dead person and their feelings for the person (Bruce, 2002). For the survivors, life must go on. Normally, feelings of grief last for about three to twelve weeks, followed by less extreme mourning that can last for a year or two.

The Biology and Neurophysiology of Aging

Why we age is one of the principal questions underlying *gerontology* - the study of the aging process and its effects. All human beings are subject to *primary aging* - the inevitable biological process of gradual and continuing changes in various body organs and systems that will eventually result in death. The rate of this primary aging process varies from individual to individual as a function of genetic factors. Primary aging is complicated by *secondary aging* - aging that is at least partially under the individual's control. Secondary aging is influenced by such factors as chronic disease, muscular atrophy from lack of exercise, and abusive practices, such as smoking, alcoholism, and poor diet.

Given our increasing knowledge of aging, it may be possible to systematically extend your own life. There is, for example, clear evidence that a regular regimen of substantial exercise can prolong life (Dubbert, 1992). You can also avoid smoking, which causes over 500,000 deaths each year, produces a 70% excess death rate from cardiovascular disorder, and is the principal cause of lung cancer, the most frequent fatal cancer (Beckett, 1993). There is also increasing evidence that antioxidants, such as vitamins C and E, commonly found in fruits and vegetables, may prolong life (see the Critical Thinker).

Further evidence comes from the Georgia Centenarian Study, which is following Georgians over 100 years of age (Siegler, Longino, & Johnson, 1992). The study points to family longevity, environmental support, life satisfaction, and health practices as factors that may contribute to long life (Poon et al., 1992). Other studies of social factors in longevity are inconsistent, with some reporting that quality-of-life, social network, and similar factors seem unrelated to long life (Shahtahmasebi, Davies, & Wenger, 1992). While the ongoing research on aging will no doubt yield further clues, one thing we do know is that there is no "magic elixir" that will help you live to a ripe old age (see the Critical Thinker).

The Life Span

Life span refers to the maximum length of life that is biologically possible. Research suggests that the maximum life span for a human being is somewhere between 100 and 140 years. There are many stories of people living very long lives, but most remain unverified. For example, it was said that the people of Vilcabamba, a village in Ecuador, lived unusually long lives, with many residents well over age 100. Careful research discovered, however, that at least some of these people had falsely inflated their ages and that the average age in the village is probably not substantially higher than that elsewhere in the world (Mazess and Forman, 1979).

Why Do We Age? Theories of Aging

What underlying biological mechanisms account for the aging process? Although many theories have been advanced to explain biological aging, there are two principal types, cellular theories and physiological theories (Balcombe & Sinclair, 2001).

Cellular theories attribute the aging process to genetic mechanisms that operate at the level of the individual cell to cause the symptoms of aging. One such theory suggests that DNA molecules of genes within the cells eventually become damaged by radiation, chemicals, or other destructive processes and begin to produce inaccurate information. The result is that body cells can no longer be repaired and replaced as efficiently, leading to such characteristic signs of aging as gray hair and aching joints (Staiano-Coico et al., 1983). An alternative cellular theory offered by Leonard Hayflick suggests a direct genetic predisposition toward eventual destruction of cells. That is, we actually have genes whose sole purpose is to activate the aging process or that change their function from promoting growth to promoting destruction, thereby programming the organism to age and eventually die (Hayflick, 1975, 1992). The study of the genetic basis for aging is still in its early stages, and future research promises to yield considerable information as to how heredity predisposes the body to age. Hayflick's interesting theory is discussed in Horizon 3.

Physiological theories suggest that aging takes place not so much in individual cells as in organ systems. One theory that has received a great deal of attention is the idea that aging results from the gradual decline of the endocrine (hormonal) system (Shock, 1977). Because that system controls a wide variety of important homeostatic mechanisms that maintain such balances as temperature, blood sugar level, and metabolic function, any decline in its functioning would certainly have effects on all body systems.

According to other physiological approaches, often referred to as wear-and-tear theories, the longer the body is used, the more wear and tear it undergoes and the less it is able to function effectively (Lee & Cerami, 1990). Like a 1980 car with 150,000 miles on it, parts eventually wear out and the body gets beyond the point where parts can be repaired or replaced. While it is certainly likely that wear and tear contribute to the aging process, wear-and-tear theories have not yet been able to explain most aspects of aging. For example, regular exercise appears to improve, not reduce, physical fitness, and damaged or worn body parts are often repaired or replaced by normal physiological processes.

Although no single theory has yet adequately explained the biological aging process, it no doubt does involve some combination of genetic coding, deteriorating endocrine and other organ functions, and wear and tear. Aging is at the very least an interactive combination of these factors and very likely several others that have not yet been discovered.

The Dying Brain

The brain contains nearly 100 billion neurons, but many of these nerve cells die every day, beginning at birth (Cook et al., 2002). Moreover, unlike cells in other body systems, neurons are not replaced; the progressive loss is permanent. Fortunately, it appears that infants have far more neurons than they need, so the decrease presents no immediate problem. Moreover, while neurons are dying, there is also a neural growth process that continues into adolescence and involves the formation of new synapses. And it also appears that the dendrites of some neurons continue to grow well into old age, possibly making up for some of the loss of other neurons.

The rate at which nerve cells are lost accelerates throughout adulthood, and by the age of fifty or so the daily toll runs into the thousands. By age 85, the brain has lost about 8% of its total neurons, but the reduction is not uniform across the brain as a whole. Rather, most of the dying neurons are found in the cortex, particularly the frontal lobes, where thought processes take place and motor activity is controlled (see Chapter 3). Such hindbrain structures as the medulla, which regulates heart function and breathing, show very little decline, allowing activities that are essential for survival to go on uninterrupted. This arrangement is consistent with an evolutionary process that works to sustain life.

The factors in neural decline are unclear. However, some recent evidence points to high levels of homocysteine as a possible factor. Homocysteine is an amino acid that contributes to high levels of LDL (bad) cholesterol and is an independent risk factor for heart disease. It also increases the tendency for blood to clot and can thus block blood vessels, including those in the brain and heart. Homocysteine is high in those with low levels of vitamins B6 and B12 and folate (folic acid), a water-soluble B vitamin (Reutens & Sachdev, 2002).

The ongoing neural decline no doubt accounts for some of the functional physiological deterioration commonly seen with aging. Studies of the electrical activity of the brain, measured with the electroencephalograph (EEG; see Chapter 3), demonstrate changes with aging that may also be associated with behavior changes. Basically, there is a slowing of EEG and a decrease in alpha frequency - the EEG frequency associated with relaxation - in the early 80s (Nakano, Miyasaka, Ohtaka, & Ohomori, 1992). Such changes appear to be related to mild cognitive decline within the normal range (Cook et al., 2002).

Conclusion

In this chapter we have seen that adolescence is not necessarily the period of struggle and turmoil it is often portrayed to be and that the generation gap between teenagers and parents is also something of a myth. We have also learned that development is an ongoing process throughout the adult years and have answered such questions as: What role does work play in our lives? How long can we hope to live? What effect does aging have on learning and memory? Does personality change over the life span? How does our society deal with death and dying? It seems clear that development is, indeed, a life-long process that is launched at the moment of conception, rides the waves that mark life's ups and downs, and ends only beneath the final, dark storm clouds of death.

Summary

Evolution and Adulthood

1. Evolutionary adaptations affect adult, as well as child, development.
2. The study of adult development involves longitudinal, cross-sectional, and sequential designs.

Adolescence: Transition to Adulthood

1. Physical development in adolescence includes the maturation of sexual organs in both males and females and the development of secondary sex characteristics.
2. Erikson has characterized the central issue of adolescence as identity versus role confusion. Although single-parent homes with lower incomes are increasingly common and the rate to teen suicide has increased, evidence suggests that most teens do not undergo a severe identity crisis.
3. Adolescent behavior is greatly influenced by peer group membership, although parents continue to be a major influence on attitudes and values. They also affect smoking, drug abuse, and delinquency.
4. Gender roles and gender identity are established during adolescence, though development begins earlier.
5. Whereas in some other cultures adolescence may be brief or nonexistent, in Western society it is a prolonged period of transition between childhood and adulthood.

Adulthood: Maturity to Old Age

1. Adulthood is that portion of the life span that occurs after biological psychological, and social maturity have been reached.
2. Several psychologists have proposed that adult development follows a series of definable stages, characterized by specific themes or developmental tasks. Major theorists include Erikson and Levinson.
3. Major biological changes during adulthood include neural decline and the onset of menopause.
4. Neo-Piagetian theories suggest the development of postformal forms of thought in cognitively advanced adults.
5. Freud said that a normal adult should be able to love and to work.
6. The social clock specifies society's expectations regarding the timely accomplishment of adult tasks such as marriage and career.

7. The age of first marriage has risen considerably in recent decades. Marital dissatisfaction is very likely to lead to divorce, and the majority of divorced persons remarry, though remarriages are even less successful than first marriages.
8. Divorce has increased because it has become more acceptable and because more women are working and financially independent.
9. Divorce has negative effects on both adults and children, but the effects on children may not last beyond childhood.
10. Most married couples have children, thereby creating the unique social system of the family. As major life events are encountered by the family, the family system is modified and the roles of members change.
11. An increasing number of women are entering the work force. Their salaries are lower, in part due to more career interruptions. Women still do more of the housework, even with both spouses working.

The Older Adult: Living Longer and Living Better

1. An increasing proportion of the population is surviving past age 65. Aging has psychological and social as well as biological components. Primary aging is the biological process of changes in body organs and systems; secondary aging involves factors that are to some degree under the control of the individual.
2. Elderly people are generally much more capable than stereotypes suggest, but they nevertheless experience discrimination.
3. An age-related decline in learning ability that accelerates after age 65 may be due to problems in pacing, motivation, and distractibility.
4. The noticeable deterioration of long-term memory with age appears to be related to problems with the input and output of memory, but not with storage.
5. For the most part, personality traits and emotionality remain stable over the course of adulthood.
6. Most older people have a positive attitude toward retirement, although this attitude depends in part on the reasons for retiring. Adjustment to retirement is heavily dependent on financial security and health status.
7. Major types of grandparents include apportioned, remote, and individualized. Whereas grandchildren tend to have uniform positive feelings toward grandparents, the reverse is not necessarily true.
8. Loss of a spouse is perhaps the most severe trauma most people ever encounter. Widowed people undergo a grieving process and then deal with the reduced social interactions and financial resources often created by loss of the spouse.
9. Death is now technically defined as brain death, rather than clinical death. In our society death has come to be hidden and avoided.
10. According to Kubler-Ross, five stages can be identified in the process of dying: denial, anger, bargaining, depression, and acceptance. This theory has not been strongly supported by research, however.

The Biology and Neurophysiology of Aging

1. Primary aging is a basic biological process, while secondary aging is partially under the individual's control.
2. The maximum life span for human beings is between 100 and 130 years.
3. Although life expectancy for those over age 65 is not much different than it was a century ago, the life expectancy at birth has increased dramatically.
4. Among biological theories of aging are cellular (physiological) approaches and wear-and-tear theories.
5. The brain begins to lose neurons at birth; they lost at an increasing rate as we age and are not replaced.

Ask Yourself

1. What are the most important aspect of physical development during adolescence and how do they affect the psychological development and functioning?

2. To what extent does development in adolescence and in the adult years involve crises as Erikson and others hypothesized? What is the evidence?

3. Who influences the teenager more, parents or peers, and in what specific ways? To what extent do teens rebel against their parents?

4. Describe the major experimental designs used in the study of development. Can you think of others that would work as well or better, at least for certain kinds of hypotheses?

5. What are the major benefits to the individual of marriage, and how would you go about selecting a marital partner and making your marriage a happy one?

6. What are the major causes and effects of divorce?

7. What are the major considerations in career choice and in job satisfaction? In what ways do you think they are related? What special considerations in these areas apply to women?

8. What are the causes of aging? Discuss the major theories. In what ways might science be able to slow the aging process? What kinds of research would be needed?

9. What changes in psychological functioning occur as the person ages? Are there ways of compensating for these changes?

10. Discuss the major myths of aging that are prevalent in Western societies. What evidence speaks against these myths?

11. What are the major definitions and meanings of death? Describe a more adaptive attitude toward death that could be taken by individuals and the society as a whole.

KEY TERMS

acculturation
androgynous
anti-oxidants
biological maturity
brain death
clinical death
cohort effects
cross-sectional study
empty nest
ethnic identity
euthanasia
free radicals
gender identity
gender role stereotype
gender role
gender schema theory
gerontology
identity crisis
life span
longitudinal study
menarche
menopause
midlife crisis
postformal thought
primary aging
psychological maturity
puberty
secondary aging
secondary sex characteristics
sequential design
social clock
social death
social maturity

KEY PEOPLE

Paul Baltes
Erik Erikson
Sigmund Freud
Leonard Hayflick
Elizabeth Kubler-Ross
Daniel Levinson
Warner Schaie

Psychology in the 21st Century

Death with Dignity or Murder in the First?

Dr. Jack Kevorkian's participation in a series of deaths has focused public attention on the important moral issue of euthanasia. Frequently called mercy killing, *euthanasia* is literally translated "good death" and refers to intentionally ending a life to prevent further suffering. In *passive euthanasia*, the person is allowed to die by either not initiating life support measures, like CPR and respirators, or by stopping them. In *active euthanasia*, the person's life is ended by some direct means requiring specific action. She may take or be given a drug, for example.

The Michigan Supreme Court ruled in 1994 that Kevorkian could not be charged with murder if he had only supplied the means of death (Helminski, 1995). He could only be charged under common law with assisting a suicide and was subsequently acquitted of any wrong-doing in a series of jury trials. Some have taken this to imply that the general public, to the extent that it is represented by these juries, favors mercy killing, at least in the form of assisted suicide. However, like most important moral issues, this one is actually a complex dilemma with strong arguments on both sides. It has been controversial for centuries.

Euthanasia was actively and loudly debated in ancient Greece and Rome for hundreds of years and the issue never fully resolved. In subsequent centuries and in various countries, it has often been a focus of public attention. In 1870, after the development of ether as a general anesthetic and morphine as a pain killer, Samuel Williams proposed the use of these drugs to intentionally end life in terminal patients. His suggestion triggered off a 35-year debate in the U.S. and Britain about the ethics of euthanasia, culminating in an Ohio bill to legalize it. The bill was finally defeated, and now, as we approach the 21ST century, we are seeing the same arguments on both sides of the issue once again being recycled.

Death With Dignity

A favorite phrase of those advocating euthanasia is "death with dignity," suggesting that the terminally ill person should be free to end his own life, even if that requires the help of others. Individual choice, it is argued, should be the rule. Advocates point out that euthanasia can relieve excruciating pain in a patient who has little or no chance of survival or end the suffering of one with a severe cognitive deficit that leaves him unable to even recognize others. The cost to the family and society of prolonged terminal care for such patients is also reduced. And the High Court of England recently ruled that the physician is required to comply with a competent patient's request to turn off a respirator, even when she knows that will result in death (Slowther, 2002).

Studies of critical-care physicians - those who frequently treat terminal or very ill patients - show that at least passive euthanasia may already be a fact. One study, for example, found that 96% of 879 such physicians say they have withheld or removed life-sustaining treatment and thereby intentionally allowed patients to die. Most reported that they do so quite frequently, and 83% indicated that they sometimes withhold treatment without consulting with the patient or family. In fact, 34% have done so *against* the wishes of the patient or family (Asch et al., 1995). And some physicians and medical ethicists clearly favor euthanasia. However, 80% of geriatric physicians believe that voluntary euthanasia is never ethically justified (Dickinson et al., 2002).

Death With Dignity Is Still Death

Those who argue against euthanasia point out that death is a final, irrevocable act, no matter the personal dignity with which it is accomplished. And there are many arguments against mercy killing. Some religions hold that it is simply wrong for any human life to be intentionally ended, even by the individual herself, and similar contentions have been made on moral grounds. There are also arguments against mercy killing based on more immediate, practical considerations. New cures may come along while a patient is still alive, and miraculous, unexpected recoveries occur with greater frequency than the public is generally aware of. The real-life case of Ruth in Chapter 3, who recovered after a judge refused the request of her husband and physicians to end her life, is an example. But doesn't the individual have a right to die, a right to end his own life?

Critics of euthanasia argue that extremely ill people are not well qualified to make such an irrevocable decision. Most have little or no detailed medical knowledge of their condition, and many are depressed, confused, distracted by pain, or drugged with sedatives or narcotic pain killers. Would you, they ask, want such a person to make a decision about *your* life?

What about family members and physicians, who may be in better positions to make the euthanasia decision? Family members usually also lack adequate medical knowledge and are often very upset by the patient's condition and the decision itself. Moreover, they may potentially have conflicts of interest, such as money from the estate, that can bias their decisions. The treating physician doesn't have these same problems, but may present others. Dealing with critically ill patients every day, he may grow so accustomed to death that he becomes insensitive to individual patients and their families, though that is obviously not true of all physicians. Death to the insensitive physician is a routine matter, and he may all too easily and too quickly make the decision to remove or refuse life support. Moreover, he is usually hurried because he is very busy, and often he is extremely tired, raising questions about his ability to make valid life-or-death decisions for the patient. He may also be biased by knowledge of the cost of treatment and the need for beds

"The Importance of Being Dead". Another bias the physician may have occurs when he knows the patient has agreed to donate her organs. Could knowing that another patient needs those organs actually sway a doctor to declare his patient dead too soon? In an article entitled "The Importance of Being Dead," Menikoff (2002) points out that organs are all too frequently harvested from donors before they are legally dead. This is obviously a serious ethical issue for medicine to address and it is at the center of a major current debate (DuBois, 2002).

The Slippery Slope

But there is an even stronger argument against euthanasia, one that led to an editorial in the journal *Neurology* entitled "The Slippery Slope in Medicine" (Kurtzke & Houff, 1994). The phrase refers to the possibility that euthanasia could easily get out of hand. Society might begin by legalizing it strictly for cases of patients who are terminally ill. Some cases of cancer, AIDS, and Alzheimer's Disease, for example, might qualify. We could then move to euthanizing patients who are not terminal, but are in severe pain, comatose for a long period of time, or unable to think or to recognize others. In fact, Kevorkian's third trial was for assisting the deaths of two women who were not terminal. The next step may be to extend euthanasia laws to cover patients who could live for fairly long periods in relative comfort, but have no chance of recovery. From there we potentially move to terminating patients whose care will be very costly even if they might live indefinitely and are able to think clearly. And, finally, society might decide that terminating the lives of "inferior" people is justifiable. Children who are retarded, deformed, or have serious diseases, for example, might be considered expendable, as might elderly adults, who appear no longer able to make significant contributions to society.

If you believe society could never slide down this slippery slope, remember the history of Nazi Germany around the time of World War II. In August, 1939, the "Reich's Commission for the Scientific Assessment of Hereditary and Genetically Determined Serious Suffering" was formed. Its job was to orchestrate the "official child-euthanasia" of sick children and adolescents, and countless children were subsequently killed (Bernhardt, 1993). In the state mental hospital at Luneburg alone, 418 of the 695 handicapped children admitted between 1941 and 1945 did not survive, most because they were killed (Suesse & Meyer, 1993). In its zeal to create a "super race," Hitler's government had slid down the slippery slope - and the larger German and world society had done nothing to stop them.

It is probably for these reasons that a majority of physicians not involved primarily in critical care do not favor euthanasia. A substantial majority of 1381 internist geriatricians surveyed in one study said they would not assist in suicide (Watts et al., 1992a). Of these physicians, only 14% believed that Kevorkian was justified. In fact, 29% said that Janet Adkins, the first patient Kevorkian assisted, was morally wrong in taking her own life. Many physicians who are against euthanasia argue that medicine should turn its attention not to methods of mercy killing but to better approaches to pain management (Kedziera, 2001). In that way, even terminal patients could live out their full lives in comfort and be able to think clearly and contribute actively (M.L. Smith et al., 1994).

Clearly, there are strong arguments on both sides of the euthanasia issue. Its emotional and moral qualities make it a complex controversy that is likely to remain unresolved well into at least the 21st century.

Research in Psychology

Probe: *Too Young to Die: Adolescent Suicide*

Suicide is the third most common cause of death among teenagers and young adults (NCHS, 2002). The suicide rate in this group has climbed rapidly in the past few decades from 4.5 deaths per 100,000 population in 1950 to 13.5 in 1992 (Health, U.S., 1996, NCHS, 1995). One study showed that 7% of adolescents now attempt suicide and 21% seriously think about killing themselves (Andrews & Lewinsohn, 1992). Look around you! Over 10,000 college students attempt suicide each year, and about 1000 are successful (Fremouw et al., 1990). Among homeless and runaway youth, these figures climb to 25%

attempting suicide and 41% seriously considering it (Feitel et al., 1992). A more detailed understanding of where adolescents stand on the suicide issue comes from a study of over 3700 high school students. Fully 25% reported some form of suicidal thought or behavior. Of these, 11% reported serious suicidal ideation, 6% said they had made specific suicidal plans, 6% made actual attempts not requiring medical care, and nearly 2% reported attempts that did require medical care (Garrison et al., 1993).

What causes adolescents to attempt suicide? Although we don't know all the answers, we do know that broken homes and lack of communication within the family are common contributing factors. The suicidal teenager is likely to be one who feels rejected by overly controlling parents who are also unsupportive (Agerbo et al., 2002). In addition, parental depression appears to contribute to teen suicide. One study showed that the offspring of parents with major depression, a serious, long-term form of depression (see Chapter 16), were more than five times as likely to attempt suicide as were teens whose parents had been diagnosed with some other disorder (Weissman et al., 1992). The strong genetic contribution to major depression is very likely a factor (Kendler et al., 1992).

Data from the National Adolescent Student Health Survey of 11,400 youth show that consuming alcohol and engaging in risky activities are also associated with increases in suicidal behavior (Windle, Miller, and Domenico, 1992). Additional factors include any form of substance abuse, being in a home with no father, having a poorly educated father, and having a mental disorder (Andrews & Lewinsohn, 1992). Finally, histories of aggressive behavior and of smoking are associated with an increased probability of suicide (Garrison et al., 1993).

Beyond these long-term factors, investigators have looked for *precipitating* factors that immediately precede the suicide. Surprisingly, general life stress may not be a significant trigger. However, there is often a major precipitating stressor that involves problems with an interpersonal relationship. In particular, the young person is more likely to commit suicide when a close relationship breaks up or cannot be established. The adolescent about to attempt suicide almost always shows a pattern of rebellion followed by withdrawal. Warning signs of impending suicide include a decrease in school achievement and attendance, difficulty with a sexual relationship, withdrawal from social relationships, and a previous suicide attempt. Even an apparently feeble attempt at suicide or simple statements of suicidal intent should always be taken seriously.

Adolescent suicide is clearly a major social problem. Only by intervening at the level of the family, the school, and the individual teenager can we hope to successfully cope with this major killer of young people. By educating adults and adolescents alike and by learning to recognize the warning signs, we may be able to reverse the steep climb in the adolescent suicide rate that has characterized recent times.

Applications of Developmental Research

The Critical Thinker: *The Fountain of Youth?*

Over 400 years ago, the Spanish explorer Ponce de Leon set out on a search for a source of eternal youth. He failed in his quest, but that has not deterred others from trying to find the secret to slowing the aging process and prolonging youth and life in general. Both quackery and serious scientific research have been applied in this effort. In the 1920s, it was widely believed that young testicles could prolong life, so a Kansas physician implanted goat testes in aging humans, while a European physician used ape testicles. Later, Swiss surgeon Paul Niehans, killed pregnant ewes and injected cells from fetal lambs into humans. A person with respiratory problems received lung cells, one with heart problems got heart cells, and so on. Many of the rich and famous - like actor Charlie Chaplin and writer W. Somerset Maugham - believed Niehans and paid well for the cellular treatment. However, there is no evidence that the therapy worked.

A more recent attempt to prolong life has involved a form of novocaine called Gerovital. Romanian physician Ana Aslan gave the drug to many people, including Mao Tse Tung and Nikita Krushchev (Aslan, 1965). Scientific study does show that Gerotival may prolong life in one strain of male rats, but it may or may not have any effect on humans.

The Basic Hypothesis or Contention

Modern, more scientific seekers of the fountain-of-youth have focused primarily on diet and certain vitamins and have formulated two related hypotheses. First, they contend that diets low in fat and high in fiber reduce disease and prolong life. Second, the modern fountain of youth spews forth antioxidants to combat *free radicals* - chemicals that damage tissue and promote both aging and disorders like cancer and heart disease (Murray et al., 2002). *Antioxidants* are vitamins that destroy free radicals and include Vitamin C (ascorbic acid), vitamin E (tocopherol), and selenium.

What Is The Evidence?

Recent studies confirm that diets high in fat and low in fiber predispose to colon cancer and heart disease. In fact, a diet with no more than 10% of its calories from fat and at least 40 grams of fiber daily may prevent up to 35% of cancers (Statland,

1992). Such a diet must basically consist of fruits, vegetables, beans, and whole grains, with little in the way of meats or dairy products. Other research shows that diets severely deficient in calories retard the aging of body tissues, reduce the likelihood of some cancers, and prolong life in animals (Meites, 1993). Researcher Roy Walford (1983) became so convinced by this evidence that he is conducting a long-term study on himself. He is attempting to extend his own life span to 140 years by restricting his intake to 1,500 calories a day, with no more than 15 percent fat and 25 percent protein. He takes vitamins to make up for the lack of a balanced diet, runs 10 or more miles each week, swims 2 miles, and lifts weights. Will his experiment be successful? We'll have to check back around the year 2080!

Some studies also support the antioxidant hypothesis, showing that low levels of these substances substantially increase the risk of heart disease and cancer (Gey et al., 1993). Correspondingly, consuming antioxidants can reduce the risk of heart disease by 20-30% (Hennekens & Gaziano, 1993) and also lower the risk of some forms of cancer. Thus far, there is evidence of an antioxidant protective effect for cancers of the colon, breast, stomach, skin, bladder, and salivary glands (Santamaria & Bianchi-Santamaria, 1992).

Is The Evidence Open To Alternative Interpretations?

Good science typically requires a long series of studies conducted by different investigators using varied methodologies over a period of time before final conclusions can be reached. The issues of diet and antioxidant consumption are certainly no exception, and thus far the research is in its relatively early stages.

After all you've read in the newspaper and heard on TV about the value of a low-fat/high-fiber diet, it may seem like heresy to suggest that this contention could prove untrue in the long run. However, scientific caution is always in order, and the low-fat gurus have already made one error: They claimed for a number of years that a low-fat/high-fiber diet keeps levels of LDL (bad) cholesterol down without any need to count calories. More recent research shows, though, that excess calories are quickly turned into fat and then LDL cholesterol by the liver - and it is very easy to eat too many calories on a low-fat diet. A further reason for caution is simply the history of the diet literature: It changes all too quickly. About thirty years ago, that literature suggested that low-carbohydrate diets were best. Later, high protein diets were advocated. And both contentions have proven to be incorrect, along with a number of other earlier diet prescriptions. Twenty years from now, the low-fat/high-fiber concept may well have to be replaced or at least substantially refined.

Caution is also in order regarding antioxidant supplements. Beta carotene was long one of the most widely touted of the antioxidants, and many people took it regularly. However, more recent, better-controlled studies find no evidence that it protects from heart disease or cancer. In addition, some studies taken as support for antioxidant theory have only shown that cultures consuming more foods high in Vitamins C, E, and beta-carotene - mainly fruits and vegetables - have less heart disease or cancer or both (Dragsted, Strube, & Larsen, 1993). However, fruits and vegetables contain many other substances that are potentially protective, and it may therefore be components other than the three vitamins that slow aging and prevent disease (van-Poppel, 1993).

Do We Need Additional Evidence?

We clearly do need more and better scientific evidence, both for low-fat/high-fiber diet theory and for antioxidant theory. Longitudinal studies in which people are randomly assigned to low-fat diet and control groups or to specific antioxidant supplement and control groups will supply some of the answers - and some of these trials are underway. More cross-sectional studies are also needed and will be carried out as we learn more about the proper controls. And sequential designs may provide even better answers, but will take time to complete.

What Conclusions Can We Reach?

Having said that scientific caution is in order, there is, in fact, already substantial evidence to support low-fat dieting and the preventive value of antioxidants, particularly tocopherol. At this point in time, medical authorities vary considerably in the advice they give, but a common recommendation is to exercise regularly and eat plenty of fruits, vegetables, beans, and whole grains in a diet that is low in fat and calories and high in fiber (van Poppel, 1993; Statland, 1992). Beyond that, mainline medicine has long maintained that vitamin supplements, though usually harmless in reasonable quantities, are unnecessary unless a specific deficiency can be demonstrated. But again, that could be wrong, and only further research will give us the answers we need about antioxidant supplements.

One thing we can be sure of: Low-fat diets and antioxidants will not be the last word on how to prevent aging and disease. We will no doubt see further developments through medical research, as well as more examples of untested and unproven approaches to slowing the aging process and prolonging life. Scientific research and technical advances have substantially increased life expectancy during this century, and further advances may gradually help us all to live to the full biological limit of well over 100 years.

Horizons in Abnormal Behavior

1) Is There a MidLife Crisis?

Forty-two-year-old Tom sat slumped over his desk, staring at nothing. After getting his MBA he had spent 20 years in a large corporation. Unhappy with his rate of progress, he had changed jobs recently, only to find that the new position seemed to be a dead end. And now he and his wife of 18 years had separated, and the divorce promised to be messy. Tom appears to be experiencing a *midlife crisis*, a traumatic period of questioning the meaning of one's life that supposedly occurs somewhere around age 40. Although long noted by philosophers, psychologists, and psychiatrists, the idea of midlife crisis was advanced in modern times by Daniel Levinson after an intensive study of 40 middle-aged men (Levinson et al., 1978, 1986). The idea was further popularized by journalist Gail Sheehey in her best-selling book *Passages: Predictable Crises of Adult Life* (1976).

Despite the popularity of the idea, research has lent little support (Waskel, 1995; Kruger, 1994). Few of the middle-class men surveyed in a research project called the California Intergenerational Studies reported the symptoms of midlife crisis. Similarly, a longitudinal study conducted at the University of Chicago found little evidence of midlife crisis in the men and women who participated (Neugarten, 1973). With the exception of some evidence of midlife marital crises (Maltas, 1992), other major studies have yielded similar results. Most researchers now believe that the midlife crisis is relatively rare (Kruger, 1994). When crises do occur, they tend to be related to specific events in the person's life that may come at midlife or at any other point in adulthood.

Horizons in Abnormal Behavior

2) Dishonoring Fathers and Mothers: Elder Abuse

Ralph Dieter was 85 years old. He spent virtually all day every day in a tiny room in his daughter's home, where she frequently yelled at him when he needed help to get to the bathroom and occasionally slapped him when his radio was too loud. He saw his substantial pension only long enough to sign the checks; it allowed his daughter and her husband to live fairly comfortably without working, so long as they didn't spend money on "the old man".

Can you imagine abusing the people who nurtured and protected you as you grew from helpless infancy to independent adulthood? Well, many people, like Ralph Dieter's daughter, apparently can - and do. Like children, many older people are relatively weak and defenseless, and, like children, they are sometimes abused. Stephen Vida (1994) points out that elder abuse takes several forms, including physical, psychological, and material abuse. The most common forms appear to be neglect (a form of psychological abuse) and depriving the individual of personal property (a form of material abuse) (I. Johnson, 1995). Among the risk factors for elder abuse are gender (women are abused more often) and cognitive condition (impaired elders are abused more). In addition, abuse is more likely when the older person and her caretaker are socially isolated from others and when the abuser drinks heavily or uses drugs. Elder abuse has been identified only recently as a social problem, but it is clearly an important one that promises to become even more significant with the continuing increase in the older population.

Horizons in Abnormal Behavior

3) The Hayflick Limit

Biologists have long hypothesized that even in the absence of any fatal disease or accident, human life has a limited span. The question is why. What is it that causes us to age and eventually, inevitably die?

The problem seems to lie at the level of the individual cell. Leonard Hayflick (1977, 1992) placed cells from a human embryo in a laboratory dish to see how long they would continue to grow and divide. As the cells grew and divided, Hayflick added enzymes to separate them, dividing the total cell population in half, then cultured the cells again. He repeated this process, dividing the culture each time cells covered the surface of the dish. After about 40 to 60 doublings, the cells stopped growing. Hayflick found individual differences in the number of times cells from different parts of the embryonic tissue would divide, but none doubled more than about 60 times. Why? Because, he concluded, the cells of each species are genetically programmed to undergo a limited number of doublings. When this genetic limit - the *Hayflick limit* - is reached, the cells die (Hayflick, 1989; Kloeden, Rossler, & Rossler, 1993).

Hayflick then took cells from adults and subjected them to a similar procedure. He found that the number of divisions for individual cells ranged from about 14 to 29. More recent research shows that the number of doublings is inversely proportional to the age of the donor and probably directly proportional to the typical longevity of the species. Thus, the younger the donor and the greater the longevity of the species, the more doublings. Turtles, which may live to be 150 years old, show up to 130 doublings, while mice, which live to a maximum of about 3-5 years, reach only 15 doublings.

These findings suggest that each cell has a limited life span, implying a limitation on the life span of the body as a whole. Studies done in a number of laboratories have provided overall support for this hypothesis (Mazin, 1993; Kloeden et al., 1993). While the weight of evidence to date supports the Hayflick model, the final word on life-span limitation may not come until well into the 21st century, by which time we may find ways to prolong life beyond what now appears to be its maximum span (Hayflick, 1989).

Further Readings

Brown, L., & Gilligan, C. (1992). *Meeting at the crossroads: Women's psychology and girls' development.* Cambridge: Harvard Univ. Press. What do girls passing from childhood through adolescence to adulthood experience? Lyn Mikel Brown and Carol Gilligan interviewed one hundred girls in depth to find out, and they tell us about the troubled crossing created by our culture.

Cleiren, M. (1993). *Bereavement and Adaptation: A comparative study of the aftermath of death.* Washington, DC: Hemisphere Publishing. Cleiren provides an in-depth coverage of how loved ones adapt to the death of a family member. Major theories of bereavement are covered, and results of a longitudinal study to 300 bereaved adults are presented.

Garrod, A., Smulyan, L., Powers, S., & Kilkenny, R. (1992). *Adolescent Portraits.* Boston: Allyn and Bacon. The authors provide a fascinating look at the lives of 15 adolescents and the challenges of growing up.

Hargrave, T., & Anderson, W. (1992). *Finishing Well: Aging and reparation in the intergenerational family.* NY: Brunner/Mazel. Although intended for therapists who deal with the elderly, this book provides insights into the challenges of late adulthood that are useful for anyone who wants to achieve a better understanding of a part of life he has not yet reached.

Hayslip, B., & Panek, P. (1993). *Adult development.* NY: HarperCollins. A thorough coverage of adulthood from biological to psychosocial aspects and the general nature of adult development.

Roy, F., & Russell, C. (1992). *The encyclopedia of aging and the elderly.* NY: Facts on File. Despite its relatively brief 300 pages, this book is quite encyclopedic in its coverage of aging. It is packed with facts and figures that provide a good idea of what is involved in the aging process.

Salthouse, T. (1992). *Mechanisms of age-cognition relations in adulthood.* Hillsdale, NJ: Lawrence Erlbaum Associates. Timothy Salthouse is a leading authority on the cognitive aspects of aging, and this book provides an excellent review of much of the work in this field.

Santrock, J. (1993). *Adolescence: An introduction.* Madison, WI: Brown & Benchmark. Santrock's up-to-date coverage tells you virtually everything you ever wanted to know about adolescence. It is written as a text on adolescent development, and the coverage is very thorough.

Additional References

U.S. Bureau of the Census (1991). *Statistical Abstract of the United States.* Washington, DC: Department of Health, Education, and Welfare.

Vemer, E., Coleman, M., Ganong, L., & Cooper, H. (1989). Marital satisfaction in remarriage: A meta-analysis. *Journal of Marriage and the Family*, 51, 713-725.

Betz, N.E. (1984). A study of career patterns of women college graduates. *Journal of Vocational Behavior, 24, 249-263.*

Tangri, S., & Jenkins, S. (1992). The women's life-paths study: The Michigan Graduates of 1967. In D. Shuster & K. Hulbert (Eds.), *Women's lives through time: Educated American women of the 20th century* (pp 20-35). San Francisco: Jossey-Bass.

Centers for Disease Control and Prevention. (1994). Deaths resulting from firearm- and motor-vehicle-related injuries - United States, 1968-1991. JAMA, 271, 495-496.

KEYS TO LATER DEVELOPMENT - 1

1. Evolution affects adult development.

A. Some examples of evolutionary effects that appear after childhood?
Human social cooperation, personality traits, heart disease.

ADOLESCENCE: TRANSITION TO ADULTHOOD

1. Adolescence begins with the onset of puberty.

A. What this is called in girls?
Menarche
B. Who develops secondary sex characteristics earlier?
Girls

2. Sexual interest and activity begin with puberty.

A. The age by which 50% of teenagers have had intercourse?
16 in boys, 17 in girls
B. What determines engagement in sexual activity?
Biology (early maturation), friends, and parents.

3. Teen pregnancy has become a major problem.

A. The percentage of nonmarital births that are to teenagers?
30%
B. Why teens get pregnant?
Lack of knowledge
Parental models and peer norms
Lack of adult supervision
Older men dating adolescent girls

4. AIDS is an increasing problem in both teens and adults.

A. The number of cases in the U.S. in 1995?
Over 513,000
B. The hopeful signs?
Increased condom use
Better AIDS education
More discussion with parents

5. Erikson and others hypothesize an identity crisis.

A. What it involves?
Answering "Who am I."
Sense of self is questioned.
Social expectations to become more independent and responsible.

B. What might suggest that this crisis does or should occur?
Increases in single-parent homes
Lower incomes
Increases in teen suicides
C. How common the crisis is?
It is relatively rare.

6. Social and emotional development continue through adolescence.

A. The advantages of the peer group?
Relaxation, enjoyment, reinforcement, etc.
B. Some types of peer groups?
Cliques
Formal organizations
C. What parents influence?
Attitudes and values
Academic achievement
Drug use, drinking, smoking, delinquency
D. Whether gender roles are different?
They are, as Eagly notes.
E. Some areas affected by gender role stereotypes?
Job choice, social behavior.
F. When gender identity begins to appear?
Age 3

KEYS TO LATER DEVELOPMENT - 2

1. Adulthood is marked by maturity.

A. The types of maturity?
Biological, psychological, social
B. The types of studies usually done?
Cross-sectional
Longitudinal
"Most efficient design"
C. The major stage theorists?
Levinson, Erikson
D. Some major biological changes during adulthood?
Neural decline
Menopause

2. Piaget hypothesized formal operational thinking in adults.

A. In what areas adults most likely use formal operations?
Areas of expertise and primary interest
B. What the Neo-Piagetians proposed?
Postformal thought in advanced adults.

3. Most adults respond to the social clock.

A. What it is?
Society's expectations regarding timing.
B. Some advantages of marriage?
Partner a source of support
Better physical and mental health
C. Some characteristics of people in happy marriages?
Men: Self-confidence
Women: Nurturance

D. The proportion of marriages that end in divorce?
50% or more
E. Whether satisfaction is greater in second marriages?
No, it is worse, and the divorce rate is 25% higher.
F. Some effects of divorce on adults?
Increased illness, suicide, homicide, and disability.
G. Some effects on children?
Lower self-esteem and grades, more depression. But the effects appear not to last indefinitely.

4. Most men and women now work.

A. The percentages of each that work?
77% of men, 59% of women.
B. Some possible reasons women's salaries are lower?
Discrimination
More work interruptions
C. Some negative effects of unemployment?
Reduced mental health
Depression
Suicide
Increased crime.

KEYS TO LATER DEVELOPMENT - 3

1. Life expectancy has increased over time.

A. What it was in ancient Greece and what it is now?
18 and 76.
B. The likely number of people over age 65 in the year 2000?
35 million.
C. What happens to life expectancy as the starting age increases?
It goes up.
D. The major types of aging?
Biological, psychological, and social

2. Gerontology studies, in part, the biology of aging.

A. The two forms of aging?
Primary, secondary
B. Some things that contribute to longevity?
Exercise, not smoking, anti-oxidants, life satisfaction, environmental support, genetics.
C. Some theories of aging?
Cellular, physiological (endocrine and wear-and-tear).

3. Cognitive processes can change with aging.

A. The major factor in the learning decline in some older people?
Pacing (slowness)
B. In what aspects of memory older people may have difficulty?
Input (encoding) and output (retrieval), but not storage.
C. Whether older people are wiser?
No, not according to Baltes.

4. Personality and psychopathology in aging have been studied.

A. How much personality changes with age?
Very little
B. What happens to overall rates of psychopathology with aging?
There is no change.
C. What form of psychopathology does increase with age?
Depression

5. Many social changes occur in old age.

A. What has happened over the years to the number of people employed beyond age 65?
It has decreased greatly.
B. Some major factors in the adjustment to retirement?
Financial security
Health status
Personality characteristics
Attitudes toward retirement
Marital status

6. Death is a reality that is often not faced.

A. The current definition of death?
Flat EEG
B. The term for artificially prolonged life?
Social death
C. The stages of dying according to Kubler-Ross?
Denial and isolation
Anger and resentment
Bargaining
Depression
Acceptance

EVOLUTION AND ADULTHOOD

KEY TERMS

cohort effects
cross-sectional design
longitudinal design
sequential design

KEY PEOPLE

Warner Schaie

ADOLESCENCE: TRANSITION TO ADULTHOOD

KEY TERMS

androgynous
ethnic identity
gender identity
gender role stereotype
gender role
gender schema theory
identity crisis
menarche
puberty
secondary sex characteristics

KEY PEOPLE

Erik Erikson
Sigmund Freud

ADULT DEVELOPMENT: MATURITY TO OLD AGE

KEY TERMS

empty nest
menopause
midlife crisis
postformal thought
psychological maturity
social clock
social maturity

KEY PEOPLE

Daniel Levinson

THE OLDER ADULT: LIVING LONGER AND LIVING BETTER

KEY TERMS

ageism
antioxidant
biological maturity
brain death
clinical death
euthanasia
gerontology
primary aging
secondary aging
social death

KEY PEOPLE

Paul Baltes
Elizabeth Kubler-Ross

THE BIOLOGY AND NEUROPHYSIOLOGY OF AGING

KEY TERMS

free radicals
life span

KEY PEOPLE

Leonard Hayflick

Chapter 12
Motivation

Outline

Networking

WHY DO PEOPLE behave the way they do? In other words, what motivates their behavior? Some behaviors are obviously motivated by physiological needs or drives; eating and sexual behaviors, for example, exist to satisfy the physical needs and support the survival of both individual and species. We will see, however, that the experience and expression of these survival drives are greatly influenced by learning and other psychological processes. The motives underlying some other behaviors, especially in humans, are more difficult to explain. Why do some people work hard to achieve, while others seem to barely get by? Why do some people actively seek out thrills and excitement, while others are content to spend their evenings watching TV? Why do some people constantly seek out the company of friends and relatives, while others strive to avoid it? Intrigued by such questions, psychologists have devoted a great deal of research to understanding how motives cause behavior and developed some fascinating theories to. We will discuss the major theories and consider a few specific motive systems, including hunger, sex, achievement, and social motivation. We will also see that the brain - particularly the hypothalamus - plays a major role in motivating our behavior.

Motivation and emotion, the topic of Chapter 13, are closely linked. Emotions like happiness and fear can be strong motivators of behavior. At the same time, aroused motives often have an emotional component, as when sexual arousal is associated with a strong feeling of love for a significant other or hatred - an emotion - motivates someone to commit murder.

A Motivated Woman

"I'm an overweight, overworked overachiever." We are eavesdropping as Cecilia munches on a chocolate chip cookie and complains to her college roommate. Indeed, she has always struggled with her weight and, at age 20, is 30 pounds above the ideal. Diet after diet has worked only temporarily, and each time she seems to regain more than she lost. This fact, she believes, has contributed to her limited success in dating, a situation she would very much like to correct. To some extent, Cecilia's frustration over her weight and dating problems is alleviated by her 3.9 GPA, her pride and joy. Indeed, she can't understand how her roommate can constantly chide her for working too hard while maintaining her own minimal 2.1 average. Since elementary school Cecilia has always worked very hard to be at or near the top of her class, and college has been no exception. She fully intends to go to medical school and has, accordingly, been gaining useful experience and building a strong application by working in two research labs at the university and on a surgical ward in a nearby hospital.

What explains Cecilia'a hard work to do well in college and go to medical school, while her roommate barely gets by? Why is she struggling with her weight? As we will see, the general answer is that Cecilia is engaging in motivated behavior.

Motivation refers to processes that energize and maintain goal-directed behavior. *Motives* are the needs and desires the goal-directed behavior attempts to satisfy. Why do you eat when you feel hungry? Why do you seek out sexual satisfaction? Why are you reading this chapter? The brief answer to all these questions is motivation.

We should note that there is by no means universal agreement on our definition of motivation - or anyone else's. In fact, when Paul and Anne Kleinginna (1981) surveyed the literature, they found 98 different definitions of the term. Nevertheless, our definition gives you a good idea of what most psychologists mean by motivated behavior.

Theories of Motivation

The lack of agreement on how to define motivation can be seen in the variety of theories that have been developed to explain it (Table 12-1). Theorists addressing motivational issues have faced three broad questions: (1) What are the major motive systems and how do they motivate behavior? (2) How do these systems relate to each other? (3) What are the underlying psychological, environmental, and physiological causes of motivated behavior and how do they interact? Attempts to answer these questions have resulted in a number of theories. Here we will discuss basic instinct, drive, incentive, and arousal theories. In addition, we will take up the more complex need hierarchy, cognitive, and evolutionary approaches.

Instinct Theory

Some behaviors are driven by *instincts* - innate, biological motives that are present in all members of a species and are expressed in a consistent way (Tinbergen, 1989; Changizi, 2003). Nest-building in birds is an innate behavior pattern triggered by a combination of internal and external events. Instinct also accounts for salmon returning to the streams where they were hatched and flocks of geese migrating south for the winter.

William McDougall (1908) hypothesized that human behavior is also motivated by instincts. He compiled a long list of automatic, inborn behavior patterns, among them curiosity, gregariousness, flight, pugnacity, and self-assertion. Following McDougall's lead, other psychologists added to the list, and by 1924 some 14,000 instincts had been invoked by various authors to explain the motivational bases for human behavior. These instinct theories soon fell into disrepute, however, because they could not explain the variability in human behavior, which was clearly influenced by learning (Tolman, 1923). The so-called human instincts simply do not fit our definition of the term instinct.

Instinct theory more generally survives today in the form of *ethology*, the study of the species-specific behaviors of animals (including humans) in their natural settings. The primary emphasis of ethology is on the origins of behaviors in lower animals (see Chapter 10). Ethologists have learned, for example, that the male stickleback fish defends its territory because its fighting behavior is triggered by the sight of the red underbelly of competing males. Ethologists are interested in behavior that is *species-specific* - meowing in cats, barking in dogs - and behavior that occurs in *fixed action patterns* - behavioral sequences that occur in exactly the same way each time because they are hard-wired into the nervous system (Elliott & Susswein, 2002). Fixed action patterns are triggered by a *releaser* - a specific stimulus that elicits the behavior. The behavior of the stickleback is one example. Flight without practice in some birds is another.

Some ethologists also point to fixed actions in human behavior, such as the smile of very early infancy that occurs without learning. Even when the automated behavior patterns characteristic of animal instincts are not present, organisms often exhibit biological preparedness, in which the animal comes equipped with the underlying biology that is necessary for a specific behavior to occur (Chapter 10). Human examples include innate facial expressions for a number of emotions (Chapter 13), walking, and language (Chapter 8).

Drive Theories

One of the most widely used concepts in theories of motivation is drive. A *drive* is a condition of arousal or tension that motivates behavior aimed at reducing that tension. Drive theories typically hypothesize that a set of physiological survival drives motivate behavior. These include hunger, thirst, sleep, pain, and sex. Additional drives can be learned on the basis of these physiological drives.

Although the drive concept was introduced by Robert S. Woodworth (1918), it was Clark Hull (1943) who first used the term in a major theory of motivation and learning. Hull and other drive theorists have suggested that a drive results from the activation of a *need* a physiological deficiency that creates a condition of disequilibrium within the body - or from intense stimuli, such as an electric shock that causes pain. The deficiency or stimulus disrupts what Walter Cannon (1929) called *homeostasis* - a state of equilibrium or stability that the body strives to sustain. Under the control of centers in the brain, homeostatic mechanisms maintain a variety of physiological balances (McCann et al., 2003). They ensure a constant internal body temperature of 98.6° even in very hot and very cold environments (Layman et al., 2003). They also maintain proper blood concentrations of oxygen, carbon dioxide, salt, sugar, and other substances (McCann et al., 2003).

Since maintaining homeostasis is essential for survival, needs must be satisfied. An activated need therefore sets up a drive to obtain some need satisfier, and obtaining the satisfier leads to *drive reduction* - the elimination of the drive state. Depriving an animal of food, for example, depletes blood glucose levels and causes other physiological changes that result in a need for food. The resulting hunger drive can be satisfied by consuming food, which produces drive reduction. In this theory a new response is learned when and only when it results in drive reduction.

Drive theory continues to guide a considerable amount of research in psychology. However, it is no longer as influential as it once was because other approaches provide better explanations for some aspects of behavior. In particular, drive theory has difficulty explaining what is motivating behavior when there is no apparent need that would activate a drive. Why did Thomas Edison work so hard on his inventions that he slept only four hours each night? Why do you eat that apple pie a-la-mode when you feel absolutely stuffed after a huge meal? Edison was certainly not thirsty or in pain, and you are certainly not hungry. Other theories, including incentive theories, explain such behaviors better.

Incentive Theories

An incentive theorist would hypothesize that you eat the apple pie because it is there: it serves as an incentive. More generally, an *incentive* is any external object or event that motivates behavior. Sometimes incentives reduce drives, but often they do not. A child may work hard to get a new toy, a student to get on A on a test, an actor to get an Oscar, or a worker to get a promotion. In each case there is an incentive but no apparent drive.

Incentive theories account for individual differences in behavior by assessing the value the incentive has for a specific individual. A student with a 4.0 average may work much harder to get an A than one with a 3.0 average, in part because he wants to maintain his perfect GPA. He values the incentive more. Value can be influenced by both biological factors and prior experience. For biological reasons, you will place much greater value on a sandwich when you last ate three days ago than when you ate three hours ago. However, based on past experience, you might prefer pizza if given a choice.

Notice the difference between drive and incentive theories: Drive theories base motivation primarily on *internal* states, such as hunger; incentive theories emphasize *external* stimuli. For that reason, drive approaches are often referred to as *push* theories and incentive approaches as *pull* theories. In the first case, you are driven or pushed by an internal state; in the second, you are enticed or pulled by an external goal. So where does the motivation for your behavior lie? Are you pushed by a hunger drive or pulled by a food incentive? The answer depends on the theory. One further implication of this difference between the two approaches is that drive theory relies more on biological factors as sources of motivation, while incentive theory is more environmental.

Optimal Arousal Theories

Arousal refers to an increase in the levels of activity of a number of physiological systems, and heightened arousal is associated with activation, alertness, and wakefulness (B. Smith et al., 2002; B. Smith, 1994). When you are aroused, you are experiencing increases in heart rate, blood pressure, respiration rate, and muscle tension, as well as changes in cortical activity (B. Smith et al., 2002). Let's consider just what these theories are, what effects arousal might have on behavior, how arousal can be measured, and how individual differences in arousal might affect behavior.

Optimizing Arousal. Arousal theories suggest that we constantly strive to maintain an *optimal* or ideal level of arousal by seeking or avoiding stimulation from the environment (B. Smith et al., 2002). When you are below your optimal arousal level, you seek stimulation. When you are above it, you avoid arousing stimuli. The sheer boredom of having nothing interesting to do on a beautiful Saturday afternoon can be so uncomfortable as to be motivating. Your arousal level is too low, and you may therefore call some friends, work out at the gym, or perhaps (if you're desperate for stimulation) try skydiving. Alternatively, the anxiety of tomorrow's exam may raise your arousal to an uncomfortable level, motivating you to look for some way of relaxing.

Optimal arousal theory hypothesizes that everyone has a physiological *need for stimulation* (Antrop et al., 2002). In fact, the theory originated in a series of experiments showing that organisms actively seek out stimulation. Harry Harlow did some classic studies in the early 1950s demonstrating that animals will learn a new response for no reward other than the opportunity to manipulate the environment. In one such study, Harlow provided monkeys with an assembled mechanical puzzle (Harlow and Meyer, 1950). Even though they received no food or other reward for disassembling the puzzle, the monkeys would work for hours taking it apart. Other researchers later showed that monkeys isolated in a box would learn to open a window simply for the visual stimulation of looking outside (Butler, 1953). The need for stimulation seen in these studies appears to have a neurological basis (Cobos et al., 2002).

Humans also have a need for stimulation. In one of the earliest sensory deprivation experiments students were paid one hundred dollars for every day they remained in a small, dimly lighted, soundproof isolation chamber. Despite the monetary incentive, few were able to stay in the chamber for more than two or three days (Bexton, Heron, and Scott, 1954). They reported a strong desire for nearly any kind of stimulation, and this desire was accompanied by restlessness, irritability, and sometimes even hallucinations (seeing or hearing things that were not actually occurring). In more recent research J. Gordon Nelson (1992) found that second and third grade children who were described as "class clowns" were seeking stimulation due to an arousal deficit. They acted up because they needed to bring their arousal levels up toward an optimal point. This human need for stimulation shows little reduction with age (Neely et al., 2002).

The Inverted-U Function. Functioning at an optimal level of arousal maximizes your *behavioral efficiency* or performance on a variety of tasks (Yoon & Jeong, 2001). This inverted-U relationship between arousal and performance was first studied by R.M. Yerkes and J. D. Dodson (1908) and is called the *Yerkes-Dodson Law* (Figure 12-1). Performance rises with arousal up to an optimum point, then decreases when arousal rises further (B. Smith et al., 1991; B. Smith, in press; Khurshid, 1993). Your performance on an exam will probably suffer if you are either totally unconcerned or extremely anxious. You should do best if you are alert, interested, and moderately concerned.

Measuring Arousal. Experiments designed to test arousal theory often involve recording one or more *psychophysiological* measures - those that assess the current functioning of a variety of internal organs and systems (Chapter 13). Such measures can be used to examine the relationship between arousal and some aspect of performance (Yoon & Jeong, 2001). They include heart rate, the electrical activity of the brain, respiration rate, blood pressure, oxygen consumption rate, and electrodermal activity (EDA; Jorgensen & Zacharia, 2002; Reynolds & Lickliter, 2002). This last measure, formerly called the galvanic skin response, is a measure of the firing of the autonomic nervous system (Gatzke-Kopp et al., 2002).

Individual Differences. Individuals differ in their optimal levels of stimulation. Some prefer noisy parties and constantly seek out social stimulation from friends, others would rather spend a quiet evening with a good book or watching TV. Hans Eysenck (1967) hypothesized that the personality dimension most centrally related to arousal level is *introversion-extraversion.* Introverts are individuals whose internal level of arousal is usually very high; as a result, they avoid the intense stimulation of interpersonal interactions in order to reduce their arousal levels. Extraverts, on the other hand, have relatively low levels of internal arousal and thus seek out other people and activities to raise their arousal levels (Smith et al., 1995). A vast body of research on this individual difference dimension has shown that extraversion-introversion is an arousal dimension based in a genetic predisposition, supplemented by experience (Ashton et al., 2002; Spirling & Persaud, 2003). It affects far more than social behavior: Learning styles, drug use, sensitivity to stimulation, and many aspects of perception are related to this individual difference variable (Fleeson et al., 2002).

Another individual difference dimension is *reactivity* or the amount of stimulus overload a person can withstand and enjoy. People who score high on a scale of reactivity developed by Hans Strelau (1972, 1980) attempt to minimize the amount of stimulation they receive, while those who score low on the scale tend to maximize incoming stimulation. People with low reactivity are more likely to be in professions that provide large amounts of stimulation (jet pilot, criminal defense attorney), have a tendency to make risky choices in experimental gambling situations, and are more likely to be involved in dangerous sports, such as mountaineering and sport parachuting (Fleeson et al., 2002).

A Need Hierarchy: Abraham Maslow

The instinct, drive, incentive, and arousal theories all assume that humans are motivated in the same ways as lower animals. Abraham Maslow theorized that some motivational forces are distinctly human. In promoting his idea, Maslow became one of the founding fathers of the *humanistic* school of psychology, which emphasizes that humans are unique in the animal kingdom. We have more to say about humanism in Chapter 14, where we discuss the personality theory of Carl Rogers.

Maslow hypothesized that human behavior is motivated by a number of competing needs that can be arranged in a hierarchy (see Figure 12-2). This *need hierarchy* is a systematic listing of needs in priority order, such that needs further up the hierarchy can be met only after more basic needs have been satisfied. The more basic needs are *deficiency needs* - needs that must be satisfied for survival. The needs at the very top are *growth needs* - needs that enhance the person's psychological functioning.

At the lowest level of the hierarchy are physiological needs, such as hunger and thirst. If these needs are not routinely fulfilled, as happens under conditions of war or famine, higher needs cannot be addressed. Safety needs, next in line when the physiological needs are met, include needs for protection, security, and freedom from anxiety. At the next two levels are social needs: the need for belongingness and the need for love. Failure to satisfy these needs can lead to feelings of loneliness and isolation. The last of the deficiency needs are the esteem needs, which include the need for self-esteem and the need for other esteem. Self-esteem is the need to maintain a perception of oneself as a generally competent, strong, independent person. The need for other esteem is the desire to have a good reputation and to obtain recognition and status. Failure to satisfy the esteem needs is likely to lead to feelings of incompetence, helplessness, and inferiority.

When all the deficiency needs are regularly satisfied, the growth needs, including needs for understanding, knowledge, and beauty, become the dominant motivators. Satisfaction of these needs moves the individual to a higher state of psychological functioning and makes him a more effective person. The very highest need - the capstone of Maslow's hierarchy - is the need for *self-actualization.* It is each individual's need to realize all her capacities, fulfill her potentials, become the best person she can be. Moreover, it is an innate drive that is part of the physiological makeup of the individual; she *must* strive to fulfill it once the other needs are satisfied. The self-actualizing person, referred to by Maslow as the fully human person, is constantly striving to achieve higher and higher levels of personal growth. He is nondefensive, open to experience, spontaneous, problem oriented, and largely autonomous from the environment (Sumerlin & Bundrick, 2000). Maslow (1954) believed that a person's position on the hierarchy is likely to rise with age, but estimated that less than one percent of the population ever achieve self-actualization.

Maslow's theory has been very influential both in practical applications and as a basis for research (Bolen et al., 2002). In the world of business it has provided a way of understanding what motivates employees and a tool to reduce turnover, increase productivity, and improve job satisfaction (Scwartz, 2000). Applications in education, nursing, consumer economics, management training, and elder care are also common (Ishikura & Tashiro, 2002; Fillit et al., 2002).

Research support, on the other hand, has been hard to come by. Complex constructs like self-actualization are difficult to define and measure, and what supportive research there is has been widely criticized (Summerlin & Bundrick, 2000). Equally as important is the repeated failure to confirm the priority ordering of the need hierarchy (Wicker et al., 1993). When subjects are asked to rank the needs in order of importance for them, the rankings typically do not conform to Maslow's hierarchy. Enduring satisfaction of physiological and security needs does not necessarily mean the person will go on to seek belongingness and love. In other cases, those needs may be pursued even in the face of chronic hunger. Moreover, the age hypothesis has not been confirmed: Position on the need hierarchy does not consistently increase with age. Maslow's theory has been influential and is widely applied in practical settings but has not been supported by research.

Cognitive Theory

Cognitive theories of motivation emphasize the role of thought processes in initiating, maintaining, and guiding behavior. We use active, conscious, decision-making processes to determine both our goals and the means by which we will achieve them. In short, thought motivates action (Erez & Isen, 2002). When the scale says you are ten pounds overweight, you *think* about the consequences, *decide* to go on a diet, and develop a *plan* for losing the weight. These are all cognitive processes, and your weight loss is thus motivated by your cognitions. In this theory, perception is a motivator and there is an important difference between extrinsic and intrinsic motivators (Niccols et al., 2003).

Perception Motivates Behavior. In cognitive theories, certain kinds of thought processes can be motivational. Theorist Bernard Weiner focuses on the role of *perception* or cognitive interpretation in behavior (Roesch & Weiner, 2001). Action is motivated by the person's perception of causality - of what is causing outcomes to occur. He hypothesizes three major dimensions of perceived causality, which he calls locus, stability, and controllability. The *locus* of perceived causality may be either inside or outside the person. When you perceive an internal locus, you see yourself as causing success or failure. If you failed a test, for example, you might conclude that you didn't study hard enough. When you perceive an external locus, you attribute success or failure to forces outside yourself. You might blame your test failure on the instructor's poor teaching. The second dimension, *stability*, refers to your perception of the consistency of the phenomenon in question. If you always do poorly on exams of this type, you might perceive failure as a stable characteristic in your life. But if such failure is unusual, you are likely to see it as an unstable characteristic. *Controllability* is your perception of the extent to which you can influence the outcome of the situation. You may feel that you can do better on your next exam by studying harder (controllable) or that nothing you can do will improve your performance (uncontrollable).

These three cognitive dimensions affect motivation in a number of ways. Locus affects self-esteem, which may be increased or decreased. Your perception of stability determines the extent to which you expect similar events to recur in the future. And your concept of controllability can affect your perceptions of other people (Cox, 2002). If you feel that others are in control of a situation, you will like them more if the outcome is positive than if it is negative. Some studies have confirmed the utility of Weiner's theory in understanding motivation and associated achievement (Shalley & Perry-Smith, 2001).

Weiner's cognitive theory of motivation is related to a broader social psychological theory called *attribution theory*, which deals with the perception of causal relationships in social situations. We discuss this approach in Chapter 19.

Extrinsic and Intrinsic Motivators. Motivation can come from outside or inside the person. *Extrinsic motivators* are those that come from the external environment and typically take the form of rewards, such as grades on tests, money, and social praise. Such external rewards are useful because they can act to modify behavior, strengthen existing behaviors, increase self-esteem, and provide helpful information about performance. A 'B' on a test, for example, can reward you for your hard work (it's better than a 'C') and also cause you to study harder in order to get an 'A' on the next exam.

Intrinsic motivators **are those that come from within you person and cause you to engage in behaviors for no apparent reward. An unknown artist works through the night to complete a painting she has no intention of selling. A scientist works fifteen-hour days for many years to understand the structure of a molecule or the function of one tiny group of neurons, with little likelihood of external reward for his efforts. What is the intrinsic motivation underlying these behaviors? Edward Deci (1975; Ryan & Deci, 2000) answers that it is a combination of stimulation and pleasure. The pleasure derives from a sense of personal competence, mastery over some aspect of the environment, and accomplishment.**

Deci hypothesizes that people have needs to feel competent and autonomous (independent), needs that are best fulfilled through intrinsically motivated activities (Deci, Vallerand, Pelletier, & Ryan, 1991). It is these activities from which the individual is most likely to derive the pleasure of personal accomplishment and the sense of competence and autonomy that comes with it. It is perhaps for that reason that people are most likely to be creative when they are intrinsically motivated (Pedersen, 2002). The most creative artists, writers, designers, and scientists appear to do their work primarily because they derive personal pleasure from it. Extrinsic rewards may eventually come as "icing on the cake," but often they never do.

Extrinsic rewards can, in fact, interfere with intrinsically motivated behaviors. Deci (1971, 1972) gave one group of participants rewards for solving puzzles and another group no rewards. When the rewards were later stopped, the original reward group decreased the time spent solving the puzzles, while the non-reward group did not. Related studies have demonstrated that children also show this reward-interference effect and that providing rewards for tasks subjects already enjoy reduces their involvement. Similar results have been found in studies of career accomplishment. Janet Spence and Robert Helmreich (1983) examined the motivations and accomplishments of college students, business people, athletes, pilots, and scientists. They found that those who were intrinsically motivated were more competent, effective, and accomplished in their fields than those working primarily for extrinsic rewards.

It seems clear that most people are motivated by both extrinsic and intrinsic rewards in their day-to-day lives. However, those who work primarily for the praise, money, and other external rewards that society makes available are likely to be less creative and to accomplish less than those whose behavior is primarily a source of personal pleasure (Chirkov et al., 2003).

Evolutionary Theory

From the evolutionary perspective, motives are seen as mechanisms that have evolved to ensure the survival and reproduction of the species. As with other evolved features, the motivational systems of current humans are those that best permitted our ancestors to adapt to their environments. They had functional utility in those early environments and were therefore passed on genetically (Deutsch, 2003)

The adaptive value of such physiological motives as hunger, thirst, pain, and sex is easy to see. All are required for the survival of either the individual or the species, and survival is basic to Darwinian theory (Thornhill & Ussery, 2000). Psychological feelings of hunger and thirst arise from bodily mechanisms triggered by the deprivation of substances basic to life itself. They cause behavior that acts to replenish these essential survival resources, whether it be hunting in the forest or driving to McDonalds. Pain is also essential because it protects the body. The feeling, or even possibility, of pain is again triggered by specific, evolved mechanisms and causes action to remove the source of the pain. You reflexively withdraw your hand from the hot stove and actively avoid the bee that might sting you. Without the pain drive, the body would be much more vulnerable to injury and death. The sex drive deals with the survival of the species through reproduction; we will discuss its evolutionary aspects when we consider sexual motivation later in the chapter.

More complex social motive systems also represent adaptations that solved specific environmental problems over the course of evolutionary history. Consider the example of the affiliation motive - the need to seek out and interact with other people. The evolutionary perspective hypothesizes that this nearly universal human motive arose because our ancestors found the company and help of others to be essential to survival. Mutual protection from predators, aid in times of illness, and help in obtaining food may all have been basic to the development of the affiliation motive.

Keys to Motivation 1

Hunger Motivation

Hunger is clearly a form of motivation. We eat because we are motivated by a physiological drive and by learning processes and events that occur in the external environment. Let's consider the roles of the stomach, the hypothalamus, and other structures in hunger and eating. We will also discuss glucostatic and set point theories of neural regulation, as well as the effects on hunger of taste and learning. Finally, we will take up obesity, dieting, and the major eating disorders.

The Role of the Stomach

Early investigators focused on the stomach as the major source of the hunger drive. One of the most famous studies was

conducted by William Beaumont, a nineteenth-century army surgeon. He studied Alexis St. Martin, a Canadian hunter who had a permanent hole in his abdominal wall resulting from a gunshot wound. Beaumont conducted a variety of digestive experiments while monitoring gastric activity through the opening. He concluded that periods without food cause gastric juice to build up in the stomach glands, distending the glands and thereby creating the sensation of hunger.

A second series of classic studies involved swallowing a balloon, then inflating it in the stomach. Sounds like a new party game, but researcher Walter Cannon had his assistant, a man named Washburn, do exactly that. Washburn swallowed a balloon with an air hose attached to it. The balloon could then be inflated, and Cannon could observe Washburn's stomach contractions simply by attaching the hose to a pressure gauge (see Figure 12-3). He had Washburn tap a telegraph key whenever he felt hunger, and these reports of hunger correlated well with the stomach contractions (Cannon and Washburn, 1912).

Most recent studies have confirmed that the stomach does have a role in hunger (Lavin et al., 2002). Receptors in the stomach and upper intestine let us know when we are hungry, help determine our appetites for specific foods, and influence the size of the meal we consume. As you eat, the stomach becomes increasingly distended, triggering the receptors and reducing or eliminating the feeling of hunger. People typically begin to report feeling hungry again when the digestive process has emptied 60% of stomach contents and are very hungry when 90% of the food is gone (Geliebter & Hashim, 2002). Recent studies suggest that the emptying of the stomach increases levels of the circulating gastric hormone **ghrelin**, which stimulates food intake (Rosicka et al., 2002; Small et al., 2002). Even early studies made it clear, however, that mechanisms in the digestive system do not act alone to regulate hunger. People whose stomachs have been surgically removed, for example, still feel hunger (Wangensteen & Carlson, 1931).

Hypothalamic Control

As early as 1904, it was discovered that damage to the hypothalamus causes humans to become obese. Subsequent research shows that two separate regions within that tiny structure are associated with hunger (Del Parigi, 2002). The *lateral hypothalamus* (LH; Figure 12-4) is thought to function as a center that produces hunger and eating behavior. When this area is electrically stimulated, the animal eats. When it is destroyed, the animal suffers *aphagia*, in which it stops eating almost entirely, then resumes eating only small amounts of highly preferred foods. Recent evidence suggests that a neural circuit connecting the lateral hypothalamus to the amygdala may cause us to eat foods we have learned to especially like, even when we are already satiated (Petrovich et al., 2002).

The second region, called the ventromedial hypothalamus (VMH), is thought to be a *satiety* center; when this area is stimulated, the animal stops eating. When it is lesioned, *hyperphagia* - nearly continuous eating - triples or quadruples normal weight (Mondo et al., 1993; see Figure 12-4). Under normal circumstances, body conditions that stimulate the lateral hypothalamus cause the animal to eat; those that stimulate the ventromedial hypothalamus cause it to stop eating.

Unfortunately, the simple idea that these two "on and off" centers alone control eating has not held up. Stimulation and destruction of the LH and VMH do not affect hunger alone. LH stimulation elicits drinking if no food is available and running if neither food nor water is present, perhaps indicating that overall arousal, rather than the hunger drive, is affected (Valenstein, 1973). VMH lesions reduce the rat's motivation to eat and the range of foods it will consume. It has, in fact, become clear that specific nuclei do not tell the whole story. Rather, several other areas of the brain, including the thalamus and frontal cortex, now appear to be involved in "hunger circuits" in the brain (Del Parigi, 2002). And neurotransmitters also play a significant role. Increases in a neurochemical called neuropeptide-Y, for example, stimulate appetite and initiate eating behavior (Blevins et al., 2002; Williams et al., 2000). The hormone Leptin also appears to be involved, acting on the neuropeptides to increase energy expenditure and decrease weight (Velkoska et al., 2003; Bagnasco et al., 2002).

Additional Brain Mechanisms

More recent research has identified a third hypothalamic hunger area, the *paraventricular nucleus* (PVN), which appears to be important in energy metabolism and the selection of specific foods. Several neurotransmitters, including serotonin, norepinephrine, and neuropeptide Y, act on the PVN to control the consumption of carbohydrates. Other neurotransmitters affect this same nucleus and others to control protein and fat consumption, as well as overall caloric intake.

Other structures involved in hunger include several areas of the cortex and the amygdala (Gautier et al., 2000). When you walk into the kitchen and see that delicious apple pie on the counter, it is amygdalar neurons that fire to whet your appetite (Del Parigi et al., 2002).

The Glucostatic Hypothesis

Glucose is a simple sugar and a major source of energy. You feel hungry when your blood glucose level is low and satiated when it is high. Moreover, injections of glucose decrease LH and increase VMH firing, suggesting that these nuclei are sensitive to glucose.

The *glucostatic theory* of Jean Mayer (1953) suggests that specialized hypothalamic neurons function as *glucostats*

- a kind of thermostat for monitoring blood glucose (Mayer, 1955). Mayer hypothesizes that these glucostats monitor glucose in the cells.

Signals to the glucostats in the VMH and LH come from the liver, which monitors the level of glucose in the blood. A drop in plasma glucose triggers the liver receptors, which signal the LH to activate the hunger drive (Penicaud et al., 2002). When enough food has been consumed, the liver senses the increase in glucose and signals the VMH to stop eating.

Set Point Theory

Some have suggested that the hypothalamus may monitor *lipids* (fats) in the blood, rather than glucose. The set-point theory of Richard Keesey and his colleagues builds on this *lipostatic hypothesis* (Keesey and Powley, 1975). A *set-point* is a biologically based weight at which your body tends to remain. Brain mechanisms keep you at that weight by monitoring the stores of fat in your fat cells. The number of fat cells is largely set, probably by genetics and early eating. However, the size of each fat cell varies, and the hypothalamus monitors this variation (Keesey, 1986). When the cells decrease in size, you feel hungry; when they increase, you stop eating. Keesey argues that lesions in the lateral hypothalamus reduce or eliminate eating behavior because they lower the set point for body weight.

Support for the theory comes from the fact that humans and other animals tend to maintain constant body weight over long periods of time, often without any specific weight monitoring (Weinsier, 2001). When you consider that eating an extra pat of butter a day would add 10 pounds a year to your body, maintaining a constant body weight seems quite remarkable. We will have more to say about set points when we consider obesity.

A recently proposed modification of set-point theory suggests that there is a "zone," rather than a point, at which weight is set by genetics and physiology (Levitsky, 2002). This newer theory is based on data showing that humans do not reduce their food intake even after consuming large amounts of food and that snacks before meals do not decrease the amount eaten at the meal. In addition, intake increases when more food is served, when a greater variety of foods is offered, and when they are eating with other people. These findings suggest that weight may easily increase within the person's set-zone based on learning and other environmental factors, partially accounting for the increasing obesity in modern times.

All in Good Taste

Taste (often combined with smell and texture) is a powerful determinant of what and how much we eat (Drewnowski, 2001). The availability of foods with particularly desirable tastes can override internal signals of satiety (Cho et al., 2002). Moreover, Barbara Rolls and her colleagues have shown that both people and rats consume far more calories when a variety of foods are offered than when just one or two are available (Rolls et al., 1984).

Taste preference is both innate and learned. Humans have broad innate preferences, such as preferences for sweet over bitter and sour tastes (Brownson et al., 2002). Beyond these general tendencies, specific tastes are largely acquired through learning. Both children and rats, for example, learn to prefer flavors that have previously been paired with foods high in fat (Ackroff & Sclafani, 2002). And foods previously associated with pleasant social interactions also come to be preferred (Touzani & Scalfani, 2001). One recent study examined identical twins discordant for obesity - one twin overweight, the other not (Rissanen et al., 2002). Learned preferences for fatty foods in the overweight twins accounted for the difference.

Taste preferences can have important adaptive functions that provide essential nutrients. Even subtle taste differences in foods can permit some animals to seek out and selectively eat nutrients they need. Early studies with ten-month-old infants showed that they could select a balanced diet when given a variety of choices (Davis, 1928). Later research indicated that animals deprived of sodium preferred sodium-rich foods (Richter, 1942) and that sodium preference decreases after a high-salt meal. As Elliot Stellar (1993) points out, the need and resulting taste for salt are innate, though this preference can be modified by learning and thus does not always involve a sodium deficit (Stasiak, 2002). It now appears, however, that selective deficiency eating is quite minimal in humans.

The Role of Learning

Learning affects not only taste preferences but also other aspects of hunger and eating. Time cues, for example, are learned. When your watch says 11:45 a.m., you may immediately begin to feel hungry. Seeing or smelling a preferred food can also trigger hunger. The sight or odor is a classically conditioned cue that causes the eating response because the association has been reinforced by the satiation of hunger and perhaps the taste of the food. Observational learning can also be a basis for eating habits. A child sees his parents repeatedly eat a certain food and learns to prefer it. This is in part how ethnic food preferences develop: A person observationally passes on to her own children ethnic preferences she learned from her parents.

Most people consume meals in the presence of others, and these social situations also provide learned cues for eating behavior (Poothullil, 2002). It's much easier to diet, for example, if the people you eat with are on successful diets. In addition, people tend to feel hungry and eat when they see others eating. A classic study showed that even chickens satiated on grain will resume eating when placed among other chickens that are eating (Bayer, 1929). Finally, the presence of others can greatly influence how <u>much</u> you eat (de Castro 2002). People eat meals that average 60 to 75 percent larger when they eat with others than when they eat alone (Redd & de Castro, 1992), and this effect is greater when the others are relatives (de Castro, 2002).

Overall, it seems clear that aspects of hunger and eating are influenced by a variety of genetic and environmental variables. Some aspects are influenced by one or the other, some by both (Figure 12-5).

Obesity

WARNING: The Surgeon General Has Determined That Eating May Be Hazardous To Your Health.

Imagine picking up a package of hamburger, a pint of ice cream, or a can of peanuts and seeing it inscribed with this slogan. Well, it probably won't happen, but it would have some basis. About 61% of all American adults are overweight, and 27% are obese - more than 30% above ideal body weight (Health, United States, 2000, NCHS, 2002). Even short of obesity, overweight is dangerous and contributes to poor health. A consensus conference of experts concluded that excessive weight contributes to morbidity and mortality from a variety of diseases and conditions, most notably high blood pressure, diabetes, and heart disease (Crepaldi et al., 1991).

Those who have the misfortune to be obese have often been subjected to humiliation and discrimination. Many people still believe that you become obese primarily because you are too "weak" to control your food intake and too lazy to exercise. "Fat and lazy" is certainly an old axiom. We now have considerable evidence, however, that the largest single factor in obesity is heredity (Frogues & Boutin, 2001). We will also consider the effects of psychological and environmental factors and learn just what is known about losing weight and keeping it off.

Genetic Factors in Obesity. One study examined 109 pairs of identical and 86 pairs of fraternal twins. Concordance for obesity was much higher in the identical twins, and heritability accounted for 85% of the variability in obesity and 50% of the variability in daily food intake (de-Castro, 1993, 2002; Figure 12-6). Studies involving adoption and family methods, as well as other twin studies, confirm this finding (Hamann & Sharma, 2002). Moreover, molecular geneticists have identified a specific gene on chromosome 11 that appears to be involved in at least one form of obesity (Bougneres, 2002). In fact, however, it is estimated that over 200 genes are involved (Zekanowski, 2001).

You actually do not inherit obesity per se, but rather a tendency to become obese (Hamann & Sharma, 2002). People with this genetic tendency store fat more efficiently and consume more food (Feinle et al., 2001). In addition, heredity may affect metabolic rate, fat cells, a weight set point, and the hypothalamus. *Metabolic rate* is essentially the speed at which the body carries out normal physiological functions. Since nearly 70% of your energy is expended in conducting these normal, internal functions, metabolic rate is an important factor in weight gain and loss.

The special cells that store fat in the body are also affected by heredity. Obese humans have far more and larger fat cells, proportional to their weight, than do normal weight people (Labib, 2003). That means more space for fat and hence a greater propensity to store it, making it easier to gain weight. It also turns out that empty fat cells just "scream" to be filled, so the overweight person who loses weight becomes extremely and chronically hungry, leading him to eat more in order to fill the fat cells.

To exacerbate the genetic problem, overeating, which also appears to be based primarily in genetics and physiology (Pearcey & de Castro, 2002), can further increase the number of fat cells you have (Rosmond, 2002). We thus have a vicious cycle in which overeating increases the number of fat cells, which increases the amount of food needed to fill them, which causes more overeating and weight gain, which produces more fat cells.

The number and size of the fat cells largely determines the hypothetical *set point* mentioned earlier (Boutin & Froguel, 2001). For example, both you and your friend might be 5'7" tall, but your set point may be 140 pounds while your friend's is 170. Your friend would have great difficulty maintaining a weight of 140, while you have no problem. In theory, your set point cannot readily be altered and is a major factor in determining your weight Hebebrand et al., 2001). You can diet stringently and get below this point, but you will regain the weight very easily. Sound familiar?

Eating Lots and Eating Wrong. You probably can't gain weight by genes alone. Some people are affected by external cues, emotional arousal, bad eating habits, and dietary restraints. All these factors increase caloric intake, but those with a genetic tendency toward obesity will gain more weight on the same number of extra calories (Kovacs et al., 2002). In addition, they may be more susceptible to some factors.

Eating on cue. Stanley Schachter (1971) compared the eating behaviors of average-weight and overweight students. Half the students in each group were fed roast beef sandwiches to fill their stomachs, while the other half were left with empty stomachs. All then took part in an alleged taste-testing task, comparing crackers of various flavors. Schachter found that the average-weight students ate few crackers if their stomachs were already full and many if they were empty. Overweight students, however, ate the same number of crackers whether they were full or empty (Schachter et al., 1968). It appeared that average-weight people responded to internal satiation cues, while overweights did not.

Other studies have also shown that overweights appear to respond primarily to external, rather than internal cues. In one case, Schachter put participants without watches in a room and set the clock to show that it was much earlier or later in the day than it actually was. Overweight participants ate far more crackers when the clock showed that it was closer to dinner time than when it showed an early-afternoon time. However, average-weight subjects ate about the same number at each time setting. Clearly, the overweight participants were responding much more to the external time cue.

Schachter concluded that obese people do not seem to regulate their eating in accordance with internal physiological needs. Instead, they are more sensitive to such external cues as the taste, smell, and sight of food. Cecilia in our example might well be munching on that chocolate chip cookie just because she saw the cookie box sitting on her dresser.

Schachter's work initiated a large body of research on the role of external cues in eating, and Judith Rodin reviewed that work in 1981. She concluded that it did *not* support the Schachter hypothesis. She found that some obese and some non-obese people are much more sensitive to external cues than others; weight seems to make no difference (Rodin & Slochower, 1976). What does seem to make a difference is the person's *insulin* response to cues. Elevated insulin is associated with feelings of hunger, and insulin level may be affected more by external cues in some people than in others. To find out, Rodin brought subjects who had not eaten for 18 hours to a lab where steak was being grilled. She found that "externals" - participants shown on prior tests to be very susceptible to environmental cues - exhibited a much larger insulin response to the steak than did "internals." However, weight had nothing to do with it (Rodin, 1981).

What can we conclude about the relationship between obesity and sensitivity to external cues? The more recent evidence appears to be more supportive of Rodin's conclusions (Mela, 2001; Bell & Rolls, 2001). However, given the conflicting results in the literature, we cannot be certain.

Memory may be a factor. Cognitive factors more generally do appear to influence eating behavior. Interestingly enough, the amount of food that a person eats at a given time may be influenced by her memory of her immediately previous meal. In one study, participants in an experimental group were given a "lunch cue" by being asked to recall what they had eaten for lunch that day, while those in a control group were not given that cue. Subjects given the cue ate significantly less food because they had been reminded of the previous meal (Higgs, 2002).

Stress and emotional arousal. If you've ever suspected that you tend to eat more when you are under stress, the evidence is on your side, and obese people are particularly susceptible to this effect (Timmerman & Acton, 2001). They may learn early in life that eating somehow decreases anxiety or their parents may reinforce that association by giving them food when they are anxious to make them feel better (Canetti et al., 2002). Either way, eating may reduce arousal, but it will increase weight.

Bad eating habits. Bad habits can be major contributors to obesity. Eating when you are not really hungry, consuming many calories shortly before bed, and eating in front of the TV or while working are all examples of poor habits. Such behaviors can contribute to weight gain, as can selecting the wrong foods - particularly those high in fat content. However, it is excessive calories that make the primary contribution to weight gain.

Restrained and unrestrained eaters. Dieting itself may contribute to obesity. Janet Polivy and Peter Herman (1983; Heatherton et al., 1988) theorize that people who are constantly dieting are *restrained eaters* - individuals who actively try to regulate their eating. Such people think about food constantly, are usually hungry, and feel guilty if they overeat. Unrestrained eaters, who are not on diets, rarely think longingly about food and don't feel guilty if they overeat. Restrained eaters consume very little food most of the time. However, when something interferes with their control, they become *disinhibited eaters* and may consume very large amounts of food in a short time. The restrained eater seems to have an all-or-none attitude: "Either I'm dieting strictly or I can eat everything in sight." Unfortunately for the guilt-ridden dieter, many conditions and events can cause disinhibition: stress, alcohol consumption, depression, and a variety of social occasions, such as Thanksgiving dinner or a banquet where "I just have to eat" (Silva et al., 2002). Polivy and Herman note that perhaps the most common cause of disinhibition, however, is simply cheating on the diet. The restrained eater may eat one ice cream cone or piece of pie and immediately decide that she has broken the diet and might as well eat anything she wants.

Restrained eaters are typically overweight people, and their ironic fate may be that dietary restraint causes frequent disinhibition, overeating, and weight gain (Figure 12-8). Obesity begets obesity, and there is certainly evidence for larger weight fluctuations in restrained than unrestrained eaters (Roemmich et al., 2002). However, evidence supporting the hypothesis is not entirely convincing. Critics point out that the theory does little to further our understanding of why people become obese to begin with. More importantly, some studies show that people of average weight fluctuate in their dietary restraint just as much as do obese people and that restrained eaters do not typically overeat (Dritschel et al., 1993). Finally, disinhibited eating in an obese person may not be an entirely psychological phenomenon as the theory suggests. It may instead involve a genetically predisposed, physiological process in which consuming a small amount of high-calorie food makes it nearly impossible for the obese person to control the physiological urge to eat more. We must conclude that the role of dietary restraint in obesity is, at best, unclear.

Losing It. As you may have noticed, it is far easier to gain weight than to lose it. In fact, dieting is a constant preoccupation of much of the populace. Between 15 and 25% of men and between 38 and 50% of women diet each year in the United States (Serdula et al., 1994), and we spend $30 billion annually in the effort (National Task Force on the Prevention and Treatment of Obesity, 1993).

There are three principal reasons overweight people don't easily get and stay thin. The first is apparent in the common outcome of that famous and often inaccurate phrase: "I'll start my diet Monday." Starting a diet is very difficult for most people because they know how frustrating the deprivation will be. (Urbszat e al., 2002). A second problem is that many dieters violate the diet either for a special occasion or simply because they get too hungry. The final - and biggest - problem is that almost everyone who loses weight regains most or all of it within one year and at best within five years (NIH Technology Assessment Conference, 1992). A "crash" diet may theoretically result in even more rapid weight gain as the brain struggles to bring you back to your set point.

You tend to lose weight slowly and gain it back quickly. Why? There are several reasons. First, the lowering of caloric intake during dieting causes metabolism to slow down, which causes you to burn less calories (Steinbeck, 2002). This means that weight loss slows progressively as you continue a diet and that stopping the diet leads to more rapid regain. Evolutionary adaptation probably explains why this happens: When it appears to the body that less food is available, it is adaptive to conserve physiological resources by expending less metabolic energy. Fortunately, the reduction in metabolic rate is not permanent (Phelan & Wadden, 2002). A second problem is that depriving the body of food tends to increase the amount consumed when the diet ends. And a related third difficulty is that you are likely to crave and hence eat specific foods of which you have been deprived. Finally, those bad eating habits play a role. Many overweight people see the diet as temporary. But such people often have poor eating behaviors, such as consuming too many high calorie foods and binge eating (Hsu et al., 2002). Moreover, life-before-diet may have revolved around food, with much time spent shopping for food, reading the food advertisements, cooking, and eating. Food had therefore become a major reinforcer. The overweight person often looks forward with fond anticipation to every meal, to going out to a restaurant, to rewarding family interactions around the dinner table, and the like. Along with the weight, a successful dieter must lose these old habits and - just as difficult - gain new ones. New rewards not involving food must be found and new activities that keep him away from food and constant thoughts of eating are essential.

Diet vodka and crocus leaves. Walk into any grocery or drug store, and you will see several current magazine covers touting the newest diets, some of them as crazy as the one in the title of this section. Which one should you choose? The answer is probably "any of them and none of them." The truth is that any diet that restricts caloric intake severely enough will take off weight, even my new and better "diet vodka and crocus leaf" regimen (except that it's really hard to find diet vodka!). On the other hand, no diet developed to date has shown long-term success for most people (Wierenga & Oldham, 2002). What about such weight loss programs as Weight Watchers, Diet Workshop, and Jenny Craig? Same answer. Many people lose weight, but almost all regain it - and often more - within a short time (Frost et al., 2002).

A successful diet has three major characteristics: It must restrict caloric intake; it must be for a lifetime; and it must be tailored to the individual. There is no consistent scientific evidence to support special diets that take off weight better than others, no special foods that "burn calories," no diets that have special properties not found in other diets. Widely touted low-fat diets, for example, do not perform as well as low-calorie diets (Pirozzo et al., 2002; Willett, 2002). Indeed, diets with moderate fat content are better (Kris-Etherton et al., 2002). There is only one secret: You must eat so few calories that you will expend more energy each day than you take in; and the number of calories you can "afford" depends on your metabolic rate, your fat cells, and, ultimately, your genetic history (de Castro, 2002). Beyond individualizing the diet and making it permanent, eating frequent, small meals appears to help (Ruidavets et al., 2002). And *behavior modification* techniques and a new combination of drugs (see the Probe), along with calorie restriction, may be more successful than other approaches (Phelan & Wadden, 2002), as may surgery to reduce the size of the stomach (Nicolai et al., 2002).

A final secret to success in weight loss and maintenance may be *exercise*. The dieter who develops and maintains a good program of predominantly aerobic exercise is more likely to be successful in the long run. Studies show that obese people who combine regular exercise with calorie restriction and behavior modification are most likely to lose abdominal fat and to maintain their reduced weights (Mayo et al., 2003). However, walking does not reduce weight; more intense exercise is necessary (Miller et al., 2002). Exercise will also improve cardiovascular health and has other positive effects as well (Schmerund & Erbel, 2003).

Unfortunately, we must conclude on the sobering note that it is not yet clear whether even the best methods are truly an improvement over simple calorie restriction without diet training. In fact, one recent study showed that 24 obese women who lost weight with no special training had regained an average of 87% of that weight within four years, with some going above 100%. These figures are very similar to those for people who lose weight on the most effective drug and exercise programs. We clealy still have more work to do.

"But I'm Too Fat": Eating Disorders

I first saw a patient with an eating disorder while I was in graduate school. Standing perhaps 5'4" tall, she weighed about 80 pounds and was standing in front of a mirror in a hospital. Thin to the point of being emaciated, she was saying to her therapist: "But I'm too fat." She was suffering from anorexia nervosa, one of the two major *eating disorders*. The other is bulimia nervosa.

Anorexia nervosa is a disorder in which the patient is usually an adolescent or young adult female (though males occasionally have this disorder) who is extremely fearful of being fat (Chambry et al., 2002). As a result, she starves herself to at least 25% below her normal body weight and refuses to maintain a higher weight. Many weigh less than 100 pounds and are almost skeletal in appearance. The disorder involves a severe distortion of body image in which the individual firmly believes she is overweight, when, in fact, she is very thin. A recent longitudinal study showed that ten years after an initial diagnosis of anorexia, about half the patients had no remaining eating disorder symptoms, though most had other psycholgical disorders involving anxiety and depression (Rastam et al., 2003).

Bulimia nervousa patients are also typically underweight, but they usually binge on huge amounts of food, after which they engage in self-induced purging (vomiting) or in laxative abuse (Bruce et al., 2003). These episodes of binging and purging occur at least twice each week and as often as twice a day. Unlike the anorexic, the bulimic is aware that her behavior is abnormal and that she is underweight, and bulimics eventually return to normal eating patterns (Quadflieg & Fichter, 2003). Attempts to divide bulimics into separate subcategories of purgers and nonpurgers have thus far failed. Another attempt has been to identify a separate disorder that involves binging but no purging and would be called simply *binge eating*, but many believe that binging is not a distinct disorder (Kerzhnerman & Lowe, 2002).

Both anorexia and bulimia are found primarily in young women from the middle and upper socioeconomic levels and typically begin between the ages of 12 and 20. The ratio of females to males is about 20:1, and the disorders have markedly increased in frequency over the past three decades to the point where perhaps as many as 15% of college women have them.

Anorexia and bulimia are both serious disorders that cause a variety of severe physical symptoms. Menstruation ceases in virtually all cases. Other serious symptoms include anemia, dehydration, vitamin and mineral deficiencies, electrolyte and endocrine disturbances, intestinal damage, dental problems, and cardiovascular disorders. Victims of anorexia nervousa are often hospitalized on an emergency basis because they are starving to death, and between 5% and 30% do die as a result of the disorder. Bulimics often also develop serious symptoms, but the disorder is.

Research on eating disorders has been quite extensive, but their causes are thus far not well understood (Steiner et al., 2003; Schmidt, 2003). It is increasingly clear that genetic and physiological factors may be involved (Allison et al., 2001). One example of a biological component is the hormone melanocortin, which appears to involved in both obesity and anorexia. On a more psycholgical level, one major hypothesis is that anorexics and bulimics are preoccupied with achievement and thinness as a result of social norms. Victims certainly are focused on achievement, with school performance well above that expected for their IQ levels, and there is little doubt about our societal "fear of fat," perhaps most obvious in advertisements for women's clothing (Gowers & Shore, 2001). There are, however, other causal factors as well. Psychoanalytic theory points to disturbances in early relationships, leading to distrust, and studies point to ongoing family conflict in which communication among members is complex and confusing (Beumont & Touyz, 2003). Others find a history of sexual abuse or other trauma. Whatever the causes, anorexia and bulimia are on the increase, and we can hope that ongoing research will turn up some more definite answers. Both disorders are typically treated with psychotherapy, though antidepressant drugs are sometimes also helpful (Casper, 2002).

Keys to Motivation 2

Sexual Motivation

Like hunger, sex is a physiological drive that is necessary for the survival of the species. Sexual behavior is thus highly motivated behavior that is based in physiology but modified by sociocultural learning processes.

A recent theoretical model incorporates genetic, neurophysiological, stimuatory, and experiential determinants of sexual behavior (Agmo, 1999). The powerful motivation of the sex drive is seen in both males and females and greatly influences behavior. Perhaps 95% of adults are sexually active in one way or another (Temple, 1993), though only 13% report having had more than one partner in the past year (Leigh et al., 1993).

In addition to intercourse, common sexual activities include masturbation and oral-genital stimulation. Studies suggest that over 90% of males and over 60% of females masturbate. Similarly, over 90% of married women had engaged in oral sex, and both men and women in another study rated receiving oral-genital sex as their most preferred activity. We will have more to say about sexual activities and particularly about safe sex in Chapter 15, where we discuss the AIDS epidemic. Here we take up the adaptive nature of gender differences in sexual behavior and the roles of biological, psychological, and sociocultural factors. We will also see that much is now known about the causes of differing sexual orientation. And we will discuss the nature, causes, and treatment of sexual dysfunction.

Sex and the Sexes: Evolved Differences in Sexual Behavior

Men are far more likely to engage in - and often to prefer - casual sexual liaisons than are women. Conversely, women are more likely to prefer commitment and to have more exacting standards for even short-term mates. These differences may be due purely to differences between the sexes in the sociocultural training they receive. However, few authorities still believe that the observed differences are due entirely or primarily to social training (Pedersen et al., 2002). Many have turned to evolutionary psychology for a deeper understanding.

Darwin (1871) proposed not only a theory of natural or survival selection, but also a theory of sexual selection, in which individuals choose characteristics on the basis of reproductive advantage. That is, those human qualities more likely to lead to reproduction of the species are selected for genetic passage to later generations. Males and females differ in the characteristics that favor reproduction, and these differences arise from the evolutionary history of the species (Buss, 1995).

Throughout human history, each sex has had several reproductive disadvantages that behavior must resolve. For men, the first is that a woman always knows the children she bears are her own, while a man can never be certain of his own paternity. Second, men cannot readily detect women who are fertile and hence valuable for reproduction, since it is difficult to know when or even whether ovulation occurs. Since men are quite reliably fertile at nearly any given moment, women have relatively little difficulty in identifying men who are reproductively valuable (Wood & Eagly, 2002).

A third obstacle for men lies in finding willing partners. In fact, you may have wondered why men are typically more willing to have casual sex than are women. The evolutionary answer is that women have a much heavier obligatory parental investment than do men. The woman's absolute minimum investment is nine months (assuming no abortion), whereas the man's is only a few minutes, and that has been true throughout evolutionary history. Therefore, men who succeeded in gaining sexual access to women historically were reproductively more successful, and their characteristics have been preserved and passed on by sexual selection (Wood & Eagly, 2002).

The disadvantages for women arise out of the reproductive benefit of casual sex for men: More partners for a man means greater potential reproductivity, fulfilling the Darwinian goal. The resulting problems for the woman have to do with the willingness and ability of the man to provide resources (Badcock, 1991, Buss, 1995). A woman first needs to identify men who are *willing* to invest resources in herself and her children. The woman who has the ability to recognize such men has a great reproductive advantage, and her characteristics will tend to be selected and passed on. The woman's second problem lies in finding men who are able to invest resources in parenthood. If a man is willing to invest but has no resources (e.g., financial) to invest, the woman and her children will still lose out.

Alice Eagly (1995) points out that evidence supporting the evolutionary position is quite substantial. On the issue of casual sex, for example, men report that they would prefer to have more than 18 lifetime sex partners, while women opt for just 4 or 5 (Buss & Schmidt, 1993). Men also show much more positive attitudes toward casual sex (Oliver & Hyde, 1993), and they behave accordingly. They have more partners, more total sexual experience, and more casual sex than do women. A further demonstration of the gender difference in promiscuity comes from a study in which men and women were approached by attractive strangers of the opposite sex. After some preliminaries, the stranger asked the subject to have sex with him or her. None of the women consented to the request, but 75% of the men did (Clark & Hatfield, 1989). The evidence clearly confirms common observation - and evolutionary theory.

Another supportive body of literature shows that women are much more particular than men about the characteristics of their short-term partners. David Buss (1989) found that women strongly prefer mates with better financial resources and the ability to provide physical protection. They reject mates who appear incapable of providing resources, such as those lacking in education or ambition. Men are far less particular. The issues raised by these findings are, however, controversial.

A final sex difference is in jealousy. Buss and his colleagues asked men and women to imagine their partners locked in passionate sexual intercourse with someone else or, alternatively, developing a deep emotional attachment for another person. Men were far more distressed by the first scenario and women by the second (Buss, Larsen, Westen, & Semmelroth, 1992). This finding has been confirmed both in our culture and in others (Buunk et al., 1994). Again it is consistent with an evolutionary approach that hypothesizes a greater emphasis on sexuality in males and commitment/security in females.

Whatever the evolutionary history, sexual arousal is a complex process that repeats in a fairly consistent, cyclical pattern. The human sexual response occurs in four stages (Masters & Johnson, 1966): excitement, plateau, orgasm, and resolution. More recent work, using magnetic resonance imaging (MRI) of the female genitalia to objectively measure sexual arousal (e.g., increases in the size of the clitoris) largely supports this model of sexual arousal (Deliganis et al., 2002). Other recent work demonstrates the involvement of both biological and psychological factors in the arousal sequence (Basson, 2001).

Biological Factors in Sexual Arousal

Sexual arousal is a product of biology modified by environment (McKenna, 2002). It is increasingly clear that sexual behavior is strongly influenced by genetic factors that are expressed in specific areas of the central nervous system and in hormones produced by the endocrine system (Emmons & Lipton, 2003).

Neurological Influences. Sexual behavior is ultimately controlled by the central nervous system. It is the brain that interprets stimuli as sexually arousing, engages in erotic fantasies, and controls the feelings of pleasure that accompany arousal and orgasm. The spinal cord also plays an important reflex role.

Erection and ejaculation are controlled at the level of the spinal cord. Stimulation of the penis generates nerve impulses that travel to a reflex center in the lower cord. This center sends signals to the muscles and arteries of the penis, causing erection. Men with spinal cords that are completely severed above this level sometimes have reflex erections, but they are not accompanied by sexual feelings. Similarly, ejaculation can be a purely reflex activity controlled by an area slightly higher on the spinal cord. Although women no doubt have similar spinal reflexes, studies have not so far revealed just how or where they take place.

The brain mechanisms involved in sexual behavior are not yet fully understood. It appears, however, that the limbic system plays a major role and that the hypothalamus is centrally involved, stimulating the pituitary gland to release sex hormones. It has been found, for example, that lesions of certain hypothalamic areas in rats eliminate sexual behavior, while stimulation of these areas produces copulation. The cortex plays an evaluative role in locating objects that are appropriate goals of sexual behavior (Arnow et al., 2002). Surgically removing the temporal lobes in a male cat leads to indiscriminate sexual mounting behavior, and cortical damage virtually anywhere in the human brain tends to interfere with sexual behavior, particularly in males. And, finally, it now appears that the neurotransmitter dopamine may be centrally involved (Giuliano & Allard, 2001).

Hormonal Influences. Sexual motivation in humans is strongly influenced by hormones (Pfaff et al., 2002). The principal hormones in women are *estrogens* (especially estradiol) and *progestins* (primarily progesterone). The male hormones are *androgens*, principally *testosterone.* Most evidence has long suggested that sexual arousal in women is stimulated, in part, by the estrogens, and higher levels of these hormones are generally associated with increased sexual desire (Wallen & Lovejoy, 1993). The chief male hormone is testosterone, which is also found in females. It is manufactured primarily by the testes in men and the ovaries in women and, as The Critical Thinker describes, is associated with sexual desire in both genders.

Psychological and Sociocultural Factors

Sexual behavior is also a product of psychological processes. It is influenced by learning and by such aspects of the immediate situation as the physical attractiveness of a partner. External stimuli and fantasy also play important roles.

The role of learning becomes evident in cross-cultural studies. Whereas American males usually find a woman's breasts sexually arousing, males in the Mangaia culture of Polynesia pay no sexual attention to the breasts at all (Mahoney, 1983). Women of the Choriti culture spit in their lover's faces during intercourse, and lovers in the Sciriono culture find biting and scratching to the point of bleeding to be highly arousing. Other studies suggest that female orgasm is heavily influenced by learning (Pfaus et al., 2001). Some societies teach their members that women are expected to enjoy coitus and to have multiple orgasms, while others teach that coitus is something that women must endure rather than enjoy, making orgasm virtually unheard of.

More immediate influences on sexual arousal and behavior include such factors as physical attractiveness, repeated exposure to arousing stimuli, and alcohol consumption. In one study, college women rated as physically attractive had both intercourse and oral-genital sex more often than did average or unattractive women (Stelzer et al., 1987). Other studies show that erotic movies produce physiological arousal responses in men (Koukounas & McCabe, 2002) and that the media, more generally, strongly influence sexual arousal and behavior (Earles et al., 2002). And a final study showed that when college men repeatedly saw the same erotic movie or engaged in the same fantasy, their levels of arousal decreased, a phenomenon called *habituation* (Koukounas & Over, 1993). When the stimulus you habituate to is your regular sexual partner, the result can be quite negative. In a final study, 35% of both men and women reported that their sexual behavior "loosened up" after drinking. As a result of drinking, many engaged in sexual intercourse or abandoned safe-sex practices (Meilman, 1993).

External Stimuli. The specific external stimuli that produce sexual arousal vary from culture to culture and, to some extent, from person to person. Studies show that such sexually explicit materials as movies and magazines are arousing for both women and men (Letourneau, 2002). Some studies have directly measured sexual arousal in women by using vaginal plethysmography, a technique in which an instrument is inserted to measure blood flow in the walls of the vagina. The walls become engorged with blood during arousal, and sexually explicit visual stimuli have been shown to produce this effect. Auditory stimuli also cause sexual arousal, as indicated by the great success of the "dial-a-porn" industry, which allows people to call a phone number and hear an arousing voice. Tactile stimulation, such as touching and stroking the genitals, is the most direct external stimulus and the most likely one to produce arousal.

Apart from touching, such simple learning processes as classical conditioning may determine what stimuli serve as sexual turn-ons for given individuals. Sounds, odors, or items of clothing may come to be arousing through their association with sexual gratification. In addition, people learn "appropriate" sources for arousal through observational learning processes by noting what is sexually arousing to peers and what kinds of stimuli are promoted by the mass media as being arousing.

---

1 See Chapter 6 for a discussion of genetic methodology.

Sexual Fantasy. It has often been said that the brain is the most powerful sex organ. In the absence of any sexual partner, pornographic video, or other external stimulus, most people readily become aroused by engaging in *autoerotic fantasy* - imagining sexual activities. The fantasizing is often accompanied by masturbation. Both men and women show increased sexual arousal when they engage in fantasy, and imagining both sexual stimuli (such as a movie star) and their own sexual responses to these stimuli increases arousal even more.

Sexual Orientation

Homosexuality refers to the preference for same-gender sexual partners, and homosexual behavior has been found in every society since the beginning of recorded history. Current terminology typically refers to male homosexuals by that term and to females as lesbians. The term gay applies to both genders. Let's consider the prevalence of homosexuality, society's attitudes toward gays, and the likely causes of same-gender preference.

Prevalence. In classic studies completed a half century ago, Alfred Kinsey and his colleagues (Kinsey et al., 1948, 1953) found that 4% of males and 2% of females are exclusively homosexual; 37% and 20% of men and women, respectively, reported at least one homosexual experience. Subsequent studies have typically yielded somewhat lower estimates, but there is some indication of an increase in recent years. Relatively recent studies prior to 1996 showed that 1.7-2.0% of males report homosexual activity within the past year, while studies done since 1996 show figures of 3.1-3.7% (Anderson & Stall, 2002).

In addition to homosexuals, some individuals are *bisexual* and have sexual contact with members of both sexes. Kinsey (1948, 1953) found that 16 percent of men and 9 percent of women were bisexual, but later estimates have varied widely. Some studies suggest that 15 to 20 percent of men and 10 to 15 percent of women are bisexual, while Masters and Johnson (1982) estimated that less than 5 percent of either gender fall in this category.

Public and Professional Attitudes. Cross-cultural data show that homosexual behavior is widely condemned in all current societies (Lim, 2002). In its extreme form, this disapproval of gay behavior is termed *homophobia* (Landen & Innala, 2002). In the United States, the attitude of the general public toward homosexuality is quite negative, with 70 to 74 percent of those surveyed in some studies saying that homosexuality is "always wrong." Other studies confirm substantial amounts of homophobia, though it may be decreasing somewhat (Pratte, 1993). Moreover, a majority of people prefer not to work around gays, and gays report frequent harassment, so that many tend to live with a degree of fear and considerable secrecy.

Even professionals who deal with homosexuality sometimes have negative attitudes. One study showed that 57% of psychiatric nurses, who often deal with gays, were classified as moderately and 20% as severely homophobic (G. Smith, 1993). Such negative views persist despite the fact that the American Psychiatric Association does not officially consider homosexuality to be a disorder and that a number of studies have found no major differences in mental health between homosexuals and heterosexuals.

The Causes of Homosexuality. Both biological and psychological explanations of homosexuality have been offered. The role of biological factors is still quite controversial (Haynes, 1995), but the fact that homosexual inclinations often appear very early in life suggests a genetic predisposition. The degree of concordance or agreement for this alternative sexual orientation is significantly higher in identical than in fraternal twins (Bailey et al., 1993; Figure 12-11).

In addition, there is evidence that a specific gene on the X chromosome influences male homosexuality (Hamer et al., 1993). Another line of research suggests that male homosexuality may be predisposed by a prenatal deficiency of androgens, while female homosexuality involves an excess of these male hormones (Meyer-Bahlberg, 1993). In addition, gays are more likely than heterosexuals to be left-handed or ambidextrous, suggesting a neural basis (Lalumiere et al., 2000). Finally, there is preliminary evidence that the hypothalamus may be structured somewhat differently in gays than in heterosexuals, suggesting a possible route of expression for the genetic predisposition (LeVay, 1993). In particular, a group of neurons in the anterior hypothalamus that is larger in men than women appears to be larger in heterosexual than in homosexual men.

Increasing knowledge of biological causes in recent years has seen a corresponding decline in the prevalence of psychological explanations of homosexuality. The two major psychological orientations that continue to receive some attention are the psychoanalytic and behavioral approaches. Freud believed that all people have latent homosexual tendencies that can be brought out by deviant parent-child relationships. While there is some supportive evidence indicating that particular kinds of family backgrounds are more likely to be associated with homosexuality, the evidence is inconsistent and inconclusive. The behavioral alternative to Freud proposes that homosexuality is the result of a conditioning process in which early homosexual thoughts, feelings, and behaviors are positively reinforced while heterosexual experiences are punished. Homosexuality may result when parents are physically or emotionally abusive or when an adolescent encounters a series of rejections and other unpleasant experiences in heterosexual contacts but has rewarding experiences in homosexual contacts (Corliss et al., 2002). Finally, there is evidence in some studies that homosexuals and bisexuals may have a higher rate of psychological disorder than heterosexuals, but this finding is not consistent, and the cause-effect relationship is unclear (Jorm et al., 2002; Schippers, 2002).

We do not yet definitively know the causes of homosexuality, but recent evidence increasingly suggests a role for genetic predispositions and associated hormonal and neurophysiological mechanisms (van Goozen et al., 2002). In fact, a majority of over 500 psychiatrists surveyed judged that homosexuality is primarily due to genetic factors (Gallagher et al., 1993). These physiological factors may well interact with psychological influences to determine the extent to which an individual will actually display partially or exclusively homosexual patterns of behavior.

Sexual Dysfunction and Its Treatment

Although 69% of women in one study (Rosen et al., 1993) and 60% of men in another (Solstad & Hertoft, 1993) report overall sexual satisfaction, the remainder do have minor to major sexual problems. We call the more chronic and serious of these conditions *sexual dysfunctions* - impairments in one or more areas of sexual performance - and 27% of women, as well as many men, have such conditions (Kadri et al., 2002). We will describe the major sexual dysfunctions, discuss their likely causes, and outline the treatments employed.

Major Sexual Dysfunctions. The major categories are defined in Table 12-2, and it is not uncommon for the same individual to have more than one of these difficulties simultaneously. Among the most common problems are erectile disorder and premature ejaculation in males and orgasmic disorder in females.

Erectile disorder (formerly referred to as impotence) is the inability to attain or maintain an erection firm enough to permit coitus. Occasional erectile failures occur in virtually every man. The problem only becomes a dysfunction if it occurs chronically, in which case it can typically be confirmed by physiological tests (Shabsigh & Anastasiadis, 2003). After initial erectile failures, the man may develop fear about his sexual performance, which further inhibits his erectile response. His partner may compound the problem by accusing him of infidelity or homosexuality, or she may feel that the problem is her fault because she is failing to arouse him. Erectile dysfunction can thus become a serious problem for the relationship as a whole.

Premature ejaculation is ejaculating too quickly during intercourse. But what is "too quickly"? After examining many cases, Masters and Johnson (1970) concluded that it is impossible to specify a minimal time duration. Rather, they consider a man to be suffering from premature ejaculation if his normally orgasmic partner does not reach orgasm at least 50 percent of the time. Female partners of premature ejaculators may experience frustration and anger and feel as though they have been "used." As with erectile problems, anxiety over premature ejaculation may contribute to the problem.

Orgasmic disorder in women is simply the failure to achieve orgasm. It may be *primary*, in which the woman has never had an orgasm; *secondary*, in which she has been orgasmic but no longer is; or *situational*, in which she is able to have orgasms in some situations but not in others, such as during masturbation but not during intercourse. Although only about 20 percent of women have never had orgasms or experience them infrequently (Hunt, 1974, Levin and Levin, 1975), orgasmic dysfunction accounts for about 90 percent of female sexual dysfunction cases seen in sex clinics (Masters et al., 1982).

Causes of Sexual Dysfunction. Some years ago it seemed clear that a vast majority of cases of sexual dysfunction - perhaps 80% - were of primarily psychosocial origin (Munjack and Ozeal, 1980; Masters et al., 1982). Current thinking has shifted toward a more organic view (Anastasiadis et al., 2002). Complicating matters is the fact that it is sometimes difficult to determine whether a given case is primarily organic or primarily psychological (Traish et al., 2002), though success in diagnosis is increasing. In women, organic factors that can affect sexual response include neurological disorders, infections, chronic illnesses, and drugs. In men, neurological problems, endocrine disorders, urogenital problems, chronic disease, alcohol and drugs are the major culprits.

There are three major classes of psychological causation: (1) developmental factors, including traumatic childhood experiences and family suggestions that sex is "dirty"; (2) personal factors, including anxiety, fear of sexual inadequacy, low self-esteem, depression, and fear of pregnancy or venereal disease; and (3) interpersonal factors within the sexual relationship, including power struggles, problems with communication, and mutual distrust or deceit (Masters, Johnson, and Kolodny, 1982). More generally, it is clear that both organic and psychological factors must be considered.

Therapy For Sexual Dysfunctions. One of the major approaches to sex therapy was developed by Masters and Johnson (1970). Typically, a dysfunctional couple is treated by male and female co-therapists. After initial discussions, a history-taking session, and physical examinations, the couple is assigned exercises in *sensate focus* - concentrating all attention on specific sensations. In initial sessions they touch each other's bodies but avoid the breasts and genitals. In later sessions the breasts and genitals are added, with each partner guiding the other in where to touch and how much pressure to apply. Further sessions finally allow intercourse. The couple is also instructed in specific techniques designed to deal with particular problems, such as premature ejaculation and orgasmic dysfunction. Several drugs, including sildenafil (Viagra) and the antidepressant drug paroxetine (Paxil) have been incorporated in updates of this treatment regimen (Basson, 2001; Laan et al., 2002; Salonia et al., 2002).

The success rates reported by the Masters and Johnson Institute are quite high. The rate for primary erectile dysfunction, for example, is 66.7 percent, while for primary orgasmic dysfunction it is 79 percent. Despite some criticisms of the early studies, more recent work confirms the success of the newer sex therapy approaches (Opsomer, 2002; Murassiz, 2003). Orgasmic dysfunction, for example, can be successfully treated by teaching the couple clitoral stimulation techniques, including the use of vibrators, and sensate focus has been combined with training in communication and the use of sexual fantasy. Current physical treatment approaches include having a man with erectile dysfunction inject drugs into his penis prior to intercourse to achieve an erection. As studies lead to greater accuracy in differentially determining the roles of physiological and psychological factors in individual cases, it is likely that we will see increasing success in applying appropriate therapeutic techniques.

Keys to Motivation 3

Achievement and Social Motivations

The hunger and sexual motives have relatively clear-cut physiological substrates that are modified by psychological processes. Other motives often involve complex cognitive and social elements that appear to be basic to their operation as motivational systems. One such drive is called achievement motivation. Although it influences the behavior of a single individual, it typically plays out in a social context. Several other clearly human motives are even more specifically social motives that influence behavior in interpersonal contexts. We will take up several such motives, including the needs for affiliation, power, and approval.

Achievement Motivation

Consider the cases of two young business executives, Angela and Charlene. Angela arrives at work promptly at 7 each morning and seldom leaves before 7 at night, always taking a loaded briefcase home with her. She works at least one day each weekend, always arrives at meetings on time, and often completes assigned work early. Charlene works the minimum hours from 9 to 5 and takes long lunches. She is often late for meetings and frequently requests extensions to complete assignments. David McClelland might suggest that the principal difference between these two people is in their levels of achievement motivation or need for achievement. The uniquely human *achievement motive* is a striving to overcome challenges, improve oneself, attain excellence, and accomplish more than others.

The Study of Achievement Motivation. McClelland and his associates define *achievement motivation* as a tendency to strive toward the attainment of goals and hypothesize that it is a a key factor important determinant of goal attainment. So important did McClelland believe achievement motivation to be that he developed an entire theory of this motive based in part on the earlier work of Henry Murray (1938). McClelland's theory views achievement motivation as a learned motive that may greatly influence the social and professional behaviors of individuals in our society. There is considerable support for his hypothesis that people differ greatly in need for achievement and that these differences are reflected in a variety of behaviors (Elliot & Harackiewicz, 1994; Rebeta et al., 1993). Moreover, the levels of achievement motivation that characterize a society have considerable impact on its technological and economic growth and on the overall success of that society as a culture.

The principal measure of the need for achievement is the Thematic Apperception Test (TAT), developed by Henry Murray. The participant is shown a series of ambiguous pictures like the one in Figure 12-12 and asked to write a story about each picture. The stories are then rated according to the degree of achievement motivation they express. McClelland developed an elaborate scoring system for the stories in order to eliminate the use of purely subjective evaluation. Cecilia, for example, would probably have a very high score on the TAT, reflecting her obvious strong desire for accomplishment, while her roommate might well have a very low score.

Numerous studies have been conducted to examine the relationship between need for achievement scores and actual behavior. It has been found that high scorers have occupational goals that are congruent with their abilities, show enhanced task performance when given specific achievement goals, work harder to attain goals, and achieve higher school grades when those grades are important for long-term success (Elliot & Harackiewicz, 1994). In addition, those who score high in the need for achievement typically perceive themselves as high in ability, take personal responsibility for their success, and choose seats near the front of college classrooms (Rebeta et al., 1993). Finally, high need achievers relax after achieving success and work harder when they fail, whereas low need achievers do just the opposite.

Theories of Achievement Motivation. One member of the original McClelland group, John W. Atkinson (1977), went on to develop a more detailed theory of achievement motivation. He hypothesizes that there are two important tendencies: a tendency to achieve success (hope of success) and a tendency to avoid failure (fear of failure). The strength of the tendency to achieve success is determined jointly by three factors: (a) the strength of the motive to achieve success, which is similar to McClelland's need for achievement; (b) the perceived probability of success in this situation; and c) the incentive value of success, which is determined by the pleasure or pride you anticipate experiencing if you are successful. The strength of the tendency to avoid failure is jointly determined by three factors that parallel those for success: (a) the strength of the motive to avoid failure; (b) the perceived probability of failure; and c) the negative incentive value of failure - how bad you believe you will feel if you fail.

Once we know the strengths of the tendencies to achieve success and to avoid failure, we can determine the *resultant achievement motivation.* It is simply the sum of the success and failure tendencies. Since the tendency to avoid failure is negative, we effectively subtract it from the tendency to achieve success. Simply put, resultant achievement motivation is the difference between the approach and avoidance tendencies. If, for example, someone challenges you to a one-on-one contest (a debate, a karate match, a tennis game), your decision to accept or reject depends on the relative strengths of the tendencies to approach and avoid the achievement situation. Taking into account how strongly you usually feel about success and failure, how likely you are to win or lose, and how good (or bad) you will feel if you win (or lose), you make the decision.

Expanding on this theory, Atkinson and David Birch (1970) have developed a *dynamics-of-action theory*, also referred to as the McClelland-Atkinson theory. It is a general theory of motivation that has been applied chiefly to achievement motivation issues. The basic assumption is that the individual is constantly in a state of activity, rather than a state of equilibrium or rest. The task of the motivation theorist is to predict the change from one activity to another, rather than predicting the change from rest to activity. For example, you may study for an exam, take a short lunch break, return to your studying, make a phone call, and then spend some time playing card with friends. Using computer simulation techniques, the dynamics-of-action theory would attempt to predict each of these changes in your behavior as a function of the relevant motivational states (Atkinson, 1982). Data support predictions that people higher in resultant achievement motivation will be more persistent in mastering a task and see goals as closer and more attainable.

Joel Raynor and Elliot Entin (1982) felt that the dynamics-of-action theory was on the right track but did not fully account for the complexity of the achievement situation. As a result, they developed a general *expectancy-value theory* that focuses on the interplay of the motives to achieve success and avoid failure as they interact with the expectancy (subjective probability) of success or failure and the incentive value of the goal to be achieved. According to this theory, we can determine the likelihood that a person will enter an achievement-oriented situation, such as a new job, and the likelihood that he will be successful if we can accurately measure four things: (1) the strength of the motive to achieve success, (2) the strength of the motive to avoid failure; (3) the subjective belief that success or failure will occur in the situation, and (4) the perceived value of the goal to be achieved. The Raynor-Entin approach represents another step in the ongoing attempt to predict behavior in achievement-oriented situations. It has been applied to the achievement behavior of both college students (Singer et al., 1993) and children (Pekrun, 1993), as well as to an understanding of how goals are developed (Wigfield, 1994).

Achievement Motivation Research. Considerable research on achievement motivation has been conducted. Among the topics it has addressed are sex differences, minority group differences, and the development of achievement motivation.

Early studies suggested to some researchers that the achievement motive is difficult to arouse in women and is probably lower than in men (Sarason and Smith, 1971). To account for these findings, Matina Horner (1968) suggested that the achievement behavior of women is highly influenced by a motive to *avoid success.* According to Horner's theory, women are trained to be less competitive and less achievement oriented than men to such an extent that they may actually strive to avoid success. Although early studies seemed to confirm this theory and some work is still underway, most later studies found either no sex differences or a higher score on success avoidance for men than for women (Tresmer, 1974). Moreover, the level of fear of success in the two sexes was found to be unstable from one study to another (Zuckerman and Wheeler, 1976). As a result, many now question whether the motive to avoid success even exists (Fleming, 1982). Furthermore, an in-depth review of the literature reveals that there is little evidence for gender differences in achievement motivation (Stewart and Chester, 1982). To the extent that there are differences, they appear to be due to differing socialization processes in the two genders (Elizur, 1994).

A classic study of the development of achievement motivation showed that mothers of high need achievement boys placed greater independence demands on their sons than did mothers of low need achievers (Winterbottom, 1953). Later studies, however, found no relationship between the age of independence training and the strength of achievement motivation, and these two factors may well be unrelated.

Other studies suggest that parental reinforcement of achievement or independence behavior plays a key role in the development of achievement motivation. Parents of high need achievement boys reward independent behavior more. In addition, children whose parents are actively involved in their schooling display higher achievement motivation (Grolnick & Slowiaczek, 1994). Finally, both achievement motivation and school performance are influenced by several aspects of parenting. Higher performance is seen in children whose parents react positively to their grades and allow the child considerable autonomy in school performance. Lower grades are found in children whose parents react negatively to their grades, maintain close surveillance over their school work, and are stylistically either over- or under-controlling (Ginsburg & Bronstein, 1993).

Achievement Motivation in Minority Groups. Although initially studied in white subjects, achievement motivation also affects the performance of members of minority groups. Steven Rakow and Andrea Bermudez (1993) studied factors in the retention and success of Hispanic Americans in technical fields. They cite achievement motivation as one of several factors that contribute to the success of this minority group in science and technology. Other studies similarly show that this motivational variable is an important determinant of academic performance in both African-American and Hispanic school children, as well as in Mexican-Americans (Menchaca, 1993).

Social Motivation

Social motives are those that are experienced and satisfied through interactions with other people. The psychology of social interaction is examined in more detail in Chapters 18 and 19; here we focus on three social motives that have received a great deal of research attention: the need for affiliation, the need for power, and the need for social approval.

The Need for Affiliation. The *affiliation motive* is a need to associate and interact with other people. The tendency to affiliate with others appears to be nearly universal among humans, and various theories have been advanced to explain why this need is so strong (McClelland et al., 1993). Some theorists suggest that it represents innate biological drives that can be satisfied only through social interaction, while others suggest that social affiliation is so powerfully rewarded in childhood that it becomes a lifelong need. Evolutionary psychology integrates these perspectives, as we have already seen. The need for human interaction and cooperation in ancient environments led to the development of neural mechanisms that both motivate and support affiliation. We are thus neurologically programmed to seek out others and motivated to reward our children for this adaptive behavior.

A classic study of affiliation was conducted by Stanley Schachter (1959). After reviewing case histories of individuals who had endured long periods of social isolation, he proposed that isolation produces *anxiety* and a consequent need to affiliate in order to reduce that anxiety. To test this hypothesis, Schachter assigned each subject in a study to one of two conditions. Those in the high-anxiety condition were shown some electronic equipment and told that they would be receiving painful electric shocks. Those in the low-anxiety condition were told that they would receive very mild shocks. All were then given an opportunity to wait their turn either alone or with other participants who would also be participating and receiving shocks. Sixty-three percent of high anxiety subjects, but only 33 percent of those in the low-anxiety condition chose to wait with others. Schachter explained these results in terms of a need for *social comparison*; the high-anxiety subjects sought out others in the same predicament who might provide clues that would help them understand their own anxieties and perhaps reduce them.

Other investigators have examined gender differences in affiliation motivation and the possible role of brain biochemistry. Elizabeth Mazur (1989) studied differences in friendship behavior between college men and women. She found no differences in the amount of pleasure and meaning derived from friendships in the two sexes, but women had significantly higher affiliation motivation than did men and were more heavily involved in their same-sex friendships. David McClelland and his colleagues studied possible biochemical correlates of affiliation. They found that arousal of the affiliation motive was associated with increased release of dopamine, which may facilitate synaptic transmission in brain areas related to social motivation (McClelland et al., 1993). This suggests a neurochemical substrate for the operation of such motives, adding to what we already know about the important functions of brain biochemistry in both normal and abnormal behaviors (see Chapters 3 and 16).

The Need for Power. The *need for power* is the need to control or influence the behavior of others. In order to study the power motive, a number of investigators have developed and validated systems for scoring power motivation on the TAT (Winter, 1973).

Researchers have found that the power motive is positively associated with assertive and aggressive behavior and can even help to predict the historical beginnings and ends of wars (Winter, 1993). In men, high power motivation is associated with a belief in the use of good will, a concern with home security, and lower dream recall. In women, it is associated with greater concerns about diet, appearance, and clothing (McClelland, 1975). Power-motivated men also engage in more verbal aggression and competitive sports and consume more liquor, and women high in power motivation tend to marry successful men (Sewards & Sewards, 2002). This latter pattern has probably changed as more women reach higher and higher positions in business and the professions.

One interesting study provided a partial basis for choosing corporate chief executive officers (CEOs), depending on whether the company would prefer to increase sales or profits. Researchers examined both power and achievement motivations in the CEOs of the 50 largest U.S. industrial firms in relation to various indicators of corporate performance. They found that high power motivation in the CEO was associated with greater growth in profits, while high achievement motivation predicted stronger growth in sales (Chusmir & Azevedo, 1992).

A large-scale national study conducted by Joseph Veroff (1982) and his associates revealed that men high in power motivation reported greater marital harmony, saw fatherhood as more important, and felt they were competent in their work. They were strongly oriented toward interpersonal roles in marriage and parenthood and tended to find leisure time unsatisfying. Women high in power motivation described themselves as competent and work oriented, expressed some concern about their image, and were heavily involved in marriage and parenthood.

Both power and achievement motivations can help us to predict some aspects of life accomplishment. David McClelland and Carol Franz (1992) interviewed 89 mothers when their sons were 5 years old to assess their child-rearing practices, then followed the sons in a longitudinal study for many years. They found that parental pressure to achieve during the first 2 years of life predicted later levels of achievement motivation, which, in turn predicted the earned income of the sons at age 31. Moderate parental encouragement of assertiveness increased the power motivation of the son, and that, in turn, was associated with higher income and greater overall work accomplishment at age 41. It thus appears that in both sexes high power motivation is associated with generally adaptive, effective patterns of behavior, although an extreme degree of this motive would very likely be maladaptive.

In an interesting study, McClelland (1985) showed how achievement, power, and affiliation motives could be assessed apart from a TAT or other formal measure. He obtained inaugural addresses of 20th-century U.S. presidents and scored them for all three motives. You might try to guess which presidents would likely be highest on each of the motives.

The Need for Social Approval. The four-year-old runs quickly to pick up the comb his mother has dropped and proudly presents it to her. The teenager decides to smoke a joint because her closest friends use marijuana regularly. The college student goes through an embarrassing and sometimes painful initiation rite in order to be accepted into a fraternity. All these individuals may be motivated by a *need for social approval.* This need may be the result of a lifetime of positive and negative reinforcements for performing socially approved and disapproved behaviors or it may reflect more generally the attitudes of one's parents.

The need for approval drives many people to display behavior primarily aimed at gaining them greater social acceptance. Participants with a high need for approval in one study cheated on a task in order to avoid disapproval (Berger et al., 1977). In another study, children with a high need for social approval did better on a task when they were attempting to attain a group standard rather than when competing against others (Cody and Brown, 1978). More generally, it seems that we often treat other people as objects that can satisfy the goal of approval.

Keys to Motivation 4

The Neurophysiology of Motivation

We have already considered the physiological mechanisms involved in hunger and sex. Ideally, we would now take up those that underlie achievement motivation and the social motives and perhaps explain how motivation more generally is mediated by neural systems. However, we noted earlier that even the neurophysiology of the hunger and sex motives is quite complex, involving several body systems and multiple areas of the brain. Imagine, then, the complexity of the mechanisms that underlie achievement motivation and the social needs. In fact, probably the best that we can reasonably say about such complicated drives is that they involve a variety of mechanisms, including the highest levels of cortical processing, those involved in thought. Because little is known about the multitude of neurophysiological factors involved in all the various drives, we will limit our discussion here to two brain centers that play key roles in motivation: the hypothalamus and the reticular activating system (Figure 12-14).

The Hypothalamus

In addition to its important role in regulating hunger and sex, the hypothalamus is involved in thermoregulation (control of body temperature), thirst, sexual arousal, and sleep. To maintain body temperature, certain hypothalamic cells activate behaviors that dissipate heat, while other cells cause behaviors that conserve heat. To control thirst and drinking behavior, one hypothalamic nucleus responds to receptors signaling low levels of body fluids by causing you to drink. At least one other nucleus responds to sexual stimulation to increase feelings of sexual arousal. And, in connection with sleep, various parts of the hypothalamus are involved in the creation of sleeping and waking states and, more generally, in the balance that we must maintain between sleep and arousal. The roles of the hypothalamus and other brain structures in sleeping and waking states are discussed in Chapter 5.

From all the evidence that the hypothalamus plays important roles in several major drive states, it is tempting to assume that this small structure is *the* motivational center in the brain. However, we must take into account the fact that each of the various drives involves somewhat different parts of the hypothalamus and that ordinarily more than one area is involved in the control of a given drive. Thus, the hypothalamus does not function as a unit in controlling drive states. More important, mechanisms elsewhere in the brain, such as the reticular activating system, play key roles in the same drive states, and the hypothalamus is thus not in complete control. Finally, research with electrical stimulation has indicated that there may be brain "reward centers" that motivate some behaviors, as outlined in our 21 for this chapter.

The Reticular Activating System

The *reticular activating system* (RAS) is a neural center for the coordination of activation or arousal arising from various sources. When multiple drives are activated, each contributes arousal input to the RAS, which coordinates an overall state of heightened arousal (Vincent, 2000).

The RAS appears to be activated by two major forms of input. One is information about sensory stimulation, which travels to the reticular formation as well as primary sensory areas like the occipital (vision) or temporal (audition) lobe. The second source of input is the cerebral cortex, which sends impulses to the reticular system when you think about something exciting.

The RAS does not act alone to create motivational states. However, it does have functions that cut across a variety of specific drives, and it is responsible for the overall coordination of a generalized drive state.

The *cerebral cortex* also plays a major role in motivation. It directly influences the hypothalamic nuclei, substantia nigra (see Chapter 3) and other nuclei that are involved in motivation. It also evaluates external motivational stimuli and responds by initiating appropriate behavior (Swanson, 2000).

Keys to Motivation 5

Conclusion

We now have some answers, albeit not final ones, to the question we raised at the beginning of the chapter: What motivates behavior? We know that there are both physiological and psychological factors in motivation. The hunger and thirst drives, like many others, are based in the physiology of the organism, but their experience, expression, and satisfaction are influenced by learning and other psychological processes. Such complex human motives as achievement and social motivation are clearly also mediated by the brain, with their development and expression perhaps even more strongly influenced by historical and current environmental factors. But the story is not yet complete. The study of motivation is complicated by the fact that emotions, such as anger and joy, can serve as motives. Indeed, emotions and motives are often intertwined in their influence on human behavior.

Summary

Theories of Motivation

1. Motivation refers to processes that energize and direct behavior in order to provide some form of satisfaction.
2. Early theories of motivation centered around the concept of instinct. Modern ethology focuses primarily on finding explanations for animal behavior.
3. Drives can be either biological or learned. Drives push behavior and incentives pull it.
4. Deficiency theories revolve around homeostasis - the tendency to maintain constant internal states.
5. Drive theory specifies that behavior is motivated by physiological or acquired drives and that learning occurs when drive reduction reinforces a stimulus-response association.
6. Incentive theories emphasize that motivation is a function of the value of an external stimulus to an individual
7. Optimal arousal approaches specify that organisms strive to optimize arousal levels, not minimize them as in drive-reduction theory.
8. Maslow envisioned a hierarchy of human needs, with deficiency needs at the bottom and growth needs at the top. All the deficiency needs must be regularly satisfied before the individual can pursue the highest need, self-actualization.
9. According to cognitive motivation theory, human action is motivated primarily by thought processes, including information seeking and perception of causality. Cause-effect perceptions have three dimensions: locus, stability, and controllability.
10. Evolutionary theory sees motives as mechanisms that have evolved to assure the survival and reproduction of the species.
11. According to Freud, unconscious motivation is the source of virtually all human behavior.

Hunger Motivation

1. Hunger is mediated by receptors in the digestive system and ultimately controlled by the hypothalamus and related neural systems. The lateral nucleus acts to produce hunger and eating behavior; the ventromedial nucleus is a satiety center; and the paraventricular nucleus appears to be important in energy metabolism.
2. The glucostatic theory holds that hypothalamic neurons called glucostats monitor blood levels of glucose in the cells to activate and deactivate the hunger drive.

3. Set point theory says that brain mechanisms (lipostats) monitor stores of fat; when fat cells decrease in size, hunger is triggered. This process tends to keep the body at a fairly constant weight - the set point.
4. Eating behavior is also affected by taste. Humans have broad, innate taste preferences; more specific tastes are learned.
5. Hunger is influenced by learning. Conditioning and social learning result in food preferences, the triggering of hunger by the sight and smell of food, eating habits, and the influence of social situations.
6. Heredity is a major contributor to obesity. It affects metabolic rate, the number and size of fat cells, your weight set point, and the functioning of the hypothalamus.
7. Schachter found that overweight people are more sensitive to external cues. However, Rodin's later research does not confirm this finding.
8. The only way to reduce weight is to burn more calories than you take in. Consuming less calories is most important, and exercise can help. Behavior modification techniques are more effective than other approaches.
9. Anorexia nervosa involves a distortion of body image in which the individual starves herself to maintain a very low weight. Bulimia nervosa involves binging followed by purging or laxative abuse.
10. Both disorders may be caused by society's preoccupation with achievement and thinness, disturbed family relationships, sexual abuse, or genetic factors.

Sexual Motivation

1. Gender differences in sexual behavior may reflect evolved differences in the characteristics that favor reproduction in the two genders. In theory, ancient environmental factors produced these differences, which were then passed on because they were adaptive.
2. Attitudes toward homosexuality are still predominantly negative. Research has increasingly suggested that a genetic predisposition may underlie sexual orientation, though psychosocial factors are likely also involved.
3. Major sexual dysfunctions include erectile dysfunction and premature ejaculation in men and orgasmic dysfunction in women.
4. Sexual dysfunctions are caused by such organic factors as neurological disorders, infections, and chronic disease. Psychological causes include developmental, personal, and interpersonal factors.
5. Masters and Johnson pioneered effective treatments for sexual dysfunction, and physical treatment approaches have now been added to these and other psychological interventions.

Achievement and Social Motivations

1. Achievement motivation, usually measured with the TAT, predicts such behaviors task performance and school grades. McClelland, Atkinson, and Raynor and Entin have developed somewhat different theories. Gender differences have been observed, and the developmental process has been studied.
2. Social motives, which are learned, experienced, and satisfied through interpersonal interaction, include the needs for affiliation, power, and social approval. All have been used to predict important aspects of human behavior.

The Neurophysiology of Motivation

1. The hypothalamus plays an important role in a number of physiological drives, including hunger, thirst, thermoregulation, and sexual behavior.
2. The reticular activating system subserves motivational functions by coordinating arousal.

Ask Yourself

1. What are the similarities and differences between instincts and drives?
2. In what important ways do the biological underplnnlngs of hunger and sexual behavior overlap?
3. Describe the physiological and psychological processes that take place in relationship to your hunger in the course of the day.

4. Discuss the major causes of obesity.
5. Discuss the results of research on the causes of homosexuality.
6. What arm the most frequent types of sexual dysfunction in men and women? What are the primary causes of these dysfunctions?
7. Discuss the several theories of achievement motivation. What are their major similarities and differences?
8. What conceptual relationships are likely to underlie the various social motives discussed in the chapter?
9. What are the major neurological mechanisms involved in motivation? Do they account for all biological aspects of motivation?

Further Readings

Alfonso, V., Allison, D., & Dunn, G. (1992). Sexual fantasy and satisfaction: A multidimensional analysis of gender differences. *J. Psych. Human Sexual.*, 5, 19-37. An interesting study of the use of fantasy in sexuality in men and women.

Boggiano, A., & Pittman, T. (1992). *Achievement and motivation: A social-developmental perspective.* NY: Cambridge University Press. This up-to-date work on achievement motivation provides chapters by a number of outstanding researchers in the field.

Byrne, W., & Parsons, B. (1993). Human sexual orientation: The biologic theories reappraised. *Archs. Genl. Psychiat.*, 1993, 228-239. A solid, readable review of genetic and hormonal studies of homosexuality.

Ferrell, R.E. (1993). Obesity: Choosing genetic approaches from a mixed menu. *Hum. Biol.*, 65, 967-975.

Kiah, C.W. (1992). The relationship of black students' achievement motivation to family cohesion and specific aspirations. In M. Lang, C. Ford, & C. Cole (Eds.). *Strategies for retaining minority students in higher education.* Springfield, IL: Charles C. Thomas. A thorough review and theoretical coverage of achievement motivation in black students.

Levine, D., & Leven, S. (1992). *Motivation, emotion, and goal direction in neural networks.* Hillsdale, NJ: Lawrence Erlbaum. This collection of chapters focuses on the application of neural networks (see Chapters 8, 9, and 10 or this text) to motivation.

Medin, D. (1993). *The psychology of learning and motivation.* San Diego: Academic Press. Edited by one of the major figures in the field, this book provides chapters by top scientists on a variety of aspects of motivation.

Reeve, J. (1992). *Understanding motivation and emotion.* Fort Worth: Harcourt. An excellent textbook on motivation. It covers all the major topics in considerable depth.

Schultz, G. (1993). Socioeconomic advantage and achievement motivation: Important mediators of academic performance in minority children in urban schools. *Urban Review.*, 25, 221-232. In this study, Schultz addresses the role of achievement motivation in the academic performance of African-American and Hispanic children.

Wigfield, A. (1994). Expectancy-value theory of achievement motivation: A developmental perspective. *Educ. Psych. Rev.*, 6, 49-78. This article applies a major theory of achievement motivation to young children and provides a model for motivational development.

Key Terms

achievement motivation
affiliation motive
androgens
anorexia nervosa
aphagia
appetitive drive

arousal
autoerotic fantasy
aversive drive
behavior modification
bulimia nervosa
deficiency motive
drive
drive stimulus
dynamics-of-action
erectile disorder
estrogens
ethology
expectancy-value
extrinsic motivation
glucostat
hedonism
homeostasis
homophobia
homosexuality
hyperphagia
incentive
instinct
intrinsic motivation
inverted-U function
lateral hypothalamus
lipostatic hypothesis
motivation
need
need hierarchy
optimal arousal level
orgasmic disorder
osmotic thirst
paraventricular nucleus
premature ejaculation
progestins
restrained eater
reticular activating system
self-actualization
sensate focus
set point
sexual dysfunction
testosterone
Thematic Apperception Test
ventromedial hypothalamus

Key People

John W. Atkinson
Walter Cannon
Hans Eysenck
Harry Harlow
Clark Hull
Richard Keesey

---

[2] **Basic research involving brain stimulation is discussed in Chapter 3.**

Abraham Maslow
David McClelland
William McDougall
Stanley Schachter
Bernard Weiner
Marvin Zuckerman

Psychology in the 21st Century

Stimulating the Human Brain

Parents are constantly trying to motivate their children, teachers their students, and bosses their employees. Suppose - just suppose - they could all directly motivate people by turning on electrodes implanted in their brains. And not only that, but suppose we could directly treat such problems as depression, excessive anxiety, and attacks of uncontrollable rage by simply stimulating a few neurons in the brain. These are interesting but somewhat frightening prospects that are already possible. The idea is to implant electrodes in very specific areas of the brain that influence or control the behavior or emotion of interest, then send electrical current through these electrodes whenever necessary.[2]

Interest in the possibility of motivating centers in the brain began with a bang in 1954 when Olds and Milner accidently discovered that electrical stimulation of certain areas of the rat's brain can be positively reinforcing. In fact, as later studies revealed, rats given the opportunity for self-stimulation would press a lever at a rate of about 1000 responses per hour to receive stimulation of the septal area of the brain and up to 7000 responses per hour to receive stimulation of an area called the medial forebrain bundle (Anderson & Miliaressis, 1994; Olds, 1961). A starving rat would even neglect food in order to stimulate this latter area. Other studies showed that electrodes placed in different brain locations caused animals to press a bar in order to *avoid* the electrical stimulation (Delgado, Roberts, and Miller, 1954).

What researchers set out to discover next was whether these reward sites relate to specific physiological drives or provide general or "pure" rewards in and of themselves. One approach was to manipulate natural need states and examine the effects of these manipulations on self-stimulation behavior. The rationale for these studies was straightforward: If the reward site is related to a natural drive, increasing or reducing that drive should correspondingly increase or reduce the self-stimulation behavior. Researchers found that reducing the hunger or sex drive by satiation or castration did indeed reduce lever-pressing for self-stimulation, while enhancing these drives through food deprivation or testosterone injection increased lever-pressing (Olds, 1978).

Other studies have isolated at least some positive reinforcement sites in the brain that may not be dependent on or directly related to any specific physiological drive. Electrodes implanted in some areas of the hypothalamus, for example, will produce self-stimulation behavior that appears to be independent of the hunger drive, even though the lateral hypothalamus can produce eating behavior when directly stimulated by the experimenter. Animals will also work to obtain stimulation of parts of the amygdala and the median forebrain bundle (Yang et al., 2002) independent of any specific drive. The implication is that these brain centers mediate a general reward or reinforcement process. Systematically giving and withholding stimulation might allow us to control a variety of behaviors - in humans as well as animals. In one demonstration of this possibility, Wanda Wyrwicka (1993) gave cats rewarding stimulation of the hypothalamus for eating bananas but not for eating meat pellets. You guessed it! The neural reward motivated the cats to choose the bananas.

Brain stimulation can also be used to elicit and control emotional responses. Of particular interest is work showing that areas of the hypothalamus and amygdala are involved in the control of aggression and rage. Stimulation of the ventromedial hypothalamus, for example, elicits aggressive behavior. Lesions of the medial hypothalamus have a similar effect, not only in laboratory animals but in humans. The amygdala can also be stimulated in different areas to produce either aggressive or submissive behavior. To make matters more interesting, Jose Delgado implanted electrodes in the amygdala of a bull. When it charged a matador, Delgado used a transmitter to send current through the electrode and stop the attack (Delgado et al., 1975). Some studies have implicated the amygdala in instances of pathological violence in humans, and some patients with temporal lobe epilepsy, which can involve damage to the amygdala, display outbursts of unprovoked violence.

If human emotion is subject to such direct neural control, could we potentially stimulate the human brain in an effort to deal with emotional problems? Is this a possibility that may be explored as we move into the 21ST century? The truth is that the first two attempts at direct stimulation of the human brain came in the 19th century (Hitzig, 1870; Bartholow, 1874). In both cases the electrical stimulus was delivered directly to exposed brain tissue during surgery. Many years later brain surgeon Wilder Penfield stimulated areas of the temporal cortex during surgery in an attempt to elicit memories (Penfield, 1975). These and other instances of human brain stimulation during surgical procedures demonstrated the possibility of eliciting and controlling behavior.

Taking human brain stimulation a giant step further, Carl Sem-Jacobsen and his colleagues have implanted electrodes to treat psychological disorders. They demonstrated that brain stimulation can be used to treat depression in human patients, who report that the stimulation produces a generally pleasurable effect (Sem-Jacobsen, 1959; Sem-Jacobsen and Torkildsen, 1960). In another application, Delgado was faced with a patient who was subject to uncontrollable attacks of rage. An electrode was implanted in his amygdala, and the patient was given a transmitter to carry with him. Whenever he felt a rage attack coming on, he could simply press the button on the transmitter, stimulate his amygdala, and abort the attack (Delgado et al., 1975). Implants have also been used to treat other emotional problems that were unresponsive to more conventional treatments and to diagnose emotional problems with underlying neurological bases. Such findings have important implications. In particular, some of the keys to understanding and even treating psychotic and other emotional disorders may lie in a more complete knowledge of the motivational and emotional areas of the brain (Greenberg, 2002). Moreover, deep brain stimulation is now being used with some success in treating a neurological disorder, Parkinson's disease (Tavella et al., 2002 Chabardes et al., 2002).

It seems clear that studies of human brain stimulation will continue in the 21st century and that we will be increasingly able to control motivated and emotional behavior through electrodes implanted in the brain. However, such possibilities raise some serious ethical questions. Under what circumstances should implantation be used? To treat intractable rage attacks, reduce depression that will not respond to other therapies, or eliminate severely psychotic behavior? Probably. To motivate students to learn or behave better? Probably not. But what about criminal behavior? Should we implant habitual criminals with electrodes that can eliminate their criminal tendencies? And who makes the decision to do an implant? The patient? The family? The psychologist or physician? A board of qualified people? Who will have the radio transmitter? Only the person? Or perhaps also a family member, the psychologist or physician, or maybe the police? Such serious ethical questions will have to be addressed because we will almost certainly be capable of using implanted electrodes to control a wide range of human motivations and emotions.

The Critical Thinker

Take it Off, Take it Off!

Behavior modification techniques can do just what the title says: They take weight off better than some other approaches. Even more important, they can help you keep that weight off.

In behavior modification, patient and therapist first identify very specifically and in detail the bad eating habits producing weight gain. The patient then learns how to change each habits. For example, if you have a habit of consuming leftovers from the evening meal, you will learn to put away or throw out all leftovers immediately after dinner. Sounds simple and obvious, but virtually all such behavior modifications are simple, and they work better than most other approaches. The therapist instructs the participant in how to monitor personal eating behavior (*self-monitoring*) and how to gain control of stimuli that tend to elicit eating (*stimulus control*). These techniques were first outlined over thirty years ago (Ferster, Nurnberger, and Lebvitt, 1962), and the first evidence for their effectiveness was provided a few years later (Stuart, 1967). Since then, many studies have demonstrated the efficacy of these methods in both adults and children, particularly when combined with diets very low in calories (Wadden et al., 1992).

An example of behavior modification is provided by a study involving the treatment of four overweight women (Fremouw et al., 1981). They were taught how to monitor their eating and keep diaries, which were collected at weekly therapy sessions. Two behavioral treatments were used. As a *stimulus control* treatment, each participant was instructed to perform behaviors that would control stimuli likely to initiate eating. Participants were told, for example, to designate one place for consuming all food and to avoid all other activities, such as reading or watching TV, while eating. They also kept snack foods out of sight and shopped from prepared lists at a time when they were not hungry. The second approach was *contingency contracting*. Here, participants deposited money and signed a contract to lose 1.5 pounds per week. They received $5.00 as reinforcement each week if they met their weekly goal and forfeited $2.50 if they did not. Two participants began with stimulus control procedures, and contingency contracting was later added; the other two participants began with contingency contracting and were later taught stimulus control procedures.

The graph for one subject shows she lost weight continuously while dieting. The second graph shows the difference between one subject who ate only in the designated place and another who ate inappropriate snacks, which was considerably reduced by the procedures.

The one approach to weight loss that may prove superior to behavior modification alone is the use of weight control drugs in combination with behavioral techniques, calorie restriction, and exercise. Most drugs used in the past have proven ineffective or dangerous or both, though newer drugs, like Meridia, may prove safe and more effective.

The Rules and Regs

Whether used alone or with drugs and exercise, there are strict behavior modification rules to be followed. Here is one version of those rules:

1. Keep close track of your caloric intake and restrict it to the level you need to lose weight or maintain weight loss.
2. Think of your diet - your change in eating habits - as permanent, not temporary.
3. Restrict your eating primarily to foods that are low in calories, low in fat, and high in fiber. Fruits, vegetables, whole grains, and beans generally fit this description.
4. Keep "fattening" foods completely out of the house.
5. Always eat your meals in the same place - for example at the kitchen table. Don't eat while reading, working or watching TV.
6. Eat at regular times, never just because you feel like it.
7. Eat a light evening meal. Food consumed earlier in the day puts on less weight.
8. Eat slowly. You will get full before you consume as much food.
9. Eat alone, but not if you tend to binge when you do so.
10. Use small plates and dishes.
11. Eat a balanced diet.
12. You can *occasionally* eat a high calorie or high fat meal, but plan it in advance and assure that you won't eat another such meal for some time.
13. Develop a regular exercise program, and spend at least 20-30 minutes three or more times each week in a hard aerobic workout. Check with your physician before starting the program to be sure it is safe for you.
14. Weigh yourself *religiously* once a week or at least once a month. Daily weights are less reliable. However, you *must* weigh yourself regularly. People who regain lost weight often do so in part because they do not realize (or admit to themselves) that they are gaining.

The Critical Thinker

Is Testosterone the Sexy Hormone?

Psychologists have long been interested in the origins of sexual desire and the physiological basis for psychological feelings of sexual arousal. As a result, a number of studies have been carried out to address a series of important questions: Why do some people have higher levels of sexual desire and interest than others? Do the levels of certain hormones increase when you become sexually aroused? Is there a chemical substance that we can use to treat people who have difficulty experiencing sexual arousal?

The Basic Hypothesis or Contention

Early investigators hypothesized that levels of the principal male sex hormone testosterone in men and of the major female sex hormone estrogen in women are largely responsible for an individual's degree of sexual desire. Men high in testosterone and women high in estrogen should exhibit stronger sexual desire and interest and become sexually aroused more easily than those low in these hormones. More recently, however, theorists have introduced a major modification of this hypothesis. The current contention is that testosterone is the primary hormone responsible for sexual desire in *both* men and women, though estrogen also has some effect in women. it has been known for some time that both genders produce both hormones, but the idea that testosterone bears primary responsibility for sexual desire in both men and women is a radical departure from earlier theories.

What Is The Evidence?

Let's first examine the evidence that testosterone influences sexual desire and arousal in men. It has consistently been found that testosterone deficiencies are associated with decreases and elevated levels with increases in sexual desire (Kolodny, Masters, and Johnson, 1979). In one study, for example, testosterone levels were determined in 7th and 8th grade boys, whose behavior was then followed for three years (Halpern et al., 1993). Higher levels predicted earlier intercourse and greater sexual activity. In another study, men between the ages of 18 and 27 saw either a sexually arousing film or a neutral film, and blood testosterone levels were measured every 10 minutes. The level of the hormone was significantly higher during and after the arousing film than the neutral one (Stoleru et al., 1993). A third study was conducted by Cesare Carani and his colleagues, who treated two groups of men with erectile dysfunction or impotence. One group had low blood levels of testosterone when they came for treatment, the other had normal levels. When Carani administered oral doses of the hormone to both groups, it improved sexual functioning in the group with low initial levels, but had no effect in the group with normal starting values (Carani et al., 1990).

Some investigators have argued that mounting evidence also supports a primary role for testosterone as a basis for sexual arousal in women. Helen Kaplan, a pioneer and major figure in human sexuality research, tested two groups of women. One group consisted of women who had undergone chemotherapy or surgery that reduced their testosterone levels. The other was a control group of women with normal levels. Those with a testosterone deficiency had significantly lower sexual desire and responsiveness (Kaplan & Owett, 1993). Other studies have shown that declines in testosterone levels are paralleled by reductions in sexual arousal and that post-menopausal women with lower levels of testosterone are less sexually active. On the other side of the coin, one study showed that women with high testosterone levels reported becoming sexually aroused more easily and more frequently and experiencing greater sexual satisfaction than did women with low levels (Persky et al., 1978). In another study Gerianne Alexander and Barbara Sherwin (1993) measured the blood testosterone levels of 19 female undergraduates and also asked them to complete daily records of their sexual behavior. Those with higher testosterone levels had greater sexual desire, engaged in more sexual activity, and responded more strongly to sexually arousing stimuli.

Is The Evidence Open To Alternative Interpretations?

We must be cautious in evaluating the testosterone evidence because the research we have discussed is correlational in nature. It tells us that there is a relationship between the hormone and sexual desire, but does not clearly demonstrate cause-effect. It is therefore possible that other factors, such as an especially good or bad relationship with a sexual partner, cause an increase or decrease in sexual arousal, which, in turn, causes a corresponding change in testosterone level. Alternatively, some third factor may cause simultaneous changes in both testosterone and sexual desire.

Along these latter lines, it is possible that the real culprit in cases of low sexual desire in women is the hypothalamus or pituitary gland, rather than testosterone level. We know that the hypothalamus is an important neural center in sexuality and that it affects pituitary functioning (Chapter 3). The pituitary, in turn, affects testosterone levels, so it is possible that the relationship of testosterone to sexual desire is actually just a sign of hypothalamic-pituitary control. Evidence comes from studies showing that 94% of women with hypothalamic-pituitary disorders do exhibit sexual problems, including reductions in sexual desire and activity (Hulter & Lundberg, 1994). It may well be, then, that testosterone level is primarily a sign of problems at higher levels of control.

Further concerns arise from studies involving the therapeutic administration of testosterone to women to raise their sexual arousal levels. If testosterone directly affects sexual arousal, giving it to women should increase their sexual desire. However, the evidence is quite mixed. Women treated with testosterone in one study reported greater pleasure from masturbation but showed no overall increase in sexual arousal or behavior (Myers et al., 1990). In another study, Michael Dow and James Gallagher (1989) treated women who reported being virtually unresponsive to sexual stimulation of any kind. Foreplay and intercourse with a partner, manual masturbation, and even stimulation of the clitoris with a vibrator failed to produce substantial sexual arousal. Dow and Gallagher assigned each woman to one of three conditions. One group received testosterone, one received sexual counseling, and one received both. Testosterone was associated with increased sexual desire only when combined with counseling; neither alone helped.

Do We Need Additional Evidence?

We clearly do need more evidence. In particular, we need more direct, experimental studies demonstrating that the administration of testosterone increases sexual arousal more than does a placebo. Such studies should be done with both men and women of various ages. They should also differentiate between those with normal levels prior to administration and those with low levels and between pre- and post-menopausal women. In addition, we will need to know whether the effects of the hormone are short-term or whether there is some long-term, continuing effect. Finally, in women it will be important to know the exact roles of both testosterone and estrogen in sexual desire and how the two hormones may interact.

What Can We Conclude?

For the moment, we can reasonably conclude that the testosterone hypothesis has strong support for males but mixed support for females. Even in men, we cannot yet be entirely certain of the causal role of the hormone in sexual desire. This is clearly one area of motivational research where the answers are not yet all in.

Horizons in Abnormal Behavior

Seeking Sensation

The person who likes to sky-dive, hang-glide, and ski is at one end of an important motivational, individual difference dimension called *sensation-seeking*. Theoretically, the high sensation-seeker is striving to raise his arousal level, which is below the optimal point (B. Smith, Perlstein, Davidson, & Gonzalez, 1991). Such thrill sports as sky-diving help to accomplish that end. Psychologist Marvin Zuckerman decided many years ago to study sensation seeking, and we are learning that it is an important motivational dimension that affects much of our behavior. It appears to have an at least partially physiological basis that may involve a genetic predisposition (Gatzke-Kopp et al., 2002). In addition, high sensation seekers have lower levels of an important brain chemical called monoamine oxidase, which may help to explain their low "natural" arousal levels and consequent need to seek stimulation (Zuckerman, 1993).

Some sensation-seekers express their need for arousal in positive ways (Neely et al., 2002); others are driven to more negative expressions, such as drug abuse and crime. In addition, police officers who are higher on this dimension are more likely to engage in high-speed pursuit (Hamant et al., 1993), and people who become pathological gamblers - unable to avoid the gaming tables - are high sensation seekers. Where do you think you stand on this important motivational dimension? Does it influence your behavior?

Older Men/Younger Women

Look around your neighborhood at the married or committed couples you know. Rarely do you see an older woman paired with a younger man, but the reverse is quite common. Ever ask yourself why this happens? Well, sociobiologists have, and their controversial theory holds that this common phenomenon is a product of the evolution of the species.

Sociobiology is a modern derivative of instinct theory (Lamb, 1993). The basic biological fact, according to this approach, is that women have fewer reproductive years than men, who can reproduce until death. As a result, women are much more concerned with the development and safety of their limited offspring, leading the two genders to use different mate selection criteria. Females select older males because they have the resources to protect them and their offspring, while males select younger females because they are maximally capable of reproducing.

Are sociobiologists right? David Buss (1991, 1994) argues strongly that they are. He says that "research by more than 50 scientists studying more than 10,000 individuals inhabiting 33 countries, 6 continents, and 5 islands supports the hypothesis...." (Buss, 1991, p. 401). If he is right, sociobiology has made a striking scientific discovery concerning the impact of evolution on social relationships and family structure. But is he? While some studies provide supportive evidence, others do not (McLellan & McKelvie, 1993), and there is certainly no lack of alternative theories that propose on a cultural learning process. Bottom line: You have to read the research literature and draw your own conclusions.

"Motivation Disappears in Cloud of Smoke"

Sounds a little like a newspaper headline, but it may be true when the cloud of smoke is coming from a marijuana cigarette. A number of studies demonstrate that regular marijuana use is often associated with the *amotivational syndrome* (Paule et al., 1992). Adolescents and others experiencing this syndrome show a lack of motivation to achieve and are often unwilling or unable to undertake any of a variety of tasks that would require effort (Thomas, 1993). Amotivational subjects have been found to be academic underachievers, to work less effectively on laboratory tasks, and to be depressive.

While it is possible that the marijuana users are people who were unmotivated to begin with, experimental studies in which monkeys are given marijuana also show the reduced motivation (Paule et al., 1992). Although a few studies have found no evidence for an amotivational syndrome, a majority do support this deleterious effect of marijuana (Paule et al., 1992. The implications? Obviously, a drug that impairs motivation could reduce ability to perform well in high school, college, and career.

Key Terms 1

arousal
behavior modification
deficiency motive
drive
ethology
extrinsic motivation

homeostasis
incentive
instinct
intrinsic motivation
inverted-U function
motivation
need
need hierarchy
optimal arousal level
self-actualization

Key People 1

Hans Eysenck
Harry Harlow
Clark Hull
William McDougall
Marvin Zuckerman

Key Terms 2

anorexia nervousa
aphagia
bulimia nervousa
glucostat
lipostatic hypothesis
restrained eater
set point

Key People 2

Walter Cannon
Richard Keesey
Stanley Schachter
Bernard Weiner

Key Terms 3

erectile disorder
estrogen
homophobia
homosexuality
orgasmic disorder
premature ejaculation
sexual dysfunction
testosterone

Key Terms 4

achievement motivation

dynamics of action
affiliation motive
Thematic Apperception Test (TAT)

Key People 4

John W. Atkinson
Abraham Maslow
David McClelland

Key Terms 5

hypothalamus
reticular activating system (RAS)

Chapter 13
Emotion

Outline

Networking

YOU SURELY already know what emotions are. You feel happy, you feel sad, and we know that these experiences are common to all human beings. So why do we need an entire chapter on emotion? The answer is that when it comes down to trying to study the emotions and understand their origins and impact on behavior, they become exceedingly elusive. We will see, in fact, that psychologists have difficulty agreeing on exactly what emotions are. Furthermore, there is no lack of theories about emotion _ how emotions are structured, where they come from, and how they affect behavior. Some theories emphasize the biological aspects of emotion; some focus on the cognitive factors in emotional experience; and some stress the role of learning. In addition, a fascinating body of research shows that the facial expressions we associate with the various emotions are innate. We will also explore one major emotion - happiness - in detail, and you will learn how happy most people are and what makes us that way. Finally, we will look at the neurophysiological underpinnings of our feeling states.

As you read this chapter, it is important to keep in mind the close association of emotion with motivation. The emotions you experience often serve to motivate behavior. Fear - an emotion - can lead to flight - a motivated behavior - and the emotional experience of strong love can motivate you to marry someone. The reverse also holds true. Motives often produce or are associated with emotion. When someone thwarts your achievement-motivated pursuit of a goal, you may experience frustration, an emotion. When your achievement motivation is fulfilled, you may experience joy.

Cat Burglar

Jennifer was awakened in the middle of the night by a strange noise coming from the living room. As she lay there listening, straining to identify the sounds, she felt her heart thumping and she began to break out in a cold sweat. What would she do if a burglar had broken in? She was all alone in the apartment. Her breathing became faster and faster, her heart pounded harder, and the butterflies in her stomach beat their wings mercilessly as she tried to mentally run through possible escape routes. She had just about made up her mind to quietly slip out of bed, when the intruder suddenly ran into the room and leaped on top of her. Reflexively, Jennifer screamed and jumped up, tangling herself in the covers and falling to the floor. Then she began to laugh and sigh in relief--the "burglar" had been her cat, Mopsy.

Have you ever had a terrifying experience like Jennifer's? Even though the danger wasn't real, she experienced real fear and all the physiological changes that accompany it. Fear is but one of many emotions we are all familiar with. Some of these emotions, such as anger and joy, are strong, while others, such as annoyance and boredom, are milder. Let's explore some definitions of emotion before we move ahead to examine major theories and bodies of research.

One of the major problems in the study of emotion has been the difficulty in defining and classifying this important human experience. Reviewers have discovered anywhere from 11 (Fantino, 1973) to 28 (Plutchik, 1980) to a whopping 92 (Kleinginna and Kleinginna, 1981) different definitions of emotion.

The Kleinginnas, who also located numerous definitions of motivation (see Chapter 12), derived a lengthy definition of emotion from their extensive review of that literature:

> Emotion is a complex set of interactions among subjective and objective factors, mediated by neural hormonal systems, which can (a) give rise to affective experiences such as feelings of arousal, pleasure/displeasure; (b) generate cognitive processes such as emotionally relevant perceptual effects, appraisals, labeling processes; ©) activate widespread physiological adjustments to the arousing conditions; and (d) lead to behavior that is often, but not always, expressive, goal directed, and adaptive. (p. 355)

It is obvious from this definition that emotion is much more than just "feelings." In fact, an emotion has at least four major components: a feeling state, cognitive processes, physiological changes, and associated behavior. In the case of Jennifer and her "burglar," the subjective *feeling state* was fear. Through *cognitive processes*, she labeled her emotion as fear, tried to identify the source of her fear, and mentally reviewed ways to deal with the situation. The *physiological changes* she experienced included a pounding heart, perspiration, and faster breathing. *Behaviorally*, she attempted to escape from the source of her fear.

One problem in defining emotion is the difficultly in separating it from motivation. Emotions can serve as motivators for behavior, and motives can be rather emotional. The motive for committing murder, for example, might be to obtain money, a concrete goal, but it might also be hatred, an emotion. Similarly, love can motivate people to engage in a number of different behaviors, from the simple acts of writing letters or making phone calls to the major steps of getting married or moving to a new city. Some theorists find this connection between emotion and motivation so significant that they see emotions as the prime motives for most behavior (Tomkins, 1963; Izard, 2002).

Emotions do not always motivate behavior, however. You may feel happy because you've done well on a test, but that happiness may not motivate you to so anything in particular. By the same token, not all motives are based in emotions. If you eat a sandwich because you are hungry and study hard so that you will do well in your courses, these behaviors can be explained in terms of the hunger motive and the achievement motive, neither of which are emotions. Carl Pribram (1980) has suggested that the main difference between emotion and motivation is that emotional reactions tend to *stop* ongoing behavior, whereas motives tend to *start* behavior. Robert Plutchik (1962) has compiled a list of further distinctions between the two concepts (Table 13-1).

Yardsticks for Emotion

Psychologists have developed a number of measures or indicators of emotion. In doing so, however, they have constantly been faced with the problem that emotions are experienced internally and must be *inferred* from observable, measurable behavior. From what behaviors can we infer the existence of a specific emotion? Using anxiety as an example, one method would be to place subjects in potentially anxiety-arousing situations, then ask them for a verbal report: "How anxious do you feel? Can you describe your anxiety?" Or we might photograph the person's facial expressions as an indication of the emotion being experienced. Or we might take various physiological measures, such as heart rate or muscle tension, as indications of the arousal that accompanies anxiety. Once we have obtained some or all of these data from a number of subjects who are supposedly experiencing anxiety, we would be faced with a number of important questions: How similar are the verbal reports of the various subjects? Are the facial expressions and other external behaviors always the same? Do the physiological indicators of anxiety follow a fairly standard pattern?

As this example suggests, psychologists have developed three main approaches to measuring emotion: self-reports, observation of external correlates of emotion, and physiological measures.

Self-Reports

Perhaps the most direct way to assess an individual's emotional functioning is to obtain a self-report - a verbal statement by the person of what she is feeling. The problem for psychologists is determining what to ask and how to ask it. The three main methods used in self-report studies are interviews, questionnaires, and self-monitoring techniques.

When *interviews* are used to obtain self-reports as a part of psychological diagnosis or treatment, they usually involve a relatively unstructured attempt to assess the client's problem. The interviewer may follow up initial answers by probing more deeply into the area covered by the question. Consider this excerpt from an initial clinical interview:

> **Psychologist:** Can you tell me what brings you here today Mr. Johnson?
> **Client:** I've been feeling real "uptight" for a long time now. Can't even concentrate on my work. I think I need some help.
> **Psychologist :** Do you feel this tension mostly at work or at other times too?
> **Client :** It's worse at work, but I'm real anxious most of the time.
> **Psychologist :** Are you mostly bothered by the anxiety itself or are there other things too?

When interviews are used in research, the person's answers are often recorded and later subjected to a content analysis. Statements such as "I cry almost every day," "I just feel that I'm not worth much," and "I never seem to have any real fun" might all contribute to a score for depression. In *content analysis*, the researcher develops a coding system, applies that system to the recorded interview of each subject, then analyzes the resulting data. A coding system for clinical interviews might include such categories as Depression, Anxiety, and Anger. Content analysis is a valuable tool because it gives a more specific, systematic basis for understanding what the interviewee has said and what it might mean (Locker, 2003).

Interviews are useful when dealing with small numbers of subjects or with individuals in a clinical setting, but they are not practical when studying large groups of people. Many investigators have therefore developed self-report inventories or *questionnaires* - sets of statements or questions designed to measure specific emotions. Among such questionnaires are the Manifest Anxiety Scale (Taylor, 1953), a self-report measure of anxiety, the Fear Survey Schedule (Geer, 1965), which assesses the anxiety evoked by particular situations, the Levels of Emotional Awareness Scale (Bydlowski et al., 2002), which measures the accuracy of the person's perception of her own emotion, and the State-Trait Anxiety Inventory (STAI), which measures both current (state) and enduring (trait) anxiety, and a similar measure for depression (Spielberger, 2002, 2003; Spielberger, Gorsuch, & Lushene, 1970). A short form of this latter measure is widely used in anxiety research (Viens, 2003; Barnes, 2002), and numerous other scales are available (Hogan, 2003).

Before reading on, pause for a minute to take the two emotion tests in Tables 13-2 and 13-3. Note, however, that *these are not "real" inventories to measure anxiety and happiness.* That is, they were not derived by following the procedures outlined in Chapter 9 for developing psychological tests. The items are similar to those found in these formal inventories, but I made them up so you could see what the tests are like.

Total up your scores on the two tests. How did you do? If the average score for college students was 5.0 on each inventory, were you above or below average in anxiety? How about happiness? If these tests were real measures of emotion, a psychologist could get a good idea of how you compare with the general population of college students. If you were going to a clinical or counseling psychologist for therapy, she could use your scores as part of an overall assessment of your personality and as an aid in planning treatment.

The sample inventories have you rate yourself on each item using a 7-point scale, and many anxiety scales adopt this approach (Wollin et al., 2003; Chapman & Kirby-Turner, 2002), but there are other approaches. Another popular method is to have subjects examine a list of descriptive adjectives and check off those that describe their emotions. The Mood Adjective Checklist (MACL), developed by Vincent and Helen Nowlis (1956), is a good example. The original, long form of the MACL contains 200 adjectives, while the short form, found in Table 13-4, contains 33 (Nowlis, 1970). The test is scored according to various sets of criteria to measure anywhere from 4 to 12 different emotion factors, including aggression, anxiety, depression, and elation. The MACL is widely used to assess mood states (Eriksson et al., 2002). Subjects in one study, for example, completed the MACL to assess daily changes in mood and to determine the effects of day of the week on emotional states (Kennedy-Moore et al., 1992). Results showed that mood did vary from day to day and was more positive on weekends than on week days. Other recent studies have used the MACL and similar instruments to evaluate the effects of pain on emotionality, the impact of physical illness on anxiety, and the perceived quality of life in patients with chronic illnesses (Dellborg et al., 2002; Engstrom et al., 2001).

The third self-report technique is to ask subjects to engage in *self-monitoring* - to monitor and record their own behavior over a period of time. A depressed patient, for example, may be asked to keep a diary indicating when, where, and under what circumstances she experiences episodes of crying, feelings of worthlessness, a sense of despair, and so on. When done carefully, such self-monitoring can provide a fairly accurate assessment of emotional functioning.

Although the self-report method for studying emotions seems simple and direct, it is fraught with a number of problems. For one thing, it is impossible to verify that subjects are giving accurate accounts. If Bob tells you he is feeling anxious, how can you verify his statement? A second problem is that people can vary in their subjective experience of the same emotion. If Joan and Bob both tell you they feel extremely anxious, how do you know that they are both reporting the same internal feelings? Another difficulty is that people may deny emotions, particularly negative ones, for a variety of reasons. An employee may be angry at his boss, for example, but deny his anger for fear of losing his job or being passed over for promotion.

A final factor that can influence the accuracy of self-report research is variability in cultural norms. One team of researchers asked professional porters in Nepal, who must carry heavy loads at high altitudes and in freezing temperatures, to describe their feelings about their work. The porters denied any feelings of pain or discomfort and, when subjected to painful electrical stimulation, reported less pain than did a group of Western mountaineers. It is possible, of course, that the Nepalese were actually experiencing less pain. However, the investigators concluded that they were probably experiencing just as much physiological pain as the Westerners but had learned to report less discomfort (Clark & Clark, 1980). Other studies have shown that certain emotions are so infrequently expressed in some cultures that the culture has no descriptive term for the emotion. Some languages, for example, have no terms for depression and therefore no self-reports of what we would call depressive affect. If the emotions have a strong biological basis, as most theories and research suggest, it is likely that some people in all cultures are experiencing the emotions but may simply have no labels with which to verbalize them.

Watch It! Direct Observation

The goal of *direct observation* techniques is to provide an objective, reliable measurement of specific overt behaviors associated with particular emotions. Suppose, for example, that you wanted to study anxiety. You would try to arrive at a constellation of behaviors that are common when anxiety is high. After you had established your behavior constellation and verified its reliability, you would be able to place subjects in various stressful conditions and have observers rate the occurrence and intensity of their anxiety behaviors.

An example of one such device for measuring anxiety is the Timed Behavioral Checklist for Performance Anxiety. It has been used to study, for example, levels of anxiety during public speaking. While subjects gave a speech, raters recorded the presence or absence of such behaviors as pacing, swaying, swallowing, and perspiring during 30-second time periods. The scores were then added to provide a behavioral measure of anxiety.

Like self-report studies, observational measures of emotion are not without problems. One difficulty is ensuring the reliability of the observations. If one observer rates a subject high in anxiety and a second observer rates the same subject moderate in anxiety, the measure is at least somewhat unreliable. Observers must therefore be carefully trained and methods for checking the reliability of their observations must be built into the procedures. The other major problem with the observational method is that the subject's underlying emotional experience is being *inferred* by an outside observer. It is difficult to be certain, for example, that a low observational rating score for anxiety does indeed mean that the subject is not feeling anxious.

Oh Heart, Be Still: Psychophysiological Measures

A pounding heart or sweaty palm can be a dead giveaway that someone is having a strong emotional reaction, and psychophysiology, a third approach to measurement, takes advantage of this observation. *Psychophysiology* involves the measurement and study of a variety of internal body states that reflect the functioning of the autonomic, skeletal, and central nervous systems and typically indicate a person's level of arousal. We can assess changes in heart rate, blood pressure, muscle tension, respiration rate, brain electrical activity, and electrodermal activity, among others. All these indicators can be recorded on a *polygraph*, a device that amplifies bioelectrical signals so that they can be observed and measured. The electroencephalogram (EEG), for example, measures the electrical activity of the brain, the electromyogram (EMG) provides an indication of neural firing in the voluntary muscles, the electrocardiogram (EKG) measures heart rate and other aspects of heart function, and electrodermal activity (EDA) is a measure of the firing of the autonomic nervous system taken at nerve endings in the sweat glands (Figure 13-1).

The psychophysiologist can use these measures to obtain an indication of emotional arousal that occurs under various stimulus conditions (Mok & Wong, 2003). In a given study, we might record heart rate and EEG activity during a time when the subject is being threatened with a series of uncomfortable electrical shocks and during another period in which he is assured that there will be no shocks. Differences in physiological activity between the two time periods will provide an indication of the impact of this stimulation on the physiological responses typically associated with fear or anxiety. To take the study a step further and examine individual differences, we might preselect subjects who are extremely high or low in anxiety to see whether the psychophysiological activity of the two groups differs when they are threatened with electric shock. Such psychophysiological measures are used in lie detection, discussed in The Critical Thinker.

It might seem that here, at last, we have a set of measures so precise and reliable that they must surely represent the ideal approach to the measurement of emotional functioning. It is certainly true that physiological measures are not influenced by the biases and inaccuracies often associated with self-reports or by the reliability problems of observational measures (Winkielman & Cacioppo, 2001). Psychophysiological measurement does, however, have its own problems.

The first difficulty is that there are definite individual differences. In our electric shock experiment, for example, one person may show a 30-beat change in heart rate while another will have only a 5-beat change. A related problem is that some people appear to be more responsive in one body system while others are more responsive in another. We may see a large change in heart rate in one person and a large change in muscle tension (EMG) in another. Indeed, the various physiological measures often show relatively low degrees of correlation with each other (Gerlach et al., 2003).

A final problem is that psychophysiological measurement may not reflect the specific underlying emotional state being investigated. In fact, each physiological measure is actually a measure of general arousal or activation, not of specific emotions. Heart rate can be increased the same amount by giving a subject a series of electric shocks, by insulting him to make him angry, by showing him sexually arousing pictures, or by playing loud tones through a pair of earphones. However, different emotions may involve differing patterns of autonomic indicators, as Horizon 1 suggests (Lang et al., 2000).

The various techniques for measuring emotional functioning have been used in a wide variety of studies. Some involve only one measure, while others use a combination of two or more. Many of these studies have been carried out in an effort to examine the structure of emotion and to test theories of emotional functioning Smith, Cranford, & Mann, 2000; Smith, Cranford, & Green, 2002; Mann & Smith, 2002; Everhart & Harrison, 2002).

Keys to Emotion 1

The Structure and Expression of Emotion

The currently dominant theories that deal with the structure and expression of human emotion hold that there are just a few basic emotions - called primary emotions - from which all others derive. These basic emotions are an innate characteristic of the human species and are experienced and expressed similarly across cultures. We will discuss the original, and currently very influential, evolutionary theory of emotion and consider the structure of primary emotions. We will then take up the major current theories dealing with the expression of emotion. These include a facial feedback theory and a theory that the facial expressions associated with the various emotions are innate and cross-culturally universal. The common theme running through all these theories is evolution: Our current emotions are genetically transmitted products of the adaptation of earlier humans to ancient environments (Abel et al., 2003). The exception comes in learning theories hypothesizing that both emotions and their expression are acquired by each individual through experience with the cultural environment in which she grows up.

Evolutionary Psychology: Innate, Universal Emotions

The first major theorist to address the issue of how emotions originate was none other than Charles Darwin. In his book The Expression of Emotions in Man and Animals (1872), Darwin argued that the facial expressions associated with specific emotions are cross-culturally universal and therefore must be innate. To gain evidence for this hypothesis, he devised a set of sixteen questions about emotional expressions and sent them to people working in a variety of cultures around the world. The questions were quite specific. For example: "Is astonishment expressed by the eyes and mouth being opened wide, and by the eyebrows being raised?" He received responses from thirty-six different observers, including some who worked with isolated peoples. On the basis of this input, Darwin determined that his hypothesis was correct - that the facial expressions associated with emotions are indeed innate and universal.

Darwin's conclusion was, of course, consistent with his more general theory of evolution. Like all other aspects of living organisms, facial expressions have evolved over time because they have survival value. Baring the teeth, for example, serves to frighten enemies because it shows that the animal is willing to fight. This facial expression remains with us as a sign of anger, even though we don't usually physically fight with the objects of our anger, much less bite them. Similarly, there is evidence that the facial expression associated with disgust was originally induced by eating something with a very bad taste. It eventually evolved to a point where it also represents displeasure over some moral or social event. For emotional expression more generally, there is considerable evidence to support Darwin's position (Segal & Blozis, 2002).

Primary Emotions

When you were very young, you learned that there are just four primary colors and that all other colors can be derived by mixing these primaries. Both artists and paint stores that mix colors right before your eyes take advantage of this well-established principle every day. Theorists like Robert Plutchik, Carroll Izard, Paul Ekman, and Jack Panksepp have adopted a similar principle for human emotion. They and others hypothesize that there are just a few *primary emotions* - basic feeling states that have evolved over the centuries because they are adaptive. All other emotional experiences arise as combinations of these primaries (Schmidt & Cohn, 2001). Moreover, the primary emotions may be linked by the genetics of evolution to specific classes of stimuli. We know that insults can lead to anger, danger to fear, rewards to happiness, and major losses to sadness. If primary emotion theorists are right, these specific emotional reactions to specific kinds of stimulus situations are inborn, based in brain circuits, and universal (Kilts et al., 2003). Let's consider the evidence for primary emotions, some criticisms, and an alternative, then turn to three specific primary emotion theories.

Primary Emotions: Pro and Con. As evidence for primary emotion theory, advocates point out that the autonomic nervous system and associated neural structures are capable of directly mediating only a few basic emotions - perhaps 4 or 5 (Dailey et al., 2002). These emotions have three characteristics. First, they have *innate neural substrates* - brain structures that are "hard-wired" to deal with the expression and perception of the specific emotion. Second, their expression is *universal*, crossing all cultures. And finally, they have unique feeling states associated with them (Gunning-Dixon et al., 2003). The wide variety of emotions that we seem to experience all derive from combinations of these few.

Primary emotion theory is not without its critics. Some researchers believe that there are no primary emotions. Instead, they hypothesize that a number of basic elements make up emotions and that all emotions are combinations of these elements. In this approach, the emotions that others call primary are created no differently than the others. Happiness might occur when three specific elements combine; anxiety might result from four other elements; anger from two others; and perhaps disgust from a combination of two of the same elements that produce anxiety with one of those found in anger. No one, complete emotion is primary. Only the elements are primary.

Despite the criticisms and alternatives, primary emotion theory has survived and continues to be influential. However, its advocates have had difficulty answering a central question: Just what are the specific primary emotions? In the 1930s, Robert Woodworth (1938) was the first to propose a structural system for the emotions, which he placed on a single continuum. Elaborating on Woodworth's work, Harold Schlosberg (1952, 1954) devised the three-dimensional structure of emotion. The three basic emotional dimensions he identified were pleasantness/unpleasantness, attention/rejection, and sleep/tension (activation level). Building on this pioneering work, Robert Plutchik (1962, 1982) has developed a more complete evolutionary model of emotional structure that attempts to show how all emotions are interrelated.

The Structure of Emotion: Robert Plutchik. Plutchik has argued that emotions can be described in terms of three different languages, which he calls subjective language, behavioral language, and functional language. *Subjective language* is the common language of emotion and includes such words as "fear," "joy," and "sorrow." *Behavioral language* tells us what action the individual takes as the result of an aroused emotion. And *functional language* indicates what the emotion does for the person. How does it help her? What function does it serve? Thus, fear (subjective language) may lead to escape behavior (behavioral language) and serve the purpose of protecting the organism (functional language).

Based on a series of studies involving judgments of emotions or emotion words, Plutchik concluded that eight basic adaptive reactions serve as prototypes for all emotions (Table 13-5). These *adaptive reactions* can best be viewed as four pairs of polar opposites: *incorporation* (taking in) is the opposite of *rejection*_(expelling); *protection* (escaping) is the opposite of *destruction* (attacking); *reproduction* (possessing) is the opposite of *reintegration* (losing); and *orientation* (stopping) is the opposite of *exploration* (starting, moving). The major opposite emotions are acceptance and disgust, fear and anger, joy and sadness, and surprise and expectancy.

According to Plutchik, emotions can vary in three important dimensions: intensity, similarity, and polarity. *Intensity* refers to degree (pleasure versus joy), *similarity* to relatedness (fear and sadness are more similar than disgust and ecstasy), and *polarity* to opposition (hate is the polar opposite of love). Plutchik used these three dimensions to construct the model shown in Figure 13-2A. This model can be sliced through at various points to yield emotion circles such as that in Figure 13-2B.

Plutchik has applied his approach to work with patient populations, evaluating the risk of suicide (Josepho & Plutchik, 1994) and showing differences in primary underlying emotions between suicide risk and violence risk. Suicide is associated with anxiety, violence with anger. He has also studied the role of emotions in psychotherapy (Plutchik et al., 1994).

A Dimensional Approach. Donald Fromme and Clayton O'Brien (1982) have proposed an alternative to Plutchik's theory that envisions a circular ordering of the emotions. Their model is based on the assumption that there are two principal underlying emotional dimensions: a hedonism or pleasure-pain dimension and an autonomic arousal dimension. A given emotional experience varies from highly positive (pleasurable) to highly negative (painful). The intensity of the emotional reaction is reflected in the amount of autonomic arousal it involves. If you compare this model, depicted in Figure 13-3, with the Plutchik circle in Figure 13-2, you will see that there are many similarities between the two as well as a number of differences. Is either model a correct representation of the structure of human emotions? The answer to this question awaits considerable further research.

Smile and You'll Be Happy: Facial Feedback Theory

You may think that you smile because you are happy, but precisely the opposite may be true: You feel happy because you are smiling. That is, the smile causes you to be happy, rather than vice versa. Hard to believe? Well, let's test the hypothesis. Before reading on, pause and smile for about a minute. Come on now, a real, big, broad smile! Do you feel happier? Well, you should according to Silvan Tomkins (1963, 1984), whose theory of emotion is based in the Darwinian, evolutionary perspective. He hypothesizes that emotion is primarily facial behavior, and the experience of a given affect or emotion *arises from* the facial expression. When you smile, you feel happy; when your brows move downward and your nostrils flare, you feel angry. The facial expression *produces* the emotion. This idea is referred to as *facial feedback theory*. Tomkins suggests that there are only nine basic, inborn emotions (see Table 13-5), each activated by specific environmental stimuli and the facial expressions they trigger.

There is considerable evidence supporting facial feedback theory, though the phenomena may be more complex than Tomkins imagined (Buck, 1994). Consider a study carried out by Ursula Hess and her colleagues at the University of Geneva in Switzerland. They had female undergraduates complete three tasks. In one they were asked to simply feel four emotions (happiness, sadness, anger, and peacefulness). In a second, they were to form facial expressions of these emotions without feeling them (e.g., smile in the happiness condition). And in the final condition, they were to both feel the emotion and form the corresponding facial expression. The finding most relevant to facial feedback theory involved the time required to self-generate the emotion. It took the subjects significantly less time to experience the emotion when they were told to both feel it and form the facial expression than when they were just told to feel it. Thus, facial feedback facilitated the experience of the emotion. On the other hand, a study of a patient who could not form facial expressions due to muscle paralysis, showed that she could nevertheless experience the emotion (Keillor et al., 2002). Despite such contrary results, a majority of studies support the hypothesis that facial expressions generate and facilitate emotional experience (de Gelder et al., 2002).

Robert Zajonc and his colleagues have identified a set of physiological processes through which a change in the facial muscles to produce a specific expression can cause you to experience the feeling state associated with the emotion. They hypothesize that differing vascular (blood vessel) reactions caused by the varied positions of the facial muscles associated with different emotions may cause the necessary physiological process to take place. According to this theory, movements of the facial muscles restrict the venous flow of blood and thereby influence the warming and cooling of the brain. The temperature of the brain tissue may, in turn, cause neurotransmitters associated with emotion to be blocked or released, generating the emotional state (Zajonc et al., 1989). Cooling the brain, Zajonc thinks, is associated with pleasant emotions; warming it produces aversive feelings.

In a fascinating test of the Zajonc hypothesis, air was blown into the nasal passages of subjects. Voila! When the air was warm, the subjects experienced negative emotions; when it was cool, they felt positive emotions. While we still have much to learn about the causal basis of the relationship between facial expression and experience, we can at least now be reasonably certain that when you smile, you should feel better.

Having said that facial expressions can generate emotional feelings, we should also note that a person's expression at the moment is often not a pure indication of an emotion. Very often, in fact, facial expression is an important part of how we communicate with others and may have little to do with internal, emotional feelings (Bolte et al., 2002). Smiling, for example, does not always mean that we are happy, as the Probe suggests.

Innate Facial Expressions

Following in Darwin's footsteps, modern-day theorist Carroll Izard (2002) suggests that the emotions have evolved in parallel with the evolution of the brain. Increases in brain complexity are associated with increases in the number of emotions and in the complexity of emotional expression. According to Izard, the neural mechanisms for both facial expressions and the perception of such expressions are innate (Izard et al., 2002). Furthermore, like Tomkins he believes that emotional experience is activated by sensory feedback from the face. Facial expression leads to subjective emotional experience - smiling results in a feeling of happiness, scowling in anger (see Table 13-5).

Consider the far-reaching importance of what Darwin and Izard have asserted: If each major emotion is associated with a specific facial expression and if facial expressions are innate, it follows that the emotions themselves are innate and that learning has a relatively minor impact on emotional experience. When you think about it, this is a fascinating idea: Despite the many other differences among peoples from different cultures, smiling, scowling, and other facial expressions of emotion may be unaffected by cultural training. They are cross-culturally universal because they are innate characteristics of the entire human species. Evidence to support this assertion has come from two kinds of research: newborn studies and cross-cultural studies.

Born to smile. Studies of newborn infants have shown that a number of emotional expressions are present at birth, including disgust, interest, startle, smiling, and distress (Izard, 2002; Montague & Walker, 2002). Expressions of anger and surprise appear by three or four months of age, and shame and fear can be observed within a month or two after that. Expressions of content are found by the end of the first year, and guilt appears early in the second year (Izard et al., 2002).

These findings have led some investigators to conclude that any emotional expression present at birth must be innate and that even those expressions that develop as a function of physiological maturation during the early months are probably in large part hereditary. However, some studies of infant facial expression have not supported Izard's hypothesis, suggesting that head or eye movement, rather than a specific emotion, may be responsible for some expressions. In addition, we have no way of directly assessing the emotion the baby is experiencing at the time the facial expression appears. When the baby smiles, is she really experiencing happiness? When she screws up her face, is she really feeling anger? Or is it possible that these facial expressions are less specific to particular emotions and that the emotional experience is later tied to the expressions through learning? Finally, some work suggests that early experience does influence facial expressions of emotion (Pollak & Kistler, 2002). Nevertheless, most of the newborn literature does lend support to the concept of innate facial emotional expression (Izard, 2002).

Cross-Cultural Studies. If facial expressions are inborn, they should be the same in all cultures. Paul Ekman (1994), another major theorist and research scientist, also believes that Darwin was right in hypothesizing cross-cultural universality. He points out that human emotions have gradually evolved over the centuries (Ekman, 1992). Those emotions with greater adaptive value in dealing with life tasks have survived and less effective emotions have dropped out. The surviving emotions have become our basic or primary emotions, and it is on these that the entire variety of human emotional experience is built (Ekman, 1993).

Darwin sought to establish cultural universality with his questionnaire, but modern researchers have developed more sophisticated methods, including computerized analysis of facial photos. Ekman (1972), for example, showed photographs like those in Figure 13-4 to college students in Brazil, Chile, Argentina, Japan, and the United States and asked them to indicate what emotion was being expressed. He found a high degree of agreement in judgment across these five cultures, though the extent of agreement varied from one emotion to another. Faces depicting happiness, for example, were rated as happy by 87 to 98 percent of the people in any given culture, while those depicting fear were rated correctly by 71 to 88 percent. Interestingly enough, however, the ability to recognize facial expressions of specific emotions declines with age (Calder et al., 2003), and the underlying neural mechanisms in men and women may be somewhat different (Lee et al., 2002).

Critics pointed out that early studies of this type involved exclusively cultures that were literate and therefore had a partially shared background. In response, Ekman and others conducted studies of isolated, preliterate cultures in places like Borneo and New Guinea. These studies have, like those of literate cultures, consistently shown high percentages of agreement in judging the emotions expressed in the pictures, thereby confirming the other cross-cultural results.

Although a few studies find no evidence for such universal emotions, most do (Huang et al., 2001). One team of reviewers examined studies spanning 37 countries and 5 continents (Schier & Wallbott, 1994). They concluded that there is consistent evidence for the cross-cultural stability of emotional response patterns. Cultures differ in how emotions are elicited and regulated, but not in how they are expressed or perceived. Another study showed that Americans accurately perceive Hindu Indian facial expressions of emotion (Hejmadi et al., 2000). Ekman (1993) has reached a similar conclusion and also points out that when subjects voluntarily form specific facial expressions, these are accompanied by systematically different patterns of firing in the autonomic and central nervous systems.

As Ekman notes, his results do not necessarily mean that emotional expression is entirely innate. In fact, evidence for the universality of expression is largely limited to the emotions studied in the Ekman research: happiness, fear, surprise, anger, disgust, and sadness. Moreover, even for these emotions, only partial facial expressions occur in certain cultural contexts, and the situations that trigger particular emotions vary from one culture to another (Cole et al., 2002; Mandal et al., 2001). What, then, can we conclude? It is reasonable to say at this point that there is good cross-cultural agreement on emotional expression and thus that it is largely innate. However, the inborn expressions can be modified to some degree by cultural experience.

The Role of Learning and Experience

Almost all theorists recognize that learning and experience play at least some role in the expression of emotion. The disagreement lies in the extent to which learning is involved. Some theorists hold that learning plays only a minor role, whereas others believe that emotions are entirely learned - that not only emotional expression but emotions themselves are acquired through experience.

The Biological View of Experience. Among theorists rooted in a biological tradition, learning has a relatively minor role in emotion. Robert Plutchik (1994), for example, believes that emotions are a direct expression of the genetic potentials of an individual and that learning simply acts to modify them in various ways. One effect of learning is to influence the *relative frequency* with which the different emotions are expressed. Some people express anger more often, while others are more likely to express sadness. Another effect of learning is to modify the *external signs* of emotion; different people may express the same emotion in different ways. One person may learn to express joy by laughing loudly, hugging loved ones, and more generally making an open display of this positive emotion; another may express joy in a more subdued fashion. Learning also affects the *strength and stability* of the mixture of emotions that develop.

Plutchik and others point out that this conceptualization of the factors in emotion is consistent with studies showing differences across cultural subgroups in the way emotions are expressed. David Matsumoto (1993), for example, studied the expression and intensity of emotion in four ethnic groups: Caucasian, African-American, Asian, and Hispanic. He found differences in the social rules and circumstances under which the various groups expressed emotion and in the typical intensity of expression, reflecting the effects of cultural learning in shaping the details of emotionality. The basic emotions were the same across all four groups; only the nuances of expression were different.

Carroll Izard (1994) takes a similar approach. He hypothesizes that "each emotion sensitizes the infant to particular features of the environment and thus facilitates the processing of particular types of information and the learning of particular relationships" (1978, p. 195). In Izard's view, ten fundamental emotions appear early in life: interest, joy, surprise, distress, anger, disgust, contempt, fear, shame/shyness, and guilt. All ten are innate and emerge over the first few months of life to influence the behavior of the infant. As the individual develops, learning influences the cues, or activators, that elicit these emotions, the cognitive processes that shape emotional reactions, and the coping responses used to deal with emotions (Izard, 1992). The result is that innate emotions become individualized in their expression by learning and by experience more generally. Everyone is born with the same basic emotion of anger, for example. However, one person learns to express it primarily through verbal responses, another through physical aggression.

Activators are stimuli or situations that may, on the basis of learning, cause an emotion to be expressed. For example, a friend of yours may have learned to be fearful of large dogs; you, on the other hand, may not be afraid of dogs but are deathly afraid of heights. Thus the same basic emotion, fear, is elicited by different activators in different individuals. *Cognitive processes* may differ from one person to another, leading to differences in the ways emotional situations are viewed. Faced with the sudden, anxiety-producing proclamation "Please put all books and papers under your desk. We're going to have a pop quiz," your friend may see his already borderline grade going off the bottom of the scale. His cognitive assessment leads him to predict disaster, and he panics as the quiz is distributed. You, on the other hand, may cognitively construe the quiz as an opportunity to improve your grade and therefore face it with calm confidence. Approaches to *coping* with emotional situations are also influenced by learning (Frazier et al., 2002). One person who is afraid of dogs may cope with his fear by avoiding them, while another might confront her fear by making it a point to visit the homes of friends with large dogs and pet the dogs.

According to biological theorists, then, the emotions are inherited givens that emerge as a function of physiological maturation. But although emotions are innate, their expression and activation are influenced by learning and experience, as are the coping responses for dealing with them (Fox, 2002).

The Learning Theory View of Experience. Countering the view that emotion is basically biological and affected by learning in only minor ways is the idea that all emotion is learned. The classic work testing this hypothesis was done by Neal Miller (1948, 1951), who studied fear as an acquired drive. Miller's position was that fear has no biological basis. There is no innate emotion called fear, and any behavior that we attribute to such an emotion must be learned. To prove his point, he devised an experiment that involved a shuttlebox with two compartments, one painted white and one painted black. Rats were placed in one compartment, where they received electric shocks. The only way to escape the shocks was to run through a door into the other compartment. Half the rats were shocked in the white compartment and ran to the black one; the other half were shocked in the black compartment and ran to the white one. At first the rats responded to the painful shocks by squealing, running and jumping, until they eventually stumbled upon the doorway and escaped into the other compartment. After a number of trials, however, rats shocked in the white compartment, for example, would run into the black compartment as soon as they were placed in the box, demonstrating that they had *learned* to fear the white compartment. That is, the color white came to serve as a cue to elicit fear.

Once the fear had been learned, Miller closed the door between the compartments and the rats had to learn to turn a wheel in order to open it and escape. Despite the fact that no further shocks were given, the animals were so afraid of being stuck in the white compartment that they quickly learned to turn the wheel and escape. Not only did they learn the emotion, but it was powerful enough to serve as a drive to motivate the learning of new behavior. We see once again how closely interrelated emotions and drives (motives) can be. Clark Hull and other learning theorists subsequently used Miller's research as a jumping-off point for explaining how secondary drives and emotions - which form the basis for most human behavior - are acquired through learning processes.

The classic case of Little Albert (Chapter 6), who learned to fear a white rat when it was paired with a loud noise, demonstrates that humans can also acquire fears through learning processes. However, there appear to be definite limits on what objects people can learn to fear. Children can quite readily be conditioned to show fear of such objects as leather boots, caterpillars, and black cats, but the same conditioning techniques cannot teach them to fear colored cloth, opera glasses, or wooden toys (Marks, 1977; Seligman, 1970, 1971). This may suggest that fear is learned but that humans are genetically more *prepared* to learn fears of some objects than of others (Seligman, 1970). This biological preparedness is discussed in Chapter 6.

Taking a somewhat different approach to the role of learning in emotion, James Averill (1980) has suggested that emotions are *social constructs.* By this he means that emotions are developed, learned, or constructed by and under the influence of *culture.* In the course of the normal learning processes, the individual acquires emotional reactions that determine all aspects of behavior. According to Averill, only a small subset of emotional reactions are biologically determined; these include startle responses to sudden noises, uneasiness at great heights, and attack behaviors in response to pain. In his view, virtually all other emotions are culturally learned.

Keys to Emotion 2

The Experience of Emotions: Major Theories

Evolutionary theory deals with the origins, structure, and expression of emotion but does not tell us what makes us feel happy on one occasion and sad on another. What is the sequence of events when we experience feelings? How does cognition relate to the subjective experience of emotion? What is the relationship between emotion and behavior? A number of theories have been developed in an effort to provide answers to these and other important questions. Although the various theoretical approaches differ in important ways, there are a few points on which all theorists agree. In particular, they agree that emotions have several major components. Klaus Scherer (1982) has identified these as: (1) subjective feelings, (2) cognitive appraisal, (3) physiological arousal, (4) motor expression (body movements), and (5) motivational tendencies (needs to act on the basis of emotions). They differ as to the relative importance of the various components and the order in which these components appear in the sequence of events that includes an emotional response. One major set of theories emphasizes the physiological basis of emotion, another the role of cognition, and a third the role of the unconscious.

Physiologically Oriented Theories

Although they agree that learning and cognition may be involved in emotion, some theorists strongly emphasize that emotion is primarily a product of the brain and nervous system. Its origins lie in physiological reactions to stimuli. The major approaches include the James-Lange, Cannon-Bard, and psychobiological theories.

The James-Lange Theory. The oldest psychological theory of the experience of emotion is that formulated in 1884 by William James.[1] Shortly thereafter it was supported by Carl Lange (1885) and became known as the *James-Lange theory*. The importance of this theory, as George Mandler (1990) points out, is that it has shaped work on emotion for an entire century. The striking hypothesis of the theory is that physiological reactions to a stimulus trigger emotions, not the other way around. This somewhat surprising idea bears repeating: Your physiological reaction to an emotional stimulus causes you to feel the emotion, not vice versa.

In our example of Jennifer's experience, the common-sense explanation would be that the mysterious noise (the stimulus) produced fear (the emotion), which caused her heart to speed up and her sweat glands to produce perspiration (the visceral response). What James and Lange proposed, however, was that stimuli cause physiological responses, which in turn trigger the subjective experience of an emotion. Jennifer heard the noise, which initiated physiological changes, which then caused her to feel afraid. William James' theory is actually more complex than this statement would imply, but its impact on the study of emotion lies in its emphasis on the primacy of the physiological reaction. In fact, there is still discussion of the James-Lange theory, and Leonard Berkowitz (1990) has integrated it with cognitive theory in his explanation of aggressive behavior.

The Cannon-Bard Theory. Although the James-Lange theory quickly gained considerable support, Walter Cannon (1927) took issue with its major hypothesis. He pointed out that the organ systems James thought provided the primary physiological basis for emotion react slowly to stimulation, whereas emotions occur very rapidly. When Jen heard the sounds in her apartment, she seemed to react almost instantly. However, the accompanying physiological changes, particularly those involving hormones, would not have taken place quickly enough to account for her rapid emotional arousal. Cannon also questioned whether the organs James specified, such as the heart and stomach, could actually produce a variety of emotions. He pointed out that under James-Lange such peripheral, visceral physiology as heart rate, blood pressure, and digestive function would have to be capable of somehow indicating just which emotion was to be experienced, and he doubted that this was possible. In fact, he noted that humans whose sympathetic nervous systems had been surgically detached from their viscera (like the heart and stomach) still reported feeling emotions.

Having punched some rather large apparent holes in the James-Lange theory, Cannon and his colleague Phillip Bard presented an alternative approach, called the *Cannon-Bard theory*. They proposed that internal or external stimuli lead to sensory impulses that are sent to the cortex of the brain. The cortex normally inhibits the action of subcortical emotional centers that would otherwise run wild and cause intense reactions. The arrival of sensory impulses at the cortex reduces the normal inhibitory action and releases activity in the thalamus. Impulses from the thalamus then travel to the brain stem, where the autonomic nervous system produces organ responses, and back to the cortex, where

---

[1] Darwin's theory of emotion is older but deals with the origins and expression of emotion, not with immediate emotional experience.

the sensation of emotion is produced. In this theory, then, a stimulus leads to both the visceral responses and the emotional sensation simultaneously. The James-Lange and Cannon-Bard theories are compared in Figure 13-5. Some studies have directly compared the two theories (Cobos et al., 2002), and research over time has provided partial support for each theory (Russell, 2003; Crucian et al., 2000).

Psychobiological Theory. Jack Panksepp (Panksepp et al., 2002) has developed a psychobiological theory of emotional functioning, which suggests that basic emotions are related to specific neural circuits. According to Panksepp, there are four basic emotions (fear, rage, panic, and expectancy), each of which is associated with a *command system* found in the brain. These four basic systems interact to produce other emotions. Panksepp also suggests that specific neurochemicals may be associated with the various emotional command systems. There is evidence, for example, that the neurotransmitter dopamine is associated with the expectancy system, while acetylcholine mediates action in the rage system (Knutson et al., 2002). Other evidence documents specific roles for the amygdala, hippocampus, and temporal cortex in the processing of emotion (Fischer et al., 2003; Hariri, 2002).

This theory has been subjected to a number of criticisms. Magdna Arnold (1982) questions the basis for the specific locations of emotion circuits, and James Averill (1982) points out that the "hardwired" circuits may not be flexible enough to serve as a neurological basis for emotion. However, the theory has generated considerable interest among investigators and has led to productive research into the neurological bases of emotional functioning (Iwase et al., 2002). Moreover, other theorists have now begun to introduce into their own work the idea that the *neural networks* discussed in Chapters 6, 7, and 8 may well underlie emotional functioning, and hemispheric differences in the recognition of facial emotion have been demonstrated (Prodan et al., 2001).

Cognitive Theories

Building on the physiological theories, some modern theorists have suggested that cognition or thought has a primary role in generating and guiding emotion. One major theory deals with the role of cognitive labeling in determining just what emotions are experienced. One derivative of this approach hypothesizes that people often misattribute an emotion to an incorrect cause. Another derivative theory shows how excitation from one source can transfer to another. Additional cognitive theories hypothesize that thought processes are primarily responsible for triggering both emotional responses and behaviors designed to cope with the emotional situation (Proudfoot et al., 2003).

Schachter's Cognitive-Labeling Theory. The most influential cognitive theory is one that returns to the James-Lange hypothesis and attempts to deal with Cannon's criticisms. It was developed by Stanley Schachter and is called *cognitive-labeling theory* (see Figure 13-5). Schachter accepts the idea that emotions follow the James-Lange sequence: stimulus --> physiological response --> felt emotion. However, he notes that the earlier theory does not account for the fact that the same physiological response pattern can be associated with a wide variety of emotions. How do we know which emotion we are experiencing? "I feel aroused, but am I happy, angry, or sad?" Schachter's solution to this puzzle was to introduce the idea of the cognitive labeling or representation of physiological responses. A *cognitive label* is an interpretation of physiological arousal, based on situational cues and past experience, that identifies the emotion associated with the arousal. When faced with an emotional stimulus, you experience general physiological arousal that does not relate to any specific emotion. Your perception of the stimulus situation then leads you to label the arousal as representing some particular emotion. If you experience a pounding heart, rapid breathing, and increased muscle tension, you might label this arousal as fear if you are facing a robber at the time. But these same physiological changes in the presence of an attractive person of the opposite sex might be labeled as love or sexual excitement. If there is no obvious explanation for your arousal, you will search for acceptable cognitions to provide the appropriate emotional labels. In situations where there is no physiological arousal, there will be no emotional experience. Both physiology and cognition are required.

To test his theory, Schachter and co-researcher Jerome Singer (1962) conducted a classic and controversial study. Subjects were told they would be part of an experiment on the effects of a vitamin compound and were subsequently given an injection. What they did not know was that they were being injected with epinephrine, which produces increased blood pressure, heart rate, respiration, and blood sugar level, causing the subject to experience such effects as palpitations, flushing, rapid breathing, and tremors. Each subject was then randomly assigned to one of four groups:

- Informed group - Subjects in this condition were told ahead of time that the injection might have side effects, including arousal symptoms.
- Misinformed group - Subjects were told that the drug would cause headaches, body itches, numb feet, and other symptoms not associated with epinephrine.
- Uninformed group - Subjects were told that there would be no side effects.
- Control group - Control subjects received an injection of saline solution, which has no physiological effects and thus acted as a placebo.

After being given the injection, subjects were instructed to wait in a room that turned out to be occupied by a confederate of the experimenters. In one experimental condition, the confederate acted elated and engaged in such activities as playing basketball with wastepaper and flying paper airplanes. In a second experimental condition, the confederate and the subject were given questionnaires to fill out; as the questions became more and more personal and insulting, the confederate acted angrier and angrier until finally he tore up the questionnaire and stalked out of the room.

Of particular interest to Schachter and Singer were the behaviors of the uninformed group. How would they react to their physiological arousal? Results showed that the uninformed subjects were more likely to be elated and to report feelings of happiness when the confederate acted elated and more likely to be angry and report feelings of anger when the confederate acted angry (Figure 13-6). The misinformed group also shifted their feelings to correspond to those of the confederate. These responses were not found in the epinephrine-informed subjects, who apparently attributed their arousal to the drug they had been given and not to the situation. The placebo group showed no particular emotional reaction to the situation.

Schachter's work has been criticized on a variety of methodological grounds, and attempts to replicate results have met with mixed success. One problem is Schachter's assumption that general arousal contributes equally and identically to all emotions. Subsequent research suggests that it does not. Moreover, it appears that arousal symptoms, such as a pounding heart, are much more likely to be interpreted in terms of negative than positive emotions. A third problem is that Schachter's cognitive labeling process seems to occur primarily or exclusively in novel situations involving moderate arousal. A fourth issue is that the labeling of emotions is often based on past experience and memory, not just immediate situational factors. And, finally, Schachter's assumption that all emotions involve essentially the same neurochemical mediating processes has proven incorrect.

Despite these criticisms and negative findings, Schachter's theory has had a considerable impact on the study of emotion. It was the primary stimulus not only for a large body of research, but also for a number of related theories and for the cognitive view of emotion more generally.

Getting It Wrong: Misattribution. The historical chain of theoretical events that began with James and Lange and moved a step further with Schachter has been extended to the development of *misattribution theory* (Winton, 1990). Schachter's cognitive labeling theory clearly suggests that the particular emotion an individual experiences is a function of the labeling process; it does not result directly from the stimulus producing the actual physiological arousal. It follows from this idea that it should be possible to misattribute the arousal from an emotional source, such as fear, to a nonemotional source, such as a drug.

A number of researchers have tried to test this possibility and to determine its potential applications, such as helping people reduce anxiety. In one of the earliest studies, all subjects were given a placebo pill that had no physiological effects. Half were assigned to a *drug-arousal* condition, in which they were told that the pill produced arousal symptoms (increased heart rate and so on). The other half formed a *drug non-arousal* group, in which they were told that the pill produced such arousal-irrelevant symptoms as numb feet. Following drug administration, all subjects were given a series of increasingly painful electric shocks. Those in the drug-arousal group tolerated significantly more intense shocks than those in the drug-non-arousal group. Why were those told that the pill would produce arousal symptoms able to tolerate more shock? Because they were misattributing part of the arousal induced by the painful stimulation to the pill.

Other studies have shown that subjects high in test anxiety are less fearful in a testing situation when they misattribute their arousal to a placebo and that physiological responses to a fearful stimulus are reduced when subjects attribute the arousal to a nonemotional source. Similarly, eyewitnesses to crimes, who are often aroused by fear or excitement, can misattribute their arousal, creating inaccurate memories of the event (Belli et al., 1994). There are also common attributions that can be inaccurate on some occasions. An example is premenstrual syndrome (PMS), in which a woman experiences physiologically induced irritability, anger, and depression during the week before her period. Although the woman has little control over her negative emotions, we often misattribute behaviors to PMS and label women without this syndrome as having it.

Misattribution has important real-life implications, in part because it can lead to conflict and violence. One study showed that Israeli-Jewish students made misattributions about the intentions of the two sides in the Arab-Israeli conflict that could easily contribute to the future of the conflict (Bizman & Hoffman, 1993). In another study aggressive and nonaggressive Latino and African-American middle-school children were read ambiguous scenarios describing negative situations initiated by a hypothetical peer, such as having someone bump into them fairly hard on the way to school. They then made judgments as to the peer's intentions, their own feelings of anger, and the likelihood that they would behave aggressively. Those in the aggressive group were more likely to perceive the peer as intentionally committing the negative act and were correspondingly more apt to respond with violence. Thus, a misattribution of the intent of the peer could easily lead to unnecessary and inappropriate aggression.

Transfer of Excitation. An interesting extension of the misattribution idea is Dolf Zillman's (1971, 1978) hypothesis that arousal from one source may influence otherwise unrelated cognitions and reactions. One study conducted in British Columbia rather dramatically illustrated his point. An experimenter asked men who had just crossed either a solid wooden bridge 10 feet above a stream or a precariously swinging bridge that spanned a deep gorge high above roaring rapids to complete a questionnaire. When the experimenter was female, the men who crossed the dangerous bridge exhibited more sexual imagery on a portion of the questionnaire dealing with that topic and were more likely to later call the woman for a date. Zillman's explanation for this result is that a *transfer of excitation* occurs. The arousal generated by crossing the swaying bridge transfers to the interaction with the female experimenter to heighten sexual arousal. When the same experimenter approached the men further down the trail, long after crossing one of the bridges, there was no difference in sexual imagery, suggesting that the effect at the bridge was, indeed, due to a transfer of excitation Dutton & Aron, 1974).

In another study, Zillman and a colleague had half their subjects ride an exercise bike until they were breathing heavily and their hearts were pounding. They were then insulted by a confederate. Those who had just ridden the bike were more aggressive toward the insulter than were subjects who had engaged in a non-arousing task prior to being insulted (Zillman and Bryant, 1974). That is, the arousal produced by riding the bicycle transferred to the insult situation, thus increasing anger. A number of other studies have confirmed the transfer-of-excitation effect and shown that some people are much more susceptible to it than others. The moral of this research? If you must make someone angry, try to do it at a time when she is otherwise calm, cool, and collected!

Cognitive Appraisal Theories. Some theories have placed an even stronger emphasis on cognitive processes than does Schachter's theory and its derivatives. These approaches focus on the role of such cognitive factors as thought, learning, memory, and perception in emotional experience. Two of the major theorists are Richard Lazarus and Magda Arnold.

According to Lazarus (1991, 1993), each emotion has three major components: cognitive appraisals, action impulses, and patterned somatic (bodily) reactions. *Cognitive appraisal* consists of evaluating the significance of stimuli in relation to one's well-being (called *primary appraisal*) and then evaluating possible coping resources and strategies for dealing with any stress that grows out of the emotional situation (*secondary appraisal*). Primary appraisal is an evaluation of the cognitive antecedents of the emotion, not the content of the emotion itself (Herrald & Tomaka, 2002). A person confronted by a mugger brandishing a gun evaluates the mugger and the gun, not the fear he is feeling. Secondary appraisal taps memory and prior experience and uses thought processes in an effort to reduce stress.

Action impulses involve cognitively processing a possible behavior - that is, thinking about taking an action. Faced with the mugger, you may contemplate grabbing the gun, yelling for help, using a defensive pepper spray, or running. *Patterned somatic reactions* are physiological responses that accompany and are a part of the overall emotional experience. In Jennifer's case, for example, her cognitive appraisal of the strange noise in the night led her to suspect a burglar. She then considered possible actions to take (action impulses). Her patterned somatic reactions were the physiological changes commonly associated with fear. A number of studies have supported the Lazarus theory as a way of understanding emotional arousal and suggested that his dimensions of appraisal appear to be similar across a variety of cultures (Skinner & Brewer, 2002).

Lazarus hypothesizes that when we are emotionally aroused, we engage in *coping processes* - thoughts and behaviors that represent attempts to reduce stress. The major coping mechanisms are palliation and direct action. *Palliation* is a defensive process in which we alter our own reactions to emotional events. We may try to ignore negative events, make ourselves believe that they will just go away, or try to modify our physiological reactions by jogging, meditating, or taking drugs. The alternative is to take *direct action* to cope with emotion. If an upcoming exam is worrying you, the alternatives are to persuade yourself not to worry because it won't be as bad as you fear (palliation) or to study harder (direct action).

Notice that the Lazarus theory contrasts sharply with Schachter's (see Figure 13-5). Lazarus essentially hypothesizes that emotions are products of cognitive activity and that specific physiological patterns are associated with specific emotions. Schachter holds that all emotions share a general state of physiological arousal that is made emotionally specific by the cognitive labeling process.

Like Schachter, Lazarus has his critics, who suggest that cognitive appraisals actually follow emotional arousal or that cognition and affect are processed separately. As a result of these and other criticisms, cognitive appraisal theory has many detractors. However, there is also considerable evidence supporting it (Waibel-Duncan & Sandier, 2002)

Magda Arnold (1960, 1970), like Lazarus, emphasizes the role of cognitive appraisal in emotion and suggests that we automatically evaluate every situation with regard to its relevance to ourselves. If the appraisal results in a tendency to engage in some action, that tendency is called emotion. Memories of related prior experience and expectations regarding the current situation guide our appraisals, and from this combination of memory and expectation we devise coping strategies. Arnold also specifies the hypothetical neural pathways that may be involved in the appraisal process. She sees the *limbic system* as controlling the outcome of cognitive processes and thereby guiding the person to engage in approach and avoidance behavior. The *hippocampus* controls the recall of relevant memories and impulses to act, and the *cerebellum* generates behavioral action patterns that are relayed to the *frontal lobe*, where the emotion is felt and the urge to act is turned into overt motor behavior. Arnold has thus attempted to combine the cognitive, feeling, and neurophysiological components of emotion to present a unified theory of how emotions take place.

It seems clear that our cognitions affect our emotions, but the opposite is also true. Emotional mood states can influence our cognitions, as the discussion of mood congruence in our 21 for this chapter makes clear.

Unconscious Origins of Emotional Experience: Psychoanalytic Theory

The physiologically and cognitively oriented theories we have discussed thus far all emphasize, or at least assume, the *conscious* nature of emotional experience. We are aware, at some point in the process, of both the stimulus eliciting the emotional reaction and the emotion itself.

Sigmund Freud and many of his students and colleagues disagreed with this understanding of emotion. In his psychoanalytic theory, Freud hypothesized that emotional experiences are largely a result of unconscious processes. The unconscious in Freudian theory is an area of the personality containing emotions, motives, and memories of past experience of which we are not aware, but which nevertheless influence behavior. Most experiences from early childhood, for example, are unconscious. As an adult, you are not aware of them, cannot attach verbal or imaginal labels to them, and therefore cannot consciously think about them. Yet the unconscious is a powerful source of emotion and motivation: It can cause you to experience emotions with no awareness of where they came from and to engage in behavior that serves no consciously obvious purpose.

The emphasis in psychoanalytic theory is on negative emotions, particularly anxiety and anger, and these emotions are typically thought to result from conflicts that occur at unconscious levels of functioning (Schussler, 2002). The powerful negative emotions that result from these unconscious conflicts are experienced in awareness as highly unpleasant and disturbing. Perhaps you have at times felt very tense and anxious for no apparent reason. You have no exams coming up, no serious disagreements with other people, no trouble at work - no good reason to feel anxious; yet, you do. Freud would say that your anxiety is the result of some unconscious conflict, often resulting from early childhood experience.

Freud's theoretical statements concerning emotion and its implications for abnormal behavior and clinical treatment served as a stimulus for considerable elaboration by many other psychoanalysts. More detailed psychodynamic theories of emotion have been proposed by a number of theorists. Several have offered revised understandings of how emotions arise from unconscious processes and suggested just how specific emotions are dealt with by unconscious mechanisms. While it is one of the oldest theories of emotional functioning, the psychoanalytic approach continues to develop and to have considerable impact on our understanding of emotion.

Theories of Emotion: Some Conclusions

The number and variety of current theories of emotion make it clear that there is by no means complete accord on the basis for emotional functioning. Most theorists agree that a physiological substrate underlies emotion. However, they disagree as to how general or specific this physiology may be and whether physiological changes cause the psychological experience of the emotion or vice versa. There is also some agreement that cognitive processes are involved in emotion. Once again, however, there is by no means total unanimity as to the relationship. Do cognitions give rise to emotions, or do the physiological or psychological components of emotion produce relevant cognitions? Do emotions arise largely from unconscious conflicts or from stimuli in the environment? We have hypothetical answers to these questions, but the answers vary from one theory to another.

Keys to Emotion 3

Happiness

"Happiness is a warm puppy." CHARLES SCHULTZ, 1962

This famous quote is the title of the equally famous book by Charles Schultz, creator of *Peanuts*. Perhaps you don't agree. Perhaps to you happiness is a perfect sunset, a little child's smile, a caring lover, or a dollar in your pocket. But whatever your sources of happiness, you would probably at least agree with Schultz and most other people that happiness is an important emotion. Here we explore some of what psychologists have learned about this most positive of emotions. In other chapters we examine emotions such as anxiety (15), depression (16), and love (19).

The Greatest Happiness Principle

People were interested in happiness long before psychology came along. Aristotle thought that happiness lies in the successful pursuit of pleasure and that we are happiest when we live well-ordered lives, doing what we enjoy and do well. His views influence research on happiness to this day. Plato, on the other hand, held that the source of all happiness is the virtuous life, since our own virtue is the only aspect of our destiny that we really control. At the other extreme is the somewhat notorious hedonistic view of the Epicureans, who were quite certain that we achieve happiness by maximizing pleasure and minimizing pain. And, finally, the Greatest Happiness Principle of 19th-century philosopher, John Stuart Mill:

> **The creed which accepts as the foundation of morals Utility, or the Greatest Happiness Principle, holds that actions are right in proportion as they tend to promote happiness, wrong as they tend to produce the reverse of happiness.** – *Utilitarianism*, 1863

So important is happiness in Mill's view that it defines the appropriateness of all behavior. A somewhat different view of happiness is presented in a recent book by famous psychologist Martin Seligman (2002), entitled *Authentic Happiness*. Seligman holds that happiness comes from identifying our strengths and using them to improve our world and thereby achieve lasting happiness.

Happiness Is Not (Just) a Warm Puppy

Beyond the pronouncements of ancient philosophers and modern cartoonists, what do we know about happiness? If it is not (for most people) a warm puppy, what is it? Well, consider these possibilities:

- Happiness is smoking a joint or snorting some "coke."
- Happiness is a home in the suburbs.
- Happiness is living in America.
- Happiness is a high income.
- Happiness is winning the lottery.

Which of these do you agree with? Let's look briefly at each of these potential sources of positive emotionality.

Even if you have experienced the "highs" that some people report from smoking marijuana or snorting cocaine, you would probably agree that drugs are not a true source of happiness. At best, they may bring temporary pleasure or relief from stress. Cocaine impairs sexual functioning, can damage the fetus during pregnancy, and causes heart attacks (Zimring et al., 1994). Marijuana can produce lung damage and be a factor in murder (Spunt et al., 1994). These are hardly the ingredients of happiness!

Well, maybe we've eliminated puppies and pot, but surely a home in the suburbs or in America more generally could be the answer. A Detroit study showed that when the happiness levels of people living in the city were compared with those of people in the suburbs, there was no difference. Both groups were equally happy. As to living in America, cross-cultural studies have indeed reported differences in happiness from one country to another (Veenhoven, 1995). Asian cultures report lower levels of happiness than others (Weaver, 2001), and the happiest people live in North America, Australia, and Europe.

Finally, we come to people with lots of money, either from high incomes or winning the lottery. Although data on the relationship between income and happiness have been somewhat inconsistent, most recent studies do show a modest correlation. Across 18,000 college students in 39 countries and nearly 5000 American adults, those with higher personal or family incomes are somewhat happier (Diener et al., 1993). However, a study of executive compensation showed that as salaries went up, happiness actually went down (Bolster & Hawthorne, 2002). And what about the lottery? If you won the lottery, you would certainly be happier. Indeed, many people play the lottery every week and dream of winning. But if they do win, they might be disappointed. One team of researchers studied 22 people, most of whom had won $100,000 or more in the Illinois State Lottery, and compared them with a control group of people who had not won anything. Just a few months after they won the newly rich were no happier than the non-winners (Brickman, Coates, and Janoff-Bulman, 1978). Obviously, even large sums of money do not necessarily make people happier. *How Happy Are We?*

> **Every one of these hundreds of millions of human beings is in some form seeking happiness.... Not one is altogether noble nor altogether trustworthy nor altogether consistent; and not one is altogether vile.... Not a single one but has at some time wept.** – H.G. Wells, *The Outline of History*, 1920

H.G. Wells, author of *The Time Machine* and *The War That Will End War*, had a point: Though we all experience sadness and all weep at times, what we constantly seek is happiness. How successful are we? The truth is that most people are quite happy. According to surveys, a majority of people in many countries are "very happy" (33%) or "pretty happy" (50%). Only a few (about 10%) are "not too happy". Similar results from other studies have shown that about 60% are moderately to very happy. And other studies confirm quite high levels of happiness (Lester, 2002), particularly in democracies (Frey, 2000). However, the populations of some countries, such as Iran, have much lower levels of happiness (Kousha, 2000). A problem with this research, however, is that "happiness" is defined and labeled differently in different studies, where it may be called life satisfaction, well-being, contentment, pleasure, or gratification, among other things. This makes it difficult to directly compare the results of different studies (Stanley & cheek, 2003).

Using somewhat different methodology, other psychologists have asked people to rate themselves on happiness rating scales and have then averaged the ratings across groups of people. One team of researchers asked college students a single question: "How elated or depressed, happy or unhappy, did you feel today?" (Wessman & Ricks, 1966) Students responded by rating themselves on a 10-point scale. A rating of 10 was labeled as: "Complete elation. rapturous joy and soaring ecstasy." A rating of 1 was: "Utter depression and gloom, completely down. All is black and leaden" (p.273). The mean (average) rating was 6.14 for women and 6.0 for men, just above the middle of the scale. A rating of six was labeled: "Feeling pretty good, 'OK'." This study is consistent with others in showing that the average person is "pretty happy."

What does this relatively high average happiness imply? Among other things, it means that the average person is probably quite well-adjusted. Robin Goodwin (1992) obtained scores on 201 married couples on a scale validated to measure overall levels of adjustment. She found that one item on the inventory was highly correlated with the total adjustment score. That item? "Overall, just how happy are you?" Thus, happiness predicts total adjustment. Better adjusted people are happier, and happier people are better adjusted.

People who have higher levels of adjustment are better at coping with the problems life throws at them. Faced with a financial shortfall, a poorly adjusted person may become anxious or depressed, throw up his hands, and do nothing constructive to solve the problem. A well-adjusted person may take a second job, contact credit holders to arrange smaller monthly payments, and stop spending money on anything but essentials. It is thus not surprising that coping styles are related to happiness, with some suggestion that those who develop more effective coping strategies tend to make themselves happier.

Factors in Happiness

According to one theory, happiness consists of two major components: long-term affective states and short-term affective states (Kozma et al., 1992). The *long-term states* represent a continuing background of emotion that is quite stable from month to month and year to year. They may well be grounded in experiences beginning in childhood, supplemented by average, continuing emotional experience over a lifetime. If you had a reasonably happy childhood and have continued to have predominantly positive emotional experiences, you are likely to have positive long-term affective states. If your history of emotionally-relevant experiences is more negative, you will have long-term affective states that are correspondingly negative. The *short-term states* are based on recent events in your life, such as the birth of a child or failing an exam. Kozma and his colleagues find support for an *additive model*, in which current happiness is an additive combination of the long-term and short-term states. If your long-term state is quite optimistic, based on a lifetime of relatively positive events, going on vacation will increase your current state of happiness, while losing your job will decrease it.

George Sand captured the essence of one of the major long-term factors in happiness: **"There is only one happiness in life, to love and be loved"** (*Letter to Lina Calamatta*, March 31, 1862). Indeed, many of the factors involved in determining long-term states have to do with social relationships. Sigmund Freud and his colleagues in the psychoanalytic school have long held, for example, that your relationship with your parents during childhood is an important determinant of later adjustment and happiness. Much of current theory in developmental psychology similarly acknowledges the central role of early parent-child relationships in adult adjustment. In addition, one study assessed many possible components of happiness and showed that personal autonomy, competence, positive social relationships, and self-esteem are the most important contributors to happiness (Sheldon et al., 2001)

Later in life, most people develop many other associations, the most central of which are love relationships. Michael Argyle and his colleagues asked nearly 500 people to rate each of a number of positive events on a 100-point scale measuring how happy each event would likely make a person (Henderson, Argyle, and Fernham, 1984). Table 13-6 shows some of their results: It may not surprise you to learn that "falling in love " was the happiest event. Making up after an argument, getting married or engaged, and going out with friends also made the top group of positive events.

Other studies further document the positive impact of ongoing love relationships. Both men and women derive considerable happiness from marriage, and married people are happier than singles. In some studies, only about 20% of divorced men and 15% of divorced women reported that they were "very happy." Among singles, 25% of women and 20% of men reached this high level of positive affect. Marrieds do best of all, with 35% of men and 41.5% of women in the "very happy" category, despite considerable variability in happiness among couples (Russell & Wells, 1994).

While a wide variety of studies have long supported the positive emotional impact of marriage, it is important to note that the cause-effect relationships here are not entirely clear. We could conclude that marriage causes happiness. However, it is also possible that the direction of causality is essentially the opposite of that: People with high, stable happiness and adjustment are more likely to marry, stay married, and remain happy in that marriage.

Marriage is usually followed by the birth of children. Are they the "bundles of joy" that tradition would have them be? While many couples report that their children are a source of joy and fulfillment, studies of marital satisfaction do not support that assertion. A clue comes from an examination of Table 13-6, which reveals that the only high-positive item mentioning children is the birth of a child. A number of studies have assessed marital satisfaction at various points in a marriage, beginning before the couple has children and going through the pre-school, school, and teen years to retirement and the death of the first spouse. In general, couples with children between the ages of 5 and 12 are happier than those with pre-schoolers or teenagers. However, they are by far the happiest before they have children and after the children leave home. Don't be disappointed. Your parents still love you!

There are, of course, many other long-term factors in happiness. They include health, friendships, work, success, recreation, and exercise, and religion (Townsend et al., 2002). Personality traits associated with greater happiness include extraversion and tendermindedness (Doyle, 2000). Some studies have shown that In addition, there may well be genetic predispositions that contribute to the typical happiness level of any given individual. We know that heredity is involved in such negative emotional states as anxiety and depression (Kendler et al., 2002), as well as in many normal personality traits (see Chapters 10 and 16). Evidence suggests that genetically based neurochemistry may be involved as well. It is therefore reasonable to entertain the hypothesis that happiness is also affected by our genes, though evidence of such a predisposition will have to await future research.

On the short-term side of the emotional equation, current and recent events are important determinants of happiness. Remember that "falling in love" tops the list in Table 13-6. Similarly positive events, such as doing well on an examination, getting promoted, or simply going out with friends, are also mood-boosters. Conversely, the breakup of a relationship, doing poorly on an examination, not getting promoted, or sitting home alone when you had hoped to go out can detract from happiness. It is important to note, however, that you can experience negative affect about a single event but be happy overall or vice versa. This is a particularly important point because it suggests that happiness is not an entirely unitary phenomenon. It has multiple positive and negative components, and these components are partially independent. For example, you may have had one day last month that was a truly bad day. You got a 'C' instead of the expected 'A' on your exam, had an argument with your boy- or girlfriend, and came down with a severe cold. However, if your ongoing level of happiness falls nears the population average of "quite happy," you probably bounced back fairly quickly. You felt bad that day and perhaps for a day or two thereafter, but gradually returned to your usual happy state.

Adaptation Level Theory

A more general theory of behavior that also applies to emotion suggests that we react to new stimuli on the basis of our present level of adaptation. Your adaptation level is your current, neutral level of functioning relative to some specific stimulus situation. We automatically establish a neutral point or adaptation for each of a variety of kinds of stimulation, and we then compare any new stimulus with this middle ground to see whether it is higher or lower. Listen to some sounds around you. If they seem neither loud nor soft, they are near your adaptation level for sound intensity. Sounds of higher intensity than these will seem loud, and less intense sounds will be evaluated as soft. If you hear mostly louder or softer sounds for a period of time, your adaptation level goes up or down accordingly.

The adaptation level concept also applies to psychological phenomena. A classic case in point is income level. If you are a working college student, you may have a low income - say $10,000 a year. When you graduate, you may start a job at $25,000 a year, which will initially seem like a very high income given your $10,000 adaptation level. However, if you look back on the $25,000 fifteen years later when you are making $50,000, it will seem very low because your adaptation level has moved up. To take the concept a step further, your sense of accomplishment, success, or positive outcome will depend on your existing level of adaptation. Should you thus become one of those still rare millionaires, you would soon adapt to having a million dollars, and perhaps ten million would be required to make you feel more successful (Groot, 2000).

Emotion operates in the same way. If you are happy now with a lover who seems to attend to all your needs, good grades in your courses, a comfortable income, and good health, you can bet that you won't continue to be happy unless things get noticeably better (Lucas et al., 2003). Your adaptation level is always a neutral point, and only something above neutral will make you feel happy. Doesn't seem fair, does it? But, that - as the adaptation-level theorist would say - is life.

Solomon's Opponent-Process Theory

Adaptation-level theory essentially suggests that the emotions tend to balance toward a neutral point over relatively long periods of time. Richard Solomon (1980) took this idea a step further, looking at immediate, as well as long-term, emotional tendencies. His *opponent-process theory* suggests that emotions balance toward a neutral point not only in the long run but also in the short run. Specifically, every emotion causes an opposite emotion to occur (Figure 13-7). Solomon hypothesizes that an emotional event first elicits a *primary* state, a largely unlearned, "automatic" response. That state, in turn, triggers an *opponent* state that is the emotional opposite of the primary state. The opponent state starts later than the primary state, lasts longer, and becomes stronger with repetition, while the primary state becomes weaker.

Solomon initially observed that highly positive emotional experiences seem almost invariably to be followed by emotional lows. You are ecstatic that you won $500 in the lottery, but a few hours or days later feel rather glum, per-

haps because you now think you have spent too much of the money too quickly. The reverse also occurs. For me, a good example is exercise. When I am doing routine jogging or biking, I find the whole thing tedious and boring, and I feel miserable; however, later I experience genuine pleasure, both in a relatively immediate sense of well-being and in the knowledge that I am improving my health. A less routine example is the sky-diving described in Chapter 2. The fear I felt as I looked down 3000 feet just before that first jump was shortly followed by an elated sense of pleasure and accomplishment as I collapsed my chute after landing. With repeated jumps, the fear grew weaker and the pleasure stronger. While my personal experience is only an anecdotal reaction, Solomon (1980) cites data demonstrating very similar reactions in other skydivers as well. The sport-parachuting example also supports the second principle from Solomon's theory: Repeating the emotional experience increases the relative strength of the opposing emotion. As you jump repeatedly, the fear lessens relative to the pleasure.

Studies based on opponent-process theory show that it may apply to a variety of phenomena. The theory has been supported by using hypnotic induction to generate emotions, by naturalistic observations of both humans and animals, by studies of the anxiety-inducing effects of certain chemical substances, and by investigation of consumer decisions (Schwartz et al., 2002; Ley, 1994). In addition, it has been used to explain the emotional "numbing" that occurs in some combat veterans and others who have undergone traumatic emotional experiences.

Keys to Emotion 4

The Neurophysiology of Emotion

Emotion clearly has a neurophysiological basis, a point driven home particularly by the evolutionary theories we discussed earlier in the chapter. When you are very happy, angry, sad, or fearful, you have a subjective feeling of the emotion, but you also experience a strong physiological reaction. Take fear, for example: Jennifer's pounding heart and rapid breathing were signs of the physiological changes that are a part of emotion. The fact that Jennifer may be more (or less) upset than you would be under the same circumstances suggests that there are important individual differences in the experience and expression of the emotion. You undoubtedly know some people who easily panic when faced with danger and others who are quite calm. Recent studies show that such differences in emotionality are heavily influenced by genetic predispositions, which are expressed in the structure and functioning of the nervous and endocrine systems. We have already mentioned these various aspects of neurophysiology in connection with some theories of emotion, like those of Arnold and Panksepp. Now we review what is known about the role of the autonomic nervous system, the endocrine system, the amygdala and limbic system more generally, the cerebral cortex, and neurochemistry.

The Autonomic Nervous System

The autonomic nervous system (ANS) is a major subdivision of the peripheral nervous system. It sends nerves into such organs as the heart, blood vessels, kidneys, stomach, and intestines. The ANS has two main subsystems, the sympathetic and the parasympathetic, both of which originate in the hypothalamus. The *sympathetic nervous system* - Cannon's "emergency" system - acts to facilitate the arousal of major functions by producing a widespread neural discharge that mobilizes the body. When you experience an intense emotion, such as fear or anger, the sympathetic system goes into action. It causes such changes as an increase in heart rate, a rise in blood pressure, and a change in blood flow pattern away from the skin and stomach and toward the muscles of the limbs (see Figure 13-8). These changes increase your level of alertness and your readiness to act. Such heightened arousal is often referred to as the *fight-or-flight* response, a term coined by Cannon (1927).

The second branch of the ANS, the *parasympathetic nervous system*, is dominant during periods of relaxation and acts primarily to conserve and store (rather than expend) energy. It tends to maintain internal states and produce calmness and rest. If you eat a large meal, then sit down to relax, your parasympathetic system is dominating visceral and glandular functions. Your heart rate will slow, blood pressure will be lowered, and relatively large amounts of blood will be routed to your stomach and skin, rather than your limb muscles. But suppose that while you are relaxing in your easy chair someone throws a rock through your window. Now the sympathetic system takes over, mobilizing your body systems for quick reaction. Digestion will be virtually halted, and you may subsequently experience uncomfortable digestive side effects.

In addition to having opposing effects, the parasympathetic and sympathetic systems differ in other ways as well. In general, the influence of the parasympathetic system on the visceral organs is more specific than that of the sympathetic system. In addition, the neurotransmitters that facilitate the flow of neural impulses to the muscles or glands differ in the two systems. In the sympathetic system the principal transmitter is norepinephrine, while in the parasympathetic system it is acetylcholine.

The Endocrine System

As pointed out in Chapter 3, the endocrine system consists of a number of glands that produce chemicals called *hormones*. The endocrine glands that play the greatest role in emotional arousal are the adrenal glands, which are perched on top of the kidneys. Among the hormones produced by the cortex of the adrenal glands are *glucocorticoids*, which promote the conversion of stored proteins and fats to glucose. Glucose is needed under conditions of arousal to increase levels of energy and to repair damaged tissue. The glucocorticoids mediate the response to stress (see Chapter 15) and are important to the normal functioning of the immune system, which wards off disease. The medulla, or inner part of the adrenals, is the source of the key hormones involved in the fight-or-flight response: *epinephrine* and *norepinephrine* (see Figure 13-8).

These hormones are instrumental in heightening levels of such body functions as heart rate and blood pressure. The increased arousal levels are in part a function of the fact that epinephrine helps break down body protein and thereby increases glucose levels in the blood. Breathing rate accelerates, increasing levels of blood oxygen, and the combination of glucose and oxygen increases heart rate, constricts blood vessels, and causes other changes associated with sympathetic dominance.

Through the hypothalamus, where the autonomic nervous system originates, stimulates the *pituitary gland*, which in turn controls the release of such substances as adrenal hormones. One of the hormones produced by the pituitary is ACTH (adrenocorticotropic hormone). This hormone is released when the pituitary is stimulated by substances produced by the hypothalamus. The ACTH circulates through the blood to reach the adrenal cortex and cause production of the glucocorticoids. Under conditions of emotional arousal, the amount of ACTH and therefore of glucocorticoids increases markedly to support the emotional reaction. There is some evidence that the pattern of hormones released varies systematically from one emotion to another. Happiness and sadness, for example, produce quite different endocrine patterns in some studies (Brown et al., 1993).

It should be apparent by now that emotional arousal is multiply determined. It is a function of both neuroelectrical activity in the autonomic nervous system and hormones produced by the endocrine system, and these two systems influence each other. In addition, the central nervous system is importantly involved in emotional arousal.

The Role of the Brain

The autonomic and endocrine systems clearly play important roles in emotion. However, it is the brain that recognizes and interprets emotional stimuli, formulates psychological and physiological reactions to those stimuli, and activates the autonomic and endocrine systems.

One of the pioneer researchers in the study of brain functions in emotion was James Papez (1937), who proposed the existence of a circuit in the brain, now known as the *Papez loop*, that mediates emotional responses. His theory was revised by Paul MacLean (1949), who gave Papez's circuit the name *limbic system* (Figure 13-9). Although research has led to modifications of the Papez theory, he was basically right in concluding that the limbic system is central to emotion, and his work provided support for the Cannon-Bard theory. The limbic system receives direct, emotionally relevant input from the senses and acts to integrate that input and send emotional information on to the cortex (Anderson & Bushman, 2002).

Earlier hypotheses suggested that the hippocampus may be the primary limbic structure in emotion. However, current work focuses principally on the *amygdala*. In fact, James LeDoux (1994), one of the major current theorists in this area, makes the amygdala central to his theory, and there is considerable evidence to support its role. The evidence comes from lesioning studies in monkeys and from observations of the results of damage to the human brain. If, for example, the amygdala is removed from aggressive animals like the lynx, they become quite docile. Similarly, removal of the amygdala eliminates the aggressive behavior that is sometimes a problem in epileptic patients. Similar studies point to a central role for this important limbic structure in fear and associated escape and avoidance behaviors, as well as anger (Zald, 2003; George et al., 1995). Further evidence comes from neurochemical studies. Claudia Farb and her colleagues studied glutamate, a neurotransmitter found in the amygdala (Farb et al., 1992). They found that it is clearly involved in the mediation of emotion and emotional learning.

Douglas Derryberry and Don Tucker (1992) point out that the amygdala and other limbic structures can hardly act alone to coordinate and process emotion. Rather, the brainstem, and particularly the cortex, are also involved in an integrated system for dealing with emotion. An ascending emotional system, taking emotional information from the autonomic nervous system and limbic areas to the cortex, triggers adaptive perceptual and cognitive processes mediated by cortical structures. A descending system permits the cortex to influence limbic structures and thereby coordinate the processing and expression of emotion through endocrine, ANS and motor functions. The specific areas of the cortex involved in emotion include parts of the frontal and temporal lobes, the cerebellum (Schutter et al., 2003), and possibly the parietal cortex as well (Veit et al., 2002). In addition, there are hemispheric differences in the processing of emotion, with some studies showing more processing by the right hemisphere than the left (Peper & Karcher, 2001).

There is also considerable current interest in the possibility that the right and left hemispheres of the brain may have somewhat different functions (see Chapter 3). Although hypotheses concerning lateralization of functions originally focused on cognitive activities, more recent work has examined the differential roles of the two hemispheres in emotion (Peper & Karcher, 2001). Studies of patients with brain lesions have shown that people with left-hemisphere damage tend to be depressed, tearful, and withdrawn, whereas those with right-hemisphere damage tend to lack emotional expression or to at times show inappropriate happiness. Other work has demonstrated lateral differences in the processing of specific emotions, such as happiness. These observations might suggest that the right hemisphere is specialized for negative mood states while the left hemisphere is specialized for positive mood states or else projects no mood state at all, a position adopted by Richard Davidson and his colleagues (Tomarken & Davidson, 1992).

Unfortunately, other studies have not been entirely consistent with these observations (B. Smith, Kline, & Meyers, 1990). One alternative possibility is that the right hemisphere may perform virtually all aspects of the processing of emotion, a hypothesis for which there is considerable support (Silberman & Weingartner, 1986). Another possibility is that we need to separate emotion into two components, content and intensity. In that case, there is evidence that the content of emotion (for example, whether it is happiness or sadness) is processed by the right hemisphere and its intensity (how strong the emotion is) is a function of the left hemisphere (B. Smith et al., 1990; R.A. Davidson et al., 1992). Which of these hypotheses is correct? Well, your guess is about as good at this point as that of the various researchers and theorists. Further research with such brain imaging techniques as PET scans and MRIs may well yield more definite answers in the near future.

Neurochemistry in Emotion

James Henry (1992) has theorized that the various emotions involve different patterns of neurochemicals in the brain. What happens, for example, when a threat appears? If you feel confident that you can overcome the threat, you may feel anger. In that case, Henry argues, the hypothalamus and amygdala signal the ANS to release norepinephrine. The combination of ANS and hormonal arousal causes your blood pressure to rise, your heart to pound, and your breathing to become shallow and fast. If you are not so confident, you may experience fear. Your fear reaction is mediated by the amygdala, which triggers the production of a different neurotransmitter, epinephrine. Other neurotransmitters and hormones are also involved in responses to stress, as Chapter 15 suggests (Henry, 1993).

Keys to Emotion 5

Conclusion

It seems clear that emotional experience is complicated. This complexity is reflected in the multiple philosophical and psychological principles that aspire to explain it and in the scientific findings. Happiness - the emotion we dealt with most fully - defies simple logic in that it cannot be predicted very effectively from such things as winning the lottery. On the other hand, we know that the average person is reasonably happy most of the time and we know something about the long-term and short-term factors that contribute to overall current happiness levels. Perhaps more importantly we can recognize that happiness is a "typical" emotion, in that its general principles apply to other emotions as well. We now know that all these emotions have both physiological and psychological components, that they are influenced by both genetics and learning, and that they interact with cognition and are related to definite facial expressions. We also know that the emotions are expressed in the physiology of the autonomic nervous system, the endocrine system, the limbic system, and other areas of the brain. And we can expect that ongoing research will help us to further understand the multiple genetic and environmental contributing factors that underlie the vast range of human emotional experience.

Summary

1. Most definitions of emotion include four components: a feeling state, cognitive processes, physiological changes, and behavior.
2. Emotion and motivation are closely related. Emotions often motivate behavior, and motives are frequently emotional.

Yardsticks for Emotion

1 Psychologists use three principal measures of emotion: self-report, direct observation, and psychophysiological measurement

2 Self-report approaches present several problems: difficulty in determining accuracy; variability in subjective experience; denial of emotions; and differences in cultural norms.

The Structure and Expression of Emotion

1. Major theories of the structure and expression of emotion include Darwin's basic theory of evolution, Plutchik's primary emotion theory, Tomkins' facial feedback theory, Izard's universal facial expressions, and learning theory.
2. Darwin concluded that facial expressions of emotion are universal because they have evolved as an adaptive species characteristic.
3. Primary emotion theorists hypothesize a small number of basic emotions that may be genetically linked through evolution to specific classes of stimuli. Characteristics of primary emotions include innate neural substrates, unique feeling states, and universality.
4. Robert Plutchik identifies eight basic adaptive reactions that serve as prototypes for all emotions. They vary in intensity, similarity, and polarity.
5. Fromme and Clayton propose a circular ordering based on two dimensions: hedonism and autonomic arousal.
6. Tomkins' facial feedback theory suggests that basic emotional facial expressions are inborn and that we infer our emotions on the basis of our expressions.
7. Izard believes that emotions have evolved with the brain and that both the major emotions and their associated facial expressions are innate and hence universal. Infant and cross-cultural studies support his theory.
8. Biological theorists hold that the role of learning is to determine the relative frequency of emotions, modify their external expression, and influence their strength and stability.
9. Learning theorists believe that all emotions are acquired. Averill hypothesizes that emotions are social constructs developed through cultural learning.

The Experience of Emotion: Major Theories

1. Physiological theories of emotional experience include the James-Lange, Cannon-Bard, and psychobiological approaches.
2. Cognitive theories include Schachter's cognitive-labeling, misattribution theory, transfer of excitation, and cognitive appraisal.
3. According to Lazarus, each emotion has three major components: cognitive appraisal, action impulses, and patterned somatic reactions. Arnold emphasizes the roles of memory and expectation in the cognitive appraisals that lead to emotion.
4. Psychoanalytic theory holds that emotions are primarily the result of unconscious processes.

Happiness

1. The sources of happiness are not always obvious. Money, in particular, does not necessarily bring lasting bliss.
2. The average person is quite happy and well-adjusted.
3. Current happiness is a combination of long-term and short-term affective states.
4. Among the major factors in happiness are genetic predispositions, relationships, health, work, success, recreation, and exercise. Current and recent events also affect happiness levels.
5. We establish and modify adaptation levels to which our emotions are relative. Opponent-process theory holds that every emotion causes an opposite emotion, which increases in strength with repetition.

The Neurophysiology of Emotion

1. Emotional arousal is a function of several physiological changes, including those in the autonomic nervous system (ANS), the endocrine system, and the brain. The sympathetic branch of the ANS acts to facilitate arousal to prepare the body for fight or flight.
2. The primary hormones involved in the fight-or-flight response are epinephrine and norepinephrine, produced by the adrenal glands.
3. Among brain areas involved in emotional functioning are the limbic system, the amygdala, and the cortex. The two cerebral hemispheres may be differentially involved in processing emotion.

Ask Yourself

1. Why has emotion been such a difficult term to define?
2. What appear to be the major components of emotion?
3. What roles do the autonomic nervous system and hormones play in emotions?
4. What are the three major methods of measuring emotion? What are the main drawbacks of each?
5. According to Plutchik, how are the various emotions related to each other?
6. Describe the role that cognition plays in the following theories: James-Lange, Cannon-Bard, cognitive labeling, Lazarus, Arnold.
7. What evidence is there for the idea that emotions are innate and universal? What is your view of the role of biology versus learning in emotion?
8. What major neural and endocrine systems are involved in emotion?
9. Discuss the major factors in happiness. How do the findings match with your personal experience?

Further Readings

Bashore, T., & Rapp, P.E. (1993). Are there alternatives to traditional polygraph procedures? *Psychol. Bull.*, 113, 3-22. This interesting review article lays out what we know about lie detection, including future possibilities.

Carlson, J., & Hatfield, E. (1992). *Psychology of Emotion.* Fort Worth: Harcourt. The authors provide and excellent detailing of the literature on emotion. If you want to go well beyond my chapter, read their book.

Ekman, P. (1993). Facial expression and emotion. *Amer. Psychol.*, 48, 384-392. Paul Ekman reviews what we know about cross-cultural similarities and differences in facial expression and their implications.

Frank, M., Ekman, P., & Friesen, W. (1993). Behavioral markers and recognizability of the smile of enjoyment. *J. Pers. Soc., Psychol.*, 64, 83-93. This study is a good example of the work of Paul Ekman and his colleagues, in this case differentiating between the basic smile of enjoyment and smiles posed for social purposes.

Graham, S., Hudley, C., & Williams, E. (1992). Attributional and emotional determinants of aggression among African-American and Latino young adolescents. *Devel., Psychol.*, 28, 731-740. This interesting study of attribution theory as it applies to minority groups is noted in the text.

LeDoux, J. (1989). Cognitive-emotional interactions in the brain. *Cognit. Emo.*, 3, 267-289. LeDoux succinctly lays out the underlying neuropsychology of emotion and cognition, focusing on the amygdala as the key to the emotion network.

Mayer, J., Gaschke, Y., Braverman, D., & Evans, T. (1992). Mood-congruent judgment is a general effect. *J. Pers., Soc., Psychol.*, 63, 119-132. In this interesting paper, John Mayer and his colleagues report three studies of the mood congruence effect discussed in our 21.

Plutchik, R. "A Psychoevolutionary Theory of Emotions," *Social Science Information.* 21(1982), 529-553.This paper contains an excellent statement of Plutchik's structural approach and reviews considerable research on emotionality.

Reeve, J. (1992). *Understanding motivation and emotion.* Fort Worth: Harcourt. Reeve provides a good overview of The psychology of emotion, integrating it with motivation.

Psychology in the 21st Century

Mood Congruence

Introductory Psychology Student: "I've just gone over my notes for this exam, and I just don't know thematerial."

Roommate: "What makes you think that?"

Student: "I couldn't even answer my own questions about the Panksepp theory, excitation transfer, or facial feedback. Obviously, I'm going to fail this one cold."

What the student has not told his roommate is that he just came back from a major fight with his girlfriend of two years and is in a very bad mood. The roommate is also unaware that the material the student doesn't know is only a small proportion of that covered in the five chapters scheduled for the exam. Considerable evidence would suggest that mood is affecting the student's evaluation of his preparation for the exam and by his self-esteem as it relates to academic performance (Tafarodi et al., 2003). He has selectively focused on what he doesn't know, rather than what he does.

We do not yet know very much about the effects of emotional mood states on cognition and behavior, but we are learning that the impact can be quite powerful. In one study, children in the third and seventh grades first underwent a mood manipulation in which they viewed line drawings and photographs that induced happy or sad mood states. They then examined a series of drawings and photos of neutral faces and were asked to indicate the expression on each face. When they were in a bad mood, they tended to call the faces sad. When they were in a good mood, the very same faces were labeled as happy (Stegge et al., 1993). Gordon Bower (1981) obtained a similar effect in another study when subjects were hypnotized and put in happy or sad moods. After the hypnotic mood induction, subjects read a passage describing an interaction between a happy man and a sad man and detailing their lives and emotions. They were then asked to indicate which character they identified with. The "sad" subjects identified with the sad character and the "happy" subjects with the happy character. And other studies support the association of mood with perception (Killgore & Cupp, 2002; Knight et al., 2002).

We know that the mood congruence effect goes beyond such self-relevant judgments to a variety of laboratory tasks and to non-laboratory settings in the community. People in good moods expect their favorite political candidate to win, taxes and violence to decrease, the economy to improve, and their own good fortunes to increase; those in bad moods are more likely to have just the opposite expectations. We have also learned that the mood congruence effect applies not only to happy and sad moods, but to a range of positive and negative mood states that appears to span the emotions (Erk et al., 2003). Angry and disgusted mood states have many of the same basic effects as sadness, and feeling relaxed or loving can have effects similar to those of happiness.

Mood congruence affects not only judgments about oneself and the world, but also the effectiveness with which learning takes place. In one study, subjects learned three paired-associate word lists that varied in how positively or negatively toned the words were. They showed better learning of lists containing words that were more consistent with their mood states (DesRosiers & Robinson, 1992). A similar effect was seen in the Bower (1981) study described above. When subjects were brought back to the laboratory a day after reading the story about the happy and sad men, they recalled more about the character they had identified with the previous day than about the other character. Previously happy subjects remembered more about the happy man, sad subjects about the sad man, even though they were now in a neutral mood. In a final study, 60 female undergraduates were subjected to a mood induction procedure, then learned 20 words that were related to either elation or depression. They later recalled more of the words that were consistent with their induced mood states (Wilson et al., 1991).

So it seems clear that mood congruence effects do occur. The question is, why? What psychological and neurophysiological mechanisms underlie these important effects of emotion on judgment, learning, and performance? We suspect that the differential availability of memories may be a key (Kano et al., 2003). To understand this explanation, we begin with the observation that it is easier to learn new material that relates to information already in memory. Suppose, for example, that in preparation for a trip to France and Germany you are trying to learn some useful phrases in those languages. If you have taken a year of French and no German, it will be far easier to learn a new phrase in the former language than in the latter. Similarly, learning to use a new piece of computer software is far easier for the experienced computer user than for the novice, even though neither of them has ever seen this particular program before. In each case, the prior experience provides a frame of reference that makes learning easier. In a similar way, a good or bad mood increases the availability of memories congruent with that mood and thereby makes it easier to acquire or recall information that is mood-consistent (Erez & Isen, 2002).

There are two problems with the availability hypothesis. First, we have very little empirical data to support this explanation of mood congruence. Second, it provides no immediate neurophysiological basis for the effect. Presumably, neural mechanisms mediate mood congruence. It is particularly important to gain some understanding of these mechanisms because they may tell us something more generally about the relationship between emotion and cognition. Research on mood congruence will be an important focus within the psychology of emotion as we move into the 21st century. It will help us to understand not only the basis for this interesting effect, but also the psychological and neural underpinnings of the emotion-cognition relationship. It is for these answers that we look to the future.

The Critical Thinker

To Catch a Thief: The Psychophysiology of Lying

"Lie detectors" - electronic devices that record physiological responses while a person is being questioned - are widely used in criminal investigations, national security operations, and employee screening. The usual procedure begins with a pretest interview. The interrogator explains the procedure, including the use of the lie detector, or *polygraph*, and goes over a list of emotionally neutral and "loaded" questions that may have relevance. Neutral questions might include: "Is your name John?" and "Is it sunny outside?" Loaded questions might include: "Were you personally acquainted with the deceased, Melissa Jones?" "Have you ever been in Melissa Jones' home?" and "Did you kill Melissa Jones?" The examiner also attempts to impress upon the subject the accuracy of the lie detection process (Lykken, 1974).

For the test session itself, electrodes are attached to the subject to measure such physiological responses as heart rate, respiration rate, and electrodermal activity (see Figure 13-1). Although there is no specific physiological response associated with lying, noticeable increases in overall arousal to loaded questions signified by changes in these measures are taken as an indication of an emotional response to lying. With the electrodes in place, the interrogator repeats the questions from the pretest interview, then compares responses to loaded questions with responses to neutral questions. A pattern of larger responses to loaded questions is taken as a sign of deception. Many polygraphers actually do not rely entirely on the psychophysiological measures. They also carefully observe the person's behavior for "obvious" signs that he is lying. One experienced polygraph administrator told the author that a suspect who entered the room, sat down, crossed one leg over the other, and began picking lint off his trousers would almost surely be judged guilty - and that was before the machine was even turned on!

The Basic Hypothesis or Contention

Police agencies and prosecutors have long contended that a lie detector test is a very good indication of whether or not a suspect is guilty. Many police agencies, in fact, try hard to persuade suspects to take a polygraph test because they believe it will make their jobs quicker and easier. Corporations interviewing potential or current employees have similarly contended that lie detection is an accurate and useful tool. That is why over 2 million people were tested annually by corporations until recently and why large numbers still are.

What Is The Evidence?

David Lykken (1984) estimates a 65% percent accuracy rate for polygraph testing and points out that an innocent person has a 50% chance of failing, though others put it far lower (Greenberg, 2002; Ben-Shakhar et al., 2002). The major problem is that the polygraph recording detects not only the arousal of lying, but also the arousal that arises simply from the stress of being tested. Imagine how aroused you would be if suddenly accused of a crime you didn't commit! Even if the test were 90% accurate, as those who make money giving it claim, many innocent people would fail. If, for example, 1,000 people are given the test and if 50 are, in fact, liars, 45 will be caught. However 95 truthful people will also fail the test, and thus 95 out of 140 failures, or 68 percent, will actually be truthful people.

Supporting Lykken's strong stance against the use of polygraph testing are a variety of studies showing that high percentages of truthful people will be polygraph "liars" (MacLaren, 2001). The Figure shows the results of one such study. Another team of investigators had polygraph experts examine the records of 100 individuals who had been suspects in thefts (Kleinmuntz & Szucko, 1984). Of the total, 50 had later confessed to the thefts, while the other 50 were innocent because in each case someone else had confessed. The experts decided that over one-third of the clearly innocent people in this second group were guilty and that nearly 25% of the confessed thieves were innocent!

It is because these and other studies demonstrate a high degree of inaccuracy that most attorneys refuse to have clients take police lie detector tests. And it is for the same reason that the American Psychological Association has advised against the use of lie detectors (Abeles, 1985), polygraph evidence is not permissible in most courts, and Congress passed the Employee Polygraph Protection Act of 1988, prohibiting virtually all nongovernmental polygraph use. Ironically, then, when the polygraph operator confidently asserts to the suspect that the test is highly accurate, the studies and resultant expert opinions would suggest that it is *he* who is lying!

An additional reason for avoiding the use of polygraphs is the occurrence of false negatives - instances in which the person is intentionally lying and is not caught by the machine. Many repeat criminals are psychopaths, who have little or no sense of guilt. It is therefore easy for them to lie without experiencing the anxiety that produces the arousal picked up by the polygraph. In addition, there are "tricks" you can learn that make it quite easy to pass a lie detector test. In fact, spies are often taught how to pass polygraph tests so that they can serve as double agents. This is precisely what happened when Fidel Castro's Cuban agents infiltrated the CIA between 1977 and 1987. They repeatedly passed CIA lie detector tests because they knew how to lie without failing the polygraph (Safire, 1989).

Is the Evidence Open to Alternative Interpretations?

Advocates of polygraph testing and the admission of lie detector evidence in the courts have long contended that the studies must somehow be flawed (Rosenfeld, 1995). In some cases, studies have used laboratory subjects who are instructed to lie (or not lie) for purposes of the research, rather than real criminal suspects. The physiological measures also vary somewhat from one study to another, as they do from one police agency to another, making it more difficult to compare some studies with others. And in some cases, the researcher conducting the polygraph interviews is less experienced than many police or corporate polygraphers, suggesting that she might not interpret the results as accurately. However, on balance the evidence is overwhelming: Lie detection is, at best, very inaccurate. And no convincing alternative interpretation of the evidence has been offered.

Do We Need More Evidence?

Although we should always be open to any new evidence that might be offered, it appears that the inaccuracy of lie detection is so well established as to make extensive additional research unwarranted. Instead, we should perhaps turn our energies to a search for more accurate and effective ways of distinguishing between truth and falsehood. In fact, a number of investigators are doing exactly that. One possible improvement on the polygraph is the voice-stress analyzer. In this approach, the person's voice or a tape of it is played into a machine and a printout shows a series of waves that represent the voice. Another method is to examine patterns of eye movement as subjects scan a series of objects and report which ones they have seen before. If the subject lies, the mismatch between the eye movements and the verbal report can be detected (Cohen et al., 1994).

A third alternative under development relies on the possibility that lying and telling the truth produce different patterns of brain electrical activity (Bashore & Rapp, 1993). A final possibility is the analysis of facial expression, sometimes combined with other measures (Ekman et al., 1991). The problem with all four of these newer approaches is that none has been shown to be any more reliable than the polygraph.

What Can We Conclude?

We must conclude that traditional polygraph lie detection, widely advocated by police agencies, is inaccurate and inadequate. It yields far too many false negatives and, more importantly, false positives. Although the search for alternative methods of lie detection has thus far not yielded a demonstrably reliable, valid method, such a method may well be developed through further research. The bottom line? We need a reliable, valid method of lie detection, and thus far we do not have one.

Probe

Smile! You're on Candid Camera

When is a smile not a smile? The rather unexciting answer to this riddle is: when it is a social cue (Sarra & Otta, 2002). Consider a personal example: When my son or daughter, at the age of 16 or 17, was about to leave on a Saturday night date, I would often sternly say something like: "Now I expect to see you back by 10:00, and *don't* be late." This harsh, parental edict caused no family conflict because they could see that I was smiling broadly. The smile served as an easily read social signal that I was kidding about the unreasonably early hour. Indeed, it completely negated the verbalization, and they knew instantly that they could believe the facial expression, rather than what I had said. This is a straightforward example of the important role of emotional expression in social communication.

Smiling is a good example of an emotional expression that may not be. What I mean is that we typically think of smiling as a simple expression of happiness - and it can be. However, studies done by Paul Ekman and others indicate that smiling is perhaps more often a method of social communication than an expression of emotion (Frank, Ekman, & Friesen, 1993; Devereux & Ginsburg, 2001). In fact, Ekman and his colleagues have identified seventeen kinds of smiles. Of these, one, called the *Duchenne smile*, after the French scientist who first noted the difference between real and posed smiles, is an expression of genuine enjoyment. The remainder are not (Messinger et al., 2001). They are smiles that are posed for such purposes as hiding sadness (called "masking smiles") or persuading another person that you are enjoying your conversation with her ("false smiles"). In these cases, the facial expression is obviously a method of social communication, not an expression of positive affect. But beware! Observers can differentiate between smiles of enjoyment and social smiles (Fernandez-Dols et al., 2002).

One investigator analyzed the timing of smiles during the course of conversations and found that smiles occur at the same points as verbal responses called *back channels* (Brunner, 1979). Such back channels are indications that the listener is involved in the conversation and understands, agrees or disagrees, or in some other ways reacts to the speaker. Just as the listener often consciously creates verbalizations such as "sure" and "uh huh" to indicate her attentiveness, she will smile as another way of facilitating the communication process. Smiling in such situations has little to do with the emotional nature of the listener's response.

The social function of smiles was also noted in a study in which people were observed in three different situations: a bowling alley, a hockey game, and walking on the street. In the bowling alley, it was found that smiling occurred more often when the person had turned toward friends (31% of the time) than when he was still facing the bowling pins (3%), whether the bowler's score was good or bad. At the hockey game, fans were seen to smile as much when socially interacting with people near them as when their team scored. Finally, pedestrians smiled regularly when talking to friends but did not smile simply because it was a nice day. The researchers concluded that smiles function as communication devices more frequently than as expressions of emotion (Kraut and Johnson, 1979).

This social function of smiling, and of emotional expression more generally, is found even in infants and primates. The social smile appears at the age of about eight to ten weeks, when it seems to be an invitation to continued social interaction (Izard, 1978). The smile can indicate familiarity and usually invites attention and care and more generally enhances the social interaction process (Baudouin et al., 2000). Beyond just smiling, the infant very soon has a wide repertoire of nonverbal emotional expressions. Carroll Izard studied infants and their mothers to see just how effective these expressions are in accomplishing their purposes. He and a colleague asked mothers to indicate what actions they typically take when their infants display a particular emotional expression (Huebner & Izard, 1988). They found that infant facial expressions are very effective social communication devices, indeed. For example, when the infant expresses physical distress, most mothers pick him up, love and cuddle him, and take care of his needs. Primates also use facial expression and gestures socially. They are used as social signals to assess the motivations of others, to maintain positive social interactions, and to ward off potentially hostile behavior.

The social function of emotional expression applies to far more than smiling. In fact, not only facial expressions of the other emotions, but also such nonverbal expressions of emotion as gesturing and posture serve to facilitate social interaction. In fact, *dynamic systems theory* of emotion suggests that emotions and their expression are created in a social context and both reflect and inform that context (Fogel et al., 1992).

When, for example, you are interacting with another person, your expressions of emotion or apparent emotion reflect your purpose in having the conversation and your "reading" of the other person. She, in turn, is reading you and using emotional expression - smiling and otherwise - to better communicate with you. Consider the socially complex situation that exists as that first, second, or third date is drawing to a close. Does your dating partner want to kiss? Is she or he willing to kiss? Do more than kiss? Neither the questions nor the answers will often be verbal. You carefully attend to each other's nonverbal expressions of emotion both to pose the questions and to learn the answers - but I guess you already knew that!

The social functions of emotional expression, including gender-differentiated expression, are initially learned in the family context as the child grows up. Some interesting research shows, in fact, that family support for the appropriate expression of emotion can have very positive outcomes. Children from such emotionally expressive families tend to be more popular in school, have more positive self-concepts, and engage in more positive social behavior.

Horizons in Abnormal Behavior

The Physiology of Feelings: Are Emotions Different?

Think of times when you have been extremely joyful, angry, sad, and frightened. Your psychological feelings were obviously very different. You feel "choked up" when sad, "hot under the collar" when angry, and the like. Moreover, different emotions produce different appearances: the downcast eyes and drooping facial muscles of sadness; the stunned, paralyzed appearance of sudden fear; and the explosive tenseness of anger are quite easily distinguished. But what of the accompanying physiology? Is that also different? This is an important question that is both old and new in the psychology of emotion.

In 1953, Albert Ax reported that anger and fear produce differing finger temperatures, but others were unable to consistently replicate these results, and research on the problem dropped off. More recently, however, studies support a physiological differentiation in terms of varied patterns of autonomic nervous system (ANS) activity. Robert Levenson, Paul Ekman, and their colleagues have used two methods in particular to look for ANS patterns. In one, subjects are taught how to "construct" specific facial expressions associated with specific emotions - anger, fear, disgust, etc. In the other, subjects are asked to vividly relive personal experiences of these same emotions. In one study Levenson and his colleagues (Levenson et al., 1990) found 14 distinctions among ANS patterns associated with 6 emotions. Common differences include heart acceleration with anger and fear, but deceleration with disgust, as well as differences in such measures as finger temperature between fear and anger (Levenson, 1992). Further knowledge of the differential physiology of the emotions through future research will greatly enhance our overall understanding of human emotional experience.

Faraway Places: Emotions in Tahiti

People who grow up in Japan, Africa, or France do not express all the same emotions in all the same ways as those who grow up in the United States. Even languages reflect these cultural differences. For example, a small culture of Philippine head hunters, the Ilongot, use one word, *liget*, for both grief and anger (Russell, 1991).

To learn more about the universe of various human characteristics, such as emotion, anthropologists often study small, isolated, preliterate cultures. In one such investigation, Robert Levy (1982, 1985), examined the way Tahitian villagers express various emotions and the words and phrases they use to label those emotions. He was able to distinguish between emotions that are subject to hypercognition and those subject to hypocognition. *Hypercognition* means that the native language includes a large number of terms for what we Westerners might label as a single state. *Hypocognition* means that relatively little distinction is made among what we would characterize as several different states.

A good example of hypercognition in Tahiti is anger. The Tahitians have separate words for a variety of forms of anger, including irritability, rage, and the ordinary feeling of anger. There is also a substantial linguistic structure dealing with how to evaluate anger, what causes it to occur, how it operates within the person, and what should be done about it. The implication is that anger is a culturally and socially important emotion in Tahiti and therefore requires detailed knowledge and explicit, unambiguous forms of expression and interpretation.

An example of hypocognition is sadness. Although the Tahitians have separate words for severe and mild grief, the concepts of longing, loneliness, and generalized sadness are not separately named. The implication is that sadness is less important in Tahitian culture than in Western society and therefore requires less clear-cut differentiation.

Vent That Anger?

In the violent American society of the 1990s, psychologists have increasingly asked just how best to deal with anger. One long-standing "treatment" has been to suggest venting the rage. In fact, if you have ever been very sad or very angry, you have probably had someone tell you that you will be better off if you "let it out." If we can vent our rage, a process called *catharsis*, we will be less angry and less violent.

Like so many other old adages, this one appears to be basically incorrect. Catharsis has, at best, a very temporary calming effect. Beyond that, it may have the opposite result. When subjects in laboratory studies are angered, then invited to repeatedly administer electric shocks to the person they believe has offended them, giving the initial shocks should reduce their anger through catharsis. Instead they *increase* the shock on later trials, suggesting that their anger is growing.

Getting out of the laboratory into the real world, it is often argued that participating in or watching violent sports should produce catharsis and thereby reduce aggressive behavior. In fact, this has been a common justification for sports like boxing and football. However, results show the opposite effect. Such sports increase anger and violence, rather than decreasing it, and cultures that are generally more belligerent emphasize more violent sports as well. Indeed, so clear is the evidence against catharsis that William Lewis and Amy Bucher (1992) advise psychologists to stop using it as a therapeutic technique. Clearly, our task in The 21st century is to look for better ways of reducing the rage that often underlies violent behavior.

Key Terms 1

psychophysiology
self-monitoring
self-report

Key Terms 2

activator
adaptive reaction
facial feedback theory
primary emotions

Key People 2

Charles Darwin

Paul Ekman
Carroll Izard
Robert Plutchik
Silvan Tomkins

Key Terms - 3

action impulse
Cannon-Bard Theory
cognitive appraisal
cognitive-labeling theory
James-Lange theory
misattribution
patterned somatic reaction
primary appraisal
secondary appraisal
psychobiological theory
transfer of excitation
unconscious

Key People 3

Magda Arnold
Sigmund Freud
William James
Carl Lange
Richard Lazarus
Neal Miller
Jerome Singer

Key Terms 4

adaptation level theory
greatest happiness principle
opponent-process theory

Key People 4

James Stuart Mill
Richard Solomon

Key Terms 5

adrenal glands
autonomic nervous system (ANS)
endocrine system
glucocorticoids
Papez loop
parasympathetic nervous system
pituitary gland
sympathetic nervous system

Key People 5

James Papez

Keys to Emotion 1

1. Most definitions of emotion include four components.
   - A. What they are?
     - Feeling state, cognitive processes, physiological changes, behavior
   - B. How emotions and motives are related?
     - Emotions often motivate
     - Motivations are often emotional.

2. To conduct studies, we must have measures of emotion.
   - A. The major types
     - Self-report, direct observation, psychophysiological.
   - B. The major self-report approaches?
     - Interviews, questionnaires, self-monitoring.
   - C. The problems with self-report measures?
     - Hard to determine accuracy
     - Variability of subjective experience
     - Denial
     - Varied cultural norms
   - D. Some psychophysiological indicators?
     - Heart rate, blood pressure, muscle tension, respiration rate, brain electrical activity, electrodermal activity.

Keys to Emotion 2

1. There are two broad types of theories of the structure and expression of emotion.
   - A. What they are?
     - Evolutionary/biological
     - Learning
   - B. Which type is better supported by research?
     - Evolutionary
2. There are several related evolutionary theories.
   - A. The first theorist to address the evolution of emotion?
     - Darwin
   - B. What the major evolutionary theories are and the names of the theorists?
     - Evolution: Darwin
     - Primary emotion: Plutchik
     - Facial feedback: Tomkins
     - Universal facial expression: Izard
   - C. Darwin's major conclusion?
     - Emotions and their facial expressions have evolved and are universal.
3. Primary emotion theory hypothesizes only a few basic emotions.
   - A. The origin of the primary emotions?
     - Inherited as a universal, species characteristic
   - B. How they are elicited?
     - By genetically-linked stimulus classes

C. Where other emotions come from?
Combinations of the primaries

D. The characteristics of primary emotions?
Innate neural substrates
Unique feeling states
Universality

4. A major theorist is Robert Plutchik.

A. The languages of emotion?
Subjective, behavioral, and functional

B. The number and nature of basic adaptive reactions?
Eight
Four pairs of polar opposites

C. Three dimensions of emotional variability?
Intensity, similarity, polarity

D. An alternative primary emotion theory?
Fromme and Clayton's circular ordering.

5. Facial feedback theory is also a derivative of Darwin.

A. The major theorist?
Tomkins

B. Why you become happy?
Because you smile

C. A mechanism that may underlie the feedback effect?
Facial muscles restrict blood flow, which produces cooling and warming of the brain, affecting neurotransmitters.

6. Facial expressions and emotions may be innate.

A. A modern theorist with this view?
Izard

B. The predicted variability of facial expression with culture?
Little or none.

C. The results of supportive infant research?
Emotional expressions are present at birth

D. The results of cross-cultural research?
All cultures associate the same expressions with the same emotions.

7. Learning plays a role in emotion.

A. Its role according to biological theorists?
Determine relative frequency
Modify external expression
Influence strength and stability

B. Izard's theory?
Emotions are innate
Learnd cues or activators elicit emotion
Cognitive processes are affected by learning.

C. Its role according to learning theorists?
Learning is the sole or primary basis for emotion and its expression.

D. Averill's theory?
Emotions are social constructs developed through cultural learning.

Keys to Emotions 3

1. Emotional experience has several agreed-upon components
   - A. What they are?
     - Subjective feelings, cognitive appraisal, physiological arousal, motor expression, motivational tendencies.
2. Some theories of emotional experience are heavily physiological.
   - A. The major theories and theorists?
     - James-Lange
     - Cannon-Bard
     - Psychobiological - Panksepp
   - B. The James-Lange theory?
     - The physiological response causes the emotional feeling.
   - C. The Cannon-Bard theory?
     - The stimulus simultaneously causes both visceral responses and emotional feelings.
   - D. Some problems with the James-Lange theory?
     - The organs respond too slowly
     - The organs may not be able to differentiate emotions.
3. Cognitive theories give thought processes a primary role in emotion.
   - A. The major theories?
     - Cognitive labeling - Schachter
     - Misattribution
     - Transfer of excitation - Zillman
     - Appraisal - Lazarus
   - B. Schachter's basic contention?
     - Physiological response produced by stimulus is cognitively labeled on the basis of the situation.
   - C. How the epinephrine-uninformed group in Schachter-Singer reacted?
     - Labeled the emotion on basis of the situation
   - D. What misattribution theory says?
     - Arousal from one source is misattributed to another.
   - E. What increased sexual imagery in the bridge study?
     - Transfer of excitation generated by crossing a dangerous bridge.
   - F. The two types of appraisal in Lazarus?
     - Primary - evaluation of stimulus
     - Secondary - evaluation of coping strategies
   - G. Two major types of coping processes?
     - Palliation
     - Direct action
4. Emotional experiences are often of unconscious origin
   - A. Whose theory this is?
     - Freud
   - B. What produces anxiety and anger?
     - Strong unconscious conflicts

Keys to Emotions 4

1. Happiness has been addressed by philosophers as well as psychologists.
   - A. Aristotle's view?
     - Happiness lies in the pursuit of pleasure.
   - B. Plato's view?
     - Happiness is a product of virtue

C. The Epicurean view?
  Hedonism - Achieve happiness by maximizing pleasure.

D. Mill's view?
  Happiness defines what is appropriate.

2. The sources of true happiness are somewhat elusive.

A. The relationship of income to happiness?
  Modestly correlated

B. What happens when someone wins the lottery?
  Increased happiness for a short time only.

3. Researchers have measured happiness in the population.

A. What proportion of people are happy?
  Probably 60 - 80%

B. How happiness relates to adjustment?
  Positively

C. What current level of happiness represents?
  A combination of long-term and short-term states.

4. A number of factors contribute to happiness.

A. What some major ones are?
  Genetic predisposition, health, exercise, work, relationships, success, recreation, recent events.

B. A major social source of happiness?
  Love relationships

C. The happiest group based on marital status?
  Married couples

D. When couples are happiest?
  Before having children and after they leave the home.

5. Adaptation level influences reactions to new stimuli.

A. How it applies to emotion?
  Emotions balance toward neutral over time.

B. What Solomon's theory says?
  Every primary emotional reaction causes an opponent state to occur.

Keys to Emotion 5

1. Emotion is a product of multiple neurophysiological systems and processes.

A. What the major ones are?
  Autonomic nervous system
  Endocrine system
  Amygdala
  Cortex
  Neurochemistry

B. The action of the sympathetic nervous system?
  Mobilizes the body for action.

C. The action of the parasympathetic system?
  Conserves energy

2. The endocrine system is important in emotion.

A. The major glands involved?
  Adrenals

B. The role of glucocorticoids?
  Produced by adrenal cortex
  Increase energy and repair damage

Bolster immune system to fight disease

C. The key hormones for fight-or-flight?
Epinephrine and norepinephrine
Produced by adrenal medulla

D. The role of the pituitary gland?
Produces ACTH, which causes adrenal cortex to produce glucocorticoids.

3. The limbic system is important in emotion.

A. The major limbic structure involved?
Amygdala

B. Some emotions influenced by the amygdala?
Anger/aggression and fear

4. The cerebral cortex is also important.

A. The major lobes involved?
Frontal, temporal, and possibly parietal.

B. Whether the two hemispheres deal with emotion differently?
Probably, but there are several different theories.

5. Neurochemistry is no doubt important in emotion.

A. Some examples of likely neurochemical involvement?
Anger may involve release of norepinephrine and fear release of epinephrine.

Chapter 14

Personality: Theory, Research, and Assessment

Outline

The Human Personality

Issues and Assumptions in Personality Theory

Personality and Evolution: Nature and Nurture

The Major Theories

Psychodynamic Theory: Sigmund Freud and His Colleagues

Psychoanalytic Theory: Sigmund Freud

Jung's Analytic Theory

The Social Analysts

Evaluating Psychodynamic Theories

Cognitive/Behavioral Approaches

Personality Through Reinforcement: B.F. Skinner

The Cognitive-Behavioral Framework

Bandura's Social Learning Theory

Rotter's Cognitive/Behavioral Theory

Evaluating Cognitive-Behavioral Theory

Humanistic Theory

Carl Rogers: The Self-Concept

Evaluating Humanistic Theories

Traits, Situations, and Their Interactions

Gordon Allport

Raymond B. Cattell

Hans Eysenck

The Big 5

Walter Mischel's Situationism

Interactionism

Evaluating Trait and Interactional Theories

The Neurophysiology of Personality

Neuroanatomy and Neurochemistry

Neural Networks

Personality Assessment

Objective Personality Tests

Projective Personality Tests

Networking

DID YOU KNOW that much of your behavior may be determined by motivations you are not even aware of? That things you see your parents do repeatedly, even at the age of 1 or 2, may affect your adult personality and behavior? That perceiving yourself as an effective person is associated with improved performance? That there may be only 3 to 5 major dimensions that can completely describe your personality? That your personality is strongly influenced by hereditary predispositions? Well, if you didn't know these things, you soon will! Beginning with Sigmund Freud, psychologists have developed numerous theories to explain what personality is and how it develops and functions. Four main approaches or schools of thought have emerged: the psychodynamic approach; the cognitive/behavioral approach; humanistic theory; and trait/interactional approaches. Each offers different insights into the nature of personality and how it is acquired. We will talk about the major theories in each of these schools and discuss research on such topics as self-concept, unconscious motivation, and the role of genetics in personality. We will also cover methods for assessing personality.

The field of personality has an especially close relationship to the fields of stress, psychopathology, and treatment - the subjects of our next three chapters. As Brendan and Winifred Maher (1994) point out, the study of personality has enhanced our understanding of psychopathology, including the effects of stress, and vice versa. Similarly, we have applied our growing understanding of both personality and pathology to the development of effective therapies, and observations made during therapy have been a major factor in the development and revision of personality theories. It will thus not be surprising to learn that such major personality theories as psychoanalytic theory and humanism deal not only with normal personality functioning but also with the effects of stress, with abnormal behavior, and with its treatment. For example, we will discuss Sigmund Freud's psychoanalytic theory of personality in this chapter because it provides a basis for understanding how the normal personality develops and functions. But it also explains how behavior becomes abnormal and how psychologists and psychiatrists might treat it, and those aspects of the theory are covered in Chapters 16 and 17.

Down and Out?

Jodi was sobbing uncontrollably. At 3:00 a.m., she was sitting alone in her dorm room contemplating suicide and had in her hand a bottle with enough pills to do it. She opened the bottle, poured half the pills into one hand, and picked up a glass of water with the other.

Jodi had twice cancelled and rescheduled an appointment with a psychologist at the University Counseling Center, but had finally, very hesitantly, gone yesterday. Very anxious and depressed, she spent much of each day crying. Her stomach in knots, she had glanced furtively about her for possible acquaintances as she approached the counseling center. When Dr. Warner asked why she was there, she had burst into tears and managed to blurt out something about depression. She told him that her middle-class parents had divorced when she was 12 and that she had missed her father terribly. Away from home for the first time, she was having a rough freshman year - low grades, no friends, no dates, no fun - "the whole nine yards," as Dr. Warner put it. When the session ended, Dr. Warner scheduled her for 12 weeks of counseling to begin the following week. Jodi had agreed, but all that seemed far away as she brought the handful of pills to her lips.... We'll return to Jodi's problems later in the chapter.

The Human Personality

Psychologists want to know. The Army wants to know. The CIA wants to know. IBM wants to know. And probably *you* want to know: Who are you? What are you like? Are you typically happy or sad? Anxious or calm? Kind or mean? Affectionate or cold? Extraverted or introverted? In other words what is your personality like? You are no doubt curious about your own personality, and you constantly assess the personalities of people you meet. Indeed, the only difference between you and a psychologist is that the psychologist does a more formal assessment based on theory and research and using carefully developed tests.

Thinkers throughout history have been interested in personality. The early Greeks tried to explain it in terms of balances among four bodily substances they called *humours*: phlegm, yellow bile, black bile, and blood. Assessing personality on the basis of such physical characteristics remained popular for several centuries, leading to such "scientific" approaches as *phrenology*, which purported to be able to determine personality characteristics by mapping the bumps on your head. If phrenology doesn't sound like your cup of tea, what about a modern-day alternative, *astrology*? Some studies suggest that up to 30% of the population believe that personality descriptions and predictions based on astrological signs are accurate (Clarke, 1991), and even skeptical people in one study became much less skeptical when given flattering astrological descriptions of themselves (Glick, 1989). There is, of course, absolutely *no* scientific evidence to support astrology (Crowe, 1990), so don't rely on your horoscope when making major decisions.

Formal, scientific theories of personality did finally come along at the beginning of this century. It was then that Sigmund Freud, whose approach we will consider shortly, developed the first of those theories. Since that time, considerable effort has been expended in conducting research on personality and in developing additional theories. While not all the theories we will discuss in this chapter are as scientifically developed or detailed as would be ideal, all are nevertheless basically scientific and hence a major step beyond speculation and casual observation. Based on what we now know, we can define *personality* as an individually unique, consistent pattern of behavioral and psychological attributes that endure over time and across situations.

How much impact has the field of personality had? Well, views vary, but many psychologists believe that personality is the field that most clearly brings psychology together (Smith & Vetter, 1991). Research in such diverse areas as perception, development, neuroscience, cognition, motivation, emotion, social psychology, and psychopathology all come together in the study of the human personality. It is in this field that psychology has most directly and clearly applied its diverse principles and research methods in an attempt to predict and understand the causes of human behavior. And it is with that focus in mind that we take up the field of personality.

The study of personality takes two forms: theory and research. Personality theorists have constructed models of personality development and functioning in an effort to understand how consistent patterns of behavior occur and what factors influence those patterns. Personality research takes many forms and represents a wide-ranging attempt to conduct empirical investigations of the major factors that underlie thought, emotion, and behavior. Some research is done in a direct attempt to test the major theories of personality, while other research is of a more exploratory nature.

Issues and Assumptions in Personality Theory

Each personality theorist addresses what he considers to be the major causes of patterns of human behavior. In order to do so, he must, directly or indirectly, deal with several sets of issues concerning the causes. In particular, any personality theory is concerned with at least four major sets of issues and assumptions: determinism versus free will, the origins of personality, the motivation of behavior, holism versus elementalism; and the continuity of personality over time.

Determinism versus Free Will. The issue of free will versus determinism has been debated for centuries. The *free will* argument holds that the individual is responsible for his own actions and has genuine free choice. *You* decide what courses to take, select a career, choose a spouse, and make daily decisions and choices. *Determinism*, on the other hand, argues that behavior can be fully explained by scientific principles. It is caused by consistent, definable factors, such as early life experiences, physiological drives, or unconscious motivating forces.

The free will argument does not lend itself to scientific theories of personality. It assumes that no scientific laws underlie behavior. We can therefore never hope to predict, understand, or control the actions of individuals because there is no way of knowing its causes. A scientific theory of personality *must* assume that it is possible to derive scientific laws specifying cause-effect relationships. Because the theories we will describe in this chapter are scientific theories, all take a deterministic viewpoint.

The Origins of Personality. Theorists have addressed two major issues relating to the origin and development of personality. The *nature-nurture* issue, outlined in Chapter 1, deals with the roles of heredity and environment in personality development. Most theorists agree that both are involved, but they differ greatly as to the relative importance of these factors.

The second issue deals with the role of *early life experience*. Some theorists believe that personality structure is largely set during the early years of life, while others see personality development as a process that continues throughout life.

Motivation. As we discuss in more detail in Chapter 12, the forces that impel people to engage in behaviors are collectively referred to as *motivation*. Two motivational issues are of particular concern in personality theory: whether motivation is primarily conscious or unconscious, and whether it is goal-oriented. Some theorists hypothesize that motivation is largely *unconscious*. In such theories, the personality includes a variety of motive systems that lie below the level of awareness but nevertheless have considerable influence on behavior. Other theories stress the conscious nature of motivation.

The second motivational issue deals with the extent to which motivation is seen as *teleological*, which means goal-oriented or purposeful. Some theorists argue that the individual is motivated primarily to reduce drives. When you become hungry, for example, you are motivated to eat, thereby reducing the hunger drive. Others believe that goals are more important motivators. We strive not to reduce drives but to realize our potentials.

Holism versus Elementalism. Some theorists assume that the individual functions as a totality or whole. This *holistic* approach argues that the person operates as a total entity and that no individual bit of behavior can be fully understood without reference to that totality. If we want to understand why some people have much more aggressive personalities than others, we would have to study aggression in the broader context of the total personality; we could not learn much from studies of aggression as an isolated characteristic. The opposing position is *elementalism*, which assumes that human behavior can best be understood by breaking it down into specific fragments that can be carefully defined and studied. Proponents of this approach would prefer to look only at aggression and study it in depth.

The Continuity of Personality. A final issue is the *continuity* of personality - the extent to which the personality of any given individual remains consistent over time. If you think back over the past ten or fifteen years of your life, you will probably conclude that you have changed somewhat - matured perhaps - but that in most ways you are the same person you have always been.

Continuity is an important assumption for personality theory because without it there would be no personality. Moreover, it is important for you as an individual to be able to count on the stability of your own personality. Consistency enhances feelings of psychological well-being and provides a sense of identity that allows you to plan for the future. While we expect people to change somewhat, we hypothesize that the central characteristics of a given individual will remain stable over all or most of a lifetime.

What evidence do we have for continuity? Actually, quite a bit, most of it from longitudinal studies in which the same people are followed for many years. Two good examples are the *Berkeley Guidance Study* and the *Oakland Growth Study*, both conducted at the Institute of Human Development at the University of California at Berkeley. Beginning in 1929 and 1932, respectively, these studies followed their subjects from childhood into middle age. Assessments of personality characteristics were conducted throughout adolescence and again in the 30s, 40s, and 50s. The results? Personality characteristics showed a high degree of continuity.

Personality and Evolution: Nature and Nurture

It is a striking observation that a vast majority of humans have entirely normal personalities. Although about 16% of people are experiencing some mental disorder in any given month, most have only mild symptoms, and only about 3% ever have the most severe disorders (Kessler et al., 1994). While this by no means suggests that psychological disorder is no problem - it is, as we discuss in Chapter 16 - it does mean that most people are reasonably well-adjusted and capable of leading productive lives most of the time. Why? Why do most people have normal personalities? Why don't we see much higher levels of severely abnormal behavior?

One theoretical answer to this scientific puzzle is that normality is a product of ancient environments and of required adaptations to those environments - a product of evolution. Remember that evolutionary psychology postulates the selective genetic passage of adaptive behavioral characteristics from species to more evolved species and from generation to generation (Weiss et al., 2002). Natural selection over millions of years has thus produced a gradually evolving and increasingly adaptive set of human personality traits.

Although it may not be obvious, many personality theorists have at least implicitly subscribed to this evolutionary view. Freud's theory, for example, is based in evolutionary concepts that were in their infancy at the time he developed psychoanalysis. Similarly, trait theorists like Eysenck and Cattell seek to discover the basic sets of human personality traits, and their theories assume that those traits may be genetically based and hence subject to evolutionary influence. And evolutionary, adaptive processes have often been used to account for the highest levels of human consciousness, unconscious functioning, and the entire process of personality development (Borkenau et al., 2001).

Nature, Nurture, and Personality. An evolutionary viewpoint requires not only a long history of environmental influences, but also evidence of genetic factors, and a growing body of research strongly confirms the role of heredity in personality. In fact, an important, though controversial, future application of personality research may make it possible to change your personality in a very direct way. The Human Genome Project (Chapter 10) has been completed, providing a full genetic map (van Ommen, 2002). With this important navigational device in hand, we will soon be able to better manipulate genes in order to change human characteristics. We might attack such problems as cancer and heart disease, modifying gene structures to prevent or treat these disorders (Stein et al., 2002). However, the ability to manipulate genetic structure means that we could eventually intervene to modify the individual human personality - providing, of course, that it is strongly influenced by heredity. Let's see if it is.

Your father is extraverted and so are you, and both you and your mother are very open to your experience and very agreeable. Moreover, studies show that you are not alone. The personality test scores of children and their parents are significantly correlated. To what extent are these trait similarities due to genetics and to what extent were you influenced by your parental environment? As in such areas as intelligence (Chapter 9), temperament (Chapter 10), and alcoholism (Chapter 5), the answer must come through careful empirical studies.

Twin studies of personality functioning suggest a substantial genetic component (Kendler, 2001; Figure 14-1). The Minnesota Study of Twins Reared Apart includes 56 pairs of twins separated on average at age 10 weeks, with no contact until 34 years later. They have been compared with identical twins reared together and with fraternal twins reared apart and together. Across a number of personality trait dimensions, the median (middle) correlation for these identical twins reared apart is .49, as compared with .52 for identical twins reared together and only .21 and .23 for fraternal twins reared apart and together, respectively (Markon et al., 2002). These studies are consistent with the results of a large-scale investigation of 30,000 twin pairs spanning four countries. It also showed a heritability of about 50% (Eaves et al., 1999), as did the Minnesota Twin Family Study (Iacono & McGue, 2002), the German Observational Study of Adult Twins (Spinath et al., 2002), and a Japanese Study (Ando et al., 2002). Such specific traits as extraversion, sensation-seeking, and sense of well-being, for example, are quite highly heritable (Miles et al., 2001; Soyka et al., 2002; Weiss et al., 2002). Moreover, molecular genetic studies have begun to identify the specific genes responsible for some normal personality traits (Bookman et al., 2002)

Adoption studies provide additional support for the heritability of traits. When we study adoptees, each participant has both biological and foster (environmental) parents. Personality similarity to the biological parents supports the role of heredity, while greater similarity to the adoptive parents would support an environmental hypothesis. Although both sets of parents clearly have some influence, studies consistently show that the personalities of adoptees are more like those of their biological parents (Tsuang & Faraone, 1995).

So there is clearly a strong genetic component in personality. In fact, we have begun to map some of the specific genes involved. However, three cautions are important. First, genetic factors clearly do not entirely account for personality. They are important, but heritability averages around 50%, leaving considerable room for environmental influence. The second caution is that the overall 50% heritability does not mean that all traits are subject to equal degrees of genetic influence. For example, it appears that distractibility and aggression are not as heritable as extraversion, neuroticism, and sensation-seeking (Miles et al., 2001; Eaves et al., 1999). The third issue, which applies specifically to twin studies, is the concern that identical and fraternal twins may be treated differently by their parents and that this difference in treatment may partially account for the higher concordances in identicals when both groups are raised together. However, studies do not support this concern.

Overall, we must conclude that personality has a strong hereditary component, but that environmental factors, interacting with genetics, are also important. What we inherit is a set of predispositions toward particular traits, not the full-blown traits themselves. The genetic predispositions interact with the environment to form the trait we see in adulthood. It is also important to remember that we must consider the heritability issue on a trait-by-trait basis. Some traits are heavily influenced by heredity, others primarily by environment.

The Major Theories

Most of the major theories of personality fall into one of four broad approaches or schools of thought: the psychodynamic school, humanism, cognitive-behavioral theory, and the trait approach. Let's consider each of these plus the neurophysiology of personality and personality assessment.

Keys to Personality 1

Psychodynamic Theory: Sigmund Freud and His Colleagues

Despite an interest in the origins of personality that has spanned many centuries, it is striking that no one was able to develop a truly scientific theory until the beginning of the twentieth century. If you don't recognize one other name in this book, you will recognize the name of the man who created that first scientific theory: It is Sigmund Freud, without doubt one of the most influential theorists in the history of psychology. In fact, a recent survey of psychologists named Freud as the second of the five most important authors in the field (the first was B.F. Skinner; Norcross & Tomako, 1994). We will discuss Freud's psychoanalytic theory, then take up, in turn, theories of Carl Jung, Alfred Adler, Karen Horney, and Harry Stack Sullivan.

Psychoanalytic Theory: Sigmund Freud

Freud published his first book, *The Interpretation of Dreams*, in 1900. It contained a scientific theory of personality, psychopathology (abnormal behavior), and psychotherapy. His approach is called psychoanalytic theory and it is now part of a broader school of thought called the psychodynamic school.

Freud had not started out to be a psychiatrist. He had studied medicine at the University of Vienna and gone into private practice as a clinical neurologist following his graduation in 1881. However, he soon found that his interest in emotional problems was greater than his interest in neurology. He therefore began to develop the basic ideas that would eventually become psychoanalytic theory. That theory, in turn, would provide the guiding principles for the first scientifically based approach to *psychotherapy* - a broad term referring to the treatment of psychological disorders by listening to and talking with a patient over a series of sessions.

By 1886, Freud was using his new therapy to treat patients, and between 1890 and 1900, he began to present his theory to groups of physicians in Vienna. They found it unacceptable, but Freud persisted and began to attract a steadily growing band of young physicians who listened with increasing respect to his ideas. The approach they were so impressed with is called *psychoanalysis* - a method of psychotherapy that emphasizes helping the patient to understand problems that she is not aware of, problems that are deeply buried in the unconscious mind. Before long, Freud's method was being taught around the world, and his small band had grown to hundreds and then thousands of followers, who formed an international group of practicing psychoanalysts. The influence of Freud's work is now so widespread, both in and beyond the fields of psychology and psychiatry, that it is difficult to say just where it stops. It is woven into the very fabric of the mental health professions and of society at large and has become not merely a theory but a way of thinking. We will outline Freud's concept of unconscious motivation, consider the structure and energy of the human personality, and discuss the conflicts and anxieties that all humans experience.

You Don't Know What You're Doing: The Unconscious. One of Freud's major contributions to our understanding of human behavior was his recognition that *unconscious* factors - those of which we are not aware - have far greater influence on our behavior than do conscious ones. He proposed a continuum of consciousness, ranging from acute awareness to the deeply unconscious, and he divided this continuum into three segments: the conscious, the unconscious, and the preconscious (Figure 14-2). In a famous analogy, Freud compared the *conscious* mind to the tip of an iceberg: It is the very small portion that is visible. It contains everything of which we are aware at any given time, and its contents change from moment to moment. The unconscious is much larger and more influential, containing powerful drives that are responsible for most aspects of human behavior (Schussler, 2002). Between the conscious and unconscious lies the *preconscious*, an area that contains thoughts, memories, and perceptions that can quite easily be brought into awareness (Ross, 2003). If, for example, you are asked for your phone number or your parents' first names, you can readily bring this information into awareness.

Freud found a number of ways to tap into the psychological treasure trove of the unconscious, and one of the most interesting is the *dream*. He hypothesized that the dream is a disguised version of a dangerous unconscious wish or impulse. As a result, psychoanalysts use dreams to gain insight into the unconscious functioning of their patients. In fact, even therapists not specifically trained in psychoanalysis interpret dreams much as Freud would (Bonime, 2002), and there is evidence that interpreting our own dreams can also increase self-understanding (da Rocha Barros, 2002). In recent studies, Robert Stickgold and his colleagues at the Harvard Medical School have recorded dream content from many participants (Stickgold et al., 1994). They have studied cognitive processes in dreams, as well as emotional content (Hobson & Stickgold, 1994). And they report that anxiety is the emotion most frequently experienced in dreams, supporting Freud's contention that the dream is a release for pent-up, negative emotions. We have much more to say about the study of dreaming in Chapter 5.

Energy Dynamics and the Structure of Personality. Freud regarded the human body as an organic system that consumes food, converts it to energy, and uses this energy to perform both physical and mental activity. The energy for mental activity is called *psychic energy* or *libido*, and there is an *energy economy*, in which the individual has only a limited amount of energy available at any given time. The energy you use for jogging is no longer available that day for studying, and the energy you use for these two activities makes less available for social interaction.

Energy is used to fuel the activities of three hypothetical personality structures - the id, ego, and superego - that together determine behavior. The *id* is a part of your biological makeup and is present at birth. It is the ultimate source of all psychic energy. A very primitive structure, it is made up of drives and operates on what Freud calls the *pleasure principle*, meaning that it attempts to satisfy drives immediately through impulsive, irrational behavior and through fantasy (Holt, 2002). Impulsively deciding to go to a party when you had planned to study for tomorrow's big exam and daydreaming that you are an astronaut or famous neurosurgeon are examples of id influence.

The immature and irrational id would not long survive on its own. Some other structure is needed to permit rationality (logical reasoning) and provide contact with external reality. These functions are served by the *ego* - the aspect of personality that controls rational thought processes and has contact with external reality. It operates on the *reality principle*, meaning that it delays the gratification of an id drive until an appropriate object is located, then obtains the object and satisfies the drive. For example, if the id's hunger drive is active, the ego will take no action to satisfy it until food (the appropriate object) is located. Through the ego, the individual learns to differentiate between fantasy and reality, to plan ahead, and to gain some control over the external environment.

Behavior is also influenced by the social and moral values of society. These values are taught to the child by the parents and eventually form the *superego*, a set of internal social controls over behavior. This third psychic structure serves primarily as a "conscience," punishing the person for acts or anticipated acts that violate social mores or norms. It may, for example, stop someone from stealing food to satisfy the hunger drive by creating feelings of guilt for considering such an immoral act. A secondary function of the superego is to provide a set of goals - the *ego ideal* - which the person strives to achieve.

Conflict and Anxiety. Energy is employed by the three psychic structures to carry out their respective functions, and their relative energy level or "power" in the personality greatly influences behavior. A dominant id will lead to irrational, impulsive acts, a powerful superego to highly moralistic behavior patterns, and a dominant ego to realistic, rational behaviors. Freud proposed that the three structures are constantly competing for psychic energy to provide them with the "power" to control behavior. The person is thus constantly in a state of internal conflict - a clash among the opposing forces represented by the three psychic structures. For example, when someone cuts in front of you in heavy traffic, the aggressive drives of the id might cause you to take revenge by making some gesture that conveys your anger. The rational ego may block this potentially dangerous impulse (he might have a gun) and the superego might impose moral sanctions (it is wrong to commit such aggressive acts). Which structure will "win?" It depends on your individual personality and on which structure has the most energy available to it.

The conflict among the psychic structures is one major source of *anxiety* - an unpleasant emotional state characterized by nervousness and apprehension (Brenner, 2002; H.F. Smith, 2003). Although *reality anxiety* (fear) may arise from events in the external world, Freud was most concerned with anxiety that develops as a result of *intrapsychic conflict* -the competition among the three structures. *Moral anxiety* (guilt) occurs when the superego punishes the individual for immoral behavior. You might feel guilty if you gestured aggressively at that driver. *Neurotic anxiety* results from a conflict between the id and the ego. It arises when dangerous id impulses threaten to break through the protective barriers of the ego to invade consciousness and cause impulsive behavior. It is the most powerful form of anxiety and the one Freud believed to be the basis for psychological disorder (see Chapter 16).

The Defense Mechanisms. Anxiety is so painful that the individual must have some means of reducing it. Otherwise, we would constantly be overwhelmed by anxiety, and it would frequently lead to abnormal behavior. Freud therefore postulated the existence of *defense mechanisms* - processes that reside in the unconscious portion of the ego and act to reduce anxiety. These mechanisms operate to distort the anxiety-producing impulse in order to reduce its threat or to block the expression of the impulse entirely.

The major defense mechanism is *repression*, in which the ego uses its energy to force anxiety-producing impulses into the unconscious. Repression does not, however, mean that the anxiety is gone. In fact, the repressed impulses will tend to reappear in consciousness, where defense mechanisms will again be needed (Talvitie & Ihanus, 2002). As a result of repression, you may experience slips of the tongue, symbolic dreams in which repressed ideas make themselves known, or forgetfulness. For example, while taking that "impossible" required math course, you may find that you frequently forget where you left your notes or textbook and when the next exam is. To Freud, this means that repression is causing you to forget things related to the math course because not thinking about math reduces your anxiety. In fact, repression is often called *selective forgetting.*

Repression and the other defenses are also involved in the development of psychological disorders. They can distort reality, causing you to function less efficiently and effectively. You may, for instance, spend hours searching for missing math books and notes over the course of the semester as a result of repression. Although the defenses always distort reality to some extent and are involved in the development of disorders, they are also a part of normal personality functioning. If you've ever unconsciously tried to protect yourself by explaining away your shortcomings or failures (rationalization), by attributing your own objectionable ideas to others (projection), or by getting angry at your dog after a run-in with your parents (displacement), you've used defense mechanisms.

In a test of the defense concept, Fraser Watts and Kieran Coyle (1993) asked people who were afraid of spiders (spider-phobics) and those who were not (non-phobics) to learn and recall a list of words relating to spider phobia. Those who were spider phobic had significantly poorer recall for the words than those who were not. Why? Probably because the anxiety of the spider phobia had caused the phobics to repress words that would elicit that anxiety.

One line of research on repression has addressed the serious issue of repressed memories of childhood sexual abuse (Chapter 7). A girl who is sexually abused may repress the abuse and not remember it until adulthood, if ever. Researchers have found that at least 19% of those reporting sexual abuse repress it until adulthood (Loftus et al., 1994). We cover this interesting in Chapter 7. Other research has shown that some people (called repressors) readily repress anxiety-producing memories, while others (nonrepressors) do not. The two groups show neurological differences, and repressors recall fewer negative childhood events than nonrepressors. It appears that at least some of Freud's insights regarding the defenses were accurate.

A final important aspect of Freudian theory deals with the development of the personality through a series of biologically determined stages. We cover that part of the theory in Chapter 10.

What would Freud say about Jodi's depression? He would likely interpret it as resulting from childhood experiences, perhaps involving her early relationship with one or both parents. The basis for the depression would be seen as largely unconscious, and the forgetfulness would be interpreted as repression.

Contemporary Psychoanalytic Theory

Psychoanalytic theory has evolved considerably since Freud's death in 1939 in the forms of ego psychology and object relations theory. Whereas Freud's emphasis was on the biological, irrational forces of the id, modern psychoanalysis revolves around the rational influences of the ego. Three major ego psychologists are Heinz Hartmann, Anna Freud (Sigmund's daughter), and Erik Erikson. Hartmann, a student and close associate of Freud during the great theorist's final years of life, began *ego psychology*, a modification of psychoanalytic theory in which the ego, rather than the id, becomes the primary basis for human development and functioning. Anna Freud and Erik Erikson (Chapter 10) emphasized a similar ego-oriented theme in their theories of personality development.

The change in emphasis from id to ego modified the psychoanalytic view of human nature markedly. In Freudian theory, human behavior is heavily influenced by the unconscious, nonrational, physiological, internal forces of the id. In the ego theory of Hartmann and his colleagues, these forces are balanced by the conscious, rational, environmental, reality-oriented forces of the ego (Wallerstein, 2002). Conscious, willful cognition and the external environment are given much greater control over behavior, and the theory is more comprehensive than was Freud's original formulation.

The currently dominant approach in psychoanalysis is called *object relations theory*. It focuses on the importance of each person's relationships with a variety of objects (Buckley, 2003). Since "objects" in Freudian theory include other people, the primary emphasis in object relations theory is on the relationship between the child and its mother, as well as other caretakers (Ogden, 2002). The principal theorists include Melanie Klein (1975), Heinz Kohut (1984), and Otto Kernberg (1976).

Object relations theory originated in the work of Klein, who led the movement to shift psychoanalytic theory toward a greater emphasis on the importance of social relationships. The theory suggests that early object relations have a considerable impact on the child's development of a sense of self or identity, as well as feelings of psychological security and sex role. In the ideal case, the child bonds securely with the mother in early infancy and subsequently develops into a strong, independent individual. However, a destructive early relationship with the mother or any other social object can contribute to the later development of psychopathology.

The impact of these psychoanalytic theories continues to be strongly felt. Ego psychologists, object-relations therapists, and classical Freudian psychoanalysts treat many thousands of patients each year. In addition, the large body of research generated by the work of Freud and his colleagues continues to grow rapidly. And further developments in psychoanalytic theory itself occur each year.

But not all theorists interested in Freud's approach followed and extended his teachings so directly. Other psychodynamic theorists after Freud basically took his theory as a starting point, then made modifications that they felt improved upon his basic conceptualizations. There are, in fact, many neo-Freudians (those whose theories are based on Freud's), but we focus here on just a few of the major ones: Jung, Adler, Horney, and Sullivan.

Carl Jung's Analytic Theory

As a young physician just completing his medical training, Carl Jung was greatly impressed by Freud's book *The Interpretation of Dreams*. In 1906 Jung began corresponding with Freud, and the two soon met and worked together. So substantial was Jung's early involvement in Freud's work that he was elected the first president of the Psychoanalytic Association in Vienna. But he and Freud later clashed over important theoretical differences, and the two parted company in 1914. Jung was uncomfortable with Freud's emphasis on sexuality and also preferred to study psychosis, whereas Freud emphasized neurosis. Jung went on to develop his own unique theory of personality. It remains even now a very influential theory, though not nearly in a class with Freud's (Astor, 2002).

Conscious and Unconscious Functioning. In Jung's theory, the ego consists of all conscious aspects of the personality, including conscious thoughts, feelings, perceptions, active memories, and self- evaluations (Figure 14-3). The ego functions to structure external reality and interacts with the outside world, while also controlling the individual's self-perception and providing a sense of personal identity. The ego is protected by a social facade or mask - a public personality - called the persona, behind which the individual lives. The persona develops as a result of social pressures and is often not an accurate reflection of the person's real feelings and attitudes. You may, for example, project to others a persona of great self-confidence, whereas you actually feel quite inadequate.

Jung's view of the unconscious differed substantially from Freud's. In particular, he hypothesized a *collective unconscious*, one of his most controversial contributions to personality theory (Peery, 2002). This part of the personality contains experiences accumulated over generations of humanity and transmitted genetically to the individual as a set of universal tendencies. These tendencies, which include fear of snakes, love for one's mother, and belief in a supreme being, exist as archetypes in the collective unconscious. An *archetype* is a prototype from which copies can be produced (McDowell, 2001). There is, for example, a mother archetype that reflects and generates universal attitudes toward mothers. The mother archetype predisposes the infant to respond in certain ways toward its mother and is also reflected in many ways in the visual art, religion, mythology, and literature of various cultures. Other archetypes include the father, God, child, power, death, the demon, the hero, and earth. Each produces a universal tendency to respond in particular ways toward individuals or situations representing the archetype (Saunders & Skar, 2001).

Attitudes and Functions. Jung postulated that there are two basic types or *attitudes* of personality, introversion and extraversion. The introvert is interested in subjective feelings and experiences, while the extravert is interested in people and the outside world. In any given person, one attitude is typically conscious and dominant, the other unconscious and subordinate. Since Jung's time, considerable research has demonstrated that the differentiation between introversion and extraversion is indeed an important one: it reflects major differences not only in social attitudes but in many other aspects of the individual's behavior.

Jung also proposed four major psychological *functions* - ways in which the personality operates to influence behavior - which exist in opposing pairs: sensation versus intuition, and thinking versus feeling. *Sensation* is a reality function through which the individual closely observes the environment and takes it in. You may observe that one person always smiles when you meet her, while another seems to scowl or look away. *Intuition* organizes the world through subjective impressions; you have a hunch that the first person likes you, while the second one may not. Thinking and feeling further elaborate on experiences acquired through sensation and intuition. *Thinking* classifies experiences according to logical, discrete categories, while *feeling* classifies information according to its pleasantness or unpleasantness and arranges it into a value structure. You classify the first individual as a friendly person who makes you feel pleasant and the second as an unfriendly person who makes you feel unpleasant.

The Social Analysts

Three other post-Freudian psychodynamic theorists - Alfred Adler, Karen Horney, and Harry Stack Sullivan - are referred to as social analytic theorists because each emphasized the influence of social factors on human behavior. All three felt that Freud had made a major contribution to the understanding of behavior and that many aspects of his theory were basically correct. However, they differed from Freud in four major respects:

- They de-emphasized the role of biological factors.
- They gave consciousness a relatively more important role.
- They introduced the self as a construct in their theories, holding that knowledge of self is an important factor in behavior.
- They introduced sociocultural factors into psychodynamic theory.

Alfred Adler. The first of the social analytic theorists was Alfred Adler. He joined Freud in 1902 but was asked to leave Freud's inner circle a few years later when he proposed what seemed to be a radically different theory of personality.

Adler suggested that nearly all aspects of personality development take place in a social context and are influenced by feelings of inferiority that develop in childhood. The individual strives throughout life to compensate for inferiority, and it is thus inferiority that serves as the basic motivation for virtually all human behavior. This motivation becomes goal-oriented as the person strives to attain a state in which he is superior to his own earlier level of functioning.

Striving to compensate for inferiority and achieve superiority or self-perfection could be socially destructive if carried out with a purely selfish orientation. To reduce the likelihood of such selfish behavior, there is an innate, biologically-predisposed tendency toward *social interest* - a striving to engage in behaviors that are directly helpful to other individuals and to society more generally. The ideal expression of social interest leads to the simultaneous satisfaction of the needs of both the individual and society.

A final emphasis in Adler's theory is on the role of *birth order* in the development of the personality. The "only" child, for example, tends to dominate the parents during the formative years and develops habits based on rewards received for this dominant behavior. The first-born child may feel insecure when later children are born, and the second-born child may initially dominate both the parents and the older sibling and thus become an ambitious, striving individual. Surveys of the literature show that the influence of Adler's birth order concept on research has not only continued but increased (Watkins, 1992).

Karen Horney. Karen Horney became a fully trained psychoanalyst only to break away from the Freudian school in 1941. Her own ideas about the causes of behavior emphasized the innate capacity for human growth. In her view, every individual constantly strives for, but never quite achieves, the fullest realization of all potentialities.

According to Horney, social influences on the personality begin in the home, where the parents act as agents of society, and her theory is thus closely related to the object relations school (Ingram, 2001). The actions of the parents are central to the psychological growth of the child, and they should ideally provide a home life characterized by warmth, understanding, and mutual respect. The worst thing that parents can do is to display a lack of love and understanding for the child as he attempts to adapt to and confront the world. When parental love is lacking, the result may be a state of *basic anxiety* in which the child has an extreme feeling of isolation and hopelessness in a hostile world. Such anxiety can lead to *neuroses* - a class of disorders centering around high levels of apprehension or anxiety and involving disordered patterns of behavior. Horney also described other disorders, such as one that we define in Chapter 16, called borderline personality disorder (Paris, 2001).

Horney hypothesized that neurosis is basically a cultural phenomenon and that some cultures are more likely than others to create high rates of neurotic disorder (Ceccoli et al., 2000). In particular, cultures in which there is emotional isolation, tension, insecurity, and feelings of helplessness increase the likelihood that any given individual will develop a neurosis.

Horney also modified Freud's theory as it applies to women and is widely cited as an early contributor to feminine psychology. In that area, as in her role in psychoanalysis more generally, Karen Horney was a pioneer.

Harry Stack Sullivan. Whereas Adler spoke of innate social interest and Horney emphasized the role of culture and family in personality functioning, Sullivan stressed the importance of *interpersonal interaction* - the social exchange or relationship between two people (Hansen, 2002). The thrust of Sullivan's approach was that the individual develops a personality in order to satisfy needs, primarily through social interaction. He emphasized two principal kinds of needs: satisfaction needs and security needs. *Satisfaction needs* are basic biological requirements for survival, such as the needs for food, water, and sleep. The infant gradually learns to satisfy these needs through interaction with the mother and others. *Security needs* develop when the person experiences anxiety that arises from social interactions. This anxiety often determines the content of dreams, as anxiety from other sources does in Freud's theory.

In order to deal with these powerful needs, the individual develops specialized mechanisms called *dynamisms*. Each dynamism is essentially a habit or pattern of behavior that has previously been associated with the satisfaction of a particular need. For example, a person who repeatedly faces dangerous situations and learns to deal with them fearlessly is said to have a "courage dynamism." Like other aspects of personality functioning, dynamisms develop and are typically expressed in interpersonal situations. One important dynamism, the *self system*, develops as a protective device to avoid and reduce anxiety. By maintaining a consistent, positive self-image, the individual can successfully defend against anxiety.

As people interact with others, they also begin to build sets of expectations as to how other people will act in particular situations. These social expectations, which Sullivan called *personifications*, guide later interpersonal interactions. The personification of the mother, for example, causes the child to expect to find her mother's characteristics in other women, such as aunts and teachers. These expectations greatly affect how she interacts with such women and may strongly influence the course of any relationships she develops with them.

The social analytic theorists would interpret Jodi's problems somewhat differently than would Freud. Although they would agree on the role of unconscious factors and early experience, they would also look to factors in the social environment. Horney, for example, would search for conflict in Jodi's family, and Sullivan would examine her early interpersonal relationships.

Evaluating Psychodynamic Theory

Despite its great impact on our attempts to understand human personality, psychodynamic theory has been widely criticized. Among the major criticisms are these:

- As Paul Meehl (1994) points out, psychodynamic theory is too complex and requires too much subjective inference about underlying causes of behavior.
- The theory lacks scientific precision; its constructs and hypotheses are antiquated and difficult to test. How do we , for example, test the hypothesis that dreams are an expression of dangerous id impulses?

- There is too much emphasis on the biological underpinnings of behavior. This criticism has abated in recent years as our knowledge concerning the substantial influence of biology on behavior has increased: Freud may have been right.
- The original Freudian theory was based on an unrepresentative sample of patients. He saw primarily neurotic, upper-class Viennese women. How can we generalize from this sample to men and to other cultures? This early concern was considerably allayed as psychoanalysis spread worldwide and came to be used in many cultures.
- The theory is too sexist. It focuses on male sexual development and implies that women are psychological second-class citizens. Karen Horney and others have corrected this flaw in their later theories.
- The view of human nature is too negative. Freud and many of his colleagues saw humans as motivated primarily by aggression and sexual desire and driven by the irrational, unconscious impulses of the id. Any good that we find in society is an indirect result of these negative motivations.

While many consider these criticisms to be valid, it is important that we also note the positive value of Freud's work. He proved that it is possible to have a scientific theory of personality and psychopathology, and he demonstrated the importance of such concepts and ideas as the unconscious, anxiety, defense mechanisms, and dream analysis. He also developed a scientifically based approach to psychotherapy that provided practitioners - for the first time in history - with a set of careful guidelines for diagnosis and therapy. Most of all, he provided a comprehensive theory of human nature and human behavior, rich in its understanding of the powerful forces of biology, reality, and society that motivate us all. It is a theory that refuses to deny the complexity of human behavior and dares to venture an explanation despite that complexity; a theory that provides a full, meaningful view of the psychological life of every human being.

It is for these reasons that Sigmund Freud is one of the most influential thinkers in the history of psychology and in the history of the world, in a class with Charles Darwin, Isaac Newton, and Albert Einstein. And it is for these reasons that Freud's theory has generated thousands of empirical studies and reached the centennial of its great influence on human thought across such diverse fields as psychology, psychiatry, medicine, education, sociology, anthropology, English literature, and religion.

Keys to Personality 2

Cognitive/Behavioral Approaches

Despite the value that many see in Freud's work, others have focused on the criticisms, and this emphasis has led to the development of new schools of thought. One of these is the cognitive/behavioral school, which traces its origins, in part, to the behaviorism of John B. Watson, B.F. Skinner, and their colleagues. Watson held, in effect, that all behavior is a product of learning processes. Skinner expanded Watson's behaviorism and focused it on operant conditioning, in which external events reinforce responses and thereby increase their frequency. And cognitive theorists, including Albert Bandura, later modified the emphasis to focus on the role of thought processes in personality and behavior. We will see how Skinner's theory, discussed more fully in Chapter 6, applies to personality, then turn to the general cognitive-behavioral framework before considering the theories of Bandura and others.

Personality Through Reinforcement: B.F. Skinner

Skinner believes that we can understand behavior without employing such unobservable constructs as "id," "ego," "anxiety," or "unconscious." He chose to ignore such constructs because they reduce the objectivity of psychology and make its research, he felt, less scientific. Rather than use constructs, Skinner employs a *functional analysis* of behavior - the determination of cause-effect relationships through the identification of antecedent or preceding events (stimuli) and the observation of behavioral consequences (responses). If we control the environment affecting an individual and carefully observe his behaviors, we can identify their causes.

In Skinner's view, the behavior patterns we often refer to collectively as personality are entirely acquired through *reinforcement* - anything that increases the probability of a response. Both simple and complex behaviors, including social behaviors, are acquired in this way. You may, for example, know someone who enjoys interacting with people, has many friends, frequently attends parties, and prefers to study in a group rather than alone. Whereas some would call this person an extravert, Skinner would avoid the extraversion construct and simply suggest that she is exhibiting outgoing behaviors for which she has been reinforced in the past. Similarly, a Skinnerian would not label Jodi's problem as depression. Rather, the focus would be on specific behaviors, such as forgetfulness and crying and the reinforcement that produced these behaviors.

The Cognitive-Behavioral Framework

Many psychologists were interested in the role of learning and of environmental influences more generally on behavior, as was Skinner. However, a growing number of these psychologists eventually became disenchanted with what they saw as Skinner's overemphasis on observable responses at the expense of any attempt to understand thought processes (Hartzler & Fromme, 2003). As a result, much of psychology moved from a focus on observable responses to a focus on cognitions (thoughts) and their impact on behavior. Over this same time period, computer hardware and software became increasingly sophisticated, making it possible to develop useful computer models of cognitive functioning and its neurological bases. As Dan Stein (1994) convincingly argues, these two forces combined to shift the focus of the field of personality—and of much of psychology—toward a cognitive-behavioral approach.

The *cognitive-behavioral* school of personality continues to recognize the importance of basic learning processes, such as operant and classical conditioning, in the development of behavior patterns. However, learning becomes a more complex and varied activity, and thought processes are seen as centrally involved in the development and functioning of the personality. The cognitive-behavioral school focuses more on how cognitions are acquired and modified and how they affect behavior than on the simple learning processes that may account for more basic behaviors (Halmi et al., 2002).

Consider the example of a patient with chronic depression. Where the Skinnerian behaviorist focuses on the reinforcement that produced such specific behaviors as crying, the cognitive theorist looks to the kinds of thoughts and expectancies that may cause the depression. Jodi, for example, may tend to blow minor events out of proportion and expect that she cannot solve her problems. Both are cognitive influences that might cause depression. We have more to say about cognitive theory in Chapter 8 and about cognitive views of depression in Chapter 16.

Bandura's Social Learning Theory

According to Albert Bandura's *social learning theory*, human personality consists of a collection of behaviors that have been acquired through the ongoing, reciprocal interaction of personal and environmental factors (Figure 14-4). Someone who is very aggressive, for example, will probably initiate new interactions in an aggressive fashion, think aggressive thoughts, and elicit responses from others that reinforce her own aggressiveness. Thoughts, behaviors, and the environment interact in the development and continued expression of aggressiveness. A key point of Bandura's theory is that responses, aggressive or otherwise, need not necessarily be performed in order to be learned: learning may occur vicariously when the person observes the behavior of others and becomes capable of repeating the observed behavior (Bandura, 1995).

It is Bandura's contention that more traditional forms of learning, including classical and operant conditioning, play a minor role in personality development. Most important are the social behaviors necessary for effective interactions with others, and these behaviors are acquired largely through social learning processes. Social learning occurs through *modeling*, in which one person displays (models) the behavior to be learned and another acquires the behavior through observation. Consider the example of extraverted behavior. Bandura would argue that the person learns outgoing behaviors by observing them in parents and other models. The child watches the parents interact with other people and imitates some of their behaviors or at least incorporates them into his repertoire of possible behaviors. He is even more likely to learn these behaviors if he sees the parents being rewarded for them.

But he need not display the behaviors immediately; often, in fact, they do not appear until adolescence or adulthood, if ever. Once they do become prominent in his overall behavior pattern, he will be perceived as an extravert. Emotional reactions, like Jodi's depression and anxiety, can be acquired in the same way: She may have observed depressive and anxious behaviors in her parents or others and not exhibited them until many years later.

In Bandura's view, the behavior patterns that make up personality do not operate at random; rather, they are under the general influence of a self system that affects most of the individual's behavior. Bandura proposes that people observe their own performance, which is followed by a judgmental process that leads to a self-response. This response includes a sense of *self-efficacy*, an evaluation of one's own effectiveness in dealing with situations (Bandura et al., 2001). Self-efficacy develops through a special form of observational learning in which the person observes her own actions in relation to the outcome of a situation. A successful outcome increases the sense of self-efficacy, while an unsuccessful outcome reduces it. Success and failure experiences across a wide variety of situations over a period of time provide a generalized sense of self-efficacy that will have a broad influence on behavior.

Scales have been developed to measure self-efficacy (Steffen et al., 2002), and studies have shown that increases in this positive sense of self can improve occupational performance, help pregnant women stop smoking, reduce the physiological effects of stressors, and enhance the process of choosing careers in college women (Tsay & Chao, 2002; Gwaltney et al., 2002). Such findings have led Bandura to make the self-efficacy concept an increasingly central part of his theory. We cover Bandura's more general theory of behavior in Chapter 6.

Rotter's Cognitive-Behavioral Theory

Other theorists have offered cognitive-behavioral alternatives to Bandura's approach. One is Julian Rotter (1954), who hypothesizes that learning experiences cause us to develop cognitive expectancies that guide our behavior. For each situation in which we must act, we develop expectancies as to what will happen following our behavior. We also place a value on the outcome, and these two cognitive factors—outcome expectancy and value—determine our behavior. Rotter goes a step further to identify two groups of people, *internals* (those who develop the general expectancy that they control their own rewards and punishments) and *externals* (those who believe that they are controlled by outside forces). He has developed a test, the *Internal-External Locus of Control Scale* (the *I-E Scale*) to identify members of these two groups. Scores on this test are correlated with a variety of behaviors (Rotter, 1990).

A final note on cognitive theories is that some of these approaches have led to the development of psychotherapies used to treat such problems as negative body image, depression, and the post-traumatic stress disorders experienced by some war veterans. There is more on these therapies in Chapter 17.

Evaluating Cognitive-Behavioral Theory

The behavioral and cognitive-behavioral approaches have contributed enormously to our understanding of how the behavior patterns that make up the human personality develop. Few would question the importance of such basic learning processes as classical and operant conditioning. In addition, the behavioral approach —which heavily dominated virtually the entire field of psychology for several decades—shaped personality psychology into a much "harder" science than it had previously been, holding it to high standards of conceptual clarity, precision, objectivity, and careful experimentation. Cognitive-behaviorism adds to these virtues a careful treatment of the role of cognitive processes in personality. And behaviorism has resulted in many practical benefits to society, providing new methods of teaching and of psychotherapy, as well as a better understanding of how learning takes place.

Despite these pluses, many have criticized the behavioral and cognitive-behavioral theories. The basic behavioral approaches are considered too simplistic and superficial. How can we possibly account for the complexities of human personality through simple reinforcement approaches? Even cognitive-behavioral personality theories place far too much emphasis on environmental factors. Despite massive evidence that behavior has biological underpinnings (see Chapters 1, 3, 10, 12 and 15), these approaches largely ignore genetics and physiology. Finally, they tend to reduce the personality to a machine that operates according to a specific set of rules or an equation into which each and every human being can be plugged. This criticism is addressed to some degree by Bandura's increasing emphasis on the role of self (Bandura, 1991, 1992), but critics are not yet satisfied.

Keys to Personality 3

Humanistic Theory

From the perspective of humanistic theorists, psychodynamic and behavioral theories have major flaws. The psychoanalytic approach views human beings purely as biological organisms that operate on a set of universal principles, while behavioral theories attempt to explain the richness and complexity of human behavior solely in terms of a few oversimplified, mechanistic learning principles and cognitive concepts. In both traditions, people are seen as little more than subjects of research to be probed, examined, and manipulated. People are thus robbed of their individuality, capacity for growth, and dignity.

Humanism offers the alternative view that human beings are unique in the animal kingdom, not merely the highest rung on the ladder of evolution. Unlike other animals, humans have a self-concept—a perception of what they are like— and more generally are not "just animals." Moreover, each and every individual is different and important in her own right, and this individuality is a central determinant of human behavior. Each person is also equipped with a set of positive potentials and an inborn drive to realize those potentials and move toward higher levels of functioning. The natural human tendency is to strive toward happiness, love, creativity, fulfillment, and goodness, though society often interferes with the attainment of these goals. The humanistic view has come to have many advocates and many applications in such disparate areas as psychotherapy and corporate employee morale enhancement (Ramsey & Calvert, 1994). The most prominent humanistic theorist is Carl Rogers.

Carl Rogers: The Self-Concept

Carl Rogers was one of the great pioneers in personality psychology. He constructed a major theory and almost single-handedly started the entire school of humanism. In addition, he developed an important new method of psychotherapy and became the first psychologist to do systematic, well-designed, empirical research to test the effectiveness of therapy.

Born in Oakpark, Illinois in 1902, Rogers received his Ph.D. from Teachers College of Columbia University in 1931. After considerable experience as a clinical psychologist, he joined the psychology department at Ohio State University in 1941 and soon began to publish his ideas about psychotherapy and personality.

The Structure of Personality. The two major structural components in Rogerian theory are the organism and the self (Rogers, 1959, 1963, 1980). The *organism* is the sum total of the person—all of one's physical and psychological attributes (Figure 14-5). The self, or *self-concept*, is an organized pattern of perceptions and evaluations of one's own characteristics. You may, for example, perceive and examine your characteristics as a student, as a son or daughter, as a worker, and so on. Your self-concept is also evaluative; you see yourself not just as a student but more specifically as a good student or a poor student.

Research supports the presence of both descriptive and evaluative components of the self-concept (Gottlieb & J.L. Rogers, 2002; Byrne, 2002), but how and when does it form? While humanistic theory insists that self-concept is uniquely human, Gordon Gallup (1977; Gallup & Suarez, 1991) hypothesized that it might also be a characteristic of primates. To test his hypothesis, he studied the ability of primates to recognize their own images in a mirror. If they could, this would imply that they had some sense of self. He exposed the animals to a mirror for ten days, then anesthetized them, painted bright red spots on the uppermost part of one eyebrow and on top of the opposite ear, let them recover from the anesthesia, and placed them once again in front of the mirror. The chimps immediately began to explore the red spots, seemingly indicating that they had learned to recognize themselves in the mirror and thus had developed some sense of self. Interestingly enough, of the animals Gallup tested, only highly evolved apes could recognize themselves. Monkeys could not, even after more than 2400 hours of mirror exposure. More recent studies, in fact, have called into question self-recognition even in apes (Heyes, 1994).

But what about infants? Some researchers have used the Gallup technique to test self-concept development in human babies. After the mother applies a dot of rouge to the infant's nose, an observer records how often he touches it. The baby is then seated in front of a mirror, and nose-touching is again observed. Results show that mirror exposure increases the frequency of nose-touching dramatically at about the age of 18 months. The infant has apparently developed enough of a sense of self by that age to recognize that his nose is not ordinarily red.

There is also evidence that the beginnings of self-recognition and self-concept formation may occur even earlier than 18 months (Himmelfarb, 2003). In fact, Gallup and others have built on Eleanor Gibson's (1987) work on infant perception (Chapter 10) to hypothesize that the sensory and perceptual apparatus includes an inherent distinction between self and non-self (Eilers & Westercamp, 2003; Gallup, 1992). The infant is actually born, they believe, with the ability to at least minimally differentiate herself from the rest of the world. This innate ability forms the basis for the development of the self-concept. Eleanor Maccoby (1980) pointed out many years ago, however, that it is not until about the age of six or seven years that any real psychological self develops.

The many and varied perceptions that make up the self-concept are not random; the self is both organized and consistent. The organizational aspect of the self-concept means that you tend to view yourself as a whole, integrating your characteristics to form a total picture of yourself. This organized pattern tends to remain highly consistent over a period of time, even in the face of information that may contradict your self-concept (Campbell et al., 2003).

The Motivation of Behavior. Rogers believes that just one motivational system, called the actualization tendency, provides the impetus for all behavior. *Actualization* is an inborn tendency of the total organism to realize all its potentials, to grow and improve, and to maintain and enhance itself. As the person interacts with the environment, each experience is evaluated to determine whether it satisfies the actualizing tendency. Experiences that promote actualization are positively valued and will be sought out in the future, while experiences that inhibit actualization are negatively valued and will be avoided. Whether positive or negative, the experience will be accurately perceived and the individual will be fully aware of its occurrence.

A portion of the actualization tendency is diverted for the specific purpose of maintaining and enhancing the self, a motive system called *self-actualization*. It causes the individual to strive for self-enhancement and to maintain the consistency of the self-concept. Self-actualization is basically a social phenomenon. It is an attempt to maintain a consistent self-concept that fulfills the conditions or values established by the society (Sumerlin & Bundrick, 2000).

Under the influence of self-actualization, experience is evaluated to determine whether it will enhance the self. Experiences that are consistent with the existing self-concept and thus self-enhancing are accurately perceived, whereas those not consistent with the self are distorted. If you see yourself as an "A" student, getting an "A" on an exam will be self-consistent, and the information will be perceived accurately. But if you get a "D" on an exam, you may tend to distort the experience: "The professor must have screwed up the grading" or "I really wasn't feeling very well the night before the exam."

When experience is distorted, the consistency of the self-concept is maintained, but a state of *incongruence*, or discrepancy, between the self-concept and the actual experience has been created. If you blame your low exam grade on your professor, you will still be able to maintain your "A" student self-concept, but it will be somewhat inaccurate, since you did indeed receive a "D". Rogers believes that we all distort experience to maintain self-consistency and to self-actualize. The result is that we all have somewhat inaccurate self-concepts. Moreover, when experiences are distorted, the actualization of the total organism—a far more important consideration for Rogers—may be impaired. Consider the example of a teenager whose friends—or those he would like to be his friends—take up smoking. His self-concept is that he is a friendly, socially acceptable person. To refuse to take up smoking would be inconsistent with this self-concept and perhaps jeopardize his group membership. In effect, the need to self-actualize might cause him to succumb to the social pressure to smoke. Since smoking would obviously have an adverse effect on the physical health of the total organism (see Chapter 15), we can conclude that self-actualization has, in this case, been harmful.

Rogerian Research

A considerable amount of research has been conducted to evaluate Rogerian theory, much of it in the context of psychotherapy. The theory suggests, for example, that a person is psychologically healthier when her self-concept is similar to her concept of the ideal person. In a classic study, Rogerian researchers had clients about to enter therapy complete a test in which they described their self-concepts and also described the ideal person. A repeat test after therapy showed that their self-concepts had moved significantly closer to their ideal concepts, while a control group of participants with no therapy showed no change (Butler & Haigh, 1953). The authors concluded that the therapy had worked and that the theory had been validated. Most studies have similarly tended to validate the major hypotheses of Rogerian theory and to demonstrate that Rogerian therapy is helpful (Barrett & Godfrey, 1994).

Beyond evaluation of the theory, literally thousands of studies have been based on the self-concept. Like Freud's concepts of unconscious motivation and defense, Rogers' self-concept has proven to be a very useful construct. One study showed, for example, that self-concept measures can help to predict educational risks in African-American youth, such as dropping out of school, (Connell et al., 1994). Others have used self-concept measures to determine how disabled people view themselves and have documented the presence of negative self-concepts in some African-American children (Owusu, 1994).

Other self-oriented theories besides that of Rogers have made important contributions. Abraham Maslow's motivational self-theory is covered in Chapter 12. The work of an important current theorist, Hazel Markus, appears in the Probe.

Evaluating Humanistic Theories

Humanism has had a considerable impact on society, and its ideas are found throughout much of contemporary culture. The great value of humanism is that it has brought to personality psychology—and to society—a much more positive view of individual human beings. People are seen as generally good and as striving to become better. To psychologists and others uncomfortable with the relatively negative and mechanistic views of the psychodynamic and behavioral theorists, humanism came as a welcome, cool breeze on a very hot day. Even beyond this valuable contribution, the Rogerian method of psychotherapy and his development of the first well-designed therapy research program have had a great impact.

No more immune to criticism than other approaches, humanism has nevertheless taken its share of punches (Phares, 1988; Smith & Vetter, 1991; Wallach & Wallach, 1983). One long-standing criticism is that the theory relies too much on self-report, which is often invalid. Who says the client in therapy or the participant in research is making accurate statements about herself? A second point is that this approach short-changes the very concepts that are so central to the theories it seeks to replace. There is little recognition of the importance of biological determinants, cognitions, situations, or learning, and unconscious motivation operates only when there is psychopathology.

Other critics believe that humanism is more philosophy than science and that it is foolishly optimistic about people and their motives. Many researchers interpret their studies as showing that behavior is often based on very negative human motives, such as aggression, revenge, and dishonesty, whereas humanists see the same results as showing that society has interfered with the positive motives of the individual. A related criticism is that the theory promotes selfishness. It encourages people to focus on their own personal needs and goals over those of others and thereby advances the welfare of the individual at the expense of that of society.

Keys to Personality 4

Traits, Situations, and Their Interaction

Each of the major personality theorists assumes that behavior is heavily influenced by *traits*—stable, consistent, internal characteristics. Walter Mischel, however, introduced *situationism*, which insists that behavior is determined primarily by external situations, not personality traits. We will consider several theorists who have made traits central to their theories, then turn to Mischel's situational view and to a further alternative, known as interactionism.

Gordon Allport

One of the trail-blazing pioneers in trait theory was Gordon Allport (1961). He believed that every personality is made up of a set of traits and that these traits shape behavior and cause it to be consistent over time and across situations. He strongly emphasized the uniqueness of each individual's personality. Every person is so different from every other person that even his specific traits are different from those of any other individual.

Allport distinguished between common and unique traits. *Common traits* are characteristics that are similar (though never identical) in many people. Examples would be friendliness, aggressiveness, and dominance. We can place everyone on a continuum of friendliness. Some people are very friendly, others moderately friendly, and still others unfriendly. *Unique traits* are those found in only one person, and it is these traits that make each person different and special. Often they involve a unique style with which the person presents herself—her particular "brand" of humor or hostility, her unique way of expressing optimism, and the like.

Allport also broke traits down in another way. He held that each common and each unique trait can be cardinal, central, or secondary. This classification indicates how important a given trait is in the personality of a particular individual. *Cardinal* traits are those that dominate the personality. Most people have only one cardinal trait, if any. If I ask you to characterize your brother's personality in a few words, you will very likely mention his cardinal trait. If you say he is dominant, this means that he has a cardinal trait of dominance that characterizes much of his behavior. He will lead class discussions, be the focus of attention at parties, be an authoritative, assertive manager, and select the restaurant when going out to eat with a group of people.

Central traits are those that are not quite as important as cardinal traits, but nevertheless influence much of the individual's behavior. If one of your brother's central traits is friendliness, he will not only be a consistently dominant personality, but will usually also be friendly. *Secondary* traits are those that we see relatively rarely in a given person. They appear in certain situations but are not a particularly important part of our description of this individual. Your brother might have a secondary trait of humor that he shows only occasionally. Since every personality is unique, the same traits might be cardinal in one person, central in another, and secondary in a third.

Raymond B. Cattell

Raymond Cattell has long held that personality consists of a set of traits (Cattell et al., 2002). Each trait is represented as a bipolar dimension with high and low ends. For example, there is an anxiety trait dimension that runs from very high to very low. As an individual, you can fall at any point on the continuum, and your trait level of anxiety will remain constant time.

Cattell's research over the past fifty years has involved primarily the application of powerful multivariate, statistical techniques, most often factor analysis (McArdle & Cattell, 1994). *Factor analysis* analyzes sets of correlations (relationships among variables) to identify groups or clusters of variables that go together, suggesting that a single, underlying factor influences all of them. The overall effect of the analysis is to reduce the information in a large number of items to something that can be understood in terms of a small number of factors.

In a factor analytic study, Cattell has large numbers of participants answer large numbers of items describing themselves and then factor analyzes these items in a search for clusters of variables that represent personality dimensions. After many studies, he has concluded that there is a set of personality trait dimensions that apply to all people from childhood through old age and across all cultural and ethnic groups. He originally derived 16 of these important trait dimensions and later expanded the list, through further studies, to 23. A second set of factors covers the domain of abnormal behavior.

Cattell believes that traits alone cannot predict behavior. He hypothesizes that the behavior you are likely to display at a given moment can best be predicted by knowing both your standing on relevant *traits* and the nature of the *situation* in which you find yourself (Cattell et al., 2002). In addition, your current *states* of functioning, such as your mood, will influence your behavior (Figure 14-6). Consider, for example, what might influence your performance on the next exam in your psychology course. Both your high score on anxiety (a relevant trait) and the fact that the test is very difficult (the situation) will influence your performance. In addition, whether you are tired or well-rested, happy or depressed (all temporary states) will have an effect. If you have very high trait anxiety, the test is very difficult, and you are overtired, you might not do well. However, a change in any one of these—lower trait anxiety, an easier test, or getting a good night's sleep—could raise your test score. Cattell and others have done extensive research to support his theory (Yap et al., 2002; Monleon et al., 2003; Cattell et al., 2002).

Hans Eysenck

British theorist Hans Eysenck, like Cattell, has used factor analysis to search for a set of personality dimensions. Rather than 16 or 23 dimensions, however, Eysenck finds just three. His theory is therefore a *typology*—an approach that focuses on a small number of very broad dimensions (Grossarth, Eysenck, & Boyle, 1995). The first dimension is a bipolar continuum running from extraversion to introversion and simply labeled *extraversion.* At one extreme are people who are very outgoing—extraverts. They have many friends, enjoy such activities as parties and study groups, and actively seek out social interaction. At the other end are people who avoid most interaction—introverts.

The second dimension is *neuroticism*, which differentiates between people who are very unemotional and those whose emotions are subject to easy arousal and rapid change (Eysenck, 1995). People in the latter group tend to be moody and are much more likely to cry, get angry, or experience other strong emotional reactions. They are also more likely to become neurotic (see Chapter 16), hence the name for the dimension. The final dimension is *psychoticism.* Those high on this trait are distant, insensitive to others, and often withdrawn and solitary (Roy, 2002).

Eysenck believes that his dimensions are heavily influenced by biological factors. All are hypothesized to have strong hereditary components, and all are theoretically controlled by specific brain structures. In fact, his personality dimensions are merely reflections of underlying biological differences among people, modified over time by learning. Studies have supported the strong influence of genetic factors on these dimensions (Famous et al., 2002; Kirk et al., 2001). Heritability for extraversion may be .70 or higher. Moreover, studies have shown that the Eysenck dimensions have substantial effects on relevant aspects of biological functioning (B. Smith et al., 1990; B. Smith et al., 1995; Knust & Stewart, 2002). Such studies, supporting Eysenck's heavily biological theory of personality, are important because they have revealed the tip of an iceberg—the fact that many personality dimensions involve varying degrees of biological influence. Eysenck was the first major theorist to hold such a strongly biological view, and current researchers interested in the biological underpinnings of other dimensions owe him a considerable debt.

Eysenck developed questionnaires to measure his dimensions and has conducted extensive research to evaluate them (Grossarth, Eysenck, & Barrett, 1993). He and others have used these inventories in a variety of studies testing hypotheses drawn from his theory (Ferguson, 2001). They have shown, for example, that those higher in neuroticism react more strongly to stressors (Korotkov & Hannah, 1994) and that the Eysenck dimensions can help predict the occurrence of cancer, coronary heart disease, and substance abuse (Eysenck, 1993; Acton, 2003).

The Big Five

The major current alternative to Cattell and Eysenck has been *The Big Five.* Rather than 3 or 23 factors, some investigators now believe the correct number is 5 (Thompson et al., 2002; Lamb et al., 2002). Paul Costa and Robert McCrae have done extensive work to isolate five central and universal factors in personality: extraversion, agreeableness, conscientiousness, neuroticism, and openness to experience (Table 14-2). The importance and generality of the five factors have been confirmed in many investigations conducted by several different research groups (McCrae & John, 1992; Paunonen & Ashton, 2001; Paulhus & Reynolds, 1995). They have been applied, for example, in evaluating the personalities of combat pilots and aged people and can be used to predict job satisfaction and behavior in close relationships and to aid in the assessment of clinical patients (Judge et al., 2002; Coker et al., 2002). Moreover, they have been found to exist in the peoples of several nations, including the U.S., Japan, China, Canada, Germany, Poland, and Finland (McCrae et al., 2002; McCrae, 2001).

Complicating matters considerably is the fact that not all studies turn up exactly the same five factors, prompting some personality psychologists to ask "Which Big 5" (John, 1989)? Table 14-3 shows several alternatives to the five Costa-McCrae factors derived in various studies. You can see that there is considerable overlap, but the lists are not exactly the same (Kentle, 2002). For example, extraversion has been otherwise labeled as warmth, gregariousness, and assertiveness. They appear to be similar factors, but they are not identical. What does this mean? Perhaps that there is a finite set of fairly universal personality factors and that there may be about 5 of these, which may be similar to those in the Costa-McCrae studies. Notice, however, that this is not a very strong or definite statement because it is too soon to know for certain. Further research should help to increase our understanding of these factors, though there is also a reasonable probability that the factors considered crucial will change as more research is done (Graziano & Tobin, 2002).

The importance of the various personality factor models—most recently the Big Five approach—is that they do point to the real possibility that all human personality structure can be described in terms of a reasonably small, universal set of traits. If that is the case—and when we are a bit more certain just which traits those are—we will be able to move further toward using these traits to predict behavior in a variety of situations. The value of these approaches is that they may ultimately lead to highly accurate predictions of complex behavior. However, there are also strong critics of the Big 5 approach (Eysenck, 1993), and Lawrence Pervin (1994) has pointed out that the growing consensus concerning the Big 5 is both premature and dangerous. We need far more evidence before we can be certain.

Walter Mischel's Situationism

In sharp contrast to the Big 5 and all the other trait theories is Walter Mischel's *situationism.* In a dramatic departure from the traditional wisdom, Mischel pointed out in 1968 that support for the existence of traits would require cross-situational consistency in human behavior. Trait theory would be supported, for example, only if a person described as an extravert were extraverted in a wide variety of situations. Mischel then went on to argue that such consistencies are rare. For instance, you probably behave very differently at a party than you do in a classroom. To support his theory, Mischel summarized a number of studies that showed a lack of cross-situational consistency in such areas as moral behavior, aggression, anxiety, and attitude toward authority figures. Following this initial summary of existing research, Mischel and his colleagues went on to conduct a number of other studies supporting the idea that behavior is primarily under the control of external situations, not internal traits. Some of these are discussed in our Critical Thinker box, where we consider the impact of Mischel's message on the practice of clinical and counseling psychology.

Mischel's work leaves us in a bit of a dilemma. Trait theorists make a strong case for stable personality characteristics, whereas situationists demonstrate the impact of situations on behavior. Where does the truth lie? Perhaps somewhere between the two extremes, in a largely cognitive-behavioral approach known as interactionism, to which Mischel and many others now subscribe (Mischel & Shoda, 1995).

Interactionism

As interactional theorist Norman Endler points out, the 1970s and early 1980s saw an active attempt by personality researchers and theorists to resolve the trait-situation debate (Endler & Kocovski, 2002). The partially acceptable compromise that has developed out of this effort is *interactionism*—the view that behavior is influenced by traits, situations, and their interactions (Bowers, 1973; Shoda, Mischel, & Wright, 1995). A person high in trait anxiety, for example, may display anxious behavior in situations that elicit anxiety, such as a test or job interview, but may exhibit considerably less anxiety in other situations. A person low in trait anxiety, on the other hand, might not exhibit much anxiety, even in situations that tend to elicit it, though he will be more anxious in those situations than in others. You may recall that Cattell had many years earlier postulated an interaction of traits and situations, as well as states; he just didn't call his theory interactionism.

Many studies have supported the interactionist view (Mendoza-Denton et al., 2001; Crooks, 2001). One investigation carried out by Endler and his colleagues investigated the effects of trait and situational factors on college examination performance. Both anxiety levels and situational factors were measured, and results showed that performance could best be predicted by the interactions of trait and situational variables (Endler et al., 1994). Similarly, Mischel and his colleagues studied the behavior of 6- to 13-year-old children in such common summer camp situations as peer teasing and adult praise and punishment. They also measured stable personality traits and found that the behavior of the children was interactively determined by traits and situations (Shoda, Mischel, & Wright, 1994). On a more applied level, consider what trait and interactional theorists might say about Jodi's problem. Both would look at patterns of personality traits that might help in understanding her depression. The interactionist would also carefully examine contributing situational factors, such as the current stresses of college life.

While Mischel's situationism was perhaps an overreaction to strict trait theories, it made a valuable contribution by stirring interest in looking beyond traits to include consideration of situational influences. The resulting interactional theory, focusing on how traits and situations both separately and jointly determine behavior, has provided us with a much more comprehensive theory of personality.

Evaluating Trait and Interactional Theories

Few personality psychologists now question the basic premise of trait theory—that people exhibit patterns of behavior that remain stable over much of their lives—and the evidence clearly supports this view (Brody, 1994). Trait theory has the value of providing us with a basis for predicting and understanding complex patterns of human behavior. Moreover, there is little doubt that further research will more clearly identify the basic trait dimensions and provide us with increasing scientific knowledge of just how each trait interacts with the others to influence behavior. And many would argue that trait theory therefore provides us with the best chance of ultimately achieving a full understanding of the causes of human behavior and underlying mental processes.

Critics, however, point to several flaws in trait theory. First, these theories seem to describe, not predict, behavior. If I give you a test and conclude that you are extraverted, anxious, agreeable, and not very open to experience, what does that allow me to predict? According to critics, very little. A second concern is that trait descriptions are too sterile. They describe a static person—a collection of dispositions; the dynamic, individual human being is somehow missing. A further criticism is that trait theory is not very explanatory. It often does not tell us where traits come from or just how they act to influence behavior. Why are you conscientious, while your friend is not? What differentiated the two of you along that trait dimension? And just how does the trait cause your behavior to differ from your friend's? Again, we must note that efforts to locate the basis for traits are ongoing and involve studies of heritability and environmentality. Finally, critics point to the failure of many trait theories to systematically take situational factors into consideration, when evidence indicates that they are clearly important. Only Cattell's theory among the major trait approaches is immune to this criticism.

Interactionism became an important alternative to trait theory because it does systematically take into account both internal and external (both trait and situational) factors. Indeed, many personality psychologists have come to see this approach as the way of the future, perhaps because it seems inherently logical: clearly, situations, traits, and their interactions all appear to affect behavior. However, we should note that interactionism, obvious and appealing though it may be, is still only a theory (Louw & Pitman, 2001). It may provide a reasonable and workable alternative to strict trait and situational positions, but it is not, in any absolute sense, "right." In fact, the history of science should lead us to guess that this theory, like others, will change as further evidence is gathered and will someday be replaced by newer theories.

Keys to Personality 5

The Neurophysiology of Personally

If personality is a product of evolution and involves genetic influences, as we saw earlier in the chapter, we assume that it must have some basis in the central nervous system. Genetic predispositions must affect certain brain structures or the neurochemical substrates of the brain (Williamson et al., 2003; Domschke et al., 2003). We can make such an assumption, but here the waters become murky. Personality functioning is complicated, involving many traits, a variety of structures, conscious and unconscious components, cognitive and emotional elements, and ongoing dynamic changes—depending upon the particular theory you subscribe to. This means that the neurophysiological bases of personality, whatever they may be, are probably also exceedingly complex. As a result, the only honest answer to the question of where the personality lies in the brain is that we really don't yet know. Perhaps ironically, in fact, we know more about the abnormal personality than the normal one (see Chapter 16). What little we do know about the neurophysiology of normal personality suggests the possible involvement of a few specific structures, certain neurochemicals, and perhaps neural networks.

Neuroanatomy and Neurochemistry

We can learn much about the neural substrates of normal personality structure and function from the study of motivation (Chapter 12), emotion (Chapter 13), stress (Chapter 15), and abnormal behavior (Chapter 16). Here we will focus on the personality more generally. It is likely that personality traits and components are mediated by a variety of cortical and subcortical structures throughout the brain (Myslobodsky et al., 1995). The one most clearly implicated is the frontal cortex (Tranel et al., 2002; Figure 14-7), where the most advanced level of integration occurs. Thought processes appear to take place here, and it is likely that the more complex aspects of personality also involve the frontal lobes (Decety & Chaminade, 2003). In fact, some work suggests that the self-concept may be "located" in the prefrontal cortex (Miller et al., 2002; Kelley et al., 2002). Remember the case of Phineas Gage (Chapter 3)? He suffered marked personality changes after an iron bar passed through his frontal lobe (Haas, 2001). More recent studies have documented many cases in which frontal damage produces selective personality change (Braun et al., 2001-2002; Dolan & Park, 2002).

The temporal and parietal lobes have also been implicated in some studies, as have certain subcortical areas (B.D. Smith, Meyers & Kline, 1989). Some people who have seizures as a result of damage to the temporal cortex, for example, exhibit quite consistent personality changes, and removal of the amygdala may also contribute to personality change. The reticular activating system (RAS) of the brain stem may be involved in at least the extraversion dimension of personality, and Eysenck's neuroticism factor may be mediated by the limbic system.

Our knowledge of neurochemical involvement in personality is even more primitive than our knowledge of its neuroanatomical substrates. One neurotransmitter that does appear to have a part in personality is dopamine (Sobell et al., 1995). Some studies have implicated it in extraversion, and others in personality functioning more generally (Cruz et al., 1995). We do not yet know just how dopamine mediates normal personality, but we may soon find some clues through its involvement in such abnormal behaviors as the anxiety disorders and schizophrenia (Cohen et al., 1993). Other neurotransmitters likely to play roles in normal personality functioning include serotonin, epinephrine, and norepinephrine (Moresco et al., 2002).

Neural Networks

We will probably have to turn to the neural network or some similar conceptualization of distributed functioning to understand the neurophysiology of personality (Wenzel & Baumart-Schmitt, 2002; Parnas & Bovet, 1995). *Neural networks* are circuits formed by sets of interconnected neurons that may be scattered through various areas of the brain (Mechelli et al., 2002). They are dealt with more fully in Chapters 6, 7. and 8, but here we can see how they apply to personality.

Consider the example of extraversion. This trait dimension has a strong hereditary component, which may affect the structure of sets of neurons in the RAS, the frontal cortex, and perhaps other areas of the brain. These scattered neurons may be joined in what we could call "extraversion circuits," which process information and events relating to the extraversion-introversion dimension. Experience and learning would modify these circuits over time to establish a stable extraversion trait by adolescence or adulthood. Each major personality trait would similarly have a neural network formed by heredity and learning. The extraversion networks would interact with these neural networks for other personality dimensions to jointly affect behavior in a variety of situations. Although neural networking is still in its infancy, some researchers have already begun to apply computer-based network models to the development of both normal and abnormal personality traits. One example is recent work showing that a neural network for the self-concept may involve areas of the frontal and prefrontal cortices (Kjaer et al., 2002).

Keys to Personality 6

Personality Assessment

An important assumption underlying personality theories is that there are individual differences among people. To test the theories and more generally gain information about individual personalities, it is necessary to measure these differences. *Personality assessment* involves systematically gathering information about a person in order to understand and predict her behavior. The overall goal is to obtain reliable, valid measures of individual differences that will permit the accurate prediction of behavior. *Reliability* refers to the dependability of the measurement—the extent to which it is consistent and stable. *Validity* is the degree to which a test measures what it purports to measure. These concepts are discussed in more detail in Chapter 9.

Differing theoretical approaches and the varied needs of clinical and counseling psychologists and researchers have led to the development of a number of different personality assessment methods. They include objective tests and projective tests.

Objective Personality Tests

Objective personality tests present the test-taker with a number of specific items to which he is asked to respond, either on paper or on a computer screen. The items are often self-descriptive and ask the participant to indicate whether or not an item applies to him or the extent to which it applies. For that reason, we often refer to objective tests as involving a *self-report* method. Typical items might include:

___ I often feel tired during the day.

___ Most people seem to like me.

___ I sometimes hear voices that others can't hear.

Once the participant has responded to the various items on the test, one or more scores can be calculated to indicate where she stands on the personality variable or variables being measured. Three major personality inventories that employ this self-report approach are the MMPI, the 16PF, and the NEO-PI.

The MMPI. The *Minnesota Multiphasic Personality Inventory (MMPI)* is the best known and most widely employed of all objective personality tests (Dahlstrom, 1992; Ito et al., 1995). It was developed in the late 1930s to provide an instrument that could be used in both clinical practice and research to identify major forms of psychopathology (Hathaway and McKinley, 1940). After a number of revisions, the test contains 566 items that are scored to yield ten clinical scales and four validity scales.

The 10 clinical scales measure specific characteristics and disorders. Most of these scales were developed using *criterion keying*—a method in which a group of people diagnosed as having a specific psychological disorder (the criterion group) is identified and their responses compared with those of normal control participants. The items that differentiate the two groups are used to make up the scale measuring that disorder. The four validity scales represent an attempt to ensure that participants are answering the questions truthfully.

In clinical use, all ten clinical scales and four validity scales are scored, and a profile of the patient's performance on the test is generated, often by computer, as our 21 describes. A clinical or counseling psychologist then interprets the meaning of the patterns of scores based on the extensive research that has been done on the MMPI since its development. Our reviews the interesting use of computer scoring and interpretation in personality assessment. Patterns of high scale scores may indicate psychopathology or poor adjustment (Keiller & Graham, 1993).

The usefulness of the MMPI scores has been documented in over ten thousand investigations. One study examined the ability of the MMPI Depression Scale to accurately diagnose depression in a sample of psychiatric inpatients. It showed substantial validity, and the author concluded that it is useful, in the assessment of depression (Boone, 1994). In other studies, the test has been employed to evaluate Desert Storm combat troops (Elhai et al., 2003) and assess airline pilot applicants to determine whether they exhibit abnormal tendencies (Butcher, 1994). In further work using MMPI items, researchers have developed specialized scales to diagnose alcoholism and drug abuse more generally and a scale to predict who will start smoking (Johnson-Greene et al., 2002; Lipkun et al., 1994).

Despite its general utility and empirical support, the MMPI does have its problems. The reliability of the test is not as high as it might be (Dahlstrom and Welsh, 1960), and the ten clinical scales are highly intercorrelated; the behavior patterns they measure are not as different as might superficially appear to be the case. In addition, the MMPI was not originally developed for the assessment of normal personality functioning, even though it is often used for that purpose. Finally, the test is by no means perfect. For example, one study showed that it is only accurate in identifying normals 70% of the time and psychotics 55% of the time. This means that MMPI findings alone cannot be safely used as a basis for clinical diagnosis—and they rarely are.

The MMPI-2. By 1980, the MMPI had been in use for nearly 40 years, and many of its items were out of date. For example, one item asks if you like to play "drop the handkerchief." Are *you* familiar with that game? It is similar to tag, and people born since the early 1950s have typically never heard of it. As a result of this problem and others, the test was revised and the new *MMPI-2* published in 1989.

The updated version still has 10 clinical scales. It has been restandardized on a sample of 2600 people intended to be representative of the population in terms of sex, race, age, and education (Johnson et al., 1996). An adolescent version, the MMPI-A, has also been published (NCS, 1992).

Comparisons between the original MMPI and the MMPI-2 have typically suggested a high degree of agreement (McGrath et al., 2002). One team of researchers, for example, gave both tests to a group of police officers and compared the scores and profiles. They found 78% overall agreement between the two versions (Hargrove et al., 1994). Another study reported 75% agreement on a different sample (Morrison et al., 1994). Of course, we would not expect perfect agreement, given that changes were made.

Critics are less than convinced that the MMPI-2 is a significant improvement. They point out, for example, that even though only 17% of the population graduate from college, 45% of the normative sample were college graduates (Adler, 1990). Reliability and validity, although reasonably high, could certainly be improved (Helmes & Reddon, 1993). And some fear that the test may not have adequate validity across cultures. Despite these concerns, the MMPI will continue to dominate objective clinical assessment for many years to come.

The 16 PF. The MMPI focuses on abnormal behavior and does not give us a broad picture of the normal personality. A widely used personality inventory that does is the *Sixteen Personality Factor Questionnaire (16 PF)*. Developed by Raymond B. Cattell (1949), whose theory you have read about, the 16 PF originally measured his 16 basic personality trait factors; the current revision measures the expanded list of 23. Each item is a statement, such as "I like to watch team games," to which the subject responds "Yes," "Occasionally," or "No." As with the MMPI, the scores are plotted on a profile sheet and interpreted on the basis of previous research (Figure 14-9). Cattell hypothesizes that these factors represent true, underlying dimensions of the personality and as such must be adequately assessed if we are to predict important areas of human behavior.

The NEO-PI. Big Five factor theorists Costa and McCrae, whose approach we discussed earlier, developed the *NEO Personality Inventory* or *NEO-PI*, now revised and termed the NEO-PI-R (Costa & McCrae, 1992). It measures the 5 normal personality trait dimensions that make up the Costa-McCrae theory (the Big Five). The authors argue that, although designed primarily to assess normal functioning, the test can be useful in clinical settings to aid in diagnosis and in treatment decisions (Berry et al., 2001). One feature of the revised version that makes this possibility more attractive is the availability of "private" and "public" profiles (Morey et al., 2002). The private profile is the one based on the client's answers to the questions. However, it is now possible to have someone who knows the person independently complete the inventory. Discrepancies between this public personality and the client's self-description can indicate clinically-relevant problems (Young & Schinka, 2001).

Projective Personality Tests

A *projective* personality test is one in which the subject is given an ambiguous stimulus and asked to respond spontaneously. His answers are then evaluated subjectively and may also be scored according to some set of rules. All projective tests are based on the *projective hypothesis*, which states that the individual's response to an ambiguous stimulus represents a projection of his own inner—often unconscious—feelings and needs. The needs are projected onto the stimulus as the person attempts to construct a response. The projective hypothesis grew out of the psychoanalytic idea that the most important human motives exist at an unconscious level of functioning. Two of the major projectives are the Rorschach and the TAT.

The Rorschach Inkblot Test. The first formal projective assessment device, and still the major one, was the *Rorschach Test*, in which the individual is asked to respond to ambiguous inkblots. Developed by Swiss psychiatrist Hermann Rorschach (1921/1942), the Rorschach test consists of ten cards, each showing a vaguely structured, bilaterally symmetrical inkblot. Most are black-and-white, but some have color. What do you see in the inkblots in the figure? Whatever you see theoretically reflects your projection of your own unconscious needs and feelings and may therefore be different from what other people see.

When an examiner administers the Rorschach, she presents the participant with each blot and asks him what it looks like, later going back and obtaining more detailed responses. She can then evaluate the test, using a formal scoring system to arrive at a picture of the subject's personality characteristics or diagnostic category. The most carefully developed approach is the currently popular Exner System (Exner, 2002). Beyond its formal scores, the test serves as a kind of structured interview in which an experienced psychologist can often learn much about the subject's personality simply from the nature and pattern of the responses as the test is being administered (Sprohge et al., 2002).

Even when subjected to formal scoring systems, the Rorschach is a highly subjective, complex assessment approach and has therefore always been a controversial instrument for assessing personality. Its reliability and validity are difficult to determine, and many studies suggest that neither is very high (Masling, 2002), although some disagree (Viglione & Taylor, 2003). On the other hand, the test is strongly advocated by many clinicians, who believe that it provides valuable insights (Mihura et al., 2003).

The Thematic Apperception Test (TAT). Like the Rorschach, the *Thematic Apperception Test (TAT)* presents the participant with a series of ambiguous stimuli, in this case, pictures. Each picture shows one or more people engaging in some vague activity, and participants are asked to tell a story about the picture (Figure 14-11). The use of the TAT in the assessment of achievement motivation is discussed in Chapter 12.

Like the Rorschach, the TAT has not demonstrated outstanding reliability or validity (Tuerlinckx et al., 2002). The test does appear to be useful in some clinical settings and its reliability can be quite high under specific conditions, but its overall utility is still open to question (Morgan, 2002).

Keys to Personality 7

Conclusion

Now that you have read the chapter, you can see just how far-reaching personality theory and research can be. When we study the personality and its interaction with the environment, we are clearly close to the core of what many psychologists define as the major goals of the entire field: to predict and understand the unique behavior patterns of the individual human being. It must be equally clear to you by now that we don't yet know all the answers. The psychodynamic, cognitive-behavioral, humanistic, trait, and interactional theories differ markedly in their approaches to understanding personality, and the extensive research completed to date has not resolved these differences. Nevertheless, we have learned much about the origins and functioning of the personality, as well as its effects on behavior. Moreover, the major personality theories have already had substantial impact beyond the field of personality, particularly in the areas of psychopathology and therapy, which we take up in Chapters 16 and 17.

And, finally, what about Jodi. Like most people who contemplate suicide, she relented, put the pills back in the bottle, and returned to the Counseling Center for her next appointment. Since psychotherapy is very effective in cases like hers (Scogin & McElreath, 1994), she was much improved after her treatment and went on to successfully finish college.

Summary

The Human Personality

1. The major issues in personality theory include determinism, nature-nurture, the role of early life experience, unconscious motivation, teleological motivation, holism, and continuity.
2. Evolutionary psychology views current personality traits as having adaptively evolved over millions of years.
3. Twin and adoption studies show that the average heritability for personality traits is about 50%. There is considerable variability from one trait to another.

Psychodynamic Theory: Sigmund Freud and His Colleagues

1. Freud emphasizes unconscious motivation and divides the continuum into unconscious, preconscious, and conscious sectors.
2. Psychic energy is the limited, dynamic force that fuels the personality and behavior.
3. The three major psychic structures are the primitive, biological id, the logical, reality-oriented ego, and the social conscience or superego.
4. These psychic structures operate in a state of intrapsychic conflict which generates moral and neurotic anxiety. Reality anxiety is caused by real events in the external environment.
5. Unconscious defense mechanisms reduce anxiety by distorting reality. The major defense is repression, which is essentially selective forgetting.
6. Modern psychoanalytic theory includes ego psychology (Hartmann, Erikson, Anna Freud) and object relations theory (Klein, Kohut, Kernberg).
7. Jung postulated a collective unconscious containing archetypes. Jung's attitudes include introversion and extraversion. His functions include sensation, intuition, thinking, and feeling.
8. The social analysts—Adler, Horney, and Sullivan—de-emphasized biological factors and gave increased weight to conscious functioning, the self, and sociocultural factors.
9. Critics believe that psychodynamic theory is too complex, lacks scientific precision, overemphasizes biology, is sexist, has a negative view of human nature, and was originally based on a biased patient sample.

Cognitive/Behavioral Approaches

1. From a Skinnerian viewpoint, the behavior patterns we call personality are acquired through reinforcement.

2. Bandura's social learning theory holds that behavior is reciprocally determined by personal and environmental factors. Rotter bases behavior in cognitive expectancies and values.
3. Cognitive\behavioral theories have been criticized as too simplistic, mechanical, and environmental.

Humanistic Theory

1. Humanism postulates that humans are unique and that every individual is different.
2. For Carl Rogers, self-actualization can lead to a discrepancy between self-concept and the reality of experience. This can interfere with the actualization of the organism, potentially leading to psychopathology.
3. Humanism has been criticized as foolishly optimistic, selfish, and relying too much on self-report. Its constructs are also said to lack clarity and be difficult to test.

Traits, Situations, and Their Interactions

1. Trait theorists like Allport, Cattell, and Eysenck, hypothesize a limited set of major traits that characterize the personality and greatly influence behavior.
2. Allport hypothesizes common and unique traits which can be cardinal, central, or secondary.
3. Situationism emphasizes the influence of situations on behavior, and interactionism holds that traits, situations, and their interactions jointly determine behavior.
4. Trait theories are criticized as merely descriptive, too sterile, and not very explanatory.

The Neurophysiology of Personality

1. The frontal cortex is most clearly implicated as a neural substrate for personality. The temporal and parietal lobes may also be involved.
2. Neurotransmitters, including dopamine, appear to mediate both normal and abnormal personality functioning. Neural networks, with neurons across the brain, may also underlie the major personality traits.

Personality Assessment

1. Objective personality tests assess personality by presenting a number of self-report items. The MMPI and MMPI-2 are the mostly widely used tests. Both include 10 clinical and 4 validity scales.
2. The 16 P.F. is Cattell's inventory and assesses the 23 normal factors in his theory. The NEO-PI-R, developed by Costa and McCrae, assesses the Big 5 personality dimensions.
3. Projective tests are designed to tap into unconscious motivations. They include the Rorschach and the TAT.

Ask Yourself

1. What is the role of unconscious motivation in the theories of Freud, Jung, and Rogers?
2. Which major theorists believe that development is a stage-wise process? How do their stage theories differ?
3. How does the role of biological factors differ in the theories of Freud, Eysenck, and Cattell?
4. How do ego psychology and object relations theory differ from Freud's original formulation?
5. What do the social analytic theorists have in common that differentiates them from Freud?
6. In what ways might social learning theory be considered superior and in what ways inferior to psychoanalytic theory?
7. Why are there such wide variations in the number of trait dimensions proposed by various theorists?
8. What are the relative advantages and disadvantages of objective and projective tests?
9. What appear to be the roles of genetic and environmental factors in personality functioning?
10. Which theory do you personally find most appealing and why?

Further Readings

Atwood, G., & Stolorow, R. (1993). *Faces in a cloud: Intersubjectivity in personality theory.* Northvale, N.J.: Jason Aronson, Inc. In this interesting book, the authors explore the influence of a theorists personality on his personality theory. Freud, Jung, and others are discussed.

Bandura, A. (1991). Social cognitive theory of self-regulation. *Orgazal. Beh. Hum. Dec. Proc.*, 50, 248-287.

Endler, N., Kantor, L., & Parker, J. (1994). State-trait coping, state-trait anxiety and academic performance. *Pers. Ind. Diffs.*, 16, 663-670. Norman Endler and his colleagues provide a good example of careful research from an interactionist perspective.

Gilligan, C. (1982/1993). *In a different voice: Psychological theory and women's development.* Cambridge, MA: Harvard University Press. This recent reprinting of Carol Gilligan's classic work on the application of psychological theory to women is well worth reading. She is one of the leading theorists in this field.

Kagan, J., Snidman, N., Arcus, D., & Reznick, J.S. (1994). *Galen's prophecy: Temperament in human nature.* N.Y.: BasicBooks. A leading psychologist, Jerome Kagan, and his colleagues provide a fascinating treatment of the role of physiological makeup (temperament) in personality, a theory originally formulated many centuries ago by Galen.

Krahe, B. (1992). *Personality and social psychology: Towards a synthesis.* London: Sage. The fields of personality and social psychology are closely related but typically receive separate treatment. Barbara Krahe does an admirable job of showing the connections.

Maher, B., & Maher, W. (1994). Personality and psychopathology: A historical perspective. *J. Abnorm. Psychol.*, 103, 72-77. In this interesting article, the Mahers explore the relationship between personality and psychopathology (Chapter 16).

Pervin, L. (1993). *Personality: Theory and research.* N.Y.: Wiley. Pervin provides a good overview of major areas of personality research and also a treatment of each major theory.

Schultz, D., & Schultz, S. (1994). *Theories of personality.* Pacific Grove, CA: Brooks/Cole. A solid personality theory book that presents each of the theories in more details.

Watts, F., & Coyle, K. (1993). Phobics show poor recall of anxiety words. *Brit. J. Med. Psychol.*, 66, 373-382. This study is a good example of the application of scientific research methods to the study of Freudian hypotheses.

Zahn, T., Kruesi, M., Leonard, H., Rapoport, J. (1994). Autonomic activity and reaction time in relation to extraversion and behavioral impulsivity in children and adolescents. *Pers Ind. Diffs.*, 16, 751-758. Ted Zahn and his colleagues at the National Institutes of Health provide a good example of a carefully designed study relating Eysenck's personality theory to psychophysiological functioning.

Key Terms

actualization
archetypes
basic anxiety
behavioral theory
big five
cognitive-behavioral
collective unconscious
cross-situational consistency
death instincts
defense mechanisms
determinism
dynamism
ego

ego psychology
extraversion
factor analysis
fixation
humanism
humours
id
interactionism
intrapsychic conflict
introversion
libido
life instincts
Minnesota Multiphasic Personality Inventory (MMPI)
neural network
object-relations theory
objective test
persona
personal unconscious
personality
personality assessment
personification
phrenology
preconscious
projective hypothesis
projective test
psychic energy
psychoanalytic theory
psychodynamic theory
reality principle
regression
reinforcement
reliability
repression
Rorschach test
self-actualization
self-concept
situationism
Sixteen Personality Factor Questionnaire (16 PF)
social analytic theory
social interest
social learning theory
superego
teleological
Thematic Apperception Test (TAT)
trait
typology
unconscious
validity

Key Names

Alfred Adler
Gordon Allport
Albert Bandura
Raymond B. Cattell
Paul Costa

Hans J. Eysenck
Sigmund Freud
Karen Horney
Carl Jung
Robert McCrae
Walter Mischel
Carl Rogers
Julian Rotter
B.F. Skinner
Harry Stack Sullivan

Psychology in the 21st Century

Computers in Personality Assessment

The availability of computer systems and associated equipment has made it possible to automate many aspects of personality assessment. First developed in the 1960s, and clearly a window to the future, automated assessment procedures gained in popularity in the 1990s. Automation has been applied to the administration, scoring, and interpretation of various objective and projective personality tests. Computers can administer tests like the MMPI by displaying each item, then accepting and storing the participant's keyboard response. At the end of the session, the computer program can automatically score the test and print out the scores and profile sheets for the psychologist to examine. Computer scoring is more accurate than hand scoring and makes possible the rapid administration of more comprehensive batteries of tests (Jemelka et al., 1992). Many hours of human work are reduced to seconds when a computer is used, freeing psychologists to do more advanced assessments or psychotherapy.

More complex is the area of automated interpretation. To make computer interpretation of test scores possible, psychologists must develop a set of interpretive statements based on previous research and clinical experience with the test being scored. The program scores the test to obtain standard scale scores, examines the profile of the test scores, and selects the appropriate interpretive statements. It then prints the scale scores, a profile, a series of interpretive statements or short paragraphs, and a variety of supplemental information. Many psychologists find the computerized reports to be highly accurate and useful, and the increase in efficiency is considerable (Modai et al., 2002).

Perhaps the most interesting of all programs are those that provide actual diagnosis and even treatment of disorders. They are referred to more generally as *expert systems*, a topic we discuss more fully in Chapter 8. One computer program called DIAGNO II has been in use for over twenty years. It uses input data to select one of 46 diagnoses based on a logical decision-making process. In even more extensive applications, automated assessment and diagnosis programs have become part of comprehensive, interlocking systems for the diagnosis of psychiatric disorders (Fred et al., 2000). Expert treatment systems provide computer algorithms defining best approaches to therapy for depression, smoking cessation, and anxiety (Kaltenthaler et al., 2002; Trivedi, 2003).

The 21st century promises rapid progress in the development of automated assessment systems. They are now used not only in clinical settings but also in many organizational contexts. For example, one computer test battery has been used recently to assess the characteristics of successful F-16 pilots. It automatically determines their cognitive capacities, personality characteristics, and potential for psychopathology (Flynn et al., 1994). In clinical use, computer-based systems are potentially capable of increasing the reliability and validity of psychiatric diagnosis and of making the system of assessment far more efficient and effective.

Probe

Hazel Markus: The Dynamic Self-Concept

One recent focus of work on the self-concept has been that of Hazel Markus and her colleagues at the University of Michigan (Markus & Wurf, 1987; Kato & Markus, 1993). Markus points out that the self-concept of earlier theories is a relatively static entity: It changes very little from moment to moment and remains stable over most of a lifetime. Her alternative view is that the self-concept is highly active: It is a powerful influence on behavior that is constantly growing and changing. She therefore refers to the self as a *dynamic self-concept*.

Markus does not imply that the dynamic self-concept is entirely unstable. Rather, it has both long-term, stable aspects and short-term, changing elements. At any given moment, some components are accessible and active in determining behavior, while others are inaccessible and dormant. The self-concept has temporary states, which Markus calls the *working self-concept*, the self that is active and accessible at the moment. The content of this working self is influenced by situational variables. For example, as you approach the first day of your first philosophy course, those aspects of your self-concept that involve your view of yourself as a student are likely to be active. Other aspects, such as your view of yourself as a son or daughter, as an athlete, or as a computer user, are probably inactive. In reference to the philosophy course, your stable self-concept says that you are a good student, and that belief may heavily influence your view of how interesting you will find the course to be and how well you will do in it. However, if you have recently gotten considerable negative feedback—low grades, parental criticism, other students saying this course is very difficult, and the like—your working self-concept as you approach the course may be somewhat less positive. Moreover, repeated negative feedback is likely to produce a gradual modification of your stable self-concept (J. Smith & Freund, 2002).

Your *possible future self-concept* can also influence your present behavior. Markus points out that we all look ahead: What will happen to me? What will I be like next year and ten or twenty years from now? This means that we have not only a current self-concept, but also imagined future self-concepts. How do you see your future? What career will you be in? Will you be successful or unsuccessful? Happily or unhappily married or single? Such self-questioning has clear implications for behavior. By at least junior high school, for example, my son and daughter began to see themselves as possibly having a future in medicine, and that aspect of their self-concepts no doubt influenced their behavior. Now they are successful young physicians.

One study found that participants differed markedly in their possible future selves. Some had positive future selves that included such characteristics as powerful, glamorous, and esteemed. Others had negative selves, emphasizing such future characteristics as fat, out-of-shape, and unwanted (Cross & Markus, 1991). Other studies have shown that possible selves can influence performance on various tasks (Kato & Markus, 1993) and that those who project positive future selves tend to outperform those who project negative ones (Ruvolo & Markus, 1992).

Where do these present and future self-concepts come from? Markus and a colleague, Shinobu Kitayama (1991), focused on the role of culture in the development of the dynamic self-concept. They note that at least some aspects of your self-concept are likely to be consistent with the culture in which you are raised. North American and European cultures, for example, place heavy emphasis on independence and self-esteem. These cultures teach you that it is good to have high self-esteem and a strong sense of self-worth (Plaut et al., 2002). It is also best to be independent and to express your individuality. Confirming the impact of these cultural ideals on individual self-concepts is an interesting study of U.S. students. In response to a questionnaire, 70% saw themselves as superior to their peers, and 60% placed themselves in the highest 10% on a wide range of personal characteristics. Did they conform to the Western cultural ideal? You bet they did!

By contrast, Japanese and Chinese children grow up in a culture that emphasizes community membership over individuality. The child is taught to work in harmony with others, be self-effacing, and not stand out (Ng et al., 2003). Kitayama & Markus (1992) point out that the Japanese word for "different" (*tigau*) also means "wrong." As a result of their cultural backgrounds, few of these children will develop self-concepts that emphasize individuality or independence. Instead, their self-concepts will stress positive relationships with others and conformity to group norms (Heine et al., 2001).

The Critical Thinker

Do Situations Produce Abnormal Behavior?

Every psychologist who diagnoses or treats patients is constantly faced with one crucial question: What is determining this patient's behavior? To diagnose the problem accurately and treat it effectively, the psychologist needs to know what causal factors underlie the problem behavior. For a long time, most clinical theory and practice was based on the assumption that abnormal patterns of behavior are a reflection of long-standing personality traits. The job of the clinical or counseling psychologist was, therefore, to modify those traits—or at least the ways in which they are expressed—in order to effectively treat the disorder. If the underlying trait assumption were found to be incorrect, considerable changes in approaches to diagnosis and treatment would be necessary.

The Basic Hypothesis or Contention

Enter Walter Mischel. In his block-busting 1968 paper, Mischel shook up the world of trait theory—and thereby clinical practice—by advocating the position that external situations, not traits, are primarily responsible for behavior. Applied to clinical settings, this meant that the psychologist would need to assess not the patient's traits, but the situational factors affecting his behavior. If the patient had a height phobia (a strong, unrealistic fear of heights), for example, the clinician would have to look for current situations that might be causing it, rather than deep-seated traits formed perhaps in childhood.

What Is The Evidence?

Mischel and his colleagues argued that the general belief in the existence of traits may stem from a tendency to distort our perceptions of events in order to support our belief in the existence of stable traits. This tendency was demonstrated in a study in which high school students formed their initial impressions of a person's traits by reading a description of the person. When they later received information inconsistent with those traits, they believed it to represent superficial, unstable behavior (Hayden and Mischel, 1976). The high school students had apparently distorted the later information to make it consistent with the impressions they had already formed.

Other studies have shown that people tend to discount discrepant observations when trying to predict behavior and that belief in the existence of a given trait in a specific person biases perceptions and memories of that person's behavior. Finally, some studies show considerable variability in the Big 5 traits when they are viewed in different situations (Van-Heck et al., 1994). In clinical settings such findings may indeed suggest that the psychologist turn from traits to situations to understand the patient's symptoms.

Is The Evidence Open To Alternative Interpretations?

If a strict situational interpretation of behavior is correct, knowledge of personality traits would be of little help in predicting behavior. However, advocates of trait theory have not just blindly accepted this argument (Brody, 1994). They note that many of the studies failing to find cross-situational consistency are flawed, that inadequate samples of behavior have been used in situational studies, and that laboratory investigations may not generalize to the real world because laboratory settings tend to involve a high degree of situational constraint. Behavioral consistency would thus be much greater in real-world situations than in the laboratory.

Trait theory proponents also point out that what may appear to be quite different behaviors in consistency studies may in fact have the same underlying basis. For example, it may be true that your behavior is different at the party than in the classroom. However, if you are an extravert and your friend is an introvert, you would be likely to ask more questions and participate more actively in class discussions than he does. You would also interact with more people and make more friends at the party. In addition, studies have shown that behavior is more consistent in some situations than in others (Monson, Hesley, and Chernisk, 1982) and that individuals are more likely to behave similarly in situations that are *perceived* to be similar. Finally, many studies have clearly demonstrated cross-situational consistency for a variety of trait dimensions (Claeys et al., 1993; Moskovitz, 1994).

Do We Need Additional Evidence?

We clearly do, and, to a considerable degree, we already have it. Many of Mischel's most vocal critics returned to the laboratory to show that both traits and situations are involved in the determination of behavior. Such abnormal behaviors as phobia and depression are often joint products of well-established traits and current situational factors (Shumacher, 1995). The evidence for such interactional determination of behavior is extensive (Seiwa & Yokoyama, 1989). The relative contributions of traits, situational factors, and their interaction vary from one instance to another, but the general principles of interactionism appear to apply to a wide variety of behaviors. Research shows that specific traits have effects only in relevant situations (Shoda et al., 1993). For example, low and high trait anxious people will react differently to threatening situations, but the anxiety trait may not affect their behavior while they are relaxing at home (Man et al., 1995). Similarly, people who show anger easily (high trait anger) do so only in anger-provoking situations (Burns, 1995). In addition, a person's traits can cause her to choose some situations over others, as when the high anxious person chooses to take an easy college course, rather than a difficult one. And a person's traits can actually modify situations: a highly trait aggressive child can quickly disrupt the peaceful play of classmates and create chaos.

Interactionism also applies directly to clinical settings. For example, people with social phobia—a strong fear of interacting with others—display very high anxiety when placed in socially threatening situations, such as therapy (Orsillo et al., 1994). Similarly, people with high trait anxiety perceive ego-involving and time-pressured situations as threatening and become highly anxious (Endler & Kocovski, 2002). Such reactions may impair their response to therapy and also indicate to clinicians the need to assess the effects of particular situations on the emotional and behavioral reactions of their patients.

But even interactionism doesn't come close to providing a complete understanding of the causes of abnormal behavior or the best approaches to treatment. Even when the most careful studies take into account the effects of traits, situations, and their interaction, they cannot readily predict behavior. In fact, together they typically account for less than half the variability in behavior, leaving the clinician—and the researcher—with many unanswered questions (Crooks, 2001).

What Can We Conclude?

It seems clear that a purely situational approach to clinical diagnosis and treatment would be very unwise. A client may tell a therapist that she has come for help with problems relating to her marriage. However, if the therapist focuses only on these immediate situational influences, he is unlikely to be very effective. At the same time, ignoring the current marital problems in favor of a strong emphasis on the client's traits, such as anxiety, aggression, and dependency, is unlike-

ly to lead to entirely satisfactory treatment.

The literature we have reviewed would suggest that the therapist look to both the traits of the person and the situations she faces. When both factors and their interaction are taken into account, diagnosis and treatment are likely to improve. In the case of the client with marital problems, the therapist may discover that she also has a trait of high aggressiveness. He can then consider how the problems in the marriage interact with her highly aggressive personality and how this combination of trait and situational factors may contribute to her reactions. Even with this interactional approach, however, he cannot always hope for complete success, since we still have so much to learn.

Horizons in Personality

Effective People: Self-Efficacy

In Bandura's view, the behavior patterns that make up personality do not operate at random; rather, they are under the general influence of a self system that affects most of the individual's behavior. Bandura proposes that people observe their own performance, which is followed by a judgmental process that leads to a self-response. This response includes a sense of *self-efficacy*, an evaluation of one's own effectiveness in dealing with situations (Bandura, 1991). Self-efficacy develops through a special form of observational learning in which the person observes her own actions in relation to the outcome of a situation. A successful outcome increases the sense of self-efficacy, while an unsuccessful outcome reduces it. Success and failure experiences across a wide variety of situations over a period of time provide a generalized sense of self-efficacy that will have a broad influence on behavior (Bandura et al., 2001).

Scales have been developed to measure self-efficacy (Lennings, 1994), and studies have shown that increases in this positive sense of self can improve occupational performance, help pregnant women stop smoking, reduce the physiological effects of stressors, and enhance the process of choosing careers in college women (Tsay & Chao, 2002; Gwaltney et al., 2002. Such findings have led Bandura to make the self-efficacy concept an increasingly central part of his theory.

"I Am Never Startled by a Fish": The Importance of Cross-Validation

Did you know that your response to the test item "I am never startled by a fish" could help determine your score on a personality trait dimension or predict your GPA? Well, maybe. When a psychologist constructs a personality scale, he gives it to a large number of participants and runs statistical analyses to determine which items should be retained. Some items in the original pool will be kept because they relate significantly to a criterion, while others will not.

The problem? Some items that show a significant relationship to the selection criterion (such as predicting depression) may not really be appropriate. That's because some items do not really measure what they are supposed to be measuring and should therefore be eliminated. This can be accomplished only by *cross-validating* the test, that is, by giving it to a second sample of participants and reexamining the items to see if the relationship to the criterion holds.

To show other psychologists what happens when cross-validation is not done, one investigator carried out a test construction procedure using Art Buchwald's tongue-in-cheek test called the *North Dakota Null Hypothesis Brain Inventory* as an item pool (Blumenfeld, 1972). The test was given to a large number of students, and each item was correlated with GPA in an effort to predict it from the test items. Nine items were found to relate significantly to the criterion and should thus be good predictors of GPA. But do you really believe that "When I look down from a high spot I want to spit" and "I am never startled by a fish" really predict GPA? To answer this question, Blumenfeld conducted a cross-validation study in which he gave the test to a new sample of students. For this sample, none of the nine items was found to be related to GPA.

Key Terms 1

humours
personality
phrenology
teleological

Key Terms 2

archetypes

basic anxiety
collective unconscious
death instinct
defense mechanism
determinism
dynamism
ego
ego psychology
fixation
id
intrapsychic conflict
libido
life instinct
object-relations theory
persona
personal unconscious
preconscious
psychic energy
psychoanalytic theory
psychodynamic theory
reality principle
regression
repression
superego
unconscious

Key People 2

Alfred Adler
Sigmund Freud
Karen Horney
Carl Jung
Harry Stack Sullivan

Key Terms 3

behavioral theory
interactionism
reinforcement
situationism
social learning theory

Key People 3

Albert Bandura
Walter Mischel
Julian Rotter
B.F. Skinner

Key Terms 4

actualization
humanism
organism

self-actualization
self-concept

Key People 4

Carl Rogers

Key Terms 5

extraversion
factor analysis
introversion
trait
typology

Key People 5

Gordon Allport
Raymond B. Cattell
Paul Costa
Hans J. Eysenck
Robert McCrae

Key Terms 6

neural network

Key Terms 7

Minnesota Multiphasic Personality Inventory (MMPI)
objective test
projective hypothesis
projective test
reliability
Rorschach test
Sixteen Personality Factor Questionnaire (16-PF)
Thematic Apperception Test
validity

References

Rorschach, H.. (1942). *Psychodiagnostics: A diagnostic test based on perception.* (P. Lemkau & B. Kronenberg, Trans.). Berne: Huber (1st German ed. published in 1921; U.S. distributor, Grune & Stratton).

Keys to Personality 1

1. Some basic issues need to be dealt with by all personality theories.

A. The major ones?
Determinism, nature-nurture, early life experience, unconscious motivation, teleological motivation, holism, continuity.

2. Personality is partially based in biology.

A. How evolutionary psychology views personality traits?
As adaptive products of evolution

B. Some theorists who implicitly subscribe to this view?
Freud, Cattell, Eysenck

3. Modern evolutionary theory postulates the genetic transmission of evolved characteristics.

A. The average heritability for personality traits?
About 50%

B. The major types of studies done to arrive at this figure?
Twin, adoption

Keys to Personality 2

1. Freud developed the first scientific theory of personality.

A. The sectors on the continuum of consciousness?
Unconscious
Preconscious
Conscious

B. What type of motivation is most important?
Unconscious

C. A term for the dynamic force that fuels personality and behavior?
Psychic energy

D. Three major psychic structures and their basic characteristics?
Id—primitive, biological, nonrational
Ego—logical, reality-oriented
Superego—social conscience

E. The relationship of the three structures to each other?
Conflict

F. The unconscious mechanisms that reduce anxiety?
The defenses, especially repression.

G. The emphases in modern, mainstream psychoanalytic theory?
Ego psychology, object-relations theory.

2. Jung and the social analysts offered psychodynamic alternatives to Freudian theory.

A. Some of Jung's major personality structures?
Persona, collective unconscious, archetypes

B. Jung's attitudes and functions?
Attitudes: Extraversion, introversion
Functions: sensation, intuition, thinking, feeling.

C. How the social analytic theories differ from Freud?
Reduced emphasis on biological factors
More emphasis on consciousness
Introduced the self
Introduced sociocultural factors

D. Who the social analysts were?
Adler, Horney, Sullivan

E. Sullivan's major needs?
Satisfaction, Security

3. Psychodynamic theories have been criticized.
   A. The major criticisms?
      Too complex
      Lack scientific precision
      Too biological
      Based originally on an unrepresentative sample
      Sexist
      Negative view of human nature

Keys to Personality 3

1. The Skinnerian view employs no constructs.
   A. Why?
      They require unwarranted inferences.
   B. How lawful cause-effects relationships are established?
      Through functional analysis
   C. The major determinant of behavior?
      Reinforcement
2. Cognitive theory is a currently powerful approach.
   A. What shifted the emphasis in personality to cognitive?
      The shift from observable responses to cognitions
      The increasing sophistication of computer modeling.
   B. The focus of the cognitive-behavioral school?
      How cognitions are acquired and modified; how they affect behavior.
   C. The emphasis in Bandura's theory?
      Social learning through modeling
   D. How personality in acquired in Bandura's view?
      Through the reciprocal interaction of personal and environmental factors.
   E. The major criticisms of cognitive-behaviorism?
      Too simplistic, mechanical, and environmental

Keys to Personality 4

1. Humanism has a very positive view of human nature.
   A. How its view of humans differs with other schools?
      Each person is unique and important
      Humans are uniquely different from all other animals.
      Humans strive for happiness, love, and goodness.
2. The major theorist is Carl Rogers.
   A. The major structures he specifies?
      Organism, self
   B. Which is more important?
      Organism
   C. His term for one's view of one's own characteristics?
      Self-concept
   D. What Gallup's research seems to show?
      That even some primates may have self-concepts.
   E. Rogers' terms for his motivational tendencies?
      Actualization, self-actualization
   F. What the distortion of experience to maintain self-consistency causes?

Incongruence between self and experience
Inaccurate self-concept
Psychopathology in extreme cases

3. Humanism has been criticized.
   A. The major criticisms?
      Too optimistic, selfish
      Relies on self-report
      Difficult to test

KEYS TO PERSONALITY—5

1. Trait theories hypothesize a limited set of traits.
   A. The kinds of traits Allport hypothesizes?
      Common, unique
      Cardinal, central, secondary
2. Cattell and Eysenck are factor analytic theorists.
   A. What factor analysis does?
      Reduces sets of correlations to clusters of variables (factors).
   B. The number of factors Cattell finds?
      23 normal, 12 pathological
   C. The number of factors Eysenck finds and what they are?
      3 factors: Extraversion, neuroticism, psychoticism.
3. A currently popular theory is the Big Five.
   A. What the factors are?
      Extraversion, agreeableness, conscientiousness, neuroticism, openness.
   B. What complicates the picture?
      Not all researchers get exactly the same five factors.
   C. Why factor theories are important?
      They may eventually identify a small, universal set of traits.
      They may help to predict behavior more accurately.
4. Situationism and interactionism question the assumptions of pure trait theories.
   A. Who the major situational theorist is?
      Walter Mischel
   B. The basic idea in interactionism?
      Behavior is affected by traits, situations, and their interactions.
   C. The major criticisms of trait theory?
      Merely descriptive, sterile, not explanatory

KEYS TO PERSONALITY—7

1. Personality assessment involves tests of personality.
   A. The necessary characteristics of these tests?
      Reliability, validity
2. Objective tests consist of self-descriptive items.
   A. The names of some major tests?
      MMPI, MMPI-2, 16PF, NEO-PI
   B. The method used in developing the MMPI?
      Criterion keying
   C. Some problems with the MMPI?
      Relatively low reliability
      Scales are intercorrelated
      Was not developed to assess normal functioning
      Not entirely accurate in its assessments
   D. What the 16 PF measures?
      Cattell's 23 traits

E. What the NEO-PI measures?

The five Costa-McCrae traits

3. Projective tests attempt to assess unconscious functioning.

A. Some major tests?

Rorschach, TAT

B. Some problems with these tests?

Very subjective and complex

Reliability and validity hard to determine

Chapter 15

Health and Stress

Outline

Health Psychology and Behavioral Medicine

Evolutionary Psychology of Health and Stress

Sources of Stress

- Life Change
- Hassles
- Oh No, It's Monday!
- When Home Is Not a Castle
- Lack of Social Support
- Catastrophe
- Acculturation

Psychological and Biological Reactions to Stress

- Psychological Reactions
- Anxiety
- Traumatic Reactions
- Suicide
- Burnout
- Biological Reactions
- The General Adaptation Syndrome
- The Neurophysiology of Stress

Stress and Physical Illness

- The Role of Life Stress
- Multifactorial Causation: Nature, Nurture, and Stress
  - Genetic Predispositions
  - Situational Factors
- Illnesses Associated With Stress
  - Stress and The Immune System
  - Coronary Artery Disease
  - Ulcers
  - Cancer
  - Other Disorders

Dealing with Stress

- Mediating Stress
  - Social Support
  - Predicting and Controlling Stress
- Coping Strategies
  - Richard Lazarus and Cognitive Appraisal
  - Self-Instruction
  - Coping Through Change
  - Increasing Social Support
  - Stress Inoculation
  - Defense Mechanisms
  - The Health Effects of Coping
- Preventing and Reducing Stress

Overview

OUR LIVES are filled with pressures and problems: We feel their impact at home, at school, and on the job and say we are "stressed out." How stress affects us and how we cope with it depends on a number of factors, including our biological and psychological makeup. Reactions to stress occur at both emotional and physiological levels and range from temporary anxiety to chronic physical disorders such as ulcers and coronary artery disease. Fortunately, there are many factors, such as the presence of social supports, that can help us to avoid or reduce the negative effects of stress. Furthermore, there are a number of techniques we can use to cope with stress, as well as therapeutic treatments.

Health and stress are closely associated with personality, abnormal behavior, and treatment or therapy. Stress can be a factor in the development of personality, and aspects of your personality influence how strongly you will react to stress and how your health will be affected. There are also direct links among physical health, stress, and abnormal behavior. In particular, stress is a strong factor in the development of some forms of abnormal behavior, and healthy behaviors can help to prevent the development of psychopathology. Finally, it is often stress that brings people into treatment settings, where either drugs or psychotherapy or a combination of the two are used to reduce the stress. Think about these associations as you read because you will gain a better overall understanding of all the topics if you see how they are linked to each other.

Stressed Out

Fay is a 30-year-old mother of two who has gone back to school to get her law degree. She also has a part-time job as a proofreader in a typesetting shop. In a recent one-week period, she had two final exams to study for, a rush project at work that required extra hours, a birthday party to plan for her daughter, and a houseful of visiting relatives. Not surprisingly, Fay found herself getting into bed each night totally exhausted yet unable to sleep. Her stomach was upset, her head hurt, and her muscles ached. These symptoms were accompanied by feelings of tension, uneasiness, and anxiety.

It is obvious that Fay's life is filled with stress. The many demands on her - from school, job, family - served as stressors, and her psychological and physical reactions to these stressors constitute a state of stress. Some stressors are external. In Fay's case, they include final exams, extra work hours, and increased family responsibilities. Others are internal and may or may not be grounded in reality. For example, Fay may have felt guilty for not giving a more elaborate party for her daughter or for wishing that her relatives would go away.

People vary greatly in what they find stressful and in how they respond to stress. Fay, for example, felt overwhelmed. Even though she managed to keep going, she was beset by a variety of physical ailments, including migraine headaches and stomach ulcers. Someone else in her situation might have reacted differently, perhaps with confusion, withdrawal, or anger. Some people might even thrive on Fay's lifestyle. Such variations in reactions depend on a number of factors, including past experiences with stress, personality structure, and ability to cope with stressful situations.

Health Psychology and Behavioral Medicine

Studying the effects of stress on the body is the job of *health psychology*. This relatively new sub-discipline examines the psychological factors that help people to stay physically healthy and those that may be causal factors in illness (Adler & Matthews, 1994). We will consider some of the principles and findings of health psychology later in the chapter.

Behavioral medicine is the larger interdisciplinary field of which health psychology is a part. It involves scientists from a number of different fields, including medicine, health education, medical sociology, physical education, and medical anthropology (Epstein, 1992). Extensive interdisciplinary research is focused on such chronic illnesses as cancer, heart disease, and AIDS (Chesney, 1993), illnesses that tend to develop slowly and are greatly affected by health behaviors that we will take up later.

The Evolutionary Psychology of Health and Stress

From an evolutionary perspective, the healthy - and unhealthy - behaviors most widely exhibited by humans are those that have evolved because they solve particular adaptive problems. For example, most humans are at least reasonably safety-conscious and engage in a wide range of safe behaviors. Most of us check the traffic flow before stepping off the curb, keep chlorine bleach out of the reach of toddlers, and carefully check our parachutes before taking off for a sky-diving trip. These safety behaviors have evolved to help ensure the survival of the species. As we will see later in the chapter, we also frequently engage in *coping* behaviors when we are faced with stress. These are behaviors designed to reduce the negative effects of the stress and sometimes also to solve problems. They are survival-oriented behaviors because they can reduce stress, which might otherwise cause a range of both psychological and physical disorders.

At the same time, we engage in such unhealthy behaviors as smoking, heavy drinking, eating high-fat diets, and putting ourselves in stressful situations. Why do these behaviors occur? From an evolutionary perspective, they may have originally been adaptive behaviors and may even now have some adaptive qualities. For example, even though we now know that tobacco and alcohol are very dangerous substances, both can temporarily reduce levels of anxiety and both can enhance an adolescent's feelings of self-worth. Indeed, alcohol in small amounts may even help to protect us from heart disease (Doll et al., 1994; Simon & Rosolova, 1994). We will also see that researchers have been able to provide at least a partial answer to the broader nature-nurture question as it relates to stress and health.

Sources of Stress

Stress does not occur uniformly across all situations and under all circumstances. Rather, it has relatively specific sources (Christensen & Jensen, 1995). Among the major sources of stress that have been identified are life change, hassles, job stress, home life, war, and natural disasters.

Life Change

Which is more stressful: divorce or a jail term? being fired or getting married? changing jobs or retiring? In order to determine which events in life are the most stressful, Thomas Holmes and his colleagues developed the *Social Readjustment Rating Scale* (SRRS; Holmes and Rahe, 1967), which is still widely used (Koh & Hong, 1993; Thompson & Morris, 1994). The scale was originally constructed by having subjects rate each of 43 events in terms of the amount of social readjustment that would be required if the event were to occur. Getting married was arbitrarily assigned an anchor value of 50, and subjects were asked to rate the remaining items by assigning values above or below 50 to reflect the relative amount of adjustment needed.

The scores on the SRRS are expressed as life change units (LCUs). It is perhaps no surprise that the most stressful event, with 100 LCUs, is death of a spouse (see Table 15-1). Also high on the list are divorce and marital separation. Marriage is half as stressful as the death of a spouse but is still among the top ten sources of stress. Note that a number of events that we usually consider to be positive, including marriage, pregnancy, retirement, and personal achievement, are among the sources of stress. And what might seem to be minor events, such as changes in recreational or social activities, also bring with them a certain amount of stress.

Early research based on the SRRS suggested that a total of 150 LCUs or less for recent events represents a normal, relatively nonstressful existence; 150-199 LCUs means mild stress; 200-299 is moderate stress; and a score of 300 or higher is indicative of a major life crisis. But what do life stress scores mean? They mean that changes in life - even positive ones - can create a considerable amount of stress. As we will see later in the chapter, this life stress can contribute subtantantially to the development of physical disorders.

Since the pioneering efforts of Holmes and Rahe, many others have developed alternative instruments. The Student-Life Stress Inventory (Gadzella, 1994) taps a variety of stressors commonly experienced by college students, and the Parenting Stress Index identifies the sources and levels of stressors experienced by parents (Lacharite et al., 1992). Measuring other aspects of the stress response, the Daily Stress Inventory assesses the difficulties commonly experienced by many people on a day-to-day basis (Waters et al., 1993), and the Coping Resources Inventory for Stress evaluates your ability to deal effectively with stressors (Matheny et al., 1994).

Hassles

Ever have one of those days that begins with the mysteriously missing shower soap and the lost car keys, continues with the traffic snarls and full parking lot that make you late to work, and ends with an empty refrigerator and a loud, all-night party next door? These are brief *hassles*. More protracted ones are noise from the airport just outside your back door (Scattarella, 1992) and that old car that repeatedly leaves you sitting beside the road.

Studies show that daily hassles contribute a significant amount to our overall stress load. Chronic headache sufferers, for example, report more frequent hassles than do control subjects, though the two groups do not differ in the occurrence of major stress events (De-Benedittis & Lorenzetti, 1992). Higher levels of daily hassles in college freshmen are predictive of both depression and physical symptoms (Lu, 1994). And, in case you've never noticed, your computer can be a significant source of stress. In one study, a Computer Hassles Questionnaire was administered to 65 regular users. Those who reported experiencing more frequent hassles - lost files, crashed disks, missing data, and the like - also had more somatic (bodily) complaints, such as muscle pain and head aches (Hudiburg et al., 1993).

Oh No, It's Monday!

Monday morning is the most likely time for myocardial infarctions (heart attacks) to occur in working people (Willich et al., 1994). This finding seems to confirm the old adage that getting up for work on Monday morning is "the pits." Why? Perhaps because work is often a highly stressful part of life. More generally, the relationship between work and stress is substantial (Mincheva et al., 1994; Holt, 1982). Work both causes and is affected by stress. Documented sources of job stress include long hours, the presence of dangers and health hazards, physically demanding work (Kasl, 1978), negative social relationships on the job (Brodsky, 1976), and boredom (Caplan et al., 1975). Not surprisingly, personality is also a factor (Fontana & Abouserie, 1993), and it is the overly anxious individual who is most susceptible to the impact of job stress (Buck, 1972). It appears, however, that the single factor most likely to lead to job stress is a poor fit between the person and the job environment (Margolis and Kroes, 1974). If you have inadequate talent or training for your job, lack interest in it, or don't do it well, the fit is poor and job-stress high.

Stress levels vary considerably from one occupation to another. After analyzing mortality statistics for a number of conditions associated with stress, including suicide, homicide, and heart disease, Charles Karther and Leonard Linden (1982) concluded that professional services and manufacturing occupations tended to have relatively low mortality rates for the stress-related conditions. Higher stress-associated mortality rates were found for agricultural and entertainment occupations. Studies also show substantial stress in teachers (Fontana & Abouserie, 1993), orchestra conductors (Fetter, 1993), construction workers (Liu & Waterbor, 1994), and homemakers (Houston et al., 1992). Since stress contributes to disease and death, the job you choose may influence not only the way you live but the way you die.

When Home Is Not a Castle

Another major source of stress is home life (Dumas & LaFreniere, 1993). Such aspects of the home environment as the physical and social structure of the neighborhood, financial problems, parent-child relationships, and interactions with roommates, family, and landlords are all potential stressors.

According to Ilfeld (1982), the two most stressful situations in a marriage are those in which one or both spouses insist on having their own way and when one or both spend money unwisely. The third most stressful situation occurs when there is an imbalance in the extent to which each partner finds it necessary to give in to the wishes of the other. Finally, home life is seen as more stressful when either marital partner feels that he or she cannot readily talk to the other about things that are of personal importance. The inverse is also true: Being able to talk to one's spouse during times of difficulty can be an effective stress reducer.

If marriage is potentially stressful, separation and divorce are even more so. With the divorce rate currently hovering around 50% (U.S. Bureau of the Census, 1991), it is clearly important to understand the impact of divorce as a stressor. Marital separation is associated with increased rates of death due to suicide, homicide, and disease, with higher rates of illness and disability, and with greater numbers of automobile accidents (Kowalski & Stack, 1992; Bloom, Asher, and White, 1978).

Parenting is also a potential source of stress for both parent and child. In particular, dealing with a child who has serious medical, behavioral, or academic problems can be stressful for the parent. On the other side of the coin is the child whose parents are sources of stress. The most obvious cases are those involving physical abuse (see Chapter). Far more common, however, are verbal abuse, criticism of the child and the imposition of unreasonable demands. We have more to say about marriage, divorce, and family in Chapter 7.

Lack of Social Support. One of the most consistent findings in the stress literature is that the lack, loss, or disruption of social support is an extremely stressful experience likely to have severe consequences. Social support is defined as the availability of other people whom one can talk with about problems, interact with more generally, and rely on for help in time of need.

The effects of reduced social support have been documented in a variety of studies. Notice, for example, that four of the five most stressful events listed in the SRRS (Table 15-1) - death of a spouse, divorce, marital separation, and the death of a close family member - involve the loss of social support. It may not be surprising to read, then, that women who serve in such multiple - and often stressful - roles as job-holder, mother, and caregiver suffer greater effects of stress when they do not have adequate social support (Stephens et al., 1994). Other research has demonstrated that 60 percent of recently widowed women suffer major health impairments (Raphael, 1977). Another line of research, conducted by Stanley Schachter (1959), showed that people confronted with a stress-inducing experience (receiving a painful electric shock) choose to await the experience with other people, rather than in social isolation. And Phillip Zimabardo (1982) found that shyness, which has the effect of producing partial social isolation, can have substantial adverse effects, including sexual dysfunction, alcoholism, depression, low job morale, and even irrational rage leading to sudden, unplanned murder (Lee, Zimbardo, and Berthold, 1977).

Other researchers have focused more directly on social isolation and social undermining. Studies consistently demonstrate that both physical and mental health are worse among socially isolated people (Cassel, 1970; Kaplan, Cassel, and Gore, 1977) and among unmarried people (Pearlin and Johnson, 1977). Heart attack victims whose spouses are unsupportive have slower recoveries (Beach et al., 1992), and those who are socially isolated are 49% more likely to die than those who are not (Jenkinson et al., 1993). Finally, a step beyond isolation is social undermining, in which others work to actively reduce your social support. One study showed that social undermining of African-Americans in work settings increases both self-reported stress and physical illness (Gant et al., 1993).

Perhaps the most convincing results come from a longitudinal study involving over 2200 men and nearly 2500 women who were followed for nine years (Berkman and Syme, 1979). The study examined the presence or absence of four types of social ties: marriage, friends, church membership, and group associations. Results showed that people with the fewest social connections were two to five times more likely to die than those with the most connections. In addition, socially isolated individuals were more likely to engage in such poor health behaviors as smoking, drinking, and overeating, although the extent of social contacts predicted mortality over and above the effects of any of these poor health practices. The striking effect of social support on stress and health becomes clearer when we consider the implications of this finding: We can actually predict the probability of death better by knowing the amount of social contact and social support a person has than by knowing her history of smoking, drinking, overeating, and other poor health habits.

Catastrophe

Wars, disasters, and domestic crises can produce symptoms commonly associated with stress (Joseph et al., 1994). A good example is the nuclear "accident" that took place at Three Mile Island (TMI) near Middletown, Pennsylvania in 1979. Pumps that circulated water to cool the reactor shut down, and the reactor began to heat up, and the problem was not properly dealt with. The result was radioactive water on the floor of the reactor building and radioactive gas trapped in the containment building surrounding the reactor. News of this crisis was inaccurate, inadequate, and unnecessarily frightening. Following the incident, area residents exhibited a number of stress symptoms (Flynn and Chalmers, 1980), and a presidential commission investigating the incident concluded that one its major effects was to produce severe stress for many people (Dohrenwend et al., 1979).

In the years since the accident, stress symptoms continue to be seen in some TMI area residents. One study sampled 35 people randomly selected from an area within 5 miles of the TMI nuclear reactor and three control groups, one within 5 miles of an undamaged nuclear power plant, one within 5 miles of an undamaged coal-fired power plant, and one from an area more than 15 miles from any type of power plant (Fleming et al., 1982). Results showed that TMI residents exhibited greater amounts of stress on psychological and biochemical measures than did subjects in any of the three control groups.

Other civilian disasters and individual traumatic experiences also produce significant symptoms of emotional distress. One study showed symptoms in 65% of the victims of a natural disaster (Lima et al., 1993), another demonstrated clinical trauma in battered women (Dutton et al., 1994), and a third showed that 84% of college undergraduates have had at least one traumatic experience, with one-third of these reporting four or more such events. Those with stronger histories of trauma have more anxiety symptoms and are more likely to be depressed (Vrana & Lauterbach, 1994).

War is, of course, an extremely stressful situation. World War II took place over fifty years ago, but its traumatic effects have persisted for many living veterans. One study showed that 70% of those who were prisoners of war and 18% of those who were in combat still suffer from traumatic anxiety and other symptoms (Sutker et al., 1993). Not surprisingly, Jewish people who lived through the Holocaust as children also still suffer the symptoms of traumatic disorders (Robinson et al., 1994).

U.S. soldiers have also experienced their share of stress and its consequences. Participation in the Vietnam War had profound effects that still linger today, as we discuss in Probe 2. Even the relatively brief Operation Desert Storm, which took U.S. troops to the Middle East, produced some traumatic effects (Southwick et al., 1993). Those whose units were deployed for battle showed more symptoms of trauma later on than did those in units that were not involved in combat (Rothberg et al., 1994), and the families of Desert Storm veterans often suffered clinically significant stress symptoms as well (Peebles-Kleiger & Kleiger, 1994).

Acculturation

A final source of stress is *acculturation* - the process of adapting to and becoming integrated with a new cultural environment (van-Willigen et al., 1995). Newly arrived immigrants must undergo a period of adjustment and adaptation, often with fairly minimal psychosocial resources to provide them with support (McKelvey & Webb, 1996). Take the example of Puerto Ricans who have settled in Hartford, Connecticut. Nearly 40 percent live below the poverty line, and as many as two-thirds of the households in some Puerto Rican neighborhoods have no employed members (Dressler and Bernal, 1982). Research on Hispanic (mostly Puerto Rican) patients seen in a Hartford public health nursing agency showed that the acculturation stress undergone by these individuals was associated with an increase in behavior problems and with poor general health status (Dressler and Bernal, 1982).

Psychological and Biological Reactions to Stress

Now that we have explored some of the major sources of stress, we turn to the psychological and biological reactions of individuals who find themselves in stressful situations. The question here is one of impact: What does stress do to the mind and what does it do to the body?

Psychological Reactions

Some people are able to react quite positively to stress and to cope well with stressful situations. They even use the experience to improve their levels of personal functioning. However, most people react in ways that are at least partially negative and potentially harmful. Some of these negative reactions are psychological, others physical. The psychological reactions can be so severe that many theorists believe stress is at least partially responsible for a number of the psychological disorders we discuss in Chapter 16. Among the major psychological responses to stress are anxiety, traumatic reactions, suicide, and burnout.

Anxiety. Perhaps the most common and obvious reaction to stress is anxiety. It is usually defined as a vague, uncomfortable feeling state involving a sense that something unpleasant is occurring or is about to occur. A variety of situations can produce anxiety, and they range from leaving home for a new life on a college campus to being given added responsibilities on the job. Whatever its source, anxiety can have a variety of negative consequences for the individual.

The relationship between anxiety and college grades has been a topic of interest to psychologists and college students alike. One early study showed, for example, that students with higher levels of anxiety have lower grade point averages (Spielberger, 1962). A further study found that students provided with counseling aimed at reducing anxiety showed greater improvement in grades than did students not provided with such counseling (Splelberger, Denny, and Witz, 1962). And more recent work confirms the negative effects of anxiety on college performance (Schreiber & Schreiber, 1995)

Any of the major sources of stress discussed earlier is likely to induce feelings of anxiety in at least some people (Gillis, 1992). It is important to note, however, that there are wide individual variations in the extent to which a given event or situation is perceived as stressful and in the amount of anxiety experienced in any given situation. Losing a job that provides the family income, for example, will produce much higher levels of anxiety in some people than in others. Interestingly enough, recent twin studies show that differences in anxiety reactions to stressful events are strongly influenced by genetic factors (Ditto, 1993). The topic of anxiety is discussed more fully in Chapter 16.

Traumatic Reactions. The sudden death of a close relative, involvement in a serious car accident, participation in armed combat, and other such severely stressful experiences can produce a psychological reaction that is much stronger than simple anxiety (Lonigan et al., 1994). Mardi Horowitz (1982) has identified two major psychological states that often characterize this traumatic reaction: intrusion and denial. During the intrusion state, the individual is extremely vigilant, experiences startle reactions to even minor stimuli, and has sleep and dream disturbances. In addition, she is confused and disorganized and may experience panic attacks and intrusive-repetitive emotions, thoughts, and behaviors relating to the traumatic event. Bodily reactions such as nausea, diarrhea, and tremors may accompany the psychological reactions. The denial state is typically characterized by complete or partial amnesia for the traumatic event, sleep disturbances, and the experience of fantasies that counteract reality. The person lacks emotional reactivity (described as "numbness") and may exhibit extreme levels of overactivity, often alternating with withdrawal. Again, physical symptoms, such as fatigue and headaches, may occur. The more general traumatic process in which the intrusion and denial states take place is diagramed in Figure 15-1.

As an example of traumatic reaction, Horowitz (1982) described the case of a young man whose close friend had committed suicide. After the initial shock, the man realized he had paid little attention to his friend lately and had on several occasions put off the friend's request to sit down and talk about some problems he was having. The young man felt that he could have been instrumental in preventing the suicide. At first he denied the whole thing and tried to put it out of his head. After a while, however, he began to experience extreme anxiety whenever he closed his eyes to wash his face (at which point he would see the face of his dead friend) and whenever he turned the lights off (at which point he would have a sense that the friend was present in the room). Sometimes the individual is eventually able to work through the trauma. In other cases, however, the traumatic reaction continues for long periods of time. Studies confirm that when it does, it is associated with a variety of symptomatology (Dutton et al., 1994).

Suicide. Just the other day, a good friend called to ask for my help because her son-in-law had committed suicide. After a brief separation, his wife had informed him that she would definitely seek a divorce. He went home alone and killed himself. Another case of suicide - one that made the national news - was that of Harvard undergraduate Sinedu Tadesse, who stabbed her roommate to death, then hung herself on May 28, 1995.

Suicide is usually associated with depression. Though it occurs more frequently in elderly people, it is the third leading cause of death among adolescents and the second among college students (Garland & Zigler, 1993). The ultimate response to stress, suicide is typically preceded by one or more precipitating events. In one study, 70% of adolescent suicides were preceded by stressful precipitating events that occurred within one month - and often with 24 hours - of death. They most often involved interpersonal separation or severe conflict, which can produce depression (Marttunen et al., 1993). Chapter 16 discusses the relationship between depression and suicide, which is substantial. In fact, although most depressed people do not commit suicide, most suicidal individuals are depressive; the suicide rate is about 25 times higher in depressed groups.

One of the ten leading causes of death in Western countries, particularly in younger populations, suicide takes 30,000 lives in the United States each year - about one every 18 minutes. Beyond these "successful" suicides, there are 200,000 attempts each year, and five million Americans will attempt suicide some time in their lives (U.S. Bureau of the Census, 1990). These statistics mean that the suicide rate in the United States is about 10-12 per 100,000 population, putting the U.S. midway in the distribution of suicide statistics. Figures from the World Health Organization indicate that nearly half a million people worldwide commit suicide each year - over 1,000 each day or about 1.4 per minute.

The peak age range for suicide is 24-44. However, its frequency is increasing in adolescents and even children (Fremouw et al., 1990), with about 9% of high school students attempting suicide each year (Spirito et al., 1989). The rate in the 15-24 age group has quadrupled in the past forty years, with 27% having thought seriously about killing themselves (Centers for Disease Control, 1991). Over 10,000 college students try to kill themselves annually, and about 1000 are successful (Fremouw et al., 1990).

Within the United States, there is considerable variation in the suicide rates of different groups. One differentiator is gender. Completed suicide is three times more common in men, who often use guns, than in women, who are more likely to employ drug overdoses. In fact, suicide ranks as the second leading cause of death among white males between the ages of 10 and 55. However, about three times as many women as men make unsuccessful suicide attempts. Age is also a factor. Suicide rates for white males increase with age, whereas those for white females peak between ages 45 and 64, then decline slightly.

Other factors that have been correlated with suicide rates include marriage, children, income, and employment status. Married people are statistically less likely to commit suicide than singles (Stack, 1982), and some data suggest that the presence of children in the home decreases the likelihood of suicide (Stack, 1980a). Studies also show a consistent inverse relationship between income level and suicide rate (Stack, 1980b) and a positive relationship between unemployment and suicide rate (Stack, 1980a). Finally, suggestion may be a factor. One series of studies showed that suicide rates increased by 3 percent in the United States and by 13 percent in Great Britain shortly after the appearance of a newspaper story on suicide (Phillips, 1974). Similarly, there was a significant increase in automobile fatalities, especially single-car accidents (which are sometimes suicides), following suicide stories (Phillips, 1979).

There are about eight suicide attempts for every successful suicide (Leenaars & Wenckstern, 1991), and some investigators have suggested that people who make unsuccessful attempts are quite different from those who are successful. The person who unsuccessfully attempts suicide often does not really want to die. Rather, the suicide attempt may be a plea for help or a ploy to gain sympathy or attention. In fact, when suicide notes are available, as is true in about 15% of cases (O'Donnell et al., 1993), it is possible to distinguish between those of genuine suicide cases and those of people who do not intend to die (Black, 1993). The genuine notes tend to display greater amounts of self-blame and hostility and to be more specific and decisive (Ammon, 1994).

One of the most famous suicide theorists, Emile Durkheim (1897), suggested that suicide is primarily a result of the impact of society on the individual. Some suicides occur because the person has too few ties with the community, others because his relationship with the society suddenly breaks down, and still others because the society requires suicide, as in the Japanese hara-kirin ritual. While some elements of Durkheim's theory have received support in empirical studies, most aspects of his model have not held up well (Stack, 1982).

Burnout. When stress is prolonged, it can lead to burnout, which is marked by a gradual increase in psychological, behavioral, and physical symptoms until the person can no longer function effectively (Bocker, 1994). He may become anxious, irritable, depressed, even withdrawn and suspicious. Behavioral changes may include loss of interest in work, reduced job performance, drug and alcohol abuse, and increased accidents on the job. Physical symptoms can be quite varied, ranging from upset stomach and periodic diarrhea to ulcers and heart attacks. There is also wide variability in the severity of burnout, from minor, periodic symptoms of exhaustion to relatively debilitating combinations of more severe symptoms.

Burnout can occur in home life and other settings but is most often observed in job environments. One study of 300 critical care nurses showed, for example, that those who were strongly committed to their careers, had difficulties dealing with others on the job, and lacked job satisfaction were quite likely to show symptoms of burnout (Stechmiller & Yarandi, 1993). College coaches also frequently show burnout (Kelley, 1994), as do physicians. Studies have found evidence of burnout in 34% of one group of surgeons (Johnson et al., 1993) and in 58% of a broader group of physicians (Deckard et al., 1994).

A final—and very serious—reaction to severe stress is a diagnosable psychological disorder termed post-traumatic stress disorder. Often seen in war veterans and other victims of trauma, it is discussed in Probe 1.

Biological Reactions to Stress

Reactions to stress are not entirely psychological. You can probably recall a stressful situation, such as a first date or a time you had to speak before a group, when you had "butterflies" in your stomach, could feel your heart racing, and broke out in a cold sweat. These are some of the immediate—and relatively minor—*somatic* (physical) effects of stress. Stress can also produce severe, long-lasting physiological problems based on biochemical changes and actual tissue damage (Abiodun, 1994).

The General Adaptation Syndrome. Over a period of 40 years, Hans Selye (1976) carried out the most important series of physiological stress studies ever done, and others have confirmed and extended his findings (Kopin, 1995; Henry, 1992; Sudakov, 1992). Based on his extensive research, Selye proposed that the body reacts to stress in a predictable response called the general adaptation syndrome (GAS). The GAS occurs in three major phases: the alarm reaction, the stage of resistance, and the stage of exhaustion.

The alarm reaction is an emergency response to a severe stressor. In Selye's view, a stressor is anything that can injure the organism; it can be either psychological (endangered security, job loss) or physiological (disease, food deprivation). The alarm reaction involves a series of complex biochemical and physical changes in the body that produce such symptoms as increased heart rate, muscle tension, and blood pressure. Bodily resistance drops, and there may be both psychological and physiological stress symptoms, including physical illness, psychological disorder, and even death if the stress is severe enough.

A continuation of the stressor produces a second phase, the stage of resistance. This stage is initiated by an increase in the secretion of certain pituitary and adrenal hormones. It involves the disappearance of the symptoms seen in the alarm stage and an apparent resumption of reasonably normal physiological functions. In fact, however, certain physiological reactions to stress carry over into this stage, and further continuation of the stressor leads to a stage of exhaustion. During this final stage, the adrenal glands lose their ability to function normally, and the organism can no longer adapt effectively to the stress. Adaptation energy is exhausted, and the symptoms initially seen in the alarm stage reappear in a more severe and now irreversible form.

The Neurophysiology of Stress. Several structural components of the central and peripheral nervous systems are directly involved in the GAS, as are a number of endocrine glands. The cortex of the brain is central to the stress response, primarily because it is involved in the perception and interpretation of stimuli as being stressful or nonstressful. A second function of this highest level of the brain in stress is cortical inhibition —the suppression of strong emotional reactions to stressful situations. If it were not for cortical inhibition, strong emotional reactions to stress arising at the subcortical level would produce potentially devastating responses (see Chapter 12). In addition to the cortex, areas of the limbic system are involved in the stress response. In particular, the hypothalamus is active in cases where stressful stimulation produces an emotional response.

The *autonomic nervous system,* which originates in the hypothalamus, is the principal peripheral mediator of the stress response. When a situation is perceived as stressful, the sympathetic branch of the ANS becomes dominant and produces such changes as increased heart rate and blood pressure and a blood flow pattern that takes blood from the skin and stomach and moves it into the skeletal muscles of the limbs.

This initial *fight-or-flight response,* as Walter Cannon (1914) called it, would be short-lived if only the autonomic nervous system were involved (see Chapter 12). Continuation of the stress response described by Selye requires endocrine involvement to maintain the physiological reactions to stress at heightened levels. The endocrine glands involved in this prolonged stress response are the adrenal medulla, the adrenal cortex, the anterior pituitary, and the thyroid. The most immediate and rapid neuroendocrine response to stress is that of the *adrenal medulla.* Neural impulses from the hypothalamus stimulate the medulla to release epinephrine and norepinephrine into the bloodstream. These two hormones produce an increase in what is called *adrenergic activity.* This activity has essentially the same effects as sympathetic stimulation, including increased heart output, elevated blood pressure, decreased blood flow in the kidneys, increased muscle tension, and heightened levels of cholesterol in the bloodstream. The adrenal medullary response is somewhat slower than that of the sympathetic system, but it is more chronic and accounts for the initial prolongation of the stress reaction during the alarm stage of the GAS.

After sympathetic and adrenal medullary involvement, the third level of response to stress occurs in the endocrine system more generally. Substances secreted by the hypothalamus stimulate the *anterior pituitary* to release *adrenocorticotropic hormone* (ACTH) and growth hormones into the bloodstream. ACTH acts on the *adrenal cortex* to cause the release of glucocorticoid, which helps increase the supply of energy available to the body. The role of growth hormones in stress is unclear, but they appear to mobilize stored fats and to increase the concentration of such energy sources as glucose and free fatty acids in the bloodstream. Another endocrine reaction is the release of the hormone thyroxine by the thyroid gland. Increases in heart rate, blood pressure, and metabolic rate appear to be among the effects of thyroxine release.

Research confirms that there is little reduction in the level of response of the hypothalamic-pituitary-adrenal cortical system with repeated stress. In addition, biochemical mechanisms that translate stress into physical illness are being identified (Licinio et al., 1995). Such findings support the idea that this system is a key to the prolonged stress response seen during the resistance stage of the GAS (Poesen et al., 1995; Nishikaze, 1994),

Stress and Physical Illness

If Selye and others are correct, the stress induced by the general adaptation syndrome can cause or contribute to a variety of physical symptoms and disorders. Galen, the Greek physician whose theories guided medical practice for thirteen centuries after his death, estimated that 60 percent of his patients had symptoms that were based primarily on emotional functioning. Not much has changed: evidence still suggests that stress is an important contributing factor in 50 to 80 percent of all physical disease (Pelletier, 1977).

That a wide variety of illnesses may be caused or aggravated by stress is convincingly supported by a study of patients suffering from various physical ailments (Luborsky, Docherty, and Penick, 1973). It was found that every patient in the group had undergone some identifiable stressful experience shortly before the onset of the illness. Stressors that induced feelings of hostility or resentment were particularly likely to be contributing factors. To understand the role of stress in physical disorders, we begin with the destructive effects of life stress, then discuss the role of genetic and situational factors in the response to stress. We will then be ready to take up the impact of stress in a series of major physical disorders.

The Role of Life Stress

A number of studies using the Holmes-Rahe Social Readjustment Rating Scale (SRRS) that we discussed earlier have shown that people with high LCU totals are more likely than others to develop some sort of physical illness in the period following their major life stresses (Rahe, Mahan. and Authur, 1971; Cline and Chosely 1972). More generally. researchers have found that from 49 to 79 percent of those with life stress scores over 300 develop some serious disease over the next two years (Holmes and Rahe, 1967; Holmes and Masuda, 1974). Among the diseases related to life stress scores are leukemia, tuberculosis, heart disease, multiple sclerosis, and diabetes.

The finding that life stress increases the probability of a number of disorders must be interpreted with some caution (Justice, 1994). First, there are individual differences in the way people respond to stress. Sensation seekers—those who especially enjoy such thrilling activities as skiing and sport parachuting—are less likely than others to show negative effects from life stress (Smith. Johnson. and Sarason, 1978). Thus, not everyone has an equal probability of developing a serious physical illness as a result of a high life stress score. A second caution is that different stresses may be associated with different kinds of health problems. One study showed, for example, that occupational stresses are associated with a variety of physical illnesses, whereas family stresses are more likely to be associated with depression (Stewart and Salt, 1981). Finally, life stress accounts for only about nine percent of the variance contributing to the development of physical illnesses (Rabkin and Struening, 1976). This means that life stresses are causal or contributing factors in disease but that other factors probably play a greater role.

Multi-Factorial Causation: Nature, Nurture, and Stress

Stress alone clearly does not cause illness. Rather, stress is one of several factors that interact to produce disorder. The others include genetic predispositions and situational conditions, such as the ability to predict or control the stressor.

Genetic Predispositions. Some people are more likely to get certain diseases as a result of genetic predispositions or "weaknesses" for these diseases. These predispositions interact with environmental agents to produce specific disorders. Tuberculosis, for example, is caused most directly and obviously by a bacterium. However, an individual who is exposed to the bacillus is more likely to contract the disease if she has a hereditary predisposition toward it (Deretic et al., 1995).

Genetic predispositions are also characteristic of some of the disorders most commonly associated with stress. Among those clearly shown to have a genetic component are hypertension (Farber, 1981), coronary artery disease (Marenberg et al., 1994; Staunton et al., 1994), asthma (Balbi, 1994; Bentley et al., 1996), and migraine headache (Elliott et al., 1996; Russell et al., 1995). In the latter case, for example, it has been found that when parents, particularly mothers, are migraine sufferers, over 70 percent of their children will experience migraines (McKusick, 1978).

The case for *multifactorial causation,* in which two or more factors work together to produce a disease state, has been made in many studies. A good example is a study of subjects who had all been exposed to approximately equal amounts of stress from such sources as job loss, financial difficulty, marriage or divorce, and death in the family (Hinkle, 1974). Two factors distinguished the subjects who developed physical illnesses from those who did not. First, those who became ill had a past history of some physical problem or weakness, such as a preexisting heart problem, stomach difficulties, or respiratory problems. Second, the ill group had a much stronger tendency toward prolonged anxiety. That is, they worried more than the well group.

Situational Factors. The situation in which stress is experienced can also affect its impact on the individual. Consider the differing situations that two business executives face. One is in a position where major stressful events occur without warning, and, having no real power, he cannot make decisions or take actions that might ward off or reduce the stress. The other is under equal stress but knows well in advance when decisions must be made and has considerable control over the decision-making process. Who is more likely to develop an ulcer? The original answer to this question came from Joseph Brady's (1958) classic "executive monkey" study. He subjected monkeys to stress in the form of periodic electric shocks. The monkeys were paired, with one monkey of each pair having access to a lever that could prevent the shocks. The monkey with the lever was able to postpone the shock for both itself and its partner by pressing the lever; failure to press the lever delivered shock to both monkeys. Brady found that the monkeys who could avoid the shock developed ulcers, while the monkeys who had no control did not. This situation might seem analogous to our two executives: Both are subjected to stressful conditions, but only one makes decisions. The decision-making executive is the one who gets the ulcers.

Unfortunately, the picture is somewhat more complicated than Brady's study would seem to suggest. Working in Neal Miller's laboratories, J. Weiss (1969) used matched triplets of rats. One rat could turn a wheel to avoid or escape the shock. The second rat was shocked whenever the first rat was and had no control. And the third rat never received a shock. All three rats heard a tone signaling the coming shock 10 seconds before it was given. The results? The rats that had control over the shock developed less severe ulcers than those that had no control.

Weiss had gotten results that were precisely the opposite of Brady's. Why? It appears that ambiguity versus certainty may be the key. That is, uncertainty about whether the coping response (lever pressing or wheel turning) is effective increases tension and thereby the probability of ulcers. To demonstrate this, Weiss (1971) trained two groups of rats to turn a wheel in order to delay the onset of a shock. One group received a signal when they had turned the wheel far enough to avoid shock, while the other group was given no signal. The second group worked harder, performed more wheel turning, and developed more severe ulcers than the first group. Confirming these findings, other studies have shown that ulcers are less severe in subjects who learn more quickly that a coping response has been effective (Tsuda and Hirai (1975).

Now think back to Brady's study. His "executive" monkeys had to constantly pay attention and press the lever in order to avoid shock, but they were uncertain as to whether their responses were effective. It thus appears that having prior knowledge of or control over aversive stimulation reduces stress if you can be reasonably certain that your responses will be effective. That situation appears to be the more common one in humans, as we will see later in the chapter.

Illnesses Associated With Stress

The particular disease processes for which stress is thought to be a major contributing factor are termed psychosomatic (mind-body) disorders or *psychophysiologic disorders.* Included among these are hypertension (high blood pressure), coronary artery disease, diabetes, ulcers, multiple sclerosis, and cancer. In addition, stress may be a significant contributing factor in a wide variety of other diseases, from arthritis to acne. We will consider here the role of stress in disorders of the immune system, coronary artery disease, cancer, and ulcers.

Stress And The Immune System. When you are exposed to someone with a sore throat and streptococcus bacteria enter your body, you might end up with a "strep" throat unless your immune system fights off the invader. In fact, it is the immune system that works to ward off any microorganism or other potentially harmful foreign substance, including bacteria like those that cause strep throat and viruses like those that cause flu and AIDS. Any impairment of immune function therefore leaves the individual more vulnerable to a variety of possible ills (Sgoutas et al., 1994).

Three components of the immune system are particularly important in fighting disease. Two of these are white blood cells called B-cell and T-cell *lymphocytes.* The main function of B-cells is to produce *antibodies,* which are protein substances that circulate in the bloodstream. Each antibody binds to a specific foreign substance, such as a virus or bacterium, and inactivates that substance. When you get a flu shot, you develop antibodies to the flu viruses in the shot; when you are later exposed to a friend who has one of those specific viruses, your antibodies will usually prevent you from getting the flu. T-cells directly attack another cell, usually a malignant or otherwise defective one, and kill it. The third type of lymphocyte is the *natural killer (NK) cell.* It is particularly active against viruses and also kills certain kinds of tumor cells.

The immune system is affected by a variety of factors. For one thing, like other body systems, it is subject to genetic influence. You can be genetically predisposed to have stronger or weaker immune functions, just as you can be predisposed toward coronary heart disease or stomach ulcers. In addition, your immune system can be weakened by an illness or a lack of proper nutrition. It can also be weakened by stress (Schlesinger et al., 1993; Snyder et al., 1993), and it is the effect of stress on immune function that concerns us here.

John Cacioppo and his colleagues directly demonstrated the effects of stress on the components of the immune system (Sgoutas et al., 1994). They drew blood samples to measure immune system activity before and after exposing subjects to a stressor consisting of loud noise and a mental arithmetic task. The stressors significantly modified the number of NK cells and the number of T-cells, demonstrating an immediate effect on the immune system. Similar changes have been found during final exam periods as compared with non-exam times (Glaser et al., 1987) and following separation and divorce (Kiecolt-Glaser & Glaser, 1992). A meta-analysis of 38 studies provided strong, general support for the effects of stress in reducing immune function (Herbert & Cohen, 1993).

If stress reduces immune function, we might expect to see an increase in infectious diseases—and we do (Benschop, 1994). Infections ranging from the common respiratory cold to herpes have been shown to increase when people are under stress (Kiecolt-Glaser & Glaser, 1992; Cohen et al., 1991). Since the immune system is also involved in much more serious diseases, including AIDS and cancer, the effects of stress can sometimes be devastating. Indeed, stress has been found to be associated with the rate at which HIV-related disorders progress; higher levels of stress cause the disease to progress more rapidly (Black, 1994).

The connection between stress and immune dysfunction lies in the brain and central nervous system (CNS). Studies point to a bi-directional association between the immune system and the CNS. Cells in the immune system synthesize hormones and neuropeptides that communicate the status of the system directly to structures in the brain (Ballieux, 1992). The brain, in turn, interprets a situation as stressful and acts to modify the activity of the immune system, making the individual more vulnerable to infection (Cacioppo, 1994). The overall result is that stress increases the likelihood that you will contract an infectious disease.

Coronary Artery Disease. The cardiovascular system can also be a stress casualty. In fact, stress can act in two ways to cause heart attacks. First, it can act over long periods of time to gradually damage the heart. Second, it can act over a very short period to trigger an attack (Cas et al., 1993; Petch, 1996).

Much of the research on the role of stress in the gradual development of coronary artery disease has focused on personality factors. In their book *Type A Behavior and Your Heart* (1974), physicians Meyer Friedman and Ray Rosenman suggested that individuals who exhibit intense, hard-driving competitiveness, easily evoked hostility, and a persistent sense of time urgency are more likely to develop coronary artery disease than are people who do not have these personality characteristics. They labeled the hard-driving personality Type A and the more laid-back, easy-going personality Type B.

A number of studies have supported the hypothesis that Type A personality is a risk factor for CHD (Etienne & Fontaine, 1994). One study followed 3200 men who were free of CHD at the outset for a number of years. Type As were twice as likely as Type Bs to show CHD symptoms within eight years of the onset of the study (Ganster et al., 1991). In other studies, Type As have been found to experience more fatal heart attacks (O'Connor et al., 1995), develop more extensive coronary atherosclerosis (Jenkins et al., 1977), and show a greater rate of heart disease even when other risk factors are controlled (Denollet, 1993; Orth-Gomer, Albhorn, and Theorell, 1980).

Despite these supportive findings, more recent studies have often contradicted the Type A hypothesis. One large-scale study, which followed 12,000 men over a period of years, showed no relationship between Type A behavior and heart attack mortality (MRFIT, 1982). Others have also failed to confirm the relationship (Langeluddecke et al., 1988), and overall findings are now quite mixed (Johnson, 1993). One possible explanation may be that coronary risk is affected by only certain components of the Type A behavior pattern. In particular, there is some indication that the hostility aspect of Type A may be the culprit (Suarez et al., 1993).

Studies focusing on the hostility component have typically used questionnaires to identify groups of high hostile and low hostile subjects, then exposed them to laboratory stressors and measured heart rate and blood pressure. Some studies do confirm that high hostile people placed under social stress in the laboratory have higher blood pressure than do low hostiles (Christensen & Smith, 1993; Suarez et al., 1993). Moreover, even adolescents who are high in hostility show greater risk for later CHD than those low in hostility (Raikkonen and Keltikangas-Jarvinen, 1991). Although not all studies confirm the role of hostility in CHD (Cas et al., 1993), a majority to date do (Baban et al., 1993; Anderson & Lawler, 1995).

Although the Type A literature is inconsistent, there is other evidence that stress is a factor in coronary disease. Studies show, for example, that *ischemia*—insufficient blood supply to the heart—can be induced by stress. In one such investigation, stress was induced in CHD patients by using mental arithmetic or emotionally arousing speech tasks. Stress produced measurable ischemia in 68% of the patients, nearly as many as the 76% who exhibited ischemia while engaging in physical exercise (Gupta & Gupta, 1993). Thus, stress does appear to play a role in the development of heart disease, possibly by elevating the levels of cholesterol circulating in the bloodstream (Lorenz, Van Doornen, and Orlebeke, 1982).

In addition to contributing to the long-term development of heart disease, stress can act as an immediate, precipitating factor in heart attacks (Petch, 1996). One study of men under age 40 who had heart attacks showed that stress was the triggering factor in 75% of cases (Badui et al., 1993). Another showed that 80 percent of middle-aged victims had been experiencing depression, often induced by stress, for varied periods of time prior to the heart attack and that at least 50 percent had been experiencing stressful situations immediately prior to the attack (Green, Goldstein, and Moss, 1972). Animal studies confirm this observation. For example, hamsters with preexisting subclinical heart disease show substantial indications of heart failure when subjected to severe stress (Tapp, Levin, and Nadleson, 1983), as do dogs (Anderson, 1982).

Nature, nurture, and CHD. Stress is not the only—or the primary—factor in coronary heart disease. Other major factors include hypertension, obesity, smoking, a high-fat diet, high blood cholesterol levels, and genetic predisposition (Kaplan & Kimball, 1982; Cas et al., 1993). In fact, CHD is a good example of the multi-factorial causal model that we discussed earlier as applying to all psychophysiologic disorders. Stress itself is an environmental factor in CHD, as are high-fat diets and smoking. At the same time, genetic factors play a major role, particularly when CHD appears at relatively early ages.

One large-scale study followed 21,000 twins born between 1886 and 1925 for 26 years. It showed a relative risk for heart attack in males of 8.1 for identical twins and 3.8 for fraternal twins. That is, if one identical twin has a heart attack, his brother has 8 times the risk of also having an attack as would someone who is not an identical twin of a heart patient. A fraternal twin also has an elevated risk, but it is only about 4 times as great as for the general population. The greater risk in identicals supports the role of genetic factors. For women, the relative risks were 15 for identicals and 2.6 for fraternals (Marenberg et al., 1994). Other behavior genetic studies have consistently confirmed the role of heredity in CHD (Staunton et al., 1994), and molecular geneticists have begun to identify specific genes that transmit at least some forms of heart disease (Bouvagnet et al., 1994). Thus, CHD is clearly an interactive product of nature and nurture.

Ulcers. Ever hear someone say "This job could give me an ulcer?" Well, he could be right. If there is one classic physical disorder in which stress has long been thought to have a role, it is ulceration. About 10% of men and women in the United States develop ulcers at some time in their lives (Lam, 1993), and evidence suggests that stress may play a role (Saggioro & Chiozzini, 1994).

An ulcer is a lesion—an open sore—on the wall of the stomach or duodenum (the upper portion of the small intestine). Ulcers form when secretions of gastric acid are very high and when stomach contractions are very intense. Strong contractions cause the protective mucous coating of the stomach wall to break down, thereby exposing delicate tissue to the excessively high levels of acid. The acid eats into the stomach wall to produce the lesion (Garrick, 1990).

The question is what causes the overproduction of acid and the increase in stomach contractions, and it appears that stress may be a part of the answer. Ulcers often form not while you are under stress but after the stressful period has ended (Desiderato et al., 1974). This rest period is characterized by a shift from the sympathetic dominance of the stress-induced general adaptation syndrome to the parasympathetic dominance of relaxation—a kind of rebound effect. The parasympathetic firing increases gastric acid secretion and can also increase stomach contractions, setting the person up for ulcers. Studies supporting this observation have shown greater ulceration in those experiencing stress. One study followed 4500 people with no history of ulcers for 13 years. Of the total group, 68% reported that they were highly stressed at baseline. When all subjects were reexamined 13 years later, 208 had developed ulcers. They included 7% of those under stress and 4.0% of those not under stress (Anda et al., 1992). Other studies suggest that it is not acute stress but rather chronic stress, lasting greater than six months, that is associated with ulceration (Piper & Tennant, 1993).

Nature, nurture, and ulcers. As with heart disease, ulcers are caused by multiple factors, and it would be a mistake to give too much weight to stress (Johnsen et al., 1994). There is, first, considerable evidence from family, twin, and molecular genetic studies that heredity is important (Pesci & Pickett, 1994; Stanchev, 1993). People with a family history of ulcers and those with Type O blood (blood type is inherited) are genetically more likely to develop ulcers than those with no family history and other blood types (Lam, 1993). Some studies suggest that the genetic predisposition is expressed as higher production of pepsinogen, a chemical involved in digestion (Levenstein et al., 1995). However, only 42 percent of those with high levels of this chemical in one study had the disease, meaning that there must be other contributing factors. In fact, there is evidence that a genetic predisposition may combine with stress to substantially raise gastric acid output (Bresnick et al., 1993).

Environmental factors other than stress include: smoking; the use of aspirin, ibuprofen, and certain other drugs; alcohol intake; and perhaps coffee consumption (Saggioro & Chiozzini, 1994; Weiner, 1982). In addition, prior abdominal surgery and low blood pressure are associated with ulceration (Saggioro & Chiozzini, 1994; Medalie et al., 1992). Of particular significance is the presence of a bacterial infection caused by Helicobacter pylori. This bacterium is now recognized as a major cause of gastric (stomach) and duodenal ulcers in 75-95% of ulcer patients (De-Lazzari et al., 1994; Wilhelmsen et al., 1994), who can be successfully treated with antibiotics.

Does stress cause ulceration? The answer is probably "yes," but only when it occurs in conjunction with a genetic predisposition and probably one or more other factors. The precise, critical combinations of factors required to produce ulcers are not yet known.

Stress and Cancer. About 1 million Americans are diagnosed with cancer each year, and many factors potentially causing it to develop and progress have been studied (Andersen et al., 1994). One of these is stress. A number of animal studies have shown that cancer spreads more rapidly when the animals are placed under stress, though this is not an entirely consistent finding (Fox, 1983). In humans a number of reports indicate that cancer occurs more frequently or becomes terminal more quickly in people who are experiencing major stressors, such as divorce or bereavement (Chen et al., 1995; Bergsma, 1994). In addition, people with depression, which brings with it considerable stress, have been found in some studies to be more likely to die from cancer (Chorot & Sandin, 1994). Again, however, the findings are not entirely consistent, and many people with chronic depression or other forms of stress never develop cancer (Stein et al., 1991). Moreover, some studies have shown that cancer development and survival are unrelated to stress or that moderate stress or long-term experience with stress may even be protective (Cooper & Faracher, 1993; Hilakivi et al., 1994).

Further evidence favoring the stress hypothesis comes from studies in which cancer patients are given supportive counseling. Daniel Spiegel and his colleagues randomly assigned breast cancer patients to either participate in a support group or not. Their intention was simply to determine whether or not the support group helped the women deal psychologically with the cancer. However, they were surprised to find that four years later all the women who had not been in support groups but only about one-third of those who were in the groups had died (Spiegel et al., 1989). A similar study showed that 90% of the cancer patients in support groups were still living 13 years later, as compared with 38% of those not receiving the counseling (Eysenck & Grossarth-Maticek, 1991).

Evidence concerning the role of stress and the countering role of supportive counseling in cancer is clearly preliminary and mixed. In fact, some reviewers have concluded that stress may have no role in cancer (Gammon & John, 1993). The danger here is that patients hearing about the findings relating stress and coping to cancer will develop false hope or blame themselves for the progression of the disease. The truth is that cancer is a purely biological disorder. Stress almost certainly does not cause cancer cells to develop, and the only thing that counseling *may* be able to do is to strengthen the immune defenses, thereby slowing the spread of the cancer (Justice, 1985). Until more evidence has been developed, we must be very cautious about the role of stress in this major disorder.

Other Disorders. A number of other common disorders are also thought to be partially caused, aggravated, or precipitated by stress.

- **Headache.** One of the most common human health problems, headache, is often induced by stress. When regular headache sufferers were asked what precipitated their headaches, a majority, 62%, cited stress (Robbins,

1994). In another study, headache patients who received stress management training achieved a 50% or better reduction in headaches, while a control group showed no improvement (Scharff & Marcus, 1994).

- **Hypertension.** Hypertension, or high blood pressure, is clearly influenced by stress (Miller & Sita, 1994). This silent, symptomless killer disease is a significant factor in heart attack and stroke. It is commonly associated with chronic stress (Haythornthwaite, 1993) and can easily be induced by laboratory stressors (Gerin et al., 1994). It is especially prevalent in African-Americans, where studies suggest that life-style changes that reduce stress can help to prevent it (Edwards, 1995).
- **Asthma.** This respiratory disease, which involves wheezing and difficulty in breathing due to bronchoconstriction, worsens under stress (Iamandescu, 1993). Attacks in asthmatic children are often triggered by family stressors, such as punishment of the child or fights between the parents (Klinnert et al., 1994).
- **Rheumatoid arthritis.** Stress may trigger episodes of arthritic pain and may also be involved in the development of the illness (Stewart et al., 1994). Stress increases muscle tension, which in turn causes flareups of the arthritic condition (Achterberg-Lawlis, 1982; Zautra et al., 1994).
- **Skin disorders.** Many skin problems, including psoriasis, acne, and eczema, are aggravated by stress (Harvima et al., 1993). Even on a short-term basis, the individual's mood state can affect the severity of skin reactions (Laidlaw et al., 1994).

Dealing with Stress

Although stress can do considerable psychological and physiological damage, many people seem virtually unaffected by it and some even appear to thrive on stressful environments. Why is it that one of two executives in similar jobs develops ulcers while the other does not or that one working mother (such as Fay in our opening example) suffers from role strain while another in the same situation does not? The basic answer is that there are factors that can serve as buffers, reducing the impact of stress, and ways of actively working to reduce stress. Let's consider these stress mediators and coping strategies.

Mediating Stress

When national or international crises strike, the United Nations or the United States has often served to mediate between the warring factions in order to reduce the conflict. Examples are mediations of conflicts between Israel and the Arab countries and of that between the Croatian and Serbian factions in Bosnia. Similarly, there are factors that can mediate between you and a stressful environment to reduce the stress. One set of mediators may reside in your personality. Research has shown that some personality characteristics serve to protect us against the onslaught of stressors, as our 21 for this chapter describes. These protective personality traits are one of a number of *stress-mediating factors*—factors that can serve to reduce the impact of stress. More generally, stress mediators are personal or situational factors that can serve as buffers between the individual and the stressor. Two major mediators are social support and the ability to predict and control stress.

Social Support. Just as lack of social support can increase negative reactions to stress, the presence of social support can help reduce its effects (Roberts et al., 1994). One study showed that both male and female alcoholic patients under stress responded positively to social support (Billings and Moos, 1982). Another study, which examined the effects of stress following the Three Mile Island incident, found that people with higher levels of social support displayed less anxiety, depression, and alienation than those low in social support (Fleming et al., 1982). A study of over 1100 spouses of soldiers deployed in Operation Desert Storm showed that many experienced very high levels of stress. However, stress effects were lowest in those with the greatest amounts of available social support (Rosen et al., 1994). Social support is also the most consistent predictor of adjustment to a diagnosis of cancer (Varni et al., 1994) and can reduce stress loads in work settings (Huebner, 1994; Morano, 1993), decrease the stresses of divorce (Garvin et al., 1993), and reduce blood pressure and cardiovascular reactivity to stress (Lepore et al., 1993; Knox, 1993).

Often the strongest and most consistent source of support is the family. Studies have shown that the family can be both a source of stress and a mechanism for alleviating its effects. On the negative side, the incidence of illnesses is consistently high in some families and consistently low in others, and genetic factors are not sufficient to account for this phenomenon (Prapp, 1976). For example, studies show that severely asthmatic children improve significantly in about half of all cases when they are removed from the family home (Weiner, 1977). Family therapy has been used with great success in cases of asthma and other psychosomatic disorders (Minuchin, Rosinart, and Baker, 1978) and is thus far the most successful form of psychotherapy for childhood psychosomatic conditions (Guman and Kniskern, 1981). Thus, the family is clearly a source of stress.

On a more positive note, the family is an important source of social support and can significantly reduce stress (Coyne and Lazarus, 1982). Both men and women are more likely to turn to a spouse than to anyone else in times of stress (Burke and Weir, 1975), and there is clear evidence that husbands and wives do provide useful emotional support for each other (Burke and Weir, 1982). Moreover, the family has been shown to act as a significant source of social support and stress reduction in circumstances such as financial hardship (Moen, 1982), chronic illness (McCubbin et al., 1982), and a variety of other anxiety-producing situations (Caplan, 1982).

Predicting and Controlling Stress. Here's a riddle: When is a stressor not a stressor? Answer? When you can control it—or at least predict it. Conversely, unpredictability and lack of control tend to increase the impact of stress. Consider the exams in your psychology course. If each exam is scheduled well in advance for a specific date, your stress will likely be lower than if the professor says exams will be given on random days scattered through the semester. Similarly, you will typically experience less stress if you perceive that you have some control over a situation than if you do not (Lazarus & Folkman, 1984). If your physician tells you that you have diabetes but that you can reduce its effects by carefully monitoring your blood sugar and taking drugs, you will have the perception that you can control the disease. However, if he tells you that you have an equally serious disease that progresses at an unpredictable rate and over which you have no control, you are likely to experience much more stress.

Both animal and human studies have supported these observations. In one study, two rats were given shocks simultaneously. The one that could turn a wheel to escape the shocks was less likely to develop ulcers than the one that had no control (Laudenslager & Reite, 1984). This finding is similar to that of Weiss, mentioned earlier, and it also applies to people. Those who feel helpless are more likely to become depressed and to experience an increase in stress and its consequences (Burns et al., 1992). Conversely, the perception that a stressor is controllable leads to more effective coping (Valentiner et al., 1994). For example, cancer patients who feel that they have no control over their disease survive for shorter periods than those who perceive that they do have control (Rodin & Salovey, 1989), and coronary bypass patients who perceive a higher degree of control before surgery have a better quality of life eight months after surgery (Fitzgerald et al., 1993). Perceived lack of control in a variety of stressful conditions tends to increase the intensity of stress and prolong it (Baum et al., 1993).

The prediction/control findings have some clear practical implications for dealing with stressful situations. They suggest that you may profit from an effort to "get a handle" on your stressors. Gather the information you need to make the stressor predictable whenever possible and do what you can to gain at least a degree of control over it.

Another factor that may mediate the stress response is physical exercise. Do you work out regularly? If not, read Probe 2 carefully.

Coping Strategies

Coping is an active effort to reduce stress by solving the problems creating it. Coping involves both cognitive and behavioral efforts to manage environmental and internal demands and stressors. Fay, in our opening example, might take some time to think about her priorities in order to reduce the number of stressors in her life. If she decides that she ranks her desire for a law degree first, her family second, and her job third, she might ask for a few days off from work and offer to help the typesetter line up some temporary proofreaders. She would thus be making both cognitive and behavioral efforts to cope with a difficult situation. *Not coping* with the situation might mean that Fay would not spend much time studying, would do a perfunctory job on her proofreading chores, and would withdraw from her family for the duration. Some of the major coping strategies include cognitive appraisal, self-instruction, and coping through change.

Richard Lazarus and Cognitive Appraisal. Richard Lazarus and his colleagues (1980) have argued that individual differences in the response to stress are a function of the person's *cognitive appraisal*—his evaluation through thought processes—of a potentially stressful event or situation. Through cognitive appraisal, the individual evaluates the extent to which the situation is threatening to his well-being. It is this process that determines how positive or negative his stress reaction will be, what emotions he will experience, and what adaptive responses he will make (Lazarus, 1992).

Appraisal takes two forms. *Primary appraisal* is a judgment of how stressful the situation is. *Secondary appraisal* is a judgment as to what can be done about the stress. It entails evaluating possible coping strategies for their probability of success and "cost" to the individual. Suppose Jeanette hears that many people in her company are about to be laid off. Her primary appraisal will focus on just how threatening or stressful this situation is for her. If she decides that it is indeed threatening, her secondary appraisal process will focus on what to do about the situation. She may decide to do nothing, to gather more information from co-workers, to talk to the boss, or to start looking for another job.

The cognitive appraisal process both affects and is affected by emotional reactions. If the situation is evaluated as stressful, there may be a negative emotional response, such as anxiety, anger, or depression. The intensity of the reaction will depend on the person's appraisal of just how threatening the situation is. Joe Tomaka and his colleagues (1993), for example, found stronger physiological and more negative psychological responses when a stress task was seen as threatening than when subjects viewed it as challenging. Strong emotional reactions like those that threatened subjects may have experienced in this study can interfere with the cognitive appraisal process, as happens when a high level of anxiety makes it difficult to think clearly about possible coping strategies. On the other hand, a good sense of humor—leading to positive emotion—can serve to increase the effectiveness of coping and thereby reduce stress (Kuiper et al., 1993).

The Lazarus model has been studied in both the experimental laboratory and a variety of real-life situations. Norman Endler and his colleagues have demonstrated the differential effectiveness of varied coping strategies in college students faced with such common stressors as exams (Endler et al., 1994). In other studies, the role of cognitive appraisal and coping in dealing with such varied stressors as breast cancer (Stanton & Snider, 1993) and the racism experienced by African-Americans (Outlaw, 1993) have been evaluated.

Self-Instruction. If a child is faced with a stressful situation, her parents may give her verbal instructions on how to cope with the stress. The adult may learn to internalize this process and give herself verbal instructions for coping with a specific situation. A four-stage approach to verbal self-instruction has been recommended by Donald Meichenbaum (1975, 1993): preparation, confrontation, coping with anxiety-producing thoughts and feelings, and self-reinforcement. *Preparation* involves such statements as "I can develop a plan to deal with the situation" and "Don't panic; be rational." *Confrontation* is exemplified by "I *can* deal with the situation. I'm in control." *Coping with anxiety* takes the form of such statements as "This is not the worst thing that could happen" and "Focus on the situation: What steps should I take?" *Self-reinforcement* is exemplified by "I did it; I should be pleased with myself."

Studies show that self-talk can improve the response to stress. In one investigation, subjects were asked to try to solve Soma, a commercially available cube puzzle. Some subjects were assigned to a rational self-talk condition where they read such statements as "There is really no logical reason why I should consider myself a less competent or worthwhile person if I make a simple mistake on this task." Other subjects were assigned an irrational self-talk condition in which they read such statements as "I am really going to look dumb in front of the experimenter if I can't do these relatively simple tasks correctly." Results showed that rational self-talk subjects were considerably less anxious while solving the puzzle than were the irrational self-talk subjects (Rosin and Nelson, 1983).

Coping Through Change. The actions that result from cognitive appraisal or self-instruction usually involve some form of change. The two major changes that the individual can readily make are to modify the environment or to change his own behavior. Sometimes referred to as "assertive coping," changing the environment involves a forthright attempt to modify the external situation in a constructive way that has a reasonably high probability of success. Fay's efforts to get someone else to fill in for her at work for a few days would be an example of coping by removing an environmental stressor, at least temporarily. Alternatively, she might attempt to cope with her situation by changing her own behavior. She might let her household chores go for awhile and encourage her family to have take-out meals or fend for themselves for a few days while she concentrates on the other responsibilities in her life.

Increasing Social Support. We saw earlier that a lack of social support can increase levels of perceived stress (Jenkinson et al., 1993; Stephens et al., 1994) and that high levels of social support decrease stress (Rosen et al., 1994; Franks & Stephens, 1996). It would seem to follow, then, that one way to decrease negative reactions when an individual is under stress would be to increase the availability of social support. Accordingly, David Valentiner and his colleagues (1994) studied stress and coping in 175 college students over a period of two years. They focused, in particular, on the availability of parental support when students were dealing with stressors. As you might expect, increasing parental support during periods of stress reduced the perception of stress and allowed students to cope more effectively. In another investigation, Leora Rosen studied 1107 spouses of men and women deployed to the Gulf in Operation Desert Storm. Those who garnered higher levels of social support were better able to cope with the stress of having their spouse exposed to the potential dangers of the war (Rosen et al., 1994).

Stress Inoculation. Getting a flu shot each year is a good idea because it immunizes you against several viruses likely to cause flu that season. Is it also possible to get psychological inoculations, "stress shots" that make you impervious to stress? Well, perhaps not impervious, but studies do show that a prior, relatively weak exposure to a stressor, sometimes accompanied by training in stress reduction, can reduce the impact of stress (Freedy & Hobfoll, 1994; Wilken, 1996). For example, one team of investigators applied an inoculation procedure to subjects with animal phobias—strong fears of specific animals, such as snakes. Some subjects were given information about their animals, while others were not. All were then exposed to the animal. Those previously "inoculated" with the information experienced significantly less anxiety when faced with the animal than those not receiving the inoculation (Steketee et al., 1989). In another study, some scuba diving students received stress inoculation training prior to actually diving, while others did not. Those receiving the training experienced lower anxiety (Deikis, 1983), as did students with test anxiety in a third study (Pruitt, 1986). It appears that stress inoculation can reduce subsequent stress. Try it, you might like it!

Defense Mechanisms. Coping is not the only way to deal with stress. Sigmund Freud pointed out that anxiety from stress is an extremely uncomfortable state that must somehow be reduced. While successful coping would reduce anxiety by eliminating the source of stress, Freud hypothesized that the first reaction to anxiety is not coping but the use of *defense mechanisms.* Defense mechanisms are unconscious psychological processes that are used, without the individual's awareness, for the sole purpose of reducing anxiety. Without consciously intending to, you may, for example, temporarily reduce your anxiety by forgetting about an upcoming exam in a difficult course. This is an example of the most basic defense mechanism, repression.

The Health Effects of Coping

In the best of all possible worlds, coping strategies that reduce stress would have positive effects on health. However, there is evidence that both negative and positive effects can occur. For instance, those classified as having Type A personalities often take actions that successfully reduce stress, but the price they pay—potentially increased risk of coronary artery disease—can be very high. Similarly, smoking, drinking, and overeating may reduce stress for some people, but once again the price is high. One particularly damaging coping strategy is *denial* of the sort seen in men who reduce the stress engendered by heart attack symptoms by denying that there is a serious problem (Yon Kugelelgen, 1975) and in women who assure themselves that a breast lump is not serious and does not require medical attention (Katz et al., 1970).

Adaptive coping, on the other hand, can have positive effects on health. One study showed that patients under stress as a result of severe rheumatoid arthritis dealt with their problem better and were happier if they displayed a high degree of coping assets and abilities (Zautra et al., 1995). Similarly, men and women with chronic cardiac disorders are less likely to be depressed if they engage in adaptive coping (Holahan et al., 1995).

While there is certainly some evidence for the positive effects of coping, more recent studies have begun to question its efficacy. Paul Bennett and Douglas Carroll (1994) carefully reviewed the scientific literature on the use of cognitive coping interventions in cardiac patients. These patients are often taught how to use specific stress-reducing strategies because stress can be a factor in heart disease and heart attacks (Gupta & Gupta, 1993). Bennett and Carroll found considerable evidence that such training does, indeed, reduce feelings of psychological distress in heart patients. They feel more relaxed and less anxious, a clear benefit in and of itself. Unfortunately, however, there is little evidence that this psychological benefit translates into any actual reduction in the likelihood of subsequent heart attacks. In most studies, subjects with and without training in coping are about equally likely to have subsequent heart attacks and about equally likely to die.

Health Psychology

In earlier centuries, the major killer diseases were primarily those over which the individual had little or no control because they were caused by bacteria and viruses. The stretoccus bacillus, which we commonly associate with sore throat, caused kidney and heart damage and frequently killed people, as did many other bacterial illnesses before antibiotics were developed. Similarly, the small pox virus caused many deaths until a vaccine was perfected. Other primary killers included tuberculosis, pneumonia, and even influenza. Now the primary causes of death are heart disease, cancer, stroke, accidents, and, in younger age groups, AIDS. All these are disorders over which the individual can exert considerable control because we can, to some degree, prevent them. In fact, fully 50% of deaths in the United States are due in large part to life style factors (USDHHS, 1990). That is why health psychology has become so important. *Health psychology* is the subdiscipline that focuses on the identification of adaptive and maladaptive health behaviors and the application of psychological concepts and principles to the development of behavioral approaches aimed at improving health. The task of health psychology is to develop principles of prevention and teach and encourage people to actively pursue such healthy behaviors as exercising, reducing stress, and eating healthy foods. We will begin by discussing some health behaviors that shorten life and the health beliefs that foster such behaviors. We will then consider the role of psychological factors in physical illness, turning finally to some major approaches to preventing and reducing the stresses that contribute to many disorders.

Killing Yourself Slowly: Destructive Health Behaviors

It was William Shakespeare who coined the phrase "death by inches" (Coriolanus, Act V, Scene IV, l 43), and he could well have been referring to some modern health behaviors. High-fat diets, having sex without condoms, lack of exercise, smoking, and excessive alcohol consumption are examples of behaviors that we know can destroy health; yet many people regularly engage in these and other destructive behaviors. Here we will look at smoking and alcohol consumption as examples of unhealthy behaviors.

Living With Your Head in a Cloud: Smoking. Smokers have their heads in a cloud in more ways than one. In fact, smoking is the prime current example of a behavior that literally destroys your health and shortens your life. It is an addictive behavior that is undoubtedly the single most dangerous practice that people routinely engage in. In fact, it is a major etiological (causal) element in the two principal current causes of death, cardiovascular disease and cancer. Smoking is directly responsible for one in every five deaths—500,000 annually—and creates one million newly diagnosed victims each year in the United States (Cresanta, 1992; Healthy People 2000, NCHS, 1995). It is responsible for

5 million years of potential life lost annually and adds $50 billion to health care costs. Even exposure to smoking by others (passive smoking) causes an estimated 53,000 deaths per year (Lesmes & Donobrio, 1992; NCHS, 1995).

Smoking is a leading factor in cardiovascular disease, producing a 70% excess death rate from coronary heart disease alone (Lakier, 1992). It is also a major factor in cancer, which is the leading cause of death between ages 35 and 64 and the second leading cause overall (Cresanta, 1992). In fact, smoking causes 123,000 of the 143,000 deaths each year from lung cancer, the single most frequent fatal cancer in both women and men (Beckett, 1993; Szabo & Mulshine, 1993). It is also a significant causal element in cancer of the bladder, kidney, pancreas, cervix, esophagus, stomach, and oral cavity (Sasco, 1992). In addition to cardiovascular disease and cancer, smoking is involved in asthma (Gorski & Tarkowski, 1992), cataracts (Christen et al., 1992), and low back pain (Skovron, 1992) and is associated with an earlier age of onset of schizophrenia (Sandyk & Kay, 1991).

Since smoking is also a causal factor in a number of other diseases, the bigger question is just how much smoking increases *all-cause mortality*—the overall risk of death from any cause. A study of 117,000 women provides one answer to this question. The women were nurses aged 30-55 when the study started in 1976. By 1992, 2847 had died. Smoking doubled all-cause mortality. That is, smokers were almost twice as likely to die as nonsmokers. For those who had formerly smoked but stopped, the risk of death decreased to the same level as that of nonsmokers after 10-14 years (Kawachi et al., 1993).

Most people who smoke start as teenagers. There is a widespread perception among adolescents that those who smoke are more mature and more sociable than nonsmokers (Barton et al., 1982), and teens often begin to smoke because those around them—other teens and parents—model smoking (Kandel & Wu, 1995; Evans et al., 1988). Those who know the dangers but continue to smoke anyway do so, in part, because of the perceived "benefits" of this deadly habit: It reduces anxiety, helps avoid weight gain, and gives the person something to do with his hands. Note that the picture here is essentially a negative one in that smoking alleviates negative states rather than producing positive ones (Shotact et al., 1981).

The fact that smoking tends to reduce negative states suggests that tobacco dependence is primarily physiological rather than psychological. This conclusion is supported by the research of Stanley Schachter (1978, 1982), who has found that while smoking does not elevate the smoker's mood or improve task performance, *not smoking* causes smokers to perform worse than nonsmokers. Other studies have shown that smokers seem to regulate their nicotine levels to avoid withdrawal symptoms, further evidence for the physiological nature of tobacco dependence (Haxby, 1995. There is clearly no good reason to smoke, and those who continue to do so in the face of overwhelming evidence of the dangers are simply addicted—as surely as are alcoholics and narcotic abusers.

Approaches to stopping smoking include hypnosis, treatment with various drugs, operant conditioning, aversive conditioning (e.g., smoking until you get sick), the nicotine patch (which supplies nicotine through the skin), and simply going "cold turkey." Recent research suggests that a drug called mecamylamine, which reduces the effects of nicotine, and the nicotine patch may be more successful than other methods (Rose et al., 1994). Other evidence suggests that the cold turkey approach may be the most successful. Many smokers can stop temporarily using nearly any of these techniques. The problem is that 80% will soon go back to smoking (Cohen et al., 1989).

The good news is that this dangerous health behavior is on the decline. Banned on domestic and many international airline flights and by McDonald's and some other restaurant chains, smoking has become more difficult. Some towns prohibit it in public places, and increasing numbers of corporations do not allow their employees to smoke, even outside their buildings. The entire state of Maryland has implemented a ban on smoking in all public places, though a last-minute political compromise gave restaurants and bars a partial exemption. As a result of these restrictions and of increased public awareness—much of it through the work of health psychologists—smoking has decreased since 1985 from 35% to 26% in males and from 28% to 22% in females (National Household Survey on Drug Abuse, SAMHSA, 1995). At the same time, however, it is on the increase among teens, especially since 1992, rising from 28% of high school seniors in that year to 31% by 1994. A similar rise from 14% to nearly 19% was seen in eighth graders. On the other hand, the smoking rate has steadily declined among African-American teens and is much lower in that group than in whites or Hispanics (Johnston, O'Malley, & Bachman, NIH, 1995). We certainly haven't licked the smoking problem yet, but it appears that there is real hope for a smoke-free future in the long run.

Alcohol Consumption. About 67% of all Americans and 81%of those in the 26-34-year age group drink (SAMSHA, 1995), and 37% of these sometimes go on binges, drinking 5 or more drinks in rapid succession (Reynolds et al., 1992). Moreover, fully 20% of all males are alcoholics at some time in their lives (Robins et al., 1984). Alcohol consumption exacts a major toll on both the drinker and the society. Alcoholics live 19 years less than nonalcoholics, and alcohol causes serious damage to the brain, liver, and other body systems. More generally, alcohol accounts for at least 100,000 deaths per year in the United States alone (McGinnis & Foege, 1993) and costs our society over five billion dollars annually (National Council on Alcoholism, 1986).

Why do people drink? What are the major biological, psychological, and social factors that cause and support such a widespread destructive behavior? We will explore these and other issues related to alcohol use and abuse when we discuss alcoholism as a form of abnormal behavior later.

The Healthier Drinker. A few years ago we would have said simply that alcohol consumption is dangerous to your health—period. A number of carefully executed studies have now clearly shown, however, that light-to-moderate consumption significantly decreases total mortality in both men and women over age 50 (Gronback et al., 1994; Fuchs et al., 1995). But these results appear not to apply equally to everyone. First, the reduction is due primarily to a decrease in deaths from cardiovascular diseases and may apply primarily to those at increased genetic or other risk for coronary heart disease (Fuchs et al., 1995). Second, some studies still show an *increase* in deaths with even small amounts of alcohol consumption in younger age groups (Fuchs et al., 1995). And finally, even light consumption is associated with an increased risk of death from cancer of the colon and mouth, stroke, cirrhosis of the liver, accidents, and suicide (Klatsky et al., 1992).

What can we conclude? Studies of the alcohol-mortality relationship are ongoing, and the answers are clearly not all in. However, a reasonable conclusion at this time appears to be that small amounts of alcohol reduce cardiovascular mortality and thereby overall mortality in those over 50 and especially in those at risk for coronary heart disease. Heavier consumption is uniformly associated with increased mortality at all ages.

Healthier Behaviors: The Health Belief Models

Smoking, excessive drinking, poor dietary habits, and lack of exercise are clearly dangerous to your health, and a reasonable question for health psychology is just how we might understand and modify these behaviors. From a cognitive perspective, the answer comes from the hypothesis that health behaviors are a product of health beliefs. A *health belief* is a thought or cognition that a person holds with regard to some aspect of her health or about a health-related behavior. For example, you may firmly believe that exercise is absolutely essential to long life and good health, that it may improve health somewhat, or that it's benefits are much overrated. These are very different beliefs about exercise as a health behavior, and *health-belief models*—cognitive theories of health behavior—hypothesize that they will strongly influence your actual behavior (Tohnai & Hata, 1994). You are theoretically much more likely to work out regularly if you believe that exercise is essential than if you believe that it is minimally useful in maintaining good health.

There are a number of different health-belief models, but the most influential has been that of Irwin Rosenstock and his colleagues (1974). They propose that the individual's decisions regarding such negative health behaviors as smoking are a product of cognitive processes and specifically of four principal beliefs or perceptions:

- The extent to which you believe that you *personally* are threatened by a specific illness that might result from the destructive health behavior. Do you believe that you personally will develop coronary heart disease (CHD) as a result of smoking?
- Your perception of the seriousness of the disorder and its consequences. How serious do you believe CHD is and how severe might be its consequences for you?
- Your belief that some specific change in your behavior will modify the threat. Will stopping smoking actually reduce the likelihood that you personally will develop CHD?
- Your perception of the cost/benefit balance—the balance between the possibility of poor future health and perceived current benefits of the practice. Will stopping smoking now reduce your future chances of CHD enough to offset its apparent current benefits, such as anxiety reduction and weight maintenance.

The individual most likely to stop smoking is the one who believes that he can and likely will develop CHD, that it is a severe, life-threatening disorder, and that the benefits of stopping smoking are far greater than the costs. If you are a non-smoker, it may be difficult to see how anyone could believe otherwise, given the evidence we've just reviewed. However, it is very easy for even an intelligent, well-educated smoker to hold cognitions that will keep her smoking. Consider these responses to the four points by a smoker:

- "It's unlikely that I will develop CHD because there is little history of it in my family, so why not smoke?"
- "CHD is a fairly serious disorder, but I'm a strong person and would probably live through a heart attack, have bypass surgery, and live a long life."
- "The causes of CHD are complex, and I'm not sure stopping smoking would really reduce my chances of getting it."
- "CHD seems like a fairly remote possibility, and besides if I stop smoking, I'll become more anxious and gain weight, which may also increase my chances of having a heart attack."

You can see how a smoker can easily rationalize her behavior by simply adopting unhealthy beliefs. Every one of her statements is incorrect or begs the question. However, the health belief model holds that these inaccurate cognitions nevertheless control her behavior.

Health belief models have been applied to a variety of health behaviors, including HIV prevention (Abraham &

Sheeran, 1994; Zimmerman & Olson, 1994), mammographic examination for breast cancer (Champion, 1994; Stein et al., 1994), and self-examination for testicular cancer (McMaster et al., 1994). They have also been studied in connection with testing for prostate cancer (Price et al., 1993), hypertension (Grant, 1993), smoking (Lee, 1993), and alcohol consumption (Hingson et al., 1990). In each case, the basic questions are the same: Do cognitive beliefs cause the health-related behavior? Can we modify the behavior by changing the health beliefs?

To make the health belief model more salient, consider just where you stand in regard to your beliefs about health behaviors and your actual health practices. Do you smoke? Drink more than two drinks a day or binge drink? Use marijuana or other drugs? Consume a diet that is too often high in fat or calories? Avoid exercise as though it were a disease? Do you always wear a seat belt? Drive at or near the speed limit? Use condoms? Avoid going to the beach or at least use a number 15 sunscreen to prevent skin cancer? Avoid walking across the campus alone at night? Depending on you age and gender, do you fail to get regular examinations for breast, cervical, and prostate cancer, heart disease, hypertension? If you exhibit any of these unhealthy behaviors, think through the four points of the health belief model. Where have *your* beliefs failed you?

Being Sick: The Psychology of Illness

Unhealthy behaviors and the beliefs that maintain them lead to illness. Moreover, even those with the healthiest habits become ill from time to time. Health psychologists are therefore interested in how we react to and deal with illness and how the ways in which we approach our ailments might be improved. They have therefore examined the factors that lead people to seek or avoid health care, studied why so many people fail to follow medical advice, and looked at how individuals play the "sick role."

Going To The Doctor. Everyone has unpleasant physical sensations from time to time: nausea, diarhhea, runny nose, sore throat, cough, headache, muscular soreness, and the like. Some people experiencing such sensations quickly get themselves to a physician, while others rarely seek medical advice. What differentiates these two gropus?

Health psychology has identified three general and several more specific variables that influence the decision to seek (or avoid) health care. One factor is the *perception* of illness. Perceived seriousness is a major determinant of who seeks health care (Cameron, Leventhal, & Leventhal, 1993). Usually a headache is just a headache, but occasionally it might be a symptom of a brain tumor. Some people tend to perceive negative sensations as minor irritants, others as significant symptoms of a potentially major illness. The second general factor is *personality*. In particular, people chronically high in anxiety and those low in self-esteem report more physical symptoms and seek medical advice more frequently (Pennebaker, 1982). And the third factor is gender: Women seek medical advice more quickly than men, visit doctors more often, and take more prescription drugs (Rosenstock & Kirscht, 1979). Why? Perhaps because it's not "macho" to seek health care: "A real man doesn't go running to the doctor for every little thing." More generally, society may teach women from early childhood to seek medical advice and men to avoid it. In addition, some of the medical attention sought by women is for gyneocological problems, pregnancy, breast examinations, and menopause, which obviously do not occur in men.

Robin DiMatteo (1991), who has studied patient behavior extensively, identifies several more specific reasons why people avoid medical attention or delay the decision to seek it: • Failure to recognize (or accept) the potential seriousness of the symptoms; • concern about imposing on their physician; • fear that they will be seen as foolish for coming in with a minor problem; • reluctance to disrupt prior plans, such as completing a task or going to dinner with friends; and • in the case of acute symptoms like chest pain, a decision to take time for such minor matters as showering and packing. Additional reasons for delay or avoidance might include: • Reluctance to take time away from work at a busy job; • concerns about the cost of the medical care; and • a belief that the physician probably can't help anyway. What unfortunately reinforces all these reasons for delaying medical attention is that symptoms are, in fact, rarely life-threatening. Why should a 60-year-old, who has ignored symptoms all his life and never been wrong, now decide to go to the doctor? How can he know that *this* time it's serious?

Disregarding Medical Advice. In addition to the many people who avoid medical advice, there are those who seek it but then disregard it. Evidence suggests that people ignore medical recommendations between 30 and 60% of the time (Kaplan & Simon, 1990). Such noncompliance is not, however, uniform across all types of advice. People are more likely to comply when: • The treatment is short-term and highly specific (for example, antibiotics for ten days); • when the treatment is simple (taking a pill); • when the symptoms are highly specific; • when they like and respect the physician; • when the treatment is not aversive (like an injection); and • when they clearly understand the instructions (Evans & Haynes, 1990).

When treatments are more general, longer-term, difficult, or aversive, compliance is unlikely. Medical counsel to lose weight or exercise, for example, is more often ignored than not. Similarly, diabetics, though apprised of the devastating effects of poorly controlled diabetes, often fail to adhere closely to the prescribed routine of blood sugar measurements and insulin injections. One task of health psychology is to find ways to increase compliance with important medical admonitions.

But don't be misled. Health psychologists do not advise that you blindly conform to every bit of medical advice. Rather, you should evaluate it carefully. If what is being prescribed or suggested seems wrong or unclear, it is very important to question it. Physicians make mistakes, just like anyone else. Moreover, they are often hurried and, at best, have probably spent only a few minutes thinking about your case. If in doubt about a treatment, ask questions, and if still in doubt, seek a second opinion.

Playing The Sick Role. At the opposite extreme from those who ignore symptoms and avoid medical care are people who just love to play "the sick role," making certain that others are well aware of their illness. Why would they do that? Because sickness confers many *secondary gains*—rewards for being ill. Society basically gives sick people a break. The ill person can stay home from work, avoid family responsibilities, and turn down such social obligations as that boring dinner party. In addition, the sick person suddenly finds that she is the center of attention. Doctors and nurses find her interesting and important, family members sit by and minister to her every need, and friends, bosses, and co-workers call, visit, and send flowers. Moreover, there may be a virtually constant flow of expressions of sympathy, concern, love, and goodwill.

The only thing wrong with secondary gains is that they reinforce illness and tend to prolong recovery (Kinsman, Dirks, & Jones, 1982). After all, who wants to give up such valuable benefits?

Preventing and Reducing Stress

A number of approaches are currently being used to treat and control stress responses. Major methods include stress management, relaxation techniques, meditation, and biofeedback, all of which can have therapeutic physiological effects (Forbes & Pekada, 1993). *Stress Management.* One way to deal with stress is to systematically apply multiple techniques to prevent or reduce it. Teaching such techniques is the focus of *stress management* programs, which have now been popular for the past two decades or so. Taught by health psychologists and others, such programs have been widely used in industrial and health settings. There is no one, absolute set of principles that is uniformly agreed upon as the key to stress management. However, the coping strategies typically advocated include facing and directly coping with stress, rather than avoiding or ignoring it, and finding outlets for negative emotions, rather than holding them inside. Studies have shown that people who hold in their anger have higher blood pressure than those who express it (Spielberger, 1985) and that talking to others about problems greatly reduces feelings of stress (Clark, 1993). Program participants are also taught to follow sound nutritional principles, exercise regularly, and joke about their problems, since humor has been shown to reduce the effects of stress (Nezu, Nezu, & Blissett, 1988).

Relaxation Techniques. The human body contains 620 skeletal muscles. When these muscles contract, glycogen is broken down and lactic acid is formed, causing fatigue. Prolonged muscle tension, seen in states of stress, can impede circulation, create more muscle fatigue products, and allow these products to build up. Evidence suggests that chronic muscle tension is therefore associated with aches and pains in muscles of the head, back, neck, and shoulders. Relaxing the muscles stops the buildup of lactic acid and other fatigue products and should therefore reduce the aches and pains.

Edmund Jacobson (1938) demonstrated that relaxation reverses the physiological effects of stress and pioneered an approach to reducing muscle tension called *progressive relaxation.* This approach is designed to teach people to systematically reduce tension in muscles throughout the body and thereby reduce the stress response. In a typical clinical application, each of 16 different muscle groups is tensed for 7 seconds and then relaxed for 15 seconds. This tension-relaxation sequence is repeated twice for each muscle group before moving on to the next one. After completing the basic relaxation program, the subject moves on to an intermediate program in which the 16 muscle groups are combined to form 7 groups. At the most advanced stage of progressive relaxation, the person is able to tense and relax the body as one large muscle group (Beach, Burns, and Sheffield, 1982).

Those who advocate progressive relaxation suggest that it has many benefits (Benson, 1975). It should help the person to behave more competently under stress and can relieve such problems as hypertension, headache, insomnia, and anxiety. It may also improve performance on the job and in social situations, reduce fatigue, and aid in recovery from certain illnesses (Burns, 1981). Some evidence shows that it is helpful in cases of insomnia (Steinmark and Borkovek, 1973), essential hypertension (Shoemaker and Taso, 1975), and chronic headache (Blanchard, 1993; Cod, Freunlick, and Meyer, 1975). However, the evidence is mixed. Neal Miller (1983) reviewed the literature and found that much of the evidence usually cited is of the case history variety and that carefully controlled studies tend to be lacking. He concluded that considerable further research is needed before we can be certain of the effectiveness of relaxation approaches in relieving stress-related problems.

Meditation. Meditation, practiced in various forms in the Orient for centuries, may have effects quite similar to those of progressive relaxation. Both involve what Herbert Benson (1975) has termed the *relaxation response*, which includes reductions in muscle tension, heart rate, blood pressure, respiration rate, and brain cortical activity. As with progressive relaxation, there is mixed evidence that meditation may produce positive physical changes, including decreased heart rate and reduced anxiety (Alexander & Swanson, 1993). Meditation and its effects are further discussed in Chapter 5.

Biofeedback. Internal bodily processes governed by the autonomic nervous system are not normally under voluntary control. You cannot decide to slow your heart down or to stop sweating. However, it may be possible to gain some control over autonomic functions through biofeedback techniques. In *biofeedback*, the individual is given information about how a particular physiological response is currently functioning and attempts to alter that functioning in a desired direction. For example, by observing a visual display of your heart rate, you may be able to learn to reduce it. One study showed that such training reduced the heart's reactivity to stress (Sharpley, 1994).

Biofeedback can be used to augment other relaxation methods or to deal with specific stress-related disorders (Blumenstein et al., 1995). Theoretically, biofeedback should make it easier for people to achieve relaxation by showing them directly how their physiological systems are functioning. In one study, college students received electromyographic (EMG) feedback of their levels of muscle tension while attempting to relax under standard relaxation instructions (Lestman and Sowa, 1983). The feedback condition produced significantly greater decreases in blood pressure and self-reported anxiety than were seen in an untreated control group.

Biofeedback techniques have also been applied to alleviate headaches and other forms of pain, as well as hypertension, but with mixed results (Elton, 1993; Weaver & McGrady, 1995). Blanchard and his colleagues have used EMG biofeedback to reduce pain in chronic headache sufferers (Blanchard et al., 1993). It has also been successfully used to reduce chronic pain, and one study showed that the effect lasted for at least two years after treatment (Flor & Birbaumer, 1993). However, findings for migraine headache sufferers are mixed (Beach et al., 1982), and the use of biofeedback to reduce blood pressure tends to produce small reductions that are rarely clinically significant (Engel, Gaardner, and Glasgow, 1981).

Conclusion

It seems clear that psychologists interested in stress and more generally in the psychology of health still have considerable work to do. Nevertheless, we have seen in this chapter that much has already been accomplished. We understand many of the major sources of stress in our lives, ranging from minor hassles to traumas. We also have increasing knowledge of just how people react to stress, both psychologically and biologically. We have learned that optimism, social support, and physical exercise, among other things, can help to reduce the impact of stress and that coping strategies can also be effective, as can stress management, biofeedback and systematic relaxation. In addition, it appears that psychology has much to contribute to such healthy behaviors as not smoking and not drinking excessively. As we move into the 21st century, the efforts of health psychologists may lead to reductions in lung cancer, heart disease, and even AIDS (Thoresen & Powell, 1992). We will also learn more about cultural differences in health behaviors (Beardsley, 1994), the effects of stress on the immune system, and the multitude of ways in which healthy behavior can prolong life.

Summary

1. According to evolutionary psychology, human behaviors, such as safety-conscious behaviors, evolved because of the demands of ancient environments.

2. Unhealthy behaviors, like smoking, may have originally been adaptive (for example, in reducing anxiety) and developed for that reason.

Sources of Stress

1. Among the major sources of stress in our lives are life change, job stress, home life, lack of social support, and such crises such as war and natural disaster.

2. SRRS studies show that the most stressful life changes include death of a spouse, divorce, marital separation, a jail term, and the death of a close family member. Also contributing to life stress are the daily hassles of living.

3. Work both causes and is affected by stress. People in boring jobs tend to have greater work-induced stress than those who have a high degree of security and interest.

4. Potential sources of stress in home life include a negative physical environment, conflict between spouses, marital separation, and parenting.

5. Lack of social support can be a source of stress. It is associated with higher rates of physical and psychological disorder and increased mortality rates.

6. Other sources of stress include wars, natural disasters, and acculturation.

Psychological and Biological Reactions to Stress

1. Major psychological reactions to stress include anxiety, traumatic reaction (characterized by the states of intrusion and denial), and suicide. Prolonged reactions to stress may take the form of posttraumatic stress syndrome.
2. Selye's general adaptation syndrome (GAS) occurs in three stages: alarm, resistance, and exhaustion.
3. The GAS begins with a reaction of the sympathetic system, which produces such changes as increased heart rate and blood pressure. Later comes the secretion of hormones by the adrenal medulla, the pituitary, the adrenal cortex, and the thyroid.

Stress and Physical Illness

1. High life stress scores are predictive of a variety of illnesses. However, there are individual differences, and life stress is a relatively small factor in illness overall.
2. Illness is multi-factorial. Stress is one contributing element in some instances. Others include genetic and situational factors.
3. Stress can reduce immune function and thereby contribute to infectious diseases.
4. One factor that may contribute to coronary artery disease is the hard-driving, competitive personality. However, it may be only certain components of Type A that are involved.
5. Stress may contribute to ulceration, but many ulcers are primarily bacterial in origin. Other factors include heredity, smoking, alcohol, use of aspirin and related drugs.
6. Stress may contribute to cancer, but the evidence is thus far mixed.
7. Other stress disorders include headache, asthma, hypertension, rheumatoid arthritis, and certain skin disorders.

Dealing with Stress

1. Among stress-mediating factors that can serve as buffers between the individual and stressors are social support, predicting and controlling stress, an adaptive or "hardy" personality style, and regular exercise.
2. Making human stressors more predictable often makes them more manageable.
3. Coping is an active effort to solve the problems creating stress.
4. Coping mechanisms include cognitive appraisal, self-instruction, making changes, increasing social support, and Inoculation. Some coping mechanisms are maladaptive and have negative effects on health, while adaptive mechanisms often have positive health effects.
5. Stress reactions can be treated with a number of therapeutic methods. Among the most widely used are progressive relaxation, meditation, and biofeedback.

Health Psychology

1. Smoking kills 500,000 people each year and contributes to a number of diseases, including cardiovascular disease.
2. Smoking doubles all-cause mortality.
3. Approaches to stopping include drugs, conditioning, the nicotine patch, and going "cold turkey." About 80% return to smoking.
4. Alcoholics live 19 years less than other people.
5. Alcohol consumption accounts for 100,000 deaths each year.
6. Health-belief models suggest that beliefs strongly influence behavior.
7. The decision to seek medical advice is influenced by perception and personality.

8. Medical advice is often disregarded when treatments are longer-term, difficult, or aversive.
9. Many people enjoy the "sick role" because it confers secondary gains.

Ask Yourself

1. What are the major sources of stress, and what work has been done to isolate these sources?
2. What are the major sources of stress in home life? What suspected sources appear not to be real stressors?
3. How does social support relate to stress?
4. What are the effects of crisis and trauma on individuals?
5. What are the major negative psychological reactions to stress?
6. Describe the 3 stages of the general adaptation syndrome and outline the underlying neurophysiological mechanisms.
7. What evidence is there that stress produces physiological disorders?
8. What role does personality play in a person's susceptibility to stress and ability to cope with it?
9. Discuss means of reducing stress, including mediating factors and active coping. What form of coping do you think is most effective?
10. How effective are relaxation, meditation, and biofeedback in reducing stress?

Further Readings

Andersen, B., Keicolt-Glaser, J., & Glaser, R. (1994). A biobehavioral model of cancer stress and disease course. *Amer. Psychol.*, 49, 389-404. This paper details data concerned with the role of stress in cancer and presents a multifactorial theory of the disease.

Bernard, L, & Krupat, E. (1994). *Health psychology: Biopsychosoical factors in health and illness.* Ft. Worth: Harcourt Brace. A good basic text that covers the field of health psychology thoroughly.

Cacioppo, J. (1994). Social neuroscience: autonomic, neuroendocrine, and immune responses to stress. *Psychophysiology*, 31, 113-128. This interesting article reviews what we know about the effects of social and psychological stressors on major body systems.

Eysenck, H.J. (1993). Prediction of cancer and coronary heart disease mortality by menas of a personality inventory: Results of a 15-year follow-up study. *Psychol. Reps.*, 72, 499-516. This interesting longitudinal study shows that personality can have strong effects on physical health.

Falloon, I., Laporta, M., Fadden, G., and Graham-Hole, V. (1993). *Managing stress in families: Cognitive and behavioural strategies for enhancing coping skills.* London: Routledge. This book reviews stress management techniques that can be used in a family context.

Henry, J.P. (1992). Biological basis of the stress response. *Integr. Psysiol. Behav. Sci.*, 27, 66-83. This helpful article pulls together much of what we know about the physiology of stress, updating Selye's work.

Humphrey, J. (1992). *Stress among women in modern society.* Springfield, il: Charles C. Thomas. Humphrey takes a close look at the stresses of modern womanhood, their effects, and their management.

Lipton, M. (1994). *Posttraumatic stress disorder.* Springfield, il: Charles C. Thomas. Written for both professionals, this book details what we know about posttraumatic disorder.

Rice, P. (1992). *Stress and health.* The impact of stress on physical health is carefully documented in this book, as are approaches to reducing the stress in our lives.

Sarafino, E. (1994). *Health psychology: Biopsychosoical interactions.* NY: Wiley. This basic text in health psychology details the nature of the field, its goals, and its accomplishments to date.

Sgoutas, E., Cacioppo, J., Uchino, B., Malarkey, W. Pearl, D., Kiecolt-Glaser, J., & Glaser, R. (1994). The effects of an acute psychological stressor on cardiovascular, endocrine, and cellular immune response: a prospective study of individuals high and low in heart rate reactivity. *Psychophysiology*, 31, 264-271. This well-designed study exposed subjects to stressors and demonstrated their effects on body functions.

Turner, J. (1994). *Cardiovascular reactivity and stress: Patterns of physiological response.* NY: Plenum. Turner provides an introductory-level look at how stress affects the cardiovascular system.

Key Terms

acculturation
anxiety
biofeedback
cognitive appraisal
coping
general adaptation syndrome
hard personality
life change units (LCUs)
meditation
postraumatic stress response (syndrome?)
progressive relaxation
psychosomatic disorders (?)
relaxation response
Social Readjustment Rating Scale (SRRS)
social support
stress
stressor
traumatic reaction
type A personality
type B personality

Psychology in the 21st Century

Tolerating Stress: Hardy and Optimistic Personalities

Stress can clearly have anywhere from minor to devastating effects on your psychological and physical health, but not all people are equally vulnerable to its effects. Wouldn't it be nice to know the secrets of those who are almost always "calm, cool, and collected," a common way of describing the stress-invulnerable person? If we knew how people become less prone to stress, perhaps we could help others to reduce their stress loads. It is this possibility, combined with a basic, scientific interest in the question of differential stress vulnerability, that has led researchers to begin a quest that will continue well into the next century. It is a quest to identify personality characteristics that make us react more positively to stressful situations (Fontaine et al., 1993).

Both general level of adjustment and specific personality characteristics influence the stress response. The better adjusted a person is, the more adaptively he can respond to stress. One study that followed 107 male Harvard graduates over a 40-year period found that of the 59 men who had excellent mental health only 2 became chronically ill or died, while 18 of the 48 men with poor mental health developed chronic illnesses or died in the same period (Vaillant, 1979). Other studies have shown that certain personalities or behavior styles are more adaptive than others. In a 30-year follow-up study of Johns Hopkins medical students, those categorized as "slow and solid" in temperament had the fewest major physical disorders, while those classified as displaying somewhat irregular, uneven behavior had the most (Betz and Thomas, 1979).

In an attempt to identify more specific personality characteristics that may be stress-protective, Suzanne Kobasa (1979) has suggested that some people have *hardy personalities* that can serve as a source of resistance to the potentially debilitating effects of stress. This personality style has three central characteristics: commitment, control, and challenge. Such a person is firmly *committed* to the accomplishment of goals and solution of problems, is largely in *control* of her life, and enjoys the *challenges* presented by change and by problems requiring action. Individuals who score high on a test of hardiness have more positive views of themselves (Allred & Smith, 1989) and a significantly lower incidence of common physical and psychological symptoms (Kobasa, Maddi, and Puccetti, 1982; Nowack, 1989) than do those with low hardiness scores. They also show less effects of job stress (Neubauer, 1992). In addition, hardiness reduced the amount of illness seen over a two-year period during which subjects in another study were monitored (Kobasa, Maddi, and Kahn, 1982) and cut in half the rate of illness in a group of business executives (Singh, 1985). Critics point out, however, that it is too soon to know whether hardiness is an important factor in stress management or in physical health (Allred & Smith, 1989).

Another stress-reducing personality characteristic may be *optimism*. The idea here is that people who are consistently optimistic may cope more effectively with stress and thereby reduce the risk, duration, or severity of illness (Horowitz et al., 1988). This hypothesis certainly accords well with the widely held belief that positive mental attitudes are healthier. In fact, one survey study showed that 77% of the general population believe that positive thinking can reduce the likelihood of illness and 94% believe it can aide in recovery from illness (Bruckbauer & Ward, 1993). In order to test the hypothesis, the Life Orientation Test (LOT) was developed to measure optimism and has been employed in a number of studies (Scheier & Carver, 1985). In one study those scoring high on the LOT had faster recoveries from coronary bypass surgery (Scheier et al., 1989). In another, optimism was predictive of a better quality of life six months after surgery (Fitzgerald et al., 1993). And other kinds of positive outcomes of the optimism trait have also been reported (Fontaine et al., 1993; Lai, 1995; Stewart et al., 1995).

Despite these findings, many are skeptical of the value of optimism for physical and mental health. Randall Colvin and Jack Block (1994) point out that hypotheses relating optimism and similar positive mental health concepts to health are not entirely logical and have not been supported by recent studies. Their view is bolstered by a longitudinal study in which the personality characteristics of over 1100 people were assessed in childhood and the subjects followed over much of their lifetimes (Friedman & Tucker, 1993). One striking finding of this study was that optimism was *inversely* related to longevity. Those who were the most optimistic had the shortest lifespans. While the simple logic that optimism should somehow promote health seems obvious and attractive, it is clear that we cannot too quickly rush to judgment. Considerable additional research will be needed to determine just how optimism relates to health outcomes, if at all. As we move into the 21st century, researchers will further study hardiness and optimism, but they will also search for other keys to the relatively stress-invulnerable personality.

Probe

Post-Traumatic Stress Disorder

The Vietnam War was a very long time ago—particularly if you are twenty-something and have only read about it in the history books. Nevertheless, many veterans of this seed bed of psychological trauma are still feeling its effects. In fact, studies show that even now over 35% of Vietnam veterans report having suicidal thoughts related to the war (Kramer et al., 1994) and many others are still experiencing *posttraumatic stress disorder (PTSD)*. Often informally termed "shell shock" or "battle fatigue," PTSD is the most prolonged and, apart from suicide, the most serious of all reactions to severe stress. It has been widely studied in Vietnam veterans (Kramer et al., 1994; Long et al., 1994) and in veterans of World War II and the Korean war (Spiro et al., 1994). However, PTSD is also common in the victims of traumatic domestic events. It is seen in 38% of burn victims (Powers et al., 1994) and 46% of those involved in motor vehicle accidents (Blanchard et al., 1994). More generally, a study of college students revealed that any of a wide variety of prior traumatic experiences could produce the symptoms of PTSD (Vrana & Lauterbach, 1994). In fact, although the formal diagnosis of this disorder is relatively recent, reports go back at least to a study of a peasant family trapped by an avalanche in the Italian Alps in 1755 (Parry & Parry, 1994).

Researchers have long attempted to document both the causes of negative emotional reactions and the details of their effects. Focusing on the Vietnam War, Arthur S. Blank (1982) has clinically evaluated more than a thousand veterans. The most obvious sources of stress were those typically experienced during war: the constant threat of death, seeing friends injured and killed, the hidden threat of guerrilla warfare and terrorism, the lack of good food and water, difficult living conditions, arduous work and continuous fatigue, and the lack of clear objectives. Less obvious stress was imposed when the war was over and the veterans returned to a cool reception from a general public that had never approved of the Vietnam conflict.

Blank has identified four major types of negative emotional reactions experienced by Vietnam veterans:

- Psychological symptoms, such as depression, nightmares, psychophysiologic disorders (ulcers, migraine headaches), and addictions to alcohol and other drugs. This syndrome sometimes also includes more severe psychological disorders, such as schizophrenia.
- Major alterations of life course. Underachievement, crime, and a wandering lifestyle in which the veteran goes from job to job and school to school with little progress are common.

- Difficulties in relating to others. Interpersonal problems with wives, children, and other relatives, as well as a more general alienation from people and society, are frequent.
- A "broken connection" with positive images of self and humanity and a loss of faith in the human capacity for goodness are also seen in many veterans.

Common symptoms of posttraumatic stress disorder more generally include high anxiety, feelings of guilt, angry outbursts with minimal provocation, depression, nightmares, and flashbacks to the traumatic experience. Difficulties in concentration and in maintaining positive emotional relationships may also occur. In addition, any stimulus that relates to the trauma can trigger off severe anxiety and even panic attacks. For example, the extensive news coverage of the Persian Gulf war stimulated vivid personal memories in many Vietnam veterans. Those with a history of PTSD often experienced severe symptoms as a result (Long et al., 1994). The symptoms of PTSD can be relatively short-lived, lasting a month or two, with flashbacks in some victims up to a year or more later (Powers et al., 1994). However, studies of combat veterans show that it can also last a lifetime (Aldwin et al., 1994). In fact, a study of over 1200 veterans of World War II and the Korean war revealed that symptoms were still common 40-50 years after the war. Those veterans who had front line combat experience were 13 times more likely to be diagnosed with PTSD than those who had not (Spiro et al., 1994).

While a variety of forms of therapy have been used, it is typically necessary to help the disturbed veteran gain assurance that his involvement in the war was important, appropriate, and moral and that the society's disapproval of the war was not a disapproval of his personal involvement in it.

Probe

Running from Stress

As we were about to leave campus at the end of each semester, my college fencing coach would strongly admonish all members of the varsity fencing team to keep in shape during the vacation. My solution was to put on my sweats and run regularly along the streets of my small home town in Pennsylvania. To say the least, I got some very strange looks from passing motorists. "What is this guy doing running along the street?" they wondered. More generally, a person out running (it wasn't called jogging then) probably stood a good chance of being arrested, offered rides by good Samaritans, or at least thought of as a little strange in those days. Since that time, however, we have learned that the benefits of exercise are substantial, and, for some, it has become a genuine American passion. But just what are the widely touted advantages of regular physical activity?

The most carefully studied effects of exercise are those that involve the cardiovascular system. Many studies have examined the impact of exercise on blood pressure, stroke, and heart attack frequency, and there is now little doubt that it is substantial. Hypertension or high blood pressure is a major risk factor for myocardial infarction (heart attack), and studies quite consistently demonstrate reductions in blood pressure with regular physical activity. Significantly reduced pressures are seen in both younger and older people who work out (Scarpace & Lowenthal, 1994) and, conversely, hypertension is associated with low levels of exercise and physical fitness (Ikeda et al., 1993). However, it appears that a long-term, regular exercise regimen may be necessary to achieve the benefit (Wijnen et al., 1994). Exercise also reduces the probability of having a stroke. The Honolulu Heart Program has followed over 8000 men since 1965. Statistics from this study show that men who do not exercise have 3 to 4 times as great a risk of having a stroke as do those who work out regularly (Abbott et al., 1994).

As you might expect, regular exercise also reduces the likelihood of having a heart attack. In fact, those who exercise vigorously at least two days each week cut their risk of heart attacks in half (Morris & Froelicher, 1993; O'Connor et al., 1995). Exercise appears to produce this benefit by increasing the diameters of coronary arteries. These are the tiny vessels—about the size of a pencil lead— that supply blood to the heart. The diameter of a coronary artery is gradually reduced over time as cholesterol deposits plaques on its walls. A myocardial infarction occurs when blood clots in the narrowed artery, cutting off the supply to heart tissue and causing it to die. Exercise widens the coronaries and effectively reduces the likelihood that they will become completely blocked (Morris & Froelicher, 1993). In addition, it may increase the levels of protective high-density lipoprotein (HDL) cholesterol in the bloodstream (Guize et al., 1995).

Exercise also has beneficial effects on other body systems and disease processes and can reduce the impact of stress. The probability of diabetes, some forms of cancer, and perhaps other diseases is decreased by regular physical activity (Ikeda et al., 1993), as is the overall amount of physical illness experienced by the individual (Kobasa et al., 1982). Some of these benefits may be achieved because exercise boosts the operation of the immune system (Mazzeo, 1994). In addition, it reverses some of the hormonal and metabolic effects of psychological stress (Graveling, 1980), increases stress tolerance (Hoffman et al, 1982; Karasek, Russel, and Theorell, 1982), and reduces feelings of stress (Pavett et al., 1987). A more general bottom line is that physical activity, when it is regular, vigorous, and continuing over time, reduces all-cause mortality (LaFontaine et al., 1994) and increases life expectancy (Rooney, 1993).

So everyone works out, right? Well, apparently the message hasn't reached quite the entire population. A majority of the population actively avoids vigorous exercise—the "couch potato" syndrome. In fact, at least 60% of U.S. adults and a similar proportion of people in other countries do not exercise at all (MMWR, 1993; Booth et al., 1993).

Horizons in Personality

If You Can't Beat 'Em...

Hopefully, you have never been a captive or hostage, either in war or in some domestic situation. However, many people have been, and reactions can be quite varied. Some have an entirely negative experience of the sort seen in victims of World War II concentration camps. Termed the *KZ syndrome*, such traumatic reactions begin with a period of *shock*, involving depersonalization and a kind of emotional paralysis, with loss of consciousness occurring in extreme cases. This initial stage gives way to an *alarm phase*, involving feelings of anxiety, doubt, and often panic, followed by an *adaptation phase*, which may include hyperactivity, depression, or indifference. The final phase is *exhaustion*, in which there is a state of fatigue and general weakness, often following some degree of successful coping with the stress (Bastiaans, 1982).

While the KZ syndrome is about what you might expect under the strain of severe, prolonged stress, a fascinating alternative reaction to captivity is the *Stockholm Syndrome*, named for a 1973 incident in which bank robbers in Stockholm, Sweden, held four hostages for six days. At the end of this period, the hostages had developed a high degree of loyalty to the robbers. In a sense, the hostages had come to love their captors, rather than hate them. Thus, the Stockholm Syndrome is characterized by loyalty to captors, often accompanied by a rejection of relatives, authorities, and others who would save their lives.

How could hostages develop such a syndrome? One explanation is that captors may lie to the hostage, telling her that her parents, the authorities, and society do not really care about her. Such lies may seem to be confirmed by the fact that she sees no evidence that anyone is trying to save her. This is exactly what happened in the case of Patty Hearst, who was first kidnapped and later joined with her captors in robbing a bank and eluding authorities (Conway and Siegelman, 1980). In other cases the prisoners may like their captors for not killing them or mistreating them and perhaps even for seeming to save their lives (McCarthy, 1980). In addition, the captors are often themselves injured, frightened, or insecure, and the hostage may feel sympathy for them (Schreiber, 1978).

"Ooh, My Tooth": Cavities and Stress

It is perhaps not surprising to learn that stress is an important factor in coronary artery disease, hypertension, and ulcers—but cavities? A series of studies done by Donald R. Morse and his colleagues (1982) suggest that stress may well contribute to dental caries or cavity formation. In one study, dental students taking a biochemistry course provided samples of saliva before and after each of a series of difficult laboratory exercises and again after the subjects meditated for 20 minutes. Excessively high levels of bacteria and protein in the saliva immediately after the lab exercises were reduced significantly following meditation. The formation of plaque and the development of tooth decay is known to be enhanced by increasing bacterial and protein levels in the mouth. This study and others thus suggest that prolonged or recurrent stress may well increase the likelihood of cavity formation (Marcenes & Sheilham, 1992).

Tranquilizing Your Stress

Progressive relaxation, meditation, biofeedback, and exercise are all approaches to reducing stress that require some effort, are time consuming, and can be expensive if administered or supervised by a therapist. How much easier it would be to take a pill. The few seconds required to pop a tranquilizer or a barbiturate would be a much quicker way to achieve relief from stress.

The primary drugs used for stress reduction are the antianxiety agents or minor tranquilizers (see Chapter 17). The principal antianxiety agents in current use belong to the benzodiazepine group, which includes diazepam (Valium), chlordiazepoxide (Librium), alprazolam (Xanax), and lorazepam (Ativan), among others. A few minor tranquilizers are not benzodiazepines. Chief among these is the recently developed drug buspirone (BuSpar). When used in moderation and for relatively short periods of time, these drugs have been very helpful in reducing anxiety and making it easier for the individual to function better in the day-to-day world. In addition, they are relatively safe drugs, with few side effects. However, there are some problems associated with the minor tranquilizers. First, the user can become dependent on the drug and feel as though he is unable to function without it, leading to withdrawal symptoms in some patients when the drugs are discontinued. Second, the body can gradually develop a tolerance for the drug, and the person has to consume larger and larger amounts to achieve the desired effects. A third problem is that the drug remains in the body for relatively long periods of time. As a result, blood levels can build up over a period of days, leading to greater depression of the central nervous system than would be expected on the basis of a single dose.

Many clinicians do prescribe tranquilizers as a form of short-term treatment for stress. Patients with acute stress symptoms can be significantly helped for a period of a few weeks by using these drugs. However, the drugs do not deal with the real problems causing the stress. Thus, long-term drug treatment of stress is inadvisable.

Chapter 16

Abnormal Behavior

Outline

Abnormal Behavior: Perspectives and Models

The Problem of Abnormal Behavior: Definition and Scope

Historical Views: Demons and Witches

Modern Views: Evolution and Neuroscience

Major Causal Models

Classification and Diagnosis

Anxiety, Somatoform, and Dissociative Disorders

Anxiety Disorders

Somatoform Disorders

Dissociative Disorders

Schizophrenia

Primary Symptoms

Principal Types

Causal Factors

The Fate of Mr. R.

Delusional and Personality Disorders

Delusional (Paranoid) Disorders

Personality Disorders

Mood Disorders

Major Depressive Disorder

Bipolar Disorder

Types of Depression

Patients At Risk: Suicide in Depression

The Causes of Mood Disorders

The Neurophysiological of Abnormal Behavior

Schizophrenia

Mood Disorders

Cognitive Disorders

Networking

FROM TIME TO TIME everyone feels anxious or depressed or disoriented. But some people experience these symptoms so severely that they are unable to function normally in their daily lives. When such people seek help for their problems, psychologists try to diagnose the specific disorder by examining the symptoms in detail. This chapter begins with an overview of just what abnormal behavior is, what its causes might be, and how we classify the major psychological disorders. We then describe each of several major types of disorder, discussing the symptoms and causes of each.

The study of abnormal behavior is closely related to that of personality, stress, and treatment. The major theories of personality that we discuss in Chapter 14 provide a basis for most psychological theories of psychopathology (abnormality), and stress, the subject of Chapter 15, is often a factor in the development of abnormal patterns of behavior. The treatment methods we take up in Chapter 17 are the ones used for the various disorders that are the subject of this chapter.

Raving Mad

It was 3:00 a.m. when the PA system outside my tiny office in the hospital echoed my name through the hallways: Dr. Smith, report to Emergency *stat* (hospital jargon for 'hurry')." I was in graduate school (not an actual "doctor" yet) and had a part-time position at a state mental institution.

As I approached the ER, I heard sounds of scuffling and a very loud male voice shouting incoherently. As I entered, I saw a hospital attendant momentarily airborne on his way to crashing into the wall. No less than four uniformed police officers were struggling to hold a man we'll call Mr. R., who was dressed in a torn, bloody tee shirt and Army fatigues. At least 6'4" tall, he was easily 275 lbs. of solid muscle and might have been Arnold Schwarzennegger's big brother. I learned later that 25-year-old Mr. R. had suddenly "gone crazy" at home, throwing his sister against a wall and breaking several windows. He had then proceeded to a nearby bar, where he had spoken of "devils" and "evils," grabbed a man and slammed his head against the bar, giving him a concussion. He had overturned a number of tables, broken several chairs, and injured three other people before the police arrived, wrestled him into a car, and brought him to the hospital.

As I entered the ER, everyone looked at me expectantly as though I would somehow know how to deal with the problem. What would *you* do? I had a nurse call the senior medical resident to prescribe an injection of a tranquilizer. Meanwhile, we took the patient to a small room with padding on the walls and floor and a very heavy door. Once there, we all held Mr. R. down while a nurse injected the drug. He soon calmed down, though he remained incoherent.

Mr. R. was a schizophrenic, and his case was fairly typical of one subtype of that disorder. We'll return to his case later in the chapter when we discuss schizophrenia.

We begin with this anecdote because the patient exhibited the kinds of bizarre, "crazy" actions that you may immediately think of as abnormal behavior or psychopathology. There are, of course, people who fit such stereotypical images. However abnormal behavior is rarely as obvious or as dramatic as the makers of movies and TV programs would have us believe. Nor is it entirely consistent from person to person, time to time, and culture to culture.

Abnormal Behavior: Perspectives and Models

Scientists who study and clinicians who treat abnormal behavior or *psychopathology* have long shared the goal of understanding its causes, as well as its manifestations. Although we have developed a vast body of knowledge about abnormality during the twentieth century, we still have a long way to go. In fact, we are still dealing with the problem of defining it. We'll first discuss definitions of abnormal behavior, then turn to historical and current approaches to understanding it and to the theoretical models that guide both research and treatment. Finally, we will take up the classification and diagnosis of psychopathological behavior.

The Problem of Abnormal Behavior: Definition and Scope

Defining abnormal behavior has proven to be a difficult task for three reasons. First, abnormality is a construct - an abstraction - and therefore subject to varied definitions (see Chapter 2). Second, psychologists often disagree as to what constitutes a specific instance of abnormal behavior. Finally, there are cultural differences in what can reasonably be considered abnormal. For example, in most parts of the United States a person who regularly has "visions" or hallucinations would be considered quite abnormal. In Hawaii, however, many believe in the existence of a helpful spirit called the Aumakua, and a person who reports seeing and communicating with this spirit is considered fortunate, not abnormal.

What Is Abnormal Behavior? Three different approaches have been used in defining abnormality: maladaptation, social deviance, and statistical variation. *Maladaptive* behaviors are those that do not further the well-being of the individual or of society. The woman who feels compelled to wash her hands every half hour, the man who is drunk much of the time, and the depressed teenager who rarely leaves her room are all clearly exhibiting patterns of maladaptive behavior.

Abnormal behavior may also be defined as any behavior that *deviates from social norms.* The person who walks naked though Times Square or wears an evening gown to mow the lawn is clearly deviating from established social norms. Fear of harmless objects (phobias), compulsive gambling, and drug abuse are also behaviors that deviate from social norms. But deviation from a norm doesn't automatically mean that a behavior is abnormal. In fact, cultural conformity as a definition of normality has become suspect: During World War II, for example, many German citizens conformed to cultural norms that sanctioned genocide and other atrocities. Would the German citizen who refused to conform to Nazi norms be abnormal? Clearly not.

A more formal scientific definition of abnormality is that it represents *statistical deviation* from an average. That is, abnormal behaviors are those that are statistically rare and therefore unusual. This approach is most commonly used in areas like mental retardation, where scientists can calculate the proportion of individuals in the population who fall below an average range on standardized IQ tests. One problem with this approach is that it does not differentiate between desirable and undesirable behavior. Geniuses are just as rare in the population as retarded people and would therefore be equally "abnormal" using this definition.

Beyond these formal attempts at definition, most professionals who deal regularly with psychological disturbance use three practical criteria: bizarreness, discomfort, and inefficiency. *Bizarre* behavior is highly unusual and deviates from accepted standards in a fairly extreme fashion. *Discomfort* can be either physical or psychological and can range from ulcers and asthma to anxiety and depression. *Inefficiency* (something all of us experience from time to time) is considered significant if a person displays a noticeable, persistent decrease in the efficiency or effectiveness of her behavior.

The Scope of the Problem. No matter how we define abnormal behavior, it is a problem of major proportions (Figure 16-1). Recent studies show that in any one-year period 28-30 percent of the U.S. population have a diagnosable mental or substance abuse disorder (Regier et al., 1993; Kessler et al., 1994). Taking the lower figure, 56 million Americans had such disorders in 1996 (Carson et al., 1996). To care for them, the Veterans Administration alone operates 140 hospitals with over 315,000 patients (Sunshine et al., 1991), and 314 private psychiatric hospitals house another 235,000 (Redick et al., 1989). Many additional patients are found in state mental hospitals or seen as outpatients by psychologists and psychiatrists in private practice.

You might guess from these statistics that the cost of psychopathology is massive - and you are right! Estimates place the overall cost of mental illness in the United States at a minimum of $103 billion per year (Rice et al., 1992), rising to perhaps $273 billion when alcohol and drug abuse are included (Rice et al., 1991). These figures give you some idea of why understanding the causes of psychopathology and developing effective treatments are important goals.

Historical Views: Demons and Witches

Modern psychologists and psychiatrists consider abnormal behaviors to be the result of a combination of physiological and psychological factors that can be determined through research. However, this scientific view of abnormality did not become common until the early twentieth century. In ancient times, people believed in *demonology* - the idea that abnormal behavior is caused by evil spirits inhabiting the person's body.

The classical Greek and Roman civilizations brought somewhat more scientific thinking to the problem. Hippocrates, Plato, Aristotle, and Galen developed explanations for psychopathology that attributed it to brain pathology and other physical problems. However, such scientific approaches were largely lost for many centuries following Galen's death in 200 A.D. and the decline of ancient Greece and Rome.

Scientific, naturalistic explanations were replaced by religious ones and a return of demonology, which dominated thinking about abnormal behavior from about the thirteenth to the eighteenth centuries. It was commonly thought that mental illness was the result of God's wrath and that the mentally ill were possessed by Satan. As a result, they were often branded as witches. In fact, the Catholic Church, under Pope Innocent VIII, prescribed ways of identifying witches, who were actively pursued and killed. Witchcraft as an explanation for psychopathology began in Europe but came to the United States, where, in 1691, eight girls in Salem, Massachusetts, were branded as witches when they exhibited bizarre gestures and postures, convulsions, and speech problems. By 1692 nineteen people had been executed as witches and by 1693, 150 people were being held on charges of witchcraft. They were released by order of the governor and the episode ended. Investigators in more recent times have suggested that those accused of witchcraft may have been poisoned with ergot, a parasitic fungus found on cereal grains, some forms of which contain lysergic acid or LSD (Caporael, 1976).

But with the coming of the Renaissance in Europe in the sixteenth century, explanations for abnormality began to once again become more scientific. In particular, scientists searched for neurological explanations for behavior disorders. However, it was not until Sigmund Freud proposed his theory of specific, unconscious determinants near the end of the 19th century that we had a truly scientific theory of psychopathology.

Modern Views: Evolution and Neuroscience

Freud hypothesized - as do most psychologists and psychiatrists today - that abnormal behavior is caused by interactive combinations of environmental and biological factors.

The major differences in views since Freud have been in the relative weights given to nature and nurture by various theorists.

Beginning in the 1920s and continuing through the 1960s, most theorists placed much heavier emphasis on environmental than on biological influence. Disorders were thought to be primarily products of learning, stress, and other environmental factors. However, the nature-nurture pendulum for psychopathology now swings near the middle of the continuum. Environment and biology are given about equal weight overall, and the major thrust of research is to determine, for each disorder, both the extent and the exact nature of each type of influence.

Biology, Environment, and Evolution. One theoretical approach that has long given roles to both biology and environment is evolution, and modern evolutionary psychology has been applied to a basic understanding of abnormal behavior. From this vantage point, psychopathology is essentially a failure of an evolutionary process that emphasizes the inter-generational preservation of adaptive behavior patterns. Abnormal behavior is not adaptive and theoretically occurs because the human organism has not yet evolved to a point where such behavior has adapted out. It may be that the maladaptive behavior patterns we take up in this chapter were in some way adaptive in ancient environments. It is also possible that they were never adaptive and have simply not yet evolved out. In either case, they are not adaptive in modern environments, so the theory predicts that the evolutionary process will eventually cause them to disappear.

As in other areas where the modern synthesis has been applied, evolution involves the genetic transmission of characteristics - in this case predispositions to develop certain patterns of abnormal behavior. We would not expect that biological and environmental influences would have the same degrees of relative influence in every type of psychopathology. Some variability would be expected from one disorder to another.

Neuroscience and Abnormal Behavior. The hereditary predispositions predicted by evolutionary psychology should be expressed largely in the structure and biochemistry of the central nervous system. This puts the biological aspect of the causal theory in the realm of the *neuroscience* model (Chapter 3), which takes into account both biological and environmental sides of the nature-nurture problem and suggests a basically evolutionary approach to understanding abnormal behavior.

Theory and research dealing with biological factors in psychopathology have focused primarily on genetics, neuroanatomy, and neurochemistry. We now have a substantial body of evidence that genetic factors, discussed more generally in Chapter 10, are heavily responsible for some forms of psychopathology and less influential in other cases. The evidence comes from both behavior genetic and molecular genetic studies. We have even begun to discover specific genes that are involved in specific disorders. The inheritance of predispositions toward psychological disorders is expressed in neuroanatomy and neurochemistry. There is evidence that certain areas of the brain are structured differently in individuals with some forms of abnormal behavior. In addition, we have considerable evidence that specific neurotransmitters may be deficient or defective in ways that may cause some disorders. Finally, such pathogens as viruses and bacteria can cause neurological and psychological symptoms. One example is Lyme's disease, a bacterial infection that can damage the brain and produce a wide range of serious psychological symptoms (Fallon & Nields, 1994). Later in the chapter, we will consider these biological factors as they relate to specific disorders.

Major Causal Models

Modern psychologists who study abnormal behavior want most of all to understand its causes so they can better prevent and treat it. They have developed several *models* of abnormality - that is, several ways of thinking about the factors that may underlie it. One approach, called the medical model, has been dominant for many years, but a number of psychological models and a modern diathesis-stress model have also been proposed.

The Medical Model. The oldest and still most widely used model for abnormal behavior, the *medical model*, suggests that psychological abnormalities, like physical ones, can be viewed as diseases. A *disease* is a pattern of symptoms that consistently occur together. A person who has chest pain, shortness of breath, and certain characteristic abnormalities in his electrocardiogram will be diagnosed as having coronary heart disease. Ideally, each psychological disorder would also be characterized by a unique set of symptoms constituting a single diagnosable disease. However, psychological diagnosis is rarely this straightforward.

Many psychologists and psychiatrists, including Thomas Szasz, believe that the medical model is not adequate for psychological disorders (Greenberg & Bailey, 1994). In his influential book *The Myth of Mental Illness* (1961) and in other writings, Szasz has outlined a different approach to. He contends that psychological disorders are not diseases: they do not involve consistent sets of symptoms (called *syndromes*); they cannot be consistently diagnosed in many cases; and treatments are not specific to particular disorders. Szasz is also concerned about calling people with psychological problems "sick," as we would a person who has had a heart attack. He believes that we should instead refer to those with psychological disorders as having "problems in living" - behavior patterns that differ from social, moral, or legal norms and interfere with the ability to function effectively.

Psychological Models. The major psychological models fall into three broad categories: psychodynamic, behavioral, and humanistic. According to the *psychodynamic* model, abnormal behavior results from unconscious conflicts that originate primarily in childhood and produce a variety of symptoms. Originally developed by Sigmund Freud, this perspective is still widely employed by psychologists and psychiatrists (see Chapter 14). A second approach is the *behavioral* model, which suggests that all behaviors, including abnormal ones, are learned. Reinforcement (reward) and observational learning are considered to be responsible for the development of abnormal behavior patterns (Chapter 6). The third approach is the *humanistic* model, which holds that abnormal behavior is largely the result of a failure to realize potentials and of difficulties in maintaining an accurate self-concept (see Chapter 14).

The Diathesis-Stress Model. A *diathesis-stress* model is one in which a predisposing influence (diathesis) combines with a current environmental factor (stress) to produce a disorder. The diathesis can be anything in the individual's background, such as a history of physical abuse in childhood, that can predispose toward certain disorders. However, usually diathesis refers to a biological predisposition and the stress is a particular set of environmental conditions

(McGuffin et al., 1994). The psychological and biological perspectives are not mutually exclusive in a diathesis-stress model. Rather, they represent different levels of analysis of behavior that can be entirely compatible. Any given disorder may have a biological basis in the genetics and biochemistry of the individual. Learning, stress, and other environmental factors may then interact with these predisposing mechanisms to produce the actual symptoms. When both diathesis and stress are present, symptoms are likely to appear. Diathesis-stress is compatible with evolutionary psychology and is currently the dominant causal model in the study of psychological disorders.

Classification and Diagnosis

The classification of mental disorders is virtually as old as civilization itself. The Greeks devised a classification system that contained a small number of broad categories and later added many specific disorders. Other civilizations continued to add categories until, by the eighteenth century, French psychiatrist Phillipe Pinel had compiled a comprehensive list of 2400 mental disorders. In the nineteenth century, the German scientist Emil Kraepelin formulated a diagnostic system that contained an orderly set of categories and subcategories. His system, with revisions, has served as the model for all diagnostic and classification manuals since.

The DSM-IV Multi-Axial Diagnostic System. In 1952, the American Psychiatric Association published its first *Diagnostic and Statistical Manual*, dubbed DSM-I. Major revisions of the manual were published in 1968 (DSM-II), 1980 (DSM-III), and 1994 (DSM-IV).

Relatively minor revisions are contained in the 1987 DSM-III-R (Revised) and in the current manual, DSM-IV-TR (Text Revision), published in 2000.

Under the DSM-IV-TR system, any given patient or client is interviewed, tested, and diagnosed in relation to five *axes*, or dimensions:

AXIS I	Clinical Syndromes
AXIS II	Personality Syndromes
AXIS III	General Medical Conditions
AXIS IV	Psychosocial and Environmental Problems
AXIS V	Global Assessment of Functioning

Axes I, II, and III describe and evaluate the diagnostic categories and subcategories. Axis I includes most major clinical disorders - those most often treated by clinical psychologists and psychiatrists - such as anxiety disorders, phobic disorders, and schizophrenia; Axis II lists personality disorders; and Axis III deals with general medical disorders that may relate to psychological disorders. Axes IV and V provide additional information about the individual's life situation and the degree to which she functions adaptively. On Axis IV the patient's psychosocial and environmental problems, such as educational, occupational, housing, or economic difficulties, are listed. On Axis V, the patient's highest level of functioning during the past year is rated on a 100-point scale, ranging from superior functioning through mild and moderate symptoms to persistent danger of hurting himself or others. The major DSM-IV-TR categories are listed in Table 16-1. Interestingly enough, an analysis of 187 cases originally reported by Kraepelin in 1908 showed that his diagnoses were about 80% accurate by current criteria (Jablensky et al., 1993).

Problems with Psychiatric Diagnosis. Critics have long pointed out that the psychiatric labeling system and the diagnoses it produces are far from perfect. Basic problems relate to the reliability and validity of the system, but some criticisms go beyond these technical problems.

Reliability and validity. The reliability of diagnosis refers to its consistency across diagnosticians (see Chapter 9). Early studies showed that psychiatric diagnosis can be quite unreliable. In one study, for example, diagnosticians agreed on specific subcategories within the general category of "neurosis" only 16 percent of the time (Schmidt and Fonda, 1956). The developers of DSM-III attempted to solve the reliability problem by providing much more detailed, specific criteria, and it appears that they have been at least somewhat successful. Studies suggest that phobias, obsessive-compulsive disorders (discussed later in the chapter), and traumatic disorders (Chapter 15) can be quite reliably diagnosed, with agreement among diagnosticians as high as 87% (Di-Nardo, et al., 1993; Watson et al., 1991). However, agreement is lower for panic disorder and much lower for generalized anxiety and personality disorders (Di-Nardo, et al., 1993; Livesley et al., 1991).

Some critics have argued that even when the diagnostic system is highly reliable, the diagnoses used may not be valid (accurate). The labels given patients on the basis of diagnosis - "schizophrenia," "paranoia," and so on - are often not accurate reflections of actual problems.

The labeling problem. A dramatic example of the misleading qualities of labels and their effects is provided by a now-classic study conducted by David Rosenhan (1962). He and eleven other people made appointments at various mental institutions and presented themselves at the admissions offices complaining that they had been hearing voices. They assumed false names but otherwise gave entirely accurate information about spouses, children, work relationships, and so on. To their surprise, Rosenhan and his associates were all admitted and all but one were diagnosed schizophrenic. Despite the fact that they behaved in perfectly normal ways after admission and openly took notes, not a single hospital staff member recognized them as impostors. On the other hand, about a third of the *real* patients did identify them as fakes. Rosenhan concluded that once a label like schizophrenia is placed on a patient, professional diagnosticians and others are unable to see beyond it.

Not only may psychiatric labels be inaccurate, they may have a variety of negative effects on the individual. Being labeled schizophrenic, for example, may cause the person to be treated differently by others even when his behavior normal. Furthermore, such labels can stigmatize the person, making it difficult for him to get jobs, bank loans, and the like (Penn et al., 1994). The stigma of psychiatric labels applies to children as well (Chiland, 1992), and some research suggests that both the label and the associated stigma may be irreversible (Witztum et al., 1992). Further research indicates that the label itself can play a prominent role in impairing the social and psychological functioning of the individual. In effect, the treatment of the disorder - or at least its diagnosis - can have the ironic result of worsening the person's problems (Link et al., 1991).

Medical Students' Disease. Self-labeling can also be a problem. *Medical students' disease* is the common tendency for students in medicine or abnormal psychology to see in themselves disorders about which they have recently learned. Knowing the labels for the various disorders permits them to relabel their own behaviors as symptoms of those disorders. So if you find that you are "obviously" suffering from one of the abnormal behaviors you read about, think twice. Don't immediately conclude that you are an emotional wreck or that you should be in therapy or in a hospital. At the same time, of course, don't ignore symptoms that may be real.

The Value of Classification and Diagnosis. Despite criticisms of the current system, it would probably be almost impossible for clinical psychology and psychiatry to function without it. Diagnostic categories are necessary for communication among professionals and are sometimes an important adjunct to treatment. They are also necessary for research. If we want to know what causes schizophrenia and how to treat it, we must be able to identify people who display the disorder. Finally, psychiatric labels are needed for such practical purposes as the determination of legal insanity and compilation of statistics about the prevalence of psychiatric disorders. The obvious alternative to eliminating diagnosis is to improve it, and the effort to do so continues.

Keys to Abnormal Behavior 1

Anxiety, Somatoform, and Dissociative Disorders

Anxiety - a vague feeling of dread, a fear with no specific object - is an emotion that everyone experiences at times. However, when it becomes very intense and continues or recurs over time, it can be a partial basis for a number of psychological disorders. Among these are the anxiety disorders, in which the symptoms are primarily psychological, and the somatoform disorders, in which the symptoms are primarily physical. Dissociative disorders are often associated with the experience of traumatic anxiety.

Anxiety Disorders

Anxiety disorders are characterized by high levels of anxiety accompanied by patterns of ineffective, inefficient, maladaptive behavior (Walley et al., 1994). They are often referred to as *neuroses*, although that term is no longer used in DSM-IV-TR. Whatever the specific terminology employed, anxiety disorders are quite common. About 16 percent of Americans will have one of these disorders at some time in their lives, and they are seen in 9 percent of the population in any given six-month period (Robins & Regier, 1991; Walley et al., 1994). One recent study showed that 13.9% of a sample of over 1000 high school boys and 31.1% of girls have such high levels of anxiety that many of them could probably be diagnosed as suffering from disorders (Angelopoulos & Economou, 1994).

Those with anxiety disorders feel threatened and insecure and are typically uncertain of their ability to function effectively in the real world. They will do whatever is necessary to avoid anxiety-arousing situations or will defensively engage in maladaptive behaviors, such as frequent hand-washing. Such individuals also experience a variety of physical symptoms, ranging from chest pain and rapid heartbeat to muscle tension, sweating, "butterflies" in the stomach, diarrhea, and headache. In many cases these symptoms are so severe that the person cannot function effectively. Moreover, men (and perhaps women) with anxiety disorders are at significantly increased risk for fatal heart attacks (Kawachi, 1994).

If you have only experienced normal levels of anxiety (for example when you have a big exam coming up), it may be very difficult to imagine just how disturbing an anxiety disorder can be. In fact, one group of patients became so frustrated by the general lack of understanding of anxiety disorders that they formed the Anxiety Disorders Association of America to promote awareness and provide self-help programs (Ross, 1991).

Included among the anxiety disorders are generalized anxiety disorder, panic disorder, obsessive-compulsive disorder, and phobic disorder.

Generalized Anxiety Disorder. Coleman (1980) describes the case of a young man experiencing generalized anxiety disorder:

> The patient was an eighteen-year-old college student who would regularly have severe anxiety attacks just before going out on dates.... Assessment and therapy revealed strong, long-standing feelings of insecurity and inferiority as well as intense, largely unconscious, hostility toward women.... His first panic attack had occurred in his car... on his way to pick up a date. ... he had been afraid that he would die. He also experienced the anxiety-producing fantasy that he would choke his date to death when they were alone. In his words, "When we are alone in the car, I can't get my mind off her nice white throat and what it would be like to choke her to death."

A *generalized anxiety disorder* is one in which the person feels anxious and apprehensive, has a sense of impending disaster, and believes he is falling apart or losing control. Much of the anxiety is called *free-floating anxiety* - anxiety that cannot be attributed to any specific, current event. Individuals with generalized anxiety disorder also typically experience fatigue, nightmares, and periodic attacks of intense anxiety that may last from a few minutes to several hours (Table 16-2).

Diagnosis of this disorder is complicated by the fact that its symptoms are often similar to those of other disorders (Maes et al., 1994). In particular, generalized anxiety disorder is sometimes confused with depression, since it is often accompanied by mild depression, and some research even suggests it may share a common genetic predisposition with that disorder (Figure 16-2).

The causes of generalized anxiety disorder are not fully understood. According to *psychoanalytic theory*, anxiety reflects internal conflicts at an unconscious level. Powerful sexual and aggressive impulses are threatening to break through to conscious expression, and this threat creates great anxiety. The *learning theory* explanation is that the individual has learned through reinforcement or observation (modeling) to respond with anxiety to a variety of situations. A final environmental explanation is the impact of traumatic early experiences. In particular, recent evidence suggests that separation from either parent in early childhood may be a factor in the later development of a generalized anxiety disorder (Kendler et al., 1992).

Biological factors may also be involved. One study showed that the concordance rate for this disorder is 41 percent for identical twins and 4 percent for fraternal twins. More recent studies confirm that genetic factors are important, accounting for perhaps 30% of the variance (Kendler et al., 2002). Moreover, there appears to be a more general genetic factor that may predispose the individual toward any of the several anxiety disorders (Kendler et al., 2001). In fact, even the ability to cope effectively with anxiety and thereby reduce it may be influenced by heredity. Just how these genetic predispositions act to cause anxiety disorders is not yet clear. However, studies show that they may well produce a dysfunction of the serotonin or norepinephrine systems in the brain. Overall, research suggests that we can inherit a broad genetic tendency toward anxiety disorders and perhaps depression, with the specific disorder that results determined by environmental factors.

Panic Disorder. Panic disorder is marked by the occurrence of panic attacks - sudden, severe states of anxiety so extreme that the individual is unable to function effectively for a time period that can range from minutes to hours. The attack is accompanied by such physical symptoms as fainting, trembling, heart palpitations, and cold sweats. Panic disorder is diagnosed when a person experiences at least three separate panic episodes within a three-week period, with evidence of at least four temporary physiological symptoms as part of the panic episodes (Okasha et al., 1994). The disorder occurs in 1.7% of women and .8% of men (Dick et al., 1994).

One problem in diagnosing panic disorder is that its symptoms are very similar to those of a hereditary heart condition called mitral valve prolapse (MVP). Like panic disorder, MVP produces heart palpitations and chest pain. Moreover, the two disorders are often found concurrently in the same person. Although there is thus far no clear evidence that they have the same or related causes, that possibility is under investigation (Alpert et al., 1991).

As with generalized anxiety disorder, there is evidence that panic disorder is subject to a genetic predisposition (Crowe, 1990). Cognitive factors also play a role because they influence how the person perceives stress and threat (Beck et al., 1992). The early death of either parent can predispose a child toward a panic disorder. And panic disorder is more likely in those whose parents suffered from chronic physical illnesses or from physical symptoms typical of anxiety (Ehlers, 1993). Taken as a whole, these and other studies suggest important roles for both heredity and environment.

Obsessive-Compulsive Disorder. Obsessive-compulsive disorder (OCD) is characterized by persistent, uncontrollable thoughts (*obsessions*), and repetitive, unavoidable, ritualistic acts (*compulsions*) that accomplish no practical end (Pigott et al., 1994). You have probably experienced minor obsessive thoughts, such as preoccupation with an upcoming vacation, an impending decision, or a tune that you can't seem to get out of your head. Obsessive thoughts of neurotic (pathological) proportions differ from common obsessions in that they are more persistent, less rational, and tend to interfere with ongoing behavior. Examples from actual case histories include thoughts about fetuses lying in the street, people being buried alive, women's buttocks, decaying teeth, and strangling people. The most common obsessive thoughts are concerned with committing a potentially immoral act, such as injuring or killing someone (Table 16-3). Common compulsions include such things as hand-washing, stepping over cracks in the sidewalk, and excessive neatness (Valleni et al., 1994).

In *obsessive-compulsive disorder*, seen in 1% of the population (Rasmussen & Eisen, 1994), the patient typically loses voluntary control over aspects of his thoughts and actions (Arts et al., 1993). A case of obsessive-compulsive disorder in a nineteen-year-old patient was described by the young man's father:

> When George wakes in the morning . . . he feels that his hands are contaminated and so he cannot touch his clothing. He won't wash in the bathroom because he feels that the carpet is contaminated and he won't go downstairs until he is dressed. Consequently, I have to dress him, having first cleaned his shoes and got out a clean shirt, underclothes, socks, and trousers. He holds his hands above his head while I pull on his underpants and trowsers and we both make sure, by proceeding very cautiously, that he doesn't contaminate the outside of his clothing. Any error or mishap and he will have to have clean clothes because he must avoid at all costs passing on the contamination to others.... Basically he has to be completely sure that there is no contamination around because if he is not sure then he will start to worry and ruminate about it later on.... (Rachman and Hodgson, 1980, pp. 66-67).

Many people engage in regular physical behaviors that could be called compulsions. Knocking on wood, throwing salt over your shoulder, and refusing to walk under ladders are common examples. But neurotic compulsions lead the individual to repeat acts over and over. One compulsive individual routinely checked windows up to 160 times to see that they were closed and felt compelled to read the license numbers of cars and the numbers appearing on manhole covers. Another engaged in handwashing an average of 100 times a day (Coleman et al., 1980).

Freud described such disorders as less threatening replacements for an original unconscious conflict. Learning theories suggest that obsessions and compulsions are conditioned responses to anxiety. That is, the person learns that anxiety can be reduced by engaging in a ritualistic act, such as handwashing. The behavior is therefore reinforcing, and the person performs it repeatedly as long as it continues to reduce anxiety (Salzman and Thaler, 1981).

Beyond these theories, we have learned a considerable amount about obsessive-compulsive disorder in the past decade or so (Jefferys, 1993), and we now know that biological factors are also involved (Insel, 1992). Obsessions and compulsions are found more frequently in the families of patients with the disorder than in the families of control participants (Black et al., 1992), and one study showed that 71% of OCD children had at least one parent with the disorder (Riddle et al., 1990). Other studies show that either a broad hereditary tendency toward neurotic disorder or a more specific genetic factor underlies the disorder (Andrews et al., 1990; Rauch, 1992). Studies of brain anatomy have implicated specific areas of the frontal lobes and underlying basal ganglia, while neurochemical studies demonstrate involvement of the serotonin system (Rauch & Jenike, 1993; Otto, 1992; Scarone et al., 1992).

Phobic Disorders. Do you feel uneasy or anxious around spiders, nonpoisonous snakes, or perhaps bodies of water? You are probably not phobic, but phobic disorders are basically more extreme cases of such anxieties. A *phobia* is an irrational fear of some object or situation that is accompanied by avoidance behavior. Here we will differentiate between simple phobias and two complex phobias, agoraphobia and social phobia.

Simple phobias. Consider the case of Kenneth E., reported by Cameron and Rychlak (1985).

> Kenneth was a twenty-two-year-old with *claustrophobia*, a fear of enclosed spaces. Kenneth could not stay in theaters because they made him feel suffocated and afraid that he would not be able to get out in case of illness or a fire. His fear generalized to elevators, buses, and downtown city streets. He sought therapeutic help because his fears were restricting his life without reducing his overall anxiety. During therapy, it became clear that his real fear was that he might lose control of himself and shout something he must hide, something that at the same time he had an impulse to proclaim. This discovery of an impulse to give himself away in public led ultimately to the origin of the phobia. The onset of his claustrophobic symptoms had followed an acute anxiety attack in a theater. The play contained a homosexual theme that Kenneth found extremely threatening.

Claustrophobia is only one kind of *simple phobia* - an irrational fear of a specific object or situation. Among the many others are acrophobia (fear of heights), hydrophobia (fear of water), hematophobia (fear of blood), and nyctophobia (fear of the dark) (Figure 16-3).

Complex phobias. Literally meaning "fear of the marketplace," *agoraphobia* is a fear of being alone or of being in public places without access to help. Agoraphobia is sometimes accompanied by panic disorder and sometimes not. Some studies suggest that these two subgroups may represent truly different disorders (Starcevii et al., 1992), though there is no overall difference in severity (Goldberg, 1993). In either case, the person with agoraphobia has a sense of helplessness in many situations and frequently experiences extreme anxiety or panic attacks as a result of the overwhelming fear that she will be psychologically abandoned. So severe is the anxiety that many agoraphobics are literally housebound.

Like agoraphobia, *social phobia* has broad implications for behavior and lifestyle. It involves a high level of anxiety associated with the possibility that others will react negatively to your behavior (Judd, 1994; Stopa & Clark, 1993). The social phobic does not like to eat at a restaurant where he could become the center of attention, is fearful of making speeches or other public presentations, and may avoid parties and other settings where he will have a substantial degree of social exposure.

If you've never met a social phobic, it may be interesting to know that this disorder affects 2.4 million people in the United States at any given time and will affect 5 million over the course of a lifetime (Ross, 1991). On the average, it begins at age 15 and is found more frequently in women and in those with less education or a lower socioeconomic level (Schneier et al., 1992).

Causes of phobia. According to the psychoanalytic approach, which worked in Kenneth's case, phobias result from unconscious sexual or aggressive conflicts that are displaced to some external object (Compton, 1992). Kenneth's therapist concluded that the claustrophobia was a defensive device that moved his conflict over homosexuality off center stage and replaced it with a group of fears.

It seems clear that both genetics and learning are involved in the development of phobias (Kendler et al., 1992; Potts & Davidson, 1992). Behavior genetic studies have demonstrated significant hereditary influence on the development of such anxieties as fear of injury and fear of small animals (Stevenson et al., 1992). At the same time, a study of dog phobia showed that people with this disorder had experienced much less contact with dogs during early childhood than had those with no phobia, suggesting that positive or neutral early experiences may have taught the non-phobics not to be fearful (Doogan & Thomas, 1992).

These results demonstrate the need for an integrative psychobiological model for phobia. One such model has been proposed for an interesting disorder called *cardiophobia.* As the term implies, patients with this problem have frequent complaints of chest pain and heart palpitations, accompanied by a strong fear that they are having a heart attack and dying. A psychobiological model explaining the development of cardiophobia begins with a genetic predisposition toward phobia. Over time the person then undergoes a series of learning experiences, perhaps modeling behavior originally observed in a parent and being rewarded for somatic complaints, including heart symptoms. He develops a set of negative cognitions, such as the firm belief that any chest discomfort must signal the onset of a heart attack. Finally, stressors in his current life trigger off cardiophobic episodes (Eifert, 1992). A similar model could be applied to other common phobias.

Somatoform Disorders

Somatoform disorders involve physical complaints and symptoms that are similar to those of medical conditions but have no underlying organic cause. Patients with these disorders are usually seen first in medical settings because their symptoms are physical. In fact, a significant proportion of patients first seen in hospital emergency rooms have no serious physical problems and are eventually diagnosed with somatoform disorders (Purcell, 1991; Kellner, 1994). The symptoms of these disorders are not under conscious or voluntary control (Kirmayer et al., 1994). Don't confuse the somatoform disorders with the psychosomatic (psychophysiologic) disorders. The latter are true physical disorders, like ulcers and heart disease, in which stress may be a contributing factor (Chapter 15). We will consider here four major categories of somatoform disorder: somatization disorder, conversion disorder, hypochondriasis, and pain disorder.

Somatization Disorder. Also known as Briquet's syndrome or hysteria, *somatization disorder* is characterized by a multitude of physical complaints with apparent psychological origins. Common symptoms include abdominal pain, vomiting, menstrual problems, lack of sexual pleasure, backaches, and headaches. Depressive symptoms often complicate the picture, as does the possibility that the individual may actually be suffering from a serious medical condition that remains undiagnosed. Somatization disorders typically begin in childhood or adolescence and are seen predominantly in women.

Conversion Disorder. Those with a *conversion disorder* exhibit a loss or impairment of physical functions involving either the sensory or the motor system. The classic conversion symptom, seen in some of Freud's patients, is glove paralysis, in which the person experiences paralysis or numbness of the hand. The paralysis is purely psychological, and the person is able to move his hand when instructed under hypnosis to do so. Other conversion symptoms include blindness, deafness, paresthesia (a tingling sensation), and paresis (a mild, partial paralysis), all without discernible physical cause (Figure 16-4).

Conversion reactions often appear suddenly under conditions of high stress (Bokey, 1994). Consider the case of Phil:

> Phil was a forty-year-old with a history of marginal work adjustment since his discharge from the army at age twenty-five (Brady and Lind, 1968). In the years since his discharge, he had depended on public assistance and financial aid from relatives to get by. His married life was characterized by almost constant harassment from his wife and mother-in-law. During the Christmas season, they were being more demanding than usual, requiring him to work nights and weekends at various chores under their supervision. Three days before Christmas, while shopping with his wife and mother-in-law, Phil suddenly became blind

in both eyes. Physical examinations found nothing to account for his blindness, and a diagnosis of conversion disorder was made.

As with somatization disorder, there is a possibility that some conversion disorders are actually based on underlying neurological problems. Some studies show that 60 percent or more of those diagnosed with conversion disorder later develop neurological diseases (Slater and Glithero, 1965; Witlock, 1967). More generally, conversion and neurological disorders are often confused (Jones & Barklage, 1990).

Hypochondriasis. Perhaps the best known somatoform disorder is *hypochondriasis*, in which the patient has excessive concerns about his health and worries constantly that he has a major physical disease (Schmidt, 1994). Hypochondriacs constantly interpret minor irregularities in body functioning as indicative of serious underlying disorder (Hitchcock & Mathews, 1992). They may visit physicians repeatedly with the same complaint, insisting that they are seriously ill, and many display genuine satisfaction when actual physical illness is found. One study showed that 45% of all internal medicine patients with ambiguous complaints have psychiatric disorders, and 40% of these are diagnosed as hypochondriacs (van-Hemert, 1993).

The disorder is typically first diagnosed somewhere between the ages of thirty and fifty (Mesiter, 1980) and tends to persist over a period of years (Barsky et al., 1993). The patient often comes from a background characterized by chronic illness of a family member and by a strong dependency relationship with a parent (Barsky et al., 1994; Van-Hout et al., 1994). In many cases the person has previously experienced a real physical illness or a hypochondriacal complaint and has been rewarded with the sympathy and attention of others, as well as a reduction in responsibilities.

Pain Disorder. Pain disorder is diagnosed when persistent, significant pain occurs in the absence of medical pathology that would explain its duration and magnitude, and it occurs in 12.3% of the population at some time in life (Grabe et al., 2003). The pain appears to be of psychological origin and is therefore sometimes called *psychogenic pain.* The pain may be chronic but is often intermittent, and it may disappear on its own without therapy after a few weeks or months. The reported pain is most often vaguely localized in a vital organ, such as the heart, or in the lower back or limbs. Chronic lower back pain, for example, is often (but not always) symptomatic of pain disorder. In one study, chronic back pain patients subjected to psychological stress reported more pain than a control group not exposed to stress (Schwartz et al., 1994). Although the discomfort of psychogenic pain is of psychological origin, the experience of pain is very real. As a result, patients often "doctor-shop," visiting numerous physicians in hopes of finding some relief from the pain and may even undergo surgery that will, of course, do no good. They may also become virtual invalids, prisoners to their psychogenic pain. Psychotherapy, however, can help (Keefe & Williams, 1989).

Causes of Somatoform Disorders. The symptoms of somatoform disorders are, in part, a way of reducing anxiety or depression by channeling these negative feelings into the body. The physical symptoms are less disturbing to the patient and easier to deal with psychologically than is the feeling of severe anxiety. There may also be underlying disturbances in the stability and organization of the self-concept (Rodin, 1991), and genetic factors are likely to play a predisposing role.

Dissociative Disorders

Dissociative disorders involve an alteration of consciousness, usually in the form of fragmentation or splitting, which interferes with the sense of personal identity. We will discuss dissociative amnesia, fugue states, and dissociative identify or multiple personality disorder here.

Dissociative Amnesia and Fugue States. Imagine the shock of suddenly discovering that you no longer know who you are. You've forgotten your name, your address, the identities of close relatives and friends, where you work - virtually everything about yourself. Though not as common as some movies and TV shows might make them seem, such amnesias do occur.

Dissociative amnesia, often called *psychogenic amnesia*, is a temporary loss of memory about one's personal characteristics and past history. The memory loss is typically selective rather than complete (van der Hart & Nijenhuis, 2001). The person may forget her own identity, family, and address but not forget how to do her job, drive a car, and perform other learned tasks (Porter et al., 2001).

Dissociative fugue is a form of amnesia in which the person not only forgets who he is but actually moves to a new area and establishes a new identity. Severe psychological stress or excessive use of alcohol or drugs is often associated with the onset of fugue states. One example of this rare disorder is the case of a 51-year-old Indianapolis man (Jasper, 2003). Another was reported by Goldstein and Palmer (1975):

> Thirty-one-year-old Barbara disappeared from her home. Picked up two weeks later by police in another city, she disheveled and dirty. She initially failed to recognize her husband, had forgotten her name, and could remember nothing about her previous. With psychotherapy, she gradually regained her memory. It turned out that she had returned to the city where she had lived as a child.

Dissociative identity disorder, formerly called multiple personality disorder, is a condition in which the person has several alternative personalities. They have quite different characteristics, and she typically switches among them quite frequently (Huntjens et al., 2003). The CRITICAL THINKER box asks you to consider whether or not this interesting but controversial disorder actually exists.

Causes of Dissociative Disorders

The causes of multiple personality disorder, assuming it exists, are poorly understood, and the same conclusion applies to the other dissociative disorders. Psychoanalytic theory suggests that dissociation involves repressed ego states. Learning theorists, on the other hand, attribute it to acquired mechanisms for avoiding stress. That is, the individual who is under stress may learn through reinforcement to dissociate by forgetting who she is or by switching personalities in order to escape the stress. A final possibility is that a single traumatic experience, combined with preexisting personality factors, may trigger a long-term dissociative disorder. There is evidence that about 20% of those who have a significant traumatic experience develop some severe, lasting disorder, in certain cases a dissociative disorder (Bron et al., 1992).

Keys to Abnormal Behavior 2

Schizophrenia

> Suspicious and frightened, the victim fears he can trust neither his own senses nor the motives of other people.... His skin prickles, his head seems to hum, and "voices" annoy him. Unpleasant odors choke him, his food may have no taste. Bright and colorful visions ranging from brilliant butterflies to dismembered bodies pass before his eyes. Ice clinking in a nearby pitcher seems to be a diabolic device bent on his destruction.
>
> When someone talks to him, he hears only disconnected words.... His attention wanders from his inner thoughts to the grotesque way the speaker's mouth moves or the loud scrape his chair makes against the floor. He cannot understand what the person is trying to tell him, nor why. When he tries to speak, his own words sound foreign to him. Broken phrases tumble out over and over again, and somewhat fail to express how frightened and worried he is (Ails, 1967, p. 42).

This is a description of a man suffering from schizophrenia, perhaps the most severe of all psychological disorders. *Schizophrenia* is a disorder in which the person displays reduced contact with reality, accompanied by thought disturbances that result in abnormal perceptual, motor, emotional, and social functioning. The ability to perceive environmental situations accurately and respond to them in an adaptive way is a severely impaired . In fact, the patient often experiences a complete or nearly complete loss of contact with reality and functions in a fantasy state in which his perception of external events is radically different from that of other people. Schizophrenia is also characterized by disturbances of cognition and therefore in the ability to process information, often accompanied by severe disturbances in emotional functioning, speech, and even motor behavior.

About 0.7 to 1.5 percent of the population - 4 million people in the United States - will be diagnosed as schizophrenic, with perhaps 1 million of these hospitalized (Keith, Regier, & Rae, 1991; Rosenstein et al., 1989; SAMSHA, 1995). Recent statistics show some changes in the makeup of the schizophrenic population, including an increase in the proportion of African-American patients (Thompson et al., 1993). Overall, schizophrenics constitute 40% of admissions to state and county mental hospitals, by far the largest single group (Manderscheid, 1985). Most first admissions occur between the ages of 15 and 45, and at least 60% of all schizophrenics will have repeated episodes of the disorder. Of the remainder, about 30% will be symptom-free for five years and 10% will be permanently disabled. Because schizophrenia is such a severe and interesting condition, we will examine several aspects of the disorder, including the primary symptoms, principal types, and possible causal factors.

Primary Symptoms

Schizophrenia is characterized by disturbances in four major areas: thought and language, perception, motor behavior, and affect (emotion).

Disturbances of Thought and Language. Schizophrenia is primarily a thought disorder - an impairment of the ability to reason and communicate (Pinkham et al., 2003). Specific symptoms of thought disorder include loosening of associations and delusions (Sharma & Antonova, 2003). *Loosening of associations* refers to the fact that thoughts and ideas shift rapidly from one subject to another without any apparent logical or meaningful association between the sequential thoughts, as in one patient's response to the question, "Can you tell me the name of this place?":

> "I have not been a drinker for 16 years. I am taking a mental rest after a `carter' assignment of `quill.' You know, a `penwrap' I had contracts with Warner Brothers Studio and Eugene broke phonograph records but Mike protested. I have been with the Police Department for 35 years. I am made of flesh and blood--See, doctor?" (pulling up her dress). (Coleman, 1980, p. 412).

Delusions are basically false or incorrect beliefs that have no basis in reality (Roesch-Ely et al., 2003). A delusion of persecution is a belief that others are plotting against you or are mistreating you in some way. A delusion of grandeur is a false belief that you are a famous or powerful person or have some great mission in life.

Accompanying the disturbances of thought processes are disturbances of language, including clanging, neologisms, and word salad. *Clanging* refers to the juxtaposition of words that are unrelated to each other except that they rhyme: "I'm fine, Stein, but I'd like to dine on the Rhine." *Neologisms* are words coined by the person or words used in a unique fashion. One patient, for example, devised the word "tiefather" to mean a relative and the word "hangages" to refer to relationships between family generations (Bootzin and Acocella, 1984). *Word salad* refers to using a series of apparently disconnected words and phrases that seem to have no relationship, as in the example quoted above.

Disturbances of Perception. Things may look, sound, taste, and smell different to the schizophrenic. Lights may seem brighter or dimmer, sounds louder or softer, smells stronger or weaker. Furthermore, the patient often experiences disorientation as to time, place, and person: he is unable to accurately judge the passage of time, is confused about where he is, and cannot accurately recall his own personal characteristics.

The schizophrenic also experiences a breakdown in selective attention, usually called an *attention deficit*, and feels that her consciousness is flooded with a mass of incoming sensory information. As one patient put it, "I am attending to everything at once and as a result I do not really attend to anything" (MeGhie and Chapman, 1961, p. 104). This may be one reason why schizophrenics are often very insensitive to social cues when interacting with other people (Corrigan & Green, 1993).

The most dramatic form of perceptual disturbance is the *hallucination* - a perception that occurs when there is no actual stimulus. Although hallucinations may occur in any sense, auditory hallucinations are by far the most common, occurring in about 75 percent of schizophrenic patients. They may take the form of bangs, clicks or music, but voices are the most common.

Disturbances in Motor Behavior. There are two kinds of motor disturbance in schizophrenia. In the first, the person engages in a variety of unusual body postures and movements, including bizarre gestures and facial expressions. In the second the person moves very fast, swinging his arms wildly and walking at a rapid pace, or very slowly, as if he were in a slow-motion video.

Disturbances of Affect. The affective (emotional) functioning of the person with schizophrenia is also disturbed in either expression or intensity or both. She may display unusually strong or weak emotions, and her emotions are often inappropriate. Given bad news, she may laugh hysterically; told a joke, she may cry. Alternatively, some schizophrenics experience *flat affect* - a blunting of emotions in which events that would arouse considerable emotion in a normal person are discussed without any apparent emotional reaction at all. Thus, a patient whose husband or wife has just died may simply describe the death in a flat, matter-of-fact fashion.

Clearly, Mr. R., the patient in our opener, was exhibiting some of the severe symptoms of schizophrenia. However, he was fortunate to be a reactive schizophrenic, rather than a process one. In fact, he was given appropriate drugs and discharged about a month after he entered. At that time, he was coherent, his behavior was quite normal, and his prognosis was good.

Principal Types

It is often difficult to diagnose schizophrenia because the symptoms can vary greatly from one patient to another. As a result, DSM-IV-TR identifies five major subcategories of the disorder:

- Disorganized - Characterized by highly inappropriate affect, often including considerable giggling, incoherent speech, and poorly organized hallucinations and delusions.
- Catatonic - Characterized by either extreme excitement and hyperactivity or extreme withdrawal and slowing of motor movement. The classic symptom of catatonia is a prolonged period of unresponsive stupor, during which the patient may maintain unusual postures for hours or exhibit "waxy flexibility," in which the body can be placed in a variety of positions and remains in such positions for long periods.
- Paranoid - Characterized by the presence of persecutory or grandiose delusions, which tend to be illogical and disorganized.
- Undifferentiated - Diagnosed when the individual shows a mixture of symptoms that do not fit any other category.

- **Residual** - Diagnosed when the person has previously experienced at least one episode of schizophrenia but is presently showing no clear signs of the disorder.

These subtypes, originally identified by Emil Kraepelin in the late 19th century, have been questioned in more recent times. Evidence of their validity is mixed, some investigators finding the subcategories unstable (Deister & Marneros, 1993), others finding them valid (McGlashan & Fenton, 1991).

Those who do not find the Kraepelinian types useful have proposed a variety of alternatives. One approach differentiates between *process schizophrenia* - a disorder with a gradual onset - and *reactive schizophrenia* - a disorder with very rapid onset. The process schizophrenic has a very poor prognosis or outlook and will often have the disorder for the rest of his life, while the reactive has a much better prognosis. Another alternative that is currently receiving considerable attention distinguishes between positive and negative symptoms (Andreasen, 1991; Axelrod et al., 1994). *Positive* symptoms represent excesses in behavior, such as hallucinations, delusions, and bizarre behavior. *Negative* symptoms include flattening of affect, apathy, lack of social interest, reduced ability to experience pleasure, and certain language deficits. Using this approach, schizophrenics can be divided into subgroups with positive, negative, and mixed symptoms, with possible implications for differential causation. However, recent investigations have called into question the validity of even this newest system, and it seems likely that we will have a fully valid way of subclassifying schizophrenia only when we better understand its causes (Marneros et al., 1992; Klinidis et al., 1993).

Causal Factors

A number of biological and environmental factors have been implicated in schizophrenia. They include genetic, biochemical, neuroanatomical, and psychological causes. We take up biological factors when we discuss neurophysiology later in the chapter. Here, let's focus on psychological influences.

According to *psychoanalytic* theorists, schizophrenia is the result of regression - going back to an early state of development - caused by intense anxiety over unconscious impulses. The regression process causes the person to lose contact with reality, display a disorganization of thought processes, and adopt the passive attitude of the infant. A variation on the psychoanalytic approach is the idea that a *schizophrenogenic mother* (one who causes schizophrenia) neglects the child's emotional needs, using him instead to satisfy her own needs. Another classic approach is the double bind hypothesis proposed by Gregory Bateson and his associates (1956). They suggested that parents induce schizophrenia by putting the child through a series of conflicts in which they provide opposing messages. For example, the parent may repeatedly say "I love you" but refuse to show physical affection and may even abuse the child. The child receives the conflicting messages "I love you" and "I don't love you" and is at a loss to resolve the conflict. The result is schizophrenic symptoms.

A major alternative to psychodynamic theory is the *social learning* approach, which says that people learn schizophrenic behaviors by imitating parents and other key figures in their environment (Watt et al., 1982). The parent may display behaviors central to schizophrenia - not attending to the external world, misinterpreting reality, unusual motor behaviors, somewhat disorganized thought patterns - which the child then imitates (Rund, 1994). Even if the parent is not actually schizophrenic, the child may later integrate a number of these modeled behaviors into a pattern that can be diagnosed as schizophrenia.

A final possibility is that schizophrenia is related to social class. A classic study, supported by later research, showed that the highest rates of schizophrenia are in the lowest socioeconomic classes (Hollingshead & Redlich, 1958). Some psychologists have drawn from this relationship a *sociogenic hypothesis*, which suggests that poor education and poor economic conditions contribute to the disorder. Supportive evidence suggests that such conditions of deprivation may, indeed, be involved (Castle et al., 1993). An alternative interpretation is that as schizophrenics develop their symptoms and are unable to hold jobs and otherwise function, they "drift" downward into poverty. This *social drift* idea has also garnered some support.

Keys to Abnormal Behavior 3

Delusional and Personality Disorders

In a somewhat different way than schizophrenia, delusional disorders affect cognitive processes and impair the ability to think clearly and rationally. Personality disorders do not center around cognitive processes; rather, they are longstanding patterns of maladaptive social behavior and emotional functioning that typically begin in childhood and continue throughout life.

Delusional (Paranoid) Disorders

Delusional disorders fall under the same DSM-IV-TR category as schizophrenia because they are also considered to be psychotic disorders. They are characterized most often by delusions of persecution or grandeur, though other types can also occur (Jorgensen, 1994). Delusions are the only major symptom; there are no hallucinations or other behaviors that would lead to a diagnosis of schizophrenia (Harper, 1994). Consider the case of Ron:

> Ron entered therapy sometime after a divorce and a series of incidents in which he had lost one old friend after another. The therapist noticed was that Ron asked for a cup of coffee, then left it untouched until the therapist drank some of it herself. Ron then described the problems he had with his wife prior to the divorce. She was constantly, he felt, trying to poison him and had left small throw rugs at the top of the stairs, hoping he would slip and fall. He was quite sure that she also had a boyfriend who was plotting with her to kill him. In addition, several people at work were conspiring to assure that he did not receive a promotion, and Ron described in detail some of the specific ways in which they had acted against him.

Although it is obvious to us that Ron was suffering from delusions, the feelings of persecution were very real to him. He was *certain* that his wife was plotting to kill him and that his coworkers were conspiring to hold him back.

Ron's diagnosis would be *delusional disorder*, also known as *simple paranoia.* His delusions are logical and well organized and his thinking is generally clear and coherent. This is one of the essential distinctions between paranoia and paranoid schizophrenia. In the latter the delusions are less logical, less well organized, and usually more difficult to believe (Jorgensen & Jensen, 1994). In addition to delusional disorder, DSM-IV-TR includes a particularly interesting category called *shared psychotic disorder*. Also known as *folie à deux*, the disorder occurs when two people experience the same psychotic delusions (Schatzle, 2002). Cases of folie a deux are described in the Probe.

Personality Disorders

Personality disorder is diagnosed when the patient exhibits rigid, extreme, dominant personality characteristics that are maladaptive and impair social functioning. Unlike other categories of disorder, the personality disorders do not involve high levels of anxiety, physical problems, reduced contact with reality, or bizarre patterns of behavior. Rather, they are pervasive, long-term behavior patterns that influence most areas of life. They usually begin in childhood and continue for many years. About 10-13 percent of the population have a personality disorder at some time in their lives (Weissman, 1993).

Major Subcategories

Among the ten personality disorders listed in DSM-IV-TR (Table 16-4) are the *dependent personality*, who lacks self-confidence and is unwilling to assume responsibilities, and the *histrionic personality*, who is demanding and behaves dramatically and flamboyantly in an effort to gain attention. Another is the *borderline personality*, who is unstable, unpredictable, moody, and has intense, stormy interpersonal relationships. However, *antisocial personality* is by far the most common type and is, in fact, among the most frequent disorders seen in clinical practice (Barrett, 1980). As a result, we will focus on this major subcategory.

Antisocial Personality Disorder

Consider the following case:

> Donald's misbehavior as a child took many forms, including lying, cheating, petty theft, and the bullying of smaller children. As he grew older, he became more and more interested in sex, gambling, and alcohol. When he was 14 he made crude sexual advances toward a younger girl, and when she threatened to tell her parents he locked her in a shed. It was about 16 hours before she was found.... He expressed no concern for the anguish experienced by the girl and her parents, nor did he give any indication that he felt morally culpable for what he had done.... The teachers [at a private boarding school] described him as an "operator" whose behavior was determined entirely by the possibility of attaining what he wanted--in most cases something that was concrete, immediate, and personally relevant.
>
> When he was 17, Donald left the boarding school, forged his father's name on a large check, and spent about a year traveling around the world.... Throughout this period he was charged with a variety of crimes...
>
> [Now, at age 30] Donald sees nothing particularly wrong with his behavior, nor does he express remorse or guilt for using others and causing them grief.... Periodic punishments do nothing to decrease his egotism and confidence in his own abilities, nor do they offset the often considerable short-term gains of which he is capable. (Hare, 1970, pp. 1-4)

Antisocial personality disorder is diagnosed when the patient displays an ongoing pattern of manipulative, impulsive, irresponsible behavior that shows a disregard for social norms and is not accompanied by feelings of guilt. The term *psy-*

chopath is often used as an alternative diagnostic label. The initial impression is that of a person who is socially skilled, charming, sincere, and outgoing. However, the friendly exterior is a front for a self-serving, manipulative personality. Antisocial personalities focus on accomplishing their own goals and obtaining the rewards they seek without concern for the effect of their behavior on others. They show little regard for social rules and moral values, commit a variety of antisocial or asocial acts, and exhibit little real guilt or remorse for their actions. A substantial proportion of criminals display antisocial personality disorder or psychopathy (Harry, 1992), and the disorder is found disproportionately in intravenous drug abusers who develop HIV infection (Brooner et al., 1993). About 2-4 percent of people in the U.S. and Canada have antisocial personality disorder (Weissman, 1993; SAMSHA, 1995).

Antisocial personalities typically lack any real sense of responsibility, have a virtually complete disregard for the truth, and tend to be impulsive. A person with this diagnosis might be walking down the street, notice a shiny red Corvette, and drive off in it just on an impulse. Antisocial personalities also tend toward aggressive behavior and are likely to get into fights and to abuse spouses and children. In addition, they do not learn from experience, even when they are severely punished for antisocial or illegal acts. They fail to learn to respond to cues that would produce anxiety in a normal person and fail to learn to inhibit responses that will lead to punishment. For example, an antisocial personality who was arrested, convicted, and jailed for stealing that red Corvette is likely to do the same thing again shortly after release from prison.

Causes of Antisocial Personality Disorder. The scientific literature suggests that antisocial personality disorder results from a combination of biological and psychological factors (Figure 16-5). Patients have dysfunctions of the frontal lobes (Gorenstein, 1982; Meyers et al., 1992), commonly display abnormalities in EEG recordings (Khannaet al., 1980), and have autonomic nervous systems that function at lower levels of arousal than those of normal people (Hare, 1982). There is also some evidence of serotonin and neuroendocrine abnormalities (G.R. Smith et al., 1991; Fishbein et al., 1992), and both twin and adoption studies have produced evidence of modest heritability (Sutker et al., 1993; Nigg & Goldsmith, 1994). These genetic findings support the case for a hereditary factor in antisocial personality.

Don Fowles has proposed that this hereditary factor may result in deficiencies in the *behavioral inhibition system* - the hypothetical neural system that mediates learning to respond to certain cues with anxiety and learning to inhibit responses to cues signalling punishment (Fowles & Missel, 1994). The deficiency may lead to the low anxiety of the psychopath and his failure to learn from punishment experiences. Fowles hypothesizes that the *behavioral activation system* - the neural system that mediates responses to cues for rewards (positive reinforcement) is normal or overactive, partially explaining why the psychopath is focused on obtaining rewards.

Among the psychological explanations, psychodynamic theorists suggest that the problem is a weak superego. Freud described the superego as the personality structure that serves as a conscience, a guide to moral action. When it fails to develop adequately, the individual will have a weak moral value structure, little conscience, and therefore minimal guilt or anxiety over committing immoral acts.

Quite different explanations have been offered by behavioral and social learning theorists. Behaviorists hypothesize that selective reinforcement of prosocial and antisocial behavior by parents may inhibit or promote the development of antisocial personality disorder. Research has shown that the parents of these patients tend to give few rewards for prosocial behaviors. Furthermore, they often provide reinforcements quite arbitrarily, so that prosocial and antisocial behaviors may be equally and randomly reinforced (Sutker et al., 1993). In addition, there is evidence that antisocial personalities are deficient in the ability to learn anxiety responses to stimuli, probably due to a defect in the neural system that underlies anxiety (Fowles & Missel, 1994). This would account for their failure to feel guilt or anxiety when they violate social norms. Other psychosocial factors include parental antisocial behavior, low socioeconomic status, and ineffective supervision and discipline during childhood (Capaldi & Patterson, 1994).

Keys to Abnormal Behavior 4

Mood Disorders

You probably know people who seem to have unusually high levels of energy and activity and who react to stress by becoming even more active. Other people seem to have low levels of energy and respond to stress with brief periods of dejection accompanied by lethargy and low levels of activity. These normal extremes of mood state have their pathological counterparts in the disorders of mania and depression. Such severe mood disturbances are called *mood disorders.* There are a number of subcategories, but the two main ones are major depressive disorder and bipolar disorder (Table 16-5).

Major Depressive Disorder

Also called unipolar disorder, *major depressive disorder* is diagnosed when there is a persistent, negative mood state that includes profound sadness accompanied by feelings of hopelessness, dejection, despair, loneliness, and boredom. Crying spells are common, and the person reports a feeling of demoralization, resulting in part from a sense of incompetence. Other symptoms of major depressive episodes include poor appetite, insomnia or hypersomnia (too much sleep), lack of energy, inability to concentrate, recurrent thoughts about death, and a reduction in the pleasure derived from common activities. Many depressed people also report somatic complaints, with pain being the most common (Greden, 2003). Patients with similar but considerably milder symptoms are given a diagnosis of *dysthymic disorder*.

Major depression may occur as a single episode, but it is more likely that there will be multiple episodes and that the disorder will be chronic (McCaffery et al., 2003; Alpert et al., 1994). Each episode usually shows a gradual onset over a period of several weeks or months and later ends as gradually as it began. The symptoms of major depression can be seen in the case of Paula, a 57-year-old widow and mother of four children:

> The patient lived in a small, five-room woodframe row house with her two younger, unmarried children, ages 18 and 22.... [Shortly before hospitalization] her younger children reported a change in their mother's usual disposition, for no apparent reason. She appeared more easily fatigued, not as cheerful, and lackadaisical about her housework.... She stopped going to church and canceled her usual weekly bingo outing with neighborhood women.... On admission [to a mental hospital], Paula was mostly mute.... She cried periodically throughout the interviews ... [and] was agitated, frequently wringing her hands, rolling her head toward the ceiling and rocking in her chair.... (Spitzer et al., 1983, p. 118).

A number of recent studies have focused on treatment-resistant depression (TRD), in which the patient fails to respond to typical therapies (Chapter 17). This is not a small problem, since 50-60% of major depressives may be resistant (Fava, 2003). Some experts suspect that TRD may actually be a unique subtype of depression, but thus far there is not enough evidence to support that hypothesis, since resistant patients have the same symptoms as those who respond to treatment. The approach to these patients is to do additional diagnostic workups and attempt alternative treatments (Fagiolini & Kupfer, 2003).

Major depression is far more common in women, in groups born in recent years, and in relatives of depressive patients (Lewinsohn et al., 1993; Rosenvinge & Rosenvinge, 2003). The lifetime *prevalence* or risk for this disorder is nearly 13 percent in men and 21 percent in women (Kessler et al., 1994). In any given month, nearly 8 percent of men and 13 percent of women exhibit major depression, with many others having significant depressive symptoms that fall short of diagnosis (Keller, 1994; Romanoski et al., 1992; Kessler et al., 1994). Risk also varies with race and ethnicity, with higher rates in whites and Hispanics than in African-Americans (Figure 16-6). Other estimates suggest that some 20 to 40 million Americans have experienced serious depression and that at least 200,000 are hospitalized each year for depressive disorders.

Bipolar Disorder

There are two types of *Bipolar I* and *Bipolar II*. The first of these involves manic episodes and usually also depressive episodes. Bipolar II patients have major depression and a milder form of mania, called hypomania. A manic episode is a distinct period of time during which the individual's mood becomes elevated and expansive. She is hyperactive and may alternate between excessive cheerfulness and heightened irritability. She is often quite sociable, but in an intrusive, domineering way. In typical cases, an initial manic episode is followed by an alternating series of depressive and manic states, with intervening periods of relative normality. Patients with such mood swings who exhibit less severe symptoms are diagnosed with *cyclothymic disorder*. The nature of bipolar disorder can be seen in the case of a 45-year-old housewife who described her manic phase as follows:

> When I start going into a high, I no longer feel like an ordinary housewife. Instead I feel organized and accomplished and I begin to feel I am my most creative self. I can write poetry easily. I can compose melodies without effort. I can paint.... I see myself as being able to accomplish a great deal for the good of people.... I feel pleasure, a sense of euphoria or elation.... The feeling of exhilaration--the high mood--makes me feel light and full of the joy of living. However, when I go beyond this stage, I become manic and ... I begin to see things in my mind that aren't real. I also experience complete terror.... When I knew that an assassination scene [in a movie] was about to take place, I cowered under the covers and became a complete shaking wreck. I went into a manic psychosis at that point. (Fieve, 1976, pp. 17-18)

Unipolar and bipolar are similar in that they tend to occur in cycles, the patient moving either from depressed to normal affect, then back to depression or from depressed to manic to normal and back (Figure 16-7). However, in other ways they are quite different. For one thing, bipolar disorders usually begin before the age of 30, whereas depression can occur at any time. Bipolar patients typically have a history of normal personality functioning, while major depressives usually have histories of dependence and low self-esteem. Bipolar disorder is more prevalent in higher socioeconomic classes, while major depression is more common at lower levels. Bipolar disorders are somewhat more likely to run in families than are major depressions. And finally, bipolar disorder is much less common than major depression. The lifetime risk is only 0.4-1.6 percent, with no sex difference (Kessler et al., 1994). These differences between the two types of affective disorders have suggested to some researchers that they may have different causes, as we will see shortly.

Types of Depression

When a depression is clearly linked to an appropriate recent event, such as a death in the family or the loss of a job, the depression is said to be *reactive*. When there is no obvious precipitating event, the depression is said to be *endogenous*. Generally, patients diagnosed as reactive show primarily cognitive and emotional symptoms, whereas those with endogenous depression may also have physical symptoms, such as weight loss and reduced interest in sexual activity. In general, endogenous patients respond better to biological treatments, such as drugs.

Depressive patients may also be differentiated in terms of activity level. Some display intense, fast-moving behavior known as *agitation*; others show slow movement and activity *retardation*. Agitated patients usually have a better prognosis. Another classification is called *mixed anxiety and depression* and recognizes that symptoms of these disorders often co-occur and may even reflect a genetic relationship between the two disorders (Boulenger & Lavallee, 1993; Kendler et al., 1992). Our 21 discusses a final category of depression called *seasonal affective disorder* or SAD. This interesting form of depression is found in those who experience greatly heightened depressive affect (feelings) primarily in the winter months (Ford, 1992).

Patients At Risk: Suicide in Depression

Figures from the World Health Organization indicate that nearly half a million people worldwide commit suicide each year - over 1,000 per day or about 1.4 per minute. Suicide attempts are seen in over 2% of men and over 4% of women at some time in their lives. Depressive patients - and particularly those just emerging from a depressive episode - are at highest risk (Rudd et al., 1994). In fact, depression is the disorder most often associated with suicide, and depressive patients have a 15% lifetime risk of dying by their own hands (Keller, 1994; Assis et al., 1993; Klerman, 1982). Although most depressed people thus do not commit suicide, most suicidal individuals are depressive; the suicide rate is about 25 times higher in depressed groups. Both schizophrenia and substance abuse, including alcoholism, also place patients at high risk for suicide (Caldwell & Gottesman, 1992; Duberstein et al., 1993).

Suicide more generally takes 30,000 lives in the United States annually - about one every 18 minutes. Beyond these "successful" suicides, there are 200,000 attempts each year, and five million Americans will attempt suicide some time in their lives (NCHS, 1995). These statistics mean that the suicide rate is about 10-12 per 100,000 population, putting the U.S. midway in the world distribution of suicide statistics (see Table 15-2).

The highest suicide rates occur in the elderly population, age 75 and beyond. However, the rate has decreased in that group over the past several decades and nearly quadrupled in the 15-24-year age range (NCHS, 1995; (Centers for Disease Control, 1991; SAMSHA, 1995; Figure 16-8). About 10% of high school students attempt suicide each year (Spirito et al., 1989), and it is now the third leading cause of death among adolescents and the second among college students (Garland & Zigler, 1993). Over 10,000 college students attempt suicide annually, and about 1000 are successful (Fremouw et al., 1990). Patterns also vary with age.

Within the United States, there is considerable diversity in the suicide rates of various groups. One differentiator is gender. Completed suicide is three times more common in men, who often use guns, than in women, who are more likely to employ drug overdoses. In fact, suicide ranks as the second leading cause of death among white males between the ages of 10 and 55. However, about three times as many women as men make unsuccessful suicide attempts. Other groups at increased risk are those who are separated or divorced and those who live alone. Certain professionals are also particularly prone to suicide, including physicians, dentists, lawyers - and psychologists.

There are about eight suicide attempts for every successful suicide (Leenaars & Wenckstern, 1991), and people who make unsuccessful attempts often do not really want to die. Rather, the attempt is a plea for help or a ploy to gain sympathy or attention. In fact, when suicide notes are available, as is true in about 15% of cases (O'Donnell et al., 1993), it is possible to distinguish between those of genuine suicide cases and those of people who do not intend to die (Black, 1993). The genuine notes tend to display greater amounts of self-blame and hostility and to be more specific and decisive (Ammon, 1994).

As the leading cause of suicide, depression has been studied carefully in an effort to predict which patients will make attempts. Results show that while suicide is a major risk in both unipolar and bipolar disorder, bipolars are more likely to be victims (Lester, 1993). The risk is also higher when depression begins at an earlier age, when there have been more episodes, and when there is a family history of suicide attempts (Roy, 1993). Aaron Beck and his colleagues have found that the single best predictor of suicide is the patient's sense of hopelessness. The more hopeless she feels, the greater the risk of suicide (Beck et al., 1993).

Causes of Mood Disorders

Affective disorders typically result from some combination of life events, long-term psychological factors, and biological predispositions. We will take up the psychological factors here and the biological factors later in the chapter.

Stressful Life Events. Depression often follows stressful events (Hammen, 2003). However, it is not the specific event itself that causes the depression so much as the individual's *interpretation* of the event. In particular, depression is more likely to occur when the person interprets a negative event as beyond his control or when he sees himself as responsible for it. Research on an elderly population shows that lack of life satisfaction and loneliness, both potentially stressful, are also important factors in the development of depression (Green et al., 1992). Interestingly enough, the same study showed that smoking significantly predisposes people to depression - one more good reason not to smoke!

Psychological Theories. Despite the apparent importance of precipitating events in depression, a number of long-term psychological factors are associated with the development of this potentially serious disorder. *Freud* suggested that depression is the result of ego loss, a situation in which the person reacts to an actual loss, such as a death in the family, by turning negative feelings about the dead person against herself.

According to the *behavioral* approach, depression occurs because the individual is deprived of the positive reinforcements to which she has become accustomed (Fester and Colbertson, 1982; Lewinsohn, 1974). People typically rely on a small number of sources for reinforcement. When any one of those sources is lost and the overall level of reinforcement thereby greatly reduced, the result is depression.

A more *cognitive* view hypothesizes that depression results from distortions in thought patterns (Beck et al., 1993). In particular, the individual tends to interpret events in ways that minimize positive achievements, magnify problems, and overgeneralize from small numbers of isolated negative events. For example, a woman with depressive tendencies might be told by her husband that her hair doesn't look quite right. She may magnify this criticism to mean that her husband no longer loves her, that coworkers must think she is a terrible dresser, and that she doesn't do her job well either. If this line of thinking continues, her negative cognitions will lead to a depressive episode.

Another cognitive view suggests that depression results from learned helplessness, a perceived lack of control over life events. The person has an accumulation of experiences in which actions he takes seem to have had no effect or a negative effect on the outcome (Seligman, 1975; Burns, Hoeksema, Girgus, & Seligman, 1992). He therefore learns to feel helpless and quickly gives up whenever faced with a new challenge. It is Martin Seligman's hypothesis that helplessness is the central feeling underlying depression. The experimental basis for his theory is discussed in Chapter 6.

Seligman has reformulated his model to provide a more complete explanation for the relationship between learned helplessness and depression (Miller and Seligman, 1982): the individual comes to expect that her actions will lead to highly aversive rather than desirable outcomes. She feels helpless, believing that no response available to her will reduce the likelihood of the aversive outcome.

In addition, she tends to attribute all her failures to factors within herself (such as low IQ or lack of ability) and any successes to external factors (such as luck or help from others). The result of this combination of feelings and attributions is that she anticipates negative outcomes, expects to be helpless in avoiding these outcomes, attributes failures to her own inadequacies, perceives her helplessness as pervasive, and understandably becomes depressed. A study done by Seligman and a colleague compared diaries and letters written in youth with answers to current questions in people with an average age of 72. Results showed that those who felt helpless in the face of negative events at about age 20 felt exactly the same way at age 72 (Burns & Seligman, 1989). Strikingly, then, the tendency toward feelings of helplessness and depression may span a lifetime.

Keys to Abnormal Behavior 5

The Neurophysiology of Abnormal Behavior

In the late 1960s and early 1970s, psychopathology researchers began to turn some of their attention to neurophysiological influences and their underlying genetic predispositions. We discussed earlier in the chapter what is known about genetic factors in the anxiety and personality disorders. However, most work in genetics and neurophysiology has focused on other disorders, notably schizophrenia, mood disorders, and what are called cognitive disorders.

Schizophrenia

Biological factors in schizophrenia include heredity, neurochemistry, and neuroanatomy.

Genetic Factors. Behavior-genetic studies have shown definitively that genetic factors are involved in schizophrenia (DeLisi et al., 1994), and molecular geneticists have tentatively identified regions of chromosome 2q and several other chromosomes as coding for schizophrenia (Lewis et al., 2003). Investigations of the families of people with this disorder show that first-degree relatives (parents, children, and full siblings) have a much greater risk for schizophrenia than do members of the general population (Figure 16-9). It has also been found that siblings of a person with schizophrenia have an 9 percent risk of developing the disorder if neither parent has it. If one parent also has schizophrenia, the risk is nearly 18 percent, and if both have it the risk rises to over 45 percent (Gottesman, 1991. These figures are much higher than the 1 percent risk in the general population. They do not prove that schizophrenia is genetically predisposed, but studies of twins and adoptees provide more definitive data.

Twin studies involve a comparison of the concordance (agreement) rates for schizophrenia in identical and fraternal twins.[1]

One recent study, which agrees with most others, reports an average concordance rate of about 48% for identical twins and only 4% for fraternal twins (Onstad et al., 1991). Some have questioned the genetic interpretation of these results, raising the possibility that parents and others treat identical twins more similarly than they do fraternal twins, in which case it might be the differences in treatment rather than genes that cause the differences in concordance. However, studies find no significant differences in the way the two twin types are treated (Kendler et al., 1993; Morris et al., 1990).

Further evidence for the genetic basis of schizophrenia comes from the study of individuals who are adopted in infancy and therefore have the genetic endowment of one family and the environmental influence of another. In one continuing series of adoption studies begun in Denmark in the 1960s, Seymour Kety and his colleagues located adoptees who had been diagnosed as schizophrenic and formed matched control groups of adoptees with no history of the disorder. The researchers found that the adoptive relatives of the two groups have about the same rates of schizophrenia. However, the biological relatives of schizophrenics are ten times more likely than the biological relatives of controls to develop the disorder (Kety & Ingraham, 1992).

A final method for studying the genetic contribution to schizophrenia is the *high-risk study*, in which individuals who appear to be at risk for schizophrenia because of their genetic background are studied from birth onward. Sarnoff Mednick and Fini Schulsinger have been following over 200 children of schizophrenic mothers and a control group of children of normal mothers in Denmark since 1962. To date, many children in the high-risk group and very few in the low-risk group have developed schizophrenia (Cannon & Mednick, 1993). In addition, high-risk children commit more crimes, show more adjustment problems, have poorer attention, and exhibit deviant EEG patterns when compared to low-risk children.

Overall, studies suggest that heritability for schizophrenia is about 70 percent, while environmental factors account for about 20 percent of the risk. More recent studies, some using the data base produced by the Human Genome Project (see Chapter 10), have found 30 loci on 14 chromosomes that appear to be specifically involved in psychiatric disorders (Jaworski & Edwards, 1991).[2]

Some of those loci appear to be specific to schizophrenia (Wang et al., 1993). Such findings do not mean that nearly everyone who has a schizophrenic parent will develop the disorder; environmental factors must still be present to foster the development of schizophrenic symptoms and shape the course of the disease.

Brain Biochemistry. Many experts believe that the genetic factor in schizophrenia may be expressed as abnormalities in brain biochemistry (Cohen et al., 1993; Wolf et al., 1993; Ulas & Cotman, 1993). That is, the biochemical substances that serve as neurotransmitters may differ in the brains of people with schizophrenia (Sachdev, 1993). The brain may have too little or too much of a biochemical, its form or structure may deviate from normal, or there may be chemicals present that are not found in normal brains.

Numerous substances have been proposed as the possible culprits in schizophrenia. The neurochemical currently receiving the most attention is dopamine, which acts as a neurotransmitter in certain parts of the brain. The principal hypothesis is that schizophrenia is the result of excessive levels of this brain biochemical (Cohen et al., 1993). Supportive evidence comes primarily from drug studies. Certain "antipsychotic" drugs that act by blocking dopamine receptors in the brain have proven highly effective in controlling schizophrenic symptoms. Furthermore, drugs that increase dopamine activity can produce psychotic states similar to schizophrenia and intensify the symptoms in patients with the disorder. Finally, research has shown a greater density of dopamine receptors in these patients and demonstrated that excess brain dopamine is present at appropriate sites in the brains of deceased schizophrenics (Wong et al., 1986; Wolf et al., 1993).

A simple excess of dopamine is probably not, however, the answer (R.S. Smith, 1992). First of all, there appears to be a dopamine imbalance in restricted areas of the brain, perhaps including the temporal lobes (Kerwin & Murray, 1992). This malfunction of the dopamine system is thought to be genetically transmitted and is supplemented by abnormalities in other neurotransmitter systems (Goldstein & Deutsch, 1992; Wolf et al., 1993). In addition, recent work sug-

---

1 The twin method and other genetic approaches are discussed in Chapter 6.

2 Every human cell contains 23 pairs of long, thin structures called chromosomes. Each is composed of thousands of genes, and each of these, in turn, is made up of deoxyribonucleic acid (DNA). The double-spiral strands of DNA, composed of sugar, phosphate, and nitrogen, carry the genetic codes that determine many of our characteristics.

gests that the problem may not be so much an excess of dopamine as a set of dopamine *receptors* that are overactive or oversensitive. Finally, it is possible that dopamine receptors in the area of the limbic system are overactive while those in the prefrontal cortex are underactive. This recent idea helps to explain the occurrence of both positive and negative symptoms. The overactivity of dopamine receptors in the limbic system may cause positive symptoms, while the underactivity of prefrontal dopamine receptors may produce the negative symptoms.

Even with these newer refinements of the dopamine hypothesis, there are still problems. For example, studies show that the major drugs used in treating schizophrenia must actually reduce dopamine to below-normal levels in order to be effective. If the dopamine hypothesis were correct, it would only be necessary to achieve normal levels. Moreover, not all schizophrenics respond to drugs that lower dopamine levels, and even when they do, the drugs often control positive but not negative symptoms. Thus, it is unlikely that dopamine and its receptors are the only culprits in schizophrenia. We will likely discover in the long run that multiple brain biochemicals are involved (Davis et al., 1991).

Brain Anatomy. Certain brain structures may be also be abnormal in schizophrenia (Cannon et al., 1994). Studies using CAT scans and MRIs (see Chapter 3) have shown that brain ventricles, which contain cerebrospinal fluid, are enlarged in people with schizophrenia (Figure 16-10). This could cause areas of the cortex and subcortex to deteriorate and impair cognitive functioning. Such deterioration has been observed particularly in the limbic system and the prefrontal cortex (Callicott et al., 2003). The latter may underlie what is called a *hypofrontality syndrome* - an impairment in frontal lobe functions - in schizophrenics, possibly accounting for such cognitive symptoms as delusions and loosening of associations. Additional problems may occur because the corpus callosum is reduced in size, particularly where it connects the temporal lobes, decreasing communication between the two hemispheres (Woodruff et al., 1993; Breier et al., 1992). Finally, abnormalities in the temporal lobes have been increasingly implicated (Kerwin & Murray, 1992; Wolf et al., 1993).

Taken together, these biological studies suggest that the genetically transmitted predisposition toward schizophrenia may affect specific brain biochemicals, specific brain structures, or both. Considerable further re search will be needed before we know just what biochemicals and what structures are involved and how they interact to produce the biological basis for this severe disorder.

Mood Disorders

Genetic and biochemical factors also play major roles in mood disorders (Levinson et al., 2003). Family studies show a 15% risk for mood disorders in first-degree relatives of major depressives (Perris, 1992) and a 19% risk in first-degree relatives of bipolar patients, much greater than for the general population. Twin studies confirm the role of genetic factors. Identical twins of major depressives are at least twice as likely to develop the disorder as fraternal twins (Katz & McGuffin, 1993). For bipolar disorder, that difference doubles, with identicals having 4 times the risk of fraternals (Faraone et al. 2003). Overall heritability for bipolar disorder is 85% (McGuffin et al., 2003). Adoption studies show that the risk of mood disorders is 8 times as high in the biological relatives of major depressive patients as in their foster relatives. Comparable work shows that 31% of the biological parents and only 2% of the foster parents of bipolar patients are at risk. Overall evidence suggests that heritability is about 40% for major depression (Kendler et al., 1992) and 85% for bipolar disorder, and recent molecular genetic studies have begun to identify chromosomes that may be involved (Segurado et al., 2003).

Many investigators suspect that the genetic factors implicated in mood disorders operate by affecting neurochemistry. Two theories have been dominant. One suggests that depression occurs when levels of *norepinephrine* are abnormally low and that mania results when they are abnormally high (Katz et al., 1993). The second theory implicates *serotonin*, rather than norepinephrine (Grimsley & Jann, 1992). This approach notes that serotonin normally acts to modulate neural activity in other neurochemical systems, keeping it balanced and consistent. The theory suggests that the serotonin level is low in mood disorders, allowing wild fluctuations in the activity of other neurochemicals, including norepinephrine.

Research showing that antidepressant drugs that increase levels of either norepinephrine or serotonin do reduce depression supports both hypotheses (Kato et al., 1993; Asniv et al., 1992). In fact, serotonin and norepinephrine reuptake inhibitors (drugs that increase brain levels of these neurochemicals) may be equally effective (Judd et al., 1993; Song et al., 1993), suggesting that both systems are involved. However, other findings indicate that abnormal alterations in the sensitivity of receptors for these neurochemicals may also be a factor and that other brain chemicals probably also have roles to play. The overall conclusion must be that findings thus far are conflicting and inconclusive. We are clearly still far from having a final answer to the neurochemical basis for depression.

Cognitive Disorders

Cognitive disorders result from structural damage to the brain or from neurochemical imbalances and involve impairment of such processes as memory, language, thinking, and perception. Because of the neurological involvement, they were formerly called *organic (brain) syndromes.* There are three general types of disorders: delirium, dementia, and amnestic syndrome. *Delirium* is an acute, rapid-onset disorder of brain chemistry in which attention, perception, memory, and cognition are impaired. It is usually brief, though symptoms can continue for months, and it can be caused by head injury, toxic substances, or oxygen deprivation (Hill et al., 1992).

Dementia is a chronic, progressive deterioration of brain functions. Severe, permanent disturbances in memory for recent events, abstract thinking, and emotional control are its hallmarks. An example is a 38-year-old man who developed organic brain syndrome as a result of exposure to the toxic chemicals he used while installing parquet floors (Bernsen et al., 1992). Other recent cases have been a result of systemic lupus erythematosus, a disease of unknown cause that affects a number of body systems (Sibley et al., 1992; Hanly et al., 1992). The dementia syndrome more generally has many causes, including cerebrovascular accident (stroke), dietary deficiencies, anoxia (lack of oxygen), alcoholism, such infectious diseases as HIV-1, meningitis and syphilis, and brain trauma that results in tissue damage. The most common cause is Alzheimer's disease (see Chapter 3).

A final disorder is *amnestic syndrome*, commonly called amnesia. Not to be confused with dissociative amnesia, amnestic syndrome is an organic disorder that involves an inability to access memory for the past. It is most often associated with alcohol or barbiturate consumption and can be either temporary or permanent.

Unless the patient arrives at the hospital with obvious signs of damage to the head, distinguishing between organic and nonorganic (also called *functional*) disorders can be difficult. There is considerable overlap in symptoms between the two types. Establishing the presence of organic impairment and determining its specific nature involves both medical and psychological assessment. So important and complex is the testing process that a subgroup of psychologists called neuropsychologists specialize in this area of diagnosis. The *neuropsychologist* is skilled in carrying out and interpreting psychological tests designed to determine the existence and location of brain damage. In addition, such physiological measures as EEG and CAT, PETT, MRI, and SPECT scanning may be used (see Chapter 3).

Keys to Abnormal Behavior 6

Conclusion

Since Sigmund Freud leaned back in his chair after interviewing a woman with conversion hysteria and decided that her problem was based on complex, unconscious drives, we have learned a tremendous amount about the nature and causes of psychological disorders. Psychology and psychiatry have been able to adopt a truly scientific approach to the study of abnormal behavior. Integrative scientific theories have been developed and numerous important studies have been carried out. As a result, we now have some idea of the causes of many disorders and recognize that they are often based on particular combinations of physiological and psychological factors. Although we are a long way from achieving a full understanding of abnormal behavior, we are moving steadily toward that goal. As a result, we have been able to develop treatment procedures that are quite effective in dealing with some kinds of disorders. These biological and psychological therapies are the subject of Chapter 17.

Summary

Abnormal Behavior: Perspectives and Models

1. General approaches to defining abnormality have included maladaptation, deviation from social norms, and statistical deviation. Practical criteria include bizarreness, discomfort, and inefficiency.
2. Prior to the Renaissance, people typically viewed abnormal behavior as caused by demons.
3. Psychopathology can be viewed as reflecting behaviors that may have been adaptive in ancient environments but now represent failures of adaptation.
4. Genetic predispositions toward disorders and their neurological expression are studied by evolutionary psychologists and neuroscientists.
5. Several models explain the causes of abnormality: The medical model, psychological models, the neuroscience model, and the diathesis-stress model.
6. The medical model views psychological disorders as disease entities. Some psychological models do not. The diathesis-stress model says that a predisposition combines with life experiences to produce the disorder.
7. The current method for classifying and diagnosing psychological disorders is DSM-IV-TR, which provides five axes upon which each patient is categorized.

8. Problems with psychiatric diagnosis include reliability, validity, and labeling. However, classification is needed for both treatment and scientific research.

Anxiety, Somatoform and Dissociative Disorder

1. Anxiety disorders are characterized by high levels of anxiety combined with patterns of ineffective, inefficient, maladaptive behavior. They include generalized anxiety disorder, panic disorder, obsessive-compulsive disorder, and phobic disorders.
2. Generalized anxiety disorder involves a continuing sense of impending disaster, accompanied by fatigue, nightmares, and free-floating anxiety.
3. In obsessive-compulsive disorder, the person loses voluntary control over thoughts and actions, becoming obsessed with persistent thoughts and engaging in ritualistic behaviors. Phobic disorders are characterized by an irrational fear of a specific object or situation, accompanied by avoidance behaviors.
4. Somatoform disorders involve physical symptoms that are similar to medical conditions but have no underlying biological cause. The four major categories are somatization disorder, conversion disorder, pain disorder, and hypochondriasis.
5. Dissociative disorders, which involve a fragmentation of consciousness, include psychogenic amnesia, fugue states, and dissociative identity disorder.
6. Amnesia involves a loss of memory about personal characteristics, while fugue involves also moving to a new area.
7. Dissociative disorders may be repressed ego states, learned mechanisms for avoiding stress, or the result of traumatic experiences.

Schizophrenia

1. In schizophrenia the individual's ability to accurately perceive and respond to the environment is severely impaired. Major symptoms include disturbances of thought and language, perception, motor behavior and affect.
2. Schizophrenia is mainly a thought disorder and includes loosening of associations, delusions, and language disturbances. Perceptual problems include hallucinations and attention deficits.
3. The five major categories of schizophrenia are disorganized, catatonic, paranoid, undifferentiated, and residual. Symptoms can be differentiated as positive and negative.
4. Theories concerning psychological-environmental influences propose regression, the schizophrenogenic mother, the double-bind situation, social learning processes, and social drift as possible factors.

Delusional and Personality Disorders

1. Delusional disorders are characterized by delusions of persecution and sometimes delusions of grandeur.
2. The delusions are more logical than those in schizophrenia, and there are no other psychotic symptoms.
3. Personality disorders occur when pervasive traits of the individual are maladaptive.
4. The most common form is antisocial personality, characterized by a disregard for social values, a need for instant gratification, and a lack of conscience.

Mood Disorders

1. Mood disorders involve extreme alterations in mood. They include major depression and bipolar disorder. Depression may be classified along various dimensions, including endogenous-reactive and agitated-retarded.
2. Major depressive disorder includes symptoms of negative mood state, as well as physical symptoms like poor appetite and insomnia. Bipolar disorder has both manic and depressive phases.
3. Hypothesized psychological causes of mood disorders include stressful events, turning negative feelings inward, distorted thought patterns, and learned helplessness.

The Neurophysiology of Abnormal Behavior

1. Twin, adoption, and high-risk genetic studies demonstrate that schizophrenia is about 70% genetic and 20% environmental.
2. A currently popular neurochemical hypothesis is that schizophrenia involves excessive levels of dopamine in certain areas of the brain, perhaps in combination with a genetically abnormal dopamine receptor system.
3. Enlarged ventricles, a small corpus callosum, and temporal abnormalities may be involved.
4. Studies of mood disorders show that about 40% of the risk for major depression and 80% for bipolar disorder is genetic. Serotonin and norepinephrine may be causal factors in mood disorders.
5. Cognitive disorders commonly involve impairments in memory, judgment, and other intellectual functions. They include delirium, dementia, and amnestic syndrome. They may be caused by brain trauma, tumors, strokes, infections, degenerative processes, nutritional deficiencies, or toxins.

Ask Yourself

1. What are some of the drawbacks to the major approaches for defining abnormal behavior?
2. What are the major advantages and disadvantages of classification and diagnosis of abnormal behavior?
3. Compare and contrast the psychodynamic and behavioral approaches to understanding the causes of abnormal behaviors using specific disorders as examples. What approach are you more comfortable with?
4. How do biological and psychosocial factors interact in the causation of psychological disorders? Which disorders seem to be most heavily influenced by biology, and which are primarily psychosocial in origin?
5. Compare and contrast obsessive-compulsive disorders and phobic disorders.
6. What do amnesia and multiple personality have in common?
7. What are the major symptoms of schizophrenia?
8. What kinds of evidence demonstrate the involvement of biological factors in such disorders as schizophrenia and alcoholism?
9. What are the primary causal explanations for affective disorders?
10. Socially inappropriate behavior seems to be a characteristic of a number of psychological disorders, including schizophrenia, personality disorder, and alcoholism. Is this behavior a cause or an effect of the disorder?

Further Readings

Aldridge, M. (1989). *Multiple personality: An exercise in deception.* Hove, England: Lawrence Erlbaum. This fascinating review of what is known about multiple personality concludes that it is basically social role-playing.

Blum, K., & Payne, J. (1991). *Alcohol and the addictive brain.* N.Y.: Free Press. Kenneth Blum and James Payne provide a clearly written overview of what we currently know about alcoholism and its treatment.

Brannon, L., & Feist, J. (1992). *Health psychology.* Belmont, CA: Wadsworth. Focusing on the interface of psychology and medicine, this book covers most of what is known about the impact behavior on physical health.

Jack, D. (1991). *Silencing the self: Women and depression.* Cambridge, MA: Harvard University Press. The title of Dana Jack's is self-explanatory. She deals in depth with the causes and consequences of depression in women.

Oltmanns, T., Neale, J., & Davison, G. (1991). *Case studies in abnormal psychology.* N.Y.: John Wiley. An excellent supplement to a chapter on abnormal psychology, this collection of case studies provides examples of individuals with nearly all of the major disorders.

Perrotto, R., & Culkin, J. (1993). *Exploring abnormal psychology.* N.Y.: HarperCollins. This is a general text in abnormal psychology that explores the major syndromes in more depth.

Schwaab, E. (1992). *Hitler's mind: A plunge into madness.* N.Y.: Praeger. Hitler is generally regarded as having had a paranoid disorder. Schwaab's book is therefore a fascinating look at paranoia and delusional disorder.

Snaith, P. (1991). *Clinical neurosis.* Oxford: Oxford University Press. This concise text on the anxiety disorders covers what is known about causes, diagnosis, and treatment.

Thornton, J. et al. (1991). *Schizophrenia simplified.* Toronto: Hogrefe & Huber. This interesting is a guide to schizophrenia written for both the families of schizophrenia and professionals. It provides a good understanding of the disorder and its treatment.

Viscusi, W. (1992). *Smoking: Making the risky decision.* N.Y.: University Press. Covering everything you ever wanted to know about smoking, this important book pulls together the empirical evidence that smoking kills.

Psychology in the 21st Century

Don't be S.A.D

Hippocrates observed centuries ago that there are seasonal variations in human mood states. Nevertheless, it was only a few short years ago that a fascinating phenomenon called *seasonal affective disorder* or *SAD* was confirmed. What clinical researchers observed was that some patients become depressed only in the winter or late fall and winter months. In the Northern Hemisphere, where most of the research has been done, the symptoms appear primarily in January and February. In the Southern Hemisphere they are more likely to be seen in July and August, which is winter in that part of the world. It appears that those who can otherwise be classified as having major depression become normal in the spring and summer, while those with bipolar disorder may shift to mania (Ford, 1992). Overall, about 10 to 20 percent of patients with mood disorders may have SAD (Faedda et al., 1993; Williams & Schmidt, 1993). A small number display a reversal of the more common pattern, with depression in the spring and summer (Faedda et al., 1993).

What causes SAD? We are not yet certain, but It appears that the lower light levels in winter are a causal factor. Light entering through the eyes may alter levels of important neurotransmitters or somehow interact with defective receptors for these biochemicals, but evidence is thus far sparse (Rudorfer et al., 1993). Another possibility currently under investigation is that SAD patients have a thyroid dysfunction, but we appear to be some years away from knowing with any certainty the underlying causal factors (Raitere, 1992).

When Norman Rosenthal and his colleagues at the National Institutes of Health were faced with trying to treat SAD, they decided to expose their patients to bright light each day during the fall and winter seasons. This *light therapy* appears to work quite well (Hawkins, 1992). It reduces depression in virtually all patients in some studies (Bielski et al., 1992) and in 36-56% of patients in others (Rosenthal et al., 1993). Research is continuing in an effort to determine the types and levels of light and the methods and times of administration of light therapy that work best.

The ongoing effort to better understand the nature and causes of seasonal affective disorder, really just getting under way, will continue well into the next century and is clearly important in its own right. It will help the millions of people who suffer from this malady to feel better, and it will provide science with a more complete body of knowledge on depression more generally. But perhaps the even greater importance of the SAD work is that it has alerted psychologists once again to be open to the possibility of new disorders with unanticipated causes and creative cures. The discovery of SAD will very likely lead to the discovery, in the 21st century, of yet unknown causal relationships between environmental factors and symptom patterns.

The Critical Thinker

Is Multiple Personality a Real Disorder?

Imagine meeting a person who introduces herself as Joan on one occasion, Jane on another, and perhaps Sam on a third. It would appear that you have met someone with the most dramatic of the dissociative pathologies, *dissociative identity disorder (DID)*, formerly called *multiple personality disorder (MPD)*, in which one individual has two or more alternative personalities.

The Basic Hypothesis or Contention

Those who believe in, study, and treat dissociative identity disorder, are convinced that their patients have undergone a sort of psychological fragmentation and thereby unintentionally developed several distinct personalities. Each personality, they contend, has its own separate identity, with a consistent set of social behaviors, habits, and personality structures (Huntjens et al., 2003).

What Is The Evidence?

Much of the evidence for DID or MPD consists of anecdotal observations and case studies. You may be familiar with some of the more famous cases. Most widely publicized (in both a book and a movie) was the case of "Eve," who initially had three separate personalities (Thigpen and Cleekley, 1957): "Eve White" was described as sad and dignified; "Eve Black" was flirtatious and sexy; and Jane emerged during therapy and was later replaced by a more mature personality, Evelyn. The real "Eve," Christine Sizemore, has since written that she actually had thirteen personalities at the time she entered therapy and that an additional nine personalities emerged during therapy, for a total of twenty-two (Sizemore and Pittllio, 1977). Another famous case was that of Sybil, reported by her psychiatrist, Flora Schriber (1973). Sybil was found to have sixteen separate personalities, two of them male.

Studies of DID patients suggest that they now have an average of 15 personalities (Merckelbach et al., 2002) and that this number has been increasing in recent years (Spanos & Burgess, 1994). There is typically a *host* or basic personality and a number *alters* - alternative personalities. The alters are aware of each other, but the host is not aware of the alters.

Perhaps the potentially most convincing evidence of the existence of MPD comes from studies that claim to demonstrate actual physiological differences among the personalities in any one patient. Investigators have found differences in blood pressure and menstrual cycles (Putnam, Zahn, & Post, 1990), as well as electrodermal activity, a measure of autonomic functioning (Chapter 13). Most dramatically, some studies seem to show differences among the personalities in brain electrical activity, as indicated by electroencephalographic (EEG) patterns (Hughes et al., 1990).

Is the Evidence Open to Alternative Interpretations?

Those who believe that MPD is not a real disorder are quick to point out that nearly all the evidence comes from case studies, which should never be used as a basis for firm conclusions. Moreover, they emphasize the possibility of *iatrogenesis*, meaning that a therapist may actually cause multiple personalities to appear through interactions with the patient (Labott & Wallach, 2002). Fascinated by the possibility of treating an MPD, she may essentially create the disorder by using hypnosis or simply suggesting it to patients who come to her initially with other disorders (Dell, 2002).

Another point of criticism is based on the dramatic recent change in the prevalence of MPD. As of 1970, a total of only 100 cases had ever been reported worldwide. However, following the widespread publicity about the case of Sybil (Schriber, 1973), the numbers began to climb rapidly, reaching 600 by the early 1980s and currently numbering at least in the tens of thousands (Gleaves et al., 2001). To some extent, this increase may reflect changes in diagnostic criteria and practices. However, critics believe it is also possible that most of these patients, now aware of the attention that MPD gets, are blatantly faking the disorder (Beahrs, 1994). In addition, far more therapists may be suggesting it to their patients now that the thousands of cases on record have made it a more acceptable diagnosis (Dorahy, 2001).

Still another blow against MPD comes from a study in which normal college students were induced, with or without hypnosis, to take on a second personality. Over 80 percent did so, adopting a new name and set of characteristics. Moreover, when they took each of two personality tests twice, the scores of their two personalities were substantially different. In short, normal students were readily able to display multiple personalities that differed just as those of MPDs appear to (Spanos et al., 1985).

But what about the studies showing different EEG patterns in different alters? Critics point out that the studies on which the claimed differences are based are largely unpublished, making them unavailable for evaluation (Miller & Triggiano, 1992). Moreover, at least some of the studies that are available are lacking in appropriate controls. To support this latter point, researchers have conducted studies in which MPD patients are compared with normal controls who are asked to act out different roles. Philip Coons and his colleagues (1982) recorded EEGs from two multiple personality patients and one control participant, who was asked to simulate various personalities of one of the patients. The researchers did indeed find significant differences in EEG patterns for different personalities in the two patients. However, they also found that the personalities simulated by the control participant showed <u>greater</u> EEG differences than the personalities of the patients. They concluded that the observed EEG changes reflected differences in emotional state but did not confirm the existence of separate personalities.

Do We Need Additional Evidence?

The answer is clearly "yes." At the moment we have two warring camps on the MPD issue, each convinced that they are right. The mere fact that MPD (now DID) is officially listed in the DSM-IV-TR and that many cases have been diagnosed certainly does not prove its existence. By the same token, there is no convincing proof that it does not exist. Whenever we have such a situation, the only answer is to further refine our theories and do more and better studies carefully designed to answer the relevant scientific questions.

What Can We Conclude?

While those who believe in and study MPD point to a number of investigations that seem to validate the multiple personality construct (Putnam, 1991), others - with at least equally convincing evidence - continue to question its existence (Beahrs, 1994). As a result, we can only conclude that we do not know whether MPD is a real disorder - joining the anxiety disorders, schizophrenia, and the others - or whether it is primarily a product of misinterpreted role-playing, faking, and iatrogenesis. Only further research will permit us to reach a firm conclusion as to the existence of this interesting construct.

Probe

Folie à Deux

Research involving primarily case studies has identified a particularly interesting form of delusional disorder called the *shared psychotic disorder* or *folie à deux*. It is a syndrome in which two people share delusional ideas and sometimes bizarre behavior patterns. The delusions in folie à deux are usually persecutory, although they may also be religious, grandiose, or of some other form. One case, reported by Robert and Kay Faguet (1982), involved a senile mother (R) and her schizophrenic daughter (M), who engaged in a joint paranoid delusion, which they describe in the following coauthored letter:

> Dear Dr.:
> M and I send you affectionate greetings. I wish we could give them to you in person, finding that you are well and able to carry on your work. We hope your family are all well, too, relieving you of that worry. There is much to tell you about us--not to good. I am afraid our neighbor, Mr. N. who had homesteaded all the canyons (where we live)--and thereby became a multimillionaire, was murdered Christmas eve by a man who entered his home through a hole they made in his roof, robbed him and attacked him. Now it is thought advisable for us to have an armed guard. Also, something is pumped in our living room. It collects on beams, wooden furniture, a large tray, etc. We sent a specimen to H in C and the report came back that our specimen consisted of eighteen (18) different pesticides. We are told that those with criminal intent are trying to drive us out of our house! We keep getting offers for it, but we are not ready to leave yet. (p. 5)

They actually included a laboratory report to support their delusion and wrote that "we're awfully glad to have those evidence and not be thought paranoid anymore."

A second interesting case involved a married couple in which the wife, a 59-year-old teacher, suffered from a skin disorder. She believed that her skin lesions were the result of neighbors shooting at her with laser beams, and her husband came to fully share in that paranoid delusion (Raulin et al., 2001).

Research on folie à deux has been applied primarily to the question of when to diagnose this disorder. What kinds of people develop it? What is their relationship to each other? Folie ‡ deux most frequently involves two relatives, who live in social isolation and have developed a strong leader-follower or dependency relationship. The more active or dominant individual originates the delusion, which the passive party then accepts and acts on.

Actually, more than two people can be involved in this kind of shared paranoid syndrome. In an interesting case of folie a famille, an entire family - father, mother, and 12-year-old son - shared several paranoid delusions. The father was the primary case, with the mother and son eventually sharing in his delusions (Wehmeier et al., 2003). Other examples of folie à trois include three members of a German family who falsely believed they were infested with parasites (Gieler & Knoll, 1990) and two cases of Soviet-Jewish immigrant families to Israel in which delusional systems were shared among two parents and a child (Maizel et al., 1990). There have also been reports of folie à quatre (4 people; Moss & Pearce, 1989) and folie a sept (6 people; Guduco-Augular and Wlntrob, 1964).

Because folie à deux is most commonly seen in blood relatives, it may involve genetic factors that produce psychotic tendencies. However, the high incidence of the disorder in husbands and wives would suggest otherwise. Experts have emphasized that while genetic makeup may play a role in cases of blood relatives, environmental factors are probably of at least equal importance (Wehmeier et al., 2003).

Horizons in Abnormal Behavior

An Abnormal Behavior May Not Be: Cultural Differences

Is a behavior that is abnormal in our culture abnormal in all cultures? We don't yet have firm and final answers to this question, but both psychologists and cultural anthropologists are addressing the issue (Berry et al., 1992). What we do

know is that certain symptoms appearing fairly frequently in some cultures do not seem to appear at all in others. A good example is *anorexia nervosa*, in which the person starves herself to remain thin (Chapter 12). It is quite common in the U.S. and Europe but is never seen in most other parts of the world. Another case in point is *running amok*, a disorder seen in Southeast Asia but not elsewhere, in which a man moves rapidly from place to place committing indiscriminate, extremely violent acts. Malaysian women experience another unique disorder called *latah*, in which they feel compelled to imitate the behaviors of others. People in Alaska and Greenland develop *pibloqtoq*, an abnormality characterized by an irresistible compulsion to remove their clothes in sub-zero temperatures. The disorder is a dangerous one that can lead to death from exposure. Finally, you will have to hope that you don't experience *brain fag*, which is quite common in West African students preparing for exams. It involves severe headaches, difficulty in concentration, and blurred vision and could significantly lower your score on the next exam! What is clear from the cross-cultural studies completed to date is that some cultures appear to exhibit unique disorders, but that the major disorders are probably universal (Arieli & Aychen, 1994; Ormel et al., 1994). What is not clear is whether the apparently unique disorders are actually just culturally differentiated ways of expressing the same disorders seen in other societies.

What a Pain!

All of us experience pain of physical origin from time to time, but some people have the added burden of a somatoform disorder simply called pain disorder. *Pain disorder* is diagnosed when persistent, significant pain occurs in the absence of medical pathology that would explain its duration and magnitude. The pain thus appears to be of psychological origin and is therefore sometimes called *psychogenic pain*. The pain may be chronic but is often intermittent, and it may disappear on its own without therapy after a few weeks or months. The reported pain is most often vaguely localized in a vital organ, such as the heart, or in the lower back or limbs. Chronic lower back pain, for example, is often (but not always) symptomatic of pain disorder. In one study, chronic back pain patients subjected to psychological stress reported more pain than a control group not exposed to stress (Schwartz et al., 1994), supporting a common clinical observation about the role of stress in pain disorder. Although the discomfort of psychogenic pain is of psychological origin, the experience of pain is very real. As a result, patients often "doctor-shop," visiting numerous physicians in hopes of finding some relief from the pain and may even undergo surgery that will, of course, do no good. They may also become virtual invalids, prisoners to their psychogenic pain. Psychotherapy, however, can help (Keefe & Williams, 1989).

Autistic Behavior

Some severe psychological disorders appear very early in life and are therefore classified as *pervasive developmental disorders*. Among the most problematic - and thankfully rare - of these disturbances is *autistic disorder*. The symptoms of autism may appear before the age of two and a half and can even be present at birth. The child exhibits an extreme form of social withdrawal, avoiding even eye contact with other people. She also displays a variety of ritualistic movements, such as flapping her hands and arms, rocking back and forth, or spinning around, in which she becomes totally absorbed. In addition, many autistic children have a speech defect known as *echolalia*, in which they repeat or echo the words and phrases of others. Mental retardation is found in 75 percent of cases, and a final symptom is the preservation of sameness, meaning that the child insists on an obsessively orderly life. He plays with the same toys in precisely the same way over and over again. He eats foods in the same order and may insist that a specific ritual be followed in putting him to bed. Any deviation from these established routines may trigger a panic attack or tantrum.

The causes of autism are not entirely understood. There is a well-established genetic factor involved (Smalley, 1991; Folstein & Pevin, 1991), but other factors are clearly also influential. The genetic factor may be expressed as an autoimmune disorder (Singh et al., 1993), and a number of studies have implicated abnormalities in several brain structures (Gedye, 1991; Lotspeich & Ciaranello, 1993; Kemper & Bauman, 1993; Courchesne et al., 1993). Treatments are only minimally effective, and autism remains one of the mysteries of abnormal psychology.

Key Terms 1

agoraphobia
antisocial personality disorder
anxiety
anxiety disorders
autistic disorder
bipolar disorder

cognitive disorders
conversion disorder
delirium
delusional disorder
delusion
dementia
demonology
diathesis-stress
dissociative amnesia
dissociative disorders
dissociative fugue
dissociative identity disorder
dopamine
DSM-IV-TR
endogenous depression
folie a deux
hallucination
humanistic model
hypochondriasis
learned helplessness
major depressive disorder
medical model
mood disorder
multiple personality disorder
neologism
obsessive-compulsive disorder
panic disorder
personality disorders
phobic disorder
prevalence
psychodynamic model
reactive depression
reliability
schizophrenia
seasonal affective disorder
somatization disorder
somatoform disorders
substance dependence
validity

Key People 1

Aaron Beck
Dorothea Dix
Sigmund Freud
Emil Kraepelin
Phillipe Pinel
Thomas Szasz

Key Terms 2

agoraphobia
anxiety disorders
conversion disorder

dissociative disorder
dissociative identity disorder
hypochondriasis
multiple personality disorder
obsessive-compulsive disorder
panic disorder
phobic disorder
somatization disorder
somatoform disorder

Key Terms 3

hallucination
neologism
schizophrenia

Key Terms 4

antisocial personality disorder
delusional disorder
delusion
personality disorder

Key Terms 5

bipolar disorder
learned helplessness
major depressive disorder
mood disorder
seasonal affective disorder (SAD)

Key People 5

Aaron Beck

Key Terms 6

cognitive disorders
delirium
dementia
dopamine

Keys to Abnormal Behavior 1

1. Abnormal behavior is not always easy to define.
   - A. Three formal approaches to defining it?
     Maladaptive, deviate from norms, statistical deviation.
   - B. Three practical criteria?
     Bizarreness, discomfort, inefficiency

2. **Abnormality has not always been viewed scientifically.**
   - A. **A common causal attribution in earlier centuries?**
     Demonology
   - B. **When scientific explanations began?**
     Renaissance
   - C. **Some major figures in reforming treatment?**
     Pinel, Dix, Rush
3. **Psychopathology may be seen as a failure of evolution.**
   - A. **The theoretical emphasis regarding causes between about 1920 and 1970?**
     Environmental
   - B. **The emphasis since 1970?**
     Much more biological; overall a balance
   - C. **Whether abnormal behavior was ever adaptive?**
     We don't know
   - D. **Whether biology and environment contribute equally to all forms of psychopathology?**
     They don't.
4. **Causal models influence approaches to theory and research.**
   - A. **The major models?**
     Medical, psychodynamic, behavioral, humanistic, evolutionary/neuroscience.
   - B. **How the medical model views disorders?**
     As disease entities or syndromes
   - C. **How the evolutionary model views it?**
     As a failure of evolution (so far)
   - D. **How the diathesis-stress model views it?**
     As caused by a predisposition combined with life experiences.
5. **The current U.S. classification system is DSM-IV-TR**
   - A. **Whose original system it is based on?**
     Kraepelin
   - B. **What the first three axes do?**
     Describe and evaluate the major disorders
   - C. **What the last two axes do?**
     List social functioning and highest functioning.
6. **The classification system is problematic.**
   - A. **Some major problems?**
     Reliability, validity, labeling.
   - B. **Why we still need it?**
     To communicate regarding treatment and to do research.

Keys to Abnormal Behavior 2

1. **Anxiety disorders can be very debilitating.**
   - A. **Their major, general symptoms?**
     High anxiety, ineffective, maladaptive, inefficient behavior.
   - B. **The major disorders?**
     Generalized anxiety disorder
     Panic disorder
     Obsessive-compulsive disorder
     Phobic Disorders (specific, complex)
   - C. **Symptoms of generalized anxiety disorder?**
     Sense of impending disaster, free-floating anxiety, nightmares, fatigue.

D. Of OCD?
    Persistent thoughts, ritualistic behaviors, loss of control over these thoughts and actions.

2. The causes are both biological and psychological.
   A. Some biological factors?
      Genetic predispositions, serotonin, norepinephrine
   B. Some psychological factors?
      Early trauma, ways of perceiving stress, replacements for more threatening unconscious conflicts, selective reinforcement.
3. Somatoform disorders involved physical complaints with psychological causes.
   A. Some major types?
      Somatization, conversion, hypochondriasis
4. Consciousness is fragmented in dissociative disorders.
   A. Some major categories?
      Amnesia, fugue state, dissociative identify disorder.
   B. What is forgotten in amnesia?
      Personal identity information
   C. Some causes?
      Repressed ego states, learned stress avoidance, trauma.

Keys to Abnormal Behavior 3

1. Schizophrenia is perhaps the most severe of all psychological disorders.
   A. Some major areas of symptomatology?
      Thought, perception, motor, emotional, social.
   B. How common it is?
      About 1-1.5% of the population
2. It is primarily a thought disorder.
   A. Some cognitive symptoms?
      Loosening of associations, delusions, clanging, word salad, neologisms
   B. The major perceptual symptoms?
      Hallucinations, attention deficits.
   C. The major types?
      Disorganized, catatonic, paranoid, undifferentiated, residual
   D. Some alternative ways of subclassifying?
      Process-reactive, positive-negative symptoms.
3. Psychological/environmental influences are partial causal factors.
   A. Some psychoanalytic hypotheses?
      Regression, the schizophrenogenic mother, the double-bind.
   B. The social learning theory hypothesis?
      Imitation of parental behaviors
   C. The sociogenic hypothesis?
      Poor educational and economic conditions contribute to causation.

Keys to Abnormal Behavior 4

1. Delusional disorders affect cognitive processes.
   A. Major symptoms of delusional disorders?
      Delusions of grandeur and of persecution

2. **Personality disorders involve rigid, maladaptive personality characteristics.**
   A. **Whether they are long- or short-term?**
      Pervasive and long-term
   B. **Some major subcategories?**
      Dependent, histrionic, borderline, antisocial
3. **Antisocial personality disorder is found in 2-3% of the population.**
   A. **The major symptoms?**
      Manipulative, impulsive, irresponsible behavior, violates social norms.
   B. **What common symptom of other disorders is <u>not</u> present?**
      Guilt or anxiety
   C. **Some possible biological causal factors?**
      Frontal lobe dysfunction, autonomic, serotonin, and neuroendocrine abnormalities, genetic influences.
   D. **Some possible psychosocial causal factors?**
      Low socioeconomic status, parental antisocial behavior, ineffective parental supervision, selective reinforcement.

Keys to Abnormal Behavior 5

1. **Major depression is far more common in women.**
   A. **The major psychological symptoms?**
      Hopelessness, sadness, loneliness, boredom, dejection, despair, crying, demoralization.
   B. **Some additional symptoms?**
      Insomnia, hypersomnia, poor appetite, thoughts of death, reduced pleasure, pain, lack of energy.

2. **Bipolar disorder means at least one episode of mania has occurred.**
   A. **The symptoms of mania?**
      Hyperactivity, elevated mood, excessively cheerful or irritable
   B. **How common it is?**
      0.4-1.6 percent risk. Much less than major depression.
3. **Depression may be subclassified in various ways.**
   A. **The type that occurs without a precipitating event?**
      Endogenous
   B. **The type that does have a precipitating event?**
      Reactive
   C. **The subcategories in terms of activity level?**
      Agitated, retarded
   D. **A form that occurs in the winter?**
      Seasonal affective disorder

4. **Suicide occurs in 2% of men and 4% of women.**
   A. **The groups most at risk?**
      Depressives, the elderly, those living alone, certain professionals
   B. **The percentage of depressives who commit suicide?**
      15%
   C. **The best predictor?**
      A sense of hopelessness
5. **Causes of mood disorders are psychological and physiological.**
   A. **Some major psychological factors?**
      Stressful events, turning negative feelings inward, learned helplessness, distorted thought patterns.

Keys to Abnormal Behavior 6

1. Schizophrenia is heavily influenced by biological factors.
   A. What proportion of the etiology is genetic?
      70%
   B. The types of genetic studies done?
      Family, twin, adoption, high-risk
   C. How consistent the genetic results are?
      Very consistent
   D. The major brain biochemical currently implicated?
      Dopamine
   E. Major brain structures that may be involved?
      Ventricles, corpus callosum, temporal cortex
2. Mood disorders are also depend on biological factors.
   A. The percentage of risk that is genetic?
      About 40% for major depression, 80% for bipolar disorder.
   B. The major neurochemicals that may be involved?
      Serotonin, norepinephrine
3. Cognitive disorders result from brain damage.
   A. Two types of underlying brain damage?
      Structural, neurochemical
   B. The major types of cognitive disorders?
      Delirium, dementia, amnestic disorder
   C. Some major causes?
      Brain trauma, tumor, stroke, infection, degeneration, nutritional deficiency, toxins.

References

Andreasen, N., Flaum, M., Swayze, V., Tyrrell, G., & Arndt, S. (1990). Positive and negative symptoms in schizophrenia: A critical reappraisal. Archives of General Psychiatry, 47, 615-621.

Beck, A.T., & Emery, G. (1985). AAnxiety disorders and phobias: A cognitive perspective. NY: Basic Books.

Blanchard, J., & Neale, J. (1994). The neuropsychological signature of schizophrenia: Generalized or differential deficit. American Journal of Psychiatry, 15, 40-48.

Blazer, D. et al. (1994). The prevalence and distribution of major depression in a national comorbidity sample: The National Comorbidity Survey. American Journal of Psychiatry, 151, 979-986.

Burke, K., Burke, J., Regier, D., & Rae, D. (1990). Age at onset of selected mental disorders in five community populations. Archieves of General Psychiatry, 47, 511-518.

Capaldi, D., & Patterson, G. (1994). Interrelated influences of contextual factors in antisocial behaivor in childhood and adolescence for males. In D. C. Fowles, P. Sutker, & H. Goodman (Eds.), Progress in experimental personaltiyi and psychopathology research. NY: Springer.

Centers for Disease Control. (1994). Update: alcohol-related traffic fatalities - United States, 1982-1993. MMWR, Dec. 2; 43:861-3.

Davis, K., Kahn, R., Ko, G., & Davidson, M. (1991). Dopamine and schizophrenia: A review and reconceptualization. American Journal of Psychiatry, 148, 1474-1486.

Fowles, D., & Missel, K. (1994). Electordermal hyporeactivity, motivation, and psychopathy: Theoretical issues. In D. C. Fowles, P. Sutker, & H. Goodman (Eds.), Progress in experimental personaltiyi and psychopathology research. NY: Springer.

Gottesman, I. I. (1991). Schizophrenia genesis. NY: W.H. Freeman.

Kessler et al. (1994). Lifetime and 12-month prevalence of DSM-III-R psychiatric disorders in teh U.S. Archieve of General Psychiatry, 51, 8-19

Lewinsohn, P.M. (1974). A behavioral approach to depression. In R. Friedman & M. Katz (Eds.). The psychology of depression: Contemporary theory and research. N.Y.: Halstead Press.

McIntosh, J.L. (1992). Suicide in the elderly. In B. Bongar (Ed.), Suicide: Guidelines for assessment, management, and treatment. NY: Oxford University Press.

National Center for Injury Prevention and Control, CDC. (1994). Programs for the prevention of suicide among adolescents and young adults. Morbidity and Mortality Weekly Report, 43 (RR-6), 3-7.

Rapoport, J.L. (1989). The biology of obsesions and compulsions. Scientific American, 268, 83-89

SAMSHA, Office of Applied Studies. (1995). Substance abuse and mental health statistics sourcebook. Washington, DC: Superintendent of Documents, U.S. Government Printing Office.+

Wittchen et al. (1994). DSM-III-R generalized anxiety disorder in the National Comorbidity Survey. Archives of General Psychiatry, 51, 355-364.

Chapter 17

Psychological and Biomedical Therapies

Outline

Networking

PERHAPS someone you know has been "in therapy." Indeed, you may have had therapy yourself and have probably wondered what this fascinating thing that some psychologists do is really all about. What is therapy? How is it done? How well does it work? Clinical and counseling psychologists, as well as psychiatrists, often attempt to help those with emotional problems by using some form of therapy. Actually, "therapy" is a very general term that, even in reference to psychological problems, covers a wide variety of treatments. There are two broad forms of therapy, psychological therapy and biological therapy. Psychological therapies include psychoanalysis, client centered therapy, and behavioral methods, among other approaches. Biological therapies include electroconvulsive therapy, psychosurgery, and drug treatment. Although the goal of all therapies is basically the same _ to help the client feel better and function more effectively _ the approaches taken can vary widely. Furthermore, the setting in which therapy is offered can range from mental institutions to community mental health centers to private offices, and therapy can be done on an individual or group basis.

Treating Stark Terror

Chapter 16 describes the case of Kenneth, the 22-year-old with phobic disorder. He experienced his fear of theaters and later elevators, buses, and even city streets as stark terror. His phobia was so debilitating that he sought therapy for the problem. In this chapter we will follow Kenneth through several therapeutic approaches in order to see the variety of ways in which one kind of psychological problem can be treated. By the end of the chapter, Kenneth may be the most thoroughly treated patient in the history of psychology!

The various psychological disorders that we describe in Chapter 16 bring misery to both individuals and society as a whole - and that has been true since the very dawn of humankind. Mental disorder has always been a common malady, and societies throughout history have sought ways to treat it.

Many people who suffer from such disorders actively seek treatment or are encouraged or forced by others to obtain treatment for their problems. Once the decision to seek help has been made, the individual is faced with a rather substantial array of possible treatments. Some approaches are biological and others are psychological. The particular therapy - the treatment - given depends on the nature of the disorder and on the training, experience, and theoretical orientation of the therapist. All current psychological therapies are based on theories of personality and abnormal behavior and on research related to them (see Chapters 14 and 16). Different theories are likely to lead to different treatments. Biomedical therapies are based on neurological theory and research dealing with brain mechanisms that underlie psychological disorders.

Mental Health Care: Perspectives and Practices

Mental disorders have been treated virtually throughout the history of the human species. Let's briefly consider historical and modern treatment approaches, then turn to biological and environmental perspectives on treatment, look at the various professions currently involved in treatment, and finally discuss the evolutionary view of therapy.

Historical Perspectives

Human beings began treating mental disorders at least a half million years ago when Stone Age cave dwellers roamed the earth. Their belief in demonology (Chapter 16) led them to treat mental illness by boring holes in the skull of the afflicted person _ a practice known as *trephining* - to release the evil spirits. Other ancient cultures, including the early Egyptians and Chinese, engaged in *exorcism* - praying, noise making, and sometimes whipping or starvation - to drive out the evil spirits. In fact, exorcism is still practiced in some cultures.

The first real progress in treating mental disorders came in about 400 B.C. with the work of the Greek physician Hippocrates. To treat psychological disorders, which he believed were based in brain pathology and an imbalance of body fluids, he and his followers prescribed exercise, kindness, a vegetable diet, and a tranquil life style. While Hippocrates was by no means entirely right, his approach was a giant leap beyond trephining and exorcism. One of his followers was the Roman physician Galen (A.D. 130-200), whose work on anatomy and physiology dominated medicine for some 13 centuries.

When the enlightened views of ancient Rome and Greece were lost following Galen's death in A.D. 200 (Chapter 16), so were humane treatments. Blood-letting, starvation, beating, torture, and exorcism became common "therapies" for the mentally disturbed, who were housed in asylums in which they were chained to the walls of filthy cells and routinely beaten.

Humanitarian treatment did not reemerge until 1792, when Phillipe Pinel became director of the La Bicetre hospital in Paris. He removed the chains, put his patients in bright, sunny rooms, permitted them to exercise on the hospital grounds, and treated then with kindness. His experiment was a resounding success: Patients who had been in chains for as much as 30 years recovered and were released. A similar, and equally successful, experiment was soon conducted by William Tuke (1732 - 1822) in England, and the humanitarian movement then spread to America. There, Benjamin Rush, the founder of American psychiatry, established humanitarian treatment as the norm at Pennsylvania Hospital, and it soon spread to other institutions. Nevertheless, there was still much work to be done, and in 1841 Dorothea Dix (1802-1887), a New England schoolteacher, began a zealous 40-year campaign to reform the treatment of the mentally ill. She is credited with establishing 32 mental hospitals and later organizing the nursing corps for the Northern armies during the Civil War.

Following Dix' lead, mental hospitals were established all over the United States. Today, they include state and county institutions, as well as the large federal Veteran's Administration hospital system, and numerous private hospitals. Many general medical hospitals also established special wards for mental patients. By 1950, these institutions housed over a half million patients, with the number threatening to grow endlessly. With the coming of the community mental health approach and the advent of psychiatric drugs, however, the early 1960s saw the beginning of a dramatic reduction in the number of patients hospitalized with mental disorders, as Figure 17-1 shows. Even with that reduction, $54 billion dollars are spent each year on mental health care (SAMHSA, 1995). The disorders that bring the largest numbers of patients into treatment are the affective disorders, schizophrenia, and substance abuse problems (Chapters 5 and 16) (Figure 17-2).

The Community Mental Health Movement

Increasing dissatisfaction with the exclusive use of large institutional settings for mental health care brought about the *deinstitutionalization* movement. This meant getting patients out of institutions and shifting much of mental health care to community mental health centers, halfway houses, and various forms of crisis intervention.

Community Mental Health Centers. In 1963, at the request of President John F. Kennedy, Congress passed the Community Mental Health Centers Act. This law provided for the establishment of one community mental health center (CMHC) for every 50,000 people. There are now a variety of kinds of centers in the community, and just how many CMHCs we now have nationally depends on how the term is defined. Using the original, formal, legal definition, there are 498 CMHCs, with an additional 135 that offer more services than required by the original Act. By alternative definitions that include, for example, rap centers and youth centers, there are 3680 (Sarver, 2003).

A CMHC typically provides outpatient, inpatient, and emergency services. The purpose of *outpatient services* is to provide psychotherapy and other forms of mental health care without forcing the client to leave family, job, or schooling. To provide *inpatient services*, the community mental health center places clients in general hospitals in the area. *Emergency services* are usually provided through store-front clinics that remain open around the clock or through workers who serve in the emergency rooms of general hospitals.

The CMHCs have not been a total success. In fact, about 13% of federally funded centers that were operating in 1981 had closed their doors by 1990, and that trend appears to be continuing (Issue Brief, Grantmakers Health, 2003). This reduction is a symptom of larger problems. Federal funds have been cut back (Sarver, 2003), and deinstitutionalization has at least partially failed (Jones et al., 2003). Many severely disordered patients need to be hospitalized, and the CMHCs are not funded or equipped to deal with them. In addition, the integration of previously hospitalized patients back into the community often does not occur. They are too ill to survive psychologically, and many soon end up back in the hospital after using up considerable amounts of the limited community resources. The resulting reduction in CMHCs is particularly unfortunate because the services they provide are used most heavily by those who live in poverty, including large numbers of African-Americans, Hispanics, and other minorities (Yang et al., 2003).

Halfway Houses. Deinstitutionalization also brought with it the development of systems of halfway houses. A *halfway house* is basically a residence in which formerly hospitalized mental patients, drug addicts, or others can be housed. The halfway house provides partial care and partial isolation from the community, rather than the full care and complete isolation typical of large mental hospitals. Halfway houses vary in size, but most hold ten to twenty patients. A resident counselor may conduct both formal and informal counseling, supervise residents in carrying out a variety of tasks, and help them learn to deal with the practical problems of everyday living.

Crisis Intervention. Psychological emergencies are common. Approximately 5 to 10 percent of all cases seen in emergency departments of hospitals are purely psychiatric, and as many as 50 percent of emergency admissions have at least attendant psychological problems.

George Voiseskos and Frederick Lowy (1980) have identified the ten most common psychiatric emergencies:

- Attempted or threatened suicide.
- Marital or family crises.
- Acute depression.
- Intoxication or delirium.
- Psychotic behavior.
- Acute anxiety or panic.
- Medical emergencies presenting as psychiatric emergencies
- Extreme confusion.
- Aggressive, assaultive behavior.
- Homicidal behavior.

Many CMHCs provide walk-in crisis services to deal with these emergencies. In addition, there are crisis intervention teams, which may include psychologists, psychiatrists, psychiatric nurses, social workers, and volunteers. These teams intervene in any psychiatric emergency, ranging from a potential suicide to a community-wide emergency (Jones et al., 2003).

Individual crises often first find their way to a *crisis hotline*, which is a 24-hour telephone service offering advice and comfort to callers with psychological problems and concerns. Those who answer the phones are trained volunteers, usually under the supervision of a psychologist or psychiatrist. Hotline volunteers try to help rape victims, those with family crises, and others involved in emergency situations by talking with them. As John Eldrid put it, the phone conversation can have the effect of "lowering the caller's emotional temperature" (Eldrid, 1993, p. 107). In addition, most hotlines provide extensive referral services that allow the caller to get professional help when necessary.

Prevention. A final aspect of community psychology is a current movement toward preventing them psychological disorders, rather than curing them (Herman, 1994). Three levels of prevention - primary, secondary, and tertiary - have been identified. In *primary prevention*, psychologists work to eliminate conditions in the home and community that foster emotional disorders and creating conditions that promote positive mental health. *Secondary prevention* focuses on detecting emotional disorders as early as possible and providing prompt treatment (Slaby & Stringham, 1994). *Tertiary prevention* means dealing as rapidly and effectively as possible with individuals identified as having already developed serious emotional problems. The attempt here is to prevent the disorder from becoming chronic. In the long run, the prevention movement may reduce the frequency of at some psychological disorders in the population.

Modern Therapy: What Is It?

In CMHCs, as well as large mental hospitals and private offices, modern therapies are used to treat psychological disorders. *Therapy* is a systematic attempt by a trained professional to eliminate or reduce a patient's symptoms or to improve his psychological or behavioral functioning and sense of well-being. There are two basic, very general approaches to therapy: psychotherapy and biological therapy. *Psychotherapy* refers to the establishment of a helping relationship between a patient (or client) and a trained professional, who applies psychological principles to the treatment of emotional or behavioral problems.[1]

Treating Failures of Evolutionary Adaptation: Therapy

Whether biomedical or psychological, therapy is likely to be most effective when it is based on a deep understanding of both the client's problems and their origins. The treatment can then be better directed toward eliminating the underlying causes of the symptoms and thereby the symptoms themselves.

Studies of a variety of psychological disorders clearly indicate that they are products of both biological and environmental factors, usually working together to produce the observed symptoms (McGuffin et al., 1994). Major depression, for example, is clearly a joint product of hereditary brain mechanisms and a series of environmental events (Chapter 16). The biological factors are based in hereditary predispositions and the environmental factors reflect negative influences of family and culture. Therapy can therefore best be seen as an attempt to deal with problems that have their origins in both nature and nurture. And one current perspective that attempts to understand therapy from this integrative viewpoint is evolutionary psychology.

The emotional problems and disorders that face the therapist can be understood as based on a mismatch between genes and current environments. Hereditary adaptive mechanisms arose in response to the demands of ancient environments as the human species evolved. However, what was adaptive millions of years ago may not be now. The environment - both physical and sociopsychological - has changed over time. Modifications in what is passed on genetically, however, result from, and therefore follow, environmental change. As a consequence, genetic mechanisms may not always be maximally adaptive in the current environment.

Such common human characteristics as jealousy, envy, the need for fair treatment, strong reliance on the family, and the desire for small group membership may no longer always be adaptive (Millon, 2003). In fact, such traits arose in response to environmental demands millions of years ago, when the focus of early humans was primarily on hunting, gathering, and day-to-day survival. Even agriculture had not yet begun, and the rise of civilization, with its complex social institutions, was far in the future. Well, the future has arrived, and such ancient adaptations as jealousy are now often maladaptive. The therapist is thus treating individuals whose evolved adaptive mechanisms - based in specialized structures and processes in the brain - are out of date and have therefore failed.

What does this theory - that abnormal behavior results from failed adaptive mechanisms - tell us about therapy? It suggests that the most effective therapies will be those designed to modify the physiological and psychological mecha-

[1] In general, the person being treated tends to be referred to as a "patient" in pschoanalysis and related approaches and in biological therapies. The term "client" is more often used in connection with behavioral, cognitive, and humanistic approaches.

nisms that are causing the adaptive failure. If evolutionary psychology is correct, these mechanisms are likely to be domain-specific. That is, they are cognitive and emotional units or modules that are designed to deal specifically with such states as anxiety and depression (Chapter 8). An effective biomedical or psychological therapy will therefore be one that focuses specifically on the appropriate module. The task of the therapist - and more generally of clinical psychology and related professions - is thus to determine which modules need to be addressed and how best to address them.

Evolutionary perspectives on therapy are by no means new. Sigmund Freud, whose theory we discuss in Chapter 14 and whose psychoanalytic therapy we will consider shortly, adopted a basically evolutionary viewpoint (Pines, 2002). Behavioral and cognitive therapies can be seen as correcting maladaptive behaviors that are caused by the mismatch between hereditary adaptive mechanisms and current environmental demands (Andersson, 1993). And biomedical therapies, such as drugs, work only when they act on specific aspects of brain function in which evolutionary adaptation is inadequate.

The Mental Health Professions

Mental health care is administered by several groups of professionals (Table 17-1). Three of these groups consist of different kinds of psychologists with doctorates. *Clinical psychologists* work with the full range of mental disorders and do psychological assessment, diagnosis, and therapy. *Counseling psychologists* engage in these same activities but are trained to work primarily with less severely disturbed clients. *School psychologists* are often trained in special programs in colleges of education and focus on the assessment of public school students and on helping those with academic or adjustment problems.

Some physicians also administer treatment to mental patients. A *psychiatrist* completes an M.D. degree then about four years of additional training in a residency program in psychiatry. He can then perform psychotherapy and can also prescribe drugs. A *psychoanalyst* is usually a psychiatrist (but can be a psychologist) who has done postdoctoral training in a psychoanalytic institute and practices a type of therapy derived from Freudian theory. *Psychiatric nurses* are trained specifically to deal with mental patients. *Psychiatric social workers* complete a two-year master of science in social work (M.S.W.) degree. They often go to patients' homes to assess their living situations and may assist them in locating community resources in.

Those mental health professionals who do therapy are faced with over 200 schools of psychotherapy from which to choose. They can be roughly divided into two major categories: insight therapy and action therapy. We will discuss several of the major insight and action approaches.

Keys to Therapy 1

Insight Therapies

In *insight therapy*, the idea is to help the patient become more aware of unconscious motives that are producing abnormal behavior and thereby help her to understand and modify the behavior. The major insight therapies are the psychodynamic and humanistic approaches.

Psychodynamic Approaches

Psychodynamic therapies are those based on Freud's psychoanalytic theory and the theories that derived from it (see Chapter 14). The original technique developed by Freud is called psychoanalysis. More recent techniques are based on ego psychology and object relations theory.

Psychoanalysis: Sigmund Freud. As we discuss in more detail in Chapter 14, Freud's personality theory revolves around unconscious drives. When dangerous unconscious impulses threaten to break through into consciousness, the ego experiences anxiety and uses defense mechanisms, most importantly repression, to keep these impulses out of conscious awareness. The result may be an anxiety disorder, and Freud believed that the appropriate treatment is to help the patient bring unconscious conflicts into awareness and confront them. This is the basis for the original Freudian version of psychoanalysis, sometimes called *orthodox psychoanalysis.* Its basic therapeutic techniques include free association, dream interpretation, and the analysis of transference.

Free association. In *free association* the patient is encouraged to relax and say whatever comes to mind. While he may initially talk about issues that are relatively conscious and thus superficial, continued free association leads him to delve more and more deeply into the unconscious (Nelson et al., 2000). As the patient reveals unconscious thoughts, the analyst interprets the associations, thereby helping him gain insight into his motivations. As Freud suggested, this approach is particularly effective in dealing with anxiety disorders and depression (Rudolfo et al., 1994).

Dream analysis. Threatening, unconscious impulses that we are not aware of during waking hours may appear symbolically in dreams (Leclaire, 2003). Consider this dream reported by a 27-year-old patient - we'll call her Cindy - in response to her psychoanalyst's inquiry:

> Well, yes doctor, I did have an interesting dream night before last. I sometimes dream about royalty. Wonder what that means (laughs)? I dreamed that I was in a coach drawn by large horses. I was with a king, who was wearing a cape and had on an elaborate, jewel-studded crown. The coach stopped outside a big castle, and we got out. For some reason, I had to climb a pole to get into the castle, and then I was in a large, beautiful skating rink. It had fancy, lace curtains on the windows and big posts in the four corners. The ice was perfectly smooth and glistening, but I was all alone. Then the king came in. We both put on ice skates and skated all around the rink together, sort of like when the pairs skate together in the Olympics. I had a really good time. And then I woke up.

Thinkers have recognized the potential importance of dreams and their interpretation for at least 2000 years, but Freud was the first to see the value of the dream as an aspect of psychotherapy. Freud's approach is to ask the patient to remember and report any dreams she has had since the last session. He then engages in *dream analysis*, a way of interpreting each dream to determine its significance for the unconscious functioning of the patient (Loden, 2003). A dream in which you are pursued and beaten by a large policeman, for example, may really be a dream about your childhood fear of your father. Freud interpreted dreams by assuming that the underlying conflict is revealed by the presence of certain common *dream symbols*. Sexual intercourse might be symbolized by such slipping, sliding activities as ice skating or skiing, the penis by such phallic symbols as snakes, candles, and telephone poles, and the vagina by tunnels and pockets. Kings and queens represent fathers and mothers, and houses are symbolic of the human body.

Freud might interpret Cindy's dream about ice skating with a king as arising from an unconscious desire to have sexual intercourse with her father - an incest dream. A man skiing with a queen is having a symbolically similar dream. The pole that Cindy climbed would probably be seen as a phallic symbol, and the skating rink with its lacy curtains and four posts may have represented a bed.

Transference and countertransference. Another method Freud used is the *analysis of transference* (Kulish & Holtzman, 2003). He observed that as analysis progressed his patients typically began to display strong feelings toward him. At times the patient would seem to fall in love with Freud and at other times display intense dislike or even hatred. Freud interpreted these strong feelings as a *transference* or shifting onto him of the patient's childhood emotional reactions to her parents. At times the analyst might be treated as though he were the patient's father, at other times as the mother. The analyst may also develop strong feelings toward the patient, which can again be either positive or negative - a phenomenon called *countertransference* (Chessick, 2003). The analyst carefully interprets both transference and countertransference feelings in an effort to gain a further understanding of the patient's deep unconscious functioning and underlying conflicts (H.F. Smith, 2003).

Putting it together: Psychoanalysis. Traditional psychoanalysis typically extends over a period of many months or even years. Throughout that time, the therapist is charged with creating and maintaining a certain set of conditions within each therapeutic hour. She must at all times be as objective and neutral as possible. She avoids imposing her own moral judgments on the patient's behavior and does not permit her own expectations and needs to affect her interpretations. This creates a psychologically safe situation in which the patient can bring up difficult, unconscious material and report behaviors without fear of retribution.

During its earliest stages, psychoanalysis is typically focused on allowing both patient and therapist to formulate hypotheses about unconscious motives and helping the patient integrate these unconscious materials into conscious awareness. As therapy progresses, there is an increasing focus on helping the patient to integrate her newfound insights into the realities of her current lifestyle and situation.

Consider how our phobic patient, Kenneth, might be treated from a Freudian perspective. The psychoanalyst who treated him concluded that Kenneth's fear of theaters, elevators, and downtown streets served as a defensive device that shifted an underlying conflict over homosexuality off center stage and put a group of expanding fears in its place. What Kenneth really feared was not public places but his own homosexual feelings. His phobias shielded him from this danger. The analyst used Freudian techniques to help Kenneth gain insight into the underlying homosexual conflict and directed him in developing constructive ways of conducting his life.

Modern Psychodynamic Therapy. The practice of psychoanalysis has changed substantially in the nearly sixty years since Freud's death in 1939. Some current analysts still practice strict orthodox psychoanalysis. However, most employ variations of Freud's original approach that are based on theories and therapeutic techniques developed by post-Freudian analysts (Wilson, 2003). Chief among these are ego psychology and, particularly, object relations theory (Kernberg, 1994).

Ego psychology. Many modern psychoanalysts use therapeutic techniques that grow out of *ego psychology* (discussed in Chapter 14). This modification of Freudian theory deemphasizes the role and power of the irrational id in favor of that of the rational ego (Wallerstein, 2002). Though ego psychologists still rely on most of the same basic Freudian therapeutic techniques, they emphasize the constructive aspects of ego functioning, stress the present over the past, and actively attempt to help the patient develop or modify social skills and deal with the world of immediate reality (Opatow, 1993).

Modern ego analysts tend to be more active in directing the analysis, to advise the client quite explicitly on a variety of aspects of his life, and to interpret more immediately and extensively than Freud did (Busch, 1993). Some even treat clients in many fewer sessions than did traditional psychoanalysis. Such brief psychotherapy is becoming increasingly common, as our 21 describes.

Object relations theory. Although ego psychology is practiced by many analysts, the dominant current school of thought is *object relations theory*. In original Freudian theory, an *object* is anything that can satisfy a particular drive. Food, for example, is the object of the hunger drive and water an object of the thirst drive. More importantly, *people* are the objects of such powerful drives as sex and aggression, and it is around this aspect of the Freudian model that object relations theory is built.

The object relations approach developed primarily because analysts realized that the problems most often causing patients to seek therapy are those involving their relationships with other people. These can be lifelong relationships with parents or relatively short current relationships. The therapist assumes there is a strong need for caring, supportive human relationships. In particular, the child forms an attachment to the mother (an object of his need for human contact), and this attachment can be either strong or weak (see Chapter 10). The mother-child bond becomes the basis for interpersonal relationships throughout life. Men and women differ in how they form and maintain these human associations, and these gender differences are taken into account in object relations therapy (Huprich & Greenberg, 2003).

As Otto Kernberg (1994) points out, this newer variant on the psychodynamic theme has caused the psychoanalyst to take a more and more active role in therapy. He first works hard to develop a positive, caring, nurturing relationship with the patient, then uses this new attachment as a basis for actively guiding the therapy. An optimal outcome is one in which the patient's major interpersonal relationships improve and therefore satisfy her needs. She becomes better able to understand her own social needs and to invest psychologically in others - a basic requirement for fulfilling interpersonal bonds.

Some have suggested that the emotional dilemmas often faced by children can be addressed by fictional stories evoke repressed, unconscious conflicts and help the child to resolve those conflicts. One currently popular fictional character, Harry Potter, may fulfill this role. Harry battles the unconscious conflicts surrounding the destruction and loss of a mother and the sense of a war between good and evil within himself (Lake, 2003).

Humanistic Approaches

Humanistic therapies developed in reaction to the inadequacies some psychologists saw in the psychoanalytic approach. Humanistic therapists begin with the premise that each human being is a unique individual with great potential for psychological growth and development. The person has considerable freedom to control her own behavior and the capacity to achieve an accurate self-image, which will help to make her behavior more effective and realistic (Lowenstein, 1993). Two of the major humanistic approaches are client-centered therapy and Gestalt therapy.

Client-Centered Therapy: Carl Rogers. Client-centered therapy was developed by Carl Rogers (1951, 1961; Chapter 14). His basic principle is that the social values (*conditions of worth*) imposed on the individual by society underlie self-actualization, which can therefore interfere with the innately motivated actualization of the total person or organism. The unrealistic, inaccurate self-image that results can become so distorted as to cause emotional and behavioral problems (Bozarth et al., 1991).

To deal with these problems, the client-centered therapist provides a safe therapeutic climate by being completely sincere or genuine and expressing real caring for the client. In addition, he shows accurate empathy, meaning that the therapist learns to understand the innermost feelings of the client by vicariously experiencing what the client is experiencing (Orlov, 1992). Ideally, the client develops trust and is able to express feelings and thoughts more openly, thereby learning to accept experiences that were previously denied or distorted. A person who has long seen herself as compassionate but who is, in fact, unkind and inconsiderate, may come accept her true characteristics. Therapy thus helps the client to move toward a self-concept that more accurately reflects real experience, and the ideal result is greater actualization or psychological growth.

In contrast to the psychodynamic therapist, the client-centered counselor does little to interpret, direct, or advise the client. Rather, the therapist listens and tries to "hear" and accurately reflect and clarify what the client is saying about her inner feelings. Rogers (1951) provides an example of how reflection and clarification are carried out:

> Alice: I was thinking about this business of standards. I somehow developed a sort of knack, I guess, of - well, habit of - trying to make people feel at ease around me, or to make things go along smoothly. . .
>
> Counselor: In other words, what you did was always in the direction of trying to keep things smooth and to make other people feel better and to smooth the situation.

Alice: Yes. I think that's what it was. Now the reason why I did it probably was - I mean, not that I was a good little Samaritan going around making other people happy, but that was probably the role that felt easiest for me to play. I'd been doing it around home so much. I just didn't stand up for my own convictions, until I don't know whether I have any convictions to stand up for.

Counselor: You feel that for a long time you've been playing the role of kind of smoothing out the frictions or differences or whatnot . . .

Alice: M-hm.

Counselor: Rather than having any opinion or reaction of your own to the situation. Is that it?

Alice: That's it. Or that I haven't been really honestly being myself, or actually knowing what my real self is, and that I've been just playing a sort of false role. Whatever role no one else was playing, and that needed to be played at the time, I'd try to fill it in. (pp. 152-153).

How would the client-centered therapist deal with Kenneth? She would begin by establishing a caring, accepting atmosphere in which he could express his feelings openly without fear of being criticized. She would listen carefully and would periodically reflect and clarify his feelings. As Kenneth developed increasing trust, he would be able to express thoughts and emotions he had previously denied or distorted. As a result, the accuracy of his self-concept would increase and he would gradually gain insight into his fears. If concerns about homosexuality were indeed an underlying problem, Kenneth might be able to express these concerns and to accept his homosexual tendencies as part of his self-concept.

Gestalt Therapy: Fritz Perls. Gestalt therapy was developed by Frederick (Fritz) Perls (1967, 1969), who was trained in both psychoanalysis and Gestalt psychology. The latter emphasizes that we act not on the basis of external reality but rather in accord with our *perceptions* of that reality. We actively organize the stimuli that make up the world into meaningful patterns or wholes (gestalts) that are based on our expectations and needs.[2] These gestalts, and perceptions more generally, are typically inaccurate even in normal people because we see the world as society teaches us to see it (Becker, 1993).

When perceptions become abnormally inaccurate, they can lead to psychopathology. A patient might, for example, firmly believe that co-workers have conspired to block his promotion when the reality is that they have not. This paranoid delusion can create or contribute to a pattern of abnormal behavior (Chapter 16). Accordingly, the emphasis in Gestalt therapy is on creating a whole person by increasing perceptual accuracy and unifying mind and body. Ideally, the patient will come to realize that his paranoid delusion is exactly that, and the accuracy of his perceptions will more generally improve. The importance of immediate, individual experience is stressed, and the therapist works hard to keep the client focused on current experience (Polster & Polster, 1993).

Keys to Therapy 2

Behavioral and Cognitive-Behavioral Therapies

Action therapies, in contrast to insight approaches, focus directly on the client's problem behaviors - the symptoms - and try to remove them; they largely ignore underlying motives. The two related schools of therapy that best fit this action category are the behavioral and cognitive-behavioral approaches, although the latter often also involves insight. Let's take a look at each in turn, then apply them to the interesting disorder called agoraphobia. Finally, we will discuss the ongoing conflict between psychoanalysts and behavior therapists.

Behavior Therapies

Behavior therapy differs from psychodynamic and humanistic therapies in both conceptual underpinnings and actual treatment approaches. All behavior therapies are based on the fundamental principle that behavior, both normal and abnormal, is *learned*. As a result, these therapies rely on learning principles and processes to change behavior. Insight is not seen as an important component of successful treatment (Overholser, 1995).

The primary interest of the therapist is the problem behavior itself. If the client has a phobic fear of water, the therapist will focus on the water avoidance behavior that this fear engenders. The anxiety the client experiences when faced with water is an *emotional* reaction, while thoughts about water constitute the *cognitive* component. The behav-

---

[2] See Chapter 4 for a more general discussion of Gestal view.

ior therapist considers these internal components to be covert responses and as such amenable to treatment with behavioral techniques based on learning principles. Overall, the water phobic's therapist would be dealing with three responses: physical behavior (avoidance), emotion (anxiety), and cognition (thoughts).

The goals and techniques of behavior therapy are relatively simple and straightforward. The behavior therapist carefully and clearly defines the problem behavior in question, identifies the stimuli that elicit the behavior, and determines how the behavior is being reinforced. He then uses learning techniques to reduce or eliminate the undesired behavior and possibly to develop an alternative behavior to replace it. He asks questions to discover the exact nature of the behavior, establishes goals for the client, and gives specific instructions for attempting to reach those goals.

Behavioral therapies have been applied to a variety of disorders and problems. In addition to obsessive-compulsive and other anxiety disorders, behavior therapists have treated adolescent obesity (Berkowitz et al., 2003; Nakatani et al., 2003), schizophrenia, interpersonal dependency, and obesity in women with negative body images, and chronic insomnia (Perlis et al., 2003). Moderate depression can also be treated quite successfully with some behavioral therapies (Thase et al., 1994).

Of the various techniques of behavior therapy, some are based primarily on classical (respondent) conditioning principles, some on operant conditioning principles, and still others on cognitive theory.

Classical Conditioning Approaches. Undesirable responses are sometimes acquired through classical conditioning and can therefore be removed with classical conditioning techniques. If anxiety, for example, has become a conditioned response to a previously neutral stimulus, behavioral techniques can either eliminate the anxiety response. Major techniques include systematic desensitization and aversion therapy.

Systematic desensitization. The most widely used form of respondent conditioning is systematic desensitization. Originally developed by Joseph Wolpe (1958), this procedure is based on the assumption that anxiety can be reduced by pairing the anxiety-provoking stimulus with a response like relaxation that is incompatible with anxiety. The therapist first trains the client in systematic muscle relaxation, typically using progressive relaxation techniques (see Chapter 15). She then constructs a hierarchy of the client's fears or anxieties (Figure 17-3). For one client with a strong fear of dying, for example, the most fearful stimulus was a dead person in a coffin, the second was being present at a burial, and the least fearful were reading an obituary notice and seeing an ambulance (Wolpe and Wolpe, 1981).

The client was asked to imagine himself in the presence of least fearful stimulus (seeing an ambulance), then apply the progressive relaxation technique. He moved up the hierarchy and again practiced relaxing at each step and was eventually able to think of the most fearful stimulus (a dead person) and relax. The phobia had been successfully treated.

Effective use of systematic desensitization has been reported for a variety of problems, including various phobias, aggressive behavior, rejection, response to authority figures, and recurrent nightmares (Ventis et al., 2001). Test anxiety in school children has also been treated (Strumpt & Fodor, 1993), as has post-traumatic stress disorder or PTSD in war veterans (Thomas & Gafner, 1993).

Ouch! Aversion therapy. In *aversion therapy* a maladaptive response is followed by some aversive stimulus, such as electric shock or a drug that produces nausea. The idea is to associate the undesired response with the negative experience and thus eliminate it. Alcoholics, for example, are often given the drug Antabuse (disulfiram), which causes them to become violently ill if they consume alcohol (Goicolea et al., 1989).

While such therapy may appear to be unkind, it is sometimes successful in cases where other techniques have failed, and the ultimate result is often positive. In one study three groups of alcoholics were treated with psychotherapy. One group received no additional therapy, one received electric shock, and one received ipecac, which causes vomiting. When all participants were followed up 17 months after the termination of therapy, it turned out that the aversion techniques more than doubled the probability that a patient would remain abstinent (Goicolea et al., 1989).

Operant Conditioning Techniques. Such undesirable behaviors as excessive aggression can be seen as arising from the long-term application of reinforcement contingencies (Skinner, 1988). In effect, a child becomes hyperaggressive because he is rewarded for his aggressive behaviors. Operant therapies are used to change the contingencies so that the undesirable behavior is no longer reinforced (Nicholas et al., 1994). Skinnerian techniques include time-out, the token economy, and stimulus control.

Time out. One widely used technique based on operant conditioning principles is referred to as *time out from positive reinforcement.* The time out approach is often used with children. If a child has a temper tantrum in a room where there are toys, a TV set, or other reinforcers, she is immediately removed from the room and placed in a room containing no reinforcers. Placement in this room constitutes time out from the positive reinforcement that is generally available to the child. In therapy, the time out technique is used dispassionately and systematically. No anger or verbal retribution is displayed by the therapist, since such attention might be positively reinforcing.

Token economies. A *token economy* is a therapeutic setting in which objects representing positive reinforcement are given to patients whenever they display a desired behavior. In this approach, hospitalized psychiatric patients are given tokens, such as poker chips, as reinforcements for performing desired behaviors (Kahng et al., 2003). They can

later exchange the tokens for any of a variety of rewards, such as candy, TV time, or going to the movies. The behaviors to be reinforced are usually defined by the hospital staff and may include such things as going to meals on time, smiling when meeting people in the hall, or making one's bed. The effectiveness of token economies was demonstrated by Ayllon and Azrin (1965) in a classic study in which hospitalized patients received tokens for doing simple tasks for 45 days (Figure 17-4). Other studies have confirmed their results in hospitals settings (Comaty et al., 2001), but they typically do not generalize well to the outside world (Corrigan, 1991). When the patient leaves the hospital, he no longer receives tokens, and the reinforcement contingencies of the real world may be substantially more complex than those of the hospital environment. As a result, the behavioral improvements achieved in the token economy may disappear (Glynn, 1990).

Stimulus control. **In the operant *stimulus control* approach, clients are taught to use external stimuli to restrict their behavior. Many undesirable behaviors are controlled by stimuli in the environment. Sitting down at the dinner table, opening the refrigerator, and watching television, for instance, may all provide stimuli that tend to produce eating behavior. To treat an overweight person, the therapist might instruct the client to eat only when seated at the dinner table and only at predesignated times. In this way, other stimuli for eating are gradually eliminated, and eating behavior is limited to the stimulus control of the dinner table.**

Cognitive and Cognitive-Behavioral Therapies

The "strict" behaviorist focuses primarily on overtly observable behaviors; the *cognitive behaviorist* focuses primarily on thought processes or cognitions. The assumption underlying cognitive behaviorism is that cognitions are the most important causes of behavior. Changes in behavior should therefore follow from changes in underlying cognitions. Although there is an action orientation in most cognitive therapies, they also, unlike the purely behavioral approaches, involve some insights (Dalton & Coyne, 2003). A variety of cognitive-behavioral techniques have been developed. They include Beck's cognitive therapy, Ellis' rational emotive therapy, and Bandura's modeling approach.

Cognitive Therapy: Aaron Beck. **Depression is a common disorder that can be treated with electroconvulsive shock therapy, drugs, and a variety of forms of psychotherapy. Aaron Beck developed the most influential cognitive theory of depression and a corresponding therapy to treat it (Beck, 1976, 1993; Alford & Beck, 1994). In *cognitive therapy*, treatment focuses on modifying perceptual and thought processes that are thought to be causing the depression. In treating depressed clients, Beck assumes that the depression is a result of a series of cognitions involving self-devaluation, a generally negative view of life, and pessimism about the future. He uses *cognitive restructuring* - changing negative thought patterns to positive ones - to alleviate the depression. The idea is to modify cognitive skills and thought patterns, thereby changing the way the individual perceives, responds to, and interacts with the external world (Dugas et al., 2003).**

One college student - we'll call her Fran - related to her therapist an instance in which she became severely depressed after her mother mildly criticized her for not adequately cleaning the living room. During the minutes and hours following the criticism, she went through a series of increasingly negative thoughts:

- **"There, I've done it again, left the room a mess."**
- **"Fact is, I've left the whole house a mess. Just can't seem to get it right."**
- **"No wonder mom thinks I'm such an idiot. She's right."**
- **"Fact is, dad and sis think the same thing. My so-called friends too. No wonder I can't ever have a boyfriend for more than five minutes. They see it right away - how stupid and klutzy I am."**
- **"And college. What a joke. I'll never get through this semester, let alone two more years. Why did I ever come to college?"**
- **(crying) "When I think about it, my life really sucks - big time. I'm just a total failure."**

Notice how a minor negative event has been blown out of proportion. A minor criticism has led to the Fran's cognition that she is a total failure. By the time Fran has been through her series of increasingly devastating self-criticisms, she is very depressed. By changing her cognitions, Fran may be able to literally think herself out of depression or avoid its onset. She will be taught to stop herself immediately before she blows things out of proportion and to think in more positive terms.

Beck's cognitive therapy has been successfully used for many years to treat depression, generalized anxiety disorders, phobias, delusional disorders, and even low back pain (Benazon et al., 2003; Haslam & Beck, 1993; Reid et al., 2003).

Rational-Emotive Therapy: Albert Ellis. Rational-emotive therapy (RET)**, developed by Albert Ellis (1962), also attempts to restructure cognitions. In particular, Ellis points out to the client that his fears or other problems are often based on irrational beliefs. Examples of such beliefs abound:**

- **"There is only one correct solution to this problem, and if I can't figure it out, the result will be disaster."**

- "To be a good person, I must be very good at everything I do."
- "People will never like me if I don't do everything just right."
- "My father (or mother) was just about perfect. I can never come up to his (or her) standards."
- "If I don't do this exactly right, I'm a worthless person."

In treating a depressed client who sees herself as a failure, Ellis will bluntly point out the irrational belief that you must be fully successful and competent in all areas in order to be a "good person." He will use a variety of techniques, including positive reinforcement, modeling, and direct teaching, to move the client toward more realistic cognitions. Ideally, she will undergo a cognitive restructuring in which she becomes able to view the world more rationally and thereby eliminate the irrational basis for her problems.

Recent work has focused on applying RET to psychophysiologic disorders, where it has proven successful in reducing the health problems they involve (Abrams & Ellis, 1994; Ziegler & Leslie, 2003). More generally, a meta-analysis of 28 studies of RET showed that it is significantly better than placebo treatments and equivalent in effectiveness to systematic desensitization and other standard approaches (Engels et al., 1993).

Modeling: Albert Bandura. According to social learning theorists, children learn much of their social behavior through *modeling*, which basically involves observing and imitating the behaviors of others. Albert Bandura and his colleagues have shown that it is often possible to treat abnormal behavior by modeling the correct behavior for the individual, then having him attempt to imitate the model (Rosenthal and Bandura, 1978). A person with a snake phobia, for example, may be shown a film or live demonstration of someone confidently approaching and calmly handling a live snake. In a series of gradual steps, the client may learn to relax as she comes closer and closer to a snake and can eventually pick it up and handle it without fear.

Modeling has also been used with other forms of anxiety. In one study a group of high school girls with high levels of test anxiety were treated. Prior to therapy, they became extremely anxious when they even thought about exam situations, and some virtually panicked when faced with an actual test. Modeling techniques provided the girls with demonstrations of how a model could prepare for and take tests without fear and with positive outcomes. Most exhibited significant reductions in test anxiety after treatment (Sud, 1993).

Other uses of modeling techniques include the treatment of aggressive behavior, submissiveness, lack of social skills, risky sexual behavior, and autism in children (LeBlanc et al., 2003; van Empelen, et al., 2003). Aggressive behavior is a major problem in our society, and much of it is seen in adolescent and young adult males. In one study, the investigators treated a group of hyperaggressive young, delinquent males. Therapists modeled the successful use of nonaggressive behaviors in situations where aggressive behavior could have been an alternative. The delinquents showed significant reductions in their aggressive behaviors (Vidyasagar & Mishra, 1993).

In *assertiveness training*, individuals who are overly submissive in social situations are taught through modeling how to be more assertive. Models demonstrate, for example, how to appropriately but assertively send back poorly prepared food and how to get your money back when the expensive item you bought yesterday goes on sale tomorrow. A final modeling technique is *social skills training*. Perhaps you know someone who has no friends or someone who never dates because he doesn't know how to ask a woman out. Both individuals might profit from social skills training, in which models demonstrate the behaviors needed to develop friendships or to date. Similar techniques are used to teach social skills to psychiatric patients (Wong et al., 1993).

Cognitive and Behavioral Techniques In Action: Agoraphobia

Agoraphobia is a disorder in which the person fears being alone or being in public settings without support (Goldberg, 1993). Using systematic desensitization, the agoraphobic client would first be taught relaxation techniques. She would then construct a hierarchy of increasingly fearful situations, vicariously experience each situations in sequence, and attempt to relax while envisioning each. In aversion therapy, she might receive mild electric shocks for turning away from a shopping mall or for expressing high anxiety as she pictures herself at a busy airport.

An operant token economy approach might give the client redeemable poker chips every time she ventured into open spaces, and a stimulus control procedure might teach her to focus on the area immediately around her. In modeling, we might show her a videotape of someone enjoying a trip to a mall and being rewarded for going. Beck or Ellis would restructure the negative cognitions that support the phobia. They would determine the thoughts that lead to anxiety, then teach her to avoid those thoughts and think instead along more positive lines. Behavioral treatment of agoraphobia is typically about 60 to 70 percent effective in producing clinically significant improvements immediately after treatment and at a six-month follow-up (Jansen and Oat, 1982).

Finally, Kenneth's phobia would be seen by behavior therapists as involving an acquired set of symptomatic behaviors. The focus of therapy would be on helping him overcome his fears of specific situations, such as being in a theater or a crowded elevator. The strict behaviorist would have no interest at all in the possibility of underlying homosexual conflicts or other unconscious motivations for behavior. In systematic desensitization, Kenneth would learn to relax as he imagines the phobic situations. Other therapists might assess Kenneth's thoughts about being in a theater or on a crowded street, then attempt to restructure those thoughts so that they are more positive and realistic.

Table 17-2 provides a summary comparison of the various schools of therapy.

Keys to Therapy 3

Group and Family Therapies

Thus far we have described psychotherapy in terms of the individual client. In traditional approaches, the therapist sits down with a client and conducts a 50-minute session. However, recent decades have seen increased emphasis on approaches in which several clients interact with each other as well as the therapist. Two types of therapy involving multiple clients are group therapy and family therapy.

Group Therapy

Group psychotherapy involves a systematic, therapeutic interaction among several people with a trained therapist as the group leader. A typical group contains seven to ten clients, who usually do not know each other, and will meet at least once a week. Interaction in the group is primarily verbal, although the therapist does take note of such nonverbal forms of communication as posture, gestures, facial expressions, and seating arrangements. The therapist encourages clients to discuss their problems openly and sincerely. Planned, professional group therapy must be carefully distinguished from the many kinds of "human relations" groups run by people not trained in psychotherapy.

Types of Therapy. There are many types of group therapy. In psychoanalytic group therapy, the therapist may use free association, dream analysis, transference, and other such techniques in the group setting. In *encounter groups*, the focus is on intensive group experiences aimed at increasing self-awareness, improving interpersonal interactions, and realizing the personal potentials of group members for change. *Behavioral groups* target specific behaviors and use social and other reinforcements to change those behaviors (Fals-Stewart & Lucente, 1994). *Cognitive-behavioral groups* focus on having group members help each other restructure negative cognitions (Blouin et al., 1994).

A quite different approach to group therapy is used in some mental hospitals. There, patients participate in a "therapeutic social club" in which they learn social competence through group interaction. The therapist plays a largely passive role, and the patients help each other to develop social skills. Another variation is the marathon group, in which sessions continue over a relatively long time, ranging from 24 hours to several days. Such an approach has been used in drug rehabilitation programs. It helps the therapist get to know the clients rapidly and also helps break down defenses so clients can begin to develop trust.

Progress in Group Therapy. Group therapy began in Boston in 1905 when a physician formed groups of tuberculosis patients who were having difficulty adjusting to their disorder. However, it was not until World War II that group approaches were used on a large scale, mainly because military hospitals were understaffed and there were numerous psychiatric casualties (Scheidlinger, 1994). This wartime use demonstrated the potential value of the therapy, and its use grew gradually until the 1960s. At that time, many community mental health centers were opened, and group therapy experienced another significant growth spurt. Group therapy conducted by professionals is now universally accepted as a major and important therapeutic modality.

More recent times have seen an extension of the group therapy concept to the creation of *self-help groups*. Such groups are now available in virtually every community, and you can find a self-help group dealing with nearly any issue you can imagine, from marital problems and overeating to the compulsive use of credit cards and social shyness. Despite the lack of evidence that self-help groups are effective (Caserta & Lund, 1993), local chapters now number in the hundreds of thousands; there are probably over 15 million participants in the U.S. at any given time.

Since its initial use with TB patients, group therapy has found a wide variety of applications (Jennings & Sawyer, 2003). It is used with alcoholic and other substance abuse patients, who share their experiences and are guided by the therapist toward an understanding of why they drink and how essential it is that they stop drinking. Children of alcoholics have been treated with object relations group therapy, in which the focus is on psychodynamic aspects of interpersonal relationships (Piper et al., 2003). Behavioral group therapy has been successfully applied to obsessive-compulsive disorder and cognitive-behavioral therapy to bulimic patients and male batterers (Diefenbeck, 2003). Group therapy has also proven helpful for Vietnam veterans with severe psychological problems and for sexually abused teenage girls (Ovaert et al., 2003).

Our old friend Kenneth could be treated in a group therapy setting with other phobics. He would learn from the group experience that he is not unique and that others are just as terrified as he is. He would most likely be confronted by other group members and perhaps by the group leader with the need to explore the nature of his fear and its basis, and he may come out of the therapy better able to accept the reality of his phobia and with considerably reduced anxiety.

Family Therapy

For many years, therapists have recognized that some clients who demonstrate significant gains in the context of individual psychotherapy later lose what they have gained because they must return to a seriously disturbed family setting (Newark & Beels, 1994). Similarly, many "problem children" who are brought in by their parents for therapy appear to reflect a broader pathology that spans the entire family. In fact, the core of the problem is often not the child but the family as a whole. *Family therapy* deals with problems involving family structure and family interaction patterns.

There are many schools of thought as to how family therapy should be carried out. Virginia Satir (1967), one of the foremost innovators in family therapy, developed an approach called *conjoint family therapy*, which emphasizes improving interactions, communications, and relationships among family members. The intent is to provide each member with a family system that better meets needs. An alternative model is Salvador Minuchin's (1974) *structured family therapy*. It is based on *systems theory* - an approach that emphasizes the influence of the larger context, or system, on the individual and his reciprocal influence on that context. Systems include the family and society as a whole. Minuchin hypothesizes that the family system has more influence on any given member than does his own personality. Because the family system therefore contributes to the development of psychopathology, it follows that therapy aimed at changing the family environment should be effective in dealing with that pathology. A major goal of structured family therapy is to modify the organization of the family so that interactions become positive and supportive.

Social Change and Family Therapy. Since the development of these early models, family therapy has evolved to reflect changes in society (Bayer, 1995). Health care reform has necessitated changes in the duration of therapy and the settings in which it is done. Family values have changed, calling for corresponding modifications in how therapy is conducted. Non-traditional family structures have become far more common, forcing family therapists to deal with the special problems that such newer configurations bring with them. Included are the single-parent family, the step family, and the extended family, in which grandparents are living with the core family or are routinely involved in child care (Sprenkle & Bischof, 1994). And family therapy has gradually become more sensitive to differences in cultural values and their implications for both the functioning of the family and the conduct of therapy.

Examples of family therapy are its use to increase marital intimacy and to treat adolescent anorexics. One study involved 22 anorexic girls, ages 12-19. Each was randomly assigned to receive either individual therapy or family therapy for 16 months. The two treatments were equally effective in modifying attitudes toward eating and self-perceptions of body shape. However, actual increases in body mass index (a measure of body size) were significantly greater following family therapy (Robin et al., 1994). Family therapy has also been used in patients with chronic depression, in child custody disputes, and in treating the caregivers of Alzheimer's Disease patients (Eisdorfer et al., 2003; Law et al., 2003; Keitner et al., 2003; Lebow, 2003). Evidence for the effectiveness of this therapeutic approach is growing, but much more research is needed (Sprenkle, 2003).

Keys to Therapy 4

Issues in Psychotherapy: Effectiveness, Diversity, Ethics, and Legalities

Every psychotherapist is faced with several issues that go beyond the immediate conduct of therapy with any given patient. One concern is with the effectiveness of the therapy. Does therapy work and are some therapies better than others? The remaining concerns are ethical and legal in nature. What ethical standards are important when performing therapy, and what are the legal requirements imposed on therapists by law?

The Effectiveness of Psychotherapy

Psychoanalysts argue that behavioral treatment is ineffective in the long run because it deals with superficial symptoms and does not treat underlying causes. Aspirin may stop a headache but will not cure an underlying brain tumor. Similarly, the behaviorist's superficial treatment of phobic symptoms like avoidance behavior will result in the phobia returning or being replaced by other symptoms because the underlying, unconscious conflict has not been resolved. [RTF bookmark start: }1[RTF bookmark end: }1Behaviorists, on the other hand, argue that psychoanalysis takes much longer to conduct and that its clinical effectiveness has never been well established. Who is right?

Determining the effectiveness of psychotherapy has proven to be a difficult task (Lutz, 2003). For one thing, the outcome of therapy is not easy to measure. We can ask the therapist to tell us whether there has been improvement, but he is biased because he wants to be successful. We can ask the client if she has been helped, but again there is bias. She may want to please the therapist, think she has spent her money wisely, or convince us that she is capable of improvement. In fact, this bias is so common that we have named it the *hello-goodbye effect* because clients tend to come into therapy saying they are feeling miserable (the "hello") and leave saying they feel better (the "goodbye"). As a result of these biases, we often try to obtain outcome information from the therapist, the client, and outsiders, such as family members, friends, or a psychologist who is not treating the client. Such standardized tests as the MMPI, the NEO-PI, the Beck Depression Inventory, or the Rorschach (see Chapter 14) are also used, with the client completing the tests before and after therapy.

A second problem in determining the effectiveness of therapy is that clients often improve over time even if they receive no therapy at all. This phenomenon is called *spontaneous remission*, and it appears to occur in as much as 30-60% of all patients (Eysenck, 1994). In conducting a therapy outcome study, we must thus ensure that any improvement in the patient is, in fact, a result of therapy, and not of spontaneous remission. We solve this problem by conducting controlled studies in which we randomly assign each patient to an experimental group that receives therapy or a control group that does not. Outcome measures are collected on both groups before and after therapy, with the expectation that the therapy group will improve more on these measures than the controls. In some studies a second control group receives a treatment that may appear to be therapy but is not (see the Probe).

A final problem is that well-designed studies may require the use of control groups of patients who are not treated for some period of time or who receive some alternative treatment. Is there is reason to believe that the patient would be harmed by such control procedures, the study would be unethical. On the other hand, without controls, there is no way to be certain that the therapy is effective (Arean & Alvidrez, 2003).

Although researchers have attempted to conduct careful studies, many have been flawed (Bechgaard, 2003). The therapist may be inexperienced, definitions of what is meant by "therapeutic improvement" vary from one study to another, therapy may not be conducted for a long enough time, control groups may be lacking or inadequate, and the client sample may be limited. Nevertheless, some excellent studies that eliminate all or most of these problems have been done.

The Sloane and NIMH Studies. One of the best therapy outcome studies was conducted in Philadelphia by R.B. Sloane and his colleagues (1975). They randomly assigned 94 outpatients, most with anxiety disorders, to receive four months of either behavioral therapy, psychoanalytic therapy, or no therapy (the control group). They matched the groups on such factors as sex and seriousness of symptoms, and the therapists were all highly trained and experienced. Measures of therapeutic outcome included standardized psychological tests as well as ratings by the clients themselves, their relatives and friends, and an independent interviewer who did not know what group the patient was in. It was found that 80 percent of clients in both therapy groups improved, while only 48 percent of those in the control group got any better. A nearly identical study a few years later yielded similar results (Cross, et al., 1982).

More recent studies have also supported the effectiveness of psychotherapy. A large-scale outcome study was a National Institutes of Mental Health (NIMH) investigation conducted by Irene Elkin and her colleagues (Elkin et al., 1989). They studied the treatment of depression by cognitive, interpersonal (focused on improving interpersonal relationships and emotional functioning), and drug (imiprimine, a common antidepressant) therapies. They also included a placebo condition. Conducted in Norman, Oklahoma, Washington, D.C., and Pittsburgh, the study involved 239 depressed clients and 28 experienced therapists. After 16 weeks, over 50% of treated patients and only 29% of controls showed significant improvement (Figure 17-5). A somewhat smaller study of 117 depressed patients treated with cognitive-behavioral or psychodynamic therapy also showed significant improvement (Shapiro et al., 1994). Moreover, there is a *dose-response* relationship: Improvement increases with the number of therapy sessions (Figure 17-6). Another study showed that therapy performed by a trained psychotherapist is more effective than the treatments typically provided by primary care physicians, which involve primarily drugs (Schulberg et al., 2002).

Meta-Analytic Studies. Meta-analysis, a statistical method that permits a reviewer to combine the results of many separate studies (Chapter 2), has been used to evaluate psychotherapy. By the late 1970s, the Sloane study had been joined by many other investigations, and Mary Lee Smith and her colleagues were able to locate 475 therapy outcome studies (Smith et al., 1980). Using meta-analysis, they found that 80% of treated patients showed greater improvement than patients in control groups receiving no therapy (Figure 17-7). Since 50% of untreated people would be more improved than the average untreated person (and 50% less improved), this finding is not quite as dramatic as it might at first appear.[3] However, it still shows that therapy is clearly better than no therapy.

Since the Smith study, there have been a number of other meta-analyses of therapy outcome. Most of the patients in these summary studies have been diagnosed with either anxiety disorders or depression, and the treatments have included primarily psychodynamic, cognitive-behavioral, and drug therapies. All have yielded essentially the same results as the Smith study: Therapy is significantly and consistently better than no therapy (Nordhus & Pallesen, 2003; Engels et al., 1993; Scogin & McElreath, 1994). Recent meta-analyses show that cognitive-behavioral and psychodynamic therapies are also reasonably effective in treating personality disorders, which are notoriously difficult to treat (Leichsenring & Leibing, 2003).

It is important to note that most of these studies have not included schizophrenic or other psychotic patients.

---

[3] See the discussion of the normal distribution in the Appendix. Since the mean and median of the distribution are the same, the score of the average person (i.e., the average or mean score) is right at the middle of the distribution, with 50% below it (less improved) and 50% above (more improved).

Early in the twentieth century, Sigmund Freud told psychoanalysts that they should never treat psychotic patients, and he may well have been right. When psychotic groups have been studied, it is typically found that psychotherapy is far less effective than it is with anxiety disorders and depression. Why? Because these are heavily biological disorders, with strong genetic contributions, which cannot be correct with "talking therapies," though such treatments may be somewhat useful as an adjunct to drug therapies (Rector & Beck, 2002).

***Which Therapy Is Best?* If a surgeon is treating breast cancer, should she perform a radical mastectomy (removing the entire breast) or a lumpectomy (removing just a small affected area)? Is it better to treat prostate cancer with surgery or drugs? These questions have led to numerous medical studies, and the availability of multiple forms of psychotherapy have similarly necessitated psychological studies of their relative effectiveness.**

Smith and her colleagues found no differences in overall effectiveness among several major types of psychotherapy, and others have confirmed this finding (Rachman & Wilson, 1980; Shapiro et al., 1994; Engels et al., 1993; Manning et al., 1992; Crits-Christoph, 1992). However, an important note of caution here is that the finding applies only to *major* forms of therapy, meaning those that have been developed and tested scientifically and are being administered by fully qualified professionals. Not all therapies or therapists meet these criteria. It is quite easy to find people who call themselves "therapists" but who have no formal, professional qualifications, and the "therapies" they offer can actually do more harm than good. It is always therefore important to ensure that a therapist has the appropriate professional credentials.

The fact that there is no *overall* difference in effectiveness among the major therapies does not mean that all work equally well for all problems. Social behavior problems were treated best in the Smith meta-analysis with cognitive-behavioral approaches, achievement problems with psychodynamic, anxiety problems with cognitive or cognitive-behavioral, and self-esteem problems with humanistic therapies. More work along these lines is needed before we can be sure that a specific approach is best for a certain problem, but other studies do support some of the differences reported by the Smith group. That is one reason why more psychologists practice *eclectic* therapy - the use two or more types of therapy - than practice within any one school of thought (Figure 17-8).

***Common Denominators.* The fact that the major therapies are equally effective overall may suggest that they have certain common ingredients, as Hans Strupp (1986), Marvin Goldfried (Goldfried & Padawer, 1982), and Jerome Frank (1982) have pointed out. Their analyses suggest that three commonalities or *nonspecific factors* are important to positive therapy outcome:**

- **A trusting, caring, supportive relationship. A good therapist, no matter what his school of thought, is caring, reassuring, and trustworthy. He is empathic and offers a safe, warm, respectful interpersonal relationship. One study showed, for example, that greater improvement occurred in patients who believed that their therapists understood them (Lafferty et al., 1989).**

- **Hope for the demoralized. Alexander Pope said that "Hope springs eternal...," but he was apparently not dealing with depressed or highly anxious patients. The therapist <u>is</u> dealing with such patients, and she offers hope to a client who had perhaps virtually lost hope. Just because the client is in therapy - and even before the therapist does anything - he may improve. We call this the *placebo effect*, and it is discussed more fully in the Probe. In drug studies, a placebo is a pill that contains an inert substance. Many patients report improvements when given placebos. Why? Because they *think* the pill contains an actual drug and should work. Hope can be a psychological placebo: The patient feels better because he believes the treatment should make him feel better.**

- **Insight. Therapy offers the patient insight into her problems. Through the therapeutic process, she comes to a better understanding of what is causing her to feel bad or behave inappropriately. Her often disturbing symptoms become more manageable because she now has some explanation for them. Whether the causal explanation is in terms of childhood experiences and repressed, unconscious desires (psychoanalysis), improved accuracy of the self-concept (humanistic), prior reinforcement (behavioral) or irrational beliefs (cognitive-behavioral), it is an explanation. It increases understanding and gives the patient some sense of control over her problems.**

***What Conclusions Can We Reach?* We can reasonably arrive at several important conclusions concerning the outcome of psychotherapy:**

- **Psychotherapy is effective for a variety of problems, including the anxiety disorders and depression. It is much less effective for schizophrenia and other psychotic disorders.**

- **The major forms of therapy are equally effective overall.**

- **There may be differences among therapies in the disorders for which they are most effective.**

- **There may be nonspecific factors that cut across schools of thought and provide a positive, therapeutic effect.**

- **Therapy is likely to be more effective when it is sensitive to the cultural background of the patient.**

Cultural Considerations in Psychotherapy

A white psychotherapist applying a standard therapeutic approach may not be as effective with a black client as with a white one, and a black therapist may not be as effective with white as black clients. Cultural diversity has increased greatly in the United States in recent decades, and psychotherapists have become much more sensitive to the issues it raises. Suppose you were to seek therapy for severe anxiety or depression in a foreign country. You locate an experienced, reputable therapist. At the first session, this therapist, dressed in a long, heavy robe and wearing an elaborate headpiece, sits cross-legged opposite you on the floor. She lights pungent incense, lays her hands on yours, throws her head back, and chants for some time before falling into an apparent trance. She ends the session by giving you a foul-smelling potion to drink each day and instructing you to return at the next crescent moon. How would you feel about this therapy? Do you think it would help you?

Although this is perhaps an extreme example, many Hispanics, Asians, African-Americans, and others have similar questions about traditional therapeutic approaches administered by majority white therapists (Lloyd & Bhugra, 1993). These approaches are based largely on white cultural values and socialization processes. For example, mainstream, middle-class American culture places heavy emphasis on individual competence, personal responsibility, and independence. David Sue (1992) points out that by contrast Asian cultures have collectivist values: children are raised to subordinate their own needs to those of others. They seek and expect direction from those in authority. This means that many Asians will have difficulty with client-centered therapy, which gives the client very little direction and expects him to accept considerable responsibility for his own treatment. In fact, Sue (1992) found that nearly two-thirds of foreign-born Asians preferred not to enter into nondirective therapies like the client-centered approach.

There are many other examples of cultural sensitivities that are important in psychotherapy and of the negative impact that the uninformed therapist can have. African-Americans and others may resent unintentional racist comments by white therapists, and Hispanics may have difficulty because their parents taught them very different values from those of the therapist (Zayas & Solari, 1994). Similarly, individuals and families transplanted from other cultures may be faced in therapy with competing cultural systems (Guernina, 1993), and the racial dynamics that take place in therapy may interfere with the development of good therapeutic relationships (Stevenson & Renard, 1993). It is for all these reasons that doctoral training programs across the United States are working hard to recruit and to educate minority psychologists and to include cultural sensitivity training in their programs (Pederson, 1994).

Ethical and Legal Issues in Treatment

Society is quite rightly concerned with the practices of psychologists, psychiatrists, and others in treating individuals with psychological disorders. As a result of this concern, the American Psychological Association has developed ethical guidelines for psychologists, and the courts and state legislatures have formulated legal standards that guide commitment and treatment.

Ethical Standards For Psychologists. The concern of psychology as a profession with the ethics of its practices is reflected in *The Ethical Standards of Psychologists*, developed and published by the American Psychological Association and revised periodically. The ethical guidelines make four major points: (1) Psychologists must observe the highest possible standards of conduct and be careful not to misuse their influence; (2) they must recognize the limitations of their competence; (3) they must always be accountable for the fulfillment of professional responsibilities and carry out their duties in ethical, moral, and legal ways; and (4) they must protect and respect their clients at all times.

These guidelines grew out of a number of ethical questions related to the treatment of clients (Claiborn & Berberoglu, 1994). To whom should treatment be administered, and from whom should it be withheld? To what extent should therapists impose their own values on clients during therapy? How can the therapist ensure that her potentially powerful influence over the behavior of an individual client will not be misused? Under what circumstances should individuals be involuntarily committed to mental hospitals? The ethical guidelines provide answers for the practicing psychologist.

Psychological Treatment and the Law. Society has not been content to let psychologists and psychiatrists monitor themselves. Legislative and judicial systems have stepped in to impose regulations on psychological treatment.

Civil commitment. For every three people who voluntarily commit themselves to mental hospitals, two are committed involuntarily. When this happens, the individual is clearly being deprived of his liberty, a potential violation of constitutional rights. Thus, commitment procedures have come under increasingly close legal scrutiny. In general, there are two legal bases for involuntary commitment: to benefit the client and to benefit society. The difficulty is in attempting to define specific circumstances under which commitment will be beneficial (Tavolaro, 1992). Civil commitment laws favored the patient between about 1960 and 1980 but have now been changed to substantially favor the community (LaFond, 1994). In the earlier decades, legal commitment required substantial proof; since that time, society has moved to protect itself by making commitment somewhat easier.

In the precedent-setting case of *Addington v. Texas* in 1979[‡] the Supreme Court ruled that individuals can be involuntarily committed when there is "clear and convincing evidence" that they do have a mental disorder and meet other legal requirements justifying commitment. The "clear and convincing evidence" criterion is a fairly stringent one, but it is not as strict as another legal standard that could have been imposed requiring proof "beyond a reasonable doubt."

Proof of mental illness requiring commitment generally hinges on expert testimony from psychologists and psychiatrists. Until recently, most states permitted involuntary commitment if it could be proven through expert testimony that the individual was "mentally ill" or had a "need for treatment." More recently, concern over the reliability of psychiatric diagnosis has led to the imposition of additional standards. In general, one or both of two standards is now likely to be applied. First, the court will ask experts to indicate whether the client is *dangerous* to himself or others. The second standard is the so-called *thank you proposition.* It holds that once a person suffering from mental illness and involuntarily committed to an institution has been successfully treated, she will very likely be thankful that the treatment was forced upon her.

The rights of patients. What rights do mental patients or potential patients have? Three major issues have arisen in the courts (Kapp, 1994). The first is whether the patient has a *right to receive treatment.* The courts discovered in cases brought by patients or former patients that conditions in mental institutions were sometimes poor and that actual psychiatric treatment was in certain cases nonexistent. In the case of *Wyatt v. Stickney*, tried in 1972 by an Alabama federal court, two hospitals were found to provide grossly inadequate treatment. The court held that each patient must receive an individual treatment program administered by skilled staff members in a reasonable, humane environment. Later, the Supreme Court, in the case of *Youngbird v. Romeo* (1982), held that institutions housing involuntarily committed mental patients must provide "conditions of reasonable care and safety, reasonably unrestricted confinement conditions, and such training as may be required by these interests." The court also held that treatment decisions made by professionals are "presumptively valid" and must not be questioned by the courts.

The second issue is whether patients have a right to refuse treatment (Teno et al., 1993). A schizophrenic patient might prefer to refuse a powerful psychiatric drug that he knows has serious side effects or a depressed patient refuse the use of electroconvulsive therapy. What are the rights of these individuals? State statutes have generally held that involuntarily committed patients may be required to submit to any "routine" form of treatment, including widely used psychiatric medications. On the other hand, when a treatment is somewhat controversial, as in the case of ECT or psychosurgery, consent from the patient or family may be required, and such treatments tend to be regulated much more closely.

The third issue is the extent to which mental patients have a *right to a humane environment.* Here, the courts have been quite clear in specifying that mental institutions must provide a humane environment and have spelled out in detail some of the requirements of such an environment. Patients must, for example, be provided with reasonable diets, have a right to wear their own clothes, and be able to engage in regular physical exercise.

Keys to Therapy 5

Neurophysiology: The Biomedical Therapies

When psychotherapy works to lift a patient's depression or cure her anxiety disorder, it is generally presumed to be producing neurophysiological changes (Caspar et al., 1992). Cognitions may be restructured, intense emotions dampened, and behavioral symptoms like phobic avoidance reduced or eliminated. Such effects, depending upon their exact nature, very likely involve anatomical, neuroelectrical, or neurochemical changes in such areas of the brain as the hypothalamus, limbic system, temporal lobe, and prefrontal cortex (Figure 17-9). However, the nature of these changes has been little studied, and it will be some time before we can be more specific about the neurophysiology of psychological therapies.

We know far more about the neurophysiology of *biomedical therapies* (also called somatic therapies), which are by no means a new idea. Remember the ancient use of trephining and blood-letting? Among modern biological approaches to treating emotional disorders are neurological and psychopharmacological (drug) treatments.

Neurological Interventions

Some biological therapies are non-drug approaches that involve direct intervention in the functioning of the brain. Principal among these are electroconvulsive therapy and psychosurgery.

Electroconvulsive Therapy. In 1785, Dr. W. Oliver, physician to the royal family of England, accidentally gave an overdose of the stimulant *camphor* to a mental patient, who went into a coma, had convulsions, and was subsequently much improved (Valenstein, 1973). Camphor, however, was often fatal, and some alternative way to induce convulsions

---

[4] Addington v. Texas, 99 S.Ct. 1804 (1979). The clear and convincing evidence standard requires 75% certainty. The criminal standard - beyond a reasonable doubt - which does not apply here, requires 90% certainty,

was needed. In 1932, Viennese physician Manfred Sakel introduced *insulin shock therapy* to treat schizophrenia. In this treatment, the patient is given increasing amounts of insulin, which reduces blood sugar and sends the person into a coma. The resulting physiological stress or shock supposedly produced significant improvement after fifty or so treatments. However, no such positive results were ever documented, and the method was abandoned.

An alternative form of shock therapy was introduced by two Italian psychiatrists, Ugo Cerletti and Lucio Bini, in 1938. They reasoned that inducing epileptic-like convulsions through the use of electric shock to the brain might cure schizophrenia. Although subsequent use of electric shock with schizophrenic patients did not prove successful, it *was* found that shock therapy significantly improved the condition of many severely depressed patients. As a result, *electroconvulsive therapy (ECT)* came into widespread use in the treatment of major depression and is also now used very effectively in treating mania (Mukherjee et al., 1994).

The basic form of ECT treatment involves applying electrodes to both of the patient's temples (called bilateral placement) and passing an electrical current of about 70-160 volts through the brain from one side of the head to the other. An alternative form involves placing an electrode on only one temple (unilateral placement). In either case, the patient immediately loses consciousness and undergoes a muscular convulsion similar to an epileptic seizure. Muscle relaxants are given to prevent severe seizures, and the patient may also be sedated prior to the procedure. He regains consciousness within a few minutes and usually has amnesia for the period immediately preceding the shock. Such treatments are typically administered three times a week for two to four weeks.

When used in depression, ECT is highly effective. Success rates in severely depressed patients run as high as 80 to 100 percent (Schwartz, 1994). Moreover, some researchers have reported complete recovery from depressive symptoms in 70 percent of cases with only four to six treatments, and a meta-analysis of recent work shows that ECT is superior to the major forms of psychotherapy (Kho et al., 2003). Another major review and meta-analysis, conducted by the United Kingdom Review Group, compared ECT with drug therapies, using simulated ECT as a control. The British reviewers found that ECT is superior to drug therapy, that higher doses of ECT are more effective than lower doses, and that bilateral ECT is better than its unilateral counterpart (UK ECT Review Group, 2003).

Although ECT is clearly effective, it is also very controversial, in part because many people have difficulty accepting the idea of delivering electric shocks to the brain - the seat of intelligence and personality. In addition, we don't know exactly how or why ECT works, and it can have side effects. These issues are explored in THE CRITICAL THINKER.

Psychosurgery. When all other treatments appear to be unsuccessful, the most drastic of biological therapies, *psychosurgery* - brain surgery - may be applied. The original technique was introduced by Antonio De Egas Moniz in 1935, and in 1949 he shared a Nobel Prize for his surgical technique, called *prefrontal lobotomy*. It involves drilling a hole in each side of the head and inserting a surgical instrument to cut the neurological connections between the frontal cortex and the lower regions of the brain, including the thalamus and hypothalamus (see Figure 17-1). The rationale was that the frontal cortex increases emotional responses originating in the subcortical areas and that cutting the connections should therefore have a calming effect.

Moniz retired in 1944, partly because he had become hemiplegic after one of his lobotomized patients shot him, but interest in lobotomy continued. The technique was introduced into the United States by neuropsychiatrist Walter Freeman and his colleagues, who performed or supervised at least 3500 lobotomies. In fact, some facilities were performing lobotomies on as many as 50 patients in a single day (Freeman, 1959), and at least 50,000 had been performed by 1960 (Bivens, 1989).

After the initial enthusiasm, it became increasingly apparent that lobotomy produced major side effects, including seizures, stupor, and listlessness (Valenstein, 1980; Poynton, 1993). The side effects and the advent of psychiatric drugs in the 1950s greatly reduced the popularity of lobotomy (Jasper, 1995). It is now performed on only a few hundred patients a year.

More recent work involves the use of precision instruments to destroy very small areas of the brain with no damage to surrounding tissue. One relatively common procedure is the cingulotomy, which involves severing the cingulum, a fiber bundle near the corpus callosum that connects the frontal lobe to the limbic system. The procedure is performed in such anxiety disorders as phobia and obsessive-compulsive disorder when these maladies prove intractable to more common psychotherapeutic and drug treatments (Rauch et al., 1995; Baer et al., 1995). Other major areas targeted for precision surgery include small areas of the frontal lobe, amygdala, thalamus, and hypothalamus. These areas are lesioned not only in treating severe anxiety disorders, but also in cases of intractable depression (Burrows et al., 1994), pain (Lichterman, 1993), schizophrenia, and extreme aggression (Valenstein, 1980).

Reviewing the results of studies on the effectiveness of psychosurgery, Valenstein (1980) found that the procedures usually result in a reduction of depressive and anxiety symptoms. In general, cingulotomy yields good to excellent results in over 85 percent of cases, and complications are rare. Post-surgical deficits in learning ability, memory, or abstract thinking are observed, but only in a small percentage of cases (Harvey et al., 1993).

Psychopharmacology

The advent of *psychopharmacology* - the use of psychiatric drugs - in the 1950s brought about a revolution in the treatment of the mentally ill (Figure 17-10). Psychiatric drugs have proven to be very effective in the reduction or elimination of symptoms. They enable patients to function better and to be more receptive to other kinds of treatment. The hospital environment has also been greatly improved for both patients and staff.

The psychopharmacological agents most commonly used in treating mental disorders include antianxiety drugs, antipsychotic drugs, antidepressants, and antimanic agents (Table 17-3).

Antianxiety Drugs. Antianxiety agents act primarily to reduce the effects of stress and make the individual feel more relaxed. The principal drugs in current use are the *benzodiazepenes* (Ashton, 1994). They include diazepam (Valium), chlordiazepoxide (Librium), alprazolam (Xanax), among others. These drugs appear to act by binding to specific sites at synapses in the brain, particularly in the hypothalamus (Humbert, 1994) and amygdala (Pesold & Treit, 1994), where they block neural transmission. Currently used by about 6% of U.S. adults (Olfson & Pincus, 1994), they are effective in treating a range of problems, including the other major anxiety disorders (Walley et al., 1994). They are also helpful in depression (Wells et al., 1994) and smoking cessation (Robbins, 1993).

Useful as they are, the benzodiazepines also have drawbacks. The side effects are relatively minor: initial nausea, dizziness, sedation, and impaired cognitive functioning. The major problem is dependence. Patients taking these drugs, especially for long periods of time or in high doses, may have great difficulty stopping them and exhibit withdrawal symptoms when they do (Pissolo & Bisserbe, 1994; Lader, 1994).

Given these problems, researchers have worked to develop alternative anxiolytics, and one recent result has been a new drug class called the *azapirones*. The first of these was buspirone (BusSpar), which appears to be reasonably effective in treating the anxiety disorders (Faludi, 1994), post-traumatic stress disorder (Duffy & Malloy, 1994), and anxiety in alcoholics (Kranzler et al., 1994). It may not be as effective as the benzodiazepines, but it appears to have fewer side effects and does not lead to dependence or withdrawal (Faludi, 1994; Cutler et al., 1994).

Our phobic patient, Kenneth, could undoubtedly get some relief from treatment with anxiolytics. We might start him off with an azapirone, since these drugs may be the safest of the tranquilizers. If he is not responsive, we might try alprazolam (Xanax) or diazepam (Valium), both of which have proven particularly effective in treating phobias (American Medical Association, Drug Evaluations Annual, 1994).

Antipsychotic Drugs. Perhaps the most significant factor in the reduction of mental hospital populations over the last few decades has been the use of antipsychotic agents or *neuroleptics.* These drugs not only calm the patient but actually reduce the intensity of major schizophrenic symptoms, including hallucinations and delusions. Under optimal conditions, they make the patient feel better, behave more normally, and become more receptive to psychotherapy.

The first major antipsychotic agents were the still widely used *phenothiazines*, of which major examples is chlorpromazine (Thorazine) and (Mellaril). Among the somewhat more recently developed agents of other drug classes, haloperidol (Haldol), has been particularly popular in treating schizophrenics (Mauri et al., 1994; Doddi et al., 1994). These drugs act to reduce psychotic symptoms by blocking the action of the neurotransmitter *dopamine* at receptor sites in the brain. One major hypothesis suggests that schizophrenia is the result of excessive dopamine at certain synapses, which would explain why drugs that block the action of dopamine reduce psychotic symptoms (see Chapter 16).

The long-term use of these drugs, often at high dosage levels, can produce significant side effects. Principal among the "nuisance symptoms" are dryness of the mouth and throat, blurred vision, jaundice, hypotension (low blood pressure), and urinary retention (Tuety, 1994). Impairment of cognitive and emotional functioning are also common (Lader, 1994), as is sedation, though less with haloperidol than with the phenothiazines (Levander, 1994). Far more serious are progressive neuromuscular symptoms, including Parkinson-like problems, such as muscular rigidity and tremor (Blaisdell, 1994).

The most serious side effect is a condition called *tardive dyskinesia* (TD), which is marked by involuntary thrusting of the tongue, facial tics, and uncontrollable movements of the body. It can develop after a few months but more often after several years of usage and is thought to be caused by brain damage resulting from depletion of the important neurotransmitter acetylcholine (Crespo & Carbonell, 1995). It occurs in at least 20% and perhaps over 50% of patients on long-term neuroleptics (Cavallaro et al., 1994). Since there is no real treatment for TD, patients are usually maintained on the lowest doses of neuroleptics that will reduce their symptoms.

Fortunately, recent years have seen the development of a number of new antipsychotics with fewer of the serious side effects of the phenothiazines and haloperidol. *Clozapine* (Clozaril) reduces psychotic symptoms even in those who have been resistant to other treatments (Lieberman et al., 1994). Moreover, it is often effective in treating both the negative symptoms (like social incompetence and disinterest) and the positive symptoms (hallucinations, delusions, irritability) of schizophrenia, where the older drugs treat only the latter (Stern et al., 1994). Clozapine has the additional advantage that it does not appear to cause motor symptoms, and no cases of TD have yet been reported (Gerlach & Peacock, 1994). However, it does cause other serious side effects in a small percentage of patients (Toth & Frankenburg, 1994). Other new neuroleptics with reduced side effects include risperadone (Risperdal; Schooler, 1994), loxapine (Loxitane; Carlyle et al., 1993), and remoxipride Vanelle et al., 1994). With these newest additions and others soon to come, we may be moving into a new era in the treatment of schizophrenia.

Antidepressants. Several classes of drugs are used in treating depression. The oldest are the monoamine oxidase (MAO) inhibitors and the tricyclics. Both increase the concentrations of important brain chemicals, particularly serotonin and norepinephrine, resulting in a reduction in depressive symptoms. The most widely used *MAO inhibitors* include tranylcypromine (Parnate), and phenelzine (Nardil). The most widely used *tricyclics* are imipramine (Tofranil), nortriptyline (Aventyl), and amitriptyline (Elavil). While the two types of drugs are equally effective, the tricyclics are more widely used because the MAO inhibitors can interact with other drugs and with certain foods to produce highly toxic side effects and are thus considerably more dangerous (Julien, 1992).

Although safer than the MAO inhibitors, the tricyclics do have significant side effects. These include drowsiness, blurred vision, tachycardia (rapid heartbeat), urinary retention, weight gain, and constipation. In addition, 25-30% of depressed patients do not respond (Sussman, 1994), while 60-70% show only partial recovery (Amsterdam et al., 1994).

More recently developed are the *selective serotonin reuptake inhibitors* or SSRIs. As the name implies, the SSRIs selectively increase levels of the neurotransmitter serotonin with little or no effect on other brain chemicals (Hyttel, 1994). The SSRIs are very effective in reducing depressive symptoms (Casey, 1994), and one of these drugs, fluoxetine (Prosac), has become the single most widely prescribed of all antidepressants (Greenberg et al., 1994). It is actually no more effective overall than the tricyclics (Nierenberg, 1994; Tollefson et al., 1994), but it has fewer bothersome side effects.

In some patients the SSRIs do produce nausea, nervousness, insomnia, or sexual dysfunction (Sussman, 1994). However, these side effects are less frequent and better tolerated than those seen with the tricyclics (Mitchell & Mitchell, 1994). As a result, patients are less likely to stop taking an SSRI (Montgomery et al., 1994; Tollefson et al., 1994), which is important for two reasons. First, any antidepressant will obviously be more effective in the short run if the patient keeps taking it, particularly since she must continue it for a period of at least 2-4 weeks before it begins to have any significant impact. Secondly, long-term continuation on antidepressant medications is important. Patients must ordinarily remain on an antidepressant for a minimum of one year (Leonard, 1993). Otherwise, at least 30-50% will have serious relapses (Montgomery et al., 1994). It is for these reasons that fluoxetine and the other SSRIs have become more popular.

On the negative side, early publicity suggested that Prosac increases the likelihood that patients will commit suicide. Fortunately, studies have now clearly demonstrated that it does not. One study of over 3000 patients, for example, showed no difference in suicide rates between patients on fluoxetine and those on other antidepressants or placebos (Tollefson et al., 1994).

Antimanic Drugs. Bipolar disorder, in which the patient experiences episodes of both depression and mania, is not only serious but life-threatening. About 80% of patients who have one manic episode will have others, and there is a cumulative, deteriorative effect of repeated periods of mania, with untreated bipolar patients having a mortality rate that is 2-3 times that of the general population. Optimal treatment of mania can add 7 years of life, 9 years of normal health, and 10 years of activity and productivity (Gelenberg & Hopkins, 1993). Thus, effective treatment is important for both psychological and medical reasons. For many years, the drug of choice in treating mania has been the mineral salt *lithium.* About 80 percent of manic patients show complete or substantial recovery from symptoms when treated with this powerful drug (Hopkins & Gelenberg, 1994). Lithium has also been successfully used in treating some depressed patients and some bipolar patients in the depressive phase of their disorder and appears to reduce suicide rates (Ahrens et al., 1995). Despite its effectiveness, lithium is used cautiously because it is a highly toxic drug. Given too high a dosage, patients develop severe vomiting and diarrhea and sometimes even coma. In addition, long-term lithium may produce kidney, thyroid, and eye damage (Jefferson & Sen, 1994).

Lithium is not the only treatment for mania. Patients who do not respond to it can be treated with ECT, which is about 80% effective, or with anticonvulsant drugs. The latter are ordinarily used in epileptic patients to control or eliminate seizures, but they can be helpful in treating mania. One anticonvulsant, carbamazepine, is effective in 60-70% of manic patients, and another, valproate, is equally as effective as lithium (Bowden & McElroy, 1995; Bowden, 1995).

Biomedical Treatments: The Pros and Cons

Many of the psychiatric drugs and other biomedical treatments are extremely effective, and most experts agree that they should be used when needed to treat a patient's symptoms. At they same time, we have seen that there are also some drawbacks, and we need to address those as well. Psychosurgery creates permanent brain damage, ECT can produce temporary memory deficits, and some neuroleptics can cause tardive dyskinesia. MAO inhibitors and lithium can lead to coma and even death, the benzodiazepines can be addictive, and all psychoactive drugs produce at least some side effects.

Despite their drawbacks, we routinely use biomedical treatments be because they work and work very well. Before the advent of psychiatric drugs and the other biological treatments, many patients - particularly those with schizophrenia or severe depression - spent 20-30 years or more in hospitals. For all practical purposes, the diagnosis of their disorder often ended their productive lives. Drugs and ECT changed this prognosis dramatically. They made it possible to release patients from the hospital in relatively short times and return at least some of them to the community (Uhlenhuth et al., 1995).

Keys to Therapy 6

Conclusion

The problem of mental disorders and their treatment has been a thorn in the side of all societies since the beginning of civilization. However, less than a century ago society had no tested, effective means of treating psychological disorders and no integrative theories to provide a basis for developing effective therapies. Given that situation, the progress made in mental health care in this century is little short of miraculous.

A veritable plethora of drugs and other biological treatments have been developed, even if not perfected. At the same time, psychoanalytic theory has not only provided a form of psychotherapy but also served as a stimulus for the development of such powerful alternative approaches as behaviorism and humanism. Each of these major schools has also yielded effective treatment approaches. Nevertheless, we have a long way to go. Advances in biomedical treatment over the next several decades are a certainty, and significant improvements in psychotherapeutic approaches are likely but will take somewhat longer. In both cases it is reasonable to predict that advances in the next century will be even more rapid than has been the case in the past century, and mental health care 100 years from now will probably be even more highly effective.

Summary

Mental Health Care: Perspectives and Practices

1. Early treatments for mental disorders were based on demonological theory. The first real progress came with the work of Hippocrates and Galen and, centuries later, that of Pinel, Dix, and others.
2. Treatment professionals include clinical, counseling, and school psychologists, psychiatrists, psychiatric nurses, and social workers.
3. The two major categories of psychotherapy are insight therapy and action therapy.

Insight Therapies

1. Traditional Freudian psychoanalysis employs primarily free association, dream analysis, and the analysis of transference to help the patient gain insight into unconscious conflicts.
2. Modern psychodynamic approaches include ego psychology and object relations theory.
3. Among the principal humanistic therapies are Carl Rogers' client-centered therapy and Fritz Perls' Gestalt therapy.
4. Group therapy involves an interaction among several people with related problems and a therapist.
5. Types of group therapy include psychoanalytic, encounter, behavioral, and cognitive-behavioral.
6. Major family therapies include Satir's conjoint and Minuchin's structured therapy.

Behavioral and Cognitive Therapies

1. Behavioral therapies focus on specific problem behaviors and use learning approaches to modify these behaviors.
2. Classical conditioning techniques include systematic desensitization, aversion therapy, and flooding.
3. Operant conditioning approaches include time out, token economies, and stimulus control techniques.
4. Cognitive-behavioral therapies include Aaron Beck's cognitive therapy, Albert Ellis' rational-emotive therapy, and Albert Bandura's modeling approach.

Issues in Psychotherapy: Effectiveness, Ethics, and Legalities

1. Difficulties in conducting therapy research include biased evaluations, spontaneous remission, and methodological

flaws.

2. The Sloane, NIMH, and meta-analytic studies show that the major forms of psychotherapy are clearly and consistently effective.
3. There is no overall difference in effectiveness among the various schools. However, some problems may be better treated with one approach than another.
4. Factors contributing to the effectiveness of all psychotherapies may include a trusting relationship, hope, and insight.
5. Cultural sensitivities are increasingly important in the conduct of psychotherapy.
6. Major ethical and legal issues include civil commitment procedures and patient rights.
7. Involuntary commitment requires "clear and convincing evidence" of a mental disorder. Other standards include dangerousness and the thank you proposition.
8. Patients who are committed have a right to receive treatment, but not a right to refuse it unless it is controversial. Patients also have a right to a humane environment.

Community Mental Health

1. CMHCs provide outpatient, inpatient, and emergency services. Halfway houses provide a gradual transition from hospital to community.
2. Crisis intervention approaches provide for emergency care.

Neurophysiology: Biomedical Therapies

1. ECT is highly effective in treating depression. It impairs memory temporarily, but otherwise appears to be safe.
2. A prefrontal lobotomy severs connections between the frontal cortex and lower centers in an effort to reduce anxiety. It was very popular for a time, but then became controversial and unpopular.
3. Psychosurgery is now relatively rare and usually involves precise destruction of small areas of the brain.
4. Psychiatric drugs are very effective but have side effects and do not treat the underlying problem.

Ask Yourself

1. Differentiate between insight and action therapies.
2. What are some of the major differences between the psychoanalytic and humanistic approaches to treatment? Which treatment would you prefer and why?
3. What are the principal similarities and differences among the major behavioral therapies? What common threads run through all these therapies?
4. What does evidence say about the difference in effectiveness between psychoanalysis and behavior therapy?
5. What are some likely future trends in psychotherapy noted in the text?
6. What is deinstitutionalization and how has it been implemented? How effective is community mental health care? What is its likely future?
7. What are the major ethical and legal guidelines for psychologists?
8. Discuss the advantages and disadvantages of ECT and psychosurgery. Under what conditions do you think each of these treatments should be used?
9. Discuss the effectiveness of the major psychiatric drugs. What are the advantages and drawbacks of using these drugs?
10. If you were subject to severe, prolonged depression, would you prefer to be treated with antidepressant drugs, ECT, psychotherapy, or some combination? Why?

Further Readings

Alford, B., & Beck, A. (1994). Cognitive therapy of delusional beliefs. *Behavior Research and Therapy.*, 32, 369-380. In this paper, theorist Aaron Beck extends his cognitive theory of depression to another disorder.

Beers, C. *A Mind That Found Itself.* New York: Longman, Green, 1908. A classic account of one individual's experience with psychosis; fascinating reading.

Bergin, A., & Garfield, S. (1994). *Handbook of psychotherapy and behavior change.* NY: Wiley. The definitive handbook in this field, Bergin and Garfield contains chapters on all the major treatment approaches.

Bloom, B. (1992). Planned short-term psychotherapy: Current status and future challenges. *Applied and Preventive Psychology*, 1, 157-164. Bloom provides a good, readable overview of progress in developing brief psychotherapies.

Chin, J., De-La-Cancela, V., & Jenkins, Y. (1993). *Diversity in psychotherapy: The politics of race, ethnicity, and gender.* Westport, CT: Praeger. A solid treatment of the importance of ethnic issues and sensitivities in psychotherapy.

Endler, N. S. *Holiday of Darkness.* New York: Wiley, 1982.Another personal account, this time of the experiences of a widely recognized psychologist who suffered from depression. He discusses the nature of his experience and the effects of various treatments.

Guttmacher, L. (1994). *Concise guide to psychopharmacology and electroconvulsive therapy.* Washington, DC: American Psychiatric Press. This small book provides a good overview of ECT and drug therapies.

Howe, D. (1993). *On being a client: Understanding the process of counseling and psychotherapy.* London: Sage. If you are considering psychotherapy, this is an excellent book to read.

Kernberg, O. (1993). The current status of psychoanalysis. *Journal of the American Psychoanalytic Association.*, 41, 45-62. A leading psychoanalyst brings us up to date on its progress.

Khan, A., Mirolo, M.H., Hughes, D., & Bierut, L. (1993). Electroconvulsive therapy. *Psychiatric Clinics of North America*, 16, 497-513. A good overview of what ECT is and how it is done.

Lloyd, K., & Bhugra, D. (1993). Cross-cultural aspects of psychotherapy. *International Review of Psychiatry*, 5, 291-304. The authors discuss the importance of cultural sensitivity in therapy.

Nietzel, M., Bernstein, D., & Milich, R. (1991). *Introduction to clinical psychology.* Englewood Cliffs, NJ: Prentice-Hall. A widely used textbook that provides a solid introduction to the entire field of clinical psychology.

Prochaska, J., & Norcross, J. (1994). *Systems of psychotherapy: A transtheoretical analysis.* Pacific Grove, CA: Brooks/Cole. The authors provide a comprehensive and widely respected overview of the major therapies.

Rogers, C.R. & Kirschenbaum, H. (1989). *The Carl Rogers reader.* Boston: Houghton Mifflin. Carl Rogers began work on this collection of his writings shortly before his death in 1987. It provides a definitive history and overview of his theory.

Skinner, B.F. (1988). The operant side of behavior therapy. *Journal of Behavior Therapy and Experimental Psychiatry.*, 19, 171-179. In one of his last publications, leading theorist B.F. Skinner provides a good overview of behavior therapy.

Neuroscience in the 21st Century

The "McTherapy Drive-Through?" Brief Psychotherapy

You may wonder just how long therapy typically takes: A month? A year? Five years? The answer for all three time periods is "yes." When Sigmund Freud and his colleagues began psychoanalysis, the expectation was that a typical patient would be in therapy for several years, with sessions occurring at least once each week. That guideline became the norm, and therapists from other schools of thought generally concurred with the analysts that therapy should be of unlimited duration. This meant that it continued until the therapist pronounced it completed. Patients who left therapy early were considered to be failures.

As we move toward the 21ST century, we can be certain that the typical length of psychotherapy will be markedly reduced. In fact, a trend toward briefer therapy began some years ago when it was observed that notable gains can often be made with many fewer sessions (Clair & Prendergast, 1994). Some patients who were in therapy for as few as 8 or 10 sessions showed significant improvement, and some studies demonstrated that perhaps 75% improve measurably within 26 sessions (Howard et al., 1986). Such observations led to the birth of what has been variously called short-term, time-limited, or *brief therapy*. The exact number of sessions varies from one therapist and one institution to another, but the span of brief therapy is typically from 2 to 6 months (Levenson et al., 1995). The therapist usually begins with a brief assessment of the problem, then sets outcome goals, shares these with the client, and contracts for a specified number of sessions, often 6 to 12. From that point on, both therapist and client know that "the clock is ticking," and advocates of brief therapy believe that both therefore work harder and in a more focused way to conclude the therapy successfully (Fraser, 1995).

The bottom line for brief therapy is that it appears to work. It has already been employed for a number of years by some practitioners of behavioral and cognitive-behavioral approaches and by others who conduct humanistic therapies. It has been used with traumatized teenagers (Holderici, 1993), adolescent suicide attempters (Rotheran-Borus & Piacentini, 1994), bulimics (Blouin et al., 1994), and a wide range of other child, adolescent, and adult clients. One typical study compared brief therapy (12 sessions) with time-unlimited therapy for 30 disturbed children and their parents. Results showed that long-term therapy had no advantage at all over short-term (Smyrnios, 1993). In a review of many studies of time-limited therapy, Bernard Bloom (1992) concluded that this result is typical. Long-term therapy appears to have no significant advantage over short-term therapy for a majority of clients. Exceptions may be patients with deep, complex, or very severe problems, and these can be entered into lengthier therapy if necessary (Barber, 1994). To assess the exceptions, one study stratified clients as more severely or less severely depressed. For most, there was no advantage of 16 weeks over 8 weeks of therapy. However, for the most severely depressed, the longer period did produce greater improvement (Shapiro et al., 1994).

What does the future hold? First, we will see the expansion of briefer therapy across all schools of thought. Even traditionally lengthy psychoanalytic treatment has begun to change. Secondly, there will be continuing efforts to determine, through research, just what the ideal length of therapy is, and we will surely find that the ideal is variable. It will likely vary with the severity of the disorder, the specific diagnosis, and the type of therapy applied. For mildly disturbed patients and for those with certain disorders, therapy may be very brief. For severely disturbed patients and those with certain other disorders, the optimal length of therapy may be greater. And some types of therapy may be more rapidly effective for some disorders. Given the cost-cutting pressures increasingly imposed by managed care organizations, the briefer therapies will be increasingly chosen over those requiring longer periods of treatment (Edbril, 1994; Stern, 1993). We may never see the day when you can go to a "McTherapy" drive-through and come out feeling that your needs are fully satisfied, but we are certainly moving in that direction!

Probe

Placebos and Double-Blinds

Remember that old question: What's wrong with this picture? Well, here's the picture: The Magic Potion Drug Company has developed Chilledoutathine (Chilled-out-a-thine), a new tranquilizer. They give it to 100 patients with high anxiety, and careful outcome measures show significant reductions. This proves the clinical utility of the new drug. Or does it? What's wrong is that Magic Potion's researchers failed to run a placebo control group or use double-blind procedures. A *placebo* in drug research is an inert substance that appears to be identical to the active drug. If Chilledoutathine is a triangular orange pill, the placebo is also a triangular orange pill, but without the drug in it. Half the participants in Magic Potion's study should be randomly assigned to get the active drug and half the placebo.

It would also be important to assure that neither the patients nor staff members who interact with them know who is on the Chilledoutathine and who is on the placebo. If the patient knows she is on the active drug, she may show anxiety reduction based on her belief that the drug will help her; if she knows she is on the placebo, she will accordingly show no anxiety reduction. Less obviously, staff members may quite inadvertently treat active drug and placebo patients differently because they expect the drug to work, and this may affect the results of the study. Designing the experiment to ensure that both patients and staff remain unaware of the drug assignments is called a *double-blind* procedure.

The reason drug researchers bother with placebos is that many patients show a strong placebo response. That is, they feel better even when given an inactive substance that they believe is a drug (Archer, 1995). If there is no placebo group, the improvement in the active drug group can be mistakenly interpreted as a response to the drug, when it is actually a placebo effect. The truth is that virtually the entire practice of medicine was based on placebo effects for centuries. Common treatments included snake oil, bleeding, trephining, camel dung, and spiders. We now know these have no medicinal value, but many patients felt better anyway. Are those days gone? Well, not entirely. You have no doubt seen and heard advertisements for products containing ginseng and other substances typically available in health food stores. These products have usually not been tested in double-blind, placebo-controlled studies. If they were, most would very likely be found to be ineffective.

Researchers have clearly demonstrated the placebo effect and studied it carefully. In one study 19% of depressive patients showed significant improvement when given a placebo, though the antidepressant fluoxetine produced greater improvement (Small et al., 1995). In other studies, patients undergoing tooth extractions reported significant reductions in pain, and patients with anxiety disorders had less anxiety and fewer symptoms when given placebos (Cottraux et al., 1995; Levine et al., 1979). These findings are consistent with an extensive literature on placebo treatment of pain. At least 35% of patients with pain respond to placebos (Bruxelle, 1994), and one recent team of reviewers concluded that the number is often far higher than that (Turner et al., 1994).

Placebos can even have side effects. Many active drugs produce such side effects as headaches, nausea, and drowsiness, and patients are often told to expect these effects. One team of researchers gave placebos to normal volunteers. The subjects were told that the pill they were taking was an active drug and that they could expect some side effects. Of the 109 subjects, 19% did report side effects. The most common one was headache, and others included drowsiness and pain (Rosenzweig et al., 1993).

So far, we have been talking about the use of placebos in drug studies, but the same basic principles apply to psychotherapy research. Placebo effects can also occur when a patient is treated with psychotherapy for an emotional disorder, and, as in drug studies, it is important to evaluate the effect of therapy over and above that of a placebo (Laporte & Figueras, 1994). Many psychotherapy outcome studies have only an experimental group receiving the therapy and a control group receiving no treatment. Some of the most sophisticated have a third group - a placebo control group. Participants in this condition receive something that may appear to them to be treatment but is not. Some studies employ an attention-control placebo in which a therapist talks with the patient but does no actual therapy. That is, he follows no systematic therapeutic approach and is careful not to "do therapy." An example is a study evaluating systematic desensitization. The researchers used a placebo control treatment that they called "systematic ventilation," in which the subject simply told a therapist about his fears. The therapist did nothing therapeutic to allay them (Kirsch et al., 1983).

We do not know just what causes the placebo effect to occur. Cognitive theory suggests that expectations may be the cause. The patient who enters therapy with positive expectations may get better because she thinks she will get better. This effect is sometimes called a *self-fulfilling prophecy*. An alternative hypothesis is that social influence may be the key. The psychotherapist or physician can be a powerful source of social influence. She is seen as an authority figure and can easily influence the susceptible patient when she tells him to expect that the treatment will produce improvement. Whatever the cause, the placebo effect is a powerful one.

The Critical Thinker

What Shock! Is ECT Safe?

Despite numerous studies and theories, it is still not known exactly how electroconvulsive therapy (ECT) acts to reduce depressive symptoms. However, it is generally agreed that the seizure induced by ECT is largely responsible for the effect). It appears that the cumulative duration of the seizures over a series of treatments contributes to effectiveness. Patients often show some improvement with less than 250 seconds of total seizure time, and 90 percent show maximum improvement with 400 seconds or less (Kramer, 1983). Some evidence points to biochemical changes at brain synapses as the mechanism through which ECT works (Mikkelsen et al., 1994), but researchers are by no means yet certain.

The Basic Hypothesis or Contention

Although it may be the most effective treatment for many depressive patients, ECT is also the most controversial, in part because of its actual and potential side effects. Critics have long contended that ECT should be abandoned because it can produce cardiac or respiratory arrest, brain damage, and permanent memory loss.

What Is The Evidence?

Extensive research on the short-term and long-term effects of ECT over the years has addressed the issues raised by its critics. Studies show that cardiac and respiratory complications occur only rarely. In addition, although ECT often causes headaches, there is no evidence that it produces brain damage (Scott, 1995; UK ECT Review Group, 2003).

The major remaining issue is memory loss. After an ECT session, the patient is typically confused for an hour or more and experiences amnesia for the time period immediately preceding and during the treatment. With repeated sessions, the confusion increases, and the patient may become disoriented until treatment is terminated. The memory impairment usually lasts a few days and can last for months but does not appear to be permanent ([RTF bookmark start: }BM-1-[RTF bookmark end: }BM-1-Kho et al., 2003). One example of research in this area is a study of depressive elderly patients. It was found that shock treatment was successful in reducing or eliminating depression in 79 percent of the patients treated, and there were no instances of such major side effects as cardiac or respiratory arrest (Gasper and Samarsilzhe, 1982). While most patients showed states of confusion and memory loss during the series of treatments, these side effects disappeared within days after therapy ended. Another study showed improvement, not deterioration, in cognitive functioning after a course of ECT (Stoudemire et al., 1995).

Other research has focused on reducing the memory side effect of shock treatments. One relatively recent development is the use of *unilateral ECT*, in which electrodes are placed on only one side of the head to avoid passing current directly through the speech and verbal memory areas of the brain. This approach is somewhat less effective than the older method and often requires a longer series of treatments, but both amnesia and confusion are greatly reduced (Lamy et al., 1994). Other electrode placements are also being studied in an effort to find the best combination of safety and effectiveness (Swartz, 1994).

Is The Evidence Open To Alternative Interpretations?

Critical examination of early evidence favoring ECT showed that some of the studies were methodologically flawed and hence could not be said to demonstrate its safety (Zwil & Belchat, 1994). However, that alternative interpretation does not apply to more recent, well-controlled studies confirming its overall safety and effectiveness (UK ECT Review Group, 2003) A second point made by critics is that shock therapy may produce brain damage so subtle that it cannot be detected with current methods of assessment. Although the failure to find damage has held up as the field moved from relatively primitive autopsy and EEG studies to the use of such modern techniques as MRI and PET, the critics could still be right on this point. More refined and sophisticated methods of brain study certainly will be developed, and it is possible that damage will then be found. Finally, critics note that although memory loss is temporary, it is still a significant problem for the patient, particularly when it extends for several months beyond ECT therapy. It interferes with the ability to function normally for an extended period of time.

Do We Need Additional Evidence?

We certainly need additional research to determine just how ECT works to reduce depression. However, it appears that most of the required evidence concerning its safety, based on currently available methodologies, is already in. Although investigators will certainly continue to conduct neuroanatomical and neurochemical studies of the effects of ECT, there is already enough evidence to permit reasonable and valid conclusions concerning the effects of this form of therapy.

What Can We Conclude?

The most reasonable conclusion based the evidence to date is that ECT is both safe and effective. It does have side effects, most notably memory loss, but they appear to be temporary. In fact, memory problems typically last for only a few days beyond the termination of therapy. In cases where they do extend considerably beyond that, they certainly represent a significant and unfortunate side effect. However, that negative must be balanced against the relief from severe depression that the patient usually experiences. Not surprisingly, most seriously depressed patients are quite willing to accept a temporary memory loss in order to experience a lifting of the depression.

Overall, it seems clear that ECT has a future as a major treatment for depression. However, it is destined to remain controversial and may eventually be eliminated if safe, effective alternatives are developed.

KEYS TERMS 1

biomedical therapy
crisis hotline
deinstitutionalization
exorcism
halfway house
psychotherapy
therapy
trephining

KEY PEOPLE

Dorothea Dix
Phillipe Pinel
Benjamin Rush
William Tuke

KEYS TERMS 2

client-centered therapy
dream analysis
ego psychology
free association
Gestalt therapy
humanistic therapy
insight therapy
object-relations therapy
psychoanalysis
transference

KEY PEOPLE 2

Sigmund Freud
Fritz Perls
Carl Rogers

KEYS TERMS 3

action therapies
aversion therapy
behavior therapy
cognitive restructuring
flooding
modeling
rational-emotive therapy
systematic desensitization
token economy

KEY PEOPLE 3

Albert Bandura
Aaron Beck
Albert Ellis

KEYS TERMS 4

family therapy

KEY PEOPLE 4

Salvador Minuchin
Virginia Satir

KEYS TERMS 5

eclectic therapy

hello-goodbye effect
spontaneous remission
thank-you proposition

KEYS TERMS 6

antianxiety agents
antidepressants
antimanic drugs
antipsychotic agents
electroconvulsive therapy (ECT)
prefrontal lobotomy
psychosurgery

KEY PEOPLE 6

Lucio Bini
Ugo Cerletti
Antonio De Egas Moniz

KEYS TO TREATMENT - 1

1. Ancient treatments for mental disorders were not always kind.

   A. How cave dwellers treated mental illness?
      Trephining
   B. Who first introduced humane treatments?
      Hippocrates, then Galen
   C. Who reinstituted human treatments much later?
      Pinel, Dix, Tuke, and Rush

KEYS TO TREATMENT - 2

1. Insight therapies make the patient aware of unconscious motives.

   A. The major insight schools?
      Psychodynamic, Humanistic

2. Psychodynamic therapy began with Freud.

   A. What Freud's therapy is called?
      Psychoanalysis
   B. The major therapeutic techniques he used?
      Free association, dream analysis, analysis of transference.
   C. The current major psychodynamic approaches?
      Orthodox psychoanalysis, ego psychology, object-relations theory.

3. Humanistic therapies emphasize the unique individuality of the client.
   A. The major humanistic theorist and his technique?
      Rogers, client-centered therapy.
   B. What the therapy aims to do?
      Help the client move toward an accurate self-concept and psychological growth.
   C. The aim of Gestalt therapy?
      Increased perceptual accuracy and creating a whole person.

4. Group and family therapies treat several people at once.

   A. Some types of group therapy?
      psychoanalytic, encounter, behavioral, and cognitive-behavioral.
   B. Some major family therapies?
      Satir - conjoint therapy, Minuchin - structured therapy.
   C. Some applications of group therapy?
      In substance abuse, obsessive-compulsive disorder, bulimia, sexual abuse, PTSD in veterans.

KEYS TO TREATMENT - 3

1. Behavioral therapies focus on specific problem behaviors.

   A. How they modify behaviors?
      Using learning techniques
   B. The major types of learning approaches?
      Classical and operant conditioning
   C. Some major classical techniques?
      Aversion therapy, flooding, systematic desensitization.
   D. Some major operant approaches?
      Covert conditioning, time-out token economy, stimulus control.

2. Cognitive therapies focus on thought processes.

A. Some major approaches?
Beck - cognitive restructuring
Ellis - rational-emotive
Bandura - modeling
B. What Beck attempts to do?
Correct negative thought patterns that cause depression.
C. What Ellis attempts to do?
Correct irrational beliefs
D. What Bandura attempts to do?
Model normal behaviors that replace abnormal behaviors.

KEYS TO TREATMENT - 4

1. Psychotherapy research is difficult.

A. The major problems?
Spontaneous remission, biased evaluations, methodological flaws.

2. The Sloane and NIMH studies were well-controlled.

A. How much improvement Sloane found?
80% in both therapy groups improved vs. 48% of controls.
B. How much improvement the NIMH study found?
50% in therapy groups, 29% in controls.

3. Findings in therapy studies are consistent.

A. How effective the major therapies are?
Much more effective than no treatment
B. Which therapy is best?
All are equally effective.
C. Some common denominators?
A trusting relationship
Hope
Insight

4. Cultural sensitivity is important.

A. Why?
It makes therapy more effective for those with a different cultural background.

5. APA publishes ethical standards for psychologists.

A. Some examples of standards?
Don't misuse influence
Recognize limitations of competence
Be accountable
Protect and respect clients.

6. Civil commitment procedures are defined by law.

A. The basis rule for involuntary commitment?
Clear and convincing evidence

B. The standard proofs through expert testimony for commitment in most states?
Mental illness
Dangerousness
The thank you proposition

7. The rights of patients have been debated in recent years.

A. Whether patients have a right to receive treatment?
They do, but professional judgment as to type is presumptively valid.
B. Whether patients have a right to refuse treatment?
Only if it is controversial or unusual
C. What else hospitals must provide?
A humane environment.

KEYS TO TREATMENT - 5

1. CMHCs were mandated by a 1963 act of Congress.

A. The services they provide?
Inpatient, outpatient, emergency
B. How effective they have been?
Not very, especially more recently
C. The trend?
Many are closing, funding is reduced.

2. Other interventions include halfway houses and crisis intervention.

A. What a halfway house does?
Houses patients before they reenter the community.
B. Some forms of crisis intervention?
Walk-in service at CMHCs, crisis intervention teams, hotlines.

KEYS TO TREATMENT - 6

1. ECT is one of the most effective treatments for depression.

A. Who developed it?
Cerletti and Bini
B. What it was originally developed to treat?
Schizophrenia
C. The treatment success rate in severe depression?
80-100%
D. How safe it is?
Usually very safe. Temporary memory impairment is the only major problem.

2. The treatment of last resort is psychosurgery.

A. Who developed prefrontal lobotomy?
Moniz
B. What lobotomy is supposed to do?
Reduce anxiety
C. Some of its side effects?
Seizures, stupor, listlessness.
D. The name of a more conservative technique currently in use?
Cingulotomy

3. Psychiatry drugs are, on the whole, very effective.

A. The major types?
Anxiolytics
Neuroleptics
Antidepressants
Antimanics

4. The anxiolytics treat primarily anxiety disorders

A. What the anxiolytics do?
Reduce muscle tension, sedate
B. Some examples of anxiolytic drugs and classes?
Propanediols - meprobamate (Miltown)
Benzodiazepenes - Diazepam (Valium)
Azapirones - buspirone (BusSpar)
C. Disorders these drugs treat?
Anxiety disorders, sometimes depression.
D. Problems they present?
Dependence

5. Neuroleptics treat primarily schizophrenia.

A. What they do?
Reduce major symptoms.
B. The side effects of these drugs?
Dry mouth, blurred vision, etc.
Neuromuscular symptoms
Tardive dyskinesia
C. How they work?
By blocking dopamine.

6. The major antidepressants are generally safe and effective.

A. The major types?
Tricyclics, tetracyclics, MAO inhibitors, SSRIs.
B. Which type is the most dangerous?
MAO inhibitors
C. Whether tricyclics or SSRIs are more effective?
They are equally effective.
C. Why SSRIs may be preferable to tricyclics?
SSRIs have less side effects and are tolerated better.

7. Antimanics are very effective in treating mania.

A. The major drugs?
Lithium, carbamazepine, valproate.
B. Why lithium is dangerous?
Slight overdoses are toxic.

Chapter 18

The Individual in Society

Outline

Attidues and Attitude Change

Attitude Formation
Cognitive Consistency
Attitudes and Behavior
Attitude Change

Social Influence

When Others Watch: Social Presence
Conformity
Compliance
Obedience

Group Processes

Theories of Social Affiliation
Sociobiology
Evolutionary Psychology is Not Sociobiology
Group Norms
Group Dynamics
Cooperation and Competition

Environmental Psychology

Personal Space
Crowding
Territoriality
Environmental Stressors

Aggression

Biological Factors in Aggression
The Role of Learning
Triggers For Agressive Behavior

Networking

SOCIAL psychology studies the behavior of people as they live in, interact with, and are affected by groups. Groups profoundly influence many aspects of our lives. They are a primary source of our attitudes and social behaviors, both through direct teaching and through more subtle processes, such as group pressure to conform. In turn, individuals can have strong effects on groups, whether by serving as leaders or by playing other roles in group processes. It is this ongoing interaction between individuals and other members of the society in which they live that is the primary focus of social psychology. In this chapter we will see how attitudes are developed and changed. We will also discuss such interesting group processes as the formation and influence of norms, the power of leaders, and the nature of group communication. And we will review what is known about conformity, compliance, and obedience, as well as environmental influences on behavior and the causes of aggression.

Attitude change, group processes, conformity, and aggression are all influenced by social cognition - thinking about other people and how you relate to them - and that topic is the focus of Chapter 19. There we will learn how we form impressions of others and compare ourselves with others. We will also learn how one person becomes attracted to another, how people fall in love, why we sometimes go out of our way or even take risks to help others - and why we don't. When you have read both these chapters, you will know much of what social psychology is all about.

The Neurophysiology of Social Behavior

Just Hang'in

The meeting began with the leader's announcement that they would meet tomorrow at 10:00 a.m. at Steve's house to "discuss some important stuff and just hang out." As Steve heard the announcement, he was worried because tomorrow was a school day - the third in two weeks that he would skip - and his parents were out of town. Now 16, Steve had felt lucky indeed to be accepted into this much respected and feared "in-group" at the early age of 14 - an achievement that had not gone unnoticed at school. He had soon discovered that the group had some definite rules: Don't associate with members of other clubs; date only outside the group; smoke; do drugs; skip school when a club activity is planned. Although Steve had obediently offered his house for the meeting, he was worried: The last house the club had met at was trashed; at least 2 members were clearly alcoholic and others were hooked on various drugs and had minor police records. But there were also advantages: Everyone at school respected members of the club; Steve's best friends were members; nearly everyone shared his views on a variety of subjects; and the 18-year-old leader was a dynamic guy who had great ideas. We'll return to see how the day at Steve's house went, but first let's take a look at social psychology, which studies groups like Steve's club, among other things.

Gordon Allport (1954) defined social psychology as the attempt to "understand and explain how the thoughts, feelings, and behaviors of individuals are influenced by the actual, imagined, or implied presence of others." Beyond this broad sense of what social psychology is, however, it becomes difficult to define the actual tasks of the social psychologist. In fact, one social psychologist has lamented the fact that his field is so difficult to define:

> My grandmother does not know what I do for a living. I don't hide my profession from her, but it's difficult to explain what a social psychologist does. I have a brother who is a physician. If he is a doctor, then despite my Ph.D. I must be something else. My uncle Frank is a clinical psychologist in private practice. Since I do not treat patients, I must not be a psychologist. How, then, can I call myself a doctor and a psychologist, but not have a medical degree and never treat patients? (Goldstein, 1980, p.2)

What, then, does a social psychologist do? Basically, he studies human interaction. The focus is not so much on the individual as on the interaction process, the variables that influence that process, and the effects of interactions on the individual and the society. We begin with the interesting question of where our attitudes - toward sports, abortion, nuclear weapons, and many other topics - come from and how they can be changed. We then look at the ways in which others influence our behavior - why we tend to conform, comply, and obey. We consider just how and why groups are formed and how their norms affect the behavior of the individual. And we review what is known about the effects of the physical environment on the person and just where aggressive behavior comes from.

Attitudes and Attitude Change

What is your position on nuclear disarmament? Abortion? Capital punishment? If you were assigned a roommate of a different race, how would you react? Do you believe in God? Are frozen vegetables better than canned ones? Your answers to these questions reveal some of your attitudes.

Attitudes are studied by social psychologists because they are important determinants of behavior (Baelter, 2002). They substantially influence our reactions in a wide variety of situations and tend to be quite stable over time. Anything that strongly influences the behavior of the individual on a continuing basis is important and needs to be understood so that we can better predict and understand that behavior. And attitudes fit that description. An *attitude* is a relatively enduring predisposition to respond in a reasonably consistent manner toward a person, object, situation, or idea. Attitudes have three basic components: (1) a cognition or *belief* about how something is or should be; (2) an *emotional* response to or evaluation of the object; and (3) a pattern of *behavior* toward the object (Figure 18-1).

Attitudes are not all created equal; some are more important than others. *Central attitudes* derive from direct experience or careful logic and are basic to the individual's self_concept. The central attitudes of one person might include a belief in racial equality, the view that human beings are basically honest, and religious beliefs. These attitudes are highly resistant to change. More *peripheral attitudes* are less basic to the self_ concept and somewhat easier to change. Peripheral attitudes might include a view favoring a particular political candidate, a preference for cats over dogs, or a distrust of people with red hair. And of course, not everyone's central and peripheral attitudes are the same.

Attitude Formation

Considerable effort has been devoted to developing a better understanding of how attitudes are formed. We need to know the sources of attitudes and the ways in which they are acquired.

Sources of Attitudes. Many attitudes are strongly influenced by our *reference groups* - the groups with which we identify most strongly. Early in life, the family is the primary reference group, and parents have the greatest influence on the developing attitudes of the child (Rice et al., 1997). Later, teachers, peers, and other reference groups begin to influence attitudes. Even an intelligent teenager aware of the hazards of smoking may smoke if her peers consider smoking to be the "cool" thing to do. A study of Israeli adolescents, for example, showed that those who did not have close relationships with their parents and who were exposed to messages valuing aggression were more likely to develop attitudes favoring aggressive behavior (Mesch et al., 2003).

Political and economic attitudes are also influenced by reference groups. A conservative Republican will tend to have many of the same political and economic attitudes as other conservative Republicans. A classic study of students at Bennington College, a politically, socially, and economically liberal institution, showed that entering freshmen typically held conservative views. By the time they graduated, however, their new reference group had made them considerably more liberal (Newcomb, 1943).

A final source of attitudes is the broader culture. The general attitudes of the culture are transmitted through the family and other reference groups and through the mass media (Deater-Deckard et al., 2003). In fact, the influence of the media, particularly television and, increasingly, the Internet, is very substantial. It is discussed in our 21 and in Chapter 6.

How Attitudes Are Acquired. Attitudes are heavily influenced by childhood experience. Some theories of just how this influence occurs have focused on classical conditioning, operant conditioning, and modeling (Chapter 6). Others suggest instead more complex processes.

Classical conditioning of attitudes has been demonstrated in studies in which Participants are taught to have positive or negative responses to previously neutral stimuli. In a series of classic studies, Arthur Staats paired the neutral names of countries (Sweden and Holland) and people (Tom and Bill) with either positive words ("happy," "gift") or negative ones ("sad," "terrible"). Positive pairings produced positive attitudes toward the previously neutral country or person; negative words yielded negative attitudes (Staats and Staats, 1958). Modern studies have supported this finding and shown that attitudes can be classically conditioned even when the participant is not aware that he is learning an attitude (Olson & Fazio, 2002).

In *operant conditioning* studies self_statements reflecting specific positive or negative attitudes are systematically reinforced. In one study, college students were either reinforced or not reinforced for making positive statements about a planned college_wide event. A week later, students whose statements had been reinforced expressed significantly more favorable attitudes than those who had not been reinforced (Insko, 1965). Many of our attitudes are no doubt acquired or at least strengthened by rewards from parents and peers for expressing attitudes of which they approve.

Another method by which attitudes are acquired is *modeling* - learning by observing and imitating the attitudes of others (Bandura, 1995). According to *social learning theory*, children acquire attitudes for which they are never directly reinforced merely by observing those attitudes in their parents. If parents quite obviously enjoy the effects of alcohol, the child may acquire a positive attitude toward drinking, even if her parents tell her that drinking is bad.

Information processing theory suggests that attitude formation is a complex cognitive process (Stratta et al., 1994). We receive a number of different pieces of information about a topic from various sources and integrate this information to form an attitude. You receive information about abortion, for example, from parents, peers, politicians, special interest groups, and the mass media. Norman Anderson (1980) suggests that you arrive at your attitude about abortion by *averaging* the information received from various sources. Other information processing theorists suggest other ways of combining the information, but all agree that it is through the complex cognitive processing of information that attitudes are formed (Fishbein and Ajzen, 1975; Massaro & Cowan, 1993).

Daryl Bem's *self-perception theory* is one information processing theory that has had a major impact (Bem, 1970, 1989). Bem believes that attitudes are developed primarily through observations of one's <u>own</u> behavior. We observe how we behave and use that observation as a basis for forming an attitude. For example, you may note that you have chosen to take a series of elective psychology courses, that you usually enjoy reading books about psychology, and that you selectively attend to psychology articles in popular magazines. From these observations, you will probably conclude that you have a positive attitude toward psychology.

A final attitude formation theory suggests that people may develop attitudes through *mere exposure* to the object of the attitude (Zajonc, 1968, 2001), and research suggests that the more familiar we become with an object, the more positive our attitude toward it will be. Zajonc and his colleagues have, in fact, shown that the mere exposure effect can occur even when the exposure is subliminal and the person is thus unaware of it (Monahan et al., 2000). Thus, a politician may get high ratings in the polls simply because she has advertised heavily and gotten name recognition. Even people who can tell you nothing about her political preferences may give her positive ratings (Marie et al., 2001). But some studies fail to support this hypothesis (Snell et al., 1995; Grube & Wallack, 1994).

So how *are* attitudes formed? It seems clear that both learning and cognitive mechanisms play important parts. Some attitudes may be formed primarily through simple learning processes, others principally through complex information processing, and still others through mere exposure. In addition, we are learning that such other factors as mood state and good old-fashioned self-interest influence the attitudes we form.

Cognitive Consistency

People tend to maintain consistent attitudes, often in the face of considerable evidence that they are inappropriate or incorrect (Simon & Holyoak, 2002). If, for instance, you strongly believe that women are nurturant and passive or that men are insensitive and aggressive, you may find it difficult to permit exceptions to your belief. And if an attitude does undergo change, related attitudes are likely to change with it to maintain overall consistency. In one study, undergraduates indicated their attitudes toward U.S. involvement in the Persian Gulf War 2 days before American military intervention began and again 2 weeks later. Their attitudes toward pacifism, isolationism, and Saddam Hussein were also assessed. Shifts in attitudes toward U.S. intervention were highly correlated with changes in attitudes toward these predictors. When one changed, the others changed in a consistent way (Spellman et al., 1993). Let's examine several theories of attitude consistency, including accessibility, cognitive dissonance, balance, and self-perception approaches.

Although attitudes tend to remain consistent, some are more consistent than others. One important factor in the degree of consistency is *accessibility* - the ease and speed with which an attitude that is stored in memory can be activated (Haddock, 2004). Inaccessible attitudes are less consistent and less stable than those that are highly accessible (Holland, 2003). Perhaps you have a strong, clear, stable attitude toward smoking that says it is always bad and a somewhat negative but weaker, less clear-cut attitude toward drinking. Your smoking attitude is more accessible and will tend to be the more consistent of the two. Similarly, a strongly held belief that aggressive behavior is inappropriate is more likely to cause you to avoid such behavior (J. Smith & Terry, 2003).

Leon Festinger's (1957) *cognitive dissonance theory* says that dissonance is aroused whenever you simultaneously hold two cognitions that are psychologically incompatible. A smoker who believes that smoking can lead to cancer will experience cognitive dissonance. Research shows that dissonance is greater in current smokers than former smokers and greater in heavier than in lighter smokers. The state of dissonance is unpleasant, and the individual is motivated to reduce it and attain a greater degree of consonance, or consistency (Goldsmith et al., 2004; Spangenberg et al., 2003).

If the dissonance is between an attitude and a behavior, there are three ways to reduce it: Change the attitude, change the behavior, or modify the perceived importance of the attitude or the behavior (Harmon-Jones et al., 2003). To reduce the dissonance, some smokers change their attitude ("The relationship between smoking and cancer is purely statistical"; or "Not everyone who smokes dies of lung cancer"); some change their behavior (they stop smoking); and some modify their thinking ("It's true that smoking causes cancer, but that doesn't really apply to me because I exercise and eat nutritiously"). Dissonance reduction has been studied in many groups. Topless dancers, for example, said that they were aware of the social stigma attached to their jobs. However, they were able to reduce the resultant dissonance by emphasizing the ease of the work and the money they made and by dividing their social worlds to separate the topless dancing from their private social lives (Thompson et al., 2003).

Striving to reduce dissonance often takes the form of seeking new information consonant with the decision you have made. If you experience doubts about your choice of an expensive sports car over an inexpensive compact, you may begin to scan motor and consumer magazines. Sure enough, you find that your car has done well in crash tests, gets good gas mileage (well, for a sports car!), and has great resale value, while the car you passed up has been recalled because the tilt mirror doesn't tilt. Obviously you made the right choice!

Both classic and recent studies show how the striving for consonance over dissonance affects behavior (Joule & Azdia, 2003). The classic experiment on dissonance reduction was conducted by Festinger and J. Merrill Carlsmith (1959). They gave students who had participated in a boring experiment either $1 or $20 to tell other students that the experiment was, in fact, interesting. Having to lie to the other students was presumed to create dissonance. The participants lied as instructed and were later asked their attitudes toward the experiment. Those who had been paid $1 had significantly more positive attitudes than those who had been paid $20. The low-paid students had reduced dissonance by modifying their attitudes toward the experiment to make them more consistent with their overt behavior; the $20 students experienced little dissonance because the high compensation justified their behavior (Figure 18-2). Recent work on terrorism and terror management has similarly demonstrated that when the threat of terrorist activity is made particularly salient to someone's own mortality, the stiving to reduce dissonance is much greater (Jonas et al., 2003).

The *balance theory* of Fritz Heider (1946) suggests that we are comfortable only if our attitudes are in balance. For example, if you are strongly opposed to abortion and your roommate is pro-choice, the overall system will be in balance only if you do not like your roommate or believe she's not too bright. If you do like your roommate, there is a state of imbalance. You will strive to gain balance by modifying either your view of your roommate or your attitude toward abortion.

Bem's *self-perception theory* has also been applied to the consistency phenomenon. Bem believes that consistency is maintained not by reducing dissonance but through an active, ongoing attempt to understand one's own behavior. In fact, he hypothesizes that observing one's own behavior leads to the development of attitudes, the opposite of earlier theories. To support his point, Bem reinterpreted the findings of the original Festinger-Carlsmith study. He pointed out that a participant who is paid only $1 looks at his behavior and reasons that making a positive statement for such a small incentive must mean that he really did enjoy the task. Thus, it was not cognitive dissonance but self-perception that caused the $1 subjects to make more positive statements about the experiment.

Attitudes and Behavior

Joan, an outspoken opponent of abortion, is pregnant with an unwanted child. Does her attitude mean she will not have an abortion? Sue decides not to end an unwanted pregnancy. Does that mean she is against abortion in general? In other words, can we use Joan's attitude to predict her behavior and Sue's behavior to predict her attitude?

Predicting Behavior from Attitudes. It seems only logical that behaviors would be consistent with attitudes. If you believe that smoking is bad for you, it certainly follows that you will not smoke. Right? Well, consider the classic study of the discrepancy between attitudes and behaviors done by Robert LaPiere in the early 1930s, when many Americans were prejudiced against Asians. He toured parts of the U.S. with a young Chinese couple, visiting 184 restaurants and visited 66 hotels. After completing the tour, LaPiere sent questionnaires to all 250 places, not mentioning that he and the Chinese couple had already been in their establishments. He asked each proprietor whether or not his restaurant or hotel would accommodate Chinese people. A whopping 90% of those responding said they would not serve Asians (LaPiere, 1934). This response documented the negative attitude he knew existed, but what about the behavior? Totally inconsistent: They were actually denied service only once!

Although other early studies supported LaPiere's finding that attitudes do not predict behavior (Minard, 1953; Wicker, 1969), later work showed that under some circumstances they may (Pilkington & Neil, 1997). For one thing, *central* attitudes are more predictive than peripheral ones (Bem and Allen, 1974). In addition, *specific* attitudes are more predictive. We can better predict how much money a person will donate if we know her attitude toward her own church or synagogue than if we only know her attitude toward religion in general. A third factor is the *salience*, or personal relevance, of the attitude. More salient attitudes are better predictors of behavior.

Suppose a major group attitude or belief were shown to be invalid. Would the group disintegrate? To find out, Leon Festinger and his colleagues (1956) joined a group called the Seekers, whose leader, Mrs. Keech, predicted that the earth would be destroyed by a great flood on December 25, 1955. What happened to group cohesiveness when this prophecy failed? Amazingly enough, cohesiveness actually increased, and group members even took credit for saving the earth from destruction! More recently, we saw evidence of cohesion under duress in militia groups pressured by government agencies and the media following the Oklahoma City bombing in 1995. More peripheral or casual members dropped out, but those at the core of each group became closer and the group therefore more cohesive.

To explain the relationship between attitudes and behavior, the *model of reasoned action*, proposed by Martin Fishbein and Icek Ajzen (1974; Ajzen & Driver, 1992), suggests that people act *rationally*, and therefore the best way to predict action is to go beyond attitudes and obtain an expression of *intention.* Intention grows out of attitudes, but a statement of intent to act is more likely to predict behavior than is the attitude itself. The intention to vote for a given candidate predicts actual voting behavior much better than do more global attitudes toward the candidate (Ajzen and Fishbein, 1980). In addition, people who express an attitude against drinking are less likely to stop drinking than those who state an intention to stop.

Going a step further, Ajzen suggests that attitudes and intentions are cognitions and that other cognitions are also involved in the decision to engage in a certain behavior. The conscious intention to behave in a specific way depends on three cognitions (Ajzen & Driver, 1992):

- *Attitude*, which is defined for this purpose as a desire to act in that way.
- *Subjective norm*, defined as the individual's belief about what other people would think of her action.
- *Perceived control*, which is basically the person's belief about his ability to carry out the action.

Let's apply the Ajzen model to LaPiere's finding that prejudiced proprietors of restaurants did not refuse to serve a Chinese couple. They probably wanted to refuse service but either perceived that others would see refusal as inappropriate (the subjective norm) or were afraid of creating a scene (perceived lack of control). The result was that attitude, which alone would have caused them to refuse service, did not determine intention.

A number of studies have supported the Ajzen theory. Sandi Smith and her colleagues assessed the intention of college students to donate their organs. They then presented them with a positive or negative persuasive message about organ donation. Regardless of the message, those who had expressed a prior intent to donate were much more likely to actually take organ donor cards (the behavior) than those with no prior intention to donate (Smith et al., 1994).
Other studies have examined the role of the three hypothesized cognitions in determining intention and behavior. In one, the attitudes, subjective norms, and perceived control of nurses discriminated clearly between those intending to care for HIV positive patients and those not intending to do so (Laschinger & Goldenberg, 1993). In another, 75 undergrad-

uates were shown six video games, then given a free-play period. The dependent variable was the amount of time they played each game. Results showed that their attitudes and perceived control, as assessed by questionnaires, were predictive of which games they spent the most time on (Doll & Ajzen, 1992). Subjective norms were not a factor, supporting another aspect of the theory, which holds that the three cognitions will not always be equally influential. Other recent studies have reported similar findings (White et al., 2002) and also shown that attitudes often affect social judgments about other people (Beckstead & Downs, 2003).

Predicting Attitudes from Behavior. Some studies have shown that we can change a person's attitude by getting him to engage in the behavior he is against. A teenager like Steve in our opener may be against smoking, but after trying it under peer pressure and getting hooked, his attitude may become much more positive. Marketing research has shown that potential customers who can be persuaded to return a simple information card develop much more positive attitudes toward a product (Armitage, 2003). Similarly, white college students had more positive attitudes toward African-Americans after they wrote a pro-black essay (Leippe & Eisenstadt, 1994).

It seems clear that we can predict behaviors from attitudes and attitudes from behaviors under certain circumstances, although the relationship is considerably more complex than psychologists originally imagined. Knowledge of this relationship has been helpful in attempting to bring about changes in attitudes, a subject to which we now turn.

Attitude Change

All sorts of individuals and groups are constantly trying to change our attitudes. Politicians, pro- and anti-abortion groups, health advocates, advertisers, and even our significant others all want to persuade us to adopt their views. Their success rate varies considerably, and social psychologists have identified several factors that influence attitude change (Bernard et al., 2003). They include the person delivering the message, the message itself, the medium of communication, and the audience.

The Communicator. We are somewhat more likely to change an attitude if the communicator has a high degree of *credibility*, meaning that he is perceived as knowledgeable, trustworthy, or believable (Guimond, 1999). Credibility increases when the communicator is perceived as an expert. People are more likely to take medical advice from a physician than from a plumber. Another important communicator characteristic is *trustworthiness*. In one study, 36 Catholic nuns were given a persuasive message concerning positive attitudes toward victims of AIDS. The message was presented by either a person with unknown credentials (neutral), one with high credibility (a physician) or one with high trustworthiness (a priest). The nuns showed the greatest attitude change when the priest presented the message (Lui & Standing, 1989). *Likeability* is another characteristic that influences attitude change (Figure 18-3).

The *name recognition* of a communicator can also affect his ability to persuade. Just before basketball star Magic Johnson announced, on November 7, 1991, that he was HIV positive, Louis Penner and Barbara Fritzsche (1993) had collected data on the willingness of students to help a person with AIDS. Willingness to help increased significantly one week after Johnson delivered his message about the need to help those with AIDS. However, when Penner and Fritzsche repeated the assessment 2.5 and 5 months later, the intent to help had dropped back to its pre-announcement level. Another lesson in attitude change: When it does occur, it isn't necessarily permanent.

The Message. The nature of the message also plays a role. *Social judgment theory* hypothesizes that attitudes are more likely to be accepted if they are not too different from those already held by the audience (Sherif and Hovland, 1961; Kyle et al., 2003). If you believe that abortion should be performed only when the mother's life is in danger, you might easily be persuaded to accept the alternative position that it should be performed only when a medical review board considers it necessary. But it would be difficult to persuade you that abortions should never be performed or that they should be available on demand. Considerable research supports social judgment theory (L. Smith et al., 2003; Harries, 2001).

Emotional aspects of a message can also affect its persuasiveness. Moderate to high levels of fear can be effective in changing attitudes and behaviors. However, positive messages are generally more effective than negative ones (Wegener et al., 1994).

The Medium. The medium or channel through which a message is communicated can have a significant impact on its effectiveness. Personal, face-to-face appeals are more effective than those that come through the mass media. One study attempted to reduce the frequency of heart disease in two California cities. Residents of Gilroy were exposed to a two-year multimedia campaign. In Watsonville the same campaign was supplemented by personal contact. The city of Tracy served as a control, receiving no persuasive appeals (Maccoby, 1980). The greatest and most immediate reduction in risks was in Watsonville. All this does not mean that the media have no influence on public opinion. It simply means that personal contact is more effective, though such media as virtual reality may prove even more so (Rothbaum et al., 1995).

The Audience. People differ in how readily they can be persuaded to change their attitudes. The individual difference factor in attitude change has been called *persuasability* - the ease with which someone will change an attitude (Sagarin et al., 2002). The most easily persuaded people are those who are low in self-esteem. People high in self-esteem seem to have their own internalized standards upon which they base attitudes that they are willing to defend. A teenager high in self-esteem might join a group like Steve's and refuse to smoke or do drugs because his persuasability was lower.

An individual difference factor that relates to and may partially determine persuasability is *argumentativeness.* Dean Kazoleas (1993) exposed groups of argumentative and non-argumentative students to messages advocating attitude change. Results showed that more argumentative participants were more likely to generate counterarguments and less likely to change their attitudes.

Another approach is the *inoculation theory* of William McGuire (1961), which suggests that persuasability is reduced when initial attempts to change attitudes are unsuccessful. Just as we can increase a person's resistance to chicken pox by injecting him with a small amount of chicken pox virus, we can increase his resistance to changing an attitude by offering a mild argument against that attitude. Research supporting McGuire's theory has shown, for example, that educational inoculation procedures can reduce smoking rates in high school students and increase advertising effectiveness (Burgoon et al., 1995). Overall, inoculation research suggests that persuaders must beware: An ineffective or mild appeal can be worse than no appeal at all.

A final audience consideration is that mood state may play a part. In particular, people in positive mood states are more prone to attitude change, and positive moods produce greater change when the message is also positive and less change when it is negative (Wegener et al., 1994).

Keys to Neuroscience - 1

Social Influence

Social influence refers to the effect of other people on the cognitions and behaviors of any given individual. Humans are obviously all subject to social influence on a daily basis. Parents, professors, significant others, and a variety of social and political institutions and organizations affect our thoughts and behaviors. Even West African chimpanzees show the effects of social influence on their behavior (Lehmann & Boesch, 2003). We will consider what the mere presence of other people does to modify behavior, then turn to the study of several related types of social influence: conformity, compliance, and obedience.

When Others Watch: Social Presence

Perhaps not surprisingly, people tend to eat less when others are present than when they eat alone (Herman et al., 2003). Thus, the simple presence of other people changes a major form of behavior - eating.

Norman Triplett (1898) was the first to discover the social presence effect in what may be the first social psychology experiment ever performed. Triplett noticed that bicycle racers performed better when racing against others than when racing against the clock. To see if this effect generalized to other situations and groups, he gave children fishing reels and asked them to wind the reels as rapidly as possible. He found that they wound faster when working in pairs than when working alone. Researchers soon showed that even when others were not actively participating in a task, their presence enhanced performance (Travis, 1925; Thomas et al., 2002). The study of *social facilitation* - the name given to this enhancement - was born (Strauss, 2002).

But nothing is ever simple, and some research soon began to demonstrate that the presence of others sometimes not only did not enhance performance, it impaired it. Floyd Allport (1920) found, for example, that students developed better arguments against the views of philosophers when working alone that when working with others present, and similar effects were seen in solving math problems (Moore, 1917). This interfering effect of others was dubbed *social inhibition* (Grior et al., 1995).

Facilitation vs. Inhibition. The next question is obvious: Why is the presence of others sometimes facilitating and sometimes inhibiting? By 1983, some 241 studies had addressed this issue. A meta-analysis of these studies, involving over 23,000 participants, showed that both social facilitation and inhibition do take place, but we still have no definitive understanding of the basis for these effects (Bond & Titus, 1983). The closest we have come is the theory of Robert Zajonc (1965), who hypothesized that the presence of others facilitates the performance of dominant responses and inhibits the performance of non-dominant responses. Dominant responses are those that are simple, heavily practiced, well-learned, or natural (reflexive or instinctual) - basically those that you know and do most easily. Non-dominant responses are more complex, less practiced, or newly learned, and they are not natural. If you regularly ride a bicycle, riding is a dominant response, and the presence of others will facilitate your performance, as it did that of the racers in Triplett's study. If you are just beginning to learn the intricacies of karate, the presence of others will inhibit your performance. Personality may also be a factor (Bengtsgard, 2001).

Why are dominant responses enhanced and non-dominant responses inhibited? Zajonc hypothesized that the key is *arousal* - the extent to which you are psychologically and physiologically activated or "keyed up." The presence of others increases arousal, and arousal is known to facilitate the performance of dominant and inhibit the performance of non-dominant responses. But how do other people increase our arousal? Zajonc answers that arousal is increased by the *mere presence* of others, but several alternative answers have been offered. One is that we expect others to evaluate our performance, causing *evaluation apprehension*, which is arousing (Gray & Heatherington, 2003). A second is that this apprehension combines with the potential for *embarrassment* to enhance arousal. When the two together raise arousal too high, which is more likely on complex tasks where failure might occur, we see a decrease in performance - a social inhibition effect.

Still another explanation suggests that the presence of others causes the individual to engage in greater *self-evaluation*, which is also arousing. A final possibility is that others who are present may pose a danger and we therefore engage in *social monitoring*, which is basically keeping an eye on anyone who is watching while we are performing. The harder it is to monitor those present, the greater the arousal and the greater the chance of inhibition. Supporting this hypothesis, it appears that studies in which the experimenter is in clear view show facilitation, while those in which she is behind the participant and thus harder to monitor are more likely to show inhibition (Guerin & Innes, 1982).

Empirical support for social facilitation and inhibition effects is substantial. High school students, for example, are more likely to engage in alcohol consumption (a simple, well-learned, dominant response) in the presence of other students (Thombs & Beck, 1994). Hispanic teenagers in another study showed peer facilitation of drinking, and their parents also facilitated the behavior by promoting it as a sign of masculinity (Beck & Bargman, 1993). Another negative behavior - crime - is also enhanced by social presence. In one study the criminal records of individuals were examined before and after they joined gangs. Their criminal activity increased significantly after joining, and they were more likely to commit crimes if others were present (Thornberry et al., 1993).

Social inhibition has also been demonstrated. In one typical study, the presence of a supervisor inhibited the performance of employees performing a complex task. In fact, even when the supervisor was not physically present but was known to be monitoring by computer, performance declined, probably due to evaluation apprehension (Dennis & Valacich, 1993). In another interesting study, Roy Baumeister and Andrew Steinhilber (1984) examined World Series records over a 59-year span to see who tended to win games, the home team or the visiting team. We might logically expect a home team advantage - the social facilitation effect typically seen during the regular season. They found that facilitation did occur for the first two games of the series, with the home team winning 60% of the time. However, the home team actually *lost* the final game 59% of the time. Why? Possibly because the arousal generated by the combined effect of a final game and the presence of the home crowd became so high that it produced social inhibition.

Social Loafing. Individuals working on a task with a group often engage in *social loafing* - putting in less effort than they would if they were working alone. This interesting phenomenon was first studied not by a social psychologist but by a French agricultural engineer named Max Ringelmann. In the 1880s he had each of 14 men pull a load, then had them pull a load as a group. He found that a man working alone pulled an average of 85.3 kg (about 187 lbs.), but that same man working as part of the group pulled only 61.4 kg (134 lbs.).

Ringelmann's finding has been replicated in more recent studies of rope-pulling. In one case 102 male students pulled a rope either individually or in groups of two to six. As compared with individual performance, there was a 9% reduction in force when two students pulled and 18% when six pulled (Ingham et al., 1974). More generally, social loafing occurs on both simple and complex tasks (Sanna, 1992). It is seen, for example, on word recognition tasks and when participants are simply asked to clap and cheer (Figure 18-4). More generally, a meta-analysis of 78 studies showed that social loafing is common (Karau & Williams, 1993).

Conformity

Groups could not exist for long without some degree of conformity from group members, and a vast majority of people do conform to group expectations much of the time. *Conformity* is basically a change in attitudes or behaviors to bring the person in line with group values and the social pressure they bring to bear, as in the case of Steve's conformity to his group (Meyer & Henslin, 2003). It occurs on two levels: outward expression of the norm in response to group pressures, and private acceptance. In the latter case, the individual not only conforms overtly to group standards but actually accepts group attitudes and behaviors as his own (Johnson et al., 2003). Such private acceptance may be in part a result of *dissonance reduction*: overtly conforming to a group norm with which you privately disagree creates dissonance, so you decide you really do agree with the group. Alternatively, private acceptance may occur when you *identify* with the group. Identification is usually accompanied by positive feelings toward the group that are enhanced by agreeing with group attitudes. Yet another explanation, that of Bem's *self-perception theory*, is that you observe your own behavior as you express normative attitudes and decide as a result that you must indeed hold those attitudes.

The classic conformity study was conducted by Solomon Asch (1951). A group of people was shown a card with three lines on it and asked which of the three matched the length of a fourth line (Figure 18-5). What the actual subjects in the group didn't know was that all the other members were confederates of the experimenter. From time to time the confederates would make clearly incorrect judgments of the lines. Asch found that a third of the real participants gave in to group norms and complied with the incorrect judgments.

Subsequent studies have shown that conformity increases as the ambiguity of the situation increases and with increases in group size up to four. Conformity decreases when group norms are extremely different from the person's individual judgment and when the "deviant" individual has at least one social supporter in the group. It has also been found that a small minority in a group can often change the opinion of the majority when the minority never waivers from its original position (Landau & Leynes, 2004). And a recent meta-analysis of 133 studies spanning 17 countries shows that culture is a significant factor in conformity (Bond & Smith, 1996).

Conformity applies to a wide range of attitudes and actions and is a powerful influence on human behavior. Such diverse and important behaviors and attitudes as drug and alcohol abuse and racial prejudice are characterized by strong conformity influences. A study of over 500 high school and college students showed, for example, that the primary cause of illicit drug use was conformity, as was the case with Steve's group (Bearden et al., 1994). Studies also show that people will often perform behaviors against their own beliefs and perceptions in order to conform to group pressures. John Duckitt (1994) studied over 300 undergraduates in South Africa and found that conformity was clearly a major basis for racial prejudice. Students perceiving more pressure to conform to the prejudice norm were more likely to be prejudiced. On a more positive note, teenagers exposed to group norms emphasizing the value of exercise are more likely to make regular exercise a part of their daily routines (Rivis & Sheeran, 2003).

The power of conformity is reflected in studies showing that people will conform to group pressures even when their behavior leads directly to punishment. In one study students working in groups were given verbal warnings not conform to group pressures and were actually punished if they did conform. They nevertheless stuck tenaciously to the norms, clearly perceiving that deviation from the norm would be worse than the punishment for conforming. Another study suggests that they were right (J. Smith & Bell, 1994). High school teachers and students were shown a picture of an unknown male student, then asked to rate him on a variety of personality traits, academic performance, social class, and interpersonal skill. The subjects were randomly assigned to two groups. In one, the male student in the photo was wearing an earring; in the second, he was not. When he was wearing the earring, he was rated as having significantly more negative characteristics. In effect, he was being punished for not conforming to group norms (Workman & Johnson, 1994).

Compliance

Although you might at first glance think compliance is synonymous with conformity, it actually has a quite different definition. *Compliance* means doing what someone else asks you to do when that person has no specific authority to make the request. Are you a compliant person? Suppose a stranger walked up to you and asked you to empty your pockets to prove that you did not take a dime from a pay phone. Would you comply? Well, 80% of the people approached in one study did exactly that (Moriarty, 1975). Compliance is also important in many real social situations (Invernizzi et al., 2003).

From the standpoint of evolutionary psychology, social compliance makes sense. It helps those whose requests you fulfill to better adapt to the environment and vice versa (Krebs & Janicki, 2004). It is, in effect, the social psychological version of the old axiom "Scratch my back and I'll scratch yours." On the other hand, some who would have you comply are not so altruistic, and they include a wide variety of people. Salespeople, for example, rely on compliance to make a living. Fund-raising organizations are successful only to the extent that they can gain your compliance to their requests. And the same is true of Army recruiters, politicians, scam artists who persuade elderly people to hand over their life savings, and the neighbor who needs help fixing his lawn mower. The question for social psychology is what the principles of compliance might be and what techniques therefore work best (Marder, 2003).

The Cognitive Dissonance Principle. Festinger's cognitive dissonance theory applies to a number of phenomena studied by social psychologists. Its basic concept - that we try to maintain consistency by striving to resolve discrepancies between beliefs and behaviors or among beliefs - provides an explanation of compliance under some circumstances.

Social psychologist Robert Cialdini (1988; 2003) has applied dissonance and other principles in an attempt to understand compliance. He began by going to those who are expert in the application of compliance: public relations experts, Army recruiters, advertising agency personnel, politicians and lobbyists. He underwent training in the sale of cars, encyclopedias, and insurance. In short, he began by studying how compliance techniques are used in the real world. He then went on to apply such theories as dissonance and to study several techniques that derive from these theories (Table 18-1).

A Foot In The Door. Consider this situation: A man stops by your desk in the office and asks to use your phone to make a local call. You naturally agree, and he then asks for a cup of coffee while he is waiting to see Mr. Jones. You give him the coffee, and he soon tells you that he is there to sell Mr. Jones an encyclopedia. It happens that he has just one other set left and can give you a special deal on these exceptional volumes. You buy the encyclopedias. You have been suckered by the *foot-in-the-door* (FITD) technique, a common sales approach based on the cognitive dissonance princi-

ple (Guadagno & Burger, 2003); Burger et al., 2004). You comply with the second request because refusing to do so after complying with the first one creates dissonance.

It is often on the basis of foot-in-the-door that people buy everything from vacuum cleaners to MX missile systems. Missile systems? Perhaps you think you've never bought a missile system, but as an American taxpayer you most certainly have, and politicians used FITD to fund it. The widely touted MX missile system began when politicians persuaded their colleagues and the public to spend just a few million dollars (a very small request by national standards) for research and development. They gradually appropriated hundreds of millions of additional dollars. How could we object after our initial compliance (Gueguen, 2002; Burger & Caldwell, 2003)?

A good example of the effectiveness of the FITD technique is an interesting study done in a bar. In this study bartenders asked 15 patrons to sign a petition against drunk driving. Over the next six weeks, each of these subjects and 15 others who had not been requested to sign were asked to take taxis home when they became too drunk to drive. Compliance was far higher in the group who had signed the petition (Taylor & Booth-Butterfield, 1993). Elliot Aronson and his colleagues also demonstrated the persuasive power of dissonance. They had college students publicly advocate safe sex to prevent AIDS, then reminded them of their own past failures to play safe. The dissonance thus created caused them to purchase more condoms (Stone et al., 1994).

***Low-Ball Technique.* A second application of dissonance theory is the *low-ball technique*, in which the person is persuaded to agree to a low price, then induced to pay a much higher price. The low-ball approach is commonly used by catalog sales companies. You look through the catalog and find an item you like at a reasonable price. Committed to the item, you fill out the order form, only to find that the "shipping and handling" charge (often well-hidden in tiny print) substantially increases the cost. A quick glance at several catalogs lying around my house proves the point: A $7.95 box of cards has a shipping and handling charge of $3.95 (a 50% increase in the cost); a $7.99 can of silicone "wonder lubricant" would cost an additional $4.50 in shipping and handling (a 56% increase); and for a $2.50 tool hanger, I would pay a total of $4.50 (an unbelievable 180% increase!).**

The low-ball technique is very effective. In one study solicitors sought a $2.00 donation to the American Cancer Society. When the $2.00 request was preceded by a request for 0.50, $1.00, or $1.50, participants were much more likely to comply (Wang et al., 1989). Most studies suggest that low-ball is more effective than foot-in-the-door. One example is a study in which 150 smokers were asked to abstain for 18 hours (Joule, 1987). Low-ball (asking initially for a shorter time) was more effective than FITD (getting agreement as to the dangers of smoking). Similarly, when phone survey participants were asked to answer questions on sensitive topics, such as sexuality, they were more likely to comply with a low-ball approach than with FITD, though both were more effective than a straight request (Hornik et al., 1991).

***A Door-In-The-Face.* Another social psychological concept that can explain some instances of compliance is the *reciprocity principle*. It says that people who receive benefits must contribute in kind; they must return the favors of others. That is the basis for the *door-in-the-face* (DITF) technique, in which your refusal of a highly unreasonable request causes you to comply with a lesser one. Perhaps you've faced a situation similar to this one, in which a guy in a fire hat appears at your door:**

> **Fire hat:** The Millville Volunteer Fire Company is asking everyone here in your neighborhood to give at least $200 toward the purchase of our new truck.
> **You:** We'd love to help, but that's a lot of money.
> **Fire hat:** Well, could you handle $50 or $100?
> **You:** Yes, I think we can give you $50.

Again you've been had, but this time for a good cause. The DITF principle often works well even though it may appear to conflict with the dissonance principle that underlies FITD and low-ball. In those cases, an initial minor request causes you to comply to the larger request in order to reduce dissonance. In DITF, the secret seems to lie in a version of the reciprocity principle. The hard-working volunteer fireman has done you a favor by letting you off the hook with his reduced request. You therefore owe him something and pay him back by agreeing to a smaller amount. In addition, there is a contrast effect: The $50 amount you agreed to seemed like a lot less after the initial $200 request than it would have if $50 were the initial request.

Research supports the effectiveness of the DITF technique, and it is often applied when charitable donations are requested. In one study 155 undergraduates were approached for donations. When an initial large request was made (the DITF), they were more likely to agree to a the second, smaller request than when that request alone was made (Abrahams & Bell, 1994).

Obedience

Even stronger than compliance is *obedience*, in which a command from an authority figure directly causes an individual to modify his behavior, sometimes against his better judgment. Steve, for example, obeyed the leader and invited

the group to his house. Obedience is a virtually universal phenomenon in society and has been carefully studied by social psychologists. A gruesome example of obedience was seen in Waco, Texas, on April 19, 1993. The Branch Davidian complex had been surrounded by agents of the FBI and Bureau of Alcohol, Tobaccco, and Firearms (ATF) for 51 days. During all that time, despite an obviously hopeless situation, most members of the sect steadfastly obeyed leader David Koresh and refused to surrender. When federal agents finally decided to storm the complex, Koresh may have ordered the Davidians to start fires and to kill themselves and each other. If that is the case, as the Justice Department says it is, they obeyed. They obeyed just as Lieutenant Calley's subordinates in the Vietnam War blindly obeyed him and killed 50 civilians in My Lai in 1969. They obeyed just as nearly 1000 members of the Jonestown, Guyana, cult obeyed Jim Jones in 1978 and killed themselves by drinking poison. And they obeyed just as the Nazis obeyed Adolf Hitler and murdered millions of helpless Jews and others during World War II.

Are these extreme examples of the behavior of a small segment of humanity, perhaps a segment too mentally ill or too intellectually deficient to resist authority? Surely *you* would not succumb. Or would you?

Some Basic Studies of Obedience. To find out just how obedient the average person is, Stanley Milgram (1963, 1974) conducted a series of experiments in which one person was ordered to cause severe pain in another. In a typical Milgram study, the participant was told that his job was to teach another participant (actually a confederate of the experimenter) a verbal learning task. The "learner" was strapped into a chair and hooked to some ominous-looking electronic equipment. The subject was then taken to a nearby room, where he was shown a machine with levers sequentially labeled from "Slight Shock" at one end to "Danger: Severe Shock" at the other end. He was told that he should give the learner up to 450 volts of electricity and that he should deliver a shock each time an incorrect answer was given. He was to increase the intensity of the shock after each mistake. Unknown to the subject, there were no actual shocks delivered. The "learner" made numerous mistakes, and as the shock level was increased, he began not only to complain about the shocks but to shout out things like "I can't stand the pain." If the participant hesitated about administering further shocks, the experimenter strongly encouraged him to go on, saying things like "It's absolutely essential that you continue."

If you were a participant in this experiment, what would you do? Would you refuse to continue, or would you go on giving shocks up to the "Severe Shock" level? If you think you would quit, you would be in the minority (Figure 18-6). A full 65 percent of the subjects in Milgram's experiment administered shocks all the way to the highest level, despite the screams and protests of the "learner." Milgram explained these results in terms of obedience to authority. The experimenter wore a white coat, looked very official, and was in charge of the study. Surely he must have known what he was doing.

Continuing The Quest. The Milgram research generated widespread interest in the study of obedience, and results have typically supported Milgram's central finding: Normal people are very obedient, even causing harm to others when ordered to do so. In one study, for example, participants interviewed a job applicant. They were ordered to make him nervous, disturb him during a test, and cause him to fail and remain unemployed. Over 90% did as instructed (Meeus & Raaijmakers, 1986). In another case an experienced nurse alone on a hospital ward received a phone call from someone unknown to her claiming to be a doctor and ordering her to administer a common drug to a specific patient. Although the "doctor" ordered a dangerously high dosage that was two to three times the maximum allowable for that drug, 95% of the nurses would have administered it if not stopped by an experimenter who was secretly watching them (Rank & Jacobson, 1977). That level of obedience is still observed (Krackow & Blass, 1995).

We can begin to see from these studies how a charismatic leader can have a devastating effect on followers. However, it is clear more generally that consistent, lasting personality traits also strongly influence behavior (Brandstatter & Farthofer, 1997) and obedience is no exception. Some people are far more likely to obey than others.

The Ethical Dilemma. Was there anything ethically wrong with the Milgram experiments and those that have followed them? The "learners" were confederates who received no actual shocks and were not concerned because they knew they would not. However, the "teachers" - the real subjects - were often in considerable psychological pain. They did not just glibly administer the shocks, but rather agonized over their task. Consider this reaction reported by Milgram as typical:

- After administering 180 volts of the possible maximum of 450, the participant says:

  > He can't stand it. I'm not going to kill that man in there. Do you hear him hollering? He's hollering. He can't stand it. What if something happens to him?....I mean, I refuse to take responsibility....I mean, who is going to take responsibility if anything happens to that gentleman?

- The experimenter agrees to take responsibility:

  > All right....

- The subject has now administered 240 volts.

  Oh, no, you mean I've got to keep going up the scale? No sir, I'm not going to kill that man. I'm not going to give him 450 volts.

- He is told that the experiment requires him to go higher:

  I know it does, but that man is hollering in there, sir.

The outcome? This subject went all the way to 450 volts, despite his obvious agony. For this reason, Milgram's critics over the years have accused him of unethical behavior. He put many normal people through a kind of personal hell as they were forced by the experimenter's orders to hurt another human being (Blass, 1995).

Those who support Milgram point out that his studies had real and important social value. They provided scientific evidence that even normal people are so obedient that they will inflict pain on others when told to do so. The results taught us something important about human behavior that has widespread implications for our understanding of such situations as Waco and Nazi Germany. Milgram has also come to his own defense. He believed, he says, that most participants would stop well short of the "danger" zone on the console. The results were thus a surprise to him but also an important scientific discovery. In addition, he points out that participants were carefully debriefed at the end of the experiment. The "learner" came into the room and interacted with them in a friendly way, and they were told that he received no actual shocks and that most people went all the way to 450 volts. Thus, Milgram argues, they did not leave the experiment believing they had hurt someone. Finally, he notes that 84% of the participants said they had learned something important and were glad they had participated.

Keys to Neuroscience - 2

Group Processes

Terrorists, such as those in Al Qaeda, are members of a group, and such terrorist groups no doubt follow the same principles of operation as do other groups. In fact, social psychology has begun to study groups of terrorists (Lawal, 2002).

Although most people are not terrorists, we all belong to a variety of groups. We are born into some groups, such as our family, our ethnic group, and our national group. We are more or less forced to belong to other groups because of where we live, such as our school and our neighborhood. And then there are groups that we purposely join, from social groups to professional groups to hobby clubs.

Theories of Social Affiliation

Psychologists have developed several theories of *social affiliation* - the need to be with other people (McGrath, 2004). They attempt to explain why human beings tend to form and join groups.

Social Exchange. The simplest explanation for social affiliation is that we form groups in order to avoid being alone, a situation that is extremely uncomfortable for most people (Cook & Rice, 2003). According to the classic *social exchange theory*, we associate with other people and with groups that provide us with *reinforcements* - rewards - of one sort or another (Thibaut and Kelley, 1959). These reinforcers may be social, psychological, or material, and they include such things as affection, prestige, business contacts, and satisfying social exchange. We evaluate groups according to the relative cost or gain of membership in them and join those that seem to offer more rewards than costs (Cropanzano et al., 2002).

Social exchange theory has been applied not only to group membership but also to an understanding of how we attempt to maximize rewards in the course of interactions with supervisors in an employment setting, in bargaining situations, and in deciding whether or not to help others (Guillet et al., 2002). It has also been supported by studies of the satisfaction of college students with their relationships and of the rejection of adolescents by peer groups (Hoff et al., 2003) .

Social Comparison. An alternative to social exchange theory is the idea that we join groups to obtain useful feedback. Originally formulated by Leon Festinger (1954), this *social comparison theory* continues to be an important stimulus for research on group processes (van Dijke & Poppe, 2003). It holds that a major function of groups is to help members assess their own attitudes, abilities, values, and behaviors. You evaluate your own scholastic abilities, for example, by comparing yourself with other college students, not with professors or steel workers. Social comparison theory also hypothesizes that a discrepancy between your attitudes or behaviors and those of your reference group is likely to lead to a change in your own position so that you move closer to the group norm (Klein, 2003). We have more to say about social comparison theory as it applies to individuals in Chapter 19.

Sociobiology

The social exchange and social comparison theories focus on the formation of human groups, but grouping is not an exclusively human phenomenon. Lower animals also form groups, and *sociobiology*, which studies the biological bases of social behavior, suggests that both human and animal groups form for evolutionary reasons (Nielsen, 1994). The basic premise is that social structures vary in the degree to which they are adaptive, and sometimes a small or large group is adaptive in the usual biological sense that it is more likely to further the survival and reproduction of the species (Zahavi, 2003). Consider the example of adaptive grouping in honeybees. It is important that bee hives be maintained at a constant temperature of about 35°C (95°F), both in the dead of winter and in the heat of summer. Temperature maintenance is accomplished through a group process: If the outside temperature is very high, the bees group together only loosely in the hive and obtain water droplets from returning worker bees to permit evaporative cooling; in cold conditions, they group together tightly, leaving fewer gaps from which heat can escape (Moritz & Dryger, 1994).

Groupings of various sizes and types in many other animal species, including humans, also have adaptive evolutionary value. The wolf pack, for example, can kill larger prey than could an individual wolf hunting alone. Similarly, humans often walk at night as a group in areas where they would not dare go alone. The bottom line from a sociobiological standpoint is that evolutionary processes work primarily toward the survival of the group, rather than that of the individual. Moreover, they work through a general, fitness-maximizing mechanism that directs all behavior toward survival and, particularly, reproduction. Whatever maximizes average survival in the group is what determines genetic fitness and what therefore survives. The groups that tend to form in any species are those that are more likely to further the survival of the group by ensuring that its genes are passed on (Wilson & Sober, 1994).

Sociobiologists hypothesize that common patterns of social behavior, even if they have a negative quality, occur because they selfishly maximized the genetic survival of the species - or at least did so in ancient times. Dominance, competitiveness, and aggression are examples of such behaviors. Why do they occur? Wouldn't it be better for everyone if people were more easygoing? The sociobiological answer to the paradox of such negative or potentially negative behavior patterns is that they provide a survival advantage. If competitiveness, for example, increases the probability of survival, it also increases the probability of reproduction by more competitive members of the society. The genes that underlie such behavior are thus more likely to be passed on to later generations.

Sociobiology provides an interesting perspective on the causes of human social behavior and has made some very creative contributions to the attempt to understand why people interact with each other in the ways that they commonly do. The theory has also, however, been highly controversial and has been subjected to criticism. Some critics say that the link between genes and social behavior is too complex and tenuous to make sociobiology even worthy of study (Dickemann, 1995). Others argue that sociobiologists virtually ignore the role of culture in determining behavior or that there is little empirical support for sociobiology as compared with other theories. Additional criticisms are that vague definitions have created a theory that is too imprecise, that the theory oversimplifies the whole area of population genetics, and that individual environment is more important than evolutionary history (Schlinger, 1996). Like other controversial theories, however, sociobiology has had a significant impact: It has forced social psychologists and others to seriously rethink their largely environmental theories of human behavior.

Evolutionary Psychology Is NOT Sociobiology

It is important not to confuse evolutionary psychology - which we outline in Chapter 1 and discuss in other chapters - with sociobiology. In fact, evolutionary psychologists regularly criticize sociobiologists for ignoring the role of psychological mechanisms in the control of behavior. Most sociobiologists hypothesize that animals - including humans - act directly on the basis of general, built-in mechanisms that maximize inclusive fitness. That is, virtually every act is undertaken to maximize the gene representation of that individual in future generations. As evolutionary psychologist David Buss (1995) points out, this should mean that men line up at sperm banks to increase the frequency with which their genes will be passed on. The sociobiological idea of such a single, domain-general (broad, content-free) mechanism that directs all individual behavior toward survival and reproduction also makes it very difficult to explain many common phenomena: Why do some people decide not to reproduce? Why do we often engage in such unhealthy habits as consuming fatty foods? And why is suicide the second leading cause of death in college students, occurring worldwide at the rate of 1.4 deaths per minute?

Evolutionary psychologists adopt a different position: They see themselves as having the same goal as that of other psychologists - the study of the psychological mechanisms, such as motives and desires, that cause behavior. These mechanisms do have a partly biologically basis, in that they are products of an adaptive, evolutionary process. However, they originally developed in response to *environmental* demands and are currently activated by stimuli in the immediate psychological environment. There is no claim that each act of each person is carried out in a fitness-maximizing effort.

The domain-general, fitness-maximizing mechanism of sociobiology is replaced, in evolutionary psychology, with many domain-specific mechanisms. Each is specialized for dealing with one narrow area of behavior, and each is represented by a specific module - a set of neuroanatomical and neurochemical mechanisms - in the brain (Cosmides & Tooby, 1994; Hernandez et al., 2003). Sandra Scarr (1995) has gone a step further to integrate evolutionary theory with genetic theory to provide for the inheritance of evolved characteristics. Social comparison processes, competition, and cooperation are among the social psychological phenomena explained through evolutionary psychology (Hantula, 2003). However, there are also critics of this theory, who argue that evolution is not a good explanation of such social phenomena (Vickers, 2003).

Norms

All groups affect the behavior of their individual members, and the members influence the standards and functioning of the group. This mutual influence is accomplished through a variety of mechanisms, the most important of which is group norms.

Norms are shared expectations about the attitudes and behaviors that should characterize the members of a group. Sloppy, tattered clothing and multicolored hair may be a norm for one group, while tailored suits and careful grooming may be the norm for another. Among high school students, members of some social groups may insist on Nike or Reebok sneakers, while members of other groups opt for shoes from Sears or Wards. And you saw some of the potentially destructive norms in Steve's group: smoking, drinking, drugs. In a classic experiment, Muzafer Sherif (1936) showed how group norms can influence individual judgments of the *autokinetic effect* - the apparent movement of a stationary point of light in a dark room (see Chapter 4). When Sherif asked subjects to judge how far the light had moved, they quickly modified their judgments to conform to the group mean.

One of the most important norms, common to virtually all groups, is the *reciprocity* norm. Another is *social equity*: social exchange within the group must be equitable for all (Newmann, 2002). Such norms as reciprocity and equity are so pervasive in our society that we see them operating not only within social groups but between groups as well (Johnston & White, 2003).

What are the effects of deviation from a group norm, and are there circumstances under which minority opinions can be influential? Stanley Schachter (1951) conducted a powerful experiment that showed what groups may do with individuals who deviate from norms. In his study, college students participated in a discussion group on what to do about "Johnny Rocco," a juvenile delinquent. In a report read by group members, the case was portrayed sympathetically, and the group typically favored leniency. Three confederates of the experimenter were planted in the group. One always conformed to the majority opinion, one argued at first for extreme discipline but then allowed himself to be persuaded to go along with the majority, and the third steadfastly insisted on recommending extreme punishment for Johnny. In all groups studied, this third confederate, "the deviate," was eventually rejected. He was isolated and ignored. When asked to name one person to exclude if the group size became too large, participants consistently named the deviant individual.

More recent studies suggest that a minority opinion in a group can have significant impact on the views of group members (Maass & Volpato, 1997). A meta-analysis of 97 studies of such minority influence demonstrated clear differences between public and private statements. Once a strong norm is established in a group, members will generally conform to that norm. If one member expresses opposition to the norm, other members will typically disagree with her in public. However, given the opportunity to express their views in a private way, some will be influenced by the minority opinion.

The influence of norms on such common, important and potentially dangerous behaviors as drinking, smoking and sex have been studied. John Baer (1994) assessed the impact of college norms on the drinking attitudes and behaviors of freshmen. He collected data just before the students entered college and again over the course of the first year. Surprisingly enough, the overall group exhibited decreasing acceptance of drinking as the year progressed. However, fraternities and sororities had norms that tended to strongly favor drinking. Students joining these organizations showed little or no decrease in drinking. Other studies show that smoking among high school students is strongly influenced by prevailing norms (Wang et al., 1997). And what about safe sex? One study tested an intervention designed to increase condom use by women in a college dormitory. The intervention consisted of training opinion leaders who would regularly talk with one group of 214 women (the experimental group), establishing a norm of condom use. A control group of 224 women did not receive the intervention. Results showed that the condom norm caused a modest increase in reported condom use.

The tendency of group members to follow norms can sometimes be detrimental to the functioning of the group. The Probe discusses one such circumstance - the interesting phenomenon of groupthink.

Group Dynamics

Stop for a moment and think about a group you have been a member of - perhaps a dorm, frat, or sorority group, a committee, a small club, or a high school clique like Steve's. What were the meetings like? What went on within the group that led to decisions? What conflicts occurred. All these questions fall in the domain of *group dynamics* - the processes involved in the internal operation of a group. Two important aspects of group dynamics are communication and cohesiveness.

Communication. In order to carry out actions, group members must communicate with each other. Social psychologists have therefore explored the nature of communication patterns in groups and tried to determine which patterns are the most effective.

In *chains* of communication, person A communicates with person B, person B communicates with C, and so on. This form of communication is found in many military organizations. An alternative is the *hierarchy* of communication: a number of people at the lowest level communicate with a smaller number at a higher level, and they, in turn, communicate with yet a smaller number at the top level. A third form is the *star pattern*, in which each individual group member communicates with a central person who is usually the leader.

Numerous attempts have been made to increase group communication. One approach is to develop training programs that draw on knowledge from social psychological research. An example is a study of 25 staff members who formed an interdisciplinary group in a rehabilitation clinic for chronic pain patients. They were taught how to recognize and reduce miscommunication, misunderstandings, and disorganization, thereby improving the effectiveness of the group (Cooley, 1994). Other approaches have focused on the overall method of communication used by a group and have focused on analyzing group dynamics in specific situations, such as the 1996 Mt. Everest tragedy, in which five climbers died (Mangione & Nelson, 2003). Traditionally, groups conduct their business, process information, and make decisions in face-to-face meetings where they exchange ideas and arrive at conclusions. More recently, however, computer communication has been introduced, and we can now differentiate at least two group communication methods. *Proximate communication* refers to the traditional group meeting format, while *distributed communication* involves communication primarily by computer, with each group member at a separate location (Slavin, 2002). Studies show that distributed communication often leads to the generation of more and better ideas and sometimes to better decision-making (Siau, 1995). Future work in this area will no doubt search for ideal combinations of proximate and distributed communication.

Cohesiveness. Cohesiveness is usually defined as the collection of forces that keep people together as group members. It can be based on external factors - those conditions outside the group that tend to keep it together - or on internal forces - those that involve the feelings and attitudes of members toward the group. External factors keep together such cohesive groups as the children in a family, hostages held by terrorist groups, soldiers in an army unit, and workers on assembly teams at the Harley-Davidson motorcycle factory (Chansler et al., 2003). In these cases, the members are forced into the group without choice. The major internal factor in group cohesiveness has been called *commitment* - the extent to which the person feels psychologically tied to the group (Abrams et al., 2003). In general, commitment is increased when the person works harder for group goals, sacrifices more, or receives more benefits from the group; it decreases when external pressures are strong. Under certain conditions conflict between two groups creates greater cohesion within each group.

High cohesiveness can increase the effectiveness of groups in a variety of ways (Wittenbaum et al., 2004). One study assessed cohesiveness in a 12-person American-Soviet team that spent 61 days trekking across the Bering Strait to Alaska, each member completing a measure of cohesiveness and effectiveness at the end of each day. The group functioned more effectively when cohesion was high, and cohesion increased when task assignments were perceived as fair, when disagreements were minimal, and when members were openly friendly and helped each other. Interestingly enough, planned stops at villages along the way to promote good international relations decreased the cohesiveness of the group (Leon et al., 1994). Other studies have shown that high degrees of cohesiveness reduce uncomfortable feelings of social pressure and increase satisfaction with the accomplishment of group goals. However, studies of groups that work together while being electronically monitored by supervisors show that group cohesiveness does not reduce the stress of such oversight (Panina, 2002).

Group Polarization. When several people who individually hold the same moderate position on a topic get together and discuss it, the group they form tends to adopt a more extreme position than the average one held by its members. Each of several people may, for example, be moderately against the use of nuclear power to generate electricity. However, if they form a group to discuss the topic, the group position is likely to be a more extreme one, perhaps advocating the absolute elimination of all nuclear power plants. This phenomenon is called *group polarization* (Figure 18-7). It is more likely to occur when arguments are presented with great confidence and when they are given repeatedly (Chen et al., 2002).

Group polarization has been documented in many studies (Flint, 2002). In one investigation, 30 active burglars were asked to evaluate potential burglary sites as to their vulnerability, then discuss the sites with other burglars. When the individual burglars were somewhat cautious about the vulnerability of a particular site, the group they formed came to a much more cautious evaluation (Cromwell et al., 1991). Other studies show that when a substantial majority of group members agree on one position, minority opinions drop out and polarization ends (Ohtsubo et al., 2002)

That polarization also applies to real-life settings was demonstrated in a study of a Jewish synagogue group. The

Rabbi announced that he supported the Palestinian rebellion in the Gaza Strip and West Bank. Some people agreed with him and others mildly or moderately disagreed. However, when these individuals formed groups, they polarized to positions either extremely favorable toward or extremely against the Rabbi's view (Hirschorn, 1992).

Cooperation and Competition

When we interact with others, our basic choices are to do what we can to help them, hoping they will reciprocate, or to compete with them for limited resources. Graduate students in my department, for example, often form cooperative study groups to prepare for exams. However, when they complete their degrees, they compete with each other for jobs. More generally, *cooperation* occurs whenever two or more people work together toward a common goal. *Competition* takes place when two or more people oppose each other by trying to attain some goal for themselves while denying it to others and lead to conflict (Sell et al., 2004). As a society we are often conflicted about cooperation and competition. Parents tend to encourage their children to cooperate with others, there is a more general norm favoring cooperation, and we tend to like cooperative people. At the same time competition is rampant, with individuals contending strongly for everything from clothing that is on sale to jobs. Researchers have worked hard to determine the principles that govern cooperation and competition, often using a research technique called the prisoner's dilemma.

The Prisoner's Dilemma. A favorite and often effective police tactic is to separate two suspects as soon as they are arrested and interrogate them. They are told that their willingness to confess may affect what the district attorney will recommend to the court. If both confess, he will recommend 15-year prison sentences. If neither confesses, he will recommend that both be convicted but get shorter sentences. If one confesses, he will recommend freedom for that prisoner and a 20-year sentence for the other. Hence, the prisoner's dilemma: Should he cooperate with his fellow suspect and refuse to confess or compete with his partner in an attempt to gain freedom by confessing?

Recognizing the potential of this situation for the study of cooperation and competition, social psychologists developed a laboratory exercise called the *prisoner's dilemma game.* In the basic version of this experiment, two participants, each at a separate laboratory console, are told that on any given trial they can choose to cooperate by pressing a green button or to compete by pressing a red button. Now here are the rules spelled out in the payoff matrix:

- If both cooperate (press the green button), they get the highest combined payoff ($1 + $1 = $2.00).
- If both compete (press the red button), they get the lowest combined payoff. In fact, in this example, they lose money (-$1 + -$1 = -$2).
- If one competes when the other cooperates, the competing participant achieves the highest individual payoff for any one trial ($5).

You can see the dilemma that each player faces. Over the course of many trials, the two players will each have the largest amount of money if they always cooperate. However, each player opens herself to a potentially large loss if she cooperates because her partner may compete on that trial. Hence, pressing the competitive red button on some trials can lead to the greatest individual gain.

There have been many prisoner's dilemma studies, including some in which participants unknowingly had human-like computers as partners. Collectively, these studies have resulted in some principles of cooperation and competition. The most basic is that, at least in our Western society, the far stronger tendency is to compete, not cooperate, even though this is ultimately a losing strategy (Kay & Ross, 2003). However, there are some circumstances in which cooperation occurs on early trials and competition on later trials. Research has also extended prisoner's dilemma to group settings. In these studies several participants work as a group, making decisions together and deciding to cooperate or compete with another group. What happens? Cooperation virtually goes out the window. The tendency to compete becomes even greater, and the groups rarely arrive at cooperative responses (Acevedo, 2002). Principles of cooperation and competition derived from prisoner's dilemma studies have been applied to the analysis of a variety of real-life situations, including international trade agreements, the operation of political parties, and the European Common Market (Harris & Madden, 2002).

Groups in Cyberspace

The growth of the Internet has created many online groups, whose members have typically never met in person, but may share certain values, interests, and preferences and communicate with each other frequently. Such Internet groups are, of course, very different in some ways from traditional groups in which the members meet face-to-face on a regular basis to communicate about their shared interests. This raises the question of whether or not our existing knowledge of group processes - based on the study of traditional groups - can be applied to cyber groups.

Social psychologists have recently begun to address this question, and some believe that past findings do not entirely apply to this new group phenomenon. A pair of studies showed, for example, that women are less likely to be

persuaded by a group communication conducted online than in person, whereas men show no difference between the two (Gudagno & Cialdini, 2002). Brian Butler (2000) reviewed the existing literature more generally and analyzed longitudinal data on cyber groups. He concludes that Internet groups differ from traditional groups in significant ways. In particular, they tend to be larger, have more diverse memberships, and be less stable than traditional groups. These differences suggest that social psychologists will need to conduct extensive research to see just how these groups are formed, how they gain and lose members, and how they are similar to and differ from traditional groups.

Keys to Neuroscience - 3

Environmental Psychology

Social psychologists have tended to ignore the physical environment in which social interaction takes place. Environmental psychologists, who are also interested in social interaction and its effects on the individual, have studied such factors. Among the areas they address are personal space, crowding, territoriality, and environmental stressors.

Personal Space

If you have ever had a stranger or a casual acquaintance stand within a few inches of your face while engaging in conversation, you know firsthand what is meant by an invasion of personal space. Most people react with discomfort and take action to increase the personal distance. Anthropologist Edward T. Hall first brought attention to the importance of personal space in his book *The Silent Language* (1959), but it was not until the publication of Robert Sommer's *Personal Space* in 1969 that psychologists, architects, designers, and others came together in earnest to study personal space and its relationship to individual and social processes. More recently, social psychologists have extended the concept to the study of space occupied by groups. *Personal space* is a definite but invisible psychological boundary that surrounds each of us and into which invaders are not comfortably allowed (Kramer, 1995). Although comfortable personal spaces can be very small in the case of intimate relationships, our conversations with friends are likely to take place at a distance of two feet or more, and less-personal conversations may occur at distances ranging from four to twelve feet.

Comfortable distance varies from one person to another and from one culture to another. Males are likely to maintain a greater distance between themselves than females, and highly anxious people maintain greater personal space than people low in anxiety. In addition, Italians and Greeks maintain less distance than the English and French during conversations (Remland et al., 1995).

When personal space is invaded, the individual person is likely to experience increased physiological arousal. Why? Perhaps because the invasion threatens a need for privacy, produces excessive sensory stimulation, or simply increases stress. At the same time, Bibb Latane has shown that once we are beyond the boundaries that define personal space, the effect of a social interaction on the individual decreases with increasing distance (Latane et al., 1995).

Crowding

In New York City, millions of people are crowded into an area of 369 square miles. Tokyo, with only 223 square miles, has even more. What are the effects of such urban crowding on individuals? In a classic study on the effects of crowding in rats, John B. Calhoun (1962) divided a 10 x 14 room into four pens, each providing comfortable living space for twelve rats. He then introduced a colony of rats into each pen and observed what happened as the population increased. Two of the pens were taken over by dominant males, each with a group of eight to ten females, while the sixty or so remaining rats were crowded into the other two pens. Antisocial behavior increased dramatically with the crowding. Female rats began to ignore their young, and males became either withdrawn or hyperaggressive.

Investigations of human crowding have yielded more mixed results. Some show, for instance, that crowding in prisons increases the frequency with which inmate problems occur (Kinkade et al., 1995). Similarly, crowding in work settings is associated with reduced frustration tolerance and reduced social interaction, as well as increased blood pressure and aggressiveness in men and decreased aggressiveness in women. And crowded home living conditions can lead to social withdrawal (Evans et al., 1996).

One series of studies conducted by Andrew Baum and his colleagues focused on the effects of crowding in college dormitories. Dorms with long-corridor designs, in which 32 to 40 residents share bathroom, lounge, and hallway spaces, are more crowded than those with short-corridor designs, in which 6 to 20 students have shared areas. Residents of long-corridor dormitories report greater stress, show a greater tendency to withdraw from social interactions, and display more helpless behavior when playing experimental games (Baum et al., 1982). On the other hand, some studies find no crowding effects (Rousseau-Francois & Standing, 1995). Overall it appears that crowding may have some negative effects on humans, although these effects have been difficult to demonstrate consistently.

Territoriality

We all tend to establish territories throughout our daily environments. One-half of that dorm room is *yours*, and you probably tend to use the same shower stall, sit at the same cafeteria table, and use the same chair in the lounge, day after day.

A number of studies have documented this tendency (Steele & Brown, 1995). College students will stake out and defend library seats, and game players in a video arcade will stand at a particular machine for long periods, even when not playing, defending their territory by keeping their hands on the machine. In some circumstances, territoriality can be a source of destructive behavior. In city environments, for example, gangs defend their territories vehemently (Goodenough, 1997).

Occupying one's own territory can have a number of positive effects. Married couples, for example, show better adaptation when each member has some separate territory within the home. People engaged in a debate are more likely to win when they are in their own personal territory. And workers are more satisfied and productive when their territories are not invaded by others (Omata, 1995). Territoriality may provide privacy, a possibly important source of comfort and productivity.

Environmental Stressors

Although maintaining personal space and establishing personal territories can help reduce stress and increase psychological comfort, many other environmental sources of stress remain, including noise and heat. Environmental psychologists have studied the effects of such stressors with an eye to structuring environments that help minimize them.

Noise. Excessive noise has become a fact of life, particularly in urban environments. Car engines, honking horns, jackhammers, sirens, and a variety of other sounds regularly pollute cities and suburbs. What are the consequences of exposure to such noise? Although noise seems to have little effect on the performance of simple tasks, it does impair performance on complex tasks (Becker et al., 1995). Noise exposure has also been associated with reductions in auditory and visual discrimination, increased blood pressure, attention deficits, poor performance on cognitive tests, and lower frustration tolerance. Information-processing ability is also impaired (Brand & Schneider, 1995).

Noise also has effects that go well beyond task performance. It reduces sensitivity to social cues, decreases the likelihood of altruistic (selfless) behavior, and increases aggressive behavior. People living on noisy streets are less likely to socialize than people living on quiet streets, and pedestrians are less helpful to others when the environment is noisy (Topf, 1995). Susan Staples (1996) has called for increased practical applications of what psychology has learned about noise and about individual differences in reactions to it.

Some DON'T Like It Hot. If you've ever tried to study for an exam during a heat wave, you know that heat can be a significant source of stress. Studies of heat as a stressor grew out of curiosity about what caused a series of riots that occurred during the long, hot, summers of the 1960s. All but one of the major riots began on days when the temperature exceeded 80 F, and there was an increase in the crime rate during particularly hot periods of the summer (Kerner Commission, 1968). The same was true in Houston in the early 1980s (Figure 18-8).

Considerable research confirms the relationship between temperature and the occurrence of riots. And heat also increases the rate of homicide and other violent crimes (Cheatwood, 1995). However, it seems unlikely that heat alone causes aggression. Rather, high temperatures in a situation that might potentially elicit aggression increases the likelihood of that aggression occurring. There is also evidence that when temperatures rise even further, crime rates may be *lower*, probably because the excessive heat makes activity of any kind too uncomfortable.

Keys to Neuroscience - 4

Aggression

The subjects in the Milgram studies we discussed earlier were displaying not only obedience to authority but also a form of aggression against another human being. One of the most disturbing, anxiety-producing, and potentially destructive of all forms of human behavior, aggression has been widely studied by social psychologists who believe that understanding it may help us control and reduce it. As reading 21 later in this chapter points out, violence is rampant in our society right now, but there are ways to reduce it.

Aggression can be defined as behavior performed with the intent of physically or psychologically hurting one or more other people. Internal feelings of anger and hostility may be involved, but externally observed aggressive behavior must occur in order to qualify as aggression. We need to distinguish aggression from *assertiveness*, which means taking a stand and letting one's views be clearly known without any intent to inflict harm.

Aggressive behavior may be *physical* (hitting, stabbing, shooting) or *verbal* (insulting, demeaning, shouting) and also active or passive. *Active* aggression involves some specific physical or verbal abuse of the other person, whereas *pas-*

sive aggression is a more subtle form in which *inaction* is used to harm another. The brother who neglects to tell his teenage sister that her boyfriend called, the supervisor who passes over a competent but disliked employee for promotion, the worker who knowingly fails to complete important work on time - all are exhibiting passive aggression. Aggression may also be *instrumental* (intended to achieve some goal) or *hostile* (with no particular goal except to hurt the other person). The soldier who shoots an enemy to save his own life is using instrumental aggression; the angry husband who hits his wife is engaging in hostile aggression. Let's look at contribution of learning to the development of patterns of aggression, the triggers that often set off this destructive behavior, and the biological factors that predispose people to become "lions" or "lambs."

The Role of Learning

The most basic learning theory that deals with aggression is the operant conditioning approach, which suggests that aggressive behavior develops as the result of a pattern of positive and negative reinforcements. Some studies have clearly demonstrated the effects of rewards on aggression. Nursery school children praised for an aggressive act against a particular child will continue to aggress against the same victim, and aggression can be quickly reduced when teachers ignore aggressive behavior and reward desirable behavior. Consistent with these results is the finding that inadequate discipline in the home - taking little or no action to reduce aggressive behavior - is associated with higher levels of aggressiveness later in life (Lynch, 2003). The child who can usually get her way by becoming angry and shouting at her mother is being rewarded for aggressive behavior. When such reinforcement experiences occur repeatedly over the course of childhood, they can contribute to a pattern of aggressive behavior in later life.

Social learning theory holds that most aggressive behavior is learned by observing such behavior in people who serve as models. A child may observe his father shouting at his mother and striking her in the course of an argument. Although the child is in no way specifically reinforced for engaging in similar actions, he may internalize the behavior and exhibit it many years later.

Albert Bandura (1965, 1973) conducted a classic series of studies to test this social learning approach. In the basic experiment that we describe in more detail in Chapter 6, a film showed an adult model performing aggressive acts against a "Bobo" doll. The model punched, clubbed, kicked and shouted at it. Children who saw the film subsequently exhibited these same aggressive behaviors. In extensions of this basic study, one group of children saw the model rewarded, another saw him punished, and a third saw him receive neither reward nor punishment. When the children later had an opportunity to play with the Bobo doll, those who saw the model punished exhibited less aggressive behavior than those in the other two groups. Moreover, children who saw a film in which the model did not behave aggressively toward the doll committed fewer aggressive acts than those who had seen the more violent version.

More recent studies in other laboratories have lent support to social learning hypotheses (Lebreton, 2003). Children who see more violence at home - for example between the parents - and those whose families include criminals are more likely to themselves be violent as adults (Heidgerken, 2003). Along these same lines, a study of over 500 kindergartners showed that those who were more harshly disciplined at home were more likely to be aggressive in school (Weiss et al., 1992). And inner-city African-American children show a similar pattern (Xie, 2003).

Moving beyond the home, one investigator studied children between ages 3 and 8 from different Zapotec communities in Mexico and rated the adult communities in which they lived for overall aggressiveness. It was found that children from more aggressive adult communities were themselves more aggressive (Fry, 1992). And a study of Anglo and Hispanic men and women showed that those exposed to more violence were more likely to be aggressive (Harris, 1996). More generally, children exposed to community violence are more aggressive (Guerra, 2003).

A final approach has involved the use of modeling techniques to reduce aggression. In a study of ten violent delinquents between ages 12 and 24, a therapist modeled nonaggressive behavior, and the delinquents showed a decrease in aggressiveness over time (Vidyasagar & Mishra, 1993). There is thus considerable evidence to support Bandura's idea that aggressive behaviors can be learned simply by observing those behaviors in others. Such findings have contributed to the controversy over whether observing violence on television can be harmful, which we discuss in Chapter 10.

Social learning processes have often been thought to contribute to gender differences in aggressive behavior. In fact, there is a widespread perception that such processes cause men to be more aggressive than women - but are they? Our CRITICAL THINKER discusses this important topic.

Triggers For Aggressive Behavior

Learning processes are also important in determining the stimuli and situations that will trigger off aggressive behavior in a given individual. Even the most aggressive person is unlikely to exhibit open hostility unless some immediate situation stimulates the behavior. Let's consider the roles of frustration, arousal, and deindividuation in triggering aggressive acts.

Frustration and Aggression. When your brother repeatedly knocked down the tower of blocks you were trying so hard to build, you probably became frustrated and may have hit him or shouted at him. In fact, some theorists believe that frustration is the primary stimulus for aggressive behavior.

Formulated by Neal Miller, John Dollard, and their colleagues (1939), the *frustration-aggression hypothesis* originally held that frustration *always* leads to aggression and that aggression is *always* the result of frustration. This hypothesis generated hundreds of studies, many of which largely or entirely supported it. At the same time, some researchers concluded that frustration and aggression do not always go together, and Leonard Berkowitz (1959, 1984) revised the theory. He suggested that we have an innate aggressive response to frustration that is expressed or released only if adequate conditions, such as an appropriate target person, a weapon, or a conducive environment, are present. Although the idea that frustration is the main cause of aggression is appealing, it has become apparent that only some kinds of frustration, such as perceived racial inequality, lead to aggression (Fox, 1999). Moreover, aggression is often triggered by situations other than those involving frustration, and those with a stronger genetic tendency are more likely to be aggressive, as we will see shortly (Lewis, 2003). .

The Role of Arousal and Cognition. Perhaps the most common form of instigation to aggression in our society is the verbal attack. Being insulted produces not only psychological feelings of hostility and negative emotions more generally, but also a state of physiological *arousal.* Changes include increases in blood pressure, heart rate, respiration rate, pupil diameter, muscular tension, and output of epinephrine and norepinephrine. This elevated physiological arousal represents a fight or flight reaction that can support or even cause aggressive behavior. In general, the greater the intensity of the verbal attack or other form of instigation, the greater will be the aggression.

Insults also activate *cognitive* processes as the person pauses to assess the source of the insult and its degree of seriousness. Many researchers have concluded that the emotional state resulting from an insult is a joint function of physiological changes and cognitive processes. The insulted person takes into consideration both the feeling of physiological arousal and the cognitions associated with the situation to arrive at the conclusion that he is angry. Thus, there must be both a state of arousal and an appropriate set of cognitions before the individual will actually experience an emotional state of anger and potentially engage in aggressive behavior.

Vladimir Konecni (1975) devised an interesting, classic study to demonstrate the interactive roles of arousal and cognition in aggression. The participant was insulted by a confederate, who made disparaging remarks about her intelligence and other personal characteristics. She was then asked to decide, on each of fifty successive trials, whether or not to give the confederate an "electric shock." During the experiment, the subject also heard a series of tones that were of either normal or aversive loudness. What effect did the loud noise and the insults have on the aggressiveness of the subject? The results were quite clear: Subjects who had not been insulted prior to the "shock" trials administered the least shocks, whether or not they were aroused by the loud noise; those who had been insulted administered by far the most shocks when they were in the loud noise situation. Thus, the loud noise considerably enhanced the aggressiveness induced by the insults. This result clearly suggests that heightened arousal - from any source - is likely to increase aggressive behavior that may be elicited by a current situation. So if you must insult, criticize, or frustrate another person, try to do it when he's not already aroused!

The arousal that enhances aggression need not come from a verbal insult. In fact, arousal of purely physical origin increases the probability and intensity of aggression, as Dolf Zillman (1978) has shown. He had participants become aroused by riding an exercise bike, then insulted them. They were more aggressive than participants insulted when they had not first ridden the bike, a finding confirmed in other studies. This *transfer of excitation* phenomenon is discussed in Chapter 12.

The Role of Deindividuation. Social psychologist Philip Zimbardo (1969), following the lead of personality theorist Carl Jung, suggested that some triggers for aggression revolve around the concept of individuation. *Individuation* refers to taking actions on the basis of an awareness of one's own distinct feelings, views, and preferences. When we are in familiar settings and interacting with those who know us, individuation is high and we are motivated to behave in accordance with our own self-concept and the expectations of others. *Deindividuation* is a breakdown of self-awareness, a reduction in feelings of self-consciousness and distinctiveness. It is likely to occur when we are away from friends and family and are therefore functioning in relative anonymity. Zimbardo believes that aggression is more likely to occur under such circumstances. The person feels less like himself and is less concerned with impressing others.

To test his hypothesis, Zimbardo divided female experimental subjects into two groups. "Individuated" participants were called by name, wore their own street clothes, and were otherwise treated in a personal manner. "Deindividuated" participants were not called by name and wore standard lab coats and hoods. It was found that deindividuated subjects administered more shocks to another person when asked to, confirming Zimbardo's hypothesis. Furthermore, the deindividuated participants gave substantial levels of shock to both pleasant and obnoxious victims, while individuated subjects gave greater shock to the obnoxious victims - a more socially acceptable act.

More recent studies confirm the effects of deindividuation. Participants who remain anonymous in a group situation administer significantly higher levels of noise than do those whose identities are known to other members of the group. In addition, when participants are exposed to cues that reduce the sense of individuation (such as being treated as a "number"), they experience an internal state of deindividuation that increases aggression. And several police officers working as a group are more violent toward suspects than is one officer alone (Wilson & Brewer, 1993). The deindividuation hypothesis has also been supported in real-world settings outside the laboratory.

Biological Factors in Aggression

Although learning processes are important, they cannot alone account for what we know about the origins of aggression. Biological factors are clearly also important. This fact was recognized by Sigmund Freud and later by evolutionary theorists and behavior geneticists.

The Psychoanalytic Theory of Aggression. Freud hypothesized that aggressive behavior is principally the result of an innate biological motive that he called the "death instinct." This inborn destructive tendency creates a drive state that must somehow be reduced. The person therefore engages in aggressive behavior that serves to satisfy and temporarily eliminate the uncomfortable drive state. Aggression resulting from the death instinct may be directed inward or outward. Inward-directed aggression can lead to feelings of worthlessness and depression, sometimes resulting in suicide; outward-directed aggression can lead to hostility toward others. The specifics of aggressive behavior patterns in a given individual are influenced by experiences and learning processes that take place during childhood, but the underlying basis for aggression is biological (Kraus, 1997).

An Evolutionary Basis. Like Freud, noted ethologist Konrad Lorenz (1966) believed that aggressive behavior is largely instinctual - a biological given, built into the organism at birth. He observed that aggression has significant adaptive value for many animal species, suggesting an *evolutionary* basis for this form of behavior. The roots of human aggression lie in the defensive aggression seen in many animal species. Most aggressive animals are equipped with natural weapons, such as powerful jaws, sharp teeth, and talons. Most animal aggression is directed toward members of *other* animal species, and animals within a given species often have "submission signals" that will stop a fight before either animal is killed.

Lorenz believes that human beings also have strong instinctual aggressive tendencies and have developed a variety of methods for dealing with them. However, humans do not appear to have adequate submission signals and, indeed, have developed long-range weapon systems that make submission signals much more difficult to send or receive.

Support for the ethological view that aggression has a biological basis comes from a variety of animal and human studies. It is possible to breed mice over the course of several generations so that one strain will be extremely aggressive and another will be quite docile. In addition, there is evidence that humans vary in aggressiveness from such an early point in life that physiological factors are almost certainly involved. Moreover, aggressive behavior is related to physiology in a number of known ways. It is increased by the use of alcohol, by low blood sugar levels, by injected male hormones, and by certain types of brain injuries (Miles & Carey, 1997).

Genetic Factors. The biological mechanisms of human aggression lie in the genetic substrate of behavior, an observation documented by numerous studies. In one investigation, the aggression-related personality traits of 191 pairs of identical and 309 pairs of fraternal twins were studied. Some pairs of each type were reared together and others apart. Concordance for assertive and aggressive traits was much higher in identicals, confirming the role of genetic factors (Coccaro et al., 1997). Other studies suggest that such traits as anger and hostility are highly heritable and that heritability for aggression is at least 50% (Cadoret et al., 1995. Moreover, we are well on the way to identifying some of the specific genes involved (Plomin, 1995). We will shortly see just how the genetic underpinnings of aggressive behavior may be expressed in the brain.

Keys to Neuroscience - 5

The Neurophysiology of Social Behavior

There is no doubt that social behavior is mediated by the central nervous system. Whether you are forming an attitude, acting on a group norm, obeying an instruction, or engaging in an aggressive behavior, neurological processes are clearly involved. However, there has thus far been little study of the neuroanatomy and neurochemistry of social behavior because the phenomenon itself is so complex. As a result, we will focus here on what we know about the neural basis of one form of social behavior, aggression.

We have already reviewed evidence showing that genetic factors underlie aggression and partially account for individual differences in aggressive behavior. The expression of these genetic factors appears to be in the hypothalamus and amygdala and in the release of specific neurochemicals (Sylwester, 1997). When certain regions of the *hypothalamus* are stimulated electrically, a cat will become aggressive. It will arch its back, snarl, and attack nearby objects, such as a mouse, a rat, or the experimenter's hand. Regions of the hypothalamus involved in aggression have been identified in rats and mice, and humans with lesions in these areas are similarly aggressive. The *amygdala* also has a role, and stimulation or ablation of certain parts of this structure can also systematically produce or eliminate aggressive behavior (Oakes & Coover, 1997).

Certain neurochemicals and hormones also help to form the biological substrate of aggressive behavior. In particular, *serotonin* is strongly implicated (Coccaro et al., 1997). An important neurotransmitter, it is found predominantly in the raphe system in the hindbrain, which controls sleeping and waking patterns, among other things.[1] Low levels of brain serotonin are associated with increases in aggressive behavior and with violent crime (Virkkunen et al., 1995). There is also evidence of abnormally low serotonin levels in patients exhibiting psychological disorders characterized by excessive aggressiveness. And other neurotransmitters that may be involved include epinephrine and norepinephrine.

Monoamine oxidase (MAO), a brain enzyme involved in breaking down a number of neurotransmitters for excretion from the body, has also been implicated in aggression, though there is thus far less evidence than that for serotonin. In addition to these neurochemicals, the male sex hormone *testosterone* appears to be involved. Both men and women who exhibit high levels of aggressive behavior have significantly higher levels of serum testosterone than do their more docile counterparts (Castrogiovanni et al., 1994).

Keys to Neuroscience - 6

Conclusion

It has become apparent in this chapter that social psychologists have cast a wide net in their ongoing attempt to better understand human social behavior and the effects of both biology and environment on that behavior. In addition to attitudes, group processes, conformity, obedience, and aggression, social psychologists also investigate the ongoing series of one-on-one interactions that we engage in from day to day. How do we form impressions of other people and make attributions about the causes of their behavior? How do our perceptions of ourselves affect our behavior toward others? What causes two people to be attracted to each other and become friends or lovers? And under what circumstances are we more or less likely to help others who are in difficulty? These and related topics covered in Chapter 19 round out our discussion of social psychology.

And what about the group "meeting" at Steve's house. As he feared, the group trashed the house, and when his parents placed him on restrictions, he rebelled. He became even more involved with the group and ended up not going to college - a sad commentary on the power of group norms, misguided leadership, and obedience.

Summary

1. Social psychology has been defined as the attempt to "understand and explain how the thoughts, feelings, and behaviors of individuals are influenced by the actual, imagined, or implied presence of others."

Attitudes and Attitude Change

1. An attitude is a relatively enduring predisposition to respond in a reasonably consistent manner toward a person, object, situation, or idea. Its major components are (a) a cognition or belief, (b) an emotional response, and ©) a behavior pattern.
2. Theories of attitude formation include classical conditioning, operant conditioning, modeling, mere exposure, and information-processing (including Bem's self-perception).
3. People have a tendency to be consistent in their central attitudes and to resist attempts to change these attitudes. Cognitive dissonance, balance, and self-perception theories offer explanations of consistency.
4. Attitudes are more likely to be changed if the *communicator* has credibility and is trustworthy, if the *message* is clearly presented and the content is close to the person's current position, if the *medium* is personal contact, and if the *audience* is high in persuasability.

---

1 Serotonin is discussed more fully in Chapter 3, where we deal with neurotransmitters more generally.

Social Influence

1. The presence of others can produce social facilitation or social inhibition. The cause may be arousal due to evaluation apprehension, embarrassment, self-evaluation, or social monitoring.
2. Social loafing is the reduction in effort shown by individuals when they work as part of a group.
3. Conformity is a change in attitudes or behavior to bring the individual in line with group norms.
4. Compliance means doing what someone without authority requests. Compliance techniques include foot-in-the-door, low-ball, and door-in-the-face.
5. Obedience means responding to a command from an authority figure even against your best judgment. It is socially trained and found almost universally.

Group Processes

1. According to social exchange theory, people join groups that promise more rewards than costs. According to social comparison theory, membership in a group helps people assess their own attitudes, abilities, values, and behaviors.
2. Among the most important and general group norms are the reciprocity norm and the social equity norm. Groups tend to reject those individuals who do not conform to group norms.
3. Some decision-making groups fall into the trap of groupthink, in which individual judgment becomes subordinated to group goals as a result of social pressure.
4. Sociobiology holds that evolutionary processes work through a general fitness-maximizing mechanism toward the survival of the group. Evolutionary psychology, by contrast, studies the evolutionary basis of psychological mechanisms that originate in environmental demands and are domain-specific.
5. Important aspects of interaction within groups include communication patterns and group cohesiveness. Cohesiveness may be a function of external factors, internal factors (commitment), or both.
6. The prisoner's dilemma paradigm studies cooperation and competition between and individuals and groups. .

Environmental Psychology

1. Maintaining personal space appears to be necessary for psychological comfort. Although crowding has been shown to produce antisocial behavior in rats, the effects of crowding on humans have yet to be consistently demonstrated in actual urban settings.
2. People tend to seek out and defend specific territories in a variety of environments.
3. Significant environmental stressors that can affect task performance and social interactions include noise and heat.

Aggression

1. Aggressive behavior may be physical or verbal, active or passive, instrumental or hostile. Theories of aggression range from the biological approaches of Freud, Lorenz, and the frustration-aggression hypothesis, to various learning approaches.
2. Aggressive behavior is often instigated by an attack that produces arousal. Insults also activate cognitive processes that interact with physiology to produce anger and resultant aggressive behavior.
3. Deindividuated people are more likely than individuated ones to engage in aggressive behaviors.

The Neurophysiology of Social Behavior

1. The neurophysiology of aggression involves the hypothalamus and amygdala.
2. The neurotransmitter serotonin, the brain enzyme monoamine oxidase, and the male sex hormone testosterone may also be important.

Ask Yourself

1. What are the major sources of attitudes and how are attitudes formed?
2. What is cognitive dissonance theory, and how does the classic Festinger-Carlsmith study support it?
3. Discuss the major factors that influence the likelihood of attitude change.
4. How can we explain the seemingly opposing phenomena of social facilitation and inhibition?
5. Discuss the similarities and differences among conformity, compliance, and obedience.
6. What do Milgram's findings tell us about obedience, and what ethical dilemma do his study present?
7. Compare the social exchange, social comparison, and sociobiological views of group processes.
8. What are the similarities and differences between views of sociobiology and evolutionary psychology.
9. What do prisoner's dilemma studies tell us about cooperation and competition in everyday life?
10. What effects do crowding, noise, and high temperature have on behavior?

Further Readings

Aronson, E., Wilson, T., & Akert, R. (1994). *Social psychology: The heart and the mind.* N.Y.: HarperCollins. An excellent undergraduate text in social psychology by one of the major figures in the field, Elliot Aronson, and his colleagues.

Baril, G., Ayman, R., & Palmiter, D. (1994). Measuring leader behavior: Moderators of discrepant self and subordinate descriptions. *Journal of Applied Social Psychology*., 24, 82-94. An interesting study of the behaviors of leaders as perceived by supervisors and their subordinates.

Baron, R., Kerr, N., & Miller, N. (1992). *Group process, group decision, group action.* Pacific Grove, CA: Brooks/Cole. The authors cover much of the literature on group processes and discuss its practical significance.

Baron, R., & Richardson, D. (1994). *Human aggression.* N.Y.: Plenum. An excellent review of what social psychology has learned about human aggression.

Berkowitz, L. (1993). *Aggression: Its causes, consequences, and control.* N.Y.: McGraw-Hill. Another outstanding treatment of what we know about aggression.

Brewer, M., & Weber, J. (1994). Self-evaluation effects of interpersonal versus intergroup social comparison. Journal of *Personality and Social Psychology*, 66, 268-275. Two studies of social comparison processes in individual and group settings. A good example of how social comparison research is done.

Cialdini, R. (1993). *Influence: Science and practice.* N.Y.: HarperCollins. A major researcher in the area of compliance, Robert Cialdini pulls together much of what we know about social influence.

Eagly, A., & Chaiken, S. (1993). *The psychology of attitudes.* Ft. Worth: Harcourt. Everything you ever wanted to know about attitudes is covered by a major figure in social psychology, Alice Eagly, and her colleague.

Eiser, J.R. (1994). *Attitudes, chaos and the connectionist mind.* Oxford, England: Blackwell Publishers. This interesting book covers our current knowledge of attitude formation, relating it to cognitive theory and neural networking.

Lippa, R. (1994). *Introduction to social psychology.* Pacific Grove, CA: Brooks/Cole. This is a general textbook in social psychology.

Lore, R., & Schultz, L. (1993). Control of human aggression: A comparative perspective. *American Psychologist*, 48, 16-25. An evolutionary perspective on aggression, discussing studies of aggressive behavior in children, adults, and lower animals.

Sims, H., & Lorenzi, P. (1992). *The new leadership paradigm: Social learning and cognition in organizations.* Newbury Park, CA: Sage. The authors apply what is known about leadership from a cognitive perspective to management practices.

Szymanski, K., & Harkins, S. (1993). The effect of experimenter evaluation on self-evaluation within the social loafing paradigm. *Journal of Experimental Social Psychology*, 29, 268-286. A well-designed study of aspects of social loafing.

Zimbardo, P., & Leippe, M. (1991). *The psychology of attitude change and social influence.* N.Y.: McGraw-Hill. You can learn in this book most of what is known about attitude from one of the central figures in social psychology, Philip Zimbardo.

Psychology in the 21st Century

Stop It! Violence Run Amok

"Violence: America's Uncivil War" was the title of C.W. Schwab's (1993) presidential address to the Eastern Association for Surgery of Trauma. Trauma surgeons see the results of a level of violence in our society that your grandparents no doubt find unbelievable. And violence is not, of course, limited to the U.S. It has left its mark in recent years in Iraq, Bosnia African countries, and England, among other places around the world (Sivarajasingam et al., 2003). Indeed, 500,000 people reportedly died in Rwanda in a single month. Violence is clearly the strongest and most destructive form of aggression. It has been the scourge of the 1980s and 1990s in our society and will surely spill over into the 21st century.

Statistics support what we all know to be true. Between 1960 and 1991, mortality from all causes decreased, but deaths from murder more than doubled from 7.7 to 16.6 per 100,000 population. Since 1991, we have begun to see a noticeable decrease in murder. However, 11% of teachers and 23% of students nationwide - nearly a quarter of all students - have been victims of violence in school. And a 4-year longitudinal study of violent injury and death in the urban African-American population of western Philadelphia, totaling 68,000 people, confirmed the high levels of aggression in society. Of the men in the sample between ages 20 and 29, 94% visited the emergency department of an area hospital at least once during the four years. Overall, violence-induced injuries accounted for 31% of all hospital admissions and 42% of deaths, both representing substantial increases from earlier years (Schwarz et al., 1994).

Although there has been some decrease in the amount of violent crime since 1991, studies still show that violent aggression has expanded in both type and location. One of the criminal innovations of the last decade or so, for example, is the drive-by shooting, in which someone fires from a car at another car or a person on the street. A review of all drive-by shootings occurring in Los Angeles in 1991 focused on children and adolescents. It yielded a total of 677 people in this age group who had been shot at, with 429 being wounded and 36 dying.

Another indication of the level of violence is its cost to society. Violent crimes against people age 12 and older produce $10 billion in health-care costs annually, lead to $23 billion in lost productivity, and cost $145 billion in reduced quality of life. The cost to society of every murder is calculated at $2.4 million. Violence has also expanded into our public schools to a degree never before seen.

How do we stop - or at least reduce - this violence? In one dramatic move, following the bombing of the federal building in Oklahoma, Pennsylvania Avenue in front of the White House was closed to all traffic in 1995. More generally, a number of solutions have been suggested. Some have been built into legislation, and a few are beginning to be implemented. The usual answers involve putting more police on the streets, eliminating assault weapons and perhaps other guns and giving stiffer sentences, including mandatory sentences without parole to violent criminals. Metal detectors can also be installed in appropriate public buildings and in schools, security can be increased, and threats of detection and punishment can be escalated. All these are practical and probably necessary steps, but their cumulative effect may be to turn the society into an armed camp - and that still may not be enough. What else can we do? In particular, what can we learn from psychological studies that may help to end the cycle of violence? There appear to be several things we can do:

- Increase penalties for violence. Many have criticized our system of justice, which often releases violent criminals to commit more violence, puts life-in-prison murderers back on the streets in a few short years, and returns serial rapists to our communities to rape again. More substantial and more meaningful punishments, such as the life-without-parole sentences that are beginning to appear, should clearly help to reduce violent crime.

- **Reduce violence on television.** There is little question that exposure to violence on TV increases the incidence of violent behavior (Cantor, 2003). Society must prevail on the media to reduce violent programming (see Chapter 10).
- **Reduce children's exposure to violence.** Child victims of abuse are far more likely to be violent as adults. Moreover, the abuse need not be physical. Psychological violence, such as constantly yelling at the child or emotionally abusing her, may actually be more destructive than physical violence (Fortin & Chamberland, 1995). In addition, many children who grow up in what James Garbarino (1995, p. 431) has called the "American war zone..." - the homes, streets, and schools of our violent communities - become the violent teens and adults of the next generation (Stein et al., 2003).
- **Reduce alcohol and drug use.** Per capita consumption of alcohol is substantially correlated with the overall crime rate, and studies show that reducing alcohol consumption by simply increasing beer taxes significantly reduces the incidence of rape and robbery. Research also supports raising the legal drinking age and escalating police interventions designed to prevent illegal use of alcohol. Drug use also increases violence (Shepherd, 1994).
- **Reduce the availability of cues for aggression.** Studies show that the sight of weapons and other objects associated with aggression can trigger violence (Chapter 6).
- **Directly instruct youth and adults to avoid violence.** This applies what we know about the nearly universal tendency toward obedience. If parents and teachers gave this simple, direct instruction to children repeatedly, violence could very likely be reduced.
- **Emphasize the "power of positive thinking."** Studies have established that happier people are better adjusted, cope more effectively with problems, and are thus less prone to violence (Rim, 1993). We can teach people to think more positively about their lives.
- **Establish anti-violence norms.** This will take considerable effort over time, but it will be worth it. The power of group norms in controlling individual behavior is well-established.
- **Instruct leaders to promote nonviolence.** An effective, charismatic leader can greatly influence large numbers of people to stop their own violent behavior and that of others around them (Scheidlinger, 1994).
- **Establish school and community anti-violence programs.** Programs that teach nonviolence have been developed and successfully used in schools and communities (Earls et al., 1994). Crisis intervention teams have also been successfully established and used. These approaches can be models for national anti-violence training programs based on psychological principles.
- **Reduce unemployment and stabilize employment.** Studies show that workers who have been laid off are 6 times as likely as others to commit violent acts (Catalano et al., 1993).

We will, of course, still have violence in the 21st century. However, if we follow the steps outlined here, we can begin to reduce the frequency and intensity of aggressive behavior and make the world a safer - and better - place to live.

Probe: Applications of Psychological Research

Groupthink

From the old axiom that "two heads are better than one," it would seem logical that three heads are better than two, four better than three, and so on. Moreover, if each of the "heads" involved in a group thought process is an intelligent, well-educated person with relevant expertise, the group should surely come up with a better solution to a problem than any one individual could on his own, right? Not necessarily.

Consider the following situation: The president of the United States is concerned with how to handle a Latin American country that appears bent on aggression against the United States. He calls together a group that includes two top experts on Latin America, a renowned economist, an intelligence expert, two famous Harvard professors, a dean with international experience, the country's three best military analysts, a topnotch statistician, a brilliant diplomat, and the secretary of state, who is an experienced diplomat and policy maker. Such a group, working together and highly motivated to arrive at a solution, should clearly make the best possible recommendation to the president. When President John F. Kennedy called such a group together in 1961, they formulated a plan to invade Cuba that became one of the greatest military and political errors the United States has ever made. The poorly trained group of Cuban exiles sent into Cuba's Bay of Pigs by the United States was quickly overpowered by clearly superior Cuban forces, the air attack by U.S. planes with false markings was immediately exposed, and the anticipated civil disorders against the Castro regime never happened.

The Bay of Pigs fiasco is by no means an isolated example of group decision making gone wrong. Among other famous group decisions that Irving Janis (1982, 1985) has attributed to what he calls groupthink are the decision of President Nixon's top advisors that led to Watergate, the decision of the Ford Motor Company to market the Edsel in 1956, and Hitler's disastrous decision to attack the Soviet Union in 1941. More recently, the NASA decision to go ahead with the launch of *Challenger* in 1986 was apparently an example of groupthink. Outside engineers pointed out dangers in the design of the rocket and in launching under low temperature conditions. However, the small group charged with the final decision at NASA convinced itself that all was well and went ahead.

Janis has defined *groupthink* as a pervasive group process in which individual moral values, thinking, and judgment are subordinated to apparent group goals by group pressures (see the Figure). It occurs when a group is functioning in a friendly, harmonious fashion and develops an unspoken norm to preserve harmony by uncritically accepting the views of others in the group (Janis, 1989). Janis believes that groups engaging in groupthink have five main characteristics that foster negative outcomes:

- **A need for unanimity that pressures individuals to conform to what appears to be the decision of the group.**
- **A growing sense of invulnerability and superiority.**
- **A belief in omniscience on the part of the leader.**
- **A pressure to yield to the opinions of those perceived as being experts.**
- **A direct pressure to conform.**

Some researchers believe that groupthink may not be as common as Janis believes it is (Shmidt, 2002). However, many others are convinced that it is a serious phenomenon that must be addressed, and some have offered alternatives to the Janis model (Ahlfinger & Easer, 2001). One current example of groupthink is seen in geriatric health care teams. These groups of health specialists evaluate patients and facilities, plan health care delivery, and treat individual patients. They work together on many geriatric cases over time, maximizing the opportunity for groupthink to set in. If it does, they may end up making poor decisions and applying misdirected care to numerous patients (Eaton, 2001).

Janis argues that groupthink can best be avoided when all members of the group are well aware of its danger and take measures to ensure that it will not occur. Such measures include breaking into subgroups, bringing in outside experts, and assigning some group members the role of devil's advocate. Recent efforts to reduce groupthink have included the use of *group support systems*, which are computer-based resources designed for the use of work teams in industrial and other settings. These systems provide guidelines and strategies designed, in part, to avoid the groupthink phenomenon. For example, members can sit at separate, networked computers and independently generate a number of alternative ideas, exchange and comment on these ideas anonymously via the network, and thereby reduce the groupthink dangers that seem to be inherent in face-to-face meetings over time (Kowert, 2002).

Research in Psychology

The Critical Thinker: *Are Men More Aggressive?*

Our social training tells us that men are more aggressive than women, and this seems to be confirmed by casual observation. After all, it is almost exclusively men who engage in such aggressive sports as football and boxing and primarily men who commit violent crimes. The question is whether these casual observations are confirmed by major theories and careful, empirical research.

The Basic Hypothesis or Contention

Early theorists in social psychology subscribed to the common assumption that males are more aggressive than females. Some ascribed the apparent gender discrepancy to biological differences between the sexes (Macoby and Jacklin, 1974), while others hypothesized that differences in social training make aggression more acceptable in males (Eron, 1980). In either case, the clear contention is that men are the aggressors across virtually all situations and ways of expressing aggression.

What Is The Evidence?

For many years, research in social psychology seemed to confirm the hypothesis. Indeed, the early research supported the deeply ingrained stereotype that women are gentle and nurturant while men are aggressive and demanding.

Well, stereotypes, whether they involve gender, race, or some other differentiating factor, are notoriously inaccurate, as we discuss in Chapter 19. It may therefore not be surprising that research has increasingly disconfirmed the stereotype: males are not always more aggressive than females (Petras et al., 2004).

Some research shows that females are more aggressive than males under some circumstances. One study of African-American undergraduates showed that only 33% of males, as compared with 50% of females, had been physically aggressive in romantic relationships (Clark et al., 1994). Confirming this finding and extending it to a broader (mixed-race) group of undergraduates, another investigation also showed greater physical aggression by women in dating relationships, even though men were more aggressive in some other contexts (Harris, 1994). Other research suggests that what sex differences there are may arise in middle childhood and continue through early adolescence, then disappear by the late teen years (Rosen, 2004).

Any gender differences that are observed also tend to evaporate when there is direct provocation or when the aggressive behavior is otherwise socially acceptable when it occurs during interactions with strangers (Staub, 2004). Other work shows that wives are more aggressive overall in marital relationships, though they are also more likely to suffer physical harm when the husband is the aggressive partner (Caetano et al., 2003). Alcohol is often a factor when spouses become violent (O'Leary & Schumacher, 2003).

After reviewing the literature prior to 1983, Jacquelyn Weygandt White (1983) concluded that males may have greater innate preparedness for aggression, but that this genetic difference is a relatively minor factor in the observed differences in aggressive behavior. This accords with the more recent conclusion that biological differences are probably present but minimal and that there are no overall gender differences in aggressiveness (Knight et al., 2002). Moreover, the fact that there are women who are more aggressive than many men and men who are less aggressive than many women suggests that socialization practices strongly influence sex differences in aggression.

Is The Evidence Open To Alternative Interpretations?

It seems clear that we have two opposing bodies of evidence concerning sex differences in aggression: Early research showed overall differences; more recent research does not. Ordinarily, we tend to accept more recent evidence as more valid. In this case, however, one could argue that the theories, research methods employed, and interpretations of the data may have been influenced by broader social theories, norms, and conditions. After all, even scientists are not entirely immune to such factors. In particular, society has substantially modified its view of sex differences in many areas with the relatively recent advent of feminist perspectives and the corresponding emphasis on gender equality. To the extent that this change has influenced the thinking and methods of scientists, the apparent difference between earlier and more recent findings may not be as clear cut as it appears to be.

A further consideration is that the gender similarity in aggressive behavior seen in recent research is an *overall* similarity. It is still quite possible that further research will turn up sex differences in types of aggression (e.g., physical vs. verbal) or in the situations in which aggression occurs. In fact, there is already some evidence for such differences (Connor, 2003). Which gender is more aggressive appears to depend on age, the nature of the aggression, the provocation, and the more general context surrounding the potential aggressive act.

Do We Need Additional Evidence?

George Knight and his colleagues (1996) certainly argue that we do. In particular, we need to ensure that interpretations

of scientific data have not been unduly influenced the research methodologies employed or by broader societal views or biases. In addition, researchers need to further study the possibility of sex differences in types of aggression and in aggression situations. Finally, the role of biology in the determination of any observed sex differences is not yet understood. We know that genetic factors contribute substantially to individual differences in aggressive behavior, but we do not know to what extent any *gender* differences might be biological. Some reviewers conclude that gender differences may have a partially genetic basis, while others insist that they do not. Appropriately designed twin and adoption studies and perhaps molecular genetic studies may be able to resolve this discrepancy.

What Can We Conclude?

Based on the most recent studies, the best conclusion to date is that there are probably no overall gender differences in amount of aggressive behavior. Nevertheless, this conclusion may well change as more research is conducted, and we may also be better able to identify differing conditions under which each sex is likely to be more aggressive.

KEYS TERMS 1

- attitude
- cognitive dissonance
- inoculation theory
- self-perception
- social psychology

KEY PEOPLE 1

- Icek Ajzen
- Gordon Allport
- Daryl Bem
- Leon Festinger
- Martin Fishbein
- Fritz Heider

KEYS TERMS 2

- obedience
- social facilitation
- social inhibition
- social monitoring

KEY PEOPLE 2

- Stanley Milgram
- Max Ringelmann
- Norman Triplett

KEYS TERMS 3

- cohesiveness
- conformity
- groupthink
- norm
- prisoner's dilemma
- reference group
- social comparison
- social exchange
- social judgment

KEY PEOPLE 3

Irving Janis

KEYS TERMS 4

environmental psychology
personal space
territoriality

KEYS TERMS 5

aggression
assertiveness
deindividuation
sociobiology

KEY PEOPLE 5

Albert Bandura
David Buss
John Dollard
Konrad Lorenz
Neal Miller
Philip Zimbardo

KEYS TERMS 6

amygdala
hypothalamus
serotonin
monoamine oxidase

KEYS TO SOCIAL PSYCHOLOGY - 1

1. Attitudes are enduring predispositions to respond consistently toward a person, situation, object, or idea.

   A. The major components?
      Cognition or belief; emotional response; behavior pattern.
   B. The major types?
      Central, peripheral
   C. The major sources?
      Reference groups
   D. The major theories of acquisition?
      Classical and operant conditioning, modeling, information-processing (including self-perception theory), and mere exposure.
   E. The major consistency theories?
      Cognitive dissonance, balance, self-perception.

2. Attitudes sometimes predict behavior.

   A. LaPiere's finding?
      Poor prediction of behavior from attitudes.
   B. When attitudes are more predictive?
      When they are central, specific, and/or salient
   C. The factors noted in the model of reasoned action?
      Attitude, subjective norm, perceived control.

3. Attitudes are more likely to change under certain circumstances.

   A. What communicator characteristics increase the likelihood of change?
      Credibility trustworthiness, name recognition
   B. What message characteristics increase the likelihood of change?
      Clarity and proximity to current position.

   C. What medium characteristic increases the likelihood of change?
      Personal contact
   D. What audience characteristic increases the likelihood of change?
      persuasability

KEYS TO SOCIAL PSYCHOLOGY - 2

1. Social presence produces social facilitation or inhibition.

   A. A possible theoretical key to these effects?
      Arousal
   B. The likely sources of arousal?
      Embarrassment, social monitoring, evaluation apprehension, self-evaluation.
   C. When social loafing occurs?
      When working in a group.

2. Conformity brings attitudes in line with a group norm.

   A. The major conformity theories?
      Self-perception, dissonance
   B. Who conducted the classic study?
      Solomon Asch

3. Compliance means doing what someone without authority requests.

   A. Whether it is consistent with evolutionary theory?
      It is.
   B. The major techniques?
      Foot-in-the-door, low-ball, door-in-the-face

4. Obedience is a response to a command from an authority figure.

   A. What Milgram and others have found?
      Most people are very obedient.
   B. The major criticism of the Milgram studies?
      The made subjects uncomfortable.

KEYS TO SOCIAL PSYCHOLOGY - 3

1. People have a strong need for social affiliation.

   A. The major theories?
      Social exchange, social comparison, sociobiology, evolutionary psychology.
   B. Why people join groups according to social exchange theory?
      To maximize rewards and minimize costs.
   C. Why people join groups according to social comparison theory?
      To assess their own attitudes and other qualities.
   D. Why people join groups according to sociobiology?
      To improve group survival through a domain-general fitness-maximizing mechanism.
   E. Why people join groups according to evolutionary psychology?
      To meet environmental demands, using domain-specific mechanisms.

2. Norms are basically group expectations.
   A. Some common, major norms?
      Reciprocity, social equity
   B. The result of not conforming?
      Rejection from the group.

3. Group dynamics refers to the internal operation of a group.

   A. The major aspects of dynamics?
      Communication, cohesiveness
   B. The major communication patterns?
      Chains, hierarchies, star patterns
   C. Factors in cohesiveness?
      External, internal.
   D. What group polarization does?
      Produces more extreme positions
   E. The experimental approach commonly used to study cooperation and competition?
      Prisoner's dilemma

KEYS TO SOCIAL PSYCHOLOGY - 4

1. Environmental psychology studies the effects of the physical environment.

   A. Some major areas addressed?
      Personal space, crowding, territoriality, stressors.
   B. What personal space is?
      A psychological boundary that defines a comfort zone.

C. The effects of crowding on rats?
Increased antisocial behavior and aggression.
D. The effects of crowding on humans?
No consistent effects.

2. Territoriality is a general tendency.

A. Some positive effects?
Marital satisfaction, winning debates, worker satisfaction.

3. Environmental stressors increase anxiety.

A. Some major stressors?
Noise, heat
B. Some effects of noise?
Decreases sensory discrimination, increases blood pressure, lowers frustration tolerance, etc.
C. The effect of heat?
Possibly increased aggression, when combined with other factors.

KEYS TO SOCIAL PSYCHOLOGY - 5

1. Aggression is behavior engaged in with the intent of hurting others.

A. Several subcategory breakdowns of aggression?
Physical or verbal; active or passive; instrumental or hostile.
B. Some major biological theorists?
Freud, Lorenz
C. The evolutionary basis of aggression?
Defensive aggression in animals
D. The heritability for aggression?
At least 50%

2. Learning also enters into aggression.

A. A major learning theory addressing aggression?
Social learning theory

3. Aggression is elicited or triggered by a variety of stimuli.

A. Some major triggers?
Frustration, arousal, deindividuation
B. Who formulated the frustration-aggression hypothesis?
Miller and Dollard
C. What increases arousal and the likelihood of aggression?
Insults, loud sounds and other strong stimuli, exercise.
D. Who first did the transfer of excitation research?
Dolf Zillman

4. Deindividuation may trigger aggression.
A. What it is?
Reduced feelings of self-distinctiveness
B. Who formulated the hypothesis?
Zimbardo

KEYS TO SOCIAL PSYCHOLOGY - 6

1. The genetic basis of aggressive behavior is expressed in the brain.

A. The major structures involved?
Hypothalamus, amygdala.
B. The major neurochemicals that may be involved?
Serotonin, Monoamine oxidase
C. What hormone is involved?
Testosterone.

Chapter 19

Social Cognition

Outline

Networking

SOCIAL COGNITION refers to the processes by which you think about other people and your relationship to them. This chapter examines the role of social cognition in the more intimate aspects of social interaction, those that occur on a one to one basis. When you meet people, you form impressions of them. How quickly do you form those impressions and on what do you base them? What steps do you take to try to influence others to form positive impressions of you? We also constantly employ social cognitive processes to make causal attributions about the behaviors of other people. How we make those attributions—and how we often err in making them—are also the province of the social psychologist. Another aspect of interpersonal interaction is your own self-concept, and we will see that it significantly affects and is affected by your experiences with others. We will ask, and try to answer, what causes you to be attracted to others, form friendships with them, and sometimes fall in love. And finally, we will address yet another special social situation—one in which you are in the position of potentially helping people in need. Will you help—engage in prosocial behavior—or will you stand by and do nothing? The answer is that many people do not help, and our analysis of altruism will provide some insight into this common lack of prosocial behavior.

Finally, industrial/organizational psychology

How To Succeed in Business...

Tom arrived early for the most important business meeting he had attended in several years. A justifiably self-confident executive, he hoped to land the largest contract—and probably the largest bonus—in the history of his company. As Tom was organizing his presentation, two young women arrived for the meeting. They introduced themselves as Gertrude and Laurelei ("Just call me Laurie") and said they were with the company with which Tom was seeking a contract. Both were dressed in conservative business suits, but Tom could not help noticing that Laurie was very attractive, with her large, blue eyes, small nose, and near-perfect figure. It turned out that Laurie was a high-ranking member of the company, while the much less attractive Gertrude was considerably lower in the hierarchy. He was immediately impressed with Laurie's obvious intelligence and her already high position in a major corporation. As they talked, both before and after the meeting, it became apparent that they had very similar backgrounds. Although Tom was eight years older, both had attended the same university and had similar families, the same basic business history, and a number of shared interests.

As the meeting got underway, Tom found that he was very impressed with Laurie's business acumen. She seemed confident and effective, and he was sure that she must be a well-adjusted young woman with unusually good social skills, unlike Gertrude, who seemed ill-at-ease and a bit too quiet. Laurie was similarly impressed with Tom, who substantially dominated the meeting. She also noted his athletic build, which was not concealed by his well-tailored suit. When they talked afterward, she complimented him on his presentation and business skills.

Nearly every day of our lives we interact with others. We form impressions of new people we meet and continue our relationships with those we like and love. We communicate our joys and sorrows, fulfill our needs, express our aggressions, and help others in need—or don't—all in a social context. It is that social context for human behavior that is the province of social psychology.

As social animals, we constantly solve problems, formulate hypotheses about the world, organize tasks, and plan ahead in a social context. These activities are most referred to as thinking or *cognition*, a topic we cover more fully in Chapter 8. When we apply our perceptual and thought processes to other people and to ourselves in relation to other people, we are engaging in *social cognition*. The importance of social cognitive processes and their role in both physical and mental health has recently been emphasized by the Basic Behavioral Science Task Force of the National Institute of Mental Health (1996).

Social cognition takes many forms. Every time you meet someone new, you form an immediate impression of that person. If you continue to interact with him over a period of time, you may add to or modify that impression. Social psychologists call this process impression formation. It is part of a larger area of study called social perception, and it can be seen as based on social cognitive processes. When you see someone engage in almost any kind of behavior, you tend to make causal attributions about the behavior: "I think she did that because...." You are using social cognition to arrive at your attributions, and we have attribution theories to explain the underlying processes. Through still other social cognitive processes, called social comparison and self-perception, you develop a self-concept as you interact with other people. You then engage in interpersonal behavior influenced by that self-concept. Social cognitions are also a major factor in choosing friends and mates. Why are you more attracted to one person than to another? Part of the answer is that you cognitively evaluate each person you meet: Is she physically and psychologically attractive by the cognitive standards you have developed? Does she meet your expectations? Does she have characteristics similar to your own. Finally, your social cognitions influence the likelihood that you will help others in need.

Evolution and Social Cognition

Although social cognition involves our thoughts about social interaction and other aspects of social discourse, that does not mean there is no biology involved. In fact, some recent theorists have argued forcefully that our social cognitions are heavily influenced by psychological evolution (Walsh, 1993). Indeed, Daniel Povinelli (1993) points out that the very ability of human beings to engage in social cognitive processes may represent the highest level of a lengthy evolutionary process. From this viewpoint, social cognition has adaptive value because the social interactive processes it permits enhance the survival of the species. The serious of failed social cognitive mechanisms are seen in schizophrenia, where the patient is unable to interact effectively with others (Penn et al., 1997). The social cognitive perspective has been applied in particular to an explanation of the role of physical attractiveness in social selection, the criteria for mate selection, and the occurrence of prosocial behavior, all of which we discuss later in the chapter. But first, let's examine the cognitive process of social perception.

Social Perception

You have just been introduced to a man by the name of Harold. You notice that he is of medium height, wears glasses,

has short, prematurely graying hair, is reasonably good looking, and has on a striped T-shirt and baggy pegged pants, with high-top tennis shoes. This visual information contributes to your perception of Harold. But your overall perception also involves other sensory stimuli (how Harold talks, how he smells), anything you might already know about Harold (his reputation), your interpretation of all the sensory information, and your integration of this information. In short, *person perception* is the way we organize information about other people in order to arrive at our own internal "picture" or impression of them.

Person perception is not objective. Rather, it is influenced by past experiences, expectations, and a wide variety of other factors, both in the other person and in ourselves. In this section we will examine how we form initial impressions of others, how we control the impression we ourselves make, and how we attribute causation to behavior, including our own.

Impression Formation

After meeting Harold, you may come away saying something like "He seemed sincere and pleasant. I hope I run into him again sometime," or "What an arrogant creep. I must remember to avoid him." Given even brief exposures to people, we are quick to form impressions, and these impressions can have a lasting impact. The process of *impression formation*—of developing an image and evaluation of another person—is complex, but even a single behavior on the part of that person can influence our overall impression. Susan Basow and Diane Kobrynowicz (1993) had undergraduates watch a videotape of a female student eating a meal. Given no other information, they rated her on a number of dimensions. She was seen by both men and women as significantly less socially desirable when eating a large meal than when eating a small one. In another experiment, students saw political advertisements (Kahn & Geer, 1994). When the ad was a negative personal attack of the "My opponent is scum" variety, students formed a much more negative impression of the attacker than when the ad was more positive and issue-focused. And the perceived negative characteristics of candidates Clinton and Bush in the 1992 presidential campaign were weighted more heavily by voters than their positive qualities (Klein, 1996). More generally, we often form impressions based on minimal information. One of the goals of social psychology is to determine just what influences those impressions.

First Impressions—Lasting Impressions. If you have ever dated someone—and perhaps fallen in love—think back to when you first met. What was your very first impression? What influenced that impression? How accurate was that initial view of your significant other? These are some of the questions social psychologists have asked about first impressions. Forming a first impression is a bit like getting pregnant: It happens quickly and can be very difficult to change. First impressions are often lasting impressions, even in the face of substantial evidence that they were inaccurate. Moreover, they can be strongly influenced by such seemingly minor factors as clothing and surroundings.

A woman wearing a suit jacket was seen in one study as more expert and more powerful than the same woman wearing other kinds of clothing, even though participants knew nothing else about her (Temple & Loewen, 1993). Similarly, undergraduate women rated a man wearing formal clothing as much less handsome, charming, and extraverted than the same man wearing casual clothing (Satrapa & Melhado, 1992). And adolescents rated a person seen in very affluent surroundings more positively than the same person seen in less lavish environs (Dittmar, 1992). This means that Tom's first impressions of Laurie and Gertrude will likely guide his future interactions with them.

The impressions we form are more generally influenced by our past experiences with other people and by a number of other psychological processes. Included among these are an implicit theories of personality, reliance on central traits, and our expectations. [RTF bookmark start: }imp[RTF bookmark end: }imp

Implicit Personality Theory. People tend to group sets of personality traits together. Such groupings are a part of each person's *implicit theory of personality*. When we observe that a person has some of the traits in a cluster, we automatically assume that he has the rest as well (Bruner and Tagiuri, 1954). If you meet warm, friendly, intelligent Charlene, you will assume that she is also trustworthy and dependable if you tend to implicitly group those characteristics together. If you believe that people who are detached and aloof are also arrogant and cold-hearted, your observation of the aloof Larry will lead you to assume that he is also arrogant and cold-hearted.

The implicit personality theory approach suggests that broad judgments about a person are made on the basis of underlying theories of intelligence, liking, or other characteristics. It is also assumed that the person making the judgment is largely unaware of the implicit theory she is applying. That may be true in some cases, but one body of research suggests that many people are quite conscious of the process by which they arrive at judgments (Kraut and Lewis, 1982). For many of us, "implicit" personality theories may actually be quite explicit.

Central Traits. A single trait, if it seems important enough, can influence our overall perception of a person. In his classic study of such *central traits*, Solomon Asch (1946) gave participants a list of traits and asked them to write a brief description of a person with these characteristics. One group was given the list: intelligent, warm, skillful, determined, practical, industrious, and cautious. A second group got the same list with the word "cold" being substituted for "warm." The differences in the essays written by the two groups were profound. The "warm" person was described as humorous, sociable, generous, good natured, and happy. The "cold," person was seen as lacking in humor and generosity and as irritable, ruthless, and unhappy. Apparently, "warm-cold" was a central trait that substantially influenced the global impression of the person.

Harold Kelley (1950) soon showed that the warm-cold dimension influenced not only the impression formed by participants but also their actual behavior toward a person. Subsequent research has demonstrated, however, that there is probably no one set list of central traits. Rather, how central a given trait turns out to be depends on other traits that are listed or otherwise presented with it. Basically, it appears that a central trait is simply one that is highly correlated with the other traits with which it is presented (Wishner, 1960). The warm-cold dimension acted as a central trait in the Asch study because the other traits on the list were all highly related to warm-cold. Honesty and intelligence have served similarly central roles in other studies (Sedikides & Skowronski, 1993).

Expectancy and Priming Effects. The impressions we form and the way we act on the basis of those impressions can be strongly influenced by our expectations. We often enter into interactions with preconceptions as to what the other person will be like, and these expectations may influence our behavior toward him. The result can be a *self-fulfilling prophecy*, in which your behavior toward the other person causes him to meet your expectations.

A controversial early study showed that when teachers were given false expectations about their pupils, the expectations came true (Rosenthal and Jacobson, 1968). Teachers at an elementary school were told that certain students were expected, on the basis of test scores, to show marked academic improvement over the course of the school year. At the end of the year, these students had improved significantly more than their classmates. In reality, the students "expected to improve" had been chosen at random. Apparently, the teachers' expectations influenced their behavior toward the students and helped bring about the predicted improvements.

Despite some early failures to replicate these results and initial criticisms of the research (Fielder et al., 1971), scores of studies have now validated the teacher expectation effect (Brophy. 1982; Cooper and Croyle, 1982). They show, for example, that teachers who expect a student to do poorly engage in less eye contact (Chaiken et al., 1974), spend less time answering his questions (Allington, 1980), and criticize him more for failure (Cooper & Baron, 1977). In fact, expectations can be more influential than later observations of actual behavior (McAnisich, 1993).

Impression formation can be influenced by prior events even when the events have nothing to do with the person you are to evaluate. The process of inducing states that can have this kind of indirect influence is called *priming*, and it is commonly seen in a variety of settings. For example, you may go to your first class with a new professor having just read an account of the horrors of the Holocaust. You leave the class feeling that the professor is tough, uncaring, and aloof (aren't we all!) and never realize that your view of him was affected by the priming—by having just read about the Holocaust.

To demonstrate priming in the laboratory, one researcher first had subjects perform a sentence-completion task in which they had to finish each of a number of partial sentences. In one condition, the sentences were friendly: "Jenny smiled broadly as she...." In the other, they were hostile: "Jenny screamed her answer...." Participants were then given an "unrelated" impression formation task in which they rated a briefly-described, unknown person on a number of traits. Hostile priming produced more negative trait descriptions than did friendly priming (Ikegami, 1993).

Primacy and Recency Effects. We have already seen that first impressions can be lasting ones. This is known as the *primacy effect*, and it was first demonstrated by Solomon Asch (1946) in another classic study. He gave participants a group of six adjectives: "intelligent, industrious, impulsive, critical, stubborn, envious." Half the participants received the list in this order, with the positive characteristics first, while the other half received it with the positive characteristics last. Asch found that impressions of the person with these six qualities were more favorable when intelligence and industriousness were listed first, demonstrating the primacy effect.

A number of subsequent studies have verified the power of primacy (Lange and Roth, 1975; McAndrev, 1981). However, there are some circumstances in which a *recency effect* occurs. For example, when subjects read a description of a person, then performed some irrelevant task, then read a second paragraph about the same person, their overall impression was based primarily on the second paragraph (Luchins, 1948). It appears that the recency effect becomes more likely when considerable time has passed or when intervening events dull a person's memory of what happened earlier (Miller and Campbell, 1959; Petty and Cacioppo, 1981).

Other Factors in Impression Formation. The impressions we form are also influenced by a variety of personal appearance cues, including race, sex, attractiveness, and clothing. Subjects in some studies have more positive first impressions of whites than of African-Americans and of males than of females (Deaux, 1976). In addition, physical attractiveness is a strong determinant of first impression (Zuckerman & Hodgins, 1993). Physically attractive people are seen as more intelligent and more friendly, as having better jobs, better marriages, and more self-esteem, and as having better prospects for the future (Adams and Houston, 1975). In addition, what a person wears can affect our impression of his emotional state, desire to be different from others, and likely behavior (Kefgen and Touchie- Specht, 1971).

Nonverbal behavior is another influence on impressions (Schneider et al., 1974). In one study, participants judged that looking toward the perceiver, opening the eyes, smiling, and raising the eyebrows create positive impressions, while looking away, staring, frowning, and yawning tend to create negative impressions (Clore et al., 1975). Other studies confirm that the facial expression of someone you meet can significantly influence the impression you form (Ohira & Kurono, 1993) and that body language is important (Kleinke, 1975). Favorable impressions are associated with a relaxed, open, direct body orientation, whereas crossed legs or arms give the impression that the person is suspicious or wants to avoid communication.

Your own mood when you meet a person can also affect your impression. You are more likely to form an initial positive impression of someone you meet just after receiving an 'A' on an exam than after learning of an unexpected 'D.' Research has confirmed this phenomenon: Mood affects the impressions you form (Abele & Petzold, 1994), and people in good moods form more positive impressions (Bohner et al., 1992).

Impression formation is clearly a complex process. It involves our implicit theories of personality, the apparent central traits of an individual, primacy and perhaps recency effects, various physical characteristics and nonverbal behaviors of the target person, and even the expectations we carry with us into the interaction. The Critical Thinker points to another possible factor: the stereotypes we hold. While social psychologists cannot yet claim to fully understand how impressions are formed, they have obviously developed a considerable body of knowledge that provides real insights into some aspects of that p[RTF bookmark start: }stereo[RTF bookmark end: }stereorocess.

Impression Management

Someone in Tom's position is typically interested in making the best possible impression—in *managing* the view other people will have of him. More generally, we are concerned not only with forming impressions of others, but with the sorts of impressions others form of us. The attempt to control the way in which we are perceived and evaluated by others is called *impression management* (Abrahams & Bell, 1994). While we may not approve of impression management, the fact is that virtually everyone engages in it to some degree. We all try to "put our best foot forward."

Irving Goffman (1959) likened impression management to a theatrical performance. He suggested that to effectively make the desired impression, we need many of the actor's techniques. The right "props" are important, as are intensive involvement in the role and the maintenance of a reasonable social distance from the audience. The physician who wants to give the impression of being expert, compassionate, and decisive may employ such props as a white coat, a stethoscope, and important-looking medical equipment, and she may maintain a certain social distance, which we sometimes describe as "professional demeanor," yet smile and generally behave in a friendly manner.

A number of impression management techniques work to some degree with some people, though universally successful approaches have yet to be developed (Schlenker, 1980). In other words, you can't fool all the people all the time! One of the more commonly used techniques is *ingratiation*. This approach involves flattery, conformity to the other person's opinions or behavior, rendering favors, and similar actions specifically designed to make a favorable impression and to try to influence another. Even overly obvious ingratiators can be successful, for the simple reason that people like to be flattered (Gordon, 1996). One study examined the impression management strategies of over 2200 college graduates in relation to career advancement. It was found that ingratiation toward supervisors was more successful over the long run than were self-promotion and other strategies (Judge & Bretz, 1994).

People often engage in outright deceit in an effort to create a good impression. College students, for example, frequently tell others that they have higher SAT scores than they actually do (Shepperd, 1993). However, the strategy can easily backfire because studies show that lying is often more obvious than you might think. Deceivers are more uncertain, vague, tense, formal, submissive, and reticent than those telling the truth. Moreover, they make a poorer impression on others who are rating them (Burgoon & Buller, 1994). If you want to make a good impression, the results of another study may be helpful. It showed that women have better impressions of men who display warmth and support; men are more impressed with women who are effective on the job. Remaining calm under stress was the single characteristic that drew consistent applause from both sexes (DuBrin, 1994).

Some research shows that *self-monitoring* is an important part of effective impression management. Mark Snyder (1979) has developed a Self-Monitoring Scale that measures the extent to which individuals are aware of the impression they create, are concerned about that impression, and are able to control it. People who score moderately high on this scale are judged to be less shy and more relaxed and friendly than those who score lower (Lippa, 1978). Interestingly enough, those who score *very* high are less effective in creating a good impression, perhaps because they seem insincere (Snyder, 1979).

Keys to Social Cognition 1

Making Attributions

Your boss yells at you, your boyfriend or girlfriend seems short-tempered, a casual acquaintance goes out of the way to help you with a problem. To what do you attribute the causes of these various behaviors? Social psychologists have long noted that we generally do tend to arrive at causal *attributions* —perceptions of why people engage in specific actions—particularly following negative events (Leigh & Aramburu, 1993). Karen Multon (1993) studied individuals who had recently gone through a marital separation. She found that they were: "Why did this happen?" "Was I partially responsible?" "Was money the big issue?" In effect, the broader question was: "To what can I attribute the failure of the marriage?"

Even as an outside observer, you often make causal attributions (Feather, 1993). Perhaps one of two strangers you see engaged in a conversation begins to shout at the other, for example. You may decide that this verbal aggression is an indication that the shouter has an aggressive personality or is short-tempered. This would be a *dispositional attribution*—attributing the behavior to factors *within* the person. Or you may assume that the other person must have said something insulting or otherwise provoked the aggressive behavior. This would be *situational attribution*—attributing the behavior to factors in the environment that are beyond the individual's control. A third approach would be to assume an *interaction* between dispositional and situational factors; that is, you may decide that the person is probably short-tempered but that situational factors triggered the outburst.

Attribution Theory

Attribution theory came into being in 1958, when Fritz Heider hypothesized that the perception of both social and nonsocial events involves an ongoing quest for meaningful explanations of the causes of these events. He distinguished between dispositional and situational attributions and suggested that although some attributions are largely based on logical analyses of events, others may reflect the person's psychological needs, expectations, and motivations.

Adopting Heider's basic principles, Edward Jones and Keith Davis (1965) extended his ideas to develop a theory of correspondent inferences. A *correspondent inference* is the assumption that a person's intent in performing a behavior can be inferred from the behavior itself. Jones and Davis noted that when behavior conforms closely to situational expectations, it provides little real information about motives or intentions. However, unusual or extreme behaviors may provide considerable information about intent and are usually subject to dispositional attributions. When a student contributes informative comments during a class discussion, it is difficult to determine whether she is responding primarily to the situation or to personal factors, but suppose she interrupts the professor to talk about something unrelated to the lecture. Then we would tend to attribute her behavior to personal (dispositional) factors because she is acting in a way that is inappropriate to the situation. Studies testing the Jones-Davis theory have shown that dispositional attributions are likely to occur only in the absence of clear situational explanations for the behavior (Weisz & Jones, 1993; Jones and McGills, 1976). As a result, most social psychologists currently believe that the vast majority of attributions we make every day are situational rather than dispositional (Aronson & Jones, 1992).

A third major influence on attribution theory has been the work of Harold Kelley, who hypothesized that individuals make attributions in much the same way that scientists analyze data (Kelley, 1967, 1992; Wymer and Kelley, 1982). In trying to determine whether a behavior should be attributed to internal or external factors, individuals tend to look for three characteristics (Figure 19-1):

- *Distinctiveness.* Is the actor's behavior distinctively associated with a particular stimulus? Is the specific situation in which the behavior is taking place eliciting that behavior?
- *Consensus.* Is the behavior similar to the responses of other people to the same stimulus?
- *Consistency*. Is the response consistent from one occasion to the next?

When there is considerable distinctiveness, consensus, and consistency, we generally attribute the causes of behavior to the environment. When these factors are weak or absent, we tend to attribute causation to the person (Kelley, 1991).

Leslie McArthur (1972) provided an excellent example to help clarify Kelley's theory. Suppose we want to know why John laughs at a comedian. Over a series of observations, we determine that John usually does not laugh at other comedians (high distinctiveness), that in the past John has always laughed at this particular comedian (high consistency), and that nearly everyone who hears this comedian laughs at his jokes (high consensus). We are thus likely to attribute John's laughter to situational factors, in this case the talent of the comedian.

The Fundamental Attribution Error

Much of the research growing out of the Jones-Davis and Kelley theories suggests that we have a tendency to overestimate the role of dispositional factors and to underestimate the role of situational factors when making attributions. This tendency has been called the *fundamental attribution error*, and it has been demonstrated in a wide variety of experiments (Tetlock & Philip, 1991; Miller et al., 1990). In a classic study of this bias, Jones and Victor Harris (1967) read essays opposing or favoring Fidel Castro's communist government in Cuba. Some participants were told that the writer had freely chosen to write the essay, others that the writer was given no choice; his position on the issue had been assigned. Surprisingly, both groups concluded that the writer actually held the view reflected in his essay. Their correspondent inference had biased them to make an unjustified dispositional attribution (Figure 19-2A).

A second example of the fundamental attribution error is seen in a study done by Lee Ross and his colleagues

(1977). One subject of a pair was asked to formulate a series of general knowledge questions in his own area of interest or expertise, such as movies, books, sports, or music. The other subject served as a contestant and had to respond to the questions formulated by his partner. When the contestant missed a question, as frequently happened, the questioner provided the correct answer.

At the conclusion of the quiz game, the participants rated themselves and their partners on their general knowledge "as compared with the average Stanford student," and objective observers in a related study rated both questioner and contestant on *general* knowledge. Both participants and outside observers rated the questioners much higher in general knowledge than they rated the contestants (Figure 19-2B). Actually, of course, strong situational factors were involved. Moreover, followup studies have shown that the immediate attributions do not necessarily hold up over time. In another "quiz" study, the contestants initially saw themselves as less knowledgeable than the questioners. However, when asked to again make attributions at a later date, they saw no difference in general knowledge between themselves and the questioners (Burger, 1991).

There is some controversy concerning the prevalence of the fundamental attribution error. Some reviewers conclude that it is common (Reader, 1982). Others argue that it may not be a valid concept at all (Harvey and Yarkin, 1981; Harvey and McGlynn, 1982). And David Funder (1982) found evidence that errors often occur in *both* situational and dispositional attributions. However, each type of attribution is sometimes accurate, and the challenge for future research is to determine which situational and dispositional errors are more likely to occur and under what circumstances.

The Actor-Observer Hypothesis

In an effort to better understand the nature of attribution errors, Edward Jones and Richard Nisbett (1971) formulated the *actor-observer hypothesis*, also termed the *divergent perspectives hypothesis*, which suggests that there are important differences in the attributional perspectives of actor and observer (Figure 19-3). Actors are likely to attribute their own behavior to *situational* influences, whereas observers are likely to attribute the same behavior to *dispositional* characteristics of the actor (Harvey et al., 1990). This tendency is seen in both casual interactions and long-term relationships where the partners know each other well (Fiedler et al., 1991)

Suppose, for example, that you get a 'D' on a test. You are quite likely to attribute the failure to situational factors: the exam was unfair; the time allowed to complete the test was too short; the professor hadn't covered this material in the lecture. The professor, on the other hand, is likely to attribute your poor showing on the test to you. She may suspect that you didn't prepare adequately, that you spent too much time partying instead of studying, or that you are not intellectually equipped to handle the material.

Jones and Nisbett proposed two basic reasons for the divergent attributions of actors and observers. First, the two possess different information. Actors are more aware of their own internal capabilities, feelings, and experience and may know that their performance on a given occasion is discrepant with their usual performance. You may know, for example, that you are normally an 'A' student and usually have little difficulty with the kind of material covered in the test. You therefore attribute the poor grade to external causes. Observers who lack this information are more likely to make dispositional attributions.

The second cause of divergent attributions is the fact that actor and observer focus on different cues in making attributions. The observer focuses on the actor's behavior as the most important cue, whereas the actor focuses on the situational cues. In one study, male college students were asked to explain how they had chosen their girlfriends and how close male friends had chosen *their* girlfriends. They explained their own choices in terms of the woman's characteristics and the friends' choices as being a function of his own dispositional characteristics (Nisbett et al., 1973).

The actor-observer bias has been supported in a number of studies (Roberts & McCready, 1987; Malle & Knowb, 1997). However, some researchers have modified it by adding several qualifications (Monson & Snyder, 1977). They point out that people vary in their inclination to make situational or dispositional attributions and that acts leading to *unintended* outcomes are more likely to be attributed to situational than to dispositional factors. They also note that actors are more likely than observers to make dispositional attributions when performing in situations that they have *chosen* but more likely than observers to make situational attributions when they are in situations they have not chosen. Extensive research supports the overall validity of the divergent perspectives hypothesis (Harvey et al., 1990).

Keys to Social Cognition 2

Self-Perception and Social Comparison

Just as we perceive others and make attributions about their behavior, so, too, we perceive and make attributions about ourselves. It was Socrates who said "Know thyself~" and Shakespeare who expanded on this theme in the famous lines from Hamlet: "To thine own self be true, and it must follow, as the night the day, Thou can'st not then be false to any man."

The Components of Self-Perception

Psychologists have long been interested in the development and functioning of the self, or self-concept, which represents a personal conceptualization, description, and evaluation of one's own characteristics. The self-concept has both physical and psychological components that may be of little or great importance in a particular person's self-evaluation (Kilbourne, 2003). Physical aspects include not only one's body image but also sex, age, race, and other biological characteristics. The psychological elements of the self-concept are a bit more complex. One component is *self-identity*, one's sense of unity, entity (separateness from others), and continuity. It is basically the recognition that you are a unique person, that you function as a whole person, and that you have continuity over time. That is, you know your own self-history and can project what you will be like in the future. One currently important aspect of self-identity is *racial identity*. Theory suggests that self-identity develops in a social context (Greenwood, 1994; Malon et al., 1994), and you view yourself, in part, as a member of a particular racial or ethnic group. Considerable attention has been devoted in recent years to the study of racial identity in African-Americans (Belgrave et al., 1994). One repeated observation is that African-American children often have more negative self-identities than do white children (Owusu-Bempau, 1994). This has led to educational programs focusing on positive aspects of black identity in hopes that African-American children will grow up with more positive self-images. The concept of racial identity has also been extended to the study of children with one black and one white parent. Such children have biracial identity, and some theorists believe that they should be encouraged and helped to developed a self-identity that emphasizes the strengths of their dual heritage (Bowles, 1993).

A second psychological component of the self-concept is *self-esteem*—the sense of personal pride. It includes your evaluation of yourself and a tendency and desire to see yourself as positive (Burnett, 1994). Self-esteem is a product of long-term life experiences—success and failure, praise and censure, acceptance and rejection, love and hate. It can be raised to its very pinnacle by the continuing devotion of a loving parent—or dashed on the rocks of despair by a critical, rejecting caretaker. Indeed, even otherwise caring parents who "play favorites" with their children may foster reduced self-esteem. One recent study showed that 62% of parents are seen as having a favored child, and the unfavored children in those families are more likely to develop low self-esteem (Zervas & Sherman, 1994).

The importance of self-esteem lies in the breadth of its influence, from school achievement and career accomplishment to success in love, marriage, and parenthood. Tom's self-confidence and likely high self-esteem in our opener are not based entirely on his success in business. Quite the opposite: They are a product of his childhood and have helped him to become a successful businessman.

Self-image is your overall picture of yourself, an evaluative perception of your own characteristics (Burnett, 1994). The self-image is perhaps the most basic aspect of the self-concept. Characteristics of central importance to your self-image can have a great impact on your attitudes, feelings, and behaviors (Stryker & Serpe, 1994). If friendliness is one of your primary self-perceived characteristics, it will likely cause you to act positively toward others in most situations; to do otherwise would be inconsistent with your self-image. If, on the other hand, you see yourself as a generally hostile person, your behavior toward others will be quite different. The image you consciously try to convey to others—your public image—can be quite different from your self-image (Rind & Benjamin, 1994). And self-image is often distorted and inaccurate.

Just as your perceptions of others are biased, your view of yourself is always somewhat distorted and inaccurate. You may see yourself as a friendly person, while other people may see you as cool and distant. You may view yourself as independent and assertive, while others might consider you to be dependent and retiring. Such inaccuracies can extend to body image as well. You may think of yourself as quite plain, yet others may find you handsome or pretty, and vice versa. A striking example of the potential inaccuracy of the self-concept is seen in people with anorexia nervosa. A young woman with this disorder may starve herself until she weighs 80 pounds or less but look in the mirror and insist that she is fat (see Chapter 12).

The Role of the Self

No matter how accurate or inaccurate the self-concept, many theorists believe it has a tremendous impact on all areas of life. Your attitudes, emotional reactions, ways of thinking about a variety of topics, career decisions, and choice of marital partner are all strongly influenced by how you perceive yourself (Banaji & Prentice, 1994). In addition, the way a certain person, situation, or event relates to your self-concept greatly influences how you will respond to that person, situation, or event. Because self-concept is such a pervasive factor, it is important that we learn as much as possible about how it influences our thoughts and behaviors.

Information-Processing and Schemas. As theorist Hazel Markus points out, much of the impact of self-concept may come through its effect on the way we process information (Markus, 1977; Ruvolo & Markus, 1992; Kato & Markus, 1993). As we interact with the environment, we are constantly taking in and processing a variety of kinds of information in an effort to make sense of the world and to take appropriate action.

The effect of the self on such information processing was demonstrated in an experiment conducted by Marcus (1977). She had individuals rate themselves in order to determine the degree to which each defined himself in terms of dependence-independence. She then chose two groups: those who rated themselves at the extremes (either highly independent or highly dependent); and those who did not (a middle group). She next asked participants to read a list of adjectives, such as "conforming" and "assertive," and to determine which of these adjectives applied to them. Those who had rated themselves as either highly independent or highly dependent made significantly more rapid judgments than those in the middle group. They were also able to predict their future behavior with more confidence.

Markus suggests that dependence-independence is a dimension that serves as a *schema*, or central theme, for collecting and organizing information. Schemas or schemata are cognitive structures that affect social processes. Stereotypes can be seen as schemas that affect the way we view the behaviors of others and the way we interact with them. On the basis of her experiments, Markus reasoned that people have well-organized schemata for those dimensions that are particularly central to their self-concepts and less-organized schemata for less important dimensions. Her theory, which has received considerable empirical support (Dohi, 1994), is related to the *gender schema theory* of Sandra Bem (1982). In a feminist analysis of social context, Bem hypothesizes that we react to a wide range of situations in terms of our gender schema—our perception of ourselves as masculine or feminine (Bem, 1993).

Organizing New Information. Theorist Carl Rogers (Chapter 14) pointed out that the self-concept may also help to organize *new* information. In one study subjects were asked to read sixty self-descriptive sentences and then shown a list containing these sixty sentences interspersed with sixty new ones. Those subjects who had been told to decide whether each of the original items had been descriptive of them were much more accurate in recognizing these items when they were embedded in the second list (Rogers, 1977). Further research confirms that this "self-referent" strategy is more effective than several other approaches in memorizing information and that the more relevant new information is to an existing schema, the more likely participants are to believe they have seen the information previously (Rogers, Rogers, and Kiper, 1977, 1979). This research clearly suggests that the self-concept has its great impact on behavior at least in part through its influence on the organization and processing of information—a social cognitive process.

Effects of Self-Awareness

Self-perception can be seen as an extension of the idea of person perception. You yourself are basically a *social object* in the environment. You perceive yourself in much the way you perceive others. Conscious attention directed toward the self as a social object is called *self-awareness.* Some individuals are more aware of themselves and have a greater tendency to focus on the self than others (Morin, 1993). One team of investigators reasoned that by measuring the degree of an individual's self-awareness they could determine some of its effects (Fenigstein et al., 1975). They therefore developed a *Self-Consciousness Scale* to measure the enduring tendency to focus attention on the self. This scale contains twenty-three items, such as "I'm often the subject of my own fantasies," "I never scrutinize myself," and "I sometimes have the feeling that I'm off somewhere watching myself." Participants are asked to score each item from zero (extremely uncharacteristic) to four (extremely characteristic). These scores can then be correlated with other aspects of the self.

Studies show that a high degree of self-awareness makes a person more aware of the alternative perspectives of others (Assendorpf et al., 1996) more sensitive to their needs and values (Richardson & Molinaro, 1996). Other work suggests that it may be possible to increase self-awareness through *self-talk.* In using self-talk, the individual basically comments to himself on his own behavior as an outsider might, thereby potentially increasing self-consciousness (Morin, 1993).

You might think that self-awareness is an entirely good thing. Wouldn't greater awareness of your own characteristics mean better adjustment and functioning? Perhaps under some circumstances, but recent research has turned up some opposing results. For example, when a group of undergraduate students were given the Self-Consciousness Scale and some other measures, it was found that a high degree of self-reflection—leading to greater self-awareness—was associated with low self esteem (Conway & Giannopoulos, 1993). Similar results were seen in a group of 1860 students making the transition to junior high school: Increased self-consciousness was associated with reduced adjustment (Lord et al., 1994). These results provide a good example of why we must do scientific research, rather than making assumptions. Greater self-awareness is not, under all circumstances, a positive indicator, even though common sense might lead us to think it is.

Robert Wicklund (1975; Steins & Wicklund, 1993) has suggested that when attention is directed toward the self, a *self-appraisal* process is immediately set in motion, increasing both self-praise and self-criticism. One team of investigators heightened self-awareness in subjects by having them listen to tape recordings of their own voices as they stood in front of a mirror (Ickes, Wicklund, and Farris, 1973). Those subjects who were given negative information about their personalities were more self-critical than control participants who were not in front of a mirror. The researchers also found that receiving positive information in front of the mirror resulted in greater self-esteem than receiving the same information without the mirror. These studies confirm Wicklund's idea that heightened self-awareness increases both positive and negative self-evaluations (Schiffmann & Wickman, 1992).

Social Comparison Theory

The self-concept develops as a self-description and evaluation of your own, specific characteristics (Burnett, 1994). You see yourself as a successful student (or an unsuccessful one), a good daughter (or a bad one), a kind person (or an unkind one). Studies show than even an infant a few months old has at least the beginnings of a self-concept (Liu et al., 1993). But where does this all-important self-concept come from? Many social psychologists currently believe that it grows out of a process in which we match our own characteristics against those of others—a process of *social comparison* (Takata, 1993).

According to theorist Charles Horton Cooley (1902), whose classic work has been very influential, the self-concept arises out of social interaction and is principally the individual's interpretation of how others view him. Cooley called it the "looking glass self." In Cooley's conception, the self is a social mirror in which we learn to see ourselves as others see us.

Sociologist George Herbert Mead (1934), another major theorist, also saw the self as a product of social interaction and hypothesized that it develops as we learn to distinguish between the "I" as perceiver of the external world and the "me" as the object of our own perceptions. The "I" acts upon the world, and the world responds with approval or disapproval, reward or punishment for behavior. Eventually the child incorporates the reactions of others, and the "me" takes over the process of reward and punishment. The self-concept in Mead's view is thus an internalization of the society's view of the individual and a mechanism for maintaining socially appropriate behavior. Building on Mead's ideas, but arriving at somewhat different conclusions, social psychologist Leon Festinger (1954) suggested that the self-concept develops as a function not so much of direct feedback as of our personal comparisons of ourselves with others. Festinger's very influential approach is the one that we call *social comparison theory*, and it holds that the self-concept grows out of a learned need for self-evaluation. Rather than using some objective standard against which to judge ourselves, we often use the behavior of others as a guideline for comparison and judgment. Ask yourself how good a student you are, how attractive you are, or how good an athlete you are. How do you answer these questions? Festinger hypothesized that it is probably through a social comparison process in which you assess how your academic performance, attractiveness, or athletic ability stacks up against that of other people with whom you interact.

Supportive Evidence. Many studies have provided support for social comparison theory. If we ask participants how attractive they are, then observe how they make that determination, we find that they compare themselves with others who may be more or less attractive (Brown et al., 1992). The subject may conclude that "I am more attractive than my roommate but somewhat less attractive than my best friend." Social comparison also appears to be a substantial basis for self-perceptions of how desirable (Heckhausen & Krueger, 1993), intelligent (Butler, 1992), and interesting (Wheeler & Riyake, 1992) we are, among many other characteristics. Moreover, when subjects perceive a change in their social comparison group, they are likely to change their own self-perceptions (Klein & Kunda, 1993).

Social comparison is particularly important in the development and maintenance of self-esteem. College students who compare themselves unfavorably with similar students have lower self-esteem, which is associated with an increase in depressive affect (Major et al., 1993). To better understand the relationship between social comparison and self-esteem, one team of researchers had subjects indicate which of their own characteristics they liked and which they did not (Ditto & Griffin, 1993). They found that participants high in self-esteem perceived their most liked attributes as relatively uncommon in others and their least-liked features as relatively common. They were clearly comparing themselves favorably with others.

If you constantly make social comparisons, it is reasonable to wonder with whom you are likely to compare yourself. You might compare your performance in basketball with that of Michael Jordan, your acting skills with those of Tom Hanks, or your musical talent with that of pianist Van Cliburn, but that is unlikely. More often we compare ourselves with people who are at least reasonably similar to us, and these people comprise our *reference groups*. Other college basketball players, actors, or musicians, for example, would be more likely reference groups than top professionals, and the comparison group you look to will depend on the issue. If, for example, you are a feminist evaluating your career potential or accomplishments, you might choose as your reference group all people in a given field, all women, or perhaps all feminists (Young, 1994). If you are evaluating changes in your cognitive skills over many years, you may look to other people in your own age group as a point of reference (Powell & Whitla, 1994). If you are deaf, other deaf people may frequently be your reference group (Bat-Chava, 1993). In any case, you are free to choose your reference groups, and the groups you choose can make a great difference in how you feel about yourself (Butler et al., 1994).
Downward comparisons, in which you look at those less fortunate or accomplished than you are can raise your self-esteem; *upward comparisons* can lower it. Lisa Aspinwall and Shelley Taylor (1993) showed that participants who are low in self-esteem have significantly improved self-evaluations and mood states after engaging in downward comparisons. Related studies show that although everyone feels better about themselves after a downward comparison, the improvement in self-evaluation is greater in those who start out with low self-esteem (Reis et al., 1993).

So, how good a student are you? Whatever your answer, studies suggest that it will be based on social comparisons that you make (Pyryt & Mendaglio, 1994; Strein, 1993).

Alternatives to Social Comparison

An alternative approach to understanding how the self develops is Daryl Bem's (1970, 1989) *self-perception theory*, which holds that we come to know ourselves by observing our own overt behavior. As we see ourselves behave, we make inferences about our characteristics in much the same way that we observe and make inferences and generalizations about others. You may note, for example, that you get good grades, can easily absorb and understand complex new material in a variety of subject areas, and always score well on tests like the SAT. From these observations you may infer that you are very intelligent, and that conclusion becomes part of your self-concept.

Another theory is that of Seymour Epstein (1973), who suggests that the self-concept is actually a *self-theory*. It is a set of hypotheses we form about our own characteristics. In Epstein's view, we observe ourselves engaging in behavior, then speculate about why we may have engaged in that behavior. The speculation leads to the formulation of hypotheses, which are then tested through further behavioral observations and may be accepted or rejected as part of the self-concept. As elementary school progresses, you notice that you usually get 'As' on spelling, reading, math, and other tests. You might formulate various explanatory hypotheses. The 'As' are due to good luck; parental help; easy subject matter; good teachers; or high intelligence. You then observe that you maintain good performance across teachers, that your peers often say the subject matter is hard, and that you perform well on standardized tests. Again you may conclude that the high intelligence hypothesis is best confirmed by the evidence.

Epstein suggests that we form a self-theory for three principal reasons: it enables us to predict our own behavior; it organizes data we derive from experience so that we can behave appropriately and cope effectively; and it provides a basis for increased self-esteem by allowing us to maintain a clear sense of personal identity. Incorporation of high intelligence as a part of your self-theory thus helps you to predict your performance on the next test, tells you how much you need to study, and boosts your self-esteem.

Social Cognition and Self-Protection

How well do you *really* know yourself? Is your self-concept accurate, your self-esteem entirely a reflection of your life experiences, your self-image solidly based in reality? The answer is a resounding "NO!" according to many psychologists who have studied the self. In fact, the self is a distorted, inaccurate structure, built on some combination of reality and illusion. The test of this distortion is to determine whether you view yourself in the same way that others view you, and studies show that virtually everyone is at least somewhat inaccurate by this criterion. How many times have you heard several people who work under a particular boss describe her in unflattering terms as overbearing, ineffectual, disorganized, helpless, or just downright nasty? Do you think the boss describes herself in those terms? Probably not. The real question is how such distortions of the self-concept arise, and one general answer to this question is that they are the result of certain social cognitive processes.

Theorists working from a variety of psychological perspectives have long held that distortions occur because we typically strive to achieve and maintain a positive self-image. This is not always an easy task. The star of the football team may have no talent for math, the math whiz-kid may have trouble getting dates, and the most popular girl in the high school may have parents who constantly criticize her. Moreover, some people have all of the above: no athletic skills, no obvious academic talents, no dates, and world's most uncaring parents. Such negative life experiences—and we all have some of them—can lower self-esteem and make for a less positive self-image. As a result, we typically adopt one or more of a variety of psychological strategies designed to protect the all-important but fragile self-concept and provide us with a positive self-image in the face of adversity. Some theorists believe that we protect the self primarily through the use of illusion and self-deception, the subject of our 21 for this chapter.

Keys to Social Cognition 3

Interpersonal Attraction and Romantic Love

We meet many people in a lifetime. Some we dislike, others become casual acquaintances, and still others become friends or close friends. A very few we love. Occasionally, we experience the romantic ideal of love at first sight: We see her or him across a crowded room; eyes meet, there is a sudden and mutual surge of emotional energy, a unique, powerful essence, a chemistry that can only be love. Such intense, instantaneous, overpowering love is something to be cherished, for very few people ever experience it. More often, love relationships develop gradually. We meet someone, perhaps have a positive initial impression, perhaps recognize that this is a person we could grow to love. We find time—make time—to interact with this special person. Liking becomes strong liking; casual friendship turns to mutual infatuation. Hearts touch. The relationship deepens and intensifies. We are in love—powerful, overwhelming, all-encompassing romantic love.

Love is the stuff that dreams are made of. It is such an intensely pleasurable, wonderful feeling that it is perhaps best left to poets, philosophers, and lyricists. Nevertheless, social psychologists have made a valiant attempt to better understand the essence of love. In that attempt, they have focused primarily on the processes that bring two people together—the processes of *interpersonal attraction*. What factors influence our attraction to and liking for another person? It turns out that some factors reside in the characteristics of the other person; others are a function of the situation in which we interact or of the relationship itself. Interestingly enough, there is increasing evidence that the factors in interpersonal attraction are similar across cultures and genders (Hatfield & Rapson, 1993). We begin our study of interpersonal attraction by considering the powerful impact of physical attractiveness, then examine psychological, situational, and relational factors. Finally, we turn to the fascinating topic of how and with whom we fall in love.

Physical Attractiveness: A Definite Plus

Numerous studies have shown that the single most important factor in finding other people appealing or likeable is physical attractiveness (Berscheid, 1994; Curtart and Lippold, 1975; Walster et al., 1966). In fact, when we perceive someone as physically attractive, we tend to ascribe all sorts of other positive characteristics to her or him. In some studies, for example, subjects are presented with photos of people previously judged to be very attractive, average, and unattractive and asked to rate the people on a variety of characteristics. The result? Attractive people are typically judged to be happier, better adjusted, more successful, more socially skilled, more desirable as marriage partners, and of higher occupational status than less attractive people (Larose et al., 1993; Erwin, 1993; Townsend, 1993. Considering that physical appearance was the only information subjects had about the people they were rating, the attractiveness effect was striking. You can see how this applies in practical settings. Tom, in our opening story, was very impressed with Laurie. Now we can guess that his positive view of her adjustment, social skills, and business acumen may have been strongly influenced by her beauty, which may also have helped her climb the corporate ladder. Studies demonstrate the advantage that attractive people have when they apply for jobs and promotions (Wade & Kinicki, 1997; Marlowe et al., 1996).

And this is only the tip of the iceberg. Elaine Hatfield and her colleagues found that your choice of a marital partner—one of the most important decisions in nearly everyone's life—is heavily based on physical attractiveness. It is the single most influential factor for both men and women, though women additionally consider earning potential to be important (Sprecher et al., 1994). Physically attractive people have more interaction with members of the opposite sex and are more satisfied with these interactions than are their unattractive counterparts (Reiss, 1980), and when in need they receive more help (Benson, Karabenick, and Lerner, 1976).

Maybe It's True. Perhaps physically attractive people actually are more likable, and some researchers have set out to test that hypothesis. In one study, students participated in three phone conversations with people they had never met and were then asked to rate each of their phone partners on likability, social skills, and desirability of future contact. Findings showed that physically attractive phone partners received higher ratings than did unattractive partners, even though the subjects had never actually seen them (Goldman and Lewis, 1977).

By now you might be asking, "If I'm unattractive, should I just go crawl in a hole?" At least four kinds of findings suggest that you need not beat too hasty a retreat. First, physical attractiveness is by no means the only characteristic influencing social preference (Eagly et al., 1991). Second, there are also individual differences in the extent to which people consider physical attractiveness important. It has been found, for example, that people with less sexist attitudes are less influenced by physical attractiveness (Touheys 1979; Anderson and Bem, 1981). Third, the weight assigned to attractiveness decreases with the age of the perceiver (Zuckerman & Hodgins, 1993). Finally, faces rated as "average" are also rated as "attractive" (Rhodes & Tremewan, 1996).

Since physical attractiveness is such an important factor in person perception, many psychologists have asked the obvious question: Why? Interestingly enough, few answers have been offered, and one of the major current ones comes from the perspective of evolutionary theory.

Physical Attractiveness: An Evolutionary Perspective

Why is it that we have such a strong preference for physically attractive people and why do certain characteristics cause one person to be perceived as more attractive than another? Perhaps the answer to both questions is that those qualities perceived as more attractive have greater adaptive value for the continuation of the species. That, at least, is the view of evolutionary theory (Gangestad, 1993).

You can quite easily divide ten people at a party into more and less attractive groups, and your ratings will probably be quite similar to those of other men and women. But what are you looking at? What influences your ratings? Part of the answer lies in the person's face. Men prefer female faces characterized by large eyes, a small nose, and a small chin (Cunningham, 1986). Women prefer men with large eyes, prominent cheekbones, and a large chin (Cunningham et al., 1990). Moreover, there is some evidence that these preferred facial features are consistent across cultures, supporting an evolutionary viewpoint (Perrett et al., 1994). Further support comes from studies involving computer programs that generate genetically-based faces, then allow participants to modify the faces over a number of generations. The beautiful faces they arrive at have been found in other studies to be associated with high fertility, and selection of sexual partners with such faces would therefore further the propagation of the species (Johnston & Franklin, 1993). Facial features found to be associated with such species-desirable characteristics as immunocompetence (the body's ability to fend off disease) and good health have also been found to be attractive, again supporting an evolutionary view of beauty (Thornbill & Gangestad, 1993). From this standpoint, beauty is not, as one research team put it, "in the eye of the beholder," but rather in the genes (Johnston & Franklin, 1993).

Body shape is an obvious second determinant of perceived attractiveness. Men generally agree that a female body shape approximating the age-old hourglass dimensions is ideal (Winnins et al., 1968), and women similarly show considerable agreement as to the most desirable male body (Beck et al., 1976). One possible explanation for these preferences is that we all grow up learning from our parents, peers, and others just what the ideal body looks like; by the time we are adults we have simply accepted these learned ideals.

An alternative view is that of evolutionary theory, which suggests that preferred body shape, like preferred facial appearance, should have adaptive value (Hatfield & Sprecher, 1995; Jones, 1995). In one study, Devendra Singh (1993) examined the role of overall thinness and of waist-to-hip (WHR) ratio to perceived beauty. The WHR is a measure of body fat distribution based on the relationship of waist size to hip size. Singh conducted a series of studies in which college students and older subjects rated the beauty of females. She found that thin female figures were not desirable. They were not rated as more attractive or as having more desirable personality characteristics. However, WHR did make a difference. Normal weight females with low WHR were judged to be the most attractive. Why? Probably because WHR is correlated with a woman's reproductive endocrinological status. Women with low WHR reproduce more readily and more frequently. In addition, they have lower long-term health risks than do high WHR women (Singh, 1993, 1994, 1995). From an evolutionary standpoint, both characteristics are selected because they have adaptive value. While not all studies are in agreement with Singh's findings, considerable literature does support this evolutionary view (Henss, 1995). We will have more to say about this viewpoint shortly when we discuss love and mate selection.

Psychological Characteristics

Although physical attractiveness is a powerful determinant of liking, several psychological characteristics are also important. We are likely to form favorable impressions of people who are friendly, warm, and personable. We also tend to be attracted to those who are intelligence, competence, and good judgment (Rubin, 1973). Personality traits have also been studied. One investigation exposed undergraduate students to potential interaction partners. In one condition, the partner acted a role in which he or she was very positive in evaluating people and situations; in a second condition, the partner was negative. Participants had a clear preference for interacting with the positive partner, suggesting a more subtle but clearly desirable and preferred characteristic (Lipkus & Rusbult, 1993). Think about this study next time you're about to complain!

A Rose by Any Other Name . . . May Not Be

Be careful when you name your children! Believe it or not, a person's first name may also influence how attractive she is perceived to be. Hortense may be seen as less attractive than Susan, and Oscar may be less appealing than David. In one study of the name effect, the investigator provided participants with photos of six young women who had previously been rated as approximately equal in attractiveness and asked them to vote for one as "queen" of the annual New Orleans St. Joseph's Day festivities (Garwood, 19??). Each photo was randomly assigned a name that had previously been rated as desirable (Kathy, Jennifer, or Christine) or undesirable (Ethel, Harriet, or Gertrude). Results were clear-cut: The three women assigned desirable names received 158 votes, while the three with undesirable names got only 39 votes. Both male and female participants engaged in the same discrimination, with 77 percent of females and 83 percent of males voting for the photos with the most desirable names.

Subjects in another study were also shown photos. For some, the person in a given photo was assigned an attractive name, for others an unattractive name, and for still others no name. The person in any one, specific photo was typically rated as more physically attractive when she was given an attractive name (e.g., Susan) than when she was given an unattractive name (e.g., Hortense) (Erwin, 1993). Other studies have shown that teachers rate hypothetical elementary students with more attractive names as better readers (Stewart & Segalowitz, 1991), that certain names are stereotypically associated with high or low intelligence (Joubert, 1993), and that undergraduates who like their own names have higher self-esteem (Joubert, 1991). What's in a name? Plenty!

Situational and Relational Characteristics

Attraction to another person is influenced not only by her characteristics but also by situational factors and by the relationship itself.

Situational Factors. Situational factors include proximity, familiarity, and arousal. *Proximity* refers to the simple fact that we are more likely to be attracted to and become friends with people who live or work close by. Many relationships begin, for example, in work settings, where the two people see each other every day (Pierce et al., 1996). Neighbors, students who have multiple classes together, and people who regularly go to the same fitness club or swimming pool also have the proximity factor working for them. Closely related to proximity is the *familiarity* effect: the more often we encounter someone, the more likely we are to like him or her. This effect does not always hold true, of course. Sometimes too much exposure to a person can produce dislike or boredom (Miller, 1976), and repeated exposure to someone you already dislike will not increase attraction (Brocknet and Swap, 1976).

Among those people we are situationally close to and familiar with, we clearly like some better than others. One of the factors contributing to this differentiation is *positive emotional arousal* (May and Hamilton, 1977). You may, for example, develop a definite liking for someone you meet while enjoying yourself at the beach or on the ski slopes, while meeting the same person in your office during a frustrating period of work overload will be less conducive to attraction.

Relational Factors. The relationship you have with a friend also affects the development and continuation of the friendship. Ellen Berscheid (1994) points out that such *relational factors* are currently of central interest to social psychologists who study interpersonal attraction. Receiving greatest attention are social cognitive processes that go on within a relationship and can strongly affect its quality and continuation. For example, a good friend asks you to go to a concert that you know you will find terminally boring. In making your decision, you think about its impact on the relationship: Will it improve the friendship if you go? Will it do serious harm to the relationship if you don't? Does your friendship obligate you to go? You are thinking about the relationship, relying on cognitive processes to make a social decision. The issue for social psychology is just what the relevant cognitive processes are, how they take place, and how they affect the relationship.

Other aspects of interpersonal interaction that can affect attraction include reciprocity, similarity, and complementarity. *Reciprocity* refers to the fact that we tend to like those who like us (Shrauger and Jones, 1968). Studies have quite consistently confirmed the role of reciprocity in the formation of relationships (Clark & Ayers, 1988). The exception to this general rule appears to be "universally likeable" people—individuals who are liked by virtually everyone they come in contact with, regardless of whether they reciprocate the positive attraction (Folkes and Sears, 1977). Such people are described as having consistently positive attitudes, and that may be part of the secret to their popularity.

Similarity is also a major factor in attraction, as in the case of Tom and Laurie in the opening scenario. A great deal of research has shown that people tend to be attracted to others with similar educational backgrounds, economic status, race, social class, politics, religion, attitudes, and values (Pilkington & Lydon, 1997; Shaikh & Kanekar, 1994; Hoyle, 1993. College dating partners have been found to be highly similar in such areas as physical attractiveness, religion, plans for graduate education, and even SAT scores (Hill, Rubin. and Peplau. 1976). In multicultural settings, it appears that attraction is based on non-cultural similarities among the people involved (Osbeck et al., 1997).

Do Opposites Attract?

It seems somehow intuitively appealing that among people, as with magnets, opposites attract. Intrigued by this possibility, researchers have compared friends and couples in physical appearance, age, race, religion, socioeconomic level, education, height, and intelligence. The findings suggest that actually we are much more attracted to similar people than to opposites (Shaikh & Kanekar, 1994). Nevertheless, Robert Lynch (1955) many years ago argued the case for *complementarity*, suggesting the needs of one marital partner are likely to complement the needs of the other. Thus, an insecure partner would be more likely to choose a secure partner, a dominant partner to choose a submissive one, and so on. Some studies have supported this view by showing that we may be attracted to those with different attitudes, beliefs, or values when we are not quite sure what is expected of us (Ross, Gold, and Stone, 1980). Others suggest that during the first 18 months of a marriage, while the relationship is still developing, similarity in values and attitudes is important; beyond that point complementary needs may become salient (Kerckhoff and Davis, 1962). However, complementarity has not more generally held up as a major, positive factor in the formation and continuation of relationships (Nowicki & Manheim, 1991). The more common and far stronger finding is that similarity attracts and difference does not.

Romantic Love

And when love speaks, the voice of all the Gods makes heaven drowsy with the harmony.
SHAKESPEARE

There is only one happiness in life, to love and be loved.
NATHANIEL HAWTHORNE

O! How this spring of love resembleth the uncertain glory of an April day!
SHAKESPEARE

The importance of love in human society is evidenced by the outpouring of literature and music with love as its central theme. Falling in love is an experience that most people have at least once and that many people have several times. The experience has sometimes been termed "indescribable," but it clearly involves an intense emotional state characterized by a confusing cacophony of deeply profound feelings. Ecstasy may alternate with pain, certainty with anxiety, and tender concern with strong sexual passion. But what exactly is love? How does it differ from liking? Are there different kinds of love? What conditions are needed for love to occur?

Types of Love: Passionate and Companionate. Ellen Berscheid and Elaine Walster (1978) distinguish two forms of love that can characterize romantic relationships. The form that perhaps comes immediately to mind is the intense emotion of someone who has fallen "head over heels" in love. Berscheid and Walster call this *passionate love.* The passionate love seen in the early stages of many love relationships may be short-lived—perhaps because it is so exhausting. However, it does not typically disappear from the relationship. One study assessed the passion in relationships of couples at three stages of marriage: just married; becoming parents; and the empty nest, when all children had left the home. There was a consistent decrease in passion across these three stages of the marriage (Tucker & Aron, 1993). However, even at the empty nest stage, passion was still moderately high.

But not all is lost when passionate love decreases; instead, companionate love takes over. *Companionate love* is a sense of deep affection accompanied by the realization that one's thoughts and emotions are inextricably intertwined with those of the other person. It is a less intense but more lasting type of love that manifests itself as a feeling of deep caring and warmth for the other person.

The Triangular Model of Love. An alternative to the Berscheid-Walster theory is Robert Sternberg's (1986) *triangular model* of love (Figure 19-4A). He collected data on feelings that occur in a variety of friendships and love relationships and concluded that three dimensions are needed to describe these feelings:

- *Passion*—This dimension describes intense feelings of need to be with the partner. Passion is the *hot* side of love, and strong sexual desire is among the intense feelings.
- *Intimacy*—Called the *warm* side of love, intimacy includes feelings of mutual understanding and closeness.
- *Decision/Commitment*—This *cold* or rational aspect of love involves a conscious decision to maintain and enhance the exclusive relationship.

Passion is the *motivational* component, intimacy the *emotional* component, and decision/commitment the *cognitive* component of love. By combining these three elements, it is possible to define a variety of kinds of love based on the relative strengths of motivation, emotion, and cognition. Romantic love, for example, involves high degrees of intimacy and passion, but low commitment, while companionate love is high in intimacy and commitment but lower in passion. Sternberg describes eight such combinations, each yielding its own variety of love (Figure 19-4b).

Sternberg hypothesizes that the relative strengths of the three components vary as the relationship continues. In fact, like a person, it develops over time, and the nature of the relationship changes as this developmental process takes place. Passion increases rapidly and dramatically as the partners initially fall in love. The rise in intimacy is somewhat more gradual, but it eventually overtakes and surpasses passion to become the primary component. Passion meanwhile decreases, reaching a level well below its early peak. And, the slow-rising sense of decision and commitment bypasses passion to join intimacy, with these two components dominating the relationship. Research has tended to confirm these patterns, particularly the decrease in passion (Tucker & Aron, 1993).

Sternberg (1988) developed an inventory to measure the dimensions of his theory. It is called the Triangular Love Scale (TLS) and has been used in a number of studies, which have shown that it is reliable and valid (Whitley, 1993). In addition, studies using the scale to test Sternberg's theory have provided at least partial support for the tripartite makeup of love that he proposes (Hassebrauck & Buhl, 1996; Grau & Kumpf, 1993).

Alternatives to Sternberg's approach include the evolutionary and cognitive-labeling theories. These perspectives are dealt with in the Probe.

The Battle Of The Sexes? If there is any area of life in which we might expect gender differences, it is in the criteria applied to developing new love relationships. However, it appears that there is actually very little difference. Douglas Kenrick and his colleagues (1993) asked male and female college students to specify their minimum criteria on each of 24 traits for dates, one-night sexual liaisons, ongoing sexual partners, exclusive dating partners, and marriage partners. Overall, the sexes were quite similar, though men did have less stringent criteria for casual sexual relationships. Consistent with this latter result is the common observation that men are more sexually promiscuous than women (Walsh, 1993) and place a higher value on the sexual aspect of a love relationship (Hong & Faedda, 1994).

Cultural differences have also been studied. Focusing on passionate love and sexual desire, Elaine Hatfield and Richard Rapson (1993) conclude that cultural differences are minimal. Major cultural groups are, in fact, quite similar in their views of love, intimacy, and sex. They also confirm the lack of gender differences in the preferred characteristics of loved ones and conclude that differences lie more in the personality of the individual than in his or her gender or cultural background.

Might Tom and Laurie fall in love? Well, they certainly meet some of the criteria[RTF bookmark start: }tom[RTF bookmark end: }tom: physical attractiveness, similarity, reciprocity, and the physiological arousal engendered by a crucial business meeting. Moreover, Tom is older, often an important element in attraction, at least from an evolutionary perspective.

Liking and Loving

Loving is simply a strong form of liking, right? Probably not. Zick Rubin (1970) hypothesized that liking and loving differ not only quantitatively but qualitatively as well. He devised a series of sentences related to liking and loving, such as "It would be hard for me to get along without______," "I have great confidence in______'s good judgment," and "I feel that I can confide in______about virtually everything." He administered seventy such items to 198 college students, asking them to respond to each statement by first filling in the name of a boyfriend or girlfriend and then the name of a platonic friend of the opposite sex. The participants responded to each of the items with a score from 1 ("not at all true") to 9 ("definitely true; agree completely"). As a result of this process, Rubin was able to derive two nine-item scales, one to assess liking and one to assess loving. Statements on the liking scale emphasize the similarity between two people and their feelings of respect and admiration. In effect, it measures friendship. The items on the love scale emphasize attachment (fulfillment of needs for dependency and affiliation), caring (concern for the other person), and intimacy (trust and absorption).

When Rubin administered his two scales to 158 dating couples, he found that liking scores were about the same for a close friend and for the dating partner but that love scale scores were much higher for the dating partner, confirming the distinction between liking and loving. He also found that those who scored high on the love scale were more likely to say they were "in love," spent more time gazing into each other's eyes, and gave higher estimates of the probability that they would marry their partner. When Rubin conducted follow-up interviews six months later, he found that those couples with higher initial love scores were more likely to still be dating and more likely to describe their relationship as of equal or greater intensity.

Even though loving and liking are different, they are by no means mutually exclusive. In fact, dating couples can quite readily distinguish between feelings of love and feelings of liking or friendship within their relationships. Research shows that many couples place considerable weight on the friendship aspect of their relationship. Having someone with mutual interests to confide in, commiserate with, and turn to for support is a valued asset of the relationship. It is no doubt for that reason that 44% of those in relationships say their romantic partner is also their closest friend (Hendrick & Hendrick, 1993). The fact is that many couples value their friendship so much that they remain friends even after the love relationship breaks up. This is particularly likely to happen if they were friends for a period of time before they became lovers (Metts et al., 1994). Thus, friendship differs qualitatively from love, but it is an important facet of most love relationships.

In the past few pages we have moved from initial interaction to passion, from simple liking to intense love. You now know that interpersonal attraction is at least as complex a process as you always thought it was. Physical attractiveness is important, but not all-important. Similarity in physical and psychological characteristics is central, but not universally necessary. Situational and relational factors moderate the influence of personal characteristics to significantly affect the entire process of interpersonal attraction. And we know that romantic love can be differentiated from simple liking.

Keys to Social Cognition 4

Prosocial Behavior

It is 3 A.M. There is a loud noise on the city street: crying, screaming, the voice of a young woman. In nearby buildings curtains are pulled aside, and shadowy figures materialize behind the windows, peering at the scene on the street. More screams. The young woman has her arms raised, her head turned to one side to avoid a male attacker with a knife. She screams and cries again, and the man runs away, afraid that someone will intervene. But no one does, and soon the screams come again—he's back! More screams for help. Again he runs—and again he returns. It is obvious to the attacker that no one will help. He stabs the woman, and she falls, bleeding, to the street. Curtains go down. No one helps.

A scene like this couldn't take place in a civilized society, could it? Well, it did. It happened in Queens, New York, in 1964. The young woman, Kitty Genovese, was murdered while people looked on from their windows. No one even called police. We still don't know why no one helped her, but the reasons given by bystanders were many and varied (Wispe, 1978; Staube, 1979). Some feared for their lives, the safety of their families, or future retaliation by the attacker; others said they were ill, infirm, too old, or too tired to help; and most felt certain that someone else would come to the rescue.

Puzzled by the Kitty Genovese murder, social psychologists began to study prosocial behavior. As a form of interpersonal interaction, *prosocial behavior*, or *altruism*, is voluntary action that shows concern for and is intended to benefit other human beings. Notice that this definition has three basic elements: (1) the behavior is performed voluntarily, (2) it is intended to benefit others, and (3) it is an end in itself, not a way of somehow benefitting the actor.

Theories of Prosocial Behavior

Why prosocial behavior occurs—and why it doesn't—has fascinated social psychologists so much that they have developed a variety of theories to explain it. One emphasizes the adaptive, evolutionary value of such behavior. Another proposes that altruism is a matter of equity or reciprocation. Still other theories focus on negative affect, empathy, or social norms as causes of for prosocial behavior.

Evolutionary Theory. Charles Darwin hypothesized that altruism occurs because it contributes to the survival of the species. Extending this idea, sociobiologist E.O. Wilson (1978, 2000) has argues that there is a genetic selection over generations for self-sacrificial behavior because such helping behavior increases the probability of species survival in the long run. The altruistic individual may sometimes die, but the species as a whole will be protected.

An alternative evolutionary hypothesis suggests that it is not altruism but *reciprocal altruism* that is selected. That is, the costs of altruism are offset by benefits to the individual, and it is this reciprocal arrangement that is genetically transmitted (Fehr & Fischbacher, 2003). We engage in prosocial behavior because evolution has programmed us to expect help from others in return.

Critics of these evolutionary views hypothesize that people engage in prosocial behavior because it is socially desirable, not in order to save the species. However, studies directly measuring the effect of social desirability on the behavior suggest otherwise. Participants appear to display prosocial behavior primarily as a true reflection of their social value orientation (Platow, 1994). This supports the evolutionary view that altruistic behavior has biologically adaptive value for the survival of the species.

Equity Theory. The *equity theory* of altruism is an environmental version of the concept of reciprocal altruism. Equity theory suggests that we help others because we expect help from them, thus achieving balance or equity in our interpersonal relationships (Dale, 1994; Walster, Walster, and Berscheid, 1978). Evidence favoring this approach includes the observation that many people donate large sums of money to charity with the statement that they are trying to help others because someone helped them at some time in the past.

Further research suggests that we tend to expect, believe in, and seek out a world in which all people are treated in an equitable manner. We are taught from early childhood that individuals must accept responsibility for their own behavior, that good behavior will be rewarded, and that bad behavior will be punished. From this understanding of the consequences of behavior, it is only a small logical step to assume that those who are rewarded *must* be good and those who suffer *deserve* the pain they bear. This *just world hypothesis* suggested to Melvin Lerner (1965, 1980) that those who see someone suffering in circumstances where they can do nothing about it will tend to believe that the suffering is justified by the person's behavior.

To test this idea, Lerner had women college students watch a female "victim" who was supposedly receiving a series of electric shocks. The victim screamed and groaned and otherwise put on a good act. After observing this torture, the subjects were asked to evaluate a number of the victim's traits, such as adjustment, attractiveness, and intelligence. It turned out that the more "pain" the victim received, the more negatively the participants evaluated her personal characteristics. Rather than feeling sympathy, participants believed the victim's suffering must have been justified and therefore negatively evaluated her characteristics.

Negative Affect and Altruism. Another theoretical position holds that altruistic behavior represents an attempt on the part of the helper to reduce the *negative affect* or emotion that is experienced when observing another person in distress (Piliavan et al., 1975). According to this theory, seeing an emergency in progress produces unpleasant physiological and emotional arousal that can be reduced by engaging in helping behavior. Some studies have indeed shown that greater negative affect produces more altruistic behavior (Rothbart et al., 1994; Cialdini and Kenrick, 1976). Others have directly contradicted this idea, showing that negative affect actually reduces helping behavior in adults (Underwood, Froming, and Moore, 1977).

We have two clues as to the possible reasons for these discrepancies. One is that negative affect increases altruistic behavior when the potential helper feels personal responsibility, but decreases it if he does not (Rogers et al., 1982). The other is that personal traits may play a role. People who are generally high in a trait of sympathy and those who exhibit good affective reasoning—an ability to understand the emotions of others—are more likely to display prosocial behavior (Knight et al., 1994).

Empathy. Denise Kreps (1975) argues that altruism is due to *empathy*—the ability to sense and deeply understand the feelings and experiences of others. Empathy produces unpleasant physiological arousal, which can be reduced by helping out. The empathy you experience when you see someone who has had an automobile accident causes you to become physiologically aroused. Calling an ambulance, comforting the victim, and providing first aid all help to reduce your arousal and make you feel good. Although this explanation suggests that empathy and altruism are ultimately self-oriented because they reduce distress, others have argued that empathy may represent a genuine feeling of concern even when it does not reduce the helper's distress (Batson et al., 1978).

Support for empathy theory comes from a study in which participants heard a tape of an interview with Carol Marcy, a university freshman. They learned that Carol had broken both legs and therefore needed volunteers to spend time going over class notes with her. Those in a high empathy condition were told to attend to Carol's *feelings* and imagine what it would be like to be in her place, while low-empathy subjects were instructed to attend to the *information* presented on the tape. Those in the high-empathy condition displayed greater empathy toward the victim and greater willingness to help, suggesting that appropriately motivated subjects can display genuine empathic understanding resulting in prosocial behavior (Poy and Batson, 1982). More generally, studies support the hypothesis that empathy is a major factor in altruism (Bagozzi & Moore, 1994; Roberts & Strayer, 1996).

Prosocial Norms. Normative theories of altruism suggest that society establishes a norm of prosocial behavior, then rewards those who conform and punishes those who don't. Altruistic behavior produces social rewards; violating the altruism norm brings social sanctions. Most research on norms for prosocial behavior has centered on reciprocity, or the *Golden Rule Norm*: "Do unto others as you would have them do unto you." You give help because you expect help will to be given in return. Studies confirm that people who have given help to a person in the past are more likely to receive help from that person in the future (Wilke and Lenzetta, 1970). However, the recipient may not reciprocate if he feels that the help was not appropriate or that it was not given voluntarily. The golden rule thus works in limited circumstances (Hay, 1994).

A second normative standard is the *social responsibility norm*, a cultural expectation that people will help those who need help and who depend on them; no specific reward is needed. Supportive studies show that most people are willing to help needy individuals without receiving any social reward (Berkowitz, 1972). However, the application of this social responsibility norm tends to be selective. We are more likely to help another person if her problem seems to stem from circumstances beyond her control than if we feel the problem is her own fault (Meyer and Muherin, 1980).

In addition to such broad social norms as reciprocity and social responsibility, Shalom Schwartz (1977) has argued that *personal norms* cause many people to feel distressed if they do not give help in at least certain situations. Those who feel generally responsible for the public good are more likely than others to make charitable donations (Fleichman, 1980), and those who feel personally obligated to donate blood are much more likely to do so than people who feel no such compunction (Zuckerman and Reis, 1978). Such personal norms can augment and sometimes override the more general cultural norms in determining the behavior of an individual. A good example is the motivation of social activists. The 1960s was an era of widespread social activism, and psychologists studied the behaviors and motivations of the activists, who were frequently selfless individuals fighting for causes that they felt would benefit others.

Carol Franz and David McClelland (1994) recently located a group of people who had been identified and studied as activists in the 1960s, as well as control participants who were not activists. Confirming the personal norm hypothesis, they found that activists were far more likely to be engaging in prosocial behavior thirty years later than were non-activists. The same personal norm that had guided their participation in the social protest movements of the 1960s continued to guide their behavior much later in adulthood.

Predicting Prosocial Behavior: Helpers, Victims, and Situations

Beyond the general theories we've just described, social psychologists have studied a number of factors that influence the probability of altruistic behavior under specific circumstances. These determinants include certain characteristics of the helper, the victim, and the situation.

Helper Characteristics. It seems obvious that the personality of the potential helper is a factor in whether he will actually engage in prosocial behavior. Despite the intuitive appeal of this idea, attempts to identify specific personality traits associated with altruism have been frustrating. Some studies show that those who have a high need for approval or believe that we live in a just world are more likely to be altruistic (Satow, 1975; Lerner et al., 1975), as are more trusting people (Cadenhead & Richman, 1996). Higher levels of moral reasoning are also associated with prosocial behavior (Carlo et al., 1996). Similarly, temperament—the physiologically based tendency to react to the environment in certain ways—is a significant factor in altruistic behavior (Farver & Branstetter, 1994). Despite these supportive findings, other studies have shown that the types of people likely to help in one situation are not likely to be helpful in others (Gergen et al., 1972). Results more generally suggest that while personality characteristics may be associated with altruism under certain circumstances, such other factors as norms, values, beliefs, and external pressures are perhaps even more important (Staub, 1979).

Temporary characteristics, such as *states* and *moods*, can also play a significant role. Many studies have shown that positive mood states increase the probability of helping behavior, whereas negative states tend to decrease it (Bateson et al., 1979; Rosenhart et al., 1981). However, negative mood states can actually lead to increased helping behavior if the cost to the helper is low and the potential benefits are high (Rothbart et al., 1994). This finding makes it clear that the effects of states and moods interact in complex ways with other factors.

Another factor in prosocial behavior is *self-awareness*, which you read about earlier in the chapter. In particular, self-awareness affects the extent to which the person acts on values relating to altruism. Self-awareness and self-reflection appear to increase the probability that a person will help when her helping values are highly related to the situation and her self-concerns have been reduced. However, under other circumstances, where her values are less relevant or she is concerned about negative consequences, self-awareness may interfere with the helping process (Gibbons and Wicklund, 1982).

Victim Characteristics. Certain features of the victim can greatly influence the likelihood that others will come to his aid. In one interesting study, the "victim" was a college student who sat in a library or lounge with several other students. When the victim left the room, a poorly dressed, unshaven confederate of the researchers came in and stole his or her books. When the victim returned, other students were more likely to help out if the victim was a woman or had initiated a conversation before the books were stolen. Physically attractive victims also received more help (Bensen et al., 1976).

Similarity and perceived responsibility are also important. The more similar the victim is to the potential helper, the greater the likelihood of prosocial behavior. Black victims are more likely to be helped by blacks and white victims by whites (Gaertner & Dovidio, 1977), and people are more like to help those of similar nationality (Feldman, 1968), attitudes (Fisher et al.), or socioeconomic level (Hensley, 1981). Potential helpers also evaluate the extent to which the victim is responsible for his own plight. In one series of studies, an apparently ill victim carrying a cane was less likely to receive help from bystanders if he reeked of alcohol and appeared to be drunk (Piliavin et al., 1969; Weiner, 1980).

Situational Factors. A variety of environmental factors can also affect altruism. People are less likely to help others in large cities than in small towns (Holahan, 1977), and even pictures of slums or blighted landscapes can reduce prosocial behavior (Shrod, 1977). In addition, loud noises tend to reduce altruism (Matthews and Cannon, 1975), while pleasant music increases it (Fried and Berkowitz, 1979). Waitresses receive higher tips on sunny days than on rainy days, although they also report that they are in a better mood on sunny days, which could affect tipping (Cunningham, 1979).

Bibb Latane and John Darley (1970) developed a decision model for prosocial behavior, which hypothesizes that a bystander goes through several stages at each of which she must decide whether or not to help (Figure 19-5). In a series of studies that followed the Kitty Genovese murder, they found that the greater the number of bystanders, the less likely it was that any one of them would help the victim (Figure 19-6A) and the longer it would take if they did (Figure 196-B). More generally, a review of fifty-six studies involving over 2000 bystanders found that approximately half of lone bystanders helped, whereas only 22 percent of those in groups helped (Latane and Nida, 1981).

Social commentators lamenting the failure to help Kitty Genovese and similar victims have often attributed the lack of altruistic behavior to cultural alienation, generalized apathy (indifference) in the populace, and even unconscious sadistic inclinations. Some bystanders in a group situation feel that the emergency is not their responsibility, that they don't really know what to do, that they would rather not get involved, or that others are more competent to deal with the problem. Some research has also suggested that bystanders in a group setting are actually less likely to interpret the situation as an emergency: "No one else is doing anything, so it must not be too serious" (Latane and Darley, 1970).

The Effects of Prosocial Behavior

Altruism may have psychological effects on both helper and victim. Helping others often improves the helper's mood (Harris, 1977). It also increases the likelihood that the person will help again in the future, probably because the initial incident produces a self-evaluation that "I am a helping person" (Freidman and Fraser, 1966). Conversely, those who fail to help a victim of suffering tend to perceive the victim as "bad" (Lerner, 1977).

It would be a logical assumption that someone who has been helped will be appreciative of the help, feel that the helper is a good person, and decide that human nature is, after all, not so bad. Actually, however, the reactions of victims are quite mixed. Aid is apparently most appreciated when it is spontaneously volunteered (Broil et al., 1974), when it is unexpected (Morse et al., 1977), and when there is an opportunity to reciprocate the favor (Cgstro, 1975). When these conditions are not present, victims may actually feel hostile toward the helper. Such negative feelings are particularly likely when the victim feels an obligation that cannot be met, when the aid is viewed as not very costly to the helper, and when the favor reduces the freedom of action of the victim (Berscheid and Walster, 1978). On an international scale, you might wonder about the value to the United States of its extensive foreign aid program. Does it pay off in good will? Apparently not—at least not in the 1970s when one study was done. Officials from over a dozen nations receiving foreign aid said that they often feel far more hostile than positive toward their benefactors (Gergen and Gergen, 1971).

Keys to Social Cognition 5

The Neurophysiology of Social Cognition

Work on the complex neural mechanisms underlying social cognition is just beginning. However, researchers have preliminary evidence for the involvement of several areas of the brain. In addition, one neurochemical has been strongly implicated.

A Neural Module For Social Cognition

Evolutionary theory hypothesizes that important psychological functions are controlled not by general brain functions but by modules specific to limited areas of behavior (Cosmides & Tooby, 1994). A given module could be located in one limited area of the brain. However, consistent with connectionist theory, it is more likely to be spread across multiple brain structures, perhaps joined by neural networks (Chapter 7).

Working from this viewpoint, Leslie Brothers and Brian Ring (1992, 1993) have proposed a neural module for social cognition. Their work at the University of California Brain Research Institute is with macaque monkeys. They have recorded from implanted electrodes while the monkeys watched videos of social behavior in macaques and humans.

Their basic finding was that the videos produce selective firing of neurons in limited areas of the temporal cortex and amygdala (Figure 19-7). In other studies, these areas are responsive to pictures of faces, facial expressions, and body movements, suggesting that they constitute at least part of a social cognition module (Brothers, 1990).

Related work in both macaques and humans has yielded similar findings. David Perrett and Nathan Emery (1994) note that certain temporal neurons quite clearly appear to code for visual information about social signals from others. They suggest that this area of the brain may well be involved when we make attributions about the intentions of others. It has also been suggested that it may be involved in generating feelings of empathy (Brothers, 1990).

An interesting extension of Brothers' work to humans is a series of studies done by Annette Karmiloff-Smith and her colleagues (1995). They presented social stimuli to patients with Williams' syndrome, a genetic disorder that produces neural deficits and is known to affect cognition. Their results were consistent with the idea of a social cognitive module in the brain, a growing conceptualization that has recently led to the development of an alternative connectionist model (Kunda & Thagard, 1996).

Frontal Cortex in Social Cognition

It is generally agreed that areas of the frontal cortex are involved in complex thought processes. Extending this assumption, some researchers have studied social cognitive processes in patients with traumatic brain damage. Patients with damage, particularly when the frontal lobe is involved, show significantly reduced social-cognitive behavior. They have difficulty interacting with others, and finding good solutions to social conflict situations (Van-Horn et al., 1992). They also show deficits in formulating self-concepts, making attributions, and more generally display social-cognitive abilities more consistent with those of adolescent or preadolescent children (Santoro & Spiers, 1994; Eslinger et al., 1992; Levine et al., 1993).

Neurochemistry: Oxytocin and Social Behavior

Oxytocin is a neuropeptide—a string of amino acids—that is manufactured in the hypothalamus and affects both the pituitary gland and areas of the brain. A number of animal studies suggest that oxytocin may be important in the initiation of social interactions. It appears to be involved in the attachment (bonding) of parent and infant (Chapter 10), in prosocial behavior, and in the formation of relationships (Insel, 1992). There are undoubtedly other brain chemicals involved in social behavior, but the work on oxytocin is an important first step in beginning to understand the neurochemistry of complex social cognition.

Keys to Social Cognition 6

Industrial/Organizational Psychology

Industrial/organizational (I/O) psychology is not a part of social psychology; in fact, it is a major subfield of psychology in its own right. However, it does share with social psychology interest in such approaches as cognitive theory and attribution theory, and both fields deal, in part, with the determinants and consequences of self-perception and social comparison.

Industrial/organizational (I/O) psychology is the branch of psychology that develops theories and conducts scientific research on the problems of human organizations and the utilization of human resources by those organizations. It also applies the principles derived from this theory and research to solving the problems of organizations and improving their functioning. A number of doctoral programs train I/O psychologists, and its major professional association, the Society for Industrial and Organizational Psychology (SIOP), currently has about 2400 members.

There is some agreement that I/O psychology began as a field on December 20, 1901, when Walter Dill Scott, a professor at Northwestern University, addressed a group of advertising executives on potential contributions of psychology to the advertising field. Some, however, prefer to credit Hugo Munsterberg, who came to the U.S. from Germany in 1892 and, as director of the psychological laboratory at Harvard, began serious work on practical applications of psychological principles. A third important early figure was James McKeen Cattell, who was chair of the psychology department at Columbia University and later founded the Psychological Corporation, which provided consulting for industry. Finally, the first person to actually receive a degree in I/O psychology was Lilian Gilbreth, who was trained at Brown University.

Modern I/O psychology divides into three principal areas: organizational psychology, personnel psychology, and human factors. Each of these is concerned with several areas of theory, research, and application.

Organizational Psychology

Organizational psychology is concerned with the structure and functioning of organizations and particularly with the social and emotional adaptations of individuals in organizational settings. It deals with the areas of job satisfaction, work motivation, and leadership.

Job Satisfaction. It seems obvious that job satisfaction—contentment with and enjoyment of one's job—is an asset for both the individual and the organization. But what produces job satisfaction and just what are its actual benefits?

These and related questions have probably produced more research in I/O psychology than any other single issue—literally thousands of studies.

To determine how satisfied employees are, most organizations—and most researchers—use questionnaires. They typically ask each worker to rate her job in a number of areas. Adequacy of pay and benefits, supervisor support and effectiveness, interest, opportunity for advancement, safety, friendliness of co-workers, and adequacy of training are common examples. The employee's collective answers to these questions provide an operational definition of job satisfaction. I/O researchers gather these data from an organization's employees, then determine what influences job satisfaction and what aspects of individual and organizational functioning it relates to.

It appears from this research that the determinants of job satisfaction are both *internal* (characteristics of the individual) and *external* (forces outside the person). Individual employees differ in the ease with which they are satisfied. Some people report high satisfaction on several different jobs they hold over a period of time, while others are dissatisfied across a variety of job settings. There is even some evidence from twin studies for a moderate genetic predisposition to be more or less satisfied (Arvey et al., 1994), which is not surprising in light of the growing evidence of genetic factors in personality (see Chapter 14). In addition, job satisfaction is higher in those who express generally higher levels of life satisfaction (Judge & Hulit, 1993). And people who either choose jobs that "fit" them well from the start or who have substantial control over the jobs they do and the schedules they keep (e.g., corporate CEOs, physicians, and college professors) tend to be more satisfied (Skolnik et al., 1993).

The job situation itself—a major external force—is also, of course, an important determinant of satisfaction. Studies show that job satisfaction is higher when the job has more positive characteristics: adequate pay and benefits, good supervision, and friendly co-workers, among others. In addition, jobs that are interesting and challenging and for which the employee is well trained yield higher levels of satisfaction.

But what are the benefits of higher job satisfaction? First, a satisfied employee is a happier employee: Increased job satisfaction makes people feel better (Crohan et al., 1989). Second, high job satisfaction tends to reduce employee absenteeism (Steel & Rentsch, 1995) and turnover (George & Jones, 1996). Third, you might expect, as many managers do, that high satisfaction leads to greater productivity. However, this turns out to be an questionable assumption. While there may be some tendency in that direction, it is a weak one, and we cannot conclude that job satisfaction and productivity are closely related (Das & Mital, 1994). The bottom line is that an organization should try to foster high satisfaction in order to make its individual employees feel better and to reduce turnover and absenteeism, but not as a path to greater productivity.

Work Motivation. I recently stood in line behind nine other people at the one and only open register in a fast food restaurant that should remain nameless—we'll just call it MacDonald's. I noticed that no less than four (count 'em, *four*!) uniformed employees sat idly in a far corner talking and joking around. Customers in the line were (believe it or not) complaining, some loudly. This was clearly a corporation that needed some I/O psychologists to study employee *work motivation*—the forces within the person that stimulate work behavior and direct it to benefit the organization. Sources of work motivation can be internal (e.g., a feeling of satisfaction with a job well done) or external (e.g., money, supervisor orders or reprimands).

A number of theories have been applied in an attempt to understand work motivation. David McClelland's theory hypothesizes greater work motivation in those high in achievement and power motivations and specifies how these motivations develop (Chapter 12). Abraham Maslow's need theory (Chapter 12) suggests that management work to gradually move each employee up the motivational hierarchy toward self-actualization—the full realization of his potentialities. McClelland's theory applies primarily to the motivation of employees at managerial levels, and there is little empirical evidence to support Maslow's hypotheses. However, two other approaches, the expectancy and equity theories, have been more widely accepted and have garnered more support.

Expectancy theory is a cognitive approach which hypothesizes that work performance results from a conscious choice to engage in the behavior that is likely to produce the greatest payoffs for the individual. The four employees at the busy fast food restaurant I was in clearly had the expectation that joking amongst themselves would be more rewarding than opening additional lines at the counter. More generally, each employee asks herself whether the reward offered for the work to be performed (e.g., pay and praise from the supervisor) is valuable enough to warrant the effort and whether there is a reasonable expectation that the reward will actually be forthcoming. If the weekly pay check is a virtual certainty but is not alone sufficient, she will assess the likelihood of supervisor praise and perhaps other rewards. Both a valued reward and a reasonable expectation of receiving it must be present if the worker is to be motivated to do the job (Peak, 1955).

Equity theory, developed primarily by J. Stacy Adams (1963) M proposes that motivation is based on the individual's assessment of the balance between input and outcome. The employee asks in effect: "Is the amount of effort I'm expending justified by the rewards (e.g., money, praise, promotion) I receive." When the two are in balance, there is *equity*, and the employee is motivated to work hard enough to maintain the balance. When workers perceive that efforts exceed rewards, there is inequity, and motivation to work decreases. Some versions of equity theory go a step further to introduce a *social comparison* hypothesis: The employee also compares the rewards she receives for the effort she expends with the apparent reward/effort balance of other people she considers relevant (Goodman, 1974).L

Leadership. A *leader* is one whose job is to structure work situations for others and to guide their behavior toward some goal. While this is actually only one of many definitions of leadership, it conveys the general sense that a leader is a person who serves as an agent of change—ideally progress—and influences the work of others. The I/O psychologist is interested in determining the characteristics of good leaders. While it is quite easy to differentiate between more and less effective leaders in organizations, determining just what makes the difference has thus far proven to be an elusive goal.

Now here's the TV game show question of the day: What did Mahatma Gandhi, Winston Churchill, and Martin Luther King have in common? The answer is, of course, that they were all *charismatic leaders*—individuals with personal characteristics that make them unusually influential and who are typically revered or held in awe by their followers. Some would add to the short list such figures as John F. Kennedy, Ronald Reagan, and Sigmund Freud—not to mention Adolf Hitler. Some I/O psychologists have studied such leaders, as well as many less famous but highly effective individuals in organizations—leaders like Lee Iacocca at Chrysler and Charles Revson at Revlon (Bass, 1985). The idea, of course, is to determine just what makes for charisma. Can we learn to recognize it in advance, predict it in selecting leaders, or even teach it?

The effort to answer these questions led Robert House (1977) to develop a theory of charismatic leadership that builds on an earlier formulation by Max Weber in the early 1900s (Weber, 1968). M House proposes that charisma requires a combination of several characteristics in the same person: self-confidence, dominance, a need to exert influence or be powerful, and a strong conviction that her beliefs and goals are both right and important. Beyond these basic characteristics, he specifies a number of additional personal qualities, behaviors, and situational factors that collectively produce a charismatic leader (Klein & House, 1995). Bernard Bass (1985) has added several more propositions to House's list to provide a fairly complete theoretical picture of charisma (Table 19-1). Although these theories are very helpful in identifying hypothetical qualities, there has thus far been little research, and we certainly have not yet developed ways to predict or foster charisma. However, I/O psychologists have developed a number of important theories of leadership that tell us much about how to select and train leaders more generally.

Early leadership theories focused on personality traits, hypothesizing that certain combinations of characteristics, such as assertiveness, flexibility, and social adeptness, are the hallmarks of leadership. With little evidence to support them, these approaches gave way to leader behavior theories, which attempted to define how leaders behave toward and interact with their subordinates. Task-oriented leaders—those who focus primarily on accomplishing organizational goals—tend to provide more structure and to be more directive. Person-oriented leaders—those who work to enhance the self-esteem and satisfaction of subordinates—tend to be somewhat less structured and directive. Interestingly enough, there has been a more recent return of interest in the personality trait approach, but with a recognition that situational factors must also be taken into account.

Several major theories of leadership have been particularly influential. *Contingency theory*, developed by Fred Fiedler (1964), lef proposes that the effectiveness of a leader depends on the interaction of his personal characteristics with the characteristics of the work situation (the contingencies) with which he must deal. Task-oriented leaders will be more effective in some settings, person-oriented leaders in others. The degree to which organizational tasks can be structured, the nature of leader-follower relationships, and the amount of power the leader has are important determinants of effectiveness. If the task is highly structured and the leader has good relationships with employees and also has high power over them, effectiveness should be high. Otherwise, it is likely to be lower. Fiedler has more recently added a cognitive element to his theory (Fiedler, 1995). It factors in the cognitive abilities of both the leader and his employees, as well as the stress the leader is under, in an effort to better predict leader effectiveness.

Victor Vroom (1974; Vroom & Jago, 1995) favors a *normative decision theory* approach, which focuses on the decision-making aspect of leadership. Individual leaders and organizations have norms or standards for making decisions. On a given occasion or across occasions, a leader can choose to make either more or less authoritarian decisions. The more authoritarian the leader chooses to be, the less the ability of others to influence decisions. Vroom believes that the best leaders are those who can be flexible enough to assess each situation to determine the extent to which others should be involved in a decision.

Attribution theory deals particularly with leader perceptions of employees and employee perceptions of leaders. Leaders observe employees and make attributions as to the causes of their performance. Seeing a poorly performing subordinate, the leader may make internal attributions (the person is lacking in ability or effort expended) or external attributions (the task is too difficult or the available resources inadequate). His effectiveness in handling the employee will clearly depend on the nature and accuracy of these attributions. By the same token, subordinates make attributions concerning the behavior of the leader, and part of her job is to behave in such a way as to positively influence those attributions.

Personnel Psychology

The basic task of personnel psychology is to fit workers to jobs and evaluate that fit. This means conducting a job analysis to determine what worker characteristics or *attributes* would be ideal for a specific job, then assessing the relevant attributes of applicants. For each job, there is theoretically an ideal set of worker attributes, including knowledge, relevant experience, social skills, job skills, motivation, and personality characteristics (Craiger & Coovert, 1994). The personnel psychologist tries to accurately assess these attributes and match them to the available jobs. Since applicants frequently do not come in with all the ideal attributes, personnel psychologists must often also develop training programs. And performance on the job must be evaluated once a person has been hired.

Job Analysis and Evaluation. My daughter was just hired as a pediatrician in a private practice. A job analysis would undoubtedly show that the job of pediatrician has many characteristics that require specific skills, bodies of knowledge, and experiences. It is unlikely that someone whose primary background is in law, plumbing, or psychology would be a good match for such a job. But this is an extreme example. Very often the detailed characteristics of a job—and hence the worker attributes it requires—are not at all obvious. *Job analysis* is a technique for ascertaining the exact characteristics of a job by breaking it down into very specific components, then determining which components are most important (Clifford, 1996). For example, we all know what the job of teacher entails—lecturing, answering questions, assigning readings, grading—because we have all had so many teachers. But do we really know the most important characteristics of the job, as opposed to those that are more peripheral? What exactly makes one teacher better than another? A job analysis can answer these questions.

A step beyond job analysis is *job evaluation*, in which each job is assessed—much as we might assess an individual employee—to see how valuable it is (Hornsby et al., 1994). How much does this job contribute to the overall goals of the organization? Is it really necessary to have this job done at all? Do we need as many people doing this job as we have now? A hospital, for example, must have doctors and nurses (though it could have too many), but does it really need full-time "community liaison" personnel. Perhaps, but this job is less obviously central than those of doctor and nurse. Job evaluation has become particularly important in relatively recent years as many corporations have "downsized" in order to streamline their operations and increase profits.

Employee Selection. Once we know what the job entails, we need procedures for selecting people who best fit it. Many large corporations and other work settings now use a number of *selection procedures*, such as tests, work samples, and interviews, to match applicants to jobs. It is the task of the personnel psychologist to conduct careful research to identify the best selection procedures for a given job setting. Standardized measures, such as intelligence, specific aptitude, motivation, and personality tests may be used. Specific work samples, such as typing tests for secretarial positions, may be developed. And interviews may be carefully structured to provide the most crucial information about the applicant (Bartram et al., 1995).

Training. The idea of training employees to do a specific job may seem simple: Secretaries at IBM may need a short course in WordPerfect; certain assembly line workers at Ford may need basic instruction in safety procedures. The question, however, is how *best* to train workers with a variety of backgrounds for a variety of jobs. Training research may be required to determine whether to offer a short course or a longer course or to use on-the-job training (OJT). Highly specific training procedures for each job must then be developed and put in place. Otherwise, poorly trained workers will do a shoddy job, turning out substandard products inefficiently. Both the worker and the organization will suffer. Considerable research indicates that carefully developing training approaches enhance both job performance and job satisfaction (Saks, 1996).

Performance Appraisal. Most organizations use some form of *performance appraisal*—a periodic evaluation of the quality of an employee's work. Performance appraisal is important to the organization because it can potentially enhance employee accomplishment and contribute to the achievement of organizational goals. It is important to the employee because it is used in determining salaries, promotions, transfers, and layoffs. But performance appraisal is not easy: Supervisors don't like to do it; employees don't like to have it done; and methods of *accurate* appraisal are difficult to develop (Sanchez & De-La-Torre, 1996).

The most common form of appraisal is a supervisor rating system. The supervisor is provided with a set of scales and must assign a numerical rating on each scale. As an example, "Completes tasks in a timely fashion" might be rated on a scale ranging from '1' (Almost Never) to '7' (Almost always). Table 19-2 provides several additional examples of appraisal items and a tongue-in-cheek interpretation of their meaning. One advantage of rating scales is that they provide evaluations on the same dimensions across supervisors and employees. A disadvantage is that they may be influenced by such extraneous factors as how much the supervisor likes the employee and whether the worker is male or female. Researchers have found, however, that reliable, valid scales can be developed and that supervisors can be trained to reduce rating errors (Conway, 1996).

Human Factors Psychology

World-War II pilots were faced with a dangerous problem: They had to fly a variety of planes in which the control consoles were not standardized. The firing controls might be to the pilot's right in a bomber, to his left in a fighter. Moreover, controls were not of any standard size, shape, or color. And identical knobs and lights performing and displaying very different functions were often located close together, making mistakes all too common. For example, pilots trying to retract the landing gear after takeoff often operated an identical knob that, instead, engaged the flaps, causing the plane to crash.

Such errors became increasingly common as equipment became more complex. Franklin Taylor points out in a classic early human factors article that military equipment frequently "...required of (pilots and other operators) too many hands, too many feet, or in the case of some of the more complex devices, too many heads" (Taylor, 1957, p. 249). Pilots had to identify nearly invisible targets, understand speech over the deafening roar of engines, and consider altimeter values that were notoriously hard to read under stress. "As a result, bombs and bullets often missed their mark, planes crashed, friendly ships were fired upon and sunk. Whales were depth-charged" (Taylor, 1957, p. 249).

Poorly designed controls have also been a factor in other kinds of accidents. In 1979, the nuclear power plant at Three Mile Island, near Harrisburg, Pennsylvania, went to critical mass and leaked large amounts of radiation into the outside air. A major factor in this disaster was the design of control consoles. When operators detected the malfunction on one of the readouts, they lost crucial time going to a distant part of the room to operate the controls necessary to correct the problem. Human factors research has since considerably improved nuclear power plant displays (Hogg et al., 1995).

Human engineering or *human factors* psychology developed in order to reduce such problems. It is concerned with human-machine and human-environment relationships and studies the best ways to design equipment and work environments to fit the abilities and limitations of humans. The myriad of buttons, lights, levers, and computer displays that populate the control panel of a space shuttle could be laid out in helter-skelter fashion. However, human engineering can determine the best sizes, shapes, colors, and locations of panel components to maximize pilot efficiency and safety and reduce frustration. In recent years, much of the focus in human factors has been on the design of computer displays because these are so heavily used in controlling equipment (Howell, 1993). However, the same principles apply to many other work environments as well.

Keys to Industrial/Organizational Psychology 7

Conclusion

We have raised many interesting questions in this chapter: How are impressions of others formed? What factors influence our causal attributions concerning the behavior of other people? How does social interaction influence and how is it influenced by the self-concept? What causes one person to be attracted to another? Why won't people help in a crisis? How can we enhance the functioning of human organizations, improve procedures for hiring and evaluating employees, and interface people with increasingly complex work environments? Many questions. And for each question we have provided answers based on extensive empirical research and carefully developed theory. Yet you must be left with the impression—the accurate impression—that we are still not close to definitive answers. For nearly every question, we have said that factors 'A','B', and 'C' may be of some importance under certain circumstances but that the question is basically a complex one requiring further research. Indeed, human interaction and human performance are nothing if not complex, and it should perhaps not be surprising that we have no final answers to the many questions we have raised. However, the strongly scientific approach of 20th-century social and industrial/organizational psychology have brought us out of the dark ages of all prior centuries, during which the vicissitudes of human interaction and performance were merely a matter of philosophical speculation. We now have scientific theory and scientific data and are hence well on the road to a day—perhaps in the 21st century—when we will have a far better understanding of the phenomena of social cognition.

Summary

Social Perception

1. Person perception is the way we organize information about other people in order to arrive at our own internal impression of them. It is influenced by past experience, expectations, and a number of other factors.

2 Impression formation is a complex process. Overall impressions are influenced by implicit personality theories, by central traits, and by stereotypes. Impression management is the attempt to control the way we are perceived by others.

Making Attributions

1. Attributions are efforts to assign causation to behavior. Dispositional attribution is assigning causation to factors within the actor; situational attribution is assigning causation to factors in the actor's environment.

2. Jones and Davis' theory of correspondent inferences suggests that whenever behavior is inappropriate to a particular situation, we attribute that behavior to dispositional factors.

3. According to Kelley, behavior is usually attributed to situational factors when distinctiveness, consensus, and consistency are high and to dispositional factors when these three characteristics are low.

4. The tendency to overestimate the role of dispositional factors and underestimate the role of situational factors is called the fundamental attribution error. The prevalence of this error is a matter of dispute.

Social Comparison And Self-Perception

1. The self-concept comprises both physical and psychological components. Psychological components include self-identity, self-esteem, and self-image. The self-concept influences information processing and therefore affects attitudes, cognitions, emotions, and behaviors.

2. Conscious attention directed toward the self as a social object is called self-awareness or self-consciousness. Heightened self-awareness can increase both positive and negative self-evaluations.

3. Cooley and Mead both envisioned the self as a product of social interaction. More recent theories have suggested that the self is a product of social comparison processes (Festinger), that aspects of the self are inferred by observations of one's own overt behavior (Bem), or that self-concept is actually a self-theory (Epstein).

Interpersonal Attraction

1. The most important factor in initial attraction to other people is physical attractiveness. Highly attractive people are perceived as happier, better adjusted, and more socially desirable. Physical attractiveness not only influences how people are treated but also how the attractive people themselves act.

2. Psychological factors that determine liking include warmth, friendliness, intelligence, competence, and good judgment.

3. Situational factors in attraction include proximity, familiarity, and physiological arousal. Relational factors include reciprocity, similarity, and complementarily.

4. Love can be differentiated into passionate love and companionate love.

5. For Rubin, liking is characterized by similarity, respect, and admiration, while loving is characterized by attachment, caring, and intimacy.

Prosocial Behavior

1. Prosocial behavior is voluntary behavior that shows concern for and is intended to benefit other human beings. Theories suggest that it is a biological mechanism contributing to species survival, an attempt to achieve equity, a striving to reduce negative affect, a result of empathy, or a response to social norms for reciprocity and social responsibility.

2. Prosocial behavior is influenced by certain characteristics of the helper and of the victim, as well as situational factors.

The Neurophysiology of Social Cognition

1. Evolutionary psychology hypothesizes neural modules that serve specific functions.

2. Parts of the temporal cortex and amygdala may be part of a social cognition module.

3. Behaviors associated with this module may include attribution and empathy.

4. Areas of the frontal cortex may also be important in social cognition. They appear to affect interaction, social conflict resolution, the formation of the self, and making attributions.

5. The neuropeptide oxytocin may be important in such behaviors as social interaction and altruism that are based on social cognition.

Industrial/Organizational Psychology

1. I/O psychology develops theories and conducts scientific research on the problems of human organizations and the utilization of human resources by those organizations.

2. Organizational psychology deals with the structure and functioning of organizations, particularly the social-emotional adjustment of employees. It studies job satisfaction, work motivation, and leadership.

3. Personnel psychology attempts to match workers to jobs and evaluate that match. It includes job analysis and evaluation, employee selection, training, and performance appraisal.

4. Human factors psychology works to interface humans with machines and job environments.

Ask Yourself

1. What are the major factors involved in forming an impression of others?

2. Outline the conditions under which dispositional and situational attributions are likely.

3. How is self-perception similar to the perception of other people and of physical objects in the environment? How is it different?

4. What role does self-concept play in determining behavior?

5. What is the role of society in the development of self-concept? How do the major theories differ on this issue?

6. What role does physical attractiveness play in interpersonal attraction?

7. Discuss the similarities and differences between liking and loving.

8. What is the theoretical basis for passionate love? Under what circumstances is someone likely to fall in love?

9. Discuss the major theories of prosocial behavior. Which theory do you find the most attractive? Why?

10. Under what circumstances is helping behavior most likely to occur? Under what circumstances is it least likely to occur? Consider the characteristics of the helper, the victim, and the situation.

Further Readings

Aronson, E., Wilson, T., & Akert, R. (1994). *Social psychology: The heart and mind.* NY: HarperCollins. This basic in social psychology is co-authored by Elliot Aronson, one of the major figures in the field. It covers all the major topics in considerable depth.

Bagozzi, R., & Moore, D. (1994). Public service advertisements: Emotions and empathy guide prosocial behavior. *Journal of Marketing*, 58, 56-70.

Duckitt, J. (1992). *The social psychology of prejudice.* NY: Praeger. This small volume will tell you everything you ever wanted to know about prejudice, covering the major theoretical and empirical literature on this important topic.

Franz, C., & McClelland, D. (1994). Lives of women and men active in the social protests of the 1960s: A longitudinal study. *Journal of Personality and Social Psychology,* 66, 196-205. In this interesting paper, Carol Franz and David McClelland report a long-term followup of people initially assessed during the social protest era of the 1960s. The question: What has happened to them since?

Hecht, M., Marston, P., & Larkey, L. (1994). Love ways and relationship quality in heterosexual relationships. *J. Social and Personal Relationships*, 11, 25-43. This study examines the influence of a variety of factors on the quality of romantic love relationships.

Hendrick, S., & Hendrick, C. (1992). *Liking, loving, and relating.* Pacific Grove, CA: Brooks/Cole. The Hendricks provide a concise, scholarly overview of what we know about close personal relationships.

Klein, W., & Kunda, Z. (1993). Maintaining self-serving social comparisons: Biased reconstruction of one's past behaviors. *Personality and Social Psychology Bulletin*, 19, 732-739. This interesting study shows how the social comparison process can be distorted to maintain a positive view of the self.

Ross, A., & Grant, M. (1994). *Experimental and nonexperimental designs in social psychology.* Madison, WI: Brown and Benchmark. The authors provide a solid coverage of the experimental side of social psychology.

Sedikides, C., & Skowronski, J. (1993). The self in impression formation: Trait centrality and social perception. *Journal of Experimental Social Psychology,* 29, 347-357. This is a well-done experimental study of the effects of honesty and intelligence (as central traits) on impression formation in college students.

Smith, P., & Bond, M. (1993). *Social psychology across cultures: Analysis and perspectives.* London: Harvester Wheatsheaf. As the title suggests, this book examines the similarities and differences in social psychological principles across cultures.

Psychology in the 21st Century

Hokus Pokus: The Self As Illusion

As we approach the end of the century, we are finally beginning to make progress in answering one of the oldest and most important questions ever asked about the self: How is it that most people maintain a positive self-image, even in the face of considerable adversity. The answer may be that we do it with smoke and mirrors; the self may be as illusory as the magician's rabbit.

Shelley Taylor and Jonathan Brown (1988) argue that the normal person engages in a substantial amount of distorted cognitive processing of self-relevant information. Rather than accept a negative self-image and low self-esteem based on the reality of disturbing life circumstances, we tend to protect the self by misinterpreting much of our experience. In effect, we engage in illusion in order to maintain a positive self-concept.

Taylor and Brown propose that we commonly engage in three principal illusions. The first is *overly positive self-evaluation*, in which you interpret some aspect of your behavior more positively than is warranted by the evidence. For example, you believe that you are a very caring person, but the reality is that you rarely do anything for others unless there is personal gain; moreover your friends would describe you as relatively uncaring. One study showed that both men and women had positive illusions regarding their own physical attractiveness and intelligence (Gabriel et al., 1994). The second illusion is *exaggerated perceptions of mastery*, in which you persuade yourself that you have far greater control over situations than you actually do. Many people believe that they are excellent drivers and can readily deal with any situation that might arise. The reality is that most of us could make a driving error at any time or run into a traffic situation that we could not control.

The third illusion is called *unrealistic optimism*, referring to unreasonably positive predictions about future self-relevant events. Most people believe that positive events, such as winning the lottery or getting a good job, are more likely to happen to them than to others; negative events, such as automobile accidents or house fires, are thought more likely to happen to others. How many people about to get married, for example, believe they will ever have an unhappy marriage, let alone a divorce? Yet this illusion occurs in the midst of a divorce rate that approximates 50% (U.S. Bureau of the Census, 1995)! Similarly, the probability of a lottery win is typically 1 in several million, and radio stations in large cities carry reports of multiple auto accidents every day of the week. Our optimism is indeed often unrealistic—and illusory.

Taylor and Brown suggest that the illusions we engage in involve normal social cognitive processes that have real adaptive value. Recall, for example, that low self-esteem is associated with depression and potential suicide (Lester, 1993). It is clearly adaptive to employ cognitive mechanisms that improve self-esteem and provide for a more positive self-image (Bates & Stevens, 1989). However, we should note that not everyone agrees with the Taylor-Brown illusion theory, and some have pointed to evidence that runs counter to it (Colvin & Block, 1994).

Other self-protective cognitive mechanisms have also been proposed. The *illusory superiority bias* allows an individual to feel that he is superior to others when, in fact, he is not (Hoorens & Buunk, 1992). This bias is often seen in work settings, where each of several employees in a group believes that she is the best. All but one is wrong! Another illusion is *unique invulnerability*, in which the individual believes she is not subject to the dangers that apply to other people. She will not get pregnant or become HIV positive, despite unprotected sex with multiple partners and will never be affected by an earthquake, despite living in California (Burger & Burns, 1988; Taylor et al., 1992). In fact, even victims of the major 1989 quake felt invulnerable to future quakes three months later (Burger & Palmer, 1992).

A final self-protective, social cognitive mechanism is *self-handicapping*. The idea here is to provide yourself with a convenient handicap that will remove the blame for failure (Rhodewalt, 1994). The student who is sure he will fail the exam doesn't study for it, providing an excuse for the failure. He can then convince himself that it is not inadequate intellect but simply lack of study that caused the failure; the self is left untouched. More generally, illness, procrastination, drinking, taking drugs, and lack of effort are among the common self-defeating behaviors that people engage in to maintain their positive self-images (Lay et al., 1992).

The illusory protection of the self has both benefits and consequences. It helps to maintain a positive self-image, which makes the person feel better and reduces anxiety and the likelihood of depression. However, these pluses come with a cost because they distort reality. Unprotected sex *does* result in pregnancy or AIDS for many people; smoking *does* cause lung cancer, heart disease, and numerous other disorders; burglars *do* enter houses with unlocked doors; people *do* die in house fires. Thus, the mentally healthy approach allows for enough illusion to protect the self-concept without placing the person in danger. As research related to self-illusion continues into the next century, we will learn more about how we can best maintain a positive self-image while functioning effectively in the real world.

Probe

Selecting A Mate: Evolution or Cognition?

Most people pair up with long-term mates. In fact, 95% of people marry at some point in their lives (Singh et al., NCHS Monthly Vital Statistics Report, 1995). But how do we fall in love, and how do we select our mates? Two theories that attempt to answer these questions are evolutionary theory and cognitive labeling theory.

We discuss the evolutionary view of physical attractiveness in the text. Not surprisingly, this perspective has also been applied to the selection of mates (Kenrick et al., 1994). Evolutionary theory holds that the criteria for mate selection are established on the basis of the adaptive value they have for the species. We select mates whose characteristics, such as fertility and good health, will further the survival and enhancement of the human race. Such characteristics might include fertility and good health. We have already seen that men are more likely to select women with facial and body shape characteristics associated with greater fertility (Singh, 1993). In addition, there is evidence that both genders prefer mates with biological features indicative of good health, which is also an adaptive characteristic likely to enhance species survival (Gangestad & Buss, 1993; Jones, 1995).

Further supporting the evolutionary view are a variety of data concerning the differential characteristics that men and women value in their mates. Both value mates who are dependable, intelligent, and kind because these characteristics promote the survival of the species (Buss et al., 1990). Beyond such broad characteristics, there are sex differences. In general, males emphasize physical attractiveness, including body shape and facial characteristics, in selecting mates. Such selection has adaptive value because it selects healthy, fertile women. Along these same evolutionary lines, men often display sexual jealousy (Buss et al., 1992) and even violent behavior (Wilson & Daly, 1993) in reaction to perceived threats not only to themselves but to the human species. Females place greater emphasis on the financial resources or potential of the male partner and on such characteristics as honesty and sincerity (Landolt et al., 1995). The Figure shows the results of a study supporting the evolutionary position.

Both men and women appear to recognize the differential selection characteristics. In one interesting study, Michael Wiederman (1993) analyzed the personal advertisements placed in newspapers by 630 men and 481 women seeking mates. In self-descriptions in their ads, the men emphasized financial resources and often mentioned honesty and sincerity. These characteristics were rarely noted in ads placed by women. Instead, they emphasized body shape and overall attractiveness and were much more likely to offer photos of themselves. Men said they were seeking attractive, younger women, while women said they were seeking financially sound, older men. Why do men seek younger women and women older men? From an evolutionary standpoint men are seeking women more likely to be fertile and able to safely bear healthy children; women are seeking older men because they are more likely to have resources that will provide security for themselves and their children.

An alternative to evolutionary psychology is Berscheid and Walster's *cognitive labeling theory*. Drawing on Stanley Schachter's work (see Chapter 12), they propose that falling in love requires a proper mixture of physiological and cognitive components. The person must first experience *physiological arousal*, which produces such symptoms as a pounding heart, rapid respiration, and a tense or fluttering stomach. Such arousal can spring from a variety of sources, including fear, frustration, joy, and sexual stimulation. The second component is a *cognitive* process in which the internal cues provided by the physiological arousal are labeled as "love." The labeling process is often quite independent of the mechanism by which the symptoms are actually aroused and is based on external, situational cues. If you experience a pounding heart and tense stomach after nearly being hit by a truck, you will probably label your emotion as "fear." However, if you experience these same symptoms in the presence of an attractive person who appears to be warm and caring and to display attitudes and values similar to your own, you may instead label the emotion as "love."

Are the evolutionary and cognitive perspectives incompatible? Probably not. Inherited social cognitive modules in the brain may mediate the cognitive processes associated with mate selection, and other modules may mediate the emotional experience of love. Since these modules are theoretically adaptive products of evolution, cognitive-labeling theory may well explain the immediate mechanisms that underlie the operation of the evolved modules.

The Critical Thinker

How Important Are Stereotypes?

The term stereotype was introduced by journalist Walter Lippman (1922), who referred to it as "the picture in the head" that you have of a particular group of people. You may think of physicians as rich, Irish people as hot-tempered, African-Americans as musical, women as nurturant, and men as competitive. Once aware that a person belongs to a particular group, you may tend to ascribe to her behaviors that you consider common in that group. A *stereotype*, then, is a set of characteristics attributed to all members of some group. It involves a *belief* that all members possess these qualities. If she is German, she must be hard-working; if Scottish, she must be thrifty.

The Basic Hypothesis or Contention

There are two widely held contentions about stereotypes. First, virtually every human being subscribes to a variety of stereotypes about different groups (Vescio et al., 2003). Second, it is argued that much of our behavior is heavily influenced by stereotypes, which contribute to the development of *prejudice*—a strong liking or disliking for the members of some group (Zanna, 1994). People often use stereotypes to justify prejudices. This leads to statements like: "I can't stand Ferugians because they're all nasty and never take showers." Well, "Ferugians" are a fictional group, but you get the point.

What Is The Evidence?

In a classic study of stereotypes, 100 Princeton students tested in the early 1930s ascribed stereotypical characteristics to each of nine different ethnic groups. Blacks were described as lazy and superstitious, Jews as shrewd and mercenary, whites as intelligent and industrious (Katz & Braly, 1933). These results also hint at another common finding: stereotypes of an in-group (your own group) are typically positive and those of out-groups are often negative (Osbeck et al., 1997). But perhaps these negative attitudes have died out in the modern, "enlightened" age? Well, later studies of Princeton students did show some weakening of the negative stereotypes (Karlins et al., 1969). However, a more recent study of 300 U.S. communities shows that the stereotypes are alive and well. A majority of respondents said that African-Americans are less intelligent, industrious, and patriotic than White Americans (*New York Times*, 1991). Similarly, the positive attitude of white Americans toward the death penalty is based in part on a stereotype of African-Americans as aggressive (Barkan & Cohn, 1994). Moreover, experimental studies confirm these observations. When participants saw one man shove another, they interpreted the shove as playful when the shover was white and aggressive when he was African-American (Duncan, 1976).

Gender stereotyping is also common (Halbert, 1997). Most people (including women) describe women as warm, dependent, sensitive, and people-oriented; most (including men) describe men as cold, independent, dominant, task-oriented, and aggressive (Colley et al., 1994; Spence et al., 1985). And these stereotypes are not new. Aristotle observed that "The courage of a man is shown in commanding, of a woman in obeying;" and the Roman historian Cicero wrote that "We should regard loveliness as the attribute of woman and dignity as the attribute of man." In modern times, gender stereotypes are prominent in such diverse areas as commercials on Music Television (MTV; Signorielli et al., 1994) and the selection of managers for jobs (McRae, 1994).

In a clever test of how gender stereotypes work, Curt Hoffman and Nancy Hurst (1990) read descriptions of "Orinthians" and "Ackmians," fictitious groups said to live on another planet. Participants were told that Ackmians are typically employed outside the home, while most Orinthians are primarily involved in child care. When asked to guess the psychological characteristics of each group, subjects described Ackmians as more forceful and competitive, Orinthians as more nurturant and compassionate (see the Figure). Once this stereotype had been formed, participants applied it uniformly, describing employed Orinthians as less competitive and assertive than employed Ackmians. Sound familiar?

Beyond race and gender, stereotypes have been applied to nearly any group you can name. There are stereotypes concerning handicapped people (Ruscello et al., 1994), elderly people (Levy & Langer, 1994), homosexuals (Monteith et al., 1993), and fat people. Like beliefs about gender differences, negative stereotypes of gays and lesbians are not only widespread but long-standing. They are even found in characters in Shakespeare's *Henry IV* (Krims, 1994). Negative stereotypes that feed a prejudice against fat people have gotten increased attention in recent years as studies have demonstrated that genetic factors are largely responsible for most extreme cases of overweight (Cardon et al., 1994). The stereotype nevertheless sees fat people as lazy, clumsy, unhealthy overeaters with no will power (Crandall, 1994).

Even children operate on the basis of stereotypes. Kimberly Powlishta and her colleagues (1994) examined the gender, ethnic, and body type (weight) biases of boys and girls in kindergarten through grade 6. They found that most of the children were biased against groups they did not belong to. Stereotyping and prejudice clearly get off to an early start.

Once established in childhood, stereotypes are strong and highly resistant to change for several reasons. First, we look for evidence that confirms stereotypes and either overlook evidence that contradicts them or consider such evidence as "the exception that proves the rule" (Snyder and Skrypnek, 1981). If you believe that all politicians are crooked, you may attend selectively to news reports about political corruption and ignore stories about honest political behavior. Second, when we do occasionally see a member of a group actually fulfilling the stereotype, the instance is rare and hence distinctive, so it stands out. An example would be seeing a known gay man displaying effeminate behavior, which many homosexuals do not. Third, studies show that people overestimate the frequency with which they have seen stereotype-fulfilling behaviors occur (Hamilton & Sherman, 1989). Fourth, we rarely have opportunities to assess non-stereotypical behaviors. How often do you take notice of homosexual men who do not display effeminate behaviors or women who are not nurturant?

Another indication of the strength of stereotypes is that people often engage in behavior that actually *makes* a stereotype come true—a self-fulfilling prophecy or expectation (Hamilton et al., 1990). Physically attractive people, for instance, are stereotyped as socially skilled and outgoing (Pilkington & Lydon, 1997). In one study men were shown a photo of an attractive or unattractive woman, then had a telephone conversation that they were told was with that woman. Men who believed they were talking to an attractive woman were more outgoing, friendly, and sociable. Moreover, judges who listened to only the woman's side of the conversation without knowing what the man had been told about her attractiveness rated women whose partners believed they were attractive as more poised, sociable, and humorous. The men thus treated the attractive and unattractive women differently and actually *elicited* the behavior they expected (Dion et al., 1972)!

Is The Evidence Open To Alternative Interpretations?

Despite evidence for stereotyping and prejudice, most people believe that they do not personally hold to or act on stereotypes. In addition, there are clearly many anecdotal instances of people who do not display the prejudiced behaviors associated with common stereotypes: the father who encourages his daughter to attend graduate school in mathematics; the white family who hire an African-American lawyer because of his excellent reputation in his field; the employer who dedicates herself to hiring and promoting people based solely on their qualifications and not their gender or ethnicity.

Such observations led Patricia Devine to offer an alternative to the idea that stereotyping and prejudice are both universal. Her recent theory builds on the classic work of Gordon Allport and W.E.B. DuBois (Gaines & Reed, 1994), as well as other theories that have often reflected the differing patterns of prejudice seen over time in various cultures (Duckitt, 1992, 1994). Devine distinguishes between automatic and controlled processing (Devine, 1989; Monteith et al., 1993). *Automatic processing* is the rapid, unconscious interpretation of information seen in the earliest stages of perception. *Controlled processing* is a more gradual perceptual activity that takes place somewhat later in time. It is under conscious control and involves an intentional, deliberate consideration of the stimulus. Devine postulates that every person in a given culture learns the major, prevailing stereotypes, which inevitably come into play during automatic processing. To that extent, at least, the stereotypes almost always affect perception. However, many people do not consciously subscribe to these stereotypes and may actually make an effort to overcome them during controlled processing. It is also controlled processing that theoretically accounts for prejudice: those who are prejudiced do consciously follow the cultural stereotypes, while unprejudiced people do not.

To test her theory, Devine (1989) first determined through a questionnaire that both prejudiced and unprejudiced white college students were equally aware of the cultural stereotype of African-Americans. She then asked each subject to stare at a spot in the center of a screen and note the location of words flashed so briefly at various locations that they could not be consciously perceived. In a *stereotype-activation* condition, the flashed words included terms like black, Negro, Africa, and ghetto. In the *nonactivation* condition, neutral words having nothing to do with any particular cultural group were flashed.

After completing this task, subjects heard a description of the behaviors of a man named Donald, some of which could be interpreted as hostile. Both prejudiced and unprejudiced subjects in the stereotype-activation condition, who presumably had an unconscious image of Donald as black, rated him as more hostile than did those in the nonactivation condition. Devine's hypotheses were thus supported. Evidence from some other laboratories also supports Devine's theory (Augoustinos et al., 1994), though the support is not universal (Locke et al., 1994).

Do We Need Additional Evidence?

We probably need no more evidence for the widespread existence of stereotypes or prejudice. However, further work based on Devine's theory is essential. Do her findings apply to a wide variety of stereotypes or only to a few? What proportion of people in any given group use controlled processing to avoid prejudiced behavior? Is it possible that automatic processing can lead to prejudiced behavior even when the conscious intent is to be unprejudiced? Might an employer who truly wants to avoid prejudice nevertheless tend to select men as managers and women as secretaries? Whites for desk jobs and African-Americans for manual labor? And we must still ask whether the Devine theory is really a valid understanding of stereotypes to begin with.

What Can We Conclude?

It seems clear that stereotypes are common if not universal and equally clear that not everyone acts on the basis of every common stereotype. Beyond these general conclusions, there is little doubt that considerable prejudice still exists in society, though it may have been reduced somewhat in recent decades. The prejudice we do see—and the stereotypes on which it is based—can be and often are destructive forces in the society.

Key Terms 1

implicit personality theory
impression management
impression formation
ingratiation
person perception
person perception
prejudice
primacy effect
priming
recency effect
self-fulfilling prophecy
self-monitoring
social cognition
stereotypes

Key People 1

Solomon Asch
Patricia Devine
Harold Kelley

Key Terms 2

actor-observer hypothesis
attribution
correspondent inference
dispositional attribution
divergent perspectives hypothesis
fundamental attribution error
situational attribution

Key People 2

Edward Jones

Key Terms 3

gender schema theory
reference group
schema
self-concept
self-perception theory
social comparison theory

Key People

Daryl Bem
Charles Horton Cooley
Seymour Epstein
Leon Festinger
Hazel Markus
George Herbert Mead
Shelley Taylor

Key Terms 4

cognitive-labeling theory
companionate love
complementarity
passionate love
triangular model of love

Key People 4

Ellen Berscheid
Elaine Hatfield
Zick Rubin
Robert Sternberg
Elaine Walster

Key Terms 5

altruism
empathy
equity theory

just-world hypothesis
norms
prosocial behavior
reciprocal altruism

Key People 5

John Darley
Bibb Latane

Key Terms 6

neural module
oxytocin

Key Terms 7

attribution theory
contingency theory
equity theory
expectancy theory
human factors psychology
industrial/organizational psychology
job analysis
job satisfaction
job evaluation
normative decision theory
organizational psychology
performance appraisal
personnel psychology
selection procedures
work motivation

Key People 7

James McKeen Cattell
Fred Fiedler
Lilian Gilbreth
Robert House
Hugo Munsterberg
Walter Dill Scott
Victor Vroom

Horizons in Social Cognition

One Moment, Please....

Nalini Ambady and Robert Rosenthal (1993) wondered just how long it takes to form an influential first impression of another person. In one study, they showed college students a silent video clip of a professor. The clip lasted less than 30 seconds and displayed only the professor's nonverbal behavior. Nevertheless, it significantly predicted end-of-semester global student evaluations of their professors. A second study showed that judgments based on similar brief views of a high school teacher's behavior predicted their principal's ratings of them. Wondering if even briefer exposures could

influence impressions, Ambady and Rosenthal conducted a third study in which some video clips were 15 seconds long and others lasted only 6 seconds. Even these brief views influenced impression formation and predicted later ratings. The moral? Don't make a bad first impression!

Attribution In Real Life: The My Lai Massacre

The American military has agonized over it for nearly three decades, philosophers have written thousands of pages on its moral implications (Linn & Gilliagn, 1990; Linn, 1993), and you have read about it in the history books: The My Lai massacre. In 1970, the entire unarmed civilian population of the village of My Lai in Vietnam was massacred by American soldiers. To whom or what can the responsibility for this massacre be attributed? Was the disaster the responsibility of the officer most immediately in charge, Lt. William Calley (eventually convicted for his part) or was it a function of circumstances beyond his control?

Kelman and Lawrence (1972) asked a representative sample of 989 American adults this question. The investigators first asked each subject whether he or she approved or disapproved of bringing Lt. Calley to trial. Of those surveyed, 35 percent approved, 58 percent disapproved, and 8 percent had no opinion. Each respondent was then asked to select one of five reasons for approving or disapproving the trial. The reasons selected by approvers and disapprovers were quite different. Among those who disapproved of the trial, two reasons accounted for 90 percent of their choices:

- It is unfair to send a man to fight in Vietnam, then put him on trial for doing his duty.
- The trial used Lt. Calley as a scapegoat; one young lieutenant shouldn't be blamed for the failures of his superiors.

Among those who approved of the trial, two reasons accounted for 45 percent of choices:

- Even a soldier in a combat situation has no right to kill defenseless civilians, and anyone who violates this rule must be brought to trial.
- The trial helps to get across the important idea that every man must bear responsibility for his own actions.

Note the difference in attributions. Those who disapproved of the trial saw Calley as a victim of circumstances—of *situational* factors. He could not have acted otherwise in the situation, given his perception of his duties. Those who approved of the trial attributed Calley's actions to *dispositional* factors. The massacre was his fault, and he must be held morally responsible. His violation of a clear moral code was intentional and morally unacceptable.

This example shows that attribution is not merely a phenomenon of the social psychology laboratory. It occurs on a day-to-day basis in connection with major and minor incidents in everyday life.

Can Altruism Be Addictive?

Voluntary blood donation without compensation or direct pressure from any external source is clearly an instance of altruistic behavior. Moreover, many people who donate blood tend to become habitual donors, making it seem as though they are in some sense "addicted" to this form of prosocial behavior. How can we explain such an addiction to altruism and understand how it occurs? According to *opponent-process theory*, if you have an initial negative reaction to the idea of giving blood, actually going through with a donation may engender a positive opposing response. This positive response, reportedly experienced by many donors as a "warm glow," helps assure that the donor will return on future occasions and eventually become psychologically addicted to donating blood.

The initial negative reaction of many potential donors was anecdotally verified when my son conducted an Eagle Scout project that involved organizing a large number of Boy Scouts to go door-to-door requesting that people sign up to give blood to the Red Cross on a specific day at a nearby location. Of the 1500 potential donors contacted, only 70 agreed. Although all 70 were reminded by phone the night before the scheduled donation, only 37 actually showed up. The anxiety behind the refusals and no-shows was clear in the many excuses given to the Scouts: "I don't think I have time that day. What day was that?" "I would, but I can't afford to feel faint that day." "I'm sorry, but I'm just not brave enough." "I think I've had hepatitis." In fact, the number of self-reported hepatitis victims suggested that there must have been a major epidemic of that disease in the area!

A more formal study involved an analysis of 1,846 questionnaires completed before and after blood donations (Piliavin et al., 1982). The researchers found that habitual donors do experience initial anxiety, which is followed by positive affect when the donation is complete. They concluded that the donor apparently becomes "hooked" on the pleasure that grows out of repeated donation. These results clearly support the opponent-process hypothesis.

Keys 1

1. Social cognition may be a product of evolution.
    - A. Why?
        - Has adaptive value; social interaction enhances species survival.

2. We form both initial and long-term impressions of others.
    - A. What perception involves?
        - Organizing information to form a picture of another person.
    - B. The importance of initial impressions?
        - They are hard to change.

3. Some psychological processes affect impression formation.
    - A. What the major ones are?
        - Implicit personality theories
        - Central traits
        - Expectations
        - Stereotypes
    - B. What implicit personality theories involve?
        - Grouping traits in clusters
    - C. What determines central traits?
        - High correlation with other traits presented with it.
    - D. What expectancies can produce when you meet another person?
        - Self-fulling prophecies
    - E. When primacy and recency effects occur?
        - Primacy: When a short time has passed
        - Recency: When a longer time has passed or events have intervened.

4. Many people employ impression management to project a certain image.
    - A. Some major techniques?
        - Ingratiation
        - Self-monitoring
        - Deceit
    - B. How well ingratiation works?
        - Very well even when fairly obvious

Keys 2

1. We tend to arrive at causal attributions to explain the behaviors of others.
    - A. The major types of attributions?
        - Dispositional
        - Situational
        - Interactional
    - B. The major theories and theorists?
        - Heider—Quest for meaningful explanations
        - Jones & Davis—Correspondent inference
        - Kelley—Attributions as scientific hypotheses

C. When dispositional attributions are most likely?
When situational explanations are unclear

D. The major characteristics in determining whether a cause is internal or external according to Kelley?
Distinctiveness
Consensus
Consistency

5. The fundamental attribution error may be a common one.

A. What it is?
The tendency to overestimate dispositional contributions and underestimate situational ones.

B. How valid it is?
Results are mixed. Errors may occur in both types of attribution.

C. What the actor-observer hypothesis suggests?
The divergent perspectives of actor and observer lead to differing attributions.

D. The more likely attributions for actors and observers?
Actors: Situational
Observers: Dispositional

E. Why actors and observers differ?
They have different information
Differential saliency

Keys 3

1. The self-concept has multiple components.

A. Some major ones?
Self-identity
Self-esteem
Self-image

B. What racial identity involves?
Development of self-identity in a social context

C. Factors that lower self-esteem?
Critical, rejecting parents
Playing favorites

D. How self-image can affect behavior?
You tend to behave in ways that are consistent with you image.

E. How objective and accurate the self-image is?
Typically quite inaccurate

2. Self-concept affects virtually all areas of life.

A. How Markus believes the self affects behavior?
By influencing information processing

B. How it affects information processing?
By acting as a set of schemata that bias perception.

C. How Rogers believes the self has its influence?
By organizing new information.

3. Self-awareness varies from one person to another.
   - A. How the self is viewed?
     As a social object
   - B. How self-awareness can be increased?
     Through self-talk
   - C. Whether greater self-awareness is better?
     Not always. It can decrease adjustment.

4. The self may develop through social comparison.
   - A. The major theorists?
     Cooley
     Mead
     Festinger
   - B. The origin of the self in Festinger's theory?
     A learned need for self-evaluation
   - C. With whom you will most likely compare yourself?
     Your reference groups—people similar to you.
   - D. What comparisons increase and decrease self-esteem?
     Downward and upward, respectively

5. There are alternatives to social comparison theory.
   - A. What the major ones are?
     Bem—self-perception
     Epstein—self-theory
   - B. The major idea in self-perception theory?
     We develop a self by observing our own behavior.
   - C. The major idea in Epstein's theory?
     The form hypotheses (a self-theory) based on past behavior, then test them on future behavior to develop a self-concept.

6. The self-concept is often distorted.
   - A. Where the distortions come from?
     They result from social cognitive processes.
   - B. Why distortions occur?
     To maintain the consistency of a fragile self.

Keys 4

1. Some factors make people more or less attractive to others.
   - A. Factors that make people more attractive?
     Physical attractiveness
     Certain psychological characteristics
     Certain relational characteristics
   - B. The most important factor?
     Physical attractiveness

2. Physical attractiveness has many benefits.
   A. The effect on rated characteristics?
      Attractive people are judged to have more desirable qualities (adjustment, intelligence, success, social skills, etc.).
   B. Some practical benefits?
      Getting jobs, getting help, selling, being treated honestly by others.
   C. Whether attractive people actually are more likable?
      Some studies suggest that they are.
   D. The evolutionary perspective on attractiveness?
      Facial features and body build characteristics considered attractive are those that have adaptive value for the survival of the species.

3. Psychological, situational, and relational characteristics are also important.
   A. Some attractive psychological qualities?
      Warmth, friendliness, personabiity, intelligence, competence, good judgment.
   B. Some major situational factors in attraction?
      Proximity
      Familiarity
      Positive emotional arousal
   C. Some important relational factors?
      Social cognitions about the effects of behaviors on the relationship.
      Reciprocity
      Complementarity
      Similarity
   D. Whether opposites attract?
      No

4. The study of love has generated opposing theories.
   A. The distinction made in the Bersheid-Walster theory?
      Passionate love: wildly emotional; early stages
      Companionate love: deep affection; more lasting
   B. The three dimensions in Sternberg's theory?
      Passion—motivational
      Intimacy—emotional
      Decision/Commitment—cognitive
   C. Schacter's components of falling in love?
      Physiological arousal
      Cognitive labeling
   D. Some characteristics of a good, lasting love relationship?
      Maturity, open communication, mutual respect, sense of committed love, equal, secure love.

5. Liking and loving may be on different dimensions.
   A. The dimensions Rubin derived?
      Friendship (similarity, respect, admiration)
      Love (dependency, affiliation, concern, intimacy)
   B. Whether loving and liking are mutually exclusive?
      No. Friendship is important in love relationships.

Keys 5

1. There are several theories of prosocial behavior.
   A. What they are?
      Evolution
      Equity
      Negative affect
      Empathy
   B. What evolution says?
      Prosocial behavior occurs because it contributes to species survival or due to reciprocal altruism.
   C. Whether reciprocal altruism can be explained from a strictly environmental perspective?
      Yes—equity theory
   D. What the just world hypothesis says?
      That people often believe suffering is justified by The person's behavior.

2. Norms may also explain prosocial behavior.
   A. The golden rule norm?
      You give help because you expect help.
   B. The responsibility norm?
      Society expects people to help those in need in order to be responsible.
   C. What the personal norms concept suggests?
      Those who feel responsible for the public good are more altruistic.

3. Several types of factors affect prosocial behavior.
   A. The major types?
      Helper characteristics
      Victim characteristics
      Situational factors
   B. Some helper characteristics that lead to altruism?
      Need for approval
      Temperament
      States
      Self-awareness
   C. Important victim characteristics
      Being female, physical attractiveness, similarity, responsibility for plight.
   D. Some situational factors?
      City vs. small town
      Loud noise
      Number of bystanders
      Cultural alienation
      Apathy

Keys 6

1. Evolutionary psychology proposes that neural modules serve specific psychological functions.
   A. Some areas of the brain that may be part of a social cognition module?
      Parts of the temporal cortex and amygdala
   B. What areas of social behavior my involve this module?
      Attribution, empathy, and probably other social-cognitive processes

2. The frontal cortex may play a role in social cognition.

A. Where the evidence comes from?

Studies of brain-damaged patients

B. The social areas in which these patients have difficulty?

Interaction, resolving social conflicts, forming self-concepts, making attributions.

3. Neurochemistry is no doubt also involved in social cognition.

A. The neurochemical identified in recent studies?

Oxytocin, a neuropeptide

B. What it appears to be involved in?

Initiating social interactions, attachment, prosocial behavior, and forming relationships.